BMDP-77

Biomedical Computer Programs

P-Series

┌─────────────────────SUGGESTIONS FOR USING THIS MANUAL─────────────────────┐
│   │
│   CHAPTER 1 (Section 1.1) contains a guide to the   │
│   entire manual.   │
│   │
│ If you   │
│   │
│   ● have not used computers before, start with Chapters 1 and 3.   │
│   │
│   ● are unfamiliar with the BMDP programs, read Chapters 1 and 2.   │
│   │
│   ● know the type of analysis you want to do, read Chapters 1   │
│   and 4 and then turn to the appropriate chapter (see Table   │
│   of Contents).   │
│   │
│   ● have used BMDP programs before, read Chapter 4 and then   │
│   turn to the appropriate analysis (see list of programs on   │
│   the inside of the front cover).   │
│   │
└───┘

┌──────────────────────────── NOTE ────────────────────────────┐
│   │
│   When references are made to results obtained from BMD program│
│   output in publications or other written material, they should│
│   contain   │
│   ● the program revision date (printed in the output)   │
│   ● a statement that the programs were developed at the Health│
│   Sciences Computing Facility, UCLA   │
│   ● a statement that Health Sciences Computing Facility is│
│   sponsored by NIH Special Research Resources Grant RR-3.│
│   │
└───┘

BMDP-77

Biomedical Computer Programs
P-Series

W. J. Dixon, Series Editor
M. B. Brown, Editor 1977 Edition

*Systems, Program and
Statistical Development*

L. Engelman
J. W. Frane
R. I. Jennrich

UNIVERSITY OF CALIFORNIA PRESS

BERKELEY · LOS ANGELES · LONDON · 1977

This publication reports work sponsored under grant RR-3 of the Biotechnology Resources Branch of the National Institutes of Health. Reproduction in whole or in part is permitted for any purpose of the United States Government.

Orders for this publication should be directed to

UNIVERSITY OF CALIFORNIA PRESS
2223 Fulton Street
Berkeley, California 94720

UNIVERSITY OF CALIFORNIA PRESS, LTD.
London, England

Comments on programs or orders for copies of the
programs should be addressed to
Health Sciences Computing Facility
as described in Appendix D.

Contents

1. Introduction   1

    1.1   A Guide to This Manual   4

2. Data Analysis -- Using the BMDP Programs   7

    2.1   Basic Terminology -- Common Features Available   8
    2.2   Scope of the Analytic Techniques   15
    2.3   Short Descriptions of the BMDP Programs   26

3. Using BMDP Programs -- An Introduction   39

    3.1   Three Annotated Examples   40
    3.2   Research Forms and Coding Sheets   47
    3.3   The Layout (Format) of the Data   51

FEATURES COMMON TO ALL PROGRAMS

4. Requirements for an Analysis -- Control Language and System Cards   55

    4.1   Control Language   56
    4.2   System Cards   67
    4.3   Common Errors   69

5. Describing Data and Variables -- In Control Language   71

    5.1   The *PROBlem* Paragraph   74
    5.2   Describing the Data: The *INPut* Paragraph   75
    5.3   Describing the Variables: The *VARiable* Paragraph   79
    5.4   The *GROUP* or *CATEGory* Paragraph   84
    5.5   An Example   87
    5.6   Summary   93

6. Data Editing -- Variable Transformation and Case Selection   95

    6.1   Control Language Transformations   97
    6.2   Case Selection and Deletion   103
    6.3   Random Numbers for Random Subsamples or for Simulations   105
    6.4   FORTRAN Transformations (Using BIMEDT)   106
    6.5   Recoding Nonnumeric Data   109
    6.6   Reading Data with a Nonstandard Format (Layout)   110
    6.7   Summary of Transformations Common to All Programs   111
    6.8   P1S -- Multipass Transformation   112
    6.9   Summary -- P1S   121

7. The BMDP File -- Saving Data and Statistics for Further Analysis   123

    7.1   Creating a BMDP File (*SAVE* Paragraph)   125
    7.2   What is Stored in a BMDP File   130
    7.3   How to Use a BMDP File as Input   132

7.4	Copying Data from a BMDP File	135
7.5	Summary	136

TYPES OF ANALYSES -- PROGRAM DESCRIPTIONS

8.	Data Description	137
8.1	P1D -- Simple Data Description	139
8.2	P2D -- Detailed Data Description, Including Frequencies	146
8.3	P4D -- Single Column Frequencies -- Numeric and Nonnumeric	155
8.4	Summary -- P1D, P2D, P4D	162

9.	Data in Groups -- Description, t Test and One-Way Analysis of Variance	167
9.1	P3D -- Comparison of Two Groups with t Tests	170
9.2	P7D -- Description of Groups (Strata) with Histograms and Analysis of Variance	185
9.3	P9D -- Multiway Description of Groups	199
9.4	Summary -- P3D, P7D, P9D	210

10.	Plots and Histograms	215
10.1	P5D -- Histograms and Univariate Plots	217
10.2	P6D -- Bivariate (Scatter) Plots	230
10.3	Summary -- P5D, P6D	241

11.	Frequency Tables	245
11.1	P1F -- Two-Way Frequency Tables -- Measures of Association	248
11.2	P2F -- Two-Way Frequency Tables -- Empty Cells and Departures from Independence	278
11.3	P3F -- Multiway Frequency Tables -- The Log-Linear Model	297
11.4	Summary -- P1F, P2F, P3F	326

12.	Missing Values -- Patterns, Estimation and Correlations	333
12.1	P8D -- Missing Value Correlation	337
12.2	PAM -- Description and Estimation of Missing Data	348
12.3	Summary -- P8D, PAM	371

13.	Regression	375
13.1	P1R -- Multiple Linear Regression	380
13.2	P2R -- Stepwise Regression	399
13.3	P9R -- All Possible Subsets Regression	418
13.4	P4R -- Regression on Principal Components	437
13.5	P5R -- Polynomial Regression	444
13.6	Summary -- P1R, P2R, P9R, P4R, P5R	453

14.	Nonlinear Regression -- And Maximum Likelihood Estimation	461
14.1	P3R -- Nonlinear Regression	464
14.2	PAR -- Derivative-Free Nonlinear Regression	484
14.3	Maximum Likelihood Estimation	499
14.4	System Cards for P3R and PAR	515
14.5	Summary -- P3R, PAR	518

15. Analysis of Variance and Covariance   521

    15.1 P1V -- One-Way Analysis of Variance and Covariance   523
    15.2 P2V -- Analysis of Variance and Covariance, Including
              Repeated Measures   540
    15.3 P3V -- General Mixed Model Analysis of Variance   581
    15.4 Summary -- P1V, P2V, P3V   599

16. Nonparametric Analysis   603

    16.1 P3S -- Nonparametric Statistics   605
    16.2 Summary -- P3S   618

17. Cluster Analysis   621

    17.1 P1M -- Cluster Analysis of Variables   623
    17.2 P2M -- Cluster Analysis of Cases   633
    17.3 P3M -- Block Clustering   643
    17.4 Summary -- P1M, P2M, P3M   649

18. Multivariate Analysis   653

    18.1 P4M -- Factor Analysis   656
    18.2 P6M -- Canonical Correlation Analysis   685
    18.3 P6R -- Partial Correlation and Multivariate Regression   697
    18.4 P7M -- Stepwise Discriminant Analysis   711
    18.5 Summary -- P4M, P6M, P6R, P7M   734

19. Survival Analysis   741

    19.1 P1L -- Life Tables and Survival Functions   743
    19.2 Summary -- P1L   769

APPENDICES

A. Computational Procedures   771

    A.1   Random Numbers   772
    A.2   Method of Provisional Means   774
    A.3   Hotelling's T^2 and Mahalanobis D^2 (P3D)   776
    A.4   Bartlett's Statistic (P9D)   778
    A.5   Tests and Measures in the Two-Way Frequency Table (P1F)   778
    A.6   Stepwise Identification of Extreme Cells (P2F)   793
    A.7   Standard Errors for Unsaturated Log-Linear Models (P3F)   796
    A.8   Orthogonal Polynomials in P3F   797
    A.9   Estimating (Smoothing) the Missing Value Correlation
           Matrix (PAM)   798
    A.10 Replacing Missing Values (PAM)   799
    A.11 Linear Regression -- Estimating the Coefficients   800
    A.12 Residual Analysis in P9R   803
    A.13 Regression on Principal Components (P4R)   805
    A.14 Polynomial Regression (P5R)   806
    A.15 Nonlinear Regression (P3R)   808
    A.16 Derivative-Free Nonlinear Regression (PAR)   811
    A.17 One-Way Analysis of Variance and Covariance (P1V)   815

A.18 Analysis of Variance and Covariance, including Repeated Measures (P2V)   818

A.19 General Mixed Model Analysis of Variance (P3V)   823

A.20 Survival Functions (P1L)   827

A.21 Maximum Likelihood Factor Analysis (P4M)   829

A.22 Canonical Analysis (P6M)   830

A.23 Stepwise Discriminant Analysis (P7M)   833

A.24 Using BMDP Programs from a Terminal   840

B. Size of Programs   841

B.1 Increasing the Capacity of BMDP Programs   841

B.2 Program Limitations   843

C. Selected Articles from *BMD Communications*   854

C.1 Detecting Outliers with Stepwise Regression (P2R)   855

C.2 It Wasn't an Accident (F-to-enter, F-to-remove)   855

C.3 Scaling for Minimum Interaction Using BMDP6M   856

C.4 Computing Predictions   857

C.5 Tolerance in Regression Analysis   857

C.6 Random Case Selection   857

C.7 Ridge Regression Using BMDP2R   858

C.8 Analysis of Multivariate Change Scores   859

C.9 Checking Order of Cards in a Data Deck   859

C.10 Alternate Form for BMDP Control Language   859

C.11 First Steps   860

C.12 Using P1D to Identify and List Cases Containing Special or Unacceptable Values   861

C.13 Maximum Likelihood Estimation by Means of P3R   862

C.14 Multivariate Analysis of Variance and Covariance Using P7M   863

C.15 Analysis of the Pattern of Missing Data   863

C.16 The Iterated Least Squares Method of Estimating Mean and Variance Components Using P3R   864

C.17 Quick and Dirty Monte Carlo   865

C.18 Lagged Variables Using Transformation Paragraph   865

C.19 Cross Validation in BMDP9R   866

C.20 Residual Analysis in BMDP9R   866

D. How To:

Request Copies of the BMD and BMDP Programs   867

Obtain Additional Manuals   867

Report Difficulties and Suspected Errors   868

Obtain *BMD Communications*   868

Obtain HSCF Technical Reports   868

REFERENCES   870

INDEX   877

TABLES

Table	Title	Page
2.1	Features common to BMDP programs	14
5.1	Werner et al. (1970) blood chemistry data	73
6.1	Control Language transformations	98
8.1	Nineteen cases of data containing nonnumeric characters	158
11.1	Data on 117 coronary patients, all males	249
11.2	Tests and measures computed by P1F	261
11.3	Incidence of peptic ulcer by blood group	273
11.4	Danish social mobility data	281
11.5	Three-year survival of breast cancer patients	300
14.1	Activity in the blood of a baboon named Brunhilda	464
14.2	Activity corresponding to levels of insulin standard	474
14.3	Data on sensitivity of *Chorda tympani* fibers in rat's tongue to four test stimulus sources	504
15.1	Data from Afifi and Azen (1972, p. 166), omitting the same cases as omitted by Kutner (1974)	542
15.2	Numerical example from Winer (1971, p. 525)	550
15.3	Numerical example from Winer (1971, p. 564)	553
15.4	Numerical example from Winer (1971, p. 546)	556
15.5	Numerical example from Winer (1971, p. 806)	560
15.6	Numerical example from Winer (1971, p. 803)	562
15.7	Life times of electronic components	588
16.1	Data from Siegal (1956, p. 253)	606
17.1	Data from Jarvik's smoking questionnaire administered to 110 subjects	624
17.2	Health indicators	633
18.1	Fisher iris data	712
19.1	Survival of lung cancer patients	745
19.2	Artificial dates giving rise to survival times in Table 19.1	764
19.3	Life table from Output 19.1	766

Preface One

This manual describes the capabilities and usage of the BMDP computer programs. These programs provide a wide variety of analytic capabilities that range from plots and simple data description to advanced statistical techniques. The first chapter outlines the organization of the manual and suggests how to use it.

This edition differs in many respects from the 1975 edition; therefore we recommend that you read Chapter 1 even if you are familiar with the previous edition.

The first BMD Biomedical Computer Programs manual appeared in 1961, and was followed by numerous editions. Each new edition included new programs with improved features, novel statistical techniques and more robust statistical algorithms. In 1968 we began to develop the English-based Control Language used with the BMDP programs described in this manual. This method of specifying instructions is more flexible than the fixed format used in the BMD programs. In addition, repeated analyses of the same data, or similar analyses of multiple sets of data, can be done by stating a minimum number of Control Language instructions.

In the first edition of the P manual twenty-six programs were described; this edition contains thirty-three. The development of new programs and revision of previously released programs is a continuing project. New options have been added to many of the programs described in the 1975 edition. The new programs in this manual are:

- Two-Way Frequency Tables -- Empty Cells and Departures from Independence (P2F) can test the independence of rows and columns using any subset of the cells in a two-way frequency table, or can identify in a stepwise manner cells that contribute to a significant chi-square test.

- Multiway Frequency Tables -- the Log-Linear Model (P3F) can form and analyze multiway frequency tables. It can fit log-linear models to the data in the table and provide methods for quickly finding models that are appropriate for the data.

- Description and Estimation of Missing Data (PAM) provides several methods for examining patterns of missing values or values out of range. It can estimate a "missing value" correlation matrix using all the observed data values, or can replace the missing values by estimates based on the observed values.

- All Possible Subsets Regression (P9R) uses an efficient algorithm to identify the "best" subsets of independent variables in terms of a criteria (such as Mallows' C_p). It also provides an extensive residual analysis including the deleted residual, weighted residual, Cook's distance and Mahalanobis distance for each case.

- Derivative-Free Nonlinear Regression (PAR) uses a new algorithm to estimate the parameters of a nonlinear function without requiring that the derivatives of the function be specified. It can also be used to obtain maximum likelihood estimates of parameters.

- General Mixed Model Analysis of Variance (P3V) estimates the parameters of any analysis of variance model by maximum likelihood or by restricted maximum likelihood and tests the significance of parameters in the model by a likelihood-ratio chi-square.

- Survival Functions (P1L) estimates the survival distribution by a life table or by the product-limit estimate.

In addition to the above new programs some of the major changes to programs that appear in the first edition are

- Description of Groups with Histograms and Analysis of Variance (P7D) prints two statistics that are not based on the assumption of homogeneity of variances. The two-way analysis of variance is obtained in an easier manner than previously.

- Two-Way Frequency Table -- Measure of Association (P1F) was substantially rewritten to include improved estimates of the standard errors of the measures of association.

- Nonlinear Regression (P3R) can now estimate parameters of nonlinear functions by maximum likelihood.

- Analysis of Variance and Covariance Including Repeated Measures (P2V) can now print the residuals and save them for further analysis. The model for the grouping factors can be specified. The assumption of compound symmetry can now be tested.

- The correlation matrix can now be pictorially printed in shaded form in Cluster Analysis of Variables (P1M) and Factor Analysis (P4M) and the distance matrix can be printed in shaded form in Cluster Analysis of Cases (P2M).

Relationship to the BMD series

The BMD series of computer programs (Dixon, 1977) was the forerunner of the BMDP series. The BMD programs use a fixed format specification for instructions, while the BMDP programs use an English-based Control Language. The BMDP programs contain many analyses that were not available in the BMD's; for example, cluster analysis, both forward and backward stepping in regression and discriminant analysis, robust location estimates, partial correlations and multivariate regression, repeated measures analysis of variance, analysis of multiway frequency tables, analysis of patterns in missing data, maximum likelihood factor analysis, general mixed model analysis of variance, etc.

The BMDP programs also have many more graphical displays and program options than the BMD's. Data and results from one BMDP program can be saved for further analysis by other BMDP programs, and the capability for transforming data has been expanded.

However, the BMD series contains several programs for spectral analysis, data patterns and the analysis of variance that are not yet available in the BMDP series. For that reason, and because some users prefer a fixed format specification, the BMD series will continue to be available (see Appendix D for how to order either the BMD or BMDP series).

Acknowledgements

It is impossible to properly credit all who have contributed to the development of these programs. Each program goes through many stages from the initial planning to the final release for distribution. In this manual we list as author(s), where possible, the person(s) who was most instrumental in the development of the program. Generally this person showed originality in the design of the program and also contributed to the statistical methodology required for the analytic technique. At the end of each program we name the designer and programmer. But these credits do not, and cannot, fully cover the contributions of our staff.

Laszlo Engelman designed the basic framework of the BMDP programs, such as the Control Language used to specify instructions, the methods used for transformations and the method of saving data and results between analyses (the BMDP (Save) File). He also programmed many of the subroutines common to all programs and several of the BMDP analyses. For many years he was supervisor of applications programming and supervised the development of many of the programs.

Robert Jennrich proposed and designed many of the programs in regression analysis, analysis of variance and discriminant analysis. He made significant contributions in nonlinear regression (P3R), factor analysis (P4M) and the analysis of variance (P2V and P3V). He supervised Mary Ralston's Ph.D. thesis, which provides the algorithm for the derivative-free nonlinear regression. He is currently involved in planning many other programs.

Jim Frane made significant contributions in the area of multivariate analysis. He designed and programmed several of the analyses at a level that makes the programs more accessible to the user; he is now supervisor of applications programming and is deeply involved in making improvements and program testing.

Morton Brown developed the frequency table programs, and John Hartigan (of Yale University) contributed greatly in the area of cluster analysis.

Other staff members, such as Al Forsythe and Ray Mickey, made significant contributions to many of the programs.

Many statisticians have made contributions and suggestions for developing the programs: R.L. Anderson in regression and analysis of variance, David Andrews in robust techniques, Virginia Clark and Robert Elashoff in survival analysis, Robert Ling in the method of pictorially representing a matrix, and John Tukey in data analysis. Valuable comments have been received from Peter Claringbold, Cuthbert Daniel, Charles Dunnett, Ivor Francis, Don Guthrie, Henry Kaiser, Sir Maurice Kendall, H.L. Lucas, John Nelder, Shayle Searle and Frank Stitt. This list is incomplete. Many statisticians have visited HSCF, and/or have discussed the programs with us at conferences. Even the list of references, is, of necessity, incomplete.

This edition of the manual was prepared by Morton Brown while he was on leave from Tel-Aviv University. His preface acknowledges the many contributions to its preparation.

W. J. Dixon

Preface Two

This edition of the BMDP manual differs from the 1975 edition in its organization (it also contains new programs and expanded program options). In this edition we attempt to integrate an extensive discussion of most program features with examples of how they are used. There are 153 input/output examples, many of which are annotated. Our emphasis is on the use of the statistical techniques and not on the numerical results obtained -- therefore we explain the terms used in the results, but do not repeat the numerical answers in the discussion of the results.

The manual is written for new users of computer programs as well as for experienced statisticians. Chapter One gives an outline of the entire manual and a guide to its use. Chapter Two describes the scope of analytical techniques available, basic terminology and a short description of each program. In chapters four through seven we discuss the specifications common to many programs and explain how they are specified in Control Language. Chapters eight through nineteen are devoted to the individual programs. The programs are discussed in relation to the analyses they perform. Each program is extensively illustrated by annotated input/output examples. Difficult formulas and computational algorithms are provided in an appendix.

This revision is based on the 1975 BMDP manual and on writeups of the seven new programs added at this time. Sections 2.2 and 2.3, Chapter 3 and many of the computational procedures in Appendix A are from the previous edition. We are grateful to the program designers and programmers for this material. Otherwise, this edition is a complete revision of the 1975 BMDP manual -- the analysis, rather than the individual program, has become the focal point.

This revision could not have been completed without the support of many Health Sciences Computing Facility staff members. Jim Frane commented at length on each draft; he also wrote and rewrote the descriptions of P2V and P3V. Jacqueline Benedetti wrote the chapter on survival analysis (Chapter 19) and helped rewrite Chapter 11. W.J. Dixon and A. Forsythe made constructive comments on large portions of the manuscript. Peter Anderson, Steve Chasen, Onelio Clark, Laszlo Engelman, Mary Ann Hill, Robert Jennrich, Mary Ralston, Paul Sampson, Lee Youkeles and other staff members read and commented on different sections.

Ellen Sommers tested and retested the programs to document how the options work and prepared the examples in this manual. Betsy Carnahan edited the computer output to the form presented.

Throughout Lyda Boyer provided strong support with her expert technical editing, improved phrasing of sentences and concern about detail. Barbra Winter, Nancy Mitton and Betsy Potter expertly typed the many drafts of the manuscript and prepared the camera-ready copy.

Appendix D contains information on ordering both the BMD and BMDP programs and the computers on which they are available. Although the programs have been under test and development for some time we know difficulties may arise in their use; these difficulties should be reported to us as described in Appendix D. Your comments and criticisms about the programs and this manual will also be appreciated.

Morton B. Brown

1

INTRODUCTION

The BMDP computer programs are designed to aid data analysis by providing methods ranging from simple data display and description to advanced statistical techniques. Data are usually analyzed by an iterative "examine and modify" series of steps. First the data are examined for unreasonable values, graphically and numerically. If unreasonable values are found they are checked and, if possible, corrected. An analysis is then performed. This analysis may identify other inconsistent observations or indicate that further analyses are needed. The BMDP programs are designed to handle all steps in an analysis, from the simple to the sophisticated.

The BMDP programs are organized so the problem to be analyzed, the variables to be used in the analysis, and the layout of the data are specified in a uniform manner for all programs. This permits different analyses of the same data with only minor changes in the instructions.

This manual is arranged by the type of analysis appropriate to the data. Included are chapters on data description and screening, plotting, frequency tables, regression, analysis of variance, multivariate analysis, etc. Each chapter describes the programs that are available to do the analysis. In the introduction to each chapter the programs are described and contrasted with each other to indicate which is preferred for a specific analysis. Programs in other chapters are cross-referenced if they provide a similar function.

The programs are loosely classified into series:

     D: data description

     F: frequency tables

     R: regression analysis

     V: analysis of variance

     M: multivariate analysis

     L: life tables and survival analysis

     S: special (miscellaneous)

Many programs cross boundaries between two series. For example, multivariate regression belongs to both the multivariate (M) and regression (R) series.

Each program is identified by a three-character code; the first is P (from BMDP) and the last is the series classification. The middle character is assigned when the programming begins; it can be 1-9 or a letter. The order does not indicate increasing complexity, and some numbers do not appear.

For example, the program "Simple Data Description" is labelled P1D since it is the first program in the Descriptive series, and "Nonlinear Regression" is labelled P3R as the third program in the Regression series. Since programs in this manual are described by content, "Multivariate Regression" (P6R) is explained in the chapter on Multivariate Analysis with programs from the M-series.

New programs are continually being developed and released. The first edition of the BMDP manual (Dixon, 1975) contained 26 programs. Thirty-three programs are in this manual -- seven are new:

     P2F -- Two-way Frequency Tables -- Empty Cells and Departures
          from Independence

     P3F -- Multiway Frequency Tables -- the Log-linear Model

     PAM -- Description and Estimation of Missing Data

     P9R -- All Possible Subsets Regression

     PAR -- Derivative-free Nonlinear Regression

     P3V -- General Mixed Model Analysis of Variance

     P1L -- Life Tables and Survival Functions

In addition, all programs are reviewed and revised in response to suggestions from users, or to correct errors. For example:

     - P1F (Two-way Frequency Tables -- Measures of Association) has been
       rewritten to correct errors and to incorporate new formulas for
       the standard errors of measures of association.

- Correlation matrices can now be printed in shaded form (pictorially) in the factor analysis program (P4M) and in the cluster analysis program (P1M).
- Blanks can now be treated uniformly either as zeros or as missing values.

Major changes in the programs and novel ways to use them are documented in the newsletter, *BMD Communications*. Articles from *BMD Communications* that describe ways to use the programs are reprinted in Appendix C.

This manual describes the current status of the programs. Since your facility may have an earlier version of the programs, we use footnotes to indicate the changes made since the first BMDP manual (Dixon, 1975) was printed. Each footnote contains the effective date of the change and the correct usage of the program before that date. Each BMDP program prints a date in the upper right hand corner of the output. When the program date is earlier than the effective date of the change, the footnote applies.

The most extensive recent changes have been to reduce the abbreviation for certain words; for example, the minimum abbreviation for

    VARIABLE

is now   VAR

instead of   VARIAB

If the programs that you have are dated before August 1977, you need to specify longer forms for many words than we require in this manual. Footnotes indicate the minimum spelling used with earlier versions of the programs. A quick way to check for proper abbreviation is to go directly to the Summary for the program you are using: it describes the current usage, and footnotes describe previous (dated) usage.

1.1 A Guide to This Manual

The scope of the statistical analyses provided by the BMDP programs is discussed in Chapter 2. Section 2.1 introduces terms used throughout this manual and describes analytical features available in more than one program. The scope of the possible analyses with the BMDP programs is outlined in Section 2.2. Abstracts of the programs are given in Section 2.3.

For readers who are using a computer for the first time, Chapter 3 gives annotated examples of simple analyses, describes how to organize your data sheets (research forms), and describes the layout (format) of your data.

Features common to all BMDP programs (Chapters 4 through 7)

Chapter 4 describes an English-based Control Language used to describe the data and specify the analysis. *The terminology and notation used throughout this manual are defined here. We recommend that you read the definitions in Section 4.1 even if you are familiar with the BMDP programs.* The Control Language instructions used to describe the data and variables are presented in Chapter 5. Methods of transforming and editing data are treated in Chapter 6. Since an analysis often requires multiple steps, the data or results from one program can be saved in a BMDP (Save) File (Chapter 7) and then used in other programs. The use of a BMDP File eliminates a repetitious description of the data.

Program descriptions (Chapters 8 through 19)

Chapters 8 through 19 describe methods of analysis and the programs available to perform them. Each chapter begins with an introduction describing alternate methods and programs. This is followed by detailed descriptions of each program. (The features described in Chapters 4 through 7 are not repeated).

Each program description begins with a short introduction. This is followed by one or more examples that illustrate the simplest or most common usage of the program. Each example consists of the Control Language instructions that are required by the program and the results produced by the program. The instructions and results are labelled Example and Output respectively and are identified by the chapter number and a sequence number within the chapter. Numbers in circles (e.g., ① , ② ,...) are used to annotate the results; the numbers on the output correspond to circled numbers in the legend or the text.

A list of program options follows the example(s) with page references to where they are discussed. Each option is described; an example is provided for many of them.

The BMDP programs can analyze large amounts of data. Near the end of each program description a statement is made of the largest problem the program can analyze without modification. A more detailed formula for determining the size of problem the program can analyze is given in Appendix B. If your problem exceeds the limit, Appendix B also contains a description of the changes needed to analyze larger problems.

The last section in the program description states the formulas and algorithms that are described in greater detail in Appendix A. The more difficult formulas and computational procedures are collected in the appendix.

Each chapter concludes with a summary. The summary consists of tables that describe the Control Language instructions used in the programs, and provides short definitions and page references to explanations of the program options. *These tables can be used as indexes to the program descriptions.*

Useful aids

An index to the manual is included in the last few pages.

On the inside front cover the programs are listed by their three-character identification codes; page references are given to program descriptions and summaries.

On the inside back cover the Control Language common to all programs (and described in Chapters 4-7) is presented in summary form. Opposite the inside back cover, space is left for you to fill in the instructions necessary to begin an analysis on your computer (see Chapters 4-7).

We recommend

If you are using computers for the first time, we recommend that you start with Chapter 3. Then read Chapters 4 and 5 for a description of the Control Language. And finally, try one of the programs in Chapters 8, 9 or 10.

If you are not familiar with the BMDP programs, but have previously used a computer, we recommend that you read Chapter 2 (Sections 2.1 and 2.2) for an overview of the programs and Chapters 4 and 5 for a description of the Control Language before turning to the specific analysis you want to do.

If you are already familiar with the BMDP programs, but not with this manual, we recommend that you skim Chapter 4. If you are already familiar with the program to be used, turn to the summary for the program (see the list of programs inside the front cover); otherwise you can either turn to the chapter describing the type of analysis that you want to do, or to Chapter 2 for an overview of all the programs.

2

DATA ANALYSIS

Using the BMDP Programs

The meaning of "data analysis" is different for each of us, depending on our level of statistical training. Techniques used in data analysis vary from the simplest display of data in a histogram or a plot and the calculation of statistics (such as the mean and standard deviation) to advanced methods of multivariate analysis. To some, data analysis involves a single display or set of computations; to others it involves a sequence of steps, each of which can suggest further analyses.

The BMDP programs provide many analytical capabilities -- from elementary to advanced. In this chapter we

- describe features that are available in more than one
  program   p. 8
- outline the scope of available analytical techniques   p. 15
- give a short description for each program   p. 26

2.1 Basic Terminology — Common Features Available

Each BMDP program is designed to provide a certain analytical capability, such as data description, plots, or regression analysis. Some statistics, plots, or other results are provided by several programs.

In this section we describe some of the common features and introduce terminology that is used throughout this manual. Table 2.1 (p. 14) lists the features and identifies the programs that contain each feature.

● DATA AND ACCEPTABLE VALUES

Data are codes representing characteristics (e.g., sex, eye color), values of measurements (e.g., height, weight) or responses to questions. Each characteristic, measurement or response is called a variable. Each case contains values for all the variables for one subject, animal, or sampling unit. A case may represent such things as responses to questions, outcomes of tests or measurements made on a subject or test animal.

Some values in a case may not be recorded. A value that is not recorded may be left blank or may be recorded with a special code; the blank or special code, whichever is used, is called a missing value code and the unrecorded value is called a missing value. Missing values are excluded from all computations.

In any program you can restrict the analysis of a variable to a specified range by assigning an upper limit (maximum) and a lower limit (minimum) for values of the variables. A value that is greater than the upper limit or less than the lower limit is out of range and is excluded from all computations.

An acceptable value is one that is not equal to a missing value code and is not out of range. A complete case is a case in which the values of all the variables are acceptable (there are no values missing or out of range).

● CASES USED IN ANALYSIS

The treatment of cases depends on the primary purpose of the analysis. For example, P1D -- Simple Data Description -- computes statistics for each variable from all acceptable values for the variable; but P2R -- Stepwise Regression -- uses only complete cases to estimate the linear regression equation.

The BMDP programs include cases in an analysis according to one of three criteria:

    A All cases are included (all acceptable values for each variable are used)

    B Cases are included only if they have acceptable values for all variables specified in the analysis

    C Only complete cases are included (cases that have acceptable values for all variables)

The difference between the above criteria can be explained in terms of an example. Suppose we have three variables, each of which has some unacceptable values, and we request means for the first two variables only. Using Method A, the mean of each variable is computed from all its acceptable values, whether or not either of the other variables have acceptable values. By Method B the means of the first two variables are computed from data in only those cases that have acceptable values for both variables. Method C allows the means to be computed from cases that have acceptable values for all three variables.

Method C may use fewer cases than either of the other methods. You can specify a list of variables to be checked by Method C. Variables that are excluded from the list are not used in any of the computations (not even their means are computed). In Chapter 5 we describe how this list is specified.

The method used by each program is shown in Table 2.1. Three programs, P3D, P8D and PAM allow you to choose explicitly between methods. The cases to be used can be further restricted by case selection in all programs.

● TRANSFORMATIONS AND CASE SELECTION

Transformations can be used to replace the value of a variable by its transformed value; e.g., weight by the logarithm of weight. Also, new variables can be created from the observed variables by transformations. For example, if pulse rate is measured before and after exercise, the difference between the two measurements can be a meaningful quantity. This difference can be specified as a new variable and can be used in the analysis. Any number of new variables can be created as functions of the observed variables. These functions, called transformations, can involve simple arithmetical operations (e.g., +, -, ÷, ×), powers, trigonometric functions, etc.

You can also select cases to be used in an analysis (e.g., data for males or data for respondents in their twenties or both).

Methods of specifying transformations and case selection are described in detail in Chapter 6.

● CLASSIFYING CASES INTO GROUPS

Some analyses, such as a t test between two groups or a one-way analysis of variance, require that the cases be classified into groups. The variable whose values are used to classify the cases into groups is called a grouping variable. Groups can be identified as codes (such as, two codes for sex) or as intervals (such as, ages 10-19, 20-29, etc.).

In all programs you can select cases belonging to specific groups (fulfilling certain criteria) by case selection (Chapter 6). The purpose of some analyses is to compare groups, such as in a plot or by a t test or by an analysis of variance. In some programs you can explicitly specify groups to be analyzed (or plotted).

● UNIVARIATE STATISTICS

Most programs compute the mean, standard deviation and frequency for each variable. In addition, other univariate statistics are computed in several BMDP programs. We review the definitions of these statistics below.

Let $x_1, x_2, \ldots x_N$ be the observed (acceptable) values for a variable in the cases used in an analysis. Then N is the <u>sample size</u>, frequency or count for the variable. The mean, $\bar{x}$, is defined as

$$\bar{x} = \Sigma\, x_j/N$$

(Other estimates of location, such as the median and more robust estimates, are available in P2D and P7D.)

The standard deviation, s, is

$$s = [\, \Sigma\, (x_j - \bar{x})^2/(N - 1)]^{\frac{1}{2}}$$

The variance is s^2 and the standard error of the mean is $s/\sqrt{N}$.

The coefficient of variation is the ratio of the standard deviation to the mean, $s/\bar{x}$. If a variable has a very small coefficient of variation, loss of computational accuracy can result due to the limited accuracy with which a number can be represented internally in the computer.

Many analyses require that the distribution of the data be normal, or at least symmetric. A measure of symmetry is skewness, and a measure of long-tailedness is kurtosis. The BMDP programs compute skewness, g_1, as

$$g_1 = \Sigma\, (x_j - \bar{x})^3/(Ns^3)$$

and kurtosis, g_2, as

$$g_2 = \Sigma\, (x_j - \bar{x})^4/(Ns^4) - 3$$

If the data are from a normal distribution, the standard error of g_1 is $(6/N)^{\frac{1}{2}}$ and of g_2 is $(24/N)^{\frac{1}{2}}$. A significant nonzero value of skewness is an indication of asymmetry. A value of g_2 significantly greater than zero indicates a distribution that is longer-tailed than the normal.

The smallest observed (acceptable) value, x_{min}, and the largest, x_{max}, are printed by several programs. The range is $(x_{max} - x_{min})$. The smallest and largest standard scores (z-scores, z_{min} and z_{max} respectively) are also printed by some programs. We define z_{min} and z_{max} as

$$z_{min} = (x_{min} - \bar{x})/s \quad \text{and} \quad z_{max} = (x_{max} - \bar{x})/s$$

● COVARIANCES AND CORRELATIONS

Covariances and correlations are used in many statistical analyses. The covariance between two variables, x and y, is

$$\text{cov}(x,y) = \Sigma\, (x_j - \bar{x})(y_j - \bar{y})/(N - 1)$$

The correlation, r, between two variables is

$$r = \frac{cov(x,y)}{s_x \, s_y} = \frac{\Sigma \, (x_j - \bar{x})(y_j - \bar{y})}{[\Sigma \, (x_j - \bar{x})^2 \, \Sigma \, (y_j - \bar{y})^2]^{\frac{1}{2}}}$$

This is also called the product-moment correlation coefficient.

The correlation can also be computed after adjusting for the linear effect of one or more other variables. For example, we may want the correlation between x and y adjusted for z and w (sometimes referred to as correlation at a fixed value of z and w). This is called the partial correlation coefficient between x and y given z and w. It is equivalent to fitting separate regression equations in z and w to x and to y, and computing the correlation between the residuals from the two regression lines.

A multiple correlation coefficient (R) is the maximum correlation that can be attained between one variable and a linear combination of other variables. This is the correlation between the first variable and the predicted value from the multiple regression of that variable on the other variables. R^2 is the proportion of variance of the first variable explained by the multiple regression relating it to the other variables.

● PLOTS AND HISTOGRAMS

An assumption of normality is required by many analyses. The assumption can be assessed by a normal probability plot. The assumption of normality is usually not with respect to the data, but with respect to the residuals, the difference between the observed value and the value predicted by the statistical model. Many programs plot the residuals in a normal probability plot.

Scatter plots of one variable against another are useful in examining the relationships between the two variables; they are also useful in assessing the fit of a statistical model (such as regression). Scatter plots of the data and results are provided in many BMDP programs.

Histograms, or bar graphs, are a basic tool in data screening. They can be used to screen for extreme values or for the shape of the distribution of the data. Several BMDP programs plot histograms as part of their analyses.

Table 2.1 indicates which programs produce plots and histograms as part of their analyses. Chapter 10 describes two programs whose primary purpose is to provide plots and histograms in final form.

● PRINTING THE DATA AND RESULTS FOR EACH CASE

Many programs can list the data for each case. Some programs print results for each case, such as predicted values and residuals from a regression.

Several programs have special capabilities for listing the data:

- P1D can print only cases with missing values or only cases that have values out of range

- PAM can print, in a compressed list, the positions of the missing values and values out of range

- P4D can print cases that contain nonnumeric symbols

- P7D can print the data after sorting the cases according to one of the variables

- P2M and P4M can print standard scores for each case

● THE BMDP FILE

A set of data is usually analyzed many times by BMDP programs. For example, the data may first be examined for extreme values (outliers) and for distributional assumptions; then necessary transformations can be performed, meaningful hypotheses tested, or relationships between the variables studied. The results of an analysis may suggest that further analyses are needed.

All programs can read a data matrix as input. All programs (except P4D) can copy the data into a BMDP File. The BMDP File is a means of storing your data or results from an analysis so you can reuse them more efficiently in other BMDP programs; the File can be created or read by any BMDP program (except P4D). There are several advantages to using a BMDP File:

- data are read efficiently from a BMDP File; the cost of reading a large amount of data from a BMDP File is substantially less than when a format statement is used

- many of the Control Language instructions specified when the BMDP File is created need not be respecified for each additional analysis

- data are stored in the BMDP File after transformation and case selection are performed

- the BMDP File is the only way to store results (such as residuals from a regression analysis or a covariance matrix) so they can be analyzed further by other BMDP programs

Table 2.1 shows that all programs (except P4D) can save the data in a BMDP File. Many programs save results, such as predicted values or residuals. Some programs can also save a covariance or correlation matrix or some other matrix of results.

All programs but P4D accept data from a BMDP File (a BMDP File can be created by one program and read by a different program). Several regression and multivariate analysis programs accept the covariance or correlation matrix from a BMDP File.

- CASE WEIGHTS

Most statistical analyses assume that the error of each observation has a constant variance. When the variance is not constant, the computations of the mean, standard deviation and other statistics are best done by weighting each case by the inverse of the variance.

Case weights can also be used to represent the frequency of an observation when the same observation is made more than once but is recorded in only one case; however, except for the frequency table programs, the sample size will be the number of cases and not the sum of weights.

You can specify case weights in many BMDP programs. The effect of the case weight on the computation of the univariate statistics, covariance and correlation is described below.

Let w_j by the case weight for the jth case. Then

$$\bar{x} = \Sigma\, w_j x_j / \Sigma w_j$$

$$s = \{\Sigma\, w_j (x_j - \bar{x})^2 / [(N - 1)\, \Sigma w_j / N]\}^{\frac{1}{2}}$$

$$cov(x,y) = \Sigma\, w_j (x_j - \bar{x})(y_j - \bar{y}) / [(N - 1)\, \Sigma w_j / N]$$

$$r = \frac{\Sigma\, w_j (x_j - \bar{x})(y_j - \bar{y})}{\{\Sigma\, w_j (x_j - \bar{x})^2 \Sigma\, w_j (y_j - \bar{y})^2\}^{\frac{1}{2}}}$$

where N is the number of acceptable observations used in the analysis with positive (nonzero) weights.

When case weights are not specified, w_j is set to one for all cases and the formulas are identical to the formulas given on p. 10.

- COMPUTATIONAL ACCURACY

The computer represents each number by a binary representation of limited accuracy. As a result there can be a loss of accuracy in certain types of computation, such as matrix inversion. Loss of accuracy is especially pronounced if a variable has a small coefficient of variation ($s/\bar{x}$) or if a variable has a very high multiple correlation with other variables.

All programs represent data values in single precision. Most programs do computations in single precision. Several programs do computations in double precision (i.e., represent each number to more digits); these programs are the ones whose computations are most likely to be affected by a loss of accuracy if the computations are done in single precision.

Table 2.1   Features common to BMDP programs

Chapter → Program → (type)	8-1	8-2	8-4	9-3	9-7	9-9	10-5	10-6	11-1	11-2	11-3	12-8	12-A	13-1	13-2	13-9	13-4	13-5	14-3	14-A	15-1	15-2	15-3	16-3	17-1	17-2	17-3	18-4	18-6	18-7	19-1	6-1
(type code)	D	D	D	D	D	D	D	D	F	F	F	D	M	R	R	R	R	R	R	R	V	V	V	S	M	M	M	M	M	R	L	S
Cases used																																
A all cases (all acceptable values)	A	A	A	A	A	A	A	A	A	A	A	A	A															A				A
B cases with acceptable values for all var. specified in analysis (see p. 8)				B											B			B				B	B		B	B		B	B		B	
C complete cases only												C	C	C	C			C	C	C	C				C	C		C				
Analytic capabilities																																
T transformations and case selection	T	T		T	T	T	T	T	T	T	T	T	T	T	T	T	T	T	T	T	T	T	T	T	T	T	T	T	T	T	T	T
W case weights									W	W	W	W	W	W	W	W	W		W	W						W		W	W	W		
D double precision													D					D		D		D		D				D	D	D	D	
Univariate statistics																																
x̄ mean	x̄	x̄		x̄	x̄	x̄	x̄	x̄	x̄	x̄	x̄	x̄	x̄	x̄	x̄	x̄	x̄		x̄	x̄	x̄				x̄	x̄	x̄	x̄	x̄	x̄		x̄
x̃ other estimates of location		x̃		x̃																												
s standard deviation	s	s		s	s	s	s	s	s	s	s	s	s	s	s	s	s		s	s	s				s	s		s	s	s		s
v coefficient of variation	v													v	v	v	v											v	v	v		
g skewness and kurtosis		g												g		g	g											g	g			
m min. and max. of the acceptable values	m	m		m	m				m	m	m			m	m	m	m		m	m				m				m	m	m		m
z z-score for min. and max. values	z													z											z	z	z					
N number of cases (sample size)	N	N		N	N	N	N	N	N	N	N	N	N	N	N	N	N	N	N	N	N	N	N	N	N	N	N	N	N	N	N	N
G above statistics computed for each group				G	G	G	G	G						G	G						G	G								G	G	
Other statistics																																
r covariances and/or correlations				r	r				r					r	r	r	r	r							r	r		r	r	r		
p partial correlations																p												p		p		
R squared multiple correlation (R² or SMC)																R	R	R										R		R		
f frequency counts, for each val. or categ.	f	f	f								f	f	f	f													f					
% frequency counts, in %	%										%	%																				
λ eigenvalues and/or eigenvectors																λ				λ								λ	λ	λ		
G above statistics computed for each group				G	G				G	G		G	G	G	G	G																
Test statistics																																
F comparison of group means (t,F)				F	F	F													F	F	F			F						F		
V comparison of group variances				V	V	V																										
χ comparison of group or cell frequencies										X		X	X	X																		
D multivariate comparison of group means (T²,D²,λ,U)				D																										D		
Plots and graphical displays																																
H histograms	H			H	H				H																							
N normal probability plots											N			N	N	N	N	N	N	N									N			
S scatter plots of data										S				S								S						S	S			
R scatter plots of results														R	R	R	R	R	R	R								R	R	R		R
O other (see program description)	O				O					O															O	O	O					O
Prints for each case																																
D data (after transformations, if any)	D		D	D										D	D	D			D	D					D			D	D	D		D
S cases with special values	S		S											S																		
z standardized scores																									z			z				
R residuals and/or predicted values											R			R	R	R			R	R					R	R				R		
F factor, princ. comp. or canon. var. scores																				F								F	F	F		
M Mahalanobis distances				M										M			M											M	M			
O other (see program description)					O									O											O	O						O
BMDP File output																																
D data (after transformations, if any)	D	D		D	D	D	D	D	D	D	D	D	D	D	D	D	D	D	D	D	D	D	D	D	D	D	D	D	D	D	D	D
R results for each case as part of data														R	R	R			R	R								R	R	R		
G codes/cutpts. saved with data	G			G	G	G	G	G	G	G	G			G	G						G	G	G							G		
C correlation and/or covariance matrix														C	C	C												C	C			
O other (see program description)														O														O		O		
Input from BMDP File																																
D data	D	D		D	D	D	D	D	D	D	D	D	D	D	D	D	D	D	D	D	D	D	D	D	D	D	D	D	D	D	D	D
C correlation or covariance matrix														C	C	C												C	C			
O other (see program description)														O														O				
Input not from BMDP File																																
D data	D	D		D	D	D	D	D	D	D	D	D	D	D	D	D	D		D	D	D	D	D	D	D	D	D	D	D	D	D	D
O other (see program description)										O	O	O				O				O					O			O	O	O		

2.2 Scope of the Analytic Techniques

The breadth of techniques available in the BMDP programs is indicated by the chapter titles:

8. Data Description
9. Data in Groups -- Description, t Tests and One-Way Analysis of Variance
10. Plots and Histograms
11. Frequency Tables
12. Missing Values -- Patterns, Estimation and Correlation
13. Regression
14. Nonlinear Regression and Maximum Likelihood Estimation
15. Analysis of Variance and Covariance
16. Nonparametric Analysis
17. Cluster Analysis
18. Multivariate Analysis
19. Survival Analysis

In this section we describe some of these techniques in general terms, and explain when the techniques are useful (see also "First Steps", Appendix C.11). Specific program options are presented in the program descriptions. Some of the more advanced techniques, such as maximum likelihood estimation, are discussed only in the program descriptions.

● DATA SCREENING AND DESCRIPTION

The first step in an analysis is to examine the data for errors and for the appropriateness of assumptions to be used in the analysis (such as normality). If errors remain in the data they can cause a "garbage-in, garbage-out" analysis. Blunders or extreme outliers in the data may need to be removed to achieve a meaningful analysis. The data may need to be transformed to fit the various assumptions (constant variance, normality, etc.) required by the statistical model.

After the original data have been recorded, various descriptive characteristics of the data can be used to detect gross errors in the observations, in coding the data, in including inappropriate cases, etc. A good place to begin screening is to check for

- symbols or characters, such as letters where numbers should be (P4D counts all distinct characters for each column of data, one column at a time); many programs will not run if nonnumeric symbols are in the data used for analysis

- outliers or blunders (P2D can be used to obtain frequency counts for all distinct values of each variable)

Listing the cases by one of the methods described on p. 12 may also locate problems in the data.

● DATA IN GROUPS

In screening, you often need to examine groups (strata or subpopulations) of the data. Unusual data values that are masked in a total population may stand out when the data are separated into groups or strata. Some variables are easily coded into groups, such as sex (males=1, females=2). Continuous variables can be categorized by a grouping variable.

P7D is especially powerful for examining groups; it prints histograms (side-by-side for each group) and statistics for each group; it also provides a choice of one-way or two-way analysis of variance to check group differences. From this output you can identify extreme outliers, obtain an idea of the distribution of data within groups, and examine whether the assumption of normality is reasonable. Heteroscedasticity (lack of constant variance over groups) can also be observed and tested, and may indicate that the input data should be transformed.

An analysis of variance using P7D can indicate whether group differences are large enough to suggest that future analyses should be stratified. More information on group differences (both univariate and multivariate) can be obtained by using P3D. It yields t statistics, Hotelling's T^2 and Mahalanobis D^2 for each pair of groups; t statistics, based on both pooled and separate variance estimates, are printed in the output.

When the cases are classified by more than one grouping variable or factor, P9D (Multiway Description of Groups) can be used to compute cell frequencies, means and standard deviations. Grouping variables can be suppressed to obtain information about marginal cells. The program tests for the equality of cell frequencies and cell means and for homogeneity of cell variances. These tests are performed on all cells or on specified marginals.

● TRANSFORMATIONS

After screening and describing your data, you should be ready to make decisions regarding transformations. Although all programs can perform simple data transformations, you may need to use P1S, the multipass transformation program, for getting the data transformed and ready for further analyses. P1S can be used when your transformation requires more than one pass through the data; for example, if you want to standardize the data it would be easier to use this program than to write your own FORTRAN program. The transformed data can be put directly on a BMDP File ready for easy input into any other BMDP program.

● PLOTS AND HISTOGRAMS

Many research workers like to see their data in graphical form; <u>scatter plots</u>, for example, are a good way to present information concisely and clearly in final reports. Scatter plots that take advantage of known information can be designed to display unusual cases or outliers -- for example, to show whether or not an individual's systolic blood pressure level is higher than his diastolic level. A scatter plot of these two variables will show if the data coding is mistakenly reversed for some cases. Or in a plot of height versus weight, a case that has a height of 72 inches and 225 lbs. will clearly stand out if the height is mispunched as 52 inches.

A grouping variable can be used in P6D to indicate group membership in the scatter plots. If age is divided into groups by years -- less than or equal to 15, 16-35, 36-55 and over 55 -- the data for one group, for example the children, may stand out in a cloud of points by themselves, indicating they should be analyzed separately in later analyses. P6D can also perform a simple regression analysis for the data in a scatter plot. This analysis may indicate whether or not an analysis of covariance should be used later. Variables can be plotted against time of entry into a study to see if observations are independent, or if a drift over time is occurring.

P5D can print a histogram for all the data or for one or more groups, each identified by a different letter. You can specify the scales of the histogram to produce a histogram suitable for a final report.

Normality can be roughly checked by looking at histograms in P7D or P5D. P5D can also print a <u>normal probability plot</u> that provides a better assessment of normality and helps to identify outliers.

● FREQUENCY TABLES

<u>Cross tabulations</u> are frequently used as a form of final reporting to give a picture of the number of cases in specified categories (or cross-classifications). Tables can be formed from data or from cell frequencies. Tables can also be formed for each level of a third variable (such as separately for males and females). Twenty-three statistics appropriate for the analysis of contingency tables are available in P1F.

P1F can test whether rows are independent of columns using the frequencies in all cells. P2F can test the same hypothesis using any subset of the cells; for example, are rows independent of the columns for all cells, excluding the cells on the diagonal? P2F can also identify cells that contribute heavily to a significant chi-square test of independence.

Multiway frequency tables are formed and analyzed by P3F. A log-linear model can be fitted to the cell frequencies and the fit tested. P3F can be used to select an appropriate model for the data and to estimate the parameters of the model.

● MISSING VALUES

   All too often the data recorded are not complete and some values are missing. These missing values are usually left blank or coded by a special code called the "missing value code". Missing values, and usually extreme values that appear to be wrong, are excluded from an analysis.

   PAM lists cases containing missing values or data to be excluded from the analysis, and reports special patterns in the data. PAM can also estimate values to replace the missing value code (or excluded values) based upon the data present in the case.

   Most regression and multivariate analyses require complete cases; i.e., no missing or excluded values in any case. Many of these analyses can begin from a correlation or covariance matrix. Both PAM and P8D can estimate correlations using cases with some data missing; the correlation matrix can then be stored in a BMDP File and used as input to other programs, including those that require complete data. PAM insures that the resulting correlation matrix is numerically appropriate (positive semidefinite) for a regression or factor analysis; P8D allows you to choose between four methods to compute the correlations.

● REGRESSION

   A regression analysis studies the relationship between a dependent variable, y, and one or more independent variables, x_i. The linear least squares model with parameters or regression coefficients, β_i, can be written

$$y = \beta_0 + \beta_1 x_1 + \ldots + \beta_p x_p + e$$

   For simple linear regression (x_1 is the only independent variable in the model), P6D, P1R and P2R can be used. If there are several independent variables, P1R, P2R or P9R can be used to perform multiple linear regression analyses.

   P1R, P2R and P9R differ in three important respects:

   - the criterion for including independent variables in the multiple linear regression

   - the ability to repeat the analysis on subgroups of the cases and compare the subgroups

   - the residual analysis available

   P1R includes all the specified independent variables in the multiple regression equation. It computes a multiple linear regression on all the data and on groups or subpopulations. If grouping is requested, P1R first analyzes all cases combined and then analyzes each group separately. After all groups have been analyzed, the regression equations are tested for equality between groups.

   P2R computes the multiple linear regression in a stepwise manner. At each step it enters into the regression equation the variable that best helps to predict y or removes the least helpful variable. Several criteria are available for entering or removing variables from the equation (see P2R program description). A stepwise procedure is useful for identifying a good set of predictor variables (separating the most important variables from those that may not be necessary at all), and when sufficient preliminary information regarding the effectiveness of the independent variables is not available. In practical applications the stepwise procedure is often a satisfactory solution.

P9R identifies "best" subsets of independent variables in terms of a criterion such as R^2, adjusted R^2 or Mallows' C_p (described in P9R program description). It also identifies alternative good subsets of the independent variables. P9R computes only a small fraction of all possible regressions to find the numerically best subset.

All three programs print and plot residuals and predicted values. The plots are useful in detecting lack of linearity, heteroscedasticity (lack of constant variance), unusual outliers, gross errors, an unusual subpopulation that should be separated from the analysis, etc. The plots may also indicate that transformations of the data are necessary or that an inappropriate model was chosen.

The residual analysis in P9R is the most extensive of the three. P9R also allows easy cross-validation of the regression model by testing it on a subset of the cases excluded from the analysis.

The relation between an independent and a dependent variable may require terms with higher powers. The model for <u>polynomial regression</u> in P5R is

$$y = \beta_0 + \beta_1 x + \beta_2 x^2 + \ldots + \beta_k x^k + e$$

P5R reports polynomials of degree one through a specified degree; this helps to determine the highest-order equation necessary for an adequate fit of the data. As higher-order terms are introduced into the model, the fitted regression curve and the original data can be plotted at each step for a visual check on how the fit is proceeding.

- NONLINEAR REGRESSION

To fit a model where the equation is not linear in the parameters you can use the <u>nonlinear regression</u> programs, P3R and PAR. These are least squares programs appropriate for a wide variety of problems that are not well-represented by equations with linear parameters. Several different functions are available in P3R by simply stating a number, including such functions as sums of exponentials

$$p_1 e^{p_2 x_1} + p_3 e^{p_4 x_1},$$

ratios of polynomials, a combination of sine and exponential functions, etc. If you want a function different from those described in the P3R program description, you can request it by FORTRAN statements in P3R or PAR. In P3R you must also specify the function's partial derivatives.

● ANALYSIS OF VARIANCE AND COVARIANCE

Analysis of variance is used to test for differences between the means of two or more groups or subpopulations. In a simple <u>one-way analysis of variance</u> each individual (or subject) is classified into one category or group -- for example, in a medical problem patients could be assigned to treatment A, B or C. The patients are grouped by the type of treatment. The model for this one-way design is

$$Y_{ik} = \mu + \alpha_i + e_{ik}$$

where α_1, α_2 and α_3 might represent the effect of treatments A, B and C, respectively on the dependent variable, Y_{ik}, a blood pressure reading for case k in group i. Programs P7D, P9D, P1V and P2V can be used to test the hypothesis

$$H_o: \text{ all } \alpha_i = 0$$

that there is no difference between treatments. Group sizes may be unequal in all three of these programs. For each group, P7D presents side-by-side histograms that give an excellent visual picture of how the groups differ.

In the medical treatment example above, if the <u>covariate</u> x (age) also affects the dependent variable (blood pressure), the one-way model becomes

$$Y_{ik} = \mu + \alpha_i + \beta(x_{ik} - \bar{x}) + e_{ik}$$

P1V could be used to examine treatment effects after adjusting for the linear effect of age. P1V also allows multiple covariates. It prints an analysis of variance table with F tests for equality of slopes, zero slopes and equality of adjusted group means (which adjusts for the effect of the covariate) and a number of residual plots.

Several factors (or characteristics) may be involved in an analysis of variance model. In a two-way factorial analysis of variance, the individuals in each group are classified by two characteristics, such as sex and treatment. The model can be written

$$Y_{ijk} = \mu + \alpha_i + \eta_j + (\alpha\eta)_{ij} + e_{ijk}$$

Here the α_i's could be treatment effect, the η_j's sex effect and $(\alpha\eta)_{ij}$ a possible interaction between sex and treatment. P7D can be used to analyze these data. The accompanying histograms give additional information.

P2V handles general fixed effects analysis of variance and covariance models. This program allows repeated responses, such as measuring a subject's blood pressure every day for a week. The repeated responses are called <u>trial factors</u> or <u>repeated measures factors</u> and need not be statistically independent. In the blood pressure example above, time could be a seven-level trial factor (e.g., a subject's blood pressure could be recorded every day of the week). In P2V the usual analysis of variance factors, such as sex and treatment, are called <u>grouping factors</u> to distinguish them from trial factors. The models may have only trial factors, only grouping factors, or both. The groups can contain an unequal number of subjects, but data for each subject must include all observations over the trial factor (a blood pressure reading must be given for each day).

- NONPARAMETRIC STATISTICS

     If your data grossly violate the usual analysis of variance normality as-
sumptions, you could try two nonparametric tests in P3S -- the Kruskal-Wallis
one-way analysis of variance test, or the Friedman two-way analysis of variance test. Nonparametric tests such as the Mann-Whitney U test, the sign test
and the Wilcoxon signed rank test can also be computed with P3S. These tests
can be used when the researcher wants to avoid t test assumptions.

- CLUSTER ANALYSIS

     Although many research studies involve multivariate observations (many
variables observed for each case), sometimes little is known about the inter-
relations between variables, between cases, or between variables and cases.
In discussing screening and data description, we emphasized that groups or
subpopulations should be examined; however, problems often arise when groups
are not clearly defined or when it is difficult to see if the data are structured. Clustering is a good technique to use in exploratory or early data
analysis when you suspect that the data may not be homogeneous and you want to
classify or reduce the data into groups. Clustering performs a display function for multivariate data similar to graphs or histograms for univariate
data; it provides a multivariate summary -- a description of characteristics
of clusters instead of individual cases.

     Three different types of clustering can be performed by BMDP programs:
clusters of variables (P1M), clusters of cases (P2M), and clusters of both
cases and variables (P3M). After deciding which program is applicable to your
problem, other questions must be answered before running P1M or P2M: How will
you measure distances between objects (variables in P1M, cases P2M)? How will
you use the distances to amalgamate or group the objects into clusters? How
will you display the resulting clusters? The best answers to these questions
are still being developed; investigators have their own preferences as to
which distance measure or which amalgamation procedure is best. You may want
to try several options given in the program descriptions to see which one
provides the best results for your problem.

     In both P1M and P2M the clustering begins by finding the closest pair of
objects (in P1M, columns, or variables; in P2M, rows, or cases) according to
the distance matrix and combining them to form a cluster. The algorithm
continues, joining pairs of objects, pairs of clusters, or an object with a
cluster, until all the data are in one cluster. These clustering steps are
shown in the output cluster diagram, or tree. The correlation or distance
matrix can also be printed in shaded form to pictorially display the clusters.

     The programs discussed above look for variables to be clustered across
all cases or for cases to be clustered (by similarity) across all variables.
However, your data may include differences between cases that do not extend
across all the variables, or your variables may not cluster across all cases.
P3M allows some of the variables (columns) to be clustered as a subset of the
cases (rows) and vice versa. This clustering by both cases and variables is
represented by a data matrix in the form of a block diagram; rows and columns
are permuted and smaller blocks (submatrices) of similar values within the

larger block are outlined. This gives a good visual representation of patterns of like values in the data matrix and can be used as a multivariate histogram. P3M is best suited to treat categorical variables that take on a small number of values.

● MULTIVARIATE ANALYSIS

Cluster analysis is not appropriate for expressing complex functional relationships. For example, if you are interested in describing the inter-relations between your variables, factor analysis is better suited to your needs, and discriminant analysis provides functions of the variables that best separate cases into predefined groups.

Factor analysis

Factor analysis is useful in exploratory data analysis. It has three general objectives: to study the correlations of a large number of variables by clustering the variables into factors, such that variables within each factor are highly correlated; to interpret each factor according to the variables belonging to it; and to summarize many variables by a few factors. The usual factor analysis model expresses each variable as a function of factors common to several variables and a factor unique to the variable:

$$z_j = a_{j1}f_1 + a_{j2}f_2 + \ldots + a_{jm}f_m + U_j$$

where

z_j = the jth standardized variable

m = the number of factors common to all the variables

U_j = the factor unique to variable z_j

a_{ji} = factor loadings

f_i = common factors

The number of factors, m, should be small and the contributions of the unique factors should also be small. The individual factor loadings, a_{ji}, for each variable should be either very large or very small so each variable is associated with a minimum number of factors.

To the extent that this factor model is appropriate for your data, the objectives stated above can be achieved. Variables with high loadings on a factor tend to be highly correlated with each other, and variables that do not have the same loading patterns tend to be less highly correlated. Each factor is interpreted according to the magnitudes of the loadings associated with it. The original variables may be replaced by the factors with little loss of information. Each case receives a score for each factor; these factor scores are computed as:

$$f_i = b_{i1}z_1 + b_{i2}z_2 + \ldots + b_{ip}z_p$$

where b_{ij} are the factor score coefficients. Factor scores can be used in later analyses, replacing the values of the original variables. Under certain circumstances these few factor scores are freer from measurement error than the original variables, and are therefore more reliable measures. The scores express the degree to which each case possesses the quality or property that the factor describes. The factor scores have mean zero and standard deviation one.

There are four main steps in factor analysis: first, the correlation or covariance matrix is computed; second, the factor loadings are estimated (initial factor extraction); third, the factors are rotated to obtain a simple interpretation (making the loadings for each factor either large or small, not in-between); and fourth, the factor scores are computed. P4M provides several methods for initial factor extraction and rotation. You can specify the methods to be used or P4M will use preassigned options. The results can be presented in a variety of plots.

Canonical correlation analysis

Canonical correlation analysis (P6M) examines the relationship between two sets of variables, and can be viewed as an extension of multiple regression analysis or of multiple correlation. Multiple regression deals with one dependent variable, Y, and p independent variables, X. The regression problem is to find a linear combination of the X variables that has maximum correlation with Y. In canonical correlation there is more than one dependent Y variable -- there is a set of them. The problem is to find a linear combination of the X variables that has maximum correlation with a linear combination of the Y variables. This correlation is called the canonical correlation coefficient. A second pair of linear combinations, with maximum correlation between the linear combinations and zero correlations with the first pair of linear combinations is found. The number of pairs of linear combinations of the X and Y sets is equal to the number of variables in the smaller set (X or Y). The technique can be used to test the independence of two sets of variables, or to predict information about a hard-to-measure set of variables from a set that is easier to measure. It can also be used to relate a combination of outcome measures to a combination of history or baseline measures. The original and canonical variables can be plotted one against the other in scatter plots.

Partial correlations and multivariate regression

Partial correlations can be computed in P6R; the correlation between each pair of dependent variables is computed after taking out the linear effect of the set of independent variables. For example, if you want to do a factor analysis on several variables (systolic blood pressure, diastolic blood pressure, blood chemistry measurements, income, etc.) but want to remove the linear effect of two variables (age and weight) from the measurements, you can state that the two variables (age and weight) are independent variables and the rest are dependent variables. The resulting partial correlation matrix (of the dependent variables with the effects of age and weight removed) can be stored as a matrix in a BMDP File, and can be used as input in P4M, the factor analysis program.

P6R can be used to regress a number of dependent variables on one set of independent variables. This multivariate regression program gives you a separate regression equation for each dependent variable, squared multiple correlation (R^2) of each independent variable with all other independent variables, R^2 of each dependent variable with the set of independent variables, and tests of significance of multiple regression.

Discriminant analysis

In discriminant analysis, the cases or subjects are divided into groups and the analysis is used to find classification functions (linear combinations of the variables) that best characterize the differences between the groups. These functions are also useful for classifying new cases.

P7M, the stepwise discriminant analysis program, is used to find the subset of variables that maximizes group differences. Variables are entered into the classification function one at a time until the group separation ceases to improve notably (this is similar to the stepwise regression program, P2R, used to find a good subset of variables for prediction). P7M is also used as a multivariate test for group differences (or multivariate analysis of variance); Wilks' lambda (U statistic) and the F approximation to lambda are printed at each step of the output for testing group differences.

A geometrical interpretation of discriminant analysis can be given by plotting each case as a point in a space where each variable is a dimension (has an axis). The points are projected onto a plane or hyperplane selected so the groups are farthest apart, giving a good visual representation of how distinct the groups are (for two groups, the points (cases) are projected onto a line where the groups are farthest apart). P7M presents plots that show such a plane. The X axis is the direction where the groups have the maximum spread; the Y axis shows the maximum spread of the groups in a direction orthogonal to the X axis - this is a plot of the canonical variables.

The canonical variables are related to canonical correlation analysis, which finds the linear combinations of the two sets of variables that are most highly correlated. The first set contains the variables in the classification function; the second set can be viewed as dummy variables used to indicate group membership. The value of the first canonical variable of the classification function set is plotted on the X axis; the value of the second on the Y axis. The coefficients for these canonical variables appear in the output. The coefficients for the second set (dummy variables) do not appear in the output. The eigenvalues and canonical correlations for all canonical variables and the canonical variable scores associated with the first and second canonical variables are also reported.

At each step, P7M uses a one-way analysis of variance F statistic (F-to-enter) to determine which variable should join the function next. At step zero, the standard univariate analysis of variance test is made for each of the variables. The variable for which the means differ most is entered first into the classification function. After step zero, the computed F-to-enter values are conditioned on the variables already present in

the function. This is like an analysis of covariance, where the previously
entered variables can be viewed as covariates and the nonentered variables
are each considered as a dependent variable.

At each step after a variable is entered, the classification functions
are recomputed including the newly entered variable. The number of classification functions is equal to the number of groups. If you have six groups,
the value of all six functions are computed for each case and the values are
used to compute the posterior probability; each case is assigned to the
group in which the value of the posterior probability is maximum. In multiple
group discriminant analysis, one function is sometimes stated in the liter-
ature for separating each pair of groups. To get this function from P7M,
you subtract the classification function coefficients of the first member
from those of the second. At each step, F statistics (the F matrix) that test
the equality of means between each pair of groups are given. These F statistics are proportional to Hotelling's T^2 and the Mahalanobis' D^2 and give an
indication of which group means are closest together and which are farthest
apart. After all variables have been entered, the program lists the
Mahalanobis' D^2 from each case to the center of each group, and the posterior
probability of the case assigned to each group. These two bits of information present a good picture of how well (or how poorly) each case has been
classified.

The discriminant analysis procedure is successful if few cases are
classified into the wrong group. If a large percentage of the cases are
classified correctly (if the posterior probability assigns them to their
original group) you know that group differences do exist and that you have
selected a set of variables that exhibit the differences. The P7M output
presents this classification information in a table of counts indicating
how many cases from each original group are assigned to each of the possible
groups. A pseudo-jackknife classification table is also printed: for each
case a classification function is computed with the case omitted from the
computations. The function is then used to classify the omitted case.
This results in a classification with less bias. (A classification function
can produce optimistic results when it is used to classify the same cases
that were used to compute it.)

● SURVIVAL ANALYSIS

The techniques described in this chapter are appropriate when outcome
measurements represent the time to occurrence of some event or response
(e.g., survival time, or time to disease recurrence). What distinguishes
the techniques of this chapter from other statistical methodology is the
ability to handle censored (incomplete) data; that is, there are cases for
which the response is not observed but the data (time in study) are included
in the analysis. This could occur in a study of survival, where an individual
remains alive at the close of the observation period or drops out before
the end.

P1L estimates the survival (time-to-response) distribution of individuals observed ober varying time periods. These estimates can be obtained
separately for different groups of patients; the equality of the distributions
for these groups can be tested by two nonparametric rank tests. Plots of the
survival, hazard and related functions can be printed.

2.3 Short Descriptions of the BMDP Programs

- ● DATA DESCRIPTION

P1D Simple Data Description: P1D computes univariate statistics, lists all data or lists selected cases (those containing missing values or values outside minimum or maximum limits) and stores the data in a BMDP File.

    For each variable, the output includes mean, standard deviation, standard error of mean, coefficient of variation, largest and smallest values, largest and smallest standardized scores (z-scores), range, and the total number of acceptable values. You can specify codes (values) or intervals (categories) for a variable; for each such variable P1D prints the number of cases with each code or in each interval.

P2D Detailed Data Description, Including Frequencies: P2D counts and lists distinct values of each variable in ascending order, and computes univariate statistics. Values of variables may be truncated or rounded by different amounts for different variables. All computations are performed on the truncated or rounded values.

    For each variable, the program prints the number of acceptable values; the maximum, minimum, range, half of the interquartile range, mean, median, mode, standard deviation, standard error of the mean, skewness and kurtosis. The computed statistics are printed on a line plot (130 characters long); a histogram is also printed. For each distinct value, the number of cases with each value, the percent of the cases counted that this number represents and the cumulative percent of cases with values $\leq$ each distinct value are printed. Optional output includes three new location estimates.

P4D Single Column Frequencies -- Numeric and Nonnumeric: P4D counts the characters (symbols) found in single column fields. The program assumes that a single column field is read for each variable in A1 format. All keypunch characters are considered legal, and the frequency of each is counted separately. P4D can be used to list the data after certain characters are replaced by specified symbols (e.g., numbers replaced by blanks). This is useful for preliminary data screening, verifying appropriate coding, and verifying (at least roughly) the kinds of data present.

- ● DATA IN GROUPS -- DESCRIPTION, t TEST AND ONE-WAY ANALYSIS OF VARIANCE

P3D Comparison of Two Groups with t Tests: P3D computes one-sample and two-sample t tests and their associated probability levels. Crude histograms, showing case distributions, are presented with each test. You can specify a grouping variable that classifies the cases into groups. If there are more than two groups the program computes two-sample t tests for each pair of groups; tests are computed for both pooled and separate variance estimates. Equality of group variances is tested. If several variables are analyzed, Mahalanobis D^2 and Hotelling's T^2 can be requested.

A one-sample t test ($H_0:\mu=0$) is computed when there is no grouping variable. A one-sample t test ($H_0:\mu=\mu_0$) or a matched pair t test may be performed.

The output includes means, standard deviations, standard error of means, maximums and minimums for each group. An F value for comparison of variances, pooled and separate t values, and two-tailed probability values for each t and F are also printed.

P7D   Description of Groups (Strata) with Histograms and Analysis of Variance: P7D groups the data into a specified number of groups based on the value of a grouping variable. For each variable the program prints histograms for each group, side by side. The number of intervals in the histograms can be specified or computed by the program. Mean, standard deviation, and frequencies are reported for each group and for all groups combined. A one-way or two-way analysis of variance is computed. Selected values for each variable can be excluded from the computations by specifying missing value codes, maximums or minimums; however, these values are displayed separately in the histogram.

Optional output includes a listing of input data after transformations or after ordering from low to high on a specified variable; correlations for each group separately and for all groups combined; and Winsorized means and 95% confidence intervals for the Winsorized means for each group.

P9D   Multiway Description of Groups: P9D provides cellwise descriptive statistics for cases when the data are classified simultaneously by several grouping variables. The program gives cell frequencies, means and standard deviations for each variable described. If requested the program yields the same information for specified marginal cells. P9D computes a chi-square test for equality of all cell frequencies, an F test for equality of all cell means (using only nonempty cells) and Bartlett's test for homogeneity of variances (using all cells with nonzero variance).

For each variable described, the program also prints a profile plot indicating how cell means shift from cell to cell. In these plots the numbers printed in the plot indicate cell frequencies; the location of the numbers indicates the deviation of cell means from the grand mean in standard deviation units.

- PLOTS AND HISTOGRAMS

P5D   Histograms and Univariate Plots: P5D prints histograms and other univariate plots. For each plot, cases belonging to one or more groups can be used. In the plots, cases from different groups can be identified by distinct letters. Plots can be printed for all groups in one plot or for each group individually. The size of the plots can be specified.

One or more of the following plots are printed for a variable: a histogram or a cumulative histogram with frequencies and percentages in each interval, a normal probability plot, a half-normal probability plot, or a cumulative distribution plot. The total frequency count, mean and standard deviation (for each group in a plot) are printed.

P6D   <u>Bivariate (Scatter) Plots</u>:   P6D prints bivariate scatter plots. Cases belonging to one or more groups can be used for each plot. The plots may have frequencies plotted for each point, or distinct letters may be used to indicate group membership. Plots can be printed for all groups in one plot or for each group in separate plots. Plots can be superimposed one on the other. You can control the size of the plots, and can request that the regression equations for regressing X on Y and Y on X be printed; inter-sections of the regression lines with the plot frame are indicated.

Optional statistics printed for each plot (for cases used in the plot) are: mean and standard deviation for each variable; equation of simple linear regression for each variable on the other variable with their residual mean square, correlation and frequency of cases.

● FREQUENCY TABLES

P1F   <u>Two-Way Frequency Tables -- Measures of Association</u>:   P1F prints a variety of two-way tables and provides estimates of many measures of association and prediction.   The tables can contain observed frequencies; expected values under independence; percentages of the table total, of each row total or of each column total; or several types of residuals. Tests and statistics that can be computed for each two-way table are: tests of independence and related measures (χ^2 test, the likelihood ratio chi-square test G^2, ϕ, the contingency coefficient and Cramer's V); tests of independence appropriate only for 2x2 tables (Fisher's exact test and Yates' corrected χ^2); measures of association appropriate for a 2x2 table (Yule's Q and Y, the cross-product ratio and the tetrachoric correlation r_t); measures of association and correlation when the categories of both factors are ordered (Goodman and Kruskal Γ, Kendall's τ_b, Stuart's τ_c, the product-moment correlation r and the Spearman rank correlation); predictive measures when the categories of both factors are ordered (Somers' D); predictive measures when either or both factors are qualitative (the Goodman and Kruskal τ, λ and λ^* and the uncertainty coefficient); McNemar's test of symmetry; and a test of a contrast on the proportions in a 2xk table. Standard errors are provided for many of the measures of association and prediction.

P2F   <u>Two-Way Frequency Tables -- Empty Cells and Departures from Independence</u>: P2F treats two special problems: First, you can exclude cells from the frequency table, such as cells with a prior probability of zero (structural zeros). P2F computes the appropriate test of independence between rows and columns (the χ^2 test of quasi-independence). This test uses all cells that are not excluded a priori and is identical to the usual χ^2 test when there are no excluded cells. Second, you can identify cells or patterns of cells that contribute to a departure from independence or quasi-independence; i.e., contribute greatly to a significant χ^2 test. You can select a criterion by which cells are identified and eliminated (treated as excluded) from the table in a stepwise manner. One such criterion is to eliminate the cell that, when excluded, minimizes the χ^2 (or likelihood ratio χ^2) test of quasi-independence performed on all cells not previously excluded. Inferences can be drawn from the data by examining the pattern of cells eliminated by this procedure.

P2F computes only the χ^2 tests of independence (or quasi-independence), expected values assuming independence, and various types of residuals. It does not provide estimates of the measures of association and prediction that are available in P1F.

P3F Multiway Frequency Tables -- The Log-Linear Model: P3F analyzes data in a multiway table. The purpose of the analysis is to obtain a description of the relationships between the factors of the table, either by forming a model for the data or by testing and ordering the importance of the interactions between the factors. The analysis is based on fitting a (hierarchical) log-linear model to the cell frequencies; that is, the logarithm of the expected cell frequency is written as an additive function of main effects and interactions in a manner similar to the usual analysis of variance model. It should be noted that the various tests for the interactions are not independent. If a two-way table were input to P3F, one possible log-linear model would include two main effects and a single interaction. The test that the interaction is zero is identical to the test for independence obtained in P1F.

You can use P3F to find an appropriate model for the data in the table by fitting specified models or by using a method to screen effects. The program tests the appropriateness of models by the likelihood ratio χ^2 (G^2) and by the usual χ^2 goodness-of-fit.

P3F prints the table of observed frequencies and can print marginal tables of the observed frequencies as well. It can test certain classes of models or specified models. For each specified model it can print the expected values and two types of residuals, estimates of the parameters of the model and their standard errors, and tests-of-fit of models that differ from the specified model by one effect.

● MISSING VALUES -- PATTERNS, ESTIMATION AND CORRELATIONS

P8D Missing Value Correlation: P8D computes correlations four different ways from data containing missing values. These computations use different cases in computing means and variances. Computations can be performed using all acceptable values -- the means are computed from all acceptable values and then deviations from these means are used to compute covariances and correlations; all acceptable pairs of values for covariances -- each element of the covariance matrix is computed from the existing pairs of values involved, which are then used to compute the correlations; all acceptable pairs of values for correlations -- each element of the correlation matrix is computed from the acceptable pairs of values involved; or all complete cases -- cases with any excluded values are not used.

Any or all of the first three types or the fourth type can be requested for each problem. Case weights may also be specified. The correlation matrix can be saved in a BMDP File and used as input to other programs. P8D can also be used to obtain a submatrix of the correlation matrix.

The output can include the mean and variance of each variable, a frequency table of acceptable values for pairs of variables, the covariance matrix, the correlation matrix, the sum of weights, the matrix of means and the matrix of variances.

PAM   Description and Estimation of Missing Values: PAM describes the pattern of missing values for multivariate data and provides estimates of the missing data.   Estimates can be means; predicted values for each missing variable derived from regressing it on the available variable with which it is most highly correlated; predicted values for each missing variable derived from its stepwise regression on some of the available variables; and predicted values for each missing variable derived from regressing it on all available variables.   The covariance matrix can be computed using complete cases only, or using all acceptable values. When the latter method is used or explicitly requested, the eigenvalues are found, and the correlation matrix is reestimated using only positive eigenvalues and their eigenvectors.   A grouping variable and case weights can be specified.   The covariance matrix and the data with estimates replacing the missing values can be saved in a BMDP File.   The matrix of pairwise frequencies of variables can also be saved and analyzed in other BMDP programs (such as factor analysis program, P4M) to further study the pattern of missing values.

PAM can print the data, the pattern of missing data, squared multiple correlations of each variable with all other variables, missing data estimates and Mahalanobis' distances for each case to the centroid of all cases, bivariate plots for specified pairs of variables, the correlation matrix, eigenvalues of the correlation matrix, and the covariance matrix.   Bivariate scatter plots can be requested for any pair of variables.   In these plots estimated values are distinguished from the original values.

For each variable in each group PAM prints the sample size, percentage missing, mean, standard deviation, coefficient of variation, maximum, minimum, maximum standard score, minimum standard score, skewness and kurtosis.

- REGRESSION

P1R   Multiple Linear Regression: P1R computes a multiple linear regression equation on all data and on groups or subsets of the data; equations with or without an intercept can be chosen.   If a grouping variable is specified to form groups, homogeneity of regression coefficients across groups is tested.   It is also possible to specify case weights.

For all data and all requested groups, the output includes mean, standard deviation, minimums and maximums, multiple R, and standard error of estimates for each variable; an analysis of variance table consisting of regression and residual sum of squares, degrees of freedom and mean squares; F statistic and probability for the regression equation; and the regression coefficients, their standard errors, and t statistics and probabilities. You can request the covariance or correlation matrix; scatter plots, normal and detrended normal probability plots of residuals, and partial residual plots; residuals, predicted values and data for each case.

P2R   Stepwise Regression: P2R estimates the parameters of multiple linear regression equations in a stepwise manner.   Four stepping algorithms are available.   Variables can be forced into the regression equation; nonforced variables can be directed in their order of entry by assigning them to different levels.   Regression equations with or without an intercept can be chosen, or the intercept can be treated as though it were an independent variable, in which case it enters the regression equation only if it is significant.   Both forward and backward stepping are possible.

Output includes the mean and standard deviation of each variable. The covariance or correlation matrix can be printed. For each step an analysis of variance table and multiple correlation is printed, and if requested, coefficients, standardized coefficients, standard errors, F ratios, partial correlations and tolerance. Other optional output includes summary tables for F ratios, partial correlations and coefficients; predicted values, residuals and data for each case; scatter plots of predicted and observed values versus selected variable values, residuals versus selected variables, and normal probability plots of residuals.

P9R   All Possible Subsets Regression: P9R identifies "best" subsets of predictor variables. Best is defined in terms of the sample R-squared, adjusted R-squared, or Mallows' C_p. For example, if adjusted R-squared is chosen, the best subset is the subset that maximizes adjusted R-squared. Note that best is defined as numerically best in terms of the observed sample and that (as for stepwise regression) no implication is made that any subset can be considered best for the population from which the sample was taken. However (as for stepwise regression) a well-chosen subset for one sample is likely to be good for similar samples.

The number of best subsets can be specified; up to ten can be requested. Thus, not only the best but also the second best, third best, etc. subsets are identified to provide several good alternatives. When M best subsets are requested, the R-squared criterion requests that the M best subsets of each subset size be determined. When the adjusted R-squared or Mallows' C_p criterion is chosen, the M best subsets are found regardless of subset size. For example, if ten best subsets are requested for 20 independent variables, the best subsets might not include any subsets of size one or twenty.

The algorithm used identifies the best subsets while computing only a small fraction of all possible regressions and is substantially more efficient than previously available algorithms. Input can be data or a correlation or covariance matrix. For up to approximately 27 variables, computer costs are comparable to costs for stepwise regression.

The output from P9R includes means, standard deviations, coefficients of variation, minimums, maximums, minimum standard scores, maximum standard scores, skewness and kurtosis, correlation matrix, covariance matrix, and bivariate plots for any pair of variables. For each of the M best subsets, the selection criterion, regression coefficients and F ratio are printed. For the best subset P9R prints R-squared, F ratio and significance; regression coefficients, standardized coefficients, standard errors, t tests, significance and tolerance; predicted values, residuals, weighted residuals, standardized residuals, deleted residuals, and Cook's measure of the influence of each case on the regression equation. Bivariate scatter plots can be requested for any pair of variables including residuals, standardized residuals, etc. A normal probability plot for the standardized residuals can be printed.

P4R   Regression on Principal Components: P4R computes a regression analysis for each dependent variable on a set of principal components computed from the independent variables.   The principal components are computed from the original variables (using the covariance matrix) or the standardized variables (using the correlation matrix).   The regression analysis is performed in a stepwise manner and the resulting coefficients are reported in terms of both principal components and the original or standardized variables.   The order of entry of components can be based on the magnitude of eigenvalues or on the absolute magnitude of correlation between the component and the dependent variable.

Output includes means, standard deviations, the covariance matrix, (the correlation matrix if standardization is requested), eigenvalues and eigenvectors (principal components), regression coefficients for principal components and for independent variables, residual sum of squares and F ratios for each step in the regression, and F ratios for each component. You may request principal component scores, scatter plots of raw data, and normal and detrended normal probability plots of residuals.

P5R   Polynomial Regression: P5R fits a polynomial in one variable to the dependent variable.   Computation is done using orthogonal polynomials.   The program reports polynomials of degree one through a degree specified by the user ($\leq$ 15).   Estimates of the regression coefficients and their standard errors are reported.   A summary table of goodness-of-fit statistics for each (except the highest degree) polynomial is printed.   For each degree a scatter plot of the predicted and observed values versus the independent variable, and residual versus the independent variable may be requested. You may also request normal and detrended normal probability plots of the residuals, the residuals listed with the data and predicted values, and a correlation matrix for the regression coefficient estimates.

● NONLINEAR REGRESSION AND MAXIMUM LIKELIHOOD ESTIMATION

P3R   Nonlinear Regression: P3R obtains a least squares fit to a nonlinear function.   It is appropriate for a wide variety of problems that are not well-represented by equations that are linear in the parameters.   Five of the most frequently used nonlinear functions are available by simply stating their code number.   Other functions can be used by stating the function and its derivatives in FORTRAN statements.   The fit is obtained by means of Gauss-Newton iterations.   Linear equality constraints on the parameters can be stated, and case weights can be used.   Parameters can also be estimated by maximum likelihood.

After each iteration the parameter values and residual sum of squares are printed.   After the last iteration the program reports the asymptotic correlations and standard deviations for the estimated parameters.   For each case after the last iteration, P3R lists the predicted and observed values for the dependent variable, residual value, and observed values for the independent variables.   You can request scatter plots of predicted and observed values versus selected variable values, residuals versus selected variables, and normal and detrended normal probability plots of residuals.

PAR   Derivative-free Nonlinear Regression: PAR computes least square estimates
of parameters in nonlinear regression. The program is used with regression
functions for which analytical expressions for the derivatives are not
provided. An iterative pseudo-Gauss-Newton algorithm is used to compute
the parameter estimates. You can specify case weights, inequality constraints on arbitrary linear combinations of parameters, and parameters to
be held fixed at initial values. Parameters can also be estimated by maximum likelihood.

After each iteration the parameter values and residual sum of squares
are printed. After the last iteration the program reports the asymptotic
correlations and standard deviations for the estimated parameters. For
each case after the the last iteration, PAR lists the predicted and observed
values for the independent variables. You can request scatter plots of
predicted and observed values versus selected variable values, residuals
versus selected variables, and normal and detrended normal probability plots
of residuals.

● ANALYSIS OF VARIANCE AND COVARIANCE

P1V   One-way Analysis of Variance and Covariance: P1V performs a one-way analysis
of variance, or a one-way analysis of covariance if covariates are specified.
Group sizes can be unequal and parallel analyses can be performed using
several dependent variables. The program tests for equality of slopes from
group to group and computes t statistics for contrasts of adjusted group
means including, in particular, all pairwise differences. The analysis of
covariance is accompanied by four types of graphs for each group: scatter
plots of each covariate versus the dependent variable and its predicted
values, each covariate versus the residuals, the residual versus the predicted values, and the squared residuals versus the predicted values.

Output from the analysis of variance on each variable includes the group
means, an analysis of variance table, pairwise t tests for group means and
t tests for contrasts of group means. For analysis of covariance on each
dependent variable P1V reports regression coefficients, their standard errors
and t values, group means, adjusted group means, standard errors of adjusted
group means, an analysis of variance table with F test for equality of adjusted group means, zero slope, equality of slopes, pairwise t test for adjusted group means, t tests for contrasts of adjusted group means, and
regression coefficients for each covariate in each group. You can also
request the correlation matrix for the regression coefficients and the
adjusted group means, maximum, minimum and mean of each variable in each
group, variance-covariance matrix, correlation matrix for each group, and
total between and within variance-covariance matrices.

P2V   Analysis of Variance and Covariance, Including Repeated Measures: P2V is
used to perform analyses of variance or covariance for general fixed
effects and repeated measures models. For each subject in repeated
measures models, the trial factors (repeated measures factors, for which
each subject is measured at each level) must have a complete factorial
structure with no missing observations. Group indices are read as data and

determine the group memberships without further specification. P2V
also handles models that contain trial factors only or grouping factors
only.

Within-subject responses need not be independent, but between-subject
responses are assumed to be. All factors, except subjects, are assumed
fixed. An orthogonal decomposition of the trial effects can be requested.
Covariates may be (but need not be) constant across trials. Unequal cell
sizes are allowed. Several distinct hypotheses can be tested, depending
on your problem. The hypotheses tested in this program are generally appropriate for experimental data.

Output includes an analysis of variance table consisting of sums of
squares, degrees of freedom, mean squares, and F statistics (with probability
values associated with each), cell means and standard deviations for the
dependent variable and covariates, adjusted cell means and regression coefficients (when covariates are present), and design information.

P3V   General Mixed Model Analysis of Variance: P3V performs a general mixed
model analysis of variance or covariance by means of maximum likelihood.
Each term of the model is given explicitly by means of a covariate index
or a set of grouping variables to denote a fixed or random ANOVA component.
Quite arbitrary unbalance is permitted, which includes (depending on the
design) missing cells.

Output from P3V includes estimates and standard deviations of the fixed
effects parameters and variance components, log-likelihood values for the
complete model and specified restricted models, variance-covariance matrix
of the parameters, predicted cell means and their standard deviations,
variance-covariance matrix of predicted cell means, pairwise tests for
equality of predicted cell means, and residual analysis including standardized residuals.

● NONPARAMETRIC STATISTICS

P3S   Nonparametric Statistics: P3S computes one or more of the following nonparametric statistics from a given set of data: sign test, Wilcoxon
signed-rank test, Kendall rank correlation coefficient, Spearman rank
correlation coefficient, Friedman two-way analysis of variance, Kendall
coefficient of concordance, Mann-Whitney U rank sum test, and Kruskal-
Wallis one-way analysis of variance.

● CLUSTER ANALYSIS

P1M   Cluster Analysis of Variables: P1M clusters similar variables by using an initial measure of association between pairs of variables (e.g., correlation) to form a cluster of the two most similar variables and then using an amalgamation (linkage) rule to form further clusters. The amalgamation rule determines the degree of association between any two clusters; a cluster consists of one or more variables. When the clustering process is finished each cluster consists of two or more variables and each variable is placed in one or more clusters. You may specify both the measure of association for the variables and the amalgamation rule for the clusters. P1M accepts a data matrix or a distance matrix (measure of association) as input.

Output includes a summary table for the clustering process, a tree diagram of clusters superimposed over a similarity or distance matrix scaled from 0 to 100, a table of similarity or distance matrix scaling, and an explanation of the tree diagram for the first problem. The correlation matrix can also be represented in shaded form after rearranging the order of the variables according to the clusters.

P2M   Cluster Analysis of Cases: P2M clusters cases according to one of four available distance measures. The two cases having the shortest distance between them are amalgamated and treated as one case and then, in turn, clustered with others. This algorithm continues until all cases and clusters are amalgamated into one cluster. The distance between cases is either the pth root of the sums of the pth powers of differences (when p = 2 this is the Euclidean distance) or χ^2 or $\phi^2(=\chi^2/N)$ where χ^2 is computed from the table formed by the two cases and the variables (the last two distance measures are useful when the data are counts).

A diagram drawn with vertical lines to indicate clustering of the cases is printed, and the order of clustering is indicated in the diagram. Optional output includes the input data matrix after standardization, the initial distance matrix between cases, and a horizontal clustering tree diagram. The distance matrix can be printed in shaded form after rearranging the cases according to the clusters.

P3M   Block Clustering: P3M simultaneously clusters cases and variables of a data matrix. Blocks (submatrices of the data matrix) are identified; the marginal rows of a block form a cluster of cases, and the marginal columns of a block form a cluster of variables. Three types of clusters are thus discovered: clusters of data values (the blocks), clusters of cases, and clusters of variables.

A block diagram completely represents the data, with relatively few printed symbols. In the block, the rows (cases) and columns (variables) of data have been permuted, and smaller blocks (or submatrices) of similar values are outlined. Similar values are left blank to give a good visual representation of like values. To prevent overlapping, the blocks form a hierarchy (that is, any pair of blocks are disjoint, or one includes the other).

At an early stage of data analysis, the program can be used as a multi-variate histogram. In one-dimensional histograms real-valued variables are separated into categories of equal length. In a sense, P3M does this too; it separates the values of each variable into a maximum of 35 intervals and codes them 1,2,...,9,A,B,...,Z. For each variable the number of categories, or intervals used, can be specified.

The output reports the number of times each variable takes each of its coded values. Two trees are printed, one reporting the joining sequence for cases (row clusters) and the other reporting the joining sequence for variables (column clusters). Also included is a block diagram on the permuted data matrix, in which a leader value and exceptions are printed for each block; values similar to the leader are blanked out.

● MULTIVARIATE ANALYSIS

P4M   Factor Analysis: P4M performs a factor analysis of either a correlation or a covariance matrix. The input can be data, correlation matrix, covariance matrix, factor loadings or factor score coefficients. Several initial communality estimates can be used, including squared multiple correlations, maximum row values and values specified by the user. Initial factor extraction can be obtained by principal components, maximum likelihood, Kaiser's Second Generation Little Jiffy, or iterated principal factor analysis. Several methods of rotation are available, including varimax and direct quartimin. Factor scores are computed for each case, and Mahalanobis distances are computed from the centroid of all cases for the factor scores, raw data, and the residuals of the original data regressed on the factor scores.

Output includes means, standard deviations, coefficients of variation, maximums and minimums, standard scores, correlation matrix, covariance matrix, factor loadings and their plots, squared multiple correlations, factor correlations, factor structure, factor scores, factor score coefficients, factor score covariances and factor score plots. The correlation matrix can be printed in shaded form after rearranging the order of the variables according to the factor loadings.

P6M   Canonical Correlation Analysis: P6M computes canonical correlation analysis for two sets of variables. Input can be a data matrix, a covariance matrix or a correlation matrix.

Output includes means, standard deviations, coefficients of variation, skewness, kurtosis, minimums, maximums, correlations, covariances, canonical correlations, eigenvalues associated with each pair of canonical variables and Bartlett's test for the significance of the remaining eigenvalues, coefficients for canonical variables, the scores of the canonical variables for each case, correlations of variables with canonical variables (loadings) and bivariate plots for original variables and canonical variables.

P6R   <u>Partial Correlation and Multivariate Regression</u>: P6R computes the partial correlations of a set of variables removing the linear effects of a second set of variables. The program can also be used for regression, especially when there are multiple dependent variables (since the computations for partial correlations include the computations of the regression coefficients for predicting the first set of variables from the second set of variables). Using double precision, P6R can be used to check computations from P1R and P2R for problems that may be ill-conditioned or involve a large number (thousands) of cases. Input can be a data matrix, a covariance matrix or a correlation matrix.

Output includes means, standard deviations, coefficients of variation, skewness, kurtosis, minimums, maximums, correlations, covariances, partial correlations, partial covariances, regression coefficients, standardized coefficients, standard errors for coefficients, covariances and correlations for regression coefficients, t tests and significance levels for regression coefficients, two types of squared multiple correlations and their significance levels (the first, of each independent variable with the other independent variables; the second, of each dependent variable with all of the independent variables), residuals from partial correlation analysis and bivariate plots for original variables and residuals.

P7M   <u>Stepwise Discriminant Analysis</u>: P7M performs a multiple group discriminant analysis. The variables used in computing the linear classification functions are chosen in a stepwise manner. At each step the variable that adds most to the separation of the groups is entered. By specifying contrasts you can state which group differences are of interest; these contrasts guide the selection of the variables. For each case the group classifications are evaluated. Based on the posterior probabilities, a classification table is computed (prior probabilities can be specified for use in these computations). In addition a jackknife-validation procedure can be requested to reduce the bias in the group classifications. The program computes canonical discriminant functions and plots the first two to give an optimal two-dimensional picture of the separation of the groups.

Output includes means, standard deviations, F statistics and degrees of freedom for each variable at each step, F statistics for distances between pairs of groups, Wilks' Λ (U statistic) for multivariate analysis of variance, Mahalanobis D^2 of each case from each group mean, classification functions, classification matrices, and percent correct classification coefficients for canonical discriminant functions, canonical correlations, canonical variables and a plot of the first two canonical variables.

● SURVIVAL ANALYSIS

P1L <u>Life Tables and Survival Functions</u>: P1L estimates the survival (time-to occurrence) curve of subjects who have been observed over successive periods of time. Two such estimates are provided: the actuarial (Cutler-Ederer) life tables, based on data grouped into time intervals; and the product-limit (Kaplan-Meier) estimate, which is based on individual survival times. Such estimates can be obtained separately for subjects in different treatment groups, or for different levels of grouping variables. Tests of equality of the survival curves are provided, using two nonparametric rank tests.

Output includes summaries of the number of occurrences and censored observations in each group and plots of the censoring patterns. Plots of survival curves, log survival hazard functions, cumulative hazard and probability density of the outcome may be requested.

● MULTIPASS TRANSFORMATION

P1S <u>Multipass Transformation</u>: P1S can be used when information from the data file is needed to compute transformations (i.e., all the data must be scanned or passed before transformations can be made; for example, missing values may need to be replaced by the mean of the values present in the sample). In each pass a further transformation of the data can be specified through FORTRAN statements. Arithmetic means, standard deviations, geometric means, harmonic means, and largest and smallest values for each variable can be computed in each transformation pass to be used in the next pass. (All the BMDP programs have the capability of doing simple transformations and data editing procedures.)

Output for each pass includes the transformed data and any of the statistics computed for each selected variable. The transformed data can be saved on a BMDP File.

3

USING BMDP PROGRAMS

An Introduction

This manual should be regarded as a reference book for the BMDP programs; it contains much more information than you need to analyze a set of data.

The programs cover a wide range of statistical techniques; they are designed to be used by research workers who may not be experienced in using a computer.

In this chapter we describe

- three examples (with extensive annotation) of how to use
  BMDP programs   p. 40

- how to organize research forms and coding sheets   p. 47

- how to describe the layout (format) of the data   p. 51

The three examples are elementary. After reading through them we recommend that you try to use one of the programs in Chapters 8, 9 or 10. To do so you will first want to read or skim through Chapters 4 and 5, which describe the language used to state instructions to the program. The more advanced programs differ from the elementary ones in the level of their statistical analyses and not in the method of stating instructions. Once you have used any program, you will be ready for all the programs.

3.1 Three Annotated Examples

● COUNTING THE FREQUENCY OF SYMBOLS IN YOUR DATA

As our first example we keypunched the following five data cards:

```
BMDP PROGRAMS ARE
EASY TO USE IF YOU
IGNORE WHAT YOU
DON'T NEED TO KNOW
1234567890$.,
```

The statement is true. BMDP programs use preassigned values for most options. The preassigned values are appropriate for a wide variety of problems. Therefore you can ignore the options that are not important to you.

One BMDP program (P4D, Section 8.3) reports the frequency of each symbol in each column of your data cards. All other programs require that all data be numeric (numbers).

In our first example we use P4D to report the frequency of each symbol in the above data cards. The following cards were submitted to the computer:

Example 3.1

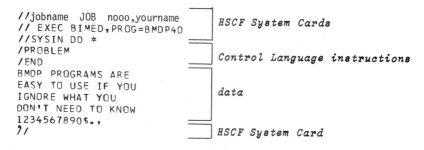

The first three cards are System Cards that are required to start an analysis by P4D; they are the cards used at the Health Sciences Computing Facility (HSCF) and may differ for your computing center. The first card is an accounting card that shows that you are a legal user of the computer. The second card names the BMDP program (BMDP4D) to be used. The third card specifies that instructions or data for the program follow immediately. Each System Card must begin in the first column of the computer card. One or more blanks must be used where each blank space is shown; blanks cannot be used where no blank is shown.

The next two cards contain the minimum Control Language instructions necessary to use P4D. No program options are specified; therefore the preassigned options are used.

The next five cards contain the data for this analysis.

The last card is a System Card that indicates the end of the instructions and data.

The computer output from the above cards is shown in Output 3.1. It correctly shows, for example, that column 1 of the data cards contains one each of the characters B, E, I, D and 1. The printed results are explained in footnotes to the output.

Output 3.1   Results produced by program P4D from Example 3.1

FREQUENCY COUNT OF CHARACTERS PER VARIABLES

CHAR	CARD CODE ②	1 ①	2	3	4	5	6	7	8	9	10	11	12	13	14	15	16	17	18	19	20
	BLANK	0	0	0	0	2	1	1	1	0	0	1	2	0	3	2	2	2	3	5	5
0	0	0	0	0	0	0	0	0	0	0	1	0	0	0	0	0	0	0	0	0	0
1	1	③ 1	0	0	0	0	0	0	0	0	0	0	0	0	0	0	0	0	0	0	0
2	2	0	1	0	0	0	0	0	0	0	0	0	0	0	0	0	0	0	0	0	0
3	3	0	0	1	0	0	0	0	0	0	0	0	0	0	0	0	0	0	0	0	0
4	4	0	0	0	1	0	0	0	0	0	0	0	0	0	0	0	0	0	0	0	0
5	5	0	0	0	0	1	0	0	0	0	0	0	0	0	0	0	0	0	0	0	0
6	6	0	0	0	0	0	1	0	0	0	0	0	0	0	0	0	0	0	0	0	0
7	7	0	0	0	0	0	0	1	0	0	0	0	0	0	0	0	0	0	0	0	0
8	8	0	0	0	0	0	0	0	1	0	0	0	0	0	0	0	0	0	0	0	0
9	9	0	0	0	0	0	0	0	0	1	0	0	0	0	0	0	0	0	0	0	0
A	12-1	0	1	0	0	0	0	0	0	0	1	1	0	0	0	1	0	0	0	0	0
B	12-2	1	0	0	0	0	0	0	0	0	0	0	0	0	0	0	0	0	0	0	0
D	12-4	1	0	1	0	0	0	0	0	0	1	0	0	0	0	0	0	0	0	0	0
E	12-5	1	0	0	0	0	1	0	1	1	0	1	0	0	0	0	1	0	0	0	0
F	12-6	0	0	0	0	0	0	0	0	0	0	0	0	0	1	0	0	0	0	0	0
G	12-7	0	1	0	0	0	0	0	0	0	1	0	0	0	0	0	0	0	0	0	0
H	12-8	0	0	0	0	0	0	0	1	0	0	0	0	0	0	0	0	0	0	0	0
I	12-9	1	0	0	0	0	0	0	0	0	0	0	0	1	0	0	0	0	0	0	0
K	11-2	0	0	0	0	0	0	0	0	0	0	0	0	0	0	1	0	0	0	0	0
M	11-4	0	1	0	0	0	0	0	0	0	0	0	1	0	0	0	0	0	0	0	0
N	11-5	0	0	2	0	0	0	0	0	0	0	0	0	0	0	1	0	0	0	0	0
O	11-6	0	1	0	1	0	0	1	1	0	0	0	0	1	1	0	0	2	0	0	0
P	11-7	0	0	0	1	0	1	0	0	0	0	0	0	0	0	0	0	0	0	0	0
R	11-9	0	0	0	0	1	0	1	0	0	1	0	0	0	0	1	0	0	0	0	0
S	0-2	0	0	1	0	0	0	0	0	0	1	0	0	1	0	0	0	0	0	0	0
T	0-3	0	0	0	0	1	1	0	0	0	0	1	1	0	0	0	0	0	0	0	0
U	0-4	0	0	0	0	0	0	0	0	1	0	0	0	0	1	0	0	1	0	0	0
W	0-6	0	0	0	0	0	0	0	1	0	0	0	0	0	0	0	0	1	0	0	0
Y	0-8	0	0	0	1	0	0	0	0	0	0	0	0	1	0	0	1	0	0	0	0
.	12-3-8	0	0	0	0	0	0	0	0	0	0	0	1	0	0	0	0	0	0	0	0
$	11-3-8	0	0	0	0	0	0	0	0	0	0	1	0	0	0	0	0	0	0	0	0
,	0-3-8	0	0	0	0	0	0	0	0	0	0	0	0	1	0	0	0	0	0	0	0
'	5-8	0	0	0	1	0	0	0	0	0	0	0	0	0	0	0	0	0	0	0	0

TOTALS

		1	2	3	4	5	6	7	8	9	10	11	12	13	14	15	16	17	18	19	20
NUMERIC	④	1	1	1	1	1	1	1	1	1	1	0	0	0	0	0	0	0	0	0	0
ALPHABETIC		4	4	4	3	2	3	3	3	4	4	3	2	4	2	3	3	3	2	0	0
SPECIAL		0	0	0	1	0	0	0	0	0	0	1	1	1	0	0	0	0	0	0	0

--- ⑤ ---

Key:

① In this example, the variable numbers are column numbers.

② The card code column indicates which holes the keypunch machine punches to represent each character; e.g., a 12 and a 1 are punched to represent A.

③ The 1's in the first column (variable) indicate that a 1, B, D, E and I were found in the first column of the 5 records.

④ The total frequency for the first column is one numeric symbol (1) and four alphabetic symbols (B, D, E and I).

⑤ The program output continues by reporting five blanks in each of the remaining columns (21-80, not shown in the above output) .

● UNIVARIATE STATISTICS FOR EACH VARIABLE

As our second example we use P1D -- Simple Data Description. P1D is described in Chapter 8; the Control Language instructions to describe the data are explained in Chapter 5. To illustrate the results of P1D we use part of the data from a study of blood chemistries. (A more complete set is shown in Table 5.1 and is used in the examples throughout this manual.) We use only the values of age and cholesterol for 188 women. The entire card deck submitted to the computer is shown in Example 3.2.

Example 3.2

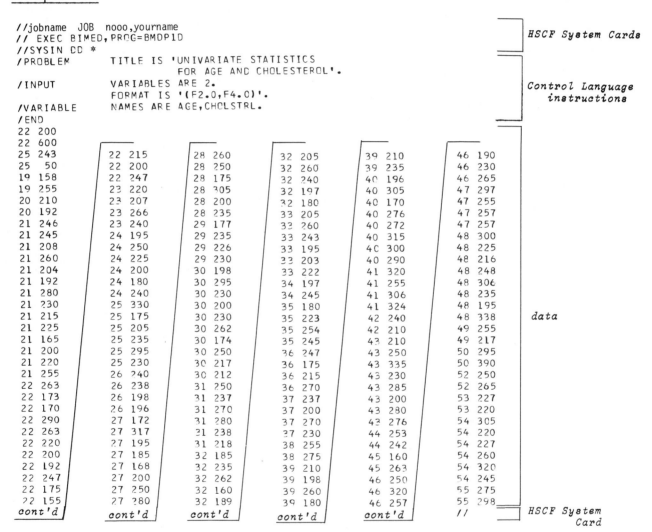

```
//jobname  JOB  nooo,yourname                              ⎤
// EXEC BIMED,PROG=BMDP1D                                  ⎬ HSCF System Cards
//SYSIN CD *                                               ⎦
/PROBLEM        TITLE IS 'UNIVARIATE STATISTICS            ⎤
                       FOR AGE AND CHOLESTEROL'.           │
/INPUT          VARIABLES ARE 2.                           ⎬ Control Language
                FORMAT IS '(F2.0,F4.0)'.                   │   instructions
/VARIABLE       NAMES ARE AGE,CHOLSTRL.                    ⎦
/END
22 200
22 600
25 243     22 215     28 260     32 205     39 210     46 190
25  50     22 200     28 250     32 260     39 235     46 230
19 158     22 247     28 175     40 196     40 196     46 265
19 255     23 220     28 305     32 197     40 305     47 297
20 210     23 207     28 200     32 180     40 170     47 255
20 192     23 266     28 235     33 205     40 276     47 257
21 246     23 240     29 177     33 260     40 272     47 257
21 245     24 195     29 235     33 243     40 315     48 300
21 208     24 250     29 226     33 195     40 300     48 225
21 260     24 225     29 230     33 203     40 290     48 216
21 204     24 200     30 198     33 222     41 320     48 248
21 192     24 180     30 295     34 197     41 255     48 306
21 280     24 240     30 230     34 245     41 306     48 235
21 230     25 330     30 200     35 180     41 324     48 195
21 215     25 175     30 230     35 223     42 240     48 338
21 225     25 205     30 262     35 254     42 210     49 255
21 165     25 235     30 174     35 245     43 210     49 217
21 200     25 295     30 250     36 247     43 250     50 295
21 220     25 230     30 217     36 175     43 335     50 390
21 255     26 240     30 212     36 215     43 230     52 250
22 263     26 238     31 250     36 270     43 285     52 265
22 173     26 198     31 237     37 237     43 200     53 227
22 170     26 196     31 270     37 200     43 280     53 220
22 290     27 172     31 280     37 270     43 276     54 305
22 263     27 317     31 238     37 230     44 253     54 220
22 220     27 195     31 218     38 255     44 242     54 227
22 200     27 185     32 185     38 275     45 160     54 260
22 192     27 168     32 235     39 210     45 263     54 320
22 247     27 200     32 262     39 198     46 250     54 245
22 175     27 250     32 160     39 260     46 320     55 275
22 155     27 280     32 189     39 180     46 257     55 298
cont'd     cont'd     cont'd     cont'd     cont'd     //
```

data

HSCF System Card

The first three System Cards are similar to those in Example 3.1 except that BMDP1D replaces BMDP4D. The Control Language instructions specify a title for the analysis, the number of variables in the data, the layout (format) of the data in each case, and names for the two variables. The format is described in detail in Section 3.3 of this chapter. The remaining instructions are explained in Chapter 5.

The results are presented in Output 3.2.

Output 3.2 Analysis of the data in Example 3.2 by P1D

```
BMDP1D - SIMPLE DATA DESCRIPTION                        PROGRAM REVISED SEPTEMBER 1977
HEALTH SCIENCES COMPUTING FACILITY                     MANUAL DATE -- 1977
UNIVERSITY OF CALIFORNIA, LOS ANGELES


PROGRAM CONTROL INFORMATION

 (1)   /PROBLEM        TITLE IS 'UNIVARIATE STATISTICS
                            FOR AGE AND CHOLESTEROL'.
       /INPUT          VARIABLES ARE 2.
                       FORMAT IS '(F2.0,F4.0)'.
       /VARIABLE       NAMES ARE AGE,CHOLSTRL.
       /END

(2) PROBLEM TITLE . . . . . . .UNIVARIATE STATISTICS FOR AGE AND CHOLESTEROL

    NUMBER OF VARIABLES TO READ IN. . . . . . . . .       2
    NUMBER OF VARIABLES ADDED BY TRANSFORMATIONS. .       0
    TOTAL NUMBER OF VARIABLES . . . . . . . . . . .       2
    NUMBER OF CASES TO READ IN. . . . . . . . . . . 1000000
    CASE LABELING VARIABLES . . . . . . . . . . . .
    LIMITS AND MISSING VALUE CHECKED BEFORE TRANSFORMATIONS
    BLANKS ARE. . . . . . . . . . . . . . . . . . .    ZEROS
    INPUT UNIT NUMBER . . . . . . . . . . . . . . .       5
    REWIND INPUT UNIT PRIOR TO READING. . DATA. . .      NO

    INPUT FORMAT
       (F2.0,F4.0)


    VARIABLES TO BE USED
            1 AGE            2 CHOLSTRL

(3) NUMBER OF CASES READ. . . . . . . . . . . . . .      188
```

```
VARIABLE              STANDARD   ST.ERR.  COEFF. OF   S M A L L E S T    L A R G E S T              TOTAL
NO. NAME       MEAN   DEVIATION  OF MEAN  VARIATION   VALUE   Z-SCORE   VALUE    Z-SCORE   RANGE    FREQUENCY

  1 AGE     (4) 33.818  10.113   0.7376    0.29904    19.000   -1.47    55.000    2.09    36.000      188
  2 CHOLSTRL   237.095  51.807   3.7784    0.21851    50.000   -3.61   600.000    7.00   550.000      188
```

Key:

(1) The Control Language instructions are printed: We are interested in the two variables punched on the data cards -- age and cholesterol count. The FORMAT statement in the INPUT paragraph describes where these variables are found on the card.

   'F2.0' says to read two columns (1-2) as the value of the first variable.
   'F4.0' says to read the next four columns (3-6) as the value of the second variable.

   F-format is for numbers; letters and special characters are not allowed (Section 3.3). The two variables are named AGE and CHOLSTRL in the VARIABLE paragraph. The names are listed in the same order as the variables in the FORMAT statement.

(2) The Control Language instructions are interpreted. Preassigned values are also reported. Since the number of cases is not specified, it is recorded as 1,000,000 and all the data are read. The other preassigned values are explained in Chapter 5.

(3) The number of cases read is reported.

(4) Univariate statistics are printed for each variable.

● COMPARING GROUPS

As our third example we use P7D -- Description of Groups (Strata) with Histograms and Analysis of Variance. P7D is described in Section 9.2.

We use the same data as in the previous example. We want to see whether the distributions of cholesterol are similar across the age groups (25 OR LESS, 26 TO 35, 36 TO 45, and OVER 45) and whether there are any unusual values or features in the data.

The card deck submitted to the computer is shown in Example 3.3. (It differs only slightly from that of Example 3.2.)

Example 3.3

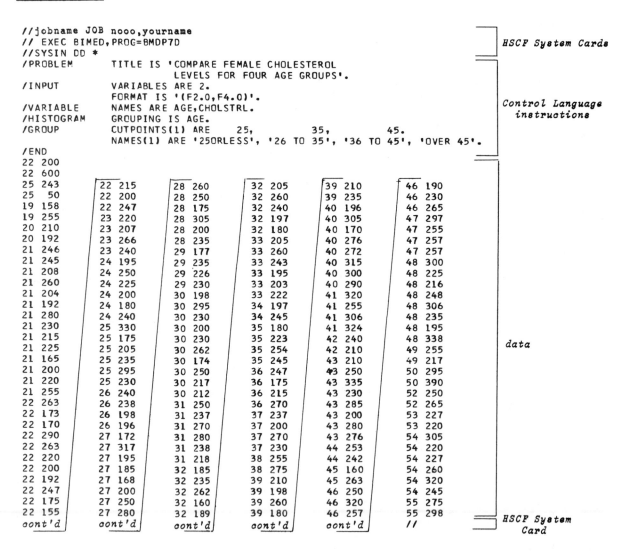

```
//jobname JOB nooo,yourname                                          }  HSCF System Cards
// EXEC BIMED,PROG=BMDP7D
//SYSIN DD *
/PROBLEM        TITLE IS 'COMPARE FEMALE CHOLESTEROL
                          LEVELS FOR FOUR AGE GROUPS'.
/INPUT          VARIABLES ARE 2.
                FORMAT IS '(F2.0,F4.0)'.                             }  Control Language
/VARIABLE       NAMES ARE AGE,CHOLSTRL.                                 instructions
/HISTOGRAM      GROUPING IS AGE.
/GROUP          CUTPOINTS(1) ARE    25,          35,          45.
                NAMES(1) ARE '25ORLESS', '26 TO 35', '36 TO 45', 'OVER 45'.
/END
22 200
22 600
25 243     22 215     28 260     32 205     39 210     46 190
25  50     22 200     28 250     32 260     39 235     46 230
19 158     22 247     28 175     32 240     40 196     46 265
19 255     23 220     28 305     32 197     40 305     47 297
20 210     23 207     28 200     32 180     40 170     47 255
20 192     23 266     28 235     33 205     40 276     47 257
21 246     23 240     29 177     33 260     40 272     47 257
21 245     24 195     29 235     33 243     40 315     48 300
21 208     24 250     29 226     33 195     40 300     48 225
21 260     24 225     29 230     33 203     40 290     48 216
21 204     24 200     30 198     33 222     41 320     48 248
21 192     24 180     30 295     34 197     41 255     48 306
21 280     24 240     30 230     34 245     41 306     48 235
21 230     25 330     30 200     35 180     41 324     48 195
21 215     25 175     30 230     35 223     42 240     48 338
21 225     25 205     30 262     35 254     42 210     49 255
21 165     25 235     30 174     35 245     43 210     49 217
21 200     25 295     30 250     36 247     43 250     50 295
21 220     25 230     30 217     36 175     43 335     50 390
21 255     26 240     30 212     36 215     43 230     52 250
22 263     26 238     31 250     36 270     43 285     52 265
22 173     26 198     31 237     37 237     43 200     53 227
22 170     26 196     31 270     37 200     43 280     53 220
22 290     27 172     31 280     37 270     43 276     54 305
22 263     27 317     31 238     37 230     44 253     54 220
22 220     27 195     31 218     38 255     44 242     54 227
22 200     27 185     32 185     38 275     45 160     54 260
22 192     27 168     32 235     39 210     45 263     54 320
22 247     27 200     32 262     39 198     46 250     54 245
22 175     27 250     32 160     39 260     46 320     55 275
22 155     27 280     32 189     39 180     46 257     55 298
cont'd     cont'd     cont'd     cont'd     cont'd     //
```

HSCF System Card

data

The first three System Cards are similar to those in the previous examples, except that BMDP7D is punched on the second card.

The Control Language instructions specify a <u>title</u> for the analysis, the number of <u>variables</u> in the data, the layout (<u>format</u>) of the data, the <u>names</u> of the variables, the <u>grouping</u> variable (the variable used to classify cases into groups), three endpoints (<u>cutpoints</u>) that define four intervals for age, and <u>names</u> for the four intervals.

The results are presented in Output 3.3.

Output 3.3 Annotated results from P7D for Example 3.3

```
BMDP7D - DESCRIPTION OF GROUPS (STRATA) WITH            PROGRAM REVISED SEPTEMBER 1977
            HISTOGRAMS AND ANALYSIS OF VARIANCE         MANUAL DATE  --  1977
HEALTH SCIENCES COMPUTING FACILITY
UNIVERSITY OF CALIFORNIA, LOS ANGELES

    PROGRAM CONTROL INFORMATION

            /PROBLEM      TITLE IS 'COMPARE FEMALE CHOLESTEROL
                             LEVELS FOR FOUR AGE GROUPS'.
            /INPUT        VARIABLES ARE 2.
                          FORMAT IS '(F2.0,F4.0)'.
 (1)        /VARIABLE     NAMES ARE AGE,CHOLSTRL.
            /HISTOGRAM    GROUPING IS AGE.
            /GROUP        CUTPOINTS(1) ARE    25,          35,          45.
                          NAMES(1) ARE '25ORLESS', '26 TO 35', '36 TO 45', 'OVER 45'.
            /END


   PROBLEM TITLE . . . . . . . .COMPARE FEMALE CHOLESTEROL LEVELS FOR FOUR AGE GROUPS
(2)
   NUMBER OF VARIABLES TO READ IN. . . . . . . . .       2
   NUMBER OF VARIABLES ADDED BY TRANSFORMATIONS. .       0
   TOTAL NUMBER OF VARIABLES . . . . . . . . . . .       2
   NUMBER OF CASES TO READ IN. . . . . . . . . . . 1000000
   CASE LABELING VARIABLES . . . . . . . . . . . .
   LIMITS AND MISSING VALUE CHECKED BEFORE TRANSFORMATIONS
   BLANKS ARE. . . . . . . . . . . . . . . . . . .    ZEROS
   INPUT UNIT NUMBER . . . . . . . . . . . . . . .       5
   REWIND INPUT UNIT PRIOR TO READING. . DATA. . .      NO

   INPUT FORMAT
        (F2.0,F4.0)


   VARIABLES TO BE USED
            1  AGE          2  CHOLSTRL

   NUMBER OF CASES READ. . . . . . . . . . . . . .     188
   PRINT DATA MATRIX . . . . . . . . . . . . . . .      NO
   PRINT DATA MATRIX AFTER ORDERING. . . . . . . .      NO
   PRINT WINSORIZING TABLE . . . . . . . . . . . .      NO
   PRINT CORRELATION TABLE . . . . . . . . . . . .      NO

                 BEFORE TRANSFORMATION                              INTERVAL RANGE
   VARIABLE      MINIMUM    MAXIMUM    MISSING   CATEGORY  CATEGORY  GREATER    LESS THAN
   NO. NAME      LIMIT      LIMIT      CODE      CODE      NAME      THAN       OR EQUAL TO

    1   AGE                                                25ORLESS             25.00000
                                                          26 TO 35  25.00000   35.00000
                                                          36 TO 45  35.00000   45.00000
                                                          OVER 45   45.00000
```

Key:

(1)   The Control Language instructions are printed. The grouping variable is age. Histograms of cholesterol values will be made for each age group. The age groups are defined by CUTPOINTS in the GROUP paragraph -- four age groups are defined as 25 or less, 26 to 35, 36 to 45, and over 45. In the GROUP paragraph, the '(1)' following CUTPOINTS and NAMES identifies the first variable (age) as the grouping variable. The group names are in apostrophes because they begin with a number or contain a special character (blank).

(2)   The Control Language instructions are interpreted.

(continued)

Output 3.3 *(continued)*

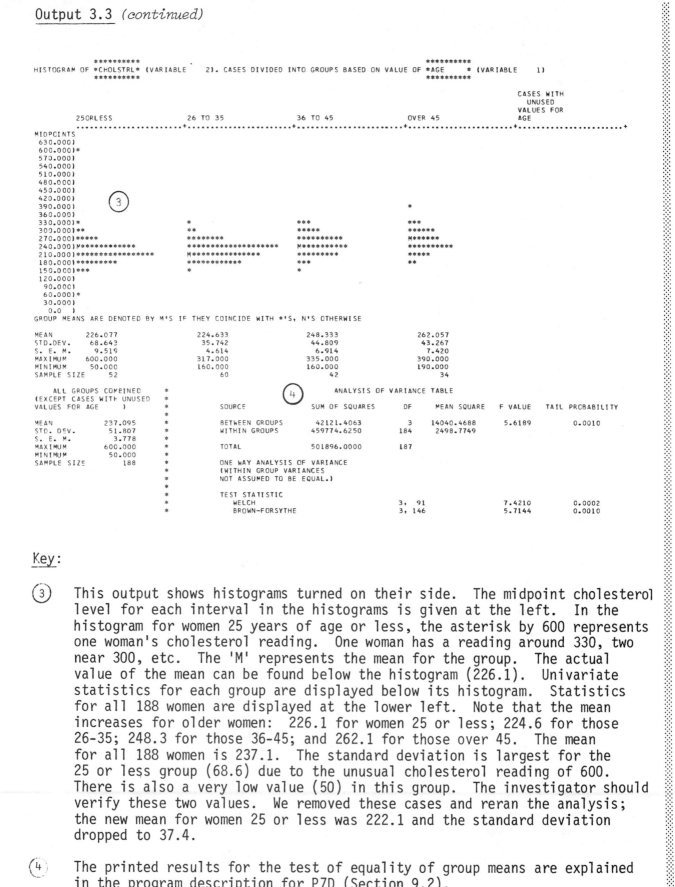

```
                ********** 
HISTOGRAM OF *CHOLSTRL* (VARIABLE     2). CASES DIVIDED INTO GROUPS BASED ON VALUE OF *AGE     * (VARIABLE     1)
                **********                                                              **********
                                                                                                          CASES WITH
                                                                                                          UNUSED
                                                                                                          VALUES FOR
            25ORLESS              26 TO 35            36 TO 45            OVER 45                           AGE
            .................+..................+..................+..................+.....................+
MIDPOINTS
 630.000)
 600.000)*
 570.000)
 540.000)
 510.000)
 480.000)
 450.000)
 420.000)
 390.000)                                                                        *
 360.000)
 330.000)*                      *                       ***                ***
 300.000)**                     **                      *****              *****
 270.000)*****                  *******                 *********          M******
 240.000)M************          ******************** M**********           **********
 210.000)****************** M************** **         *********            *****
 180.000)*********           *************             ***                  **
 150.000)***                 *                         *
 120.000)
  90.000)
  60.000)*
  30.000)
    0.0  )
GROUP MEANS ARE DENOTED BY M'S IF THEY COINCIDE WITH *'S, N'S OTHERWISE

MEAN        226.077                224.633            248.333            262.057
STD.DEV.     68.643                 35.742             44.809             43.267
S. E. M.      9.519                  4.614              6.914              7.420
MAXIMUM     600.000                317.000            335.000            390.000
MINIMUM      50.000                160.000            160.000            190.000
SAMPLE SIZE      52                     60                 42                 34
```

ALL GROUPS COMBINED (EXCEPT CASES WITH UNUSED VALUES FOR AGE)		ANALYSIS OF VARIANCE TABLE					
	*	SOURCE	SUM OF SQUARES	DF	MEAN SQUARE	F VALUE	TAIL PROBABILITY
MEAN 237.095	*	BETWEEN GROUPS	42121.4063	3	14040.4688	5.6189	0.0010
STD. DEV. 51.807	*	WITHIN GROUPS	459774.6250	184	2498.7749		
S. E. M. 3.778	*						
MAXIMUM 600.000	*	TOTAL	501896.0000	187			
MINIMUM 50.000	*						
SAMPLE SIZE 188	*	ONE WAY ANALYSIS OF VARIANCE (WITHIN GROUP VARIANCES NOT ASSUMED TO BE EQUAL.)					
	*						
	*	TEST STATISTIC					
	*	WELCH		3, 91		7.4210	0.0002
	*	BROWN-FORSYTHE		3, 146		5.7144	0.0010

Key:

③   This output shows histograms turned on their side. The midpoint cholesterol level for each interval in the histograms is given at the left. In the histogram for women 25 years of age or less, the asterisk by 600 represents one woman's cholesterol reading. One woman has a reading around 330, two near 300, etc. The 'M' represents the mean for the group. The actual value of the mean can be found below the histogram (226.1). Univariate statistics for each group are displayed below its histogram. Statistics for all 188 women are displayed at the lower left. Note that the mean increases for older women: 226.1 for women 25 or less; 224.6 for those 26-35; 248.3 for those 36-45; and 262.1 for those over 45. The mean for all 188 women is 237.1. The standard deviation is largest for the 25 or less group (68.6) due to the unusual cholesterol reading of 600. There is also a very low value (50) in this group. The investigator should verify these two values. We removed these cases and reran the analysis; the new mean for women 25 or less was 222.1 and the standard deviation dropped to 37.4.

④   The printed results for the test of equality of group means are explained in the program description for P7D (Section 9.2).

3.2 Research Forms and Coding Sheets

The data must be recorded before an analysis can be performed. The method that you choose to record the data will depend on its quantity and source.

When the data collection is not automated, the data are usually recorded on either a research form designed for the study or a coding sheet.

- DESIGN OF RESEARCH FORMS

A proper research form can save both time and money. A form designed with foresight can mean the difference between a smoothly run study and one that becomes a disaster.

The following rules should be considered when designing a research form:

- Make an outline of all data to be collected.

- Make a rough draft of the form. Include a space for indicating the card columns used for specific data on the form, preferably on the right-hand margin; this will simplify coding and keypunching, and the correct transfer of data to the assigned fields will be insured. Consult the keypunch supervisor and statistician for suggestions. Revise the form and check with them again. When the form is completed and approved, have it printed for use.

- Include a subject or case number on each form and each card that identifies each subject individually; this number is used to identify all data pertaining to one subject. Examples are hospital patient numbers, social security numbers or sequence numbers. If you question the data on a card, the identification number allows you to refer back to the form to check for errors. A sequence number on each card allows for the cards to be ordered by machine if they are dropped or otherwise disordered.

- Assign a number to each card if more than one form is involved or if there is more than one card per case. This number identifies the data on the card.

- Include explicit instructions at the beginning of each form specifying how it should be filled out. If the form is misunderstood the data may not be entered properly and the study may be useless. Forms that are filled out by subjects must be simple, easily understood and ordered conveniently.

A sample of one research form is given in Figure 3.1.

- CODING SHEETS

The research form in Figure 3.1 gives one example of a coding sheet -- the data to be keypunched are organized in a column to the right of the form. Below or beside each line appears the card columns into which the numbers are keypunched. If weight is recorded and can be either two digits (<100 lbs.) or three digits (>100 lbs.), three columns must be allowed for the number. Values less than 100 should be written with a leading zero (e.g., 095) or right-justified (a blank followed by 95).

Figure 3.1 Example of a research form

MULTIPLE CHOICE FORM

UCLA Operation _____   Name of Coder: _Esmeralda_   Col.

Patient Name _Henrietta Smithson_   Patient I.D. _653_ $\underline{653}$
1-3

Operation Date _11_ / _06_ / _74_ $\underline{110674}$
4-9

Type of Operation (Check One):

1) Hemiarthroplasty - AM .... [ ]	8) THR - McKee .... [ ]	$\underline{05}$
2) Hemiarthroplasty - FR Thompson... [ ]	9) THR - Zimmer....... [ ]	10-11
3) Hemiarthroplasty - Zimmer .... [ ]	10) THR - Other .... [ ]	
4) Cup Arthroplasty .... [ ]	11) Girdlestone .... [ ]	
5) Trochanteric Arthroplasty......... [✓]	12) Osteotomy .... [ ]	
6) Hemiarthroplasty - Other .... [ ]		
7) Total Hip Replacement - Charnley.... [ ]		

Surgeon:

1) Resident _____ [ ]	4) _Berlicz_ [✓	$\underline{4}$
2) HCA _____ [ ]	5) _____ [ ]	12
3) AC _____ [ ]	6) _____ [ ]	

Position:

1) Supine [ ]	3) Prone [ ]	$\underline{2}$
2) Lateral [✓]	4) Other (Specify)_____ [ ]	13

Type of Anesthesia:

1) Halothane [ ]	3) Nitrous & Pentothal [ ]	$\underline{2}$
2) Pentothane [✓]	4) Other (Specify)_____ [ ]	14

Greater Trochanter:

1) No Osteotomy [ ]	3) Mod. Secure Reattachment [✓]	$\underline{3}$
2) Secure Reattachment [ ]	4) Insecure Reattachment [ ]	15

Fixation Method:

2-Criss-crossed Superior Wire through Bone   2-Parallel $\underline{1}$
16

1) Stainless #18.................[✓]	4) Stainless #18 .....[ ]
2) Stainless #17.................[ ]	5) Stainless #17 .....[ ]
3) Vitallium .040 ....[ ]	6) Vitallium .040....[ ]

7) Other (Specify)_____ [ ]

Transverse Fasciotomy:

	1) Yes	2) No		
Iliotibal Band	[✓]	[ ]	(17)	1
Section Iliopsoas	[ ]	[✓]	(18)	2
Resuture Iliopsoas	[ ]	[✓]	(19)	2
Adductor Subcutaneous Tenotomy	[✓]	[ ]	(20)	1

A second type of coding sheet is one that contains lines divided into 80 columns; each column on the form represents one card column. An example of this form is shown in Figure 3.2. The values for each variable are recorded in a fixed position (set of columns) on the sheet. Each line is keypunched as a computer card.

Coding sheets should be prepared with care to avoid common keypunch errors. If the decimal point location is the same for every case, they need not be punched; and plus signs need not be punched. Care should be taken to avoid ambiguity in the use of letters, numbers and symbols. For example, the letter O may be written with a slash through it (Ø) to distinguish it from the number zero. Other number-letter pairs that may be confused are 1 and I, 2 and Z, 6 and G, and 7 and T.

Always use numbers when coding information (assigning numbers to represent race, age, sex, etc.), so they can be included in computations (e.g., to represent groups or categories). For example, sex can be coded 1 for male and 2 for female. One column should be used for each digit in the number: 1-9, one column; 10-99, two columns; 100-999, three columns, etc. Additional columns are needed if decimal points or signs are used with the numbers.

● KEYPUNCHING CARDS

Data information is punched on a card as small rectangular holes in specific locations. The standard IBM card has 80 vertical columns and 12 horizontal rows. This gives 12 punching positions in each column. One or more punches in a single column represent a character. There are two kinds of keypunch machines: the 026 character set has 47 acceptable characters, and the 029 character set has 62 acceptable characters. The BMDP programs accept Control Language and data from both kinds of keypunch machines. However, System Cards at HSCF must be punched on an 029 keypunch machine. To see how the keypunch works, insert a card in the machine and type every key on the keyboard: each letter, symbol or number is represented on the card by a specific combination of holes in one column.

Figure 3.2   Example of a coding sheet

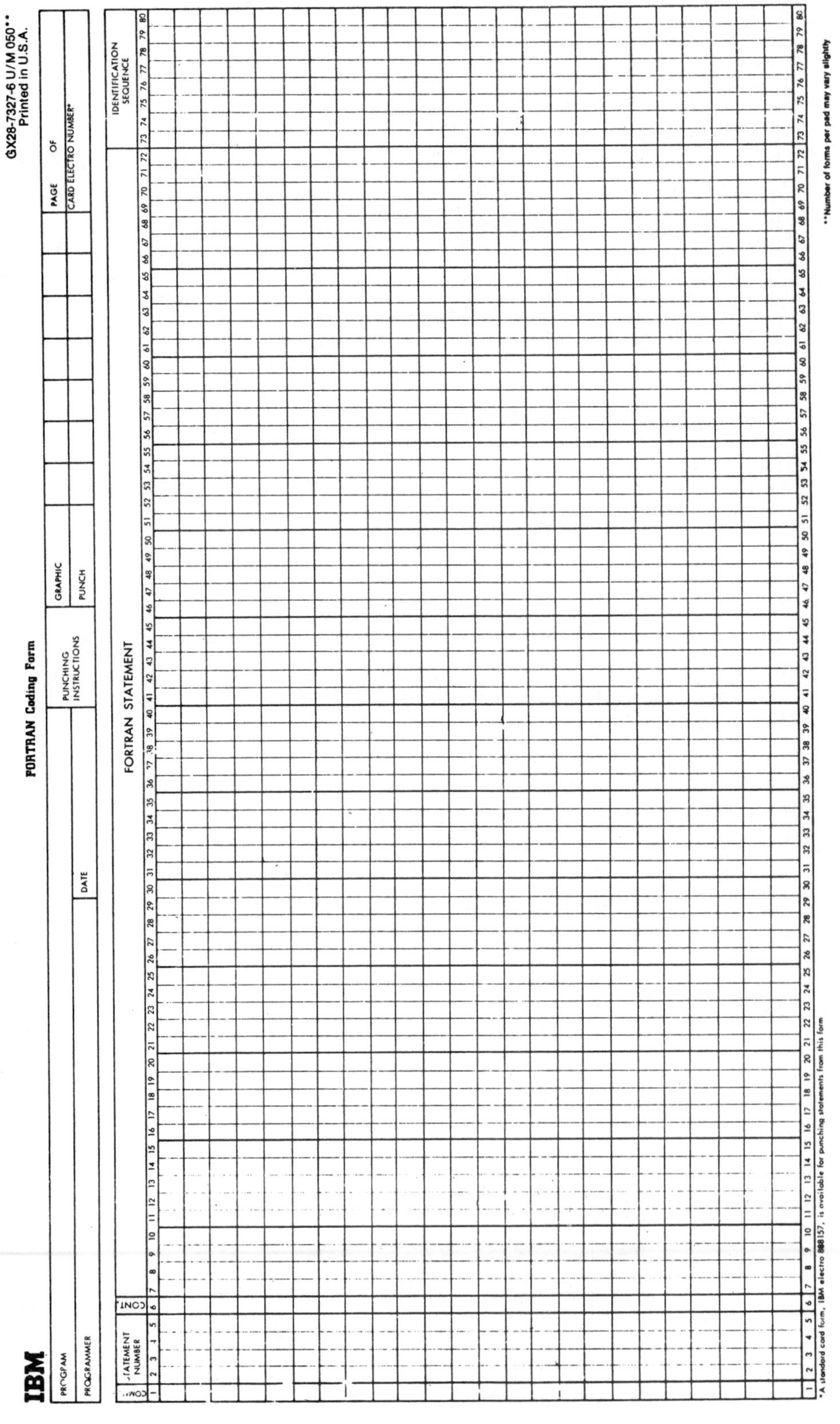

3.3 The Layout (Format) of the Data

Each BMDP program reads the data one case at a time. Each variable must be located in the same columns on the data card or in the data record for all cases. The layout of the data card or record is described by a format statement.

The word "format" refers to the arrangement of information on a data card or record. The format specifications tell the program which columns of the record to skip, which columns to group together as one number, and which columns to treat as numbers in a row. For example, the format statement tells the program whether "345890021" is to be read as

"34.5, 890.0, 0.21"

"34., 9002.1"

"589.002"

or "3, 4, 58, 90, 0, 2, 1"

A format specification indicates the size of a field (the number of columns) and the method of handling that field (skipping, entering it into the computer as a whole number, entering it into the computer as a number with two decimal digits, etc.). Each case is assumed to have the same format as other cases in the same analysis.

The BMDP programs are written to allow you to vary the format according to the requirements of the data -- this is called "variable format". A Control Language statement specifies the format the program should use. It allows considerable freedom in how to read the data.

A complete description of formats can be found in FORTRAN programming manuals. The features required for the BMDP programs are described below.

● F—TYPE FORMAT

The F-type format is used when all data input values are signed (+ or -) or unsigned <u>numbers</u> with or without a decimal point punched. *Letters and special characters are not allowed.*

The following examples illustrate F-type format:

F2.0 specifies that the number is a whole number (zero digits after the decimal point) and has at most two digits (e.g., 21,99,02, 2)

F5.1 specifies that the number has at most five digits and the decimal point precedes the last digit (e.g., 12345 is read as 1234.5, 1234 is read as 123.4)

2F5.1 describes two numbers, each with the format F5.1, and that one number follows the other in the data record

That is,

- a number before the F specifies how many consecutive variables are described by this format specification

- the first number after the F specifies the maximum number of columns in which the number can appear (be written)

- the last number specifies the number of digits after the decimal point

When a data value being read contains a decimal point, it overrides the position for the decimal point stated in the F-type format. When a data value is being written by an F-type format, the decimal point is always printed and the number of digits printed is determined by the format (e.g., the number 12.345 printed under the format F5.1 will appear as 12.3 -- only one digit is printed after the decimal point); the number of columns specified for printing must allow for the decimal point and the minus sign if the number is negative.

● SKIPPING COLUMNS AND RECORDS

Columns in the record can be skipped (ignored) by specifying the number to be skipped followed by an "X" (alphabetic X). For example, 20X specifies that 20 columns are to be skipped.

A slash (/) instructs the program to skip the remainder of the card and begin the next card. Any number of slashes can be used. Slashes are used if the data for a case are recorded on more than one card.

● A-TYPE FORMAT

The A-type format is required when alphabetical, numerical or special characters (or a combination of the three) are in the data, and is usually used for labeling cases (names, for example). Data using the A-type format specification cannot be used in computations. The following examples illustrate certain rules:

Punched Data	Format Specification	Stored Data
AGE	A3	AGEƀ
$	A1	$ƀƀƀ
GERTRUDE	2A4	GERTRUDE

Each specification of a field results in a computer word consisting of exactly 4 characters. When the specified width is less than 4, the characters are positioned in the left of the field and the remaining characters are filled in with blanks (indicated by ƀ). In the third example GERTRUDE is stored in two consecutive variables (GERT in the first, RUDE in the second).

The A-type format is used only for variables that contain case identification, such as patient name, and are not used in computations. P4D -- Single Column Frequencies - Numeric and Nonnumeric -- is the only program that uses the A-type format for purposes other than case identification.

● THE FORMAT STATEMENT

The format statement begins with a left parenthesis followed by a sequence of specifications, and closes with a right parenthesis. Each specification is followed by a comma. Blank columns in the format statement are ignored.

In the Control Language instructions, the format is specified as a sentence starting with FORMAT IS, continuing with the format enclosed in apostrophes and terminating with a period.

- FORMAT IS '(12F3.0,F4.0,11F2.0)'.

describes twenty-four variables recorded in twelve three-column numbers, followed by one four column number, and followed by eleven two-column numbers. Each data card will be read according to this format, beginning in column one of each card.

- FORMAT IS '(5X,2F6.0,F1.0,3X,F5.0/5X,F6.0)'.

describes five variables recorded on a pair of cards as follows:

1. Skip five columns in the first card.
2. Pick up two six-digit numbers in columns 6-11 and 12-17.
3. Pick up a one-digit number in column 18.
4. Skip three columns (columns 19-21).
5. Pick up a five-digit number in columns 22-26.
6. Go to the second card.
7. Skip the first five columns of the second card.
8. Pick up a six-digit number in columns 6-11 of the second card.

- FORMAT IS '(12F3.0,F4.0,11F2.0/)'.

describes the same twenty-four variables as in the first example but the program will read the data in one card and then skip the next card (because of the slash). The next case will then begin in the third card, etc.

Format statements are frequent sources of clerical errors. They should be checked very carefully.

4

REQUIREMENTS FOR AN ANALYSIS

Control Language and System Cards

Laszlo Engelman, HSCF

An English-based language, called Control Language, is used to specify an analysis to the BMDP programs. Control Language uses statements and commands organized as sentences and paragraphs. For example,

```
PLOT   YVARIABLES ARE HEIGHT, WEIGHT.
       XVARIABLES ARE   AGE , HEIGHT.
```

specifies that HEIGHT is to be plotted against AGE, and WEIGHT against HEIGHT. The Control Language rules and terms used throughout this manual are described in Section 4.1. We recommend that you read Section 4.1 even if you are familiar with the first BMDP manual (Dixon, 1975).

You must give instructions to the operating system (computer) to specify the BMDP program to use, and to verify that you are a legitimate user of the computer. The instructions are given on System Cards and are discussed in Section 4.2.

Common errors and how to deal with them are described in Section 4.3.

4.1 Control Language

The analysis to be performed is described in an English-based <u>Control Language</u>. Control Language instructions are read and interpreted by all BMDP programs, and are used to

- describe the data <u>input</u>
- name the <u>variables</u>, and state missing value codes and upper and lower limits for the variables
- specify the analysis, such as <u>regression</u>
- request optional results to be <u>printed</u>
- specify variables to be <u>plotted</u>

The following example from P6D -- Bivariate (Scatter) Plots -- demonstrates some Control Language instructions.

```
/PROBLEM        TITLE IS 'WERNER BLOOD CHEMISTRY DATA'.
/INPUT          VARIABLES ARE 9.
                FORMAT IS '(A4,5F4.0,3F4.1)'.
/VARIABLE       NAMES ARE ID,AGE,HEIGHT,WEIGHT,BRTHPILL,
                        CHOLSTRL,ALBUMIN,CALCIUM,URICACID.
                LABEL IS ID.
                BLANKS ARE MISSING.
/PLOT           YVARIABLES ARE CHOLSTRL,WEIGHT.
                XVARIABLES ARE AGE      ,HEIGHT.
/END
```

The Control Language instructions specify a <u>title</u> (Werner blood chemistry data) for the analysis; the number of <u>variables</u> in the data (9); the <u>format</u> (layout) of the data in a case; <u>names</u> for the 9 variables (ID is the name of the first variable, AGE the second, etc.); that the variable containing case <u>labels</u> is ID; that <u>blanks</u> are <u>missing</u> value codes; and the pairs of variables to be plotted (CHOLSTRL against AGE and WEIGHT against HEIGHT).

● SYNTAX AND PUNCTUATION

The Control Language instructions are written in sentences that are grouped into paragraphs. In the above example PROBLEM, INPUT, VARIABLE, PLOT and END are paragraph names.

Sentences end with a period. Paragraphs are separated by a slash (/); we prefer to put the slash before the paragraph name so it is not forgotten.

Values or names in a list are separated by commas.

Each word or value must be separated from the following word or value either by one or more blanks or by the appropriate punctuation (slash, period, comma or equal sign).

The Control Language instructions can be typed in columns 1 through 80 on each card (record). It can be typed continuously, or an arbitrary number of blanks can be used between words, sentences or paragraphs to make the Control Language easier to read (as in Example 4.1).

● PARAGRAPHS

Several paragraphs are common to all BMDP programs and are described in Chapters 5, 6 and 7. Paragraphs specific to a program are described in the individual program descriptions.

The paragraph name must be the first word in the paragraph; the name may also be repeated before any sentence or command in the paragraph. Paragraphs must be separated by a slash (/). We recommend that the slash be placed immediately before the paragraph name at the beginning of the paragraph, as shown in Example 4.1. Paragraphs can be typed continuously; they do not need to begin on separate cards (lines) as in our example.

A given paragraph can be used only once in each problem unless otherwise stated in the program description. Some paragraphs can be repeated to allow additional analyses of the same data. Except where noted, paragraphs can be stated in any order in the Control Language instructions.

The PROBLEM paragraph is required in each analysis (problem). It need not contain any sentences, and can be placed in any order among the paragraphs (but must precede the END paragraph).

The END paragraph has a special function; it terminates the Control Language instructions for a problem. It consists only of the paragraph name; i.e., /END. No other Control Language should be typed after END on the same card. (If the Control Language is keypunched on cards, END should not be punched in columns 78-80.)

BMDP programs dated before August 1977 require a FINISH paragraph when the data are not on cards or when the number of cases is specified. The FINISH paragraph consists only of

        /FINISH

and is placed immediately before the System Card that terminates the job. The FINISH paragraph must not be used when the number of cases is not specified and data are on cards. The FINISH paragraph is not necessary in BMDP programs dated August 1977 or later.

● SENTENCES

Paragraphs are composed of sentences that are commands (e.g., CORRELATION) or make assignments (e.g., VARIABLES ARE 9). The sentences can be typed in any order within the paragraph. Each sentence is terminated by a period.

Commands

A command is given either as

        command.
    or
        NO command.

depending on whether or not the command is to be executed. Each command must be followed by a period. The command must be specified as described in the program description. For example, the command

        CORRELATION.

is specified in the PRINT paragraph of many regression programs. It requests that the correlation matrix be printed. The command

        NO CORRELATION.

states that the correlation matrix is <u>not</u> to be printed.

You may also be asked to choose between mutually exclusive commands, such as

        BEFORE. or AFTER.

Then you need only specify the command that you want, the other command is automatically negated.

Assignments

The general form of an assignment sentence is

$$\text{item name} \left\{ \begin{array}{c} = \\ \text{IS} \\ \text{ARE} \end{array} \right\} \text{value(s) assigned to the specified item.}$$

The item names (or options) are specified in the program descriptions. Examples of item names are TITLE, FORMAT, NAMES, and XVARIABLES. Each assignment statement must end with a period.

IS and ARE are special words that are interchangeable with the equal sign (=). They can be used only in this context unless they are enclosed in apostrophes. The values can be numbers, names, titles, etc., according to the item's definition.

Examples of assignment statements that require one or more <u>numbers</u> (but not names) are

        VARIABLES ARE 9.
        CASES=188.
        CONTRAST=-1, 1, 1, -1.

In our program descriptions we write the definition of VARIABLE as

        VARIABLE=#.

to indicate that only one value (a number) is permissible. In the definition of CONTRAST we write

CONTRAST=$\#_1$,$\#_2$,$\cdots$.

to indicate that more than one number can be assigned.

Examples of assignment statements that require one or more values that can be either a <u>variable name</u> or a <u>variable subscript</u> are

```
GROUPING IS AGE.
LABEL IS ID.
XVARIABLES ARE AGE, WEIGHT.
XVARIABLES ARE  2,     4.
XVARIABLES ARE AGE,    4.
```

A variable <u>subscript</u> is the sequence number of the variable: 1 is the subscript for the first variable, 2 the second, etc. Variable names and subscripts are interchangeable and may be mixed in the same statement. In the above example all XVARIABLE statements mean the same thing when the variables are ordered as in the example on p. 56. In the definition of GROUPING we specify

GROUPING=v.

to show that only one grouping variable is possible. For XVARIABLES we specify

XVARIABLES=v_1,v_2,$\cdots$.

to indicate that more than one variable can be specified.

Examples of statements that require one or more <u>names</u> (but not numbers) are

```
CODE IS MYDATA.
NAMES ARE ID, AGE, HEIGHT, WEIGHT.
```

When only one name is possible as for CODE, the definition is written as

CODE=c.

When one or more names are possible, we specify

NAMES=c_1,c_2,$\cdots$.

Each name is limited to a maximum of eight characters. The name may need to be enclosed in apostrophes.

<u>Note</u>: Names, labels and titles <u>must</u> be enclosed in apostrophes (') when

- *they do not begin with a letter*

- *they contain a character (symbol) that is not a letter or a number (i.e., blank, parenthesis, comma, etc.)*

Apostrophes can be used around names even when they are not required. Apostrophes must <u>not</u> be used when the value is a number. Formats must <u>always</u> be enclosed in apostrophes.

Numbers can be used as names if they are enclosed in apostrophes.

Examples of statements that contain a <u>title</u>, <u>lengthy label</u> or <u>format</u> are

        TITLE IS 'WERNER BLOOD CHEMISTRY DATA'.
        FORMAT IS '(A4, 5F4.0, 3F4.1)'.

Formats always must be enclosed in apostrophes since they contain parentheses and other characters that are not letters or numbers; therefore we write

        FORMAT='c'.

in our definitions. Titles and labels that are longer than eight characters are likely to contain one or more blanks (to separate words); therefore they require apostrophes (see note above). To remind you that apostrophes are probably needed, we write the definition as

        TITLE='c'.

The maximum length of the title, label or format is specified in the program description.

We use c in definitions when apostrophes are probably not needed, and 'c' when they are likely to be required. However, it is not an error to use apostrophes to enclose a name even when they are not required.

For some options the item name requires a subscript. For example, codes can be specified for a grouping variable that classifies cases into groups. Names can be assigned to the codes. An example is

        CODES(5) ARE   1,   2.
        NAMES(5) ARE NOPILL,PILL.

In this example the fifth variable can take on two codes. These codes define two groups that are named NOPILL and PILL. These statements have the general form

        CODES(#)=$\#_1$,$\#_2$,$\cdots$.
        NAMES(#)=c_1,c_2,$\cdots$.

where # is the subscript of a variable or is a number specified in the definition of the item; # <u>must</u> be a number and cannot be a variable name.

Therefore in our definitions of item names (options) we use one of the following forms.

item name =
#.	one number
$\#_1$,$\#_2$,$\cdots$.	one or more numbers
v.	one variable name or subscript
v_1,v_2,$\cdots$.	one or more variable names or subscripts
c.	one name, not exceeding 8 char.
c_1,c_2,$\cdots$.	one or more names, not exceeding 8 char. each
'c'.	format, title or label that probably requires apostrophes

When the item names, such as BLANKS, are limited to specific names or values, we write

> item name = *(one only)* list of names or values.

> item name = *(one or more)* list of names or values.

depending on whether <u>only one</u> or <u>more than one</u> option can be selected.

● USING CONTROL LANGUAGE

Complete or abbreviated item names

The longer a word is, the greater chance it will be misspelled.   To minimize errors, many long words need not be punched <u>in toto</u>. For example, the following abbreviations can be used.[1]

VAR	(VARIABLES)
PROB	(PROBLEM)
CASE	(CASES)
MAX	(MAXIMUMS), etc.

Words can be further abbreviated by omitting vowels (except when the vowel is the first letter of the word), e.g., VR, PRB, CS, MX.

In the rest of this manual small letters are used in the text and summary tables to denote letters that are <u>not</u> checked by the computer.   LARGE CAPITALS are used to denote letters that are checked in item names; and *LARGE ITALIC CAPITALS* for letters that are checked in paragraph names. We include vowels in the checked letters to make the words easier to read, but they can be omitted. Therefore in this manual

VARIABLES	is typed	*VARiables* (paragraph)
	or	VARIABLES (item)
PROBLEM	is typed	*PROBlem*
CASES	is typed	CASEs
MAXIMUM	is typed	MAXIMum

Since the program checks only the part of the word we show in LARGE CAPITALS, any suffix can be added to make the word more understandable, such as completing the word or writing it in the plural rather than singular.

In <u>examples</u> we uniformly use CAPITAL LETTERS as the words appear on punch cards and in the printed output.

---

[1] BMDP programs dated before August 1977 require more letters in their abbreviated form than are shown in this manual. The Summary for each program description includes a note at the bottom that shows the minimum required abbreviation for earlier versions of the BMDP programs.

Preassigned values

Need all items and paragraphs be specified? No. Very few specifications are necessary to run a program. The specifications are used to

- describe the data
- improve the labeling of the output
- select different analyses, etc.

If not specified, many items are given <u>preassigned values</u> that are appropriate for most problems. Other specifications may not be necessary for the program to run.

The <u>preassigned value</u> is the value used for an item (option) when you do not specify its value. The definition of each item includes a statement in brackets, {}, to describe the preassigned value used for the item.

When you use a program for more than one analysis (problem) or subanalysis (subproblem), many items do not need to be respecified; once specified, the same value(s) is reused until respecified. In definitions we write

{value(s)/prev.}

if the value(s) once specified remains unchanged until respecified (i.e., the value(s) specified in the previous problem(s) is used); and we write

{value(s)}

if each time an item is not specified, the preassigned values are used (<u>not</u> the values specified in the previous problem).

Definitions

In this manual the following format is used to define a new item or option:

```
Paragraph name
    STATEMENT OR COMMAND    {preassigned value(s)}    restriction, if any
        Definition.
```

For example, in the definition of the missing value code,

```
VARiable
    MISSING=#₁,#₂,···.      {none/prev.}                one per variable
        Definition of MISSING.
```

MISSING is an item name in the VARiable paragraph. Its abbreviated form is MISS. {none/prev.} indicates that there are <u>no</u> codes for missing values unless stated. Once stated, the specified codes <u>are</u> used until changed. The restriction "one per variable" means that only one code can be specified for each variable.

Therefore if we specify

      MISSING=9,99,9.

the missing value code for the first variable is 9, for the second 99, and for the third 9.

    Another example of a definition is

```
VARiable
    BLANK= (one only)  ZERO,MISSING.            {ZERO /prev.}
        Definition of BLANK.
```

    There are only two correct forms.

      BLANK=ZERO.

or

      BLANK=MISSING.

The name on the right side of the equal sign must be spelled exactly as shown. No abbreviation is possible. BLANKs are ZERO unless otherwise specified. An assignment for BLANK remains unchanged until a new assignment is made.

    Our last example is

```
VARiable
    USE= v₁,v₂,···.                            {all variables}
        Definition of USE.
```

    USE selects a subset of the original variables to be used in the analysis. The preassigned value specifies that all variables are used unless otherwise specified. Each time a new problem begins, USE is reset to the preassigned value (since /prev. is not stated).

Summary tables

    At the end of each chapter we review the definitions of paragraphs, assignment statements and commands. The form used is

/ *Paragraph name*

    STATEMENT OR COMMAND {Preassigned value}   Definition, restriction   See page:

    When more than one program is discussed in a chapter, statements and commands common to all BMDP programs are summarized on one page. Statements and commands specific to each program described in the chapter are summarized separately on the pages following the common summary.

● ADDITIONAL CONVENTIONS IN CONTROL LANGUAGE

Blanks

Blanks can be used freely to space words, but cannot be used in the middle of numbers or names (unless the name is enclosed in apostrophes). We use blanks to space sentences and paragraphs so they are easy to read.

```
/INPUT   VARIABLES ARE 2.
         CASES ARE 10.
         FORMAT IS '(2F5.0)'.
```

is easier to read than

```
/INPUT VARIABLES ARE 2.  CASES ARE 10.  FORMAT IS
'(2F5.0)'.
```

but both are correct.

Repetition

Repetition of the same numerical values (but not names) in a list can be specified by the notation: number*value.

> 1, 2, 3, 3, 3, 3, 5, 5, 5, 5, 11.

> can be written

> 1, 2, 4*3, 4*5, 11.

This notation is often useful; e.g., when the same missing value code is used for 20 variables.

Implied list

When cutpoints or codes are used to partition a variable into groups or categories, the values are often equally spaced. To facilitate the specification of such a list, you can state

> $\#_1$ TO $\#_2$ BY $\#_3$.

For example, the list of values

> 1, 2, 3, 4, 6, 8, 10, 15, 20, 25.

can also be written

> 1 TO 4 BY 1, 6, 8, 10 TO 25 BY 5.

or as

> 1 TO 4, 6, 8, 10 TO 25 BY 5.

If BY is not specified, the difference between values is assumed to be 1. Any of the numbers can be negative or zero. As shown in the example implied list(s) can be used interchangeably with values. An implied list can be used in any list of numbers.

Because TO and BY are given a special meaning in the implied list they cannot be used as names or in any other context unless they are enclosed in apostrophes.

Tab feature

To avoid specifying all items in a list (such as names or maximums for all variables), you can tab directly to the selected item. Tabbing is necessary to specify MAXIMUMs (upper limits) or NAMEs for some variables but not for all. A number k in parentheses followed by a name or value means that the following name or number is the kth in the list.

For example,

NAMES=AGE, SEX, (15)WEIGHT, (20)PULSE, PRESSURE.

means that the 1st, 2nd, 15th, 20th and 21st names are AGE,SEX,WEIGHT,PULSE, PRESSURE respectively. The names for the other variables remain unchanged (either their preassigned names or names specified previously).

Repeated assignment of numbers

To specify that the maximums for 20 variables are 99, except for the 7th and 16th whose maximums are 9, the statement can be

MAXIMUM=6*99, 9, 8*99, 9, 4*99.

and also

MAXIMUM=20*99, (7)9, (16)9.

That is, by using the tab feature a value can be reassigned; the last value assigned in a statement is the value that is used.

Repeated sentences

If two sentences in the same paragraph refer to the same item, only the first is interpreted as specifying the item unless the program description explicitly states otherwise.

Numbers

Numbers can be either integers or real numbers (numbers with a decimal point). In addition, numbers can be in E-notation (scientific notation). That is, .000218 can also be written as 21.8E-5, or as .218E-3. And 218000 can be written as 218000.0 or as 2.18E5.

Matching elements in lists

Lists of two or more elements in the same paragraph can be stated in a form that matches and tabulates elements.

For example,

```
VARIABLE   NAMES=  AGE, WEIGHT, SEX, CHANGE.
           MINIMUMS=0,    0  , 1 ,   -10 .
           MAXIMUMS=20, 275  , 2 ,    10 .
```

can be stated as

```
VARIABLE   NAMES,         MINIMUMS,         MAXIMUMS=
           AGE,               0,               20,
           WEIGHT,            0,              275,
           SEX,               1,                2,
           CHANGE,          -10,               10.
```

Item names must be separated by commas. The matching element form cannot be used with the repetition, implied list and tab features described above, nor when the item name has a subscript.

Paragraph and item names not required by a program are ignored

When data from one program are used in another, items that are not required in the second program do not need to be removed. They are automatically ignored. For example, the same set of control cards can be used for running both P6D and P3D. If P6D uses the *PLOT* paragraph it does not need to be removed to run P3D (which does not include a *PLOT* paragraph). *PLOT* is simply ignored in P3D. *Caution: Misspelled items and paragraphs are also ignored; no warning is given when you put an item in the wrong paragraph.*

Remarks and comments

Comments can be used freely in Control Language if they do not interfere with the sentences and paragraphs required by the program. A safe procedure is to place them after a slash (/) to keep them out of other paragraphs. Since *COMMENT* is not a valid paragraph name, the *COMMENT* paragraph will be ignored in the analysis.

```
/COMMENT = 'THIS IS A COMMENT OF ANY KIND.  IT IS ENCLOSED
   IN SINGLE APOSTROPHES BECAUSE IT INCLUDES BLANKS.  IT
   COULD ALSO INCLUDE SPECIAL CHARACTERS ("$+-...ETC.)'.
```

A comment must not be used in a *TRANsformation* paragraph.

Reserved words and symbols

IS, ARE, TO and BY are special words in the Control Language, used as explained above. Therefore they should not be used except in their special context. If they are used in any other way, they must be enclosed in apostrophes (').

The apostrophe (') is a reserved symbol and should not be otherwise used. Unfortunately, on some keypunches the @ symbol is keypunched on a card in an identical manner to an apostrophe on other keypunches. Therefore, the @ symbol should not be used in Control Language statements.

4.2 System Cards

When you begin an analysis with a BMDP program at your computing facility, you must satisfy three requirements.

- You must identify yourself as a legitimate user of the computer.
- You must state the BMDP program to be used.
- You must state that the Control Language instructions for the BMDP program come next.

When the Control Language is keypunched on cards, these three functions are also specified on cards, which we call System Cards. If you are using a terminal, the same information is required but the form of specifying it is different.

Here we describe the three System Cards used at Health Sciences Computing Facility (HSCF) to start a BMDP analysis.

The first card has the form

        //jobname Ƃ JOB Ƃ (accounting information),yourname

where Ƃ indicates one or more blank spaces. The minimum required accounting information is your computer account number, which has the form nooo where n is a letter and ooo a three-digit number. Therefore in our examples we use the standard form

        //jobname   JOB   nooo,yourname

The second card specifies the program to be executed. It has the form

        // Ƃ EXEC Ƃ BIMED,PROG=BMDPxx

where xx is the two-character identification code for the BMDP program.

The third card is

        //SYSIN Ƃ DD Ƃ *

This tells the computer that the Control Language for the BMDP program follows immediately.

For example

        //P123   JOB   P123,EASY
        //   EXEC   BIMED,PROG=BMDP6D
        //SYSIN   DD   *

specifies that the user, EASY, with job number P123 (and the same jobname) wants to run program P6D. Note that blanks can only be used where shown.

If your data input is on a disk or tape, or if the program writes results to be saved on a tape or disk, it is also necessary to describe the tape or disk file to be used. This is discussed in Chapter 7.

At the end of your job another System Card is necessary to tell the computer that you are finished. At HSCF this card is

      //

in columns 1 and 2. On IBM computers this card serves as an end-of-file indicator.

The BMDP programs check for an end-of-file indicator to know when the reading of your Control Language or data (if on cards) is completed.

The exact form of all System Cards depends on your computing facility. Throughout this manual we describe the cards used at HSCF. Before running a BMDP program elsewhere you should check on the appropriate System Cards for your facility. The last page in this manual, facing the back cover, has space for you to fill in the System Cards used at your facility.

4.3 Common Errors

Several kinds of errors may cause your program to run improperly or fail to finish; these may be errors in the System Cards, in the Control Language instructions, or possibly in the program itself (called a bug). An error message is often written in the output to locate where an error occurs. Since one error may trigger others, it is always wise to <u>look for the first error message and try to correct the indicated error.</u>

If the BMDP heading (the program number and name -- e.g., BMDP4D SINGLE COLUMN FREQUENCIES - NUMERIC AND NONNUMERIC) is not printed in the output, your error is probably in the System Cards; if the system finds the program you specify, the heading is always printed before anything else is done.

When the mistake is in the syntax (punctuation) of your Control Language instructions, an error message will usually point to the place in the instructions where the error was sensed; the error will be at, or before, that place. Check the statement where the error is indicated and the previous statements (if necessary) to see if you used the Control Language correctly. Have you

- included periods at the end of each sentence?

- included a slash between paragraphs?

- used matching pairs of apostrophes and parentheses?

- put commas between all items in lists of numbers or names?

- put apostrophes around names that do not begin with a letter or that contain a character that is not a letter or a number (i.e., blank, parenthesis, comma, etc.)?

- used a reserved name (IS, ARE, TO, BY) or symbol (', @) in the wrong context?

Remember that misspelled or misplaced items, sentences or paragraphs are ignored and no warning is given.

In addition to error messages printed by the BMDP programs, the computing system may generate its own messages. If the system is one of the IBM 360 or 370 series, the following messages are typical, but may vary in different facilities. The IBM code for the error is given in parentheses.

- Computer operator cancelled your job; see the operator. (122 or 222)

- The amount of time for your job has been exceeded; check to see if you misspecified some option; if not, find out how to increase the time on your System Cards. (322)

- The program you are calling for was not found; is the program name spelled correctly? (806)

- More region or memory space in the computer is required for your job; you may need to specify a larger region size on your System Cards. (804 or 80A)

- The amount of computer disk space required for your data is too large or the allotted space that the program needs for temporary storage must be increased. (B37 or D37)

- The program stopped because of a program error; if you added any FORTRAN statements (Chapters 6 and 14) you should check them carefully. (OC0)

The following FORTRAN error messages may also be encountered:

- Error in your FORMAT statement. (IHC 211 I)

- Your FORMAT tried to read more data than you have on a card or in a record. (IHC 212 I)

- Illegal character in input; e.g., nonnumeric character found instead of a number; use P4D to identify the case(s) containing the nonnumeric data. (IHC 215 I)

- The data or Control Language instructions terminated unexpectedly; this can be caused by omitting the *FINISH* paragraph in programs dated before August 1977. (IHC 217 I)

- The computer grumbles because the argument of a function is incorrect; e.g., calculating the logarithm of zero or the square root of a negative number, or a result has an exponent that is too large, etc. This is a rare error since the BMDP programs are designed to avoid it. (IHC 25n)

If you can't locate your error after checking for all the errors described above, ask a consultant at the computing facility to help you.

5

DESCRIBING DATA AND VARIABLES

In Control Language

The BMDP programs allow great flexibility in the form and source of the data and in labeling the variables and the cases. This flexibility is achieved by allowing you to specify (or not specify) many options, depending on the analysis desired.

The Control Language used to describe the data and variables is common to all BMDP programs. In this chapter we describe the following Control Language paragraphs and how they are used:

- the *PROBlem* paragraph to give a title to the analysis   p. 74

- the *INPut* paragraph to describe the input data (number of cases, number of variables and format), to tell where the data are located (cards, terminal, tape or disk) and whether or not the data are in a BMDP File   p. 75

- the *VARiable* paragraph to name the variables, state upper and lower limits for each variable, specify missing value codes, select variables to be used in an analysis, and identify the variables that contain case labels   p. 79

- the *GROUP* or *CATEGory* paragraph to stratify or classify the cases into groups or categories (this paragraph is used primarily in BMDP programs that compare groups or form frequency tables)   p. 84

We conclude this chapter with an example of the results produced by program P3D -- Comparison of Two Groups with t Tests -- to illustrate how labeling makes the results easier to read.

Data editing and case selection are available in all BMDP programs. The data can be modified and new variables can be formed by transforming the data (e.g., the analysis may require the logarithm of height when the height is recorded). Methods for case selection and transformation are described in Chapter 6.

Data and results (such as covariance matrix) can be transferred from one BMDP program to another by using a BMDP File. The BMDP File is a means of storing data or results from a BMDP program on disk or magnetic tape. The data or results can then be used as input to other BMDP programs. The advantages of using a BMDP File are

- it greatly reduces the Control Language instructions needed to describe the data and the variables

- it is more efficient to read than data read with a format specification and can reduce the costs of reading a large amount of data

- it is the only method of transferring results from one BMDP program to another

The creation and use of a BMDP File is described in detail in Chapter 7.

● THE WERNER BLOOD CHEMISTRY DATA

We illustrate how to use Control Language by analyzing the Werner blood chemistry data (Werner et al., 1970) shown in Table 5.1. The data are physical (age, weight, height) and blood chemistry (cholesterol, albumin, calcium, uric acid) measurements on 188 women: 94 women take birth control pills and 94 do not. The data are organized as 94 pairs (one on, one off the pill in each pair) of age-matched women. The age matching is used in only one example.

Table 5.1 Werner et al. (1970) Blood Chemistry Data[1]

ID Number	Age	Height	Weight	Birthpill[2]	Cholesterol	Albumin[3]	Calcium[3]	Uric Acid[3]
2381	22	67	144	1	200	43	98	54
1946	22	64	160	2	600	35		72
1610	25	62	128	1	243	41	104	33
1797	25	68	150	2	50	38	96	30
561	19	64	125	1	158	41	99	47
2519	19	67	130	2	255	45	105	83
225	20	64	118	1	210	39	95	40
2420	20	65	119	2	192	38	93	50
1649	21	60	107	1	246	42	101	52
3108	21	65	135	2	245	34	106	48
1375	21	63	100	1	208	38	98	54
2936	21	64	120	2	260	47	106	38
988	21	67	134	1	204	40	108	34
408	21	67	145	2	192	39	95	49
913	21	63	138	1	280	41	102	41
2373	21	64	113	2	230	39	99	38
736	21	63	160	1	215	39	96	39
2334	21	64	115	2	225	44	105	44
3035	21	68	125	1	165	48	105	28
1883	21	62	106	2	200	38	95	40
2729	21	68	150	1	220	47	102	75
1848	21	64	130	2	255	34	102	40
1890	22	62	135	1	263	43	98	47
266	22	62	110	2	173	42	97	37
2125	22	57	105	1	170	46	98	45
2092	22	64	120	2	290	37	98	59
1291	22	64	115	1	263	42	102	47
1922	22	59	94	2	220	47	105	46
307	22	67	125	1	200	43	100	44
1790	22	62	97	2	192	38	95	43
239	22	58	100	1	247	42	104	52
3096	22	66	130	2	175	44	106	58
1068	22	60	100	1	155	41	96	45
2730	22	65	135	2	215	40	93	43
51	22	60	95	1	200	47	99	34
2648	22	67	124	2	247	44	102	45
906	23	63	125	1	220	32	92	42
97	23	64	105	2	207	42	100	40
649	23	63	125	1	266	42	103	47
3014	23	63	120	2	240	43	101	39
962	24	68	125	1	195	49	106	52
1912	24	64	130	2	250	39	103	46
957	24	65	130	1	225	50	108	39
338	24	65	148	2	200	37	104	49
1819	24	64	135	1	180	37	96	49
420	24	71	156	2	240	42	102	51
494	25	62	107	1	330	48	101	53
2779	25	67	175	2	175	39	93	51
477	25	66	112	1	205	46	101	33
2870	25	63	120	2	235	44	103	40
3	54	62	120	1	227		86	25
2077	54	67	127	2	260	44	106	57
3095	25	67	135	1	295	46	106	47
2363	25	67	141	2	230	38	101	52
2698	26	66	135	1	240	48	103	51
3006	26	64	118	2	238	40	99	46
796	26	65	125	1	198	44	96	43
2351	26	65	120	2	196	38	95	43
1627	27	64	120	1	172	43	98	60
152	27	64	180	2	317	37	98	84
2305	27	69	137	1	195	46	101	42
2121	27	64	125	2	185	36	94	54
883	27	63	125	1	168	42	97	41
1882	27	64	124	2	200	40	96	52
416	27	60	140	1	250	36	98	68
16	27	65	155	2	280	42	103	52
1637	28	65	108	1	260	48	106	51
3138	28	62	110	2	250	44	105	38
457	28	65	120	1	175	48	100	47
2830	28	66	113	2	305	41	93	24
1083	28	62	135	1	200	43	97	37
3359	28	65	160	2	235	42	101	41
1255	29	61	142	1	177	39	99	46
3256	29	61	115	2	235	45	98	47
1207	29	68	155	1	226	38	94	43
3210	29	65	118	2	230	44	99	44
2871	30	66	143	1	198	45	107	65
1775	30	63	110	2	295	45	98	46
1274	30	61	99	1	230	43	99	39
2365	30	63	132	2	200	37	96	34
949	30	62	125	1	230	46	104	48
3519	30	63	110	2	262	33	99	41
609	30	64	135	1	174	40	95	35
3021	30	66	112	2	250	44	100	35
1668	30	64	160	1	217	35	95	31
2877	30	68		2	212	38	100	66
3349	31	65	125	1	250	43	98	39
2454	31	66	120	2	237	34	91	49
2098	31	65	115	1	270	41	111	64
1916	31	63	110	2	280	44	99	49
782	31	66	123	1	238	37	96	33
2947	31	67	136	2	218	38	95	42
2996	32	67	132	1	185	39	103	37
441	32	68	203	2	235	38	99	37
3506	32	62	155	1	262	37	99	43
2617	32	65	126	2	160	41	97	40
2522	32	63	125	1	189	40	94	40
2400	32	71	170	2	205	37	90	60
1249	32	62	120	1	260	43	107	38
2367	32	62	145	2	240	45	108	42
57	32	66	140	1	197	44	106	58
2267	32	68	133	2	180	32	95	40
63	54	67	145	1	320	39		
234	54	67	140	2	245	39	104	56
3334	33	64	115	1	205	47	100	54
480	33	60	118	2	260	38	99	38
828	33	67	137	1	243	41	106	55
3019	33	68	130	2	195	40	95	58
61	33	65	130	1	203	44	101	48
2062	33	69	138	2	222	40	104	42
1770	34	62	112	1	197	37	93	44
3208	34	63	125	2	245	38	95	41
1140	35	62	115	1	180	40	91	59
3194	35	67	125	2	223	40	100	37
216	35	66	138	1	254	39	107	41
2501	35	66	140	2	245	39	105	56
1309	36	62	135	1	247	34	90	44
2942	36	67	120	2	175	46	103	39
819	36	66	112	1	215	43	104	42
3277	36	65	121	2	270	43	98	35
2456	37		141	1	237		105	45
2254	37	67	125	2	200	45	99	66
46	37	65	116	1	270	42	100	48
1803	37	63	129	2	230	36	91	22
2811	38	64	165	1	255	44	102	62
2341	38	65	151	2	275	38	94	46
2349	39	64	135	1	210	40	95	46
523	39	64	108	2	198	44	90	38
2675	39	63	195	1	260	40	108	42
2153	39	69	132	2	180	39	94	30
1111	39	62	100	1	210	45	91	27
1959	39	62	110	2	235	41	99	35
1701	40	63	110	1	196	39	97	42
1910	40	64	151	2	305	39	99	48
1571	40	65	145	1	170	45	100	43
2818	40	66	140	2	276	46	100	55
544	40	65	140	1	272	41	91	44
3312	40	65	137	2	315	37	96	99
383	40	67	130	1	300	40	106	52
48	40	62	117	2	290	42	99	42
263	41	62	116	1	320	44	111	61
77	41	68	215	2	255	43	105	45
564	41	64	125	1	306	45	98	62
2709	41	69	170	2	324	40	99	55
1715	42	60	105	1	240	41	101	51
1896	42	63	129	2	210	40	100	46
1326	43	66	167	1	210	40	100	52
1965	43	68	145	2	250	36	98	42
1317	43	66	138	1	335	44	105	58
1837	43	66	132	2	230	42	98	48
2220	43	64	125	1	285	45	105	50
2437	43	62	113	2	200	40	93	36
221	43	64	126	1	280	45	106	38
3286	43	65	148	2	276	41	105	50
520	55	64	124	1	275	40	98	53
22	55	64	165	2	298	36	100	63
59	44	62	118	1	253	43	94	44
2497	44	63	133	2	242	47	104	49
56	45	67	180	1	160	38	97	59
15	45	65	140	2	263	45	107	52
5	46	66		1	250	41	101	73
850	46	67	145	2	320	40	101	37
1218	46	63	138	1	257	40	90	61
132	46	62	118	2	190	38	95	43
695	46	62	103	1	230	43	102	33
541	46	65	190	2	265	41	108	85
473	47	67	135	1	297	42	100	45
2657	47	67	143	2	255	41	100	40
164	47	61	132	1	257	39	96	38
2865	47	59	94	2	257	41	103	53
554	48	62	120	1	300	39	94	51
644	48	66	143	2	225	40	100	62
852	48	67	143	1	216	40	96	47
629	48	65	134	2	248	42	102	42
1241	48	65	164	1	306	44	100	78
156	48	66	120	2	235	36	97	35
1251	48	60	125	1	195	41	95	53
64	48	64	138	2	338	37	100	58
2102	49	64	126	1	255	41	102	48
1932	49	69	158	2	217	36	106	65
44	50	69	135	1	295	43	105	63
3134	50	66	140	2	390	46	97	55
1250	52	68	150	1	250	42	97	59
1789	52	62	107	2	265	46	104	64
1149	53		178	1	227	39		50
575	53	65	140	2	220	40	107	46
2271	54	66	158	1	305	42	103	48
39	54	60	170	2	220	35	88	63

continued *continued*

[1] Two values of cholesterol (cases 2 and 4) have been deliberately modified to represent extreme values to be excluded from the analysis. Eight other values were left blank to represent missing data. Each case is recorded in columns 1 to 36 of a card; each variable uses 4 columns. The appropriate format to read the data is (A4,5F4.0,3F4.1).

[2] Birth control pill user: 1 no pill; 2 pill

[3] Albumin, calcium and uric acid are recorded to the nearest 1/10 of a unit. Other measurements are to the nearest unit.

5.1 The Problem Paragraph

The BMDP programs can analyze several sets of data, one after the other. When the description of the data (or of the analyses) is similar, many Control Language specifications need not be repeated because after they are stated they remain unchanged until restated. This is especially useful when you want to do the same analysis for subsets of the data; e.g., the same analysis for each hospital.

The analysis of a single set of data is called a problem. A second analysis of the same data is called a subproblem. The *PROBlem* paragraph must be present in the Control Language instructions for each problem (set of data). It need not be followed by statements (e.g., TITLE). That is,

/PROBLEM or /PROB

is sufficient.

• TITLE: A Label for the Output

A title can be specified in the *PROBlem* paragraph to label the output. For example, an appropriate title for our data is 'Werner blood chemistry data'. This is specified as

TITLE IS 'WERNER BLOOD CHEMISTRY DATA'.

The title cannot exceed 160 characters (two cards) in length. If omitted, the title on the output is left blank. Using the form for definitions described in Section 4.1, we write the definition of TITLE as

---

PROBlem
    TITLE='c'.   {blank}

    c is a title for the output not exceeding 160 characters in length.
    The title must be enclosed in apostrophes if it does not begin with a
    letter or if it contains a symbol that is neither a letter nor a num-
    ber, e.g., blank, comma, period, etc.

The *PROBlem* paragraph that we use for the data in Table 5.1 is

/PROBLEM   TITLE IS 'WERNER BLOOD CHEMISTRY DATA'.

5.2 Describing the Data: The Input Paragraph

The *INPut*[1] paragraph is required for the first problem (analysis). When the data are on cards or are read from a terminal, the number of VARIABLES and the FORMAT (layout) of the data are the only required specifications. When the data are on a disk or magnetic tape or in a BMDP File, the UNIT where the data are located must be specified. The Control Language used to read data from a BMDP File is described in Section 7.3.

● VARIABLE: THE NUMBER OF VARIABLES

The Werner blood chemistry data contain nine variables -- a variable containing a case label (ID), three physical measurements, a variable indicating whether the woman is taking the pill, and four blood chemistry variables. Therefore we specify

        VARIABLES ARE 9.

in the *INPut* paragraph.

Although the meaning of "variable" is usually clear, at times it is worth dividing a variable into parts so you can refer to each part separately. For example, dates are commonly written with six digits, such as 010276 or 081277. These observations can be read as a six digit number called DATE or as <u>three</u> variables called MONTH, DAY and YEAR, each two-digits long. It is easier to compute time differences between dates if they are read as three separate variables.

INPut
    VARIABLE= #.   {none/prev.}

    The number of VARIABLES[2] in each case. This is required for the first problem unless the data are from a BMDP File. The value assigned in the first problem is used in subsequent problems unless the number of VARIABLES is respecified.

The data need not be read as input. You may want to generate data using random numbers within a BMDP program or you may want to read data that is in nonstandard form (cannot be read in the same manner for each case). You will then want to specify that there are zero variables to be read as input and use one of the methods described in Chapter 6 to generate or read your data. When
        VARIABLE=0.
is specified, you must state the number of cases and you can omit the format.

---

[1] In BMDP programs dated before August 1977,
   the minimum required abbreviation is *INPUT* (not *INP*).

[2] In BMDP programs dated before August 1977,
   the minimum required abbreviation is VARIAB (not VAR).

● FORMAT: THE LAYOUT OF THE DATA

The FORMAT[3] describes the layout of the data in each case. If you are
not familiar with the format statement used in FORTRAN or in the BMD or BMDP
programs, we recommend that you read Section 3.3.

The format must describe all variables (except those containing case
labels) as floating point numbers (in F-format). The variables identified as
case labels must be described in A-format. I-format must not be used. The
format statement for the Werner data is

FORMAT IS '(A4,5F4.0,3F4.1)'.

The first variable contains the case identification and is used as a case
label; it is read using an A4 specification.

The format must begin with an open parenthesis and end with a closed
parenthesis. Therefore to conform to Control Language rules it must be
enclosed in apostrophes.

```
INPut
    FORMAT='c'.          {none/prev.}        cannot exceed 800 characters

        The format c specifies the layout of the data in a single case.  Data
        must be read in F-format (not in I-format) in all programs except P4D.
        Up to two variables may be read in A-format and used as case labels
        but not as data.  The usual FORTRAN rules for the format are appli-
        cable.  The format must be stated unless the data are from a BMDP
        File.
```

● CASE: THE NUMBER OF CASES

The number of cases must be specified when the data are followed by more
Control Language instructions; e.g., when the data are read from cards and more
than one set of data is analyzed.

The number of cases need not be specified (but can be) when all the data
are read and are not followed by more Control Language instructions. If fewer
cases are specified than are in the data, only the specified number of cases
is read. Each BMDP program checks for an end-of-file indicator and stops
reading the data when one is found. When the data are on cards, any System
Card immediately following the data cards serves as an end-of-file indicator.
Data from BMDP Files are terminated by an end-of-file indicator that is recognized by the BMDP program.

In our example we have 188 cases. This is specified as

CASES ARE 188.

---

[3] In BMDP programs dated before August 1977,
    the minimum required abbreviation is FORMAT (not FORM).

```
INPut
    CASE= #.                    {end-of-file/prev.}
```

The number of cases or observations to be read. Not required when
the data are from a BMDP File or are terminated by an end-of-file
indicator or System Card.

● UNIT: THE UNIT NUMBER

When the data are on a disk or magnetic tape you must specify where they
can be found. In Control Language a UNIT number specifies where the data are
stored. (The same UNIT number is also specified on a System Card that describes to the computer where the data are stored.) There are some restric-
tions in the choice of a unit number: 5 signifies card input, 6 is the usual
printer for output, and the BMDP programs use units 1 and 2 to save data temporarily. The most common units available are 3, 4, 7 and 8 although others
are possible.

```
INPut
    UNIT=#.                {5(cards)/prev.}      # cannot be 1, 2 or 6
```

The unit number from which the data are to be read by the program.
Not required if data are on cards.
*Note: When a UNIT number other than 5 is specified, an extra
System Card must be included to describe the location of the data
to the computer.*

● REWIND: POSITIONING THE UNIT

When the data are on a disk or magnetic tape, the data to be used in an
analysis need not start with the first data record; they may start at some
other record. The BMDP programs assume that the data begin with the first
record and position the disk or tape accordingly (REWIND). But sometimes the
data may be in sequential subsets; the first subset is used in the first analysis,
the second in the second analysis, etc. In this situation you would not want to
reposition to the beginning of the data after completing the first analysis --
you would want the disk or tape to remain positioned exactly where it is left by
the previous problem (NO REWIND). This is a rarely used option.

```
INPut
    REWIND.        {REWIND/prev. }     use only when data are from disk or tape
```

REWIND positions UNIT at the beginning (first case) of the data.
NO REWIND leaves the UNIT positioned where it is.

The Control Language instructions we use to describe the Werner data (Table 5.1) when read from cards are

<pre>
/INPUT   VARIABLES ARE 9.
                  FORMAT IS '(A4,5F4.0,3F4.1)'.
                  CASES ARE 188.
</pre>

In many examples in this manual, the CASE statement is omitted since the data are followed by a System Card. Both UNIT and REWIND are unnecessary when the data are from cards.

5.3 Describing the Variables: The Variable Paragraph

In the *VARiable*[4] paragraph

- variables can be NAMED   p. 79
- upper and lower limits (MAXIMUM and MINIMUM) can be specified for the data in each variable   p. 80
- MISSING value codes can be specified   p. 81
- variables can be selected (to be USED) for the analysis   p. 82
- variables containing case LABELS can be identified   p. 83

In addition the *VARiable* paragraph is used to indicate whether new variables are created by transformations. This is described in Chapter 6 where transformations are treated in depth.

The *VARiable* paragraph is optional and can be omitted if the above features are not needed.

● NAME: NAMING THE VARIABLES

Variables often have short names that are easy to remember such as SEX, AGE, HEIGHT, WEIGHT, ID, etc. Your results can be interpreted more easily if these names are printed in the output.

For the Werner data in Table 5.1, we specify variable names as

```
NAMES ARE ID,AGE,HEIGHT,WEIGHT,BRTHPILL,
          CHOLSTRL,ALBUMIN,CALCIUM,URICACID.
```

The first name is that of the first variable, the second that of the second variable, etc.

Variable names are restricted to eight characters. Therefore we omit several vowels to shorten names in our example:

         BRTHPILL is used in place of birthpill

and   CHOLSTRL is used in place of cholesterol.

Names do not need to be specified for all of the variables. Tabbing (p. 65) can be used to skip variables. The preassigned name for each variable is X(subscript) where <u>subscript</u> is the sequence number of the variable; e.g., X(1) is the preassigned name for the first variable. The preassigned names cannot be used in Control Language instructions except in the *TRANsform* paragraph.

---

[4] In BMDP programs dated before August 1977,
     the minimum required abbreviation is *VARIAB* (not *VAR*).

```
VARiable
    NAME= c₁,c₂,···.          {X(1),X(2),.../prev.}      one per variable
```

> Names for the variables. Each name is restricted to eight characters. Variable names are used to label the output. They (or the variable subscripts) are used in the Control Language instructions to identify the variable. However, if the NAME is not specified the variable can be identified only by its subscript (1,2,... etc.) in Control Language, i.e., the preassigned name X(subscript) cannot be used in Control Language instructions except in the *TRANsform* paragraph (Chapter 6).

Variable names, as all names in Control Language, must be enclosed in apostrophes if they do not begin with a letter or if they contain a symbol (blank, comma, etc.) that is neither a letter or a number.

● MAXIMUM and MINIMUM: UPPER AND LOWER LIMITS FOR EACH VARIABLE

Upper and lower limits can be specified to eliminate extreme values or errors and to restrict the range of data used in an analysis.

In Table 5.1 two erroneous values were deliberately entered into the data (600 for cholesterol in the second case and 50 for cholesterol in the fourth case). We eliminate both from the analysis by specifying

    MAXIMUM IS (6) 400.
    MINIMUM IS (6) 150.

Since cholesterol is the sixth variable, we tabbed to (6) (p. 65) and set limits only for cholesterol. Either limit can be specified without the other.


```
VARiable
    MAXIMUM=#₁,#₂,···.   {none/prev.}           one per variable
```

> #₁ is the upper limit for the first variable, #₂ for the second variable, etc. Limits for any or all variables can be specified. Values of a variable greater than its upper limit are excluded from all computations.

```
    MINIMUM=#₁,#₂,···.   {none/prev.}           one per variable
```

> #₁ is the lower limit for the first variable, #₂ for the second variable, etc. Limits for any or all variables can be specified. Values of a variable less than its lower limit are excluded from all computations.

● MISSING VALUES AND BLANKS

In many experiments some of the data values are not recorded for various reasons. The unrecorded values are called missing values. When the data are coded, we recommend that a special code be assigned to indicate a missing value; the missing value code can then be identified and missing values eliminated from the analysis.

The code can be a blank field; i.e., no value is recorded. The use of blank fields to denote missing values depends on your computer facility. You must check to see whether blank fields can be differentiated from zero. (Facilities with an IBM 360/370 that receive the BMDP programs as load modules can differentiate blanks from zeros.)

We deliberately left several data values blank in Table 5.1 to illustrate the problem of missing values. To specify whether blank fields denote missing values or zeros, either

BLANKS ARE MISSING.

or   BLANKS ARE ZERO.

can be specified.[5] The latter is the preassigned method of treating blank fields if neither is specified. The former is appropriate for the Werner data in Table 5.1.

VARiable
    BLANK= *(one only)* ZERO,MISSING.   {ZERO /prev.}

Unless MISSING is specified, all blank fields are treated as numeric ZEROs (0.0). If MISSING is specified, all blank fields are treated as missing value codes and are eliminated from all analyses. Check with your computing facility whether blank fields are differentiated from zeros before using the latter option.

Numbers can also be used as missing value codes for the variables. If you use a number as your missing value code, it should be an integer since computers do not represent fractions exactly and so the missing value code may not be recognized.

VARiable
    MISSING=$\#_1$,$\#_2$,$\cdots$.   {none/prev.}   one per variable

$\#_1$ is the missing value code for the first variable, $\#_2$ for the second, etc. Missing value codes are not used in the analyses.

Tabbing (p. 65) can be used to skip variables. Repetition of the same number (p. 64) is useful when the same code is used for many variables.

---

[5] In BMDP programs dated before February 1976,
     BLANK=ZERO is assumed and cannot be changed.

● USE: SELECTING VARIABLES FOR ANALYSIS

All programs allow you to select the variables to be analyzed. In many programs variables can be selected by a USE statement in the *VARiable* paragraph. The selection can also be done by specifying the variables in a manner specific to the program; e.g., by specifying the XVARIABLES and YVARIABLES for scatter plots in P6D or by specifying the ROW and COLUMN variables for two-way frequency tables in P1F.

Cases that contain values equal to the missing value code or out of range (above a specified upper limit or below a specified lower limit) are handled in three different ways by the BMDP programs:

A all cases are used (all acceptable values are included in the computations)

B cases used in the analysis must have acceptable values for all variables specified in the analysis; other cases are not used

C cases used in the analysis must have acceptable values for all variables selected by the USE statement (or all variables when there is no USE statement)

Programs using method C are P1R, P2R, P3R, P4R, PAR, P1V, P3S, P1M, P2M, P4M, and P7M. For these programs you may want to exclude irrelevant variables by a USE statement even if the variables to be analyzed are explicitly speci-fied by other instructions.

In some programs, such as those that compute univariate statistics, including an extra variable in the analysis does not affect the results. However, including an extra variable in a regression or factor analysis can severely affect the results. Therefore you should specify the variables to be analyzed when some of the variables in the data should be excluded.

For example, if we wanted to include only the blood chemistry measure-ments from Table 5.1 in an analysis, we would specify

USE = CHOLSTRL, ALBUMIN, CALCIUM, URICACID.

or   USE = 6 TO 9.

VARiable
   USE= $v_1, v_2, \cdots$.   {all variables}

Names or subscripts of variables to be used in the analysis. This should include all variables needed, such as the variable containing case weights (if any) or a variable used to classify the cases into groups (if any). Variables omitted from a USE statement can be used only to label cases; they are not used in any computations and no results are printed for the omitted variables.

● LABEL: CASE IDENTIFICATION

　　　Many BMDP programs print the data. When each case contains identifying information (a case label), such as a patient ID or name, the case label can be printed to identify the data. One or two variables (not exceeding four characters each) can be specified as a case label. These variables must be read under A-format (p. 52) and cannot be used as data in the analysis.

　　　In the Werner data (Table 5.1) the first variable is an identification (ID) number. Therefore we specify

　　　　　LABEL IS ID.

VARiable
　　LABEL=v_1, v_2 .　　　　　　　　{none/prev.}　　　　one or two variables, each
　　　　　　　　　　　　　　　　　　　　　　　　　　　　　not exceeding four characters

　　　Names or subscripts of one or two variables that are used to label the cases in the output. They must be read under A-format and are excluded from all computations. No LABEL statement or LABEL=0,0 specifies that there are no case labels.

　　　The *VARiable* paragraph we use for the Werner data (Table 5.1) and in many of our examples is

　　　　　/VARIABLE NAMES ARE ID,AGE,HEIGHT,WEIGHT,BRTHPILL,
　　　　　　　　　　　　CHOLSTRL,ALBUMIN,CALCIUM,URICACID.
　　　　　　　MAXIMUM IS (6)400.
　　　　　　　MINIMUM IS (6)150.
　　　　　　　BLANKS ARE MISSING.
　　　　　　　LABEL IS ID.

The USE statement is included in some examples.

5.4 The Group or Category Paragraph

Two paragraph names, *GROUP* and *CATEGory*, can be used interchangeably. We use *GROUP* when the purpose of the paragraph is to stratify (group) the cases so that each group can be analyzed separately, or so the groups can be compared (as in the analysis of variance). We use *CATEGory* when the paragraph defines intervals (categories) for the variable; the intervals are used to form frequency (contingency) tables.

The *GROUP* (*CATEGory*) paragraph is used to

- specify values of a discrete variable that are used as codes to define group membership for each case

- define intervals for a continuous variable that are used in the same manner as codes to identify group membership

- assign names to the groups

- combine codes or intervals to define a single group

The *GROUP* (or *CATEGory*) paragraph is not used in BMDP programs that do not group cases or form frequency tables. The paragraph can be omitted in other programs if the preassigned method of assigning codes also provides the necessary grouping. The usual method of assigning codes is to use up to <u>ten</u> values for the variable. If the variable used to identify groups takes on fewer than ten values (such as sex or the answer to a multiple choice question) there may be no need for a *GROUP* paragraph unless you want to name the groups. If the variable used to identify groups is continuous, the *GROUP* paragraph is required.

● CODE: GROUPING CASES ACCORDING TO A DISCRETE VARIABLE

A variable that takes on only a few values (such as SEX) is often used to identify groups in an analysis. The values of the variable are codes that identify the groups. For example, BRTHPILL in the Werner data takes on two values: 1 if the woman is not on the pill (NOPILL) and 2 if the woman is on the pill (PILL). Cases can be classified into two groups according to the value of BRTHPILL by specifying

       CODES(5) ARE 1 , 2.

where 5 is the subscript of the variable BRTHPILL that contains the codes. The variable name (BRTHPILL) <u>cannot</u> be used to the left of the equal sign (IS or ARE), only the variable subscript can be used as a subscript for the item name (to designate the variable).

The two groups can then be named by specifying

       NAMES(5) ARE NOPILL,PILL.

The first name (NOPILL) is the name of the group formed by the first code (1) and the second name (PILL) is the name of the group formed by the second code (2).

CODEs can be stated in any order and can be any number (positive, zero or negative). If you specify NAMEs, the number of CODEs and NAMEs should agree.

- CUTPOINTS: SPECIFYING INTERVALS FOR A VARIABLE

    A variable that is continuous (such as AGE) can also be used to define groups in an analysis. Suppose we want to classify the cases into four groups according to the AGEs of the women. We can specify

    CUTPOINTS(2) ARE 25, 35, 45.

where 2 is the subscript for the variable AGE in the Werner data. The four intervals formed are

- up to and including 25

- above 25 but less than or equal to 35

- above 35 but less than or equal to 45

- above 45

The CUTPOINTS are the upper limits for each interval. The first interval is from the specified lower limit, if any, up to and including the first cutpoint. The last interval is from above the last cutpoint to the specified upper limit, if any. That is, k cutpoints define (k+1) intervals since the endpoints are not stated as cutpoints.

    The groups formed by using these groupings for AGE can be NAMEd. The number of NAMEs must be one greater than the number of CUTPOINTs. For example,

    NAMES(2) ARE '25ORLESS', '26 TO 35', '36 TO 45', 'OVER 45'.

Apostrophes are required because each name either starts with a number or includes a blank or both.

GROUP
    CODE($\#$)=$\#_1$,$\#_2$,$\cdots$.   {up to 10 observed values/prev.}

    $\#_1$,$\#_2$,... are values of the variable that has subscript ($\#$). The values are used as codes to identify group (or category) membership. Cases containing values for the specified variable that are not equal to $\#_1$,$\#_2$,... will not be included in the groups (or categories) formed. CODE($\#$) can be repeated in the same *GROUP* paragraph for different variables. ($\#$) must be a variable subscript and not a variable name.

    CUTPOINT($\#$)=$\#_1$,$\#_2$,$\cdots$.   {same as CODE /prev.}

    $\#_1$,$\#_2$,... are the upper limits of intervals for variable ($\#$). Each interval contains its upper limit. k cutpoints define (k+1) intervals; i.e., the endpoints should not be stated. Each interval

(continued)

is treated as a code to identify group (or category) membership. *Do not specify both a* CODE *and a* CUTPOINT *statement for the same variable.* CUTPOINT(#) can be repeated in the same *GROUP* paragraph for different variables. (#) must be a variable subscript, not a name.

NAME(#)=c_1,c_2,$\cdots$.   { CODE or CUTPOINT values/prev.} one per

                                                           code or

                                                           interval

c_1 is the name of the first code or interval specified by a CODE(#) or CUTPOINT(#) statement, c_2 the name of the second, etc. A CODE or CUTPOINT statement must also be specified for the variable (#). *Groups or categories with the same* NAME *are combined into the same group or category.* This has the same effect as recoding the values of the variable. Preassigned names for groups or intervals cannot be used in Control Language instructions and are reset in each problem.

● RESET: CANCELLING PREVIOUS ASSIGNMENTS

Any CODE or CUTPOINT assignment remains until changed in a subsequent *GROUP* or *CATEGory* paragraph. At times you may want to cancel all previous assignments and respecify only what is necessary. This can be done by specifying

     RESET.

GROUP
    RESET.   {no}

    When RESET[6] is specified, all assignments made in previous *GROUP* or *CATEGory* paragraphs are cancelled.

Since the *GROUP* paragraph depends on the BMDP program being used, we use the following paragraph, or part of it, to illustrate several programs.

```
/GROUP
     CODES(5) ARE       1,    2.
     NAMES(5) ARE NOPILL, PILL.
     CUTPOINTS(2) ARE     25,              35,              45.
     NAMES(2) ARE '25ORLESS', '26 TO 35', '36 TO 45', 'OVER 45'.
```

---

[6] In BMDP programs dated before August 1977,
    when a *GROUP* paragraph is found, RESET is assumed and cannot be changed.

5.5 An Example

The following example illustrates how variables and groups are labeled by program P3D -- Comparison of Two Groups with t Tests. In P3D it is necessary to specify the variable used to classify the cases into groups. We compare the two groups NOPILL and PILL in the Werner data (Table 5.1).

The Control Language instructions used in this chapter to describe the Werner data are used in Example 5.1.

Example 5.1

```
/PROBLEM      TITLE IS 'WERNER BLOOD CHEMISTRY DATA'.

/INPUT        VARIABLES ARE 9.
              FORMAT IS '(A4,5F4.C,3F4.1)'.

/VARIABLE     NAMES ARE ID,AGE,HEIGHT,WEIGHT,BRTHPILL,
                    CHOLSTRL,ALBUMIN,CALCIUM,URICACID.
              MAXIMUM IS (6)400.
              MINIMUM IS (6)150.
              BLANKS ARE MISSING.
              LABEL IS ID.
              GROUPING IS BRTHPILL.

/GROUP        CODES(5) ARE      1,    2.
              NAMES(5) ARE NOPILL, PILL.

/END
```

The Control Language must be preceded by System Cards to initiate the analysis by P3D. At HSCF, the System Cards are

```
//jobname  JOB  nooo,yourname
//   EXEC  BIMED,PROG=BMDP3D
//SYSIN  DD  *
```

The Control Language is immediately followed by the data (Table 5.1). The analysis is terminated by another System Card. At HSCF, this System Card is

```
//
```

The GROUPING *statement in the* VARIABLE *paragraph describes the variables used to classify the cases into groups.*

The results of the analysis by P3D are presented in Output 5.1. The circled numbers below correspond to those in the output.

(1) In all BMDP programs the Control Language read by the computer is printed in the output exactly as read. In case of an error this allows you to examine the Control Language that was used.

(2) The *PROBlem, INPut* and *VARiable* paragraphs are interpreted. This interpretation is common to all BMDP programs. Preassigned values are shown for items not specified in the Control Language instructions. For example, the input unit number is 5 (i.e., the data are on cards). "Variables to be used" list all variables except the case label (ID). The number of cases to be read is set at 1,000,000 since it is not specified. Note (5) shows the number of cases actually read (found by the computer).

Output 5.1 An example of the effect of labelling variables and groups when using P3D. Circled numbers correspond to those in the text.

```
BMDP3D - COMPARISON OF TWO GROUPS WITH T TESTS          PROGRAM REVISED SEPTEMBER 1977
HEALTH SCIENCES COMPUTING FACILITY                      MANUAL DATE -- 1977
UNIVERSITY OF CALIFORNIA, LOS ANGELES

        PROGRAM CONTROL INFORMATION

                /PROBLEM     TITLE IS 'WERNER BLOOD CHEMISTRY DATA'.

        (1)     /INPUT       VARIABLES ARE 9.
                             FORMAT IS '(A4,5F4.0,3F4.1)'.

                /VARIABLE    NAMES ARE ID,AGE,HEIGHT,WEIGHT,BRTHPILL,
                                 CHOLSTRL,ALBUMIN,CALCIUM,URICACID.
                             MAXIMUM IS (6)400.
                             MINIMUM IS (6)150.
                             BLANKS ARE MISSING.
                             LABEL IS ID.
                             GROUPING IS BRTHPILL.

                /GROUP       CODES(5) ARE     1,    2.
                             NAMES(5) ARE NOPILL, PILL.

                /END
```

```
        PROBLEM TITLE . . . . . . .WERNER BLOOD CHEMISTRY DATA

 (2)    NUMBER OF VARIABLES TO READ IN. . . . . . . .      9
        NUMBER OF VARIABLES ADDED BY TRANSFORMATIONS. .    0
        TOTAL NUMBER OF VARIABLES . . . . . . . . . .      9
        NUMBER OF CASES TO READ IN. . . . . . . . . . 1000000
        CASE LABELING VARIABLES . . . . . . . . . .      ID
        LIMITS AND MISSING VALUE CHECKED BEFORE TRANSFORMATIONS
        BLANKS ARE. . . . . . . . . . . . . . . . . . MISSING
        INPUT UNIT NUMBER . . . . . . . . . . . . . .      5
        REWIND INPUT UNIT PRIOR TO READING. . DATA. . .   NO

        INPUT FORMAT
            (A4,5F4.0,3F4.1)


        VARIABLES TO BE USED
                    2  AGE        3  HEIGHT      4  WEIGHT      5  BRTHPILL      6  CHOLSTRL
                    7  ALBUMIN    8  CALCIUM     9  URICACID
 (3)    TEST TITLE. . . . . . . . .WERNER BLOOD CHEMISTRY DATA
        INDEXES OF VARIABLES TO BE ANALYZED . . . . . .   2   3   4   6   7   8   9
        USE COMPLETE CASES ONLY . . . . . . . . . . .    NO
        PRINT GROUP CORRELATION MATRICES. . . . . . . .  NO
        COMPUTE HOTELLINGS T SQUARE . . . . . . . . . .  NO
        INDEX OF GROUPING VARIABLE. . . . . . . . . .     5
        GROUPS USED IN COMPUTATIONS . . . . . . . . .    1   2
        PROGRAM NOTES
```

```
 (4)    1. THE T(POOLED) STATISTIC TESTS THE HYPOTHESIS THAT THE
        MEANS FOR THE TWO GROUPS ARE EQUAL ASSUMING THAT THE
        VARIANCES FOR THE TWO GROUPS ARE EQUAL.

        2. THE T(SEPARATE) STATISTIC TESTS THE HYPOTHESIS THAT THE
        MEANS FOR THE TWO GROUPS ARE EQUAL WITHOUT THE ASSUMPTION
        OF EQUAL VARIANCES.  SINCE THERE IS LITTLE LOSS IN USING
        THE SEPARATE VARIANCE T EVEN WHEN THE POOLED T MAY BE
        APPROPRIATE AND SINCE THE ERROR IN USING THE POOLED T WHEN
        VARIANCES ARE NOT EQUAL CAN BE VERY SERIOUS, THE SEPARATE
        VARIANCE T SHOULD BE USED IN MOST APPLICATIONS.

        3. THE F(FOR VARIANCES) STATISTIC TESTS THE HYPOTHESIS THAT
        THE VARIANCES FOR THE TWO GROUPS ARE EQUAL.

        4. THE P VALUES ARE THE TWO-TAIL SIGNIFICANCE LEVELS.

        5. FOR ONE SAMPLE TESTS, THE F(FOR VARIANCES) SHOULD BE
        IGNORED AND THE T(SEPARATE) AND T(POOLED) ARE THE SAME.
```

```
        NUMBER OF CASES READ. . . . . . . . . . . . .    188
 (5)
                         BEFORE TRANSFORMATION                            INTERVAL RANGE
        VARIABLE      MINIMUM    MAXIMUM    MISSING   CATEGORY  CATEGORY   GREATER   LESS THAN
        NO. NAME      LIMIT      LIMIT      CODE      CODE      NAME       THAN      OR EQUAL TO

 (6) 5    BRTHPILL                                    1.00000   NOPILL
                                                      2.00000   PILL
```

(continued)

EXAMPLE 5.5

Output 5.1 *(continued)*

⑦ FOR DIFFERENCES ON SINGLE VARIABLES.

⑧

```
**********
*AGE    * VARIABLE NUMBER   2      GROUP    1 NOPILL  2 PILL      1 NOPILL  (N=  94)      2 PILL    (N=  94)
**********                                MEAN        33.8188   33.8188
          STATISTICS    P VALUE  D. F.    STD DEV     10.1400   10.1400    H                      X
                                          S.E.M.       1.0459    1.0459    H                      X
T (SEPARATE)    0.0   1.000  186.0        SAMPLE SIZE      94        94    H    HH   H            X   XX   X
T (POOLED)      0.0   1.000  186          MAXIMUM     55.0000   55.0000    HHHHHHH  H H HH  H     XXXXXX  X X XX  X
                                          MINIMUM     19.0000   19.0000    HHHHHHHHHHHHHHHHHHH    XXXXXXXXXXXXXXXXXXXX
F(FOR VARIANCES) 1.00  1.000   93,  93                                     MIN----------------MAX MIN----------------MAX
                                                                              AN H =   3.0 CASES     AN X =   3.0 CASES


**********
*HEIGHT * VARIABLE NUMBER   3      GROUP    1 NOPILL  2 PILL      1 NOPILL  (N=  92)      2 PILL    (N=  94)
**********                                MEAN        64.0866   64.9252
          STATISTICS    P VALUE  D. F.    STD DEV      2.4924    2.4196    H                     XX
                                          S.E.M.       0.2599    0.2496    H  H                  XX  X
T (SEPARATE)   -2.33  0.021  183.5        SAMPLE SIZE      92        94    HH HHH H             XX XXX  X
T (POOLED)     -2.33  0.021  184          MAXIMUM     69.0000   71.0000    HH HHH H             XX XXX  XX
                                          MINIMUM     57.0000   59.0000    H  HH HHH HH         XX XXX XX X
F(FOR VARIANCES) 1.06  0.776   91,  93                                     HH  HH HH HHH HH H   X XX XX XXX XX X X
                                                                          MIN----------------MAX MIN----------------MAX
                                                                              AN H =   3.0 CASES     AN X =   3.0 CASES


**********
*WEIGHT * VARIABLE NUMBER   4      GROUP    1 NOPILL  2 PILL      1 NOPILL  (N=  93)      2 PILL    (N=  93)
**********                                MEAN       130.1502  133.1932
          STATISTICS    P VALUE  D. F.    STD DEV     18.8869   22.2926    H                     X
                                          S.E.M.       1.9585    2.3116    HH                    XXXXX
T (SEPARATE)   -1.00  0.317  179.2        SAMPLE SIZE      93        93    HHH                   XXXXXX X
T (POOLED)     -1.00  0.317  184          MAXIMUM    195.0000  215.0000    H HHHHHHH H           XXXXXXX X
                                          MINIMUM     95.0000   94.0000    HHHHHHHHHHHHHHHH H    XXXXXXXXXXXXXXXX  XX
F(FOR VARIANCES) 1.39  0.114   92,  92                                     MIN----------------MAX MIN----------------MAX
                                                                              AN H =   4.0 CASES     AN X =   4.0 CASES


**********
*CHOLSTRL* VARIABLE NUMBER   6     GROUP    1 NOPILL  2 PILL      1 NOPILL  (N=  94)      2 PILL    (N=  92)
**********                                MEAN       232.9678  239.4019
          STATISTICS    P VALUE  D. F.    STD DEV     43.4914   41.5620          H
                                          S.E.M.       4.4858    4.3331    H   H                 X XXXX
T (SEPARATE)   -1.03  0.304  183.9        SAMPLE SIZE      94        92    H HHHHHHH             X XXXX
T (POOLED)     -1.03  0.304  184          MAXIMUM    335.0000  390.0000    HHHHHHHHH  H          XXXXXXXXX
                                          MINIMUM    155.0000  160.0000    HHHHHHHHHHHHH HH      XXXXXXXXXXXXXX   X
F(FOR VARIANCES) 1.10  0.665   93,  91                                     MIN----------------MAX MIN----------------MAX
                                                                              AN H =   3.0 CASES     AN X =   3.0 CASES


**********
*ALBUMIN * VARIABLE NUMBER   7     GROUP    1 NOPILL  2 PILL      1 NOPILL  (N=  92)      2 PILL    (N=  94)
**********                                MEAN         4.1978    4.0266
          STATISTICS    P VALUE  D. F.    STD DEV      0.3451    0.3517    H H H                X X
                                          S.E.M.       0.0360    0.0363    HH HHHH              X X   X
T (SEPARATE)    3.35  0.001  184.0        SAMPLE SIZE      92        94    HH HHHH             XXXX XX X
T (POOLED)      3.35  0.001  184          MAXIMUM      5.0000    4.7000    HH HHHHHH H         XXXXX XX XX
                                          MINIMUM      3.2000    3.2000    HHHH HHHHHHH        X XXXXX XXXXXXX
F(FOR VARIANCES) 1.04  0.857   93,  91                                     H HHHHHH HHHHHHHHHH  XXXXXXXX XXXXXXX
                                                                          MIN----------------MAX MIN----------------MAX
                                                                              AN H =   2.0 CASES     AN X =   2.0 CASES


**********
*CALCIUM * VARIABLE NUMBER   8     GROUP    1 NOPILL  2 PILL      1 NOPILL  (N=  92)      2 PILL    (N=  93)
**********                                MEAN         9.9891    9.9355
          STATISTICS    P VALUE  D. F.    STD DEV      0.5035    0.4558          H              X X
                                          S.E.M.       0.0525    0.0473    H   H   H            X  XX    X
T (SEPARATE)    0.76  0.449  180.8        SAMPLE SIZE      92        93    H H H  H             X XXX   X
T (POOLED)      0.76  0.448  183          MAXIMUM     11.1000   10.8000    H  HHHHHHHHHHHHHH H  X X XXXXXXXXXXXX
                                          MINIMUM      8.6000    8.8000    H  HHHHHHHHHHHHHH H  X X XXXXXXXXXXXX
F(FOR VARIANCES) 1.22  0.343   91,  92                                     MIN----------------MAX MIN----------------MAX
                                                                              AN H =   3.0 CASES     AN X =   3.0 CASES


**********
*URICACID* VARIABLE NUMBER   9     GROUP    1 NOPILL  2 PILL      1 NOPILL  (N=  93)      2 PILL    (N=  94)
**********                                MEAN         4.7419    4.7989    H                    X
          STATISTICS    P VALUE  D. F.    STD DEV      1.0352    1.2715    HH                   XX X
                                          S.E.M.       0.1073    0.1311    HHHH                 XXXXX
T (SEPARATE)   -0.34  0.737  178.4        SAMPLE SIZE      93        94    HHHHH                XXXXX
T (POOLED)     -0.34  0.737  185          MAXIMUM      7.8000    9.9000    HHHHHHHHH            XXXXXXX
                                          MINIMUM      2.5000    2.2000    HHHHHHHHHHHH HH      X XXXXXXXXXXX  XX  X
F(FOR VARIANCES) 1.51  0.050   93,  92                                     MIN----------------MAX MIN----------------MAX
                                                                              AN H =   3.0 CASES     AN X =   3.0 CASES
```

③ This is an interpretation of Control Language instructions that are specific to P3D. Except for the index (subscript) of the grouping variable, all of them use preassigned values.

④ Explanatory notes about the program P3D.

⑤ The number of cases read.

⑥ An interpretation of the *GROUP* paragraph. This is common to many BMDP programs.

⑦ Each panel presents the analysis of a different variable. The variable name is printed.

⑧ The names of the groups being compared are printed.

We reran the same analysis using as few Control Language instructions as possible.

Example 5.2

```
/PROBLEM

/INPUT          VARIABLES ARE 9.
                FORMAT IS '(A4,5F4.C,3F4.1)'.

/VARIABLE       MAXIMUM IS (6)400.
                MINIMUM IS (6)150.
                BLANKS ARE MISSING.
                LABEL IS 1.
                GROUPING IS 5.

/END
```

The Control Language must be preceded by System Cards to initiate the analysis by P3D. At HSCF, the System Cards are

```
//jobname  JOB  nooo,yourname
//   EXEC  BIMED,PROG=BMDP3D
//SYSIN  DD  *
```

The Control Language is immediately followed by the data (Table 5.1). The analysis is terminated by another System Card. At HSCF, this System Card is

```
//
```


Output 5.2 presents the results for each variable. The circled numbers in Output 5.2 correspond to the notes above for Output 5.1. It is now more difficult to interpret the results since both the variable and group identifications are missing.

If we had not deliberately inserted incorrect values and missing values (blanks) in the data in Table 5.1, the MAXIMUM, MINIMUM and BLANK statements would not be necessary in the above two examples.

EXAMPLE 5.5

Output 5.2 An example of results without variable and group names (compare with Output 5.1).

```
BMDP3D - COMPARISON OF TWO GROUPS WITH T TESTS          PROGRAM REVISED SEPTEMBER 1977
HEALTH SCIENCES COMPUTING FACILITY                      MANUAL DATE --  1977
UNIVERSITY OF CALIFORNIA, LOS ANGELES
```

```
        PROGRAM CONTROL INFORMATION

                /PROBLEM

                /INPUT         VARIABLES ARE 9.
                               FORMAT IS '(A4,5F4.0,3F4.1)'.
        ①
                /VARIABLE      MAXIMUM IS (6)400.
                               MINIMUM IS (6)150.
                               BLANKS ARE MISSING.
                               LABEL IS 1.
                               GROUPING IS 5.

                /END
```

② PROBLEM TITLE . . . .
```
    NUMBER OF VARIABLES TO READ IN. . . . . . . . .         9
    NUMBER OF VARIABLES ADDED BY TRANSFORMATIONS. .         0
    TOTAL NUMBER OF VARIABLES . . . . . . . . . .           9
    NUMBER OF CASES TO READ IN. . . . . . . . . . . 1000000
    CASE LABELING VARIABLES . . . . . . . . . . . .      X(1)
    LIMITS AND MISSING VALUE CHECKED BEFORE TRANSFORMATIONS
    BLANKS ARE. . . . . . . . . . . . . . . . . .     MISSING
    INPUT UNIT NUMBER . . . . . . . . . . . . . . .         5
    REWIND INPUT UNIT PRIOR TO READING. . DATA. . .       NO

    INPUT FORMAT
         (A4,5F4.0,3F4.1)
```

```
    VARIABLES TO BE USED
             2  X(2)           3  X(3)         4  X(4)         5  X(5)         6  X(6)
             7  X(7)           8  X(8)         9  X(9)
```
③ TEST TITLE. . . . .
```
    INDEXES OF VARIABLES TO BE ANALYZED . . . . . .    2  3   4  6  7  8  9
    USE COMPLETE CASES ONLY . . . . . . . . . . . .       NO
    PRINT GROUP CORRELATION MATRICES. . . . . . . .       NO
    COMPUTE HOTELLINGS T SQUARE . . . . . . . . . .       NO
    INDEX OF GROUPING VARIABLE. . . . . . . . . . .        5
```

④ PROGRAM NOTES
```
1. THE T(POOLED) STATISTIC TESTS THE HYPOTHESIS THAT THE
MEANS FOR THE TWO GROUPS ARE EQUAL ASSUMING THAT THE
VARIANCES FOR THE TWO GROUPS ARE EQUAL.

2. THE T(SEPARATE) STATISTIC TESTS THE HYPOTHESIS THAT THE
MEANS FOR THE TWO GROUPS ARE EQUAL WITHOUT THE ASSUMPTION
OF EQUAL VARIANCES.  SINCE THERE IS LITTLE LOSS IN USING
THE SEPARATE VARIANCE T EVEN WHEN THE POOLED T MAY BE
APPROPRIATE AND SINCE THE ERROR IN USING THE POOLED T WHEN
VARIANCES ARE NOT EQUAL CAN BE VERY SERIOUS, THE SEPARATE
VARIANCE T SHOULD BE USED IN MOST APPLICATIONS.

3. THE F(FOR VARIANCES) STATISTIC TESTS THE HYPOTHESIS THAT
THE VARIANCES FOR THE TWO GROUPS ARE EQUAL.

4. THE P VALUES ARE THE TWO-TAIL SIGNIFICANCE LEVELS.

5. FOR ONE SAMPLE TESTS, THE F(FOR VARIANCES) SHOULD BE
IGNORED AND THE T(SEPARATE) AND T(POOLED) ARE THE SAME.
```

⑤ NUMBER OF CASES READ.   188

VARIABLE NO. NAME	BEFORE TRANSFORMATION					INTERVAL RANGE	
	MINIMUM LIMIT	MAXIMUM LIMIT	MISSING CODE	CATEGORY CODE	CATEGORY NAME	GREATER THAN	LESS THAN OR EQUAL TO
⑥ 5 X(5)				1.00000	* 1.0000		
				2.00000	* 2.0000		

NOTE--CATEGORY NAMES BEGINNING WITH * WERE GENERATED BY THE PROGRAM.

    GROUPS USED IN COMPUTATIONS   1   2

(continued)

Output 5.2 *(continued)*

FOR DIFFERENCES ON SINGLE VARIABLES

⑦   ⑧

```
************
* X(2)   * VARIABLE NUMBER   2      GROUP     1 * 1.0000   2 * 2.0000    1 * 1.0000(N=  94)        2 * 2.0000(N=  94)
************                         MEAN        33.8188     33.8188
           STATISTICS  P VALUE  D.F. STD DEV     10.1400     10.1400    H                         X
                                    S.E.M.        1.0459      1.0459    H                         X
T (SEPARATE)   0.0   1.000   186.0  SAMPLE SIZE      94          94    H      HH    H             X   XX   X
T (POOLED)     0.0   1.000   186    MAXIMUM     55.0000     55.0000    HHHHHHH    H H HH  H       XXXXXX   X X XX  X
                                    MINIMUM     19.0000     19.0000    HHHHHHHHHHHHHHHHHHHH       XXXXXXXXXXXXXXXXXXX
F(FOR VARIANCES) 1.00  1.000   93, 93                                 MIN----------------MAX MIN----------------MAX
                                                                          AN H =   3.0 CASES        AN X =   3.0 CASES


************
* X(3)   * VARIABLE NUMBER   3      GROUP     1 * 1.0000   2 * 2.0000    1 * 1.0000(N=  92)        2 * 2.0000(N=  94)
************                         MEAN        64.0866     64.9252    H                         X
           STATISTICS  P VALUE  D.F. STD DEV      2.4924      2.4196    H   H                     XX
                                    S.E.M.        0.2599      0.2496    HH HHH  H                 XX  X
T (SEPARATE)  -2.33  0.021   183.5  SAMPLE SIZE      92          94    HH HHH  H                 XX XXX  XX
T (POOLED)    -2.33  0.021   184    MAXIMUM     69.0000     71.0000    H  HH HHH HH              XX XXX XX X
                                    MINIMUM     57.0000     59.0000    HH  HH HH HHH HH H        X XX XX XXX XX X X
F(FOR VARIANCES) 1.06  0.776   91, 93                                 MIN----------------MAX MIN----------------MAX
                                                                          AN H =   3.0 CASES        AN X =   3.0 CASES


************
* X(4)   * VARIABLE NUMBER   4      GROUP     1 * 1.0000   2 * 2.0000    1 * 1.0000(N=  93)        2 * 2.0000(N=  93)
************                         MEAN       130.1502    133.1932
           STATISTICS  P VALUE  D.F. STD DEV     18.8869     22.2926    H                         X
                                    S.E.M.        1.9585      2.3116    HH                        XXXXXX
T (SEPARATE)  -1.00  0.317   179.2  SAMPLE SIZE      93          93    HHH                       XXXXXX X
T (POOLED)    -1.00  0.317   184    MAXIMUM    195.0000    215.0000    H HHHHHHH H               XXXXXXXXXXXXXX XX
                                    MINIMUM     95.0000     94.0000    HHHHHHHHHHHHHHHH H        XXXXXXXXXXXXXXXXX  XX
F(FOR VARIANCES) 1.39  0.114   92, 92                                 MIN----------------MAX MIN----------------MAX
                                                                          AN H =   4.0 CASES        AN X =   4.0 CASES


************
* X(6)   * VARIABLE NUMBER   6      GROUP     1 * 1.0000   2 * 2.0000    1 * 1.0000(N=  94)        2 * 2.0000(N=  92)
************                         MEAN       232.9678    239.4019
           STATISTICS  P VALUE  D.F. STD DEV     43.4914     41.5620              H
                                    S.E.M.        4.4858      4.3331    H  H                      X XXXX
T (SEPARATE)  -1.03  0.304   183.9  SAMPLE SIZE      94          92    H HHHHHHH                 X XXXX
T (POOLED)    -1.03  0.304   184    MAXIMUM    335.0000    390.0000    HHHHHHHHHH   H            XXXXXXXXXX
                                    MINIMUM    155.0000    160.0000    HHHHHHHHHHHHH HH          XXXXXXXXXXXXXXX   X
F(FOR VARIANCES) 1.10  0.665   93, 91                                 MIN----------------MAX MIN----------------MAX
                                                                          AN H =   3.0 CASES        AN X =   3.0 CASES


************
* X(7)   * VARIABLE NUMBER   7      GROUP     1 * 1.0000   2 * 2.0000    1 * 1.0000(N=  92)        2 * 2.0000(N=  94)
************                         MEAN         4.1978      4.0266
           STATISTICS  P VALUE  D.F. STD DEV      0.3451      0.3517                             X
                                    S.E.M.        0.0360      0.0363    HH H  H                  X X    X
T (SEPARATE)   3.35  0.001   184.0  SAMPLE SIZE      92          94    HH HHHH                   XXXX XX X
T (POOLED)     3.35  0.001   184    MAXIMUM      5.0000      4.7000    H HH HHHHH H             XXXXX XX XXX
                                    MINIMUM      3.2000      3.2000    H HHHHHHH HHHHHHHHHH      XXXXXXXXX XXXXXXX
F(FOR VARIANCES) 1.04  0.857   93, 91                                 MIN----------------MAX MIN----------------MAX
                                                                          AN H =   3.0 CASES        AN X =   3.0 CASES


************
* X(8)   * VARIABLE NUMBER   8      GROUP     1 * 1.0000   2 * 2.0000    1 * 1.0000(N=  92)        2 * 2.0000(N=  93)
************                         MEAN         9.9891      9.9355
           STATISTICS  P VALUE  D.F. STD DEV      0.5035      0.4558            H                   X   X
                                    S.E.M.        0.0525      0.0473    H  H    H                X XXX   X
T (SEPARATE)   0.76  0.449   180.8  SAMPLE SIZE      92          93    H H H   H                X XXX   X
T (POOLED)     0.76  0.448   183    MAXIMUM     11.1000     10.8000    H  HHHHHHHHHHHHH         X X XXXXXXXXXX
                                    MINIMUM      8.6000      8.8000    H HHHHHHHHHHHHHHH H       X X XXXXXXXXXXX
F(FOR VARIANCES) 1.22  0.343   91, 92                                 MIN----------------MAX MIN----------------MAX
                                                                          AN H =   3.0 CASES        AN X =   3.0 CASES


************
* X(9)   * VARIABLE NUMBER   9      GROUP     1 * 1.0000   2 * 2.0000    1 * 1.0000(N=  93)        2 * 2.0000(N=  94)
************                         MEAN         4.7419      4.7989    H                         X
           STATISTICS  P VALUE  D.F. STD DEV      1.0352      1.2715    HH                        XX X
                                    S.E.M.        0.1073      0.1311    HHHH                      XXXXX
T (SEPARATE)  -0.34  0.737   178.4  SAMPLE SIZE      93          94    HHHHH                     XXXXXX
T (POOLED)    -0.34  0.737   185    MAXIMUM      7.8000      9.9000    HHHHHHHHH                 XXXXXXXXX
                                    MINIMUM      2.5000      2.2000    HHHHHHHHHHHH HH           X XXXXXXXXXX  XX  X
F(FOR VARIANCES) 1.51  0.050   93, 92                                 MIN----------------MAX MIN----------------MAX
                                                                          AN H =   3.0 CASES        AN X =   3.0 CASES
```

5.6 Summary

To conclude we summarize all the definitions from this chapter. Other items in the *INPut* and *VARiable* paragraphs are introduced in Chapters 6 and 7. This table is repeated on the inside back cover of this manual and at the end of each chapter.

Paragraph STATEMENT[1] {Preassigned value[2]}		Definition, restriction	See pages:
/PROBlem		Required, each problem	74
TITLE='c'.	{blank}	Problem title, $\leq$ 160 char.	74
/INPut		Required, first problem. VARIABLE and FORMAT are required unless input is from a BMDP File (see Chapter 7).	75
VARIABLE=#.	{none/prev.}	No. of variables in input data	75
FORMAT='c'.	{none/prev.}	Format of input data, $\leq$ 800 char.	76
CASE=#.	{end-of-file/prev.}	No. of cases in data	76-77
UNIT=#.	{5(cards)/prev.}	Input unit if data are not on cards	77
REWIND.	{REWIND/ prev.}	Rewind input unit	77
/VARiable		Optional. For input from a BMDP File, items in this paragraph may be previously set, see Chapter 7.	79
NAME=$c_1,c_2,\cdots$.	{X(subscript)/prev.}	Variable names, one per variable	79-80
MAXIMUM=$\#_1,\#_2,\cdots$.	{none/prev.}	Upper limits, one per variable	80
MINIMUM=$\#_1,\#_2,\cdots$.	{none/prev.}	Lower limits, one per variable	80
BLANK= *(one only)* ZERO, MISSING.	{ZERO/ prev.}	Blanks treated as zeros or as missing value codes	81
MISSING=$\#_1,\#_2,\cdots$.	{none/prev.}	Missing value codes, one per variable	81
USE=$v_1,v_2,\cdots$.	{all variables}	Variables used in the analysis	82
LABEL=v_1,v_2.	{none/prev.}	Variable(s) used to label cases, read under A-format, one or two variables	83
/GROUP or *CATEGory*		Optional	84
CODE(#)=$\#_1,\#_2,\cdots$.	{10 smallest values/prev.}	Codes for variable #, may be repeated	84-85
CUTPOINT(#)=$\#_1,\#_2,\cdots$.	{see CODE/prev.}	Cutpoints to define intervals for variable #, may be repeated	84-85
NAME(#)=$c_1,c_2,\cdots$.	{CODES or CUTPOINTS /prev.}	Code or interval names for variable #, may be repeated	84-85
RESET.	{not RESET}	If RESET, all assignments in prev. *GROUP* or *CATEGory* are reset to preassigned values	86

Key: # number   v variable name or subscript
     'c' title, label or format   c name not exceeding 8 char., apostrophes may be required (p. 59)

[1] In BMDP programs dated before August 1977, the minimum required abbreviations are: *INPUT* (not *INP*), *VARIAB* (not *VAR*), VARIAB (not VAR) and FORMAT (not FORM); when a *GROUP* paragraph is used, RESET is implicitly specified and cannot be changed. In BMDP programs dated before February 1976, BLANK=ZERO is assumed and cannot be changed.

[2] "/prev." means that any assignment remains the same as that specified in the previous problem or paragraph until changed. Otherwise, the assignment returns to its preassigned value each time a new problem begins or when the paragraph is used again.

6

DATA EDITING

Variable Transformation and Case Selection

Laszlo Engelman, HSCF

The simplest form of data editing is to exclude data values from an analysis because they are either equal to a missing value code or outside specified upper and lower limits. Section 5.3 describes how to specify missing value codes (BLANK and MISSING) and upper and lower limits (MAXIMUM and MINIMUM).

If additional editing is unnecessary for your data, this chapter can be skipped. However, you may find that some data editing will be required as a result of your initial data screening.

In this chapter we describe methods of variable transformation and case selection that are common to all BMDP programs.

Variable transformation may be necessary to

- combine two or more variables into a single variable (for example, if height is recorded as FEET and INCHES, then either FEET can be replaced by FEET + INCHES/12 or INCHES can be replaced by 12 * FEET + INCHES; time differences and meaningful ratios are often formed from two or more separate measurements)

- transform the data to a preferred scale (for example, TIME may be recorded but the analysis requires RATE = 1/TIME)

- replace a data value by a corrected value

- recode the values of a variable

Case selection may be necessary to omit cases because only a subgroup of the cases are needed in the analysis (such as women under thirty), or to exclude a random subsample of cases against which the results of the analysis can be verified.

Variable transformations and case selection are described by Control Language statements in the *TRANsform* paragraph or by FORTRAN statements in a FORTRAN subroutine.

In this chapter we describe

- Control Language transformations   p. 97

- case selection and deletion   p. 103

- how to generate random numbers that can be used to choose random subsamples, or used in simulation studies   p. 105

- FORTRAN transformations (the BIMEDT procedure)   p. 106

- how to recode nonnumeric data   p. 109

- how to read data that are in a nonstandard form, such as data with two formats, or from two sources, or in binary form   p. 110

The above features are available in <u>all</u> BMDP programs (but are unlikely to be useful in P4D). Variable transformations and case selection use data from one case at a time. It is possible to compute differences between data in successive cases (lagged differences, Appendix C.18). However, more complicated functions that require data from several cases (such as a mean) are difficult if not impossible to perform by the above transformations.

A special program, P1S -- Multipass Transformation -- is available to help with more complicated functions. P1S reads the data as often as specified and additional transformations can be performed at each reading. Therefore, means can be computed during the first reading and used in a transformation during a subsequent reading. P1S is described in Section 6.8.

6.1 Control Language Transformations

Control Language transformations are stated in a *TRANsform*[1] paragraph in terms of simple expressions and are evaluated one case at a time.

Transformations specified in a *TRANsform* paragraph are applied to each case read in the problem. If you want to apply the same transformations to the data in a subsequent problem, you may specify only

     /TRANSFORM

without repeating the entire previous *TRANsform* paragraph. However, if <u>any</u> instructions are specified in the *TRANsform* paragraph, only these <u>new</u> instructions are performed; those in the previous *TRANsform* paragraph are ignored.

● SIMPLE EXPRESSIONS

The <u>simple expressions</u> used in Control Language transformations are:

- assignment; e.g.,   X(1) = X(10).
- arithmetic; e.g.,   X(3) = X(1) + X(2).
- function evaluation; e.g.,   X(3) = SQRT(X(3)).
- logical operation; e.g.,   X(7) = X(1) LT X(2).
- random number generation; e.g.,   X(1) = RNDU(73461).

The list of permissible transformations is given in Table 6.1.

The following names have a special meaning in the *TRANsform* paragraph:

- KASE is the sequence number of the case in the data read by the BMDP program.
- XMIS is the name assigned to the value used internally by the BMDP program as a code for values that are excluded because they are either equal to a missing value code or are out of range.
- USE indicates whether or not a <u>case</u> should be included in an analysis.
- OMIT and DELETE are item names that also indicate that specified cases should not be included in the analysis.

USE, OMIT and DELETE are discussed in Section 6.2. *The reserved words cannot be names of variables;* KASE *and* XMIS *cannot be used on the left side of the equal sign.*

---

[1] In BMDP programs dated before August 1977, the minimum required abbreviation is *TRANSF* (not *TRAN*).

Table 6.1   Control language transformations

Kind of Transformation	Usage[1]	Result	Example	Result is missing[2]
Assignment[3]	y = a.	a	X(7) = X(1). X(7) = 5.0.	
Arithmetic	y = a + b. y = a - b. y = a * b. y = a/b. y = a ** b. y = a MOD b.	a + b (addition) a - b (subtraction) a · b (multiplication) a/b (division) a^b (exponentiation) a MOD b = a - [a/b] · b The remainder of (a divided by b). For example, 14 MOD 4 yields 2 as result.	X(3) = X(1) + X(2). WEIGHT = WEIGHT - X(3). DIST = RATE * TIME. X(1) = 1 /TIME. X(1) = HEIGHT ** 3. MONTH = AGE MOD 12.	 b = 0 a < 0 and b ≠ integer
Function	y = LOG(a). y = SQRT(a). y = EXP(a). y = ABS(a). y = SIN(a). y = COS(a). y = ATAN(a). y = INT(a). y = SIGN(a). y = NONB(a).	$\log_{10}(a)$ (base 10 log) √a (square root) e^a (exponential) |a| : absolute value for a sin(a) (trigonometric sine, a in radians) cos(a) (trigonometric cosine, a in radians) arctan(a) (trigonometric arc tangent) [a]; integer part of a -1 if a < 0; 0 if a = 0; 1 if a > 0 Blank field detection (a if a ≠ "negative zero" and missing otherwise); blank field detection is computer dependent. Check with your computer center for the availability of this option.	WEIGHT = LOG (WEIGHT). INCOME = SQRT (INCOME). X(1) = EXP(X(2)). CHANGE = ABS(X(17)). X(1) = SIN(X(1)). X(2) = COS(X(2)). X(3) = ATAN(X(3)). AGE = INT (AGE). CHANGE = SIGN(X(1)). X(7) = NONB(X(7)).	a ≤ 0 a < 0 |a| > 174 a is "negative zero"
Logical operation[4]	y = a LE b. y = a LT b. y = a GE b. y = a GT b. y = a NE b. y = a EQ b. y = a AND b. y = a OR b. y = a IF b.	true if a ≤ b, false if a > b true if a < b, false if a ≥ b true if a ≥ b, false if a < b true if a > b, false if a ≤ b true if a ≠ b, false if a = b true if a = b, false if a ≠ b true if a ≠ 0 (true) and b ≠ 0 (true) true if a ≠ 0 (true) or b ≠ 0 (true) a if b ≠ 0 (true) (conditional re- placement, y = a IF b means that if b ≠ 0 (or true), set y to the value a; otherwise, leave y as it was)	USE = WT72 LE WT73. X(1) = X(2) LT X(3). USE = WEIGHT GE 50. TEMP = WEIGHT GT 50. USE = X(2) NE X(3). X(1) = X(2) EQ X(3). USE = TEMPA AND TEMPB. TEMP = TEMPA OR TEMPB. USE = XMIS IF TEMP.	
Random number Functions	y = RNDU(i). y = RNDG(i).	uniform (0,1) random number normal (0,1) random number	X(2) = RNDU(76347). X(3) = RNDG(46791).	} described on p. 105

Key: [1] y may be a variable name or X(#), or USE.

   a and b may be a variable name or X(#), a constant, KASE, USE, or XMIS.

   [2] If a or b is flagged as missing, the result is missing except for the logical operations NE, EQ, AND, OR, IF (see p.101)

   [3] If the argument in a "result = argument." statement is an integer, both a decimal point and a terminating period must be present; e.g., X(1) = 1.0. or X(1) = 1..

   [4] The result of any logical operation is either one if true, zero if false, or missing (XMIS). Logical operations that require true and false arguments, e.g., AND, OR and IF, treat zero as false; 'not equal zero' as true and XMIS as missing.

Note: A blank must precede and follow MOD, LE, LT, GE, GT, NE, EQ, AND, OR and IF.

● CREATING NEW VARIABLES

You can create new variables by transformation and use them in addition to the original variables; you must inform the BMDP program that new variables are created. For example, to create a new variable RATIO that is the ratio of WEIGHT to HEIGHT in the Werner blood chemistry data (Table 5.1) you would specify

        /TRANSFORM   RATIO = WEIGHT / HEIGHT.

To use RATIO in an analysis, RATIO must be added to the list of VARiable NAMEs and the number of variables must be increased by an ADD statement in the VARiable paragraph. Therefore, in the VARiable paragraph you would specify the NAMEs of the nine original variables plus the NAME(s) of added variable(s).

        /VARIABLE
          NAMES = ID, AGE, HEIGHT, WEIGHT, BRTHPILL,
                  CHOLSTRL, ALBUMIN, CALCIUM, URICACID, RATIO.
          ADD   = 1.

VARiable
    ADD=#.   {0/prev.}

The number of variables added by transformation (created either in the TRANsform paragraph or in the FORTRAN subroutine). If ADD is negative, variables are deleted. The total number of variables (largest subscript of any variable) used in an analysis is the sum of ADD and the number of VARIABLES specified in the INPut paragraph. If ADD is positive, the new variables are added to the variables read in as data; the subscripts of the new variables are integers beginning at one greater than the number of VARIABLES specified in the INPut paragraph. If ADD is negative, the last variable(s) are eliminated.

If ADD is positive, the number of NAMEs that can be specified in the VARIable paragraph is the sum of ADD and the number of VARIABLES in the INPut paragraph. That is, NAMEs can be specified for variables added by transformation.

● VARIABLE NAMES AND SUBSCRIPTS

You can use two types of variables in the TRANsform paragraph:

- variables read as input or added by transformation. (In the TRANsform paragraph you can refer to them either by their NAMEs assigned in the VARiable paragraph or by the form X(subscript).)

- temporary variables created and used in the TRANsform paragraph but not referred to in other Control Language paragraphs and not used in the analysis. (You can refer to them by any name that you do not specify in the VARiable paragraph. Up to 15 temporary variables can be used.)

All variables can be used in the Control Language transformations; even variables omitted from the USE list in the VARiable paragraph (p. 82).

• PUNCTUATION

Control Language transformations follow rules similar to other paragraphs. Each statement must be terminated by a period. A variable name must be stated on the left of the equal sign (=, IS or ARE). One or two variable names or numbers and the name of a function or operation must be stated on the right side. The examples in Table 6.1 show the correct punctuation.

A blank must precede and follow MOD, LE, LT, GE, GT, NE, EQ, AND, OR and IF. If only one value (a number) is specified on the right side of the equal sign, the number requires both a decimal point and a terminal period; e.g., X(1)=1.. or X(1)=1.0. A minus sign cannot immediately follow the equal sign; X(2)=0-X(1). must be used and not X(2)=-X(1).

• DATA CHECKING -- BEFORE OR AFTER TRANSFORMATION

As the data are read they are checked for values that are equal to the missing value code or are outside the upper and lower limits, if specified. The values that are missing or out of range are recoded. In the Control Language transformations the recoded values are called XMIS. If you do not want the values recoded to XMIS as the data are read, you must specify

AFTER.

in the *VARiable* paragraph. When AFTER[2] is specified, the data values are recoded after the Control Language transformations (and the FORTRAN subroutine) are processed. (This does not affect the recoding of blanks to missing values when BLANK=MISSING is specified in the *VARiable* paragraph.)

```
VARiable
    BEFORE. or AFTER.              {BEFORE/prev.}

        The data are recoded to internal codes for missing data or data
        out of range BEFORE or AFTER processing the transformations in
        both the TRANsform paragraph and the FORTRAN subroutine. AFTER
        is a rarely used option.
```

• TRANSFORMATIONS MUST BE STATED AS SIMPLE EXPRESSIONS

The permissible Control Language transformations are shown in Table 6.1 They must be specified in simple expressions. Some transformations may require a sequence of simple expressions; they are executed in the order stated. For example, if height is recorded as FEET and INCHES, height can be stated in feet as FEET + INCHES/12. However

FEET = FEET + INCHES / 12.

cannot be used as a transformation because it is not a simple expression. But it can be specified in two simple statements that make it a permissible transformation.

```
/TRANSFORM    INCHES = INCHES / 12.
              FEET   = FEET + INCHES.
```

---

[2] In BMDP programs dated before August 1977, the minimum required abbreviations are AFTERT (not AFT) and BEFORET (not BEF).

A more complicated example is that of a normalizing transformation for data from a Poisson distribution, such as COUNTS of radioactivity (COUNTS is the variable name). The usual transformation is

$$\sqrt{COUNTS} + \sqrt{COUNTS + 1}$$

This transformation can be stated as a sequence of simple expressions by using two temporary variable names (TEMPA and TEMPB); the result is recorded in a variable named ANSWER.

```
/TRANSFORM      TEMPA   = SQRT(COUNTS).
                TEMPB   = COUNTS +1.
                TEMPB   = SQRT(TEMPB).
                ANSWER  = TEMPA + TEMPB.
```

● READING YOUR OUTPUT

When Control Language transformations are specified, they are interpreted and the interpretation is printed as part of the output. For the above example the interpretation printed is

```
CONTROL LANGUAGE TRANSFORMATIONS ARE

TEMPA     = SQRT (     COUNTS   )  .
TEMPB     = COUNTS    +     1.0000 .
TEMPB     = SQRT (    TEMPB    )  .
ANSWER    = TEMPA    +     TEMPB   .

TEMPORARY NAMES USED IN TRANSFORMATIONS
    TEMPA      TEMPB
```

If this message does not appear, the paragraph name *TRANSform* is incorrectly specified. If you mispunch a variable name, forget to NAME your variables or to specify ADD in the *VARiable* paragraph, the variable names will be listed as temporary names.

● MISSING VALUES

Missing value rules

- Arithmetic: if the required arithmetic cannot be performed (e.g., $\sqrt{-1}$) or if any argument is missing or exceeds the upper or lower bounds for the variable, the result is missing.

- Logical: if any argument is missing, the result is set equal to the missing value code except in the following cases:

    false AND missing   yields false

    true OR missing   yields true

If one of the arguments for EQ or NE is XMIS the result is true or false depending on the value of the other arguments; e.g., in the statement X(1)=X(2) EQ XMIS, if X(2) is missing, X(1) is true; otherwise X(1) is false.

- The result in an expression involving IF is unchanged unless the condition is true. For example,

> TEMP=X(1) EQ 7.
> X(1)=XMIS IF TEMP.

leaves X(1) unaltered unless TEMP is true.

- If USE is equal to the missing value code after all the Control Language transformations have been performed, USE is set equal to zero; e.g., if USE=X(7) and X(7) is missing, USE is set equal to zero.

Blank fields on data cards can be used to denote missing values by specifying that they are to be used this way. If you want blanks to denote missing values for all variables, specify BLANK=MISSING in the _VARiable_ paragraph (Section 5.3). If you want blanks to denote missing values for some variables and zero for other variables, the NONB transformation must be used.

> /TRANSFORM   X(7) = NONB(X(7)).

That is, X(7) is missing whenever the seventh variable is recorded as a blank. _The detection of blanks is computer dependent and you should check with your computer center as to whether this feature is available._

Recoding a value to XMIS. You can set the value of a variable to XMIS (the missing value code) by using Control Language transformations. For example, if the variable (say STATUS) has more than one code for missing values (say 7 and 8), both can be recoded to missing by the following statements in the _TRANsform_ paragraph.

> /TRANSFORM   TEMP   = STATUS EQ 7.
> STATUS = XMIS IF TEMP.
> TEMP   = STATUS EQ 8.
> STATUS = XMIS IF TEMP.

The first pair of statements code TEMP as true when STATUS is equal to 7, and then recode STATUS to XMIS if TEMP is true. The second pair does the same for the value 8.

You can recode one data value to another value in a similar manner by specifying the recoded value in place of XMIS in the above example.

6.2 Case Selection and Deletion

The value of USE is unity (1) for each case unless you reset it. If the value of USE is

- positive (1), or true — the data for the case are used in the analysis and included in the BMDP File, if one is being created (Chapter 7).

- zero (0), or false — the data for the case are not used in the analysis, but if a BMDP File is being created, the data for the case will be included in the BMDP File.

- negative (-1) — the data for the case is not used in the analysis and is not included in a BMDP File if one is being created.

Note: If a BMDP File is being created (Chapter 7) the value of USE for the case is also included in the BMDP File (Section 7.2).

As described here for the *TRANsform* paragraph, USE specifies case selection. (USE in the *VARiable* paragraph (Section 5.3) selects variables to be used in the analysis.)

For example, if we want to include only subjects aged 20 to 30 in an analysis, we specify

```
/TRANSFORM       TEMPA = AGE GE 20.
                 TEMPB = AGE LE 30.
                 USE   = TEMPA AND TEMPB.
```

TEMPA is true only if AGE is greater than or equal to 20. TEMPB is true if AGE is less or equal to 30. USE is true (1) only if both TEMPA and TEMPB are true.

Note: Do not state

```
USE=AGE GE 20.
USE=AGE LE 30.
```

These instructions will include all cases for which AGE is less than or equal to 30 since the value of USE after the first statement is reset by the second statement.

Two statements, OMIT and DELETE, can be used to simplify case selections when the sequence numbers of cases not to be analyzed are known.

OMIT = list of case numbers.

has the same effect as setting USE=0 for each case in the list.

DELETE = list of case numbers.

has the same effect as setting USE=-1 (a negative value) for each case in the list. The OMIT and DELETE statements should follow any transformation statements that contain USE.

   Implied lists using TO and BY (p. 64) make it easy to list the case numbers.   For example

           /TRANSFORM   DELETE = 1 TO 50, 61, 63.

deletes the first 50 cases and the 61st and 63rd case.

   To omit odd numbered cases from an analysis that contains 100 cases, you can state

           /TRANSFORM   OMIT = 1 TO 99 BY 2.

TRANSform
   USE=#.   {1}

      If USE is 1 (positive or true), the case is used in the analysis
      and copied into a BMDP File if one is created. If USE is 0 (false),
      the case is not used in the analysis but is copied into a BMDP File.
      If USE is -1 (negative), the case is not used and not copied into
      a BMDP File.

   OMIT=$\#_1,\#_2,\cdots$.   {none}

      Sequence numbers of cases that are to be omitted from the analysis
      but included in a BMDP File if one is created. It sets USE to
      zero for each case specified. If only one case is specified, the
      case number must be followed by two periods; e.g., OMIT= 51..

   DELETE=$\#_1,\#_2,\cdots$.   {none}

      Sequence numbers of cases that are to be omitted from the analysis
      and not copied into a BMDP File if one is created. It sets USE
      to -1 for each case specified. If only one case is specified, the
      case number must be followed by two periods; e.g., DELETE= 51..

   Note: If you want to omit or delete many cases, the USE *statement
   is more efficient than* OMIT *or* DELETE.

6.3 Random Numbers for Random Subsamples or for Simulations

Two random number functions can be specified in the *TRANsform* paragraph.

- RNDU(i)   generates uniform random numbers on the interval from zero to one (0.1)

- RNDG(i)   generates random numbers from a normal distribution with mean zero and variance one

In both functions i is a large positive integer that is used to start the random number sequence (it is not used as a random number). If RNDU or RNDG are specified more than once, the value of i should be different for each. The random number generators are described in Appendix A.1.

Suppose you want a random sample of the cases -- deleting about 25% from the analysis. You can specify

```
/TRANSFORM     TEMP = RNDU(768245).
               USE  = TEMP GE 0.25.
```

The first statement sets TEMP equal to a uniform random number from zero to one. If TEMP is less than 0.25 (i.e., in about 25% of the cases), USE is set to zero.

Data can be generated using two random number generators. This is useful if you want to see the effect of violating an assumption of a test. For example, suppose you want to generate data for two groups from normal distributions with mean zero: the first group has standard deviation 1.0 and comprises about 70% of the cases; the second group has standard deviation 3.0. You can do it this way.

```
/TRANSFORM     GROUP  = 1.0.
               TEMP   = RNDU(762381).
               TEMPA  = TEMP LT 0.3.
               GROUP  = 2 IF TEMPA.
               RANDOM = RNDG(24573).
               TEMPB  = 3 * RANDOM.
               RANDOM = TEMPB IF TEMPA.
```

In the *TRANsform* paragraph GROUP is set equal to one. If the value of a uniform random number is less than 0.3 (approximately 30% of the cases), TEMPA is set to true and GROUP to 2. RANDOM is first set to a random number generated from a normal distribution with mean zero and standard deviation one. If TEMPA is true (i.e., GROUP is 2), RANDOM is multiplied by 3; i.e., it will be from a normal distribution with mean zero and standard deviation three.

When all variables are generated by transformations, the number of cases <u>must</u> be stated. In the above example you are generating your own variables; therefore specify zero variables and 1000 cases in the *INPut* paragraph. In the *VARiable* paragraph specify that two variables are ADDED by transformation and are NAMED GROUP and RANDOM.

Data appropriate to a regression model with a normal (or uniform) error distribution can be generated in a similar manner. Quick and dirty Monte Carlo is described in Appendix C.17 and random case selection in Appendix C.6.

6.4 FORTRAN Transformations (Using BIMEDT)

FORTRAN transformations are more economical than Control Language transformations when you have large quantities of data, when complicated transformations are necessary or when the transformations are applied to many variables. The FORTRAN statements are processed by the FORTRAN compiler and temporarily become part of the BMDP program. *Transformations specified in FORTRAN are processed before those specified in the TRANsform paragraph if both types are used.*

Any legitimate FORTRAN statements, such as READ, WRITE, DATA, DIMENSION, FUNCTION and SUBROUTINE, can be used. The FORTRAN subroutine in which the transformations are included starts with the following two statements:[3]

```
SUBROUTINE TRANSF(X,KASE,NPROB,USE,NVAR,XMIS)
DIMENSION X(NVAR)
```

where the following values should not be changed:

KASE   is the sequence number of the case being processed.

NPROB   is the sequence number of the problem (*PROBlem* paragraph) being processed.

NVAR   is the greater of the number of variables read or the number of variables after transformation (i.e., the number of variables read plus the number of variables ADDED by transformation, p. 99).

XMIS   is the missing value code used internally by the BMDP program. Values that are less than the lower limit or greater than the upper limit specified for a variable are recoded to values greater in absolute value than XMIS. The values are recoded BEFORE the transformations are processed unless AFTER is specified in the *VARiable* paragraph (p.100).

You can change the values of X and USE.

X   is the vector containing the data for the case being processed. The values for all variables read in the data are present. X(1) is the value of the first variable, X(2) the second, etc. The values of X can be modified to contain the transformed values.

USE   is a flag for case selection. Its interpretation is identical to that of USE in the *TRANsform* paragraph (p. 104). If USE is positive (1), the case is used in the analysis; if zero (0), the case is not used but is included in a BMDP File if one is created; if negative (-1) the case is not used and is not copied into a BMDP File.

---

[3] In BMDP programs dated before August 1977, the first three cards of the FORTRAN subroutine are

```
SUBROUTINE TRANSF(X,KASE,NPROB,USE)
COMMON/GETCMB/PAD(17),XMIS,PAD1(4)
DIMENSION X(1)
```

NVAR cannot be used in the subroutine.

Note: FORTRAN transformations do not follow Control Language rules -- they comply with FORTRAN rules. (For example, there are no periods at the end of statements.) Variable names are not recognized in the FORTRAN subroutine and cannot be used in place of X(subscript). You must check for missing values; they are not automatically excluded from the transformation computations.

If new variables are added by the transformation, ADD must be stated in the *VARiable* paragraph. The definition of ADD is given on p. 99. The data can be checked for missing value codes BEFore or AFTER the transformations are processed. The programs are preset to BEFore; AFTER must be specified when needed (p. 100).

We use the Control Language transformation examples (Sections 6.1 to 6.3) to illustrate how the same variable transformations and case selection can be done with FORTRAN statements.

The first example (p. 99) creates a new variable RATIO (the 10th variable) from the ratio of WEIGHT (the 4th variable) to HEIGHT (the 3rd variable). If you know that both WEIGHT and HEIGHT are always recorded, in FORTRAN you can specify

```
X(10) = X(4) / X(3)
```

However, if either WEIGHT or HEIGHT can be missing or out of range, you must first check whether the value is present by specifying

```
X(10) = XMIS
IF(ABS(X(3)).LT.XMIS .AND. ABS(X(4)).LT.XMIS) X(10)=X(4)/X(3)
```

The first statement specifies that X(10), RATIO, is missing unless reset by the second statement. Before computing the value of X(10) you first check that both X(3) and X(4) are not missing and not out of range. *It is necessary to compare the absolute values of the variables against XMIS since values out of range are set to internal codes more extreme than XMIS and can be positive (if greater than the upper bound) or negative (if less than the lower bound).*

The second example (p. 100) converts FEET and INCHES to height. Suppose FEET is variable 4, X(4), and INCHES is variable 5, X(5). You can specify

```
IF(ABS(X(4)).LT.XMIS .AND. ABS(X(5)).LT.XMIS) X(4)=X(4)+X(5)/12.
```

The third example (p. 101) transforms COUNT data. Suppose COUNT is X(2) and ANSWER is X(3). Your statement is

```
X(3) = XMIS
IF(ABS(X(2)).LT.XMIS) X(3)=SQRT(X(2))+SQRT(X(2)+1.0)
```

You can recode data to the missing value code. For example, if STATUS (p. 102) is X(4), then

```
IF(X(4).EQ.7.0 .OR. X(4).EQ.8.0) X(4) = XMIS
```

transforms STATUS to the missing value code if it is either 7 or 8.

You can select cases by setting the value of USE. Since AGE is the second variable, we can select the cases of subjects aged 20 to 30 (p. 103) by stating

```
        USE = 0
        IF(X(2).GE.20.0 .AND. X(2).LE.30.0) USE = 1
```

The statements OMIT and DELETE cannot be used in the FORTRAN subroutine.

To randomly select cases or generate data you can call the FORTRAN functions that generate uniform or normal random numbers (Appendix A.1).

● SYSTEM CARDS FOR FORTRAN TRANSFORMATIONS

When you specify transformations in the FORTRAN subroutine, the System Cards must be altered. The subroutine containing the FORTRAN statements must be compiled and integrated with the previously compiled BMDP program to form a modified program that will transform the data and perform the analysis.

At HSCF we have a simple procedure to compile the subroutine and execute the BMDP program.

- First you must specify three System Cards

```
//jobname  JOB  nooo,yourname
//   EXEC  BIMEDT,PROG=BMDPxx
//TRANSF DD  *
```

(Note the T at the end of BIMEDT; xx must be replaced by the two character identification of the BMDP program.)

- This is followed by the FORTRAN statements that define the transformations. *The SUBROUTINE and DIMENSION cards at the beginning and the RETURN and END cards at the end must be omitted; they are automatically supplied at HSCF. Check at your facility whether these cards are required.*

- This is followed by a System Card

```
//GO.SYSIN  DD  *
```

- This is followed by the Control Language instructions for the BMDP program and the data, if on cards.

- This is terminated by a final System Card.

```
//
```

If data are read from a disk or magnetic tape, or if a BMDP File is created, the System Cards that describe the location of the data are placed immediately before the //GO.SYSIN DD *.   See page opposite back cover.

If your computer facility does not maintain the BMDP programs in a manner similar to HSCF, check with your facility consultant for the required System Cards. A space is provided on the page opposite the inside back cover for you to record the System Cards used at your facility.

6.5 Recoding Nonnumeric Data

Nonnumeric data can be recoded as follows in any BMDP program except P4D. To illustrate how the data are recoded, let SEX be one of the variables, coded M, F; and MONTH be a second variable coded 1,2,3,4,5,6,7,8,9,0,A,B. (Many old data sets code Nov. as "-" and Dec. as "+". The same method can be used to recode these symbols.) If SEX is variable 5 and MONTH variable 7, they can be recoded by the following FORTRAN statements.

<u>COMMENTS</u>

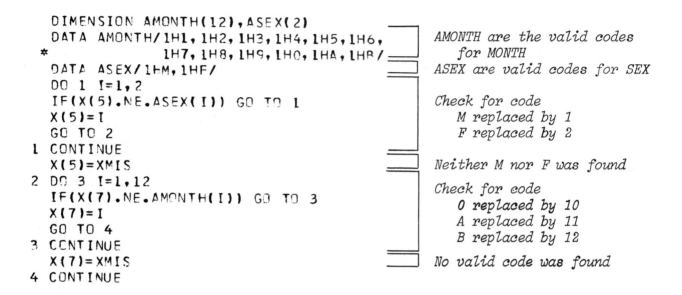

```
      DIMENSION AMONTH(12),ASEX(2)
      DATA AMONTH/1H1,1H2,1H3,1H4,1H5,1H6,
     *            1H7,1H8,1H9,1H0,1HA,1HB/
      DATA ASEX/1HM,1HF/
      DO 1 I=1,2
      IF(X(5).NE.ASEX(I)) GO TO 1
      X(5)=I
      GO TO 2
    1 CONTINUE
      X(5)=XMIS
    2 DO 3 I=1,12
      IF(X(7).NE.AMONTH(I)) GO TO 3
      X(7)=I
      GO TO 4
    3 CONTINUE
      X(7)=XMIS
    4 CONTINUE
```

AMONTH are the valid codes for MONTH

ASEX are valid codes for SEX

*Check for code
  M replaced by 1
  F replaced by 2*

Neither M nor F was found

*Check for code
  0 replaced by 10
  A replaced by 11
  B replaced by 12*

No valid code was found

In Control Language specifications, the two variables SEX and MONTH must each be read with format specification A1. In addition, you must specify

AFTER.

in the *VARiable* paragraph so the data in SEX and MONTH will not be checked until they are transformed to legitimate values.

The above FORTRAN statements must be used with the System Cards described on the previous page (the BIMEDT procedure).

6.6 Reading Data with a Nonstandard Format (Layout)

The data are usually read by the program according to the specifications in the *INPut* paragraph. Unfortunately, not all data can be read by a single format statement in the cases-by-variable form that the BMDP programs expect.

Data not in standard format can be read by the FORTRAN subroutine. To do this, set

```
/INPUT          VARIABLE = 0.
                CASE     = number of cases.
                ADD      = number of variables to be
                           read by FORTRAN subroutine.
```

Since the data are not read in the usual manner by the BMDP program, the number of cases must be stated.

The data are read in the FORTRAN subroutine and passed to the program as the vector X. For example, if the data (5 variables) were keypunched in two different formats -- the first 10 cases as (5F5.0) and the last 15 cases as (1X,5F5.0) -- the data can be read by

```
      IF(KASE.GT.10) GO TO 2
      READ(5,10) (X(I),I=1,5)
   10 FORMAT(5F5.0)
      RETURN
    2 READ(5,11) (X(I),I=1,5)
   11 FORMAT(1X,5F5.0)
```

The data records may have been collected from different sources -- for example, clinics where each clinic used its own format. However, if the clinic ID was uniformly recorded in the same place in each data record, the record can be read in A-format except for the clinic ID; it could then be written to a temporary unit and reread under the appropriate format for a specific clinic.

Another use of this feature is when each subject's data have a common first record but vary in other regards, such as number of followup records or type of record. The first record can be read for each subject and then each of the followup records can be read by an appropriate format. This feature can be used to merge data from two different locations.

You can also read data from tape or disk that was written in binary and therefore must be read in binary. To do this you specify a binary (unformatted) read statement in FORTRAN and add an extra System Card that points to the location of the data.

6.7 Summary of Transformations Common to All Programs

Control Language Transformations in all BMDP Programs (except P4D and P1S)

Paragraph STATEMENT[1] {Preassigned value}		Definition, restriction	See pages:
/TRANsform		Optional, Control Language transformations or case selection	97-105
v=simple expression.	{none}	Expression from Table 6.1	98
USE=#. or simple expression.	{1}	Case used in analysis if USE=1 (positive or true), not used otherwise	103-104
OMIT=#$_1$,#$_2$,···.	{none}	Cases to be omitted (sets USE=0)	103-104
DELETE=#$_1$,#$_2$,···.	{none}	Cases to be deleted (sets USE=-1)	103-104
/VARiable		Optional, in addition to that described in Section 5.3	
ADD=#.	{0/prev.}	No. of variables added by transformation	99
BEFORE. or AFTER.	{BEFORE/prev.}	Data checked for acceptable values before or after transformations	100

Key: # number
      v variable name or X(subscript)

[1] In BMDP programs dated before August 1977, the minimum required abbreviations are *TRANSF* (not *TRAN*), *VARIAB* (not *VAR*), BEFORET (not BEF) and AFTERT (not AFT). In programs dated before February 1976, OMIT and DELETE are not available.

- **Order of Input** (standard procedure)

  (1) System Cards, at HSCF these are

  ```
  //jobname  JOB  nooo,yourname
  //  EXEC  BIMED,PROG=BMDPxx
  //SYSIN  DD  *
  ```

  (2) Control Language instructions and data, if on cards   `see program description`

  (3) System Card, at HSCF this is   `//`

- **Order of Input** (when transformations are specified in FORTRAN)

  (1) System Cards, at HSCF these are

  ```
  //jobname  JOB  nooo,yourname
  //  EXEC  BIMEDT,PROG=BMDPxx
  //TRANSF  DD  *
  ```

  (2) Transformations in FORTRAN   `FORTRAN statements`

  (3) System Card, at HSCF this is   `//GO.SYSIN  DD  *`

  (4) Control Language instructions and data, if on cards   `see program description`

  (5) System Card, at HSCF this is   `//`

P1S

6.8 Multipass Transformation

    P1S can pass (read) the data many times. At each pass P1S can compute univariate statistics, perform variable transformations, or edit the data using statistics computed in a previous pass. For example, data can be standardized to z-scores by computing the mean and standard deviation in the first pass and then in the second pass calculating $z_j=(x_j-\bar{x})/s$ for each case. Means, standard deviations, geometric means, harmonic means and largest and smallest values for the variables can be computed in one pass and used in the next pass.

    Transformations that are computed from each case individually require only one reading of the data. They are available in all BMDP programs.

● CONTROL LANGUAGE

    The Control Language used to describe the data and variables is explained in Chapter 5; the *PROBlem*, *INPut*[4] and *VARiable* paragraphs are used in P1S. The *TRANsform* paragraph cannot be used in P1S.

    P1S usually transforms or edits data before they are analyzed by other BMDP programs. The transformed data can be saved in a BMDP File, which can then be read by all BMDP programs (except P4D). Data from a BMDP File can be used as input to P1S. The BMDP File is discussed in detail in Chapter 7.

● FORTRAN TRANSFORMATIONS

    Before reading this section you should read Section 6.4. The rules for using the FORTRAN transformations in P1S are the same as described in Section 6.4 for all BMDP programs. The major difference is in the first two records of the subroutine.

    Transformations in P1S <u>must</u> be specified by FORTRAN statements in a subroutine that is called once for each case. The first two records of the subroutine for P1S are[5]

```
      SUBROUTINE TRANSF(X,KASE,NPROB,USE,NPS,NV,NVAR,XB,SD,HM,GM,
     *          XMIN,XMAX,K1,K2,XMIS)
      DIMENSION X(NVAR),XB(NVAR),SD(NVAR),HM(NVAR),GM(NVAR),
     *          XMIN(NVAR),XMAX(NVAR),K1(NVAR),K2(NVAR)
```

---

[4] BMDP programs dated before August 1977 require more letters in their permissible abbreviated form (the capitalized letters). Their minimum required abbreviations are specified in footnotes to the Summary (p. 121).

[5] In BMDP programs dated before August 1977, the first two records of the subroutine are

```
      SUBROUTINE TRANSF(X,KASE,NPROB,USE,NPS,NV,NVAR,XB,SD,HM,GM,K1,K2,XMIS)
      DIMENSION X(NVAR),XB(NVAR),SD(NVAR),HM(NVAR),GM(NVAR),K1(NVAR),K2(NVAR)
```

XMIN and XMAX <u>cannot</u> be used.

where the following values should not be changed :

KASE   is the sequence number of the case being processed

NPROB   is the sequence number of the problem (*PROBlem* paragraph) being processed

NPS   is the sequence number of the *PASS* paragraph being processed (each pass involves one reading of the data)

NV   is the number of variables read as input

NVAR   is the larger of NV and the number of variables after transformation

XB   contains the means of the variables from the previous pass

SD   contains the standard deviations of the variables from the previous pass

HM   contains the harmonic means of the variables from the previous pass

GM   contains the geometric means of the variables from the previous pass

XMIN   contains the minimums of the variables from the previous pass

XMAX   contains the maximums of the variables from the previous pass

K1   contains the numbers of acceptable values for the variables from the previous pass

K2   contains the numbers of <u>positive</u> (acceptable) values for the variables from the previous pass

XB, SD, HM, GM, XMIN, XMAX, K1 and K2 are vectors. The first value (e.g., XB(1),SD(1),...) refers to the first variable; the second value (e.g., XB(2),SD(2),...) refers to the second variable, etc. XB and SD are computed unless NO MEAN is specified in the COMPute paragraph. HM, GM, XMIN and XMAX are computed only if specified in the COMPute paragraph. K1 and K2 are always computed.

XMIS   is the value of the missing value code used internally by the BMDP program. Values that are less than the lower limit or greater than the upper limit specified for a variable are recoded to values greater in <u>absolute value</u> than XMIS. The values are recoded BEFORE the transformations unless AFTER is specified in the *VARiable* paragraph (p. 100). *It is necessary to compare the absolute values of the variables against XMIS since values out of range are set to internal codes more extreme than XMIS that can be positive (if greater than the upper limit) or negative (if less than the lower limit).*

You may change the values of X and USE.

X   is the vector containing the data for the case being processed. X(1) is the value of the first variable, X(2) the second, etc. The values of X can be modified to contain the transformed values.

USE   is a flag for case selection. Its interpretation is identical to that of USE in the *TRANsform* paragraph (p. 103). If USE is positive (1), the case is used in the analysis; if zero (0), the case is not used but is included in a BMDP File if one is created; if negative (-1) the case is not used and is not copied into a BMDP File. When USE is negative, the case is discarded but the sequence numbers (KASE) of the remaining cases are not changed.

● RESULTS

The Werner data (Table 5.1) are used to illustrate how the blood chemistry measurements can be transformed to z-scores. A z-score is the ratio of (observed value minus mean) to the standard deviation. We specify the FORTRAN subroutine and Control Language instructions in Example 6.1.

Example 6.1

```
      IF(NPS.EQ.1) RETURN
C
      DO 2 I=6,9
      IF(ABS(X(I)).GE.XMIS) GO TO 2
      X(I)=(X(I)-XB(I))/SD(I)
    2 CONTINUE
```
FORTRAN statements describing the transformation at the second pass (NPS=2)

```
/PROBLEM     TITLE IS 'WERNER BLOOD CHEMISTRY DATA'.
/INPUT       VARIABLES ARE 9.
             FORMAT IS '(A4,5F4.0,3F4.1)'.
             CASES ARE 188.
/VARIABLE    NAMES ARE ID,AGE,HEIGHT,WEIGHT,BRTHPILL,
                     CHOLSTRL,ALBUMIN,CALCIUM,URICACID.
             MAXIMUM IS (6)400.
             MINIMUM IS (6)150.
             BLANKS ARE MISSING.
             LABEL IS ID.

/PASS        TITLE IS 'COMPUTE MEANS AND STANDARD DEVIATIONS'.

/END
```
Control Language instructions to describe the data and the first pass

                --- *the data (Table 5.1) go here* ---   *data*

```
/PASS        TITLE IS 'COMPUTE Z-SCORES'.

/PRINT       DATA.

/END
```
Control Language instructions to describe the second pass

When the transformations are specified by FORTRAN statements, the FORTRAN statements must be preceded by System Cards to initiate the analysis by P1S. At HSCF, the System Cards are

```
//jobname  JOB  nooo,yourname
//  EXEC  BIMEDT,PROG=BMDP1S
//TRANSF  DD  *
```

The FORTRAN statements are immediately followed by another System Card. At HSCF, this card is

```
//GO.SYSIN  DD  *
```

This System Card is followed by the Control Language instructions. The Control Language instructions are in turn followed by the data (Table 5.1). The analysis is terminated by a final System Card. At HSCF, this System Card is

```
//
```

The System Cards are discussed in greater detail in Section 6.4.

A *PASS* paragraph is required for each reading of the data. If the data are on cards all *PASS* paragraphs but the first are placed after the data. The order of the Control Language instructions and the data are shown in the summary (p. 122).

We specify that the data be printed to demonstrate how the transformed data look in the output (Output 6.1). Circled numbers in the output correspond to those in the text.

Output 6.1 z-scores computed by P1D. Results not reproduced are indicated in italics.

BMDP1S - MULTIPASS TRANSFORMATION
HEALTH SCIENCES COMPUTING FACILITY
UNIVERSITY OF CALIFORNIA, LOS ANGELES

PROGRAM REVISED SEPTEMBER 1977
MANUAL DATE -- 1977

--- *Control Language read by P1S is printed and interpreted* ---

① NUMBER OF CASES READ.   188

PASS TITLE................COMPUTE MEANS AND STANDARD DEVIATIONS

		2 AGE	3 HEIGHT	4 WEIGHT	5 BRTHPILL	6 CHOLSTRL	7 ALBUMIN	8 CALCIUM	9 URICACID
②	MEAN	33.818	64.510	131.67	1.5000	236.15	4.1112	9.9621	4.7705
	STAND	10.113	2.4851	20.661	0.50133	42.555	0.35796	0.47955	1.1572

PROGRAM CONTROL INFORMATION

③
```
/PASS        TITLE IS 'COMPUTE Z-SCORES'.
/PRINT       DATA.
/END
```

PASS TITLE................COMPUTE Z-SCORES

④ DATA MATRIX AFTER TRANSFORMATION. VALUES MISSING OR OUT OF RANGE ARE INDICATED BY 0.21268E 38

		2 AGE	3 HEIGHT	4 WEIGHT	5 BRTHPILL	6 CHOLSTRL	7 ALBUMIN	8 CALCIUM	9 URICACID
1	2381	22.000	67.000	144.00	1.0000	-0.84948	0.52730	-0.33807	0.54393
2	1946	22.000	64.000	160.00	2.0000	0.21268E 38	-1.7076	0.21268E 38	2.0994
3	1610	25.000	62.000	128.00	1.0000	0.16097	-0.31421E-01	0.91310	-1.2707
4	1797	25.000	68.000	150.00	2.0000	0.21268E 38	-0.86950	-0.75512	-1.5300
5	561	19.000	64.000	125.00	1.0000	-1.8364	-0.31421E-01	-0.12954	-0.60959E-01

---- cases 6 to 184 ----

		2 AGE	3 HEIGHT	4 WEIGHT	5 BRTHPILL	6 CHOLSTRL	7 ALBUMIN	8 CALCIUM	9 URICACID
185	1149	53.000	0.21268E 38	178.00	1.0000	-0.21501	-0.59014	0.21268E 38	0.19828
186	575	53.000	65.000	140.00	2.0000	-0.37950	-0.31078	1.5387	-0.14737
187	2271	54.000	66.000	158.00	1.0000	1.6179	0.24794	0.70457	0.25453E-01
188	39	54.000	60.000	170.00	2.0000	-0.37950	-1.7076	-2.4234	1.3216

		2 AGE	3 HEIGHT	4 WEIGHT	5 BRTHPILL	6 CHOLSTRL	7 ALBUMIN	8 CALCIUM	9 URICACID
⑤	MEAN	33.818	64.510	131.67	1.5000	0.17286E-04	0.11922E-03	0.86743E-04	0.39920E-04
	STAND	10.113	2.4851	20.661	0.50133	1.0000	1.0000	1.0000	0.99999

(1)   Number of cases read. All acceptable values are used in the computations. An acceptable value is one that is not equal to the missing value code or outside the specified lower or upper limits for the variable.

(2)   Means and standard deviations computed at the first pass of the data.

(3)   The second *PASS* paragraph is printed.

(4)   The data matrix, after computing all transformations specified in the first (none) and second (z-scores for variables 6 to 9) passes of the data.

(5)   Mean and standard deviations computed at the second pass of the data. The means for variables 6 to 9 are zero, except for rounding error, and the standard deviations are one.

● PASSING THE DATA

During the first pass the data are read one case at a time, specified transformations are performed, and the transformed data are copied onto a temporary unit. At each subsequent pass the data are read from the last temporary unit onto which they were copied, specified transformations are performed and the transformed data are copied onto the other temporary unit (two temporary units are used alternately to store the data).

A *PASS* paragraph is required for each pass of the data. If the data are on cards all but the first *PASS* paragraph must follow the data (see order of input in the summary, p. 122).

A TITLE can be specified to identify each pass. However, it is sufficient to specify only

        /PASS

without a title.

```
PASS
   TITLE ='c'.              {blank}                    < 160 char.
        c is a title for this pass of the data.
```

● THE *COMPute* PARAGRAPH

The *COMPute*[6] paragraph specifies the statistics to be computed at each pass and used in the transformations of the <u>next</u> pass. The *COMPute* paragraph can be repeated for each *PASS* paragraph.

The statistics are

   - mean: $\bar{x} = \Sigma\, x_j/N$

_____

[6] In BMDP programs dated before August 1977,
     the minimum required abbreviation is *COMPUTE*   (not *COMP*).

where $x_1, x_2, \ldots$ are acceptable values for a variable and N the frequency of the acceptable values

- standard deviation: $s = [\Sigma (x_j - \bar{x})^2/(N-1)]^{\frac{1}{2}}$

- harmonic mean: $\bar{x}_h = (\Sigma^+ \frac{1}{x_j} /N^+)^{-1}$

  where Σ^+ is the sum over positive values only and N^+ is the frequency of the positive values

- geometric mean: $\bar{x}_g = (\Pi^+ x_j)^{1/N^+}$

  where Π^+ is the product of the positive values only

- minimum: $\min_j x_j$

- maximum: $\max_j x_j$

- K1 and K2 in the FORTRAN subroutine are N and N^+ respectively

The means and standard deviations are computed unless

      NO MEANS.

is specified in the *COMPute* paragraph. The HARMONIC[7] mean is computed if

      HARMONIC.

is specified and the GEOMETRIC[8] mean if

      GEOMETRIC.

is specified. Both the minimum and maximum[9] are computed if

      EXTREMES.

is specified.

COMPute
    MEAN.   {MEAN/prev.}

        The means and standard deviations are computed and can be used in transformations in the next pass of the data. To negate, specify NO MEAN.

    HARMONIC.   {no/prev.}

        The harmonic means are computed and can be used in transformations in the next pass of the data.

                                    (continued)

---

[7] In BMDP programs dated before August 1977, the minimum required abbreviation is HARMONIC (not HARM).

[8] In BMDP programs dated before August 1977, the minimum required abbreviation is GEOMETRIC (not GEOM).

[9] In BMDP programs dated before August 1977, the minimum and maximum are not computed.

```
COMPute
    GEOMETRIC.   {no/prev.}

        The geometric means are computed and can be used in transformations
        in the next pass of the data.

    EXTREMES.    {no/prev.}

        The minimums and maximums are computed and can be used in trans-
        formations in the next pass of the data.
```

If you want to select the VARIABLES to be used in the computations you can specify which ones to use. If not specified all variables are used.

```
COMPute
    VARIABLE=v_1,v_2,····.    {all variables/prev.}

        Names or subscripts of variables for which statistics are to be
        computed.
```

● THE *PRINT* PARAGRAPH

In addition to the statistics requested in the *COMPute* paragraph, you can request additional statistics in the *PRINT* paragraph.

In the *PRINT* paragraph you can specify that the DATA are to be printed (as in our examples), and that the data and statistics for selected variables are to be printed.

The *PRINT* paragraph can be repeated for each *PASS* paragraph.

```
PRINT
    DATA.                  {no/prev.}
      The transformed data are printed.

    MEAN.                  {as in COMPute}
      The mean and standard deviation are printed.

    HARMONIC.              {as in COMPute}
      The harmonic means are printed.

    GEOMETRIC.             {as in COMPute}
      The geometric means are printed.

    EXTREMES.              {as in COMPute}
      The minimums and maximums are printed.

    VARIABLE=v_1,v_2,····. {as in COMPute}
      Names or subscripts of variables for which the data or statistics
      are printed.
```

● SAVING THE DATA IN A BMDP FILE

P1S performs complex transformations that are not possible in other BMDP programs. The transformed data matrix is usually saved in a BMDP File, and can then be analyzed by other BMDP programs. The BMDP File is discussed in detail in Chapter 7; you need to read Chapter 7 before using a BMDP File.

You must specify the sequence number of the PASS at which a BMDP File is to be created. In Example 6.2 the transformed z-scores are created in the second pass of the data (PASS=2). Therefore to create a BMDP File we use the following example.

Example 6.2

```
        IF(NPS.EQ.1) RETURN
C
        DO 2 I=6,9
        IF(ABS(X(I)).GE.XMIS) GO TO 2
        X(I)=(X(I)-XB(I))/SD(I)
      2 CONTINUE
```
FORTRAN statements describing the transformation at the second pass (NPS=2)

```
/PROBLEM      TITLE IS 'WERNER BLOOD CHEMISTRY DATA'.
/INPUT        VARIABLES ARE 9.
              FORMAT IS '(A4,5F4.0,3F4.1)'.
              CASES ARE 188.
/VARIABLE     NAMES ARE ID,AGE,HEIGHT,WEIGHT,BRTHPILL,
                     CHOLSTRL,ALBUMIN,CALCIUM,URICACID.
              MAXIMUM IS (6)400.
              MINIMUM IS (6)150.
              BLANKS ARE MISSING.
              LABEL IS ID.

/SAVE         UNIT IS 4.
              NEW.
              CODE IS WERNER.
              PASS IS 2.

/PASS         TITLE IS 'COMPUTE MEANS AND STANDARD DEVIATIONS'.

/END
```
Control Language instructions to describe the data and the first pass

--- the data (Table 5.1) go here ---   *data*

```
/PASS         TITLE IS 'COMPUTE Z-SCORES'.

/PRINT        DATA.

/END
```
Control Language instructions to describe the second pass

The System Cards for this example are identical to those for Example 6.1, except that a System Card to describe where to store the BMDP File must be inserted before the

```
//GO.SYSIN  DD  *
```

This additional System Card is described in Section 7.1.

The creation of a BMDP File produces the messages shown in Output 6.2.

SAVE
    PASS=#.   {none/prev.}

    Sequence number of the pass at which the BMDP File is created. The
    data at this pass are copied into a BMDP File. If PASS is not
    stated, or this pass is not reached, a BMDP File is not created.

● SIZE OF PROBLEM

    P1S can read and transform data in as many as 350 variables at one time.
Appendix B describes how to increase the capacity of the program.

● COMPUTATIONAL METHOD

    In the first pass the data are read, transformed, and written onto a
temporary unit. At each subsequent pass the data are read from one temporary
unit, transformed, and written onto a second temporary unit.

    Means and standard deviations at each pass are computed by the method of
provisional means (Appendix A.2).

ACKNOWLEDGEMENT

P1S was programmed by Caroline Ho. It supersedes BMD09S and BMD13S.

Output 6.2   z-scores computed by P1S are saved. The printed results are
                similar to those in Output 6.1 except for a message that the
                BMDP File is created. Only the message is shown below.

```
PASS TITLE.................COMPUTE Z-SCORES

BMDP FILE WRITTEN ON UNIT 4.
                     CODE. . . IS      WERNER
                     CONTENT . IS      DATA
                     LABEL . . IS
                     VARIABLES     1  ID        2  AGE      3  HEIGHT     4  WEIGHT     5  BRTHPILL
                                   6  CHOLSTRL  7  ALBUMIN  8  CALCIUM    9  URICACID

BMDP FILE ON UNIT 4 HAS BEEN COMPLETED.
```

6.9 Summary—P1S

P1S -- Multipass Transformation

Paragraph STATEMENT[1] {Preassigned value[2]}		Definition, restriction	See pages:
/PROBlem		Required each problem	74
TITLE='c'.	{blank}	Problem title, $\leq$ 160 char.	74
/INPut		Required first problem. Either VARIABLE and FORMAT or UNIT and CODE required.	75
VARIABLE=#.	{none/prev.}	No. of variables in input data	75
FORMAT='c'.	{none/prev.}	Format of input data, $\leq$ 800 char.	76
CASE=#.	{end-of-file/prev.}	No. of cases in data	76-77
UNIT=#.	{5(cards)/prev.}	Input unit if data are not on cards	77
REWIND.	{REWIND/prev.}	Rewind input unit	77
CODE=c.	{none}	BMDP File identification	132
CONTENT=c.	{DATA}	BMDP File identification	132
LABEL=c.	{none}	BMDP File extended identification, $\leq$ 40 char.	132
/VARiable		Optional. For input from a BMDP File, items in this paragraph may be previously set, see Section 7.2.	79
NAME=$c_1,c_2,\cdots$.	{X(subscript)/prev.}	Variable names, one per variable	79-80
MAXIMUM=$\#_1,\#_2,\cdots$.	{none/prev.}	Upper bounds, one per variable	80
MINIMUM=$\#_1,\#_2,\cdots$.	{none/prev.}	Lower bounds, one per variable	80
BLANK= *(one only)* ZERO, MISSING	{ZERO/prev.}	Blanks treated as zeros or as missing value codes	81
MISSING=$\#_1,\#_2,\cdots$.	{none/prev.}	Missing value codes, one per variable	81
USE=$v_1,v_2,\cdots$.	{all variables}	Variables used in the analysis	82
LABEL=v_1,v_2.	{none/prev.}	Variable(s) used to label cases, read under A-format, one or two variables	83
ADD=#.	{0/prev.}	No. of variables added through transformation	99
BEFore. or AFTER.	{BEFORE/prev.}	Data checked for limits before or after transformation	100
/SAVE		Optional, required to create BMDP File	125
CODE=c.	{none}	Code to identify BMDP File, required	125-126
LABEL='c'.	{blank}	Label for BMDP File, $\leq$ 40 char.	125-126
UNIT=#.	{none}	Unit on which to write BMDP File, not 1, 2, 5 or 6	126-127
NEW.	{not NEW}	NEW if this is first BMDP File in system file	126-127
PASS=#.	{none/prev.}	Sequence number of *PASS* in which to create BMDP File, required	119-120
/PASS		Required	116
TITLE='c'.	{blank}	Title for this pass, $\leq$ 160 char.	116
/COMPute		Optional, statistics to be used in transformations at next pass	116
MEAN.	{MEAN/prev.}	Compute means and standard deviations	117
HARMONIC.	{no/prev.}	Compute harmonic means	117
GEOMETRIC.	{no/prev.}	Compute geometric means	117-118
EXTREMES.	{no/prev.}	Compute minimums and maximums	117-118
VARIABLE=$v_1,v_2,\cdots$.		Variables for which statistics are computed	118
/PRINT		Optional, applies to current *PASS*	118
DATA.	{no/prev.}	Print data after transformation	118
MEAN.	{as in *COMPute*}	Print means and standard deviations	118
HARMONIC.	{as in *COMPute*}	Print harmonic means	118
GEOMETRIC.	{as in *COMPute*}	Print geometric means	118
EXTREMES.	{as in *COMPute*}	Print minimums and maximums	118
VARIABLES=$v_1,v_2,\cdots$.	{as in *COMPute*}	Variables for which data and statistics are printed	118
/END		Required	57

Key: # number   v variable name or subscript
     'c' title, label or format   c name not exceeding 8 char., apostrophes may be required (p. 59)

[1] In BMDP programs dated before August 1977, the minimum required abbreviations are *INPUT* (not *INP*), VARIAB (not VAR), FORMAT (not FORM), CONTENT (not CONT), *VARIAB* (not *VAR*), BEFORET (not BEF), AFTERT (not AFT), *COMPUTE* (not *COMP*), HARMONIC (not HARM) and GEOMETRIC (not GEOM); BLANK=MISSING is not available.

[2] "/prev." means that any assignment remains the same as that specified in the previous problem or subproblem until changed. Otherwise, the assignment returns to its preassigned value each time a new problem begins or the paragraph is used again.

(continued)

● <u>Order of input</u>

(1) System Cards, at HSCF these are

```
//jobname  JOB  nooo,yourname
//  EXEC  BIMEDT,PROG=BMDP1S
//TRANSF  DD  *
```

(2) Transformations specified in FORTRAN, at HSCF do <u>not</u> include SUBROUTINE and DIMENSION statements at beginning and RETURN and END at the end.

```
FORTRAN statements
```

(3) System Card, at HSCF this is

```
//GO.SYSIN  DD  *
```

(4) Control Language instructions

```
PROBLem paragraph, required
INPut paragraph, required first problem
VARiable  paragraph
SAVE paragraph
PASS paragraph, required
COMPute paragraph
PRINT paragraph
END paragraph, required at end of Control Language
```

(5) Data, if on cards

```
data
```

(6) Control Language instructions for each pass

```
PASS paragraph, required each pass
COMPute paragraph
PRINT paragraph
END  paragraph, required to terminate each batch of
     Control Language
```

(7) System Card(s), at HSCF this is

```
//
```

(6) can be repeated for additional passes of the data.
(4), (5) and (6) can be repeated to analyze additional data with the same transformations.

7

THE BMDP FILE

Saving Data and Statistics for Further Analysis

Laszlo Engelman, HSCF

A set of data is usually analyzed many times by BMDP programs. For example, the data may first be examined for extreme values (outliers) and for distributional assumptions; then necessary transformations can be performed, meaningful hypotheses tested, or relationships between the variables studied. The results of an analysis may suggest that further analyses are needed.

The BMDP (Save) File is a means of storing your data or results from an analysis so you can reuse them in other BMDP programs; the File can be created or read by any BMDP program (except P4D). There are several advantages to storing data in a BMDP File:

- Data are read efficiently from a BMDP File; the cost of reading a large amount of data from a BMDP File is substantially less than when a FORMAT statement is used (the BMDP File is unformatted).

- Most of the information specified in the *INPut, VARiable* and *GROUP* (or *CATEGory*) paragraphs when the BMDP File is created is stored in the File and need not be respecified for each analysis.

- Data are stored in the BMDP File after transformation and case selection are performed.

- The BMDP File is the only way to store results (such as residuals from a regression analysis or a covariance matrix) so they can be analyzed further by other BMDP programs.

In Example 5.1 (p. 87) the Werner blood chemistry data are analyzed by P3D (Comparison of Two Groups with t Tests). If the same analysis is made using data previously stored in a BMDP File, only the following Control Language instructions are necessary.

```
/PROBLEM       TITLE IS 'WERNER BLOOD CHEMISTRY DATA'.
/INPUT         UNIT IS 7.
               CODE IS WERNER.
/VARIABLE      GROUPING IS BRTHPILL.

/END
```

The *INPut* paragraph specifies how the program identifies the BMDP File, and the *VARiable* paragraph states which variable is used to classify the cases into groups for this analysis. The five other statements in the *VARiable* paragraph in Example 5.1, the VARIABLE and FORMAT statements in the *INPut* paragraph and the entire *GROUP* paragraph do not need to be respecified. Using a BMDP File shortens and simplifies the Control Language instructions needed for subsequent analyses.

7.1 Creating a BMDP File (Save Paragraph)

"BMDP File" is a term used to describe a set of data or results that are stored (either on a disk or magnetic tape) in a manner recognizable to BMDP programs. A BMDP File is generated when you specify (in a *SAVE* paragraph) what is to be stored in the File. In addition to the information in the *SAVE* paragraph, you must specify to the computer (on a System Card) where the BMDP File is to be stored.

● THE *SAVE* PARAGRAPH

The *SAVE* paragraph is used to create a BMDP File and to specify what to store in it, how to label it, and where to write it.

In all BMDP programs (except P4D) you can create a BMDP File to store your data. Each case in the File contains the data, or transformed data when transformations are specified; several programs also store the results computed in the analysis, such as residuals and predicted values from the regression programs.

In BMDP programs that compute a covariance or correlation matrix, the matrix can usually be saved in a separate BMDP File. Several of the multivariate programs permit other matrices to be stored as well.

The CONTENT[1] statement is used to specify what to save in a BMDP File. It is preset to DATA (that is, data are saved after transformations are performed). The program descriptions specify whether any matrices, in addition to DATA, can be saved in a BMDP File; when only DATA can be saved, CONTENT is _not_ included in the program description and need not be specified.

Each BMDP File should be uniquely identified. It must be assigned a CODE in the *SAVE* paragraph. This CODE must be specified each time the BMDP File is used as input. When more than one BMDP File is created in the same analysis, each File is assigned the same CODE; both CODE and CONTENT are necessary to uniquely identify the File.

In addition to CODE and CONTENT a BMDP File can be further identified with a LABEL. This label is printed each time the File is read. Two BMDP Files with the same CODE and CONTENT can be differentiated by specifying a LABEL.

---

[1] In BMDP programs dated before August 1977,
the minimum required abbreviation is CONTENT (not CONT).

```
SAVE
    CONTENT=c₁,c₂,···.              { DATA }

        CONTENT is required only in programs that save results (such as a
        covariance or correlation matrix) in a BMDP File in addition to the
        DATA.  When CONTENT is necessary, the program description states
        which matrices can be saved; i.e., c₁,c₂,···.

    CODE=c.                         {none}                    required, ≤ 8 char.
        A CODE used to name the BMDP File.  The name assigned to CODE in
        this paragraph must be specified each time the BMDP File is used as
        input.

    LABEL='c'.                      {blank}                   optional, ≤ 40 char.
        A lengthier label for the BMDP File.  It is printed in the output
        each time the BMDP File is used.  When two BMDP Files have the same
        CODE and CONTENT but differ in their LABELs, the LABEL can be
        used to uniquely identify the File to be read.
```

● THE LOCATION OF THE BMDP FILE

    The BMDP File is uniquely identified to the BMDP program by the CODE,
CONTENT and LABEL. When creating the File you must also specify in the
SAVE paragraph a number for the UNIT to which the File is written.

    The BMDP File is stored in a system file on a disk or magnetic tape. A
system file is any block of information that is uniquely identified by the
computer on disk or tape. The computer identifies system files by a filename
specified on a System Card; the computer cannot use Control Language instructions to identify a system file. The number of the UNIT specified in the
SAVE paragraph is also specified on the System Card; in this way the computer
connects the BMDP File with the system file.

    Several BMDP Files can be written into one system file. For example, all
the BMDP Files (one or more) created in a single analysis are written in the
same system file -- one BMDP File after another. You can also write BMDP
Files from different analyses into the same system file; new BMDP Files are
placed last.

    You must indicate when the BMDP File created in an analysis is to be
placed in a NEW system file. A NEW system file is one in which BMDP Files
have not been written previously. You can also specify that the system file
is NEW in order to write over existing BMDP Files. When NEW is specified,
the BMDP File created is placed at the beginning of the system file; all BMDP
Files previously written in this system file are deleted.

SAVE
   UNIT= #.   {none}   required, not 1,2,5 or 6

      The number of the UNIT on which the BMDP File is written.
      This number must also appear on the System Card describing the
      location of the File.

   NEW.   {not NEW }

      NEW is stated when the BMDP File you are creating is written into a
      system file that contains no previous BMDP Files or when you want to
      erase all previous BMDP Files in the system file. If the BMDP File
      is added to previous Files in the system file, NEW must not be
      specified.

• ALLOCATING SPACE FOR A BMDP FILE

      Before a NEW system file can be written, space on a disk or a magnetic
tape must be reserved for it. *The method of reserving the space depends on*
your computing facility. We describe the method used at HSCF. Check with
your facility for the method that you should use.

      At HSCF BMDP Files are usually stored on a disk. To allocate space on a
disk you must specify five cards:

```
//jobname  JOB  nooo,yourname
// EXEC  FSPROC                          HSCF
//SYSIN  DD  *                           File Service
   ALLOCATE  DSNAME=FS.nooo.filename,NVAR=(m,n)   procedure
//
```

where

   - nooo is your computer job number

   - ALLOCATE should not start before column 2 (column 1 must be blank)

   - filename is a name for your system file (it can be the same as the
     CODE for your BMDP File) not exceeding 8 characters

   - m is the number of variables

   - n is the number of cases

      For example, space can be allocated for the Werner blood chemistry data
(188 cases, 9 variables) by specifying

```
//jobname  JOB   nooo,yourname
//EXEC  FSPROC                          HSCF
//SYSIN  DD  *                          File Service
   ALLOCATE DSNAME=FS.nooo.WERNER,NVAR=(9,188)   procedure
//
```

If a covariance matrix is being saved, both m and n are the number of variables. If more than one BMDP File is to be saved in the same system file, m and n should be specified so that m·n (their product) is approximately the sum of the products for the individual BMDP Files.

If you are not using HSCF's computing system, you should consider the following when preparing System Cards to save a BMDP File:

- BMDP Files are written as sequential files

- BMDP Files are written with binary FORTRAN WRITE statements (RECFM=VBS)

- to increase efficiency, BMDP File records should be blocked as large as possible

- if the system file is to contain more than one BMDP File, sufficient space should be allocated to accommodate all Files

- the BMDP File should not be deleted when the job that created it is completed; it should be retained

The preferred way to allocate and maintain a BMDP File changes from system to system. Consult your facility for exact instructions.

● A SYSTEM CARD DESCRIBING THE UNIT

The UNIT stated in the *SAVE* paragraph tells the BMDP program where to write the BMDP File. A System Card must also describe the system file into which the BMDP File is written.

The form of the System Card depends on your facility. At HSCF this card has the form

        //FTyyF001   DD   DSNAME=FS.nooo.filename,DISP=OLD

where

- yy   is the number of the UNIT in the *SAVE* paragraph, and
- filename   is the filename (name of the system file) that appeared on the ALLOCATE card.

For example, if the *SAVE* paragraph used with the Werner blood chemistry data was specified as

        /SAVE   CODE IS WERNER.
                         UNIT IS 4.
                         NEW.

the System Card would be

        //FT04F001   DD   DSNAME=FS.nooo.WERNER,DISP=OLD

The filename and the BMDP File CODE need not be the same. However, the same name can be used for both.

The System Card should immediately precede

        //SYSIN DD *

(When transformations are specified in FORTRAN, the order of the System Cards is described in the summary, p. 136.)

    We illustrate the above by saving the Werner blood chemistry data in a BMDP File using the Control Language instructions in Example 5.1 (p. 87) and the *SAVE* paragraph described above.

Example 7.1

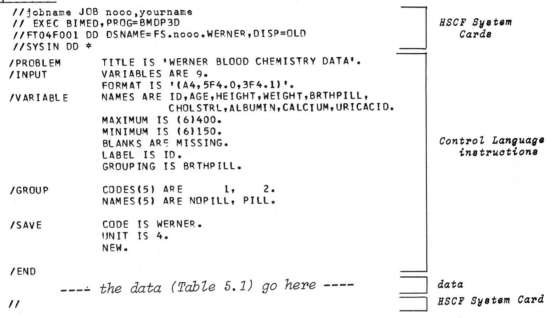

```
//jobname JOB nooo,yourname
// EXEC BIMED,PROG=BMDP3D              HSCF System
//FT04F001 DD DSNAME=FS.nooo.WERNER,DISP=OLD    Cards
//SYSIN DD *
/PROBLEM      TITLE IS 'WERNER BLOOD CHEMISTRY DATA'.
/INPUT        VARIABLES ARE 9.
              FORMAT IS '(A4,5F4.0,3F4.1)'.
/VARIABLE     NAMES ARE ID,AGE,HEIGHT,WEIGHT,BRTHPILL,
                  CHOLSTRL,ALBUMIN,CALCIUM,URICACID.
              MAXIMUM IS (6)400.                 Control Language
              MINIMUM IS (6)150.                    instructions
              BLANKS ARE MISSING.
              LABEL IS ID.
              GROUPING IS BRTHPILL.

/GROUP        CODES(5) ARE      1,    2.
              NAMES(5) ARE NOPILL, PILL.

/SAVE         CODE IS WERNER.
              UNIT IS 4.
              NEW.

/END
              ---- the data (Table 5.1) go here ----    data
//                                               HSCF System Card
```

    Output 7.1 shows the message printed by all BMDP programs when a BMDP File is created.   All lines but the last are printed when the program <u>begins</u> to write the BMDP File. The last line is written when the BMDP File is completed. The last message may be separated from the first part by some program results. If a BMDP program terminates with an error, you should check if the last line has been printed to be sure the BMDP File is complete.

Output 7.1 The messages printed by the BMDP program when a BMDP File is created.[2]

```
BMDP FILE WRITTEN ON UNIT 4.
  ①      CODE. . . IS     WERNER
          CONTENT . IS     DATA
          LABEL . . IS
          VARIABLES    1  ID       2  AGE      3  HEIGHT   4  WEIGHT   5  BRTHPILL
                       6  CHOLSTRL 7  ALBUMIN  8  CALCIUM  9  URICACID

        --- some results may appear here ---

② BMDP FILE ON UNIT 4 HAS BEEN COMPLETED.
```

Note: ① is printed when the program begins to write the BMDP File.

       ② is printed when the program finishes writing the BMDP File.

_____

[2] In BMDP programs dated before August 1977,
     the term Save File is used instead of BMDP File.

7.2 What is Stored in a BMDP File

● DATA

When you create a BMDP File to save your data, the data are written into a File <u>after</u>

- all transformations are performed, if any are specified (i.e., the transformed data are saved)
- values of any variable equal to its missing value code are recoded to a unique missing value code (called XMIS) recognized by all BMDP programs
- values of any variable outside the upper (MAXIMUM) and lower (MINIMUM) limits are recoded to codes (similar to XMIS) recognized by all BMDP programs

The original data containing the observed missing value codes and extreme values are <u>not</u> kept in the BMDP File. In addition, cases for which USE is set to a negative value by case selection or transformation (Section 6.2) are <u>not</u> copied into the File; the value of USE (zero or one) is recorded for each case written into the BMDP File.

When the BMDP File is created the number of VARIABLES (after transformations, if any) is recorded. If the BMDP program that creates the File adds results (such as residuals) to each case, the number of variables recorded in the File is increased to include all additional variables.

The data in the BMDP File are <u>not</u> written or read with a FORMAT statement; they are written as binary records. *The FORMAT statement must be omitted from the INPut paragraph; the absence of FORMAT and presence of CODE signal to the program that a BMDP File is read as input.*

The number of CASEs need not be specified when input is from a BMDP File. A record is written at the end of each File that is recognized by each program as the end of the data.

Therefore, when reading a BMDP File the FORMAT <u>must not</u> be stated, and the number of VARIABLES and the number of CASEs <u>need not be</u> stated.

When the BMDP File is being created, the NAMEs of the variables and the identity of the case LABEL variables are written in the File. As described above, missing values and values out of range are recoded to special values that are recognized by every BMDP program.

When data are stored in a BMDP File, the USE statement in the *VARiable* paragraph, if specified, does not affect the BMDP File. All variables are copied into the File.

If a *GROUP* or *CATEGory* paragraph is specified when a BMDP File is created, the CODEs, CUTPOINTs and NAMEs are included in the File.[3]

If your input is from a BMDP File and you are creating a new BMDP File, the CODEs, CUTPOINTs and NAMEs from the first File are copied into the new File unless you update the *GROUP* or *CATEGory* paragraph.

● A COVARIANCE OR CORRELATION MATRIX

Several BMDP programs allow you to save a covariance or correlation matrix that can then be used as input to subsequent analyses by other BMDP programs. Since a covariance matrix can be converted to a correlation matrix, and conversely, the two matrices are equivalent for the purpose of analysis.

When a covariance or correlation matrix is saved in a BMDP File, each row is written as a separate record. Although each record has the same length (i.e., contains p values if p is the number of variables in the matrix), only the lower triangular part of the matrix is filled with values. That is, the first record contains one value, the second two values,..., and the last contains all values. The remainder of each record is padded. After the covariance or correlation matrix, the variance, mean, frequency and sum of case weights for each variable is recorded in the File. When the correlations or covariances are computed by a missing value formula as in P8D or PAM this fact is also recorded in the File.

The covariance or correlation matrix saved is the one used in the analysis by the BMDP program. Therefore only variables used in the analysis are saved. The number of VARIABLEs saved is recorded, and the NAMEs of the variables and their original subscripts are saved.

A correlation or covariance matrix can be punched onto cards from a BMDP File. To do so, you must read the BMDP File into a program such as P1D that only accepts data as input. (The CONTENT must be correctly specified as it is in the BMDP File.) Then you can use the method described in Section 7.4 to copy the data (the covariance or correlation matrix) into your own data file or onto the punch unit. Remember that the lower triangular matrix contains the covariances and correlations.

● OTHER MATRICES

Other results that can be saved in a BMDP File are described in the individual program descriptions.

---

[3] In BMDP programs dated before August 1977,
the *GROUP* or *CATEGory* information is not included in the BMDP File.

7.3 How to Use a BMDP File as Input

The *INPut* paragraph is used to describe the BMDP File that is to be read as input. In addition, a System Card is necessary to describe the location of the system file to the computer.

The BMDP File is described by its CODE name and CONTENT (when the CONTENT is not DATA). If there are two BMDP Files with the same CODE and CONTENT, you can also specify the LABEL of the File that you want (provided you have given the two files different LABELs).

Since the BMDP File is on a disk or magnetic tape, the UNIT from which to read the File must be specified; the program searches for the BMDP File specified in the *INPut* paragraph.

INPut

    CONTENT=c.   { DATA }

        Required only if the CONTENT[4] of the BMDP File to be read is not DATA. If specified, it must be identical to the CONTENT speci- fied in the *SAVE* paragraph when the File was created.

    CODE=c.   {none}   required

        The CODE name assigned to the BMDP File when the File was created.

        Note: If you specify CODE='Б', where Б is a blank, the first BMDP File is read as input and the CODE is reported in the output.

    LABEL='c'.   {blank}   optional

        The LABEL is required only if two BMDP Files in the same system file have identical CODEs and CONTENTs. If specified it must be identical to the LABEL specified when the File was created.

        Note: The FORMAT must not be specified.

    UNIT=#.   {required to read a BMDP File/prev.}   not 1,2,5 or 6

        The UNIT from which to read the BMDP File. *A System Card is also necessary to describe the location of the system file containing the BMDP File to the computer. See order of input in the summary (p. 136).*

If the BMDP File created in Example 7.1 is read as input to the same program (P3D, but it could be a different program), the entire order of input is shown below.

---

[4] In BMDP programs dated before August 1977,
    CONTENT should be specified if there is more than one BMDP File in the system file.

Example 7.2

```
//jobname JOB nooo,yourname
// EXEC BIMED,PROG=BMDP3D
//FT04F001 DD DSNAME=FS.nooo.WERNER,DISP=OLD        HSCF System
//SYSIN DD *                                          Cards

/PROBLEM        TITLE IS 'WERNER BLOOD CHEMISTRY DATA'.
/INPUT          UNIT IS 4.
                CODE IS WERNER.                    Control Language
/VARIABLE       GROUPING IS BRTHPILL.               instructions

/END
//                                                 HSCF System Card
```

In Output 7.2 we reproduce the message that the BMDP File is used as input.

● READING THE BMDP FILE

You must retrieve a BMDP File from the system file into which it was written if you want to use it for input. The System Card to identify the system file must be similar to the System Card used when the File was created.

At HSCF the System Card to identify the system file is

    //FTyyF001   DD   DSNAME=FS.nooo.filename,DISP=OLD

where

    yy   is the UNIT specified in the *INPut* paragraph

    nooo.filename is identical to that on the System Card when the
                    BMDP File was created

For example, if the *INPut* paragraph is

    /INPUT   UNIT IS 7.
             CODE IS WERNER.

the appropriate HSCF System Card is

    //FT07F001   DD   DSNAME=FS.nooo.WERNER,DISP=OLD

Output 7.2 The message ① printed by the BMDP program when a BMDP File is read as input.

```
PROBLEM TITLE . . . . . . .WERNER BLOOD CHEMISTRY DATA

NUMBER OF VARIABLES TO READ IN. . . . . . . . .       9
NUMBER OF VARIABLES ADDED BY TRANSFORMATIONS. .       0
TOTAL NUMBER OF VARIABLES . . . . . . . . . .         9
NUMBER OF CASES TO READ IN. . . . . . . . . . 1000000
CASE LABELING VARIABLES . . . . . . . . . . .        ID
LIMITS AND MISSING VALUE CHECKED BEFORE TRANSFORMATIONS
BLANKS ARE. . . . . . . . . . . . . . . . . .     ZEROS
INPUT UNIT NUMBER . . . . . . . . . . . . . .         4
REWIND INPUT UNIT PRIOR TO READING. . DATA. . .     YES

INPUT FORMAT
BMDP FILE . . . CODE. . . IS    WERNER
                CONTENT . IS    DATA
   ①            LABEL . . IS
                VARIABLES   1  ID        2  AGE       3  HEIGHT     4  WEIGHT     5  BRTHPILL
                            6  CHCLSTRL  7  ALBUMIN   8  CALCIUM    9  URICACID
```

-133-

The System Card should immediately precede

        //SYSIN DD *

You can use a BMDP File as input and also create another BMDP File in the same problem. The two BMDP Files must have the same UNITs (in the *SAVE* and *INPut* paragraphs) if they are in the same system file, and different UNITs if they are in different system files. When you create a BMDP File to store your DATA and the BMDP program you are using does not add additional statistics to the File (such as residuals or predicted values), the BMDP File being created cannot be in the same system file as the BMDP File read as input.

When you are using input and output in BMDP Files that are in two system files, two System Cards are necessary. The System Card with the smaller UNIT number must precede that with the larger UNIT number and both must be placed before the

        //SYSIN DD *

System Card.

● RESPECIFYING INFORMATION CONTAINED IN THE BMDP FILE

In Section 7.2 we described the Control Language information that is stored in or with the BMDP File. It is possible to modify that information for a particular analysis, or to copy the BMDP File into a second File with slightly different specifications. *When data are from a BMDP File the* FORMAT *must not be specified. The number of* CASEs *and number of* VARIABLES *need not be specified.*

You can specify a smaller number of CASEs than there are in the BMDP File; only the number of cases specified will be read.

You can reNAME the variables, but you cannot respecify the case LABEL variable(s). You can reduce the upper limit (MAXIMUM) or increase the lower limit (MINIMUM) for any variable; increasing the upper limit or lowering the lower limit does not affect the data since values out of range have been recoded and are not used in the analysis. You can specify additional MISSING value codes; the missing values already recoded will still be treated as missing. A USE statement in the *VARiable* paragraph can be specified to select variables for individual analysis.

You can perform additional transformations and add new variables to the data. You can respecify which cases are to be used by case selection.

You can add to or change the *GROUP* or *CATEGory* information contained in the BMDP File by specifying another *GROUP* or *CATEGory* paragraph.

7.4 Copying Data from a BMDP File

If the data are in a BMDP File and you want to use them in your own program or in a program that does not accept the BMDP File as input, the data can be copied or punched by inserting a WRITE statement in the FORTRAN transformation subroutine (Section 6.4). This WRITE statement follows all the rules of FORTRAN. For example

```
        WRITE(7,1000)  (X(I),I=1,NVAR)
1000    FORMAT(5F6.0)
```

where 7 is the UNIT to which the data are copied using the format statement 1000. *Note: System Cards are required to describe the BMDP File and the file to which the data are copied. See the order of input when FORTRAN transformations are specified (p. 136).*

This feature can also be used to subdivide your data file into several subfiles according to any condition you want to specify (in FORTRAN). Depending upon the condition, each subfile can be written to a different FORTRAN unit using your own format. Remember that System Cards are needed to describe the FORTRAN units if the data on each unit are to be saved.

When copying the data into your own file, you may recode any missing values and values out of range to other codes. You can recode these values as follows:

```
    DO  1I=1,NVAR
    IF(X(I).EQ.XMIS) X(I)=    your code for missing values
    IF(X(I).GT.XMIS) X(I)=    your code for values greater than the upper
                                limit
    IF(X(I).LT.(-XMIS))X(I)= your code for values less than the lower
                                limit
  1 CONTINUE
```

If you have any case LABEL variables, they should not be included in the above recoding loop; they should be skipped. The FORTRAN statements to check for XMIS and values out of range should be placed before the WRITE statement above.

Note that this method recovers the data and not the Control Language information in the BMDP File (such as variable names).

BMDP Files can be read into or written by the SAS and PSTAT systems.

7.5 Summary

Control Language Specific to BMDP Files

Paragraph STATEMENT[1]	{Preassigned value}	Definition, restriction	See pages:
/SAVE		Required to create a BMDP File	125
CODE=c.	{none}	Code to identify BMDP File, required	125-126
LABEL='c'.	{blank}	Label for BMDP File, $\leq$ 40 char.	125-126
UNIT=#.	{none}	Unit on which to write BMDP File, not 1, 2, 5 or 6	126-127
NEW.	{not NEW}	NEW if this is first BMDP File in system file	126-127
/INPut		Required to read BMDP File as input	132
CONTENT=c.	{DATA}	Data or matrix in BMDP File	132
CODE=c.	{blank}	Code to identify BMDP File, required	132
LABEL='c'.	{blank}	Label for BMDP File	132
UNIT=#.	{none/prev.}	Unit from which to read BMDP File, $\neq$ 1, 2, 5 or 6	132

CONTENT, CODE and LABEL, *if specified, must be identical to that when BMDP File was created.*
FORMAT *must not be specified.*

Key:
  #   number
  c   name not exceeding 8 char., apostrophes may be required (p. 59)
  'c'   title, label or format

[1] In BMDP programs dated before August 1977, the minimum required abbreviations are CONTENT (not CONT) and *INPUT* (not *INP*).

- Order of input to read or create a BMDP File (standard procedure)

  (1) System Cards, at HSCF these are
  ```
  //jobname  JOB  nooo,yourname
  //  EXEC  BIMED,PROG=BMDPxx
  //FTyyF001  DD  DSNAME=FS.nooo.filename,DISP=OLD
  //SYSIN  DD  *
  ```

  (2) Control Language instructions
  and data, if on cards
  ```
  see program description
  ```

  (3) System Card, at HSCF this is
  ```
  //
  ```

- Order of input to read or create a BMDP File (when transformations are specified in FORTRAN)

  (1) System Cards, at HSCF these are
  ```
  //jobname  JOB  nooo,yourname
  //  EXEC  BIMEDT,PROG=BMDPxx
  //TRANSF  DD  *
  ```

  (2) FORTRAN statements
  ```
  FORTRAN transformations
  ```

  (3) System Cards, at HSCF these are
  ```
  //GO.FTyyF001  DD  DSNAME=FS.nooo.filename,DISP=OLD
  //GO.SYSIN  DD  *
  ```

  (4) Control Language instructions
  and data, if on cards
  ```
  see program description
  ```

  (5) System Card, at HSCF this is
  ```
  //
  ```

8

DATA DESCRIPTION

The first step in an analysis is to examine the data for recording, transcribing or keypunching errors and for outliers or extreme values. Many powerful statistical techniques can be severely affected by errors or extreme values in the data and do not provide a warning that the data fail to fulfill the assumptions of the analysis. Pitfalls caused by faulty data can often be avoided by examining the data closely, either one variable at a time or one variable in relation to another.

The three BMDP programs discussed in this chapter provide descriptions of the data one variable at a time.

P1D -- Simple Data Description   p. 139
P2D -- Detailed Data Description Including Frequencies   p. 146
P4D -- Single Column Frequencies -- Numeric and Nonnumeric   p. 155

Computations in P1D and P2D use all _acceptable_ values for each variable; i.e., values that are not equal to the missing value code and are not outside specified upper and lower limits. The data that are not used are called _excluded_ values.

P1D provides a compact summary of the data. For each variable, P1D computes the mean, standard deviation, coefficient of variation and the largest and smallest standard scores (z-scores). It reports the number of acceptable values, and can also list all the cases, or only the cases that contain one or more values excluded from the computations. PAM, described in Section 12.2, prints the position of each excluded value in a compressed list.

P2D plots a histogram of the values for each variable, counts the frequency of each distinct value, and computes the relative frequency distribution (percent of cases less than or equal to each value). When you have many cases, these results are difficult to interpret (and costly to compute) for a continuous variable; therefore, the values for each variable can be rounded or truncated to provide fewer distinct values in the analysis. P2D computes the mean, standard deviation, skewness and kurtosis for each variable. It calculates the median and can estimate three new robust measures of location. The mean, mode, quartiles and measures of location are plotted on a line graph.

P4D is the only BMDP program that accepts nonnumeric data (except as case labels). It counts the frequency of each distinct character (letter, number, symbol) found in each column of the data records (cards). It can list all the cases, or only the cases that contain specified kinds of characters (such as numbers, letters, or symbols). This feature can be used to identify cases that contain nonnumeric data due to a recording or keypunching error.

The three programs (P1D, P2D, P4D) complement each other in data screening and description. P1D is inexpensive and often indicates errors, such as extreme values. P4D is especially useful when there is a possibility that nonnumeric characters are in the data. (When the nonnumeric characters represent codes for a variable, such as M and F for SEX , they can be recoded to numeric codes in any BMDP program, see Section 6.5.) P4D is also useful when many of the variables are coded into single columns; i.e., have values from 1 to 9. P2D produces a wider variety of results than P4D. P1D can be used before P2D to find the range of values for each continuous variable. You can then specify values to round or truncate the data to produce fewer distinct values for an analysis by P2D.

Histograms are a valuable method of examining the data for extreme values and distributional assumptions (e.g., symmetry or normality). P2D plots a small histogram for each variable. Larger and better labelled histograms are printed by P5D (Section 10.1). When the cases are grouped, as by SEX, side-by-side histograms (one for each group) give you a better picture of the data; these histograms are available in P7D (Section 9.2).

P1D

8.1 Simple Data Description

P1D computes univariate statistics for each variable, including the largest and smallest standard scores. The data can be listed for all cases or selectively for cases containing excluded values. P1D can count the frequency of specified codes or intervals for any variable.

- CONTROL LANGUAGE

    The Control Language instructions to describe the data and variables are common to all BMDP programs and are explained in Chapter 5: the *PROBlem*, *INPut*,[1] *VARiable* and *GROUP* are used in P1D.

    If data editing or transformations are necessary, the methods described in Chapter 6 can be used. Data can be read using a FORMAT statement or from a BMDP File (Chapter 7). If a BMDP File is read as input and a new BMDP File is created in the same problem, the two Files must be in different system files and must have different UNIT numbers.

    A summary of the Control Language instructions common to all BMDP programs is on p. 162; a summary of the Control Language instructions specific to P1D follows the general summary. The summary can be used as an index to the program:

- RESULTS

    In the examples below we use P1D to analyze the Werner blood chemistry data (Table 5.1). Example 8.1 shows the Control Language instructions that are used to obtain a compact summary of the data. These Control Language instructions are described in Chapter 5.

Example 8.1

```
/PROBLEM     TITLE IS 'WERNER BLOOD CHEMISTRY DATA'.
/INPUT       VARIABLES ARE 9.
             FORMAT IS '(A4,5F4.0,3F4.1)'.
/VARIABLE    NAMES ARE ID,AGE,HEIGHT,WEIGHT,BRTHPILL,
                   CHOLSTRL,ALBUMIN,CALCIUM,URICACID.
             MAXIMUM IS (6)400.
             MINIMUM IS (6)150.
             BLANKS ARE MISSING.
             LABEL IS ID.

/END
```

---

[1] BMDP programs dated before August 1977 require more letters in their permissible abbreviated form (the capitalized letters). The minimum required abbreviations are specified in the footnotes to the summary (p. 162).

The Control Language must be preceded by System Cards to initiate the analysis by P1D. At HSCF, the System Cards are

```
//jobname  JOB  nooo,yourname
//   EXEC  BIMED,PROG=BMDP1D
//SYSIN  DD  *
```

The Control Language is immediately followed by the data (Table 5.1). The analysis is terminated by another System Card. At HSCF, this System Card is

```
//
```

The results of the analysis by P1D are presented in Output 8.1. Circled numbers below correspond to those in the output.

(1)   The number of cases read is 188. The number of cases is not specified in the Control Language instructions, so all the cases are read. All computations by P1D use all acceptable values for each variable -- i.e., all values that are not missing and not out of range.

For each variable P1D prints its

(2)   mean

(3)   standard deviation

(4)   standard error of the mean

(5)   coefficient of variation

(6)   smallest acceptable value observed in the data and its standard score (z-score)

(7)   largest acceptable value observed in the data and its standard score (z-score)

(8)   range

(9)   total frequency of the acceptable values

These statistics are defined in Section 2.1.

Output 8.1   Univariate statistics computed by P1D. Circled numbers correspond to those in the text. Results not reproduced are indicated in italics.

BMDP1D - SIMPLE DATA DESCRIPTION
HEALTH SCIENCES COMPUTING FACILITY
UNIVERSITY OF CALIFORNIA, LOS ANGELES

PROGRAM REVISED SEPTEMBER 1977
MANUAL DATE -- 1977

--- *Control Language read by P1D is printed and interpreted* ---

(1) NUMBER OF CASES READ.   188

VARIABLE NO. NAME	MEAN	STANDARD DEVIATION	ST.ERR. OF MEAN	COEFF. OF VARIATION	SMALLEST VALUE	SMALLEST Z-SCORE	LARGEST VALUE	LARGEST Z-SCORE	RANGE	TOTAL FREQUENCY
2 AGE	33.818	10.113	0.7376	0.29904	19.000	-1.46528	55.000	2.09449	36.000	188
3 HEIGHT	64.510	2.485	0.1822	0.03852	57.000	-3.02207	71.000	2.61155	14.000	186
4 WEIGHT	131.671	20.661	1.5149	0.15691	94.000	-1.82335	215.000	4.03323	121.000	186
5 BRTHPILL	1.500	0.501	0.0366	0.33423	1.000	-0.99726	2.000	0.99743	1.000	188
6 CHOLSTRL	236.150	42.555	3.1203	0.18020	155.000	-1.90693	390.000	3.61529	235.000	186
7 ALBUMIN	4.111	0.358	0.0262	0.08707	3.200	-2.54565	5.000	2.48281	1.800	186
8 CALCIUM	9.962	0.480	0.0353	0.04814	8.600	-2.84041	11.100	2.37280	2.500	185
9 URICACID	4.771	1.157	0.0846	0.24258	2.200	-2.22129	9.900	4.43252	7.700	187

(2)   (3)   (4)   (5)   (6)   (7)   (8)   (9)

There are several very large standard scores, such as 4.0 computed for a weight of 215 pounds and 4.4 computed for a uric acid reading of 9.9. All variables except AGE and BRTHPILL have total frequencies less than 188; i.e., have one or more excluded values.

● OPTIONAL RESULTS

In addition to the above results, you can

- list all cases in the data or only cases containing excluded values   p. 141

- request the frequencies of codes or intervals specified for a variable   p. 143

- store the data in a BMDP File to be used as input to other BMDP programs   p. 144

Appendix C.12 describes how P1D can be used to identify special or unacceptable values.

● PRINTING THE DATA

Any one or all of the following can be printed:

- cases in which a value is equal to a missing value code specified in the *VARIable* paragraph

- cases in which the value for any variable is less than its specified lower limit (MINIMUM in the *VARiable* paragraph)

- cases in which the value for any variable is greater than its specified upper limit (MAXIMUM in the *VARiable* paragraph)

- all cases

In any listing of the cases, missing values are replaced by the word MISSING, values less than the lower limit are replaced by TOO SMALL, and values greater than the upper limit are replaced by TOO LARGE.

The data are printed only if a *PRINT* paragraph is specified with one or more of the commands MISSING, MINIMUM, MAXIMUM or DATA, which correspond to the four options described above. To illustrate the *PRINT* paragraph, we add

```
/PRINT MISSING.
       MINIMUM.
       MAXIMUM.
```

to Example 8.1.

Example 8.2

```
/PROBLEM      TITLE IS 'WERNER BLOOD CHEMISTRY DATA'.
/INPUT        VARIABLES ARE 9.
              FORMAT IS '(A4,5F4.0,3F4.1)'.
/VARIABLE     NAMES ARE ID,AGE,HEIGHT,WEIGHT,BRTHPILL,
                   CHOLSTRL,ALBUMIN,CALCIUM,URICACID.
              MAXIMUM IS (6)400.
              MINIMUM IS (6)150.
              BLANKS ARE MISSING.
              LABEL IS ID.

/PRINT        MISSING.
              MINIMUM.
              MAXIMUM.

/END
```

The cases listed in Output 8.2 are obtained by this analysis in addition to the results shown in Output 8.1. Each of the eight cases listed contains one or more values replaced by MISSING, TOO SMALL or TOO LARGE. The criteria used to select the cases are printed above the list.

You can save residuals (or other results) from a BMDP program in a BMDP File and use P1D to select and print cases with large values for the residuals (or other results).

PRINT

   MISSING.   {no/prev.}

   List cases in which at least one variable has a value equal to a missing value code.

   MINIMUM.   {no/prev.}

   List cases in which at least one variable has a value less than its specified lower limit.

                                              (continued)

Output 8.2   P1D lists cases containing values excluded from the computations.

```
PRINT CASES CONTAINING MISSING VALUES.

PRINT CASES CONTAINING VALUES GREATER THAN THE STATED MAXIMA.

PRINT CASES CONTAINING VALUES LESS THAN THE STATED MINIMA.
```

CASE LABEL NO.	2 AGE	3 HEIGHT	4 WEIGHT	5 BRTHPILL	6 CHOLSTRL	7 ALBUMIN	8 CALCIUM	9 URICACID
1946	2	22.0000	64.0000	160.0000	2.0000	TOO LARGE	3.5000	MISSING	7.2000
1797	4	25.0000	68.0000	150.0000	2.0000	TOO SMALL	3.8000	9.6000	3.0000
3	51	54.0000	62.0000	120.0000	1.000	227.0000	MISSING	8.6000	2.5000
2877	86	30.0000	68.0000	MISSING	2.0000	212.0000	3.8000	10.000	6.6000
63	103	54.0000	67.0000	145.0000	1.000	320.0000	3.9000	MISSING	MISSING
2456	121	37.0000	MISSING	141.0000	1.000	237.0000	MISSING	10.5000	4.5000
5	161	46.0000	66.0000	MISSING	1.000	250.0000	4.1000	10.1000	7.3000
1149	185	53.0000	MISSING	178.0000	1.000	227.0000	3.9000	MISSING	5.0000

```
NUMBER OF CASES READ. . . . . . . . . . . . .    198
```

--- statistics printed in Output 8.1 appear here ---

PRINT
    MAXIMUM.   {no/prev.}

        List cases in which at least one variable has a value greater than its specified upper limit.

    DATA.   {no/prev.}

        List all cases.

● FREQUENCIES OF SPECIFIED CODES

    CODEs and CUTPOINTs can be specified for each variable in the *GROUP* paragraph (Section 5.4). The frequency of acceptable values for each distinct code or interval is printed. For example, we specify CODEs for BRTHPILL, and CUTPOINTs for AGE in Example 8.3.

Example 8.3

```
/PROBLEM     TITLE IS 'WERNER BLOOD CHEMISTRY DATA'.
/INPUT       VARIABLES ARE 9.
             FORMAT IS '(A4,5F4.0,3F4.1)'.
/VARIABLE    NAMES ARE ID,AGE,HEIGHT,WEIGHT,BRTHPILL,
                   CHOLSTRL,ALBUMIN,CALCIUM,URICACID.
             MAXIMUM IS (6)400.
             MINIMUM IS (6)150.
             BLANKS ARE MISSING.
             LABEL IS ID.

/GROUP       CODES(5) ARE      1,    2.
             NAMES(5) ARE NOPILL, PILL.
             CUTPOINTS(2) ARE     25,          35,          45.
             NAMES(2) ARE '25ORLESS', '26 TO 35', '36 TO 45', 'OVER 45'.

/END
```

Output 8.3 P1D counts the frequencies of codes or intervals specified in a *GROUP* paragraph.

NUMBER OF CASES READ.   188

VARIABLE NO. NAME	BEFORE TRANSFORMATION MINIMUM LIMIT	MAXIMUM LIMIT	MISSING CODE	CATEGORY CODE	CATEGORY NAME	INTERVAL RANGE GREATER THAN	LESS THAN OR EQUAL TO
2 AGE					25ORLESS		25.00000
					26 TO 35	25.00000	35.00000
					36 TO 45	35.00000	45.00000
					OVER 45	45.00000	
5 BRTHPILL				1.00000	NOPILL		
				2.00000	PILL		

--- statistics printed in Output 8.1 appear here ---

	CATEGORY NAME	CATEGORY FREQUENCY	NO. OF VALUES MISSING OR OUTSIDE THE RANGE	TOTAL FREQUENCY
AGE			0	188
	25ORLESS	52		
	26 TO 35	60		
	36 TO 45	42		
	OVER 45	34		
BRTHPILL			0	188
	NOPILL	94		
	PILL	94		

Output 8.3 shows how the *GROUP* paragraph is interpreted and the frequencies for the categories (codes or intervals) specified by the CODEs and CUTPOINTs.

Any number of variables can be assigned codes or cutpoints in the *GROUP* paragraph.

● STORING DATA IN A BMDP FILE

A BMDP File is an efficient way to save the data on a disk or magnetic tape so it can be used as input to other BMDP programs. The creation and use of a BMDP File is described fully in Chapter 7. When a BMDP File is used as input to a program, much of the information specified in the *INPut*, *VARiable* and *GROUP* paragraphs need not be repeated (Section 7.2).

P1D is often the first program used to analyze a set of data. In Example 8.4 we illustrate how to create a BMDP File to save your data by adding a *SAVE* paragraph to Example 8.3.

Example 8.4

```
/PROBLEM      TITLE IS 'WERNER BLOOD CHEMISTRY DATA'.
/INPUT        VARIABLES ARE 9.
              FORMAT IS '(A4,5F4.0,3F4.1)'.
/VARIABLE     NAMES ARE ID,AGE,HEIGHT,WEIGHT,BRTHPILL,
                     CHOLSTRL,ALBUMIN,CALCIUM,URICACID.
              MAXIMUM IS (6)400.
              MINIMUM IS (6)150.
              BLANKS ARE MISSING.
              LABEL IS ID.

/GROUP        CODES(5) ARE        1,     2.
              NAMES(5) ARE NOPILL, PILL.
              CUTPOINTS(2) ARE      25,          35,          45.
              NAMES(2) ARE '25ORLESS', '26 TO 35', '36 TO 45', 'OVER 45'.

/SAVE         UNIT IS 4.
              NEW.
              CODE IS WERNER.

/END
```

Note: The System Cards that precede the Control Language must contain a card describing where to store the BMDP File (Section 7.1). At HSCF, the System Cards are

```
//jobname  JOB  nooo,yourname
//  EXEC  BIMED,PROG=BMDP1D
//FT04F001  DD  DSNAME=FS.nooo.filename,DISP=OLD
//SYSIN  DD  *
```

In addition space must be allocated for the system file (Section 7.1).

The messages printed by P1D are shown in Output 8.4; they tell you that a BMDP File has been created and the data are saved. The message about the code, content, label and variables is printed before the BMDP File is written. Always be sure there is also a message that says the BMDP File has been completed.

The BMDP File contains the data, the variable NAMEs, the identity of the variables containing case LABELs, and the CODEs, CUTPOINTs and NAMEs from the *GROUP* paragraph. The data excluded from the computations are recoded on the BMDP File to internal codes for missing values or values out of range. Therefore much of the Control Language need not be respecified when the data in the BMDP File are used for other analyses (Section 7.2).

● SIZE OF PROBLEM

P1D can simultaneously analyze over 300 variables. Appendix B describes how to increase the capacity of the program.

● COMPUTATIONAL METHOD

P1D computes the means and standard deviations in single precision by a provisional means algorithm described in Appendix A.2.

ACKNOWLEDGEMENT

P1D was programmed by Koji Yamasaki. It supersedes BMD01D.

Output 8.4 Messages printed by P1D to indicate that a BMDP File is created.

```
BMDP FILE WRITTEN ON UNIT 4.

           CODE. . . IS      WERNER
           CONTENT . IS      DATA
           LABEL . . IS
           VARIABLES     1  ID         2  AGE        3  HEIGHT     4  WEIGHT     5  BRTHPILL
                         6  CHOLSTRL   7  ALBUMIN    8  CALCIUM    9  URICACID




BMDP FILE ON UNIT 4 HAS BEEN COMPLETED.




NUMBER OF CASES READ. . . . . . . . . . . . .    188
```
--- statistics printed in Output 8.1 appear here ---

P2D

8.2 Detailed Data Description, Including Frequencies

P2D counts and lists distinct values of each variable in the analysis. It computes univariate statistics, including the mean, median, standard deviation, skewness and kurtosis. P2D plots a histogram for each variable and plots the positions of several estimates of location on a line. P2D also computes three new robust estimates of location. The data values can be truncated or rounded before the statistics are computed.

● CONTROL LANGUAGE

The Control Language instructions to describe the data and variables are common to all BMDP programs and are explained in Chapter 5: the *PROBlem*, *INPut*[2] and *VARiable* paragraphs are used in P2D.

If data editing or transformations are necessary, the methods described in Chapter 6 can be used. Data can be read using a FORMAT statement or from a BMDP File (Chapter 7). If a BMDP File is read as input and a new BMDP File is created in the same problem, the two Files must be in different system files and must have different UNIT numbers.

A summary of the Control Language instructions common to all BMDP programs is on p. 162; a summary of the Control Language instructions specific to P2D follows the general summary. The summary can be used as an index to the program description.

● RESULTS

We use P2D to analyze the Werner blood chemistry data (Table 5.1). Example 8.5 shows the Control Language instructions used to obtain a detailed description for each variable. These Control Language instructions are described in Chapter 5.

---

[2] BMDP programs dated before August 1977 require more letters in their permissible abbreviated form (the capitalized letters). The minimum required abbreviations are specified in the footnotes to the summary (p. 162).

Example 8.5

```
/PROBLEM        TITLE IS 'WERNER BLOOD CHEMISTRY DATA'.
/INPUT          VARIABLES ARE 9.
                FORMAT IS '(A4,5F4.0,3F4.1)'.
/VARIABLE       NAMES ARE ID,AGE,HEIGHT,WEIGHT,BRTHPILL,
                        CHOLSTRL,ALBUMIN,CALCIUM,URICACID.
                MAXIMUM IS (6)400.
                MINIMUM IS (6)150.
                BLANKS ARE MISSING.
                LABEL IS ID.

/END
```

The Control Language must be preceded by System Cards to initiate the analysis
by P2D. At HSCF, the System Cards are

```
//jobname  JOB  nooo,yourname
//  EXEC  BIMED,PROG=BMDP2D
//SYSIN  DD  *
```

The Control Language is immediately followed by the data (Table 5.1). The
analysis is terminated by another System Card. At HSCF, this System Card is

```
//
```

       The results of the analysis by P2D are presented in Output 8.5. Circled
numbers below correspond to those in the output.

(1)   Program notes specific to P2D.

(2)   Number of cases read is 188. The number of cases is not specified in the
Control Language instructions, so all the cases are read. The computations
use all acceptable values for each variable; i.e., values not equal to a
missing value code and not outside specified upper and lower limits.

(3)   Each variable is analyzed in a separate panel. We present only the results
for CHOLSTRL in Output 8.5.

(4)   There are 188 cases in the Werner data. Two values for CHOLSTRL are
excluded from the analysis by the MINIMUM and MAXIMUM specification
in the *VARiable* paragraph. Therefore 186 cases are counted (N). Since
CHOLSTRL is continuous, there are many distinct values (80).

(5)   Univariate statistics contain

- the maximum observed value (not out of range)

- the minimum observed value (not out of range)

- the range

- the variance (s^2)

- the interquartile range: $(Q_3-Q_1)/2$

      where Q_1 and Q_3 correspond to the 25th and 75th percentiles
respectively.

(6)   Location estimates and their standard errors include

- the mean ($\bar{x}$) and the standard error of the mean ($s/\sqrt{N}$)

<u>Output 8.5</u> Detailed description of a variable printed by P2D. Circled numbers correspond to those in the text. Results not reproduced are indicated in italics.

```
BMDP2D - DETAILED DATA DESCRIPTION, INCLUDING FREQUENCIES          PROGRAM REVISED SEPTEMBER 1977
HEALTH SCIENCES COMPUTING FACILITY                                MANUAL DATE -- 1977
UNIVERSITY OF CALIFORNIA, LOS ANGELES
```

--- Control Language read by P2D is printed and interpreted ---

(1) THREE LOCATION ESTIMATES ARE PRINTED & PLOTTED FCR COMPARISON.
     WHEN ANY ESTIMATES ARE TOO CLOSE TOGETHER FOR BOTH TO APPEAR ON THE
     PLOT, THE PRIORITY OF PLOTTING IS THE ORDER IN WHICH THE ESTIMATES
     ARE LISTED.

     Q1 AND C3 ARE THE 1ST & 3RD QUARTILES. S- AND S+ REPRESENT THE
     QUANTITIES (MEAN-ST.DEV.) AND (MEAN+ST.DEV.).

(2)   NUMBER OF CASES READ.   188

--- analysis of variables 2 to 5 ---

```
(3)  VARIABLE NUMBER . . . . . .       6    (5)  MAXIMUM    390.0000000          H    H                    
             NAME . . . . . . . CHOLSTRL         MINIMUM    155.0000000          H    H         EACH ''H''
(4)  NUMBER OF DISTINCT VALUES .      80         RANGE      235.0000000          H    H         REPRESENTS
     NUMBER OF VALUES COUNTED. .     186         VARIANCE  1810.9609375          H  HHH          2.60
     NUMBER OF VALUES NOT COUNTED      2         ST.DEV.     42.5553894          H HHHH         COUNTS
                                                 (Q3-Q1)/2   30.0000000          H HHHHHHH   H
     LOCATION ESTIMATES                          ST.ERROR                        H  HHHHHHH  H
              MEAN         236.1505280            3.1203117                       HHHHHHHHH  H
(6)           MEDIAN       235.0000000            3.4641027                      HHHHHHHHHHH H H
              MODE         200.0000000                                        HHHHHHHHHHHHHHHHH
                                                                              MIN----------------MAX   (8)
                                                                                             Q1=  200.0000000
                                                                              DIV. BY S.E.   Q3=  26C.0000000
                                          (7) SKEWNESS  0.4703844  2.6189890   S-=  193.5951385
                                              KURTOSIS  0.1034966  0.2881222   S+=  278.7058105
                                                                              EACH . =   1.8217049
```

```
          (10)       S    Q                            Q     S
M                    -    M              MM             3     +                                          M
I..................................O.........EE.........................................................A
N                    D                DA                                                                X
                     E                IN
```

```
           PERCENTS                PERCENTS                 PERCENTS                 PERCENTS
VALUE COUNT CELL  CUM    VALUE COUNT CELL  CUM    VALUE COUNT CELL  CUM    VALUE COUNT CELL  CUM
155.   1   0.5   0.5     200.   10  5.4  25.8     237.   2   1.1  52.2     272.   1   0.5  82.3
158.   1   0.5   1.1     203.   1   0.5  26.3     238.   2   1.1  53.2     275.   2   1.1  83.3
160.   2   1.1   2.2     204.   1   0.5  26.9     240.   5   2.7  55.9     276.   2   1.1  84.4
165.   1   0.5   2.7     205.   3   1.6  28.5     242.   1   0.5  56.5     280.   4   2.2  86.6
168.   1   0.5   3.2     207.   1   0.5  29.0     243.   2   1.1  57.5     285.   1   0.5  87.1
170.   2   1.1   4.3     208.   1   0.5  29.6     245.   4   2.2  59.7     290.   2   1.1  88.2
172.   1   0.5   4.8     210.   5   2.7  32.3     246.   1   0.5  60.2     295.   3   1.6  89.8
173.   1   0.5   5.4     212.   1   0.5  32.8     247.   3   1.6  61.8     297.   1   0.5  90.3
174.   1   0.5   5.9     215.   3   1.6  34.4     248.   1   C.5  62.4     298.   1   0.5  90.9
175.   4   2.2   8.1     216.   1   0.5  34.9     250.   8   4.3  66.7     300.   2   1.1  91.9
177.   1   0.5   8.6     217.   2   1.1  36.0     253.   1   0.5  67.2     305.   3   1.6  93.5
180.   4   2.2  10.8     218.   1   0.5  36.6     254.   1   0.5  67.7     306.   2   1.1  94.6
185.   2   1.1  11.8     220.   5   2.7  39.2     255.   6   3.2  71.0     315.   1   0.5  95.2
189.   1   0.5  12.4     222.   1   0.5  39.8     257.   3   1.6  72.6     317.   1   0.5  95.7
190.   1   0.5  12.9     223.   1   0.5  40.3     260.   6   3.2  75.8     320.   3   1.6  97.3
192.   3   1.6  14.5     225.   3   1.6  41.9     262.   2   1.1  76.9     324.   1   0.5  97.8
195.   4   2.2  16.7     226.   1   0.5  42.5     263.   3   1.6  78.5     330.   1   0.5  98.4
196.   2   1.1  17.7     227.   2   1.1  43.5     265.   2   1.1  79.6     335.   1   0.5  98.9
197.   2   1.1  18.8     230.   8   4.3  47.8     266.   1   0.5  80.1     338.   1   0.5  99.5
198.   3   1.6  20.4     235.   6   3.2  51.1     270.   3   1.6  81.7     390.   1   0.5 100.0
```

(11) appears at left of VALUE column.

--- analysis of variables 7 to 9 ---

- the median: the 50th percentile (when there is an even number of observations, the two observations nearest the 50th percentile are averaged). The standard error for the median is computed as $(x_{(i)} - x_{(j)})/(2\sqrt{3})$ (pseudostandard error formula proposed by J.W. Tukey in a personal communication) where $x_{(i)}$ and $x_{(j)}$ are the ith and jth order statistics (values of rank i and j),

  i is defined as the integer part of $\frac{1}{2}(N + \sqrt{3N}) + 1$ and

  j is defined as the integer part of $\frac{1}{2}(N - \sqrt{3N}) + 1$.

- mode: the value with the maximum frequency

(7) Skewness, g_1, and kurtosis, g_2

The expected value of the skewness, g_1, is zero for a symmetric distribution. The standard error of g_1 is $(6/N)^{\frac{1}{2}}$ under the assumption of normality. The ratio of skewness to its standard error (labelled DIV. BY S.E. in Output 8.5) is a test of normality. (For CHOLSTRL this ratio is 2.6, which indicates that the distribution is skewed to the right.)

The expected value of the kurtosis, g_2, is zero for a normal distribution, positive for a distribution with heavier tails than the normal and negative for a distribution with lighter tails. The standard error of g_2 is $(24/N)^{\frac{1}{2}}$. The ratio of kurtosis to its standard error (labelled DIV. BY S.E. in Output 8.5) is a test of normality.

The formulas for the standard errors of g_1 and g_2 are from Cramer (1946, p. 375).

(8) Quartiles and mean ± standard deviation include

  - Q_1: the 25th percentile
  - Q_3: the 75th percentile
  - S-: $\bar{x} - s$
  - S+: $\bar{x} + s$

  All four are plotted in a line plot ((10) below).

(9) The data are plotted in a histogram that is limited to a maximum height of 10 lines and a maximum width of 40 characters. The width is the minimum of 40 and $10 \log_{10} N$. As a result it may be necessary for an "H" in the histogram to represent more than one observation. This is indicated in a note to the right of the histogram.

(10) The location estimates (such as the mean, median, mode, quartiles and S+ and S-) are plotted on a line 130 characters wide. If two measures coincide in their plotting positions, the one listed first in the statistics is plotted.

In Output 8.5 the measures are plotted from left to right in the following order: minimum, S-, Q_1 and the mode, median, mean, Q_3, S+ and maximum.

(11) A table is printed in which each distinct observed value is listed with its frequency, the percent of observations with this distinct value, and the cumulative percent of observations less than or equal to this distinct value. For example, 10.8 percent of the women have a CHOLSTRL value less than or equal to 180. This table is not very informative because it contains too many distinct values -- which also makes it costly to compute. Fewer distinct values can be obtained by rounding or truncating the CHOLSTRL values before the analysis.

● OPTIONAL RESULTS

You can

- compute three new robust estimates of location   p. 150

- truncate or round values of the variables to produce
  fewer distinct values in the analysis   p. 152

● ROBUST MEASURES OF LOCATION

Three robust measures of location can be estimated in P2D.[3] We name them trimmed mean, Hampel and biweight (Andrews et al., 1972). These measures estimate the location (mean) of a symmetric distribution with less variability than the mean or median when the data come from a long-tailed symmetric distribution, such as data with outliers or extreme values.

The mean is an estimate of location in which each observation is given the same weight. These three new measures do <u>not</u> weight observations equally.

The trimmed mean omits the largest 15 percent of the acceptable values and the smallest 15 percent and computes the mean using the remaining observations (the middle 70 percent). That is, each observation in the middle 70 percent has weight one and the extreme observations (large or small) have weight zero.

Both the Hampel and biweight estimates assign higher weights to the observations near the estimate than to those far from the estimate. The two diagrams below show the weights used as a function of

$$u = \frac{\text{observed value - estimate of location}}{\text{estimate of dispersion}}$$

where the estimate of dispersion is the median of |observed value - estimate of location|.

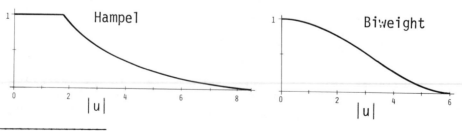

---

[3] BMDP programs dated before August 1977 compute three other robust measures and <u>not</u> those described here; skewness and kurtosis are computed only where the robust estimates are requested.

Since the estimate of location is used in the formula for u, the estimate of location must be found by iteration.

To obtain these robust measures the paragraph *COUNT* and the command ESTIMATE must be added to the above Control Language.

COUNT
   ESTIMATE   {no}

     If ESTIMATE is specified, the trimmed mean, Hampel and biweight estimates of location are computed and plotted on a line plot.

We use Example 8.6 to obtain the three robust measures.

Example 8.6

```
/PROBLEM      TITLE IS 'WERNER BLOOD CHEMISTRY DATA'.
/INPUT        VARIABLES ARE 9.
              FORMAT IS '(A4,5F4.C,3F4.1)'.
/VARIABLE     NAMES ARE ID,AGE,HEIGHT,WEIGHT,BRTHPILL,
                  CHOLSTRL,ALBUMIN,CALCIUM,URICACID.
              MAXIMUM IS (6)400.
              MINIMUM IS (6)150.
              BLANKS ARE MISSING.
              LABEL IS ID.

/COUNT        ESTIMATES.

/END
```

Output 8.6 Three robust estimates of location for CHOLSTRL are printed and plotted by P2D.

```
VARIABLE NUMBER . . . . . .     6      MAXIMUM    390.0000000       H   H
       NAME . . . . . . . CHOLSTRL     MINIMUM    155.0000000       H   H
NUMBER OF DISTINCT VALUES .     80      RANGE      235.0000000       H   H
NUMBER OF VALUES CCUNTED. .    186      VARIANCE  1810.9609375       H  HHH                         EACH ''H''
NUMBER OF VALUES NOT COUNTED     2      ST.DEV.     42.5553894       H HHHH                        REPRESENTS
LOCATION ESTIMATES                      (Q3-Q1)/2   30.0000000      H HHHHHH   H                       2.60
                                                  ST.ERROR          H FHHHHHH  H                     COUNTS
          MEAN       236.1505280       3.1203117    HHHHHHHHHH  H
          MEDIAN     235.0000000       3.4641027    HHHHHHHHHHH H H
          MODE       200.0000000                    HHHHHHHHHHHHHHHHH
     SOME NEW LOCATION ESTIMATES                    MIN------------------MAX
          HAMPEL     233.6557312                                              Q1=  200.0000000
 (12)     TRIMMED    233.5522156                            DIV. BY S.E.      Q3=  26C.C000000
          BIWEIGHT   233.7855072    (13)          SKEWNESS  0.4703844  2.6189890   S-=  193.5951385
                                                  KURTOSIS  0.1034966  0.2881222   S+=  278.7058105
            S  Q                                                          EACH . =   1.8217049
            -  M                    HMM          Q   S
  M         O                       AEE          3   +                                             M
  I.........................O.................MDA.....................................................A
  N         D                       PIN                                                            X
            E
```

		PERCENTS				PERCENTS				PERCENTS				PERCENTS	
VALUE	COUNT	CELL	CUM	VALUE	COUNT	CELL	CUM	VALUE	COUNT	CELL	CUM	VALUE	COUNT	CELL	CUM
155.	1	0.5	0.5	200.	10	5.4	25.8	237.	2	1.1	52.2	272.	1	0.5	82.3
158.	1	0.5	1.1	203.	1	0.5	26.3	238.	2	1.1	53.2	275.	2	1.1	83.3
160.	2	1.1	2.2	204.	1	0.5	26.9	240.	5	2.7	55.9	276.	2	1.1	84.4
165.	1	0.5	2.7	205.	3	1.6	28.5	242.	1	0.5	56.5	280.	4	2.2	86.6
168.	1	0.5	3.2	207.	1	0.5	29.0	243.	2	1.1	57.5	285.	1	0.5	87.1
170.	2	1.1	4.3	208.	1	0.5	29.6	245.	4	2.2	59.7	290.	2	1.1	88.2
172.	1	0.5	4.8	210.	5	2.7	32.3	246.	1	0.5	60.2	295.	3	1.6	89.8
173.	1	0.5	5.4	212.	1	0.5	32.8	247.	3	1.6	61.8	297.	1	0.5	90.3
174.	1	0.5	5.9	215.	3	1.6	34.4	248.	1	0.5	62.4	298.	1	0.5	90.9
175.	4	2.2	8.1	216.	1	0.5	34.9	250.	8	4.3	66.7	300.	2	1.1	91.9
177.	1	0.5	8.6	217.	2	1.1	36.0	253.	1	0.5	67.2	305.	3	1.6	93.5
180.	4	2.2	10.8	218.	1	0.5	36.6	254.	1	0.5	67.7	306.	2	1.1	94.6
185.	2	1.1	11.8	220.	5	2.7	39.2	255.	6	3.2	71.0	315.	1	0.5	95.2
189.	1	0.5	12.4	222.	1	0.5	39.8	257.	3	1.6	72.6	317.	1	0.5	95.7
190.	1	0.5	12.9	223.	1	0.5	40.3	260.	6	3.2	75.8	320.	3	1.6	97.3
192.	3	1.6	14.5	225.	3	1.6	41.9	262.	2	1.1	76.9	324.	1	0.5	97.8
195.	4	2.2	16.7	226.	1	0.5	42.5	263.	3	1.6	78.5	330.	1	0.5	98.4
196.	2	1.1	17.7	227.	2	1.1	43.5	265.	2	1.1	79.6	335.	1	C.5	98.9
197.	2	1.1	18.8	230.	8	4.3	47.8	266.	1	0.5	80.1	338.	1	0.5	99.5
198.	3	1.6	20.4	235.	6	3.2	51.1	270.	3	1.6	81.7	390.	1	0.5	100.0

The three measures are printed in Output 8.6.

(12) The Hampel, trimmed mean and biweight estimates of location are printed.

(13) The three estimates can also be plotted along the line. Only the Hampel estimate is plotted since it coincides with the other two estimates in their plotting positions. The statistic listed first in the results takes precedence in the line plot when two or more values coincide.

● ROUNDING OR TRUNCATING VALUES

When a variable is continuous and there are many cases in the data, the table of distinct values and frequencies may have too many entries. P2D produces a large but not very useful table that is time-consuming (costly) to build. Rounding or truncating values to fewer digits produces fewer distinct values and, hence, a smaller table that is easier to interpret and much faster to construct.

All computations use the rounded or truncated values if either is specified. The choice between rounding, truncating or leaving the data unmodified depends upon whether or not the variable is continuous.

Rounding and truncating are specified by ROUND and TRUNCATE assignments in the *COUNT* paragraph.

If you examine the distinct values of CHOLSTRL in Example 8.6, you see that 98 of the 186 values end with the last digit 0 or 5. Therefore it is reasonable to round the values to the nearest 5 or 10 units. In the following example we round CHOLSTRL to the nearest 10 units, i.e.,

        ROUND = (6)10.

specifies that the values for CHOLSTRL (the sixth variable in the Werner data) are to be rounded to the nearest number divisible by 10. Tabbing (p. 65) is necessary to skip variables. If both ROUND and TRUNCATE are specified for the same variable, the ROUND specification takes precedence.

Example 8.7

```
/PROBLEM      TITLE IS 'WERNER BLOOD CHEMISTRY DATA'.
/INPUT        VARIABLES ARE 9.
              FORMAT IS '(A4,5F4.0,3F4.1)'.
/VARIABLE     NAMES ARE ID,AGE,HEIGHT,WEIGHT,BRTHPILL,
                  CHOLSTRL,ALBUMIN,CALCIUM,URICACID.
              MAXIMUM IS (6)400.
              MINIMUM IS (6)150.
              BLANKS ARE MISSING.
              LABEL IS ID.

/COUNT        ESTIMATES.
              ROUND IS (6)10.

/END
```

The rounded results for CHOLSTRL are shown in Output 8.7. Compare these results with those in Output 8.6. There are 10 distinct values instead of 80, and each distinct value is divisible by 10. All computations in Output 8.7 are performed using the rounded data. The mean is now 237.8 instead of 236.2; the median is 240 instead of 235.

COUNT

ROUND=#$_1$,#$_2$,$\cdots$.　　　　{no rounding}　　　　one per variable

　　The units to which the variables are to be rounded. For example, setting #$_2$ to 10 specifies that the second variable is to be rounded to the nearest number divisible by 10. Data can be rounded to any positive value, including values less than one; e.g., 0.1, 0.05, etc. Tabbing (p. 65) can be used to skip variables.

TRUNCATE=#$_1$,#$_2$,$\cdots$.　　　{no truncation}　　　one per variable

　　The units to which the variables are to be truncated. For example, setting #$_2$ to 10 requests that the second variable be truncated to the nearest lower number divisible by 10. Data can be truncated to any positive value including values less than one; e.g., 0.1, 0.05, etc. Tabbing (p. 65) can be used to skip variables. If both ROUND and TRUNCATE are specified for the same variable, the ROUND specification takes precedence.

Output 8.7　Effect of rounding the values of CHOLSTRL to the nearest 10 units. Compare these results with those in Output 8.6 using the original values.

```
VARIABLE NUMBER . . . . . .       6        MAXIMUM    390.0000000          H
         NAME . . . . . . . CHOLSTRL        MINIMUM    160.0000000         HH
NUMBER OF DISTINCT VALUES .      20         RANGE      230.0000000        HH   HH
NUMBER OF VALUES COUNTED. .     186         VARIANCE  1825.9228516        HH  HHH                    EACH ''H''
NUMBER OF VALUES NOT COUNTED      2         ST.DEV.     42.7308197       HHHHHHH                     REPRESENTS
***VALUES ARE ROUNDED TO. .   10.0000       (Q3-Q1)/2   30.0000000       HHHHHH                          2.50
LOCATION ESTIMATES                          ST.ERROR                    H HHHHHH                       COUNTS
              MEAN        237.7956848        3.1331749               HHHHHHHHHH H
              MEDIAN      240.0000000        2.8867521              HHHHHHHHHHH HHH
              MODE        200.0000000                               HHHHHHHHHHHHHHHH
                                                                 MIN-------------------MAX
        SOME NEW LOCATION ESTIMATES                                                         Q1=  200.0000000
              HAMPEL      235.2883606                               DIV. BY S.E.   Q3=  260.0000000
              TRIMMED     235.1612854        SKEWNESS    0.4663235   2.5963793     S-=  195.0648651
              BIWEIGHT    234.7217255        KURTOSIS    0.062111'9  0.1729121     S+=  280.5263672
                                                                           EACH . =    1.7829456
          S Q                                          Q           S
M         - M                    H MM                  3           +                                        M
I.................0...............A.EE.....................................................................A
N         D                    M AD                                                                        X
          E                    P NI
```

| | | PERCENTS | | | | PERCENTS | | | | PERCENTS | | | | PERCENTS | |
VALUE	COUNT	CELL	CUM	VALUE	COUNT	CELL	CUM	VALUE	COUNT	CELL	CUM	VALUE	COUNT	CELL	CUM
160.	4	2.2	2.2	210.	11	5.9	32.8	260.	20	10.8	78.5	310.	5	2.7	94.6
170.	7	3.8	5.9	220.	14	7.5	40.3	270.	7	3.8	82.3	320.	6	3.2	97.8
180.	9	4.8	10.8	230.	14	7.5	47.8	280.	8	4.3	86.6	330.	1	0.5	98.4
190.	7	3.8	14.5	240.	18	9.7	57.5	290.	3	1.6	88.2	340.	2	1.1	99.5
200.	23	12.4	26.9	250.	19	10.2	67.7	300.	7	3.8	91.9	390.	1	0.5	100.0

● SIZE OF PROBLEM

Frequencies for approximately 250 variables can be counted at the same time if each requested variable has relatively few distinct values (less than 25). If frequencies for only one variable are counted, the variable can have approximately 6,800 distinct values. Appendix B describes how to increase the capacity of the program.

● COMPUTATIONAL METHOD

The data for each variable are read and the frequency table of distinct values is constructed. All statistics are computed from the frequency table (not from the original data). Therefore, when the data are rounded or truncated, the statistics are affected. The formulas for the statistics use the frequency of each distinct value. First the mean is computed, and then the variance, skewness and kurtosis are calculated using differences from the mean.

ACKNOWLEDGEMENT

P2D was designed and programmed by Laszlo Engelman. An earlier version was prepared by Dan Frumkes.

P4D

8.3 Single Column Frequencies — Numeric and Nonnumeric

P4D counts the frequency of each character (number, letter or symbol) in single column fields. It can be used to list the data as read or after replacing sets of characters with specified symbols (e.g., replacing numbers with blanks).

P4D is useful in preliminary data screening to verify the kinds of data present, to count frequencies of single column data, and to indicate extreme values and outliers. It is limited to analyzing only single column data.

● CONTROL LANGUAGE

P4D describes the data and variables in the *PROBlem*, *INPut*[4] and *VARiable* paragraphs described in Chapter 5. However, most specifications are not necessary or relevant. Therefore we quickly review definitions of items that are most useful in P4D.

The *PROBlem* paragraph is required.

- a TITLE can be specified for the analysis.

The *INPut* paragraph is optional. (It is not required as it is in all other BMDP programs.)

- VARIABLES refer to single columns of data (except for one or two case label variables that can be up to four characters each). Therefore there are up to 80 variables in the data on each card. The preassigned number of VARIABLES is 80. You can analyze up to 200 variables.

- FORMAT, if specified, must be in A1 format for each variable (column) that is not a case label variable. The preassigned FORMAT is (80A1); i.e., the whole data card is to be counted column by column. This is the only BMDP program with a preassigned format and the only program that uses A1 format; all other BMDP programs use F format. The FORMAT need not be specified unless you wish to skip columns or use case LABELs.

- CASEs, UNIT and REWIND are the same as described in Section 5.2, and need not be used when the data are on cards.

---

[4] BMDP programs dated before August 1977 require more letters in their permissible abbreviated form (the capitalized letters). The minimum required abbreviations are specified in the footnotes to the summary (p. 165).

The *VARiable* paragraph can be used to NAME variables or to specify one or two variables that LABEL cases. The remainder of the *VARiable* paragraph is not relevant to P4D.

● RESULTS

For our first example we use P4D to analyze the Werner blood chemistry data (Table 5.1). Example 8.8 presents the Control Language instructions used; the only specification is a TITLE for the analysis.

Example 8.8

```
/PROBLEM        TITLE IS 'WERNER BLOOD CHEMISTRY DATA'.
/END
```

The Control Language must be preceded by System Cards to initiate the analysis by P4D. At HSCF, the System Cards are

```
//jobname  JOB  nooo,yourname
//  EXEC  BIMED,PROG=BMDP4D
//SYSIN  DD  *
```

The Control Language is immediately followed by the data (Table 5.1). The analysis is terminated by another System Card. At HSCF, this System Card is

```
//
```

The results of the analysis by P4D are presented in Output 8.8. The circled numbers below correspond to those in the output.

(1) Each variable represents the data in a single column. The term "variable" does not have the same meaning as variable in other BMDP programs. For example, AGE is coded in columns 7 and 8 of the data cards. Therefore P4D reads AGE as two variables (the 7th and 8th). The frequency of the 10's digit is reported as variable 7 and the frequencies of the unit's digit are reported as variable 8. Fourteen women are aged 50-59 (5 in the 10's digit) and none are 60 or over.

(2) The Werner data is entirely numeric except for several blank codes inserted in the data. Therefore the characters printed are zero to nine and blank. When nonnumeric data are present, this list is expanded.

(3) BRTHPILL is coded in column 20 of the data card. Here we see that variable (column) 20 has 94 ones and 94 twos.

(4) The data for CHOLSTRL are in columns 22 to 24 of the data card. Therefore variable 22 contains the distribution of the 100's digit of CHOLSTRL. This column contains one 6 (a value for CHOLSTRL of 600 or over) and one blank but the remaining values are between 1 and 3. This kind of examination can identify unusual values.

Output 8.8 Frequency counts of each column by P4D for the data in Table 5.1. Circled numbers correspond to those in the text. Results not reproduced are indicated in italics.

```
BMDP4D - SINGLE COLUMN FREQUENCIES -- NUMERIC AND NONNUMERIC        PROGRAM REVISED SEPTEMBER 1977
HEALTH SCIENCES COMPUTING FACILITY                                 MANUAL DATE --  1977
UNIVERSITY OF CALIFORNIA, LOS ANGELES
```

--- Control Language read by P4D is printed and interpreted ---

FREQUENCY COUNT OF CHARACTERS PER VARIABLES

CHAR	CARD CODE	1	2	3	4 ①	5	6	7	8	9	10	11	12	13	14	15	16	17	18	19	20
	BLANK	68	18	2	0	188	188	0	0	188	188	2	2	188	7	2	2	188	188	188	③0
0	0	0	13	17	18	0	0	0	22	0	0	0	8	0	0	15	54	0	0	0	0
1	1	47	15	24	21	0	0	2	24	0	0	0	6	0	179	31	5	0	0	0	94
2	2	51	25	18	16	0	0	72	30	0	0	0	26	0	2	43	10	0	0	0	94
3	3	22	21	18	14	0	0	54	20	0	0	0	20	0	0	39	12	0	0	0	0
4 ②	4	0	15	22	17	0	0	46	16	0	0	0	31	0	0	25	9	0	0	0	0
5	5	0	14	23	17	0	0	14	16	0	0	4	28	0	0	11	54	0	0	0	0
6	6	0	15	18	22	0	0	0	14	0	0	180	21	0	0	8	8	0	0	0	0
7	7	0	14	18	23	0	0	0	16	0	0	2	25	0	0	5	10	0	0	0	0
8	8	0	20	11	16	0	0	0	16	0	0	0	13	0	0	2	20	0	0	0	0
9	9	0	18	17	24	0	0	0	14	0	0	0	8	0	0	7	4	0	0	0	0
TOTALS NUMERIC		120	170	186	188	0	0	188	188	0	0	186	186	0	181	186	186	0	0	0	188

FREQUENCY COUNT OF CHARACTERS PER VARIABLES

CHAR	CARD CODE	21	22	23 ④	24	25	26	27	28	29	30	31	32	33	34	35	36	37	38	39	40
	BLANK	188	1	0	0	188	188	2	2	188	95	3	3	188	188	1	1	188	188	188	188
0	0	0	0	25	74	0	0	0	24	0	0	91	22	0	0	0	17	0	0	0	0
1	1	0	38	15	0	0	0	0	18	0	93	2	18	0	0	0	15	0	0	0	0
2	2	0	131	17	10	0	0	0	19	0	0	0	11	0	0	5	25	0	0	0	0
3	3	0	17	21	9	0	0	62	16	0	0	0	15	0	0	36	21	0	0	0	0
4	4	0	0	17	4	0	0	123	21	0	0	0	16	0	0	78	18	0	0	0	0
5	5	0	0	22	50	0	0	1	15	0	0	0	26	0	0	43	20	0	0	0	0
6	6	0	1	18	10	0	0	0	16	0	0	0	24	0	0	17	14	0	0	0	0
7	7	0	0	18	18	0	0	0	17	0	0	0	14	0	0	4	16	0	0	0	0
8	8	0	0	12	12	0	0	0	21	0	0	2	22	0	0	3	24	0	0	0	0
9	9	0	0	23	1	0	0	0	19	0	0	90	17	0	0	1	17	0	0	0	0
TOTALS NUMERIC		0	187	188	189	0	0	186	186	0	93	185	185	0	0	187	187	0	0	0	0

--- similar counts for variables (columns) 41-60 and 61-80, which report all blanks ---

Table 8.1 Nineteen cases of data containing nonnumeric characters. The data
are in columns 1-26 of each card.

```
0456375825403175328 4.63754
130567851540637251 70.65W19
8125705614352358264 0.32734
1236547825007315604 5.63245
5    452076 020713548.32540
452037525265055334283.65024
43MISTAKE6508351  65.65883
85135237 73066234598.60H53
7162705610858832510 0.65027
81257.56143534561756.40335
13056.851540YES63524.62755
71627.56108512573256.77215
12365.78250053027616.64'32
45203.52526544321565.98325
812576.6143545443212.96352
12365.78250053324132.537 6
13056.85154013725689.53408
45203.52526563041255.64325
71627.56108511356405.65310
```

As a second example of a P4D analysis we use the data in Table 8.1. To
reduce the output we specify the number of variables (26 columns) in Example 8.9.

Example 8.9

```
/PROBLEM        TITLE IS 'DATA WITH NONNUMERIC SYMBOLS'.
/INPUT          VARIABLES ARE 26.

/END
```

The results are presented in Output 8.9. The characters found in the
data include letters (A,E,H, etc.) and symbols (.,'). This example is
described in greater detail in Section 3.1.

● OPTIONAL RESULTS

You can identify cases containing data (characters) that are not numeric.

You can print the data with different kinds of characters transformed to
blanks.

● PRINTING DATA: THE *PRINT* PARAGRAPH

P4D can print all the data or parts of the data. If only

    /PRINT

is specified, all the data are printed in the order read with a space inserted
after every 10th variable (column). Records that are completely blank are not
printed.

A subset of the data can be printed by modifying types of characters (such as letters, numbers or symbols) into blanks. The characters are divided into seven types:

1. letters of the alphabet
2. numbers (numeric data)
3. period or decimal point
4. plus and minus sign
5. blanks
6. symbols; i.e., comma, slash and any nonnumeric and nonalphabetic characters not listed above
7. illegal characters; i.e., characters not read under A1 format

Each type of character can be printed unchanged or replaced by a single character of your choice. For example

```
/PRINT NUMERIC=' '.
       BLANK='*'.
```

requests that numbers be recoded to blanks and blanks in the input data be recoded to asterisks. All records that are not entirely blank after recoding will be printed.

The *PRINT* paragraph in P4D is used in Example 8.10 to analyze the data in Table 8.1.

Output 8.9 Frequency counts by P4D for the data in Table 8.1

THERE WERE ONLY   19 CASES PRIOR TO END OF FILE.

FREQUENCY COUNT OF CHARACTERS PER VARIABLES

CHAR	CARD CODE	1	2	3	4	5	6	7	8	9	10	11	12	13	14	15	16	17	18	19	20
	BLANK	0	1	1	1	0	0	0	0	1	0	1	0	0	0	0	0	1	1	0	0
0	0	1	0	3	3	0	2	0	1	0	3	3	10	1	1	2	0	0	1	2	3
1	1	6	6	1	0	0	0	0	0	9	0	0	0	3	2	1	2	3	3	2	0
2	2	0	3	6	3	0	1	1	3	4	3	0	0	2	1	1	6	1	5	1	2
3	3	0	4	3	1	4	0	1	0	0	0	4	0	2	8	4	2	5	0	1	1
4	4	4	1	0	0	1	1	0	0	3	4	0	2	2	1	2	3	1	3	2	5
5	5	1	4	1	6	4	1	9	3	3	7	1	9	2	2	5	3	3	4	3	3
6	6	0	0	3	4	3	1	0	6	0	2	3	0	3	1	0	2	2	3	2	0
7	7	3	0	0	0	6	3	3	1	1	1	0	0	1	0	4	1	1	1	1	0
8	8	4	0	0	0	0	0	3	4	0	0	3	0	2	1	0	1	0	0	3	2
9	9	0	0	0	0	0	0	0	0	0	0	0	0	0	0	0	0	0	0	1	1
A	12-1	0	0	0	0	0	0	1	0	0	0	0	0	0	0	0	0	0	0	0	0
E	12-5	0	0	0	0	0	0	0	0	1	0	0	0	0	1	0	0	0	0	0	0
H	12-8	0	0	0	0	0	0	0	0	0	0	0	0	0	0	0	0	0	0	0	0
I	12-9	0	0	0	1	0	0	0	0	0	0	0	0	0	0	0	0	0	0	0	0
K	11-2	0	0	0	0	0	0	0	1	0	0	0	0	0	0	0	0	0	0	0	0
M	11-4	0	0	1	0	0	0	0	0	0	0	0	0	0	0	0	0	0	0	0	0
O	11-6	0	0	0	0	0	0	0	0	0	0	0	0	0	0	1	0	0	0	0	0
S	0-2	0	0	0	0	1	0	0	0	0	0	0	0	0	0	0	0	0	0	0	0
T	0-3	0	0	0	0	0	1	0	0	0	0	0	0	0	0	0	0	0	0	0	0
W	0-6	0	0	0	0	0	0	0	0	0	0	0	0	0	0	0	0	0	0	0	0
Y	0-8	0	0	0	0	0	0	0	0	0	0	0	0	1	0	0	0	0	0	0	0
.	12-3-8	0	0	0	0	0	9	1	0	0	0	0	0	0	0	0	0	0	0	0	0
,	5-8	0	0	0	0	0	0	0	0	0	0	0	0	0	0	0	0	0	0	0	0
TOTALS																					
	NUMERIC	19	18	17	17	18	9	17	18	17	19	18	19	18	18	18	19	18	18	19	19
	ALPHABETIC	0	0	1	1	1	1	1	1	1	0	0	0	1	1	0	0	0	0	0	0
	SPECIAL	0	0	0	0	0	9	1	0	0	0	0	0	0	0	0	0	0	0	0	0

--- similar analysis for variables (columns) 21-26 ---

Example 8.10

```
    /PROBLEM      TITLE IS 'DATA WITH NONNUMERIC SYMBOLS'.
    /INPUT        VARIABLES ARE 26.

    /PRINT        NUMERIC IS ' '.
                  BLANK   IS '*'.

    /END
```

The results are shown in Output 8.10. These results are in addition to the column frequencies printed in Output 8.9.

Note that no numbers appear in Output 8.10. The asterisks show where blanks previously occurred. One decimal point appears to be out of line. Letters and the apostrophe are quickly located.

The possible assignments[5] are explained below. Any symbol, number or letter can be used in place of each c. Any assignment that is not made leaves the data unchanged.

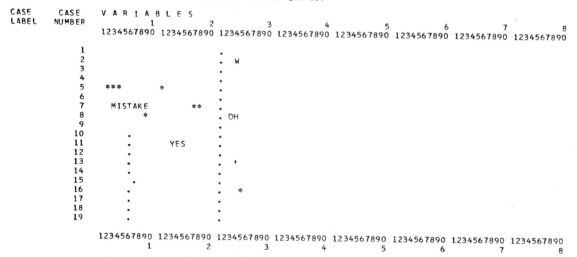

<u>Output 8.10</u>   P4D lists the cases after substituting blanks for numbers and asterisks for blanks.

```
LISTING OF FIRST CHARACTER OF EACH VARIABLE AFTER CHARACTER REPLACEMENT AS REQUESTED IN 'PRINT' PARAGRAPH.
CASES THAT BECOME ALL BLANK AFTER REPLACEMENT ARE NOT LISTED.

CASE     CASE     V A R I A B L E S
LABEL    NUMBER          1          2          3          4          5          6          7          8
                  1234567890 1234567890 1234567890 1234567890 1234567890 1234567890 1234567890 1234567890

          1                             .
          2                             .  W
          3                             .
          4                             .
          5       ***          *        .
          6                             .
          7       MISTAKE         **    .
          8            *                 .  OH
          9                             .
         10            .                 .
         11            .       YES        .
         12            .                 .
         13            .                 . '
         14            .                 .
         15          .                   .
         16            .                 .  *
         17            .                 .
         18            .                 .
         19            .                 .

                  1234567890 1234567890 1234567890 1234567890 1234567890 1234567890 1234567890 1234567890
                       1          2          3          4          5          6          7          8

THERE WERE ONLY    19 CASES PRIOR TO END OF FILE.
```

--- results in Output 8.9 appear here ---

[5] If your P4D is dated before August 1977, SIGN, PERIOD and SYMBOL cannot be used. In their place SPECIAL='c'. must be used, which recodes the plus and minus signs, periods and all symbols to c; if dated before February 1976, ILLEGAL is not available.

```
PRINT
    NUMERIC='c'.          {unchanged}                                    1 char.
       All numeric data are replaced by the character c.

    ALPHABETIC='c'.       {unchanged}                                    1 char.
       All letters are replaced by the character c.

    PERIOD='c'.           {unchanged}                                    1 char.
       All periods are replaced by the character c.

    SIGN='c'.             {unchanged}                                    1 char.
       The plus (+) and minus (-) signs are replaced by the character c.

    BLANK='c'.            {unchanged}
       All blanks are replaced by the character c.

    SYMBOL='c'.           {unchanged}                                    1 char.
       All symbols are replaced by the character c.  Symbols are those
       commonly available on a keypunch machine but not a number, letter,
       sign, period or blank.  They include ()&/¢!$,=*<>%@'_:;|¬?" and
       several punches that have no printed characters associated with
       them.  Since some punches can not be printed, their position in
       the data can be identified by assigning a printable character to
        SYMBOL.

    ILLEGAL='c'.          {unchanged}                                    1 char.
       All illegal characters are replaced by the symbol c.  Illegal
       characters are characters that occur by reading the data under
       a FORMAT other than A1, or by keypunching a card with more than
       one character in the same column.
```

*Note: When a PRINT paragraph is specified, all data records are printed
that are not entirely blank after the above substitutions, if any,
are performed.*

● SIZE OF PROBLEM

   The frequencies of characters in 200 variables (columns) can be counted
at the same time. Appendix B describes how to increase the capacity of the
program.

ACKNOWLEDGEMENT

*P4D was designed by W.J. Dixon and Laszlo Engelman and programmed by
Laszlo Engelman. It supersedes BMD04D.*

8.4 Summary — P1D, P2D, P4D

The Control Language on this page is common to all programs except P4D. See also the Control Language specific to

P1D -- Simple Description	p. 163
P2D -- Detailed Description Including Frequencies	p. 164

All Control Language for P4D is on p. 165.

Paragraph STATEMENT[1] {Preassigned value[2]}		Definition, restriction	See pages:
/PROBlem		Required each problem	74
TITLE='c'.	{blank}	Problem title, $\leq$ 160 char.	74
/INPut		Required first problem. Either VARIABLE and FORMAT, or UNIT and CODE required.	75
VARIABLE=#.	{none/prev.}	No. of variables in input data	75
FORMAT='c'.	{none/prev.}	Format of input data, $\leq$ 800 char.	76
CASE=#.	{end-of-file/prev.}	No. of cases in data	76-77
UNIT=#.	{5(cards)/prev.}	Input unit if data are not on cards; not 1, 2, 6	77
REWIND.	{REWIND/prev.}	Rewind input unit	77
CODE=c.	{none}	Code to identify BMDP File	132
CONTENT=c.	{DATA}	Data or matrix in BMDP File	132
LABEL=c.	{none}	Label of BMDP File, $\leq$ 40 char.	132
/VARiable		Optional. For input from a BMDP File, items in this paragraph may be previously set, see Chapter 7.	79
NAME=$c_1,c_2,\cdots$.	{X(subscript)/prev.}	Variable names, one per variable	79-80
MAXIMUM=$\#_1,\#_2,\cdots$.	{none/prev.}	Upper limits, one per variable	80
MINIMUM=$\#_1,\#_2,\cdots$.	{none/prev.}	Lower limits, one per variable	80
BLANK= (one only) ZERO, MISSING.	{ZERO/prev.}	Blanks treated as zeros or as missing value codes	81
MISSING=$\#_1,\#_2,\cdots$.	{none/prev.}	Missing value codes, one per variable	81
USE=$v_1,v_2,\cdots$.	{all variables}	Variables used in the analysis	82
LABEL=v_1,v_2.	{none/prev.}	Variable(s) used to label cases, read under A-format, one or two	83
ADD=#.	{0/prev.}	No. of variables added through transformation	99
BEFORE. or AFTER.	{BEFORE/prev.}	Data checked for limits before or after transformation	100
/TRANsform		Optional, Control Language transformations and case selection	97-105
/SAVE		Optional, required to create BMDP File	125
CODE=c.	{none}	Code to identify BMDP File, required	125-126
LABEL='c'.	{blank}	Label for BMDP File, $\leq$ 40 char.	125-126
UNIT=#.	{none}	Unit on which BMDP File is written; not 1, 2, 5 or 6	126-127
NEW.	{not new}	NEW if this is first BMDP File written in the system file	126-127

Key: # number
     'c' title, label or format
    v variable name or subscript
    c name not exceeding 8 char., apostrophes may be required (p. 59)

[1] In BMDP programs dated before August 1977, the minimum required abbreviations are *INPUT* (not *INP*), VARIAB (not VAR), FORMAT (not FORM), CONTENT (not CONT), *VARIAB* (not *VAR*), BEFORET (not BEF), AFTERT (not AFT), *TRANSF* (not *TRAN*). If dated before February 1976, BLANK=ZERO and cannot be changed.

[2] "/prev." means that any assignment remains the same as that specified in the previous problem or subproblem until changed. Otherwise, the assignment returns to its preassigned value each time a new problem begins or the paragraph is used again.

P1D -- Simple Data Description

(in addition to that on p. 162)

Paragraph STATEMENT [1] {Preassigned value}		Definition, restriction	See pages:
/PRINT		Optional, required to print data	141
MISSING.	{no/prev.}	Print cases containing missing value codes	141-142
MINIMUM.	{no/prev.}	Print cases containing values < lower limit	141-142
MAXIMUM.	{no/prev.}	Print cases containing values > upper limit	141-143
DATA.	{no/prev.}	Print all cases	141-143
/GROUP		Optional, required if you want frequencies of codes or intervals	143-144
CODE(#)=$\#_1,\#_2,\cdots$.	{10 smallest values/prev.}	Codes for variable #, may be repeated	84-85
CUTPOINT(#)=$\#_1,\#_2,\cdots$.	{see CODE/prev.}	Cutpoints to form intervals for variable #, may be repeated	84-85
NAME(#)=$c_1,c_2,\cdots$.	{CODEs or CUTPOINTs /prev.}	Code or interval names for variable #, may be repeated	84-85
RESET.	{not RESET}	If RESET, all assignments in prev. *GROUP* paragraph are reset to preassigned values	86
/END		Required	57

Key: # number
      c name not exceeding 8 char., apostrophes may be required (p. 59)

[1] In BMDP programs dated before August 1977, RESET is implicitly specified and cannot be changed.

- Order of input

    (1) System Cards, at HSCF these are
```
//jobname  JOB  nooo,yourname
//  EXEC  BIMED,PROG=BMDP1D
//SYSIN  DD  *
```

    (2) Control Language instructions
```
PROBlem paragraph, required
INPut paragraph, required first problem
VARiable paragraph
TRANsform paragraph
SAVE paragraph
PRINT paragraph
GROUP paragraph
END paragraph, required at end of Control Language
```

    (3) Data, if on cards   data

    (4) System Card, at HSCF this is   //

   Control Language instructions and data (2 and 3) can be repeated for additional problems.

P2D -- Detailed Data Description
Including Frequencies

(in addition to that on p. 162)

Paragraph STATEMENT {Preassigned value}		Definition, restriction	See pages:
/COUNT		Optional	
ESTIMATE.	{no}	Three robust estimates of location are printed	150-152
TRUNCATE=$\#_1,\#_2,\cdots$.	{no truncation}	Used to truncate data values, one per variable	152-153
ROUND=$\#_1,\#_2,\cdots$.	{no rounding}	Used to round data values, one per variable	152-153
/END		Required	57

Key: # number

- Order of input

  (1) System Cards, at HSCF these are
  ```
  //jobname  JOB  nooo,yourname
  //   EXEC  BIMED,PROG=BMDP2D
  //SYSIN  DD  *
  ```

  (2) Control Language instructions
  ```
  PROBlem paragraph, required
  INPut paragraph, required first problem
  VARiable paragraph
  TRANsform paragraph
  SAVE paragraph
  COUNT paragraph
  END paragraph, required at end of Control Language
  ```

  (3) Data, if on cards
  ```
  data
  ```

  (4) System Card, at HSCF this is
  ```
  //
  ```

  Control Language instructions and data (2 and 3) can be repeated for additional problems.

P4D -- Single Column Frequencies
-- Numeric and Nonnumeric

Paragraph STATEMENT[1] {Preassigned value[2]}		Definition, restriction	See pages:
/PROBlem		Required each problem	74
TITLE='c'.	{blank}	Problem title, ≤ 160 char.	74
/INPut		Optional	155
VARIABLE=#.	{80/prev.}	Number of variables in input data, < 200 var.	155
FORMAT='c'.	{(80A1)/prev.}	Format of input data, ≤ 800 char., use only A1 format	155
CASE=#.	{end-of-file/prev.}	Number of cases in data	76-77
UNIT=#.	{5(cards)/prev.}	Input unit, if data are not on cards	77
REWIND.	{REWIND/ prev.}	Rewind input unit	77
/VARiable		Optional	156
NAME=c₁,c₂,···.	{X(subscript)/prev.}	Variable names, one per variable	79-80
LABEL=#₁,#₂.	{none/prev.}	Variable(s) used to label cases, one or two	83
/PRINT		Optional, required to print data	158
ALPHABETIC='c'.	{none}	Replaces letters in the data, 1 char.	158-161
NUMERIC='c'.	{none}	Replaces numbers in the data, 1 char.	158-161
BLANK='c'.	{none}	Replaces blank char. in the data, 1 char.	158-161
PERIOD='c'.	{none}	Replaces period (decimal point) in the data, 1 char.	158-161
SIGN='c'.	{none}	Replaces plus, minus in the data, 1 char.	158-161
SYMBOL='c'.	{none}	Replaces symbols in the data, 1 char.	158-161
ILLEGAL='c'.	{none}	Replaces illegal values in the data, 1 char.	158-161
/END		Required	57

Key: # number | c name not exceeding 8 char., apostrophes may be required (p. 59)
      'c' title, label, format or character

[1] In BMDP programs dated before August 1977, the minimum required abbreviations are *INPUT* (not *INP*), *VARIAB* (not *VAR*), VARIAB (not VAR), FORMAT (not FORM), ALPHA (not ALP), and NUMERIC (not NUM); instead of PERIOD, SIGN and SYMBOL, the statement SPECIAL='c'. must be used. If dated before February 1976, ILLEGAL is not available.

[2] "/prev." means that any assignment remains the same as that specified in the previous problem or subproblem until changed. Otherwise, the assignment returns to its preassigned value each time a new problem begins or the paragraph is used again.

● Order of input

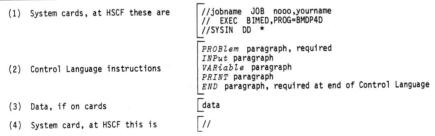

(1) System cards, at HSCF these are
```
//jobname JOB nooo,yourname
//   EXEC  BIMED,PROG=BMDP4D
//SYSIN DD  *
```

(2) Control Language instructions
```
PROBlem paragraph, required
INPut paragraph
VARiable paragraph
PRINT paragraph
END paragraph, required at end of Control Language
```

(3) Data, if on cards   ⌈data

(4) System card, at HSCF this is   ⌈//

Control Language instructions and data (2 and 3) can be repeated for additional problems.

9

DATA IN GROUPS

Description, t Tests and One-Way Analysis of Variance

Data are often classified into groups -- such as by sex, by age or by treatment. Unusual data values may be recognized when the data are examined separately for each group. For example, if the data are classified by age, a a height of six feet in the under-ten group is almost certainly an error, but six feet in an over-twenty group is not suspicious. Histograms of the data in each group are a convenient way to screen the data for unusual values and for normality.

Group means can be compared by a t test when there are only two groups, or by a one-way analysis of variance (ANOVA) when there are more than two groups. The choice of t test or ANOVA statistic depends primarily on whether the variances in the groups are equal or unequal.

In this chapter we discuss three BMDP programs that summarize data in groups, and compare the groups.

P3D -- Comparison of Two Groups with t Tests   p. 170
P7D -- Description of Groups (Strata) with Histograms and
          Analysis of Variance   p. 185
P9D -- Multiway Description of Groups   p. 199

P3D analyzes data in one or two groups. If the cases are classified into more than two groups, pairs of groups can be compared -- or all possible pairings of the groups can be compared. Univariate statistics and a histogram are printed for each variable in each group. If there is only one group, the one-sample t test is computed to test if the mean is zero. If there are two groups, their means are compared by two two-sample t tests -- with and without the assumption of the equality of variances; the equality of variances is tested by an F test. The means of several variables can be simultaneously tested for equality between two groups by Hotelling's T^2 and Mahalanobis D^2. The correlations between the variables in each group can be printed.

P7D analyzes data for each variable in any number of groups and plots side-by-side histograms of the data in each group. The intervals of the histograms are labelled. Values that are equal to a missing value code or are out of range are tallied separately. A one-way (or two-way) analysis of variance is performed to test the equality of means between groups. In addition to the classical one-way analysis of variance, P7D also computes two statistics that do not assume the equality of variance in each group. The input data, including any transformations, can be listed in the original order or after sorting the cases according to the values of a variable. P7D can also compute Winsorized means for each group and confidence limits for the Winsorized means. The correlations between the variables for each group and for all groups combined can be printed.

P9D analyzes data for each variable in any number of groups; the groups can be defined as all combinations of the levels of several variables. Univariate statistics are provided for each group. A one-way ANOVA is computed to test the equality of the means of all the groups. To test for homogeneity (equality) of variances, Bartlett's statistic is evaluated. A plot that shows the shift in means from group to group is an option. P9D also tests for the equality of group frequencies. If tests of the frequencies are your primary interest, the frequency table programs, Chapter 11, may be more appropriate.

Many other programs also present or analyze data in groups. For example, more than one group can be plotted in the same histogram in P5D (Section 10.1); more complex analysis of variance models, including the one-way ANOVA with covariates, are considered in Chapter 15; and nonparametric tests to compare groups are treated in Chapter 16.

● CONTROL LANGUAGE

The Control Language instructions to describe the data and variables are common to all BMDP programs and are explained in Chapter 5: the *PROBlem*, *INPut*[1], *VARiable* and *GROUP* paragraphs are used in the programs discussed in this chapter.

---

[1] BMDP programs dated before August 1977 require more letters in the permissible abbreviated form (the capitalized letters). The minimum required abbreviations are specified in the footnotes to the summary (p. 210).

If data editing or transformations are necessary, the methods described in Chapter 6 can be used. Data can be read using a FORMAT statement or from a BMDP File (Chapter 7). If a BMDP File is read as input and a new BMDP File is created in the same problem, the two Files must be in different system files and must have different UNIT numbers.

A summary of the Control Language instructions common to all BMDP programs is on p. 210; summaries of the Control Language instructions specific to each program described in this chapter follow the general summary. These summaries can be used as indexes to the program descriptions.

P3D

9.1 Comparison of Two Groups with t Tests

P3D analyzes data in one or two groups. If the cases are classified into more than two groups, pairs of groups can be compared or all possible pairings of the groups can be compared. Univariate statistics and a histogram are printed for each variable in each group. If there is only one group, the one-sample t test is computed to test if the mean is zero. If there are two groups, the group means are compared by two two-sample t tests -- with and without the assumption of the equality of variances. The equality of variances is tested by an F test. The means of several variables can be simultaneously tested for equality between two groups by Hotelling's T^2 and Mahalanobis D^2. The correlations between the variables in each group can be printed.

- RESULTS

We use P3D to analyze the Werner blood chemistry data (Table 5.1). The analysis compares two groups of women -- those on the pill with those not on the pill. Except for GROUPING IS BRTHPILL the Control Language instructions in Example 9.1 are described in Chapter 5.

Example 9.1

```
/PROBLEM      TITLE IS 'WERNER BLOOD CHEMISTRY DATA'.
/INPUT        VARIABLES ARE 9.
              FORMAT IS '(A4,5F4.0,3F4.1)'.
/VARIABLE     NAMES ARE ID,AGE,HEIGHT,WEIGHT,BRTHPILL,
                    CHOLSTRL,ALBUMIN,CALCIUM,URICACID.
              MAXIMUM IS (6)400.
              MINIMUM IS (6)150.
              BLANKS ARE MISSING.
              LABEL IS ID.
              GROUPING IS BRTHPILL.

/GROUP        CODES(5) ARE        1,    2.
              NAMES(5) ARE NOPILL, PILL.

/END
```

The Control Language must be preceded by System Cards to initiate the analysis by P3D. At HSCF, the System Cards are

```
//jobname   JOB  nooo,yourname
//  EXEC  BIMED,PROG=BMDP3D
//SYSIN  DD  *
```

The Control Language is immediately followed by the data (Table 5.1). The analysis is terminated by another System Card. At HSCF, this System Card is

```
//
```

The results of the above analysis using P3D are shown in Output 9.1. Circled numbers below correspond to those in the output.

(1) Interpretation of the *TEST* paragraph and items specific to P3D. No *TEST* paragraph is specified; therefore preassigned values are printed.

-170-

Output 9.1 Comparison of two groups by P3D. Circled numbers correspond to
those in the text. Results not reproduced are indicated in italics.

```
BMDP3D - COMPARISON OF TWO GROUPS WITH T TESTS          PROGRAM REVISED SEPTEMBER 1977
HEALTH SCIENCES COMPUTING FACILITY                      MANUAL DATE -- 1977
UNIVERSITY OF CALIFORNIA, LOS ANGELES
```

--- Control Language read by P3D is printed and interpreted ---

```
① TEST TITLE. . . . . . . . . .WERNER BLOOD CHEMISTRY DATA
   INDEXES OF VARIABLES TO BE ANALYZED . . . . . .   2  3   4   6  7  8  9
   USE COMPLETE CASES ONLY . . . . . . . . . . .        NO
   PRINT GROUP CORRELATION MATRICES. . . . . . .        NO
   COMPUTE HOTELLINGS T SQUARE . . . . . . . . .        NO
   INDEX OF GROUPING VARIABLE. . . . . . . . . .         5
   GROUPS USED IN COMPUTATIONS . . . . . . . . .      1  2

② PROGRAM NOTES

   1. THE T(POOLED) STATISTIC TESTS THE HYPOTHESIS THAT THE
   MEANS FOR THE TWO GROUPS ARE EQUAL ASSUMING THAT THE
   VARIANCES FOR THE TWO GROUPS ARE EQUAL.

   2. THE T(SEPARATE) STATISTIC TESTS THE HYPOTHESIS THAT THE
   MEANS FOR THE TWO GROUPS ARE EQUAL WITHOUT THE ASSUMPTION
   OF EQUAL VARIANCES. SINCE THERE IS LITTLE LOSS IN USING
   THE SEPARATE VARIANCE T EVEN WHEN THE POOLED T MAY BE
   APPROPRIATE AND SINCE THE ERROR IN USING THE POOLED T WHEN
   VARIANCES ARE NOT EQUAL CAN BE VERY SERIOUS, THE SEPARATE
   VARIANCE T SHOULD BE USED IN MOST APPLICATIONS.

   3. THE F(FOR VARIANCES) STATISTIC TESTS THE HYPOTHESIS THAT
   THE VARIANCES FOR THE TWO GROUPS ARE EQUAL.

   4. THE P VALUES ARE THE TWO-TAIL SIGNIFICANCE LEVELS.

   5. FOR ONE SAMPLE TESTS, THE F(FOR VARIANCES) SHOULD BE
   IGNORED AND THE T(SEPARATE) AND T(POOLED) ARE THE SAME.

③ NUMBER OF CASES READ. . . . . . . . . . . . .   188
```

```
                    BEFORE TRANSFORMATION                              INTERVAL RANGE
   VARIABLE    MINIMUM   MAXIMUM   MISSING   CATEGORY  CATEGORY   GREATER    LESS THAN
④ NO. NAME     LIMIT     LIMIT     CODE      CODE      NAME       THAN       OR EQUAL TO

   5  BRTHPILL                               1.00000   NOPILL
                                             2.00000   PILL
```

FOR DIFFERENCES ON SINGLE VARIABLES

```
   **********
⑤ *AGE     *  VARIABLE NUMBER   2      GROUP      1 NOPILL   2 PILL        1 NOPILL  (N=  94)        2 PILL    (N=  94)
   **********                                      MEAN        33.8188    33.8188
              STATISTICS    P VALUE  D. F.         STD DEV     10.1400    10.1400    H                         X
                                                   S.E.M.       1.0459     1.0459    H                         X
   T (SEPARATE)    0.0    1.000  186.0    SAM SIZ         94         94    H     HH  H                 X    XX  X
   T (POOLED)      0.0    1.000  186      MAXIMUM     55.0000    55.0000    HHHHHHH   H H HH  H         XXXXXXX   X X XX  X
                                          MINIMUM     19.0000    19.0000    HHHHHHHHHHHHHHHHHHHHH      XXXXXXXXXXXXXXXXXXXX
   F(FOR VARIANCES)  1.00  1.000   93,  93                                 MIN------------------MAX MIN------------------MAX
                                                                             AN H =    3.0 CASES        AN X =    3.0 CASES


   **********
⑤ *HEIGHT  *  VARIABLE NUMBER   3      GROUP      1 NOPILL   2 PILL        1 NOPILL  (N=  92)        2 PILL    (N=  94)
   **********                                      MEAN        64.0866    64.9252                              XX
              STATISTICS    P VALUE  D. F.         STD DEV      2.4924     2.4196    H                         XX  X
                                                   S.E.M.       0.2599     0.2496    H  H                      XX XXX  X
   T (SEPARATE)  -2.328   0.021  183.5    SAM SIZ         92         94    HH HHH  H                  XX XXX  XX
   T (POOLED)    -2.33    0.021  184      MAXIMUM     69.0000    71.0000    HH HHH  H                  XX XXX  XX
                                          MINIMUM     57.0000    59.0000    H  HH HHH HH              XX XXX XX X
   F(FOR VARIANCES)  1.06  0.776   91,  93                                 HH  HH HH HHH HH H        X XX XX XXX XX X X
                                                                           MIN------------------MAX MIN------------------MAX
                                                                             AN H =    3.0 CASES        AN X =    3.0 CASES


   **********
⑤ *WEIGHT  *  VARIABLE NUMBER   4      GROUP      1 NOPILL   2 PILL        1 NOPILL  (N=  93)        2 PILL    (N=  93)
   **********                                      MEAN       130.1502   133.1932    H
              STATISTICS    P VALUE  D. F.         STD DEV     18.8869    22.2926    HH                        X
                                                   S.E.M.       1.9585     2.3116    HHH                       XXX  X
   T (SEPARATE)  -1.004   0.317  179.2    SAM SIZ         93         93    HHHHHH                    XXXXXXX
   T (POOLED)    -1.00    0.317  184      MAXIMUM    195.0000   215.0000    H HHHHHH  H               XXXXXXX X
                                          MINIMUM     95.0000    94.0000    HHHHHHHHHHHHHHHH H        XXXXXXXXXXXXXX  XX
   F(FOR VARIANCES)  1.39  0.114   92,  92                                 MIN------------------MAX MIN------------------MAX
                                                                             AN H =    3.0 CASES        AN X =    3.0 CASES


   **********                                                                                 ⑥                         ⑦
⑤ *CHOLSTRL*  VARIABLE NUMBER   6      GROUP      1 NOPILL   2 PILL        1 NOPILL  (N=  94)        2 PILL    (N=  92)
   **********                                      MEAN       232.9678   239.4019    H   H                     X  XXX
              STATISTICS    P VALUE  D. F.         STD DEV     43.4914    41.5620    HH   H                    X  XXXX
                                                   S.E.M.       4.4858     4.3331    H  HHHHHHH                X  XXXX
⑧ T (SEPARATE)  -1.032   0.304  183.9    SAM SIZ         94         92    H  HHHHHH   H              X  XXXXXX
   T (POOLED)    -1.03    0.304  184      MAXIMUM    335.0000   390.0000    HHHHHHHHHHHHH H          XXXXXXXXXXX
                                          MINIMUM    155.0000   160.0000    HHHHHHHHHHHHH HH         XXXXXXXXXXXXXXX   X
   F(FOR VARIANCES)  1.10  0.665   93,  91                                 MIN------------------MAX MIN------------------MAX
                                                                             AN H =    2.0 CASES        AN X =    2.0 CASES
```

--- analysis for variables 7-9 ---

(2) Program notes. Explanatory notes about the tests computed by P3D.

(3) Number of cases read. The number of cases is not specified in our example, so all the cases are read. The computations use all acceptable data; i.e., values not equal to a missing value code and not outside specified upper and lower limits.

(4) Interpretation of the *GROUP* paragraph.

(5) The names of the variables being analyzed. Each variable is analyzed in turn.

(6) For each group (identified by the group subscript and group name) P3D prints

- mean: $\bar{x}$

- standard deviation: s

- S.E.M. (standard error of the mean): $s/\sqrt{N}$

- sample size (frequency): N

- maximum observed value (not out of range)

- minimum observed value (not out of range)

(7) A histogram of the data for each group. The histogram is a maximum of six lines high and 20 characters wide. These histograms provide a quick look at the shape of the distribution. Both histograms are plotted on the same scale extending from the minimum value to the maximum value in all the groups analyzed in the subproblem. The label under the histogram specifies how many observations each H or X represents. (The number of H's or X's to be plotted is raised to the next highest integer. That is, when there is only one observation to be plotted, an H or X is printed.)

(8) Three tests are computed to compare the two groups.

- t (separate variances). This is a two-sample t statistic in which the variance of each group is estimated separately. It is appropriate whenever the population variances are <u>not</u> assumed to be equal. The t statistic is

$$t = (\bar{x}_1 - \bar{x}_2)\left/\left(\frac{s_1^2}{N_1} + \frac{s_1^2}{N_2}\right)^{\frac{1}{2}}\right.$$

where the subscripts 1 and 2 refer to the two groups. The degrees of freedom are approximated (Brownlee, 1965, p. 299) by

$$f = \left[\frac{c^2}{N_1-1} + \frac{(1-c)^2}{N_2-1}\right]^{-1}$$

where

$$c = \frac{var(\bar{x}_1)}{var(\bar{x}_1+\bar{x}_2)} = \frac{s_1^2/N_1}{s_1^2/N_1 + s_2^2/N_2}$$

- t (pooled variances). When the population variances in the two groups are assumed to be equal, the estimate of the variance can be obtained by pooling (averaging) the two estimates of the variance. This two-sample t statistic is

$$t = (\bar{x}_1 - \bar{x}_2) \bigg/ \left[\left(\frac{(N_1-1)s_1^2 + (N_2-1)s_2^2}{N_1 + N_2 - 2} \right) \left(\frac{1}{N_1} + \frac{1}{N_2} \right) \right]^{\frac{1}{2}}$$

The degrees of freedom are $N_1 + N_2 - 2$. When N_1 and N_2 differ and the two population variances are not equal, the distribution of this t statistic can be strongly affected and may not resemble a t distribution.

- F (for variances). A test of equality of variances is

$$F = s_1^2/s_2^2 \text{ or } s_2^2/s_1^2$$

whichever is larger. The degrees of freedom are N_1-1 and N_2-1 or N_2-1 and N_1-1 respectively.

The p-values for the above three statistics correspond to two-sided tests of significance (i.e., test inequality in either direction) when the samples are drawn from normal distributions. For all but small sample sizes the p-values for the t tests are not greatly affected by moderate departures from normality (Armitage, 1971, p. 119). However, the distribution of the F statistic to test the equality of variances is sensitive to departures from normality (Armitage, 1971, p. 143).

● OPTIONAL RESULTS

In addition to the results described above you can

- select pairs of groups to be compared when the data are classified into more than two groups   p. 174

- simultaneously test the equality of the means of several variables (Hotelling's T^2)   p. 177

- request correlations between the variables in each group   p. 179

- test whether the mean of one group (as occurs in a paired t test) is zero (or equal to a constant)   p. 182

● GROUPING (CLASSIFYING) CASES

To classify the cases into groups you must specify a GROUPING variable in the *VARiable* paragraph. In Example 9.1 we specify

GROUPING IS BRTHPILL.

and also include a *GROUP* paragraph to name the groups. The *GROUP* paragraph can be omitted when the values of the GROUPING variable contain ten or fewer distinct values (as in our example) and you do not want to name the groups.

When no grouping variable is specified, a one-sample t test is performed (p. 182).

VARiable
    GROUPING=v.   {no grouping var./prev.}

   Name or subscript of the variable used to classify the cases into groups. If GROUPING is not specified or is set to zero, there is no grouping variable. If a GROUPING variable has more than ten distinct values, CODEs or CUTPOINTs must be specified for it in the *GROUP* paragraph (Section 5.4).

● THE *TEST* PARAGRAPH

   The *TEST* paragraph is used to specify
   - the groups to be compared   p. 174
   - the variables to be analyzed   p. 174
   - that Mahalanobis D^2 and Hotelling's T^2 be computed   p. 177
   - a title for the analysis   p. 175
   - whether all data or only data in complete cases are to be used in the computations   p. 178
   - whether correlations are to be printed   p. 179

   More than one *TEST* paragraph can be placed <u>before</u> the *END* paragraph to describe additional analyses of the same data.

● CHOOSING AND LABELLING YOUR RESULTS

   When the GROUPING variable classifies the cases into more than two groups, all possible pairs of the groups are compared, unless you explicitly state which groups are to be compared in the *TEST* paragraph.

   In addition, you can select the variables to be compared.

   To illustrate both group and variable selection we use the following Control Language instructions.

Example 9.2

```
/PROBLEM     TITLE IS 'WERNER BLOOD CHEMISTRY DATA'.
/INPUT       VARIABLES ARE 9.
             FORMAT IS '(A4,5F4.0,3F4.1)'.
/VARIABLE    NAMES ARE ID,AGE,HEIGHT,WEIGHT,BRTHPILL,
                 CHOLSTRL,ALBUMIN,CALCIUM,URICACID.
             MAXIMUM IS (6)400.
             MINIMUM IS (6)150.
             BLANKS ARE MISSING.
             LABEL IS ID.
             GROUPING IS AGE.
```

```
/GROUP          CUTPOINTS(2) ARE     25,            35,            45.
                NAMES(2) ARE '25ORLESS', '26 TO 35', '36 TO 45', 'OVER 45'.

/TEST           VARIABLE IS CHOLSTRL.
                GROUPS ARE 1 TO 3.

/TEST           VARIABLES ARE CHOLSTRL,ALBUMIN,CALCIUM,URICACID.
                GROUPS ARE 1,4.

/END
```

We use AGE as the GROUPING variable; AGE classifies the cases into four groups. The results are presented in Output 9.2.

Two *TEST* paragraphs are used. The first paragraph specifies that only the variable CHOLSTRL is to be analyzed and that three groups (with subscripts 1, 2 and 3) are to be compared. These groups are named 25ORLESS, 26 TO 35 and 36 TO 45. There are three possible pairings of three groups. Therefore three analyses of CHOLSTRL are computed, each using a different pair of groups.

The second *TEST* paragraph specifies that two groups (with subscripts 1 and 4) are to be compared using the data from the four blood chemistry measurements. This analysis follows the interpretation of the second *TEST* paragraph.

A title can be specified in each *TEST* paragraph to label the analysis.

TEST

    VARIABLE= $v_1,v_2,\cdots$.   {all variables except the GROUPING variable/prev.}

    Names or subscripts of the VARIABLES[2] to be analyzed. When USE is stated in the *VARiable* paragraph, VARIABLES in the *TEST* paragraph must be included in the USE list.

    GROUP= $g_1,g_2,\cdots$.   {all groups/prev.}

    The groups to be compared. $g_1,g_2,\ldots$ are the GROUP NAMEs or group subscripts. A group subscript is the sequence number of the group in the list of CODEs or CUTPOINTs specified in the *GROUP* paragraph, or, if not specified in a *GROUP* paragraph, the rank order of the group. If more than two GROUPs are specified, each possible pair of groups is compared.

    TITLE='c'.   {blank} $\leq$ 80 char.

    A title for the analysis.

---

[2] If your BMDP programs are dated before August 1977, the minimum required abbreviation is VARIAB (not VAR).

<u>Output 9.2</u> An analysis by P3D using two *TEST* paragraphs

```
TEST TITLE. . . . . . . . .WERNER BLOOD CHEMISTRY DATA
INDEXES OF VARIABLES TO BE ANALYZED . . . . . .   6
USE COMPLETE CASES ONLY . . . . . . . . . . . .       NO
PRINT GROUP CORRELATION MATRICES. . . . . . . .       NO
COMPUTE HOTELLINGS T SQUARE . . . . . . . . . .       NO
INDEX OF GROUPING VARIABLE. . . . . . . . . . .        2
GROUPS USED IN COMPUTATIONS . . . . . . . . . .    1   2   3
```

FOR DIFFERENCES ON SINGLE VARIABLES

```
**********
*CHOLSTRL*  VARIABLE NUMBER   6       GROUP     1 250RLESS   2 26 TO 35      1 250RLESS(N=  50)       2 26 TO 35(N=  60)
**********                            MEAN       222.1198    224.6331
         STATISTICS     P VALUE  D. F.  STD DEV    37.4441     35.7419           H                        X
                                        S.E.M.      5.2954      4.6143           H                        X   X
T (SEPARATE)   -0.358  0.721  102.6    SAM SIZ         50          60           H           H   H        X X   XXXX
T (POOLED)     -0.36   0.720  108     MAXIMUM     330.0000    317.0000          HH HHHHHHHH              XXXXXXXXXX
                                      MINIMUM     155.0000    160.0000          HHH HHHHHHHHHHHH    H    XXXXXXXXXXXXX XXX
F(FOR VARIANCES)  1.10  0.728   49,  59                                 MIN------------------MAX MIN------------------MAX
                                                                            AN H =   2.0 CASES       AN X =   2.0 CASES
```

```
**********************************************************************************************************************
```

FOR DIFFERENCES ON SINGLE VARIABLES

```
**********
*CHOLSTRL*  VARIABLE NUMBER   6       GROUP     1 250RLESS   3 36 TO 45      1 250RLESS(N=  50)       3 36 TO 45(N=  42)
**********                            MEAN       222.1198    248.3332
         STATISTICS     P VALUE  D. F.  STD DEV    37.4441     44.8088           H
                                        S.E.M.      5.2954      6.9141           H
T (SEPARATE)   -3.010  0.003   80.1    SAM SIZ         50          42           H   H   H                X
T (POOLED)     -3.06   0.003   90     MAXIMUM     330.0000    335.0000          HH HHHHHHH             X  X  XXXXXX   X
                                      MINIMUM     155.0000    160.0000          HHH HHHHHHHHHHHH    H   XXX X X XXXXXXX XXXX
F(FOR VARIANCES)  1.43  0.228   41,  49                                 MIN------------------MAX MIN------------------MAX
                                                                            AN H =   2.0 CASES       AN X =   2.0 CASES
```

```
**********************************************************************************************************************
```

FOR DIFFERENCES ON SINGLE VARIABLES

```
**********
*CHOLSTRL*  VARIABLE NUMBER   6       GROUP     2 26 TO 35   3 36 TO 45      2 26 TO 35(N=  60)       3 36 TO 45(N=  42)
**********                            MEAN       224.6331    248.3332
         STATISTICS     P VALUE  D. F.  STD DEV    35.7419     44.8088           H
                                        S.E.M.      4.6143      6.9141           H   H
T (SEPARATE)   -2.851  0.006   75.3    SAM SIZ         60          42           H H  HHHH                 X
T (POOLED)     -2.97   0.004  100     MAXIMUM     317.0000    335.0000          HHHHHHHHHH             X X XXXXXX   X
                                      MINIMUM     160.0000    160.0000          HHHHHHHHHHHHHH HHH       XXX X X XXXXXXX XXXX
F(FOR VARIANCES)  1.57  0.110   41,  59                                 MIN------------------MAX MIN------------------MAX
                                                                            AN H =   2.0 CASES       AN X =   2.0 CASES
```

```
**********************************************************************************************************************
```

```
TEST TITLE. . . . . . . . .WERNER BLOOD CHEMISTRY DATA
INDEXES OF VARIABLES TO BE ANALYZED . . . . . .   6   7   8   9
USE COMPLETE CASES ONLY . . . . . . . . . . . .       NO
PRINT GROUP CORRELATION MATRICES. . . . . . . .       NO
COMPUTE HOTELLINGS T SQUARE . . . . . . . . . .       NO
INDEX OF GROUPING VARIABLE. . . . . . . . . . .        2
GROUPS USED IN COMPUTATIONS . . . . . . . . . .    1   4

NUMBER OF CASES READ. . . . . . . . . . . . .        188
```

FOR DIFFERENCES ON SINGLE VARIABLES

```
**********
*CHOLSTRL*  VARIABLE NUMBER   6       GROUP     1 250RLESS   4 OVER 45      1 250RLESS(N=  50)       4 OVER 45 (N=  34)
**********                            MEAN       222.1198    262.0566
         STATISTICS     P VALUE  D. F.  STD DEV    37.4441     43.2672           H
                                        S.E.M.      5.2954      7.4203           H  H  H                  X
T (SEPARATE)   -4.381  0.000   64.0    SAM SIZ         50          34           HHH  H               X X  X   X
T (POOLED)     -4.50   0.000   82     MAXIMUM     330.0000    390.0000          HH HHHHHHH            XX X   X
                                      MINIMUM     155.0000    190.0000          HHHHHHHHHHHH  H       XX XXXXXXXX XX   X
F(FOR VARIANCES)  1.34  0.352   33,  49                                 MIN------------------MAX MIN------------------MAX
                                                                            AN H =   2.0 CASES       AN X =   2.0 CASES
```

```
**********
*ALBUMIN *  VARIABLE NUMBER   7       GROUP     1 250RLESS   4 OVER 45      1 250RLESS(N=  52)       4 OVER 45 (N=  33)
**********                            MEAN         4.1538      4.0394           HH   H                   X  X
         STATISTICS     P VALUE  D. F.  STD DEV     0.4118      0.2680          HH   H                   XX  X
                                        S.E.M.      0.0571      0.0467          HH  HHHH   H             XX  XX
T (SEPARATE)    1.552  0.124   82.9    SAM SIZ         52          33          HHH  HHHH  HH            X  XX  XX
T (POOLED)      1.42   0.161   83     MAXIMUM       5.0000      4.6000         H  HHHH HHHH HHH         X   XX XXXX X
                                      MINIMUM       3.2000      3.5000         H HH HHHH HHHHHHHHHH     XXXXXX XXXX X
F(FOR VARIANCES)  2.36  0.011   51,  32                                 MIN------------------MAX MIN------------------MAX
                                                                            AN H =   1.0 CASES       AN X =   1.0 CASES
```

--- similar analyses for variables 8 and 9 ---

● HOTELLING'S T^2 AND MAHALANOBIS D^2

The equality of means of several variables can be tested simultaneously by the multivariate Hotelling's T^2 (Morrison, 1967, p. 120) and Mahalanobis D^2. The statistics are equivalent and can be transformed to an F statistic when there are one or two groups.

In matrix notation let $\bar{X}_1$ be a column vector that contains the means of the variables in one group, $\bar{X}_2$ the corresponding means in a second group, and S a square matrix representing the pooled within-groups covariance matrix for the two groups being compared. Mahalanobis D^2 is a measure of the distance between the means of the two groups

$$D^2 = (\bar{X}_1 - \bar{X}_2)' \, S^{-1}(\bar{X}_1 - \bar{X}_2)$$

where the prime indicates the transpose of a matrix.

Hotelling's T^2 is

$$T^2 = D^2 \bigg/ \left(\frac{1}{N_1} + \frac{1}{N_2} \right)$$

Both Mahalanobis D^2 and Hotelling's T^2 can be transformed to an F statistic.

$$F = \frac{T^2(N_1 + N_2 - v - 1)}{v(N_1 + N_2 - 2)}$$

where v is the number of variables in the analysis.

When there is only <u>one group</u>, the formulas are

$$D^2 = \bar{X}_1' \, S^{-1} \, \bar{X}_1 \quad , \quad T^2 = N_1 D^2 \quad \text{and} \quad F = T^2 \frac{(N_1 - v)}{v(N_1 - 1)}$$

When the group means are unequal both T^2 and F increase as N_1 (and N_2) increases, while D^2 does not. Therefore D^2 is a better description of the distance between groups when distances are compared.

The above formulas assume that the data are available in each case for all the variables compared. If some data values are equal to missing value codes or are out of range, observations for all variables may not be present in each case. Then N_1 and N_2 are replaced by the harmonic means of the frequencies of variables of the first and second groups respectively; this provides an approximate test of the equality of means. The formula is given in Appendix A.3.

TEST
    HOTELLING.   {no/prev.}
        When HOTELLING is specified, Hotelling's T^2 and Mahalanobis D^2
        are computed.

● Values Out of Range or Missing -- COMPLETE Cases

Usually an analysis of a single variable uses all the acceptable values for the variable whether or not the value of any other variable is acceptable. Conversely, the usual definition of Hotelling's T^2 requires that the data values be acceptable for all the variables for any case that is included in the computations.

Cases containing acceptable data values for all variables that are included in the analysis are called complete cases.

In P3D you can specify whether all the computations are to be based on COMPLETE cases only, or on all acceptable values. If COMPLETE is specified, the univariate statistics and the t statistics are also computed using only complete cases.

To illustrate the effect COMPLETE has on the results, we specify two analyses that differ only in the command COMPLETE.

Example 9.3a

```
/PROBLEM        TITLE IS 'WERNER BLOOD CHEMISTRY DATA'.
/INPUT          VARIABLES ARE 9.
                FORMAT IS '(A4,5F4.0,3F4.1)'.
/VARIABLE       NAMES ARE ID,AGE,HEIGHT,WEIGHT,BRTHPILL,
                     CHOLSTRL,ALBUMIN,CALCIUM,URICACID.
                MAXIMUM IS (6)400.
                MINIMUM IS (6)150.
                BLANKS ARE MISSING.
                LABEL IS ID.
                GROUPING IS BRTHPILL.

/GROUP          CODES(5) ARE      1,    2.
                NAMES(5) ARE NOPILL, PILL.

/TEST           VARIABLES ARE CHOLSTRL,ALBUMIN,CALCIUM,URICACID.
                HOTELLING.

/END
```

Example 9.3b

```
/PROBLEM        TITLE IS 'WERNER BLOOD CHEMISTRY DATA'.
/INPUT          VARIABLES ARE 9.
                FORMAT IS '(A4,5F4.0,3F4.1)'.
/VARIABLE       NAMES ARE ID,AGE,HEIGHT,WEIGHT,BRTHPILL,
                     CHOLSTRL,ALBUMIN,CALCIUM,URICACID.
                MAXIMUM IS (6)400.
                MINIMUM IS (6)150.
                BLANKS ARE MISSING.
                LABEL IS ID.
                GROUPING IS BRTHPILL.

/GROUP          CODES(5) ARE      1,    2.
                NAMES(5) ARE NOPILL, PILL.

/TEST           VARIABLES ARE CHOLSTRL,ALBUMIN,CALCIUM,URICACID.
                HOTELLING.
                COMPLETE.

/END
```

The results for the two analyses are presented in Outputs 9.3a and 9.3b. The small differences between the two results are due to the fact that we have only eight cases containing unacceptable data. Note the different frequencies (sample sizes) and degrees of freedom used in the two analyses.

A large difference between the two analyses would indicate that the results may be biased due to the pattern of missing values or values out of range. If your analyses show a large difference, you may want to examine the data by using PAM (Section 12.2) to study the pattern of values excluded from the analysis.

TEST

    COMPLETE.   {no/prev.}

        When COMPLETE[3] is specified, only complete cases are used in all the computations. Complete cases are cases in which the data are acceptable (not missing or out of range) for all variables specified in the USE statement of the *VARiable* paragraph (all variables if USE is not specified). COMPLETE or NO COMPLETE can be specified in only the first *TEST* paragraph of any problem. It cannot be altered until a new problem begins.

● CORRELATIONS

        The CORRELATIONS[4] between the variables in each group are printed when

        CORRELATION.

is specified in the *TEST* paragraph. The method of computing correlations depends on whether COMPLETE cases or all acceptable data are used. When COMPLETE cases are used, the correlation between two variables (i and k) is

$$r_{ik} = \frac{\Sigma_j (x_{ij} - \bar{x}_i)(x_{kj} - \bar{x}_k)}{[\Sigma_j (x_{ij} - \bar{x}_i)^2 \Sigma_j (x_{kj} - \bar{x}_k)^2]^{\frac{1}{2}}}$$

where the summations are over all complete cases in the group. When all available data are used, the covariance of variables i and k is computed using complete pairs of observations; i.e.,

$$cov_{ik} = \Sigma_j (x_{ij} - \bar{x}_{i(k)})(x_{kj} - \bar{x}_{k(i)})/(N_{ik} - 1)$$

---

[3] If your BMDP programs are dated before August 1977,
    COMPLETE is in the *INPUT* paragraph, and not in *TEST*.

[4] If your BMDP programs are dated before August 1977,
    CORRELATION is in the *PRINT* paragraph, and not in *TEST*.

Output 9.3 a and b The Mahalanobis D^2 (a) using all acceptable values and (b) complete cases only

9.3a

```
TEST TITLE. . . . . . . .WERNER BLOOD CHEMISTRY DATA
INDEXES OF VARIABLES TO BE ANALYZED . . . . . .  6   7   8   9
USE COMPLETE CASES ONLY . . . . . . . . . . .        NO
PRINT GROUP CORRELATION MATRICES. . . . . . . .      NO
COMPUTE HOTELLINGS T SQUARE . . . . . . . . .       YES
INDEX OF GROUPING VARIABLE. . . . . . . . . .         5
GROUPS USED IN COMPUTATIONS . . . . . . . . .      1   2


FOR DIFFERENCES AMONG GROUP MEANS USING ALL VARIABLES

    MAHALANOBIS D SQUARE          0.2819
    HOTELLING T SQUARE           13.0364
    F VALUE                       3.1882        P VALUE     0.015
       DEGREES OF FREEDOM      4,  179


FOR DIFFERENCES ON SINGLE VARIABLES


**********
*CHOLSTRL*  VARIABLE NUMBER   6      GROUP    1 NOPILL  2 PILL    1 NOPILL  (N= 94)     2 PILL    (N= 92)
**********                                    MEAN   232.9678  239.4019    H    H               X   XXX
            STATISTICS   P VALUE  D. F.       STD DEV 43.4914   41.5620    HH    H              X  XXXX
                                              S.E.M.   4.4858    4.3331    H HHHHHHH            X  XXXX
T (SEPARATE)   -1.032  0.304  183.9           SAM SIZ     94        92    H HHHHHHH   H         X  XXXXX
T (POOLED)     -1.03   0.304  184             MAXIMUM 335.0000  390.0000  HHHHHHHHHHHHH H       XXXXXXXXXXXX
                                              MINIMUM 155.0000  160.0000  HHHHHHHHHHHHH HH      XXXXXXXXXXXXXX  X
F(FOR VARIANCES) 1.10  0.665  93,   91                                   MIN-----------------MAX MIN-----------------MAX
                                                                          AN H =   2.0 CASES         AN X =   2.0 CASES


**********
*ALBUMIN *  VARIABLE NUMBER   7      GROUP    1 NOPILL  2 PILL    1 NOPILL  (N= 92)     2 PILL    (N= 94)
**********                                    MEAN     4.1978    4.0266    H    H               X  X
            STATISTICS   P VALUE  D. F.       STD DEV  0.3451    0.3517    HH  HHH             X  X    X
                                              S.E.M.   0.0360    0.0363    HH  HHHH            XXXX XX  X
T (SEPARATE)    3.351  0.001  184.0           SAM SIZ     92        94     HH  HHHHHH H        XXXXX XX XX
T (POOLED)      3.35   0.001  184             MAXIMUM  5.0000    4.7000    HHHH  HHHHHHHH      X  XXXXX XXXXXXX
                                              MINIMUM  3.2000    3.2000    H HHHHHHH HHHHHHHHHH XXXXXXXX XXXXXXX
F(FOR VARIANCES) 1.04  0.857  93,   91                                   MIN-----------------MAX MIN-----------------MAX
                                                                          AN H =   2.0 CASES         AN X =   2.0 CASES
```

--- similar analyses for variables 8 and 9 ---

9.3b

```
TEST TITLE. . . . . . . .WERNER BLOOD CHEMISTRY DATA
INDEXES OF VARIABLES TO BE ANALYZED . . . . . .  6   7   8   9
USE COMPLETE CASES ONLY . . . . . . . . . . .       YES
PRINT GROUP CORRELATION MATRICES. . . . . . . .      NO
COMPUTE HOTELLINGS T SQUARE . . . . . . . . .       YES
INDEX OF GROUPING VARIABLE. . . . . . . . . .         5
GROUPS USED IN COMPUTATIONS . . . . . . . . .      1   2


FOR DIFFERENCES AMONG GROUP MEANS USING ALL VARIABLES

    MAHALANOBIS D SQUARE          0.2864
    HOTELLING T SQUARE           13.0284
    F VALUE                       3.2028        P VALUE     0.014
       DEGREES OF FREEDOM      4,  177


FOR DIFFERENCES ON SINGLE VARIABLES


**********
*CHOLSTRL*  VARIABLE NUMBER   6      GROUP    1 NOPILL  2 PILL    1 NOPILL  (N= 90)     2 PILL    (N= 92)
**********                                    MEAN   232.0886  239.4019    H    H               X   XXX
            STATISTICS   P VALUE  D. F.       STD DEV 43.4700   41.5620    HH    H              X  XXXX
                                              S.E.M.   4.5821    4.3331    H HHH HHH            X  XXXX
T (SEPARATE)   -1.160  0.248  179.2           SAM SIZ     90        92    H HHH HHH  H          X  XXXXXX
T (POOLED)     -1.16   0.248  180             MAXIMUM 335.0000  390.0000  HHHHHHHHHHHHH         XXXXXXXXXXXX
                                              MINIMUM 155.0000  160.0000  HHHHHHHHHHHHH HH      XXXXXXXXXXXXXX  X
F(FOR VARIANCES) 1.09  0.671  89,   91                                   MIN-----------------MAX MIN-----------------MAX
                                                                          AN H =   2.0 CASES         AN X =   2.0 CASES


**********
*ALBUMIN *  VARIABLE NUMBER   7      GROUP    1 NOPILL  2 PILL    1 NOPILL  (N= 90)     2 PILL    (N= 92)
**********                                    MEAN     4.2044    4.0348    H H H               X  X
            STATISTICS   P VALUE  D. F.       STD DEV  0.3461    0.3503    H  HHH              X  X    X
                                              S.E.M.   0.0365    0.0365    HH  HHHH            XXXX XX  X
T (SEPARATE)    3.287  0.001  180.0           SAM SIZ     90        92     HH  HHHHHH H        XXXXX XX XX
T (POOLED)      3.29   0.001  180             MAXIMUM  5.0000    4.7000    HHHH  HHHHHHHH      X  XXXXX XXXXXXX
                                              MINIMUM  3.2000    3.2000    H HHHHHHH HHHHHHHHHH XXXXXXXX XXXXXXX
F(FOR VARIANCES) 1.02  0.908  91,   89                                   MIN-----------------MAX MIN-----------------MAX
                                                                          AN H =   2.0 CASES         AN X =   2.0 CASES
```

--- similar analyses for variables 8 and 9 ---

where $\bar{x}_{i(k)}$ is the mean of variable i for cases that also contain variable k. The summation is over the cases in the group for which data for both variables are present (N_{ik} cases). The correlation is computed as

$$r_{ik} = cov_{ik}/(s_i s_k)^{\frac{1}{2}}$$

where s_i and s_k are the standard deviations for each variable (that is, they are each based on all acceptable data for the variable in the group). It is therefore possible that the correlation matrix will not be positive definite (for a definition of positive definite, see Scheffé, 1959, p. 398), and that a correlation will be greater than one.

TEST

   CORRELATION.   {no/prev.}

     Print the correlation matrix used.

    Example 9.4 requests the correlation matrix that is printed in Output 9.4.

Example 9.4

```
/PROBLEM      TITLE IS 'WERNER BLOOD CHEMISTRY DATA'.
/INPUT        VARIABLES ARE 9.
              FORMAT IS '(A4,5F4.0,3F4.1)'.
/VARIABLE     NAMES ARE ID,AGE,HEIGHT,WEIGHT,BRTHPILL,
                  CHOLSTRL,ALBUMIN,CALCIUM,URICACID.
              MAXIMUM IS (6)400.
              MINIMUM IS (6)150.
              BLANKS ARE MISSING.
              LABEL IS ID.
              GROUPING IS BRTHPILL.

/GROUP        CODES(5) ARE     1,    2.
              NAMES(5) ARE NOPILL, PILL.

/TEST         VARIABLES ARE CHOLSTRL,ALBUMIN,CALCIUM,URICACID.
              CORRELATIONS.

/END
```

The correlation matrix is presented in Output 9.4.

● THE ONE-SAMPLE T TEST (OR PAIRED T TEST)

The Werner data (Table 5.1) consist of 94 pairs of age-matched women. In each pair the first woman is <u>not</u> on the pill and the second woman is. In Example 9.5 we perform a paired <u>t</u> test by reading each <u>pair</u> of data records as a single case. We then use Control Language transformations to form <u>four</u> new variables that represent differences in the blood measurement variab<u>les</u>. The Control Language rules for the *TRANsform* paragraph are described in Chapter 6. We request a one-sample t test for each new variable (those representing differences) by <u>not</u> specifying a GROUPing variable.

<u>Output 9.4</u> Correlation matrices for each group

```
TEST TITLE. . . . . . . . . .WERNER BLOOD CHEMISTRY DATA
INDEXES OF VARIABLES TO BE ANALYZED . . . . . .   6   7   8   9
USE COMPLETE CASES ONLY . . . . . . . . . . . .        NO
PRINT GROUP CORRELATION MATRICES. . . . . . . .       YES
COMPUTE HOTELLINGS T SQUARE . . . . . . . . . .        NO
INDEX OF GROUPING VARIABLE. . . . . . . . . . .         5
GROUPS USED IN COMPUTATIONS . . . . . . . . . .    1   2
```

```
CORRELATION MATRIX FOR GROUP     1 NOPILL


                 CHOLSTRL    ALBUMIN    CALCIUM    URICACID
                    6           7          8          9

CHOLSTRL    6     1.0000
ALBUMIN     7     0.0296     1.0000
CALCIUM     8     0.2874     0.4452     1.0000
URICACID    9     0.2739     0.0858     0.2009     1.0000



CORRELATION MATRIX FOR GROUP     2 PILL


                 CHOLSTRL    ALBUMIN    CALCIUM    URICACID
                    6           7          8          9

CHOLSTRL    6     1.0000
ALBUMIN     7     0.1160     1.0000
CALCIUM     8     0.2153     0.4258     1.0000
URICACID    9     0.2473    -0.0485     0.1916     1.0000
```

--- analysis of variables 6 to 9 as in Output 9.1 ---

Example 9.5

```
/PROBLEM      TITLE IS 'WERNER BLOOD CHEMISTRY DATA'.
/INPUT        VARIABLES ARE 13.
              FORMAT IS '(A4,5F4.0,3F4.1/20X,F4.0,3F4.1)'.
/VARIABLE     NAMES ARE ID,AGE,HEIGHT,WEIGHT,BRTHPILL,
                 CHOL1,ALB1,CAL1,URIC1,
                 CHOL2,ALB2,CAL2,URIC2,
                 CHOLDIFF,ALBDIFF,CALDIFF,URICDIFF.
              MAXIMUMS ARE (6)400,(10)400.
              MINIMUMS ARE (6)150,(10)150.
              BLANKS ARE MISSING.
              LABEL IS ID.
              ADD IS 4.

/TRANSFORM    CHOLDIFF = CHOL1 - CHOL2.
              ALBDIFF  = ALB1  - ALB2.
              CALDIFF  = CAL1  - CAL2.
              URICDIFF = URIC1 - URIC2.

/TEST         VARIABLES ARE 14 TO 17.
              HOTELLING.

/END
```

Output 9.5 shows that the results for ALBDIFF (the difference in ALBUMIN measurements) are significant. When there is only one group, the two t tests are identical and the F (for variances) is meaningless.

To test that a variable mean is equal to a constant, the constant can be subtracted from each value of the variable in the *TRANsform* paragraph. For example, to subtract 125 from a variable named XYZ, you can specify

/TRANSFORM XYZ=XYZ-125.

The one-sample t test on the new XYZ is equivalent to a test that the mean of XYZ is 125.

● SIZE OF PROBLEM

P3D can analyze very large problems; it is not limited by the number of cases in the data. The maximum number of variables V depends on the number of groups G. The following table can be used as a guide.

G	2	3	4	5	10
V without HOTEL and CORR	240	160	120	96	48
V with HOTEL or CORR	53	42	36	31	21

Appendix B describes how to increase the capacity of the program.

● COMPUTATIONAL METHOD

Means, standard deviations and covariances are computed in single precision using the method of provisional means (Appendix A.2). The formulas for Hotelling's T^2 and Mahalanobis D^2 are given in Appendix A.3.

ACKNOWLEDGEMENT

P3D was programmed by Sandra Fu and Jerry Douglas. Recent revisions were made by Lanaii Kline. P3D supersedes BMD13D.

Output 9.5 Paired t test by P3D

```
CONTROL LANGUAGE TRANSFORMATIONS ARE

        CHOLDIFF = CHOL1   -   CHOL2  .
        ALBDIFF  = ALB1    -   ALB2   .
        CALDIFF  = CAL1    -   CAL2   .
        URICDIFF = URIC1   -   URIC2  .


VARIABLES TO BE USED
             2  AGE          3  HEIGHT     4  WEIGHT     5  BRTHPILL    6  CHOL1
             7  ALB1         8  CAL1       9  URIC1     10  CHOL2      11  ALB2
            12  CAL2        13  URIC2     14  CHOLDIFF  15  ALBDIFF    16  CALDIFF
            17  URICDIFF


TEST TITLE. . . . . . . . .WERNER BLOOD CHEMISTRY DATA
INDEXES OF VARIABLES TO BE ANALYZED . . . . . .  14 15  16  17
USE COMPLETE CASES ONLY . . . . . . . . . . .      NO
PRINT GROUP CORRELATION MATRICES. . . . . . . .    NO
COMPUTE HOTELLINGS T SQUARE . . . . . . . . . .    YES
INDEX OF GROUPING VARIABLE. . . . . . . . . . .     0
GROUPS USED IN COMPUTATIONS . . . . . . . . . .    1   2


NUMBER OF CASES READ. . . . . . . . . . . . .      94



FOR DIFFERENCES AMONG GROUP MEANS USING ALL VARIABLES

    MAHALANOBIS D SQUARE        0.1303
    HOTELLING T SQUARE         11.8567
    F VALUE                     2.8329      P VALUE     0.029
      DEGREES OF FREEDOM      4,  86



FOR DIFFERENCES ON SINGLE VARIABLES


**********
*CHOLDIFF*  VARIABLE NUMBER  14
**********
                          MEAN        -6.1848                    H
    T STATISTIC  P VALUE  D. F.   STD DEV    55.5390              H  H
                          S.E.M.       6.2074              H  H
        -1.00     0.322    91     SAM SIZ     92          HHHHH H H
                          MAXIMUM    155.0000            HHHHHHHH H
                          MINIMUM   -145.0000         HHHHHHHHHHHHHHHHH  H
                                                    MIN------------.------MAX
                                                    AN H =    3.0 CASES


**********
*ALBDIFF *  VARIABLE NUMBER  15
**********
                          MEAN         0.1804                    H
    T STATISTIC  P VALUE  D. F.   STD DEV     0.5315              HH
                          S.E.M.       0.0554           H   HHH  H
         3.26     0.002    91     SAM SIZ     92        HHHHHHH HH
                          MAXIMUM      1.3000        HHHHHHHHHHHHHH H
                          MINIMUM     -1.2000      HHHHHHHHHHHHHHHHH H
                                                    MIN-----------------MAX
                                                    AN H =    2.0 CASES
```

--- *similar analyses for CALDIFF and URIDIFF* ---

P7D

9.2 Description of Groups (Strata) with Histograms and Analysis of Variance

W.J. Dixon, HSCF

P7D analyzes data for each variable in any number of groups and plots side-by-side histograms for each group. The intervals of the histograms are labelled. Values that are missing or out of range are tallied separately. A one-way (or two-way) analysis of variance is performed to test the equality of means between groups. In addition to the classical one-way analysis of variance, P7D also computes two statistics that do not assume the equality of variances in each group. The input data, including any transformations, can be listed in the original order or after sorting the cases according to the values of a variable. P7D can also compute Winsorized means for each group and confidence limits for the Winsorized means. The correlations between the variables for each group and for all groups combined can be printed.

● RESULTS

We use P7D to analyze the Werner blood chemistry data (Table 5.1). In our first example we compare four groups of women, classified according to their ages. Except for the *HISTogram* paragraph, the Control Language instructions are explained in Chapter 5.

Example 9.6

```
/PROBLEM       TITLE IS 'WERNER BLOOD CHEMISTRY DATA'.
/INPUT         VARIABLES ARE 9.
               FORMAT IS '(A4,5F4.0,3F4.1)'.
/VARIABLE      NAMES ARE ID,AGE,HEIGHT,WEIGHT,BRTHPILL,
                     CHOLSTRL,ALBUMIN,CALCIUM,URICACID.
               MAXIMUM IS (6)400.
               MINIMUM IS (6)150.
               BLANKS ARE MISSING.
               LABEL IS ID.

/GROUP         CUTPOINTS(2) ARE    25,        35,        45.
               NAMES(2) ARE '25ORLESS', '26 TO 35', '36 TO 45', 'OVER 45'.

/HISTOGRAM     GROUPING IS AGE.

/END
```

The Control Language must be preceded by System Cards to initiate the analysis by P7D. At HSCF, the System Cards are

```
//jobname  JOB   nooo,yourname
//   EXEC   BIMED,PROG=BMDP7D
//SYSIN  DD *
```

The Control Language is immediately followed by the data (Table 5.1). The analysis is terminated by another System Card. At HSCF, this System Card is

```
//
```

The results of the above analysis by P7D are shown in Output 9.6. Circled numbers below correspond to those in the output.

(1)   Number of cases read. The number of cases is not specified in our example, so all the cases are read. The computations use all acceptable data; i.e., values not equal to a missing value code and not outside specified upper and lower limits.

(2)   Interpretation of Control Language options in the *PRINT* paragraph specific to P7D. As no *PRINT* paragraph is specified, all options take their preassigned values (NO).

(3)   Interpretation of the *GROUP* paragraph.

(4)   Side-by-side histograms of the data in each group. We present the histograms for the variable CHOLSTRL. (Histograms are also plotted for all the other variables.) The base of each histogram is the vertical axis. The frequencies are plotted horizontally with the groups offset from one another. Each asterisk represents an observation. All observations are plotted in one example. When there are too many observations to be plotted in the available space, the number of observations are printed at the right end of the line of asterisks (all observations are plotted in our example). The M in the histogram represents the group mean; when the group mean does <u>not</u> coincide with an observation, an N is plotted instead of an M.

Values excluded from the computations are tallied above the histogram in the appropriate group or in the rightmost group if the grouping variable does not have an acceptable value. Two values are excluded from the first group in our example.

The midpoint for each interval is printed to the left of the histograms. Each interval includes its upper limit. For example, 210.0 and 225.0 are successive midpoints, so the value 217.5 would be classified into the interval with midpoint 210.0.

(5)   For each group, P7D prints

  - mean: $\bar{x}$

  - standard deviation: s

  - standard error of the mean (S.E.M.)

  - maximum observed value (not out of range)

  - minimum observed value (not out of range)

  - sample size (frequency): N

(6)   For all groups combined, P7D prints the mean, standard deviation, standard error of the mean, maximum, minimum and frequency. The standard deviation is computed from the overall mean for the variable (<u>not</u> from the group means).

Output 9.6 Comparison of groups by P7D. Circled numbers correspond to those in the text. Results not reproduced are indicated in italics.

BMDP7D - DESCRIPTION OF GROUPS (STRATA) WITH
        HISTOGRAMS AND ANALYSIS OF VARIANCE
HEALTH SCIENCES COMPUTING FACILITY
UNIVERSITY OF CALIFORNIA, LOS ANGELES

PROGRAM REVISED SEPTEMBER 1977
MANUAL DATE -- 1977

--- Control Language read by P7D is printed and interpreted ---

(1) NUMBER OF CASES READ.   188
    PRINT DATA MATRIX . . . .   NO
(2) PRINT DATA MATRIX AFTER ORDERING. . . . . . .   NO
    PRINT WINSORIZING TABLE . . . .   NO
    PRINT CORRELATION TABLE . . . .   NO

VARIABLE NO. NAME	BEFORE TRANSFORMATION MINIMUM LIMIT	MAXIMUM LIMIT	MISSING CODE	CATEGORY CODE	CATEGORY NAME	INTERVAL RANGE GREATER THAN	LESS THAN OR EQUAL TO
(3) 2 AGE					25ORLESS		25.00000
					26 TO 35	25.00000	35.00000
					36 TO 45	35.00000	45.00000
					OVER 45	45.00000	

--- analyses of variables 2 to 5 similar to that below for CHOLSTRL ---

HISTOGRAM OF CHOLSTRL(VARIABLE   6). CASES DIVIDED INTO GROUPS BASED ON VALUE OF AGE   (VARIABLE   2)

				CASES WITH INVALID GROUP SPECIFICATION AGE
25ORLESS	26 TO 35	36 TO 45	OVER 45	

```
                25ORLESS           26 TO 35            36 TO 45            OVER 45             AGE
     .....................+...................+...................+...................+..................+
VAR  6
EXCLUDED
VALUES
      **
          TABULATIONS AND COMPUTATIONS WHICH FOLLOW EXCLUDE VALUES LISTED ABOVE
MIDPOINTS
 435.000)
 420.000)
 405.000)
 390.000)                                                        *
 375.000)
 360.000)
 345.000)                                                        *
 330.000)*                                   **
 315.000)                     *              **                 **
 300.000)*                    **             ***                ******
 285.000)**                   **             ***
 270.000)***                  *              *******            ***
 255.000)****                 *********       M****              M********
 240.000)********             ***********      ****               **
 225.000)M******              M******          **                 ******
 210.000)******               *****            *****              **
 195.000)********             ***********       ****              **
 180.000)****                 *******          **
 165.000)***                  ***              **
 150.000)*
 135.000)
 120.000)
GROUP MEANS ARE DENOTED BY M'S IF THEY COINCIDE WITH *'S, N'S OTHERWISE
```

	25ORLESS		26 TO 35	36 TO 45	OVER 45
MEAN	222.120	(5)	224.633	248.333	262.057
STD.DEV.	37.444		35.742	44.809	43.267
S. E. M.	5.295		4.614	6.914	7.420
MAXIMUM	330.000		317.000	335.000	390.000
MINIMUM	155.000		160.000	160.000	190.000
SAMPLE SIZE	50		60	42	34

```
     ALL GROUPS COMBINED      *                    ANALYSIS OF VARIANCE TABLE
  (CASES THAT CONTAIN SPECIAL *
     CODES ARE EXCLUDED)      *   SOURCE  (7)    SUM OF SQUARES    DF    MEAN SQUARE    F VALUE    TAIL PROBABILITY
                             *
MEAN          236.150        *   BETWEEN GROUPS    46854.3438      3    15618.1133     9.8639       0.0000
STD. DEV.      42.555        *   WITHIN GROUPS    288171.3750    182     1583.3591
S. E. M.        3.120        *
MAXIMUM (6)   390.000        *   TOTAL            335025.6875    185
MINIMUM       155.000        *
SAMPLE SIZE       186        *   ONE WAY ANALYSIS OF VARIANCE
                             *   WITHIN GROUP VARIANCES ARE
                             *   NOT ASSUMED TO BE EQUAL.
                             *
                             *   TEST STATISTIC
                             *      WELCH          (8)            3,  90                  9.1072       0.0000
                             *      BROWN-FORSYTHE                3, 150                  9.4182       0.0000
```

--- similar analyses for variables 7 to 9 ---

⑦   A one-way analysis of variance (ANOVA) that tests the equality of group means.

Let x_{ij} represent the jth observation in the ith group and $\bar{x}_i$ the mean and N_i the number of observations in the ith group. Then

- between sum of squares: $BSS = \Sigma_i \ N_i(\bar{x}_i-\bar{x})^2$

  where $\bar{x} = \underset{i}{\Sigma} \ N_i\bar{x}_i/\Sigma \ N_i$

- between degrees of freedom = g-1
  where g is the number of groups
- between mean square = BSS/(g-1)
- within sum of squares: $WSS = \Sigma_i\Sigma_j \ (x_{ij} - \bar{x}_i)^2$

- within degrees of freedom = $\Sigma_i \ (N_i-1)$

- within mean square = WSS / $\Sigma_i \ (N_i-1)$

- F value = (between mean square)/(within mean square)

- tail probability is the probability of exceeding the F ratio when the group means are equal (the probability reported is appropriate when the data are sampled from normal populations with equal population variances; the distribution of the F ratio is sensitive to the assumption of equal population variances, Brown and Forsythe, 1974a)

The F value (analysis of variance) is a test of the equality of group means. When the groups are ordered (as in this example), you may want to test contrasts on the group means, such as a linear trend. Both contrasts and covariates can be used in P1V (Section 15.1).

⑧   Two additional one-way analysis of variance statistics are computed. Neither statistic assumes the equality of variances in each group. The two are:

Welch statistic:

$$W = \frac{\Sigma_i \ w_i(\bar{x}_i - \tilde{x})^2/(g - 1)}{\left[1 + \dfrac{2(g - 2)}{g^2 - 1} \ \Sigma_i \ (1 - w_i/u)^2/(N_i - 1)\right]}$$

where

$$w_i = N_i/s_i^2 \ , \quad u = \Sigma_i \ w_i \ , \quad \text{and } \tilde{x} = \Sigma \ w_i\bar{x}_i/u$$

When all population means are equal (even if the variances are unequal), W is approximately distributed as an F statistic with g-1 and f degrees of freedom, where f is implicitly defined as

$$1/f = (3/(g^2 - 1)) \ \Sigma_i \ (1 - w_i/u)^2/(N_i - 1)$$

Brown-Forsythe statistic:

$$F^* = \Sigma_i \ N_i(\bar{x}_i - \bar{x})^2 / \Sigma_i \ (1 - N_i/N)s_i^2$$

Critical values are obtained from the F distribution with g-1 and f degrees of freedom where f is implicitly defined by the Satterthwaite approximation

$$\frac{1}{f} = \Sigma_i \ c_i^2/(N_i - 1)$$

and

$$c_i = (1 - N_i/N)s_i^2/[\Sigma_i \ (1 - N_i/N)s_i^2] \ .$$

When there are only two groups both F* and W reduce to the separate variance t test computed by P3D (p. 172). W and F* weight the sums of squares in the numerator differently. The two statistics are described by Brown and Forsythe (1974a).

A robust test of the equality of variances is provided by a one-way analysis of variance computed on the absolute values of the deviations from the group means (Brown and Forsythe, 1974b). This test, named after Levene, will soon be included in the results printed by P7D (it is not at this printing).

● OPTIONAL RESULTS

In addition to the results described above, you can

- list the input data or the data ordered by the GROUPING variable — p. 193

- print correlations between variables for all groups combined and for each group separately — p. 195

- compute Winsorized means and their confidence limits — p. 196

- compute a two-way ANOVA by specifying two GROUPING variables — p. 191

● THE *HISTogram* PARAGRAPH

The *HISTogram* paragraph is required and may be repeated before the *END* paragraph to specify additional analyses of the same data.

In the *HISTogram* paragraph you must specify a GROUPING variable to classify the cases into groups.

You may also

- select variables to be analyzed — p. 190

- scale the histogram — p. 190

- describe whether the analysis of variance is one-way or two-way — p. 191

- GROUPING (CLASSIFYING THE CASES)

    Cases are classified into groups by a GROUPING[5] variable as in Example 9.6. If two GROUPING variables are specified, groups are formed for each combination of the two grouping variables and a two-way ANOVA is computed as described in detail on p. 191.

HISTogram
    GROUPING=v_1,v_2.   {none/prev.}   required, one or two variables

      Names or subscripts of one or two GROUPING variables. When one GROUPING variable is specified, the cases are classified according to the GROUPING variable and a one-way ANOVA is computed. When two GROUPING variables are specified, the cases are classified simultaneously by both GROUPING variables and a two-way ANOVA is computed.

      If a GROUPING variable has more than ten distinct values, CODES or CUTPOINTS must be specified for it in the *GROUP* paragraph (Section 5.4).

- SELECTING VARIABLES TO BE ANALYZED

    When you do not want to analyze all the variables, you can select the variables you want by a USE statement in the *VARiable* paragraph or by a VARIABLE[6] statement in the *HISTogram* paragraph. When a USE statement is specified, it remains effective for all analyses of the same set of data. A VARIABLE statement in the *HISTogram* paragraph can be altered in any additional analysis of the same set of data.

HISTogram
    VARIABLE=v_1,v_2,$\cdots$.   {all variables/prev.}

      Names or subscripts of the variables to be analyzed. That is, histograms, the ANOVA and all results are computed only on the specified variables.

- SCALING THE HISTOGRAMS

    Unless otherwise specified, the histograms are scaled to an INCREMENT (step size) of

$$\frac{\text{maximum value} - \text{minimum value}}{\text{no. of intervals}}$$

---

[5] If your BMDP programs are dated before August 1977, and two or more variables are specified for GROUPING, P7D analyzes the data separately for each GROUPING variable.

[6] If your BMDP programs are dated before August 1977, the minimum required abbreviation is VARIAB (not VAR).

where the number of INTERVALs is the smaller of 30 and 10 $\log_{10}$ (number of cases read). If the data are single digit data (e.g., the integers 0 to 9), the scale of the histograms can be improved by setting the INCREMENTs for the single digit variables to one. Similarly, the scale of histograms for data with a few equally spaced values is improved by specifying the increment.

HISTogram
  INCREMENT=$\#_1$,$\#_2$,$\cdots$. $\left\{\dfrac{\text{max. - min.}}{\text{no. of intervals}}\right\}$ one per variable

  The difference between the points on the base of the histogram is set to INCREMENT. The first number is the INCREMENT for the first variable, etc.

  INTERVAL=$\#_1$,$\#_2$,$\cdots$.   {zero/prev.}   one per variable

  The maximum number of intervals in the histogram. If zero, INTERVAL is the smaller of 30 and 10 $\log_{10}$ (no. of cases). If both INCREMENT and INTERVAL are specified for a variable, INCREMENT is used if it does not yield more intervals than specified by INTERVAL; otherwise INCREMENT is computed from INTERVAL.

• THE TWO-WAY ANOVA

A two-way ANOVA is computed when two GROUPING variables are stated. For example, if

     /HISTOGRAM GROUPING IS BRTHPILL,AGE.

is specified the cases are classified into eight groups (2 BRTHPILL codes x 4 AGE groupings).

The following Control Language instructions request the two-way ANOVA.

Example 9.7

```
/PROBLEM      TITLE IS 'WERNER BLOOD CHEMISTRY DATA'.
/INPUT        VARIABLES ARE 9.
              FORMAT IS '(A4,5F4.0,3F4.1)'.
/VARIABLE     NAMES ARE ID,AGE,HEIGHT,WEIGHT,BRTHPILL,
                   CHOLSTRL,ALBUMIN,CALCIUM,URICACID.
              MAXIMUM IS (6)400.
              MINIMUM IS (6)150.
              BLANKS ARE MISSING.
              LABEL IS ID.

/GROUP        CODES(5) ARE      1,    2.
              NAMES(5) ARE NOPILL, PILL.
              CUTPOINTS(2) ARE    25,          35,          45.
              NAMES(2) ARE '25ORLESS', '26 TO 35', '36 TO 45', 'OVER 45'.

/HISTOGRAM    GROUPING ARE BRTHPILL,AGE.

/END
```

The results for CHOLSTRL are presented in Output 9.7. Eight groups are formed and a two-way ANOVA is computed. The levels of the first grouping variable (BRTHPILL) represent the rows and those of the second grouping variable (AGE) represent columns in the analysis of variance calculations.

The sums of squares in the one-way ANOVA are well known. The sums of squares in the two-way ANOVA depend upon the hypothesis of interest unless there are the same number of observations in each group or the rows are independent of the columns in the two-way table of group (cell) frequencies. We test hypotheses that are not dependent on the group frequencies.

Let $\mu_{ij} = E(Y_{ij})$, where Y_{ij} is an observation of the group (i,j). The test of equality of row means is the test that

$$\sum_j \mu_{ij} = \sum_j \mu_{kj} \quad \text{for all } i, k.$$

Output 9.7 Two-way analysis of variance by P7D. The results for CHOLSTRL only are shown.

```
HISTOGRAM OF CHOLSTRL(VARIABLE   6).

                                                                                                          CASES WITH
                                                                                                          INVALID GROUP
BRTHPILL NOPILL       NOPILL       NOPILL       NOPILL       PILL         PILL         PILL         PILL   SPECIFICATION
AGE      25ORLESS     26 TO 35     36 TO 45     OVER 45      25ORLESS     26 TO 35     36 TO 45     OVER 45  PILL.AGE
         ......+........+........+........+........+........+........+........+........+........+........+............+
VAR  6
EXCLUDED
VALUES
                                                                **
         TABULATIONS AND COMPUTATIONS WHICH FOLLOW EXCLUDE VALUES LISTED ABOVE
MIDPOINTS
 435.000)
 420.000)
 405.000)
 390.000)                                                                                   *
 375.000)
 360.000)
 345.000)                                                                                   *
 330.000)*             *                                                     *              *
 315.000)              *                                       *             *              *
 300.000)*             **          *****                       **            *              *
 285.000)*             **                          *           **            *              *
 270.000)***     *     **          *                                         *****          **
 255.000)        ****** M**        M****           ****        ****          M*             M***
 240.000)***     ***    ***                        *****       M*******      **             **
 225.000)M**     ***                 ***           M***        ****          **             ***
 210.000)*****   M**   ****          *             **          **            *              *
 195.000)****    *******  *          *             *****       ****          ***            *
 180.000)*       *****                             ***         **            **
 165.000)***     **    **                          *
 150.000)*
 135.000)
 120.000)
GROUP MEANS ARE DENOTED BY M'S IF THEY COINCIDE WITH *'S, N'S OTHERWISE

MEAN      221.654   214.767   249.095   262.470   222.625   234.500   247.571   261.646
STD.DEV.   43.265    31.865    47.226    36.690    30.853    37.179    43.411    50.146
S. E. M.    8.485     5.818    10.306     8.899     6.298     6.788     9.473    12.162
MAXIMUM   330.000   270.000   335.000   320.000   290.000   317.000   324.000   390.000
MINIMUM   155.000   168.000   160.000   195.000   173.000   160.000   175.000   190.000
SAMPLE SIZE    26        30        21        17        24        30        21        17
```

```
     ALL GROUPS COMBINED     *            ANALYSIS OF VARIANCE TABLE
(CASES THAT CONTAIN SPECIAL  *
     CODES ARE EXCLUDED)     *    SOURCE        SUM OF SQUARES   DF    MEAN SQUARE   F VALUE   TAIL PROBABILITY
                             *
                             *
MEAN           236.150       *    BRTHPILL         936.9470      1     936.9470      0.5908        0.4431
STD. DEV.       42.555       *    AGE            46813.0742      3   15604.3555      9.8395        0.0000
S. E. M.         3.120       *    INTERACTION     4133.9453      3    1377.9817      0.8689        0.4584
MAXIMUM        390.000       *    ERROR         282288.9375    178    1585.8928
MINIMUM        155.000       *
SAMPLE SIZE        186       *    ONE WAY ANALYSIS OF VARIANCE
                             *    WITHIN GROUP VARIANCES ARE
                             *    NOT ASSUMED TO BE EQUAL.
                             *
                             *    TEST STATISTIC
                             *      WELCH             7,  70                4.8242        0.0002
                             *      BROWN-FORSYTHE    7, 140                4.5432        0.0001
```

The test of equality of column means is the test that

$$\sum_i \mu_{ij} = \sum_i \mu_{i\ell} \quad \text{for all } j, \ell.$$

The test of no interaction is the test that

$$\mu_{ij} + \mu_{k\ell} = \mu_{i\ell} + \mu_{jk} \quad \text{for all } i \neq k \text{ and } j \neq \ell.$$

The model can also be expressed as

$$E(Y_{ij}) = \mu + \alpha_i + \beta_j + \gamma_{ij}$$

with constraints

$$\sum_i \alpha_i = 0 \quad ; \quad \sum_j \beta_j = 0 \quad ; \quad \text{and} \quad \sum_i \gamma_{ij} = \sum_j \gamma_{ij} = 0.$$

The hypotheses tested are

$$\alpha_i = 0$$

$$\beta_j = 0$$

$$\gamma_{ij} = 0$$

This formulation of the model and hypotheses is equivalent to the one above.

The hypotheses tested here are the same for equal or unequal cell size problems. In particular, the hypotheses tested are not affected by the loss of some of the cases. It should be noted that although the hypotheses tested are orthogonal, the sums of squares for unequal cell size problems are not in general orthogonal. Orthogonal sums of squares methods (or "sequential" methods) test hypotheses that are functions of cell sizes, and are not given here. For more detailed discussions see Kutner (1974) and Speed and Hocking (1976).

Computationally, the sums of squares that test these hypotheses can be obtained as the difference in fitting two regression models. In one model the effects corresponding to the rows, columns and interaction are fitted. In the second model the effects corresponding to row or column or interaction (whichever is being tested) are set to zero.

LISTING THE DATA

The data can be listed in the same order as read by specifying

DATA.

in the *PRINT* paragraph. The data can also be listed after the cases are ordered (or sorted) according to the GROUPING variable by specifying

ORDER.

in the *PRINT* paragraph.

The Control Language instructions to specify both these options are shown in Example 9.8.

Example 9.8

```
/PROBLEM        TITLE IS 'WERNER BLOOD CHEMISTRY DATA'.
/INPUT          VARIABLES ARE 9.
                FORMAT IS '(A4,5F4.0,3F4.1)'.
/VARIABLE       NAMES ARE ID,AGE,HEIGHT,WEIGHT,BRTHPILL,
                     CHOLSTRL,ALBUMIN,CALCIUM,URICACID.
                MAXIMUM IS (6)400.
                MINIMUM IS (6)150.
                BLANKS ARE MISSING.
                LABEL IS ID.

/GROUP          CUTPOINTS(2) ARE    25,        35,        45.
                NAMES(2) ARE '25ORLESS', '26 TO 35', '36 TO 45', 'OVER 45'.

/HISTOGRAM      GROUPING IS AGE.

/PRINT          DATA.
                ORDER.

/END
```

The results are presented in Output 9.8. The first listing of the data is the order in which the data were read. The second listing is ordered according to the GROUPING variable AGE. (The case numbers are not in sequence.)

Output 9.8 Data matrix printed as read and after ordering by AGE

```
NUMBER OF CASES READ. . . . . . . . . . . . . .    188
PRINT DATA MATRIX . . . . . . . . . . . . . .      YES
PRINT DATA MATRIX AFTER ORDERING. . . . . . . .    YES
PRINT WINSORIZING TABLE . . . . . . . . . . . .    NO
PRINT CORRELATION TABLE . . . . . . . . . . . .    NO
```

DATA MATRIX AFTER TRANSFORMATION (EXCLUDED VALUES ARE PRINTED AS ASTERISKS, IF ANY)

CASE NO.		AGE	HEIGHT	WEIGHT	BRTHPILL	CHOLSTRL	ALBUMIN	CALCIUM	URICACID
1	2381	22.00000	67.00000	144.00000	1.00000	200.00000	4.30000	9.80000	5.40000
2	1946	22.00000	64.00000	160.00000	2.00000************		3.50000************		7.20000
3	1610	25.00000	62.00000	128.00000	1.00000	243.00000	4.10000	10.40000	3.30000
4	1797	25.00000	68.00000	150.00000	2.00000************		3.80000	9.60000	3.00000
5	561	19.00000	64.00000	125.00000	1.00000	158.00000	4.10000	9.90000	4.70000

--- cases 6 to 183 ---

CASE NO.		AGE	HEIGHT	WEIGHT	BRTHPILL	CHOLSTRL	ALBUMIN	CALCIUM	URICACID
184	1789	52.00000	62.00000	107.00000	2.00000	265.00000	4.60000	10.40000	6.40000
185	1149	53.00000************		178.00000	1.00000	227.00000	3.90000************		5.00000
186	575	53.00000	65.00000	140.00000	2.00000	220.00000	4.00000	10.70000	4.60000
187	2271	54.00000	66.00000	158.00000	1.00000	305.00000	4.20000	10.30000	4.80000
188	39	54.00000	60.00000	170.00000	2.00000	220.00000	3.50000	8.80000	6.30000

DATA MATRIX AFTER TRANSFORMATION AND ORDERING ON VARIABLE 2 AGE
(EXCLUDED VALUES ARE PRINTED AS ASTERISKS, IF ANY)

CASE NO.		AGE	HEIGHT	WEIGHT	BRTHPILL	CHOLSTRL	ALBUMIN	CALCIUM	URICACID
5	561	19.00000	64.00000	125.00000	1.00000	158.00000	4.10000	9.90000	4.70000
6	2519	19.00000	67.00000	130.00000	2.00000	255.00000	4.50000	10.50000	8.30000
7	225	20.00000	64.00000	118.00000	1.00000	210.00000	3.90000	9.50000	4.00000
8	2420	20.00000	65.00000	119.00000	2.00000	192.00000	3.80000	9.30000	5.00000
13	988	21.00000	67.00000	134.00000	1.00000	204.00000	4.00000	10.80000	3.40000

--- remainder of cases after ordering ---

CASE NO.		AGE	HEIGHT	WEIGHT	BRTHPILL	CHOLSTRL	ALBUMIN	CALCIUM	URICACID
187	2271	54.00000	66.00000	158.00000	1.00000	305.00000	4.20000	10.30000	4.80000
103	63	54.00000	67.00000	145.00000	1.00000	320.00000	3.90000************************		
188	39	54.00000	60.00000	170.00000	2.00000	220.00000	3.50000	8.80000	6.30000
155	520	55.00000	64.00000	124.00000	1.00000	275.00000	4.00000	9.80000	5.30000
156	22	55.00000	64.00000	165.00000	2.00000	298.00000	3.60000	10.00000	6.30000

--- histograms and analyses for each variable ---

```
┌─────────────────────────────────────────────────────────────────────┐
│  PRINT                                                               │
│     DATA.               {no/prev.}                                  │
│                                                                      │
│        Print the input data in the order they are read into the computer. │
│                                                                      │
│     ORDER.              {no/prev.}                                  │
│                                                                      │
│        Print the input data after reordering according to the GROUPing │
│        variable.                                                     │
└─────────────────────────────────────────────────────────────────────┘
```

- CORRELATIONS

    The correlations between the variables are computed when

        CORRELATION.

is specified in the *PRINT* paragraph. The correlations are computed for all
the data combined and for the cases in each group separately.

    Each correlation is computed using only cases containing acceptable
values for both of the variables.

    The correlations are requested in Example 9.9.

Example 9.9

```
        /PROBLEM      TITLE IS 'WERNER BLOOD CHEMISTRY DATA'.
        /INPUT        VARIABLES ARE 9.
                      FORMAT IS '(A4,5F4.0,3F4.1)'.
        /VARIABLE     NAMES ARE ID,AGE,HEIGHT,WEIGHT,BRTHPILL,
                          CHOLSTRL,ALBUMIN,CALCIUM,URICACID.
                      MAXIMUM IS (6)400.
                      MINIMUM IS (6)150.
                      BLANKS ARE MISSING.
                      LABEL IS ID.

        /GROUP        CUTPOINTS(2) ARE    25,         35,         45.
                      NAMES(2) ARE '25ORLESS', '26 TO 35', '36 TO 45', 'OVER 45'.

        /HISTOGRAM    GROUPING IS AGE.

        /PRINT        CORRELATION.

        /END
```

    The correlations in Output 9.9 are printed immediately after the histo-
grams for CHOLSTRL. Each correlation is between the variable specified in the
left-hand column and CHOLSTRL. First the correlation based on data from all
groups is printed and then the correlations within each group. The correlation for all groups uses the means for the variables, not the group means.
The number of cases from which the correlations are computed is printed in
parentheses under the correlations.

    The correlations are not printed as the usual correlation matrix. Each
panel of correlations contains all possible pairings of variables with the
variable presented in the histograms above.

> *PRINT*
>
> CORRELATION.   {no/prev.}
>
>   Correlations are computed between the variables for each group
>   and for all groups combined by using the data in complete pairs.

● WINSORIZED MEANS

The usual formula for the mean assigns an equal weight to each observation. This estimate is known to be sensitive to outliers. Therefore in more robust estimates of the mean, extreme observations are assigned less weight than observations nearer the center. The Winsorized mean is a robust estimate. Other robust estimates are provided in P2D (Section 8.2).

The Winsorized mean is similar to the arithmetic mean except that an equal number of observations, say g, in each tail are set equal to the (g+1)st observation in the tail. This is known as g-level Winsorization. Dixon and Tukey (1968) studied the Winsorized mean and its approximate standard error. The zero-level Winsorized mean is the arithmetic mean. If

        WINSOR.

is specified in the *PRINT* paragraph, P7D computes the g-level Winsorized means for g=0,1,2,3,4,5 and the half-length of the 95% confidence limit. The latter is defined as

Output 9.9 Panel of correlations printed by P7D. Only the results for CHOLSTRL are shown.

```
NUMBER OF CASES READ. . . . . . . . . . . . . .    198
PRINT DATA MATRIX . . . . . . . . . . . . . .      NO
PRINT DATA MATRIX AFTER ORDERING. . . . . . . .    NO
PRINT WINSORIZING TABLE . . . . . . . . . . .      NO
PRINT CORRELATION TABLE . . . . . . . . . . .      YES
```

--- *histograms and analysis of CHOLSTRL* ---

CORRELATIONS WITH VARIABLE 6 CHOLSTRL   (COUNTS IN PARENTHESES)

VARIABLE	ALL GROUPS	25ORLESS	26 TO 35	36 TO 45	OVER 45
2 AGE	0.3678 (186)	0.1947 (50)	-0.0221 (60)	0.1312 (42)	0.0705 (34)
3 HEIGHT	0.0199 (184)	-0.0281 (50)	-0.1342 (60)	-0.0352 (41)	0.2606 (33)
4 WEIGHT	0.1474 (184)	0.0195 (50)	0.0299 (59)	0.1065 (42)	0.1235 (33)
5 BRTHPILL	0.0758 (186)	0.0131 (50)	0.2784 (60)	-0.0172 (42)	-0.0097 (34)
7 ALBUMIN	0.0534 (184)	0.0680 (50)	0.0227 (60)	0.0320 (41)	0.3170 (33)
8 CALCIUM	0.2515 (184)	0.3431 (50)	0.2889 (60)	0.3426 (42)	0.1462 (32)
9 URICACID	0.2660 (185)	0.1804 (50)	0.0643 (60)	0.4202 (42)	0.1801 (33)

-196-

$$c_j = t_{N-2g-1} \cdot \frac{N-1}{N-2g-1} \cdot \sqrt{\frac{S_g^2}{N(N-1)}}$$

where N is the number of observations for a variable in a group, S_g^2 is the sum of squares using the Winsorized observations, and t_k is the 97.5 percentile of the Student t statistic with k degrees of freedom.

The following Control Language instructions request the Winsorized means.

Example 9.10

```
/PROBLEM      TITLE IS 'WERNER BLOOD CHEMISTRY DATA'.
/INPUT        VARIABLES ARE 9.
              FORMAT IS '(A4,5F4.0,3F4.1)'.
/VARIABLE     NAMES ARE ID,AGE,HEIGHT,WEIGHT,BRTHPILL,
                  CHOLSTRL,ALBUMIN,CALCIUM,URICACID.
              MAXIMUM IS (6)400.
              MINIMUM IS (6)150.
              BLANKS ARE MISSING.
              LABEL IS ID.

/GROUP        CUTPOINTS(2) ARE     25,        35,        45.
              NAMES(2) ARE '25ORLESS', '26 TO 35', '36 TO 45', 'OVER 45'.

/HISTOGRAM    GROUPING IS AGE.

/PRINT        WINSORIZED.

/END
```

The results for CHOLSTRL are presented in Output 9.10. The leftmost column indicates the level of Winsorization. The remaining columns contain the results for each group (identified at the top of the column). Four horizontal panels are printed. The uppermost contains the Winsorized means, the second the half-length of the 95% confidence interval, the third the six largest values in the group, and the last the six smallest values in the group. The mean corresponding to the shortest confidence interval in each group is indicated by ** and the mean corresponding to the next shortest is indicated by *.

PRINT
   WINSORIZED.   {no/prev.}

   The g-level Winsorized means for g=0,1,...,5 are printed; also the half-lengths of the 95% confidence intervals and the maximum and minimum observations <u>after</u> Winsorization.

● SIZE OF PROGRAM

Unlike most BMDP programs, P7D keeps the data in computer memory. The number of cases (C) that it can analyze depends on the number of variables (V). The following table provides a guide:

V	2	3	4	5	10	20	50
C	4700	3500	2800	2350	1250	670	275

Appendix B describes how the capacity of the program can be increased.

● COMPUTATIONAL METHOD

Means, standard deviations and covariances are computed in single precision using the method of provisional means (Appendix A.2).

ACKNOWLEDGEMENT

P7D was programmed by Paul Sampson. Recent revisions were made by Peter Mundle. P7D supersedes BMD07D whose design was proposed by W.J. Dixon.

Output 9.10 Winsorized means computed by P7D. Only the results for CHOLSTRL are shown.

```
NUMBER OF CASES READ. . . . . . . . . . . . .        188
PRINT DATA MATRIX . . . . . . . . . . . . . .        NO
PRINT DATA MATRIX AFTER ORDERING. . . . . . .        NO
PRINT WINSORIZING TABLE . . . . . . . . . . .        YES
PRINT CORRELATION TABLE . . . . . . . . . . .        NO
```

--- histograms and analysis of CHOLSTRL ---

WINSORIZATION OF VARIABLE 6 CHOLSTRL   UNDEFINED VALUES ARE PRINTED AS   999.9988

	25ORLESS	26 TO 35	36 TO 45	OVER 45
MEAN	**INDICATES THE MEAN CORRESPONDING TO THE SHORTEST CONFIDENCE INTERVAL, * TO THE NEXT SHORTEST CONFIDENCE INTERVAL			
0	222.1198	224.6331**	248.3332**	262.0569
1	221.4708 *	224.5665	248.3094 *	260.6743 *
2	221.5598	224.3664	248.3570	260.8506**
3	221.2598	223.7164 *	248.3569	260.9387
4	220.3797**	223.7831	249.0236	259.6443
5	220.2797	223.1164	249.1426	259.4971
(LENGTH OF .95 CONFIDENCE INTERVAL)/2				
0	10.6448	9.2363	13.9666	15.0969
1	10.5505	9.3722	14.3935	14.5522
2	10.7526	9.4554	14.9352	14.0431
3	10.7344	9.3558	15.3759	15.0855
4	10.5060	9.7006	14.8904	14.8998
5	10.7898	9.5936	15.6736	16.1549
MAXIMUM				
0	330.0000	317.0000	335.0000	390.0000
1	295.0000	305.0000	324.0000	338.0000
2	290.0000	295.0000	320.0000	320.0000
3	280.0000	280.0000	315.0000	320.0000
4	266.0000	280.0000	306.0000	306.0000
5	263.0000	270.0000	305.0000	305.0000
MINIMUM				
0	155.0000	160.0000	160.0000	190.0000
1	158.0000	168.0000	170.0000	195.0000
2	165.0000	172.0000	175.0000	216.0000
3	170.0000	174.0000	180.0000	217.0000
4	173.0000	175.0000	196.0000	220.0000
5	175.0000	177.0000	198.0000	220.0000

P9D

9.3 Multiway Description of Groups

Laszlo Engelman, HSCF

P9D analyzes data for each variable in any number of groups; the groups can be defined as all combinations of the levels of several variables. Univariate statistics are provided for each group. A one-way ANOVA is computed to test the equality of the means of all the groups. To test for homogeneity (equality) of variances, Bartlett's statistic is evaluated. P9D also tests for the equality of group frequencies. A plot that shows the shift in means from group to group is an option.

● RESULTS

We use P9D to analyze the Werner blood chemistry data (Table 5.1). In our first example we classify the cases both by the age of the woman and by whether or not she is on the pill. Except for the *TABULate* paragraph, the Control Language instructions in Example 9.11 are described in Chapter 5.

Example 9.11

```
/PROBLEM      TITLE IS 'WERNER BLOOD CHEMISTRY DATA'.
/INPUT        VARIABLES ARE 9.
              FORMAT IS '(A4,5F4.0,3F4.1)'.
/VARIABLE     NAMES ARE ID,AGE,HEIGHT,WEIGHT,BRTHPILL,
                   CHOLSTRL,ALBUMIN,CALCIUM,URICACID.
              MAXIMUM IS (6)400.
              MINIMUM IS (6)150.
              BLANKS ARE MISSING.
              LABEL IS ID.

/GROUP        CODES(5) ARE      1,    2.
              NAMES(5) ARE NOPILL, PILL.
              CUTPOINTS(2) ARE     25,        35,        45.
              NAMES(2) ARE '25ORLESS', '26 TO 35', '36 TO 45', 'OVER 45'.

/TABULATE     GROUPING ARE AGE,BRTHPILL.
              VARIABLES ARE CHOLSTRL,URICACID.

/END
```

The Control Language must be preceded by System Cards to initiate the analysis by P9D. At HSCF, the System Cards are

```
//jobname  JOB  nooo,yourname
//   EXEC  BIMED,PROG=BMDP9D
//SYSIN  DD  *
```

The Control Language is immediately followed by the data (Table 5.1). The analysis is terminated by another System Card. At HSCF, this System Card is

```
//
```

The results of the above analysis are shown in Output 9.11. Circled numbers below correspond to those in the output.

Output 9.11   An analysis by P9D using two grouping variables.   Circled numbers correspond to those in the text.   Results not reproduced are indicated in *italics*.

```
BMDP9D - MULTIWAY DESCRIPTION OF GROUPS              PROGRAM REVISED SEPTEMBER 1977
HEALTH SCIENCES COMPUTING FACILITY                  MANUAL DATE -- 1977
UNIVERSITY OF CALIFORNIA, LOS ANGELES
```

--- Control Language read by P9D is printed and interpreted ---

① NUMBER OF CASES READ.   188

②
VARIABLE	BEFORE TRANSFORMATION					INTERVAL RANGE	
NO. NAME	MINIMUM LIMIT	MAXIMUM LIMIT	MISSING CODE	CATEGORY CODE	CATEGORY NAME	GREATER THAN	LESS THAN OR EQUAL TO
2 AGE					25ORLESS		25.00000
					26 TO 35	25.00000	35.00000
					36 TO 45	35.00000	45.00000
					OVER 45	45.00000	
5 BRTHPILL				1.00000	NOPILL		
				2.00000	PILL		
6 CHOLSTRL	150.00000	400.00000					

③ CELL DEFINITIONS FOR MARGINALS OVER INDICES INDICATED BY POINTS IN ' '.
FOR GROUPING VARIABLES WITH CUTPOINTS 'VALUE' IS THE INCLUSIVE UPPER LIMIT OF THE INTERVAL.

```
CELL        AGE        BRTHPILL
NUMBER       2            5
  1       25ORLESS     NOPILL
  2       26 TO 35     NOPILL
  3       36 TO 45     NOPILL
  4       OVER 45      NOPILL
  5       25ORLESS     PILL
  6       26 TO 35     PILL
  7       36 TO 45     PILL
  8       OVER 45      PILL
```

DESCRIPTIVE STATISTICS FOR NON-EMPTY CELLS OF ' '

④
CELL NUMBER	VARIABLE 6 CHOLSTRL			VARIABLE 9 URICACID		
	FREQ.	MEAN	STD.DEV.	FREQ.	MEAN	STD.DEV.
1	26.	221.65384	43.2647	26.	4.51153	0.9488
2	30.	214.76666	31.8647	30.	4.66666	0.9897
3	21.	249.09523	47.2259	21.	4.81904	0.8835
4	17.	262.47046	36.6898	16.	5.15624	1.3574
5	24.	222.62500	30.8528	26.	4.73461	1.1164
6	30.	234.50000	37.1787	30.	4.59333	1.1274
7	21.	247.57143	43.4115	21.	4.65714	1.5416
8	17.	261.64697	50.1460	17.	5.43529	1.2777

⑤
```
EQUALITY    CHI-SQUARE        8.06451              8.89305
OF CELL        D.F.           7.                   7.
FREQ.     ALPHA(CHI-SQ)       0.3269               0.2604

WITHIN   SUM OF SQUARES    282288.93750          235.83162
            D.F.             178.                 179.
         MEAN SQUARE       1585.89282             1.31749

BETWEEN  SUM OF SQUARES     52740.32031            13.25559
            D.F.             7.                    7.
         MEAN SQUARE       7534.32813             1.89365

EQUALITY      F-VALUE          4.75084             1.43731
OF MEANS     D.F.-S         7.   178.           7.   179.
           ALPHA(F)           0.0001              0.1929

HOMOG.    BARTLETT TEST       9.48999            10.75478
  OF       APPROX. F          1.33224             1.50981
VARIANCE    D.F.-S        7. 28708.            7. 28597.
           ALPHA(F)           0.2302              0.1586
```

①   Number of cases read. The number of cases is not specified in our example, so all cases are read. The computations use all acceptable data; i.e., values not equal to a code for missing values and not outside the specified upper and lower limits.

②   Interpretation of the *GROUP* paragraph.

③   P9D analyzes data in cells formed by all possible combinations of the GROUPING variable specified in the *TABULate* paragraph. In our example AGE (4 intervals) and BRTHPILL (2 codes) are the GROUPING variables. The eight possible combinations of these two variables are listed. For example, cell 4 is OVER45 and NOPILL. The cell numbers are used to identify the eight combinations in the results.

④   For each cell (identified in ③), P9D prints

- the frequency of acceptable data in the ith cell: N_i

- the mean: $\bar{x}_i = \Sigma_j x_{ij}/N_i$

     where x_{ij} is the jth observation in the ith cell

- the standard deviation: $s_i = \{\Sigma_j (x_{ij}-\bar{x}_i)^2/(N_i-1)\}^{\frac{1}{2}}$

⑤   The data in the cells are compared by

- a χ^2 test of the equality of cell frequencies; i.e.,

$$\text{CHI-SQUARE} = \Sigma_i (N_i-\bar{N})^2/\bar{N}$$

     where $\bar{N} = \Sigma N_i/g$ and g is the number of groups.

$$\text{D.F.} = g - 1$$

$$\text{ALPHA(CHI-SQ)} = \text{probability of exceeding this } \chi^2$$

- a test of the equality of group means; i.e., a one-way analysis of variance. The components are

$$\text{WITHIN SUM OF SQUARES} = \Sigma_i \Sigma_j (x_{ij}-\bar{x}_i)^2$$

$$\text{D.F.} = \Sigma_i (N_i-1)$$

$$\text{MEAN SQUARE} = \text{within sum of squares/D.F.}$$

$$\text{BETWEEN SUM OF SQUARES} = \Sigma_i N_i (\bar{x}_i-\bar{x})^2$$

     where $\bar{x} = \Sigma N_i \bar{x}_i / \Sigma N_i$

$$\text{D.F.} = g - 1$$

     where g is the number of nonempty groups

$$\text{MEAN SQUARE} = \text{between sum of squares/D.F.}$$

$$\text{F-VALUE} = \text{between mean square/within mean square}$$

$$D.F.-S = (g-1), \Sigma \, (N_i-1)$$

$$ALPHA(F) = \text{probability of exceeding this } F$$

The computation of ALPHA(F) assumes that the data are sampled from normal populations with equal variances. When the samples sizes (N_i) of the cells and the population variances are not equal, the distribution of F can be strongly affected and the ALPHA(F) may not be meaningful. In this case the Welch or Brown-Forsythe statistics in P7D (Section 9.2) or a transformation of the data should be considered.

The F value (analysis of variance) is a test of the equality of group means. When the groups are ordered (as in this example), you may want to test contrasts on the group means, such as a linear trend. Both contrasts and covariates can be used in P1V (Chapter 15).

- Bartlett's test of equality (homogeneity) of variances for groups with nonzero variances. Its formula is in Appendix A.4. The significance of Bartlett's test, ALPHA(F), is evaluated using Box's approximation (Dixon and Massey, 1969, p. 308). The test is sensitive to the asumption of normality and may improperly reject the null hypothesis too often when the distribution of the data is nonnormal. P7D computes Levene's test, which is less sensitive to the assumption of normality.

● OPTIONAL RESULTS

In addition to the above results, you can

- compactly plot the cell means relative to the overall mean   p. 203
- request a similar analysis for marginal subsets of the cells p. 204

● THE *TABULate* PARAGRAPH

The *TABULate*[7] paragraph is used to specify the GROUPING[8] variables to be used to classify the cases, the VARIABLES[9] to be analyzed, MARGINAL subsets of the cells to be studied, and to state whether the means are to be plotted (PLOTMEAN[10]).

---

[7] If your BMDP programs are dated before August 1977, the minimum required abbreviation is *TABULATE* (not *TABUL*).

[8] If your BMDP programs are dated before August 1977, INDEX= must be used in place of GROUPING=.

[9] If your BMDP programs are dated before August 1977, DESCRIBE= must be used in place of VARIABLE= and is required.

[10] If your BMDP programs are dated before August 1977, HISTOGRAM. must be used in place of PLOTMEAN.

The *TABULate* paragraph is required and can be repeated for additional analyses. If repeated, it must be placed <u>after</u> the data (if on cards). The order of input in the summary (p. 213) shows where to place the paragraph.

TABULate
    GROUPING=v_1,v_2,$\cdots$.   {none/prev.}   required

        Names or subscripts of the variables used to classify the cases into groups (cells) for the analysis. The cells are formed from all possible combinations of the levels of v_1,v_2,$\cdots$; the levels for each variable are the intervals or codes assigned in the *GROUP* paragraph.

        If a GROUPING variable has more than ten distinct values, CODEs or CUTPOINTS must be specified for it in the *GROUP* paragraph (Section 5.4).

    VARIABLE=v_1,v_2,$\cdots$.   {all variables}

        Names or subscripts of the variables to be analyzed. If not specified, all variables except the GROUPING variables are analyzed.

● PLOTMEAN -- PLOTTING THE MEAN OF EACH CELL

The means of the cells are plotted relative to the overall mean in a compact plot when PLOTMEAN is specified in the *TABULate* paragraph. If PLOTMEAN is added to Example 9.11, the following plots are printed after the results in Output 9.11.

```
GROUPED DISTRIBUTIONS OF VARIABLES AT CELLS OF  'AB'
IN THE GRAPHS BELOW POSITIONS ARE DETERMINED BY CELL MEAN VALUES, CHARACTERS INDICATE CELL FREQUENCIES.
WHEN POSITIONS COINCIDE FREQUENCIES ARE SUMMED.

            VARIABLE   6 CHOLSTRL       VARIABLE   9 URICACID
    MEAN            236.1505                    4.7706
 ST.DV.             42.555                      1.157

 CELL  *-  S    S   M    S    S   +**-  S    S   M    S    S   +*
   1   * )        B             ( ** )        B             ( *
   2   * )      C               ( ** )        C             ( *
   3   * )            B         ( ** )        B             ( *
   4   * )             A        ( ** )             A        ( *
   5   * )        B             ( ** )        B             ( *
   6   * )          C           ( ** )        C             ( *
   7   * )           B          ( ** )        B             ( *
   3   * )             A        ( ** )             A        ( *
```

There are two plots (one for CHOLSTRL and one for URICACID). The vertical scale is the cell identification number. The horizontal axis contains an M for the overall mean and S's that represent differences in one standard deviation along the horizontal axis. The letters in the graph are codes for the number of observations in the cell (see definition below). The letters are plotted at the position of the mean of the cell.

TABULate
    PLOTMEANS.   {no/prev.}

> Plots of the means for each group. Each group is represented in a plot by its frequency plotted at its group mean. The following symbols are used for the frequencies.

Symbol	Frequency	Symbol	Frequency	Symbol	Frequency
blank	0	A	10-19	J	100-199
1	1	B	20-29	K	200-299
2	2	C	30-39	L	300-399
3	3	D	40-49	M	400-499
4	4	E	50-59	N	500-599
5	5	F	60-69	O	600-699
6	6	G	70-79	P	700-799
7	7	H	80-89	Q	800-899
8	8	I	90-99	R	900-999
9	9			S	≥ 1000

- ● MARGINAL SUBSETS OF THE CELLS

In Example 9.11 we requested results for each cell and tests between cells. You may want the same results for marginal subsets of the cells -- such as AGE groupings only, or BRTHPILL codes only.

Marginal subsets are specified as follows: When there are two GROUPING variables, the statement

        MARGIN='AB','A.','.B','..'.

specifies

- 'AB': two letters. All possible combinations of the two GROUPING variables are used.

- 'A.': a letter in the first position and a period in the second. A period is interpreted as "average over." Therefore classification is by the first GROUPING variable only.

- '.B': a period in the first position and a letter in the second. Classification is by the second GROUPING variable only.

- '..': two periods. There is no GROUPING variable by which to classify cases. Only one cell is formed.

The number of letters and periods between the apostrophes must be the same as the number of GROUPING variables. The position of the letters and periods between the apostrophes instructs P9D to classify by GROUPING variable according to the positions. Therefore 'X..Y.Z' specifies that all three-way combinations (marginals) of the first, fourth and sixth GROUPING variables are to be used.

By specifying PLOTMEANS, we obtain each cell mean plotted in the same line as the other cell means in its subset.

To demonstrate this option we use Example 9.12.

Example 9.12

```
/PROBLEM      TITLE IS 'WERNER BLOOD CHEMISTRY DATA'.
/INPUT        VARIABLES ARE 9.
              FORMAT IS '(A4,5F4.0,3F4.1)'.
/VARIABLE     NAMES ARE ID,AGE,HEIGHT,WEIGHT,BRTHPILL,
                    CHOLSTRL,ALBUMIN,CALCIUM,URICACID.
              MAXIMUM IS (6)400.
              MINIMUM IS (6)150.
              BLANKS ARE MISSING.
              LABEL IS ID.

/GROUP        CODES(5) ARE       1,    2.
              NAMES(5) ARE NOPILL, PILL.
              NAMES(2) ARE '25ORLESS', '26 TO 35', '36 TO 45', 'OVER 45'.
              CUTPOINTS(2) ARE     25,         35,          45.

/TABULATE     GROUPING ARE AGE,BRTHPILL.
              VARIABLES ARE CHOLSTRL,URICACID.
              MARGINS ARE 'AB', 'A.', '.B', '..'.
              PLOTMEANS.

/END
```

The results are shown in Output 9.12. The first page of the output corresponds to the specification 'AB', the second to 'A.' and the third to '.B'. The results for 'A.' classify the data only by AGE before doing the statistical analysis. The plots contain one or two letters on each line. These letters are plotted at the cell means of the two-way classification 'AB'. If two cell means coincide in their plotting position, the letter printed corresponds to the total frequency of the two groups. The plots for '.B' contain up to four cell means on each line.

TABULate
  MARGIN=$'c_1'$,$'c_2'$,$\cdots$.   {cells as defined by all GROUPING variables}

  Each c_1, c_2 represents a marginal subset of cells to be analyzed. The number of characters including periods in each c_i must be equal to the number of variables in the GROUPING statement. A period in place of a character means "averaged over."

● SIZE OF PROBLEM

P9D can analyze very large amounts of data. Appendix B describes how the capacity of the program can be increased.

Output 9.12   Results of specifying MARGINALs in P9D. The first page corresponds to the marginal 'AB', the second page to 'A.', and the third page to '.B'.

CELL DEFINITIONS FOR MARGINALS OVER INDICES INDICATED BY POINTS IN 'AB'.
FOR GROUPING VARIABLES WITH CUTPOINTS 'VALUE' IS THE INCLUSIVE UPPER LIMIT OF THE INTERVAL.

```
CELL        AGE         BRTHPILL
NUMBER       2             5
  1        25ORLESS      NOPILL
  2        26 TO 35      NOPILL
  3        36 TO 45      NOPILL
  4        OVER 45       NOPILL
  5        25ORLESS      PILL
  6        26 TO 35      PILL
  7        36 TO 45      PILL
  8        OVER 45       PILL
```

DESCRIPTIVE STATISTICS FOR NON-EMPTY CELLS OF 'AB'

```
CELL      VARIABLE  6 CHOLSTRL        VARIABLE  9 URICACID
NUMBER   FREQ.    MEAN    STD.DEV.    FREQ.    MEAN    STD.DEV.

  1       26.   221.65384  43.2647     26.    4.51153   0.9488
  2       30.   214.76666  31.8647     30.    4.66666   0.9897
  3       21.   249.09523  47.2259     21.    4.81904   0.8835
  4       17.   262.47046  36.6898     16.    5.15624   1.3574
  5       24.   222.62500  30.8528     26.    4.73461   1.1164
  6       30.   234.50000  37.1787     30.    4.59333   1.1274
  7       21.   247.57143  43.4115     21.    4.65714   1.5416
  8       17.   261.64697  50.1460     17.    5.43529   1.2777
```

```
EQUALITY   CHI-SQUARE        8.06451              8.89305
OF CELL      D.F.            7.                   7.
FREQ.     ALPHA(CHI-SQ)      0.3269               0.2604


WITHIN   SUM OF SQUARES  282288.93750           235.83162
             D.F.           178.                 179.
          MEAN SQUARE      1585.89282              1.31749

BETWEEN  SUM OF SQUARES   52740.32031            13.25559
             D.F.           7.                    7.
          MEAN SQUARE      7534.32813              1.89365

EQUALITY     F-VALUE         4.75084              1.43731
OF MEANS     D.F.-S       7.   178.            7.    179.
            ALPHA(F)         0.0001               0.1929


HOMOG.   BARTLETT TEST       9.48999             10.75478
  OF       APPROX. F         1.33224              1.50981
VARIANCE    D.F.-S        7. 28708.            7. 28597.
            ALPHA(F)         0.2302               0.1586
```

GROUPED DISTRIBUTIONS OF VARIABLES AT CELLS OF 'AB'
IN THE GRAPHS BELOW POSITIONS ARE DETERMINED BY CELL MEAN VALUES, CHARACTERS INDICATE CELL FREQUENCIES.
WHEN POSITIONS COINCIDE FREQUENCIES ARE SUMMED.

```
             VARIABLE  6 CHOLSTRL        VARIABLE  9 URICACID
  MEAN           236.1505                   4.7706
ST.DV.            42.555                    1.157

CELL   *-  S   S   M   S   S   +**-  S   S   M   S   S   +**
  1    * )         B        ( ** )         B        ( *
  2    * )        C         ( ** )        C         ( *
  3    * )           B      ( ** )           B      ( *
  4    * )             A    ( ** )             A    ( *
  5    * )         B        ( ** )         B        ( *
  6    * )          C       ( ** )          C       ( *
  7    * )           B      ( ** )           B      ( *
  8    * )             A    ( ** )             A    ( *
```

(continued)

Output 9.12   *(continued)*

CELL DEFINITIONS FOR MARGINALS OVER INDICES INDICATED BY POINTS IN 'A.'.
FOR GROUPING VARIABLES WITH CUTPOINTS 'VALUE' IS THE INCLUSIVE UPPER LIMIT OF THE INTERVAL.

```
                         ALL
CELL        AGE          BRTHPILL
NUMBER       2              5
   1       25ORLESS
   2       26 TO 35
   3       36 TO 45
   4       OVER 45
```

DESCRIPTIVE STATISTICS FOR NON-EMPTY CELLS OF 'A.'

```
        CELL      VARIABLE  6 CHOLSTRL          VARIABLE   9 URICACID
       NUMBER   FREQ.    MEAN     STD.DEV.    FREQ.     MEAN    STD.DEV.

          1      50.   222.12000   37.4442     52.    4.62307   1.0320
          2      60.   224.63333   35.7420     60.    4.62999   1.0524
          3      42.   248.33333   44.8089     42.    4.73809   1.2437
          4      34.   262.05859   43.2673     33.    5.29999   1.3038
```

```
EQUALITY   CHI-SQUARE        7.97849                   8.87165
OF CELL        D.F.          3.                        3.
FREQ.      ALPHA(CHI-SQ)     0.0465                    0.0310

WITHIN   SUM OF SQUARES   288172.06250              237.47621
            D.F.             182.                    183.
          MEAN SQUARE      1583.36279                 1.29768

BETWEEN SUM OF SQUARES    46857.34766                11.61095
            D.F.             3.                       3.
          MEAN SQUARE     15619.11328                 3.87031

EQUALITY      F-VALUE         9.86452                  2.98248
OF MEANS      D.F.-S        3.   192.                3.   183.
             ALPHA(F)         0.0000                   0.0327

HOMOG.    BARTLETT TEST       3.35889                  3.58682
  OF        APPROX. F         1.10897                  1.18421
VARIANCE    D.F.-S         3.  54058.               3.  53838.
             ALPHA(F)         0.3439                   0.3140
```

GROUPED DISTRIBUTIONS OF VARIABLES AT CELLS OF 'A.'
IN THE GRAPHS BELOW POSITIONS ARE DETERMINED BY CELL MEAN VALUES, CHARACTERS INDICATE CELL FREQUENCIES.
WHEN POSITIONS COINCIDE FREQUENCIES ARE SUMMED.

```
           VARIABLE   6 CHOLSTRL          VARIABLE   9 URICACID
  MEAN          236.1505                      4.7706
 ST.DV.          42.555                       1.157

CELL   *-  S   S    M   S    S   +**-  S    S    M   S   S    +*
  1    * )          E             ( ** )           BB          ( *
  2    * )        C   C           ( ** )           CC          ( *
  3    * )            BB          ( ** )           D           ( *
  4    * )              C         ( ** )             AA        ( *
```

(continued)

Output 9.12   *(continued)*

CELL DEFINITIONS FOR MARGINALS OVER INDICES INDICATED BY POINTS IN '.B'.
FOR GROUPING VARIABLES WITH CUTPOINTS 'VALUE' IS THE INCLUSIVE UPPER LIMIT OF THE INTERVAL.

```
            ALL
CELL        AGE        BRTHPILL
NUMBER       2            5
  1                     NOPILL
  2                     PILL
```

DESCRIPTIVE STATISTICS FOR NON-EMPTY CELLS OF '.B'

```
CELL       VARIABLE   6 CHOLSTRL        VARIABLE   9 URICACID
NUMBER   FREQ.    MEAN     STD.DEV.    FREQ.    MEAN     STD.DEV.

  1       94.   232.96808   43.4915     93.    4.74192   1.0352
  2       92.   239.40216   41.5621     94.    4.79893   1.2715


EQUALITY    CHI-SQUARE        0.02151              0.00535
OF CELL        D.F.           1.                   1.
FREQ.    ALPHA(CHI-SQ)        0.8834               0.9417


WITHIN   SUM OF SQUARES   333104.37500          248.93524
            D.F.             184.                 185.
         MEAN SQUARE       1810.34985             1.34560

BETWEEN  SUM OF SQUARES     1924.76099            0.15191
            D.F.             1.                   1.
         MEAN SQUARE       1924.76099             0.15191

EQUALITY    F-VALUE           1.06320             0.11289
OF MEANS    D.F.-S         1.   184.            1.   185.
         ALPHA(F)            0.3038               0.7373


HOMOG.    BARTLETT TEST        0.18945              3.88025
  OF       APPROX. F          0.18843              3.85950
VARIANCE   D.F.-S          1.101536.            1.102667.
          ALPHA(F)            0.6642               0.0495
```

GROUPED DISTRIBUTIONS OF VARIABLES AT CELLS OF '.B'
IN THE GRAPHS BELOW POSITIONS ARE DETERMINED BY CELL MEAN VALUES, CHARACTERS INDICATE CELL FREQUENCIES.
WHEN POSITIONS COINCIDE FREQUENCIES ARE SUMMED.

```
            VARIABLE   6 CHOLSTRL        VARIABLE   9 URICACID
MEAN            236.1505                    4.7706
ST.DV.           42.555                     1.157

CELL   *-  S    S    M   S    S   +**-  S    S    M    S    S   +*
  1    * )         CB   BA       ( ** )              BE  A       ( *
  2    * )        B CB  A        ( ** )              CD  A       ( *
```

--- analysis for the marginal '..' ---

● COMPUTATIONAL METHOD

P9D computes means and standard deviations in single precision by a provisional means algorithm (Appendix A.2). The formula for Bartlett's test is in Appendix A.4.

P9D copies the data to a temporary unit and determines how many variables (V = 1, 2, 3 or 4) to analyze at one time. It then rereads the data from the temporary unit as many times as necessary to analyze all the variables.

ACKNOWLEDGEMENT

P9D was designed and programmed by Laszlo Engelman. Recent revisions were made by Peter Mundle.

9.4 Summary — P3D, P7D, P9D

The Control Language on this page is <u>common</u> to all programs. This is followed by the Control Language specific to

P3D -- Comparison of Two Groups with t Tests	p. 211	
P7D -- Description of Groups (Data) with Histograms and Analysis of Variance	p. 212	
P9D -- Multiway Description of Groups	p. 213	

Paragraph STATEMENT[1] {Preassigned value[2]}		Definition, restriction	See pages:
/PROBlem		Required each problem	74
TITLE='c'.	{blank}	Problem title, $\leq$ 160 char.	74
/INPut		Required first problem. Either VARIABLE and FORMAT, or UNIT and CODE required.	75
VARIABLE=#.	{none/prev.}	No. of variables in input data	75
FORMAT='c'.	{none/prev.}	Format of input data, $\leq$ 800 char.	76
CASE=#.	{end-of-file/prev.}	No. of cases in data	76-77
UNIT=#.	{5(cards)/prev.}	Input unit if data are not on cards; not 1, 2, 6	77
REWIND.	{REWIND/prev.}	Rewind input unit	77
CODE=c.	{none}	Code to identify BMDP File	132
CONTENT=c.	{DATA}	Data or matrix in BMDP File	132
LABEL=c.	{none}	Label of BMDP File, $\leq$ 40 char.	132
/VARiable		Optional. For input from a BMDP File, items in this paragraph may be previously set, see Chapter 7.	79
NAME=$c_1,c_2,\cdots$.	{X(subscript)/prev.}	Variable names, one per variable	79-80
MAXIMUM=$\#_1,\#_2,\cdots$.	{none/prev.}	Upper limits, one per variable	80
MINIMUM=$\#_1,\#_2,\cdots$.	{none/prev.}	Lower limits, one per variable	80
BLANK= *(one only)* ZERO, MISSING.	{ZERO/ prev.}	Blanks treated as zeros or as missing value codes	81
MISSING=$\#_1,\#_2,\cdots$.	{none/prev.}	Missing value codes, one per variable	81
USE=$v_1,v_2,\cdots$.	{all variables}	Variables used in the analysis	82
LABEL=v_1,v_2.	{none/prev.}	Variable(s) used to label cases, read under A-format, one or two	83
ADD=#.	{0/prev.}	No. of variables added through transformation	99
BEFORE. *or* AFTER.	{BEFORE/prev.}	Data checked for limits before or after transformation	100
/TRANsform		Optional, Control Language transformations and case selection	97-105
/SAVE		Optional, required to create BMDP File	125
CODE=c.	{none}	Code to identify BMDP File, required	125-126
LABEL='c'.	{blank}	Label for BMDP File, $\leq$ 40 char.	125-126
UNIT=#.	{none}	Unit on which BMDP File is written; not 1, 2, 5 or 6	126-127
NEW.	{not new}	NEW if this is first BMDP File written in the system file	126-127

Key: #   number
'c' title, label or format

v variable name or subscript
c name not exceeding 8 char., apostrophes may be required (p. 59)

[1] In BMDP programs dated before August 1977, the minimum required abbreviations are *INPUT* (not *INP*), VARIAB (not VAR), FORMAT (not FORM), CONTENT (not CONT), *VARIAB* (not *VAR*), BEFORET (not BEF), AFTERT (not AFT), *TRANSF* (not *TRAN*). If dated before February 1976, BLANK=ZERO and cannot be changed.

[2] "/prev." means that any assignment remains the same as that specified in the previous problem or subproblem until changed. Otherwise, the assignment returns to its preassigned value each time a new problem begins or the paragraph is used again.

P3D -- Comparison of Two Groups with t Tests

(in addition to that on p. 210)

Paragraph STATEMENT[1] {Preassigned value}	Definition, restriction	See pages:
VARiable	Specify as part of *VARiable* paragraph, p. 210	
GROUPing=v. {no grouping/prev.}	Variable used to classify cases into groups	173-174
/GROUP	Optional, required if GROUPING variable has	
	more than 10 distinct values	84
CODE(#)=$\#_1,\#_2,\cdots$. {10 smallest values/prev.}	Codes for variable #, may be repeated	84-85
CUTPOINT(#)=$\#_1,\#_2,\cdots$. {see CODE /prev.}	Cutpoints to form intervals for variable #,	
	may be repeated	84-85
NAME(#)=$c_1,c_2,\cdots$. {CODEs or CUTPOINTs /prev.}	Code or interval names for variable #, may be	
	repeated	84-85
RESET. {not RESET }	If RESET, all assignments in prev. *GROUP*	
	paragraph are reset to preassigned values	86
/TEST	Optional, may be repeated	174
TITLE='c'. {blank}	Title for this analysis, $\leq$ 80 char.	174-175
VARIABLE=$v_1,v_2,\cdots$. {all variables}	Variables for which groups are compared	174-175
GROUP=$g_1,g_2,\cdots$. {all groups}	Groups to be compared in all pairwise	
	combinations	174-175
HOTELLING. {no/prev.}	Compute Hotelling's T^2 and Mahalanobis D^2	177
COMPLETE. {no/prev.}	Use all acceptable data or COMPLETE cases	178-179
CORRELATION. {no/prev.}	Print correlation matrix of each group	179-181
/END	Required each problem	57

Key: v   variable name or subscript   g   group name (assigned in *GROUP* paragraph) or group subscript
       'c' title   c   name not exceeding 8 char., apostrophes may be required (p. 59)

[1] In BMDP programs dated before August 1977, CORRELATION is specified in a *PRINT* paragraph (not in *TEST*) and COMPLETE in the *INPut* paragraph (not in *TEST*); the minimum required abbreviation is VARIAB (not VAR); when a *GROUP* paragraph is used, RESET is implicitly specified and cannot be changed.

- Order of input

  (1) System Cards, at HSCF these are
  ```
  //jobname  JOB  nooo,yourname
  //  EXEC  BIMED,PROG=BMDP3D
  //SYSIN  DD  *
  ```

  (2) Control Language instructions
  ```
  PROBlem paragraph, required
  INPut paragraph, required first problem
  VARiable paragraph
  TRANsform paragraph
  SAVE paragraph
  GROUP paragraph
  TEST paragraph, may be repeated
  END paragraph, required at end of Control Language
  ```

  (3) Data, if on cards
  ```
  data
  ```

  (4) System Card, at HSCF this is
  ```
  //
  ```

  Control Language instructions and data (2 and 3) can be repeated for additional problems.

P7D -- Description of Groups (Strata) with Histograms and Analysis of Variance

(in addition to that on p. 210)

Paragraph STATEMENT[1] {Preassigned value}	Definition, restriction	See pages:
/HISTogram	Required	189
GROUPING=v. *or* v_1,v_2. {none }	Variables used to classify cases. If v, one-way ANOVA; if v_1,v_2, two-way ANOVA.	190, 191-193
VARIABLE=v_1,v_2,···. {all variables/prev.}	Variables for which groups are compared	190
INCREMENT=$\#_1$,$\#_2$,···. {(max-min)/ INTERVAL}	Scale for base of histogram, one per variable	190-191
INTERVAL=$\#_1$,$\#_2$,···. {zero/prev.}	Number of intervals in histogram. If zero, set to minimum (30, 10 $\log_{10}$N). One per variable.	190-191
/GROUP	Optional, required if GROUPING variable has more than 10 distinct values	84
CODE(#)=$\#_1$,$\#_2$,···. {10 smallest values/prev.}	Codes for variable #, may be repeated	84-85
CUTPOINT(#)=$\#_1$,$\#_2$,···. {see CODE/ prev.}	Cutpoints to form intervals for variable #, may be repeated	84-85
NAME(#)=c_1,c_2,···. {CODEs or CUTPOINTs/prev.}	Code or interval names for variable #, may be repeated	84-85
RESET. {not RESET }	If RESET, all assignments in prev. *GROUP* paragraph are reset to preassigned values	86
/PRINT	Optional	
DATA. {no/prev.}	Print input data	193-195
ORDER. {no/prev.}	Print input data ordered by the grouping variable	193-195
CORRELATION. {no/prev.}	Print correlations between all variables	195-196
WINSOR. {no/prev.}	Print Winsorized means	196-197
/END	Required each problem	57

Key: # number c name not exceeding 8 char., apostrophes may be required (p.59)
     v variable name or subscript

[1] In BMDP programs dated before August 1977, if more than one GROUPING variable is specified, each is used in turn to classify cases; the minimum required abbreviation is VARIAB (not VAR); when a *GROUP* paragraph is used, RESET is implicitly specified and cannot be changed.

- Order of Input

    (1) System Cards, at HSCF these are
```
//jobname JOB nooo,yourname
//  EXEC  BIMED,PROG=BMDP7D
//SYSIN  DD  *
```

    (2) Control Language instructions
```
PROBlem paragraph, required
INPut paragraph, required first problem
VARiable paragraph
TRANsform paragraph
SAVE paragraph
HISTogram paragraph, required, may be repeated
GROUP paragraph
PRINT paragraph
END paragraph, required at end of Control Language
```

    (3) Data, if on cards
```
data
```

    (4) System Card, at HSCF this is
```
//
```

Control Language instructions and data (2 and 3) can be repeated for additional problems.

P9D -- Multiway Description of Groups

(in addition to that on p. 210)

Paragraph STATEMENT[1] {Preassigned value}		Definition, restriction	See pages:
/TABULate		Required	202-203
GROUPING=$v_1,v_2,\cdots$.	{none/prev.}	Variables used to classify cases, required	202-203
VARIABLE=$v_1,v_2,\cdots$.	{all variables}	Variables to be analyzed	202-203
PLOTMEANS.	{no/prev.}	Plot means of each group	203-204
MARGIN='c_1','c_2',$\cdots$.	{all groups}	Marginal description of groups to be described	204-205
/GROUP		Optional, required if any GROUPING variable has more than 10 distinct values	84
CODE(#)=$\#_1,\#_2,\cdots$.	{10 smallest values/prev.}	Codes for variable #, may be repeated	84-85
CUTPOINT(#)=$\#_1,\#_2,\cdots$.	{see CODE/prev.}	Cutpoints to form intervals for variable #, may be repeated	84-85
NAME(#)=$c_1,c_2,\cdots$.	{CODEs or CUTPOINTs /prev.}	Code or interval names for variable #, may be repeated	84-85
RESET.	{not RESET}	If RESET, all assignments in prev. GROUP paragraphs are reset to preassigned values	86
/END		Required each problem	57

Key: v variable name or subscript   c name not exceeding 8 char., apostrophes may be required (p. 59)
      'c' marginal configurations (see p. 205)

[1] In BMDP programs dated before August 1977, INDEX must be used in place of GROUPING and DESCRIBE in place of
PLOTMEANS in the *TABULATE* (not *TABUL*) paragraph; when a *GROUP* paragraph is used, RESET is implicitly specified and <u>cannot</u> be changed.

- Order of input

     (1) System Cards, at HSCF these are
```
//jobname  JOB  nooo,yourname
//   EXEC  BIMED,PROG=BMDP9D
//SYSIN DD  *
```

     (2) Control Language instructions
```
PROBlem paragraph, required
INPut paragraph, required first problem
VARiable paragraph
TRANsform paragraph
SAVE paragraph
TABULate paragraph, required
GROUP paragraph
END paragraph, required at end of Control Language
```

     (3) Data, if on cards
```
data
```

     (4) Control Language instructions
         to specify an additional
         analysis of the same data
```
TABULate paragraph
GROUP paragraph
END paragraph, required at end of Control Language
```

     (5) System Card, at HSCF this is
```
//
```

     Control Language instructions *TABULate*, *GROUP* and *END*, terminated by *END* (4), can be repeated for additional
analyses of the same data.

     Control Language instructions and data (2 - 4) can be repeated for analyses of additional data sets.

10

PLOTS AND HISTOGRAMS

A graphical display is a very useful way to describe data, reveal unusual values or discover relationships between variables. The data for a variable can be plotted as a histogram of the frequency distribution or of the cumulative distribution, or as a graph of the data values in a normal or half-normal probability plot. To demonstrate relationships between two variables the data for one variable can be plotted against the data for the other variable in a scatter plot.

In this chapter we describe two programs that produce graphical displays.

P5D -- Histograms and Univariate Plots   p. 217
P6D -- Bivariate (Scatter) Plots   p. 230

P5D prints histograms of the frequency distribution and of the cumulative distribution function. The cases can be classified into groups and plotted in a single figure using different symbols for each group. The frequency distribution and cumulative distribution are printed beside each histogram, both as frequencies and as percentages.

P5D prints normal or half-normal probability plots of the data. The linear trend can be removed from a normal probability plot before printing it; this produces a detrended normal probability plot. Normal probability plots can be used to screen data or residuals for nonnormality or for the presence of outliers. P5D also plots cumulative frequencies against the data values. When the cases are classified into groups, the data for several groups can be plotted in the same graph; each group is uniquely identified. The frequency, mean and standard deviation are printed for each group.

P6D plots one variable against another variable in a scatter plot. It computes and prints equations of the simple linear regressions relating each variable to the other, and indicates the intersections of the regression lines with the frame of the plot. The cases can be classified into groups; the data for one or more groups can be plotted in a single frame and the data points identified by group. More than one pair of variables can be plotted in a single plot. The size of the plots can be specified.

Histograms are plotted in three BMDP programs other than P5D:

- P2D (Section 8.2) produces a compact histogram (a maximum of 40 characters wide and 10 characters high) for each variable

- P3D (Section 9.1) plots two side-by-side compact histograms (each a maximum of 20 characters wide and 6 characters high) for each variable when the cases are classified into two groups.

- P7D (Section 9.2) plots side-by-side histograms for each variable when the cases are classified into one or more groups. The bases of the histograms are plotted vertically and a scale is printed along the base.

Normal probability plots of residuals are available in all regression programs (Chapters 13 and 14, and in P6R, Section 18.3).

Scatter plots are produced by many BMDP programs as an aid in interpreting the analysis. For example, the regression programs (Chapters 13 and 14) plot residuals and predicted values against the observed data. However, you may want to plot one variable against another variable (where variable may refer to a residual, predicted value, factor score or any function of the data) in a manner not permitted by the BMDP program you are using to perform an analysis. The data matrix, augmented by the residuals, predicted values or factor scores, can be saved in a BMDP File and then input to P6D to produce the desired plots.

● CONTROL LANGUAGE

The Control Language instructions to describe the data and variables are common to all BMDP programs and are explained in Chapter 5: the *PROBlem*, *INPut*[1], *VARiable* and *GROUP* paragraph are used in the programs discussed in this chapter. If data editing or transformations are necessary, the methods described in Chapter 6 can be used. Data can be read using a FORMAT statement or from a BMDP File (Chapter 7). If a BMDP File is read as input and a new BMDP File is created in the same problem, the two Files must be in different system files and must have different UNIT numbers.

A summary of the Control Language instructions common to all BMDP programs is on p. 241; summaries of the Control Language instructions specific to each program described in this chapter follow the general summary. These summaries can be used as indexes to the program descriptions.

---

[1] BMDP programs dated before August 1977 require more letters than are shown in this manual in their permissible abbreviated form (the capitalized letters). The minimum required abbreviations for earlier versions are specified in footnotes to the summary (p. 241).

P5D

10.1 Histograms and Univariate Plots

Steve Chasen, HSCF

P5D prints histograms of the frequency distribution and of the cumulative distribution function. The cases can be classified into groups and plotted in a single figure using different symbols for each group. The frequency distribution and cumulative distribution are printed beside each histogram, both as frequencies and as percentages.

P5D prints a normal or half-normal probability plot of the data. The linear trend can be removed from a normal probability plot before printing it; this produces a <u>detrended</u> normal probability plot. Normal probability plots can be used to screen data or residuals for nonnormality or for the presence of outliers. P5D also plots cumulative frequencies against the data values.

When the cases are classified into groups, the data for any number of groups can be plotted in the same graph with each group uniquely identified. For example, you can request separate histograms for each group and one histogram for all groups combined. The frequency, mean and standard deviation are printed for each group.

● THE *PLOT* PARAGRAPH

The *PLOT* paragraph is required in P5D. If all you want are histograms for each variable as in Example 10.1 below, you can specify only

        /PLOT

since histograms are the preassigned option.

If you want additional plots, the *PLOT* paragraph can be used to specify
   - the types of plots   pp. 217-224
   - the variables plotted   p. 224
   - the groups plotted when the cases are
     classified into groups   p. 224
   - the size and scale of plots   p. 227

The *PLOT* paragraph can be repeated before *END* to specify more than one set of plots.

● HISTOGRAMS

We use the Werner blood chemistry data (Table 5.1) to illustrate the plots produced by P5D. The Control Language instructions in Example 10.1 are described in Chapter 5. Preassigned options are used in the *PLOT* paragraph.

10.1 PLOTS AND HISTOGRAMS

Example 10.1

```
/PROBLEM       TITLE IS 'WERNER BLOOD CHEMISTRY DATA'.
/INPUT         VARIABLES ARE 9.
               FORMAT IS '(A4,5F4.C,3F4.1)'.
/VARIABLE      NAMES ARE ID,AGE,HEIGHT,WEIGHT,BRTHPILL,
                  CHOLSTRL,ALBUMIN,CALCIUM,URICACID.
               MAXIMUM IS (6)400.
               MINIMUM IS (6)150.
               BLANKS ARE MISSING.
               LABEL IS ID.

/PLOT

/END
```

The Control Language must be preceded by System Cards to initiate the analysis by P5D. At HSCF, the System Cards are

```
//jobname  JOB  nooo,yourname
//  EXEC  BIMED,PROG=BMDP5D
//SYSIN  DD  *
```

The Control Language is immediately followed by the data (Table 5.1). The analysis is terminated by another System Card. At HSCF, this System Card is

```
//
```

The Control Language instructions in Example 10.1 produce one histogram for each variable. In Output 10.1 only the histogram produced for CHOLSTRL is presented.

Output 10.1 Example of a histogram printed by P5D. Results not reproduced are indicated in italics.

```
BMDP5D - HISTOGRAMS AND UNIVARIATE PLOTS          PROGRAM REVISED SEPTEMBER 1977
HEALTH SCIENCES COMPUTING FACILITY                MANUAL DATE  —  1977
UNIVERSITY OF CALIFORNIA, LOS ANGELES
```

--- Control Language read by P5D is printed and interpreted ---

```
NUMBER OF CASES READ. . . . . . . . . . . . .     188
```

--- table of contents to the plots (histograms) is printed ---

--- histograms for variables 2 to 5 ---

```
HISTOGRAM OF VARIABLE    6 CHOLSTRL
                          SYMBOL   COUNT      MEAN      ST.DEV.
                            X       186     236.150     42.555
INTERVAL                                                                        FREQUENCY PERCENTAGE
NAME       5   10   15   20   25   30   35   40   45   50   55   60   65   70   75   80   INT. CUM. INT.  CUM.
         +----+----+----+----+----+----+----+----+----+----+----+----+----+----+----+----+
* 150.00 +                                                                          0    0    0.0   0.0
* 165.00 +XXXXX                                                                     5    5    2.7   2.7
* 180.00 +XXXXXXXXXXXXXXX                                                          15   20    8.1  10.8
* 195.00 +XXXXXXXXXXX                                                              11   31    5.9  16.7
* 210.00 +XXXXXXXXXXXXXXXXXXXXXXXXXXXXX                                            29   60   15.6  32.3
* 225.00 +XXXXXXXXXXXXXXXXXX                                                       18   78    9.7  41.9
* 240.00 +XXXXXXXXXXXXXXXXXXXXXXXXXX                                               26  104   14.0  55.9
* 255.00 +XXXXXXXXXXXXXXXXXXXXXXXXXXXX                                             28  132   15.1  71.0
* 270.00 +XXXXXXXXXXXXXXXXXXXX                                                     20  152   10.8  81.7
* 285.00 +XXXXXXXXXX                                                               10  162    5.4  87.1
* 300.00 +XXXXXXXXX                                                                 9  171    4.8  91.9
* 315.00 +XXXXXX                                                                    6  177    3.2  95.2
* 330.00 +XXXXX                                                                     6  183    3.2  98.4
* 345.00 +XX                                                                        2  185    1.1  99.5
* 360.00 +                                                                          0  185    0.0  99.5
* 375.00 +                                                                          0  185    0.0  99.5
* 390.00 +X                                                                         1  186    0.5 100.0
* 405.00 +                                                                          0  186    0.0 100.0
* 420.00 +                                                                          0  186    0.0 100.0
* 435.00 +                                                                          0  186    0.0 100.0
         +----+----+----+----+----+----+----+----+----+----+----+----+----+----+----+----+
           5   10   15   20   25   30   35   40   45   50   55   60   65   70   75   80
```

--- histograms for variables 7 to 9 ---

The base of the histogram is the vertical axis. The number of X's printed in a line (horizontally) is the frequency of cases. Each value on the vertical axis represents the upper limit of the interval. Therefore there are five cases greater than 150 and less than or equal to 165.

The frequency of observations in each interval and the cumulative frequency of observations up to and including the interval, as well as the percents of observations represented by the frequency and the cumulative frequency, are printed to the right of the histogram.

When there are more observations than can be printed in a single line, the entire line is filled with X's terminated by an asterisk; the exact frequency is printed to the right of the line.

● NORMAL PROBABILITY PLOTS

Three types of normal probability plots are produced by P5D. All three types are requested in Example 10.2. The SIZE of each plot is also specified. If SIZE is not specified, each plot fills a computer page (80 characters wide and 50 lines high); we have reduced the size of the plots to 40 characters wide and 25 lines high.

Example 10.2

```
/PROBLEM      TITLE IS 'WERNER BLOOD CHEMISTRY DATA'.
/INPUT        VARIABLES ARE 9.
              FORMAT IS '(A4,5F4.0,3F4.1)'.
/VARIABLE     NAMES ARE ID,AGE,HEIGHT,WEIGHT,BRTHPILL,
                  CHOLSTRL,ALBUMIN,CALCIUM,URICACID.
              MAXIMUM IS (6)400.
              MINIMUM IS (6)150.
              BLANKS ARE MISSING.
              LABEL IS ID.

/PLOT         TYPES ARE NORM,HALFNORM,DNORM.
              SIZE IS 40,25.

/END
```

The three probability plots are printed for each variable. In Output 10.2 we present only the plots for CHOLSTRL.

Normal probability plots

The observed values are plotted along the horizontal axis. The data values are ordered before plotting: the vertical axis corresponds to the expected normal value based on the rank of the observation. Let $x_{(1)}, x_{(2)}, \ldots$ represent the data values after ordering from smallest to largest. The subscript (j) is the rank order of the observation. If N is the total frequency, the vertical plotting position corresponds to the expected normal value for the relative rank (j out of N) of the observation. The expected normal value is estimated as

$$\Phi^{-1}[(3j-1)/(3N+1)],$$

Output 10.2 Normal probability plots printed by P5D. Only those for CHOLSTRL are shown.

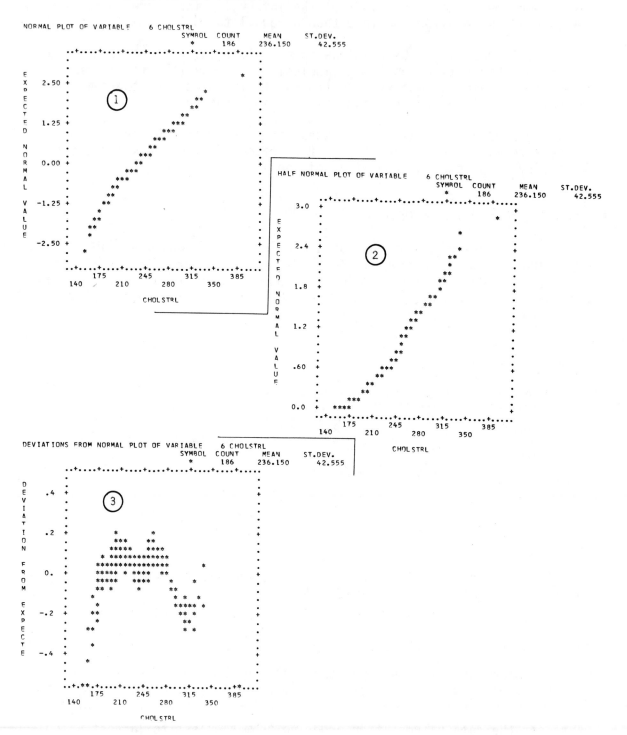

Key: ① Normal probability plot
      ② Half-normal probability plot
      ③ Detrended normal probability plot

the standard normal value corresponding to the probability $(3j-1)/(3N+1)$. If the data are from a normal distribution, this line will be straight, except for random fluctuations.

Detrended normal probability plot

This is similar to the normal probability plot except that the linear trend is removed before the plot is printed. The vertical scale represents the differences between the expected normal values and the standardized values of the observations. That is, each observation is transformed into a standardized value by subtracting the mean and dividing by the standard deviation; i.e., $z_{(j)} = (x_{(j)} - \bar{x})/s$. We then compute

$$\Phi^{-1}[(3j-1)/(3N+1)] - z_{(j)} \quad .$$

Half-normal plot

This is also similar to the normal plot; however, the expected values are computed by using only the positive half of the normal distribution. The expected value of the jth observation (after ordering) is estimated by

$$\Phi^{-1}[(3N+3j-1)/(6N+1)]$$

This plot is primarily used in residual plots when you want to ignore the sign of the residual; for example, when the residual is proportional to the square root of a chi-square variate with one degree of freedom (Daniel, 1959).

● A CUMULATIVE FREQUENCY PLOT

In a cumulative frequency plot the cumulative frequency distribution is plotted against the data values. P5D prints a cumulative frequency plot when

TYPE=CUM.

is specified in the *PLOT* paragraph.

Example 10.3

```
/PROBLEM     TITLE IS 'WERNER BLOOD CHEMISTRY DATA'.
/INPUT       VARIABLES ARE 9.
             FORMAT IS '(A4,5F4.0,3F4.1)'.
/VARIABLE    NAMES ARE ID,AGE,HEIGHT,WEIGHT,BRTHPILL,
                  CHOLSTRL,ALBUMIN,CALCIUM,URICACID.
             MAXIMUM IS (6)400.
             MINIMUM IS (6)150.
             BLANKS ARE MISSING.
             LABEL IS ID.

/PLOT        TYPE IS CUM.
             SIZE IS 40,25.

/END
```

The cumulative frequency plot for CHOLSTRL is presented in Output 10.3. The cumulative frequency distribution is plotted on the vertical axis and the data values on the horizontal axis. This plot is similar to a cumulative histogram (see Output 10.4) except that the area under the curve is not filled with asterisks.

- ● A CUMULATIVE HISTOGRAM

A cumulative histogram shows the frequencies accumulated over all data values less than or equal to the plotted frequency. P5D prints a cumulative histogram when

         TYPE=CHIST.

is specified in the *PLOT* paragraph.

Output 10.3 Cumulative frequency plot printed by P5D. Only the plot for CHOLSTRL is shown.

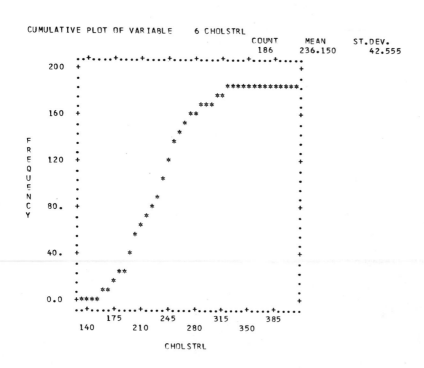

Example 10.4

```
/PROBLEM       TITLE IS 'WERNER BLOOD CHEMISTRY DATA'.
/INPUT         VARIABLES ARE 9.
               FORMAT IS '(A4,5F4.0,3F4.1)'.
/VARIABLE      NAMES ARE ID,AGE,HEIGHT,WEIGHT,BRTHPILL,
                   CHOLSTRL,ALBUMIN,CALCIUM,URICACID.
               MAXIMUM IS (6)400.
               MINIMUM IS (6)150.
               BLANKS ARE MISSING.
               LABEL IS ID.

/PLOT          TYPE IS CHIST.

/END
```

The cumulative histogram for CHOLSTRL is presented in Output 10.4 (and again in Output 10.6 with a different, and improved, scale). The base is the vertical axis. The number of X's printed in a line corresponds to the cumulative frequency of cases up to and including the value printed on the vertical axis. Therefore, there are twenty cases less than or equal to 180. The same four columns of frequencies and percents as in the histogram shown in Output 10.1 are printed to the right of the cumulative histogram.

When there are more observations than can be printed in a single line, the entire line is filled with X's terminated by an asterisk. The cumulative frequency can be read from the second column of frequencies to the right of the plot.

Output 10.4   Cumulative histogram printed by P5D. Only the histogram for
              CHOLSTRL is shown.

```
CUMULATIVE HISTOGRAM OF VARIABLE    6 CHOLSTRL
                           SYMBOL  COUNT      MEAN       ST.DEV.
                             X      186      236.150      42.555
INTERVAL                                                                        FREQUENCY PERCENTAGE
NAME        5   10   15   20   25   30   35   40   45   50   55   60   65   70   75   80    INT. CUM.  INT.  CUM.
          +----+----+----+----+----+----+----+----+----+----+----+----+----+----+----+----+
* 150.00  +                                                                                 0    0    0.0    0.0
* 165.00  +XXXXX                                                                            5    5    2.7    2.7
* 180.00  +XXXXXXXXXXXXXXXXXXXX                                                             15   20    8.1   10.8
* 195.00  +XXXXXXXXXXXXXXXXXXXXXXXXXXXXXXX                                                  11   31    5.9   16.7
* 210.00  +XXXXXXXXXXXXXXXXXXXXXXXXXXXXXXXXXXXXXXXXXXXXXXXXXXXXXXXXXXXXXXX                  29   60   15.6   32.3
* 225.00  +XXXXXXXXXXXXXXXXXXXXXXXXXXXXXXXXXXXXXXXXXXXXXXXXXXXXXXXXXXXXXXXXXXXXXXXXXX       18   78    9.7   41.9
* 240.00  +XXXXXXXXXXXXXXXXXXXXXXXXXXXXXXXXXXXXXXXXXXXXXXXXXXXXXXXXXXXXXXXXXXXXXXXXXXXX*     26  104   14.0   55.9
* 255.00  +XXXXXXXXXXXXXXXXXXXXXXXXXXXXXXXXXXXXXXXXXXXXXXXXXXXXXXXXXXXXXXXXXXXXXXXXXXXX*     28  132   15.1   71.0
* 270.00  +XXXXXXXXXXXXXXXXXXXXXXXXXXXXXXXXXXXXXXXXXXXXXXXXXXXXXXXXXXXXXXXXXXXXXXXXXXXX*     20  152   10.8   81.7
* 285.00  +XXXXXXXXXXXXXXXXXXXXXXXXXXXXXXXXXXXXXXXXXXXXXXXXXXXXXXXXXXXXXXXXXXXXXXXXXXXX*     10  162    5.4   87.1
* 300.00  +XXXXXXXXXXXXXXXXXXXXXXXXXXXXXXXXXXXXXXXXXXXXXXXXXXXXXXXXXXXXXXXXXXXXXXXXXXXX*      9  171    4.8   91.9
* 315.00  +XXXXXXXXXXXXXXXXXXXXXXXXXXXXXXXXXXXXXXXXXXXXXXXXXXXXXXXXXXXXXXXXXXXXXXXXXXXX*      6  177    3.2   95.2
* 330.00  +XXXXXXXXXXXXXXXXXXXXXXXXXXXXXXXXXXXXXXXXXXXXXXXXXXXXXXXXXXXXXXXXXXXXXXXXXXXX*      6  183    3.2   98.4
* 345.00  +XXXXXXXXXXXXXXXXXXXXXXXXXXXXXXXXXXXXXXXXXXXXXXXXXXXXXXXXXXXXXXXXXXXXXXXXXXXX*      2  185    1.1   99.5
* 360.00  +XXXXXXXXXXXXXXXXXXXXXXXXXXXXXXXXXXXXXXXXXXXXXXXXXXXXXXXXXXXXXXXXXXXXXXXXXXXX*      0  185    0.0   99.5
* 375.00  +XXXXXXXXXXXXXXXXXXXXXXXXXXXXXXXXXXXXXXXXXXXXXXXXXXXXXXXXXXXXXXXXXXXXXXXXXXXX*      0  185    0.0   99.5
* 390.00  +XXXXXXXXXXXXXXXXXXXXXXXXXXXXXXXXXXXXXXXXXXXXXXXXXXXXXXXXXXXXXXXXXXXXXXXXXXXX*      1  186    0.5  100.0
* 405.00  +XXXXXXXXXXXXXXXXXXXXXXXXXXXXXXXXXXXXXXXXXXXXXXXXXXXXXXXXXXXXXXXXXXXXXXXXXXXX*      0  186    0.0  100.0
* 420.00  +XXXXXXXXXXXXXXXXXXXXXXXXXXXXXXXXXXXXXXXXXXXXXXXXXXXXXXXXXXXXXXXXXXXXXXXXXXXX*      0  186    0.0  100.0
* 435.00  +XXXXXXXXXXXXXXXXXXXXXXXXXXXXXXXXXXXXXXXXXXXXXXXXXXXXXXXXXXXXXXXXXXXXXXXXXXXX*      0  186    0.0  100.0
          +----+----+----+----+----+----+----+----+----+----+----+----+----+----+----+----+
            5   10   15   20   25   30   35   40   45   50   55   60   65   70   75   80
```

```
PLOT
    TYPE= (one or more) HIST,NORM,HALFNORM,
          DNORM,CUM,CHIST.                         {HIST/ prev. }

        The types of plots to be printed, where

            HIST      ≡ histogram
            NORM      ≡ normal probability plot
            HALFNORM  ≡ halfnormal plot
            DNORM     ≡ detrended normal probability plot
            CUM       ≡ cumulative frequency distribution plot
            CHIST     ≡ cumulative histogram

        These plots are illustrated in Outputs 10.1-10.4.  The desired
        types must be spelled exactly as shown above, separated by commas
        and terminated by a period.
```

● SELECTING VARIABLES TO BE PLOTTED

All variables are plotted unless a selection is specified. Specification can be made by either USE in the *VARiable* paragraph (Section 5.3) or by VARIABLE[2] in the *PLOT* paragraph.

In Outputs 10.1 to 10.4 we present only the plots for CHOLSTRL although plots for all the variables are printed. If we add

            VARIABLE IS CHOLSTRL.

to the *PLOT* paragraph in each example, only the plot for CHOLSTRL is printed.

```
PLOT
    VARIABLE=v₁,v₂,···.                  {all variables/prev.}

        Names or subscripts of variables to be plotted.
```

● SELECTING GROUPS TO BE PLOTTED

Cases can be classified into groups by specifying a GROUPING variable in the *VARiable* paragraph. For example

            GROUPING IS BRTHPILL.

in the *VARiable* paragraph specifies that cases are classified according to the values of BRTHPILL. A *GROUP* paragraph is required when the GROUPING variable is continuous or takes on more than 10 distinct values. A *GROUP* paragraph is also used to name the groups.

---

[2] If your BMDP programs are dated before August 1977,
      the minimum required abbreviation is VARIAB (not VAR).

When a GROUPING variable is specified, each group can be printed in an individual plot or specified groups can be combined into a single plot. Each group can be identified by a different symbol. We use the following example to demonstrate the effect of grouping cases.

Example 10.5

```
/PROBLEM      TITLE IS 'WERNER BLOOD CHEMISTRY DATA'.
/INPUT        VARIABLES ARE 9.
              FORMAT IS '(A4,5F4.0,3F4.1)'.
/VARIABLE     NAMES ARE ID,AGE,HEIGHT,WEIGHT,BRTHPILL,
                    CHOLSTRL,ALBUMIN,CALCIUM,URICACID.
              MAXIMUM IS (6)400.
              MINIMUM IS (6)150.
              BLANKS ARE MISSING.
              LABEL IS ID.
              GROUPING IS BRTHPILL.

/GROUP        CODES(5) ARE      1,    2.
              NAMES(5) ARE NOPILL, PILL.

/PLOT         VARIABLE IS CHOLSTRL.
              TYPES ARE HIST,NORM.
              GROUP IS NOPILL.
              GROUPS ARE NOPILL,PILL.
              SIZE IS 40,25.

/END
```

In the *PLOT* paragraph we specify that HISTOGRAMS and NORMAL probability plots are to be printed for CHOLSTRL. Each GROUP statement describes a different plot. Therefore first the group NOPILL is plotted by itself and then the groups NOPILL and PILL are plotted together.

The plots are shown in Output 10.5. The first histogram and normal plot contain only A's, the symbol assigned to the first group (NOPILL). The second histogram and normal plot contain both A's and B's (PILL). Above each plot are the names of the groups printed, their symbols, frequencies, mean and standard deviations. In the normal plots each group is plotted separately; asterisks indicate group overlap.

VARiable
  GROUPING= v.   {no grouping/prev.}

  Name or subscript of the variable used to classify the cases into groups. If not specified or if set to zero, the cases are not grouped. If the GROUPING variable takes on more than 10 distinct values or codes, CODEs or CUTPOINTS for the variable must be specified in the *GROUP* paragraph (Section 5.4).

Output 10.5 Histograms and probability plots with symbols representing groups.

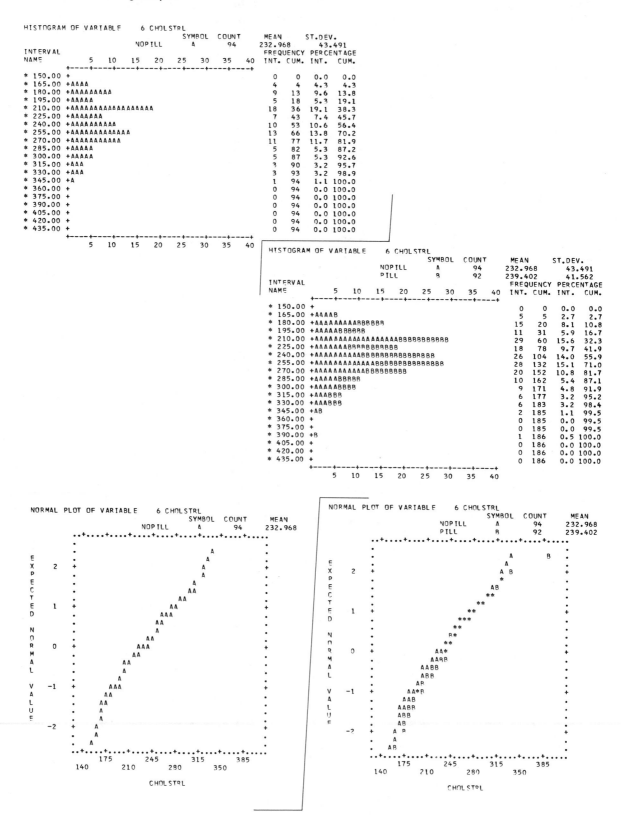

```
PLOT
    GROUP=g_1,g_2,···.        {all groups}              can be repeated

        g_1,g_2,··· are the group NAMEs (from the GROUP paragraph) or
        group subscripts. The specified groups are plotted in the same
        graph. A group subscript is the sequence number of the group as
        specified in the GROUP paragraph. The GROUP statement can be
        repeated in the PLOT paragraph. Each GROUP statement defines a
        separate plot.
```

● THE SIZE AND SCALE OF PLOTS

In Examples 10.2 and 10.3 we specify

SIZE=40,25.

in the PLOT paragraph. The first number (40) determines the number of characters for the horizontal axis (width) and the second the number of lines for the vertical axis (height) of the normal probability plots and the cumulative frequency plot. If not specified, SIZE is preassigned to 80 characters wide and 50 lines high.

The width of the histogram and of the cumulative histogram is also determined by the first number assigned to SIZE (40 in our example). The height of the histogram is the number of codes or intervals specified for the variable in the GROUP paragraph (each line represents a code or an interval); if neither is specified the height is determined by $8 \log_{10}(N) + 2$, where N is the number of cases read.

You can specify upper and lower limits for the scale printed along the horizontal axis of the normal probability plots and the cumulative frequency plot, and along the vertical axis of the histograms. Upper and lower limits are specified by setting MAXIMUMS[3] and MINIMUMS[3] for the variables in the PLOT paragraph. Observations greater than the maximum or less than the minimum for a variable are not plotted and are <u>not</u> used in computations.

```
PLOT
    MINIMUM= #_1,#_2,···.      {none/prev.}          one per variable

        Lower limits for the variables. #_1 is the lower limit for the first
        variable, #_2 for the second, etc. If a lower limit is specified, it
        is used as the lower limit of the plot's scale and values less than
        the lower limit are omitted from the plot and from all computations.
```

(continued)

---

[3] If your BMDP programs are dated before August 1977,
    MINIMUMS and MAXIMUMS specified in the VARiable paragraph are used
    as limits for the plots; MINIMUMS and MAXIMUMS cannot be specified in
    the PLOT paragraph.

```
PLOT
   MAXIMUM= #₁,#₂,···.              {none/prev.}              one per variable
```

$$MAXIMUM= \#_1,\#_2,\cdots. \qquad \{none/prev.\} \qquad \text{one per variable}$$

Upper limits for the variables. $\#_1$ is the upper limit for the first variable, etc. If an upper limit is specified, it is used as the upper limit of the plot's scale and values greater than the upper limit are omitted from the plot and from all computations.

The scale for the horizontal axis of the histograms is the integers 1,2,... up to the width of the plot. This scale can be reset by specifying the origin and the frequency represented by each symbol. For example

SCALE=0,3.

specifies that 0 is the frequency at the base of the histogram and each symbol represents three units. This is demonstrated in the following example.

Example 10.6

```
/PROBLEM      TITLE IS 'WERNER BLOOD CHEMISTRY DATA'.
/INPUT        VARIABLES ARE 9.
              FORMAT IS '(A4,5F4.0,3F4.1)'.
/VARIABLE     NAMES ARE ID,AGE,HEIGHT,WEIGHT,BRTHPILL,
                   CHOLSTRL,ALBUMIN,CALCIUM,URICACID.
              MAXIMUM IS (6)400.
              MINIMUM IS (6)150.
              BLANKS ARE MISSING.
              LABEL IS ID.

/PLOT         VARIABLE IS CHOLSTRL.
              TYPE IS CHIST.
              SCALE IS 0,3.

/END
```

The cumulative histogram with a reset scale is printed in Output 10.6. Compare this with the one in Output 10.4, which uses the preassigned scale.

Output 10.6 Cumulative histogram for CHOLSTRL with a modified scale. Compare this with Output 10.4.

```
CUMULATIVE HISTOGRAM OF VARIABLE    6 CHOLSTRL
                                  SYMBOL   COUNT      MEAN      ST.DEV.
                                    X       186     236.150     42.555
INTERVAL                                                                                      FREQUENCY  PERCENTAGE
NAME        15   30   45   60   75   90  105  120  135  150  165  180  195  210  225  240      INT. CUM.  INT.  CUM.
            +----+----+----+----+----+----+----+----+----+----+----+----+----+----+----+----+
* 150.00 +                                                                                      0    0    0.0    0.0
* 165.00 +XX                                                                                    5    5    2.7    2.7
* 180.00 +XXXXXX                                                                               15   20    8.1   10.8
* 195.00 +XXXXXXXXXX                                                                           11   31    5.9   16.7
* 210.00 +XXXXXXXXXXXXXXXXXXXX                                                                 29   60   15.6   32.3
* 225.00 +XXXXXXXXXXXXXXXXXXXXXXXXX                                                            18   78    9.7   41.9
* 240.00 +XXXXXXXXXXXXXXXXXXXXXXXXXXXXXXXXXXXX                                                 26  104   14.0   55.9
* 255.00 +XXXXXXXXXXXXXXXXXXXXXXXXXXXXXXXXXXXXXXXXXXXXXXX                                      28  132   15.1   71.0
* 270.00 +XXXXXXXXXXXXXXXXXXXXXXXXXXXXXXXXXXXXXXXXXXXXXXXXXXXXXXX                              20  152   10.8   81.7
* 285.00 +XXXXXXXXXXXXXXXXXXXXXXXXXXXXXXXXXXXXXXXXXXXXXXXXXXXXXXXXXXX                          10  162    5.4   87.1
* 300.00 +XXXXXXXXXXXXXXXXXXXXXXXXXXXXXXXXXXXXXXXXXXXXXXXXXXXXXXXXXXXXXXX                        9  171    4.8   91.9
* 315.00 +XXXXXXXXXXXXXXXXXXXXXXXXXXXXXXXXXXXXXXXXXXXXXXXXXXXXXXXXXXXXXXXXXX                     6  177    3.2   95.2
* 330.00 +XXXXXXXXXXXXXXXXXXXXXXXXXXXXXXXXXXXXXXXXXXXXXXXXXXXXXXXXXXXXXXXXXXXXX                  6  183    3.2   98.4
* 345.00 +XXXXXXXXXXXXXXXXXXXXXXXXXXXXXXXXXXXXXXXXXXXXXXXXXXXXXXXXXXXXXXXXXXXXXXX                2  185    1.1   99.5
* 360.00 +XXXXXXXXXXXXXXXXXXXXXXXXXXXXXXXXXXXXXXXXXXXXXXXXXXXXXXXXXXXXXXXXXXXXXXX                0  185    0.0   99.5
* 375.00 +XXXXXXXXXXXXXXXXXXXXXXXXXXXXXXXXXXXXXXXXXXXXXXXXXXXXXXXXXXXXXXXXXXXXXXX                0  185    0.0   99.5
* 390.00 +XXXXXXXXXXXXXXXXXXXXXXXXXXXXXXXXXXXXXXXXXXXXXXXXXXXXXXXXXXXXXXXXXXXXXXXX               1  186    0.5  100.0
* 405.00 +XXXXXXXXXXXXXXXXXXXXXXXXXXXXXXXXXXXXXXXXXXXXXXXXXXXXXXXXXXXXXXXXXXXXXXXX               0  186    0.0  100.0
* 420.00 +XXXXXXXXXXXXXXXXXXXXXXXXXXXXXXXXXXXXXXXXXXXXXXXXXXXXXXXXXXXXXXXXXXXXXXXX               0  186    0.0  100.0
* 435.00 +XXXXXXXXXXXXXXXXXXXXXXXXXXXXXXXXXXXXXXXXXXXXXXXXXXXXXXXXXXXXXXXXXXXXXXXX               0  186    0.0  100.0
            +----+----+----+----+----+----+----+----+----+----+----+----+----+----+----+----+
                15   30   45   60   75   90  105  120  135  150  165  180  195  210  225  240
```

PLOT

    SIZE=$\#_1$,$\#_2$.   {80,50/prev.} $\#_1 \leq 100$

        $\#_1$ is the number of characters in the horizontal axis (width) of all six types of plots. $\#_2$ is the number of characters (lines) in the vertical axis (height) of the normal plots and cumulative frequency plot.

    SCALE=$\#_1$,$\#_2$.   {0,1/prev.}

        $\#_1$ is the value of the frequency at the base of the histograms. $\#_2$ is the number of units represented by each symbol plotted in the histogram.

- SIZE OF PROBLEM

    P5D copies the data to a temporary unit and rereads it as many times as necessary to form the specified plots. Each time the data are read P5D constructs as many plots as it can fit into memory (about 10 if the plots are the preassigned size, more if the plots are smaller). The largest single plot that can be printed is about 100 x 150.

- COMPUTATIONAL METHOD

    Computations of the means and standard deviations are in single precision by the method of provisional means (Appendix A.2).

ACKNOWLEDGEMENT

    P5D was designed and programmed by Steve Chasen. P5D and P6D supersede BMD05D.

P6D

10.2 Bivariate (Scatter) Plots

Steve Chasen, HSCF

P6D displays one variable against another variable in a scatter plot. It computes and prints equations of the simple linear regression relating each variable to the other, and indicates the intersections of the regression lines with the frame of the plot. The cases can be classified into groups; the data for one or more groups can be printed in a single frame and the data points identified by group. More than one pair of variables can be plotted in a single plot. The size of the plots can be specified.

● THE *PLOT* PARAGRAPH

The *PLOT* paragraph specifies the variables to be plotted vertically (YVAR) and horizontally (XVAR), the SIZE of the plot and the GROUPs to be plotted if the cases are classified into groups. *PLOT* can be repeated several times before the *END* paragraph to specify different combinations of variables to be plotted or to modify the size of the plots.

● SCATTER PLOTS

The Werner blood chemistry data (Table 5.1) are used to illustrate the plots produced by P6D. In the first example we specify the variables to be plotted along the Y-axis (YVAR) and the X-axis (XVAR). The other Control Language instructions are described in Chapter 5.

Example 10.7

```
/PROBLEM      TITLE IS 'WERNER BLOOD CHEMISTRY DATA'.
/INPUT        VARIABLES ARE 9.
              FORMAT IS '(A4,5F4.0,3F4.1)'.
/VARIABLE     NAMES ARE ID,AGE,HEIGHT,WEIGHT,BRTHPILL,
                    CHOLSTRL,ALBUMIN,CALCIUM,URICACID.
              MAXIMUM IS (6)400.
              MINIMUM IS (6)150.
              BLANKS ARE MISSING.
              LABEL IS ID.

/PLOT         YVAR ARE CHOLSTRL,URICACID.
              XVAR ARE AGE      ,WEIGHT.
              SIZE IS 40,25.

/END
```

The Control Language must be preceded by System Cards to initiate the analysis by P6D. At HSCF, the System Cards are

```
//jobname  JOB  nooo,yourname
//   EXEC  BIMED,PROG=BMDP6D
//SYSIN DD  *
```

The Control Language is immediately followed by the data (Table 5.1). The analysis is terminated by another System Card. At HSCF, this System Card is

```
//
```

Output 10.7   Scatter plots printed by P6D.

BMDP6D – BIVARIATE (SCATTER) PLOTS
HEALTH SCIENCES COMPUTING FACILITY
UNIVERSITY OF CALIFORNIA, LOS ANGELES

PROGRAM REVISED SEPTEMBER 1977
MANUAL DATE -- 1977

--- Control Language read by P6D is printed and interpreted ---

NUMBER OF CASES READ.   188

TABLE OF CONTENTS

HORIZONTAL VARIABLE NO. NAME	VERTICAL VARIABLE NO. NAME	GROUP NAME	PLOT SYMBOL	PAGE NO.
2 AGE	6 CHOLSTRL		. . . .	3
4 WEIGHT	9 URICACID		. . . .	4

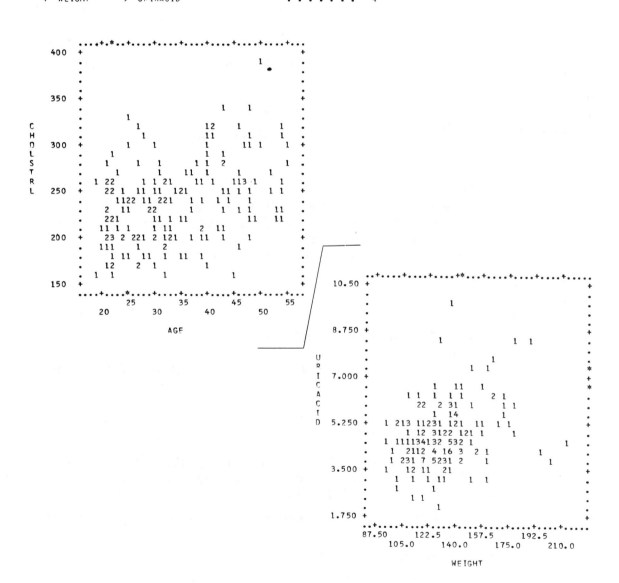

Two plots are printed in Output 10.7: CHOLSTRL against AGE and URICACID against WEIGHT. Numbers in the plots are the frequencies of points plotted at the same positions. SIZE is specified in Example 10.7 to reduce the size of the plots from a full computer page to a more convenient size.

On all plots asterisks (*) plotted on the frame correspond to values that are equal to the missing value code or are out of range (less than the specified MINIMUM or greater than the specified MAXIMUM). These values are <u>not</u> used in the computations.

All possible pairings of the YVAR and XVAR variables are plotted when

        CROSS.

is specified in the *PLOT* paragraph.

PLOT
    YVAR=v_1,v_2,$\cdots$.   {last variable/prev.}

      Names or subscripts of variables to be plotted vertically (along the Y-axes).

    XVAR=v_1,v_2,$\cdots$.   {first variable/prev.}

      Names or subscripts of variables to be plotted horizontally (along the X-axes).

    PAIR. *or* CROSS.   { PAIR }

      The program is preset to PAIR the YVAR variables with the XVAR variables, the first YVAR against the first XVAR , etc., and plot each pair in a separate graph. If CROSS is specified, all possible pairings of the YVAR and XVAR variables are plotted, each in a separate graph.

• STATISTICS AND SIMPLE LINEAR REGRESSION

The statistics listed below are optional in P6D. They are computed and printed when

        STATISTICS.

is specified in the *PLOT* paragraph.

- frequency (N) of points plotted. Points are plotted for all cases that contain acceptable values for both variables; i.e., values that are not missing or out of range.

- correlation (r) between the two variables computed using all pairs of acceptable values.

- mean for each variable: $\bar{x}$ and $\bar{y}$

- standard deviation for each variable: s_x and s_y

- the regression lines of X on Y (i.e., X=b'Y+a') and of Y on X (i.e., Y=aX+b)

$$b' = rs_x/s_y \quad ; \qquad a' = \bar{x} - b\bar{y}$$

$$b = rs_y/s_x \quad ; \qquad a = \bar{y} - b\bar{x}$$

- the residual mean square error (labelled RES.MS. in the results):

$$s^2_{x|y} = \Sigma(x_j - \hat{x}_j)^2/(N-2) \quad \text{where} \quad \hat{x}_j = b'y_j + a$$

and

$$s^2_{y|x} = \Sigma(y_j - \hat{y}_j)^2/(N-2) \quad \text{where} \quad \hat{y}_j = bx_j + a$$

In Example 10.8 we specify the variables to be plotted, the size of the plots, and request that statistics be computed and printed.

Example 10.8

```
/PROBLEM      TITLE IS 'WERNER BLOOD CHEMISTRY DATA'.
/INPUT        VARIABLES ARE 9.
              FORMAT IS '(A4,5F4.0,3F4.1)'.
/VARIABLE     NAMES ARE ID,AGE,HEIGHT,WEIGHT,BRTHPILL,
                      CHOLSTRL,ALBUMIN,CALCIUM,URICACID.
              MAXIMUM IS (6)400.
              MINIMUM IS (6)150.
              BLANKS ARE MISSING.
              LABEL IS ID.

/PLOT         YVAR ARE CHOLSTRL,URICACID.
              XVAR ARE AGE        ,WEIGHT.
              SIZE IS 40,25.
              STATISTICS.

/END
```

The statistics and plots are printed in Output 10.8. On the frame of each plot are two X's and two Y's. The X's show where the line X=b'Y+a' intersects the frame of the plot, and the Y's show where the line Y=bX+a intersects the frame. Asterisks (*) on the frame represent values that were excluded from the computations because one or both of the values for the two variables were missing or out of range.

PLOT

STATistics.   {no/prev.}

If STATistics is specified, the following are computed: the mean and standard deviation for each variable, the correlation and the two regression lines

X = b'Y+a
Y = bX+a

In addition, the intersections of the two lines with the frame of the plot are indicated by "X"s and "Y"s respectively. All computations are based on data from the plotted cases.

● SIZE ᴀɴᴅ SCALE ᴏꜰ ᴛʜᴇ Pʟᴏᴛꜱ

You can reduce the size of the plots as in the examples above or request plots that require several pages. The size of the plot can be specified as the number of characters for the X-axis (the width) and the number of lines for the Y-axis (height). The width is stated first; the program is preset to 70,42 if SIZE is not specified. In Examples 10.7 and 10.8 we reduced the figures to 40 characters wide and 25 lines high by specifying

    SIZE=40,25.

Output 10.8 Scatter plots with estimates of regression lines

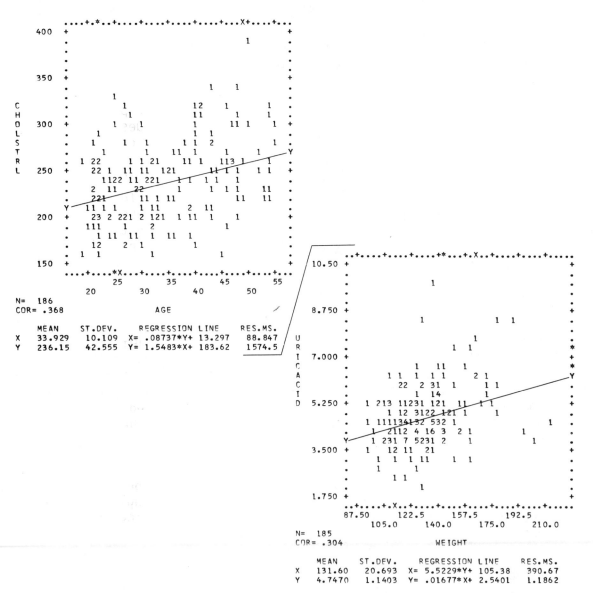

Note: In the above plots we have drawn a line between the two Y's on the frames of the plots. This shows the least squares regression line Y = bX + a. Similar lines can be drawn joining the two X's.

```
PLOT
    SIZE=#₁,#₂.              {70,42}                    #₁ ≤ 100
```
$\#_1$ is the number of characters for the X-axis (the width) and $\#_2$ is the number of lines for the Y-axis (the height). The width is stated first.

You can specify the scale on each axis by setting a MINIMUM[4] and MAXIMUM[4] limit for the variable in the *PLOT* paragraph. If limits are not specified, the observed minimum and maximum are used. If groups are plotted in separate graphs each group may have a different observed minimum and maximum. Therefore, if MINIMUM and MAXIMUM are not specified, the scales may differ from graph to graph.

```
PLOT
    MINIMUM= #₁,#₂,···.        {none/prev.}          one per variable
```
Lower limits for the variables. $\#_1$ is the lower limit for the first variable, $\#_2$ for the second, etc. If a lower limit is specified, it is used as the lower limit of the plot's scale and values less than the lower limit are omitted from the plot and from all computations.

```
    MAXIMUM= #₁,#₂,···.        {none/prev.}          one per variable
```
Upper limits for the variables. $\#_1$ is the upper limit for the first variable, etc. If an upper limit is specified, it is used as the upper limit of the plot's scale and values greater than the upper limit are omitted from the plot and from all computations.

● SELECTING GROUPS TO BE PLOTTED

Cases can be classified into groups by specifying a GROUPING variable in the *VARiable* paragraph. For example

GROUPING IS BRTHPILL.

in the *VARiable* paragraph specifies that cases are classified according to the values of BRTHPILL. A *GROUP* paragraph is required when the GROUPING variable is continuous or takes on more than 10 distinct values. A *GROUP* paragraph can also be used to name the groups.

When a GROUPING variable is specified, each group can be printed in an individual plot or specified groups can be combined into a single plot. Each group is identified by a different symbol. We use the following example to demonstrate the effect of grouping cases.

---

[4] If your BMDP programs are dated before August 1977, MINIMUMS and MAXIMUMS specified in the *VARiable* paragraph are used as limits for the plots; MINIMUMS and MAXIMUMS cannot be specified in the *PLOT* paragraph.

Example 10.9

```
/PROBLEM      TITLE IS 'WERNER BLOOD CHEMISTRY DATA'.
/INPUT        VARIABLES ARE 9.
              FORMAT IS '(A4,5F4.0,3F4.1)'.
/VARIABLE     NAMES ARE ID,AGE,HEIGHT,WEIGHT,BRTHPILL,
                   CHOLSTRL,ALBUMIN,CALCIUM,URICACID.
              MAXIMUM IS (6)400.
              MINIMUM IS (6)150.
              BLANKS ARE MISSING.
              LABEL IS ID.
              GROUPING IS BRTHPILL.

/GROUP        CODES(5) ARE       1,     2.
              NAMES(5) ARE NOPILL, PILL.

/PLOT         YVAR IS CHOLSTRL.
              XVAR IS AGE.
              SIZE IS 40,25.
              STATISTICS.

/PLOT         YVAR IS URICACID.
              XVAR IS WEIGHT.
              GROUP IS NOPILL.
              GROUPS ARE NOPILL,PILL.

/END
```

There is no GROUP statement in the first *PLOT* paragraph; therefore frequencies are printed in the first plot in Output 10.9. Two GROUP statements are specified in the second *PLOT* paragraph; the symbol A in Output 10.9 represents the cases in the first group (NOPILL) and B the cases in the second group (PILL). Computations are performed using all data plotted without regard to group membership.

Since MINIMUM and MAXIMUM limits are not specified for WEIGHT, WEIGHT has different scales in the last two plots.

VARiable

   GROUPING= v.   {no grouping/prev.}

     Name or subscript of the variable used to classify the cases into groups. If GROUPING is not specified or is set to zero, the cases are not grouped. If the GROUPING variable takes on more than 10 distinct values or codes, CODES or CUTPOINTS for the variable must be specified in the *GROUP* paragraph (Section 5.4).

PLOT

   GROUP=$g_1,g_2,\cdots$.   {all groups}   can be repeated

     $g_1,g_2,\ldots$ are the group NAMEs (from the *GROUP* paragraph) or group subscripts. The specified groups are plotted in the same graph. A group subscript is the sequence number of the group as specified in the *GROUP* paragraph. The GROUP statement can be repeated in the *PLOT* paragraph. Each GROUP statement defines a separate graph.

<u>Output 10.9</u> Scatter plots printed by P6D. In two plots symbols are used to represent group membership.

TABLE OF CONTENTS

HORIZONTAL VARIABLE NO. NAME	VERTICAL VARIABLE NO. NAME	GROUP NAME	PLOT SYMBOL		PAGE NO.
2 AGE	6 CHOLSTRL			· · · · · · ·	4
4 WEIGHT	9 URICACID	NOPILL	A	· · · · · · ·	5
4 WEIGHT	9 URICACID	NOPILL PILL	A B	· · · · · · ·	6

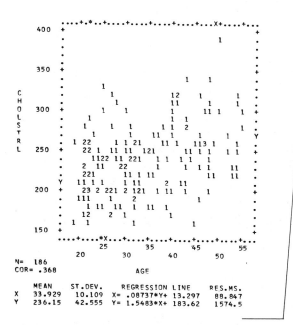

N= 186
COR= .368

	MEAN	ST.DEV.	REGRESSION LINE	RES.MS.
X	33.929	10.109	X= .08737*Y+ 13.297	88.847
Y	236.15	42.555	Y= 1.5483*X+ 183.62	1574.5

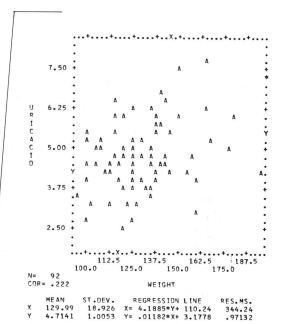

N= 92
COR= .222

	MEAN	ST.DEV.	REGRESSION LINE	RES.MS.
X	129.99	18.926	X= 4.1885*Y+ 110.24	344.24
Y	4.7141	1.0053	Y= .01182*X+ 3.1778	.97132

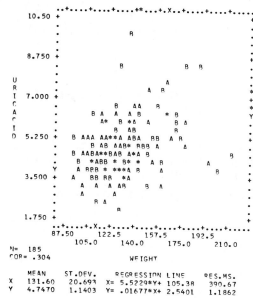

N= 185
COR= .304

	MEAN	ST.DEV.	REGRESSION LINE	RES.MS.
X	131.60	20.693	X= 5.5229*Y+ 105.38	390.67
Y	4.7470	1.1403	Y= .01677*X+ 2.5401	1.1862

● MULTIPLE PLOTS IN THE SAME FRAME

More than one pair of variables can be plotted in the same frame.[5] This is useful when several variables represent the same type of measurements or the same variable is measured at different times, and all are to be plotted against a common variable. To allow flexibility you can specify whether all the XVARIABLES are to be plotted in a common X-axis (XCOMMON), whether all the YVARIABLES are to be plotted on a common Y-axis (YCOMMON), or whether all plots are to be made in a common frame (COMMON). For any of these instructions each pair of variables is plotted using a different symbol.

PLOT

    XCOMMON.   {no}

       All the XVARIABLES specified in this *PLOT* paragraph are plotted on a common X-axis.

    YCOMMON.   {no}

       All the YVARIABLES specified in this *PLOT* paragraph are plotted on a common Y-axis.

    COMMON.   {no}

       All plots specified in this *PLOT* paragraph are plotted in a common frame.

● IDENTIFYING PAIRS OF VARIABLES AND GROUPS

If only one pair of variables is plotted in a frame and a GROUP statement is not specified, the frequency of the points are plotted (e.g., Output 10.6). You can specify that a uniform symbol be plotted, such as an asterisk for all points, by stating

        SYMBOL='*'.

in the *PLOT* paragraph; when a symbol is specified, the frequency is <u>not</u> printed.

If two or more pairs of variables are plotted in a common frame, or if a GROUP statement is specified, each group for each pair of variables is assigned a unique letter (A,B,...) to identify its points. You can specify the degree of labelling you want by any combination of the following:

---

[5] If your BMDP programs are dated before August 1977, only one pair of variables can be plotted in the same frame; XCOMMON, YCOMMON and COMMON are not available.

$$CHARACTER = \begin{cases} FREQ. & \text{frequency is plotted at each point} \\ GROUP. & \text{groups } \underline{only} \text{ are uniquely identified} \\ VAR. & \text{pairs of variables } \underline{only} \text{ are uniquely} \\ & \qquad \text{identified} \\ GROUP,VAR. & \text{both groups and pairs of variables are} \\ & \qquad \text{uniquely identified} \end{cases}$$

The preassigned values are described in the two paragraphs above.

When CHARACTER=GROUP[6] is stated and group NAMEs are specified in the *GROUP* paragraph, the symbols plotted are the first letters of the group names. When CHARACTER=VAR is stated and variable NAMEs are specified in the *VARiable* paragraph, the first letters of the XVARIABLE names are plotted if XCOMMON and the first letters of the YVARIABLE names are plotted if YCOMMON. Otherwise, the letters A,B,... are used.

You may specify the SYMBOLs[7] to be used in place of A,B,... by stating

SYMBOL='c_1','c_2',$\cdots$.

where c_1 is the symbol that replaces A, c_2 replaces B, etc. If only one SYMBOL is specified, it is used uniformly for all the points. Otherwise, the number of SYMBOLs, if specified, must be equal to the number of groups if CHARACTER=GROUP is stated; equal to the number of pairs of variables in the frame if CHARACTER=VAR is stated; and equal to the product of the number of groups and number of pairs of variables if CHARACTER=GROUP,VAR. is stated.

PLOT
   CHARACTER=FREQ.
or CHARACTER= *(one or both)* GROUP,VAR.

    See above for explanation.

   SYMBOL='c_1','c_2',$\cdots$.

    See above for explanation

{FREQ if no GROUP statement and only one pair of variables per frame; GROUP, VAR otherwise}

{1,2,... if CHAR=FREQ; A,B,... otherwise}

---

[6] If your BMDP programs are dated before August 1977, only FREQ or GROUP can be assigned to CHARACTER; SYMBOL is not available.

[7] If your BMDP programs are dated before August 1977, SYMBOL is not available.

- SIZE OF PROBLEM

    P6D copies the data and rereads it as many times as necessary to form the specified plots. Each time the data are read, P6D constructs as many plots as it can fit into memory (about 10 if the plots are the preassigned size (70,42), more if the plots are smaller). The largest single plot can have 24,000 plot positions (length of X-axis x length of Y-axis).

- COMPUTATIONAL METHOD

    Computation of the means, standard deviations and covariances are in single precision by the method of provisional means (Appendix A.2).

    When MINIMUMS and MAXIMUMS are not specified in the *PLOT* paragraph for any variable to be plotted, the data are first read to find the observed minimums and maximums and then reread to construct the scatter plots.

ACKNOWLEDGEMENT

    P6D was designed and programmed by Steve Chasen.   P5D and P6D supersede BMD05D.

10.3 Summary — P5D, P6D

The Control Language on this page is <u>common</u> to all programs. Summaries on the next two pages show the Control Language specific to

P5D -- Histograms and Univariate Plots   p. 242
P6D -- Bivariate (Scatter) Plots   p. 243

Paragraph STATEMENT[1] {Preassigned value[2]}		Definition, restriction	See pages:
/PROBlem		Required each problem	74
TITLE='c'.	{blank}	Problem title, $\leq$ 160 char.	74
/INPut		Required first problem. Either VARIABLE and FORMAT, or UNIT and CODE required.	75
VARIABLE=#.	{none/prev.}	No. of variables in input data	75
FORMAT='c'.	{none/prev.}	Format of input data, $\leq$ 800 char.	76
CASE=#.	{end-of-file/prev.}	No. of cases in data	76-77
UNIT=#.	{5(cards)/prev.}	Input unit if data are not on cards; not 1, 2, 6	77
REWIND.	{REWIND/prev.}	Rewind input unit	77
CODE=c.	{none}	Code to identify BMDP File	132
CONTENT=c.	{DATA}	Data or matrix in BMDP File	132
LABEL=c.	{none}	Label of BMDP File, $\leq$ 40 char.	132
/VARiable		Optional. For input from a BMDP File, items in this paragraph may be previously set, see Chapter 7.	79
NAME=$c_1,c_2,\cdots$.	{X(subscript)/prev.}	Variable names, one per variable	79-80
MAXIMUM=$\#_1,\#_2,\cdots$.	{none/prev.}	Upper limits, one per variable	80
MINIMUM=$\#_1,\#_2,\cdots$.	{none/prev.}	Lower limits, one per variable	80
BLANK= *(one only)* ZERO, MISSING.	{ZERO/prev.}	Blanks treated as zeros or as missing value codes	81
MISSING=$\#_1,\#_2,\cdots$.	{none/prev.}	Missing value codes, one per variable	81
USE=$v_1,v_2,\cdots$.	{all variables}	Variables used in the analysis	82
LABEL=v_1,v_2.	{none/prev.}	Variable(s) used to label cases, read under A-format, one or two	83
ADD=#.	{0/prev.}	No. of variables added through transformation	99
BEFORE. *or* AFTER.	{BEFORE/prev.}	Data checked for limits before or after transformation	100
/TRANsform		Optional, Control Language transformations and case selection	97-105
/SAVE		Optional, required to create BMDP File	125
CODE=c.	{none}	Code to identify BMDP File, required	125-126
LABEL='c'.	{blank}	Label for BMDP File, $\leq$ 40 char.	125-126
UNIT=#.	{none}	Unit on which BMDP File is written; not 1, 2, 5 or 6	126-127
NEW.	{not new}	NEW if this is first BMDP File written in the system file	126-127

<u>Key:</u>   #   number   v   variable name or subscript
      'c'   title, label or format   c   name not exceeding 8 char., apostrophes may be required (p. 59)

[1] In BMDP programs dated before August 1977, the minimum required abbreviations are *INPUT* (not *INP*), VARIAB (not VAR), FORMAT (not FORM), CONTENT (not CONT), *VARIAB* (not *VAR*), BEFORET (not BEF), AFTERT (not AFT), *TRANSF* (not *TRAN*). If dated before February 1976, BLANK=ZERO and cannot be changed.

[2] "/prev." means that any assignment remains the same as that specified in the previous problem or subproblem until changed. Otherwise, the assignment returns to its preassigned value each time a new problem begins or the paragraph is used again.

P5D -- Histograms and Univariate Plots

(in addition to that on p. 241)

Paragraph STATEMENT[1] {Preassigned value}		Definition, restriction	See pages:
VARiable		Specify as part of *VARiable* paragraph, p. 241	
GROUPING=v.	{no grouping/prev.}	Variable used to classify cases into groups	224-225
/GROUP		Optional, required if GROUPING variable has more than 10 distinct values	84
CODE(#)=#$_1$,#$_2$,···.	{10 smallest values/prev.}	Codes for variable #, may be repeated	84-85
CUTPOINT(#)=#$_1$,#$_2$,···.	{see CODE/ prev.}	Cutpoints to form intervals for variable #, may be repeated	84-85
NAME(#)=c$_1$,c$_2$,···.	{CODEs or CUTPoints /prev.}	Code or interval names for variable #, may be repeated	84-85
RESET.	{not RESET}	If RESET, all assignments in prev. *GROUP* paragraph are reset to preassigned values	86
/PLOT		Required, may be repeated	217
TYPE= *(one or more)* HIST,NORM,DNORM,HALFNORM, CUM,CHIST.	{HIST/prev.}	Type of plot	217-224
VARIABLE=v$_1$,v$_2$,···.	{all variables/prev.}	Variables to be plotted	224
GROUP=g$_1$,g$_2$,···.	{all groups in one plot}	Groups used in one plot, may be repeated	224-227
MINIMUM=#$_1$,#$_2$,···.	{none/prev.}	Lower limits for the variables, one per variable	227
MAXIMUM=#$_1$,#$_2$,···.	{none/prev.}	Upper limits for the variables, one per variable	227-228
SIZE=#$_1$,#$_2$.	{80,50/prev.}	Length of horizontal axis (#$_1$) for all plots and vertical axis (#$_2$) for all but HIST, CHIST	228-229
SCALE=#$_1$,#$_2$.	{0,1}	Origin of scale and number of observations per character in HIST, CHIST	228-229
/END		Required	57

Key: # number
    g group name (from *GROUP* paragraph) or group subscript
    v variable name or subscript

[1] In BMDP programs dated before August 1977, the minimum required abbreviation is VARIAB (not VAR); MINIMUM and MAXIMUM for the plot scales are stated in the *VARiable* paragraph (not the *PLOT* paragraph).

- Order of input

    (1) System Cards, at HSCF these are
```
//jobname  JOB  nooo,yourname
//  EXEC  BIMED,PROG=BMDP5D
//SYSIN  DD  *
```

    (2) Control Language instructions
```
PROBlem paragraph, required
INPut paragraph, required first problem
VARiable paragaraph
TRANsform paragraph
SAVE paragraph
GROUP paragraph
PLOT paragraph, required, may be repeated for additional plots
END paragraph, required at end of Control Language
```

    (3) Data, if on cards
```
data
```

    (4) System Card, at HSCF this is
```
//
```

    Control Language instructions (2) and data (3) can be repeated for additional problems.

P6D -- Bivariate (Scatter) Plots

(in addition to that on p. 241)

Paragraph STATEMENT[1] {Preassigned value}		Definition, restriction	See pages:
VARiable		Specify as part of *VARiable* paragraph, p. 241	
GROUPing=v.	{no grouping/prev.}	Variable used to classify cases into groups	235-236
/GROUP		Optional, required if GROUPing variable has more than 10 distinct values	84
CODE(#)=$\#_1,\#_2,\cdots$.	{10 smallest values/prev.}	Codes for variable #, may be repeated	84-85
CUTPOINT(#)=$\#_1,\#_2,\cdots$.	{see CODE /prev.}	Cutpoints to form intervals for variable #, may be repeated	84-85
NAME(#)=$c_1,c_2,\cdots$.	{CODES or CUTPOINTS /prev.}	Code or interval names for variable #, may be repeated	84-85
RESET.	{not RESET}	If RESET, all assignments in prev. *GROUP* paragraph are reset to preassigned values	86
/PLOT		Required, may be repeated	230
XVAR=$v_1,v_2,\cdots$.	{first var. only/prev.}	Variables for X-axes of plots	230-232
YVAR=$v_1,v_2,\cdots$.	{last var. only/prev.}	Variables for Y-axes of plots	230-232
PAIR. *or* CROSS.	{PAIR }	If CROSS, each XVAR vs each YVAR; if PAIR, 1st XVAR vs 1st YVAR, 2nd vs 2nd, etc.	230-232
STATISTICS.	{no/prev.}	Print statistics and regression lines for each plot	232-233
MINIMUM=$\#_1,\#_2,\cdots$.	{none/prev.}	Lower limits for the variables, one per variable	235
MAXIMUM=$\#_1,\#_2,\cdots$.	{none/prev.}	Upper limits for the variables, one per variable	235
SIZE=$\#_1,\#_2$.	{70,42/prev.}	Length of X and Y axes	234-235
XCOMMON.	{no}	All XVARs are plotted on a common X-axis	238
YCOMMON.	{no}	All YVARs are plotted on a common Y-axis	238
COMMON.	{no}	All plots are plotted in a common frame	238
CHARACTER=FREQ.	{see p. 238}	Frequencies, <u>group</u> or <u>variable</u> identification is plotted	238-239
or CHARACTER= *(one or both)* GROUP,VAR.			
SYMBOL='c_1','c_2',$\cdots$.	{1,2,... if CHAR=FREQ; A,B,... otherwise}	Symbols used for group or variable identification	238-239
GROUP=$g_1,g_2,\cdots$.	{all groups in one plot}	Groups used in each plot, may be repeated	235-236
/END		Required	57

Key: #   number   g   group name (from *GROUP* paragraph) or group subscript
     v   variable name or subscript   c   name not exceeding 8 char., apostrophes may be required (p. 59)
    'c'   character

[1] In BMDP programs dated before August 1977, when a *GROUP* paragraph is found, RESET is implicitly specified and cannot be changed; the minimum required abbreviation is VARIAB (not VAR); MINIMUM and MAXIMUM for the plot scales are stated in the *VARiable* paragraph (not the *PLOT* paragraph); XCOMMON, YCOMMON, COMMON and SYMBOL cannot be used; CHARACTER can be FREQ or GROUP (but not VAR).

- Order of input

     (1)   System Cards; at HSCF these are
```
//jobname  JOB   nooo,yourname
//    EXEC  BIMED,PROG=BMDP6D
//SYSIN  DD  *
```

     (2)   Control Language instructions
```
PROBlem paragraph, required
INPut paragraph, required first problem
VARiable paragraph
TRANsform paragraph
SAVE paragraph
GROUP paragraph
PLOT paragraph, required, may be repeated for additional plots
END paragraph, required at end of Control Language
```

     (3)   Data, if on cards   data

     (4)   System Card; at HSCF this is   //

    Control Language instructions (2) and (3) can be repeated for additional problems.

11

FREQUENCY TABLES

Frequency tables (or cross-tabulations) are used to summarize results from surveys, clinical studies and experiments. These tables are appropriate when the data are qualitative or categorical (e.g., sex, treatment or outcome group, or an answer to a multiple choice question), discrete but ordered (e.g., number of pregnancies, level of education attained, or a judgement on an ordered scale) or continuous but grouped into intervals (e.g., ranges of age, weight or height).

In this chapter we discuss the formation of frequency tables, statistics appropriate to categorical data and tests of hypotheses about the data. The tables can be two-way, multiway, or cross sections of a multiway table. The tabulation of disease severity by drug treatment is an example of a two-way table. If the tabulation is performed for each sex separately, then each table formed (one for males and one for females) is a cross section of a three-way table (disease by drug by sex). Similarly a four-way table can be separated into cross sections that are three-way tables or two-way tables. Often it is useful to examine the multiway table as well as cross sections.

In this chapter we describe three programs.

P1F -- Two-way Frequency Tables--Measures of Association   p. 248
P2F -- Two-Frequency Tables--Empty Cells and Departures
      from Independence   p. 278
P3F -- Multiway Frequency Tables--The Log-Linear Model   p. 297

P1F prints a variety of two-way tables and provides estimates of many measures of association and prediction. You can request tables of observed frequencies; expected values under independence; percentages of the table total, of each row total, or of each column total; and several types of residuals. Tests and statistics that can be computed for each two-way table are

- tests of independence and related measures: χ^2 test, likelihood ratio chi-square test G^2, ϕ, contingency coefficient and Cramer's V

- tests of independence appropriate only for 2x2 tables: Fisher's exact test and Yates' corrected χ^2

- measures of association appropriate for a 2x2 table: Yule's Q and Y, cross-product ratio and tetrachoric correlation r_t

- measures of association and correlation when the categories of both factors are ordered: Goodman and Kruskal Γ, Kendall's τ_b, Stuart's τ_c, product-moment correlation r and Spearman rank correlation r_s

- predictive measures when the categories of both factors are ordered: Somers' D

- predictive measures when either or both factors are qualitative: Goodman and Kruskal τ, λ and λ^* and uncertainty coefficient

- McNemar's test of symmetry

- a test of a contrast on the proportions in a 2xk table

Standard errors are provided for many of the measures of association and prediction.

P2F analyzes two special problems:

- You can use P2F to exclude cells from the frequency table, such as cells with a prior probability of zero (structural zeros). P2F computes the appropriate test of independence between rows and columns (the χ^2 test of quasi-independence, Goodman, 1968; Bishop et al., 1975). This test of independence uses all cells that are not excluded a priori and is identical to the usual χ^2 test when there are no excluded cells.

- You can use P2F to identify cells or patterns of cells that contribute to a departure from independence or quasi-independence, i.e., contribute greatly to a significant χ^2 test. You can select a criterion by which cells are identified and eliminated (treated as excluded) from the table in a stepwise manner. One such criterion is to eliminate the cell that, when excluded, minimizes the χ^2 (or G^2) test of quasi-independence performed on all cells not previously excluded. Inferences can be drawn from the data by examining the pattern of cells eliminated by this procedure (see Brown, 1974).

P2F computes only the χ^2 tests of independence (or quasi-independence), expected values assuming independence, and various types of residuals. It does not provide estimates of the measures of association and prediction that are available in P1F. P2F prints the observed and expected frequencies and various types of residuals, but does not print tables of percentages as P1F does.

P3F analyzes data in a multiway table. The purpose of the analysis is to obtain a description of the relationships between the factors of the table, either by forming a model for the data or by testing and ordering the importance of the interactions between the factors. The analysis is based on fitting a (hierarchical) log-linear model to the cell frequencies; that is, the logarithm of the expected cell frequency is written as an additive function of main effects and interactions in a manner similar to the usual analysis of variance model. It should be noted that the various tests for the interactions are not independent. If a two-way table is input to P3F, one possible log-linear model includes two main effects and a single interaction. The test that the interaction is zero is identical to the test for independence obtained in P1F.

You can use P3F to find an appropriate model for the data in the table either by fitting specified models or by using a method of screening effects explained on p. 303. The program tests the appropriateness of models by the likelihood ratio χ^2 (G^2) and by the usual χ^2 goodness-of-fit.

If you want means, standard deviations and other statistics for the observations in each cell of a table, we recommend P9D (Section 9.3).

● CONTROL LANGUAGE

The Control Language instructions to describe the data and variables are common to all BMDP programs and are explained in Chapter 5: the *PROBlem*, *INPut*[1], *VARiable* and *CATEGory* paragraphs are used in the frequency table programs discussed in this chapter.

If data editing or transformations are necessary, the methods described in Chapter 6 can be used. Data can be read using a FORMAT statement or from a a BMDP File (Chapter 7). If a BMDP File is read as input and a new BMDP File is created in the same problem, the two Files must be in different system files and must have different UNIT numbers.

A summary of the Control Language instructions common to all BMDP programs is on p. 326; summaries of the Control Language instructions specific to each program described in this chapter follow the general summary. These summaries can be used as indexes to the program descriptions.

● FORMS OF DATA INPUT

Usually a case contains data for a single observation. The frequency table programs can also accept tabulated data, such as a table from a government or scientific report. The use of previously tabulated data as input is described on p. 271.

---

[1] BMDP programs dated before August 1977 require more letters than are shown in this manual in their permissible abbreviated form (the capitalized letters). The minimum required abbreviations for earlier versions are specified in footnotes to the summary (p. 326).

P1F

11.1 Two-Way Frequency Tables — Measures of Association

Morton Brown, HSCF
Jacqueline Benedetti, HSCF

P1F prints a variety of two-way tables and provides estimates of many measures of association and prediction. You can request tables of observed frequencies; expected values under independence; percentages of the table total, of each row total or each column total; or several types of residuals. Tests and statistics that can be computed are

- tests of independence and related measures: χ^2 test, likelihood ratio chi-square test (G^2), ϕ, contingency coefficient and Cramer's V

- tests of independence appropriate only for 2x2 tables: Fisher's exact test and Yates' corrected χ^2

- measures of association appropriate for a 2x2 table: Yule's Q and Y, cross-product ratio and tetrachoric correlation r_t

- measures of association and correlation when the categories of both factors are ordered: Goodman and Kruskal Γ, Kendall's τ_b, Stuart's τ_c, product-moment correlation r and Spearman rank correlation r_s

- predictive measures when the categories of both factors are ordered: Somers' D

- predictive measures when either or both factors are qualitative: the Goodman and Kruskal τ, λ and λ^* and uncertainty coefficient

- McNemar's test of symmetry

- a test of a contrast on the proportions in a 2xk table

Standard errors are provided for many of the measures of association and prediction.[2]

- RESULTS

The Kasser coronary data presented in Table 11.1 (Kasser and Bruce, 1969; Kronmal and Tarter, 1973) are used to illustrate the results printed by P1F. In Example 11.1 we specify (in the *TABLE* paragraph) the formation of two two-way frequency tables: the first is ACTIVE classified against FUNCTION, and the second is ANGINA classified against INFARCT. The *CATEGory* paragraph is used to name the CODEs; when there are 10 or fewer codes (distinct values) for each categorical variable this paragraph can be omitted (Section 5.4).

---

[2] P1F was rewritten and reissued in August 1976. The description in this manual is of the <u>revised</u> program. Minor changes in item names as of August 1977 are described in a footnote to the summary (p. 327).

Table 11.1 Data on 117 coronary patients, all males, from a study by Kasser and Bruce (1969) as presented in Kronmal and Tarter (1973)

AGE	FUNCTION	ACTIVE	INFARCT	ANGINA	HIGHBP
42	2	2	1	1	0
66	2	2	1	1	0
56	2	0	1	1	0
55	2	2	1	1	0
41	2	2	1	1	1
62	0	0	1	0	1
46	2	2	1	1	1
44	2	1	0	1	1
50	1	2	0	1	1
73	3	3	0	1	0
48	2	2	1	1	0
53	2	2	1	1	0
51	3	1	1	1	1
59	0	0	0	1	1
54	3	3	1	1	1
41	2	2	1	1	1
56	2	2	1	0	1
38	0	2	0	1	1
40	3	3	1	1	0
42	1	2	1	1	0
51	1	2	0	1	0
52	1	0	1	1	0
37	0	1	0	1	0
48	1	2	1	0	0
35	0	0	1	1	0
35	1	1	1	0	0
48	3	3	0	1	1
52	2	2	0	1	1
46	2	3	0	1	1
51	3	0	0	1	0
50	0	0	0	1	0
72	3	3	0	1	1
56	3	3	1	1	0
56	3	3	1	1	0
63	2	2	1	1	0
53	1	2	1	1	0
53	0	1	1	0	0
57	3	2	0	1	0
57	1	2	0	1	1

cont'd

AGE	FUNCTION	ACTIVE	INFARCT	ANGINA	HIGHBP
62	2	2	1	1	0
73	2	2	0	1	0
44	2	0	0	1	0
63	3	2	1	1	0
59	1	1	0	1	0
51	1	0	1	0	0
52	3	0	1	1	0
64	0	0	1	0	0
53	2	2	1	0	0
58	1	2	0	1	0
53	0	2	1	1	1
58	2	2	0	1	0
45	1	2	1	1	1
42	3	2	0	1	0
60	2	2	0	1	1
34	1	0	1	0	1
64	2	2	1	1	0
35	1	2	1	0	1
42	2	2	0	1	0
53	2	2	1	0	0
58	1	2	1	0	1
38	1	2	0	1	0
35	2	2	1	1	0
34	2	3	1	1	0
68	3	2	1	1	0
49	3	2	0	1	0
55	2	2	0	1	1
58	0	2	1	1	0
43	2	2	1	1	0
39	2	1	0	1	0
66	3	3	0	1	1
50	2	2	1	1	0
45	3	3	0	1	0
53	0	0	0	1	0
56	3	3	1	1	1
49	2	2	1	1	1
49	0	0	1	0	0
56	2	2	1	1	0
38	0	0	1	1	0

cont'd

AGE	FUNCTION	ACTIVE	INFARCT	ANGINA	HIGHBP
39	0	0	1	1	0
62	2	2	1	1	0
70	3	2	1	1	1
53	2	0	1	1	1
68	2	2	1	1	0
50	2	0	0	0	1
46	2	2	0	1	0
58	3	2	1	1	0
57	2	2	0	0	0
55	3	3	1	0	0
52	0	0	1	1	0
61	2	2	0	0	0
45	2	2	0	1	0
51	2	0	1	1	0
55	3	3	1	1	1
51	1	0	0	1	0
46	1	0	1	1	0
69	1	2	0	1	0
51	3	3	1	1	1
49	1	1	0	1	1
58	3	3	1	1	0
38	3	3	1	1	0
50	1	1	1	0	0
38	1	3	1	1	0
58	1	0	1	0	0
69	0	0	0	1	0
66	0	0	0	1	0
49	2	2	0	1	0
62	0	0	1	1	0
44	0	0	1	1	1
58	3	0	1	1	0
45	2	2	1	1	0
58	3	3	1	1	1
54	2	2	1	1	0
55	2	2	1	1	1
68	2	2	1	1	0
68	2	2	1	1	0
47	1	2	1	1	1
55	0	0	0	1	0

Key: AGE (in years)

FUNCTION -- functional class: 0 none, 1 minimal, 2 moderate, 3 more than moderate
(3 is a combination of two groups)

ACTIVE: 0 unknown, 1 very, 2 normal, 3 limited

INFARCT -- history of past myocardial infarctions: 0 none, 1 present

ANGINA -- history of angina pectoris: 0 none, 1 present

HIGHBP -- history of high blood pressure: 0 none, 1 present

AGE is recorded in columns 3 and 4; the other variables are recorded in columns 8, 12, 16, 20 and 24.

Example 11.1

```
/PROBLEM       TITLE IS 'KASSER CORONARY DATA'.
/INPUT         VARIABLES ARE 6.
               FORMAT IS '(6F4.0)'.
/VARIABLE      NAMES ARE AGE,FUNCTION,ACTIVE,INFARCT,ANGINA,HIGHBP.

/TABLE         COLUMN IS FUNCTION, INFARCT.
               ROW    IS ACTIVE , ANGINA .

/CATEGORY      CODES(2) ARE    0,      1,      2,      3.
               NAMES(2) ARE NONE, MINIMAL, MODERATE, SEVERE.
               CODES(3) ARE    1,      2,      3.
               NAMES(3) ARE VERY, NORMAL, LIMITED.
               CODES(4) ARE    0,      1.
               NAMES(4) ARE NONE, PRESENT.
               CODES(5) ARE    0,      1.
               NAMES(5) ARE NONE, PRESENT.

/END
```

The Control Language must be preceded by System Cards to initiate the analysis by P1F. At HSCF, the System Cards are

```
//jobname  JOB  nooo,yourname
//   EXEC  BIMED,PROG=BMDP1F
//SYSIN DD *
```

The Control Language is immediately followed by the data (Table 11.1). The analysis is terminated by another System Card. At HSCF, this System Card is

```
//
```

The frequency tables specified in the *TABLE* paragraph are printed in Output 11.1. Circled numbers below correspond to those in the output.

(1) Number of cases read. Each table is formed using all acceptable values for the categorical variables; that is, values that are not missing or out of range. When CODEs are specified for a categorical variable, only values of the variable equal to one of the specified CODEs are used in the analysis.

(2) For each variable, P1F prints the

- mean
- frequency of acceptable values
- standard deviation
- smallest observed value (not out of range)
- largest observed value (not out of range)

(3) The two-way frequency table is printed. Around the border of the table P1F prints the row and column marginal totals. If necessary, additional rows and columns are printed to report the numbers of values that are missing, out of range, or not equal to any specified CODE.

In the table of ACTIVE by FUNCTION, the row labelled NOT COUNTED reports the number of values not equal to any specified code (equal to the code zero).

(4) Rows or columns that are entirely zero are excluded from all computations. Under the hypothesis of independence between row and column variables, the expected value of cell (i,j) is $e_{ij} = r_i c_j / N$, where r_i is the row total, c_j the column total and N the total frequency in

<u>Output 11.1</u> Two-way frequency tables formed by P1F. Circled numbers corre-
spond to those in the text. Results not reproduced are indicated
in italics.

BMDP1F - TWO-WAY FREQUENCY TABLES -- MEASURES OF ASSOCIATION   PROGRAM REVISED SEPTEMBER 1977
HEALTH SCIENCES COMPUTING FACILITY   MANUAL DATE -- 1977
UNIVERSITY OF CALIFORNIA, LOS ANGELES

--- Control Language read by P1F is printed and interpreted ---

(1) NUMBER OF CASES READ.   117

	VARIABLE NO. NAME	MEAN	FREQ	S.D.	SMALLEST	LARGEST
(2)	1 AGE	52.32	117	9.47	34.00	73.00
	2 FUNCTION	1.68	117	1.01	0.0	3.00
	3 ACTIVE	1.59	117	1.04	0.0	3.00
	4 INFARCT	0.63	117	0.48	0.0	1.00
	5 ANGINA	0.84	117	0.37	0.0	1.00
	6 HIGHBP	0.31	117	0.46	0.0	1.00

TABLE NO.   1   ACTIVE VAR(3) VS FUNCTIONVAR(2)

CELL FREQUENCY COUNTS
----

(3)
```
                                 FUNCTION(VAR   2)

                       NONE     MINIMAL  MODERATE SEVERE
              EQ./EQ.   0.00      1.00     2.00     3.00     TOTAL

ACTIVE   VERY  1.00       2         4        2         1   I    9
(VAR  3) NORMAL 2.00      3        13       37         7   I   60
         LIMITED 3.00     0         1        2        16   I   19
                       --------  -------- -------- --------
              TOTAL       5        18       41        24        88
         NOT  COUNTED    15         6        5         3
```
....

(4) MINIMUM NONZERO EXPECTED VALUE IS   0.511
----- ALL STATISTICS ARE COMPUTED USING THE ORIGINAL CELL FREQUENCIES
           EXCLUDING ROWS AND/OR COLUMNS WHICH ARE ZERO.

(5)
STATISTIC	VALUE	D.F.	PROB.
PEARSON CHISQUARE	48.365	6	0.0000

....

TABLE NO.   2   ANGINA VAR(5) VS INFARCT VAR(4)

CELL FREQUENCY COUNTS

```
                                 INFARCT (VAR   4)

                       NONE     PRESENT
              EQ./EQ.   0.00      1.00     TOTAL

ANGINA   NONE   0.00      3        16     I   19
(VAR  5) PRESENT 1.00    40        58     I   98
                       --------  --------
              TOTAL      43        74        117
```
....

MINIMUM NONZERO EXPECTED VALUE IS   6.983
----- ALL STATISTICS ARE COMPUTED USING THE ORIGINAL CELL FREQUENCIES
           EXCLUDING ROWS AND/OR COLUMNS WHICH ARE ZERO.

STATISTIC	VALUE	D.F.	PROB.	STATISTIC	VALUE	D.F.	PROB.
PEARSON CHISQUARE	4.288	1	0.0384	YATES' CORRECTED CHISQUARE	3.279	1	0.0702

....

the table. The minimum expected value is printed. A very small minimum expected value indicates that the chi-square test of independence may be poorly approximated by a chi-square distribution.

The minimum expected value in the table of ACTIVE by FUNCTION is 0.511. With this small an expected value you may want to combine categories of one of the variables (see p. 258).

(5)   The Pearson chi-square statistic is a test of independence between rows and columns. It is computed for every frequency table and is defined as

$$\chi^2 = \Sigma \ \Sigma \ (a_{ij} - e_{ij})^2 / e_{ij}$$

where a_{ij} is the observed frequency in cell (i,j). P1F prints the values of the χ^2 statistic, its degrees of freedom (D.F.) and its probability (the probability of a more extreme result under the hypothesis of independence, i.e., its p-value). If you choose to test a hypothesis at a given level of significance (say .05), a probability less than this level is a significant result.

The table of INFARCT vs ANGINA is 2x2 (2 rows and 2 columns). In addition to the χ^2 test, Yates' corrected chi-square and its probability are also printed (see p. 262).

● OPTIONAL RESULTS AND INPUT

You must specify the categorical variables that define the tables. You can also

- request separate tables at each level of a third categorical variable (cross sections)   p. 253
- combine or stack two or more categorical variables into a single variable   p. 254
- print tables of expected values and percentages   p. 256
- add a constant to each cell's frequency before computing statistics   p. 258
- collapse (combine) adjacent rows or columns until the minimum expected value exceeds a specified constant   p. 258
- specify the statistics to be calculated for each table   p. 260
- print tables of residuals or tables adjusted to have constant row and column marginal totals   p. 268
- input data one case at a time or in a tabulated form   p. 271

● DESCRIBING TABLE(S) TO BE FORMED

As shown in the above example, the tables are specified by ROW and COLUMN variables in the *TABLE* paragraph. The *TABLE* paragraph can be repeated before the *END* paragraph to create additional tables.

In Example 11.1 two tables are specified. The first ROW variable is paired with the first COLUMN variable; the second ROW variable with the second COLUMN variable. To form tables from all possible pairings of the ROW and COLUMN variables, specify

CROSS.

in the *TABLE* paragraph. If CROSS were specified in Example 11.1, four tables would be printed:

ACTIVE	against	FUNCTION
ACTIVE	against	INFARCT
ANGINA	against	FUNCTION
ANGINA	against	INFARCT

TABLE
ROW= $v_1,v_2,\cdots$.   {none}   required

Names or subscripts of variables that define the row categories (index). If a ROW variable has more than 10 distinct values, you must specify its CODEs or CUTPOINTs in the *CATEGory* paragraph.

COLUMN= $v_1,v_2,\cdots$.   {none}   required

Names or subscripts of variables that define the column categories (index). If a COLUMN variable has more than 10 distinct values, you must specify its CODEs or CUTPOINTs in the *CATEGory* paragraph.

PAIR. *or* CROSS.   { PAIR }

If CROSS is specified, tables are formed from all possible combinations of the ROW and COLUMN variables. Otherwise, the first ROW variable and first COLUMN variable define the first table, the second ROW variable and second COLUMN variable the second table, etc.

● CROSS SECTIONS OF A TABLE

You may want to form a two-way frequency table for each level of a third variable. For example, this third variable might be sex or age grouping or treatment group.

The two tables printed in Output 11.1 can be formed at each of three AGE groupings if you specify three intervals for AGE in the *CATEGory* paragraph and state

CONDITION IS AGE.

in the *TABLE* paragraph. In Example 11.2 we request these cross sections of the two tables by adding this statement and CUTPOINTS for AGE to the previous example.

Example 11.2

```
/PROBLEM      TITLE IS 'KASSER CORONARY DATA'.
/INPUT        VARIABLES ARE 6.
              FORMAT IS '(6F4.0)'.
/VARIABLE     NAMES ARE AGE,FUNCTION,ACTIVE,INFARCT,ANGINA,HIGHBP.

/TABLE        COLUMN IS FUNCTION, INFARCT.
              ROW    IS ACTIVE  , ANGINA .
              CONDITION IS AGE.

/CATEGORY     CUTPOINTS(1) ARE    50,       60.
              NAMES(1) ARE 'UNDER 51', '51-60', 'OVER 60'.
              CODES(2) ARE     0,      1,      2,      3.
              NAMES(2) ARE NONE, MINIMAL, MODERATE, SEVERE.
              CODES(3) ARE     1,      2,      3.
              NAMES(3) ARE VERY, NORMAL, LIMITED.
              CODES(4) ARE     0,      1.
              NAMES(4) ARE NONE, PRESENT.
              CODES(5) ARE     0,      1.
              NAMES(5) ARE NONE, PRESENT.

/END
```

Six tables are created by the above Control Language instructions: ACTIVE against FUNCTION at each of three AGE groupings and ANGINA against INFARCT at the same AGE groupings. Three of the six tables are presented in Output 11.2.

TABLE

CONDITION$= v_1, v_2, \cdots$.   {none}

Names or subscripts of CONDITION variables. Each CONDITION variable is used in turn to form three-way tables with each pair of ROW and COLUMN variables. For each category of the CONDITION variable a two-way cross section of the table (ROW classified against COLUMN) is printed and analyzed. If a CONDITION variable takes on more than 10 distinct values, you must specify CODEs or CUTPOINTS for it in the *CATEGory* paragraph.

● STACKING OR COMBINING INDEX VARIABLES

ROW, COLUMN and CONDITION all use one variable at a time to create a table. Sometimes it is appropriate to use all possible combinations of two or more variables as a ROW, COLUMN or CONDITION variable. For example, you may want to form a table for each combination of AGE and HIGHBP groupings.

A new categorical variable that contains each combination can be created by a transformation. The new variable can also be formed in P1F by stating

DEFINE(7)=AGE,HIGHBP.

in the *VARiable* paragraph, where 7 is greater than the subscript of any other variable and is used as the subscript of the new variable. The new variable has six categories: three age categories for each level of HIGHBP. The new categories are AGE UNDER 51 with HIGHBP NONE, AGE 51-60 with HIGHBP NONE, AGE OVER 60 with HIGHBP NONE, AGE UNDER 51 with HIGHBP PRESENT, etc.

Output 11.2   Two-way frequency tables formed for each age interval. The age interval used is shown by an arrow.

```
              THE ANALYSIS IS OF THE DATA
              IN LEVEL UNDER 51 OF     AGE     (VAR   1)

              TABLE NO.   1              ACTIVE  VAR(   3) VS FUNCTIONVAR(   2)


              CELL FREQUENCY COUNTS
              --------------------

                                FUNCTION(VAR   2)

                          NONE    MINIMAL  MODERATE SEVERE
                  EQ./EQ.  0.00    1.00     2.00    3.00    TOTAL

ACTIVE  VERY    1.00        1        3        2       0  I    6
(VAR  3) NORMAL  2.00       1        7       14       2  I   24
        LIMITED 3.00        0        1        2       4  I    7
                          _____ _____ _____ _____
                TOTAL        2       11       18       6        37
        NOT    COUNTED       6        2        2       0
```
....

```
MINIMUM NONZERO EXPECTED VALUE IS      0.324

STATISTIC                VALUE   D.F.   PROB.
PEARSON CHISQUARE        13.703     6  0.0331
```
....

```
              THE ANALYSIS IS OF THE DATA
              IN LEVEL 51-60    OF    AGE     (VAR   1)

              TABLE NO.   2              ACTIVE  VAR(   3) VS FUNCTIONVAR(   2)


              CELL FREQUENCY COUNTS
              --------------------

                                FUNCTION(VAR   2)

                          NONE    MINIMAL  MODERATE SEVERE
                  EQ./EQ.  0.00    1.00     2.00    3.00    TOTAL

ACTIVE  VERY    1.00        1        1        0       1  I    3
(VAR  3) NORMAL  2.00       2        5       13       2  I   22
        LIMITED 3.00        0        0        0       9  I    9
                          _____ _____ _____ _____
                TOTAL        3        6       13      12        34
        NOT    COUNTED       4        4        3       3
```
....

```
MINIMUM NONZERO EXPECTED VALUE IS      0.265

STATISTIC                VALUE   D.F.   PROB.
PEARSON CHISQUARE        27.217     6  0.0001
```
....

```
              THE ANALYSIS IS OF THE DATA
              IN LEVEL OVER 60  OF     AGE     (VAR   1)

              TABLE NO.   3              ACTIVE  VAR(   3) VS FUNCTIONVAR(   2)


              CELL FREQUENCY COUNTS
              --------------------

                                FUNCTION(VAR   2)

                          NONE    MINIMAL  MODERATE SEVERE
                  EQ./EQ.  0.00    1.00     2.00    3.00    TOTAL

ACTIVE  VERY    1.00        0        0        0       0  I    0
(VAR  3) NORMAL  2.00       0        1       10       3  I   14
        LIMITED 3.00        0        0        0       3  I    3
                          _____ _____ _____ _____
                TOTAL        0        1       10       6        17
        NOT    COUNTED       5        0        0       0
```
....

```
MINIMUM NONZERO EXPECTED VALUE IS      0.176

STATISTIC                VALUE   D.F.   PROB.
PEARSON CHISQUARE         6.679     2  0.0355
```
....

--- this is followed by three tables for ANGINA by INFARCT ---

---

VARiable
    DEFINE(#)=$v_1,v_2,\cdots$.   {none}   may be repeated

    Names or subscripts of variables to be stacked (or combined) into a
    single index that defines a new variable. DEFINE constructs an
    index made up of all possible combinations of the levels (codes or
    categories) of the specified variables; # must be greater than any
    variable subscript. CODES or CUTPOINTS must be specified in the
    CATEGory paragraph for each variable, $v_1,v_2,\cdots$. The levels of v_1
    are the fastest changing, v_2 the next fastest, etc., in the new index
    variable created by the DEFINE statement. If more than one variable
    is DEFINED, each must be given a different subscript.

● TABLES OF EXPECTED VALUES AND PERCENTAGES

    Tables of percentages and the table of expected values are often desired.
The *PRINT* paragraph in the following example demonstrates how to request
these tables.

Example 11.3

```
/PROBLEM      TITLE IS 'KASSER CORONARY DATA'.
/INPUT        VARIABLES ARE 6.
              FORMAT IS '(6F4.0)'.
/VARIABLE     NAMES ARE AGE,FUNCTION,ACTIVE,INFARCT,ANGINA,HIGHBP.

/TABLE        COLUMN IS FUNCTION, INFARCT.
              ROW    IS ACTIVE  , ANGINA .

/CATEGORY     CODES(2) ARE    0,       1,       2,       3.
              NAMES(2) ARE NONE, MINIMAL, MODERATE, SEVERE.
              CODES(3) ARE    1,       2,       3.
              NAMES(3) ARE VERY, NORMAL, LIMITED.
              CODES(4) ARE    0,       1.
              NAMES(4) ARE NONE, PRESENT.
              CODES(5) ARE    0,       1.
              NAMES(5) ARE NONE, PRESENT.

/PRINT        EXPECTED.
              ROWPERCENT.
              COLPERCENT.
              TOTPERCENT.

/END
```

    The tables are presented in Output 11.3. Circled numbers below corres-
pond to those in the output. The tables are:

(6)   percentages of the total frequency: $100\ a_{ij}/N$

(7)   percentages of the row marginal frequencies: $100\ a_{ij}/r_i$

(8)   percentages of the column marginal frequencies: $100\ a_{ij}/c_j$

(9)   expected values (e_{ij}) calculated under the hypothesis of independence:
      $r_i c_j/N$

Output 11.3   Tables of percentages and of expected values printed by P1F.

--- results in Output 11.1 for ACTIVE by FUNCTION appear here ---

PERCENTAGES OF THE TOTAL FREQUENCY
----

⑥

		EQ./EQ.	FUNCTION(VAR 2)				
			NONE 0.00	MINIMAL 1.00	MODERATE 2.00	SEVERE 3.00	TOTAL
ACTIVE	VERY	1.00	2.27	4.55	2.27	1.14	10.23
(VAR 3)	NORMAL	2.00	3.41	14.77	42.05	7.95	68.18
	LIMITED	3.00	0.0	1.14	2.27	18.18	21.59
	TOTAL		5.68	20.45	46.59	27.27	100.00

PERCENTAGES OF THE ROW TOTALS
----

⑦

		EQ./EQ.	FUNCTION(VAR 2)				
			NONE 0.00	MINIMAL 1.00	MODERATE 2.00	SEVERE 3.00	TOTAL
ACTIVE	VERY	1.00	22.22	44.44	22.22	11.11	100.00
(VAR 3)	NORMAL	2.00	5.00	21.67	61.67	11.67	100.00
	LIMITED	3.00	0.0	5.26	10.53	84.21	100.00
	TOTAL		5.68	20.45	46.59	27.27	100.00

PERCENTAGES OF THE COLUMN TOTALS
----

⑧

		EQ./EQ.	FUNCTION(VAR 2)				
			NONE 0.00	MINIMAL 1.00	MODERATE 2.00	SEVERE 3.00	TOTAL
ACTIVE	VERY	1.00	40.00	22.22	4.88	4.17	10.23
(VAR 3)	NORMAL	2.00	60.00	72.22	90.24	29.17	68.18
	LIMITED	3.00	0.0	5.56	4.88	66.67	21.59
	TOTAL		100.00	100.00	100.00	100.00	100.00

EXPECTED CELL VALUES
----

⑨

		EQ./EQ.	FUNCTION(VAR 2)			
			NONE 0.00	MINIMAL 1.00	MODERATE 2.00	SEVERE 3.00
ACTIVE	VERY	1.00	0.51	1.84	4.19	2.45
(VAR 3)	NORMAL	2.00	3.41	12.27	27.95	16.36
	LIMITED	3.00	1.08	3.89	8.85	5.18

....

--- similar analysis for ANGINA by INFARCT ---

```
PRINT
   OBSERVED.              { OBSERVED}

      Table of observed frequencies (a_{ij}) is printed unless
      NO OBSERVED is specified.

   EXPECTED.              {no}

      Table of expected frequencies is printed: $e_{ij} = r_i c_j / N$.  The
      expected frequencies are computed after adding DELTA to each
      cell (see below).

   ROWPERCENT.            {no}

      Table of row percentages is printed: $100\ a_{ij}/r_i$.

   COLPERCENT.            {no}

      Table of column percentages is printed: $100\ a_{ij}/c_j$.

   TOTPERCENT.            {no}

      Table of percentages of total frequency is printed: $100\ a_{ij}/N$.
```

- ## DELTA: ADDING A CONSTANT TO EACH CELL

  When the observed cell frequencies contain many values near zero, some
data analysts add a constant to each cell before computing the x^2 test.
A constant (such as 0.5) can be added in P1F by specifying

          DELTA=0.5.

in the *TABLE* paragraph. Many statistics and tables are affected by the value
of DELTA.

  The constant is not added to rows or columns that are entirely zero.

```
TABLE
   DELTA=#.               {0.0}

      A constant added to the frequency in each cell of the table.  The
      definition of the Control Language instruction for each statistic
      or table states whether the value of DELTA affects the computation.
```

- ## COLLAPSING ADJACENT ROWS OR COLUMNS

  Low frequencies can be avoided by reducing the number of rows or columns.
This can be done in the *CATEGory* paragraph by modifying the CUTPOINTS
or by using the same NAMES for several codes or intervals.

P1F can automatically collapse rows or columns based on the minimum expected frequency. If the minimum expected frequency is less than a specified constant (1.0 or 5.0 is often used), the row or column (whichever has a smaller frequency) containing the cell is combined with a neighboring row or column (the neighbor with the smaller frequency). The minimum expected frequencies are computed for the collapsed tables and additional rows or columns are combined until all expected frequency values exceed the specified constant. Because this automatic collapsing involves only adjacent rows and columns, it may ignore logical collapsing of nonordered categories. Depending on the problem at hand, it may be more reasonable to run the program twice -- once to determine the expected cell values, and a second time to collapse by modifying cutpoints or names in the *CATEGory* paragraph.

The following example illustrates how rows and columns are collapsed by the addition of a MINIMUM statement in the *TABLE* paragraph.

Example 11.4

```
/PROBLEM     TITLE IS 'KASSER CORONARY DATA'.
/INPUT       VARIABLES ARE 6.
             FORMAT IS '(6F4.0)'.
/VARIABLE    NAMES ARE AGE,FUNCTION,ACTIVE,INFARCT,ANGINA,HIGHBP.

/TABLE       COLUMN IS FUNCTION, INFARCT.
             ROW    IS ACTIVE  , ANGINA .
             MINIMUM IS 1.

/CATEGORY    CODES(2) ARE     0,       1,       2,      3.
             NAMES(2) ARE NONE, MINIMAL, MODERATE, SEVERE.
             CODES(3) ARE     1,       2,      3.
             NAMES(3) ARE VERY, NORMAL, LIMITED.
             CODES(4) ARE     0,       1.
             NAMES(4) ARE NONE, PRESENT.
             CODES(5) ARE     0,       1.
             NAMES(5) ARE NONE, PRESENT.

/PRINT       EXPECTED.

/END
```

The observed frequency table in Output 11.4 has an extra row and column that indicate which rows and columns are combined before some tests and statistics are computed. The row COLLAP.GROUP contains the indices of the collapsed categories; that is, the first and second columns (NONE and MINIMAL) are combined prior to the computation of the Pearson χ^2 test. (This is indicated by the 1's in the row COLLAP.GROUP for the first two columns.) To see the effect of collapsing, the χ^2 test in this output can be compared with that in Output 11.1.

TABLE
  MINImum= #.   {zero}

    If the minimum expected frequency in the table is less than
    MINImum, adjacent rows or columns are combined (see above for
    method) before the χ^2 test, G^2, ϕ, contingency coefficient C and
    Cramer's V are computed; the other statistics and all tables are
    not affected.

- ### STATISTICS: TESTS AND MEASURES

The most familiar test for the independence of the rows and columns in a two-way table is the (Pearson) χ^2 test. When the table has two rows or two columns χ^2 is also a test for equality of proportions. If this is the only statistic you want, the *STATistics* paragraph is not needed.

A variety of tests of independence and measures of the relationships between the row and column variables are available in P1F. These tests and measures are described in Table 11.2. The columns in Table 11.2 are

- the name of the test or measure

- an indication of whether the test or measure assumes that the levels of the categorical variables are ordered

- the size of the table (any size (RxC) or square (RxR) or 2x2)

- the range of possible values for the statistics

- the formula (the formulas for all statistics and their standard errors, if computed, are given in Appendix A.5)

Output 11.4   Automatic collapsing performed by P1F. The first two columns are combined because cell (1,1) has an expected frequency less than the value specified for MINIMUM (1.0).

```
       TABLE NO.   1                      ACTIVE  VAR(   3) VS  FUNCTIONVAR(   2)


       CELL FREQUENCY COUNTS
       --------------------


                                FUNCTION(VAR   2)

                             NONE     MINIMAL  MODERATE SEVERE                   COLLAP.
                    EQ./EQ.  0.00     1.00     2.00     3.00      TOTAL          GROUP

     ACTIVE   VERY    1.00     2        4        2        1    I    9              1
     (VAR  3) NORMAL  2.00     3       13       37        7    I   60              2
              LIMITED 3.00     0        1        2       16    I   19              3
                              -------- -------- -------- --------
                    TOTAL      5       18       41       24        88
              NOT    COUNTED  15        6        5        3
              COLLAP. GROUP    1        1        2        3                        0
```
....

```
     MINIMUM NONZERO EXPECTED VALUE IS        0.511


     STATISTIC                  VALUE    D.F.   PROB.
     PEARSON CHISQUARE          47.014      4   0.0000
```
....

```
          EXPECTED CELL VALUES
          --------------------


                                FUNCTION(VAR   2)

                             NONE     MINIMAL  MODERATE SEVERE
                    EQ./EQ.  0.00     1.00     2.00     3.00

     ACTIVE   VERY    1.00    0.51     1.84     4.19     2.45
     (VAR  3) NORMAL  2.00    3.41    12.27    27.95    16.36
              LIMITED 3.00    1.08     3.89     8.85     5.18
```
....

Table 11.2 Tests and measures computed by P1F

Table 11.2

Tests and Measures Computed by P1F

Test or measure	Indices ordered?	Table	Range of values	Formula	Test that measure is zero	Interpretation
χ^2 test	no	RxC	$0,\infty$	$\chi^2 = \Sigma\Sigma \dfrac{(a_{ij}-e_{ij})^2}{e_{ij}}$	Chisquare with $(R-1)(C-1)$df	Tests of independence of rows and columns or equality of proportions between rows or columns
G^2 likelihood ratio test	no	RxC	$0,\infty$	$G^2 = 2\Sigma\Sigma\, a_{ij}\,\ell n\left(\dfrac{a_{ij}}{e_{ij}}\right)$	Chisquare with $(R-1)(C-1)$df	
χ_y^2 (Yates corrected χ^2)	no	2x2	$0,\infty$	$\chi_y^2 = \dfrac{N(\lvert ad-bc\rvert-\frac{N}{2})^2}{r_1 r_2 c_1 c_2}$	Chisquare with 1 df	
Fisher's exact test	no	2x2	$0,1$	probability of more extreme configuration (1-tail or 2-tail)		
ϕ (phi)	no	RxC	$0,m$	$\phi = (\chi^2/N)^{\frac{1}{2}}$	use χ^2 test	Same as χ^2 but not dependent on N. Used to compare tables.
		2x2	$-1,1$	$\phi = \dfrac{ad-bc}{(r_1 r_2 c_1 c_2)^{\frac{1}{2}}}$	use χ^2 test	
Contingency coefficient, C	no	RxC	$0,1$	$C = \left[\dfrac{\chi^2}{N+\chi^2}\right]^{\frac{1}{2}}$	use χ^2 test	
Cramer's V	no	RxC	$0,1$	$V = \left[\dfrac{\chi^2}{N(m-1)}\right]^{\frac{1}{2}}$	use χ^2 test	
Yule's Q	no	2x2	$-1,1$	$Q = \dfrac{ad-bc}{ad+bc}$	use χ^2 test	Probability of similar (dissimilar) ranking on two ordered indices among cases with different values for both indices
Yule's Y	no	2x2	$-1,1$	$Y = \dfrac{\sqrt{ad}-\sqrt{bc}}{\sqrt{ad}+\sqrt{bc}}$	use χ^2 test	Similar to Q but less weighting for similar and dissimilar rankings
Cross-product ratio α		2x2	$0,\infty$	$\alpha = \dfrac{ad}{bc}$	to test $\alpha=1$ use χ^2 test	odds-ratio $\cdot$ ratio of two proportions
Tetrachoric correlation, r_t		2x2	$-1,1$	Appendix A.5	$r_t/s_0(r_t)$	Correlation of bivariate normal with the probabilities a/N, b/N, c/N, d/N in the four quadrants.
Gamma, Γ	yes	RxC	$-1,1$	$\Gamma = \dfrac{P-Q}{P+Q}$	$\Gamma/s_0(\Gamma)$	Probability of similar (dissimilar) ranking on two indices among cases with different values for both indices
Kendall's τ_b	yes	RxC	$-1,1$	$\tau_b = \dfrac{P-Q}{[(N^2-\Sigma r_i^2)(N^2-\Sigma c_j^2)]^{\frac{1}{2}}}$	$t_b/s_0(t_b)$	Numerator as in Γ, denominator $\geq$ that of Γ
Stuart's τ_c	yes	RxC	$-1,1$	$\tau_c = \dfrac{P-Q}{N^2}\left[\dfrac{m}{m-1}\right]$	$t_c/s_0(t_c)$	Numerator as in Γ, τ_b. Denominator $\geq$ that of Γ, τ_b.
Product-moment correlation, r	yes	RxC	$-1,1$	$r = \dfrac{\Sigma\Sigma\, a_{ij}(i-\bar{i})(j-\bar{j})}{[\Sigma r_i(i-\bar{i})^2 \Sigma c_j(j-\bar{j})^2]^{\frac{1}{2}}}$	$r/s_0(r)$	Correlation using values of the indices with frequencies as number of replicates
Spearman rank correlation, r_s	yes	RxC	$-1,1$	$r_s \equiv r$ applied to ranks	$r_s/s_0(r_s)$	As in r except ranks of the indices are the values
Somers' D	yes	RxC	$-1,1$	$D_{j\mid i} = \dfrac{P-Q}{N^2-\Sigma r_i^2}$	$D/s_0(D)$	Probability of similar (dissimilar) ranking on two indices among cases with different values for row index. Note: $\tau_b^2 = D_{j\mid i}\cdot D_{i\mid j}$
Goodman and Kruskal τ	no	RxC	$0,1$	$\tau_{j\mid i} = \dfrac{N\,\Sigma\Sigma\, a_{ij}^2/r_i - \Sigma c_j^2}{N^2 - \Sigma c_j^2}$	use χ^2 test	Compares random proportional prediction of one index with conditional proportional prediction based upon knowledge of second index.
Optimal prediction λ	no	RxC	$0,1$	$\lambda_{j\mid i} = \dfrac{\Sigma\limits_i \max\limits_j a_{ij} - \max\limits_j c_j}{N - \max\limits_j c_j}$		Measure of predictive association--relative degree of success with which one index can be used to predict second index
Optimal prediction λ^*	no	RxC	$0,1$	$\lambda_{j\mid i}^* = \dfrac{\Sigma(\max\limits_j a_{ij})/r_i - \max\limits_j \Sigma(a_{ij}/r_i)}{R - \max\limits_j \Sigma(a_{ij}/r_i)}$		Similar to λ but adjusted to have common row marginals
Uncertainty coefficient, U	no	RxC	$0,1$	$U_{j\mid i} = \dfrac{\Sigma\Sigma\, a_{ij}\ell n[r_i c_j/(a_{ij}N)]}{\Sigma c_j\,\ell n\,[c_j/N]}$	use G^2 test	Relative reduction in uncertainty about one index when the second index is known
McNemar's test of symmetry	no	RxR (square)	$0,\infty$	$\chi_{MC}^2 = \Sigma\Sigma\limits_{i<j} \dfrac{(a_{ij}-a_{ji})^2}{a_{ij}+a_{ji}}$	chisquare with $R(R-1)/2$ df	Test of symmetry by comparing each pair of cells about diagonal

Note: The columns are more fully described on p. 260.
The notation is defined in Appendix A.5.

- the test that the measure is zero (many tests are equivalent either to the χ^2 test or likelihood ratio G^2; for several measures, a t-like statistic is used, Brown and Benedetti, 1977a)

- an interpretation of the test or measure's meaning or usage

The statistics are discussed according to their use. *The computation of the statistics does not include rows and columns that are entirely zero.*

Tests of independence between rows and columns, or of the equality of proportions

An alternative to the usual (Pearson) χ^2 test is the likelihood ratio chi-square statistic G^2. This test is based on maximum likelihood estimation, and is used more than any other test statistic in the analysis of multiway frequency tables. It can be requested by the command

LRCHI.

in the *STATistics* paragraph.

When the table is 2x2, two statistics are often used -- the Yates' corrected χ^2 (χ^2_y) and Fisher's exact test. Yates' correction is thought to provide an improved approximation to the chi-square distribution, and is automatically printed when the table is 2x2.

P1F computes Fisher's exact test for a 2x2 table when the minimum expected value is less than 20. The two-tail probability is the sum over all configurations (e.g., patterns of cell frequencies) whose probability assuming independence is less than or equal to the probability of the observed configuration (each pattern must preserve the observed row and column totals). The one-tail probability is the sum over the configurations in the same tail as the one observed that have a probability less than or equal to that observed. If your hypothesis is one-sided the tail needed to test the hypothesis may differ from the one-tail probability computed; if it does differ, its probability exceeds 0.5 and is therefore nonsignificant.

STATistics

CHISQUARE.   {CHISQUARE/ prev.}

The χ^2 test and (if the table is 2x2) Yates' corrected χ^2 (χ^2_y) are computed. The χ^2 test is computed after collapsing, if any, and after adding the constant DELTA. χ^2_y is computed after adding DELTA.

LRCHI.   {no/prev.}

The likelihood ratio chi-square G^2 is computed after collapsing, if any, and after adding DELTA.

FISHER.   {no/prev.}   2x2 table only

Fisher's exact probabilities, both 1-tail and 2-tail, are computed. See above for a definition, and Appendix A.5 for the exact formula.

Measures related to the χ^2 test

The χ^2 statistic is dependent on the sample size N; that is, when the model of independence is not appropriate (i.e., the row variable is related to the column variable), the expected value of the χ^2 statistic is proportional to the sample size N. Other statistics, such as the contingency coefficient C, ϕ and Cramer's V, are functions of χ^2 that do not show dependence on N. These measures are useful in comparing results between tables based on different sample sizes, and are of a descriptive nature only.

When the table is 2x2, ϕ corresponds to Cramer's V. Otherwise V is always less than or equal to unity, but ϕ can exceed unity. C is normalized differently from ϕ and V. All three measures are zero if (and only if) the χ^2 test is zero. Therefore the hypothesis that they are equal to zero can be tested by the χ^2 test for independence.

If the row and column totals are held fixed, the totals determine the maximum value that these measures can attain. In the 2x2 table ϕ_{max} and C_{max} are printed, where ϕ_{max} is the largest positive value of ϕ attainable when the observed ϕ is positive, and the largest negative value of ϕ attainable when the observed ϕ is negative. C_{max} is obtained from ϕ_{max}.

Measures appropriate to a 2x2 table

The odds-ratio, Yule's Q and Y and the tetrachoric correlation are measures developed specifically for a 2x2 table. The measures are zero if (and only if) the χ^2 test for independence is zero. Therefore the hypothesis that a measure is zero can be tested by the χ^2 test or by the ratio of the statistic to its estimated standard error.

The tetrachoric correlation is appropriate when the 2x2 table is formed by dividing two continuous variables, each into two parts, and counting the frequencies (number of cases) in the four quadrants formed by the division. If the frequency in one cell is zero, it is set to ½ and all other frequencies are altered to preserve row and column totals. This provides a lower limit on the correlation. See Brown and Benedetti (1977b) for a discussion of the tetrachoric correlation.

In addition to the odds-ratio, the natural logarithm of the odds-ratio and its standard error are also printed. The use of the odds ratio in retrospective and prospective studies is discussed by Mantel and Haenszel (1959) and by Fleiss (1973, Chapters 5 and 6).

STATistics
CONTINGENCY.   {no/prev.}

The contingency coefficient C, ϕ, Cramer's V and, if the table is 2x2, Yule's Q and Y, C_{max}, ϕ_{max} and the odds-ratio α are computed. C, V and ϕ are computed from the value of the χ^2 test. The others are computed only if the observed table is 2x2; they are computed after adding the constant DELTA.

```
STATistics
    TETRACHORIC.            {no/prev.}

    The tetrachoric correlation $r_t$ is computed for a 2x2 table only.
    See Appendix A.5 for an exact definition.  It is computed
    after the addition of DELTA.
```

Measures of association and correlation

The measures Γ, τ_b, and τ_c are appropriate when both indices of the table have ordered categories. They differ only in their denominator; that is, in how ties are treated ($|\tau_c| < |\tau_b| < |\Gamma|$). Tests that these measures, the correlation r, and the Spearman rank correlation r_s are zero are discussed by Brown and Benedetti (1977a). They use the ratio of the estimate of the measure to its approximate asymptotic standard error (s_0) under the hypothesis that the measure is zero. For sufficiently large samples, the ratio is approximately a t statistic. Also, for sufficiently large samples, confidence limits can be constructed for the measure by using the asymptotic standard error formula developed by Goodman and Kruskal (1972).

Somers' D is an asymmetric measure of association. Table 11.2 shows how it is related to τ_b.

```
STATistics
    GAMMA.                  {no/prev.}

    $\Gamma$, Kendall's $\tau_b$, Stuart's $\tau_c$ and Somers' D are computed.

    CORRELATION.            {no/prev.}

    The product-moment correlation is computed.

    SPEARMAN.               {no/prev.}

    The Spearman rank correlation is computed.
```

Measures of prediction and uncertainty

Goodman and Kruskal's τ, λ, λ^* and the uncertainty coefficient U all measure the gain in predicting one categorical variable of the table when the value of the second categorical variable is known, relative to when it is not known. The conditions imposed on the frequencies differ between statistics. See Goodman and Kruskal (1954) for a discussion of the first three measures.

These measures assume no ordering of the categories. They are inherently asymmetric. Each categorical variable can be predicted from the other one. P1F computes both asymmetric forms for each statistic. You must choose the one appropriate to your problem. Both λ and U also have a symmetric form created by summing the numerators and denominators of the two asymmetric forms and then calculating the ratio.

```
STATistics
    TAUS.                    {no/prev.}

    Goodman and Kruskal's τ is printed.

    LAMBDA.                  {no/prev.}

    Goodman and Kruskal's λ, both asymmetric and symmetric, are
    printed.

    LSTAR.                   {no/prev.}

    Goodman and Kruskal's λ* is printed.

    UNCERTAINTY.             {no/prev.}

    The uncertainty coefficients, both asymmetric and symmetric,
    are printed.
```

In Example 11.5 we request all the statistics discussed above.

Example 11.5

```
/PROBLEM      TITLE IS 'KASSER CORONARY DATA'.
/INPUT        VARIABLES ARE 6.
              FORMAT IS '(6F4.0)'.
/VARIABLE     NAMES ARE AGE,FUNCTION,ACTIVE,INFARCT,ANGINA,HIGHBP.

/TABLE        COLUMN IS FUNCTION, INFARCT.
              ROW    IS ACTIVE  , ANGINA .

/CATEGORY     CODES(2) ARE    0,       1,       2,       3.
              NAMES(2) ARE NONE, MINIMAL, MODERATE, SEVERE.
              CODES(3) ARE    1,       2,       3.
              NAMES(3) ARE VERY, NORMAL, LIMITED.
              CODES(4) ARE    0,       1.
              NAMES(4) ARE NONE, PRESENT.
              CODES(5) ARE    0,       1.
              NAMES(5) ARE NONE, PRESENT.


/STATISTICS   LRCHI.
              FISHER.
              CONTINGENCY.
              TETRACHORIC.
              GAMMA.
              CORRELATION.
              SPEARMAN.
              TAUS.
              LAMBDA.
              LSTAR.
              UNCERTAINTY.

/END
```

The statistics are printed in Output 11.5. Circled numbers below
correspond to those in the output. The statistics are presented in two
panels.

(10) If computed, the chi-square tests and related measures and Fisher's
exact test are printed in the top panel. For each chi-square test, its
degrees of freedom (D.F.) and its tail probability (PROB) are also printed.

Output 11.5. Measures and tests computed by P1F.

```
        TABLE NO.   1              ACTIVE  VAR(  3) VS  FUNCTIONVAR(  2)


        CELL FREQUENCY COUNTS
        --------------------

                                 FUNCTION(VAR  2)

                           NONE   MINIMAL  MODERATE SEVERE
                   EQ./EQ.  0.00    1.00     2.00    3.00    TOTAL

  ACTIVE   VERY    1.00      2       4        2       1   I    9
  (VAR  3) NORMAL  2.00      3      13       37       7   I   60
           LIMITED 3.00      0       1        2      16   I   19
                         ------- ------- ------- -------
                  TOTAL      5      18       41      24       88
            NOT  COUNTED    15       6        5       3
```

```
  MINIMUM NONZERO EXPECTED VALUE IS      0.511
  ----- ALL STATISTICS ARE COMPUTED USING THE ORIGINAL CELL FREQUENCIES
            EXCLUDING ROWS AND/OR COLUMNS WHICH ARE ZERO.
```

	STATISTIC	VALUE	D.F.	PROB.	STATISTIC	VALUE	D.F.	PROB.
(10)	PEARSON CHISQUARE	48.365	6	0.0000	LIKELIHOOD RATIO CHISQ.	43.906	6	0.0000
	PHI	0.741						
	CONTINGENCY COEF. C	0.596			CRAMER'S V	0.524		

	STATISTIC	VALUE	ASE1	T-VALUE	DEP.	STATISTIC	VALUE	ASE1	T-VALUE	DEP.
(11)	GAMMA	0.785	0.100	5.368		STUART'S TAU-C	0.453	0.084	5.368	
						KENDALL'S TAU-B	0.536	0.086	5.368	
	SOMER'S D	0.632	0.097	5.368	2	SOMER'S D	0.455	0.082	5.368	3
	PRODUCT MOMENT CORRELATION	0.551	0.087	4.538		SPEARMAN RANK CORRELATION	0.574	0.089	5.537	
						LAMBDA-SYMMETRIC	0.333	0.096	2.948	
	LAMBDA-ASYMMETRIC	0.340	0.085	3.484	2	LAMBDA-ASYMMETRIC	0.321	0.141	1.915	3
	LAMBDA-STAR-ASYMMETRIC	0.432	0.109	3.477	2	LAMBDA-STAR-ASYMMETRIC	0.253	0.117	2.032	3
	TAU-ASYMMETRIC	0.231	0.060	3.936	2	TAU-ASYMMETRIC	0.317	0.089	3.273	3
						UNCERTAINTY-NORMED	0.247	0.066	3.599	
	UNCERTAINTY-ASYM.-NORMED	0.208	0.058	3.599	2	UNCERTAINTY-ASYM.-NORMED	0.302	0.079	3.599	3

```
        TABLE NO.   2              ANGINA  VAR(  5) VS  INFARCT VAR(  4)


        CELL FREQUENCY COUNTS
        --------------------

                              INFARCT (VAR  4)

                         NONE   PRESENT
                 EQ./EQ.  0.00    1.00    TOTAL

  ANGINA  NONE    0.00     3       16   I    19
  (VAR  5) PRESENT 1.00    40       58   I    98
                        -------- --------
                 TOTAL    43       74      117
```

```
  MINIMUM NONZERO EXPECTED VALUE IS      6.983
  ----- ALL STATISTICS ARE COMPUTED USING THE ORIGINAL CELL FREQUENCIES
            EXCLUDING ROWS AND/OR COLUMNS WHICH ARE ZERO.
```

	STATISTIC	VALUE	D.F.	PROB.	STATISTIC	VALUE	D.F.	PROB.
(10)	FISHER EXACT TEST(1-TAIL)			0.0309	FISHER EXACT TEST(2-TAIL)			0.0413
	PEARSON CHISQUARE	4.288	1	0.0384	YATES' CORRECTED CHISQUARE	3.279	1	0.0702
	LIKELIHOOD RATIO CHISQ.	4.778	1	0.0288				
	PHI=CRAMER'S V	-0.191			MAXIMUM VALUE FOR PHI	-0.336		
	CONTINGENCY COEF. C	0.188			MAXIMUM VALUE FOR C	0.318		

	STATISTIC	VALUE	ASE1	T-VALUE	DEP.	STATISTIC	VALUE	ASE1	T-VALUE	DEP.
(11)	YULE'S Q	-0.572	0.222	-2.202		YULE'S Y	-0.315	0.149	-2.420	
	CROSS-PRODUCT RATIO	0.272				LOG(CROSS-PRODUCT RATIO)	-1.302	0.662	-2.505	
	TETRACHORIC CORRELATION	-0.396	0.166	-2.231						
	GAMMA	-0.572	0.222	-2.359		STUART'S TAU-C	-0.136	0.058	-2.359	
						KENDALL'S TAU-B	-0.191	0.075	-2.359	
	SOMER'S D	-0.250	0.097	-2.359	4	SOMER'S D	-0.146	0.062	-2.359	5
	PRODUCT MOMENT CORRELATION	-0.191	0.075	-2.359		SPEARMAN RANK CORRELATION	-0.191	0.075	-2.359	
						LAMBDA-SYMMETRIC	0.0	0.0	0.0	
	LAMBDA-ASYMMETRIC	0.0	0.0	0.0	4	LAMBDA-ASYMMETRIC	0.0	0.0	0.0	5
	LAMBDA-STAR-ASYMMETRIC	0.0	0.0	0.0	4	LAMBDA-STAR-ASYMMETRIC	0.0	0.0	0.0	5
	TAU-ASYMMETRIC	0.037	0.028	1.286	4	TAU-ASYMMETRIC	0.037	0.029	1.188	5
						UNCERTAINTY-NORMED	0.037	0.031	1.180	
	UNCERTAINTY-ASYM.-NORMED	0.031	0.026	1.180	4	UNCERTAINTY-ASYM.-NORMED	0.046	0.038	1.180	5

⑪ The remaining statistics are printed in the second panel. Two asymptotic standard errors are computed for each statistic. One asymptotic standard error s_1, labelled ASE1 in the output, can be used to form confidence intervals for the statistics. The other standard error s_0 can be used to test the null hypothesis that the measure is zero; the value of the statistic divided by s_0 is labelled T-VALUE in the output. The two asymptotic standard errors are discussed in greater detail by Brown and Benedetti (1977a).

For each asymmetric measure (Somers' D, λ, λ^*, τ, and the uncertainty coefficient), two asymmetric statistics are printed. These are predictive measures; the dependent (predicted) variable is listed under the heading DEP. in the output.

McNemar's test of symmetry

When the same subjects are measured at two different times, square frequency tables are produced; the two categorical variables represent the results. For such frequency tables it may be more appropriate to test for change around the diagonal rather than for independence. One diagonal test is McNemar's test of symmetry, which tests the equality of frequencies in all pairs of cells that are symmetric about the diagonal. In the 2x2 table this reduces to the test of equality of the two off-diagonal cells.

STATistics
　　MCNEMAR　　　　　　　{no}　　　　　　　　　　　　RxR tables only

　　　McNemar's test of symmetry is printed. It is computed after adding the constant DELTA.

● TESTING A CONTRAST ON THE PROPORTIONS

When one categorical variable is dichotomous (i.e., the table is 2xC or Rx2), hypotheses can be specified about linear combinations of the proportions. Cochran (1954) proposed a test of the linear trend of the proportions on an arbitrary set of weights. This is equivalent to testing the slope of a simple linear regression where the dependent variable is the proportion.

The weights (COEFFICIENTS) are specified for each categorical variable for which the test of slope is desired. The test is computed whenever the other categorical variable in the two-way table has two levels (i.e., the table is 2xC or Rx2).

CATEGory
　　COEFFICIENTS(#)=$\#_1,\#_2,\cdots$.　　　{none}　　2xC or Rx2 table only

　　　The coefficients of variable (#) are used in testing the probabilities in a dichotomy for a linear trend. The formula for the 1 degree of freedom χ^2 test is in Appendix A.5.

In the following example we specify a linear trend for the three AGE groupings by adding a COEFFICIENT statement in the *CATEGory* paragraph. We request tables of AGE by INFARCT and AGE by ANGINA; both are 3x2.

Example 11.6

```
/PROBLEM     TITLE IS 'KASSER CORONARY DATA'.
/INPUT       VARIABLES ARE 6.
             FORMAT IS '(6F4.0)'.
/VARIABLE    NAMES ARE AGE,FUNCTION,ACTIVE,INFARCT,ANGINA,HIGHBP.

/TABLE       ROW    IS AGE.
             COLUMN IS INFARCT, ANGINA.
             CROSS.

/CATEGORY    CODES(4) ARE     0,       1.
             NAMES(4) ARE NONE, PRESENT.
             CODES(5) ARE     0,       1.
             NAMES(5) ARE NONE, PRESENT.
             CUTPOINTS(1)    ARE        50,       60.
             NAMES(1)        ARE 'UNDER 51', '51-60', 'OVER 60'.
             COEFFICIENTS(1) ARE          1,       2,          3.

/END
```

The results are presented in Output 11.6. A test of the linear regression is provided for each table.

● RESIDUALS

Residuals are measures of the differences between the observed and expected values of the cells. P1F can be used to help you examine residuals; it can compute and print

DIFFERENCES: $(a_{ij} - e_{ij})$

STANDARDIZED residuals: $(a_{ij} - e_{ij})/\sqrt{e_{ij}}$

ADJUSTED standardized residuals:

$$(a_{ij} - e_{ij})/ \left[e_{ij} \left(1 - \frac{r_i}{N} \right) \left(1 - \frac{c_j}{N} \right) \right]^{\frac{1}{2}}$$

FREEMAN-Tukey residuals:

$$\sqrt{a_{ij}} + \sqrt{a_{ij}+1} - \sqrt{4e_{ij}+1}$$

The standardized residuals are the square roots of the components of the χ^2 statistic; the sum of squares of the standardized residuals is the χ^2 statistic. Haberman (1973) proposed using an adjusted standardized residual since it has equal variance for all cells. The Freeman-Tukey residual (Bishop et al.,1975) is based on a transformation that normalizes variables with a Poisson distribution.

<u>Output 11.6.</u> Test of a trend in proportions for 2xC or Rx2 tables. The test
is indicated by an arrow.

```
        TABLE NO.    1                    AGE     VAR(  1) VS  INFARCT VAR(   4)

        CELL FREQUENCY COUNTS
        ---------------------

                                      INFARCT (VAR    4)

                            NONE     PRESENT
                   LE./EQ.  0.00      1.00     TOTAL

AGE        UNDER 51  50.0     20        27    I     47
(VAR  1) 51-60       60.0     15        33    I     48
           OVER 60  MAX.       8        14    I     22
                                    -------- --------
                   TOTAL       43        74        117
```
....

```
    MINIMUM NONZERO EXPECTED VALUE IS       8.085

    STATISTIC                    VALUE    D.F.   PROB.
    PEARSON CHISQUARE            1.307       2  0.5202
    CHISQ FOR REGRESSION COEFF.  0.534       1  0.4648  ↖
```
....


```
        TABLE NO.    2                    AGE     VAR(  1) VS  ANGINA VAR(   5)

        CELL FREQUENCY COUNTS
        ---------------------

                                      ANGINA (VAR    5)

                            NONE     PRESENT
                   LE./EQ.  0.00      1.00     TOTAL

AGE        UNDER 51  50.0      7        40    I     47
(VAR  1) 51-60       60.0      9        39    I     48
           OVER 60  MAX.       3        19    I     22
                                    -------- --------
                   TOTAL       19        98        117
```
....

```
    MINIMUM NONZERO EXPECTED VALUE IS       3.573

    STATISTIC                    VALUE    D.F.   PROB.
    PEARSON CHISQUARE            0.395       2  0.8209
    CHISQ FOR REGRESSION COEFF.  0.000       1  0.9838  ↖
```
....

PRINT

    DIFFERENCES.   {no}

        Table of differences; $d_{ij} = a_{ij} - e_{ij}$

    STANDARDIZED.   {no}

        Table of standardized residuals ; $d_{ij} = (a_{ij}-e_{ij})/\sqrt{e_{ij}}$

    ADJUSTED.   {no}

        Table of adjusted standardized residuals   (Haberman, 1973);

$$d_{ij} = (a_{ij}-e_{ij})/ \left[e_{ij} \left(1 - \frac{r_i}{N} \right) \left(1 - \frac{c_j}{N} \right) \right]^{\frac{1}{2}}$$

    FREEMAN.   {no}

        Table of Freeman-Tukey residuals; $d_{ij} = \sqrt{a_{ij}} + \sqrt{a_{ij}+1} - \sqrt{4e_{ij}+1}$

Note: The above tables are computed after adding DELTA *to each cell.*

• ADJUSTED MARGINALS

    Mosteller (1968) smoothed the values in a two-way frequency table by adjusting the marginals iteratively so that each row total is 100/R and each column total is 100/C, where R is the number of rows, and C is the number of columns. P1F smoothes your frequency table when

        SMOOTH.

is specified in the *PRINT* paragraph.

PRINT

    SMOOTH.   {no/prev.}

      Table of "smoothed" values. Table frequencies are iteratively adjusted until the row totals are 100/R and column totals are 100/C. The computation of these values is described in Appendix A.5.

    To illustrate how to request several of the above tables we use the following example.

Example 11.7

```
/PROBLEM       TITLE IS 'KASSER CORONARY DATA'.
/INPUT         VARIABLES ARE 6.
               FORMAT IS '(6F4.0)'.
/VARIABLE      NAMES ARE AGE,FUNCTION,ACTIVE,INFARCT,ANGINA,HIGHBP.

/TABLE         COLUMN IS FUNCTION, INFARCT.
               ROW    IS ACTIVE  , ANGINA .

/CATEGORY      CODES(2) ARE    0,      1,      2,      3.
               NAMES(2) ARE NONE, MINIMAL, MODERATE, SEVERE.
               CODES(3) ARE    1,      2,      3.
               NAMES(3) ARE VERY, NORMAL, LIMITED.
               CODES(4) ARE    0,      1.
               NAMES(4) ARE NONE, PRESENT.
               CODES(5) ARE    0,      1.
               NAMES(5) ARE NONE, PRESENT.

/PRINT         STANDARDIZED.
               ADJUSTED.
               FREEMAN.
               SMOOTH.

/END
```

The tables are presented in Output 11.7.

● FORMS OF DATA INPUT

Usually a case contains data for a single observation. In the frequency table programs you can also input tabulated data, such as a table from a government or scientific report. Each case can represent data from a cell of the table; the number of observations (frequency) in the cell is recorded as one of the variables. The data can also be input as frequency tables.

We use P1F to illustrate two forms of data input: frequency table input and data input as cell indices and frequencies. These forms of data input are identical for all three frequency table programs.

If the data have already been accumulated into a (multiway) frequency table, it is more efficient to use the table as input than to return to the original data. Consider a frequency table that has two rows and three columns, such as

```
        10   20   30
        40   50   60
```

This table can be read by P1F in either of two ways. You can record only the frequencies on your data card; e.g.,

```
        10   20   30   40   50   60
```

You then need to specify the dimensions of the TABLE in the *INPut* paragraph; e.g.,

```
        TABLE=3,2.
```

where 3 is the number of levels of the index that changes more rapidly (columns in our example) and 2 of the index that changes more slowly (rows). Or you can record each cell frequency with the indices of the cell; e.g.,

11.1 FREQUENCY TABLES

<u>Output 11.7.</u> Residuals and smoothed values printed by P1F.

--- results in Output 11.1 for ACTIVE by FUNCTION appear here ---

STANDARDIZED DEVIATIONS =(OBSERVED-EXPECTED)/SQRT(EXPECTED)

```
                           FUNCTION(VAR   2)
                     NONE    MINIMAL  MODERATE SEVERE
             EQ./EQ.  0.00    1.00     2.00    3.00

ACTIVE  VERY   1.00    2.08    1.59    -1.07   -0.93
(VAR 3) NORMAL 2.00   -0.22    0.21     1.71   -2.31
        LIMITED 3.00  -1.04   -1.46    -2.30    4.75
```

ADJUSTED STANDARDIZED DEVIATIONS =(OBSERVED-EXPECTED)/STANDARD DEVIATION OF THE NUMERATOR

```
                           FUNCTION(VAR   2)
                     NONE    MINIMAL  MODERATE SEVERE
             EQ./EQ.  0.00    1.00     2.00    3.00

ACTIVE  VERY   1.00    2.26    1.88    -1.55   -1.15
(VAR 3) NORMAL 2.00   -0.40    0.41     4.15   -4.81
        LIMITED 3.00  -1.21   -1.85    -3.56    6.29
```

FREEMAN/TUKEY DEVIATES

```
                           FUNCTION(VAR   2)
                     NONE    MINIMAL  MODERATE SEVERE
             EQ./EQ.  0.00    1.00     2.00    3.00

ACTIVE  VERY   1.00    1.40    1.34    -1.07   -0.87
(VAR 3) NORMAL 2.00   -0.09    0.27     1.63   -2.68
        LIMITED 3.00  -1.31   -1.65    -2.89    3.46
```

SMOOTHED VALUES

```
                           FUNCTION(VAR   2)
                     NONE    MINIMAL  MODERATE SEVERE
             EQ./EQ.  0.00    1.00     2.00    3.00    TOTAL

ACTIVE  VERY   1.00   18.01   11.10    3.38    0.84    33.33
(VAR 3) NORMAL 2.00    6.84    9.14   15.86    1.49    33.33
        LIMITED 3.00   0.0     4.71    5.74   22.88    33.33

        TOTAL         24.85   24.94   24.98   25.22   100.00
```

CONVERGENCE REACHED AFTER 7 ITERATIONS.

--- similar analysis for ANGINA by INFARCT ---

```
1 1  10
1 2  20
1 3  30
2 1  40
2 2  50
2 3  60
```

and treat each cell as a case. Then in the *TABLE* paragraph you would specify

COUNT=3.

to indicate that the cell frequencies are recorded as variable 3.

As a more complex example we use the following 2x2x3 table from Woolf (1955) (Table 11.3).

Table 11.3   Incidence of Peptic Ulcer by Blood Group (Woolf, 1955)

Blood Group	LONDON		MANCHESTER		NEWCASTLE	
	0	A	0	A	0	A
Illness						
ULCER	911	579	361	246	396	219
CONTROL	4578	4219	4532	3775	6598	5261

Input as a multiway table

The multiway table can be written as

911   579 4578 4219   361   246 4532 3775   396   219 6598 5261

where the frequencies are ordered so that Blood Group is the fastest varying index, Illness the next fastest, and City the slowest. That is, if i represents Blood Group, j is Illness, k is City and f_{ijk} is the frequency in cell (i,j,k), the order of cells is

$$f_{111}, f_{211}, f_{121}, f_{221}, f_{112}, f_{212}, f_{221}, f_{222}, f_{113}, f_{213}, f_{123}, f_{223}.$$

To read this table as input you must specify

TABLE=2,2,3.

in the *INPut* paragraph, where the first 2 is the number of levels of the fastest varying index, the second 2 is the number of levels of the next fastest varying index and 3 is the number of levels of the slowest varying index.

In the following example we present the Control Language instructions and the data; the data are read as a multiway table.

Example 11.8

```
/PROBLEM     TITLE IS 'BLISS BLCCDGROUPING DATA -
                 EXAMPLE OF MULTIWAY TABLE INPUT'.
/INPUT       VARIABLES ARE 3.
             TABLE IS 2,2,3.
             FORMAT IS '(4F5.0)'.
/VARIABLE    NAMES ARE BLOODGRP,ILLNESS,CITY.

/TABLE       ROW IS ILLNESS.
             COLUMN IS BLOODGRP.

/CATEGORY    NAMES(1) ARE 'GROUP O','GROUP A'.
             NAMES(2) ARE ULCER,CONTROL.
             NAMES(3) ARE LONDON,MANCHSTR,NEWCASTL.

/END
   911  579 4578 4219
   361  246 4532 3775
   396  219 6598 5261
```

*Control
Language
instructions*

*input is
multiway
table*

The number of VARIABLES in the input is the number of categorical variables in the table (3 in our example). The FORMAT describes the entire table (the entire table is read at one time).

In the above example the 12 cell frequencies are punched on 3 cards. (They could be punched on one card.) P1F determines the number of values to read from the TABLE statement in the *INPut* paragraph (2x2x3=12). The FORMAT (4F5.0) is equivalent to (4F5.0/4F5.0/4F5.0) since the format specification is repeated until all 12 values are read.

The table shown in Output 11.8 is obtained from Example 11.8. The frequencies in the table ILLNESS by BLOODGRP are the results of summing the observed frequencies over the index CITY. That is, the table to be analyzed can be a subtable of the table read as input.

Output 11.8   Example of using a multiway frequency table as input to P1F

```
          TABLE NO.   1              ILLNESS VAR(  2) VS  BLOODGRPVAR(   1)


          CELL FREQUENCY COUNTS
          --------------------

                              BLOODGRP(VAR    1)

                         GROUP O  GROUP A
                EQ./EQ.   1.00     2.00     TOTAL

ILLNESS   ULCER    1.00    1668    1044   I 2712
(VAR  2)  CONTROL  2.00   15708   13255   I28963

                 TOTAL    17376   14299   31675
..................................................................

  MINIMUM NONZERO EXPECTED VALUE IS   1224.274
  ----- ALL STATISTICS ARE COMPUTED USING THE ORIGINAL CELL FREQUENCIES
          EXCLUDING ROWS AND/OR COLUMNS WHICH ARE ZERO.


STATISTIC                VALUE   D.F.  PROB.    STATISTIC                   VALUE   D.F.  PROB.
PEARSON CHISQUARE        52.921     1  0.0000   YATES' CORRECTED CHISQUARE  52.628     1  0.0000
..................................................................
```

```
┌─
│ INPut
│    TABLE=#₁,#₂,····.        {none}        required if data are input as a
│                                           multiway table
│
│    #₁,#₂,... are the number of levels of each of the categorical
│    variables (factors) in the table; their product is the number of
│    cells in the table.  #₁ is the number of levels of the fastest vary-
│    ing index, #₂ of the next fastest, etc.  A maximum of seven indices
│    can be used.  The number of VARIABLES should be specified as
│    the number of factors;  the number of CASEs is not used; and the
│    FORMAT should describe the entire table.  Transformations and
│    data editing cannot be used with this form of input.
└─
```

Input as cell indices and frequencies

The tabulated data can also be organized as sets of cell indices and
frequency count, such as

1	1	1	911	2	1	1	361	3	1	1	396
1	1	2	579	2	1	2	246	3	1	2	219
1	2	1	4578	2	2	1	4532	3	2	1	6598
1	2	2	4219	2	2	2	3775	3	2	2	5261

The data are typed as 12 records, where each record is a set of (3) cell
indices and the observed frequency for that cell. The first three numbers
represent the categories for CITY, ILLNESS and BLOODGRP respectively; the
fourth number is the frequency.

To read the data, the following Control Language instructions are used.

Example 11.9

```
/PROBLEM      TITLE IS 'BLISS BLOODGROUPING DATA — EXAMPLE OF
                  CELL INDICES AND FREQUENCIES INPUT'.
/INPUT        VARIABLES ARE 4.
              CASES ARE 12.
              FORMAT IS '(3F2.0,F5.0)'.
/VARIABLE     NAMES ARE CITY,ILLNESS,BLOODGRP,FREQ.

/TABLE        ROW IS ILLNESS.
              COLUMN IS BLOODGRP.
              COUNT IS FREQ.

/CATEGORY     NAMES(1) ARE LONDON,MANCHSTR,NEWCASTL.
              NAMES(2) ARE ULCER,CONTROL.
              NAMES(3) ARE 'GROUP O','GROUP A'.

/END
```

*Control
Language
instructions*

(continued)

```
1  1  1    911
1  1  2    579
1  2  1   4578
1  2  2   4219
2  1  1    361
2  1  2    246
2  2  1   4532
2  2  2   3775
3  1  1    396
3  1  2    219
3  2  1   6598
3  2  2   5261
```

*input is in
form of cell
indices and
frequencies*

Each categorical variable and the "frequency count" variable are treated as variables (VARIABLE=4). The format describes a case (there are 12 cases, one for each cell in the table) which consists of a set of indices and its frequency count. Therefore, the data are described in the same manner as when each case is an observation. When COUNT=FREQ is specified in the *TABLE* paragraph, the program accumulates frequencies in the COUNT variable (FREQ) instead of treating each case as one observation.

The table is printed in Output 11.9. The frequencies are the same as in Output 11.8.

TABLE
    COUNT=v_1,v_2,$\cdots$.   {none}   required <u>only</u> when data are
                                                               input as <u>cell</u> indices and
                                                               frequency counts

    Names or subscripts of variables that contain frequency counts. If
    more than one variable is specified, tables are formed for each
    variable separately.

<u>Output 11.9</u> Example of using cell indices and frequencies as input to P1F

```
THE ANALYSIS IS OF THE DATA
USING THE FREQUENCY COUNTS IN  FREQ    (VAR   4)


TABLE NO.   1              ILLNESS VAR(   2) VS  BLOODGRPVAR(   3)


CELL FREQUENCY COUNTS
---------------------

                              BLOODGRP(VAR   3)

                     GROUP O  GROUP A
            EQ./EQ.   1.00     2.00    TOTAL

ILLNESS  ULCER    1.00   1668    1044   I 2712
(VAR  2) CONTROL  2.00  15708   13255   I28963
                        -------- --------
                 TOTAL  17376   14299    31675
```

```
MINIMUM NONZERO EXPECTED VALUE IS    1224.274
----- ALL STATISTICS ARE COMPUTED USING THE ORIGINAL CELL FREQUENCIES
        EXCLUDING ROWS AND/OR COLUMNS WHICH ARE ZERO.
```

STATISTIC	VALUE	D.F.	PROB.	STATISTIC	VALUE	D.F.	PROB.
PEARSON CHISQUARE	52.921	1	0.0000	YATES' CORRECTED CHISQUARE	52.628	1	0.0000

● SIZE OF PROBLEM

P1F can analyze any combination of tables with less than 10,000 cells in all the tables combined plus in the largest table (the cells in the largest table are counted twice). The largest single table must have less than 5,000 cells. The size of a table is (R+6)(C+6) to allow space for recording row and column totals, number of values out of range and missing, etc.

Note: The size of a table depends on whether CODEs or CUTPOINTS are specified for the categorical variables. When not specified, the program assumes that there can be 10 levels to the variable for the purpose of allocating space for the table.

If the problem is too large, the programs forms and analyzes as many tables as possible in a single reading of the data.

Appendix B describes how to increase the capacity of the program.

● COMPUTATIONAL METHOD

The formulas for the test statistics and the measures, as well as their standard errors, are in Appendix A.5. All computations are performed in single precision.

ACKNOWLEDGEMENT

P1F was designed by Morton Brown and programmed by Morton Brown and Koji Yamasaki. It supersedes BMD02S.

P2F

11.2 Two-Way Frequency Tables — Empty Cells and Departures from Independence

Morton Brown, HSCF

P2F analyzes two special problems:

- You can use P2F to exclude cells from the frequency table, such as cells with a prior probability of zero (structural zeros). P2F computes the appropriate test of independence between rows and columns (the χ^2 test of quasi-independence, Goodman, 1968; Bishop et al., 1975). This test of independence uses all cells that are not excluded a priori and is identical to the usual χ^2 test when there are no excluded cells.

- You can use P2F to identify cells or patterns of cells that contribute to a departure from independence or quasi-independence; i.e., contribute greatly to a significant χ^2 test. You can select a criterion by which cells are identified and eliminated (treated as excluded) from the table in a stepwise manner. One such criterion is to eliminate the cell that, when excluded, minimizes the χ^2 (or likelihood ratio χ^2) test of quasi-independence performed on all cells not previously excluded. Inferences can be drawn from the data by examining the pattern of cells eliminated by this procedure (see Brown, 1974).

P2F computes only the χ^2 tests of independence (or quasi-independence), expected values assuming independence, and various types of residuals. It does not provide estimates of the measures of association and prediction that are available in P1F. P2F prints the observed and expected frequencies and various types of residuals, but does not print tables of percentages, as does P1F.

In most instances the above two problems are treated <u>after</u> the data have been tabulated. P2F allows previously tabulated data as input; we use tabulated data as input in all examples but Example 11.10 below.

- RESULTS

P2F forms two-way frequency tables from data in the same manner as P1F. As our first example we repeat the Control Language instructions from Example 11.1 to form two two-way tables[3]

---

[3] P2F was originally distributed in August 1976. Minor changes in item names as of August 1977 are described in a footnote to the summary (p. 329).

Example 11.10

```
/PROBLEM         TITLE IS 'KASSER CORONARY DATA'.
/INPUT           VARIABLES ARE 6.
                 FORMAT IS '(6F4.0)'.
/VARIABLE        NAMES ARE AGE,FUNCTION,ACTIVE,INFARCT,ANGINA,HIGHBP.

/TABLE           COLUMN IS FUNCTION, INFARCT.
                 ROW    IS ACTIVE  , ANGINA .

/CATEGORY        CODES(2) ARE     0,       1,       2,       3.
                 NAMES(2) ARE NONE, MINIMAL, MODERATE, SEVERE.
                 CODES(3) ARE     1,       2,       3.
                 NAMES(3) ARE VERY, NORMAL, LIMITED.
                 CODES(4) ARE     0,       1.
                 NAMES(4) ARE NONE, PRESENT.
                 CODES(5) ARE     0,       1.
                 NAMES(5) ARE NONE, PRESENT.

/END
```

The Control Language must be preceded by System Cards to initiate the analysis by P2F. At HSCF, the System Cards are

```
//jobname  JOB  nooo,yourname
//   EXEC  BIMED,PROG=BMDP2F
//SYSIN DD  *
```

The Control Language is immediately followed by the data (Table 11.1). The analysis is terminated by another System Card. At HSCF, this System Card is

```
//
```

The frequency tables specified in the *TABLE* paragraph are printed in Output 11.10. Circled numbers below correspond to those in the output.

(1) Number of cases read. Each table is formed using all acceptable values for the categorical variables; that is, values that are not missing or out of range. When CODEs are specified for a categorical variable, only values of the variable equal to one of the specified CODEs are used in the analysis.

(2) For each variable, P2F prints the

- mean
- frequency of acceptable values
- standard deviation
- smallest observed value (not out of range)
- largest observed value (not out of range)

(3) Interpretations of options specific to P2F. The options shown are preassigned and are discussed in the program description.

(4) The two-way frequency table is printed. Around the border of the table P2F prints the row and column marginal totals. If necessary, additional rows and columns are printed to report the numbers of values that are missing, out of range, or not equal to any specified CODE.

In the table of ACTIVE by FUNCTION, the row labelled NOT COUNTED reports the number of values not equal to any specified code (equal to the code zero).

<u>Output 11.10</u> Two-way frequency tables formed by P2F. Circled numbers corre-
spond to those in the text. Results not reproduced are indicated
in italics.

```
BMDP2F - TWO-WAY FREQUENCY TABLES -- EMPTY CELLS              PROGRAM REVISED SEPTEMBER 1977
        - AND DEPARTURES FROM INDEPENDENCE                    MANUAL DATE -- 1977
HEALTH SCIENCES COMPUTING FACILITY
UNIVERSITY OF CALIFORNIA, LOS ANGELES
```

--- Control Language instructions read by P2F are printed and interpreted ---

(1) NUMBER OF CASES READ.   117

(2)
```
VARIABLE           MEAN      FREQ      S.D.    SMALLEST   LARGEST
NO. NAME
  1 AGE            52.32     117       9.47     34.00      73.00
  2 FUNCTION        1.68     117       1.01      0.0        3.00
  3 ACTIVE          1.59     117       1.04      0.0        3.00
  4 INFARCT         0.63     117       0.48      0.0        1.00
  5 ANGINA          0.84     117       0.37      0.0        1.00
  6 HIGHBP          0.31     117       0.46      0.0        1.00
```

(3)
```
ADDED TO EACH CELL IS . . . . . . . . . . . .         0.0
MAX. NO. OF ITERATION TO OBTAIN FIT IS. . . .          20
TOLERANCE FOR CONVERGENCE IS. . . . . . . . .      0.05000
NO. OF CELLS SPECIFIED AS EMPTY IS. . . . . .           0
**********************************************************************************************
TABLE NO.   1                    ACTIVE (VAR   3) VS FUNCTION(VAR   2)
```

(4) CELL FREQUENCY COUNTS

```
                                      FUNCTION(VAR   2)

                        NONE    MINIMAL  MODERATE  SEVERE
              EQ./EQ.   0.00     1.00      2.00     3.00      TOTAL

ACTIVE  VERY   1.00       2        4         2        1   I     9
(VAR 3) NORMAL 2.00       3       13        37        7   I    60
        LIMITED 3.00      0        1         2       16   I    19
                        -------  --------  -------  --------
              TOTAL       5       18        41       24        88
        NOT
        COUNTED          15        6         5        3
```

(5) CHISQUARE   PROBABILITY   D.F.
        48.36   0.0000   6

```
ADDED TO EACH CELL IS . . . . . . . . . . . .         0.0
MAX. NO. OF ITERATION TO OBTAIN FIT IS. . . .          20
TOLERANCE FOR CONVERGENCE IS. . . . . . . . .      0.05000
NO. OF CELLS SPECIFIED AS EMPTY IS. . . . . .           0
**********************************************************************************************
TABLE NO.   2                    ANGINA (VAR   5) VS INFARCT (VAR   4)
```

CELL FREQUENCY COUNTS

```
                                   INFARCT (VAR   4)

                        NONE    PRESENT
              EQ./EQ.   0.00     1.00     TOTAL

ANGINA  NONE   0.00       3       16    I    19
(VAR 5) PRESENT 1.00     40       58    I    98
                        -------  -------
              TOTAL      43       74        117
```

CHISQUARE   PROBABILITY   D.F.
   4.29   0.0384   1

(5)   The Pearson chi-square statistic is a test of independence between rows and columns. It is computed for every frequency table and is defined as

$$\chi^2 = \Sigma\,\Sigma\,(a_{ij}-e_{ij})^2/e_{ij}$$

where a_{ij} is the observed frequency in cell (i,j) and e_{ij} is the expected value as defined on p. 289. P2F prints the values of the χ^2 statistic, its degrees of freedom (D.F.) and its probability (the probability of a more extreme result under the hypothesis of independence, i.e., its p-value). If you choose to test a hypothesis at a given level of significance (say .05), a probability less than this level is a significant result.

A second example

Danish social mobility data (Svalastoga, 1959; Bishop et al., 1975, p. 210) presented in Table 11.4 are used in the remaining examples for P2F The tabulated data are read by specifying

     TABLE=5,5.

in the *INPut* paragraph (5 is the number of levels of each categorical variable). The input of tabulated data is described for P1F on p. 271, and is identical for P2F.

Table 11.4 Danish Social Mobility Data (Svalastoga, 1959, and Bishop et al., 1975, p. 210)

	Son's Status				
Father's Status	1	2	3	4	5
1	18	17	16	4	2
2	24	105	109	59	21
3	23	84	289	217	95
4	8	49	175	348	198
5	6	8	69	201	246

In Example 11.11 we specify that the diagonal cells are EMPTY. This excludes the diagonal cells from the test of independence; the test is computed using the remaining cells. Therefore, this is a test of the hypothesis that if a change in a son's status occurs, the change is independent of the father's social class.

Example 11.11

```
/PROBLEM      TITLE IS 'DANISH SOCIAL MOBILITY DATA'.
/INPUT        VARIABLES ARE 2.
              FORMAT IS '(5F4.0)'.
              TABLE IS 5,5.
/VARIABLE     NAMES ARE SON,FATHER.

/TABLE        ROW IS FATHER.
              COLUMN IS SON.
              EMPTY ARE 1,1, 2,2, 3,3, 4,4, 5,5.

/END
```

*Control
Language
instructions*

(continued)

```
18   17   16    4    2                              ⎤   input is
24  105  109   59   21                              │   multiway
23   84  289  217   95                              │   table
 8   49  175  348  198                              │
 6    8   69  201  246                              ⎦
```

The results are presented in Output 11.11. The chi-square test of quasi-independence is highly significant (270.25 with 11 degrees of freedom); i.e., even without the diagonal cells, there is still an association between fathers' and sons' statuses. Before the diagonal cells were excluded from the analysis, the chi-square test of independence was 754.10 with 16 degrees of freedom.

A third example

When the χ^2 test of independence is highly significant, it is of interest to examine whether the lack of independence can be attributed to a few cells. This knowledge can be useful in drawing inferences from the data. P2F identifies particular cells that contribute most heavily to the lack of independence. As with any automatic method it should be used in conjunction with your knowledge of the subject matter. For example, you may observe that the lack of independence is explained by a pattern of cells in the table, for example the cells on the diagonal or those in a row. P2F can identify in a stepwise manner cells that contribute heavily to the χ^2 test. Therefore we add a *STEP* paragraph to Example 11.11.

Output 11.11   A test of quasi-independence by P2F

```
ADDED TO EACH CELL IS . . . . . . . . . . . .        0.0
MAX. NO. OF ITERATION TO OBTAIN FIT IS. . . .         20
TOLERANCE FOR CONVERGENCE IS. . . . . . . . .      0.05000
NO. OF CELLS SPECIFIED AS EMPTY IS. . . . . .         5
INDICES(ROW,COL) OF CELLS SPECIFIED AS EMPTY. ( 1, 1) ( 2, 2) ( 3, 3) ( 4, 4) ( 5, 5)
*************************************************************************************************
TABLE NO.   1                  FATHER (VAR   2) VS SON      (VAR    1)


CELL FREQUENCY COUNTS

                                    SON      (VAR   1)


                 EQ./EQ.    1.00    2.00    3.00    4.00    5.00    TOTAL

FATHER            1.00        18      17      16       4       2   I    57
(VAR   2)         2.00        24     105     109      59      21   I   318
                  3.00        23      84     289     217      95   I   708
                  4.00         8      49     175     348     198   I   778
                  5.00         6       8      69     201     246   I   530
                            _____  _____  _____  _____  _____
                  TOTAL       79     263     658     829     562      2391
```

```
CHISQUARE   PROBABILITY   D.F.   ITERATIONS     EMPTY      OBSERVED    FITTED
                                   TO FIT     ROW  COL     VALUES     VALUES
 270.25        0.0         11         4         1    1       18.0       1.31
                                                2    2      105.0      22.00
                                                3    3      289.0     158.32
                                                4    4      348.0     284.35
                                                5    5      246.0      71.74
```

Example 11.12

```
/PROBLEM        TITLE IS 'DANISH SOCIAL MOBILITY DATA'.
/INPUT          VARIABLES ARE 2.
                FORMAT IS '(5F4.0)'.
                TABLE IS 5,5.
/VARIABLE       NAMES ARE SON,FATHER.

/TABLE          ROW IS FATHER.
                COLUMN IS SON.
                EMPTY ARE 1,1, 2,2, 3,3, 4,4, 5,5.

/STEP           CRITERION IS CHISQ.

/END
```

In the *STEP* paragraph we specify the criterion used to identify extreme cells. The CRITERION CHISQ excludes cells from the analysis that contribute greatly to the chi-square test of independence (or quasi-independence).

The results are presented in Output 11.12. Circled numbers below correspond to those in the output.

⑥ An explanatory note. At any step cells can be divided into two groups: those still included in the test of quasi-independence and those excluded by an EMPTY statement or at a previous step. A quasi-independent model (model of independence between row and column variables) is fit to the data in the included cells. For each included cell the stepping criterion is evaluated. The cell with the maximum value of the criterion is

Output 11.12 Stepwise identification of cells by P2F

```
            ADDED TO EACH CELL IS . . . . . . . . . . .       0.0
            MAX. NO. OF ITERATION TO OBTAIN FIT IS. . . .      20
            TOLERANCE FOR CONVERGENCE IS. . . . . . . .     0.05000
            NO. OF CELLS SPECIFIED AS EMPTY IS. . . . . .      5
            INDICES(ROW,COL) OF CELLS SPECIFIED AS EMPTY. ( 1, 1) ( 2, 2) ( 3, 3) ( 4, 4) ( 5, 5)
*************************************************************************************************
            TABLE NO.   1            FATHER  (VAR   2) VS SON       (VAR   1)


            CELL FREQUENCY COUNTS

                                          SON      (VAR   1)


                   EQ./EQ.   1.00    2.00    3.00    4.00    5.00      TOTAL

FATHER             1.00       18      17      16       4       2   I    57
(VAR  2)           2.00       24     105     109      59      21   I   318
                   3.00       23      84     289     217      95   I   708
                   4.00        8      49     175     348     198   I   778
                   5.00        6       8      69     201     246   I   530
                           _____ _____ _____ _____ _____
                   TOTAL      79     263     658     829     562     2391
```

```
++++++++++++++++++++++++++++++++ STEP PARAGRAPH  1 FOR TABLE NO.  1 ++++++++++++++++++++++++++++++++
```

⑥ FOR EACH NON-EMPTY CELL OF THE PREVIOUSLY FITTED (ESTIMATED) TABLE, THE VALUE OF THE CRITERION CHOSEN IS COMPUTED AND THE CELL THAT YIELDS THE LARGEST ABSOLUTE VALUE (IN CASE OF CHISQUARE THE SMALLEST VALUE WHEN THAT CELL IS ASSUMED EMPTY) IS DELETED. THE TABLE IS THEN RE-FITTED FOR THE NEXT STEP.

⑦
```
    MAX. NUMBER OF STEPS IS . . . . . . . . . . .       16
    MAX. PROBABILITY FOR CHISQ. IS. . . . . . . .    0.05000
    MIN. LEVEL OF THE CRITERION FOR DELETION IS .    2.00000
    MAX. LEVEL OF THE CRITERION FOR REENTER IS. .    1.00000
```

(continued)

Output 11.12 *(continued)*

```
**********************************************************************
THE CRITERION FOR IDENTIFYING AN EXTREME CELL AND DELETING IT IS CHISQUARE
----------------------------------------------------------------------
```

STEP NO.	CHISQUARE	PROBABILITY	D.F.	ITERATIONS TO FIT		DELETED CELL ROW COL	OBSERVED VALUES	FITTED VALUES	CRITERION IF RE-INCLUDED
⑧ 0	270.25	0.0	11	4		1 1	18.0	1.31	
						2 2	105.0	22.00	
						3 3	289.0	158.32	
						4 4	348.0	284.35	
						5 5	246.0	71.74	

STEP NO.	CHISQUARE	PROBABILITY	D.F.	ITERATIONS TO FIT		DELETED CELL ROW COL	OBSERVED VALUES	FITTED VALUES	CRITERION IF RE-INCLUDED
1	185.51	0.0000	10	7		1 1	18.0	1.48	264.04
						2 2	105.0	25.68	267.38
						3 3	289.0	221.53	196.45
						4 4	348.0	188.23	226.48
				CELL DELETED FOR THIS STEP IS		5 4 *	201.0 *	51.57 *	317.04
						5 5	246.0	34.81	460.24

⑨ THE CRITERION TO DELETE THIS CELL WAS   215.34

STEP NO.	CHISQUARE	PROBABILITY	D.F.	ITERATIONS TO FIT		DELETED CELL ROW COL	OBSERVED VALUES	FITTED VALUES	CRITERION IF RE-INCLUDED
2	72.90	0.0000	9	9		1 1	18.0	1.61	146.09
						2 2	105.0	28.63	145.52
						3 3	289.0	373.94	75.74
						4 4	348.0	95.93	240.80
				CELL DELETED FOR THIS STEP IS		4 5 *	198.0 *	40.43 *	246.14
						5 4	201.0	34.32	266.71
						5 5	246.0	14.47	615.93

THE CRITERION TO DELETE THIS CELL WAS   106.40

STEP NO.	CHISQUARE	PROBABILITY	D.F.	ITERATIONS TO FIT		DELETED CELL ROW COL	OBSERVED VALUES	FITTED VALUES	CRITERION IF RE-INCLUDED
3	38.19	0.0000	8	3		1 1	18.0	1.02	159.88
				CELL DELETED FOR THIS STEP IS		1 2 *	17.0 *	2.78 *	75.67
						2 2	105.0	25.70	131.64
						3 3	289.0	390.61	44.61
						4 4	348.0	96.07	200.93
						4 5	198.0	40.49	207.93
						5 4	201.0	34.37	229.87
						5 5	246.0	14.48	577.44

THE CRITERION TO DELETE THIS CELL WAS   37.95

STEP NO.	CHISQUARE	PROBABILITY	D.F.	ITERATIONS TO FIT		DELETED CELL ROW COL	OBSERVED VALUES	FITTED VALUES	CRITERION IF RE-INCLUDED
4	10.54	0.1598	7	4		1 1	18.0	0.71	182.40
						1 2	17.0	2.72	48.74
				CELL DELETED FOR THIS STEP IS		2 1 *	24.0 *	6.13 *	39.11
						2 2	105.0	23.37	122.53
						3 3	289.0	395.13	20.08
						4 4	348.0	100.08	163.03
						4 5	198.0	42.18	172.18
						5 4	201.0	35.81	192.17
						5 5	246.0	15.09	534.26

THE CRITERION TO DELETE THIS CELL WAS   10.89

STEPPING IS TERMINATED. THE PROBABILITY FOR CHISQUARE IS   0.160, WHICH IS GREATER THAN THE ALPHA   0.050

```
*********************************************************************************************
                                    SUMMARY TABLE
```

⑩

	DELETED CELL ROW COL	STEP NO.	CHISQUARE VALUE	PROBABILITY	WHEN DELETED FITTED	CRITERION TO DELETE	CURRENT FITTED	CRITERION TO REENTER
1	1 1				1.31	0.0	0.71	182.40
2	2 2				22.00	0.0	23.37	122.53
3	3 3				158.32	0.0	395.13	20.08
4	4 4				284.35	0.0	100.08	163.03
5	5 5				71.74	0.0	15.09	534.26
6	5 4	1	185.51	0.0000	51.57	215.34	35.81	192.17
7	4 5	2	72.90	0.0000	40.43	106.40	42.18	172.18
8	1 2	3	38.19	0.0000	2.78	37.95	2.72	48.74
9	2 1	4	10.54	0.1598	6.13	10.89	6.13	39.11

excluded and the stepping is repeated. When the CRITERION is CHISQ, the cell excluded is the one whose exclusion would reduce the χ^2 test the most. The stepping terminates when the χ^2 test of quasi-independence is nonsignificant; you can specify the size of the test (the size is 0.05 if not specified).

(7) Values that can be specified in the *STEP* paragraph. Preassigned values are shown. The terms are explained on p. 292.

(8) At step 0 the chi-square test for quasi-independence is computed omitting <u>only</u> cells excluded by an EMPTY statement. The tail probability of the $\overline{\chi^2}$ and its degrees of freedom are printed. Quasi-independent models are fitted by an iterative algorithm (Appendix A.6); the number of iterations is printed.

The cells excluded are called "deleted cells". For each deleted cell P2F prints the observed frequency and the fitted (expected) value based on the quasi-independent model.

(9) At step 1 cell (5,4) is identified by the criterion and excluded from the cells to which the quasi-independent model is fitted. The χ^2 test printed is for the quasi-independent model with six cells excluded (the five original cells and the new one) The degrees of freedom are reduced by 1. For each cell P2F prints the observed value, the fitted value computed from the new quasi-independent model, and the value of the criterion as though each cell were reincluded in the table (cells can be reincluded, see p. 290).

Both the value of the criterion for the cell being excluded and the value of the criterion if the cell were reincluded are estimated <u>without</u> refitting a quasi-independent model. These values are only approximate. For example the value of the criterion to delete cell (4,5) is 215.34 but the χ^2 test of quasi-independence is 185.51. These two numbers would agree if the value of the criterion CHISQ were calculated by fitting a different quasi-independent model for each cell that can be excluded. The definitions of the criteria are on p. 291 .

(10) After the last step a summary table is printed. The four cells excluded are (5,4), (4,5), (1,2) and (2,1). By examining the table of observed frequencies, we interpret this to mean that there is substantial cross-over between status 4 and 5 and between status 1 and 2.

In the summary table P2F prints for each step

- the χ^2 statistic
- the fitted value and the criterion to delete at the step when a cell is deleted (the criterion to delete is not printed for cells excluded by an EMPTY specification)
- the current fitted value using the quasi-independent model at the last step and the value of the criterion to reenter (if the cell were reincluded).

● OPTIONAL RESULTS AND INPUT

You must specify the categorical variables that define the tables. You can

- request the tables at each level of a third categorical variable   p. 287

- combine or stack two or more categorical variables into a single variable   p. 287

- add a constant to the frequency in each cell before fitting the quasi-independent model   p. 288

- exclude cells from the analysis   p. 288

- print the expected values for the observed table   p. 290

- identify cells in a stepwise manner according to a criterion that you specify   p. 290

- accept tabulated data as input   p. 295

● DESCRIBING TABLE(S) TO BE FORMED

As shown in the above examples, tables are specified as ROW and COLUMN variables in the *TABLE* paragraph. The *TABLE* paragraph can be repeated before the *END* paragraph to create additional tables.

Tables are formed in a manner similar to P1F (p. 252). We repeat only the Control Language definitions.

TABLE

    ROW= $v_1, v_2, \cdots$.   {none}   required

        Names or subscripts of variables that define the row categories (index). If a ROW variable takes on more than 10 distinct values, you must specify its CODEs or CUTPOINTS in the *CATEGory* paragraph.

    COLUMN= $v_1, v_2, \cdots$.   {none}   required

        Names or subscripts of variables that define the column categories (index). If a COLUMN variable takes on more than 10 distinct values, you must specify its CODEs or CUTPOINTS in the *CATEGory* paragraph.

    PAIR. *or* CROSS.   { PAIR }

        If CROSS is specified, tables are formed from all possible combinations of the ROW and COLUMN variables. Otherwise, the first ROW variable and first COLUMN variable define the first table, the second ROW variable and second COLUMN variable the second table, etc.

● CROSS SECTIONS OF A TABLE

You may want to form a frequency table for each level of a third variable; for example, for each sex, for each age grouping, for each treatment group, etc.

This is described in greater detail for P1F (p. 253). We repeat only the definition.

TABLE
    CONDITION=v_1,v_2,$\cdots$.   {none}

> Names or subscripts of CONDITION variables. Each CONDITION variable is used in turn to form three-way tables with each pair of ROW and COLUMN variables. For each category of the CONDITION variable a two-way cross section of the table (ROW classified against COLUMN) is printed and analyzed. If a CONDITION variable takes on more than 10 distinct values, you must specify its CODES or CUTPOINTS in the *CATEGory* paragraph.

● STACKING OR COMBINING INDICES

ROW, COLUMN and CONDITION all use one variable at a time to create a table. Sometimes it is appropriate to use all possible combinations of two or more variables as a ROW, COLUMN or CONDITION variable. For example, you may want to form a table for each combination of AGE and HIGHBP groupings in the Kasser data (Table 11.1).

A new variable that contains each combination can be created by a transformation. The new variable can also be formed in P2F by stating

        DEFINE(7)=AGE, HIGHBP.

in the *VARiable* paragraph, where 7 is greater than the subscript of any other variable and is used as the subscript of the new variable. The new variable would be made up of six categories: three age categories for each level of HIGHBP.

VARiable
    DEFINE(#)=v_1,v_2,$\cdots$.   {none}   may be repeated

> Names or subscripts of variables to be stacked (or combined) into a single index, which defines a new variable. DEFINE constructs an index made up of all possible combinations of the levels (codes or categories) of the specified variables; # must be greater than any variable subscript. CODES or CUTPOINTS must be specified in the *CATEGory* paragraph for each variable v_1,v_2,$\cdots$. The levels of v_1 are the fastest changing, v_2 the next fastest, etc., in the new index variable created by the DEFINE statement. If more than one DEFINE statement is present, each new defined variable must be given a different subscript.

- DELTA: ADDING A CONSTANT TO EACH CELL

When the observed cell frequencies contain many values near zero some data analysts add a constant to each cell before computing the χ^2 test.   A constant (such as 0.5) can be added in P2F by specifying

DELTA=0.5.

in the *TABLE* paragraph.   This affects <u>all</u> computations including the χ^2 tests and the criterion values.

The constant is not added to rows or columns that are entirely zero.

TABLE
DELTA=#.   {0.0}

A constant added to the frequency in each cell of the table before computing the χ^2 tests and the criterion values.

- EXCLUDING CELLS FROM AN ANALYSIS

Cells can be excluded from the hypothesis of quasi-independence, for example when the probability is zero that an observation occurs in the cell (a structural zero).   Cells are excluded by specifying that they are EMPTY in the *TABLE* paragraph.   In Example 11.11 the diagonal cells are excluded.

TABLE
EMPTY(#)=$\#_{11},\#_{12},\#_{21},\#_{22},\cdots$.   {none}

$(\#_{11},\#_{12})$, $(\#_{21},\#_{22})\ldots$ are the pairs of row and column indices of the cells to be excluded from the analysis.   They are the numbers 1 to R or 1 to C and not the code, cutpoint or category name.   # is the sequence number of the table if more than one table is described in this *TABLE* paragraph;   EMPTY= can be used when only a single table is described.

Any number of excluded cells may be specified in the *TABLE* paragraph. When the remaining cells can be arranged into two or more distinct subtables that have no rows and no columns in common, the table is called separable.   An example of a separable table is

10	--	--	20
--	30	40	--
--	50	60	--
70	--	--	80

which can be reordered into

10	20	--	--
70	80	--	--
--	--	30	40
--	--	50	60

where -- represents an excluded cell.

When the table is <u>not</u> separable, both the χ^2 and the degrees of freedom are computed correctly. When the table <u>is</u> separable, the χ^2 is computed correctly but the degrees of freedom are overestimated. The correct degrees of freedom are the sum of the degrees of freedom associated with the χ^2 test in each distinct subtable.

● THE TEST OF INDEPENDENCE BETWEEN ROWS AND COLUMNS

When all cell frequencies are used in the test of independence (no cells are EMPTY), the expected (also called fitted) value of cell (i,j) is

$$e_{ij} = r_i c_j / N.$$

The χ^2 test is

$$\chi^2 = \Sigma \Sigma (a_{ij} - e_{ij})^2 / e_{ij}$$

and the likelihood ratio chi-square (G^2) is

$$G^2 = 2 \Sigma \Sigma a_{ij} \, ln(a_{ij} / e_{ij})$$

where the summations are over all the cells.

When one or more cell frequencies are excluded from the test of independence, the model

$$e_{ij} = \alpha_i \beta_j$$

is fitted to the observed frequencies a_{ij} in the remaining cells (those that are not excluded). The estimates of α_i and β_j are obtained by iteration (Appendix A.6). The χ^2 test of quasi-independence is

$$\chi^2 = \Sigma \Sigma (a_{ij} - e_{ij})^2 / e_{ij}$$

and the likelihood ratio χ^2 is

$$G^2 = 2 \Sigma \Sigma a_{ij} \, ln(a_{ij} / e_{ij})$$

where the summations are over the nonexcluded cells.

Since the estimates of α_i and β_j are obtained by iteration, there must be a way to decide when to stop iterating. We use the following criteria to stop iteration: Stop when the maximum change in the estimated expected values for all cells is less than CONVERGE, or when the number of iterations exceeds ITERATION. We preassign CONVERGE to 0.05 and ITERATION to 20.0, which should be adequate for most problems. Other values can be used.

TABLE
   CONVERGE=#.   {0.05}

   The iteration to estimate α_i and β_j is terminated when the change in expected values is less than CONVERGE. This is more precisely defined in Appendix A.6.

```
TABLE
    ITERATION=#.                {20}

        Maximum number of iterations.  The algorithm to estimate expected
        values is terminated by this iteration even if the convergence
        criterion (CONVERGE) is not yet satisfied.
```

● TABLES OF OBSERVED AND FITTED FREQUENCIES

The table of OBSERVED frequencies is printed unless

NO OBSERVED.

is stated in the *TABLE* paragraph.

The table of FITTED values can be printed by specifying

FIT.

in the *TABLE* paragraph. The FITTED values are the e_{ij} estimated by the model of independence or quasi-independence.

```
TABLE
    OBServed.                {OBServed}

        The table of observed frequencies is printed unless  NO OBServed
        is specified.

    FITted.                  {no}

        Print the table of expected (fitted) values under the model of
        independence or quasi-independence.  Fitted values for the EMPTY
        cells using the model of quasi-independence are also printed.
```

● *STEP* -- IDENTIFYING CELLS IN A STEPWISE MANNER

Cells whose observed values differ greatly from their expected values, according to a specified criterion, can be identified in a stepwise manner (Brown, 1974). Cells so identified are eliminated from the computation of the χ^2 (or G^2) test of independence and are treated in a manner similar to cells declared EMPTY a priori. At each step, cells that have not been eliminated are examined for possible elimination according to the criterion. Cells already eliminated are reviewed to see if they are eligible to be reentered. A cell is eligible for reentry when its observed value is similar to its expected value estimated by the new model of quasi-independence. Cells declared EMPTY are not eligible for reentry, although their criteria for reentry are computed and printed.

The criteria for identifying the cells for elimination (or reentry) can be divided conceptually into three groups: CHISQUARE and LRCHI (likelihood ratio chi-square); DIFFERENCE, STANDARDIZED, and ADJUSTED; and QUSTAN (quasi-standardized) and QUADJ (quasi-adjusted).

In the first group the cell identified for elimination is the one that, when eliminated, reduces the χ^2 (or G^2) test of independence the most. The printed value of the criterion is the resulting χ^2 (or G^2). To determine whether a cell should be entered or eliminated, the change in χ^2 (or G^2) is compared with the values of REENTER or ELIMINATE.

In the second group the criteria are residuals: DIFferences, STANdardized residuals, and Haberman's ADJusted standardized residuals (Haberman, 1973).

In the first two groups, the criterion used to select a cell for elimination depends upon its expected value, which is computed using the observed value for that cell. After a cell has been eliminated, computation of its expected value no longer depends on the original frequency in that cell. Hence, the criterion for reentry may differ greatly from the criterion for elimination.

In the third group (QUSTAN and QUADJ), the expected values and variances used to compute the criterion do not depend on the cell that is being tested. Therefore the value of the criterion to eliminate and to reenter are similar at the step where the cell is first eliminated. All criteria are precisely defined in Appendix A.6.

To describe the stepping algorithm, let E be the set of cells that are empty a priori or have been eliminated before the kth step. At the kth step the value of the criterion for each cell in E is evaluated and compared with REENTER. If any cell previously eliminated has a value less than REENTER, the cell with the lowest value is reentered in the observed table. Otherwise, the cell not in E with the largest value of the criterion for elimination is identified and, if this value exceeds ELIMINATE, it is eliminated from the table; i.e., added to E. If any tables are requested at this step they are printed. Zeros denote cells that have already been eliminated.

A *STEP* paragraph must be used for stepwise elimination. Example 11.11 illustrates how a *STEP* paragraph is used. It can be repeated for additional analyses. If more than one *TABLE* paragraph is specified, the *STEP* paragraph applies to the *TABLE* paragraph preceding it.

STEP

CRITERION= *(one or more)* CHISQ,LRCHI,DIF, {none} required
STAN,ADJ,QUSTAN,QUADJ.

The criteria are:

CHISQ	chooses the cell whose elimination minimizes the χ^2 test
LRCHI	chooses the cell whose elimination minimizes the likelihood ratio chi-square G^2
DIF	chooses the cell that has the maximum absolute difference $\lvert a_{ij} - e_{ij} \rvert$
STAN	chooses the cell that has the maximum absolute standardized residual $\lvert a_{ij} - e_{ij} \rvert / \sqrt{e_{ij}}$

(continued)

(continued from previous page)

ADJ   chooses the cell that has the maximum absolute adjusted standardized residual

$$|a_{ij}-e_{ij}|/\left[\, e_{ij}\,\left(1-\frac{r_i}{N}\right)\,\left(1-\frac{c_j}{N}\right)\right]^{\frac{1}{2}}$$

QUSTAN   chooses the cell that has the maximum absolute standardized residual after elimination

QUADJ   chooses the cell that has the maximum absolute adjusted standardized residual after elimination

The criteria CHISQ or LRCHI are recommended. If more than one criterion is stated, the analysis is repeated using each criterion in turn. When LRCHI is chosen, the χ^2's printed at each step and in the summary table are likelihood ratio χ^2 (G^2); otherwise the χ^2 test is printed. More precise definitions of the criteria are in Appendix A.6.

Several constants can be adjusted in the stepping procedure, but usually need not be. The constants are:

STEP
   MAXSTEP= #.   {(R-1)(C-1)}

   The maximum number of steps (cells identified) before the stepwise procedure is terminated.

   ALPHA= #.   {0.05}

   Stepping is terminated when the (tail) probability of the χ^2 exceeds ALPHA.

   ELIMINATE= #.   {2.0}

   Stepping is terminated when the largest value of the criterion over all cells is less than ELIMINATE.

   REENTER=#.   {1.0}

   A cell previously eliminated is reentered if its value for the criterion is less than REENTER. To avoid loops, REENTER must be less than ELIMINATE.

Note: For the CHISQ *and* LRCHI *criteria,* ELIMINATE *and* REENTER *refer to changes in the* χ^2 *when the cell is eliminated or reentered. Stepping is terminated when no cell can pass the* ELIMINATE *or* REENTER *limits, when the probability passes the* ALPHA *limit, or when* MAXSTEP *is reached.*

● PRINTING TABLES DURING STEPPING

    Tables of the values of any of the criteria or of the fitted values can be printed at steps specified in the *STEP* paragraph. In Example 11.13 we request a table of the chi-square test and a table of the fitted values at steps 0 and 3.

Example 11.13

```
/PROBLEM     TITLE IS 'DANISH SOCIAL MOBILITY DATA'.
/INPUT       VARIABLES ARE 2.
             FORMAT IS '(5F4.0)'.
             TABLE IS 5,5.
/VARIABLE    NAMES ARE SON,FATHER.

/TABLE       ROW IS FATHER.
             COLUMN IS SON.
             EMPTY ARE 1,1, 2,2, 3,3, 4,4, 5,5.

/STEP        CRITERION IS CHISQ.
             PRINT = 0,3.
             FITTED.
             CHISQUARE.

/END
```

    The extra tables produced by this example are shown in Output 11.13. Note that PRINT=0 specifies that the tables are printed before the first step.

STEP

    PRINT=$\#_1$,$\#_2$,$\cdots$. *or* ALL.   {none}

      The steps at which the tables specified from the list below are to be printed. PRINT=ALL specifies that the tables are to be printed at ALL steps. PRINT=0 specifies printing before the first step; i.e., based on the observed frequencies.

    FITTED.   {no}

      The table of fitted values: e_{ij}. Values are estimated for the excluded cells.

    CHISQUARE.   {no}

      The table of the χ^2 test, when each cell in turn is excluded.

    LRCHI.   {no}

      The table of the likelihood ratio statistic G^2, when each cell in turn is excluded.

    DIFFERENCE.   {no}

      Table of differences: $a_{ij} - e_{ij}$

    STANDARDIZED.   {no}

      Table of standardized residuals: $(a_{ij} - e_{ij})/\sqrt{e_{ij}}$

Output 11.13 Tables printed during stepping by P2F

STEP NO. 0	CHISQUARE 270.25	PROBABILITY 0.0	D.F. 11	ITERATIONS TO FIT 4	DELETED CELL ROW	COL	OBSERVED VALUES	FITTED VALUES
					1	1	18.0	1.31
					2	2	105.0	22.00
					3	3	289.0	158.32
					4	4	348.0	284.35
					5	5	246.0	71.74

THE FITTED (EXPECTED OR ESTIMATED) CELL VALUES

SON   (VAR   1)

	EQ./EQ.	1.00	2.00	3.00	4.00	5.00
FATHER (VAR 2)	1.00	1.31	3.77	11.05	16.04	8.13
	2.00	7.62	22.00	64.45	93.54	47.39
	3.00	18.71	54.05	158.34	229.81	116.42
	4.00	23.15	66.88	195.92	284.35	144.06
	5.00	11.53	33.30	97.56	141.60	71.74

CHISQUARE VALUES WHEN EACH CELL IN TURN IS CONSIDERED EMPTY A PRIORI

SON   (VAR   1)

	EQ./EQ.	1.00	2.00	3.00	4.00	5.00
FATHER (VAR 2)	1.00	0.0	226.22	278.98	240.46	255.38
	2.00	235.25	0.0	235.18	235.27	241.04
	3.00	273.48	259.81	0.0	269.95	263.89
	4.00	246.70	252.68	266.33	0.0	223.49
	5.00	262.21	235.09	254.30	215.33	0.0

STEP NO. 1	CHISQUARE 185.51	PROBABILITY 0.0000	D.F. 10	ITERATIONS TO FIT 7	DELETED CELL ROW	COL	OBSERVED VALUES	FITTED VALUES	CRITERION IF RE-INCLUDED
					1	1	18.0	1.48	264.04
					2	2	105.0	25.68	267.38
					3	3	289.0	221.53	196.45
					4	4	348.0	188.23	226.48
		CELL DELETED FOR THIS STEP IS			5	4 *	201.0 *	51.57 *	317.04
	THE CRITERION TO DELETE THIS CELL WAS 215.34				5	5	246.0	34.81	460.24

--- *results for steps 2 and 3* ---

THE FITTED (EXPECTED OR ESTIMATED) CELL VALUES

SON   (VAR   1)

	EQ./EQ.	1.00	2.00	3.00	4.00	5.00
FATHER (VAR 2)	1.00	1.02	2.78	12.44	6.72	2.83
	2.00	9.40	25.69	115.16	62.22	26.22
	3.00	31.89	87.15	390.59	211.05	88.94
	4.00	14.52	39.67	177.81	96.07	40.49
	5.00	5.19	14.19	63.61	34.37	14.48

CHISQUARE VALUES WHEN EACH CELL IN TURN IS CONSIDERED EMPTY A PRIORI

SON   (VAR   1)

	EQ./EQ.	1.00	2.00	3.00	4.00	5.00
FATHER (VAR 2)	1.00	0.0	0.0	36.18	36.64	37.85
	2.00	10.89	0.0	36.41	37.52	36.30
	3.00	27.72	37.87	0.0	37.43	37.02
	4.00	31.27	34.96	38.13	0.0	0.0
	5.00	38.46	34.95	37.20	0.0	0.0

STEP

    ADJUSTED.   {no}

        Table of adjusted standardized residuals:

$$(a_{ij}-e_{ij})/\left[\, e_{ij}\,\left(1-\frac{r_i}{N}\right)\left(1-\frac{c_j}{N}\right)\right]^{\frac{1}{2}}$$

    QUSTANDARDIZED.   {no}

        Table of quasi-standardized residuals; i.e., standardized
        residuals computed by excluding each cell in turn.

    QUADJUSTED.   {no}

        Table of quasi-adjusted standardized residuals; i.e., adjusted
        standardized residuals computed by excluding each cell in turn.

More precise definitions are given in Appendix A.6.

Any of the above tables can be printed for the original table (PRINT=0) when stepping is <u>not</u> wanted. To do so specify ALPHA=-1.0. in the *STEP* paragraph. Since the size (probability level) of any test is positive, it exceeds -1.0 and therefore stepping is not performed.

● FORMS OF DATA INPUT

    Usually each case contains data for a single observation. In the frequency table programs you can also input tabulated data, such as a table from a government or scientific report. Each case can represent data from a cell of the table; the number of observations (frequency) in the cell is recorded as one of the variables. The data can also be input as frequency tables.

    We discuss how to use tabulated data as input for P1F on p. 271; only the Control Language definitions are repeated here.

INPut
    TABLE=#$_1$,#$_2$,···.   {none}   required if data are input
                                              as a multiway table

        #$_1$,#$_2$,... are the <u>number of levels</u> of each of the categorical variables (factors) in the table; their product is the number of cells in the table. #$_1$ is the number of levels of the fastest varying index, #$_2$ of the next fastest, etc. A maximum of seven indices can be used. The number of VARIABLES should be specified as the number of factors; the number of CASES is not used; and the FORMAT should describe the entire table. Transformations and data editing cannot be used with this form of input.

```
TABLE
    COUNT=v₁,v₂,···.          {none}          required only when data are input
                                              as cell indices and frequency
                                              counts
        Names or subscripts of variables that contain the frequency counts.
        If more than one variable is specified, tables are formed for
        each variable separately.
```

- SIZE OF PROBLEM

    P2F can analyze any single frequency table that has less than 3,500 cells or any combination of tables where the total number of cells in all the tables combined plus twice the number of cells in the largest table (the cells in the largest table are counted twice) does not exceed 10,000 cells. The size of a table is $(R+6)(C+6)$.

    The size of a table depends on whether CODEs or CUTPOINTs are specified. When they are not specified, P2F assumes that there can be 10 levels to the categorical variable for the purpose of allocating space for the table.

    The program will form and analyze as many tables as possible at one time.

    Appendix B describes how to increase the capacity of the program.

- COMPUTATIONAL METHOD

    The algorithm to find expected values when any cell is empty or eliminated, the stepping algorithm, and the criteria are described in Appendix A.6. All computations are performed in single precision.

ACKNOWLEDGEMENT

    P2F was designed by Morton Brown and programmed by Morton Brown and Koji Yamasaki.

P3F

11.3 Multiway Frequency Tables — The Log-Linear Model

Morton Brown, HSCF

P3F analyzes data in a multiway table. The purpose of the analysis is
to obtain a description of the relationships between the factors of the table,
either by forming a model for the data or by testing and ordering the importance of the interactions between the factors. The analysis is based on
fitting a (hierarchical) log-linear model to the cell frequencies; that is,
the logarithm of the expected cell frequency is written as an additive function
of main effects and interactions in a manner similar to the usual analysis of
variance model. It should be noted that the various tests for the interactions
are not independent. If a two-way table were input to P3F, one possible log-
linear model would include two main effects and a single interaction. The
test that the interaction is zero is identical to the test for independence
obtained in P1F.

You can use P3F to find an appropriate model for the data in the table
either by fitting specified models or by using a method of screening effects
explained on p. 303. The program tests the appropriateness of models by the
likelihood ratio χ^2 (G^2) and by the usual χ^2 goodness-of-fit.

Unless you are interested in testing particular models, the appropriate
analysis of a multiway frequency table usually involves several runs of P3F.
In a first run of the program, methods for screening effects can be used to
suggest interesting models for further investigation.

● RESULTS

P3F can be used to form and print a multiway frequency table, to screen
for an appropriate model, or to fit specified models. We use three examples
to illustrate the capabilities of P3F.[4]

Creating and printing a multiway table

We use the Kasser coronary data (Table 11.1) in the first example
A three-way frequency table is formed by the Control Language instructions
in Example 11.14; the three categorical variables are INFARCT, ANGINA and
HIGHBP.

The *TABLE* paragraph is used to specify the categorical variables that
define the table (the INDICES and SYMBOLS used to identify the categorical
variables). Because P3F can form multiway tables, this specification differs
from that in P1F and P2F. The remaining Control Language instructions are
common to all BMDP programs.

---

[4] P3F was originally distributed in August 1976. Minor changes in item names
as of August 1977 are described in a footnote to the summary (p. 331).

Example 11.14

```
/PROBLEM        TITLE IS 'KASSER CORONARY DATA'.
/INPUT          VARIABLES ARE 6.
                FORMAT IS '(6F4.0)'.
/VARIABLE       NAMES ARE AGE,FUNCTION,ACTIVE,INFARCT,ANGINA,HIGHBP.

/TABLE          INDICES ARE INFARCT, ANGINA, HIGHBP.
                SYMBOLS ARE I,       A,       H.

/CATEGORY       CODES(4) ARE     0,       1.
                NAMES(4) ARE NONE, PRESENT.
                CODES(5) ARE     0,       1.
                NAMES(5) ARE NONE, PRESENT.
                CODES(6) ARE     0,       1.
                NAMES(6) ARE NORMAL, HYPERTEN.

/END
```

The Control Language must be preceded by System Cards to initiate the analysis by P3F.
At HSCF, the System Cards are

```
//jobname  JOB  nooo,yourname
//   EXEC   BIMED,PROG=BMDP3F
//SYSIN  DD  *
```

The Control Language is immediately followed by the data (Table 11.1). The analysis
is terminated by another System Card. At HSCF, this System Card is

```
//
```

The results are presented in Output 11.14. Circled numbers below
correspond to those in the output.

(1)   Number of cases read. Each table is formed using all acceptable values
for the categorical variables; that is, all values that are not missing
or out or range. When CODEs are specified for a categorical variable,
only values of the variable equal to one of the specified CODEs are
used in the analysis.

(2)   For each variable, P3F prints the

- mean
- frequency of acceptable values
- standard deviation
- smallest observed value (not out of range)
- largest observed value (not out of range)

(3)   The *TABLE* paragraph is interpreted. Some of the values listed were not
specified; preassigned values are reported.

(4)   The frequency table formed is printed. The first categorical variable
(INDEx) is printed horizontally; the others are printed vertically.

The total frequency in the table is printed below the table. Since all
cases contain acceptable values for the three categorical variables, the
total frequency is equal to the number of cases read.

Marginal subtables of the frequency table can be printed, if you request
them (p. 310).

(5)   The last two tables are explained in greater detail in the following
example.

Output 11.14   A multiway contingency table formed by P3F. Circled numbers
correspond to those in the text. Results not reproduced are
indicated in italics.

BMDP3F - MULTIWAY FREQUENCY TABLES -- THE LOG-LINEAR MODEL   PROGRAM REVISED SEPTEMBER 1977
HEALTH SCIENCES COMPUTING FACILITY   MANUAL DATE -- 1977
UNIVERSITY OF CALIFORNIA, LOS ANGELES

--- Control Language read by P3F is printed and interpreted ---

(1) NUMBER OF CASES READ.   117

(2) VARIABLE   MEAN   FREQ   S.D.   SMALLEST   LARGEST
     NO. NAME
      4 INFARCT   0.63   117   0.48   0.0   1.00
      5 ANGINA   0.84   117   0.37   0.0   1.00
      6 HIGHBP   0.31   117   0.46   0.0   1.00

     TABLE NO. 1

(3) VARIABLE INDICES.   4   5   6
     SYMBOLS FOR INDICES   I   A   H
     NUMBER OF LEVELS.   2   2   2
     MAXIMUM NUMBER OF ITERATIONS.   20
     MAXIMUM PERMISSIBLE DIFFERNCE BETWEEN
     AN OBSERVED & FITTED MARGINAL TOTAL 0.100
     CONSTANT TO BE ADDED TO EACH FREQUENCY. 0.0
     NUMBER OF MODELS SPECIFIED.   0

           THE FOLLOWING TABLE IS ANALYZED.
     HIGHBP   ANGINA   I   INFARCT (I)
(4)   H   A   I   NONE   PRESENT

     NORMAL   NONE   I   2   11
               PRESENT I   26   42
                        I
     HYPERTEN NONE   I   1   5
               PRESENT I   14   16

           THE TOTAL FREQUENCY IS   117

(5) THE RESULTS OF FITTING ALL K-FACTOR MARGINALS.
     THIS IS A SIMULTANEOUS TEST THAT ALL K+1 AND HIGHER FACTOR INTERACTIONS ARE ZERO

     K-FACTOR   D.F.   LR CHISQ   PROB.   PEARSON CHISQ   PROB.   ITERATIONS
     0(MEAN)   7   89.86   0.0000   91.07   0.0000
     1   4   5.40   0.2488   4.93   0.2950   2
     2   1   0.03   0.8579   0.03   0.8587   3

     A SIMULTANEOUS TEST THAT ALL K-FACTOR INTERACTIONS ARE ZERO.
     THE ENTRIES ARE DIFFERENCES IN THE ABOVE TABLE.

     K-FACTOR   D.F.   LR CHISQ   PROB.   PEARSON CHISQ   PROB.
     1   3   84.46   0.0000   86.14   0.0000
     2   3   5.37   0.1469   4.89   0.1797
     3   1   0.03   0.8579   0.03   0.8587

If you only want to form and print a multiway frequency table and do not want to test any hypotheses, you may skip the following examples and turn to p. 306.

Model screening

In the second example we use data from the Morrison (1973) study on the Survival of Breast Cancer Patients (Table 11.5). The data are treated by Bishop et al. (1975, p. 103) as a four-way frequency table where one variable (INFL.APP) has four categories:

> Minimal Inflamation and Malignant Appearance
> Minimal Inflamation and Benign Appearance
> Greater Inflamation and Malignant Appearance
> Greater Inflamation and Benign Appearance

Table 11.5   Three-Year Survival of Breast Cancer Patients According to Two Histologic Criteria, Age and Diagnostic Center (Morrison et al., 1973; Bishop et al., 1975, p. 103)

Diagnostic Center	Age	Survived	Minimal Inflammation		Greater Inflammation	
			Malignant Appearance	Benign Appearance	Malignant Appearance	Benign Appearance
Tokyo	Under 50	No	9	7	4	3
		Yes	26	68	25	9
	50-69	No	9	9	11	2
		Yes	20	46	18	5
	70 or over	No	2	3	1	0
		Yes	1	6	5	1
Boston	Under 50	No	6	7	6	0
		Yes	11	24	4	0
	50-69	No	8	20	3	2
		Yes	18	58	10	3
	70 or over	No	9	18	3	0
		Yes	15	26	1	1
Glamorgan	Under 50	No	16	7	3	0
		Yes	16	20	8	1
	50-69	No	14	12	3	0
		Yes	27	39	10	4
	70 or over	No	3	7	3	0
		Yes	12	11	4	1

In Example 11.15 we read the table in as a multiway frequency table in a manner similar to P1F and P2F. In the *INPut* paragraph we specify

TABLE=4, 2, 3, 3.

to indicate that the fastest varying categorical variable (INFL.APP) has four levels, the next fastest (SURVIVED) has two levels, the next fastest (AGE) has three levels and the slowest changing (CENTER) also has three levels.

In the *TABLE* paragraph, in addition to specifying the categorical variables whose levels are the INDICES of the table, we specify the option

ASSOCIATION.

This option prints tests that can be used in screening for an appropriate model.

In this example we add 0.5 to each cell (DELTA=0.5) so that no cell will have an expected value of zero.

Example 11.15

```
/PROBLEM      TITLE IS 'MORRISON BREAST CANCER DATA'.
/INPUT        VARIABLES ARE 4.
              FORMAT IS '(8F4.0)'.
              TABLE IS 4,2,3,3.
/VARIABLE     NAMES ARE 'INFL.APP',SURVIVED,AGE,CENTER.

/TABLE        INDICES ARE 'INFL.APP', SURVIVED, AGE, CENTER.
              SYMBOLS ARE  I,        S,       A,   C.
              ASSOCIATION.
              DELTA IS 0.5.

/CATEGORY     NAMES(1) ARE 'MIN.MAL', 'MIN.BEN', 'GRT.MAL', 'GRT.BEN'.
              NAMES(2) ARE NO, YES.
              NAMES(3) ARE UNDER50, '50-69', OVER69.
              NAMES(4) ARE TOKYO, BOSTON, GLAMORGN.

/END
   9    7    4    3   26   68   25    9
   9    9   11    2   20   46   18    5
   2    3    1    0    1    6    5    1
   6    7    6    0   11   24    4    0
   8   20    3    2   18   58   10    3
   9   18    3    0   15   26    1    1
  16    7    3    0   16   20    8    1
  14   12    3    0   27   39   10    4
   3    7    3    0   12   11    4    1
```

Control Language instructions

input is multiway table

Before discussing the results it may be helpful to review some standard terminology. Consider a four-way IxJxKxL contingency table, where the four indices pertain to categorical variables A,B,C,D, respectively. Let $f_{ijk\ell}$ be the observed frequency in cell (i,j,k,ℓ) of the table.

P3F performs an analysis of the data based on the assumption that the logarithm of the expected values is a linear function of certain parameters. That is, as in the analysis of variance, the log-linear model may be written as

$$\ln F_{ijk\ell} = \theta + \lambda_i^A + \lambda_j^B + \lambda_k^C + \lambda_\ell^D + \lambda_{ij}^{AB} + \lambda_{ik}^{AC} + \lambda_{i\ell}^{AD} + \lambda_{jk}^{BC} + \lambda_{j\ell}^{BD}$$

$$+ \lambda_{k\ell}^{CD} + \lambda_{ijk}^{ABC} + \lambda_{ij\ell}^{ABD} + \lambda_{ik\ell}^{ACD} + \lambda_{jk\ell}^{BCD} + \lambda_{ijk\ell}^{ABCD}$$

where $F_{ijk\ell} = E(f_{ijk\ell})$ is the expected value of the observed frequencies and the λ's satisfy the constraints

$$\Sigma_i \lambda_i^A = 0,\dots, \qquad \Sigma_i \lambda_{ij}^{AB} = \Sigma_j \lambda_{ij}^{AB} = 0,\dots,$$

$$\Sigma_i \lambda_{ijk}^{ABC} = \Sigma_j \lambda_{ijk}^{ABC} = \Sigma_k \lambda_{ijk}^{ABC} = 0,\dots,$$

$$\Sigma_i \; \lambda_{ijk\ell}^{ABCD} = \Sigma_j \; \lambda_{ijk\ell}^{ABCD} = \Sigma_k \; \lambda_{ijk\ell}^{ABCD} = \Sigma_\ell \; \lambda_{ijk\ell}^{ABCD} = 0$$

The λ's are called <u>effects</u>, with the superscripts indicating the variables to which the effect refers. For example, λ^A means that the effect is due to variable A alone. In identifying an effect, the subscript is omitted. The <u>order</u> of the effect is the number of factors in the superscript. Hence, λ^A is a first order effect.

The log-linear model written above is referred to as the <u>saturated</u> model, since it contains all possible effects. By setting certain effects equal to zero, different models are formed. In a <u>hierarchical</u> model a higher order effect cannot be present unless all lower order effects whose factors are subsets of the higher order effect are also included in the model: e.g., if λ^{ABC} is stated (nonzero), it means that λ^{AB}, λ^{BC}, λ^{AC}, λ^A, λ^B, λ^C, θ are all present. Since only hierarchical models are considered, models are described by a minimal set of effects. For example, the full second-order model includes the terms with superscripts [θ,A,B,C,D,AB,AC,AD,BC,BD,CD] while all the three-factor and four-factor terms are set to zero. This model can be described by the minimal set of effects [AB,AC,AD,BC,BD,CD]. Including a higher order effect automatically implies including the lower order effects contained by it. That is, [AB] implies [AB,A,B,θ].

Let $F_{ijk\ell}$ be the fitted frequency (expected value) for cell (i,j,k,ℓ) for a particular model under consideration. The goodness-of-fit of the model can be tested using either the usual Pearson goodness-of-fit chi-square statistic

$$\chi^2 = \sum_{i,j,k,\ell} (f_{ijk\ell} - F_{ijk\ell})^2 / F_{ijk\ell}$$

or the likelihood ratio statistic

$$G^2 = 2 \sum_{i,j,k,\ell} f_{ijk\ell} \; \ln (f_{ijk\ell}/F_{ijk\ell})$$

Both are asymptotically distributed as chi-square, with n-p degrees of freedom (df), where n is the number of cells, and p is the number of estimated independent parameters.

The likelihood ratio chi-square (G^2) is additive under partitioning for nested models. Two models, M_1 and M_2, are said to be nested if all of the λ effects in M_1 are a subset of the λ's contained in M_2. The difference in G^2 between the two models is a test of the additional effects in M_2 conditional on the effects in M_1. This difference also has an asymptotic chi-square distribution with degrees of freedom equal to the difference in the number of parameters fitted to the two models. This property does not hold for the Pearson χ^2. Therefore, for some of the tests described below, only the likelihood ratio test (G^2) is computed.

Zero counts or frequencies. Both "0 $\ln(0/c)$" and "0 $\ln(0/0)$" are set to zero in the computation of G^2. When a fitted (expected) value is zero, G^2 is correctly computed, but its degrees of freedom are overestimated. A warning message is printed when any expected value is zero. To avoid zero expected frequencies you may choose to group the categories of an index or to add a constant (DELTA) to each cell (p. 312).

The results from Example 11.15 are presented in Output 11.15. Circled numbers below correspond to those in the output.

⑥ The results of fitting models of full order, for example of order k. This is a test that all interactions of order k+1 and higher are zero. When k=2, the model fitted is the full second order model; this tests whether all three-factor and four-factor interactions are zero.

⑦ A test that all interactions of a given order k are zero. This test is the difference between the fits of two models of full order (the models of order k-1 and k).

The tests resulting from fitting models of a given order indicate how complex a model must be to fit the data adequately.

From the output we see that the test of the second order interaction is highly significant, but the third order interactions are nonsignificant. Therefore a model that is appropriate for the data will include 2-factor interactions but may not require 3-factor interactions.

⑧ Tests of partial and marginal association for each subset of factors (Brown, 1976).

The test of any effect in a log-linear model depends on which other effects are included in the model. Therefore no single test determines the relative importance of an effect. Brown (1976) suggested the use of two tests --marginal and partial association --to screen effects.

The hypothesis that the partial association of k factors is zero is a test of whether a significant difference exists between the fit of two hierarchical models -- one is the full model of order k, and the other the model that differs from it in that the specified k-factor interaction is excluded. For example, to test the partial association of A and B (i.e., two factors), the full second order model is fitted and then the same model with λ^{AB} set to zero. The difference in the tests-of-fit is a test of partial association.

The hypothesis that the marginal association of k factors is zero is a test that the k factor interaction is zero in the marginal subtable formed by the k factors (i.e., summed over all other factors). For example, to test the marginal association of A and B (i.e., two factors), the two-way table indexed by A and B is formed and the two-factor interaction is tested.

The tests of marginal and partial association can be simultaneously used to screen the various interactions to determine whether they are necessary in the model for the data being used, whether they are not necessary, or whether they are questionable. In a second pass of P3F

Output 11.15   Model screening by P3F

```
TABLE NC.  1

VARIABLE INDICES. . . . . . . . . . . . . . . . .     1    2    3    4
SYMBOLS FCR INDICES . . . . . . . . . . . . . . .     I    S    A    C
NUMBER CF LEVELS. . . . . . . . . . . . . . . . .     4    2    3    3
MAXIMUM NUMBER OF ITERATIONS. . . . . . . . . .          20
MAXIMUM PERMISSIBLE CIFFERNCE BETWEEN
AN OBSERVED & FITTED MARGINAL TOTAL . . . . . .   0.100
CONSTANT TO BE ACCED TO EACH FREQUENCY. . . . .   C.500
NUMBER OF MOCELS SPECIFIED. . . . . . . . . . .       0
```

```
        THE FOLLCWING TABLE IS ANALYZED.
   CENTER      AGE      SURVIVEDI  INFL.APP(I)
     C          A.        S    I   MIN.MAL  MIN.BEN  GRT.MAL  GRT.BEN
   ----------------------------------------------------------------------
   TOKYC     UNDER50     NO    I      9        7        4        3
                        YES    I     26       68       25        9
                               I
             50-69       NO    I      9        9       11        2
                        YES    I     20       46       18        5
                               I
             OVER69      NO    I      2        3        1        0
                        YES    I      1        6        5        1
             ------------------I-------------------------------------------
   BOSTON    UNDER50     NO    I      6        7        6        0
                        YES    I     11       24        4        0
                               I
             50-69       NO    I      8       20        3        2
                        YES    I     18       58       10        3
                               I
             OVER69      NO    I      9       18        3        0
                        YES    I     15       26        1        1
             ------------------I-------------------------------------------
   GLAMORGN  UNDER50     NO    I     16        7        3        0
                        YES    I     16       20        8        1
                               I
             50-69       NO    I     14       12        3        0
                        YES    I     27       39       10        4
                               I
             OVER69      NO    I      3        7        3        0
                        YES    I     12       11        4        1
   ----------------------------------------------------------------------
   **FOR ANALYSIS,    0.500 IS ADDED TO EACH CELL ABCVE

       THE TOTAL FREQUENCY IS     764
```

⑥ THE RESULTS OF FITTING ALL K-FACTOR MARGINALS.
THIS IS A SIMULTANEOUS TEST THAT ALL K+1 AND HIGHER FACTOR INTERACTIONS ARE ZERO

K-FACTOR	D.F.	LR CHISQ	PROB.	PEARSON CHISQ	PPROB.	ITERATIONS
0(MEAN)	71	806.49	C.0	1062.63	0.0	
1	63	174.34	0.0002	181.39	0.0002	2
2	40	39.92	0.4738	40.16	0.4630	5
3	12	9.01	0.7020	8.93	0.7091	4

⑦ A SIMULTANEOUS TEST THAT ALL K-FACTOR INTERACTIONS ARE ZERO.
THE ENTRIES ARE DIFFERENCES IN THE ABOVE TABLE.

K-FACTOR	D.F.	LR CHISQ	PROB.	PEARSON CHISQ	PPCR.
1	8	632.15	0.0	881.24	0.0
2	23	134.42	C.0001	141.22	C.0001
3	28	30.91	0.3212	31.24	0.3067
4	12	9.01	0.7020	8.93	0.7091

A TEST OF PARTIAL ASSOCIATION OF THE FACTORS.
IT IS CALCULATED AS THE DIFFERENCE BETWEEN THE FULL K-TH
ORDER MODEL AND THAT WHICH EXCLUDES ONLY THE SPECIFIED
EFFECT. K IS THE NUMBER OF FACTORS IN THE EFFECT.

A TEST OF MARGINAL ASSOCIATION OF THE FACTORS.
THE TABLE IS SUMMED OVER THE UNSPECIFIED INDICES
AND THEN THE EFFECT IS TESTED TO BE ZERO.

⑧

EFFECT	D.F.	LR CHISQ	PROB.	ITERATIONS	LR CHISQ	PPDB.	ITERATIONS
I	3	370.15	0.0				
S	1	152.85	0.0000				
A	2	100.21	0.0000				
C	2	8.94	0.0115				
IS	3	10.18	0.0171	4	9.49	0.0235	2
IA	6	1.47	C.9613	4	3.09	0.7974	2
IC	6	34.23	0.0000	4	35.41	0.0000	2
SA	2	4.17	0.1241	4	7.72	0.0211	2
SC	2	7.79	0.0204	4	10.89	0.0043	2
AC	4	66.81	C.0000	4	72.22	0.0000	2
ISA	6	4.83	0.5657	4	7.71	0.260C	4
ISC	6	4.13	0.6595	4	5.19	0.5200	4
IAC	12	11.41	0.4945	4	12.35	0.4180	4
SAC	4	7.48	0.1126	4	8.73	0.0683	4
ISAC	12	9.01	0.7020	4			

the models that contain all the necessary terms and relevant combinations of the questionable terms can be defined, and an appropriate model (or models) for the data can be rapidly chosen. This is further explained in Brown (1976).

From the output we see that the third order interactions are not significant when tested for either partial or marginal association. Therefore they are not needed in the final model. The tests of marginal and partial association are both highly significant for AC and IC; therefore AC and IC belong in the model. Both tests are moderately significant for IS and SC; therefore IS and SC probably belong in the model. One test (marginal association) is significant and the other is not significant for SA; therefore it is doubtful whether SA is needed in the model. Both tests are nonsignificant for IA; therefore IA is not needed in the model. These results give guidelines on the relative importance of the two-factor interactions. In our next example we use these guidelines to choose the models to be tested.

When the table is two-or three-way, you can obtain tests of all possible hierarchical models (p. 314).

Testing specified models

Using the guidelines provided by the results of the above analysis, we select several models to be fitted to the data. They are

    [AC, IC, S]
    [AC, IC, SC]
    [AC, IC, IS]
    [AC, IC, SC, IS]
    [AC, IC, SC, IS, SA]

The first model contains the two most significant two-factor interactions and all the main effects; since the model is hierarchical the main effects for A, I and C are implicitly specified by AC and IC. The next three models contain the first model and all possible combinations of the two moderately large interactions. The last model includes an interaction (SA) that is unlikely to be necessary.

The models are specified in the *FIT* paragraph, as shown in Example 11.16.

Example 11.16

```
/PROBLEM      TITLE IS 'MORRISON BREAST CANCER DATA'.
/INPUT        VARIABLES ARE 4.
              FORMAT IS '(8F4.0)'.
              TABLE IS 4,2,3,3.
/VARIABLE     NAMES ARE 'INFL.APP',SURVIVED,AGE,CENTER.

/TABLE        INDICES ARE 'INFL.APP', SURVIVED, AGE, CENTER.
              SYMBOLS ARE I,        S,        A,   C.
              DELTA IS 0.5.

/CATEGORY     NAMES(1) ARE 'MIN.MAL', 'MIN.BEN', 'GRT.MAL', 'GRT.BEN'.
              NAMES(2) ARE NO, YES.
              NAMES(3) ARE UNDER50, '50-69', OVER69.
              NAMES(4) ARE TOKYO, BOSTON, GLAMORGN.
```

(continued)

```
/FIT          MODEL IS AC, IC, S.
              MODEL IS AC, IC, SC.
              MODEL IS AC, IC, IS.
              MODEL IS AC, IC, SC, IS.
              MODEL IS AC, IC, SC, IS, SA.

/END
```

The tests of the models are presented in Output 11.16. For each model the G^2 and χ^2 tests-of-fit are computed, as well as the probability of exceeding the computed test statistic. D.F. are the degrees of freedom for both tests.

The fit of the model [AC, IC, S] is nonsignificant; therefore this model is sufficient to explain the relationships between the factors. The difference between the fits of this model [AC, IC, SC] is a test of the two-factor interaction λ^{SC}; G^2 for this test is 66.71 - 55.83 = 10.88 with 53 - 51 = 2 degrees of freedom. This is a significant result and therefore we may decide to include λ^{SC} in the model although the test-of-fit of the first model is not significant. Similar comparisons can be made for the other effects.

● OPTIONAL RESULTS AND INPUT

Using the flexibility P3F offers in forming and analyzing frequency tables you can

- form and analyze tables that are cross sections of a multiway table — p. 308
- print marginal subtables of the table of observed frequencies — p. 310
- add a constant to each cell before fitting log-linear models — p. 312
- request tests of partial and marginal association — p. 313
- request that all possible models be fitted when the table is two-way or three-way — p. 314

Output 11.16 Fitting specified models by P3F

--- all results but ⑧ in Output 11.15 appear here ---

```
THE FOLLOWING MODEL WAS FIT.
NO.     MODEL                    D.F.   LR CHISQ   PROB.    PEARSON CHISQ   PROB.    ITERATIONS
 1    AC,IC,S.                    53     66.71     0.0977       67.85       0.0825        2

THE FOLLOWING MODEL WAS FIT.
NO.     MODEL                    D.F.   LR CHISQ   PROB.    PEARSON CHISQ   PROB.    ITERATIONS
 2    AC,IC,SC.                   51     55.83     0.2982       57.53       0.2464        2

THE FOLLOWING MODEL WAS FIT.
NO.     MODEL                    D.F.   LR CHISQ   PROB.    PEARSON CHISQ   PROB.    ITERATIONS
 3    AC,IC,IS.                   50     57.23     0.2245       57.52       0.2168        2

THE FOLLOWING MODEL WAS FIT.
NO.     MODEL                    D.F.   LR CHISQ   PROB.    PEARSON CHISQ   PROB.    ITERATIONS
 4    AC,IC,SC,IS.                48     45.61     0.5713       45.36       0.5818        4

THE FOLLOWING MODEL WAS FIT.
NO.     MODEL                    D.F.   LR CHISQ   PROB.    PEARSON CHISQ   PROB.    ITERATIONS
 5    AC,IC,SC,IS,SA.             46     41.39     0.6654       41.83       0.6476        4
```

- modify the criterion for convergence of the algorithm
  that estimates expected (fitted) values   p. 315

- specify that any hierarchical model be fitted to the
  data and request expected values, residuals (standardized or Freeman-Tukey), estimates of the parameters
  of the model, and test-of-fit models that differ from
  the specified model by one effect.   p. 315

- use tabulated results as input   p. 323

● FORMING MULTIWAY TABLES -- THE *TABLE* PARAGRAPH

   The tables to be formed are specified in the *TABLE* paragraph; the *TABLE*
paragraph is required and may be repeated before the *END* paragraph to specify
additional tables.

   Since multiway tables can be formed by P3F, it is not sufficient to
specify only the row and column variables. The INDEX (categorical) variables must be specified, as well as one character SYMBOLs that are used to
label the variables in the output and to specify models.

   In Output 11.14, we used

```
/TABLE          INDICES ARE INFARCT, ANGINA, HIGHER.
                SYMBOLS ARE I,      A,      H.
```

The first categorical variable (INDEX) is printed horizontally, the second is
printed vertically and its categories vary most rapidly, the third is also
printed vertically and its categories vary next to most rapidly, and so on.
In the output, effects are described by their superscripts (SYMBOLs):
I for INFARCT, etc.

TABLE
   INDEX=v_1,v_2,$\cdots$.   {none}   required, $\leq$ 7 categorical variables

   Names or subscripts of variables used as categorical variables to
   form the multiway table. If any variable takes on more than 10
   distinct values, CODEs or CUTPOINTS must be specified for it in
   the *CATEGory* paragraph. If CODEs or CUTPOINTS are not specified, P3F allocates space for 10 levels; this may cause you to exceed
   the maximum size for a table (p. 325) if your table is five-way or
   higher or if you form many four-way tables at one time.

   SYMBOL=c_1,c_2,$\cdots$.   {none}   required, one per INDEX variable,
                                                   one character each

   The SYMBOLs are used as labels for the INDEX variables in the
   output and to describe models. The first SYMBOL is used for the
   first INDEX variable, etc.

If only INDEX and SYMBOLS are specified in the *TABLE* paragraph, the table is formed and printed and the models of full order are tested (see Output 11.14).

Cross-sections of a higher-way table

Sometimes you may want separate multiway tables for each variable such as sex, treatment group, or age group. As in P1F and P2F, this is accomplished by specifying a categorical variable that is used to stratify the cases. We call this CONDITIONING the tables on an additional variable. For example, we reanalyze the data from the survival of breast cancer patients (Table 11.4) to produce three tables and analyses, one for each CENTER.

Example 11.17

```
/PROBLEM      TITLE IS 'MORRISON BREAST CANCER DATA'.
/INPUT        VARIABLES ARE 4.
              FORMAT IS '(8F4.0)'.
              TABLE IS 4,2,3,3.
/VARIABLE     NAMES ARE 'INFL.APP',SURVIVED,AGE,CENTER.

/TABLE        INDICES ARE 'INFL.APP', SURVIVED, AGE.
              SYMBOLS ARE  I,          S,        A.
              CONDITION IS CENTER.
              DELTA IS 0.5.

/CATEGORY     NAMES(1) ARE 'MIN.MAL', 'MIN.BEN', 'GRT.MAL', 'GRT.BEN'.
              NAMES(2) ARE NO, YES.
              NAMES(3) ARE UNDER50, '50-69', OVER69.
              NAMES(4) ARE TOKYO, BOSTON, GLAMORGN.

/END
```

Results for one of the tables are presented in Output 11.17.

TABLE
    CONDITION= $v_1, v_2, \cdots$.   {none}

    Names or subscripts of variables used to stratify the cases. If more than one is specified, each one is used in turn. A table is formed and analyzed at each level (code or category) of this variable. If the variable takes on more than 10 distinct values, CODEs or CUTPOINTS must be specified for it in the *CATEGory* paragraph.

Stacking or combining variables

INDEX and CONDITION use each categorical variable as a separate index or factor. At times it is appropriate to use all possible combinations of two or more variables as a single factor, most likely as a CONDITION variable. See P1F (p. 254) for a more detailed explanation.

<u>Output 11.17</u> Results for each center. The arrow points to the message
describing the center.

TABLE NC. 1

```
VARIABLE INDICES. . . . . . . . . . . . . . . . .    1    2    3
SYMBOLS FOR INDICES . . . . . . . . . . . . . . .    I    S    A
NUMBER OF LEVELS. . . . . . . . . . . . . . . . .    4    2    3
MAXIMUM NUMBER OF ITERATIONS. . . . . . . . . .         20
MAXIMUM PERMISSIBLE CIFFERNCE BETWEEN
AN OBSERVED & FITTED MARGINAL TOTAL . . . . . .      0.100
CONSTANT TO BE ADDED TO EACH FREQUENCY. . . . .      0.500
NUMBER OF MODELS SPECIFIED. . . . . . . . . .           0
```

***ANALYSIS IS PERFORMED ON THE DATA
  FOR THE LEVEL TOKYO   OF VARIABLE CENTER   ⬅——————

```
        THE FOLLCWING TABLE IS ANALYZED.
  AGE     SURVIVEDI  INFL.APP(I)
    A        S   I   MIN.MAL  MIN.BEN  GRT.MAL  GRT.BEN
  --------------------------------------------------------
  UNDER50   NO   I       9        7        4        3
            YES  I      26       68       25        9
                 I
  50-69     NO   I       9        9       11        2
            YES  I      20       46       18        5
                 I
  OVER69    NO   I       2        3        1        0
            YES  I       1        6        5        1
  --------------------------------------------------------
```

**FOR ANALYSIS,   0.500 IS ADDED TO EACH CELL ABOVE

        THE TOTAL FREQUENCY IS   290

THE RESULTS OF FITTING ALL K-FACTOR MARGINALS.
THIS IS A SIMULTANEOUS TEST THAT ALL K+1 AND HIGHER FACTOR INTERACTIONS ARE ZERO

K-FACTOR	D.F.	LR CHISQ	PROB.	PEARSON CHISQ	PROB.	ITERATIONS
0(MEAN)	23	339.77	0.0	467.75	0.0	
1	17	22.53	0.1651	22.50	0.1662	2
2	6	4.24	0.6445	4.20	0.6495	4

A SIMULTANEOUS TEST THAT ALL K-FACTOR INTERACTIONS ARE ZERO.
THE ENTRIES ARE DIFFERENCES IN THE ABOVE TABLE.

K-FACTOR	D.F.	LR CHISQ	PROB.	PEARSON CHISQ	PROB.
1	6	317.24	0.0	445.24	0.0
2	11	18.29	0.0750	18.30	0.0749
3	6	4.24	0.6445	4.20	0.6495

--- similar results are printed for the other centers ---

VARiable
>   DEFINE(#)=v$_1$,v$_2$,···.   {none}   may be repeated
>
>   Names or subscripts of variables to be stacked (or combined) into a
>   single index, that defines a new variable. DEFINE constructs
>   a categorical variable made up of all possible combinations of the
>   levels (codes or categories) of the specified variables; # must
>   be greater than any variable subscript, and becomes the subscript
>   of the new variable. CODEs or CUTPOINTS must be specified in
>   the *CATEGory* paragraph for each variable stacked by a DEFINE
>   statement. The levels of v$_1$ are the fastest changing, v$_2$ the
>   next fastest, etc., in the newly created variable.

● PRINTING THE OBSERVED FREQUENCIES AND MARGINAL SUBTABLES

The table of observed frequencies is printed unless

NO OBSERVED.

is specified in the *TABLE* paragraph.

Marginal subtables of the observed frequencies can also be printed. For
example, if you specify

MARGINAL=2.

in the *TABLE* paragraph, all one-way and two-way marginal subtables are printed.
To illustrate the results we added this statement to Example 11.15.

Example 11.18

```
/PROBLEM     TITLE IS 'MORRISON BREAST CANCER DATA'.
/INPUT       VARIABLES ARE 4.
             FORMAT IS '(8F4.0)'.
             TABLE IS 4,2,3,3.
/VARIABLE    NAMES ARE 'INFL.APP',SURVIVED,AGE,CENTER.

/TABLE       INDICES ARE 'INFL.APP', SURVIVED, AGE, CENTER.
             SYMBOLS ARE I,        S,        A,   C.
             MARGINAL IS 2.
             DELTA IS 0.5.

/CATEGORY    NAMES(1) ARE 'MIN.MAL', 'MIN.BEN', 'GRT.MAL', 'GRT.BEN'.
             NAMES(2) ARE NO, YES.
             NAMES(3) ARE UNDER50, '50-69', OVER69.
             NAMES(4) ARE TOKYO, BOSTON, GLAMORGN.

/END
```

The resulting marginal subtables are printed in Output 11.18.

Output 11.18 Marginal subtables printed by P3F

--- observed frequency table is printed ---

```
     MARGINAL TOTALS
INFL.APP(I)
  MIÑ.MAL  MIN.BEN  GRT.MAL  GRT.BEN
---------------------------------------
    222      388      122       32
---------------------------------------
```

```
     MARGINAL TOTALS
SURVIVED(S)
   NO       YES
------------------
   210      554
------------------
```

```
       MARGINAL TOTALS
AGE     (A)
    UNDER50   50-69    OVER69
------------------------------
     280      351      133
------------------------------
```

```
      MARGINAL TOTALS
CENTER  (C)
   TOKYO    BOSTON   GLAMORGN
------------------------------
    290      253      221
------------------------------
```

```
       MARGINAL TOTALS
SURVIVEDI  INFL.APP(I)
   S   I    MIN.MAL  MIN.BEN  GRT.MAL  GRT.BEN
----------------------------------------------
NO     I      76       90       37        7
YES    I     14€      298       85       25
----------------------------------------------
```

```
       MARGINAL TOTALS
AGE      I  INFL.APP(I)
   A   I    MIN.MAL  MIN.BEN  GRT.MAL  GRT.BEN
----------------------------------------------
UNDER50 I     84      133       50       13
50-69   I     96      184       55       16
OVER69  I     42       71       17        3
----------------------------------------------
```

```
         MARGINAL TOTALS
CENTER  I  INFL.APP(I)
   C    I    MIN.MAL  MIN.BEN  GRT.MAL  GRT.BEN
-----------------------------------------------
TOKYO   I     67      139       64       20
BOSTON  I     67      153       27        6
GLAMORGNI     88       96       31        6
-----------------------------------------------
```

```
        MARGINAL TOTALS
AGE      I  SURVIVED(S)
   A    I    NO       YES
--------------------------
UNDER50 I     68      212
50-69   I     93      258
OVER69  I     49       84
--------------------------
```

```
        MARGINAL TOTALS
CENTER  I  SURVIVED(S)
   C    I    NO       YES
--------------------------
TOKYO   I     60      230
BOSTON  I     82      171
GLAMORGNI     68      153
--------------------------
```

```
         MARGINAL TOTALS
CENTER  I  AGE      (A)
   C    I    UNDER50   50-69    OVER69
---------------------------------------
TOKYO   I     151      120       19
BOSTON  I      58      122       73
GLAMORGNI      71      109       41
---------------------------------------
```

--- results are printed for the analysis of the frequency table ---

```
TABLE
    OBServed.                      { OBSERVED/prev.}

        The table of observed frequencies formed by the INDEx variables
        is printed unless NO OBServed is specified.

    MARGINAL=#.                    {0/prev.}

        Print all marginal subtables that have this many (#) or fewer
        categorical variables.  A marginal subtable is the sum of the
        observed frequencies over all levels of the categorical variables
        that are not used to form the marginal subtable.
```

● ADDING A CONSTANT TO EACH CELL

When the expected values of the cell frequencies are small, some investigators add a constant (usually 0.5) to each cell. Alternatively, the cells can be combined to increase the observed frequencies.

```
TABLE
    DELTA=#.                       {zero/prev.}

        A constant (DELTA) is added to each cell frequency before
        fitting models.
```

● TESTS OF MODELS OF FULL ORDER

The tests of all effects of a given order, or greater than a given order, (⑥ and ⑦ in Output 11.15, p. 304) are computed unless

        NO SIMULTANEOUS.

is specified in the *TABLE* paragraph.

A test that all effects greater than order 2 are zero is performed by fitting the model that includes all 0, 1st and 2nd order effects; i.e., [AB,AC,AD,BC,BD,CD] using the notation on p. 301. To test that all effects greater than order 1 are zero, the model fitted includes all 0 and 1st order marginals; i.e., [A,B,C,D].

A simultaneous test that all effects of order k are zero is obtained from differences between the above simultaneous tests. That is, a test that all effects of order 2 are zero is the difference between tests of fit of the full second order model [AB,AC,AD,BC,BD,CD] and the full first order model [A,B,C,D].

```
┌─────────────────────────────────────────────────────────────┐
│  TABLE                                                        │
│     SIMULTANEOUS.                        {yes/prev.}          │
│                                                               │
│     Tests of all effects of a given order are printed unless  │
│     NO SIMULTANEOUS is specified.                             │
│                                                               │
└─────────────────────────────────────────────────────────────┘
```

● TESTS OF PARTIAL AND MARGINAL ASSOCIATION

For every subset of factors the tests of partial and marginal association are printed if

                ASSOCIATION.
is specified in the *TABLE* paragraph.

Partial association tests that the partial association between a
set of factors in an effect λ is zero: this is the difference between fitting a model containing all marginals of the same order as λ, and the model
containing all marginals of that order except the one being tested. For
example, to test that the partial association of A with B is zero, the
difference is taken between the fit of the model [AB,AC,BC,AD,BD,CD] and
the model [AC,BC,AD,BD,CD] (i.e., λ^{AB} is excluded). The degrees of freedom
for this test are the same as for the corresponding test of marginal association. Since this is a test of differences of all of the nested models, only
the likelihood ratio test G^2 is appropriate.

Marginal association tests that the marginal association between
a set of factors in an effect λ is zero. For example, let λ^{AB} be the effect
of interest. From the marginal table for variables A and B (i.e., the table
is summed over the levels of the remaining categorical variables), the test
that $\lambda^{AB}=0$ is performed by fitting the model [A,B] to the resulting two-
dimensional table; (i.e., the model containing all effects except the effect
of interest). If λ^{ABC} is to be tested, the table is summed over the levels
of variable D, and the model [AB,AC,BC] is fitted to the three-dimensional
table with elements f_{ijk+}.

The tests of marginal association are equal to those of partial association for the main effects and the highest-order interaction.

The degrees of freedom associated with the chi-square test of both
marginal association and partial association of an effect Z is

$$(I-1)^{\delta^{ZA}} (J-1)^{\delta^{ZB}} (K-1)^{\delta^{ZC}} (L-1)^{\delta^{ZD}}$$

where $\delta^{ZA}=1$ if A is part of Z, and zero otherwise; this is the same formula
as for interactions in the analysis of variance.

This option is illustrated by ⑧ in Output 11.15, and the use of these
tests is described on p. 303.

```
   TABLE
       ASSOCIATION.              {no/prev.}
           For each effect, print the tests that the partial and marginal
           association are each zero.  Each test requires the fitting of a
           model by iteration, which can be time-consuming in high-
           dimensional tables (5-way or more).
```

● FITTING ALL HIERARCHICAL MODELS

When the table is two- or three-way, all hierarchical models are printed if

        ALL.

is specified (four models in the two-way table, and 18 in the three-way table). We illustrate this by adding ALL to Example 11.14.

Example 11.19

```
/PROBLEM      TITLE IS 'KASSER CORONARY DATA'.
/INPUT        VARIABLES ARE 6.
              FORMAT IS '(6F4.0)'.
/VARIABLE     NAMES ARE AGE,FUNCTION,ACTIVE,INFARCT,ANGINA,HIGHBP.

/TABLE        INDICES ARE INFARCT, ANGINA, HIGHBP.
              SYMBOLS ARE I,        A,       H.
              ALL.

/CATEGORY     CODES(4) ARE    0,        1.
              NAMES(4) ARE NONE, PRESENT.
              CODES(5) ARE    0,        1.
              NAMES(5) ARE NONE, PRESENT.
              CODES(6) ARE    0,        1.
              NAMES(6) ARE NORMAL, HYPERTEN.

/END
```

Output 11.19 Fitting all models to the data in a three-way table by P3F

--- results in Output 11.14 appear here ---

ALL MODELS ARE REQUESTED--

MODEL	DF	LIKELIHOOD-RATIO CHISQ	PROB.	PEARSON CHISQ	PROB.
I	6	81.55	0.0000	81.66	0.0
A	6	31.47	0.0000	32.83	0.0000
H	6	72.10	0.0000	62.78	0.0000
I,A	5	23.16	0.0003	22.33	0.0005
I,H	5	63.79	0.0000	56.73	0.0
A,H	5	13.71	0.0176	12.81	0.0253
I,A,H	4	5.40	0.2488	4.93	0.2950
IA	4	18.38	0.0010	17.84	0.0013
IH	4	63.25	0.0000	55.73	0.0000
AH	4	13.70	0.0083	12.80	0.0123
IA,H	3	0.62	0.8917	0.62	0.8912
IH,A	3	4.86	0.1821	4.39	0.2220
AH,I	3	5.39	0.1453	4.93	0.1772
IA,IH	2	0.09	0.9583	0.09	0.9578
AI,AH	2	0.61	0.7358	0.62	0.7343
HI,HA	2	4.86	0.0882	4.37	0.1124
IA,IH,AH	1	0.03	0.8579	0.03	0.8587

The models fitted and tested are shown in Output 11.19. Each model is described by its minimal hierarchical form. That is, [AI,IH] represents the log-linear model

$$\theta + \lambda^A + \lambda^I + \lambda^H + \lambda^{AI} + \lambda^{IH} \; .$$

The model [I, A, H] is nonsignificant, therefore we conclude that the model of independence between factors provides an adequate fit to the data.

TABLE
ALL.   {none/prev.}

    Fit all hierarchical models in a two- or three-way table.
    If the table is more than three-way, ALL is not available.

● CONVERGENCE OF THE MODEL-FITTING

Each model is fitted by an algorithm published by Haberman (1972) called iterative proportional fitting. To control the accuracy of the final fit and to limit the maximum number of iterations, the CONVERGENCE criterion and the maximum number of ITERATIONS can be stated. In general, pre-assigned values can be used.

TABLE
CONVERGENCE=#.   {0.1/prev.}

    Maximum permitted difference between every observed and fitted marginal total in the model.

ITERATION=#.   {20/prev.}

    Maximum number of iterations used to fit any model. An error message is printed if this number is reached.

● SPECIFYING YOUR OWN MODELS -- THE *FIT* PARAGRAPH

If your study is designed to test specific hypotheses, you will have certain models you may want to test. Or if you used the screening capabilities in P3F, you may want to test models identified during the screening.

You can specify the models you want to test in the *FIT* paragraph; the *FIT* paragraph can be repeated to test additional models. The models are fitted to the tables described in the last *TABLE* paragraph preceding the *FIT* paragraph.

In Output 11.16 we illustrate the results of fitting several models to the data from the breast cancer survival study.

The statement

        MODEL=AC,IC,S.

specifies the hierarchical model

$$\theta + \lambda^A + \lambda^I + \lambda^C + \lambda^S + \lambda^{AC} + \lambda^{IC}$$

That is, a model is described by a sequence of superscripts. You need not specify superscripts that are subsets of other superscripts. Therefore A, I and C are not specified in the above example. MODEL is repeated in the *FIT* paragraph in Example 11.16 to test additional models.

FIT

    MODEL=c_1,c_2,$\cdots$.   {none}   may be repeated

        c_1,c_2,... are the superscripts of the effects that define the hierarchical model to be fitted to the data. Each superscript must contain <u>only</u> SYMBOLS specified in the *TABLE* paragraph. The superscripts are separated by commas and terminated by a period. For example, the model $\theta + \lambda^A + \lambda^B + \lambda^C + \lambda^D + \lambda^{AC} + \lambda^{BD}$ can be specified as MODEL= AC,BD. More than one model can be specified in one *FIT* paragraph, each model must be stated in a separate MODEL= statement.

● EXPECTED VALUES AND RESIDUALS

        Expected values ($F_{ijk\ell}$) are the frequencies for every cell estimated by the fitted model. They are printed for each MODEL if

        EXPECTED.

is specified in the *FIT* paragraph.

        Two types of residuals are available in P3F. For standardized residuals, specify

        STANDARDIZED.

in the *FIT* paragraph; the residual

$$(f_{ijk\ell} - F_{ijk\ell})/F_{ijk\ell}^{\frac{1}{2}}$$

is printed for each cell. The sum of squares of these residuals is the χ^2 test. A second type of residual is the Freeman-Tukey residual, which is defined as

$$f_{ijk\ell}^{\frac{1}{2}} + (f_{ijk\ell} + 1)^{\frac{1}{2}} - (4F_{ijk\ell} + 1)^{\frac{1}{2}} .$$

This residual is obtained by specifying

        FREEMAN.

in the *FIT* paragraph.

To illustrate these results we use the following example.

Example 11.20

```
/PROBLEM      TITLE IS 'MORRISON BREAST CANCER DATA'.
/INPUT        VARIABLES ARE 4.
              FORMAT IS '(8F4.0)'.
              TABLE IS 4,2,3,3.
/VARIABLE     NAMES ARE 'INFL.APP',SURVIVED,AGE,CENTER.

/TABLE        INDICES ARE 'INFL.APP', SURVIVED, AGE, CENTER.
              SYMBOLS ARE  I,          S,        A,  C.
              DELTA IS 0.5.

/CATEGORY     NAMES(1) ARE 'MIN.MAL', 'MIN.BEN', 'GRT.MAL', 'GRT.BEN'.
              NAMES(2) ARE NO, YES.
              NAMES(3) ARE UNDER50, '50-69', OVER69.
              NAMES(4) ARE TOKYO, BOSTON, GLAMORGN.

/FIT          MODEL IS AC, IC, SC.
              EXPECTED.
              STANDARDIZED.
              FREEMAN.

/END
```

The expected values and residuals are printed in Output 11.20.

FIT

    EXPECTED.   {no}

        Expected values (F_{ijkl}) are printed for each MODEL.

    STANDARDIZED.   {no}

        Standardized residuals are printed for each MODEL.

    FREEMAN.   {no}

        Freeman-Tukey residuals are printed for each MODEL.

● ESTIMATES OF THE PARAMETERS OF THE MODEL

When LAMBDA is specified in the *FIT* paragraph, estimates of the parameters of the log-linear model (λ) are printed for each MODEL. Standard deviations of the estimates are also computed; the ratio of the estimate of λ to its standard error is printed.

Let

$$x_{ijkl} = \ln F_{ijkl} .$$

The estimates of the effects are similar to the calculation of main effects and interactions in a factorial analysis of variance, for example,

Output 11.20   Expected (fitted) values and residuals printed by P3F

--- results in Output 11.15 except ⑧ appear here ---

THE FOLLOWING MODEL WAS FIT.

NO.	MODEL		D.F.	LR CHISQ	PROB.	PEARSON CHISQ	PROB.	ITERATIONS
1	AC,IC,SC.		51	55.83	0.2982	57.53	0.2464	2

THE FITTED VALUES

CENTER C	AGE A	SURVIVED S	I	INFL.APP(I) MIN.MAL	MIN.BEN	GRT.MAL	GRT.BEN
TOKYO	UNDER50	NO	I	7.852	15.928	7.515	2.580
		YES	I	28.076	56.953	26.872	9.225
	50-69	NO	I	6.281	12.742	6.012	2.064
		YES	I	22.460	45.563	21.498	7.380
	OVER69	NO	I	1.165	2.363	1.115	0.383
		YES	I	4.166	8.451	3.988	1.369
BOSTON	UNDER50	NO	I	5.439	12.120	2.331	0.699
		YES	I	10.939	24.378	4.688	1.406
	50-69	NO	I	11.052	24.631	4.737	1.421
		YES	I	22.231	49.542	9.527	2.858
	OVER69	NO	I	6.754	15.052	2.895	0.868
		YES	I	13.585	30.276	5.822	1.747
GLAMORGN	UNDER50	NO	I	9.303	10.121	3.476	0.920
		YES	I	19.989	21.746	7.468	1.977
	50-69	NO	I	14.017	15.249	5.237	1.386
		YES	I	30.117	32.764	11.252	2.979
	OVER69	NO	I	5.582	6.073	2.086	0.552
		YES	I	11.993	13.048	4.481	1.186

STANDARDIZED RESIDUALS = (OBSERVED-FITTED)/SQRT(FITTED)

CENTER C	AGE A	SURVIVED S	I	INFL.APP(I) MIN.MAL	MIN.BEN	GRT.MAL	GRT.BEN
TOKYO	UNDER50	NO	I	0.588	-2.112	-1.100	0.573
		YES	I	-0.297	1.530	-0.265	0.091
	50-69	NO	I	1.284	-0.908	2.238	0.304
		YES	I	-0.414	0.139	-0.647	-0.692
	OVER69	NO	I	1.237	0.739	0.364	0.189
		YES	I	-1.306	-0.671	0.757	0.112
BOSTON	UNDER50	NO	I	0.455	-1.327	2.731	-0.238
		YES	I	0.170	0.025	-0.087	-0.764
	50-69	NO	I	-0.768	-0.832	-0.568	0.905
		YES	I	-0.791	1.273	0.315	0.380
	OVER69	NO	I	1.056	0.889	0.356	-0.395
		YES	I	0.519	-0.686	-1.791	-0.187
GLAMORGN	UNDER50	NO	I	2.360	-0.824	0.013	-0.438
		YES	I	-0.780	-0.267	0.377	-0.339
	50-69	NO	I	0.129	-0.704	-0.759	-0.753
		YES	I	-0.477	1.177	-0.224	0.882
	OVER69	NO	I	-0.881	0.579	0.979	-0.070
		YES	I	0.146	-0.428	0.009	0.288

FREEMAN-TUKEY DEVIATES

CENTER C	AGE A	SURVIVED S	I	INFL.APP(I) MIN.MAL	MIN.BEN	GRT.MAL	GRT.BEN
TOKYO	UNDER50	NO	I	0.630	-2.390	-1.107	0.628
		YES	I	-0.252	1.487	-0.218	0.166
	50-69	NO	I	1.211	-0.886	1.922	0.410
		YES	I	-0.367	0.174	-0.610	-0.630
	OVER69	NO	I	1.073	0.759	0.469	0.341
		YES	I	-1.397	-0.611	0.778	0.261
BOSTON	UNDER50	NO	I	0.518	-1.380	2.075	-0.017
		YES	I	0.237	0.074	0.022	-0.642
	50-69	NO	I	-0.726	-0.812	-0.474	0.867
		YES	I	-0.766	1.249	0.378	0.466
	OVER69	NO	I	1.029	0.893	0.445	-0.183
		YES	I	0.560	-0.658	-2.123	-0.020
GLAMORGN	UNDER50	NO	I	2.064	-0.787	0.132	-0.232
		YES	I	-0.752	-0.215	0.441	-0.179
	50-69	NO	I	0.191	-0.664	-0.693	-0.626
		YES	I	-0.439	1.157	-0.151	0.873
	OVER69	NO	I	-0.838	0.625	0.936	0.141
		YES	I	0.212	-0.366	0.116	0.409

$$\hat{\lambda}_i^A = \bar{x}_{i...} - \bar{x}_{....}$$

$$\hat{\lambda}_{ij}^{AB} = \bar{x}_{ij..} - \bar{x}_{i...} - \bar{x}_{.j..} + \bar{x}_{....}$$

$$\hat{\lambda}_{ijk}^{ABC} = \bar{x}_{ijk.} - \bar{x}_{ij..} - \bar{x}_{i.k.} - \bar{x}_{.jk.} + \bar{x}_{i...} + \bar{x}_{.j..} + \bar{x}_{..k.} - \bar{x}_{....},$$

where a period (.) indicates the mean of the omitted subscript.

For a particular λ in the saturated model, say λ^Z, the variance is given by

$$\sigma^2(\lambda_{i'j'k'\ell'}^Z) = \left(\frac{1}{IJKL}\right)^2 \sum_{ijk\ell} \frac{[(I-1)^{\delta_{ii'}^{ZA}} (J-1)^{\delta_{jj'}^{ZB}} (K-1)^{\delta_{kk'}^{ZC}} (L-1)^{\delta_{\ell\ell'}^{ZD}}]^2}{f_{ijk\ell}}$$

where $\delta_{ii'}^{ZA} = 1$ if A is a factor in effect Z and $i=i'$; otherwise, $\delta_{ii'}^{ZA} = 0$. Similar definitions are used for $\delta_{jj'}^{ZB}$, $\delta_{kk'}^{ZC}$, and $\delta_{\ell\ell'}^{ZD}$.

S.K. Lee (1977) gives a method for finding variances of the $\hat{\lambda}$'s when the model is not saturated and the expected value of the cells can be expressed in closed form; i.e., the model is direct. His method is implemented for direct models. When the model is indirect, a direct model is found for which the indirect model is a subset. Lee's method is then applied to the direct model, providing an upper bound on the variance of estimates. The ratio $\hat{\lambda}/\sigma(\lambda)$ is printed for all the estimates. The model used to computed $\sigma(\lambda)$ is printed in the output.

Both $\ln(0)$ and $\ln(1/0)$ are set to zero. Therefore, when there are values equal to zero, both $\hat{\lambda}$ and $s_{\hat{\lambda}}$ are undefined if a zero occurs in a marginal table; then the estimates of the parameters ($\hat{\lambda}$) are undefined for that marginal table.

FIT

LAMBDA.   {no}

    Print the estimates of the parameters of the log-linear model, and the estimates divided by their standard error. These estimates are printed only if the tail probability of the test-of-fit of the model exceeds PROBABILITY; i.e., the test-of-fit is nonsignificant.

BETA.   {no}

    Print the estimates of the multiplicative parameters ($\beta=e^\lambda$). These estimates are printed only if the tail probability of the test-of-fit of the model exceeds PROBABILITY.

```
FIT

    PROBability=#.        {0.05}

        The level of significance against which the test-of-fit is
        compared.  If the test-of-fit of the model is nonsignificant,
        the estimates of the log-linear model ( LAMBDA and  BETA )
        are printed if requested.
```

Example 11.21

```
/PROBLEM        TITLE IS 'MORRISON BREAST CANCER DATA'.
/INPUT          VARIABLES ARE 4.
                FORMAT IS '(8F4.0)'.
                TABLE IS 4,2,3,3.
/VARIABLE       NAMES ARE 'INFL.APP',SURVIVED,AGE,CENTER.

/TABLE          INDICES ARE 'INFL.APP',  SURVIVED, AGE, CENTER.
                SYMBOLS ARE I,           S,        A,   C.
                DELTA IS 0.5.

/CATEGORY       NAMES(1) ARE 'MIN.MAL', 'MIN.BEN', 'GRT.MAL', 'GRT.BEN'.
                NAMES(2) ARE NO, YES.
                NAMES(3) ARE UNDER50, '50-69', OVER69.
                NAMES(4) ARE TOKYO, BOSTON, GLAMORGN.

/FIT            MODEL IS AC, IC, SC.
                LAMBDA.
                BETA.

/END
```

The resulting estimates are printed in Output 11.21.

● ORTHOGONAL DECOMPOSITION OF THE LOG-LINEAR PARAMETERS

    When the ORTHOGONAL statement is used, coefficients of the linear,
quadratic, etc., orthogonal polynomials are generated for each specified
symbol assuming that the levels of the categorical variables are equally spaced.
The polynomial coefficients (and all products of them) are applied to the logarithms of the expected values of the cells estimated by the specified MODEL;
i.e.,

$$\sum_{i,j,k,\ell} c_{ijk\ell} \; \ln F_{ijk\ell}$$

When the model is a saturated model, the asymptotic variance is

$$\sigma^2 = \Sigma \frac{c^2_{ijk\ell}}{f_{ijk\ell}}$$

where $c_{ijk\ell}$ is the value of the polynomial for cell (i,j,k,ℓ); the ratio of
the coefficient to its asymptotic standard error is computed and printed.

Output 11.21   Estimates of the log-linear parameters by P3F

```
THE FOLLOWING MODEL WAS FIT.
NO.     MODEL
 1    AC,IC,SC.
```

D.F.	LR CHISQ	PROB.	PEARSON CHISQ	PROB.	ITERATIONS
51	55.83	0.2982	57.53	0.2464	2

THETA (MEAN) ------- 1.826

ESTIMATES OF THE LOG-LINEAR PARAMETERS
INFL.APP(I)

MIN.MAL	MIN.BEN	GRT.MAL	GRT.BEN
0.480	1.011	-0.145	-1.346

ESTIMATES OF THE LOG-LINEAR PARAMETERS
SURVIVED(S)

NO	YES
-0.456	0.456

ESTIMATES OF THE LOG-LINEAR PARAMETERS
AGE   (A)

UNDER50	50-69	OVER69
0.145	0.444	-0.589

ESTIMATES OF THE LOG-LINEAR PARAMETERS
CENTER (C)

TOKYO	BOSTON	GLAMORGN
0.049	0.001	-0.050

ESTIMATES OF THE LOG-LINEAR PARAMETERS
CENTER I INFL.APP(I)

C	I	MIN.MAL	MIN.BEN	GRT.MAL	GRT.BEN
TOKYO	I	-0.368	-0.191	0.214	0.345
BOSTON	I	0.044	0.315	-0.178	-0.181
GLAMORGN	I	0.323	-0.123	-0.036	-0.164

ESTIMATES OF THE LOG-LINEAR PARAMETERS
CENTER I SURVIVED(S)

C	I	NO	YES
TOKYO	I	-0.181	0.181
BOSTON	I	0.107	-0.107
GLAMORGN	I	0.074	-0.074

ESTIMATES OF THE LOG-LINEAR PARAMETERS
CENTER I AGE   (A)

C	I	UNDER50	50-69	OVER69
TOKYO	I	0.565	0.043	-0.609
BOSTON	I	-0.454	-0.043	0.497
GLAMORGN	I	-0.111	-0.000	0.112

THE STANDARDIZED ESTIMATES ARE COMPUTED USING ASYMPTOTIC VARIANCES
BASED ON THE GIVEN MODEL.

ESTIMATES OF THE LOG-LINEAR PARAMETERS DIVIDED BY ITS STANDARD ERROR

INFL.APP(I)

MIN.MAL	MIN.BEN	GRT.MAL	GRT.BEN
6.775	15.730	-1.718	-10.150

SURVIVED(S)

NO	YES
-11.548	11.548

AGE   (A)

UNDER50	50-69	OVER69
2.627	8.634	-8.649

CENTER (C)

TOKYO	BOSTON	GLAMORGN
0.596	0.014	-0.586

CENTER I INFL.APP(I)

C	I	MIN.MAL	MIN.BEN	GRT.MAL	GRT.BEN
TOKYO	I	-3.862	-2.292	2.012	2.121
BOSTON	I	0.425	3.385	-1.400	-0.910
GLAMORGN	I	3.199	-1.287	-0.289	-0.827

CENTER I SURVIVED(S)

C	I	NO	YES
TOKYO	I	-3.207	3.207
BOSTON	I	1.958	-1.959
GLAMORGN	I	1.304	-1.304

CENTER I AGE   (A)

C	I	UNDER50	50-69	OVER69
TOKYO	I	7.348	0.576	-5.648
BOSTON	I	-5.755	-0.618	5.757
GLAMORGN	I	-1.419	-0.003	1.194

THETA (MEAN) ------- 6.209

ESTIMATES OF THE MULTIPLICATIVE PARAMETERS
INFL.APP(I)

MIN.MAL	MIN.BEN	GRT.MAL	GRT.BEN
1.616	2.748	0.865	0.260

ESTIMATES OF THE MULTIPLICATIVE PARAMETERS
SURVIVED(S)

NO	YES
0.634	1.578

ESTIMATES OF THE MULTIPLICATIVE PARAMETERS
AGE   (A)

UNDER50	50-69	OVER69
1.156	1.559	0.555

ESTIMATES OF THE MULTIPLICATIVE PARAMETERS
CENTER (C)

TOKYO	BOSTON	GLAMORGN
1.050	1.001	0.951

ESTIMATES OF THE MULTIPLICATIVE PARAMETERS
CENTER I INFL.APP(I)

C	I	MIN.MAL	MIN.BEN	GRT.MAL	GRT.BEN
TOKYO	I	0.692	0.826	1.238	1.412
BOSTON	I	1.045	1.370	0.837	0.834
GLAMORGN	I	1.382	0.884	0.965	0.849

ESTIMATES OF THE MULTIPLICATIVE PARAMETERS
CENTER I SURVIVED(S)

C	I	NO	YES
TOKYO	I	0.835	1.198
BOSTON	I	1.113	0.899
GLAMORGN	I	1.077	0.929

ESTIMATES OF THE MULTIPLICATIVE PARAMETERS
CENTER I AGE   (A)

C	I	UNDER50	50-69	OVER69
TOKYO	I	1.760	1.044	0.544
BOSTON	I	0.635	0.958	1.644
GLAMORGN	I	0.894	1.000	1.118

FIT

ORTHOGONAL=c_1,c_2,$\cdots$.　　　{none}　　SYMBOLS as specified in *TABLE*

> For each SYMBOL specified, the linear, quadratic, etc., orthogonal contrasts are generated; they and their products are fitted to the logarithms of the expected cell frequencies estimated from the MODEL.
>
> When all SYMBOLS are not listed, the polynomials are fitted at each combination of the levels of the unspecified SYMBOLS. The asymptotic standard error for each polynomial is computed when the MODEL is saturated.
>
> When the tail probability of the test-of-fit of the model is less than PROBABILITY (i.e., is significant), orthogonal decomposition is not performed.

● STEPPING -- ADDING OR DELETING AN EFFECT FROM THE MODEL

The ADD command is used to form models that include MODEL and differ from it by only one effect. That is, the following calculation is performed for each MODEL. Let [Z] be the minimal set of effects. All hierarchical models that include Z and differ from it in only one effect are fitted. For example, let [Z] = [AB,AC]; that is, the model

$$ln\, F_{ijk\ell} = \theta + \lambda_i^A + \lambda_j^B + \lambda_k^C + \lambda_{ij}^{AB} + \lambda_{ik}^{AC}$$

The following models include [Z] and differ from it by only one effect: [AB,AC,D] and [AB,AC,BC]. Therefore they are fitted and tested.

The DELETE command is used to form models that are included by MODEL and differ from it by only one effect. That is, the following calculation is performed for each model specified by the user: Let [Z] be the minimal set of effects. All hierarchical models that are included in Z and differ from it by only one effect are fitted. For example, let [Z] = [AB,AC]. The following models are included in [Z] and differ from it by one effect: [AB,C] and [AC,B]. Therefore they are fitted and tested.

ADD and DELETE can be used to search for a model in a stepwise manner or to compute the tests of marginal and partial association when the design requires that an interaction be included in all models (see Benedetti and Brown, 1976).

In the following example we specify only two of the models requested in Example 11.16. The remaining models requested in that example are formed by adding or deleting an effect from the model.

Example 11.22

```
/PROBLEM      TITLE IS 'MORRISON BREAST CANCER DATA'.
/INPUT        VARIABLES ARE 4.
              FORMAT IS '(8F4.0)'.
              TABLE IS 4,2,3,3.
/VARIABLE     NAMES ARE 'INFL.APP',SURVIVED,AGE,CENTER.

/TABLE        INDICES ARE 'INFL.APP', SURVIVED, AGE, CENTER.
              SYMBOLS ARE  I,         S,        A,   C.
              DELTA IS 0.5.

/CATEGORY     NAMES(1) ARE 'MIN.MAL', 'MIN.BEN', 'GRT.MAL', 'GRT.BEN'.
              NAMES(2) ARE NO, YES.
              NAMES(3) ARE UNDER50, '50-69', OVER69.
              NAMES(4) ARE TOKYO, BOSTON, GLAMORGN.

/FIT          MODEL IS AC, IC, S.
              ADD.

/FIT          MODEL IS AC, IC, SC, IS, SA.
              DELETE.

/END
```

The results are presented in Output 11.22. First the specified model [AC, IC, S] is fit to the data. Then each model that contains it and differs from it by one effect is formed and tested. The first model formed is [IS, AC, IC] which differs from the specified model by the interaction λ^{IS}. Two lines are printed for the model [IS, AC, IC]. The first line is a test of the model; the second line is a test of the interaction λ^{IS} obtained as the difference between the fits of the specified model and the model formed.

The two results presented for each model indicate a problem in their interpretation. The test-of-fit of the model is a test that many interactions are simultaneously zero. The test of a specific interaction has greater power and can be significant even when the tests-of-fit of both models (whose difference was computed) are nonsignificant. For example, the test of λ^{IS} is highly significant, whereas the tests of both [AC, IS, S] and [IS, AC, IC] are non-significant.

FIT

    ADD.   {no}

        Form and test all hierarchical models that include MODEL and differ from it by only one effect.

    DELETE.   {no}

        Form and test all hierarchical models that are included in MODEL and differ from it by only one effect.

● FORMS OF DATA INPUT

Usually each case contains data for a single observation. In the frequency table programs you can also input tabulated data, such as a table from a government or scientific report. Each case can represent data from a cell of the table; the number of observations (frequency) in the cell is recorded as one of the variables. The data can also be input as frequency tables.

We discuss how to use tabulated data as input for P1F on p. 271; only the Control Language definitions are repeated here.

INPut
    TABLE=$\#_1$,$\#_2$,$\cdots$.   {none}   required if data are input
                                             as a multiway table

$\#_1$,$\#_2$,... are the number of levels of each of the categorical variables (factors) in the table; their product is the number of cells in the table. $\#_1$ is the number of levels of the fastest varying index, $\#_2$ of the next fastest, etc. A maximum of seven indices can be used. The number of VARIABLES should be specified as the number of factors; the number of CASEs is not used; and the FORMAT should describe the entire table. Transformations and data editing cannot be used with this form of input.

Output 11.22   Adding and deleting effects from a model

A SIMULTANEOUS TEST THAT ALL K-FACTOR INTERACTIONS ARE ZERO.
THE ENTRIES ARE DIFFERENCES IN THE ABOVE TABLE.

K-FACTOR	D.F.	LR CHISQ	PROB.	PEARSON CHISQ	PROB.
1	8	632.15	0.0	881.24	0.0
2	23	134.42	0.0001	141.22	0.0001
3	28	30.91	0.3212	31.24	0.3067
4	12	9.01	0.7020	8.93	0.7091

THE FOLLOWING MODEL WAS FIT.

NO.	MODEL		'EFFECT'	D.F.	LR CHISQ	PROB.	PEARSON CHISQ	PROB.	ITERATIONS
1	AC,IC,S.			53	66.71	0.0977	67.85	0.0825	2

ADD--THE FOLLOWING MODELS INCLUDE THE ABOVE MODEL AND DIFFER FROM IT BY ONLY ONE 'EFFECT'

MODEL		'EFFECT'	D.F.	LR CHISQ	PROB.	PEARSON CHISQ	PROB.	ITERATIONS
IS,AC,IC.		IS	50	57.23	0.2245	57.52	0.2168	2
	DIFFERENCE DUE TO	IS	3	9.48	0.0235	10.33	0.0160	
IA,AC,IC,S.		IA	47	65.20	0.0406	65.91	0.0357	4
	DIFFERENCE DUE TO	IA	6	1.52	0.9583	1.93	0.9256	
SA,AC,IC.		SA	51	59.00	0.2063	63.47	0.1130	2
	DIFFERENCE DUE TO	SA	2	7.71	0.0211	4.38	0.1120	
SC,AC,IC.		SC	51	55.83	0.2982	57.53	0.2464	2
	DIFFERENCE DUE TO	SC	2	10.88	0.0043	10.32	0.0057	

THE FOLLOWING MODEL WAS FIT.

NO.	MODEL		'EFFECT'	D.F.	LR CHISQ	PROB.	PEARSON CHISQ	PROB.	ITERATIONS
2	AC,IC,SC,IS,SA.			46	41.39	0.6654	41.83	0.6476	4

DELETE--THE FOLLOWING MODELS ARE INCLUDED IN THE ABOVE MODEL AND DIFFER FROM IT BY ONLY ONE 'EFFECT'

MODEL		'EFFECT'	D.F.	LR CHISQ	PROB.	PEARSON CHISQ	PROB.	ITERATIONS
IC,SC,IS,SA.		AC	50	110.11	0.0001	108.48	0.0001	4
	DIFFERENCE DUE TO	AC	4	68.72	0.0000	66.66	0.0000	
AC,SC,IS,SA.		IC	52	77.53	0.0125	79.92	0.0078	4
	DIFFERENCE DUE TO	IC	6	36.14	0.0000	38.09	0.0000	
AC,IC,IS,SA.		SC	48	49.29	0.4214	51.41	0.3416	3
	DIFFERENCE DUE TO	SC	2	7.90	0.0193	9.59	0.0083	
AC,IC,SC,SA.		IS	49	51.61	0.3720	54.72	0.2664	4
	DIFFERENCE DUE TO	IS	3	10.22	0.0168	12.90	0.0049	
AC,IC,SC,IS.		SA	48	45.61	0.5713	45.36	0.5818	4
	DIFFERENCE DUE TO	SA	2	4.22	0.1213	3.53	0.1712	

TABLE
     COUNT=v_1,v_2,$\cdots$.   {none}   required <u>only</u> when data are input
                                                     as cell indices and frequency
                                                     counts

     Names or subscripts of variables that contain the frequency counts.
     If more than one variable is specified, tables are formed for each
     variable separately.

● SIZE OF PROBLEM

P3F can form and print a frequency table containing about 12,000 cells,
but cannot analyze it; the sum of the cells in all tables formed in a single
problem cannot exceed approximately 12,000.   When frequency table input is not
used and if neither cutpoints nor codes are specified, the program will
initially assign 10 levels to the index and allocate the size of the table
based upon this assignment; therefore a four-way table could be allocated
10,000 cells where, in reality, it uses far fewer.

The program can analyze any single table that contains less than 3,000
cells.   The upper limit depends on the number of marginal tables formed.

● COMPUTATIONAL METHOD

All models are fitted by an iterative proportional fitting algorithm
published by Haberman (1972).

The computation of standard errors for the estimates of parameters of the
log-linear model is described in Appendix A.7.

The use of orthogonal polynomials is described in Appendix A.8.   All
computations are performed in single precision.

ACKNOWLEDGEMENT

*P3F was designed by Morton Brown and programmed by Morton Brown and
Koji Yamasaki.*

11.4 Summary — P1F, P2F, P3F

The Control Language on this page is common to all programs. This is followed by the Control Language specific to

P1F -- Two-way Frequency Tables -- Measures of Association   p. 327
P2F -- Two-way Frequency Tables -- Empty Cells and
       Departures from Independence   p. 329
P3F -- Multiway Frequency Tables -- the Log-Linear Model   p. 331

Paragraph STATEMENT[1] {Preassigned value[2]}		Definition, restriction	See pages:
/PROBlem		Required each problem	74
TITLE='c'.	{blank}	Problem title, $\leq$ 160 char.	74
/INPut		Required first problem. Either VARIABLE and FORMAT, or UNIT and CODE required.	75
VARIABLE=#.	{none/prev.}	No. of variables in input data	75
FORMAT='c'.	{none/prev.}	Format of input data, $\leq$ 800 char.	76
CASE=#.	{end-of-file/prev.}	No. of cases in data	76-77
UNIT=#.	{5(cards)/prev.}	Input unit if data are not on cards; not 1, 2, 6	77
REWIND.	{REWIND/prev.}	Rewind input unit	77
CODE=c.	{none}	Code to identify BMDP File	132
CONTENT=c.	{DATA}	Data or matrix in BMDP File	132
LABEL=c.	{none}	Label of BMDP File, $\leq$ 40 char.	132
/VARiable		Optional. For input from a BMDP File, items in this paragraph may be previously set, see Chapter 7.	79
NAME=$c_1,c_2,\cdots$.	{X(subscript)/prev.}	Variable names, one per variable	79-80
MAXIMUM=$\#_1,\#_2,\cdots$.	{none/prev.}	Upper limits, one per variable	80
MINIMUM=$\#_1,\#_2,\cdots$.	{none/prev.}	Lower limits, one per variable	80
BLANK= (one only) ZERO, MISSING.	{ZERO/prev.}	Blanks treated as zeros or as missing value codes	81
MISSING=$\#_1,\#_2,\cdots$.	{none/prev.}	Missing value codes, one per variable	81
USE=$v_1,v_2,\cdots$.	{all variables}	Variables used in the analysis	82
LABEL=v_1,v_2.	{none/prev.}	Variable(s) used to label cases, read under A-format, one or two	83
ADD=#.	{0/prev.}	No. of variables added through transformation	99
BEFore. or AFTer.	{BEFore/prev.}	Data checked for limits before or after transformation	100
/TRANsform		Optional, Control Language transformations and case selection	97-105
/SAVE		Optional, required to create BMDP File	125
CODE=c.	{none}	Code to identify BMDP File, required	125-126
LABEL='c'.	{blank}	Label for BMDP File, $\leq$ 40 char.	125-126
UNIT=#.	{none}	Unit on which BMDP File is written; not 1, 2, 5 or 6	126-127
NEW.	{not new}	NEW if this is first BMDP File written in the system file	126-127

Key: #   number   v variable name or subscript
     'c' title, label or format   c name not exceeding 8 char., apostrophes may be required (p. 59)

[1] In BMDP programs dated before August 1977, the minimum required abbreviations are *INPUT* (not *INP*), VARIAB (not VAR), FORMAT (not FORM), CONTENT (not CONT), *VARIAB* (not *VAR*), BEFORET (not BEF), AFTERT (not AFT), *TRANSF* (not *TRAN*). If dated before February 1976, BLANK=ZERO and cannot be changed.

[2] "/prev." means that any assignment remains the same as that specified in the previous problem or subproblem until changed. Otherwise, the assignment returns to its preassigned value each time a new problem begins or the paragraph is used again.

P1F -- Two-way Frequency Tables -- Measures of Association

(in addition to that on p. 326)

Paragraph STATEMENT[1] {Preassigned value}		Definition, restriction	See pages:
INPut		Specify as part of *INPut* paragraph, p. 326	
TABLE=$\#_1,\#_2,\cdots$.	{none}	When input is a multiway frequency table, number of levels for each index (fastest moving index first)	273-275
VARiable		Specify as part of *VARiable* paragraph, p. 326	
DEFINE($\#$)=$v_1,v_2,\cdots$.	{none}	Define new index by combining variables	254, 256
/TABLE		Required, may be repeated	252
ROW=$v_1,v_2,\cdots$.	{none}	Variables defining row categories	253
COLUMN=$v_1,v_2,\cdots$.	{none}	Variables defining column categories	253
PAIR. *or* CROSS.	{PAIR}	Pair or cross ROW and COLUMN variables	253
CONDITION=$v_1,v_2,\cdots$.	{none}	Tables formed for each level of each CONDITION variable	253-254
COUNT=$v_1,v_2,\cdots$.	{none}	Variables containing frequency counts when input is cell indices and frequency counts	275-276
DELTA=$\#$.	{0}	Constant added to each cell frequency before calculating statistics	258
MINIMUM=$\#$.	{0}	Adjacent rows or columns combined if minimum expected frequency is less than MINIMUM	258-259
/CATEGory		Required if any ROW, COLUMN or CONDITION variable has more than 10 distinct values	84
CODE($\#$)=$\#_1,\#_2,\cdots$.	{10 smallest values/prev.}	Codes for variable $\#$, may be repeated	84-85
CUTPOINT($\#$)=$\#_1,\#_2,\cdots$.	{see CODE /prev.}	Cutpoints to form intervals for variable $\#$, may be repeated	84-85
NAME($\#$)=$c_1,c_2,\cdots$.	{CODEs or CUTPOINTs /prev.}	Code or interval names for variable $\#$, may be repeated	84-85
RESET.	{not RESET}	If RESET, all assignments in previous *CATEGory* paragraph are reset to pre-assigned values	86
COEFFICIENT($\#$)=$\#_1,\#_2,\cdots$.	{none/prev.}	Values assigned to categories when table is 2x2 or Rx2 to test for trend in probabilities	267-268
/PRINT		Optional, tables to be printed	
OBSERVED.	{OBS/ prev.}	Print table of observed frequencies	258
EXPECTED.	{no/prev.}	Print table of expected values	256-258
ROWPERCENT.	{no/prev.}	Print table of row percentages	256-258
COLPERCENT.	{no/prev.}	Print table of column percentages	256-258
TOTPERCENT.	{no/prev.}	Print table of percentages of total frequency	256-258
DIFFERENCE.	{no/prev.}	Print table of differences	268-270
STANDARDIZED.	{no/prev.}	Print table of standardized deviations	268-270
ADJUSTED.	{no/prev.}	Print table of adjusted standardized deviations	268-270
FREEMAN.	{no/prev.}	Print table of Freeman-Tukey deviates	270
SMOOTHED.	{no/prev.}	Print table of smoothed values	
/STATistics		Optional, tests and measures to be computed	
CHISQUARE.	{CHISQ/ prev.}	χ^2 test and Yates' corrected χ^2 (2x2 table)	262
CONTINGENCY	{no/prev.}	C, ϕ, Cramer's V and (for 2x2 table) α, Yule's Q and Y, C_{max}, ϕ_{max}	263 262
LRCHI.	{no/prev.}	Likelihood ratio test G^2	262
FISHER.	{no/prev.}	Fisher's exact probabilities	263-264
TETRACHORIC.	{no/prev.}	Tetrachoric correlation	264
CORRELATION.	{no/prev.}	Product-moment correlation	264
SPEARMAN.	{no/prev.}	Spearman rank correlation	264
GAMMA.	{no/prev.}	Γ, Kendall's τ_b, Stuart's τ_c, Somers' D	264-265
LAMBDA.	{no/prev.}	λ	264-265
LSTAR.	{no/prev.}	$\lambda*$	264-265
TAUS.	{no/prev.}	Goodman and Kruskall's τ	264-265
UNCERTAINTY.	{no/prev.}	Uncertainty coefficients	267
MCNEMAR.	{no/prev.}	McNemar's test of symmetry	
/END		Required	57

Key: # number   c name not exceeding 8 char., apostrophes may be required (p. 59)
     v variable name or subscript

[1] P1F was substantially revised in August 1976 -- versions dated before August 1976 are not longer supported. In BMDP programs dated before August 1977, when a *CATEGory* paragraph is used, RESET is implicitly specified and cannot be changed.

(continued)

● <u>Order of input</u>

    (1) System Cards, at HSCF these are

```
//jobname  JOB  nooo,yourname
//  EXEC  BIMED,PROG=BMDP1F
//SYSIN  DD  *
```

    (2) Control Language instructions

```
PROBlem paragraph, required
INPut paragraph, required first problem
VARiable paragraph
TRANsform paragraph
SAVE paragraph
TABLE  paragraph, required, may be repeated
CATEGory paragraph
PRINT paragraph
STATistics paragraph
END paragraph, required at end of Control Language
```

    (3) Data, if on cards   data

    (4) System Card, at HSCF this is   //

Control Language instructions and data (2 and 3) can be repeated for additional problems.

P2F -- Two-way Frequency Tables -- Empty Cells and Departures from Independence

(in addition to that on p. 326)

Paragraph STATEMENT[1] {Preassigned value}	Definition, restriction	See pages
INPut	Specify as part of *INPut* paragraph, p. 326	
TABLE=$\#_1$,$\#_2$,$\cdots$. {none}	When input is a multiway frequency table, number of levels for each index (fastest moving index first)	295
VARiable	Specify as part of *VARiable* paragraph, p. 326	
DEFINE(#)=v_1,v_2,$\cdots$. {none}	Define new index by combining variables	287
/TABLE	Required, may be repeated	286
ROW=v_1,v_2,$\cdots$. {none}	Variables defining row categories	286
COLUMN=v_1,v_2,$\cdots$. {none}	Variables defining column categories	286
PAIR. *or* CROSS. {PAIR}	Pair or cross ROW and COLUMN variables	286
CONDITION=v_1,v_2,$\cdots$. {none}	Tables formed for each level of each CONDITION variable	287
COUNT=v_1,v_2,$\cdots$. {none}	Variables containing frequency counts when input is cell indices and frequency counts	295-296
OBSERVED. {OBS}	Print table of observed frequencies	290
FITTED. {no}	Print table of fitted (expected) values	290
DELTA=#. {0}	Value added to cell frequencies before analysis	288
EMPTY(#)=$\#_{11}$,$\#_{12}$,$\#_{21}$,$\#_{22}$,$\cdots$. {none}	Cell indices to be excluded	288-289
CONVERGENCE=#. {0.05}	Convergence criterion for iteration	289
ITERATION=#. {20}	Maximum no. of iterations	289-290
/STEP	Optional, may be repeated, applies to preceding *TABLE* paragraph	290-291
CRITERION=(*one or more*) CHISQ,LRCHI, DIF,STAN,ADJ,QUSTAN,QUADJ. {none}	Required, criterion for cell elimination	290-292
MAXSTEP=#. {(R-1)(C-1)}	Maximum number of steps	292
ALPHA=#. {0.05}	Stepping stops when χ^2 test nonsignificant at ALPHA level	292
ELIMINATE=#. {2.0}	Lower limit of criterion to eliminate a cell	292
REENTER=#. {1.0}	Upper limit of criterion to reenter a cell	292
PRINT=$\#_1$,$\#_2$,$\cdots$. *or* ALL. {none}	Steps at which tables below are printed	293-295
FITTED. {no}	Table of fitted (expected) values	293
CHISQUARE. {no}	Table of χ^2 values when each cell in turn is eliminated	293
LRCHI. {no}	Table of G^2 values when each cell in turn is eliminated	293
DIFFERENCE. {no}	Table of differences (observed-fitted)	293
STANDARDIZED. {no}	Table of standardized residuals	293
ADJUSTED. {no}	Table of adjusted standardized residuals	293-295
QUSTAN. {no}	Table of quasi-standardized residuals when each cell in turn is eliminated	293-295
QUADJ. {no}	Table of quasi-adjusted standardized residuals when each cell in turn is eliminated	293-295
/CATEGory	Required if any ROW, COLUMN or CONDITION variable has more than 10 distinct values	84
CODE(#)=$\#_1$,$\#_2$,$\cdots$. {10 smallest values/prev.}	Codes for variable #, may be repeated	84-85
CUTPOINT(#)=$\#_1$,$\#_2$,$\cdots$. {see CODE/prev.}	Cutpoints to form intervals for variable #, may be repeated	84-85
NAME(#)=c_1,c_2,$\cdots$. {CODEs or CUTPOINTS/ prev.}	Code or interval names for variable #, may be repeated	84-85
RESET. {not RESET}	If RESET, all assignments in prev. *CATEGory* paragraph are reset to preassigned values	86
/END	Required	57

Key: # number
      v variable name or subscript
      c name not exceeding 8 char., apostrophes may be required (p. 59)

[1] P2F was originally released in August 1976. In BMDP programs dated before August 1977, when a *CATEGory* paragraph is used, RESET is implicitly specified and cannot be changed.

(continued)

- <u>Order of input</u>

(1) System Cards, at HSCF these are

```
//jobname  JOB  nooo,yourname
//   EXEC  BIMED,PROG=BMDP2F
//SYSIN  DD *
```

(2) Control Language instructions

```
PROBlem paragraph, required
INPut paragraph, required first problem
VARiable paragraph
TRANsform paragraph
SAVE paragraph
TABLE  paragraph, required, may be repeated
STEP   paragraph, may be repeated
CATEGory paragraph
END   paragraph, required at end of Control Language
```

(3) Data, if on cards

```
data
```

(4) System Card, at HSCF this is

```
//
```

Control Language instructions and data (2 and 3) can be repeated for additional problems.

P3F -- Multiway Frequency Tables -- the Log-Linear Model

(in addition to that on p. 326)

Paragraph STATEMENT[1] {Preassigned value}		Definition, restriction	See pages:
INPut		Specify as part of *INPut* paragraph, p. 326	
TABLE=$\#_1$,$\#_2$,$\cdots$.	{none}	When input is a multiway frequency table, number of levels for each index (fastest moving first)	323-324
VARiable		Specify as part of *VARiable* paragraph, p. 326	
DEFINE(#)=v_1,v_2,$\cdots$.	{none}	Define new index by combining variables	308-310
/TABLE		Required, may be repeated	307
INDEX=v_1,v_2,$\cdots$.	{none}	Required, variables used as indices for table, ≤ 7 variables	307
SYMBOL=c_1,c_2,$\cdots$.	{none}	Required, symbols to denote INDEX variables in analysis, 1 char.	307
CONDITION=v_1,v_2,$\cdots$.	{none}	Tables formed for each level of each CONDITIONING variable	308
COUNT=v_1,v_2,$\cdots$.	{none}	Variables containing frequency counts when input is cell indices and frequency counts	323-325
OBSERVED.	{OBS/ prev.}	Print table of observed frequencies	310-312
MARGINAL=#.	{0/prev.}	Print all marginal subtables up to order #	310-312
DELTA=#.	{0.0/prev.}	Added to each frequency before analysis	312
SIMULTANEOUS.	{SIMUL/prev.}	Tests-of-fit of models of full order	312-313
ASSOCIATION.	{no/prev.}	Tests of marginal and partial association	313-314
ALL.	{no/prev.}	All models in 2- or 3-way table	314-315
CONVERGENCE=#.	{0.1/prev.}	Criterion for convergence of model-fitting algorithm	315
ITERATION=#.	{20/prev.}	Maximum no. of iterations	315
/FIT		Optional, may be repeated, applies to preceding *TABLE* paragraph	315
MODEL=c_1,c_2,$\cdots$.	{none}	Required, hierarchical model to be fitted, may be repeated	315-316
EXPECTED.	{no}	Table of fitted (expected) values	316-317
STANDARDIZED.	{no}	Table of standardized residuals	316-317
FREEMAN.	{no}	Table of Freeman-Tukey deviates	316-317
LAMBDA.	{no}	Estimate log-linear parameters of MODEL	317-320
BETA.	{no}	Estimate multiplicative parameters of MODEL	317-320
ORTHOGONAL=c_1,c_2,$\cdots$.	{no}	Fit orthogonal contrast to LAMBDA for SYMBOLs specified	320-322
PROBABILITY=#.	{.05}	LAMBDA, BETA, ORTHOGONAL printed only if test-of-fit of MODEL exceeds PROBABILITY (is nonsignificant)	317-320
ADD.	{no}	Form models containing MODEL as subset	322-323
DELETE.	{no}	Form models contained by MODEL	322-323
/CATEGory		Required if any ROW, COLUMN or CONDITION variable has more than 10 distinct values	
CODE(#)=$\#_1$,$\#_2$,$\cdots$.	{10 smallest values/prev.}	Codes for variable #, may be repeated	84-85
CUTPOINT(#)=$\#_1$,$\#_2$,$\cdots$.	{see CODE/prev.}	Cutpoints to form intervals for variable #, may be repeated	84-85
NAME(#)=c_1,c_2,$\cdots$.	{CODEs or CUTPOINTs/prev.}	Code or interval names for variable #, may be repeated	84-85
RESET.	{not RESET}	If RESET, all assignments in prev. *CATEGory* paragraph are reset to preassigned values	86
/END		Required	57

Key: # number   c name not exceeding 8 char., apostrophes may be required (p. 59)

[1] P3F was originally released in August 1976. In BMDP programs dated before August 1977, the minimum required abbreviations are INDEX (not IND) and SYMBOL (not SYMB); when a *CATEGory* paragraph is used, RESET is implicitly specified and cannot be changed.

(continued)

● <u>Order of input</u>

(1) System Cards, at HSCF these are

```
//jobname  JOB  nooo,yourname
//   EXEC  BIMED,PROG=BMDP3F
//SYSIN  DD  *
```

(2) Control Language instructions

PROBlem paragraph, required
INPut paragraph, required first problem
VARiable paragraph
TRANsform paragraph
SAVE paragraph
TABLE paragraph, required, may be repeated
FIT paragraph , may be repeated
CATEGory paragraph
END paragraph, required at end of Control Language

(3) Data, if on cards

data

(4) System Card, at HSCF this is

//

Control Language instructions and data (2 and 3) can be repeated for additional problems.

12

MISSING VALUES

Patterns, Estimation and Correlations

In even the best designed and monitored experiments, observations can be recorded incorrectly or not recorded at all. For example, an animal may die from a cause unrelated to the experiment, a patient may not return for a follow-up visit, a blood sample may be ruined, or the recording equipment may malfunction. When an entire case is missing, the analysis must accommodate the resulting imbalance.

When values for one or more variables are not recorded in some cases, the problem is far more complex. Two possible choices are

- to eliminate all the data for cases that contain any missing values
- to use acceptable values from all cases, including the incomplete cases

The second choice requires a more difficult analysis, but may be necessary when more than a few cases are incomplete.

Cases with known errors (or univariate outliers) can be treated in a similar manner to those with missing values. Univariate outliers may be identified in a preliminary data screening, or they may violate specified limits. Ordinarily they are eliminated from statistical analysis by specifying MINIMUM and MAXIMUM limits for the variables.

In this chapter missing values usually refer to observations that are not recorded, or are improperly recorded. Cases with missing values are those that have one or more observations equal to the missing value code or out of range (as specified in the *VARiable* paragraph or set during data editing, Chapter 6).

Many classical statistical analyses require complete cases (i.e., no missing values). When doing exploratory data analysis, this restriction can be circumvented. For example, regression or factor analysis can start from a correlation matrix rather than from the original data; methods are available to estimate the correlations from all acceptable values. A second approach is to reestimate missing observations and then use the "completed" data in an analysis.

In this chapter we describe two programs.

P8D -- Missing Value Correlation		p. 337
PAM -- Description and Estimation of Missing Data		p. 348

Both can be used to estimate a correlation matrix when there are missing values in some cases; the resulting matrix can then be input to a subsequent analysis, such as regression or factor analysis. In addition, PAM can replace missing values with estimates based on data present for the case.

P8D computes correlations from data containing missing values in any of four different ways. Computations can be performed using

- only complete cases (COMPLETE); cases with any missing values or values out of range are not used

- all pairs of acceptable values for correlations (CORPAIR); the correlation for each pair of variables is computed using only cases that have acceptable values for both variables

- all pairs of acceptable values for covariances (COVPAIR); the covariance for each pair of variables is computed as in CORPAIR, but variances are computed separately from all acceptable values for each variable (this differs from CORPAIR in the variances used)

- all acceptable values (ALLVALUE); the means and variances are computed from all acceptable values for each variable and the covariances are computed using deviations from these means (this differs from COVPAIR in the means used for the covariances)

The method COMPLETE is the only method of the four that guarantees a correlation matrix that can be inverted (one that is positive semidefinite), and that can be used in factor analysis and for multiple regression. In addition,

P8D tabulates the frequencies of existing pairs of variables. The mean and variance of each variable are printed. Case weights can be used in the computations.

PAM can estimate covariances or correlations by either of two methods. It can also replace missing values by estimates based on the acceptable values. To better understand the implication of estimating either the missing values or correlations and using them in an analysis, the extent and the pattern of the missing values can also be examined with PAM. If the pattern of missing data is not random,an analysis of the data can be severely affected.

PAM estimates covariances or correlations using only complete cases (COMPLETE), or using all acceptable values (as in the ALLVALUE option in P8D). When the latter method is used, the eigenvalues are found and, when any eigenvalues are negative, the correlation matrix is reestimated using only positive eigenvalues and their eigenvectors. This guarantees that the correlation matrix is positive semidefinite and can be used in multiple regression and factor analysis.

PAM can replace missing values by means or by predicted values using regression equations that are computed by any of several methods. In one method (REGR) the squared multiple correlations of each variable with all the other variables are computed; they are a measure of multicollinearity and indicate how well each variable can be estimated from the other variables.

The pattern of missing values is described in a number of ways including a cases-by-variables plot of the location of the missing data. PAM also computes the Mahalanobis distance of each case (including those having missing values) to the mean of all cases (or the group mean when the cases are grouped). PAM prints the frequency and percentage of missing data for each pair of variables. Specified pairs of variables can be plotted against each other. Cases can be grouped and case weights assigned. For each variable in each group PAM computes the sample size, percentage missing, and univariate statistics.

Both P8D and PAM can be used for data description to enhance your understanding of the effect of missing data. Also, they can be used to prepare the data for further analysis

- by computing and saving a covariance or correlation matrix, which is then used as input for further analyses (such as regression or factor analysis)

- by estimating the missing values; the "completed" data are saved and used as input to additional analyses

Subsequent analyses <u>are affected</u> by either of these procedures, as are the usual tests of significance reported. However, the results can be useful in exploratory data analysis.

● CONTROL LANGUAGE

The Control Language instructions to describe the data and variables are common to all BMDP programs and are explained in Chapter 5: the *PROBlem*, *INPut*[1] and *VARiable* paragraphs are used in the programs discussed in this chapter; the *GROUP* paragraph can be used in PAM.

If data editing or transformations are necessary, the methods described in Chapter 6 can be used. Data can be read using a FORMAT statement or from a BMDP File (Chapter 7).

A summary of the Control Language instructions common to all BMDP programs is on p. 371; summaries of the Control Language instructions specific to each program described in this chapter follow the general summary. These summaries can be used as indexes to the program descriptions.

---

[1] BMDP programs dated before August 1977 require more letters than are shown in this manual in their permissible abbreviated form (the capitalized letters). The minimum required abbreviations for earlier versions are specified in footnotes to the summary (p. 371).

P8D

12.1 Missing Value Correlation

When the data contain missing values or values out of range, P8D computes covariances and correlations by any of four methods. The covariance or correlation matrix can be saved in a BMDP File to be read as input by other BMDP programs. Case weights can be used in the computations.

To explain the difference between the methods of estimating the correlation, we use the following notation:

x_{ij} = the value of the ith variable in the jth case

$\delta_j^{ik} = \begin{cases} 1 & \text{if } x_{ij} \text{ and } x_{kj} \text{ are both acceptable values} \\ 0 & \text{otherwise} \end{cases}$

N = number of complete cases (cases that have acceptable values for all variables)

n_i = number of acceptable values for the ith variable ($\Sigma_j \, \delta_j^{ii}$)

n_{ik} = number of cases for which both variables (i and k) have acceptable values ($\Sigma_j \, \delta_j^{ik}$)

The method COMPLETE uses only complete cases in the computation of the correlations; values from the incomplete cases are not used in any computations.

The method CORPAIR uses the n_{ik} pairs of acceptable values to compute the correlation between variables i and k. Let

$$\bar{x}_{i(k)} = \Sigma_j \, \delta_j^{ik} \, x_{ij}/n_{ik} \quad \text{(i.e., the mean of variable i when variable k also has an acceptable value).}$$

Then the covariance between variables i and k is

$$\text{cov}_{ik}^{(1)} = \Sigma_j \, \delta_j^{ik} \, (x_{ij} - \bar{x}_{i(k)})(x_{kj} - \bar{x}_{k(i)})/(n_{ik} - 1)$$

and the variance of variable i is

$$\text{var}_{i(k)} = \text{cov}_{ii}^{(1)} = \Sigma_j \, \delta_j^{ik} \, (x_{ij} - \bar{x}_{i(k)})^2/(n_{ik} - 1) \, .$$

The correlation is

$$r_{ik} = \text{cov}_{ik}^{(1)} / (\text{var}_{i(k)} \cdot \text{var}_{k(i)})^{\frac{1}{2}} \, .$$

The method COVPAIR differs from CORPAIR in that it computes the variance of a variable using all acceptable values of the variable but computes the covariance as in CORPAIR. That is,

$$\text{var}_i = \Sigma \, \delta_j^{ii} \, (x_{ij} - \bar{x}_i)^2 / (n_i - 1)$$

where

$$\bar{x}_i = \Sigma \, \delta_j^{ii} \, x_{ij}/n_i$$

and

$$r_{ik} = cov_{ik}^{(1)} / (var_i \cdot var_k)^{\frac{1}{2}} \, .$$

The last method (ALLVALUE) uses all acceptable values in the computation of the mean, variance and covariance. That is, $\bar{x}_i$ and var_i are defined as in COVPAIR and

$$cov_{ik}^{(2)} = \Sigma \, \delta_j^{ik} \, (x_{ij} - \bar{x}_i)(x_{kj} - \bar{x}_k)/(n_{ik} - 1) \, .$$

Then

$$r_{ik} = cov_{ik}^{(2)} / (var_i \cdot var_k)^{\frac{1}{2}} \, .$$

When case weights are used the above formulas are modified as described on p. 345.

Of the four methods, only ALLVALUE uses all the available data in computing a correlation; COMPLETE uses the least data. ALLVALUE and COVPAIR are not restricted to using the same cases in both the covariances and variances for a correlation, therefore the estimate of a correlation can exceed unity. Only COMPLETE guarantees a correlation matrix that is positive semidefinite (one that can be inverted except for variables that are exact linear functions of other variables). However, COMPLETE may be a poor choice when too many cases are omitted from the computations. PAM (Section 12.2) modifies the correlation estimates produced by ALLVALUE to guarantee that the correlation matrix is positive semidefinite. If the pattern of missing data is not random (see PAM), all of the methods may give misleading results.

The methods differ in the maximum number of variables for which a correlation matrix can be formed. COMPLETE can handle up to 160 variables, ALLVALUE and COVPAIR 70, and CORPAIR 60.

● RESULTS

In our first example P8D computes a correlation matrix for the variables in the Werner blood chemistry data (Table 5.1). The Control Language instructions used in Example 12.1 are described in Chapter 5. CORPAIR is the preassigned method to estimate the correlations.

Example 12.1

```
/PROBLEM      TITLE IS 'WERNER BLOOD CHEMISTRY DATA'.
/INPUT        VARIABLES ARE 9.
              FORMAT IS '(A4,5F4.0,3F4.1)'.
/VARIABLE     NAMES ARE ID,AGE,HEIGHT,WEIGHT,BRTHPILL,
                  CHOLSTRL,ALBUMIN,CALCIUM,URICACID.
              MAXIMUM IS (6)400.
              MINIMUM IS (6)150.
              BLANKS ARE MISSING.
              LABEL IS ID.

/END
```

The Control Language must be preceded by System Cards to initiate the analysis by P8D.
At HSCF, the System Cards are

```
//jobname  JOB   nooo,yourname
//    EXEC  BIMED,PROG=BMDP8D
//SYSIN  DD  *
```

The Control Language is immediately followed by the data (Table 5.1). The analysis
is terminated by another System Card. At HSCF, this System Card is

```
//
```

The results are presented in Output 12.1. Circled numbers below correspond to those in the output.

① Interpretation of Control Language instructions specific to P8D. No
such instructions are specified in Example 12.1; therefore preassigned
options are shown.

② Number of cases read. P8D allows you to specify the method used to
compute correlations. The method chosen determines whether data are
used or not used from a case that contains missing values or values out
of range.

③ For each variable the mean, variance, standard deviation and coefficient
of variation are computed using all acceptable values for the variable.
The number of acceptable values (frequency) is also printed. The last
column is titled SUM OF WEIGHTS: when case WEIGHTs are specified,
this column records the sum of the case weights for the observations
present; otherwise this column is identical to the FREQUENCY column.

④ The frequency n_{ik} of cases for which both variables have acceptable
values is reported for each pair of variables.

⑤ Estimates of the correlations by the CORPAIR method (the preassigned
method of computing the correlations); any of the methods can be
specified.

● OPTIONAL RESULTS

Results that can be requested include:
  - the covariance matrix computed by any of the methods   p. 342
  - the matrix of means, $\bar{x}_{i(k)}$; i.e., the mean of variable i
    for cases when variable k has acceptable values   p. 342

Output 12.1   Results of an analysis of the Werner data by P8D. Circled
numbers correspond to those in the text. Results not reproduced are indicated in italics.

BMDP8D - MISSING VALUE CORRELATION   PROGRAM REVISED SEPTEMBER 1977
HEALTH SCIENCES COMPUTING FACILITY   MANUAL DATE -- 1977
UNIVERSITY OF CALIFORNIA, LOS ANGELES

--- *Control Language read by P8D is printed and interpreted* ---

①
```
    WEIGHT VARIABLE . . . . . . . . . . . . . . . .        0
    CORRELATION TYPE(S)
        USE ALL EXISTING VALUES. . . . . . . . . .        NO
        USE ALL EXISTING PAIRS FOR CROSS PRODUCTS. .       NO
        USE ALL EXISTING PAIRS FOR CORRELATIONS. . .      YES
        USE ONLY COMPLETE CASES. . . . . . . . . . .       NO
    PRINT MATRIX OF FREQUENCIES . . . . . . . . . .       YES
    PRINT MATRIX OF SUM OF WEIGHTS. . . . . . . . .        NO
    PRINT MATRIX OF MEANS . . . . . . . . . . . . .        NO
    PRINT MATRIX OF VARIANCES . . . . . . . . . . .        NO
    PRINT COVARIANCE MATRIX . . . . . . . . . . . .        NO
    PRINT CORRELATION MATRIX. . . . . . . . . . . .       YES
```

② NUMBER OF CASES READ.   188

③
VARIABLE NO.	LABEL	MEAN	VARIANCE	STANDARD DEVIATION	COEFF. OF VARIATION	FREQUENCY	SUM OF WEIGHTS
2	AGE	33.81914	102.26572	10.11265	0.29902	188.00000	188.00000
3	HEIGHT	64.51074	6.17545	2.48505	0.03852	186.00000	186.00000
4	WEIGHT	131.67204	426.85327	20.66043	0.15691	186.00000	186.00000
5	BRTHPILL	1.50000	0.25133	0.50133	0.33422	188.00000	188.00000
6	CHOLSTRL	236.15053	1810.94702	42.55522	0.18020	186.00000	186.00000
7	ALBUMIN	4.11123	0.12814	0.35796	0.08707	186.00000	186.00000
8	CALCIUM	9.96208	0.22997	0.47955	0.04814	185.00000	185.00000
9	URICACID	4.77051	1.33919	1.15723	0.24258	187.00000	187.00000

FREQUENCY TABLE

④
		AGE 2	HEIGHT 3	WEIGHT 4	BRTHPILL 5	CHOLSTRL 6	ALBUMIN 7	CALCIUM 8	URICACID 9
AGE	2	188							
HEIGHT	3	186	186						
WEIGHT	4	186	184	186					
BRTHPILL	5	188	186	186	188				
CHOLSTRL	6	186	184	184	186	186			
ALBUMIN	7	186	185	184	186	184	186		
CALCIUM	8	185	184	183	185	184	183	185	
URICACID	9	187	185	185	187	185	185	185	187

ESTIMATES OF CORRELATIONS - CORPAIR

⑤
		AGE 2	HEIGHT 3	WEIGHT 4	BRTHPILL 5	CHOLSTRL 6	ALBUMIN 7	CALCIUM 8	URICACID 9
AGE	2	1.0000							
HEIGHT	3	0.0807	1.0000						
WEIGHT	4	0.2521	0.4759	1.0000					
BRTHPILL	5	0.0	0.1692	0.0738	1.0000				
CHOLSTRL	6	0.3678	0.0199	0.1474	0.0758	1.0000			
ALBUMIN	7	-0.0719	-0.0208	-0.2533	-0.2398	0.0534	1.0000		
CALCIUM	8	-0.0325	0.1485	0.0703	-0.0561	0.2515	0.4534	1.0000	
URICACID	9	0.1776	0.1335	0.3043	0.0247	0.2660	0.0072	0.1949	1.0000

- the matrix of variances, $var_{i(k)}$; i.e., the variance of
   variable i for cases when variable k has acceptable values   p. 342

- the case weight matrix; i.e., the sum of the weights for
   cases for which the values of variables i and k are both
   acceptable   p. 342

P8D also allows a rectangular submatrix to be specified and
computed. This is valuable when there are so many variables that
the computation of all correlations is very expensive.   p. 343

   You can specify a case weight variable.   p. 345

   You can store the correlation or covariance matrix in a BMDP
File to be used as input to other BMDP analyses.   p. 345

● *CORRelation* -- SPECIFYING THE METHOD (TYPE) OF COMPUTATION

   The method of computation is specified in the *CORRelation* paragraph
by a TYPE statement: COMPLETE, CORPAIR, COVPAIR and ALLVALUE can
be used. If COMPLETE is not specified, any or all of the other methods can
be requested in one analysis. That is, either

         /CORRELATION TYPE IS COMPLETE.
   or
         /CORRELATION TYPES ARE ALLVALUE,COVPAIR,CORPAIR.

is correct. However, COMPLETE cannot be used with any other method. If
more than one method is specified, each is used in turn to compute covariances
and correlations; if a matrix is to be saved in a BMDP File, only the matrix
computed by the first method specified is saved.

```
CORRelation
   TYPE= (one or more) CORPAIR, COVPAIR,ALLVALUE.  {CORPAIR/prev.}
     or
   TYPE=COMPLETE.

   The method used to estimate correlations:
      COMPLETE -- only complete cases are used
      CORPAIR  -- only cases that have acceptable values for both
                  variables are used to compute correlations
      COVPAIR  -- covariances are computed from cases that have accep-
                  table values for both variables but variances are
                  computed from all acceptable values
      ALLVALUE -- all acceptable values are used
   These terms are defined more precisely on p. 337.
```

● Specifying Matrices to be Printed

The correlation matrix and matrix of pairwise frequencies (n_{ik}) are printed automatically. You can request additional results such as

- the covariance matrix
- the matrix of means, $\bar{x}_{i(k)}$
- the matrix of variances, $var_{i(k)}$
- the matrix of sums of case weights

The *PRINT* paragraph is used to specify the desired results.

PRINT
>   FREQUENCY.   { FREQUENCY /prev. }
>
>   The matrix of pairwise frequencies, n_{ik}, is printed unless you specify NO FREQUENCY.
>
>   CORRELATION   { CORRELATION /prev. }
>
>   The correlation matrices computed by the methods specified in TYPE are printed unless you specify NO CORRELATION.
>
>   COVARIANCE.   {no/prev.}
>
>   Print the covariance matrix computed by the same method(s) as described for CORRELATION.
>
>   MEAN.   {no/prev.}
>
>   Print the matrix of means, $\bar{x}_{i(k)}$. This is computed only if TYPE is COVPAIR or CORPAIR.
>
>   *Note: Univariate means and standard deviations are always printed.*
>
>   VARIANCE.   {no/prev.}
>
>   Print the matrix of variances, $var_{i(k)}$. This is only computed if TYPE is CORPAIR .
>
>   SUMWEIGHT.   {no/prev.}
>
>   Print the matrix of sums of weights.[2] This is ignored if a WEIGHT variable is not specified.

To demonstrate these results we use the following example.

---

[2] If your BMDP programs are dated before August 1977, the minimum required abbreviation is SUMWTS (not SUMW).

Example 12.2

```
/PROBLEM     TITLE IS 'WERNER BLOOD CHEMISTRY DATA'.
/INPUT       VARIABLES ARE 9.
             FORMAT IS '(A4,5F4.0,3F4.1)'.
/VARIABLE    NAMES ARE ID,AGE,HEIGHT,WEIGHT,BRTHPILL,
                 CHOLSTRL,ALBUMIN,CALCIUM,URICACID.
             MAXIMUM IS (6)400.
             MINIMUM IS (6)150.
             BLANKS ARE MISSING.
             LABEL IS ID.

/PRINT       MEAN.
             VARIANCE.
             COVARIANCE.

/END
```

Output 12.2 contains the matrices of means ⑥, variances ⑦ and covariances ⑧ in addition to the results in Output 12.1.

● SELECTING A SUBSET OF THE VARIABLES

In common with most BMDP programs, a subset of the variables can be selected for analysis by P8D; the variables to be USEd are specified in the *VARiable* paragraph. You can also request the computation of a portion of the correlation (or covariance) matrix by specifying ROW and COLUMN variables in the *VARiable* paragraph.

When ROW and/or COLUMN is specified, P8D computes either the specified rectangular portion of the matrix or the entire (triangular) matrix that contains correlations between all the variables specified as ROW and COLUMN variables. The entire (triangular) matrix is computed and printed when the TYPE is COMPLETE or when fewer correlations are computed in the triangular matrix than there are in the rectangular portion. For example, if

ROWS ARE AGE,HEIGHT,WEIGHT.

COLUMNS ARE CHOLSTRL,ALBUMIN,CALCIUM,URICACID.

is added to Example 12.1, a correlation matrix with three rows and four columns is computed and printed. When TYPE is COMPLETE, all correlations between the seven ROW and COLUMN variables are computed.

VARiable
    ROW= $v_1,v_2,\cdots$.   {all variables/prev.}

    Names or subscripts of variables used as the rows for the matrices printed.

    COLUMN=$v_1,v_2,\cdots$.   {all variables/prev.}

    Names or subscripts of variables used as columns for the matrices printed.

    Note: The covariance and correlation matrices cannot be saved in a BMDP File when ROW or COLUMN is specified.

Output 12.2   Optional results printed by P8D. Results not reproduced are
              indicated in italics.

--- *univariate statistics* ---

ESTIMATE OF MEAN OF COLUMN VARIABLE FOR USE WITH ROW VARIABLE

(6)

		AGE 2	HEIGHT 3	WEIGHT 4	BRTHPILL 5	CHOLSTRL 6	ALBUMIN 7	CALCIUM 8	URICACID 9
AGE	2	33.819	64.511	131.672	1.500	236.151	4.111	9.962	4.771
HEIGHT	3	33.699	64.511	131.370	1.505	236.196	4.112	9.959	4.771
WEIGHT	4	33.774	64.484	131.672	1.500	236.207	4.113	9.961	4.747
BRTHPILL	5	33.819	64.511	131.672	1.500	236.151	4.111	9.962	4.771
CHOLSTRL	6	33.930	64.495	131.418	1.495	236.151	4.116	9.964	4.767
ALBUMIN	7	33.694	64.524	131.685	1.505	236.196	4.111	9.967	4.784
CALCIUM	8	33.670	64.500	131.191	1.503	235.745	4.117	9.962	4.756
URICACID	9	33.711	64.497	131.600	1.503	235.697	4.112	9.962	4.771

--- *frequency table of pairs of variables* ---

ESTIMATE OF VARIANCE OF COLUMN VARIABLE FOR USE WITH ROW VARIABLE

(7)

		AGE 2	HEIGHT 3	WEIGHT 4	BRTHPILL 5	CHOLSTRL 6	ALBUMIN 7	CALCIUM 8	URICACID 9
AGE	2	102.266	6.175	426.853	0.251	1810.947	0.128	0.230	1.339
HEIGHT	3	101.313	6.175	419.223	0.251	1830.273	0.129	0.230	1.353
WEIGHT	4	102.488	6.164	426.853	0.251	1826.499	0.129	0.232	1.300
BRTHPILL	5	102.266	6.175	426.853	0.251	1810.947	0.128	0.230	1.339
CHOLSTRL	6	102.183	6.175	425.233	0.251	1810.947	0.127	0.231	1.305
ALBUMIN	7	101.099	6.175	430.298	0.251	1830.276	0.128	0.221	1.325
CALCIUM	8	98.939	6.208	416.480	0.251	1791.697	0.128	0.230	1.321
URICACID	9	100.614	6.175	428.204	0.251	1782.373	0.129	0.230	1.339

--- *correlation matrix* ---

ESTIMATES OF COVARIANCES - COVPAIR

(8)

		AGE 2	HEIGHT 3	WEIGHT 4	BRTHPILL 5	CHOLSTRL 6	ALBUMIN 7	CALCIUM 8	URICACID 9
AGE	2	102.266							
HEIGHT	3	2.019	6.175						
WEIGHT	4	52.730	24.192	426.853					
BRTHPILL	5	0.0	0.211	0.765	0.251				
CHOLSTRL	6	158.215	2.116	129.923	1.617	1810.947			
ALBUMIN	7	-0.259	-0.019	-1.887	-0.043	0.814	0.128		
CALCIUM	8	-0.155	0.177	0.692	-0.013	5.112	0.076	0.230	
URICACID	9	2.062	0.386	7.181	0.014	12.826	0.003	0.107	1.339

● CASE WEIGHTs

Case weights can be used in the computation of means, variances, covariances and correlations. If a case WEIGHT variable is specified, the formulas on p. 337 are modified as follows. Let

w_j = weight for case j $(w_j \geq 0)$

n_{ik} = number of cases in which both variables (i and k) have acceptable values and w_j is positive

Then replace δ_j^{ik} by $\delta_j^{ik} w_j$ and $(n_{ik} - 1)$ by $(n_{ik} - 1) \Sigma_j \delta_j^{ik} w_j / n_{ik}$ in the formulas for the variances and covariances, The formulas for the means are

$$\bar{x}_i = \Sigma_j \delta_j^{ii} w_j x_{ij} / \Sigma_j \delta_j^{ii} w_j$$

and

$$\bar{x}_{i(k)} = \Sigma_j \delta_j^{ik} w_j x_{ij} / \Sigma_j \delta_j^{ik} w_j$$

The formula for complete cases is given in Section 2.1.

VARiable
    WEIGHT=v.   {no case weights var./prev.}

 Name or subscript of the variable that contains case weights. The effect case weights have on the computations is explained above. If WEIGHT is not specified or is set to zero, there are no case weights.

● SAVING RESULTS IN A BMDP FILE

P8D can save the correlation matrix, the covariance matrix, or the data (after transformations are performed) in a BMDP File (Chapter 7). The results saved in a BMDP File can be further analyzed by other programs.

When a covariance or correlation matrix is saved and further analyzed, the effective sample size recorded in the BMDP File is the harmonic mean of the sample sizes of the individual variables (unless TYPE=COMPLETE is specified).

SAVE
    CONTENT= *(one or more)*   DATA,COVA,CORR.   {DATA}

 The matrices to be saved in a BMDP File. If COVA (covariances) or CORR (correlations) is specified, and more than one method of computing the correlation matrix is specified, only the covariances or correlations computed by the first method stated in *CORRelation* TYPE is saved. COVA and CORR are not saved if *VARiable* ROW or COLUMN is specified.

When a BMDP File is read as input and you are creating a second BMDP File to save the data, the two Files must be in different system files and assigned different UNIT numbers.

Example 12.3 shows the Control Language instructions (the *SAVE* paragraph) required to save the correlation matrix. Any BMDP program that accepts a correlation matrix as input also accepts a covariance matrix (and conversely).

Example 12.3

```
/PROBLEM      TITLE IS 'WERNER BLOOD CHEMISTRY DATA'.
/INPUT        VARIABLES ARE 9.
              FORMAT IS '(A4,5F4.0,3F4.1)'.
/VARIABLE     NAMES ARE ID,AGE,HEIGHT,WEIGHT,BRTHPILL,
                        CHOLSTRL,ALBUMIN,CALCIUM,URICACID.
              MAXIMUM IS (6)400.
              MINIMUM IS (6)150.
              BLANKS ARE MISSING.
              LABEL IS ID.

/SAVE         UNIT IS 4.
              NEW.
              CODE IS WERNER.
              CONTENT IS CORR.

/CORRELATION  TYPES ARE ALLVALUE,COVPAIR.

/END
```

Note: The System Cards that precede the Control Language must contain a card describing where to store the BMDP File (Section 7.1). At HSCF, the System Cards are

```
//jobname  JOB  nooo,yourname
//   EXEC  BIMED,PROG=BMDP8D
//FT04F001  DD  DSNAME=FS.nooo.filename,DISP=OLD
//SYSIN  DD  *
```

In addition space must be allocated for the system file (Section 7.1).

Output 12.3 shows that a BMDP File has been created by P8D to contain the correlation matrix. Although the correlation matrix is computed by two methods (TYPE=ALLVALUE,COVPAIR.), only the correlation matrix computed by the first method (ALLVALUE) is saved.

● SIZE OF PROBLEM

The maximum number of variables that can be analyzed by P8D depends on the method used to compute the correlations. Up to 160 variables can be used when the method is COMPLETE, 60 variables when it is CORPAIR , and 70 variables otherwise. Appendix B describes how to increase the capacity of the program.

When the number of variables exceeds these limits, the capacity of the program can be increased (Appendix B) or P8D can reread the data and calculate the matrix in manageable blocks. Since the latter may be expensive, it is done only when SEGMENT is specified in the *CORRelation* paragraph.[3]

---

[3] If your BMDP programs are dated before August 1977, SEGMENT is not available.

CORRelation
    SEGMENT.   {no/prev.}

    When the number of variables exceeds the number that can be
    analyzed at one time, the correlation or covariance matrix is
    computed in manageable segments.

● COMPUTATIONAL METHOD

    When the method COMPLETE is used to compute correlations, the means,
variances and covariances are computed by the method of provisional means
described in Appendix A.2. When the correlations are computed by a
method other than COMPLETE , the method of provisional means is modified
to keep track of the extra matrices needed, such as $\bar{x}_{i(k)}$ or $var_{i(k)}$. All
computations are performed in single precision.

ACKNOWLEDGEMENT

P8D was programmed by Peter Mundle. It supersedes BMD12D.

Output 12.3 Creating a BMDP File to save results from P8D

```
                 ESTIMATES OF CORRELATIONS - COVPAIR

              AGE      HEIGHT    WEIGHT   BRTHPILL  CHOLSTRL  ALBUMIN   CALCIUM   URICACID
               2         3         4         5         6         7         8         9

AGE       2   1.0000
HEIGHT    3   0.0804   1.0000
WEIGHT    4   0.2524   0.4712   1.0000
BRTHPILL  5   0.0      0.1692   0.0738   1.0000
CHOLSTRL  6   0.3676   0.0200   0.1478   0.0758   1.0000
ALBUMIN   7  -0.0715  -0.0208  -0.2552  -0.2398   0.0534   1.0000
CALCIUM   8  -0.0319   0.1488   0.0698  -0.0561   0.2505   0.4434   1.0000
URICACID  9   0.1762   0.1342   0.3003   0.0247   0.2605   0.0072   0.1936   1.0000


                 ESTIMATES OF CORRELATIONS - ALLVALUE

              AGE      HEIGHT    WEIGHT   BRTHPILL  CHOLSTRL  ALBUMIN   CALCIUM   URICACID
               2         3         4         5         6         7         8         9

AGE       2   1.0000
HEIGHT    3   0.0804   1.0000
WEIGHT    4   0.2524   0.4713   1.0000
BRTHPILL  5   0.0      0.1692   0.0738   1.0000
CHOLSTRL  6   0.3676   0.0200   0.1478   0.0758   1.0000
ALBUMIN   7  -0.0715  -0.0208  -0.2552  -0.2398   0.0534   1.0000
CALCIUM   8  -0.0319   0.1488   0.0699  -0.0561   0.2505   0.4436   1.0000
URICACID  9   0.1762   0.1342   0.3004   0.0247   0.2605   0.0072   0.1936   1.0000

BMDP FILE WRITTEN ON UNIT 4.

        CODE. . . IS      WERNER
        CONTENT . IS      CORR
        LABEL . . IS
        VARIABLES     2   AGE      3   HEIGHT   4   WEIGHT   5   BRTHPILL  6   CHOLSTRL
                      7   ALBUMIN  8   CALCIUM  9   URICACID

    MATRIX TYPE SAVED IS     ALLVALUE


BMDP FILE ON UNIT 4 HAS BEEN COMPLETED.
```

PAM

12.2 Description and Estimation of Missing Data

James Frane, HSCF

PAM is designed to fulfill two primary functions:

- To describe the pattern of missing data -- Where are the missing values located? How extensive are they? Do pairs of variables tend to have values missing in the same cases? Are cases with missing values extreme (far from the mean)?

- To prepare input for other BMDP programs -- PAM can estimate the covariance and correlation matrices by either of two computational methods or it can replace missing values or values out of range by estimated values (using one of several methods). The covariance matrix and the "completed" data matrix can be saved in a BMDP File for further analysis by other programs.

The first function is a preliminary step to the second. Usually you will want to use PAM twice; first to look at the pattern and extent of the missing values and then to compute covariances or provide estimates for the missing values.

● RESULTS

PAM provides a variety of results to describe the pattern of missing values. In our first example the Werner blood chemistry data (Table 5.1) are analyzed by PAM. The Control Language instructions in Example 12.4 are described in Chapter 5. There are no instructions in Example 12.4 specific to PAM; only preassigned options are used. [4]

Example 12.4

```
/PROBLEM      TITLE IS 'WERNER BLOOD CHEMISTRY DATA'.
/INPUT        VARIABLES ARE 9.
              FORMAT IS '(A4,5F4.0,3F4.1)'.
/VARIABLE     NAMES ARE ID,AGE,HEIGHT,WEIGHT,BRTHPILL,
                  CHOLSTRL,ALBUMIN,CALCIUM,URICACID.
              MAXIMUM IS (6)400.
              MINIMUM IS (6)150.
              BLANKS ARE MISSING.
              LABEL IS ID.

/END
```

The Control Language must be preceded by System Cards to initiate the analysis by PAM. At HSCF, the System Cards are

```
//jobname  JOB  nooo,yourname
//  EXEC  BIMED,PROG=BMDPAM
//SYSIN  DD  *
```

The Control Language is immediately followed by the data (Table 5.1). The analysis is terminated by another System Card. At HSCF, this System Card is

```
//
```

---

[4] PAM was distributed originally in August 1976. If your version is dated before August 1977, there are minor changes in the abbreviations and item names; these changes are described in the footnotes to the summary (p. 373).

The results of the analysis are presented in Output 12.4. Circled numbers below correspond to those in the output.

① Interpretation of Control Language instructions specific to PAM. No such instructions are specified in Example 12.4; therefore preassigned options are shown.

② For cases that contain missing values or values out of range, a cases-by-variables plot showing the location of missing values (M--missing), values less than the lower limit (S--too small) and values greater than the upper limit (B--too big). In our example, the second case has a value larger than the upper limit for CHOLSTRL and a missing value for CALCIUM.

③ Number of cases read. You can specify whether computations use only complete cases (cases with no data missing and positive case weight) or all acceptable values.

④ For variables with missing values or values out of range, the percent of values that are missing or out of range.

⑤ Univariate statistics for each variable, including the sample size (number of acceptable observations), mean, standard deviation, coefficient of variation, smallest observed value (not out or range), largest observed value (not out of range), smallest standard score, largest standard score, skewness and kurtosis. (These statistics are defined in Section 2.1.)

⑥ Data from the first five cases are printed. The word MISS replaces missing values, SMAL replaces values less than the lower limit and BIG replaces values greater than the upper limit (see cases 1 and 2). You can request that the data be printed for any number of cases.

⑦ For each pair of variables, the sample size (number) of cases containing acceptable values for both variables. Variables having acceptable values for all cases or no acceptable values are omitted from the table. For example, there are 184 cases with acceptable values for both HEIGHT and WEIGHT.

⑧ Pairwise percentage of missing data.

For each pair of variables in ⑦, PAM prints the percentage of cases in which either variable has a missing value or value out of range. The diagonal elements are the percentages for the individual variables.

⑨ Correlations of dichotomized variables. The correlation of each pair of variables in ⑦ is computed using a dichotomy for each variable; one represents an acceptable value, and zero a value that is missing or out of range. Variables that contain only acceptable values or no acceptable values are not included in this matrix. This correlation matrix (CORRDICH) can be saved in a BMDP File and used in other programs such as factor analysis to further study the pattern of missing values. (*Note: all other computations are based on the acceptable observations and not on these dichotomies.*)

<u>Output 12.4</u>   Results of an analysis of the Werner data by PAM. Circled numbers correspond to those in the text. Results not reproduced are indicated in italics.

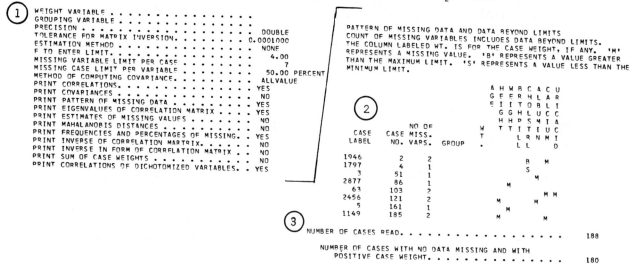

BMDPAM — DESCRIPTION AND ESTIMATION OF MISSING DATA
HEALTH SCIENCES COMPUTING FACILITY   PROGRAM REVISED SEPTEMBER 1977
UNIVERSITY OF CALIFORNIA, LOS ANGELES   MANUAL DATE -- 1977

--- Control Language read by PAM is printed and interpreted ---

(1) WEIGHT VARIABLE . . . .
    GROUPING VARIABLE . . . .
    PRECISION . . . . DOUBLE
    TOLERANCE FOR MATRIX INVERSION. 0.0001000
    ESTIMATION METHOD . . . . NONE
    F TO ENTER LIMIT. 4.00
    MISSING VARIABLE LIMIT PER CASE 7
    MISSING CASE LIMIT PER VARIABLE . . . . 50.00 PERCENT
    METHOD OF COMPUTING COVARIANCE. . . . . ALLVALUE
    PRINT CORRELATIONS. . . . . YES
    PRINT COVARIANCES . . . . NO
    PRINT PATTERN OF MISSING DATA . . . . YES
    PRINT EIGENVALUES OF CORRELATION MATRIX . . . YES
    PRINT ESTIMATES OF MISSING VALUES . . . . . . NO
    PRINT MAHALANOBIS DISTANCES . . . . NO
    PRINT FREQUENCIES AND PERCENTAGES OF MISSING. YES
    PRINT INVERSE OF CORRELATION MATRIX . . . . . NO
    PRINT INVERSE IN FORM OF CORRELATION MATRIX . NO
    PRINT SUM OF CASE WEIGHTS . . . . NO
    PRINT CORRELATIONS OF DICHOTOMIZED VARIABLES. YES

PATTERN OF MISSING DATA AND DATA BEYOND LIMITS
COUNT OF MISSING VARIABLES INCLUDES DATA BEYOND LIMITS.
THE COLUMN LABELED WT. IS FOR THE CASE WEIGHT, IF ANY. 'M'
REPRESENTS A MISSING VALUE. 'B' REPRESENTS A VALUE GREATER
THAN THE MAXIMUM LIMIT. 'S' REPRESENTS A VALUE LESS THAN THE
MINIMUM LIMIT.

(2)
```
                                          A H W B C A C U
                                          G E F R H L A R
                                          E I I T O B L I
                                          I G G H L U C C
                              NO OF    W   H H P S M I A
         CASE    CASE MISS.       .    T   T T I U C I C
         LABEL   NO.  VARS.  GROUP          L R N M T D
                                               L L       D

         1946     2     2                           B   M
         1797     4     1                           S
            3    51     1                       M
         2877    86     1               M
           63   103     2                           M M
         2456   121     2         M         M
            5   161     1               M
         1149   185     2               M       M
```

(3) NUMBER OF CASES READ. 188

    NUMBER OF CASES WITH NO DATA MISSING AND WITH
        POSITIVE CASE WEIGHT. 180

(4) PERCENTAGES OF MISSING DATA FOR EACH VARIABLE IN EACH GROUP

    THESE PERCENTAGES ARE BASED ON SAMPLE SIZES AND GROUP SIZES
    REPORTED WITH THE UNIVARIATE SUMMARY STATISTICS BELOW.
    VARIABLES WITHOUT MISSING DATA ARE NOT INCLUDED.

```
                        1
    HEIGHT     3      1.1
    WEIGHT     4      1.1
    CHOLSTRL   6      1.1
    ALBUMIN    7      1.1
    CALCIUM    8      1.6
    URICACID   9      0.5
```

UNIVARIATE SUMMARY STATISTICS

(5) VARIABLE	SAMPLE SIZE	MEAN	STANDARD DEVIATION	COEFFICIENT OF VARIATION	SMALLEST VALUE	LARGEST VALUE	SMALLEST STANDARD SCORE	LARGEST STANDARD SCORE	SKEWNESS	KURTOSIS
2 AGE	188	33.81915	10.11269	0.299023	19.00000	55.00000	-1.47	2.09	0.41	-1.00
3 HEIGHT	186	64.51075	2.48507	0.038522	57.00000	71.00000	-3.02	2.61	-0.14	-0.07
4 WEIGHT	186	131.67204	20.66058	0.156909	94.00000	215.00000	-1.82	4.03	1.00	1.71
5 BRTHPILL	188	1.50000	0.50134	0.334223	1.00000	2.00000	-1.00	1.00	0.00	-2.01
6 CHOLSTRL	186	236.15054	42.55551	0.180205	155.00000	390.00000	-1.91	3.62	0.47	0.10
7 ALBUMIN	186	4.11129	0.35797	0.087070	3.20000	5.00000	-2.55	2.48	-0.03	-0.36
8 CALCIUM	185	9.96216	0.47956	0.048138	8.60000	11.10000	-2.84	2.37	-0.11	-0.40
9 URICACID	187	4.77059	1.15723	0.242576	2.20000	9.90000	-2.22	4.43	1.07	2.36

DATA AFTER TRANSFORMATIONS FOR FIRST   5 CASES

'MISS' DENOTES A MISSING VALUE, 'BIG' DENOTES A
VALUE THAT EXCEEDS THE MAXIMUM LIMIT, AND 'SMAL'
DENOTES A VALUE THAT IS LESS THAN THE MINIMUM LIMIT.

(6)
```
       CASE
LABEL  NUMBER    WEIGHT    GROUP    2 AGE      3 HEIGHT   4 WEIGHT    5 BRTHPILL  6 CHOLSTRL  7 ALBUMIN
                8 CALCIUM 9 URICACID
2381     1      1.00000
                9.80000   5.40000  22.00000   67.00000   144.00000   1.00000     200.00000   4.30000
1946     2      1.00000
                MISS      7.20000  22.00000   64.00000   160.00000   2.00000     BIG         3.50000
1610     3      1.00000
                10.40000  3.30000  25.00000   62.00000   128.00000   1.00000     243.00000   4.10000
1797     4      1.00000
                9.60000   3.00000  25.00000   68.00000   150.00000   2.00000     SMAL        3.80000
561      5      1.00000
                9.90000   4.70000  19.00000   64.00000   125.00000   1.00000     158.00000   4.10000
```

(continued)

Output 12.4 *(continued)*

```
SAMPLE SIZES FOR EACH PAIR OF VARIABLES
(NUMBER OF TIMES BOTH VARIABLES ARE AVAILABLE)
IN ORDER TO SAVE SPACE, VARIABLES WITH NO MISSING
DATA OR THAT HAVE NO DATA ARE NOT INCLUDED.
```

(7)

		HEIGHT 3	WEIGHT 4	CHOLSTRL 6	ALBUMIN 7	CALCIUM 8	URICACID 9
HEIGHT	3	186					
WEIGHT	4	184	186				
CHOLSTRL	6	184	184	186			
ALBUMIN	7	185	184	184	186		
CALCIUM	8	184	183	184	183	185	
URICACID	9	185	185	185	185	185	187

```
PAIRWISE PERCENTAGES OF MISSING DATA

DIAGONAL ELEMENTS ARE THE PERCENTAGES THAT EACH VARIABLE
IS MISSING.  OFF-DIAGONAL ELEMENTS ARE THE PERCENTAGES
EITHER VARIABLE IS MISSING.  THESE PERCENTAGES DO NOT INCLUDE
CASES WITH MISSING GROUP OR WEIGHT VARIABLES, CASES WITH
ZERO WEIGHTS, CASES EXCLUDED BY SETTING USE EQUAL TO A
NON-POSITIVE VALUE BY TRANSFORMATIONS, OR CASES WITH GROUPING
VALUES NOT USED.  VARIABLES WITH NO MISSING DATA OR THAT
HAVE NO DATA ARE NOT INCLUDED HERE.
```

(8)

		HEIGHT 3	WEIGHT 4	CHOLSTRL 6	ALBUMIN 7	CALCIUM 8	URICACID 9
HEIGHT	3	1.1					
WEIGHT	4	2.1	1.1				
CHOLSTRL	6	2.1	2.1	1.1			
ALBUMIN	7	1.6	2.1	2.1	1.1		
CALCIUM	8	2.1	2.7	2.1	2.7	1.6	
URICACID	9	1.6	1.6	1.6	1.6	1.6	0.5

```
CORRELATIONS OF THE DICHOTOMIZED VARIABLES WHERE FOR EACH
VARIABLE ZERO INDICATES THAT THE VALUE WAS MISSING AND ONE
INDICATES THAT THE VALUE WAS PRESENT.  VARIABLES WITH NO
MISSING DATA OR WHICH ARE COMPLETELY MISSING ARE NOT
INCLUDED.
```

(9)

		HEIGHT 3	WEIGHT 4	CHOLSTRL 6	ALBUMIN 7	CALCIUM 8	URICACID 9
HEIGHT	3	1.000					
WEIGHT	4	-0.011	1.000				
CHOLSTRL	6	-0.011	-0.011	1.000			
ALBUMIN	7	0.495	-0.011	-0.011	1.000		
CALCIUM	8	0.401	-0.013	0.401	-0.013	1.000	
URICACID	9	-0.008	-0.008	-0.008	-0.008	0.574	1.000

```
NOTE THAT THE REMAINING OUTPUT IS FOR THE ORDINARY
CORRELATIONS, NOT THE CORRELATIONS FOR THE
DICHOTOMIZED VARIABLES.
```

```
CORRELATIONS
```

(10)

		AGE 2	HEIGHT 3	WEIGHT 4	BRTHPILL 5	CHOLSTRL 6	ALBUMIN 7	CALCIUM 8	URICACID 9
AGE	2	1.000							
HEIGHT	3	0.080	1.000						
WEIGHT	4	0.252	0.471	1.000					
BRTHPILL	5	0.0	0.169	0.074	1.000				
CHOLSTRL	6	0.368	0.020	0.148	0.076	1.000			
ALBUMIN	7	-0.072	-0.021	-0.255	-0.240	0.053	1.000		
CALCIUM	8	-0.032	0.149	0.070	-0.056	0.250	0.444	1.000	
URICACID	9	0.176	0.134	0.300	0.025	0.260	0.007	0.194	1.000

```
EIGENVALUES OF ORIGINAL CORRELATION MATRIX
```

(11)
```
2.0016
1.6239
1.1923
0.9613
0.8031
0.5862
0.4686
0.3729
```

(10)   Correlations. This analysis (Example 12.4) uses the preassigned method of computing correlations, which is ALLVALUE (see P8D, pp. 337-338). When this method is used it is possible that the correlation matrix will not be positive semidefinite. If negative eigenvalues are found, the correlation matrix is recomputed using the positive eigenvalues and their eigenvectors (see below for details).

(11)   Eigenvalues of the correlation matrix.

● OPTIONAL RESULTS

When preassigned options only are used as in Example 12.4, the missing values are not replaced by estimates based on the acceptable values.

You can

- specify how correlations are to be computed   p. 352
- request that missing values be replaced by estimates and specify the method to be used   p. 353
- state whether values out of range are to be replaced by estimates   p. 355
- specify a *GROUPing* variable to classify the cases   p. 363
- specify that there are case weights   p. 364
- state the number of cases to be printed   p. 359
- request optional printed results or delete some of the printed results   p. 359
- request bivariate (scatter) plots of the variables and of the estimates of the missing values   p. 361
- save results in a BMDP File   p. 367

● UNIVARIATE STATISTICS, COVARIANCES AND CORRELATIONS

The univariate statistics, covariances and correlations can be computed using

- all acceptable values (ALLVALUE): the mean of each variable is computed from all acceptable values of the variable; deviations from the means are used to compute covariances and correlations (see P8D, pp. 337-338)

- complete cases only (COMPLETE): cases with missing values or or values out of range are not used in the computations

When all acceptable values (ALLVALUE) are used, the correlation between two variables can exceed unity since the variances may be computed using more values than the covariances. More generally, the correlation matrix may not be positive semidefinite (i.e., the estimated correlation matrix is not a proper correlation matrix). When the correlation matrix is not positive semidefinite, one or more eigenvalues will be negative, the correlation matrix is then recomputed from the positive eigenvalues and corresponding eigenvectors (Appendix A.9). This guarantees that the "smoothed" correlation matrix is positive semidefinite and can be used in regression and factor analysis.

ALLVALUE is the preassigned method and is preferred when missing values are not concentrated into a very few cases. However, a check on the effect of the missing data can be made by comparing correlations computed by both methods.

ESTimate
    TYPE= *(one only)* ALLVALUE,COMPLETE.   {ALLVALUE/prev.}

    ALLVALUE uses all acceptable values for each variable wherever possible. See P8D (p. 338) for a more exact definition. When ALLVALUE is used, the correlation matrix may have to be smoothed to eliminate negative eigenvalues as explained above.

    When COMPLETE is specified, only cases that have valid data for all variables are used in the computations of the mean and all other univariate statistics, and in the covariances.

● METHODS OF ESTIMATING MISSING VALUES

PAM can replace missing values and values out of range by estimates computed by any of the following methods.

MEAN   -- The mean of the variable is substituted for the missing values. If the cases are classified into groups, the group mean of the variable is substituted.

SINGLE   -- Each missing value for a variable is estimated by regressing that variable on the variable with which it is most highly correlated, provided the F-to-enter limit is met (see below); otherwise the (group) mean is used.

TWOSTEP -- Each missing value for a variable is estimated by regressing that variable on up to two variables selected by stepwise regression (see below). If the F-to-enter limit is <u>not</u> met for either variable, the SINGLE method is <u>used</u>.

STEP   -- Each missing value for a variable is estimated by regressing that variable on <u>all</u> variables that meet the F-to-enter criterion. Stepwise regression is used to select among the variables that have acceptable values in the case with the missing value.

REGR   -- Each missing value for a variable is estimated by regressing that variable on all variables that have acceptable values in the case with the missing value. The F-to-enter criterion is not used.

The F-to-enter criterion is motivated by an approximate test of the coefficient of any predictor variable. That is, the square of the ratio of the predictor's regression coefficient to its standard error is approximately distributed as an F statistic with one degree of freedom for the numerator. The square of this ratio is compared with the F-to-enter limit (ENTER). This test is affected by the missing values and the procedure of variable selection. We suggest that ENTER not be less than 4.0 to avoid using too many predictor variables (overfitting).

In a stepwise regression of a dependent variable on several others, the variable that has the highest correlation with the dependent variable is chosen first for the regression equation. The variable chosen next is the one with the highest partial correlation with the dependent variable conditional on the variable(s) already in the equation. Additional variables are chosen in the same manner until all variables with acceptable values are used or the F-to-enter criterion is not satisfied.

The choice of method depends on the number of cases, the magnitude of the correlations, the number of missing values, the purpose of estimating the data, the pattern of missing values, etc. When all the correlations are very low it is usually difficult to improve on MEAN . If each variable is highly correlated with another variable and economy is essential, SINGLE may be appropriate. When the number of cases is large and there are many large correlations, REGR is appropriate but may use too many predictor variables (overfitting). STEP or TWOSTEP is appropriate when the correlation matrix contains clusters of moderate or high correlations.

You may prefer STEP to other methods for the same reasons that ordinary stepwise regression is preferred. However, substantially more computation is required than for the other methods. The REGR method is notably cheaper than the STEP, but requires more computation than MEAN, SINGLE and TWOSTEP.

Before estimating missing values it is necessary to thoroughly screen the data and to study the pattern of missing data and correlations; the correlations can be severely affected by extreme values. We suggest that you use P2D (Section 8.2) or P7D (Section 9.2) as well as the screening output from PAM before you choose a method of estimation.

```
ESTimate
    METHOD= (one only)   MEAN,SINGLE,TWOSTEP,STEP,
                         REGR, NONE.                {NONE/prev.}

    The method used to estimate and replace missing values and values
    out of range (see below). NONE means that there is no estimation
    of missing values.  Therefore, to estimate missing values a method
    must be specified.  The methods are described in detail above.
    Some of the results described in the PRINT paragraph are available
    only for specific methods due to the computational techniques used.
```

● ESTIMATING AND REPLACING VALUES OUT OF RANGE

Unless you request otherwise, only observations that are equal to the missing value code are estimated. Values out of range are estimated when

and
MAXIMUM.

MINIMUM.

are specified in the *ESTimate* paragraph. MAXIMUM specifies that values greater than the upper limit for the variables are to be estimated; and MINIMUM specifies that values that are less than the lower limit for the variables are to be estimated. (Values greater than the upper limit or less than the lower limit are not used in any computations whether or not they are estimated.)

ESTimate
MAXIMUM.   {no/prev.}

Reestimate and replace values that are greater than the specified upper limits for the variables. The values are replaced by the same METHOD as missing values.

MINIMUM.   {no/prev.}

Reestimate and replace values that are less than the specified lower limits for the variables. The values are replaced by the same METHOD as missing values.

In the following example we specify that the missing values and values out of range are to be replaced by estimates provided by the METHOD REGR.

Example 12.5

```
/PROBLEM     TITLE IS 'WERNER BLOOD CHEMISTRY DATA'.
/INPUT       VARIABLES ARE 9.
             FORMAT IS '(A4,5F4.0,3F4.1)'.
/VARIABLE    NAMES ARE ID,AGE,HEIGHT,WEIGHT,BRTHPILL,
                CHOLSTRL,ALBUMIN,CALCIUM,URICACID.
             MAXIMUM IS (6)400.
             MINIMUM IS (6)150.
             BLANKS ARE MISSING.
             LABEL IS ID.

/ESTIMATE    METHOD IS REGR.
             MINIMUM.
             MAXIMUM.

/END
```

The results are presented in Output 12.5. Circled numbers below correspond to those in the output.

⑫ Squared multiple correlations of each variable with all other variables. These indicate approximately the extent that each variable can be estimated from the others by multiple regression. In addition to the

<u>Output 12.5</u>   Estimation of missing values by PAM using METHOD=REGR

--- results shown in Output 12.4 appear here ---

SQUARED MULTIPLE CORRELATIONS OF EACH VARIABLE WITH ALL OTHER VARIABLES
(MEASURES OF MULTICOLLINEARITY OF VARIABLES)
AND TESTS OF SIGNIFICANCE OF MULTIPLE REGRESSION
DEGREES OF FREEDOM FOR F-STATISTICS ARE   7 AND   180

(12)

VARIABLE NO.	NAME	SMC	F-STATISTIC	SIGNIFICANCE (P LESS THAN)
2	AGE	0.198751	6.38	0.00000
3	HEIGHT	0.272510	9.63	0.00000
4	WEIGHT	0.378877	15.69	0.00000
5	BRTHPILL	0.102934	2.95	0.00597
6	CHOLSTRL	0.240848	8.16	0.00000
7	ALBUMIN	0.323993	12.32	0.00000
8	CALCIUM	0.305248	11.30	0.00000
9	URICACID	0.155962	4.75	0.00006

*** WARNING ***   WHEN THE ALLVALUE OPTION IS USED, THE
DEGREES OF FREEDOM USED IN COMPUTING THE ABOVE F STATISTICS
INCLUDE CASES WITH MISSING VALUES. IF THE AMOUNT OF
MISSING DATA IS VERY LARGE, THE SIGNIFICANCE OF THE
F STATISTICS IS EXAGGERATED.

ESTIMATES THAT ARE LESS THAN THE MINIMUMS
STATED IN THE VARIABLE PARAGRAPH ARE FLAGGED BY THE
LETTER 'S' (SMALL) AFTER THE ESTIMATE. ESTIMATES
GREATER THAN THE MAXIMUMS ARE FLAGGED BY THE LETTER
'B' (BIG).

MAHALANOBIS DISTANCES ARE COMPUTED FROM EACH CASE TO THE
CENTROID OF ITS GROUP. ONLY THOSE VARIABLES WHICH WERE
ORIGINALLY AVAILABLE ARE USED--ESTIMATED VALUES ARE NOT USED.

SIGNIFICANCE LEVELS FOR MAHALANOBIS DISTANCES (CHI-SQUARES)
THAT ARE LESS THAN .001 ARE FLAGGED WITH AN ASTERISK.

ESTIMATES OF MISSING DATA, MAHALANOBIS D-SQUARED (CHI-SQUARED)
AND SQUARED MULTIPLE CORRELATIONS WITH AVAILABLE VARIABLES

(13)

CASE LABEL	CASE NUMBER	MISSING VARIABLE	ESTIMATE	R-SQUARED	GROUP	CHI-SQ	CHISQ/DF	D.F.	SIGNIFICANCE
2381	1					5.699	0.712	8	0.6810
1946	2	6 CHOLSTRL	237.1477	0.194		11.877	1.979	6	0.0648
1946	2	8 CALCIUM	9.8462	0.262		11.877	1.979	6	0.0648
1610	3					6.299	0.787	8	0.6137
1797	4	6 CHOLSTRL	205.1026	0.241		7.366	1.052	7	0.3918

--- similar statistics for cases 5 to 184 ---

CASE LABEL	CASE NUMBER	MISSING VARIABLE	ESTIMATE	R-SQUARED	GROUP	CHI-SQ	CHISQ/DF	D.F.	SIGNIFICANCE
1149	185	3 HEIGHT	66.6956	0.265		9.453	1.575	6	0.1497
1149	185	8 CALCIUM	9.8471	0.298		9.453	1.575	6	0.1497
575	186					11.891	1.486	8	0.1561
2271	187					7.625	0.953	8	0.4709
39	188					23.223	2.903	8	0.0031

ESTIMATION OF MISSING DATA COMPLETED

squared multiple correlation (R^2), the F statistics corresponding to R^2 and the tail probabilities are printed.

(13) Estimates of the missing values and values out of range. The squared multiple correlation (R^2) of the variable estimated with the variables used in the regression equation is printed beside each estimate. For each case, the Mahalanobis D^2 (distance) of the case from the mean is computed; this is labelled CHISQ since for large multivariate normal samples the distribution of D^2 is approximately χ^2. CHISQ/DF is the value of D^2 divided by the number of acceptable values in the case; for large degrees of freedom these values are easier to inspect than the values of CHISQ since their distributions are similar for different degrees of freedom.

As an aid to screening these values, PAM prints the tail area (p-value or probability of exceeding the value of CHISQ) and flags values less than 0.001 with an asterisk. This is not an exact test but can aid in identifying suspicious cases that need to be rechecked. An unusually large number of outliers can indicate that a transformation of the data is necessary; the skewness and kurtosis can also suggest the need for a transformation.

● OPTIONS THAT AFFECT THE METHOD OF ESTIMATION

The F-to-enter limit for three METHODS (SINGLE, TWOSTEP and STEP) can be changed. The preassigned value is 4.0 to avoid fitting too many predictor variables.

ESTimate
     ENTER= #.   {4.0/prev.}

     The F-to-enter limit for three METHODS (SINGLE, TWOSTEP, and STEP). The F-to-enter value for a variable must exceed ENTER for the variable to enter the regression equation. F-to-enter is the square of the ratio of the coefficient, if entered into the regression equation, to its standard error.

The regression equation will include a constant term (intercept) to be estimated unless ZERO is specified.

ESTimate
     ZERO.   {not ZERO/prev.} Not available when a GROUPING
                                                        variable is specified.

     If ZERO is specified, the regression equation used will not have an intercept; i.e., it will pass through the origin. The correlation matrix, covariance matrix, regression statistics, and all but the univariate statistics are computed assuming variable means are zero. *Note: this option is rarely used.*

The regression equation is formed by stepwise inverting (sweeping) the correlation matrix. The TOLERANCE checks that the variable about to be included is <u>not</u> a linear combination of variables already in the regression equation.

ESTimate
   TOLERANCE=#.   {0.0001/prev.}   between 0.0 and 1.0

   No variable is entered into the regression equation whose squared multiple correlation is greater than 1.0-TOLERANCE. A variable is also not entered if, by being entered, it would cause one of the variables already in the regression equation to violate the TOLERANCE check. For IBM 360 and 370 computers, TOLERANCE should not be less than 10^{-7}.

- CASES AND VARIABLES FOR WHICH MISSING VALUES ARE ESTIMATED

   If a case contains too many missing values or values out of range, you may not want to include that case in the computations, or to estimate the missing values for the case. To eliminate such cases, you can specify:

ESTimate
   VLIM=#.   {no. of var.-1}

   The maximum number of variables with missing values or values out of range permitted in a case. When the limit is exceeded, the case is not used in any computations (means, covariances, etc.) and the missing values in the case are not estimated.

   If any variable has too many missing values or values out of range, you may not want to compute statistics for it or estimate its missing values. If a pair of variables has too many cases where one or both observations are not acceptable, the estimate of the covariance or correlation for this pair of variables may be poor. Therefore, you can specify the maximum percentage of cases that can have unacceptable observations and yet the computations are performed. If not specified, the preassigned percentage is 50%.

ESTimate
   CLIM=#.   {50.0}

   The maximum percentage of cases that can have missing values or values out of range for any variable or pair of variables in any group. If this limit is exceeded, estimation of missing values is <u>not</u> performed. If the COMPLETE method of computing covariances is used, this limit is applied to the cases with <u>any</u> missing values or values out of range.

● Results Printed by PAM

     Outputs 12.4 and 12.5 illustrate many of the results that are printed by PAM. Several matrices, such as the covariance matrix and the inverse of the correlation matrix, can also be printed. Some of the matrices, such as those in Output 12.5, depend on whether missing values are estimated, and possibly on the method of estimation. If the preassigned options only are desired (as in Outputs 12.4 and 12.5), the *PRINT* paragraph need not be used.

     In Output 12.4 the first five cases of the data are printed (⑥). If more (or fewer) cases are wanted,

        CASE=number of cases to print.

can be specified.

PRINT
    CASE=#.   {5/prev.}

    Number of cases for which the data are to be printed. In the output missing values are replaced by MISS, values greater than the upper limit by BIG and values less than the lower limit by SMAL. The data are printed after transformations, if any, are performed.

     You can request any of the following MATRICES. However, if you specify any matrices, only those specified are printed.

PRINT
    MATRICES= *(one or more)* PAT,FREQ,CORRDICH,   {PAT,FREQ,
                              CORR,EIGEN,EST,   CORRDICH,CORR,
                              DIS,COVA,CREG,RREG,   EIGEN,EST,
                              SUMW.   DIS/prev.}

    The list of matrices to be printed. The matrices are

      PAT   -- the pattern of missing data and values beyond limits (② in Output 12.4). If the number of variables exceeds 100, only the first 100 variables are used.

      FREQ   -- the sample sizes and percentage missing or out of range for each variable and for each pair of variables (⑦ and ⑧). It is printed for pairs of variables only if TYPE is ALLVALUE.

    CORRDICH -- correlations computed using the dichotomies: 1.0 if the value is acceptable and 0.0 otherwise (⑨). Variables that contain only acceptable values or contain no acceptable values are not included in CORRDICH.

      CORR   -- correlations computed from the acceptable values or complete cases using the ALLVALUE or COMPLETE methods (⑩). If the method is ALLVALUE and the

                                            (continued)

(continued from previous page)

> correlation matrix is <u>not</u> positive semidefinite, the correlation matrix is smoothed (recomputed) using only the positive eigenvalues and the associated eigenvectors (see Appendix A.9).

EIGEN   --   eigenvalues of the correlation matrix (⑪). If the method of computing correlations is ALLVALUE and the correlation matrix is <u>not</u> positive semidefinite, both the eigenvalues of the original correlation matrix and the eigenvalues of the smoothed (recomputed) correlation matrix are printed.

EST   --   the estimates of the missing data (this option is not available if the METHOD used is MEAN). If the METHOD used is REGR, the Mahalanobis distance from the mean is also reported for cases that contain estimated values.

DIS   --   the distance of each case from the mean is computed (EST reports distances for only those cases in which values are estimated). Both EST and DIS are shown in ⑬ in Output 12.5. DIS is available only when the METHOD used is REGR.

COVA   --   the matrix of covariances.

CREG   --   the inverse of the correlation matrix. This is available only if the method of estimating missing values is REGR.

RREG   --   the inverse of the correlation matrix standardized to have ones on the diagonal (in the same way that a covariance matrix is converted to a correlation matrix). This is available only if the method of estimating missing values is REGR.

SUMW   --   matrix of the sum of case weights for each pair of variables. It is printed only if a case WEIGHT variable is specified and if ALLVALUE is used to compute correlations.

The preassigned matrices that are printed if no specification is given are PAT, FREQ, CORRDICH, CORR, EIGEN, EST, and DIS. However, if you want only the univariate statistics and pattern of missing values, you can specify

/PRINT MATRICES ARE PAT,FREQ.

Since the covariance and correlation matrices are not needed, they are not computed and a lot of computation is avoided.

Note: If the correlation matrix is not to be printed and the ESTimation METHOD is NONE or MEAN, then the correlation matrix, covariance matrix, sample sizes for pairs of variables, etc. will not be computed and cannot be output to BMDP File. This results in a considerable reduction in the computational and computer memory requirements; e.g., several hundred variables can be screened when the correlation matrix is not needed.

- *PLOTting* PAIRS OF VARIABLES

    You can request scatter plots of any pairs of variables. Two plots are formed for each pair, one showing cases with acceptable values for both variables, the second showing cases with an estimated value for at least one variable.

    The equations for the two regression lines

    $$Y = a + bY$$
    $$X = a' + b'Y$$

are printed below each plot.

    The lengths of both axes of the plot can be adjusted.

PLOT
    XVAR=$v_1,v_2,\cdots$.   {none}

      Names or subscripts of variables to be plotted along the X-axis (horizontally).

    YVAR=$v_1,v_2,\cdots$.   {none}

      Names or subscripts of variables to be plotted along the Y-axis (vertically).

      The first variable in XVAR is plotted against the first in YVAR, the second against the second, etc. Two plots are printed for each pair of variables, the first showing cases with acceptable values for both variables, and the second showing cases with an estimated value for at least one of the variables.

    SIZE=$\#_1,\#_2$.   {50,50/prev.}

      The first number is the length of the X-axis, and the second is the length of the Y-axis.

We demonstrate these plots by the following example.

Example 12.6

```
/PROBLEM      TITLE IS 'WERNER BLOOD CHEMISTRY DATA'.
/INPUT        VARIABLES ARE 9.
              FORMAT IS '(A4,5F4.0,3F4.1)'.
/VARIABLE     NAMES ARE ID,AGE,HEIGHT,WEIGHT,BRTHPILL,
                    CHOLSTRL,ALBUMIN,CALCIUM,URICACID.
              MAXIMUM IS (6)400.
              MINIMUM IS (6)150.
              BLANKS ARE MISSING.
              LABEL IS ID.

/ESTIMATE     METHOD IS REGR.
              MINIMUM.
              MAXIMUM.

/PLOT         XVAR IS AGE.
              YVAR IS CHOLSTRL.
              SIZE IS 40,25.

/END
```

Output 12.6   Plots printed by PAM

--- results shown is Output 12.5 appear here ---

ON THE FOLLOWING PAGES TWO PLOTS APPEAR FOR EACH PAIR OF VARIABLES
FOR WHICH PLOTS HAVE BEEN REQUESTED.   THE FIRST PLOT CONTAINS
CASES FOR WHICH NEITHER VARIABLE HAS BEEN ESTIMATED.   THE
SECOND PLOT CONTAINS CASES FOR WHICH EITHER OR BOTH VARIABLES
HAVE BEEN ESTIMATED.   IF THE VARIABLE FOR THE X-AXIS HAS BEEN
ESTIMATED BUT NOT THE VARIABLE FOR THE Y-AXIS, THE CASE IS
PLOTTED WITH AN 'X'.   IF THE VARIABLE FOR THE Y-AXIS HAS BEEN
ESTIMATED BUT NOT THE VARIABLE FOR THE X-AXIS, THE CASE IS
PLOTTED WITH A 'Y'.   IF BOTH VARIABLES HAVE BEEN ESTIMATED, A
'B' IS USED.   WHEN TWO OR MORE CASES ARE PLOTTED IN THE SAME
POSITION AND IF THEY WOULD RECEIVE DIFFERENT PLOT CHARACTERS,
THEN AN ASTERISK IS USED.

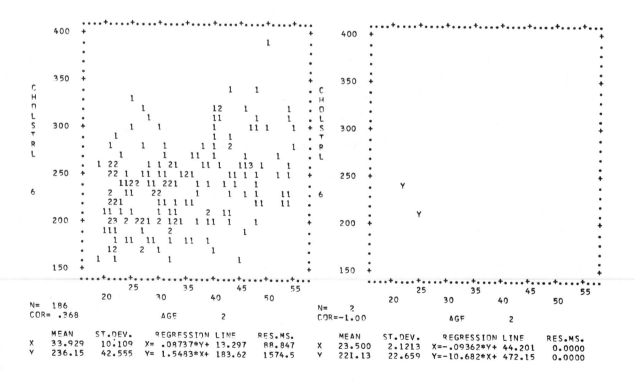

	MEAN	ST.DEV.	REGRESSION LINE	RES.MS.		MEAN	ST.DEV.	REGRESSION LINE	RES.MS.
X	33.929	10.109	X= .08737*Y+ 13.297	88.847	X	23.500	2.1213	X=-.09362*Y+ 44.201	0.0000
Y	236.15	42.555	Y= 1.5483*X+ 183.62	1574.5	Y	221.13	22.659	Y=-10.682*X+ 472.15	0.0000

The plots are presented in Output 12.6. The plot on the left contains only cases that have acceptable values for both variables; the plot on the right presents only those points for which at least one value is estimated.

● CLASSIFYING CASES INTO GROUPS

Cases can by classified into groups by specifying a GROUPING variable in the *VARiable* paragraph. The GROUPING variable must be discrete (have a limited number of values). CODEs must be specified in the *GROUP* paragraph for the GROUPING variables. If the groups are NAMED, distinct names must be specified for each group. *(Note: these requirements are more restrictive than in other programs.)*

A GROUPING variable modifies the following computations:

- Sample sizes, number of complete cases and percent of "incomplete" cases are printed for each group.

- For each variable the sample size and percent missing data are printed for each group.

- For each group a panel of univariate statistics is printed.

- Covariances are computed by using deviations from the group means to produce a pooled within-groups covariance matrix.

- Correlations are computed from the within-groups covariance matrix.

- The pooled (within-groups) covariance matrix and group means are used in the various methods of estimating missing values.

- The group means are used for all the methods of estimating missing values.

- The Mahalanobis distance is computed from each case to the mean of its group.

Cases in which the grouping variable is missing (i.e., cases that cannot be assigned to groups) are eliminated from all computations. If the GROUPING variable is missing and GROUP is specified in the *ESTimate* paragraph the missing value of the GROUPING variable is estimated and the other missing values in that case are estimated as if the GROUPING variable were known to be equal to its estimated value.

VARiable
    GROUPING= v.   {no grouping/prev.}

    The name or subscript of the variable used to classify the cases into groups. A *GROUP* paragraph (Section 5.4) <u>must</u> be included to specify <u>CODE</u>s (not CUTPOINTs) for the GROUPING variable. If the groups are named each name must be distinct. Grouping the cases modifies the computations as described above. If GROUPING is not specified or is set to zero, there is no grouping variable.

ESTimate
   GROUP.   {no}

   If GROUP is specified, missing values of the GROUPING variable
   are estimated. An estimate for a missing value is first obtained
   by the METHOD specified; the nearest CODE is used as the value
   of the GROUPING variable.

We demonstrate the effect of a GROUPING variable by the following
example.

Example 12.7

```
/PROBLEM     TITLE IS 'WERNER BLOOD CHEMISTRY DATA'.
/INPUT       VARIABLES ARE 9.
             FORMAT IS '(A4,5F4.0,3F4.1)'.
/VARIABLE    NAMES ARE ID,AGE,HEIGHT,WEIGHT,BRTHPILL,
                  CHOLSTRL,ALBUMIN,CALCIUM,URICACID.
             MAXIMUM IS (6)400.
             MINIMUM IS (6)150.
             BLANKS ARE MISSING.
             LABEL IS ID.
             GROUPING IS BRTHPILL.

/GROUP       CODES(5) ARE      1,    2.
             NAMES(5) ARE NOPILL, PILL.

/ESTIMATE    METHOD IS REGR.
             MINIMUM.
             MAXIMUM.

/END
```

The results are presented in Output 12.7. They can be compared with those
in Outputs 12.4 and 12.5, for which a GROUPING variable was not specified.

● CASE WEIGHTs

   Cases can be weighted by specifying a WEIGHT variable in the *VARiable*
paragraph. The effect the weight variable has on computing means, covariances
and correlations is described in P8D (p. 345). The weighted correlation
matrix is used in estimating missing data; its inverse is used in computing
the Mahalanobis distance.

VARiable
   WEIGHT=v.   {no case weights/prev.}

   Name or subscript of the variable containing weights for each case.
   The effect case weights have on computations is described in P8D
   (p. 345). If WEIGHT is not specified or is set to zero, there is
   no case weight variable.

Output 12.7   Effect of a GROUPING variable on an analysis by PAM. Compare
this output with Outputs 12.4 and 12.5.

```
WEIGHT VARIABLE . . . . . . . . . . . . . . .
GROUPING VARIABLE . . . . . . . . . . . . . . .          5 BRTHPILL
```

```
PATTERN OF MISSING DATA AND DATA BEYOND LIMITS
COUNT OF MISSING VARIABLES INCLUDES DATA BEYOND LIMITS.
THE COLUMN LABELED WT. IS FOR THE CASE WEIGHT, IF ANY.  'M'
REPRESENTS A MISSING VALUE.  'B' REPRESENTS A VALUE GREATER
THAN THE MAXIMUM LIMIT.  'S' REPRESENTS A VALUE LESS THAN THE
MINIMUM LIMIT.

                                A H W C A C U
                                G E E H L A R
                                F I I O B L I
                                  G G L U C C
                                  H H S M I A
                       NO OF    W T T T I U C
          CASE   CASE  MISS.    T   R N M I
          LABEL  NO.  VARS.   GROUP .     L     D

          1946     2    2 PILL              B     M
          1797     4    1 PILL              S
             3    51    1 NOPILL                M
          2877    86    1 PILL           M
            63   103    2 NOPILL                    M M
          2456   121    2 NOPILL        M     M
             5   161    1 NOPILL              M
          1149   185    2 NOPILL        M          M


          NUMBER OF CASES READ. . . . . . . . . . . . . . . . . .      188

            NUMBER OF CASES WITH NO DATA MISSING AND WITH
               POSITIVE CASE WEIGHT. . . . . . . . . . . . . .      180
```

```
                         BEFORE TRANSFORMATION                          INTERVAL RANGE
          VARIABLE      MINIMUM   MAXIMUM    MISSING    CATEGORY  CATEGORY   GREATER   LESS THAN
          NO. NAME      LIMIT     LIMIT      CODE       CODE      NAME       THAN      OR EQUAL TO

          5   BRTHPILL                                  1.00000   NOPILL
                                                        2.00000   PILL
```

```
TABLE OF SAMPLE SIZES
(PERCENTAGES OF MISSING INCLUDE CASES WITH ANY VARIABLE
MISSING OR BEYOND MAXIMUM OR MINIMUM LIMITS)

      GROUP     SIZE    COMPLETE CASES    PERCENT MISSING

    NOPILL       94          89               5.3
    PILL         94          91               3.2
```

```
SAMPLE SIZES FOR EACH VARIABLE IN EACH GROUP
VARIABLES WITHOUT MISSING DATA ARE NOT INCLUDED.
                NOPILL   PILL
                   1      2

    HEIGHT     3     92      94
    WEIGHT     4     93      93
    CHOLSTRL   6     94      92
    ALBUMIN    7     92      94
    CALCIUM    8     92      93
    URICACID   9     93      94
```

```
PERCENTAGES OF MISSING DATA FOR EACH VARIABLE IN EACH GROUP

THESE PERCENTAGES ARE BASED ON SAMPLE SIZES AND GROUP SIZES
REPORTED WITH THE UNIVARIATE SUMMARY STATISTICS BELOW.
VARIABLES WITHOUT MISSING DATA ARE NOT INCLUDED.

                NOPILL   PILL
                   1      2

    HEIGHT     3    2.1     0.0
    WEIGHT     4    1.1     1.1
    CHOLSTRL   6    0.0     2.1
    ALBUMIN    7    2.1     0.0
    CALCIUM    8    2.1     1.1
    URICACID   9    1.1     0.0
```

(continued)

Output 12.7 *(continued)*

UNIVARIATE SUMMARY STATISTICS

GROUP IS NOPILL   SIZE IS   94

VARIABLE	SAMPLE SIZE	MEAN	STANDARD DEVIATION	COEFFICIENT OF VARIATION	SMALLEST VALUE	LARGEST VALUE	SMALLEST STANDARD SCORE	LARGEST STANDARD SCORE	SKEWNESS	KURTOSIS
2 AGE	94	33.81915	10.13984	0.299825	19.00000	55.00000	-1.46	2.09	0.41	-1.00
3 HEIGHT	92	64.08696	2.49242	0.038891	57.00000	69.00000	-2.84	1.97	-0.24	-0.07
4 WEIGHT	93	130.15054	18.88693	0.145116	95.00000	195.00000	-1.86	3.43	0.73	1.71
6 CHOLSTRL	94	232.96809	43.49155	0.186685	155.00000	335.00000	-1.79	2.35	0.29	-2.01
7 ALBUMIN	92	4.19783	0.34513	0.082217	3.20000	5.00000	-2.89	2.32	-0.05	0.10
8 CALCIUM	92	9.98913	0.50349	0.050404	8.60000	11.10000	-2.76	2.21	-0.12	-0.36
9 URICACID	93	4.74194	1.03518	0.218303	2.50000	7.80000	-2.17	2.95	0.50	-0.40

--- univariate statistics for the second group ---

--- ⑤ to ⑧ from Output 12.4 appear here ---

CORRELATIONS
(COMPUTED FROM POOLED WITHIN GROUPS COVARIANCE MATRIX)

		AGE 2	HEIGHT 3	WEIGHT 4	CHOLSTRL 6	ALBUMIN 7	CALCIUM 8	URICACID 9
AGE	2	1.000						
HEIGHT	3	0.079	1.000					
WEIGHT	4	0.252	0.464	1.000				
CHOLSTRL	6	0.368	0.008	0.143	1.000			
ALBUMIN	7	-0.071	0.020	-0.245	0.073	1.000		
CALCIUM	8	-0.031	0.160	0.075	0.256	0.441	1.000	
URICACID	9	0.176	0.132	0.299	0.259	0.011	0.195	1.000

SQUARED MULTIPLE CORRELATIONS OF EACH VARIABLE WITH ALL OTHER VARIABLES
(MEASURES OF MULTICOLLINEARITY OF VARIABLES)
AND TESTS OF SIGNIFICANCE OF MULTIPLE REGRESSION
DEGREES OF FREEDOM FOR F-STATISTICS ARE   6 AND   180

VARIABLE NO.	NAME	SMC	F-STATISTIC	SIGNIFICANCE (P LESS THAN)
2	AGE	0.197489	7.38	0.00000
3	HEIGHT	0.248362	9.91	0.00000
4	WEIGHT	0.373320	17.87	0.00000
6	CHOLSTRL	0.235604	9.25	0.00000
7	ALBUMIN	0.280552	11.70	0.00000
8	CALCIUM	0.301196	12.93	0.00000
9	URICACID	0.154925	5.50	0.00003

EIGENVALUES OF ORIGINAL CORRELATION MATRIX

```
1.9758
1.5360
1.1881
0.8093
0.6169
0.4832
0.3907
```

ESTIMATES OF MISSING DATA, MAHALANOBIS D-SQUARED (CHI-SQUARED)
AND SQUARED MULTIPLE CORRELATIONS WITH AVAILABLE VARIABLES

CASE LABEL	CASE NUMBER	MISSING VARIABLE	ESTIMATE	R-SQUARED	GROUP	CHI-SQ	CHISQ/DF	D.F.	SIGNIFICANCE
2381	1				NOPILL	4.677	0.668	7	0.6993
1946	2	6 CHOLSTRL	237.3527	0.188	PILL	10.793	2.159	5	0.0556
1946	2	8 CALCIUM	9.8481	0.258	PILL	10.793	2.159	5	0.0556
1610	3				NOPILL	5.267	0.752	7	0.6274
1797	4	6 CHOLSTRL	205.2696	0.236	PILL	6.342	1.057	6	0.3860

--- similar statistics for cases 5 to 184 ---

1149	185	3 HEIGHT	66.6665	0.241	NOPILL	8.419	1.684	5	0.1346
1149	185	8 CALCIUM	9.8471	0.294	NOPILL	8.419	1.684	5	0.1346
575	186				PILL	10.813	1.545	7	0.1470
2271	187				NOPILL	6.594	0.942	7	0.4724
39	188				PILL	22.041	3.149	7	0.0025

ESTIMATION OF MISSING DATA COMPLETED

- SAVING THE DATA, ITS COVARIANCE MATRIX, OR THE CORRELATION
  MATRIX OF THE DICHOTOMIZED VARIABLES

PAM can be used to prepare data for another program. The BMDP File
(Chapter 7) can be used to save the "completed" data matrix, including the
estimates for the missing data, the COVARIANCE matrix and the correlation
matrix formed from the dichotomized values (CORRDICH, p. 359). The data or
matrices can be further analyzed by other BMDP programs.

PAM is primarily intended to serve as a preprocessor for multivariate
analysis. For example, the missing values can be replaced by estimates and
then a factor analysis, discriminant analysis, repeated measures analysis of
variance or cluster analysis can be requested. The grouping variable, if it
is missing, should not ordinarily be estimated. If PAM is used as a preprocessor for regression, estimates of missing data for the independent variables should not be made if the independent variables are fixed. If some
independent variables are random, they should be estimated from other random
predictors but not from the dependent variable. Missing values of the dependent variable should not ordinarily be estimated prior to regression analysis
since the R^2 in the regression analysis would then be inflated. If you
estimate missing values of the dependent variable for regression, analysis of
variance or analysis of covariance, care should be taken in making inferences
on the data with the estimates since the residual mean square will be too
small and R^2 too big. Thus, while estimation of missing values may allow exploratory data analysis, rigorous hypothesis testing cannot be performed.

When there are missing data for the dependent variable in a repeated
measures analysis of variance (P2V), an entire case is deleted if any dependent variable is missing. PAM may be used to estimate the dependent variable,
but bias enters the analysis. However, the bias will be small if the number
of missing values is small. In some studies it may be preferable to eliminate
cases with missing data; in others, the number of levels of the repeated
measures factors may be so large that the number of cases with some missing
data may be very large, and so it may be better to estimate missing data.
Methods of treating missing data problems are discussed by Frane (1976) and
Beale and Little (1975).

```
SAVE
    CONTENT= (one or more)  DATA,COVA,CORRDICH.       {DATA}
       The matrix to be saved.
          DATA       -- the data with missing values replaced by estimates.
                          if any.
          COVA       -- the covariance matrix.  If a GROUPING variable
                          is specified, the pooled within-group covariance
                          matrix is saved.
          CORRDICH -- the correlation matrix for the dichotomies (see p. 359)
```

In our final example we save the data and the covariance matrix in a BMDP
File and then further analyze COVA by P4M (Factor Analysis, Section 18.1).

Example 12.8a

```
/PROBLEM      TITLE IS 'WERNER BLOOD CHEMISTRY DATA'.
/INPUT        VARIABLES ARE 9.
              FORMAT IS '(A4,5F4.0,3F4.1)'.
/VARIABLE     NAMES ARE ID,AGE,HEIGHT,WEIGHT,BRTHPILL,
                  CHOLSTRL,ALBUMIN,CALCIUM,URICACID.
              MAXIMUM IS (6)400.
              MINIMUM IS (6)150.
              BLANKS ARE MISSING.
              LABEL IS ID.

/ESTIMATE     METHOD IS REGR.
              MINIMUM.
              MAXIMUM.

/SAVE         UNIT IS 4.
              NEW.
              CODE IS WERNER.
              CONTENT IS DATA,COVA.

/END
```

Note: The System Cards that precede the Control Language must contain a card describing where to store the BMDP File (Section 7.1). At HSCF, the System Cards are

```
//jobname  JOB  nooo,yourname
//  EXEC  BIMED,PROG=BMDPAM
//FT04F001  DD  DSNAME=FS.nooo.filename,DISP=OLD
//SYSIN  DD  *
```

In addition space must be allocated for the system file (Section 7.1).

Example 12.8b

```
/PROBLEM      TITLE IS 'WERNER BLOOD CHEMISTRY DATA'.
/INPUT        UNIT IS 4.
              CODE IS WERNER.
              CONTENT IS COVA.

/END
```

The Control Language must be preceded by System Cards to initiate an analysis by P4M and to specify the system file containing the BMDP File (Section 7.3).

```
//jobname  JOB  nooo,yourname
//  EXEC  BIMED,PROG=BMDP4M
//FT04F001  DD  DSNAME=FS.nooo.filename,DISP=OLD
//SYSIN  DD  *
```

where filename is the same filename as in Example 12.8a. The Control Language is terminated by another System Card. At HSCF, this System Card is

```
//
```

● SIZE OF PROBLEM

When correlations are computed or when missing values are estimated by any METHOD except MEAN, about 60 variables and 10 groups can be analyzed. If METHOD is MEAN or NONE and a correlation matrix is not computed, about 130 variables and 10 groups can be analyzed or about 400 variables when there is no grouping variable. Appendix B describes how to increase the capacity of the program.

<u>Outputs 12.8 a and b.</u> Creating a BMDP File with PAM (a) and using
                          it in P4M (b).

<u>12.8a</u>

```
BMDPAM - DESCRIPTION AND ESTIMATION OF MISSING DATA        PROGRAM REVISED SEPTEMBER 1977
HEALTH SCIENCES COMPUTING FACILITY                         MANUAL DATE --  1977
UNIVERSITY OF CALIFORNIA, LOS ANGELES


    REQUESTED OUTPUT BMDP FILE . . . UNIT. . .        4
                                     CODE. . .    WERNER
                                     LABEL . .
                                     CONTENT .
                                                 COVA
                                                 DATA
```

--- results in Output 12.4 are printed here ---

```
BMDP FILE WRITTEN ON UNIT      4
                     CODE. . . IS      WERNER
                     CONTENT . IS      COVA
                     LABEL . . IS
                     VARIABLES     2  AGE       3  HEIGHT     4  WEIGHT     5  BRTHPILL     6  CHOLSTRL
                                   7  ALBUMIN   8  CALCIUM    9  URICACID

    BMDP FILE ON UNIT 4 HAS BEEN COMPLETED.

BMDP FILE WRITTEN ON UNIT      4
                     CODE. . . IS      WERNER
                     CONTENT . IS      DATA
                     LABEL . . IS
                     VARIABLES     1  ID        2  AGE        3  HEIGHT     4  WEIGHT       5  BRTHPILL
                                   6  CHCLSTRL  7  ALBUMIN    8  CALCIUM    9  URICACID
```

--- ⑬ from Output 12.5 appears here ---

```
    BMDP FILE ON UNIT 4 HAS BEEN COMPLETED.
```

<u>12.8b</u>

```
BMDP4M - FACTOR ANALYSIS                                   PROGRAM REVISED SEPTEMBER 1977
HEALTH SCIENCES COMPUTING FACILITY                         MANUAL DATE --  1977
UNIVERSITY OF CALIFORNIA, LOS ANGELES


    INPUT FORMAT
            BMDP FILE . . . . . CODE. . . IS     WERNER
                                CONTENT . IS     COVA
                                LABEL . . IS
                                VARIABLES    2  AGE      3  HEIGHT     4  WEIGHT     5  BRTHPILL     6  CHOLSTRL
                                             7  ALBUMIN  8  CALCIUM    9  URICACID

VARIABLES TO BE USED
             2  AGE       3  HEIGHT      4  WEIGHT     5  BRTHPILL     6  CHOLSTRL
             7  ALBUMIN   8  CALCIUM     9  URICACID

NUMBER OF VARIABLES TO BE USED. . . . . . . .    8

INPUT CORRELATION OR COVARIANCE MATRIX COMPUTED WITH MISSING DATA.

    VARIABLE
NO.       NAME     SAMPLE SIZE    SUM OF WEIGHTS

    2  AGE              188.          188.000
    3  HEIGHT           186.          186.000
    4  WEIGHT           186.          186.000
    5  BRTHPILL         188.          188.000
    6  CHOLSTRL         186.          186.000
    7  ALBUMIN          186.          186.000
    8  CALCIUM          185.          185.000
    9  URICACID         187.          187.000

HARMONIC MEAN OF SAMPLE SIZES    186
```

```
CORRELATION MATRIX
              AGE      HEIGHT    WEIGHT   BRTHPILL  CHOLSTRL  ALBUMIN   CALCIUM   URICACID
               2         3         4         5         6         7         8         9

AGE       2   1.000
HEIGHT    3   0.080    1.000
WEIGHT    4   0.252    0.471    1.000
BRTHPILL  5   0.0      0.169    0.074    1.000
CHOLSTRL  6   0.368    0.020    0.148    0.076    1.000
ALBUMIN   7  -0.072   -0.021   -0.255   -0.240    0.053    1.000
CALCIUM   8  -0.032    0.149    0.070   -0.056    0.250    0.444    1.000
URICACID  9   0.176    0.134    0.300    0.025    0.260    0.007    0.194    1.000
```

---results of the factor analysis are also printed ---

● COMPUTATIONAL METHOD

The data are read in single precision. Computations are performed in double precision except for the matrix of sum of weights (SUMW), which is computed in single precision.

The data are read in casewise and written on a scratch file. Univariate statistics and the covariance matrix are computed using either complete cases only or using all values as in the ALLVALUE option in P8D. (The covariance matrix is not computed when it is not required in any computations or for printing.)

If the ALLVALUE option is selected, the data are read twice. During the first reading, the univariate statistics are computed using the method of provisional means (Appendix A.2); during the second pass, the covariance matrix is computed. Two passes are required in order to conserve computer memory. If complete cases only are used, the data are read once and the covariance matrix is also computed by the method of provisional means. When a grouping variable is specified, the pooled within-groups covariance matrix is computed.

If case weights are used, weights are adjusted so that the average nonzero weight is one.

The methods of estimating missing values are described in Appendix A.10.

ACKNOWLEDGEMENT

PAM was designed and programmed by James Frane.

The Control Language on this page is common to all programs. Summaries on the next two pages show the Control Language specific to

P8D -- Missing Value Correlation   p. 372
PAM -- Description and Estimation of Missing Data   p. 373

Paragraph STATEMENT[1] {Preassigned value[2]}		Definition, restriction	See pages:
/PROBlem		Required each problem	74
TITLE='c'.	{blank}	Problem title, $\leq$ 160 char.	74
/INPut		Required first problem. Either VARIABLE and FORMAT, or UNIT and CODE required.	75
VARIABLE=#.	{none/prev.}	No. of variables in input data	75
FORMAT='c'.	{none/prev.}	Format of input data, $\leq$ 800 char.	76
CASE=#.	{end-of-file/prev.}	No. of cases in data	76-77
UNIT=#.	{5(cards)/prev.}	Input unit if data are not on cards; not 1, 2, 6	77
REWIND.	{REWIND/prev.}	Rewind input unit	77
CODE=c.	{none}	Code to identify BMDP File	132
CONTENT=c.	{DATA}	Data or matrix in BMDP File	132
LABEL=c.	{none}	Label of BMDP File, $\leq$ 40 char.	132
/VARiable		Optional. For input from a BMDP File, items in this paragraph may be previously set, see Chapter 7.	79
NAME=c_1,c_2,$\cdots$.	{X(subscript)/prev.}	Variable names, one per variable	79-80
MAXIMUM=$\#_1$,$\#_2$,$\cdots$.	{none/prev.}	Upper limits, one per variable	80
MINIMUM=$\#_1$,$\#_2$,$\cdots$.	{none/prev.}	Lower limits, one per variable	80
BLANK= (one only) ZERO, MISSING.	{ZERO/prev.}	Blanks treated as zeros or as missing value codes	81
MISSING=$\#_1$,$\#_2$,$\cdots$.	{none/prev.}	Missing value codes, one per variable	81
USE=v_1,v_2,$\cdots$.	{all variables}	Variables used in the analysis	82
LABEL=v_1,v_2.	{none/prev.}	Variable(s) used to label cases, read under A-format, one or two	83
ADD=#.	{0/prev.}	No. of variables added through transformation	99
BEFORE. or AFTER.	{BEFORE/prev.}	Data checked for limits before or after transformation	100
/TRANSform		Optional, Control Language transformations and case selection	97-105
/SAVE		Optional, required to create BMDP File	125
CODE=c.	{none}	Code to identify BMDP File, required	125-126
LABEL='c'.	{blank}	Label for BMDP File, $\leq$ 40 char.	125-126
UNIT=#.	{none}	Unit on which BMDP File is written; not 1, 2, 5 or 6	126-127
NEW.	{not new}	NEW if this is first BMDP File written in the system file	126-127

Key: #   number   v   variable name or subscript
     'c'   title, label or format   c   name not exceeding 8 char., apostrophes may be required (p. 59)

[1] In BMDP programs dated before August 1977, the minimum required abbreviations are INPUT (not INP), VARIAB (not VAR), FORMAT (not FORM), CONTENT (not CONT), VARIAB (not VAR), BEFORET (not BEF), AFTERT (not AFT), TRANSF (not TRAN). If dated before February 1976, BLANK=ZERO and cannot be changed.

[2] "/prev." means that any assignment remains the same as that specified in the previous problem or subproblem until changed. Otherwise, the assignment returns to its preassigned value each time a new problem begins or the paragraph is used again.

P8D -- Missing Value Correlation

(in addition to that on p. 371)

Paragraph STATEMENT[1] {Preassigned value}		Definition, restriction	See pages:
VARiable		Specify as part of *VARiable* paragraph, p.371	
ROW=$v_1,v_2,\cdots$.	{all variables/prev.}	Row variables for covariance or correlation matrix	343
COLUMN=$v_1,v_2,\cdots$.	{all variables/prev.}	Column variables for covariance or correlation matrix	343
WEIGHT=v.	{no weight var./prev.}	Variable containing case weights	345
SAVE		Specify as part of *SAVE* paragraph, p. 371	
CONTENT= *(one or more)* DATA,COVA,CORR.	{DATA/prev.}	Matrices to be saved in BMDP File	345-346
/CORRelation		Optional	
TYPE= *(one or more)* ALLVALUE,COVPAIR,CORPAIR. *or* TYPE=COMPLETE.	{CORPAIR/prev.}	Method to compute correlations	341
SEGMENT.	{no/prev.}	Matrices too large to be processed at one time are processed in segments	346-347
/PRINT		Optional	
FREQUENCY.	{FREQUENCY/prev.}	Print table of pairwise frequencies	342
CORRELATION.	{CORRELATION/prev.}	Print correlation matrix	342
COVARIANCE.	{no/prev.}	Print covariance matrix	342
MEAN.	{no/prev.}	Print matrix of pairwise means	342
VARIANCE.	{no/prev.}	Print matrix of pairwise variances	342
SUMWEIGHT.	{no/prev.}	Print matrix of sums of weight	342
/END		Required	57

Key: v variable name or subscript

[1] In BMDP programs dated before August 1977, the minimum required abbreviation is SUMWTS (not SUMW); SEGMENT is not available.

- Order of input

(1) System Cards, at HSCF these are
```
//jobname JOB nooo,yourname
//   EXEC  BIMED,PROG=BMDP8D
//SYSIN DD  *
```

(2) Control Language instructions
```
PROBLem paragraph, required
INPut paragraph, required first problem
VARiable paragraph
TRANsform paragraph
SAVE paragraph
CORRelation paragraph
PRINT paragraph
END paragraph, required at end of Control Language
```

(3) Data, if on cards
```
data
```

(4) System Card, at HSCF this is
```
//
```

Control Language instructions and data (2 and 3) can be repeated for additional problems.

PAM -- Description and Estimation of Missing Data

(in addition to that on p. 371)

Paragraph STATEMENT[1] {Preassigned value}		Definition, restriction	See pages:
VARiable		Specify as part of *VARiable* paragraph, p.371	
WEIGHT=v.	{no weight var./prev.}	Variable containing case weights	364
GROUPING=v.	{no grouping var./prev.}	Variable used to classify cases into groups	363
/GROUP		Required if GROUPING variable is specified	363
CODE(#)=$\#_1,\#_2,\cdots$	{none}	Codes for variable #, required	84-85
NAME=(#)=$\#_1,\#_2,\cdots$.	{CODEs }	Group names for variable #. If specified, each must be distinct.	84-85
RESET.	{not RESET }	If RESET, all assignments in previous *GROUP* paragraph are reset to preassigned values	86
SAVE		Specify as part of *SAVE* paragraph, p.371	
CONTENT= (one or more) DATA,COVA,CORRDICH.	{DATA /prev. }	Matrices to be saved in BMDP File	367
/ESTimate		Optional	
TYPE= (one only) ALLVALUE,COMPLETE.	{ALLVALUE /prev.}	Method to compute covariances and correlations	352-353
METHOD= (one only) NONE,MEAN,SINGLE,TWOSTEP, STEP,REGR.	{NONE/prev.}	Method to estimate missing data	353-354
MAXIMUM.	{no/prev.}	Reestimate values greater than specified upper limit	355
MINIMUM.	{no/prev.}	Reestimate values less than specified lower limit	355
GROUP.	{no/prev.}	Reestimate missing group code.	364
ENTER=#.	{4/prev.}	F-to-enter criterion	357
ZERO.	{no/prev.}	Compute estimates from regression equation without intercept	357
TOLERANCE=#.	{0.0001/prev.}	Tolerance for matrix inversion	358
VLIMIT=#.	{no. of var.-1/prev.}	Case dropped if number of variables exceeds VLIM	358
CLIMIT=#.	{50/prev.}	Maximum percentage of missing cases permitted for any variable	358
/PRINT		Optional	
CASE=#.	{5/prev.}	No. of cases for which data are printed	359
MATRICES= (one or more) PAT,FREQ,CORRDICH,CORR, EIGEN,EST,DIS,COVA,CREG,RREG,SUMW.	{PAT,FREQ,CORRDICH,CORR, EIGEN,EST,DIS/prev.}	Matrices to be printed	359-361
/PLOT			
XVAR=$v_1,v_2,\cdots$.	{none}	Variables for X-axes of plots	361
YVAR=$v_1,v_2,\cdots$.	{none}	Variables for Y-axes of plots	361
SIZE=$\#_1,\#_2$.	{50,50/prev.}	Length of X and Y axes	361
/END		Required	57

Key: # number
     v variable name or subscript

[1] PAM was originally released in August 1976. In BMDP programs dated before August 1977, the minimum required abbreviation is CONTENT (not CONT); in the CONTENT statement, use CORRF (not CORRDICH); in the METHOD statement, use SIMPLE (not SINGLE), STEPWISE (not STEP) and REGRES (not REGR); in the MATRICES statement, use CORRF (not CORRDICH), INVCV (not CREG) and INVCR (not RREG); when a *GROUP* paragraph is used, RESET is implicitly specified and cannot be changed.

- Order of input

(1) System Cards, at HSCF these are

```
//jobname JOB nooo,yourname
//   EXEC  BIMED,PROG=BMDPAM
//SYSIN  DD  *
```

(2) Control Language instructions

```
PROBlem paragraph, required
INPut paragraph, required first problem
VARiable paragraph
GROUP paragraph
TRANsform paragraph
SAVE paragraph
ESTimate paragraph
PRINT paragraph
PLOT paragraph
END paragraph, required at end of Control Language
```

(3) Data, if on cards

```
data
```

(4) System Card, at HSCF this is

```
//
```

Control Language instructions and data (2 and 3) can be repeated for additional problems

13

REGRESSION

Regression is used to quantify the relationship between variables when the value of one variable is affected by changes in the values of other variables. The affected variable is the dependent (predicted) variable and the others are the independent (predictor) variables. The correlation between two variables can indicate whether an increase in one variable is associated with an increase in the other variable.

The relationship between a dependent variable y and an independent variable x is linear if the expected value of y can be expressed as $\alpha + \beta x$; i.e.,

$$E(y) = \alpha + \beta x$$

where α and β are the coefficients (parameters) of the regression equation. α is called the intercept and β the slope of the regression.

When there is one independent variable, as in the above equation, the regression is called simple linear regression. The program P6D -- Bivariate (Scatter) Plots -- (Section 10.2) can plot one variable against the other, estimate the regression equation relating the variables, and indicate on the frame of the plot where to draw the regression line. Two programs described in this chapter (P1R and P2R) can also be used to estimate the parameters of a simple linear regression.

A model of multiple linear regression is written as

$$E(y) = \alpha + \beta_1 x_1 + \beta_2 x_2 + \ldots$$

where $x_1, x_2, \ldots$ are the independent variables and $\beta_1, \beta_2, \ldots$ their regression coefficients. When the model has this form, the selection of variables to be in the model can be a major problem; data may have been collected on more variables than are necessary in the model, or an important variable that is needed in the model may have been omitted from the study.

In this chapter we describe

P1R --	Multiple Linear Regression	p. 380
P2R --	Stepwise Regression	p. 399
P9R --	All Possible Subsets Regression	p. 418
P4R --	Regression on Principal Components	p. 437

These programs differ in three important respects: the criterion for including independent variables in the multiple linear regression, the ability to repeat the analysis on subgroups of the cases and compare the subgroups, and the residual analysis available.

We also describe a fifth program

P5R --	Polynomial Regression	p. 444

P5R is used when the expected value of the dependent variable can be approximated by a polynomial expression in terms of a single independent variable.

P1R estimates the multiple linear regression equation using all the independent variables. Results are reported only for the equation containing all the variables. The regression can be estimated from all the cases, and also from cases in separate groups if specified. When the cases are in groups, the regression equations are tested for equality across groups. Equality of slopes (with possibly different intercepts) is tested in P1V (Section 15.1).

P2R enters and removes variables from a multiple linear regression equation in a stepwise manner. That is, at each step variables are removed and/or entered into the equation, according to one of four criteria. Forward stepping (beginning with no predictors) and backward stepping (beginning with all predictors) are possible. The order of entry of the variables can be predetermined, partially specified or determined only by the criteria for entry and removal of variables.

P9R identifies "best" subsets of predictor variables. Best is defined in terms of the sample R-squared, adjusted R-squared, or Mallows' C_p. For example, if adjusted R-squared is chosen, the best subset is the subset that maximizes adjusted R-squared. The number of best subsets (up to ten) can be specified. Thus, not only the best but also the second best, third best, etc. subsets are identified to provide several good alternatives.

P4R computes a regression analysis for the dependent variable on a set of principal components computed from the independent variables. The principal components are computed from the original variables (using the covariance matrix). The regression analysis is performed in a stepwise manner and the resulting coefficients are reported in terms of both the principal components and the original or standardized variables. The order of entry of components can be based on the magnitude of eigenvalues or on the absolute value of correlation between the component and the dependent variable.

The methods of variable selection differ in P2R, P9R and P4R. P9R optimizes a criterion by searching the relevant subsets of the variables (not all subsets are computed) by the Furnival and Wilson (1974a,b) algorithm. It can treat at most 27 independent variables and is about as fast as stepwise regression for this number of variables. P2R can treat a much larger problem (about 150 variables) but reports a simple series of solutions (at different steps). P4R is most valuable when subsets of the independent variables are highly correlated or when the number of variables is large relative to the number of cases; the principal components provide linear combinations of the independent variables to be entered stepwise into the regression equation.

The solutions obtained by P2R, P9R and P4R are all based on the data supplied. Other samples from the same population can be expected to lead to other "optimal" solutions that will differ to some degree from each other. This problem is common to all statistical procedures, including these variable selection methods. The alternative subsets provided by P9R may help the analyst evaluate the "uniqueness" of the solution.

P9R uses double precision for many of its computations. The other programs use only single precision. The precision can be important when the coefficient of variation is very small or when the correlation matrix for the predictor variables is nearly singular.

Programs P1R, P2R, P4R and P9R estimate the regression coefficients and their standard errors and print the covariance and correlation matrices. They all print and plot predicted values and residuals against the variables. P9R can perform more extensive analyses of residuals than the other programs: it can compute and plot standardized residuals, the residual for each case based upon omitting the case from the regression analysis, and Cook's measure of the influence of each case on the regression equation.

Each program can begin an analysis from the data or from a covariance or correlation matrix. A BMDP File can be created that contains a covariance matrix or that contains residuals and predicted values as well as the data.

Cases with missing values or values out of range are not used by these programs. If too many cases are affected by this restriction, you may first want to read Chapter 12 and use a missing value covariance or correlation matrix as input to these regression programs.

P5R is used when the dependent variable has a nonlinear relationship with one independent variable that can be approximated by a low order polynomial. The degree of the polynomial is determined in a stepwise manner. Orthogonal polynomials are used in the computation. Goodness-of-fit statistics are printed for each polynomial, except the one with the highest degree. The predicted values and residuals can be plotted against the independent variable.

In the regression equations described above we wrote the expected value of y, E(y), rather than y. If we write y, then an error term must be added. That is,

$$E(y) = \alpha + \beta x$$

is equivalent to

$$y = \alpha + \beta x + \varepsilon$$

where ε represents an error term (with mean zero). If the error term has a constant variance across all cases, least squares regression (used by these programs) is the usual method of estimating the coefficients. If the error term's variance is not constant, weighted least squares regression is more appropriate; the data in each case are weighted by the inverse of the variance for that case. All regression programs except P4R allow case weights to be specified.

Some apparently nonlinear relationships between x and y can also be analyzed by linear regression. For example,

$$E(y) = \alpha + \beta/x$$

is nonlinear in x but linear in $z = 1/x$ and

$$E(y) = \alpha + \beta e^X$$

is nonlinear in x but linear in $z = e^X$. The transformation $z = 1/x$ or $z = e^X$ can be done as part of the analysis.

Case weights may be required when a nonlinear function is transformed into a linear function by modifying the dependent variable. For example

$$E(y) = \alpha e^{\beta X} \qquad \text{or} \qquad y = \alpha e^{\beta X} + \varepsilon$$

is often transformed to

$$ln(y) = \alpha' + \beta x + \varepsilon'$$

where $\alpha' = ln(\alpha)$ and ε' is the error term for $ln(y)$. However, if ε in the original equation has constant variance across cases, then ε' <u>cannot</u> have constant variance and case weights are desirable for the latter analysis.

Many nonlinear functions cannot be transformed to linear, such as the sum of two exponentials

$$E(y) = \beta_1 e^{\beta_2 X} + \beta_3 e^{\beta_4 X}$$

Methods of estimating the coefficients of nonlinear regressions are described in Chapter 14.

When there is more than one dependent variable, the interrelations of the variables can be studied by multivariate methods (Chapter 18). Categorical (multinomial) data can be fitted by a log-linear model (Section 11.3).

● CONTROL LANGUAGE

The Control Language instructions to describe the data and variables are common to all BMDP programs and are explained in Chapter 5: the *PROBlem*, *INPut*[1] and *VARiable* paragraphs are used in all the regression analysis programs; the *GROUP* paragraph can be used in P1R.

---

[1] BMDP programs dated before August 1977 require more letters in their permissible abbreviated form (the capitalized letters). Their minimum required abbreviations are specified in footnotes to the summary (p. 453).

If data editing or transformations are necessary, the methods described in Chapter 6 can be used. Data can be read using a FORMAT statement or from a BMDP File (Chapter 7).

A summary of the Control Language instructions common to all BMDP programs is on p. 453; summaries of the Control Language instructions specific to each program described in this chapter follow the general summary. These summaries can be used as indexes to the program descriptions.

P1R

13.1 Multiple Linear Regression

P1R estimates a multiple linear regression that relates a dependent variable to several independent variables. Let y represent the value of the dependent variable and $x_1, x_2, \ldots, x_p$ the values of the independent variables. P1R estimates by least squares the coefficients $\beta_1, \beta_2, \ldots, \beta_p$ in the equation

$$y = \alpha + \beta_1 x_1 + \beta_2 x_2 + \ldots + \beta_p x_p + \epsilon$$

where ϵ represents the error. That is, it finds $a, b_1, b_2, \ldots, b_p$ (the estimates of $\alpha, \beta_1, \beta_2, \ldots, \beta_p$) that minimize

$$\Sigma \, (y - a - b_1 x_1 - b_2 x_2 - \ldots - b_p x_p)^2$$

where the summation is over the cases used in the analysis. When case weights are specified,

$$\Sigma \, w(y - a - b_1 x_1 - b_2 x_2 - \ldots - b_p x_p)^2$$

is minimized, where w is the case weight.

When the cases are grouped by a GROUPING variable, P1R first estimates the regression for all groups combined, and then separately for each group. The equality of the regression lines across groups is tested.

● RESULTS

In our first example we use P1R to analyze the Werner blood chemistry data (Table 5.1). We specify that CHOLSTRL is the dependent variable and that AGE, WEIGHT and URICACID are independent variables. Only the *REGRess* paragraph is specific to P1R, the remaining Control Language instructions are common to all BMDP programs and are described in Chapter 5.

Example 13.1

```
/PROBLEM     TITLE IS 'WERNER BLOOD CHEMISTRY DATA'.
/INPUT       VARIABLES ARE 9.
             FORMAT IS '(A4,5F4.0,3F4.1)'.
/VARIABLE    NAMES ARE ID,AGE,HEIGHT,WEIGHT,BRTHPILL,
                       CHOLSTRL,ALBUMIN,CALCIUM,URICACID.
             MAXIMUM IS (6)400.
             MINIMUM IS (6)150.
             BLANKS ARE MISSING.
             LABEL IS ID.

/REGRESS     DEPENDENT IS CHOLSTRL.
             INDEPENDENT ARE AGE,WEIGHT,URICACID.

/END
```

The Control Language must be preceded by System Cards to initiate the analysis by P1R. At HSCF, the System Cards are

```
//jobname  JOB  nooo,yourname
//  EXEC  BIMED,PROG=BMDP1R
//SYSIN  DD  *
```

The Control Language is immediately followed by the data (Table 5.1). The analysis is terminated by another System Card. At HSCF, this System Card is

```
//
```

The results of the above analysis are presented in Output 13.1. Circled numbers below correspond to those in the output.

The model fitted by P1R is

$$y = a + b_1x_1 + b_2x_2 + \ldots + b_px_p + \varepsilon$$

where

y is the dependent variable

$x_1,\ldots,x_p$ are the independent variables

$b_1,\ldots,b_p$ are the regression coefficients

a is the intercept

p is the number of independent variables

ε is the error with mean zero

The predicted value $\hat{y}$ for each case is

$$\hat{y} = a + b_1x_1 + b_2x_2 + \ldots + b_px_p$$

The residual for each case is $(y-\hat{y})$. We have omitted from the formulas a subscript indicating case number.

(1) Only complete cases are used in the computations; i.e., cases that have no missing values or values out of range. Therefore only 180 of the original 188 cases are used. All variables are checked for invalid values unless USE is specified in the *VARiable* paragraph (Section 5.3), in which case only the variables in the USE statement are checked.

(2) Univariate statistics are computed for each variable using the complete cases

- mean

- standard deviation

- coefficient of variation

- minimum observed value (not out of range)

- maximum observed value (not out of range)

(3) The multiple correlation R is printed (i.e., the correlation of the dependent variable with the predicted value) as well as

- the multiple R^2

- standard error of the estimate: $\{\Sigma (y_j-\hat{y}_j)^2/(N-p)\}^{\frac{1}{2}}$

<u>Output 13.1</u> Multiple linear regression by P1R. Circled numbers correspond to those in the text. Results not reproduced are indicated in italics.

```
BMDP1R - MULTIPLE LINEAR REGRESSION                    PROGRAM REVISED SEPTEMBER 1977
HEALTH SCIENCES COMPUTING FACILITY                     MANUAL DATE -- 1977
UNIVERSITY OF CALIFORNIA, LOS ANGELES
```

--- Control Language read by P1R is printed and interpreted ---

```
REGRESSION INTERCEPT. . . . . . . . . . . . . .NON-ZERO
GROUPING VARIABLE . . . . . . . . . . . . . .
WEIGHT VARIABLE . . . . . . . . . . . . . . .
PRINT COVARIANCE MATRIX . . . . . . . . . . .          NO
PRINT CORRELATION MATRIX. . . . . . . . . . .          NO
PRINT RESIDUALS . . . . . . . . . . . . . . .          NO
PROBIT PLOT . . . . . . . . . . . . . . . . .          NO
```

(1)
```
NUMBER OF CASES READ. . . . . . . . . . . .          188
    CASES WITH DATA MISSING OR BEYOND LIMITS . .        8
        REMAINING NUMBER OF CASES . . . . . . .        180
```

(2)

VARIABLE	MEAN	STANDARD DEVIATION	COEFFICIENT OF VARIATION	MINIMUM	MAXIMUM
2 AGE	33.53819	9.89836	0.29514	19.00000	55.00000
3 HEIGHT	64.46597	2.48213	0.03850	57.00000	71.00000
4 WEIGHT	131.09384	20.49977	0.15637	94.00000	215.00000
5 BRTHPILL	1.50551	0.50136	0.33302	1.00000	2.00000
6 CHOLSTRL	235.83821	42.74364	0.18124	155.00000	390.00000
7 ALBUMIN	4.12052	0.35871	0.08706	3.20000	5.00000
8 CALCIUM	9.96773	0.47279	0.04743	8.80000	11.10000
9 URICACID	4.75551	1.12111	0.23575	2.20000	9.90000

```
REGRESSION TITLE. . . . . . . . . . . . . . .WERNER BLOOD CHEMISTRY DATA
DEPENDENT-VARIABLE. . . . . . . . . . . . . .       6 CHOLSTRL
TOLERANCE . . . . . . . . . . . . . . . . . .     0.0100
ALL DATA CONSIDERED AS A SINGLE GROUP
```

(3)
```
MULTIPLE R              0.4175      STD. ERROR OF EST.      39.1698
MULTIPLE R-SQUARE       0.1743
```

ANALYSIS OF VARIANCE

(4)

	SUM OF SQUARES	DF	MEAN SQUARE	F RATIO	P(TAIL)
REGRESSION	57004.242	3	19001.414	12.385	0.00000
RESIDUAL	270032.000	176	1534.273		

(5)

VARIABLE		COEFFICIENT	STD. ERROR	STD. REG COEFF	T	P(2 TAIL)
INTERCEPT		151.420				
AGE	2	1.390	0.309	0.322	4.497	0.000
WEIGHT	4	0.003	0.153	0.001	0.019	0.985
URICACID	9	7.871	2.769	0.206	2.843	0.005

④ The analysis of variance table for the regression is printed. It contains

    - the regression sum of squares: $\Sigma \, (\hat{y}_j - \bar{y})^2$

    - the residual sum of squares: $\Sigma \, (y_j - \hat{y}_j)^2$

    - the F ratio that tests significance of the regression

⑤ A summary table for the regression is printed. It contains

    - the coefficient: b_i

    - the standard error of the coefficient: $s(b_i)$ (Appendix A.11)

    - the standardized regression coefficient: $b_i s_x / s_y$
      (the regression coefficient for standardized variables)

    - t test for the coefficient, $b_i / s(b_i)$, and the associated two-tailed probability value

● Optional Results and Input

In addition to the above results, you can request

- the covariance and correlation matrices	p. 384
- the correlation matrix of the regression coefficients	p. 384
- residual, predicted value and data for each case	p. 384
- scatter plots, normal probability plots of residuals and partial residual plots	p. 387

Cases can be classified into groups. Each group is analyzed separately and the regression equations tested for equality between groups.   p. 391

P1R can perform weighted least squares regression.   p. 394

Input can be data, a covariance matrix or a correlation matrix. If it is a covariance or correlation matrix, it must be from a BMDP File.   p. 394

The data (including residuals and predicted values) and the covariance matrix can be saved in a BMDP File and used as input to other programs.   p. 395

● Specifying the Regression -- The *REGRess* Paragraph

The *REGRess*[2] paragraph describes the dependent (predicted) variable and the independent (predictor) variables. This paragraph can be repeated <u>before</u> the *END* paragraph to specify additional analyses of the same data.

---

[2] In BMDP programs dated before August 1977, the minimum required abbreviation is *REGRES* (not *REGR*).

The dependent variable must be specified in the first *REGRess* paragraph. If the independent variables are not specified, all other variables are considered as independent except the GROUPING variable, the case WEIGHT variable, or variables not included in a USE statement, if one is specified.

Each regression analysis can be given a separate title.

REGRess

DEPENDENT=v.   {none/prev.}   required

Name or subscript of the dependent (predicted) variable.

INDEPENDENT=$v_1,v_2,\cdots$.   {all var./prev.}

Names or subscripts of the independent (predictor) variables. If not specified all variables are used as independent variables except those specified as the DEPENDENT, GROUPING or case WEIGHT variable.

TITLE='c'.   {blank} $\leq$ 80 char.

Title for the regression analysis.

● PRINTING THE DATA, COVARIANCES AND CORRELATIONS

The data, residuals and predicted values are printed for each case when DATA is specified in the *PRINT* paragraph. In addition the serial correlation of the residuals is printed. The serial correlation is defined as

$$\frac{\Sigma\ (w_j w_{j-1})^{\frac{1}{2}}(y_j-\hat{y}_j)(y_{j-1}-\hat{y}_{j-1})}{\{\ \Sigma\ w_j(y_j-\hat{y}_j)^2 \Sigma\ w_{j-1}(y_{j-1}-\hat{y}_{j-1})^2\}^{\frac{1}{2}}}$$

where the summation is for j=2 to N and w_j is the case weight for the jth case (1.0 if there is no case weight). A large serial correlation indicates a pattern in the residuals. When the data are ordered, such as by time, the pattern can be a result of a change in the method of data collection or an omission of a variable from the regression equation.

P1R can also print the correlation matrix and covariance matrix of the variables and the correlation matrix of the regression coefficients.

PRINT

DATA.   {no/prev.}

The data (after transformation), residuals and predicted values are printed. The serial correlation of the residuals is also computed.

(continued)

PRINT

> CORRELATION.   {no/prev.}
>
> The correlation matrix of the variables is printed.
>
> COVARIANCE.   {no/prev.}
>
> The covariance matrix of the variables is printed.
>
> RREGRESSION.   {no/prev.}
>
> The correlation matrix of the regression coefficients is printed.[3]
> See Appendix A.11 for the formula.

We use the following example to illustrate these additional results.

Example 13.2

```
/PROBLEM     TITLE IS 'WERNER BLOOD CHEMISTRY DATA'.
/INPUT       VARIABLES ARE 9.
             FORMAT IS '(A4,5F4.0,3F4.1)'.
/VARIABLE    NAMES ARE ID,AGE,HEIGHT,WEIGHT,BRTHPILL,
                   CHOLSTRL,ALBUMIN,CALCIUM,URICACID.
             MAXIMUM IS (6)400.
             MINIMUM IS (6)150.
             BLANKS ARE MISSING.
             LABEL IS ID.

/REGRESS     DEPENDENT IS CHOLSTRL.
             INDEPENDENT ARE AGE,WEIGHT,URICACID.

/PRINT       DATA.
             CORRELATION.
             COVARIANCE.
             RREG.

/END
```

Output 13.2 presents the additional output requested by the instructions in the *PRINT* paragraph.

(6)   The covariance matrix of the variables.

(7)   The correlation matrix of the variables.

(8)   The correlation matrix of the regression coefficients.

(9)   The residual $(y_j - \hat{y}_j)$, predicted value $\hat{y}_j$, and data for each case. A negative case number denotes a case with a missing value; the missing values are replaced by a series of asterisks. Asterisks are also printed when the predicted value or residual cannot be computed due to a missing value in the case. The number of standard deviations that a value is from the overall mean for the variables is reported by zero, one, two or three asterisks after the value; three asterisks represent three or more standard deviations.

---

[3] In BMDP programs dated before August 1977,
RREG is not available.

Output 13.2 Optional results printed by P1R

```
REGRESSION INTERCEPT. . . . . . . . . . . . .NON-ZERO
GROUPING VARIABLE . . . . . . . . . . . . . . .
WEIGHT VARIABLE . . . . . . . . . . . . . . . .
PRINT COVARIANCE MATRIX . . . . . . . . . . .      YES
PRINT CORRELATION MATRIX. . . . . . . . . . .      YES
PRINT RESIDUALS . . . . . . . . . . . . . . .      YES
PROBIT PLOT . . . . . . . . . . . . . . . . .      NO

NUMBER OF CASES READ. . . . . . . . . . . .        188
    CASES WITH DATA MISSING OR BEYOND LIMITS . .      8
    REMAINING NUMBER OF CASES . . . . . . . .       180
```

--- univariate statistics are printed ---

COVARIANCE MATRIX

(6)

		AGE 2	HEIGHT 3	WEIGHT 4	BRTHPILL 5	CHOLSTRL 6	ALBUMIN 7	CALCIUM 8	URICACID 9
AGE	2	97.9776							
HEIGHT	3	2.1922	6.1610						
WEIGHT	4	51.7972	24.0917	420.2407					
BRTHPILL	5	0.2793	0.2041	0.8236	0.2514				
CHOLSTRL	6	154.5264	1.2157	128.1221	1.9649	1827.0183			
ALBUMIN	7	-0.2802	-0.0052	-1.7253	-0.0423	0.8819	0.1287		
CALCIUM	8	-0.0404	0.1676	0.6272	-0.0149	5.1487	0.0768	0.2235	
URICACID	9	2.3143	0.3489	6.9781	0.0086	13.1294	0.0120	0.0881	1.2569

CORRELATION MATRIX

(7)

		AGE 2	HEIGHT 3	WEIGHT 4	BRTHPILL 5	CHOLSTRL 6	ALBUMIN 7	CALCIUM 8	URICACID 9
AGE	2	1.0000							
HEIGHT	3	0.0892	1.0000						
WEIGHT	4	0.2553	0.4735	1.0000					
BRTHPILL	5	0.0563	0.1640	0.0801	1.0000				
CHOLSTRL	6	0.3652	0.0115	0.1462	0.0917	1.0000			
ALBUMIN	7	-0.0789	-0.0058	-0.2346	-0.2352	0.0575	1.0000		
CALCIUM	8	-0.0086	0.1428	0.0647	-0.0629	0.2548	0.4529	1.0000	
URICACID	9	0.2085	0.1254	0.3036	0.0154	0.2740	0.0299	0.1662	1.0000

--- regression analysis, (3) to (5) from Output 13.1, is printed ---

CORRELATION MATRIX OF REGRESSION COEFFICIENTS

(8)

		AGE 2	WEIGHT 4	URICACID 9
AGE	2	1.0000		
WEIGHT	4	-0.2060	1.0000	
URICACID	9	-0.1422	-0.2648	1.0000

(9)

CASE LABEL	NO.	RESIDUAL	PREDICTED VALUE	VARIABLES 2 AGE / 8 CALCIUM	3 HEIGHT / 9 URICACID	4 WEIGHT	5 BRTHPILL	6 CHOLSTRL	7 ALBUMIN
2381	1	-24.9135	224.9135	22.0000* / 9.8000	67.0000* / 5.4000	144.0000	1.0000*	200.0000	4.3000
1946	-2	********** ***	239.1275	22.0000* / **********	64.0000* / 7.2000**	160.0000*	2.0000	**********	3.5000*
1610	3	30.4927	212.5073	25.0000 / 10.4000	62.0000* / 3.3000*	128.0000	1.0000	243.0000	4.1000
1797	-4	********** ***	210.2096	25.0000 / 9.6000	68.0000* / 3.0000*	150.0000	2.0000	**********	3.8000
561	5	-57.1798 *	215.1798	19.0000* / 9.9000	64.0000 / 4.7000	125.0000	1.0000	158.0000*	4.1000

--- similar statistics for cases 6 to 185 ---

CASE LABEL	NO.	RESIDUAL	PREDICTED VALUE	VARIABLES 2 AGE / 8 CALCIUM	3 HEIGHT / 9 URICACID	4 WEIGHT	5 BRTHPILL	6 CHOLSTRL	7 ALBUMIN
575	186	-41.6860 *	261.6860	53.0000* / 10.7000*	65.0000 / 4.6000	140.0000	2.0000	220.0000	4.0000
2271	187	40.2979 *	264.7021	54.0000** / 10.3000	66.0000 / 4.8000	158.0000*	1.0000*	305.0000*	4.2000
39	188	-56.5432 *	276.5432	54.0000** / 8.8000**	60.0000* / 6.3000*	170.0000	2.0000	220.0000	3.5000*

```
NOTE - NEGATIVE CASE NUMBER DENOTES A CASE WITH MISSING VALUES.
       THE NUMBER OF STANDARD DEVIATIONS FROM THE MEAN IS DENOTED BY UP TO 3 ASTERISKS TO THE RIGHT
         OF EACH RESIDUAL OR VARIABLE.
       MISSING VALUES ARE DENOTED BY MORE THAN THREE ASTERISKS.


SERIAL CORRELATION OF RESIDUALS = -0.0781
```

● PLOTS

In Example 13.3 we request the plots that can be printed by P1R.

Example 13.3

```
/PROBLEM      TITLE IS 'WERNER BLOOD CHEMISTRY DATA'.
/INPUT        VARIABLES ARE 9.
              FORMAT IS '(A4,5F4.0,3F4.1)'.
/VARIABLE     NAMES ARE ID,AGE,HEIGHT,WEIGHT,BRTHPILL,
                         CHOLSTRL,ALBUMIN,CALCIUM,URICACID.
              MAXIMUM IS (6)400.
              MINIMUM IS (6)150.
              BLANKS ARE MISSING.
              LABEL IS ID.

/REGRESS      DEPENDENT IS CHOLSTRL.
              INDEPENDENT ARE AGE,WEIGHT,URICACID.

/PLOT         RESIDUALS.
              VARIABLE IS URICACID.
              PREP IS AGE.
              NORMAL.
              DNORMAL.
              SIZE IS 40,25.

/END
```

The plots are presented in Output 13.3. Circled numbers below correspond to those in the output.

(10) The residuals $(y_j-\hat{y}_j)$ are plotted against the predicted values (estimates) $\hat{y}_j$. The number of points plotted at each position is printed.

(11) The residuals squared $(y_j-\hat{y}_j)^2$ are plotted against the predicted values (estimates) $\hat{y}_j$. The number of points plotted at each position is printed.

(12) The observed values of the dependent variable (y_j) and the predicted values $(\hat{y}_j)$ are plotted against the observed values of an independent variable (x_{ij}) (URICACID in our example). O and P represent observed and predicted values respectively, and $*$ represents overlap between observed and predicted values.

(13) The residuals $(y_j-\hat{y}_j)$ are plotted against the observed values of the same independent variable (x_{ij}) as in (12). The number of points plotted at each position is printed.

(14) A partial residual plot (PREP) of an independent variable is printed. This is a plot of the residual plus the contribution of the independent variable to the regression $(y_j - \hat{y}_j + b_ix_{ij})$ against the observed values of that variable (x_{ij}). This type of plot is described by Larsen and McCleary (1972). The number of points plotted at each position is printed.

(15) A normal probability plot of the residuals is printed. The residual $(\hat{y}_j-y_j)$ is plotted against the expected normal deviate corresponding to its rank. The computation of the expected normal deviate is explained in Section 10.1 (p. 219).

(16) A detrended normal plot of the residuals (described in Section 10.1, p. 221).

Output 13.3 Plots available in P1R

```
REGRESSION INTERCEPT. . . . . . . . . . . . . .NON-ZERO
GROUPING VARIABLE . . . . . . . . . . . . . . .
WEIGHT VARIABLE . . . . . . . . . . . . . . .
PRINT COVARIANCE MATRIX . . . . . . . . . . .      NO
PRINT CORRELATION MATRIX. . . . . . . . . . .      NO
PRINT RESIDUALS . . . . . . . . . . . . . . .      NO
PROBIT PLOT . . . . . . . . . . . . . . . . .      YES

NUMBER OF CASES READ. . . . . . . . . . . . . .    188
    CASES WITH DATA MISSING OR BEYOND LIMITS . .     8
         REMAINING NUMBER OF CASES . . . . . . . .  180
```

--- regression analysis, ③ *to* ⑤ *in Output 13.1, is printed ---*

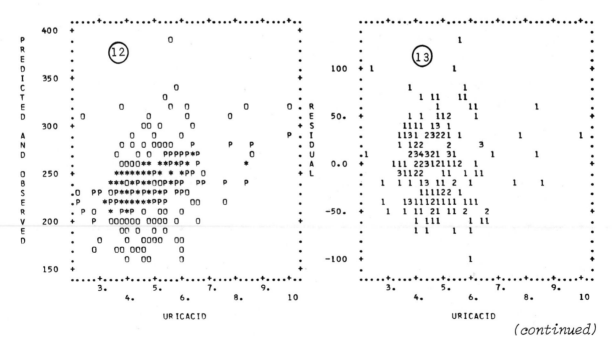

PREDICTD

URICACID

(continued)

Output 13.3 *(continued)*

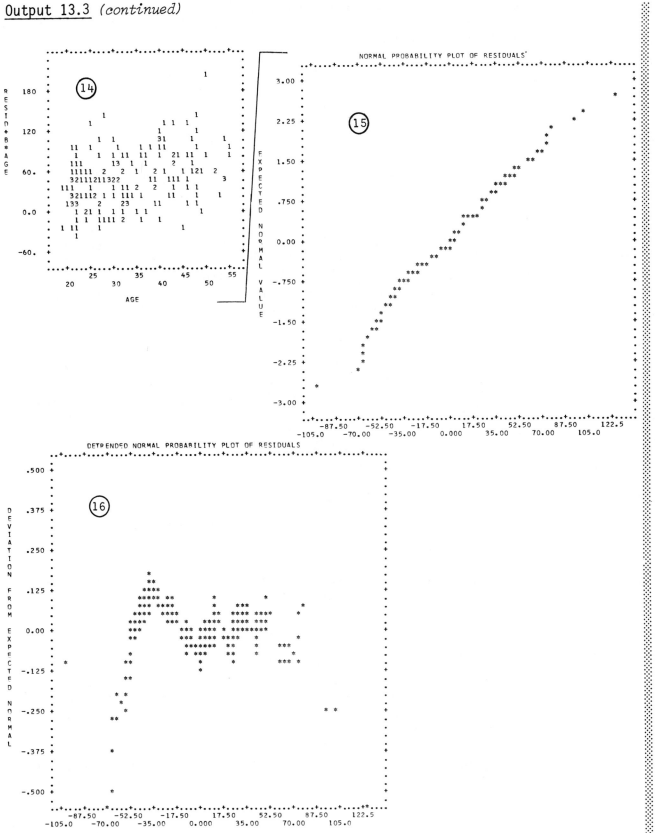

The size of all the plots can be scaled. Those in Output 13.3 are smaller than the preassigned size (50 characters wide and 50 lines high); they are 40 characters wide and 25 lines high; i.e.,

SIZE=40, 25.

is specified in Example 13.3.

PLOT

RESIDUAL. {no/prev.}

Plot the residuals $(y-\hat{y})$ and residuals squared $(y-\hat{y})^2$ in separate graphs against the predicted values $\hat{y}$.

VARIABLE= $v_1,v_2,\cdots$. {none/prev.}

Names or subscripts of variables against which the observed values of the dependent variable y and the predicted values $\hat{y}$ are plotted. Overlaps between observed and predicted values are indicated by asterisks. The residuals $(y-\hat{y})$ are also plotted against the same variables. Each variable is plotted in a separate graph.

PREP= $v_1,v_2,\cdots$. {none/prev.}

Names or subscripts of variables plotted in partial residual plots. This is a plot of the (residual + coefficient · observed value of independent variable) against the observed value of that independent variable; i.e., $(y - \hat{y} + bx)$ against x.

NORMAL. {no/prev.}

Plot a normal probability plot of the residuals.[4]

DNORMAL. {no/prev.}

Plot a detrended normal probability plot of the residuals.[4]

SIZE= $\#_1,\#_2$. {50,50/prev.}

$\#_1$ is the number of characters (width) in the horizontal axis and $\#_2$ is the number of lines (height) in the vertical axis.

● THE INTERCEPT IN THE REGRESSION EQUATION

The regression equation usually contains an intercept (a constant term), e.g., in

$$y = a + b_1x_1 + b_2x_2 + \ldots + b_px_p$$

a is the intercept. In some problems the intercept must be zero; this can be specified by

TYPE=ZERO.

---

[4] In BMDP programs dated before August 1977, PROBIT is used in place of both NORMAL and DNORMAL.

in the *REGRess* paragraph. When this option is specified, the covariances are the sums of products of observed values instead of the sums of products of deviations from the sample means.

REGRess
   TYPE= *(one only)* ZERO,NONZERO.   { NONZERO /prev.}

   If ZERO is specified, the intercept in the regression equation is set to zero. TYPE can be stated only in the first *REGRess* paragraph in any problem; it cannot be changed until a new problem begins. *Note: This option is rarely used.*

● TOLERANCE: INVERTING THE COVARIANCE MATRIX

   To estimate the parameters of the regression equation P1R must invert the covariance matrix (Appendix A.11). The matrix inversion is performed in a stepwise manner -- at each step an additional independent variable is entered into the regression equation. The variable chosen for entry is the variable with the highest partial correlation with the dependent variable. All independent variables are entered into the regression equation except those that fail the TOLERANCE limit defined below. Use P9R if you need a lower tolerance limit.

REGRess
   TOLERANCE=#.   {0.01/prev.}   between 0.01 and 1.0

   An independent variable is not entered into the regression equation if it fails to pass the TOLERANCE limit; i.e., if its squared multiple correlation (R^2) with independent variables already in the equation exceeds 1.0-TOLERANCE or if its entry will cause the squared multiple correlation of any previously entered variable with the independent variables in the equation to exceed 1.0-TOLERANCE.

● GROUPING CASES

   Cases can be classified into groups by specifying a GROUPING variable in the *VARiable* paragraph. When a GROUPING variable is stated, the data are first analyzed for all groups combined and then reanalyzed for each group separately. The GROUPING variable is not used as an independent variable.

   The analysis terminates with a test of equality of the regression lines between groups. When the regression lines (intercepts and slopes) are identical, the total of the sum of squares (SS) of the residuals over the groups will be equal to the SS of the residuals for the analysis of the data prior to grouping. A test of equality of the regression lines is as follows.

Residual SS within groups = $\displaystyle\sum_{(\text{groups})}$ Residual SS of the group

Total SS = Residual SS of data prior to grouping

Regression SS over groups = Total SS - Residual SS within group

This leads to the F test for equality of regression lines across groups

$$F = \frac{\text{Regression SS over groups}/\sum p_i}{\text{Residual SS within groups}/(N - g - \sum p_i)}$$

where

p_i = number of independent variables in the regression equation for the ith group

g = number of groups

N = number of cases in all the groups combined

The p_i's can differ between groups only if one or more variables do not pass the tolerance limit.

VARiable

GROUPING= v.   {no grouping var./prev.}

Name or subscript of the variable used to classify the cases into groups. If GROUPING is not stated or is set to zero, the cases are not grouped. If the GROUPING variable takes on more than 10 distinct values or codes, CODEs or CUTPOINTs for the variable must be specified in the *GROUP* paragraph (Section 5.4).

In Example 13.4 we use BRTHPILL as a GROUPING variable.

Example 13.4

```
/PROBLEM     TITLE IS 'WERNER BLOOD CHEMISTRY DATA'.
/INPUT       VARIABLES ARE 9.
             FORMAT IS '(A4,5F4.0,3F4.1)'.
/VARIABLE    NAMES ARE ID,AGE,HEIGHT,WEIGHT,BRTHPILL,
                   CHOLSTRL,ALBUMIN,CALCIUM,URICACID.
             MAXIMUM IS (6)400.
             MINIMUM IS (6)150.
             BLANKS ARE MISSING.
             LABEL IS ID.
             GROUPING IS BRTHPILL.

/GROUP       CODES(5) ARE      1,     2.
             NAMES(5) ARE NOPILL, PILL.

/REGRESS     DEPENDENT IS CHOLSTRL.
             INDEPENDENT ARE AGE,WEIGHT,URICACID.

/END
```

<u>Output 13.4</u> Separate analyses of groups by P1R. Results not reproduced are indicated in italics.

```
REGRESSION INTERCEPT. . . . . . . . . . . . . .NON-ZERO
GROUPING VARIABLE . . . . . . . . . . . . . . .BRTHPILL
```

--- *univariate statistics for all variables* ---

VARIABLE		BEFORE TRANSFORMATION					INTERVAL RANGE	
NO. NAME		MINIMUM LIMIT	MAXIMUM LIMIT	MISSING CODE	CATEGORY CODE	CATEGORY NAME	GREATER THAN	LESS THAN OR EQUAL TO
5	BRTHPILL				1.00000	NOPILL		
					2.00000	PILL		

```
REGRESSION TITLE. . . . . . . . . . . . . . .WERNER BLOOD CHEMISTRY DATA
DEPENDENT VARIABLE. . . . . . . . . . . . . .      6 CHOLSTRL
TOLERANCE . . . . . . . . . . . . . . . . . .   0.0100
```
(17) ALL DATA CONSIDERED AS A SINGLE GROUP

```
MULTIPLE R             0.4175        STD. ERROR OF EST.        39.1698
MULTIPLE R-SQUARE      0.1743
```

ANALYSIS OF VARIANCE

	SUM OF SQUARES	DF	MEAN SQUARE	F RATIO	P(TAIL)
REGRESSION	57004.242	3	19001.414	12.385	0.00000
RESIDUAL	270032.000	176	1534.273		

VARIABLE		COEFFICIENT	STD. ERROR	STD. REG COEFF	T	P(2 TAIL)
INTERCEPT		151.420				
AGE	2	1.390	0.309	0.322	4.497	0.000
WEIGHT	4	0.003	0.153	0.001	0.019	0.985
URICACID	9	7.871	2.769	0.206	2.843	0.005

```
REGRESSION FOR GROUPS  1  NOPILL
    REGRESSION INTERCEPT. . . . . . . . . . . . . .NON-ZERO
(18) GROUPING VARIABLE . . . . . . . . . . . . . . .BRTHPILL
```

--- *univariate statistics for group NOPILL* ---

```
REGRESSION TITLE. . . . . . . . . . . . . . .WERNER BLOOD CHEMISTRY DATA
DEPENDENT VARIABLE. . . . . . . . . . . . . .      6 CHOLSTRL
TOLERANCE . . . . . . . . . . . . . . . . . .   0.0100

MULTIPLE R             0.4601        STD. ERROR OF EST.        39.4559
MULTIPLE R-SQUARE      0.2117
```

ANALYSIS OF VARIANCE

	SUM OF SQUARES	DF	MEAN SQUARE	F RATIO	P(TAIL)
REGRESSION	35528.281	3	11842.758	7.607	0.00014
RESIDUAL	132325.438	85	1556.770		

VARIABLE		COEFFICIENT	STD. ERROR	STD. REG COEFF	T	P(2 TAIL)
INTERCEPT		149.810				
AGE	2	1.721	0.459	0.379	3.751	0.000
WEIGHT	4	-0.142	0.238	-0.060	-0.595	0.554
URICACID	9	9.217	4.416	0.210	2.087	0.040

```
REGRESSION FOR GROUPS  2  PILL
```

--- *univariate statistics for group PILL* ---

```
REGRESSION TITLE. . . . . . . . . . . . . . .WERNER BLOOD CHEMISTRY DATA
DEPENDENT VARIABLE. . . . . . . . . . . . . .      6 CHOLSTRL
TOLERANCE . . . . . . . . . . . . . . . . . .   0.0100

MULTIPLE R             0.3825        STD. ERROR OF EST.        39.1795
MULTIPLE R-SQUARE      0.1463
```

ANALYSIS OF VARIANCE

	SUM OF SQUARES	DF	MEAN SQUARE	F RATIO	P(TAIL)
REGRESSION	22885.969	3	7628.656	4.970	0.00313
RESIDUAL	133548.125	87	1535.036		

VARIABLE		COEFFICIENT	STD. ERROR	STD. REG COEFF	T	P(2 TAIL)
INTERCEPT		157.630				
AGE	2	1.070	0.423	0.261	2.533	0.013
WEIGHT	4	0.102	0.203	0.054	0.501	0.618
URICACID	9	6.726	3.594	0.200	1.871	0.065

ANALYSIS OF VARIANCE OF REGRESSION COEFFICIENTS OVER GROUPS
(= REDUCTION OF RESIDUALS DUE TO GROUPING)

	SUM OF SQUARES	DF	MEAN SQUARE	F RATIO	P(TAIL)
(19) REGRESSION OVER GROUPS	4158.438	4	1039.609	0.673	0.61187
RESIDUAL WITHIN GROUPS	265873.563	172	1545.776		

A SIGNIFICANT F RATIO INDICATES THAT THE SLOPES AND/OR INTERCEPTS DIFFER BEYOND CHANCE BETWEEN THE GROUPS

The results are presented in Output 13.4.   Three regression analyses are performed.   First P1R analyzes the data in all groups combined ⑰ and then analyzes each group separately ⑱ .   Finally there is a test of the equality of the regression lines ⑲ ; the F ratio is nonsignificant in our example and therefore we conclude that the two BRTHPILL groups have similar regression equations.

● CASE WEIGHTs

When the error variance is not homogeneous but varies from case to case, weighted least squares estimation is more appropriate; the weight (w) for each case is proportional to the inverse of the variance.   In weighted least squares, estimates of the parameters minimize

$$\Sigma \; w_j(y_j - \hat{y}_j)^2$$

where w_j is the weight for case j.

You can estimate predicted values for cases not used to compute the regression equation by setting their case weights to zero (see Appendix C.4).

Case weights affect the computation of the means, variances, covariances and correlations (see Section 2.1).

VARiable
    WEIGHT=v.   { no weight var./prev.}

    Name or subscript of the variable containing case weights.   The
    weights should be greater than or equal to zero.   If WEIGHT
    is not stated or is set to zero, there are no case weights.

● *INPut* FROM A BMDP FILE

Only data can be read by P1R unless a BMDP File (Chapter 7) is used as input: DATA, a COVARIANCE matrix, or a CORRELATION matrix can be input from a BMDP File.

In the following example we use the CORRELATION matrix computed by P8D (see Example 12.3, p. 346).

Example 13.5

```
/PROBLEM     TITLE IS 'WERNER BLOOD CHEMISTRY DATA'.

/INPUT       UNIT IS 4.
             CODE IS WERNER.
             CONTENT IS COVA.

/COMMENT     'BMDP FILE WAS CREATED BY EXAMPLE 12.3'.

/REGRESS     DEPENDENT IS CHOLSTRL.
             INDEPENDENT ARE AGE,WEIGHT,URICACID.

/END
```

Note: The System Cards that precede the Control Language must contain a card describing where to find the BMDP File (Section 7.3). At HSCF, the System Cards are

```
//jobname  JOB  nooo,yourname
//   EXEC  BIMED,PROG=BMDP1R
//FT04F001  DD  DSNAME=FS.nooo.filename,DISP=OLD
//SYSIN  DD  *
```

where filename is the name given to the system file when the BMDP File was created.

The results are presented in Output 13.5. Note that the results differ from those in Output 13.1 since the correlation matrix in this example also uses data from the incomplete cases.

When the input is not data, the CONTENT of the BMDP File must be specified.

INPut

    CONTENT= c.   { DATA}   used only when input is from a BMDP File

       When the input is not DATA, CONTENT must be specified. It must be identical to the CONTENT stated in the *SAVE* paragraph when the BMDP File was created.

When the CONTENT is DATA, COVA or CORR, P1R recognizes how the input is to be analyzed. Several BMDP programs create BMDP Files with a different CONTENT that is not recognized by P1R. You can use other Files as input to P1R but you must specify in a TYPE statement how they are to be analyzed (as DATA, a COVARIANCE or a CORRELATION matrix).

INPut

    TYPE=*(one only)* DATA,COVA,CORR.   {same as CONTENT} used only if
                                                  input is from
                                                  BMDP File

      TYPE specifies how the input is analyzed. It must be specified when a BMDP File is read as input and the CONTENT is not one of the three TYPES -- DATA, COVA or CORR.

● STORING THE DATA AND COVARIANCE MATRIX IN A BMDP FILE

Both the DATA (including predicted values and residuals) and the COVARIANCE matrix from P1R can be saved in a BMDP File to use as input to a further analysis. Saving the COVARIANCE matrix allows subsequent analyses to start from the computed means and covariances, which may result in a substantial reduction of computer costs. Chapter 7 describes BMDP Files and how they are used.

Output 13.5 Using a covariance matrix as input to P1R

```
INPUT FORMAT
        BMDP FILE . . . . . CODE. . . IS      WERNER
                            CONTENT . IS      COVA
                            LABEL . . IS
                            VARIABLES     2  AGE        3  HEIGHT     4  WEIGHT      5  BRTHPILL    6  CHOLSTRL
                                          7  ALBUMIN    8  CALCIUM    9  URICACID


        REGRESSION INTERCEPT. . . . . . . . . . . . . .NON-ZERO
        GROUPING VARIABLE . . . . . . . . . . . . . . .
        WEIGHT VARIABLE . . . . . . . . . . . . . . . .
        PRINT COVARIANCE MATRIX . . . . . . . . . . . .        NO
        PRINT CORRELATION MATRIX. . . . . . . . . . . .        NO
        PRINT RESIDUALS . . . . . . . . . . . . . . . .        NO
        PROBIT PLOT . . . . . . . . . . . . . . . . . .        NO

INPUT CORRELATION OR COVARIANCE MATRIX COMPUTED WITH MISSING DATA.

        VARIABLE
    NO.     NAME    SAMPLE SIZE    SUM OF WEIGHTS

      2 AGE             188.          188.000
      3 HEIGHT          186.          186.000
      4 WEIGHT          186.          186.000
      5 BRTHPILL        188.          188.000
      6 CHOLSTRL        186.          186.000
      7 ALBUMIN         186.          186.000
      8 CALCIUM         185.          185.000
      9 URICACID        187.          187.000

HARMONIC MEAN OF SAMPLE SIZES    186


VARIABLE                MEAN  STANDARD DEVIATION  ST.DEV/MEAN
      2 AGE          33.81914         10.11265       0.29902
      3 HEIGHT       64.51074          2.48505       0.03852
      4 WEIGHT      131.67204         20.66043       0.15691
      5 BRTHPILL      1.50000          0.50133       0.33422
      6 CHOLSTRL    236.15053         42.55522       0.18020
      7 ALBUMIN       4.11123          0.35796       0.08707
      8 CALCIUM       9.96208          0.47955       0.04814
      9 URICACID      4.77051          1.15723       0.24258




        REGRESSION TITLE. . . . . . . . . . . . . . . .WERNER BLOOD CHEMISTRY DATA
        DEPENDENT VARIABLE. . . . . . . . . . . . . . .       6 CHOLSTRL
        TOLERANCE . . . . . . . . . . . . . . . . . . . . . 0.0100
ALL DATA CONSIDERED AS A SINGLE GROUP

MULTIPLE R              0.4180          STD. ERROR OF EST.        38.9769
MULTIPLE R-SQUARE      0.1747

ANALYSIS OF VARIANCE
                    SUM OF SQUARES   DF    MEAN SQUARE    F RATIO   P(TAIL)
        REGRESSION      58531.270     3     19510.422     12.843   0.00000
        RESIDUAL       276493.875   182      1519.197

                                          STD. REG
    VARIABLE    COEFFICIENT STD. ERROR     COEFF        T    P(2 TAIL)

INTERCEPT          152.724
AGE          2       1.394      0.295      0.331      4.732    0.000
WEIGHT       4       0.008      0.149      0.004      0.052    0.958
URICACID     9       7.391      2.612      0.201      2.830    0.005
```

```
SAVE
   CONTENT= (one or both) DATA,COVA.      {DATA }
```

   The matrices to be saved in a BMDP File. If DATA is specified,
   the predicted values are saved as variable (VT+1) and named
   PREDICTD and the residuals are saved as variable (VT+2) and named
   RESIDUAL where VT is the total number of variables (after transformation, if any).

   _Note: When a GROUPING variable is specified, the predicted values,
   residuals and covariances are saved only from the analysis using all
   groups combined. When the REGRess paragraph is repeated before END,
   the predicted values and residuals from the first regression only are
   saved._

In Example 13.6 we create a BMDP File to save the data and covariance
matrix.

Example 13.6

```
/PROBLEM     TITLE IS 'WERNER BLOOD CHEMISTRY DATA'.
/INPUT       VARIABLES ARE 9.
             FORMAT IS '(A4,5F4.0,3F4.1)'.
/VARIABLE    NAMES ARE ID,AGE,HEIGHT,WEIGHT,BRTHPILL,
                   CHOLSTRL,ALBUMIN,CALCIUM,URICACID.
             MAXIMUM IS (6)400.
             MINIMUM IS (6)150.
             BLANKS ARE MISSING.
             LABEL IS ID.
/REGRESS     DEPENDENT IS CHOLSTRL.
             INDEPENDENT ARE AGE,WEIGHT,URICACID.
/SAVE        UNIT IS 4.
             NEW.
             CODE IS WERNER.
             CONTENT IS DATA,COVA.
/END
```

Note: The System Cards that precede the Control Language must contain a card describing
where to store the BMDP File (Section 7.1). At HSCF, the System Cards are

```
//jobname  JOB  nooo,yourname
//  EXEC  BIMED,PROG=BMDP1R
//FT04F001  DD  DSNAME=FS.nooo.filename,DISP=OLD
//SYSIN  DD  *
```

In addition space must be allocated for the system file (Section 7.1).

The messages printed by P1R to indicate that the BMDP Files are created
appear in Output 13.6.

● SIZE OF PROBLEM

   P1R can estimate a regression equation containing 145 independent variables. Appendix B describes how the capacity of the program can be increased.

● COMPUTATIONAL METHOD

All computations are performed in single precision. Means, standard deviations and covariances are computed by the method of provisional means (Appendix A.2). The sum of cross-products matrix is swept (pivoted) on all independent variables except those that fail the tolerance limit (Appendix A.11). The independent variables are entered into the regression equation one at a time according to the size of their partial correlations; the independent variable with the largest partial correlation is chosen at each step.

ACKNOWLEDGEMENT

P1R was programmed by Douglas Jackson and Jerry Douglas. Recent revisions were made by Lanaii Kline. P1R supersedes BMD01R.

Output 13.6 Saving the covariance matrix and data in BMDP Files

```
NUMBER OF CASES READ. . . . . . . . . . . . . .    188
     CASES WITH DATA MISSING OR BEYOND LIMITS . .      8
         REMAINING NUMBER OF CASES . . . . . . . .    180


BMDP FILE WRITTEN ON UNIT 4.

          CODE. . . IS     WERNER
          CONTENT . IS     COVA
          LABEL . . IS
          VARIABLES      2  AGE       3  HEIGHT    4  WEIGHT    5  BRTHPILL   6  CHOLSTRL
                         7  ALBUMIN   8  CALCIUM   9  URICACID


    BMDP FILE ON UNIT 4 HAS BEEN COMPLETED.
```

--- univariate statistics and regression analysis appear here ---

```
BMDP FILE WRITTEN ON UNIT 4.

          CODE. . . IS     WERNER
          CONTENT . IS     DATA
          LABEL . . IS
          VARIABLES      1  ID        2  AGE       3  HEIGHT    4  WEIGHT     5  BRTHPILL
                         6  CHOLSTRL  7  ALBUMIN   8  CALCIUM   9  URICACID  10  PREDICTD
                        11  RESIDUAL


    BMDP FILE ON UNIT 4 HAS BEEN COMPLETED.
```

P2R

13.2 Stepwise Regression

P2R computes estimates of the parameters of a multiple linear regression equation in a stepwise manner. That is, the variables are entered (forward stepping) or removed (backward stepping) from the equation one at a time according to any of four possible criteria. The order of entry or removal can be specified entirely or in part. The regression equation can be estimated with or without an intercept.

● RESULTS

The Werner blood chemistry data (Table 5.1) are used to illustrate the results produced by P2R. In Example 13.7 we request that a stepwise regression be performed with CHOLSTRL as the dependent variable. Only the *REGRess* paragraph is specific to P2R. The remaining Control Language instructions are described in Chapter 5.

Example 13.7

```
/PROBLEM     TITLE IS 'WERNER BLOOD CHEMISTRY DATA'.
/INPUT       VARIABLES ARE 9.
             FORMAT IS '(A4,5F4.0,3F4.1)'.
/VARIABLE    NAMES ARE ID,AGE,HEIGHT,WEIGHT,BRTHPILL,
                 CHOLSTRL,ALBUMIN,CALCIUM,URICACID.
             MAXIMUM IS (6)400.
             MINIMUM IS (6)150.
             BLANKS ARE MISSING.
             LABEL IS ID.

/REGRESS     DEPENDENT IS CHOLSTRL.

/END
```

The Control Language must be preceded by System Cards to initiate the analysis by P2R. At HSCF, the System Cards are

```
//jobname  JOB  nooo,yourname
//  EXEC  BIMED,PROG=BMDP2R
//SYSIN  DD  *
```

The Control Language is immediately followed by the data (Table 5.1). The analysis is terminated by another System Card. At HSCF, this System Card is

```
//
```

The results of the regression analysis are presented in Output 13.7. The circled numbers below correspond to those in the output.

① Complete cases only are used in the computations; i.e., cases that have no missing values or values out of range. Therefore only 180 of the original 188 cases are used. All variables are checked for invalid values unless USE is specified in the *VARiable* paragraph (Section 5.3); in which case only the variables specified in the USE statement are checked for acceptable values.

②   Univariate statistics for each variable (computed from the complete cases)

- mean
- standard deviation
- coefficient of variation
- skewness
- kurtosis
- smallest observed value (not out of range)
- largest observed value (not out of range)
- smallest standard score
- largest standard score

These statistics are discussed in greater detail in Section 2.1.

③   The interpretation of the *REGRess* paragraph. Since only the DEPENDENT variable is specified in Example 13.7, the remainder of the options take their preassigned values.

- the stepping algorithm is "F"; that is, the entry or removal of the variables from the equation is based on F-to-enter or F-to-remove limits (explained in ⑥ below).

The regression model fitted to the data is

$$y = a + b_1x_1 + b_2x_2 +...+ b_px_p + \epsilon$$

where

y is the dependent variable

$x_1,...,x_p$ are the independent variables

$b_2,...,b_p$ are the regression coefficients

a is the intercept

p is the number of independent variables

ϵ is the error with mean zero

The predicted value $\hat{y}$ for each case is

$$\hat{y} = a + b_1x_1 + b_2x_2 +...+ b_px_p$$

We have omitted a subscript (j) indicating case number from the formulas. The residual for each case is $(y_j-\hat{y}_j)$. The number of parameters in the model p' is $p+1$ if the intercept is present and p if the intercept is set to zero.

④   Results are printed at each step. We describe the results at Step 1. The multiple correlation R is printed (i.e., the correlation of the dependent variable y with the predicted value $\hat{y}$) as well as

Output 13.7 Stepwise regression by P2R. Circled numbers correspond to those
in the text. Results not reproduced are indicated in italics.

BMDP2R - STEPWISE REGRESSION
HEALTH SCIENCES COMPUTING FACILITY
UNIVERSITY OF CALIFORNIA, LOS ANGELES

PROGRAM REVISED SEPTEMBER 1977
MANUAL DATE -- 1977

--- Control Language read by P2R is printed and interpreted ---

```
REGRESSION INTERCEPT. . . . . . . . . . . . . . .NON ZERO
WEIGHT VARIABLE . . . . . . . . . . . . . . . .
PRINT COVARIANCE MATRIX . . . . . . . . . . . .     NO
PRINT CORRELATION MATRIX. . . . . . . . . . . .     NO
PRINT ANOVA AT EACH STEP. . . . . . . . . . . .     YES
PRINT STEP OUTPUT . . . . . . . . . . . . . . .     YES
PRINT REGRESSION COEFFICIENT SUMMARY TABLE. . .     YES
PRINT PARTIAL CORRELATION SUMMARY TABLE . . . .     NO
PRINT F-RATIO SUMMARY TABLE . . . . . . . . . .     NO
PRINT SUMMARY TABLE . . . . . . . . . . . . . .     YES
PRINT RESIDUALS AND DATA. . . . . . . . . . . .     NO

NUMBER OF CASES READ. . . . . . . . . . . . .     188
    CASES WITH DATA MISSING OR BEYOND LIMITS . . .     8
    REMAINING NUMBER OF CASES . . . . . . . . .     180
```

① ②

VARIABLE NO. NAME	MEAN	STANDARD DEVIATION	COEFFICIENT OF VARIATION	SKEWNESS	KURTOSIS	SMALLEST VALUE	LARGEST VALUE	SMALLEST STD SCORE	LARGEST STD SCORE
2 AGE	33.5382	9.8984	0.2951	0.4039	-0.9908	19.0000	55.0000	-1.4687	2.1682
3 HEIGHT	64.4660	2.4821	0.0385	-0.1185	-0.0402	57.0000	71.0000	-3.0079	2.6324
4 WEIGHT	131.0938	20.4998	0.1564	1.0572	1.9389	94.0000	215.0000	-1.8095	4.0930
5 BRTHPILL	1.5055	0.5014	0.3330	-0.0220	-2.0106	1.0000	2.0000	-1.0083	0.9863
6 CHOLSTRL	235.8382	42.7436	0.1812	0.4578	0.0640	155.0000	390.0000	-1.8912	3.6067
7 ALBUMIN	4.1205	0.3587	0.0871	-0.0678	-0.3606	3.2000	5.0000	-2.5662	2.4518
8 CALCIUM	9.9677	0.4728	0.0474	-0.0287	-0.5804	8.8000	11.1000	-2.4699	2.3949
9 URICACID	4.7555	1.1211	0.2358	1.1759	2.9185	2.2000	9.0000	-2.2794	4.5887

NOTE - KURTOSIS VALUES GREATER THAN ZERO INDICATE A DISTRIBUTION WITH HEAVIER TAILS THAN NORMAL DISTRIBUTION

③
```
REGRESSION TITLE. . . . . . . . . . . . . . .WERNER BLOOD CHEMISTRY DATA
STEPPING ALGORITHM. . . . . . . . . . . . . .F
MAXIMUM NUMBER OF STEPS . . . . . . . . . . .     18
DEPENDENT VARIABLE. . . . . . . . . . . . .     6 CHOLSTRL
MINIMUM ACCEPTABLE F TO ENTER . . . . . . . .     4.000,   4.000
MAXIMUM ACCEPTABLE F TO REMOVE. . . . . . . .     3.900,   3.900
MINIMUM ACCEPTABLE TOLERANCE. . . . . . . . . 0.01000

STEP NO.   0

MULTIPLE R            0.0
MULTIPLE R-SQUARE     0.0
ADJUSTED R-SQUARE     0.0
STD. ERROR OF EST.   42.7436

ANALYSIS OF VARIANCE
                   SUM OF SQUARES    DF    MEAN SQUARE    F RATIO
    REGRESSION     0.0               0   0.0             0.0
    RESIDUAL       327036.19       179   1827.018
```

VARIABLES IN EQUATION

VARIABLE	COEFFICIENT	STD. ERROR OF COEFF	STD REG COEFF	TOLERANCE	F TO REMOVE
(Y-INTERCEPT	235.838)				

VARIABLES NOT IN EQUATION

LEVEL.	VARIABLE		PARTIAL CORR.	TOLERANCE	F TO ENTER	LEVEL
.	AGE	2	0.365	1.00000	27.399	1
.	HEIGHT	3	0.011	1.00000	0.023	1
.	WEIGHT	4	0.146	1.00000	3.889	1
.	BRTHPILL	5	0.092	1.00000	1.509	1
.	ALBUMIN	7	0.058	1.00000	0.591	1
.	CALCIUM	8	0.255	1.00000	12.356	1
.	URICACID	9	0.274	1.00000	14.446	1

④
```
STEP NO.   1
VARIABLE ENTERED   2 AGE

MULTIPLE R            0.3652
MULTIPLE R-SQUARE     0.1334
ADJUSTED R-SQUARE     0.1285
STD. ERROR OF EST.   39.9024

ANALYSIS OF VARIANCE
                   SUM OF SQUARES    DF    MEAN SQUARE    F RATIO
⑤  REGRESSION     43624.605         1   43624.61        27.399
    RESIDUAL       283411.63       178   1592.200
```

VARIABLES IN EQUATION

VARIABLE	COEFFICIENT	STD. ERROR OF COEFF	STD REG COEFF	TOLERANCE	F TO REMOVE
(Y-INTERCEPT	182.943)				
AGE 2	1.5772	0.3013	0.365	1.000	27.40

⑥

VARIABLES NOT IN EQUATION

LEVEL.	VARIABLE		PARTIAL CORR.	TOLERANCE	F TO ENTER	LEVEL
1 .	HEIGHT	3	-0.023	0.99204	0.092	1
.	WEIGHT	4	0.059	0.93484	0.616	1
.	BRTHPILL	5	0.077	0.99683	1.043	1
.	ALBUMIN	7	0.093	0.99377	1.545	1
.	CALCIUM	8	0.277	0.99993	14.719	1
.	URICACID	9	0.217	0.95651	8.770	1

(continued)

Output 13.7 *(continued)*

```
STEP NO.    2
VARIABLE ENTERED    8 CALCIUM

MULTIPLE R              0.4471
MULTIPLE R-SQUARE       0.1999
ADJUSTED R-SQUARE       0.1909
STD. ERROR OF EST.     38.4482

ANALYSIS OF VARIANCE
                     SUM OF SQUARES     DF     MEAN SQUARE    F RATIO
          REGRESSION   65382.938         2     32691.47       22.115
          RESIDUAL    261653.25        177      1478.267
```

		VARIABLES IN EQUATION					.		VARIABLES NOT IN EQUATION			
VARIABLE		COEFFICIENT	STD. ERROR OF COEFF	STD REG COEFF	TOLERANCE	F TO REMOVE	LEVEL .	VARIABLE	PARTIAL CORR.	TOLERANCE	F TO ENTER	LEVEL
(Y-INTERCEPT		-49.830)					1 . HEIGHT	3	-0.066	0.97141	0.770	1
AGE	2	1.5868	0.2903	0.367	1.000	29.87	1 . WEIGHT	4	0.041	0.93036	0.302	1
CALCIUM	8	23.3203	6.0785	0.258	1.000	14.72	. BRTHPILL	5	0.098	0.99294	1.702	1
							. ALBUMIN	7	-0.038	0.78926	0.256	1
							. URICACID	9	0.179	0.92827	5.842	1

```
STEP NO.    3
VARIABLE ENTERED    9 URICACID

MULTIPLE R              0.4750
MULTIPLE R-SQUARE       0.2256
ADJUSTED R-SQUARE       0.2124
STD. ERROR OF EST.     37.9329

ANALYSIS OF VARIANCE
                     SUM OF SQUARES     DF     MEAN SQUARE    F RATIO
          REGRESSION   73789.250         3     24596.41       17.094
          RESIDUAL    253246.94        176      1438.903
```

		VARIABLES IN EQUATION					.		VARIABLES NOT IN EQUATION			
VARIABLE		COEFFICIENT	STD. ERROR OF COEFF	STD REG COEFF	TOLERANCE	F TO REMOVE	LEVEL .	VARIABLE	PARTIAL CORR.	TOLERANCE	F TO ENTER	LEVEL
(Y-INTERCEPT		-49.738)					1 . HEIGHT	3	-0.083	0.96406	1.221	1
AGE	2	1.4359	0.2932	0.333	0.955	23.99	1 . WEIGHT	4	-0.005	0.86875	0.004	1
CALCIUM	8	20.7920	6.0876	0.230	0.970	11.67	1 . BRTHPILL	5	0.097	0.99272	1.655	1
URICACID	9	6.3444	2.6248	0.166	0.928	5.84	. ALBUMIN	7	-0.032	0.78831	0.185	1

```
F-LEVELS(   4.000,   3.900) OR TOLERANCE INSUFFICIENT FOR FURTHER STEPPING
```

STEPWISE REGRESSION COEFFICIENTS

⑦

VARIABLES STEP	0 Y-INTCPT	2 AGE	3 HEIGHT	4 WEIGHT	5 BRTHPILL	7 ALBUMIN	8 CALCIUM	9 URICACID
0	235.8382*	1.5772	0.1973	0.3049	7.8169	6.8533	23.0333	10.4459
1	182.9431*	1.5772*	-0.3668	0.1182	6.0835	10.3523	23.3203	7.8848
2	-49.8298*	1.5868*	-1.0313	0.0801	7.4891	-4.5760	23.3203*	6.3444
3	-49.7384*	1.4359*	-1.2847	-0.0098	7.2891	-3.8369	20.7920*	6.3444*

```
NOTE-
    1) REGRESSION COEFFICIENTS FOR VARIABLES IN THE EQUATION ARE INDICATED BY AN ASTERISK
    2) THE REMAINING COEFFICIENTS ARE THOSE WHICH WOULD BE OBTAINED IF THAT VARIABLE WERE TO ENTER IN THE NEXT STEP
```

SUMMARY TABLE

⑧

STEP NO.	VARIABLE ENTERED	REMOVED	MULTIPLE R	RSQ	INCREASE IN RSQ	F-TO- ENTER	F-TO- REMOVE	NUMBER OF INDEPENDENT VARIABLES INCLUDED
1	2 AGE		0.3652	0.1334	0.1334	27.3989		1
2	8 CALCIUM		0.4471	0.1999	0.0665	14.7188		2
3	9 URICACID		0.4750	0.2256	0.0257	5.8421		3

- the multiple R^2

- the adjusted R^2: $R^2 - p(1-R^2)/(N-p')$

- the standard error of the estimate: $\{\Sigma \, (y_j - \hat{y}_j)^2/(N-p')\}^{\frac{1}{2}}$ where N is the number of cases

⑤ The analysis of variance table for the regression is printed containing

- the regression sum of squares: $\Sigma \, (\hat{y}_j - \bar{y})^2$

- the residual sum of squares: $\Sigma \, (y_j - \hat{y}_j)^2$

- the F ratio: this is a test of the significance of the coefficients of the independent variables in the regression equation. Since variables are selected for inclusion in the equation in a manner that maximizes the F ratio, the level of significance of the F ratio cannot be obtained from an F distribution. When important variables have <u>not</u> as yet been included in the regression equation, the denominator of the F ratio (the residual mean square error) is inflated.

⑥ Statistics for each independent variable. To the left of the table are the independent variables already entered into the equation (AGE is the only one at Step 1) and to the right are those not yet entered.

For the independent variables in the equation, P2R prints

- regression coefficient: b_i

- standard error of the coefficient: $s(b_i)$

- standardized regression coefficient: $b_i s_i/s_y$ (the regression coefficient for standardized variables)

- tolerance (described on p. 410)

- F-to-remove: this is a test of the regression coefficient. It is equal to $[b_i/s(b_i)]^2$. It is also the ratio

$$\frac{SS(\text{residuals if variable is removed from equation}) - SS(\text{residuals})}{SS(\text{residuals})/(N-p')}$$

where SS is the sum of squares.

In two of the criteria for entering and removing variables (p. 405) F-to-remove is compared with the maximum acceptable F-to-remove (in ③) and if it is less than the acceptable limit, the variable is removed from the equation.

The F-to-remove values are affected by the process of variable selection (variables with large F-to-enter values are selected). Therefore, if an F-to-remove is compared to the critical values of the F distribution, the size of the test is biased (it will usually appear more significant than it really is). The F's-to-remove are helpful in determining the relative importance of the selected variables and as indications of the statistical accuracy with which the coefficients are estimated.

- level (described on p. 409)

For each independent variable not in the equation P2R prints

- partial correlation: the correlation of each independent variable with the dependent variable removing the effect of variables already in the equation (see Appendix A.11)

- tolerance: a check that the variable is not <u>too</u> highly correlated with one or more variables already in the equation (described on p. 410)

- F-to-enter: F-to-enter tests the coefficient for each variable as if it were entered separately into the equation at the next step. Let SS(residuals) be the sum of squares of residuals at this step and SS(next) be the residual sum of squares after the next independent variable is entered. Then

$$\text{F-to-enter} = \frac{\text{SS(residuals) - SS(next)}}{\text{SS(next)}/(N-p'-1)}$$

The F-to-enter for the variable actually entered at the next step is equal to F-to-remove for that variable immediately after being entered.

The distribution of the largest F-to-enter is affected by the number of variables available for selection. Therefore, if the largest F-to-enter is compared with the critical values of the F distribution, the size of the test is likely to be more significant than it really is. See Appendix C.2 for further discussion of the F-to-enter and F-to-remove.

- level: used to predetermine the order of entry of variables (described on p. 409).

⑦ Stepwise regression coefficients. This table shows the values of the regression coefficients of the variables in the equation (those with asterisks) at each step, and the coefficients of the other variables as if each had been entered separately into the regression equation.

⑧ A summary table reporting the variable entered, the multiple R and the F-to-enter at each step.

● OPTIONAL RESULTS AND INPUT

In addition to the above results you can request that P2R print

- the data, covariances, and correlations   p. 412

- summary tables of the partial correlations and of the F-to-enter and F-to-remove values   p. 412

- scatter plots, normal probability plots and partial residual plots   p. 414

P2R accepts input as data, a covariance matrix or a correlation matrix as input. The input must be from a BMDP File if it is a covariance or correlation matrix.   p. 416

Both the data and the covariance matrix can be saved in a BMDP
File and used as input to other programs.   p. 416

P2R can perform weighted least squares regression.   p. 415

● *REGRess:* SPECIFYING THE REGRESSION

The *REGRess*[5] paragraph describes the dependent and independent variables,
the method of entering and removing variables and the method of treating the
intercept. This paragraph can be repeated before the *END* paragraph to
specify additional analyses of the same data.

The dependent variable must be specified in the first *REGRess* paragraph. If the independent variables are not specified, all other variables
are considered as independent except the case WEIGHT variable and variables
omitted from a USE statement if specified. The independent variables can
be specified and the order of their entry into the regression equation
partially or completely predetermined by an assignment of LEVELs to the
variables (p. 409).

Each regression analysis can be given a separate title.

REGRess
   DEPENDENT=v.   {none/prev.}   required
      Name or subscript of the dependent (predicted) variable.

   INDEPENDENT=$v_1,v_2,\cdots$.   {all vars./prev.}
      Names or subscripts of the independent (predictor) variables.[6] If
      LEVELs are assigned to the variables (p. 409), the LEVELs
      determine both the order of entry of the independent variables and
      which variables are to be entered. If neither INDEPENDENT nor
      LEVEL is specified, all variables are used except the
      DEPENDENT variable and the case WEIGHT variable, if any.

   TITLE='c'.   {blank} $\leq$ 80 char.
      A title for the regression analysis.

● METHODS OF ENTERING AND REMOVING VARIABLES

Any one of four methods can be used for entering or removing variables
into or from the equation at each step. The methods are:
   F   The variable with the smallest F-to-remove is removed if its
           F-to-remove is less than the F-to-remove limit. If no variable

---

[5] In BMDP programs dated before August 1977,
    the minimum required abbreviation is *REGRES* (not *REGR*).

[6] In BMDP programs dated before August 1977,
    only LEVEL can be used (INDEP is not available).

meets this criterion, the variable with the largest F-to-enter is entered if the F-to-enter exceeds the F-to-enter limit. (F-to-remove and F-to-enter are described on pp. 403-404.)

FSWAP The variable with the smallest F-to-remove is removed if its F-to-remove is less than the F-to-remove limit. When no variable meets this criterion, a variable in the equation is exchanged with a variable not yet in the equation if the exchange increases the multiple R. If no variable can be exchanged, a variable is entered as in F.

R The variable with the smallest F-to-remove is removed if its removal results in a larger multiple R than was previously obtained for the same number of variables. If no variable meets this criterion, a variable is entered as for F.

RSWAP The variable with the smallest F-to-remove is removed by the criterion R. When no variable meets this criterion, a variable in the equation is exchanged with a variable not yet in the equation if the exchange increases the multiple R. If no variable can be exchanged, a variable is entered as in F.

The method F requires the fewest computations (is cheapest), R the next fewest. FSWAP and RSWAP require many more computations; you may want to use P9R (Section 13.3) instead.

REGRess
  METHOD= *(one only)* F,FSWAP,R,RSWAP.   {F/prev.}

  The METHOD used to enter or remove variables.[7] The methods are described above.

● FORWARD AND BACKWARD STEPPING

Since all four methods begin with no variables in the equation, they appear to describe a <u>forward</u> stepping algorithm. They can also be used for a <u>backward</u> stepping algorithm. The F-to-enter and F-to-remove limits can each be assigned two values. The first pair is used until all variables that meet the criteria have been entered; the second pair of limits is then used to remove the variables (backward stepping). By assigning very low values to the first pair of values, all (or almost all) variables can be entered into the equation. By assigning high values to the second pair, the variables in the equation can be removed.

---

[7] In BMDP programs dated before August 1977,
    the minimum required abbreviation is METHOD (not METH).

```
REGRess
    ENTER=#₁,#₂.                          {4.0,4.0/prev.}
```

F-to-enter limits. The first number is used until no more variables can be entered. The second number is then used to remove variables. We describe above how to set them to obtain backward stepping. If only one number is specified, the second number is set equal to it.

```
    REMOVE=#₁,#₂.                         {3.9,3.9/prev.}
```

F-to-remove limits. The first number is used until no more variables can be entered. The second number is then used to remove variables. We describe above how to set them to obtain backward stepping. REMOVE must be less than ENTER, or a variable could be entered and removed at alternate steps. If only one number is specified, the second number is set equal to it.

We request both forward and backward stepping in the following example.

Example 13.8

```
/PROBLEM      TITLE IS 'WERNER BLOOD CHEMISTRY DATA'.
/INPUT        VARIABLES ARE 9.
              FORMAT IS '(A4,5F4.0,3F4.1)'.
/VARIABLE     NAMES ARE ID,AGE,HEIGHT,WEIGHT,BRTHPILL,
                      CHOLSTRL,ALBUMIN,CALCIUM,URICACID.
              MAXIMUM IS (6)400.
              MINIMUM IS (6)150.
              BLANKS ARE MISSING.
              LABEL IS ID.

/REGRESS      DEPENDENT IS CHOLSTRL.
              TITLE IS 'FORWARD STEPPING FOLLOWED BY BACKWARD STEPPING'.
              ENTER  = 1,50.
              REMOVE = 0,49.

/END
```

The results are presented in Output 13.8. First the five variables that pass the F-to-enter limit are entered into the regression. Two variables (WEIGHT and ALBUMIN) do not pass the limit. At the sixth step HEIGHT is removed since it had the smallest F-to-remove at the previous step. At subsequent steps the other independent variables are removed.

In this example the variables are removed from the equation by backward stepping in the reverse order from which they were entered. The orders of entry and of removal may not coincide.

• THE INTERCEPT

The intercept, a, is usually part of a regression equation; however, in a few problems the intercept must be equal to zero because the regression line must pass through the origin. The intercept can be treated in three ways:

- always in the equation (NONZERO)
- never in the equation (ZERO)

- initially in the equation but may be removed if its F-to-remove is very small (FLOAT)

The adjusted R^2 is printed only when there is an intercept in the regression equation.

REGRess
   TYPE= *(one only)* NONZERO,ZERO,FLOAT.   { NONZERO/prev.}

The intercept is assumed to be in the equation (NONZERO) unless a ZERO intercept or FLOAT is specified. If FLOAT is specified, the intercept is initially entered into the equation but can be removed as any other independent variable. *Note: The options* ZERO *and* FLOAT *are rarely used.*

Output 13.8 Forward and backward stepping by P2R

```
REGRESSION TITLE. . . . . . . . . . . . . . . .FORWARD STEPPING FOLLOWED BY BACKWARD STEPPING
STEPPING ALGORITHM. . . . . . . . . . . . . .F
MAXIMUM NUMBER OF STEPS . . . . . . . . . . .    18
DEPENDENT VARIABLE. . . . . . . . . . . . . .     6 CHOLSTRL
MINIMUM ACCEPTABLE F TO ENTER . . . . . . . .  1.000,  50.000
MAXIMUM ACCEPTABLE F TO REMOVE. . . . . . . .  0.0  ,  49.000
MINIMUM ACCEPTABLE TOLERANCE. . . . . . . . . 0.01000
```

--- results for steps 0 to 4 ---

```
     STEP NO.   5
  VARIABLE ENTERED   3 HEIGHT

  MULTIPLE R              0.4907
  MULTIPLE R-SQUARE       0.2408
  ADJUSTED R-SQUARE       0.2190
  STD. ERROR OF EST.     37.7742

  ANALYSIS OF VARIANCE
                       SUM OF SQUARES      DF     MEAN SQUARE     F RATIO
          REGRESSION    78756.938          5      15751.39       11.039
          RESIDUAL     248279.19         174       1426.892
```

```
                     VARIABLES IN EQUATION                                  .              VARIABLES NOT IN EQUATION
                                 STD. ERROR  STD REG              F TO       .                     PARTIAL                F TO
      VARIABLE     COEFFICIENT   OF COEFF     COEFF    TOLERANCE  REMOVE  LEVEL. VARIABLE          CORR.  TOLERANCE  ENTER  LEVEL
  (Y-INTERCEPT      21.526 )                                              .
  AGE          2    1.4415       0.2929      0.334     0.948     24.22    1 . WEIGHT      4    0.039   0.68591   0.259    1
  HEIGHT       3   -1.5854       1.1757     -0.092     0.936      1.82    1 . ALBUMIN     7   -0.014   0.74640   0.034    1
  BRTHPILL     5    8.6071       5.7359      0.101     0.964      2.25    1 .
  CALCIUM      8   22.4556       6.1354      0.248     0.947     13.40    1 .
  URICACID     9    6.5983       2.6238      0.173     0.921      6.32    1 .

  F-LEVELS(   1.000,   0.0   ) OR TOLERANCE INSUFFICIENT FOR FURTHER STEPPING
```

--- results for steps 6 to 9 ---

```
  SUMMARY TABLE
  STEP           VARIABLE            MULTIPLE      INCREASE     F-TO-      F-TO-    NUMBER OF INDEPENDENT
  NO.     ENTERED       REMOVED     R       RSQ     IN RSQ      ENTER      REMOVE   VARIABLES INCLUDED
    1     2 AGE                    0.3652  0.1334   0.1334     27.3989                      1
    2     8 CALCIUM               0.4471  0.1999   0.0665     14.7188                      2
    3     9 URICACID              0.4750  0.2256   0.0257      5.8421                      3
    4     5 BRTHPILL              0.4826  0.2329   0.0073      1.6554                      4
    5     3 HEIGHT                0.4907  0.2408   0.0079      1.8183                      5
    6                  3 HEIGHT   0.4826  0.2329  -0.0079                 1.8183            4
    7                  5 BRTHPILL 0.4750  0.2256  -0.0073                 1.6554            3
    8                  9 URICACID 0.4471  0.1999  -0.0257                 5.8421            2
    9                  8 CALCIUM  0.3652  0.1334  -0.0665                14.7187            1
```

● ORDERING THE ENTRY OF VARIABLES

The order of entering independent variables into an equation is specified in a LEVEL statement. If LEVEL is not specified, the independent variables are entered as described in the METHOD discussion (p. 405). It is possible to specify complete ordering or partial ordering for the variables. LEVEL can also be used to eliminate variables from an analysis.

In the LEVEL statement you can assign positive numbers (integers) or zeros to the variables. Variables assigned a level of zero are excluded from the analysis; the level of the DEPENDENT variable is set to zero. Variables assigned a positive value are entered into the equation -- variables with smaller values are entered before variables with larger values. Variables with the same value compete for entry according to the METHOD specified. P2R begins stepping with the lowest positive value of LEVEL and enters all possible variables with that LEVEL before considering variables at the next higher level. Variables not assigned any value for LEVEL are set to a value greater than the maximum value assigned (one if no LEVEL statement is present).

When variables are eliminated by setting LEVEL=0, the F-to-enter statistic is printed for these variables at each step. When variables are eliminated from the analysis by omitting them from the USE statement in the *VARiable* paragraph, not even their F-to-enter values are computed and printed.

REGRess
LEVEL=#$_1$,#$_2$,$\cdots$. {highest level stated +1}   one per variable

The first number is the level for the first variable, the second is the level for the second variable, etc. Note that the levels are matched to the variable subscripts (that is, the variables read as data) and not to the order of variables in the *VARiable* USE statement (if given). The effect of LEVEL is described above.

The use of LEVEL is illustrated by Example 13.9. The statement FORCE=1 is explained in the content of the example and the definition below.

Example 13.9

```
/PROBLEM     TITLE IS 'WERNER BLOOD CHEMISTRY DATA'.
/INPUT       VARIABLES ARE 9.
             FORMAT IS '(A4,5F4.0,3F4.1)'.
/VARIABLE    NAMES ARE ID,AGE,HEIGHT,WEIGHT,BRTHPILL,
                   CHOLSTRL,ALBUMIN,CALCIUM,URICACID.
             MAXIMUM IS (6)400.
             MINIMUM IS (6)150.
             BLANKS ARE MISSING.
             LABEL IS ID.

/REGRESS     DEPENDENT IS CHOLSTRL.
             TITLE IS 'SPECIFYING ORDER OF ENTRY
                   OF VARIABLES INTO EQUATION'.
             LEVELS ARE 0,3,2*2,2*0,3*1.
             FORCE IS 1.

/END
```

The variables are divided into four groups:

level 1 - ALBUMIN, CALCIUM, URICACID
      2 - HEIGHT, WEIGHT
      3 - AGE
      0 - ID, BRTHPILL, CHOLSTRL (these are not used as independent variables)

Output 13.9 presents the results from the above analysis. AGE has the highest F-to-enter at Step 0 (and logically would be the first entered), but it is not entered because other variables have a lower LEVEL assigned. First URICACID enters since it has the largest F-to-enter at Step 0 of the three variables at level one (i.e., among ALBUMIN, CALCIUM or URICACID). In the following two steps, CALCIUM and ALBUMIN are entered. ALBUMIN is entered although it violates the F-to-enter limit because FORCE=1 is stated. Variables with a LEVEL less than or equal to FORCE are forced into the equation without regard to the F-to-enter limit and are not removed. Neither HEIGHT nor WEIGHT are entered because they violate the F-to-enter limit and their LEVEL exceeds FORCE. AGE is finally entered.

REGRess
    FORCE=#.   {zero/prev.}

   If FORCE is not specified or is set to zero, there is no forcing.
   If FORCE is nonzero, variables that are assigned a LEVEL less than
   or equal to FORCE are forced into the equation, whether or not their
   F-to-enters are greater than the F-to-enter limit. Only the TOLERANCE
   test can be used to stop a forced variable from entering the equation.

● TOLERANCE: INVERTING THE COVARIANCE MATRIX

   To estimate the parameters of the regression equation P2R inverts the covariance matrix in a stepwise manner (Appendix A.11). A variable is not entered into the regression equation if it does not pass the TOLERANCE limit defined below. Use P9R if you need a lower tolerance limit.

REGRess
    TOLERANCE=#.   {0.01/prev.}   between 0.01 and 1.0

   An independent variable is not entered into the regression equation
   if it does not pass the TOLERANCE limit; i.e., if its squared
   multiple correlation (R^2) with independent variables already in the
   equation exceeds 1.0-TOLERANCE, or if its entry will cause the
   squared mutliple correlation of any previously entered variable
   with the independent variables in the equation to exceed
   1.0-TOLERANCE.

● STEP: LIMITING THE NUMBER OF STEPS

Usually the stepping ends when the F-to-enter, F-to-remove or tolerance limits are violated for all the remaining independent variables. However, it is possible to specify a maximum number of steps; stepping ends when this number is reached.

REGRess
    STEP=#.   {twice the number of var./prev.}

    The maximum number of forward and backward steps allowed.

Output 13.9 Determining the order of entry of variables by a LEVEL statement in P2R

```
REGRESSION TITLE. . . . . . . . . . . . . . . .SPECIFYING ORDER OF ENTRY OF VARIABLES INTO EQUATION
STEPPING ALGORITHM. . . . . . . . . . . . . . .F
MAXIMUM NUMBER OF STEPS . . . . . . . . . . . .    18
DEPENDENT VARIABLE. . . . . . . . . . . . . . .     6 CHOLSTRL
MINIMUM ACCEPTABLE F TO ENTER . . . . . . . . . 4.000,  4.000
MAXIMUM ACCEPTABLE F TO REMOVE. . . . . . . . . 3.900,  3.900
MINIMUM ACCEPTABLE TOLERANCE. . . . . . . . . . 0.01000
FORCED LEVELS . . . . . . . . . . . . . . . .     1
```

```
STEP NO.   0

MULTIPLE R              0.0
MULTIPLE R-SQUARE       0.0
ADJUSTED R-SQUARE       0.0
STD. ERROR OF EST.     42.7436

ANALYSIS OF VARIANCE
                    SUM OF SQUARES      DF    MEAN SQUARE    F RATIO
          REGRESSION   0.0              0     0.0            0.0
          RESIDUAL   327036.19        179    1827.018
```

	VARIABLES IN EQUATION							VARIABLES NOT IN EQUATION				
		STD. ERROR	STD REG		F TO				PARTIAL		F TO	
VARIABLE	COEFFICIENT	OF COEFF	COEFF	TOLERANCE	REMOVE	LEVEL.	VARIABLE		CORR.	TOLERANCE	ENTER	LEVEL
(Y-INTERCEPT	235.838)					.	AGE	2	0.365	1.00000	27.399	3
						.	HEIGHT	3	0.011	1.00000	0.023	2
						.	WEIGHT	4	0.146	1.00000	3.889	2
						.	BRTHPILL	5	0.092	1.00000	1.509	0
						.	ALBUMIN	7	0.058	1.00000	0.591	1
						.	CALCIUM	8	0.255	1.00000	12.356	1
						.	URICACID	9	0.274	1.00000	14.446	1

```
STEP NO.   1
VARIABLE ENTERED    9 URICACID
```

--- *results for steps 1 to 4* ---

```
SUMMARY TABLE
STEP          VARIABLE            MULTIPLE    INCREASE      F-TO-     F-TO-   NUMBER OF INDEPENDENT
NO.    ENTERED    REMOVED       R      RSQ     IN RSQ       ENTER    REMOVE   VARIABLES INCLUDED
  1    9 URICACID            0.2740  0.0751   0.0751      14.4463                     1
  2    8 CALCIUM             0.3465  0.1201   0.0450       9.0560                     2
  3    7 ALBUMIN             0.3505  0.1229   0.0028       0.5607                     3
  4    2 AGE                 0.4759  0.2264   0.1036      23.4297                     4
```

- *PRINTing* TABLES AND MATRICES

    Output 13.7 presents results that are printed automatically. In the
following example we illustrate additional tables that can be printed; they are
requested in the *PRINT* paragraph.

Example 13.10

```
/PROBLEM      TITLE IS 'WERNER BLOOD CHEMISTRY DATA'.
/INPUT        VARIABLES ARE 9.
              FORMAT IS '(A4,5F4.0,3F4.1)'.
/VARIABLE     NAMES ARE ID,AGE,HEIGHT,WEIGHT,BRTHPILL,
                   CHOLSTRL,ALBUMIN,CALCIUM,URICACID.
              MAXIMUM IS (6)400.
              MINIMUM IS (6)150.
              BLANKS ARE MISSING.
              LABEL IS ID.

/REGRESS      DEPENDENT IS CHOLSTRL.

/PRINT        DATA.
              COVARIANCE.
              CORRELATION.
              RREG.
              PARTIAL.
              FRATIO.

/END
```

    The additional results are presented in Output 13.10. Circled numbers
below correspond to those in the output.

⑨   COVARIANCE matrix of the variables.

⑩   CORRELATION matrix of the variables.

⑪   Correlation matrix of the regression coefficients of the final regression
equation (RREG): defined in Appendix A.11.

⑫   F-to-enter and F-to-remove for each variable at each step (FRATIO):
Asterisks indicate variables in the equation (F-to-remove); values
without asterisks are F's-to-enter.

⑬   Partial correlations at each step (PARTIAL): Asterisks indicate variables in the equation. The partial correlation of a variable in the
equation is its correlation with the dependent variable after removing
the effect of the remaining variables in the equation.

⑭   The residual $(y_j - \hat{y}_j)$, predicted value $\hat{y}_j$, and data for each case. A negative case number denotes a case with a missing value; the missing values
are replaced by a series of asterisks. Asterisks are also printed when
the predicted value or residual cannot be computed due to a missing value
in the case. The number of standard deviations that a value is from the
overall mean for the variables is reported by zero, one, two or three
asterisks after the value; three asterisks represent three or more standard deviations.

Output 13.10 Optional results printed by P2R. Results not reproduced are
             indicated in italics.

--- univariate statistics ---

--- covariance matrix ---

⑨

CORRELATION MATRIX

⑩

		AGE 2	HEIGHT 3	WEIGHT 4	BRTHPILL 5	CHOLSTRL 6	ALBUMIN 7	CALCIUM 8	URICACID 9
AGE	2	1.0000							
HEIGHT	3	0.0892	1.0000						
WEIGHT	4	0.2553	0.4735	1.0000					
BRTHPILL	5	0.0563	0.1640	0.0801	1.0000				
CHOLSTRL	6	0.3652	0.0115	0.1462	0.0917	1.0000			
ALBUMIN	7	-0.0789	-0.0058	-0.2346	-0.2352	0.0575	1.0000		
CALCIUM	8	-0.0086	0.1428	0.0647	-0.0629	0.2548	0.4529	1.0000	
URICACID	9	0.2085	0.1254	0.3036	0.0154	0.2740	0.0299	0.1662	1.0000

--- results for steps 0 to 4 ---

CORRELATION MATRIX OF REGRESSION COEFFICIENTS

⑪

		AGE 2	CALCIUM 8	URICACID 9
AGE	2	1.0000		
CALCIUM	8	0.0449	1.0000	
URICACID	9	-0.2130	-0.1718	1.0000

--- stepwise regression coefficients ---

F-TO-ENTER OR F-TO-REMOVE OF EACH VARIABLE AT EACH STEP

⑫

VARIABLES STEP	2 AGE	3 HEIGHT	4 WEIGHT	5 BRTHPILL	7 ALBUMIN	8 CALCIUM	9 URICACID
0	27.3989	0.0234	3.8888	1.5091	0.5908	12.3559	14.4464
1	27.3989*	0.0920	0.6156	1.0428	1.5454	14.7188	8.7697
2	29.8695*	0.7697	0.3023	1.7017	0.2564	14.7188*	5.8421
3	23.9881*	1.2211	0.0043	1.6554	0.1849	11.6655*	5.8421*

PARTIAL CORRELATIONS

⑬

VARIABLES STEP	2 AGE	3 HEIGHT	4 WEIGHT	5 BRTHPILL	7 ALBUMIN	8 CALCIUM	9 URICACID
0	0.3652	0.0115	0.1462	0.0917	0.0575	0.2548	0.2740
1	0.3652*	-0.0228	0.0589	0.0765	0.0930	0.2771	0.2173
2	0.3800*	-0.0660	0.0414	0.0979	-0.0381	0.2771*	0.1792
3	0.3463*	-0.0832	-0.0050	0.0968	-0.0325	0.2493*	0.1792*

SUMMARY TABLE

STEP NO.	VARIABLE ENTERED REMOVED	MULTIPLE R	RSQ	INCREASE IN RSQ	F-TO- ENTER	F-TO- REMOVE	NUMBER OF INDEPENDENT VARIABLES INCLUDED
1	2 AGE	0.3652	0.1334	0.1334	27.3989		1
2	8 CALCIUM	0.4471	0.1999	0.0665	14.7188		2
3	9 URICACID	0.4750	0.2256	0.0257	5.8421		3

LIST OF PREDICTED VALUES, RESIDUALS, AND VARIABLES
(- INDICATES A CASE CONTAINING ONE OR MORE VARIABLES OUT OF RANGE OR MISSING)

⑭

CASE NO. LABEL	PREDICTED	RESIDUAL	WEIGHT	VARIABLES 6 CHOLSTRL	2 AGE	3 HEIGHT	4 WEIGHT	5 BRTHPILL	7 ALBUMIN
1 2381	219.8721	-19.8721	1.000	200.0000	22.0000	67.0000	144.0000	1.0000	4.3000
-2 1946	***********	***************	1.000	***********	22.0000	64.0000	160.0000	2.0000	3.5000
3 1610	223.3316	19.6684	1.000	243.0000	25.0000	62.0000	128.0000	1.0000	4.1000
-4 1797	204.7949	***************	1.000	***********	25.0000	68.0000	150.0000	2.0000	3.8000
5 561	213.2025	-55.2025*	1.000	158.0000	19.0000	64.0000	125.0000	1.0000	4.1000

--- similar statistics for cases 6 to 185 ---

186 575	278.0215	-58.0215*	1.000	220.0000	53.0000	65.0000	140.0000	2.0000	4.0000
187 2271	272.4094	32.5906	1.000	305.0000	54.0000	66.0000	158.0000	1.0000	4.2000
188 39	250.7381	-30.7381	1.000	220.0000	54.0000	60.0000	170.0000	2.0000	3.5000

EACH ASTERISK REPRESENTS ONE STANDARD DEVIATION

LIST OF PREDICTED VALUES, RESIDUALS, AND VARIABLES (CONTINUED)

--- values for variable 8 are printed in a separate panel ---

PRINT

    COVARIANCE.   {no/prev.}

       Print the covariance matrix of the variables.

    CORRELATION.   {no/prev.}

       Print the correlation matrix of the variables.

    ANOVA.   {ANOVA /prev.}

       An analysis of variance table at each step is printed unless you
       specify NO ANOVA.

    STEP.   {STEP/prev.}

       The results at each step are printed unless you specify NO STEP.

    RREGRESSION.   {no/prev.}

       Print the correlation matrix of the regression coefficients.[8]

    COEFFICIENTS.   {COEFFICIENT /prev.}

       The summary table of regression coefficients is printed unless you
       specify NO COEFFICIENTS.

    FRATIO.   {no/prev.}

       Print the summary table of F-to-enter and F-to-remove values.

    PARTIAL.   {no/prev.}

       Print the summary table of partial correlations.[9]

    SUMMARY   {SUMMARY/prev.}

       A summary table with the multiple R, R^2, F-to-enter and F-to-remove
       at each step is printed unless you specify NO SUMMARY. [10]

    DATA.   {no/prev.}

       Print the input data, residuals and predicted values.

● *PLOTs* AVAILABLE IN P2R

    The plots available in P2R are the same as those in P1R. Examples are
presented in Output 13.3 (p. 388). For a discussion of the plots, please
read p. 387. We repeat only the definitions.

---

[8] In BMDP programs dated before August 1977,
   RREG is not available.

[9] In BMDP programs dated before August 1977,
   the minimum required abbreviation is PARTIAL (not PART).

[10] In BMDP programs dated before August 1977,
   the minimum required abbreviation is SUMMARY (not SUM).

PLOT

RESIDUAL.   {no/prev.}

Plot the residuals $(y-\hat{y})$ and residuals squared $(y-\hat{y})^2$ in separate graphs against the predicted values $\hat{y}$.

VARIABLE=$v_1,v_2,\cdots$.   {none/prev.}

Names or subscripts of variables against which the observed values of the dependent variable y and the predicted values $\hat{y}$ are plotted. Overlaps between observed and predicted values are indicated by asterisks. The residuals $(y-\hat{y})$ are also plotted against the same variables. Each variable is plotted in a separate graph.

PREP=$v_1,v_2,\cdots$.   {none/prev.}

Names or subscripts of variables plotted in partial residual plots. This is a plot of the (residual + coefficient $\cdot$ observed value of independent variable) against the observed value of that independent variable; i.e., $(y - \hat{y} + bx)$ against x.

NORMAL.   {no/prev.}

Plot a normal probability plot of the residuals.[11]

DNORMAL.   {no/prev.}

Plot a detrended normal probability plot of the residuals.[11]

SIZE=$\#_1,\#_2$.   {50,50/prev.}

$\#_1$ is the number of characters (width) in the horizontal axis and $\#_2$ is the number of lines (height) in the vertical axis

● CASE WEIGHTS

When the error variance is not homogeneous but varies from case to case, weighted least squares estimation is more appropriate; the weight (w) for each case is proportional to the inverse of the variance. In weighted least squares, estimates of the coefficients minimize

$$\sum_j w_j(y_j-\hat{y}_j)^2$$

where w_j is the weight for case j.

You can estimate predicted values for cases not used to compute the regression equation by setting their case weights to zero (See Appendix C.4).

Case weights affect the computation of the means, variances, covariances and correlations (see Section 2.1).

---

[11] In BMDP programs dated before August 1977,
    PROBIT is used in place of both NORMAL and DNORMAL.

```
┌─────────────────────────────────────────────────────────────────────┐
│ VARiable                                                              │
│    WEIGHT=v.                              {no weight var./prev.}       │
│                                                                       │
│       Name or subscript of the variable containing case weights. The  │
│       weights should be greater than or equal to zero.  If WEIGHT      │
│       is not stated or is set to zero, there are no case weights.      │
│                                                                       │
└─────────────────────────────────────────────────────────────────────┘
```

● *INPut* FROM A BMDP FILE

Only data can be read by P2R unless a BMDP File (Chapter 7) is used as input: DATA, a COVARIANCE matrix, or a CORRELATION matrix can be input from a BMDP File.

Example 13.5 (p. 394) illustrates how to use a CORRELATION matrix as input for P1R; it can also be used for P2R.

When the input is not data, the CONTENT of the BMDP File must be specified.

```
┌─────────────────────────────────────────────────────────────────────┐
│ INPut                                                                 │
│    CONTENT= c.    { DATA }       used only when input is from a BMDP File │
│       When the input is not DATA, CONTENT must be specified.  It must  │
│       be identical to the CONTENT stated in the SAVE paragraph when the│
│       BMDP File was created.                                          │
│                                                                       │
└─────────────────────────────────────────────────────────────────────┘
```

When the CONTENT is DATA, COVA or CORR, P2R recognizes how the input is to be analyzed. Several BMDP programs create BMDP Files with a different CONTENT that is not recognized by P2R. You can use other Files as input to P2R but you must specify by a TYPE statement how they are to be analyzed (as DATA, a COVARIANCE or a CORRELATION matrix).

```
┌─────────────────────────────────────────────────────────────────────┐
│ INPut                                                                 │
│    TYPE= (one only) DATA,COVA,CORR.  {same as CONTENT } used only if  │
│                                                           input is from│
│                                                           BMDP File    │
│       TYPE specifies how the input is analyzed.  It must be specified  │
│       when a BMDP File is read as input and the CONTENT is not one of  │
│       the three TYPEs -- DATA, COVA or CORR.                           │
│                                                                       │
└─────────────────────────────────────────────────────────────────────┘
```

● STORING THE DATA AND COVARIANCE MATRIX IN A BMDP FILE

Both the DATA (including predicted values and residuals) and the COVARIANCE matrix from P2R can be saved in a BMDP File to use as input to a further analysis. Saving the COVARIANCE matrix allows subsequent analyses to start from the computed means and covariances, which may result in a substantial reduction of computer costs. Chapter 7 describes BMDP Files and how they are used.

The *SAVE* paragraph is illustrated for P1R in Example 13.6, and is the same for P2R. The definition is repeated below.

SAVE

   CONTENT=*(one or both)* DATA,COVA.   { DATA }

     The matrices to be saved in a BMDP File. If DATA is specified, the predicted values are saved as variable (VT+1) and named PREDICTD and the residuals are saved as variable (VT+2) and named RESIDUAL where VT is the total number of variables (after transformation, if any).

● SIZE OF PROBLEM

P2R can analyze a problem with up to 150 variables included in the analysis. Appendix B describes how to increase the capacity of the program.

● COMPUTATIONAL METHOD

All computations are performed in single precision. Means, standard deviations and covariances are computed by the method of provisional means (Appendix A.2). The independent variables are entered into the regression equation or removed from it in a stepwise manner (Appendix A.11) according to the specified (or preassigned) options that you select.

ACKNOWLEDGEMENT

P2R was programmed by Jerry Douglas. Recent revisions were made by Lanaii Kline. P2R supersedes BMDO2R; Robert Jennrich guided the development of BMDO2R.

P9R

13.3 All Possible Subsets Regression

James Frane, HSCF

P9R estimates regression equations for "best" subsets of predictor variables and does extensive residual analysis. Best is defined in terms of the sample R-squared, adjusted R-squared, or Mallows' C_p. For example, if adjusted R-squared is chosen, the best subset is the subset that maximizes adjusted R-squared. A specified number of best subsets (M--up to ten) is identified. Thus, not only the best but also the second best, third best, etc., subsets are identified to provide several good alternatives. The R-squared criterion identifies the M best subsets of each subset size. (Subset size is the number of independent variables included in the equation.) When the adjusted R-squared or Mallows' C_p criterion is chosen, the M best subsets are identified without regard to subset size; for example, if ten best subsets are requested for 20 independent variables, the best subsets might not include subsets of size one or twenty.

Extensive residual analysis is available. Statistics that can be printed, plotted or saved in a BMDP File include predicted values, residuals, standardized (Studentized) residuals, a residual for each case obtained by deleting that case from the estimation of the regression equation, weighted residuals and Cook's (1977) distance. The statistics aid in assessing the fit of the data to the regression, the dependence on the independent variables and the sensitivity of the regression equation to the data for each case.

FORTRAN coding for the best subset algorithm was obtained from G.M. Furnival and R.W. Wilson (1974a and 1974b). This algorithm identifies the best subsets while computing only a small fraction of all possible regressions and is substantially more efficient than previously available algorithms. P9R (without modification) can analyze problems containing up to 27 variables -- computer costs are comparable to costs for stepwise regression. Up to 100 variables can be analyzed by P9R when you request multiple linear regression without subset selection.

● RESULTS

The Werner blood chemistry data (Table 5.1) are analyzed to illustrate the results reported by P9R. In Example 13.11 the *REGRess* paragraph is specific to P9R; the other Control Language instructions are described in Chapter 5.

<u>Example 13.11</u>

```
/PROBLEM      TITLE IS 'WERNER BLOOD CHEMISTRY DATA'.
/INPUT        VARIABLES ARE 9.
              FORMAT IS '(A4,5F4.0,3F4.1)'.
/VARIABLE     NAMES ARE ID,AGE,HEIGHT,WEIGHT,BRTHPILL,
                     CHOLSTRL,ALBUMIN,CALCIUM,URICACID.
              MAXIMUM IS (6)400.
              MINIMUM IS (6)150.
              BLANKS ARE MISSING.
              LABEL IS ID.

/REGRESS      DEPENDENT IS CHOLSTRL.
              INDEPENDENT ARE 2 TO 4, 7 TO 9.

/END
```

The Control Language must be preceded by System Cards to initiate the analysis by P9R.
At HSCF, the System Cards are

```
//jobname  JOB  nooo,yourname
//  EXEC  BIMED,PROG=BMDP9R
//SYSIN  DD  *
```

The Control Language is immediately followed by the data (Table 5.1). The analysis
is terminated by another System Card. At HSCF, this System Card is

```
//
```

Output 13.11 presents the results of the analysis by P9R. Circled
numbers below correspond to those in the output.

(1) Interpretation of the *REGRess* paragraph and Control Language instructions specific to P9R. Many of the options listed are preassigned.

(2) Data for the first five cases (after transformation, if any). Only
cases used in the computations are printed. If you want other cases
printed, you can request them in the *PRINT* paragraph.

(3) Only complete cases are used in the computations; i.e., cases that have
no missing values or values out of range. Therefore only 180 of the
original 188 cases are used. The DEPENDENT and INDEPENDENT variables only are checked for acceptable values.

(4) Univariate statistics for each variable (computed from the complete
cases)

- mean

- standard deviation

- coefficient of variation

- smallest observed value (not out of range)

- largest observed value (not out of range)

- smallest standard score

- largest standard score

- skewness

- kurtosis

These statistics are described in Section 2.1.

Output 13.11 Results of a regression analysis by P9R. Circled numbers
correspond to those in the text. Results not reproduced
are indicated in italics.

BMDP9R – ALL POSSIBLE SUBSETS REGRESSION
HEALTH SCIENCES COMPUTING FACILITY
UNIVERSITY OF CALIFORNIA, LOS ANGELES

PROGRAM REVISED SEPTEMBER 1977
MANUAL DATE -- 1977

--- *Control Language read by P9R is printed and interpreted* ---

(1)
```
INDEPENDENT VARIABLES ARE
        2  AGE          3  HEIGHT      4  WEIGHT      7  ALBUMIN     8  CALCIUM
        9  URICACID

DEPENDENT VARIABLE. . . . . . . . . . . . . . . .   6 CHOLSTRL
NUMBER OF 'BEST' REGRESSIONS. . . . . . . . . . .   5
SELECTION CRITERION . . . . . . . . . . . . . .    CP
WEIGHT VARIABLE . . . . . . . . . . . . . . . .
PRECISION . . . . . . . . . . . . . . . . . . .    DOUBLE
TOLERANCE FOR MATRIX INVERSION. . . . . . . .      0.0001000

PRINT CORRELATION MATRIX. . . . . . . . . . . .    YES
PRINT COVARIANCE MATRIX . . . . . . . . . . . .    NO
PRINT RESIDUALS . . . . . . . . . . . . . . . .    NO
PRINT COVARIANCE MATRIX FOR REGRESSION COEFS. .    NO
PRINT CORRELATION MATRIX FOR REGRESSION COEFS .    NO
```

(2)
```
DATA AFTER TRANSFORMATIONS FOR FIRST    5 CASES
CASES WITH ZERO WEIGHTS AND MISSING DATA NOT INCLUDED.

   CASE
LABEL   NUMBER      WEIGHT    2 AGE     3 HEIGHT   4 WEIGHT   7 ALBUMIN   8 CALCIUM   9 URICACID   6 CHOLSTRL

2381      1        1.00000   22.00000   67.00000   144.00000   4.30000    9.80000     5.40000     200.00000

1610      3        1.00000   25.00000   62.00000   128.00000   4.10000   10.40000     3.30000     243.00000

 561      5        1.00000   19.00000   64.00000   125.00000   4.10000    9.90000     4.70000     158.00000

2519      6        1.00000   19.00000   67.00000   130.00000   4.50000   10.50000     8.30000     255.00000

 225      7        1.00000   20.00000   64.00000   118.00000   3.90000    9.50000     4.00000     210.00000
```

(3)
```
NUMBER OF CASES READ. . . . . . . . . . . . . .    188
CASES WITH DATA MISSING OR BEYOND LIMITS . .        8
     REMAINING NUMBER OF CASES . . . . . . . .     180
```

(4)
```
UNIVARIATE SUMMARY STATISTICS
```

VARIABLE	MEAN	STANDARD DEVIATION	COEFFICIENT OF VARIATION	SMALLEST VALUE	LARGEST VALUE	SMALLEST STANDARD SCORE	LARGEST STANDARD SCORE	SKEWNESS	KURTOSIS
2 AGE	33.53889	9.89801	0.295120	19.00000	55.00000	-1.47	2.17	0.40	-0.99
3 HEIGHT	64.46667	2.48211	0.038502	57.00000	71.00000	-3.01	2.63	-0.12	-0.04
4 WEIGHT	131.09444	20.49982	0.156374	94.00000	215.00000	-1.81	4.09	1.06	1.94
7 ALBUMIN	4.12056	0.35872	0.087057	3.20000	5.00000	-2.57	2.45	-0.07	-0.36
8 CALCIUM	9.96778	0.47280	0.047433	8.80000	11.10000	-2.47	2.39	-0.03	-0.58
9 URICACID	4.75556	1.12111	0.235748	2.20000	9.90000	-2.28	4.59	1.18	2.92
6 CHOLSTRL	235.83889	42.74377	0.181241	155.00000	390.00000	-1.89	3.61	0.46	0.06

(5)
```
CORRELATIONS
              AGE      HEIGHT    WEIGHT    ALBUMIN   CALCIUM   URICACID  CHOLSTRL
               2         3         4         7         8         9         6

AGE       2   1.000
HEIGHT    3   0.089    1.000
WEIGHT    4   0.255    0.473    1.000
ALBUMIN   7  -0.079   -0.006   -0.235    1.000
CALCIUM   8  -0.009    0.143    0.065    0.453    1.000
URICACID  9   0.209    0.125    0.304    0.030    0.166    1.000
CHOLSTRL  6   0.365    0.011    0.146    0.057    0.255    0.274    1.000
```

(6)
```
NOTE THAT THE CRITERIA (R-SQUARED, ADJUSTED R-SQUARED
AND CP), THE REGRESSION COEFFICIENTS, AND THEIR
T-STATISTICS ARE REPORTED FOR THE    5 BEST SUBSETS.
THE CRITERIA ARE EVALUATED FOR MANY OTHER SUBSETS, SOME OF
WHICH MAY ALSO BE QUITE GOOD.  THESE OTHER SUBSETS ARE NOT
NECESSARILY BETTER THAN ANY SUBSET WHICH HAS NOT BEEN
PRINTED.
```

(continued)

Output 13.11 *(continued)*

⑦   ********* REGRESSIONS WITH 1 VARIABLES *********

```
  R-SQUARED ADJ R-SQ     CP      VARIABLES IN SUBSET

   0.13339  0.12852    19.40      2
   0.07506  0.06987    32.55      9
   0.06490  0.05965    34.84      8
   0.02138  0.01588    44.65      4
   0.00331 -0.00229    48.73      7
   0.00013 -0.00549    49.44      3
```

                               ********* REGRESSIONS WITH 2 VARIABLES *********

```
  R-SQUARED ADJ R-SQ     CP      VARIABLES IN SUBSET

   0.19992  0.19088     6.40      2  8
   0.17430  0.16497    12.17      2  9
   0.14089  0.13118    19.71      2  7
   0.13639  0.12663    20.72      2  4
   0.13384  0.12405    21.30      2  3
```

--- *regressions with 3 to 5 variables appear here* ---

                               ********* REGRESSIONS WITH 5 VARIABLES *********

```
  R-SQUARED ADJ R-SQ     CP      VARIABLES IN SUBSET

   0.23213  0.21007     5.13      2  3  7  8  9
                                  THIS IS ONE OF THE   5 BEST SUBSETS.

                                  VARIABLE          COEFFICIENT     T-STATISTIC
                                  2 AGE             0.144852D 01       4.91
                                  3 HEIGHT         -0.132644D 01      -1.14
                                  7 ALBUMIN        -0.454807D 01      -0.51
                                  8 CALCIUM         0.232669D 02       3.37
                                  9 URICACID        0.655939D 01       2.48
                                    INTERCEPT       0.283964D 02

   0.23207  0.21001     5.15      2  3  4     8  9
   0.22661  0.20439     6.38      2     4  7  8  9
   0.20904  0.18631    10.34      2  3  4  7  8
   0.18429  0.16085    15.92      2  3  4  7     9
   0.13286  0.10795    27.51      3  4  7     8  9
```

                               ********* REGRESSIONS WITH 6 VARIABLES *********

```
  R-SQUARED ADJ R-SQ     CP      VARIABLES IN SUBSET

   0.23272  0.20611     7.00      2  3  4  7  8  9
```

```
        12 REGRESSIONS COMPUTED IN THE PROCESS OF FINDING BEST SUBSETS.
        69 MULTIPLICATIONS AND DIVISIONS WERE USED IN FINDING BEST
           SUBSETS (NOT INCLUDING COMPUTATION OF COVARIANCE MATRIX).
```

⑧
```
STATISTICS FOR 'BEST' SUBSET
MALLOW'S CP                      2.60
SQUARED MULTIPLE CORRELATION     0.22562
MULTIPLE CORRELATION             0.47500
ADJUSTED SQUARED MULT. CORR.     0.21242
RESIDUAL MEAN SQUARE          0.143992D 04
STANDARD ERROR OF EST.        0.379332D 02
F-STATISTIC                     17.09
NUMERATOR DEGREES OF FREEDOM       3
DENOMINATOR DEGREES OF FREEDOM   176
SIGNIFICANCE                     0.0000
```

```
  VARIABLE    REGRESSION      STANDARD   STAND.   T-    2TAIL      TOL-
  NO.  NAME   COEFFICIENT      ERROR     COEF.   STAT.   SIG.     ERANCE

      INTERCEPT -0.497409D 02  0.606922D 02  -1.164  -0.82  0.414
   2 AGE        0.143596D 01   0.293183D 00   0.333   4.90  0.000   0.954582
   8 CALCIUM    0.207918D 02   0.608754D 01   0.230   3.42  0.001   0.970402
   9 URICACID   0.634439D 01   0.262485D 01   0.166   2.42  0.017   0.928274
```

(5) The correlation matrix with the dependent variable listed last.

(6) Since no criterion (METHOD) is specified in Example 13.11, the criterion used is Mallows' C_p. The five best subsets of variables according to Mallows' C_p are reported (5 is the preassigned number of subsets to be identified).

(7) Not all subsets of the independent variables are evaluated. At each subset size, P9R reports for up to 10 subsets of independent variables

- squared multiple correlation (R^2): the square of the correlation between the dependent variable y and the predicted value $\hat{y}$

- adjusted R^2: $R^2 - p(1-R^2)/(N-p')$

  where N is the number of cases and p' is the number of independent variables p (when the intercept is set to zero) or $p+1$ (when the intercept is not zero)

- Mallows' C_p: $RSS/s^2 - (N-2p')$

  where RSS is the residual sum of squares based on the selected independent variables and s^2 is the residual mean square based on the regression using all independent variables

The coefficient of each variable and the coefficient divided by its standard error (the t statistic) are also reported for the best subsets chosen by the criterion.

(8) An analysis of the "best" subset selected by the criterion (the criterion is C_p in our example). For the best subset P9R prints

- the squared multiple correlation (R^2)

- adjusted R^2

- standard error of estimate ($RMS^{\frac{1}{2}}$)

- F statistic (test of the significance of the regression coefficients; however, its level of significance is sensitive to the method by which the best subset is selected)

For each variable in the best subset P9R prints

- the regression coefficient: b_i

- its standard error: $s(b_i)$ (see Appendix A.11)

- the standardized regression coefficient: $b_i s_i/s_y$ (the regression coefficient for standardized variables)

- t statistic: $b_i/s(b_i)$

- the two-tail level of significance of the t statistic (the level of significance of the test that the coefficient is zero)

- tolerance (described on p. 432)

● OPTIONAL RESULTS AND INPUT

In addition to the above results, the following are available on request:

- the covariance matrix of the variables   p. 426
- residuals and predicted values   p. 426
- correlations of estimates of the regression coefficients   p. 426
- scatter plots and normal probability plots   p. 429

Weighted least squares regression can be performed. Case weights can also be used to cross-validate your results.   p. 432

Input to P9R can be data, a covariance or a correlation matrix. The input need <u>not</u> be from a BMDP File. (Other regression programs can accept a covariance or correlation matrix as input only if the matrix is in a BMDP File.)   p. 433

The data (including predicted values, residuals and related measures) and the covariance matrix can be saved in a BMDP File for input to another program.   p. 434

● *REGRess:* SPECIFYING THE REGRESSION

The *REGRess* paragraph is <u>required</u> to describe the dependent (predicted) and independent (predictor) variables.[12] This paragraph <u>cannot</u> be repeated in P9R.

REGRess
    DEPENDENT= v.   {none}   required
      Name or subscript of the dependent (predicted) variable.

    INDEPENDENT=$v_1, v_2, \cdots$.   {none}
      Names or subscripts of the independent (predictor) variables. At least 3 variables must be specified unless METHOD=NONE is specified as described below.

● METHOD: CHOOSING THE BEST SUBSET

Any of three METHODs can be used as the criterion for the best subset (see Hocking, 1972).

- CP: Mallows' C_p (Daniel and Wood, 1971, p. 86) is defined as

$$C_p = \frac{RSS}{s^2} - (N - 2p')$$

---

[12] P9R was originally distributed in August 1976. If your version is dated before August 1977, there are some minor changes in the abbreviated forms and item names; previous form is given as a footnote to the summary (p. 457).

where

RSS   is the residual sum of squares for the best subset being tested

p' is the number of variables in the subset (including the intercept, if any)

s^2 is the residual mean square based on the regression using all independent variables

Best is defined as the smallest C_p.

- RSQ: multiple correlation squared (R^2)

Best is defined as the largest R^2.

- ADJ: adjusted R^2 is defined as

$$R^2 - p(1-R^2)/(N-p')$$

Best is defined as the largest adjusted R^2.

If you do not want P9R to search for the best subsets, you can specify

- NONE: an ordinary regression is performed using all independent variables. This option is used when the primary interest is in the residual analysis that is not available in other programs, or when you need computations done in double precision.

When CP is the METHOD used, the criterion

$$C_p = \frac{RSS}{s^2} - (N-2p')$$

can be modified by specifying a value for PENALTY. Without this specification, when an additional variable is entered p increases by one and $-(N-2p)$ increases by two -- two is a penalty for adding a variable. The value specified for PENALTY becomes the coefficient of p in the above formula.

REGRess
   METHOD= *(one only)* CP,RSQ,ADJ,NONE   {CP /prev.}

   Criterion for choosing the best subset. The methods are described above. If NONE is specified, a multiple linear regression analysis is performed using all independent variables (no subsets are identified).

PENALTY=#.   {2/prev.}

   The penalty for entering an additional variable when the METHOD is CP. Penalty is defined above. Mallows' C_p corresponds to a penalty of 2.

NUMBER=#.   {5/prev.}   cannot exceed 10

   The number of best subsets to be identified. For CP and ADJ, this number is found for all subset sizes combined. For RSQ this number is found for each subset size.

● STRATEGIES FOR VARIABLE SELECTION

Several strategies can be used to select independent variables. One strategy is to screen a large set of variables and delete those that appear definitely redundant with respect to predicting the dependent variable. Another sample can then be taken and a subset of the first subset chosen. This process might be repeated. The number of variables in the subset and the criterion for selection is highly dependent upon the stage of the research. It is suggested that in any final selection of variables all the t statistics for the coefficients be highly significant from both the statistical and practical points of view.

The t statistics for the coefficients of the variables for the subset that maximizes adjusted R-squared are all greater than one in absolute value. Maximizing adjusted R-squared is equivalent to minimizing the residual mean square. In the language of stepwise regression, the subset that maximizes adjusted R-squared is such that each variable in the subset has an F-to-remove value greater than one and the remaining variables have F-to-enter values less than one. Subsets larger than the subset that maximizes the adjusted R-squared are not likely to be very good.

The t statistics for the coefficients of the variables for the subset that minimizes C_p tend to be greater than $\sqrt{2}$ in absolute value. In the language of stepwise regression, the subset that minimizes C_p is such that the F-to-remove values for variables in the subset tend to be greater than two and the F-to-enter values for the remaining variables tend to be less than two.

The preassigned F-to-enter and F-to-remove limits in the stepwise program P2R are 4 and 3.9. This F-to-enter limit suggests that the t statistics for the regression coefficients should be at least two. In P9R this type of restriction can be imposed (approximately) on the coefficients by means of the PENALTY statement in the *REGRess* paragraph. The F-to-remove values tend to be greater than the specified value of PENALTY for the best subset.

The problem of variable selection increases as the number of redundant and irrelevant variables increases. Inclusion of such variables permits artifacts in the data to produce spuriously high t statistics, R-squared values and adjusted R-squared values, and spuriously low C_p statistics -- just as spuriously optimistic statistics can result in a stepwise regression. As a general rule of thumb, a smaller number of variables is likely to provide better results in a cross-validation (application of the regression coefficients to new data). A cross-validation can easily be made in this program by means of the case weight variable. The "training" set should be assigned weights of one and the cross-validation set should be assigned weight zero. If you request that the residuals be printed or plotted, the residual mean square for the training set and the average squared residual for the cross-validation set are printed and can be compared. (See Appendix C.19).

● *PRINTing* THE DATA, RESIDUALS AND MATRICES

You can specify the number of CASEs to print. If not specified, five cases are printed.

```
PRINT
    CASE=#.                          {5/prev.}

    Number of cases of data (after transformations, if any) to be
    printed.
```

The CORRELATIONS and COVARIANCES between the variables, and the correlations of the estimates of the regression coefficients (RREG) can be printed. In addition, residuals, predicted values and related values can be printed.

Some of these tables are requested in the following example.

Example 13.12

```
/PROBLEM      TITLE IS 'WERNER BLOOD CHEMISTRY DATA'.
/INPUT        VARIABLES ARE 9.
              FORMAT IS '(A4,5F4.0,3F4.1)'.
/VARIABLE     NAMES ARE ID,AGE,HEIGHT,WEIGHT,BRTHPILL,
                  CHOLSTRL,ALBUMIN,CALCIUM,URICACID.
              MAXIMUM IS (6)400.
              MINIMUM IS (6)150.
              BLANKS ARE MISSING.
              LABEL IS ID.

/REGRESS      DEPENDENT IS CHOLSTRL.
              INDEPENDENT ARE 2 TO 4, 7 TO 9.

/PRINT        MATRICES ARE COVA,RREG,RESI.

/END
```

The results of the analysis appear in Output 13.12. Circled numbers below correspond to those in the output.

⑨   The covariance matrix of the variables (the dependent variable is last).

⑩   Correlations of the estimates of the regression coefficients (defined in Appendix A.11) calculated for the best subset.

⑪   The request to print residuals yields the following for each case

   - the value of the dependent variable: y

   - the predicted value for the dependent variable (predicted from the best subset): $\hat{y}$

   - the residual: $y-\hat{y}$

   - case weight: w (one if a case WEIGHT is not specified)

- weighted residual: $\sqrt{w}$ $(y-\hat{y})$ (if w is zero or one, $y-\hat{y}$ is printed)

- standardized (Studentized) residual (Prescott, 1975): $(y-\hat{y})/$(standard error)

- deleted residual: the residual that would be obtained if the case were omitted from the computation of the regression line (see Appendix A.12 for the formula)

- Mahalanobis distance: the distance of each case from the mean of all cases used to estimate the regression equation (computed from the values of the independent variables in the best subset, see Append'x A.12 for the formula); a large distance indicates that the case is an outlier in the space defined by the independent variables.

- Cook's (1977) distance: a measure of the change in the coefficients of the regression that would occur if the case were omitted from the computation of the coefficients (see Appendix A.12 for the formula)

See Appendix C.20 for further discussion of the residual analysis.

(12) Summary statistics for the residuals for cases with positive weights:

- average residual: Σ $(y-\hat{y})/N$

- residual mean square: Σ $(y-\hat{y})^2/(N-p)$

- average deleted residual: Σ deleted residual$/N$

- average squared deleted residual: Σ (deleted residual)$^2/N$

If case weights are specified, the above formulas are modified to include the case weights. These summary statistics are reported separately for cases with zero case weight (see Appendix C.19).

(13) Numerical consistency check: the residual mean square is computed both from the residuals and from the covariance matrix.

```
PRINT
   MATRICES= (one or more) CORR,COVA,RREG,RESI.    { CORR /prev.}

   Matrices to be printed.  If any MATRICES are specified, only those
   requested are printed.

      CORR :  correlation matrix

      COVA :  covariance matrix

      RREG :  correlations of the estimates of the regression coefficients

      RESI :  residuals, predicted values and related measures as
              described in (11) , (12) and (13)  above.
```

Output 13.12 Optional printed results by P9R

```
PRINT CORRELATION MATRIX. . . . . . . . . . . . .  NO
PRINT COVARIANCE MATRIX . . . . . . . . . . . . .  YES
PRINT RESIDUALS . . . . . . . . . . . . . . . . .  YES
PRINT COVARIANCE MATRIX FOR REGRESSION COEFS. .    NO
PRINT CORRELATION MATRIX FOR REGRESSION COEFS .    YES
```

--- *univariate statistics appear here* ---

⑨

COVARIANCES		AGE 2	HEIGHT 3	WEIGHT 4	ALBUMIN 7	CALCIUM 8	URICACID 9	CHOLSTRL 6
AGE	2	0.979705E 02						
HEIGHT	3	0.218845E 01	0.616089E 01					
WEIGHT	4	0.517924E 02	0.240898E 02	0.420242E 03				
ALBUMIN	7	-0.280412E 00	-0.517689E-02	-0.172541E 01	0.128681E 00			
CALCIUM	8	-0.406390E-01	0.167635E 00	0.627083E 00	0.768113E-01	0.223537E 00		
URICACID	9	0.231403E 01	0.348790E 00	0.697796E 00	0.120360E-01	0.881130E-01	0.125690E 01	
CHOLSTRL	6	0.154517E 03	0.120968E 01	0.128116E 03	0.881543E 00	0.514841E 01	0.131291E 02	0.182703E 04

--- *best subset selected and best subset analyzed* ---

CORRELATIONS OF THE ESTIMATES OF THE REGRESSION COEFFICIENTS

⑩

		AGE 2	CALCIUM 8	URICACID 9
AGE	2	1.000		
CALCIUM	8	0.045	1.000	
URICACID	9	-0.213	-0.172	1.000

```
IN THE TABLE BELOW, THE STANDARDIZED RESIDUAL IS THE RESIDUAL
DIVIDED BY ITS STANDARD ERROR.  THE COLUMN LABEL DELETED
RESIDUAL CONTAINS THE RESIDUAL FOR EACH CASE FROM
PREDICTING THAT CASE FROM THE OTHER CASES, I.E, THE
RESIDUAL FOR THE CASE AFTER REMOVING THE EFFECT OF
THAT CASE FROM THE REGRESSION COEFFICIENTS.
```

⑪

CASE LABEL	CASE NO.	OBSERVED CHOLSTRL	PREDICTED VALUE	RESIDUAL	CASE WEIGHT	WEIGHTED RESIDUAL	STAND-ARDIZED RESIDUAL	DELETED RESIDUAL	MAHALA-NOBIS DISTANCE	COOK'S DISTANCE
2381	1	200.0000	219.8697	-19.8697	1.000	-19.8697	-0.53	-20.2452	2.33	0.00
1610	3	243.0000	223.3295	19.6705	1.000	19.6705	0.52	20.1547	3.31	0.00
561	5	158.0000	213.2000	-55.2000	1.000	-55.2000	-1.47	-56.2248	2.27	0.01
2519	6	255.0000	248.5149	6.4851	1.000	6.4851	0.18	7.1211	14.99	0.00
225	7	210.0000	201.8782	8.1218	1.000	8.1218	0.22	8.3037	2.93	0.00

--- *similar statistics for cases 8 to 185* ---

575	186	220.0000	278.0215	-58.0215	1.000	-58.0215	-1.57	-60.7439	7.03	0.03
2271	187	305.0000	272.4094	32.5904	1.000	32.5904	0.87	33.7344	5.08	0.01
39	188	220.0000	250.7384	-30.7384	1.000	-30.7384	-0.84	-33.1994	12.27	0.01

SUMMARY STATISTICS FOR RESIDUALS

⑫ (CASES WITH POSITIVE WEIGHT)

```
AVERAGE RESIDUAL                        -0.0000
RESIDUAL MEAN SQUARE                  1438.92452742
AVERAGE DELETED RESIDUAL                 0.0324

AVE. SQUARED DELETED RESIDUAL         1474.14341152
```

```
        0.08 IS THE MAXIMUM VALUE OF COOK'S DISTANCE AMONG CASES
WITH POSITIVE WEIGHT.  THIS OCCURRED FOR CASE NUMBER    60 152
```

NUMERICAL CONSISTENCY CHECK

⑬ RESIDUAL MEAN SQUARES ARE COMPUTED FROM BOTH COVARIANCE MATRIX AND RESIDUALS, AND
RELATIVE DIFFERENCE (DIFFERENCE DIVIDED BY SMALLER OF TWO ESTIMATES) IS COMPUTED.

RESIDUAL MEAN SQUARES COMPUTED FROM

COVARIANCE MATRIX	RESIDUALS	RELATIVE DIFFERENCE
0.143892D 04	0.143892D 04	0.790082D-16

● PLOTS AVAILABLE IN P9R

We use the following example to illustrate the plots available in P9R.

Example 13.13

```
/PROBLEM     TITLE IS 'WERNER BLOOD CHEMISTRY DATA'.
/INPUT       VARIABLES ARE 9.
             FORMAT IS '(A4,5F4.0,3F4.1)'.
/VARIABLE    NAMES ARE ID,AGE,HEIGHT,WEIGHT,BRTHPILL,
                     CHOLSTRL,ALBUMIN,CALCIUM,URICACID.
             MAXIMUM IS (6)400.
             MINIMUM IS (6)150.
             BLANKS ARE MISSING.
             LABEL IS ID.

/REGRESS     DEPENDENT IS CHOLSTRL.
             INDEPENDENT ARE 2 TO 4, 7 TO 9.

/PLOT        YVAR ARE CHOLSTRL,RESIDUAL,CHOLSTRL,RESIDUAL,RESIDUAL.
             XVAR ARE AGE     ,URICACID,PREDICTD,PREDICTD,DELRESID.
             NORMAL.
             SIZE IS 40,25.

/END
```

The plots are presented in Output 13.13. Circled numbers below correspond to those in the output. The types of plots shown are:

(14) One variable against another variable.

(15) Residuals against a variable.

(16) A variable against predicted values.

(17) Residuals against predicted values.

(18) Residuals against deleted residuals (this plot should be inspected for cases that have a large discrepancy between the residual and deleted residual).

(19) A normal probability plot of the standardized residuals.

The predicted values, residuals and related values are derived variables and are available for plotting. Suppose there are VT variables (after transformations, if any). Then

- the predicted value is kept as variable VT+1 and named PREDICTD

- the residual is kept as variable VT+2 and named RESIDUAL

- the standardized residual is kept as variable VT+3 and named STRESIDL

- the weighted residual is kept as variable VT+4 and named WRESIDUL

- Mahalanobis distance is kept as variable VT+5 and named DISTANCE

- the deleted residual is kept as variable VT+6 and named DELRESID

- Cook's distance is kept as variable VT+7 and named COOKDIST

These new variables can be plotted against each other or against any variable by specifying their name (or subscript) as an XVAR or YVAR variable.

PLOT

   YVAR=$v_1,v_2,\cdots$.   {none}

     Names or subscripts of variables for the Y axes of plots.

   XVAR=$v_1,v_2,\cdots$.   {none}

     Names or subscripts of variables for the X axes of plots. The first YVAR variable is plotted against the first XVAR variable, the second against the second, etc. Residuals and predicted values can be specified as either XVAR or YVAR. See above for how they are named.

   SIZE=$\#_1,\#_2$.   {50,50/prev.}

     $\#_1$ is the number of characters (width) in the horizontal axis and $\#_2$ is the number of lines (height) in the vertical axis.

   NORMAL.   {no/prev.}

     Print a normal probability plot for the <u>standardized</u> residuals.

Output 13.13   Plots printed by P9R

```
NORMAL PROB. PLOT OF STANDARDIZED RESIDUALS . . YES
NUMBER OF PAIRS OF VARIABLES TO BE PLOTTED. . .        5
```

IN THE BIVARIATE PLOTS WHICH FOLLOW, A = 10 CASES, B = 11 CASES, ..., AND * = 20 OR MORE CASES.

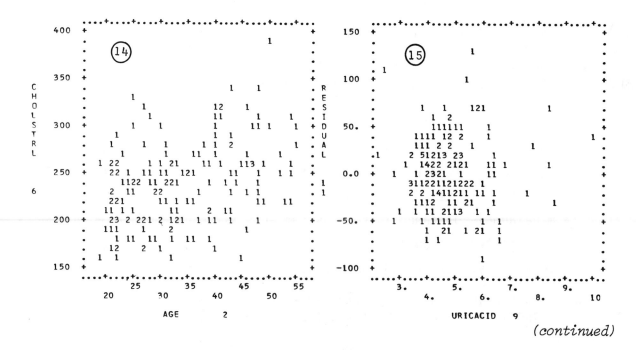

AGE   2

URICACID   9

(continued)

Output 13.13 *(continued)*

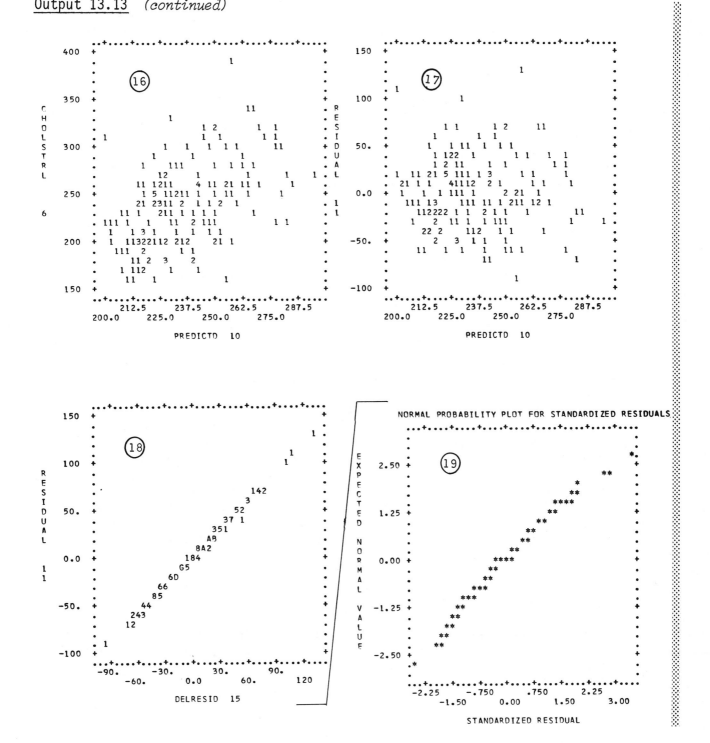

- THE INTERCEPT IN THE REGRESSION EQUATION

    The regression equation usually contains an intercept (a constant term); e.g., in

$$y = a + b_1x_1 + b_2x_2 + \ldots + b_px_p$$

a is the intercept. In some problems, the intercept must be zero; this can be specified by

    ZERO.

in the *REGRess* paragraph. This is a <u>rarely</u> used option that affects the computations as described in Appendix A.11.

REGRess
    ZERO.   { not ZERO/prev.}

    If ZERO is specified, the intercept in the regression equation is set to zero. *Note: this is a rarely used option that affects the computations (see Appendix A.11).*

- TOLERANCE: INVERTING THE COVARIANCE MATRIX

    The covariance matrix must be inverted to compute the residual mean square (required for C_p); the equation containing all the independent variables is used. If the squared multiple correlation (R^2) of any independent variable with the other independent variables is too high, the computation of the inverse loses numerical accuracy. Therefore the TOLERANCE limit is used as a check on the largest multiple correlation (TOLERANCE= $1-R^2$). If the limit is violated, P9R reports a list of the variables in violation and terminates the computations unless the METHOD is NONE. In the latter case, P9R reports a regression equation for a nonredundant subset of predictor variables.

REGRess
    TOLERANCE=#.   {0.0001/prev.}

    If the R^2 of any independent variable with the other independent variables exceeds 1-TOLERANCE, the computations are terminated unless the METHOD is NONE. For IBM 360 and 370 computers, we suggest that TOLERANCE be at least 10^{-4}.

- CASE WEIGHTS

    When the error variance is not homogeneous but varies from case to case, weighted least squares estimation is more appropriate; the weight (w) for each case is proportional to the inverse of the variance. In weighted least squares, estimates of the coefficients minimize

$$\Sigma\ w_j(y_j - \hat{y}_j)^2$$

where w_j is the weight for case j.

You can estimate predicted values for cases not used to compute the regression equation by setting their case weights to zero. The use of zero case weights to perform a cross-validation is explained in Appendix C.19.

Case weights affect the computation of the means, variances, covariances and correlations (see Section 2.1).

VARiable
    WEIGHT=v.   {no weight var./prev.}

> Name or subscript of the variable containing case weights. The weights should be greater than or equal to zero. If WEIGHT is not stated or is set to zero, there are no case weights.

● FORMS OF DATA INPUT

DATA, a CORRELATION matrix or a COVARIANCE matrix can be used as input to P9R. The input can be from a BMDP File (Chapter 7) but need not be. (In other regression programs the correlation and covariance matrices can only be input from a BMDP File.)

The input of a CORRELATION matrix from a BMDP File is illustrated in Example 13.5 for P1R; it is similar for P9R.

When P9R reads as input a COVARIANCE or CORRELATION matrix that is <u>not</u> in a BMDP File, it assumes that the matrix is SQUARE unless

    SHAPE=LOWER.

is specified in the *INPut* paragraph. The matrix is read one row at a time whether it is SQUARE or LOWER. When LOWER is specified, the lower triangular matrix is read. That is, the first value in the first case is read as the first row, the first two values in the second case as the second row, etc. The TYPE of the input must be specified.

INPut
    CONTENT=c.   {DATA}   used only when input is
                                              from a BMDP File

> If the input is not DATA, CONTENT must be specified. It must be identical to the CONTENT stated in the *SAVE* paragraph when the BMDP File was created.
>
>   *(continued)*

> INPut
>   TYPE= *(one only)* DATA,COVA,CORR.   {same as CONTENT ;
>   otherwise DATA}
>
>   The type of input. TYPE must be specified when a covariance or
>   correlation matrix is input that is not in a BMDP File. TYPE
>   must also be specified when a BMDP File is input and the CONTENT
>   is <u>not</u> one of the three TYPES: DATA, COVA or CORR.
>
>   SHAPE= *(one only)* SQUARE,LOWER.   { SQUARE /prev.}
>
>   SHAPE is required only when a covariance or correlation matrix is
>   input that is not a BMDP File. LOWER means that a lower triangu-
>   lar matrix is input. Each row is read separetely and must begin
>   in a new record. The FORMat statement must describe the longest
>   (last) row in the matrix.

● SAVE -- THE DATA AND THE COVARIANCE MATRIX

Both the DATA (including predicted values, residuals and related
measures) and the COVARIANCE matrix can be saved in a BMDP File to be used
for input to a subsequent analysis. Chapter 7 describes BMDP Files and how
they are used.

When DATA are saved, the following statistics are also saved:

- the predicted values as variable (VT+1) named PREDICTD

- residuals as variable (VT+2) named RESIDUAL

- standardized residuals as variable (VT+3) named STRESIDL

- weighted residuals as variable (VT+4) named WRESIDUL

- Mahalanobis distances as variable (VT+5) named DISTANCE

- deleted residuals as variable (VT+6) named DELRESID

- Cook's (1977) distances as variable (VT+7) named COOKDIST

where VT is the number of variables (after transformations, if any). (See
pp. 426-427 for a more detailed description of these terms.)

> SAVE
>   CONTENT= *(one or both)* DATA,COVA.   {DATA}
>
>   The matrices to be saved in a BMDP File. If DATA is specified, the
>   data and the seven additional variables described above are saved.
>   If COVA is specified, the covariance matrix is saved.

Example 13.14 requests that P9R save both the data and covariance matrix.

Example 13.14

```
    /PROBLEM        TITLE IS 'WERNER BLOOD CHEMISTRY DATA'.
    /INPUT          VARIABLES ARE 9.
                    FORMAT IS '(A4,5F4.0,3F4.1)'.
    /VARIABLE       NAMES ARE ID,AGE,HEIGHT,WEIGHT,BRTHPILL,
                            CHOLSTRL,ALBUMIN,CALCIUM,URICACID.
                    MAXIMUM IS (6)400.
                    MINIMUM IS (6)150.
                    BLANKS ARE MISSING.
                    LABEL IS ID.

    /REGRESS        DEPENDENT IS CHOLSTRL.
                    INDEPENDENT ARE 2 TO 4, 7 TO 9.

    /SAVE           UNIT IS 4.
                    NEW.
                    CODE IS WERNER.
                    CONTENT IS DATA,COVA.

    /END
```

Note: The System Cards that precede the Control Language must contain a card describing where to store the BMDP File (Section 7.1). At HSCF, the System Cards are

```
    //jobname JOB  nooo,yourname
    //  EXEC  BIMED,PROG=BMDP9R
    //FT04F001  DD  DSNAME=FS.nooo.filename,DISP=OLD
    //SYSIN DD  *
```

In addition space must be allocated for the system file (Section 7.1).

The messages indicating that the BMDP Files are created are shown in Output 13.14. When the CONTENT is DATA, seven variables are saved in addition to the original variables.

● SIZE OF PROBLEM

When METHOD is NONE, 100 independent variables can be included in the analysis; otherwise, up to 27 variables can be used. Appendix B describes how to increase the capacity of the program.

● COMPUTATIONAL METHOD

Data are read in single precision. The covariance matrix is computed by the method of provisional means (Appendix A.2) in double precision. FORTRAN coding for the best subset algorithm was obtained from Furnival and Wilson (1974a,b). The best subset algorithm uses a mixture of single and double precision and employs both forward and reverse pivots (sweeps, see Appendix A.11). Excessive roundoff error may occur in the best subset algorithm if the R-squared for the dependent variable exceeds .9999 or if the tolerance for any independent variable is less than .0001. To check the results for the best subset, the computations are repeated in double precision with forward pivots only, using a fresh copy of the covariance matrix.

The residuals and related statistics computed for the residual analysis are defined in Appendix A.12.

ACKNOWLEDGEMENT

P9R was designed and programmed by James Frane.   FORTRAN coding for the best subset algorithm was obtained from Furnival and Wilson.

:::

<u>Output 13.14</u> Saving the covariance matrix and data in BMDP Files by P9R

```
REQUESTED OUTPUT BMDP FILE
    UNIT    =        4
    CODE    = WERNER
    LABEL   =
    CONTENT =
              DATA
              COVA




BMDP FILE WRITTEN ON UNIT 4.
                    CODE. . . IS      WERNER
                    CONTENT . IS      COVA
                    LABEL . . IS
                    VARIABLES    2  AGE       3  HEIGHT     4  WEIGHT     7  ALBUMIN    8  CALCIUM
                                 9  URICACID  6  CHOLSTRL


    BMDP FILE ON UNIT 4 HAS BEEN COMPLETED.


NUMBER OF CASES READ. . . . . . . . . . . . .      188
    CASES WITH DATA MISSING OR BEYOND LIMITS . .      8
        REMAINING NUMBER OF CASES . . . . . . .      180
```

--- *analysis of best subset appears here* ---

```
    BMDP FILE WRITTEN ON UNIT 4.
                    CODE. . . IS      WERNER
                    CONTENT . IS      DATA
                    LABEL . . IS
                    VARIABLES    1  ID        2  AGE       3  HEIGHT     4  WEIGHT     5  BRTHPILL
                                 6  CHOLSTRL  7  ALBUMIN   8  CALCIUM    9  URICACID  10  PREDICTD
                                11  RESIDUAL 12  STRESIDL 13  WRESIDUL  14  DISTANCE  15  DELRESID
                                16  COOKDIST

SUMMARY STATISTICS FOR RESIDUALS

(CASES WITH POSITIVE WEIGHT)

AVERAGE RESIDUAL                   -0.0000
RESIDUAL MEAN SQUARE          1438.92452742
AVERAGE PREDICTED RESIDUAL         0.0324
AVERAGE SQUARED PRED. RESID.  1474.14341152


    BMDP FILE ON UNIT 4 HAS BEEN COMPLETED.
```

P4R

13.4 Regression on Principal Components

P4R computes a regression analysis for a dependent variable on a set of principal components computed from the independent variables. The principal components are computed from the original variables (using the covariance matrix) or the standardized variables (using the correlation matrix). The regression analysis is performed in a stepwise manner and the resulting coefficients are reported in terms of both the principal components and the original or standardized variables. The magnitude of the eigenvalues or of the correlations between the components and the dependent variable determines the order of entry of components.

● RESULTS

The Werner blood chemistry data (Table 5.1) are used to illustrate the results produced by P4R. In the following example the *REGRess* paragraph is specific to P4R; the other Control Language instructions are described in Chapter 5.

Example 13.15

```
/PROBLEM      TITLE IS 'WERNER BLOOD CHEMISTRY DATA'.
/INPUT        VARIABLES ARE 9.
              FORMAT IS '(A4,5F4.0,3F4.1)'.
/VARIABLE     NAMES ARE ID,AGE,HEIGHT,WEIGHT,BRTHPILL,
                    CHOLSTRL,ALBUMIN,CALCIUM,URICACID.
              MAXIMUM IS (6)400.
              MINIMUM IS (6)150.
              BLANKS ARE MISSING.
              LABEL IS ID.

/REGRESS      DEPENDENT IS CHOLSTRL.
              INDEPENDENT ARE 2 TO 4, 7 TO 9.

/END
```

The Control Language must be preceded by System Cards to initiate the analysis by P4R. At HSCF, the System Cards are

```
//jobname  JOB  nooo,yourname
//   EXEC  BIMED,PROG=BMDP4R
//SYSIN  DD  *
```

The Control Language is immediately followed by the data (Table 5.1). The analysis is terminated by another System Card. At HSCF, this System Card is

```
//
```

The results are presented in Output 13.15. Circled numbers below correspond to those in the output.

① Control Language instructions specific to P4R are interpreted. Preassigned values are reported for some options.

-437-

Output 13.15 Regression on principal components by P4R. Circled numbers correspond to those in the text. Results not reproduced are indicated in italics.

```
BMDP4R - REGRESSION ON PRINCIPAL COMPONENTS          PROGRAM REVISED SEPTEMBER 1977
HEALTH SCIENCES COMPUTING FACILITY                   MANUAL DATE -- 1977
UNIVERSITY OF CALIFORNIA, LOS ANGELES
```

--- *Control Language read by P4R is printed and interpreted* ---

(1)
```
DEPENDENT VARIABLE(S) . . . . . . . . . . . . . .  6
INDEPENDENT VARIABLES . . . . . . . . . . . . .   2  3  4  7  8  9
COMPUTATION BASED ON CORRELATION MATRIX OF INDEPENDENT VARIABLES
PRINCIPAL COMPONENTS ARE ENTERED IN ORDER OF MAGNITUDE OF CORRELATIONS WITH DEP. VAR
MAXIMUM NUMBER OF COMPONENTS TO ENTER . . . . .    6
NUMBER OF COMPONENTS TO ENTER LIMITED BY MAGNITUDE OF CORRELATIONS GREATER THAN   0.0100
```

(2)
```
NUMBER OF CASES READ. . . . . . . . . . . . . .     188
   CASES WITH DATA MISSING OR BEYOND LIMITS . .       8
        REMAINING NUMBER OF CASES . . . . . . .     180
```

(3)

VARIABLE NO.	NAME	MEAN	STANDARD DEVIATION	COEFFICIENT OF VARIATION
2	AGE	33.53819	9.89836	0.29514
3	HEIGHT	64.46597	2.48213	0.03850
4	WEIGHT	131.09384	20.49977	0.15637
5	BRTHPILL	1.50551	0.50136	0.33302
6	CHOLSTRL	235.83821	42.74364	0.18124
7	ALBUMIN	4.12052	0.35871	0.08706
8	CALCIUM	9.96773	0.47279	0.04743
9	URICACID	4.75551	1.12111	0.23575

(4)

CORRELATION MATRIX

		AGE 2	HEIGHT 3	WEIGHT 4	CHOLSTRL 6	ALBUMIN 7	CALCIUM 8	URICACID 9
AGE	2	1.0000						
HEIGHT	3	0.0892	1.0000					
WEIGHT	4	0.2553	0.4735	1.0000				
CHOLSTRL	6	0.3652	0.0115	0.1462	1.0000			
ALBUMIN	7	-0.0789	-0.0058	-0.2346	0.0575	1.0000		
CALCIUM	8	-0.0086	0.1428	0.0647	0.2548	0.4529	1.0000	
URICACID	9	0.2085	0.1254	0.3036	0.2740	0.0299	0.1662	1.0000

(5)

EIGENVALUES

```
   1.80863     1.50590     0.97973     0.76741     0.53500     0.40330
```

CUMULATIVE PROPORTION OF TOTAL VARIANCE OF INDEPENDENT VARIABLES

```
   0.30144     0.55242     0.71571     0.84361     0.93278     1.00000
```

(6)

EIGENVECTORS

		1	2	3	4	5	6
2	AGE	0.3724	-0.1154	-0.6265	-0.6646	-0.0295	0.1136
3	HEIGHT	0.5001	0.0703	0.5903	-0.1985	-0.4307	0.4143
4	WEIGHT	0.6195	-0.1382	0.2035	0.0495	0.2966	-0.6821
7	ALBUMIN	-0.1144	0.6950	-0.0593	-0.1904	-0.4790	-0.4844
8	CALCIUM	0.1592	0.6761	0.0367	-0.0406	0.6520	0.2991
9	URICACID	0.4348	0.1501	-0.4612	0.6918	-0.2668	0.1611

```
DEPENDENT VARIABLE    6 CHOLSTRL
```
(7)
```
                                   TOTAL SUM OF SQUARES    327036.25
                                   DEGREES OF FREEDOM         179.
                                          MEAN SQUARE      1827.0181
```

(8) CORRELATION BETWEEN PRINCIPAL COMPONENTS AND DEPENDENT VARIABLE
```
        0.28661     0.15631     -0.31596     -0.07933     0.12731     0.06137
```

(9)
```
REGRESSION COEFFICIENTS OF PRINCIPAL COMPONENTS
CONSTANT     COMPONENTS
(MEAN OF Y)
 235.83821    9.10922     5.44471    -13.64436    -3.87068     7.43944     4.13043
```

COEFFICIENTS OF VARIABLES OBTAINED FROM REGRESSION ON PRINCIPAL COMPONENTS

(10)

INDEX OF COMPONENTS ENTERING	RESIDUAL SUM OF SQUARES	F-VALUES REGRESSION MODEL	COMPONENT TO ENTER	R2	CONSTANT	2 AGE	3 HEIGHT	4 WEIGHT	7 ALBUMIN	8 CALCIUM	9 URICACID
3	294387.68750	19.74	19.74	0.0998	408.3735	0.8636	-3.2449	-0.1354	2.2571	-1.0590	5.6134
1	267523.93750	19.69	17.77	0.1820	207.0804	1.2064	-1.4097	0.1398	-0.6481	2.0087	9.1459
2	259533.00000	15.26	5.42	0.2064	79.5347	1.1429	-1.2555	0.1031	9.9004	9.7949	9.8749
5	254232.81250	12.53	3.65	0.2226	96.4812	1.1207	-2.5463	0.2108	-0.0343	20.0537	8.1048
4	252174.75000	10.33	1.42	0.2289	68.6193	1.3806	-2.2367	0.2014	2.0198	20.3858	5.7163
6	250943.12500	8.74	0.85	0.2327	34.7177	1.4280	-1.5473	0.0640	-3.5584	22.9987	6.3098

② Complete cases only are used in the computations; i.e., cases that have no missing values or values out of range. Therefore only 180 of the original 188 cases are used. All variables are checked for acceptable values unless USE is specified in the *VARiable* paragraph (Section 5.3), in which case only variables specified in the USE statement are checked.

③ Univariate statistics are computed for each variable using the complete cases

  - mean
  - standard deviation
  - coefficient of variation

④ The matrix of correlations.

⑤ Eigenvalues from the correlation matrix of the independent variables. The cumulative proportion of the total variance is the cumulative sum of eigenvalues divided by the total sum of all the eigenvalues.

⑥ Eigenvectors corresponding to the eigenvalues.

⑦ The total sum of squares $\qquad \Sigma_j (y_j - \bar{y})^2$

and mean square $\qquad \Sigma_j (y_j - \bar{y})^2 / (N-1)$

for the dependent variable y before the regression analysis.

⑧ The correlation between each principal component and the dependent variable.

⑨ The regression coefficients of the principal components. Since the principal components are mutually orthogonal, these coefficients do <u>not</u> depend on the order of entry of the components.

⑩ Coefficients of the variables

  - index of the entering component: the component entered at each step
  - the residual sum of squares at each step: $\Sigma_j (y_j - \hat{y}_j)^2$

    where $\hat{y}$ is the predicted value

  - F-value for the regression model:

        mean square regression/mean square residuals

    The degrees of freedom for this F-value are p and N-p-1 where p is the number of components in the regression. This is an overall test of significance for the regression equation.

  - F-value component to enter: this is a test of the significance of the coefficient of this component only; the degrees of freedom for this F-value are 1 and N-p-1
  - R^2: multiple correlation squared
  - the intercept and coefficients of the original independent variables corresponding to the components already entered

These terms are more precisely explained in Appendix A.13.

● Optional Results and Input

In addition to the above results, you can request

- principal component scores for each case   p. 441
- scatter plots and normal probability plots   p. 442

The data can be saved in a BMDP File for input to other programs. p. 443

● *REGRess:* Specifying the Regression

The *REGRess* paragraph describes the dependent (predicted) variable and the independent variables.[13] This paragraph can be repeated before the *END* paragraph to specify additional analyses of the same data.

The dependent variable must be specified in the first *REGRess* paragraph. If the independent variables are not specified, all variables are treated as independent variables unless a USE statement is specified; only variables listed in the USE statement are included in the analysis.

Each regression analysis can be given a separate title.

```
REGRess
   DEPENDENT=v.                    {none/prev.}              required
      Name or subscript of the dependent (predicted) variable.

   INDEPENDENT=v₁,v₂,···.          {all var./prev.}
      Names or subscripts of the independent (predictor) variables.  If
      not specified, all variables are used as independent variables
      except that specified as the DEPENDENT variable.

   TITLE='c'.                      {blank}                  ≤ 80 char.
      Title for the regression analysis.
```

The regression can be performed using principal components from either the covariance or correlation matrix: the former corresponds to using the original data, and the latter to standardizing each independent variable by subtracting its mean and then dividing by its standard deviation.

```
REGRess
   STANDARDIZE.                    {STAND /prev.}

      The independent variables are standardized before performing the
      principal components analysis unless you specify NO STANDARDIZE.
```

---

[13] In BMDP programs dated before August 1977,
       the minimum required abbreviation is *REGRES* (not *REGR*).

Either of two criteria determine the order of entry of the principal components (eigenvectors):

- Components are entered in the order of the magnitude of the absolute value of their correlations with the dependent variable, the largest is entered first.

- Components are entered in the order of magnitude of the eigenvalues, the largest is entered first.

REGRess

CORRELATION. *or* EIGENVALUE.   {CORR/prev.}

Criterion for entering components into the regression equation. CORR enters the component(s) with the largest correlation(s) first; and EIGEN the component(s) with the largest eigenvalue(s).

The number of components entered into the regression can be restricted by specifying a minimum limit for a component value (correlation or eigenvalue) as an entry requirement. For IBM 360 and 370 computers, the eigenvalue limit should not ordinarily be lowered.

REGRess

LIMIT=$\#_1$,$\#_2$.   {0.01,0.01/prev.}

A component is <u>not</u> entered into the regression equation if its correlation (if the criterion is CORR) is less than $\#_1$ or its eigenvalue (for either criterion) is less than $\#_2$. Either limit can be changed.[14] To change the limit for eigenvalue without changing that of correlation, specify LIMIT= (2)$\#_2$.

- *PRINT* SCORES FOR EACH CASE

Principal component scores for each case are printed if you specify

/PRINT SCORE.

We request the scores in the following example.

Example 13.16

```
/PROBLEM      TITLE IS 'WERNER BLOOD CHEMISTRY DATA'.
/INPUT        VARIABLES ARE 9.
              FORMAT IS '(A4,5F4.0,3F4.1)'.
/VARIABLE     NAMES ARE ID,AGE,HEIGHT,WEIGHT,BRTHPILL,
                     CHOLSTRL,ALBUMIN,CALCIUM,URICACID.
              MAXIMUM IS (6)400.
              MINIMUM IS (6)150.
              BLANKS ARE MISSING.
              LABEL IS ID.

/REGRESS      DEPENDENT IS CHOLSTRL.
              INDEPENDENT ARE 2 TO 4, 7 TO 9.

/PRINT        SCORE.

/END
```

---

[14] In BMDP programs dated before August 1977, LIMIT=#. is used and the limit applies to the criterion for entering components (CORR or EIGEN).

The scores are printed in Output 13.16. For each case the coefficients of each principal component are multiplied by the values of variables and the sum is printed. The first seven columns in the output correspond to the seven principal components. The last column contains the values of the dependent variable.

PRINT

SCORE.   {no/prev.}

   Print the principal component scores and the dependent variable for each case.

- *PLOTs* AVAILABLE IN P4R

   The plots available in P4R are
   - residuals $(y-\hat{y})$ plotted against the predicted values $\hat{y}$
   - residuals squared $(y-\hat{y})^2$ plotted against the predicted values $\hat{y}$
   - the observed values of the dependent variable y and the predicted value $\hat{y}$ plotted against the observed values of an independent variable x_i
   - the residuals $(y-\hat{y})$ plotted against the observed values of the same independent variable x_i
   - a normal probability plot of the residuals
   - a detrended normal probability plot of the residuals

   All the plots are illustrated in Output 13.3 for P1R (p. 388). (Only the partial residual plot of P1R is unavailable in P4R.)

PLOT

RESIDUAL.   {no/prev.}

   Plot the residuals $(y-\hat{y})$ and residuals squared $(y-\hat{y})^2$ in separate graphs against the predicted values $\hat{y}$.

(continued)

Output 13.16 Principal component scores printed by P4R

```
CASE        PRINCIPAL COMPONENT SCORES AND ORIGINAL DEPENDENT VARIABLE(S)
 1             0.4481    0.2554    1.1651    1.0502   -1.1524   -0.6216   200.0000
 2            -0.9844    0.3537    0.5648   -0.1842    1.8845   -0.4955   243.0000
 3            -0.6416    0.0434    0.7778    1.1199   -0.0229   -0.1023   158.0000
 4             1.0136    1.8087    0.0326    3.0946   -1.4059    0.9859   255.0000
 5            -1.0255   -0.7859    0.9367    0.6912   -0.3267    0.1510   210.0000

           --- similar statistics for cases 6 to 177 ---

178           0.9917    0.4247   -0.8847   -1.6240    1.6213    0.9759   220.0000
179           1.4841    0.2108   -0.6758   -1.6834    0.5517   -0.4648   305.0000
180           1.0778   -2.6831   -2.6211    0.5251    0.1744   -2.3368   220.0000
```

PLOT

VARIABLE= $v_1, v_2, \cdots$.   {none/prev.}

Names or subscripts of variables against which the observed values of the dependent variable y and the predicted values $\hat{y}$ are plotted. Overlaps between observed and predicted values are indicated by asterisks. The residuals $(y-\hat{y})$ are also plotted against the same variables. Each variable is plotted in a separate graph.

NORMAL.   {no/prev.}

Plot a normal probability plot of the residuals.[15]

DNORMAL.   {no/prev.}

Plot a detrended normal probability plot of the residuals.[15]

SIZE= $\#_1, \#_2$.   {50,50/prev.}

$\#_1$ is the number of characters (width) in the horizontal axis and $\#_2$ is the number of lines (height) in the vertical axis.

- SAVING THE DATA IN A BMDP FILE

    The data (after transformation) can be saved in a BMDP File for further analysis by other programs (Chapter 7). When the data are read from a BMDP File and a new BMDP File is created by P4R, the two Files must be in different system files and on different UNITs.

- SIZE OF PROBLEM

    This program can analyze up to 55 variables. Appendix B describes how to increase the capacity of the program.

- COMPUTATIONAL METHOD

    All computations are performed in single precision. Means, standard deviations and covariances are computed by the method of provisional means (Appendix A.2). The computational procedure for P4R is described in Appendix A.13.

ACKNOWLEDGEMENT

P4R was programmed by Jerry Douglas and Laszlo Engelman. It supersedes BMD02M.

---

[15] In BMDP programs dated before August 1977, PROBIT is used in place of both NORMAL and DNORMAL.

P5R

13.5 Polynomial Regression

P5R fits a polynomial in one independent variable to the dependent variable. The form of the regression equation is

$$y = \beta_0 + \beta_1 x + \beta_2 x^2 + \ldots + \beta_p x^p + e$$

Computation is done using orthogonal polynomials based on an algorithm by Forsythe (1957). The program reports polynomials of degree one through a degree specified by the user (≤ 15). Goodness-of-fit statistics for each (except the highest degree) polynomial are printed. A weighted least squares regression can also be performed.

● RESULTS

In our first example we use P5R to fit a polynomial regression in AGE to CHOLSTRL using the Werner blood chemistry data (Table 5.1). In Example 13.17 the *REGRess* paragraph is specific to P5R; the other Control Language instructions are described in Chapter 5.

Example 13.17

```
/PROBLEM      TITLE IS 'WERNER BLOOD CHEMISTRY DATA'.
/INPUT        VARIABLES ARE 9.
              FORMAT IS '(A4,5F4.0,3F4.1)'.
/VARIABLE     NAMES ARE ID,AGE,HEIGHT,WEIGHT,BRTHPILL,
                    CHOLSTRL,ALBUMIN,CALCIUM,URICACID.
              MAXIMUM IS (6)400.
              MINIMUM IS (6)150.
              BLANKS ARE MISSING.
              LABEL IS ID.

/REGRESS      DEPENDENT IS CHOLSTRL.
              INDEPENDENT IS AGE.

/END
```

The Control Language must be preceded by System Cards to initiate the analysis by P5R. At HSCF, the System Cards are

```
//jobname  JOB  nooo,yourname
//   EXEC  BIMED,PROG=BMDP5R
//SYSIN  DD  *
```

The Control Language is immediately followed by the data (Table 5.1). The analysis is terminated by another System Card. At HSCF, this System Card is

```
//
```

The results of this analysis are presented in Output 13.17. Circled numbers below correspond to those in the output.

(1) Interpretation of the Control Language instructions specific to P5R. Preassigned values are reported for some options.

Output 13.17 Polynomial regression by P5R. Circled numbers correspond to those in the text. Results not reproduced are indicated in italics.

BMDP5R - POLYNOMIAL REGRESSION
HEALTH SCIENCES COMPUTING FACILITY
UNIVERSITY OF CALIFORNIA, LOS ANGELES

PROGRAM REVISED SEPTEMBER 1977
MANUAL DATE -- 1977

--- Control Language read by P5R is printed and interpreted ---

```
    REGRESSION TITLE. . . . . . . . . . . . . .
①  INDEPENDENT VARIABLE. . . . . . . . . . . .    2 AGE
    DEPENDENT VARIABLE. . . . . . . . . . . . .    6 CHOLSTRL
    WEIGHT VARIABLE . . . . . . . . . . . . . .    0
    DEGREEE OF POLYNOMIAL . . . . . . . . . . .    3
    PRINT CORRELATION MATRIX. . . . . . . . . .    NO
    PRINT ORTHOGONAL POLYNOMIAL . . . . . . . .    NO

    NUMBER OF CASES READ. . . . . . . . . . . .    188
②    CASES WITH DATA MISSING OR BEYOND LIMITS . .    2
        REMAINING NUMBER OF CASES . . . . . . . .    186
```

RESULTS FOR POLYNOMIAL OF DEGREE 1

POLYNOMIAL COEFFICIENTS	ORTHOGONAL POLYNOMIAL			POLYNOMIAL IN X		
DEGREE	REGRESSION COEFFICIENT	STANDARD ERROR	T VALUE	REGRESSION COEFFICIENT	STANDARD ERROR	T VALUE
0	3220.66394	39.68010	81.166	183.61520	10.21529	17.975
1	212.88457	39.68010	5.365	1.54834	0.28860	5.365

RESIDUAL MEAN SQUARE =   1574.51057 (D.F. = 184)

RESULTS FOR POLYNOMIAL OF DEGREE 2

POLYNOMIAL COEFFICIENTS	ORTHOGONAL POLYNOMIAL			POLYNOMIAL IN X		
DEGREE	REGRESSION COEFFICIENT	STANDARD ERROR	T VALUE	REGRESSION COEFFICIENT	STANDARD ERROR	T VALUE
0	3220.66394	39.75879	81.005	202.80670	38.16605	5.314
1	212.88457	39.75879	5.354	0.38407	2.24922	0.171
2	20.75262	39.75879	0.522	0.01621	0.03106	0.522

RESIDUAL MEAN SQUARE =   1580.76106 (D.F. = 183)

RESULTS FOR POLYNOMIAL OF DEGREE 3

③ POLYNOMIAL COEFFICIENTS

POLYNOMIAL COEFFICIENTS	ORTHOGONAL POLYNOMIAL			POLYNOMIAL IN X		
DEGREE	REGRESSION COEFFICIENT	STANDARD ERROR	T VALUE	REGRESSION COEFFICIENT	STANDARD ERROR	T VALUE
0	3220.66394	39.80178	80.918	311.19559	144.50856	2.153
1	212.88457	39.80178	5.349	-9.47715	12.87791	-0.736
2	20.75262	39.80178	0.521	0.29917	0.36515	0.819
3	-30.95494	39.80178	-0.778	-0.00258	0.00331	-0.778

RESIDUAL MEAN SQUARE =   1584.18168 (D.F. = 182)

④ GOODNESS OF FIT TEST. (A SIGNIFICANT F FOR A GIVEN DEGREE IS AN INDICATION THAT A HIGHER ORDER POLYNOMIAL SHOULD BE CONSIDERED.)

DEGREE	SUM OF SQUARES	D.F.	MEAN SQUARE	F
0	46708.71852	3	15569.57284	9.82815
1	1388.87933	2	694.43966	0.43836
2	958.20816	1	958.20816	0.60486
RESID.	288321.06643	182	1584.18168	

② Cases used in the analysis are those that have acceptable values for both the dependent and independent variables; the other variables are not checked for acceptable values. Only 186 of the 188 cases are used in the analysis.

③ Results for polynomial of degree 3:

- regression coefficient for each orthogonal polynomial and the standard error of the coefficient (orthogonal polynomials are defined in Appendix A.14)

- the regression coefficient for each power of the independent variable and the standard error of each coefficient

- for all coefficients, a t value equal to the ratio of the coefficient to its standard error. This can be considered a two-sided test of significance for the coefficient. The regression coefficients of the powers of the independent variable are highly correlated; therefore the estimates of the coefficients may not be stable and the t tests may lack power.

- residual mean square: $\Sigma_j (y_j - \hat{y}_j)^2 / (N-p-1)$

  where

  y_j is the value of the dependent variable

  $\hat{y}_j$ is the predicted value estimated by the regression

  p is the degree of the polynomial

  N is the number of cases with a nonzero weight

④ Goodness-of-fit test. This is a test of the lack of fit of the model at each degree, relative to the residual mean square from fitting the polynomial of highest degree. A high value for F is an indication of a poor fit; i.e., more terms are needed.

This run of P5R terminates with a polynomial of degree 3; this is the preassigned maximum degree.

● OPTIONAL RESULTS

In addition to the above results, the following statistics and plots can be requested:

- residuals and fitted polynomial values   p. 447
- correlations of the coefficients of the polynomial   p. 447

- plots of the dependent variable, predicted values and
  residuals against the independent variable   p. 450
- normal probability plots   p. 450
Case weights can be specified.   p. 451

● *REGRess:* SPECIFYING THE REGRESSION

The *REGRess* paragraph specifies the dependent and independent variables and, if desired, the maximum degree of the polynomial.[16] It can be repeated after the data cards for additional analyses of the same data (see order of input in the summary, p. 459).

Both the dependent and independent variables must be specified. If the degree is not specified, the maximum degree is cubic (of order three).

```
REGRess
    DEPENDENT=v.              {none/prev.}              required
       Name or subscript of the dependent (predicted) variable.

    INDEPENDENT=v.           {none/prev.}              required
       Name or subscript of the independent (predictor) variable.

    DEGREE=#.                {3/prev.}                 ≤ 15
       Maximum degree of the polynomial.

    TITLE='c'.               {blank}                   ≤ 80 char.
       Title for the analysis.
```

● *PRINTing* THE RESIDUALS AND CORRELATION MATRIX OF THE REGRESSION COEFFICIENTS

In the following example we request optional results available in P5R.

Example 13.18

```
/PROBLEM      TITLE IS 'WERNER BLOOD CHEMISTRY DATA'.
/INPUT        VARIABLES ARE 9.
              FORMAT IS '(A4,5F4.0,3F4.1)'.
/VARIABLE     NAMES ARE ID,AGE,HEIGHT,WEIGHT,BRTHPILL,
                    CHOLSTRL,ALBUMIN,CALCIUM,URICACID.
              MAXIMUM IS (6)400.
              MINIMUM IS (6)150.
              BLANKS ARE MISSING.
              LABEL IS ID.

/REGRESS      DEPENDENT IS CHOLSTRL.
              INDEPENDENT IS AGE.
              DEGREE IS 5.

/PRINT        RREG.
              DEGREE IS 5.
              ORTHPOL.

/END
```

---

[16] In BMDP programs dated before August 1977, the minimum required abbreviation is *REGRES* (not *REGR*).

The results are shown in Output 13.18. Circled numbers below correspond to those in the output.

⑤ The correlation matrix of the regression coefficients is printed at each step. These are correlations of the coefficients of the powers of the original variable (and not of the orthogonal polynomials). Note the high correlations between the coefficients.

⑥ For each case the following statistics are printed:

- the case weight, if specified
- the value of the independent variable, x_j
- the value of the dependent variable, y_j
- the predicted value, $\hat{y}_j$
- the residual, $y_j - \hat{y}_j$
- the value of the orthogonal polynomial

Blanks in the table are printed when the value is missing or out of range. This table is printed at specified steps (DEGREEs of the polynomial specified in the *PRINT* paragraph).

⑦ Orthogonal polynomial expansion. Each line in the table shows the coefficients of the powers of the independent variable (x) that are used in the orthogonal polynomial. This is obtained by specifying ORTHPOL in the *PRINT* paragraph.

Output 13.18   Optional printed results by P5R

```
REGRESSION TITLE. . . . . . . . . . . . . . . . .
INDEPENDENT VARIABLE. . . . . . . . . . . . . . .    2 AGE
DEPENDENT VARIABLE. . . . . . . . . . . . . . . .    6 CHOLSTRL
WEIGHT VARIABLE . . . . . . . . . . . . . . . . .    0
DEGREEE OF POLYNOMIAL . . . . . . . . . . . . . .    5
PRINT CORRELATION MATRIX. . . . . . . . . . . . .  YES
PRINT ORTHOGONAL POLYNOMIAL . . . . . . . . . . .  YES
PRINT RESIDUALS AT DEGREE(S). . . . . . . . . .   5

NUMBER OF CASES READ. . . . . . . . . . . . . . .  188
    CASES WITH DATA MISSING OR BEYOND LIMITS . .    2
        REMAINING NUMBER OF CASES . . . . . . . .  186
```

```
            RESULTS FOR POLYNOMIAL OF DEGREE  1


⑤    CORRELATION MATRIX FOR THE REGRESSION COEFFICIENT(BETA) ESTIMATES


              OTH DEG    1ST DEG
                1          2

OTH DEG   1    1.0000
1ST DEG   2   -0.9586    1.0000
```

POLYNOMIAL COEFFICIENTS		ORTHOGONAL POLYNOMIAL			POLYNOMIAL IN X		
	DEGREE	REGRESSION COEFFICIENT	STANDARD ERROR	T VALUE	REGRESSION COEFFICIENT	STANDARD ERROR	T VALUE
	0	3220.66394	39.68010	81.166	183.61520	10.21529	17.975
	1	212.88457	39.68010	5.365	1.54834	0.28860	5.365
RESIDUAL MEAN SQUARE =		1574.51057 (D.F. = 184)					

--- results for polynomials of degrees 2 to 4 ---

(continued)

Output 13.18 *(continued)*

RESULTS FOR POLYNOMIAL OF DEGREE 5

CORRELATION MATRIX FOR THE REGRESSION COEFFICIENT(BETA) ESTIMATES

		0TH DEG 1	1ST DEG 2	2ND DEG 3	3RD DEG 4	4TH DEG 5	5TH DEG 6
0TH DEG	1	1.0000					
1ST DEG	2	-0.9984	1.0000				
2ND DEG	3	0.9936	-0.9984	1.0000			
3RD DEG	4	-0.9861	0.9938	-0.9985	1.0000		
4TH DEG	5	0.9763	-0.9868	0.9943	-0.9986	1.0000	
5TH DEG	6	-0.9649	0.9779	-0.9879	0.9949	-0.9988	1.0000

POLYNOMIAL COEFFICIENTS		ORTHOGONAL POLYNOMIAL			POLYNOMIAL IN X		
DEGREE		REGRESSION COEFFICIENT	STANDARD ERROR	T VALUE	REGRESSION COEFFICIENT	STANDARD ERROR	T VALUE
0		3220.66394	39.78279	80.956	-2887.89075	2292.39126	-1.260
1		212.88457	39.78279	5.351	462.26328	343.87828	1.344
2		20.75262	39.78279	0.522	-26.65226	20.08098	-1.327
3		-30.95494	39.78279	-0.778	0.74445	0.57116	1.303
4		-32.18981	39.78279	-0.809	-0.01007	0.00792	-1.271
5		49.03323	39.78279	1.233	0.00005	0.00004	1.233

RESIDUAL MEAN SQUARE = 0.15827D 04 (D.F. = 180)

⑥

CASE NO.	CASE LABEL	CASE WEIGHT	X VALUE	Y VALUE	PREDICTED VALUE	RESIDUAL	5TH DEG ORTH. POLY. VALUE
1	2381	1.00000	22.00000	200.00000	223.34681	-23.34680	0.05583
2	1946	1.00000	22.00000		223.34681		
3	1610	1.00000	25.00000	243.00000	227.01349	15.98651	0.06458
4	1797	1.00000	25.00000		227.01349		
5	561	1.00000	19.00000	158.00000	198.79582	-40.79581	-0.30192

--- similar statistics for cases 6 to 185 ---

186	575	1.00000	53.00000	220.00000	261.72439	-41.72438	-0.07877
187	2271	1.00000	54.00000	305.00000	264.90981	40.09018	0.03287
188	39	1.00000	54.00000	220.00000	264.90981	-44.90981	0.03287

GOODNESS OF FIT TEST. (A SIGNIFICANT F FOR A GIVEN DEGREE IS AN
INDICATION THAT A HIGHER ORDER POLYNOMIAL SHOULD BE CONSIDERED.)

DEGREE	SUM OF SQUARES	D.F.	MEAN SQUARE	F
0	50149.15995	5	10029.83199	6.33729
1	4829.32076	4	1207.33019	0.76284
2	4398.64959	3	1466.21653	0.92642
3	3440.44143	2	1720.22072	1.08691
4	2404.25769	1	2404.25769	1.51911
RESID.	284880.62500	180	1582.67014	

⑦ ORTHOGONAL POLYNOMIAL EXPANSION

COEFFICIENTS FOR POWERS OF X

POLYNOMIAL / POWERS OF X

	0TH POW	1ST POW	2ND POW	3RD POW	4TH POW	5TH POW
0TH DEG	0.0733235					
1ST DEG	-0.2467785	0.0072731				
2ND DEG	0.9247749	-0.0561021	0.0007812			
3RD DEG	-3.5015049	0.3185670	-0.0091410	0.0000832		
4TH DEG	14.6876279	-1.7796249	0.0776644	-0.0014499	0.0000098	
5TH DEG	-55.6009521	8.4525251	-0.4986706	0.0142833	-0.0001989	0.0000011

PRINT
    RREG.   {no/prev.}

    Print the correlation matrix of the regression coefficients of the powers of the independent variable.[17]

    DEGREE=#$_1$,#$_2$,$\cdots$.   {none/prev.}

    Print the table of predicted values and residuals at the polynomial DEGREEs specified.

    ORTHPOL.   {no/prev.}

    Print the coefficients of the powers of the independent variable corresponding to the orthogonal polynomials.[18]

● PLOTs AVAILABLE IN P5R

    The plots available in P5R are

    - the observed values of the dependent variable (y_j) and the predicted values ($\hat{y}_j$) plotted against the observed value of the independent variable (x_j)

    - the residuals ($y_j - \hat{y}_j$) plotted against the observed value of the independent variable (x_j)

    - a normal probability plot of the residuals

    - a detrended normal probability plot of the residuals

These plots are illustrated in Output 13.3 (p. 388) and are similar for P5R.

PLOT
    DEGREE=#$_1$,#$_2$,$\cdots$.   {none/prev.}

    The degree(s) of the regression at which the plots of the dependent variable, predicted values, and residuals are plotted against the independent variable. If normal plots are requested (see NORMAL and DNORMAL below), they are also plotted at these DEGREEs.

    NORMAL.   {no/prev.}

    Print the normal probability plot of the residuals (at the DEGREEs specified in the PLOT paragraph).[19]

                                                      (continued)

---

[17] In BMDP programs dated before August 1977,
     CORR is used in place of RREG.

[18] In BMDP programs dated before August 1977,
     the minimum required abbreviation is ORTHPOL (not ORTH).

[19] In BMDP programs dated before August 1977,
     PROBIT is used in place of both NORMAL and DNORMAL.

PLOT
DNORMAL.   {no/prev.}

    Print the detrended normal probability plot of the residuals
    (at the DEGREEs specified in the *PLOT* paragraph).[20]

    SIZE=$\#_1$,$\#_2$.   {50,50/prev.}

        $\#_1$ is the number of characters (width) in the horizontal axis and
        $\#_2$ is the number of lines (height) in the vertical axis.

● CASE WEIGHTs

    The data can be weighted by the values of a WEIGHT variable specified
in the *VARiable* paragraph. The WEIGHT variable is not used as an independent (predictor) variable.

    If w_j is the value of the WEIGHT variable for case j, the weight affects
the computation of the mean and covariances (see Section 2.1).

VARiable
    WEIGHT=v.   { no weight var./prev.}

    Name or subscript of the variable containing case weights. The
    weights should be greater than or equal to zero. If WEIGHT
    is not stated or is set to zero, there are no case weights.

● *INPut*

    P5R can accept only data as input.

● SAVING THE DATA IN A BMDP FILE

    When the DATA are saved, the predicted values and residuals are also
saved in a BMDP File. The predicted values are saved as variable VT+1 with
the name PREDICTD , and the residuals are saved as variable VT+2 with the
name RESIDUAL (where VT is the number of variables after transformations).

● SIZE OF PROBLEM

    The data are kept in memory. P5R can accommodate a maximum of 1000
cases. The maximum degree of the polynomial is 15. Appendix B describes how
to increase the capacity of the program.

---

[20] In BMDP programs dated before August 1977,
    PROBIT is used in place of both NORMAL and DNORMAL.

● COMPUTATIONAL METHOD

The data are read in single precision and the computations are performed in double precision. The computational procedure is described in Appendix A.14.

ACKNOWLEDGEMENT

P5R was designed by Robert Jennrich and programmed by Peter Mundle. It supersedes BMD05R.

The Control Language on this page is common to all programs. This is followed by the Control Language specific to

P1R -- Multiple Linear Regression	p. 454
P2R -- Stepwise Regression	p. 455
P9R -- All Possible Subsets Regression	p. 457
P4R -- Regression on Principal Components	p. 458
P5R -- Polynomial Regression	p. 459

Paragraph STATEMENT[1] {Preassigned value[2]}		Definition, restriction	See pages:
/PROBlem		Required each problem	74
TITLE='c'.	{blank}	Problem title, $\leq$ 160 char.	74
/INPut		Required first problem. Either VARIABLE and FORMAT, or UNIT and CODE required.	75
VARIABLE=#.	{none/prev.}	No. of variables in input data	75
FORMAT='c'.	{none/prev.}	Format of input data, $\leq$ 800 char.	76
CASE=#.	{end-of-file/prev.}	No. of cases in data	76-77
UNIT=#.	{5(cards)/prev.}	Input unit if data are not on cards; not 1, 2, 6	77
REWIND.	{REWIND/prev.}	Rewind input unit	77
CODE=c.	{none}	Code to identify BMDP File	132
CONTENT=c.	{DATA}	Data or matrix in BMDP File	132
LABEL=c.	{none}	Label of BMDP File, $\leq$ 40 char.	132
/VARiable		Optional. For input from a BMDP File, items in this paragraph may be previously set, see Chapter 7.	79
NAME=$c_1,c_2,\cdots$.	{X(subscript)/prev.}	Variable names, one per variable	79-80
MAXIMUM=$\#_1,\#_2,\cdots$.	{none/prev.}	Upper limits, one per variable	80
MINIMUM=$\#_1,\#_2,\cdots$.	{none/prev.}	Lower limits, one per variable	80
BLANK= (one only) ZERO, MISSING.	{ZERO/prev.}	Blanks treated as zeros or as missing value codes	81
MISSING=$\#_1,\#_2,\cdots$.	{none/prev.}	Missing value codes, one per variable	81
USE=$v_1,v_2,\cdots$.	{all variables}	Variables used in the analysis	82
LABEL=v_1,v_2.	{none/prev.}	Variable(s) used to label cases, read under A-format, one or two	83
ADD=#.	{0/prev.}	No. of variables added through transformation	99
BEFORE. or AFTER.	{BEFORE/prev.}	Data checked for limits before or after transformation	100
/TRANsform		Optional, Control Language transformations and case selection	97-105
/SAVE		Optional, required to create BMDP File	125
CODE=c.	{none}	Code to identify BMDP File, required	125-126
LABEL='c'.	{blank}	Label for BMDP File, $\leq$ 40 char.	125-126
UNIT=#.	{none}	Unit on which BMDP File is written; not 1, 2, 5 or 6	126-127
NEW.	{not new}	NEW if this is first BMDP File written in the system file	126-127

Key: # number   v variable name or subscript
     'c' title, label or format   c name not exceeding 8 char., apostrophes may be required (p. 59)

[1] In BMDP programs dated before August 1977, the minimum required abbreviations are *INPUT* (not INP), VARIAB (not VAR), FORMAT (not FORM), CONTENT (not CONT), *VARIAB* (not *VAR*), BEFORET (not BEF), AFTERT (not AFT), *TRANSF* (not *TRAN*). If dated before February 1976, BLANK=ZERO and cannot be changed.

[2] "/prev." means that any assignment remains the same as that specified in the previous problem or subproblem until changed. Otherwise, the assignment returns to its preassigned value each time a new problem begins or the paragraph is used again.

P1R -- Multiple Linear Regression

(in addition to that on p. 453)

Paragraph STATEMENT[1] {Preassigned value}		Definition, restriction	See pages:
INPut		Specify as part of *INPut* paragraph, p. 453	
CONTENT=c.	{DATA }	Content of BMDP File, can be data, covariance or correlation matrix	394-395
TYPE= *(one only)* DATA,COVA,CORR.	{CONTENT }	Type of input, required only if BMDP File CONTENT is not DATA, COVA or CORR	395
VARiable		Specify as part of *VARiable* paragraph, p. 453	
WEIGHT=v.	{no weighting/prev.}	Variable containing case weights	394
GROUPing=v.	{no grouping var./prev.}	Variable used to group cases	391-394
/GROUP		Required if GROUPing var. specified and it has more than 10 distinct values	84
CODE(#)=$\#_1$,$\#_2$,$\cdots$.	{10 smallest values/prev.}	Codes for variable #	84-85
CUTPOINT(#)=$\#_1$,$\#_2$,$\cdots$.	{see CODE/prev.}	Cutpoints to define intervals for variable #	84-85
NAME(#)=c_1,c_2,$\cdots$.	{CODEs or CUTPOINTs /prev.}	Codes or interval names for variable #	84-85
RESET.	{not RESET}	If RESET, all assignments in prev. *GROUP* paragraph are reset to preassigned values	86
SAVE		Specify as part of *SAVE* paragraph, p. 453	
CONTENT= *(one or both)* DATA,COVA.	{DATA }	Data and/or covariances to be saved in BMDP File	395, 397
/REGRess		Required, may be repeated	383
DEPENDENT=v.	{none/prev.}	Dependent variable, required 1st *REGRess* para.	384
INDEPENDENT=v_1,v_2,$\cdots$.	{all possible var./prev.}	Independent variables	384
TITLE='c'.	{blank}	Title for analysis, < 80 char.	384
TOLERANCE=#.	{0.01/prev.}	Guards against singularity, .00001 < # < 1.0	391
TYPE= *(one only)* NONZERO,ZERO	{NONZERO/prev.}	NONZERO - intercept included in equation ZERO - intercept set to zero	390-391
/PRINT		Optional	384
DATA.	{no/prev.}	Print input data, residuals and predicted values	384
COVARIANCE.	{no/prev.}	Print covariance matrix	384-385
CORRELATION.	{no/prev.}	Print correlation matrix	384-385
RREG.	{no/prev.}	Print correlations between reg. coefficients	384-385
/PLOT		Optional	
VARIABLE=v_1,v_2,$\cdots$.	{none/prev.}	Variables against which predicted and observed values and residuals are plotted	387-390
RESIDUAL.	{no/prev.}	Residuals and residuals squared plotted against predicted values	387-390
PREP=v_1,v_2,$\cdots$.	{none/prev.}	Variables used in partial residual plots	387-390
NORMAL.	{no/prev.}	Print normal probability plot of residuals	387-390
DNORMAL.	{no/prev.}	Print detrended normal probability plot of residuals	387-390
SIZE=$\#_1$,$\#_2$.	{50,50/prev.}	Length of X and Y variables	387-390
/END		Required	57

Key: # number   v variable name or subscript
'c' title, label or format   c name not exceeding 8 char., apostrophes may be required (p. 59)

[1] In BMDP programs dated before August 1977, the minimum required abbreviations are *REGRES* (not *REGR*), CONTENT (not CONT); RREG is not available; PROBIT is used in place of NORM and DNORM; and when a *GROUP* paragraph is used, RESET is implicitly specified and cannot be changed.

- Order of input

(1) System Cards; at HSCF these are
```
//jobname JOB nooo,yourname
// EXEC BIMED,PROG=BMDP1R
//SYSIN DD *
```

(2) Control Language instructions
```
PROBlem paragraph, required
INPut paragraph, required first problem
VARiable paragraph
TRANsform paragraph
SAVE paragraph
GROUP paragraph
REGRess paragraph, required, may be repeated
PRINT paragraph
PLOT paragraph
END paragraph, required at end of Control Language
```

(3) Data, if on cards
```
data
```

(4) System Card; at HSCF this is
```
//
```

Control Language instructions and data (2 and 3) can be repeated to analyze additional problems.

P2R -- Stepwise Regression

(in addition to that on p. 453)

Paragraph STATEMENT[1] {Preassigned value}	Definition, restriction	See pages:
INPut	Specify as part of *INPut* paragraph, p. 453	
CONTENT=c. {DATA}	Content of BMDP File, can be data, covariance or correlation matrix	416
TYPE= *(one only)* DATA,COVA,CORR. {CONTENT}	Type of input, required only if BMDP File CONTENT is not DATA, COVA or CORR	416
VARiable	Specify as part of *VARiable* paragraph, p. 453	
WEIGHT=v. {no weighting/prev.}	Variable containing case weights	415-416
SAVE	Specify as part of *SAVE* paragraph, p. 453	
CONTENT= *(one or both)* DATA,COVA. {DATA}	Data and/or covariances to be saved in BMDP File	416-417
/REGRess	Required, may be repeated	405
DEPENDENT=v. {none/prev.}	Dependent variable, required 1st *REGRess* para.	405
INDEPENDENT=$v_1,v_2,\cdots$. {all possible var./prev.}	Independent variables	405
TITLE='c'. {blank}	Title for analysis, $\leq$ 80 char.	405
METHOD=*(one only)* F,FSWAP,R,RSWAP. {F/prev.}	Criterion for entering or removing variables	405-406
ENTER=$\#_1,\#_2$. {4,4/prev.}	F-to-enter for forward and then backward stepping	406-407
REMOVE=$\#_1,\#_2$. {3.9,3.9/prev.}	F-to-remove for forward and then backward stepping	406-407
TYPE=*(one only)* NONZERO,ZERO,FLOAT. { NONZERO/prev.}	Intercept is included (NONZERO), ZERO or free to enter (FLOAT)	407-408
LEVEL=$\#_1,\#_2,\cdots$. {highest + 1}	Ordering of variables for entry, lowest nonzero first, one per variable	409-410
FORCE=#. {no forcing/prev.}	Highest LEVEL for which variables are forced into equation	409-410
TOLERANCE=#. {0.01/prev.}	Guards against singularity, $0.00001 < \# < 1.0$	410
STEP=#. {2 x no. of var./prev.}	Maximum number of steps	411
/PRINT	Optional	
ANOVA. {ANOVA /prev.}	Analysis of variance printed at each step	412-414
STEP. {STEP /prev.}	Full step output printed	412-414
COEFFICIENT. {COEF /prev.}	Summary table of regression coefficient printed	412-414
SUMMARY. {SUM /prev.}	Summary table of multiple R, R^2, F-to-enter and F-to-remove printed	412-414
COVARIANCE. {no/prev.}	Print covariance matrix	412-414
CORRELATION. {no/prev.}	Print correlation matrix	412-414
DATA. {no/prev.}	Print input data, residuals and predicted values	412-414
PARTIAL. {no/prev.}	Print summary table of partial correlations	412-414
FRATIO. {no/prev.}	Print summary table of F-to-enter and F-to-remove	412-414
RREG. {no/prev.}	Print correlations between reg. coefficients	412-414
/PLOT	Optional	
VARIABLE=$v_1,v_2,\cdots$. {none/prev.}	Variables against which predicted and observed values and residuals are plotted	414-415
RESIDUAL. {no/prev.}	Residuals and residuals squared plotted against predicted values	414-415
PREP=$v_1,v_2,\cdots$. {none/prev.}	Variables used in partial residual plots	414-415
NORMAL. {no/prev.}	Print normal probability plot of residuals	414-415
DNORMAL. {no/prev.}	Print detrended normal probability plot of residuals	414-415
SIZE=$\#_1,\#_2$. {50,50/prev.}	Length of X and Y variables	414-415
/END	Required	57

Key: #   number   v   variable name or subscript
    'c'   title, label or format   c   name not exceeding 8 char., apostrophes may be required (p. 59)

[1] In BMDP programs dated before August 1977, the minimum required abbreviations are CONTENT (not CONT), *REGRES* (not *REGR*), METHOD (not METH), PARTIAL (not PART), and SUMMARY (not SUM); INDEPENDENT and RREG are not available; and PROBIT is used in place of NORMAL and DNORMAL.

(continued)

● Order of input

(1) System Cards; at HSCF these are

```
//jobname JOB nooo,yourname
//  EXEC  BIMED,PROG=BMDP2R
//SYSIN  DD  *
```

(2) Control Language instructions

PROBlem paragraph, required
INPut paragraph, required first problem
VARiable paragraph
TRANsform paragraph
SAVE paragraph
REGRess paragraph, required, may be repeated
PRINT paragraph
PLOT paragraph
END paragraph, required at end of Control Language

(3) Data, if on cards

data

(4) System Card; at HSCF this is

//

Control Language instructions and data (2 and 3) can be repeated to analyze additional problems.

P9R -- All Possible Subsets Regression

(in addition to that on p. 453)

Paragraph STATEMENT[1] {Preassigned value}	Definition, restriction	See pages:
INPut	Specify as part of *INPut* paragraph, p. 453	
CONTENT= c.　　　　{DATA }	Content of BMDP File, can be data, covariance or correlation matrix	433
TYPE= *(one only)* DATA,COVA,CORR.　{CONTENT }	Type of input, required only if BMDP File CONTENT is not DATA, COVA or CORR	433-434
SHAPE= *(one only)* SQUARE,LOWER.　{SQUARE/prev.}	Shape of covariance or correlation matrix input when not in BMDP File	433-434
VARiable	Specify as part of *VARiable* paragraph, p. 453	
WEIGHT=v.　　　　{no weighting/prev.}	Variable containing case weights	432-433
SAVE	Specify as part of *SAVE* paragraph, p. 453	
CONTENT= *(one or both)* DATA,COVA. {DATA }	Data and/or covariances to be saved in BMDP File	434
/REGRess	Required	423
DEPENDENT=v.　　　　{none}	Dependent variable, required	423
INDEPendent=$v_1,v_1,\cdots$. {none}	Independent variables (at least 3), required	423
METHod= *(one only)* CP,RSQ,ADJ,NONE. { CP /prev.}	Criterion for best subset	423-424
PENALTY=#.　　　　{2/prev.}	Penalty for adding variable when METHOD=CP. PEN=2 for Mallows' C_p	424
NUMBER=#.　　　　{5/prev.}	Number of best subsets to find, ≤ 10	424
TOLERANCE=#.　　{0.0001/prev.}	Guards against singularity, $0 \leq \# \leq 1$.	432
ZERO.　　　　{not ZERO/prev.}	Regression equation with intercept or without intercept	432
/PRINT	Optional	
CASE=#.　　　　{5/prev.}	Number of cases of data to print	426
MATRices= *(one or more)* CORR,COVA,RESI,RREG. {CORR /prev.}	Matrices to print	426-427
/PLOT	Optional	
XVAR=$v_1,v_2,\cdots$.　　{none}	Variables for X axes of plots	429-430
YVAR=$v_1,v_2,\cdots$.　　{none}	Variables for Y axes of plots. Both Xvar and Yvar can be residuals or predicted values or related measures	429-430
NORMAL.　　　　{no/prev.}	Normal probability plot for standardized residuals	429-430
SIZE=$\#_1,\#_2$.　　　{50,50/prev.}	Length of X and Y axes	429-430
/END	Required	57

Key:　#　number　　　　　　v　variable name or subscript
　　　'c'　title, label or format　　c　name not exceeding 8 char., apostrophes may be required (p. 59)

[1] P9R was originally released in August 1976. In BMDP programs dated before August 1977, the minimum required abbreviations are CONTENT (not CONT) and *REGRES* (not *REGR*); INVCR is used in place of RREG in the MATRICES statement; PROBIT is used in place of NORMAL.

- Order of input

(1) System Cards; at HSCF these are	//jobname JOB nooo,yourname
	//　EXEC　BIMED,PROG=BMDP9R
	//SYSIN　DD　*

(2) Control Language instructions	*PROBlem* paragraph, required *INPut* paragraph, required first problem *VARiable* paragraph *TRANsform* paragraph *SAVE* paragraph *REGRess* paragraph, required *PRINT* paragraph *PLOT* paragraph *END* paragraph, required at end of Control Language
(3) Data, if on cards	data
(4) System Card; at HSCF this is	//

　　Control Language instructions and data (2 and 3) can be repeated to analyze additional problems.

P4R -- Regression on Principal Components

(in addition to that on p. 453)

Paragraph STATEMENT[1]	{Preassigned value}	Definition, restriction	See pages:
/REGRess		Required, may be repeated	440
DEPENDENT=v.	{none/prev.}	Dependent variable, required 1st REGRess para.	440
INDEPENDENT=$v_1,v_2,\cdots$.	{all possible var./prev.}	Independent variables	440
TITLE='c'.	{blank}	Title for analysis, $\leq$ 80 char.	440
STANDARDIZED.	{no/prev.}	Regression on standardized or original vars.	440
CORRELATION. or EIGEN.	{CORR/prev.}	Criterion for entering components	441
LIMIT=$\#_1,\#_2$.	{0.01,0.01/prev.}	Smallest correlation and eigenvalue that allows component to enter regression model	441
/PRINT		Optional	
SCORE.	{no/prev.}	Print standardized principal component scores for each case	441-442
/PLOT		Optional	
VARIABLE=$v_1,v_2,\cdots$.	{none/prev.}	Variables against which predicted and observed values and residuals are plotted	442
RESIDUAL.	{no/prev.}	Residuals and residuals squared plotted against predicted values	442
NORMAL.	{no/prev.}	Print normal probability plot of residuals	442-443
DNORMAL.	{no/prev.}	Print detrended normal probability plot of residuals	442-443
SIZE=$\#_1,\#_2$.	{50,50/prev.}	Length of X and Y variables.	442-443
/END		Required	57

Key: #   number   v variable name or subscript
    'c' title, label or format   c name not exceeding 8 char., apostrophes may be required (p. 59)

[1] In BMDP programs dated before August 1977, the minimum required abbreviation is REGRES (not REGR); PROBIT is used in place of NORM and DNORM; and LIMIT=#. (not $\#_1,\#_2$).

- Order of input

(1) System Cards; at HSCF these are
```
//jobname JOB nooo,yourname
//  EXEC  BIMED,PROG=BMDP4R
//SYSIN  DD  *
```

(2) Control Language instructions
```
PROBlem paragraph, required
INPut paragraph, required first problem
VARiable paragraph
TRANsform paragraph
SAVE paragraph
REGRess paragraph, required, may be repeated
PRINT paragraph
PLOT paragraph
END paragraph, required at end of Control Language
```

(3) Data, if on cards   data

(4) System Card; at HSCF this is   //

Control Language instructions and data (2 and 3) can be repeated to analyze additional problems.

P5R -- Polynomial Regression

(in addition to that on p. 453)

Paragraph STATEMENT[1]	{Preassigned value}	Definition, restriction	See pages:
VARiable		Specify as part of *VARiable* paragraph, p. 453	
WEIGHT=v.	{no weighting/prev.}	Variable containing case weights	451
/*REGRess*		Required	447
DEPENDENT=v.	{none/prev.}	Dependent variable, required 1st *REGRess* para.	447
INDEPENDENT=v.	{none/prev.}	Independent variable, required 1st *REGRess* para.	447
TITLE='c'.	{blank}	Title for analysis, $\leq$ 80 char.	447
DEGREE=#.	{3/prev.}	Maximum degree (power) of final polynomial, $\leq$ 15	447
/*PRINT*		Optional	
RREG.	{no/prev.}	Print correlation matrix of regression coefficients	447-450
DEGREE=$\#_1,\#_2,\cdots$.	{none/prev.}	Degree of polynomial at which residuals are printed	447-450
ORTHPOL.	{no/prev.}	Print coefficient of orthogonal polynomials	447-450
/*PLOT*		Optional	450
DEGREE=$\#_1,\#_2,\cdots$.	{none/prev.}	Degrees of polynomial at which predicted values and residuals are plotted against independent variable	450
NORMAL.	{no/prev.}	Normal probability plot printed at specified DEGREEs	450-451
DNORMAL.	{no/prev.}	Detrended normal probability plot printed at specified DEGREEs	450-451
SIZE=$\#_1,\#_2,\cdots$.	{50,50/prev.}	Length of X and Y axes	450-451
/*END*			57

Key: # number   v variable name or subscript
     'c' title, label or format

[1] In BMDP programs dated before August 1977, the minimum required abbreviations are *REGRES* (not *REGR*) and ORTHPOL (not ORTH); CORR is used in place of RREG; PROBIT is used in place of NORM and DNORM.

- Order of input

    (1) System Cards; at HSCF these are
```
//jobname JOB nooo,yourname
// EXEC BIMED,PROG=BMDP5R
//SYSIN DD *
```

    (2) Control Language instructions
```
PROBlem paragraph, required
INPut paragraph, required first problem
VARiable paragraph
TRANsform paragraph
SAVE paragraph
REGRess paragraph, required
PRINT paragraph
PLOT paragraph
END paragraph, required at end of Control Language
```

    (3) Data, if on cards
```
data
```

    (4) Control Language instructions to reanalyze the same data
```
REGRess paragraph, required
PRINT paragraph
PLOT paragraph
END paragraph, required at end of each batch of Control Language
```

    (5) System Card; at HSCF this is
```
//
```

     (4) can be repeated for additional analyses of the same data
     Control Language instructions and data (2-4) can be repeated to analyze additional problems

14

NONLINEAR REGRESSION

And Maximum Likelihood Estimation

A regression model is used to quantify a relationship when the value of a variable can be explained by the values of other variables. This chapter discusses methods of estimating the parameters of a <u>nonlinear</u> regression model. Nonlinear models that are linear in the parameters can be fitted as linear regression models; also some nonlinear models can be transformed to linear models. <u>Linear</u> regression models and polynomial models are described in Chapter 13.

In this chapter we describe two programs that are used to estimate parameters in nonlinear models by least squares.

P3R -- Nonlinear Regression   p. 464
PAR -- Derivative-free Nonlinear Regression   p. 484

Both programs can also be used to compute maximum likelihood
estimates of the parameters of your model.   p. 499

P3R estimates the parameters of any of five frequently used nonlinear functions when you specify a code number for the function and the number of parameters in the model. Other functions can be fitted to the data by specifying both the function and its derivatives by FORTRAN statements. The parameters are estimated by a Gauss-Newton algorithm. Exact linear constraints can be placed on the parameters of the model.

PAR estimates the parameters of any function that can be specified by FORTRAN statements. The derivatives of the function are not used (required). The parameters are estimated by a pseudo-Gauss-Newton algorithm (Ralston and Jennrich, 1977). Upper and lower limits can be specified for linear combinations of the parameters.

Both P3R and PAR can compute weighted least squares estimates. The parameters are estimated by an iterative algorithm. At each iteration the programs print the residual sum of squares and estimates of the parameters. Once parameter estimates are determined, the programs print estimates of the asymptotic standard deviations of the parameter estimates, and of the correlations between them. The residuals, predicted values and observed values of all the variables are listed.

Both programs can plot the residuals and predicted values against other variables and print normal probability plots of the residuals. The predicted values and data can be saved in a BMDP File to be further analyzed by other programs.

We recommend that you use P3R if your function is one of the five functions available by specifying a code number. A common error in P3R is the incorrect specification of derivatives; so when the derivatives are difficult to specify, we suggest you use PAR. If you expect your parameter estimates to be highly correlated, PAR is preferable because it uses double precision for its computations. P3R can analyze larger amounts of data than PAR (see p. 482 and 498).

An alternative to least squares is maximum likelihood estimation -- estimation of the parameters by maximizing the likelihood function of the data. Section 14.3 describes how P3R and PAR can be used to obtain maximum likelihood estimates of the parameters.

In PAR the function to be fitted to the data must be specified in a FORTRAN subroutine; in P3R the function and its derivatives may be specified in a FORTRAN subroutine. This affects the System Cards required to use the program. The System Cards are discussed in detail in Section 14.4.

● CONTROL LANGUAGE

The Control Language instructions to describe the data and variables are common to all BMDP programs and are explained in Chapter 5: the *PROBlem*, *INPut*[1] and *VARiable* paragraphs are used in the nonlinear regression programs.

If data editing or transformations are necessary, the methods described in Chapter 6 can be used. Data can be read using a FORMAT statement or from a BMDP File (Chapter 7).

---

[1] BMDP programs dated before August 1977 require more letters than are shown in this manual in their permissible abbreviated form (the capitalized letters). The minimum required abbreviations for earlier versions are specified in footnotes to the summary (p. 518).

A summary of the Control Language instructions common to all BMDP programs is on p. 518; summaries of the Control Language instructions specific to each nonlinear regression program follow the general summary. These summaries can be used as indexes to the program descriptions.

P3R

14.1 Nonlinear Regression

Robert Jennrich, HSCF

P3R estimates the parameters of a nonlinear function by least squares using a Gauss-Newton algorithm (Jennrich and Sampson, 1968). P3R is appropriate for a wide variety of functions that are not linear in the parameters. Any of five frequently used nonlinear functions can be specified by a Control Language statement. Other nonlinear functions, as well as their derivatives, must be specified by FORTRAN statements; when the derivatives are difficult to specify, you should consider using PAR.

● RESULTS

The data for our first example are given in Table 14.1. The data (Table 14.1) represent radioactivity counts in the blood of a baboon sampled at specified times after an initial bolus injection containing radioactive sulphate.

Table 14.1 Activity in the blood of a baboon named Brunhilda (personal communication from Shires as reported by Jennrich and Bright, 1976).

Counts x 10^{-4}	Case Weights	Time
15.1117	.004379	2
11.3601	.007749	4
9.7652	.010487	6
9.0935	.012093	8
8.4820	.013900	10
7.6891	.016914	15
7.3342	.018591	20
7.0593	.020067	25
6.7041	.022249	30
6.4313	.024177	40
6.1554	.026393	50
5.9940	.027833	60
5.7698	.030039	70
5.6440	.031392	80
5.3915	.034402	90
5.0938	.038540	110
4.8717	.042135	130
4.5996	.047267	150
4.4968	.049453	160
4.3602	.052600	170
4.2668	.054928	180

The counts are recorded in columns 2-8, case weights in columns 10-16 and time in columns 22-24.

In our first example we fit the sum of two exponentials

$$y = p_1 e^{p_2 x} + p_3 e^{p_4 x}$$

to the data in Table 14.1. This function is one of the five functions available in P3R by stating Control Language instructions. To obtain it we specify

> NUMBER IS 1.
> PARAMETERS ARE 4.

in the *REGRess* paragraph.

This function is fit by using the instructions given in Example 14.1.

Example 14.1

```
/PROBLEM      TITLE IS 'RADIOACTIVE SULFATE DATA'.
/INPUT        VARIABLES ARE 3.
              FORMAT IS '(F8.4,F8.6,F8.0)'.
/VARIABLE     NAMES ARE COUNT,CASEWT,TIME.

/REGRESS      DEPENDENT IS COUNT.
              INDEPENDENT IS TIME.
              NUMBER IS 1.
              PARAMETERS ARE 4.
              WEIGHT IS CASEWT.

/PARAMETER    INITIAL ARE 10, -.1, 5, -.01.

/END
```

When the function is <u>not</u> specified by FORTRAN statements, the Control Language must be preceded by System Card to initiate the analysis by P3R. At HSCF, the System Cards are

```
//jobname  JOB  nooo,yourname
//   EXEC  BIMED,PROG=BMDP3R
//SYSIN  DD  *
```

The Control Language is immediately followed by the data (Table 14.1). The analysis is terminated by another System Card. At HSCF, this System Card is

```
//
```

The *REGRess* and *PARAMeter* paragraphs are specific to P3R. In the *REGRess* paragraph we specify the DEPENDENT variable, the INDEPENDENT variable, the number of PARAMETERS in the model, the NUMBER identifying the function to be fit, and the variable that contains case WEIGHTs. INITIAL values for the parameters are specified in the *PARAMeter* paragraph. The remaining Control Language instructions are a general description of the data and variables, as explained in Chapter 5.

The results of the analysis are presented in Output 14.1. Circled numbers below correspond to those in the output.

(1) Interpretation of the *REGRess* paragraph. Most of the values reported are preassigned values for the program.

(2) Number of cases read. P3R uses only complete cases in all computations. That is, if the value of any variable in a case is missing or out of range, the case is omitted from all computations. If a USE statement is specified in the *VARiable* paragraph, only the values of variables in the USE statement are checked for missing value codes and values out of range.

(3) The means, standard deviations, minimums and maximums for all variables except the case WEIGHT variable. When a case WEIGHT variable is specified, weighted means and standard deviations are computed.

(4) Upper and lower limits for the parameters specified in the *PARAMeter* paragraph. As we did not specify limits, asterisks are printed.

(5) At each iteration P3R prints

  - the number of the iteration

  - the number of increment halvings (explained on p. 482)

  - the residual sum of squares

  $$RSS = \Sigma \; w \; (y-f)^2$$

  where y is the observed value of the dependent variable, f is the evaluation of the function, and w is the value of the case weight (the case weight value is 1 if there is no weighting); the summation is over all cases used in the analysis.

  - the estimates of the parameters (at step zero they are the initial estimates)

(6) The iteration at which the smallest residual sum of squares occurs. The smallest may not be at the last iteration since P3R terminates the iteration when the relative change in the sum of squares during five successive iterations is less than a specified (or preassigned) limit. Small differences between the parameter values at the last iteration and at the iteration that produces the smallest residual sum of squares can be attributed to round-off error; large differences can indicate that a saddle-point or local minimum was found. If the maximum number of iterations is reached, the derivatives may be incorrectly specified.

Note: The remaining computations use the parameter estimates from the iteration printed in the results or, when no iteration is printed, from the last iteration.

(7) The asymptotic correlation matrix of the parameter estimates. This is obtained by inverting the matrix of the sums of cross products of the derivatives. When the derivatives are too highly correlated, it may not be possible to invert the matrix completely (see Appendix A.15).

<u>Output 14.1</u> An analysis of the radioactive sulfate data using P3R. The function is the sum of two exponentials. Circled numbers correspond to those in the text. Results not reproduced are indicated in italics.

```
BMDP3R - NONLINEAR REGRESSION                                          PROGRAM REVISED SEPTEMBER 1977
HEALTH SCIENCES COMPUTING FACILITY                                     MANUAL DATE  --  1977
UNIVERSITY OF CALIFORNIA, LOS ANGELES
```

--- Control Language read by P3R is printed and interpreted ---

```
    REGRESSION TITLE

(1) REGRESSION NUMBER . . . . . . . . . . . . . . .       1
    INDEPENDENT VARIABLE(FOR BUILT-IN FUNCTION) . .   TIME
    DEPENDENT VARIABLE. . . . . . . . . . . . . . .   CCUNT
    WEIGHTING VARIABLE. . . . . . . . . . . . . . .   CASEWT
    NUMBER OF PARAMETERS. . . . . . . . . . . . . .       4
    NUMBER OF CONSTRAINTS . . . . . . . . . . . . .       0
    TOLERANCE FOR PIVOTING. . . . . . . . . . . . . 0.00100
    TOLERANCE FOR CONVERGENCE . . . . . . . . . . . C.00001
    MAXIMUM NUMBER OF ITERATIONS. . . . . . . . . .     100
    MAXIMUM NUMBER OF INCREMENT HALVINGS. . . . . .      10

    USING THE ABOVE SPECIFICATIONS THIS PROGRAM COULD PROCESS 1844 CASES.

(2) NUMBER OF CASES READ. . . . . . . . . . . . . .      21

    VARIABLE                              STANDARD
(3) NO. NAME                MEAN          DEVIATION         MINIMUM          MAXIMUM

     1  CCUNT             5.750695        1.711861         4.266800        15.111699
     3  TIME             97.933350       60.915985         2.000000       180.000000

(4) PARAMETER MAXIMA. . . . . . . . . . . .  ************** ************** ************** **************
    PARAMETER MINIMA. . . . . . . . . . . .  ************** ************** ************** **************

    ITERATION   INCREMENT    RESIDUAL SUM
     NUMBER     HALVINGS      OF SQUARES          P(   1)         P(   2)         P(   3)        P(   4)

       0           0          5.592529         1C.000000      -0.100000       5.000000      -0.010000
(5)    1           1          0.379748          9.907279      -0.101483       4.947064       0.000353
       2           0          0.058246          8.301581      -0.130405       6.940267      -0.00308C
       3           C          0.018951          9.233945      -0.178250       7.336724      -0.003128
       4           0          0.013453         1C.542834      -0.211034       7.343435      -0.003137
       5           0          0.012897         11.124450      -0.223769       7.364382      -0.00316C
       6           0          0.012850         11.290751      -0.227774       7.374455      -0.003170
       7           0          0.012846         11.336523      -0.228964       7.377789      -0.003174
       8           0          0.012845         11.349527      -0.229309       7.378793      -0.003175
       9           0          0.012845         11.353253      -0.229409       7.379086      -0.003175
      10           1          0.012845         11.353786      -0.229423       7.379128      -0.003176
      11           0          0.012845         11.354477      -0.229442       7.379182      -0.003176
      12           0          0.012845         11.354672      -0.229447       7.379197      -0.003176
      13           1          0.012845         11.354701      -0.229448       7.379200      -0.003176

    ITERATION    13 HAS THE SMALLEST RESIDUAL SUM OF SQUARES(SUBJECT TO CONSTRAINTS, IF ANY).
(6) REMAINING CALCULATIONS ARE BASED ON THE RESULTS OF THIS ITERATION.

    STANDARD FUNCTION FORM USED WITH IND =     3

    F= P(1) EXP( P(2) X(IND) ) + P(3) EXP( P(4) X(IND) ) + ....


    ASYMPTOTIC CORRELATION MATRIX OF THE PARAMETERS
(7)                      P(   1)     P(   2)     P(   3)     P(   4)
                            1           2           3           4

    P(   1)   1       1.0000
    P(   2)   2      -C.8140      1.000C
    P(   3)   3       0.1459     -0.5026      1.0000
    P(   4)   4      -0.1139      0.4184     -0.8689      1.0000

(8) COMPUTEC VALUE OF RESIDUAL MEAN SQUARE IS      0.001

    ASYMPTOTIC STANDARD DEVIATIONS OF THE PARAMETERS ASSUMING    17 DEGREES OF FREEDOM
                 P(   1)      P(   2)      P(   3)      P(   4)

             0.86583E 00 0.18740E-01 C.10660E 00 C.13630E-03

     CASE              PREDICTED    STD DEV OF       OBSERVED
(9)  NO. LABEL         COUNT        PRED VALUE       COUNT        RESIDUAL       CASEWT          TIME

      1                14.508443     0.36262        15.111699     0.603256      0.004379       2.C00000
      2                11.821134     0.17204        11.360100    -0.461034      0.007749       4.000000
      3                10.106014     0.14471         9.765200    -0.340815      0.010487       6.C000CC
```

--- similar statistics for cases 4 to 18 ---

```
     19                 4.439628     0.05193         4.496799     0.057172      C.049453     16C.00000C
     20                 4.300858     C.05506         4.360200     0.059341      0.052600     17C.000000
     21                 4.166427     0.05814         4.266800     0.100373      0.054928     180.000000

(10) SERIAL CORRELATION OF RESIDUALS=SUM(R(I)*R(I-1))/SQRT(SUM(R(I)**2)*SUM(R(I-1)**2))

     SERIAL CORRELATION    RESIDUALS ORDERED ON
          0.36600          CASE NUMBER
```

⑧ The residual mean square is the residual sum of squares divided by (N-p) where N is the number of cases with nonzero weight and p is the number of independent parameters estimated.

This is followed by the asymptotic standard deviations of the parameter estimates. A zero indicates a problem with the estimate: the estimate may lie on a boundary of the permissible parameter space (equal to its specified upper or lower limit), there may be extremely high correlations among the estimated parameters, or the estimate is so poor that if it is changed the value of the function is not affected.

⑨ For each case, P3R prints

- the predicted value (value of the function)
  $f = f(x_1, x_2, \ldots, p_1, p_2, \ldots)$
- the standard deviation of the predicted value (Appendix A.15).
- the observed value of the dependent variable y
- the residual (y-f)
- the case weight, w
- the values of the independent variables $x_1, x_2, \ldots$

⑩ The serial correlation of the residuals

$$\sum_{j=2}^{N} (w_j w_{j-1})^{\frac{1}{2}} (y_j - f_j)(y_{j-1} - f_{j-1}) / \{ \sum_{2}^{N} w_j (y_j - f_j)^2 \sum_{1}^{N-1} w_j (y_j - f_j)^2 \}^{\frac{1}{2}}$$

• SPECIFICATIONS FOR AN ANALYSIS AND OPTIONAL OUTPUT

To fit a nonlinear function to the data you must specify

- a code number indicating a function available in P3R   p. 469

                        or

  a function and its derivatives specified by FORTRAN
  statements   p. 471
- the number of parameters in the function   p. 471
- the dependent variable   p. 471

You can obtain estimates by weighted least squares regression.   p. 475

Usually you can suggest better initial estimates for the parameters than those supplied by P3R. The preassigned estimates are zero for all parameters. You must provide initial estimates if the function is undefined or all derivatives are zero when the parameter estimates are zero.   p. 477

In addition to the above, you may

- request plots of the residuals and predicted values
  against each other and against specified variables   p. 477
- request normal probability plots of the residuals   p. 477

- state upper and lower limits for the parameters   p. 478

- name the parameters   p. 478

- specify exact linear constraints on the parameters   p. 479

- request that residuals and data not be printed   p. 480

- save the data, residuals and predicted values in a BMDP File   p. 481

- alter preset values for the Gauss-Newton algorithm, such as the maximum number of iterations and the criterion for convergence   p. 481

- specify any of three options, MEANSQUARE, LOSS and PASS, that are used primarily with maximum likelihood estimation; they are discussed in Section 14.3   p. 499

● DESCRIBING THE NONLINEAR FUNCTION -- THE *REGRess* PARAGRAPH

    The *REGRess*[2] paragraph describes the function, the dependent variable and number of parameters. It is required and can be repeated after the data to describe additional analyses of the same data (see order of input in the summary, p. 519).

● FUNCTIONS AVAILABLE IN CONTROL LANGUAGE

    Five functions (and their derivatives) are available in P3R by specifying their code NUMBER[3] in the *REGRess* paragraph. The five are:

Code Number	Function
1	$f_1 = \begin{cases} p_1 e^{p_2 x} + p_3 e^{p_4 x} + \ldots + p_{m-1} e^{p_m x} & \text{if } m \text{ is even} \\[2ex] p_1 e^{p_2 x} + p_3 e^{p_4 x} + \ldots + p_m & \text{if } m \text{ is odd} \end{cases}$
2	$f_2 = 1/f_1$
3	$f_3 = p_1 + p_2 e^{p_3 x} + (p_4 + p_5 e^{p_6 x}) \sin(p_7 + p_8 x) \qquad m = 8$

---

[2] If your BMDP programs are dated before August 1977, the minimum required abbreviation is *REGRES* (not *REGR*).

[3] If your BMDP programs are dated before August 1977, the minimum required abbreviation is NUMBER (not NUMB).

Code Number	Function	

$$f_4 = \begin{cases} \dfrac{p_1 + p_3x + p_5x^2 + \ldots + p_m x^{(m-1)/2}}{1 + p_2x + p_4x^2 + \ldots + p_{m-1}x^{(m-1)/2}} & \text{if } m \text{ is odd} \\[4ex] \dfrac{p_1 + p_3x + p_5x^2 + \ldots + p_{m-1}x^{(m/2)-1}}{1 + p_2x + p_4x^2 + \ldots + p_m x^{(m/2)}} & \text{if } m \text{ is even} \end{cases}$$

4

5 $\qquad f_5 = p_1 x^{p_2} e^{p_3 x^{p_4}} + p_5 x^{p_6} e^{p_7 x^{p_8}} + \ldots$

if m is not a multiple of 4, the additional parameters are treated as zero[4]

where

m = number of parameters

x = the value of the independent variable

You must specify the DEPENDENT variable, the INDEPENDENT[5] variable and the number of PARAMETERS in addition to the code NUMBER for each function. You can fix or restrict values of the parameters by specifying upper and lower limits for them. A TITLE can also be given.

In Example 14.1 we specify

```
/REGRESS        DEPENDENT IS COUNT.
                INDEPENDENT IS TIME.
                NUMBER IS 1.
                PARAMETERS ARE 4.
```

as well as a WEIGHT variable

```
                WEIGHT IS CASEWT.
```

Note: The System Cards for any of the five functions are the same as in Example 14.1. If the function is specified by FORTRAN statements, the System Cards are described in Section 14.4.

---

[4] If your BMDP programs are dated before August 1977, m must be a multiple of 4.

[5] If your BMDP programs are dated before August 1977, INDEP is preset to 1 and cannot be changed.

REGRess
   NUMBER=#.   {none/prev.}

     The code NUMBER of one of the five nonlinear functions available
     in P3R. The number must be specified in the first *REGRess* para-
     graph when one of the five nonlinear functions is desired. When you
     specify a nonlinear function by FORTRAN statements, NUMBER is
     passed to the subroutine that evaluates the function, and can then
     be used as an index in your subroutine. NUMBER need not be speci-
     fied when your function is stated in FORTRAN.

   DEPENDENT=v.   {none/prev.}   required
     Name or subscript of the dependent (predicted) variable.

   INDEPENDENT=v.   {1/prev.}

     Name or subscript of the independent (predictor) variable; needed
     only if you request any of the five nonlinear functions available
     in P3R. It is ignored (not used even if stated) if you specify the
     function by FORTRAN statements.

   PARAMETER=#.   {none/prev.}   required
     The number of parameters in the regression function.

   TITLE='c'.   {blank} $\leq$ 160 char.
     Title for the analysis.

● Specifying a Regression Function by FORTRAN Statements

     You are not limited to using one of the five functions described above.
Any function can be fitted to the data if you can specify, in FORTRAN, both
the function and its derivatives with respect to the parameters. The FORTRAN
subroutine that contains the function and its derivatives temporarily becomes
part of program P3R and replaces the subroutine containing the five functions
described above. (You cannot use both -- one of the five functions and a
function specified in FORTRAN -- in the same job.)

     The FORTRAN subroutine is called once for each case during each itera-
tion (or halving). The calling sequence of the subroutine is[6]

        SUBROUTINE FUN(F,DF,P,X,N,KASE,NVAR,NPAR,IPASS,XLOSS)
        DIMENSION DF(NPAR),P(NPAR),X(NVAR)

where the following values should not be changed

        NPAR - the number of parameters in the function
        NVAR - the total number of variables (not the number of indepen-
              dent variables); the sum of the variables read as data
              and those added by transformations, if any.

---

[6] If your BMDP programs are dated before August 1977,
    the first two statements in the FORTRAN subroutine are
        SUBROUTINE FUN(F,DF,P,X,N)
        DIMENSION DF(1),P(1),X(1)

KASE - the sequence number of the case for which the function is being evaluated

IPASS - pass number; this is used only when the function evaluation requires more than one pass at the data (IPASS is primarily useful with maximum likelihood estimation and is explained in Section 14.3; otherwise it can be ignored).

P(1),P(2),...,P(NPAR) - the current values of the parameters

The following values are usually not changed

X(1),X(2),...,X(NVAR) - the observed values of <u>all</u> the variables in the order that they appear in the data matrix

N   - the NUMBER specified in the *REGRess* paragraph. It can be used to select functions in your FORTRAN subroutine.

XLOSS - a utility or loss function to replace the residual sum of squares as a criterion for convergence (XLOSS is primarily useful for maximum likelihood estimation and is explained in Section 14.3; otherwise it can be ignored)

The following <u>must</u> be evaluated in the subroutine

F   - the value of the function for this case (f)

DF(1),DF(2),...,DF(NPAR) - the values of the derivatives of the function with respect to the parameters ($\partial f/\partial p_i$)

The rules of FORTRAN apply in the subroutine (and <u>not</u> the rules of Control Language). Any FORTRAN statements and functions can be used.

An example. We fitted the sum of two exponentials to the data in Table 14.1 by using one of the nonlinear functions available in P3R. Now we repeat the analysis by specifying the function and its derivatives in FORTRAN. The sum of two exponentials is

$$f = p_1 e^{p_2 t} + p_3 e^{p_4 t}$$

The derivatives are

$$\frac{\partial f}{\partial p_1} = e^{p_2 t} \qquad\qquad \frac{\partial f}{\partial p_2} = p_1 t e^{p_2 t} = p_1 t \frac{\partial f}{\partial p_1}$$

$$\frac{\partial f}{\partial p_3} = e^{p_4 t} \qquad\qquad \frac{\partial f}{\partial p} = p_3 t e^{p_4 t} = p_3 t \frac{\partial f}{\partial p_3}$$

Note that $f = p_1 \frac{\partial f}{\partial p_1} + p_3 \frac{\partial f}{\partial p_2}$.

In our data the independent variable TIME is the third variable X(3). Therefore we write the function and derivatives as shown in Example 14.2.

Example 14.2

```
        DF(1)=EXP(P(2)*X(3))
        DF(2)=P(1)*X(3)*DF(1)
        DF(3)=EXP(P(4)*X(3))
        DF(4)=P(3)*X(3)*DF(3)
        F=P(1)*DF(1)+P(3)*DF(3)
```
FORTRAN statements to define function and derivatives

```
/PROBLEM        TITLE IS 'RADIOACTIVE SULFATE DATA'.
/INPUT          VARIABLES ARE 3.
                FORMAT IS '(F8.4,F8.6,F8.C)'.
/VARIABLE       NAMES ARE COUNT,CASEWT,TIME.

/REGRESS        DEPENDENT IS COUNT.
                PARAMETERS ARE 4.
                WEIGHT IS CASEWT.

/PARAMETER      INITIAL ARE 10, -.1, 5, -.01.

/END
```
Control Language instructions

When the function and its derivatives are specified by FORTRAN statements, the FORTRAN statements must be preceded by System Cards to initiate the analysis by P3R. At HSCF, the System Cards are

```
//jobname  JOB  nooo,yourname
//   EXEC  BIMEDT,PROG=BMDP3R
//FUN  DD  *
```

The FORTRAN statements are immediately followed by another System Card. At HSCF, this card is

```
//GO.SYSIN  DD  *
```

This System Card is followed by the Control Language instructions. The Control Language instructions are in turn followed by the data (Table 14.1). The analysis is terminated by a final System Card. At HSCF, this System Card is

```
//
```

The System Cards are discussed in greater detail in Section 14.4.

In the above Control Language instructions NUMBER and INDEPENDENT are not specified, as they were in Example 14.1.

The results are presented in Output 14.2. The small differences between Output 14.1 and 14.2 are due to the limited accuracy of computations performed on the computer (slightly different round-off error).

A second example. As a second example we use data from an insulin radio-immunoassay that are presented in Table 14.2 (Brown et al., 1974). The empirical function appropriate to the data is

$$f = \frac{1}{p_1 x + p_2} + p_3$$

(Täljedal and Wold, 1970). The derivatives are

$$\frac{\partial f}{\partial p_1} = -\frac{x}{(p_1 x + p_2)^2} \quad ; \quad \frac{\partial f}{\partial p_2} = -\frac{1}{(p_1 x + p_2)^2} \quad ; \quad \frac{\partial f}{\partial p_3} = 1.$$

The independent variable x is the first variable.

Table 14.2   Activity corresponding to levels of insulin standard (Brown et al., 1974).

Insulin Standard	Counts x 10^{-3}
0	9.274
0	9.522
5	8.082
5	8.354
10	7.296
10	7.518
25	5.864
25	5.974
50	4.396
50	4.110
100	2.830
100	2.674
200	1.798
200	1.566

The insulin standard is recorded in columns 4-6 and counts in columns 8-12.

Note that the function is not defined unless p_1 or p_2 is not zero; therefore initial estimates of the parameters must be specified.

The function and its derivatives are specified in Example 14.3.

Output 14.2   A similar analysis to that in Output 14.1 except that the function is defined by FORTRAN statements. Note the similarity between the two analyses.

ITERATION NUMBER	INCREMENT HALVINGS	RESIDUAL SUM OF SQUARES	P(1)	P(2)	P(3)	P(4)
0	0	5.592529	10.000000	-0.100000	5.000000	-0.010000
1	1	0.379747	9.907277	-0.101484	4.947069	0.000353
2	0	0.058245	8.301600	-0.130406	6.940269	-0.003080
3	0	0.018951	9.233960	-0.178250	7.336722	-0.003128
4	0	0.013453	10.542832	-0.211034	7.343433	-0.003137
5	0	0.012897	11.124449	-0.223769	7.364382	-0.003160
6	0	0.012850	11.290749	-0.227774	7.374455	-0.003170
7	0	0.012846	11.336525	-0.228964	7.377789	-0.003174
8	0	0.012845	11.349529	-0.229309	7.378792	-0.003175
9	0	0.012845	11.353253	-0.229409	7.379086	-0.003175
10	0	0.012845	11.354321	-0.229437	7.379169	-0.003176
11	0	0.012845	11.354629	-0.229446	7.379193	-0.003176
12	6	0.012845	11.354630	-0.229446	7.379193	-0.003176
13	7	0.012845	11.354630	-0.229446	7.379193	-0.003176

ITERATION   13 HAS THE SMALLEST RESIDUAL SUM OF SQUARES(SUBJECT TO CONSTRAINTS, IF ANY).
REMAINING CALCULATIONS ARE BASED ON THE RESULTS OF THIS ITERATION.

ASYMPTOTIC CORRELATION MATRIX OF THE PARAMETERS

		P(1) 1	P(2) 2	P(3) 3	P(4) 4
P(1)	1	1.0000			
P(2)	2	-0.8140	1.0000		
P(3)	3	0.1459	-0.5026	1.0000	
P(4)	4	-0.1139	0.4185	-0.8689	1.0000

COMPUTED VALUE OF RESIDUAL MEAN SQUARE IS   0.001

ASYMPTOTIC STANDARD DEVIATIONS OF THE PARAMETERS ASSUMING   17 DEGREES OF FREEDOM

P(1)	P(2)	P(3)	P(4)
0.86583E 00	0.18740E-01	0.10660E 00	0.13630E-03

Example 14.3

```
        DF(3)=1.0
        A=P(1)*X(1)+P(2)
        IF(A.LE.0.0) A=0.000001
        F=1.0/A+P(3)
        DF(2)=-1.0/A**2
        DF(1)=X(1)*DF(2)
```
FORTRAN statements
to define function
and derivatives

```
/PROBLEM        TITLE IS 'INSULIN DATA'.
/INPUT          VARIABLES ARE 2.
                FORMAT IS '(F6.0,F6.3)'.
/VARIABLE       NAMES ARE STANDARD,COUNT.

/REGRESS        DEPENDENT IS COUNT.
                PARAMETERS ARE 3.

/PARAMETER      INITIAL ARE 0.01, 0.1, 5.

/END
```
Control Language
instructions

The System Cards required for this analysis are the same as described for Example 14.2 and are discussed in greater detail in Section 14.4. The data for this example are in Table 14.2.

The results of the analysis are presented in Output 14.3.

● CASE WEIGHTs

When the error variance is not homogeneous but varies from case to case, weighted least squares estimation is more appropriate; the weight (w) for each case is proportional to the inverse of the variance. In weighted least squares, the quantity minimized is

$$\Sigma \ w \ (y-f)^2$$

where the sum is over all cases read.

The variance may be expressed in terms of the function f; the case weight will vary from iteration to iteration as the estimates of the parameter change. The variable $X(i)$, where i is the subscript of the case WEIGHT variable, can be modified in the FORTRAN subroutine describing the function. This is known as iteratively reweighted least squares and is used in maximum likelihood estimation (Section 14.3).

In P3R, the case WEIGHTs are specified in the REGRess paragraph.

REGRess
    WEIGHT=v.   {no weight var./prev.}

    Name or subscript of the variable containing case weights. If
    WEIGHT is not stated or is set to zero, there are no case weights.

Output 14.3   An analysis of the insulin radioimmunoassay data by P3R

NUMBER OF CASES READ.   14

VARIABLE NO. NAME	MEAN	STANDARD DEVIATION	MINIMUM	MAXIMUM
1 STANDARD	55.714249	69.637985	0.0	200.000000
2 CCUNT	5.661283	2.773079	1.566000	9.521999

PARAMETER MAXIMA. . . . . ************** ************** **************
PARAMETER MINIMA. . . . . ************** ************** **************

ITERATION NUMBER	INCREMENT HALVINGS	RESIDUAL SUM OF SQUARES	P(1)	P(2)	P(3)
0	0	168.067749	C.010000	0.100000	5.000000
1	0	7.070244	0.002958	0.120813	1.312509
2	0	0.319402	0.002667	0.107693	0.137630
3	0	0.249153	0.002693	0.108966	0.138170
4	0	0.249144	0.002694	0.108981	0.138057
5	4	0.249144	0.002694	0.108981	0.138056
6	10	0.249144	0.002694	0.108981	0.138056
7	10	0.249144	C.002694	0.108981	0.138056
8	10	0.249144	0.002694	0.108981	0.138056
9	10	0.249144	0.002694	0.108981	0.138056

ITERATION   9 HAS THE SMALLEST RESIDUAL SUM OF SQUARES(SUBJECT TO CONSTRAINTS, IF ANY).
REMAINING CALCULATIONS ARE BASED ON THE RESULTS OF THIS ITERATION.

ASYMPTOTIC CORRELATION MATRIX OF THE PARAMETERS

		P(1) 1	P(2) 2	P(3) 3
P(1)	1	1.0000		
P(2)	2	0.7446	1.0000	
P(3)	3	0.9357	0.8830	1.0000

COMPUTED VALUE OF RESIDUAL MEAN SQUARE IS   0.023

ASYMPTOTIC STANDARD DEVIATIONS OF THE PARAMETERS ASSUMING   11 DEGREES OF FREEDOM
             P(1)   P(2)   P(3)

        0.22034E-03 0.20704E-02 0.18634E 00

CASE NO. LABEL	PREDICTED COUNT	STD DEV OF PRED VALUE	OBSERVED COUNT	RESIDUAL	STANDARD
1	9.313986	0.08801	9.273999	-0.039987	0.0
2	9.313986	0.08801	9.521999	0.208014	0.0
3	8.304734	0.05688	8.082000	-0.222734	5.000000

--- similar statistics for cases 4 to 11 ---

12	2.781171	C.05920	2.674000	-0.107171	100.000000
13	1.681975	0.09110	1.797999	0.116024	200.000000
14	1.681975	0.09110	1.566000	-0.115975	200.000000

SERIAL CORRELATION OF RESIDUALS=SUM(R(I)*R(I-1))/SQRT(SUM(R(I)**2)*SUM(R(I-1)**2))

SERIAL CORRELATION	RESIDUALS ORDERED ON	
-0.42374	CASE NUMBER	ALL SUMS ARE FOR I=2,NUMBER OF CASES

● *PLOTs* OF THE RESIDUALS AND PREDICTED VALUES

In the *PLOT* paragraph you can specify the following plots:

- predicted and observed values of the dependent variable and residuals against specified variables

- residuals and residuals squared against the predicted values

- a normal probability plot of the residuals

- a detrended normal probability plot of the residuals

The residuals and predicted values plotted are those printed in the results. These plots are illustrated in Output 13.3 (p. 388). Normal probability plots are described in Section 10.1 (p. 219). The plots are specified as follows:

PLOT
RESIDUAL.   {no/prev.}

The residuals (y-f) and residuals squared $(y-f)^2$ are plotted against the predicted values (the value of the function f) in separate plots.

VARIABLE= $v_1,v_2,\cdots$. {none/prev.}

Names or subscripts of variables against which the observed values of the dependent variable y and the predicted values f are plotted in one graph. In a second graph the residuals (y-f) are plotted against these variables.

NORMAL.   {no/prev.}
Normal probability plot of the residuals is printed. [7]

DNORMAL.   {no/prev.}
Detrended normal probability plot of the residuals is printed. [7]

SIZE=$\#_1,\#_2$.   {50,50/prev.}
$\#_1$ is the number of characters (width) in the horizontal axis and $\#_2$ is the number of lines (height) in the vertical axis.

● DESCRIBING THE *PARAMeters*

The *PARAMeter* paragraph is used to specify initial estimates for the parameters. An upper and a lower limit and a name can be specified for each parameter. Exact linear constraints can be imposed on the parameters.

---

[7] If your BMDP programs are dated before August 1977, PROBIT is used in place of NORM and DNORM.

P3R provides initial values for the parameters (zeros for all). These values may be a very poor starting point. For example, in the insulin radioimmunoassay, Example 14.3, the function is undefined when the parameters are all zero. Initial values must be specified when the function is undefined, or all the derivatives are zero when all parameters are zero.

Usually you can specify improved initial values by a little forethought. Improved values reduce the computation required to find a solution, and increase the likelihood of finding a global solution when there are local minimums to the residual sum of squares. Here are some suggestions to help you provide reasonable initial values:

- use the solution from a similar analysis or from an analysis by a different method

- if you cannot choose an exact value, choose a reasonable range for the parameter and pick a value close to the limit nearer zero (but preferably not zero and not a specified boundary); this is the limit that is usually more precisely estimated

- if you still cannot decide, use arbitrary nonzero numbers such as ± 1, ± 2, ± 3,... depending on whether you think the parameters are positive or negative

---

PARAMeter
   INITIAL= $\#_1, \#_2, \cdots$.   {0.0,0.0,.../prev.}   one per parameter

   Initial values for the parameter estimates. The values must satisfy specified lower and upper limits for the parameters. Good initial estimates are important to avoid saddlepoints or local minimums of the residual sum of squares.

   Note: If the final sum of squares seems too large, if there appear to be unusual features in the estimates of the parameters or residuals, or if system error messages, such as underflow, overflow or divide check are printed, you should check

   - *the formulas of your derivatives*

   - *the FORTRAN statements that specify the function and derivatives*

   - *whether the function (or derivatives) evaluated using the initial values of the parameters and at the largest or smallest data values is extremely large or small*

   If no error is found, you should try different initial values.

You can specify upper and lower limits for the parameters. Limits can be used to restrict a parameter to a given range in order to avoid a local minimum, a value of the parameter for which the function is undefined, or an interval where a change in the parameter does not affect the function (i.e., its estimated derivative is zero). You can fit the value of a parameter by setting its upper and lower limits to the fixed value.

You can specify names for the parameters to be used in the printed results.

You can specify upper and lower limits and names for any subset of the parameters by using the tab feature (p. 65).

PARAMeter
 MAXIMUM= $\#_1,\#_2,\cdots$. {none/prev.}   one per parameter
  Upper limits for the parameters.

 MINIMUM= $\#_1,\#_2,\cdots$. {none/prev.}   one per parameter
  Lower limits for the parameters.

 NAME= $c_1,c_2,\cdots$.   {P(1),P(2),.../prev.}   one per parameter
  Names for the parameters.

● CONSTRAINTS ON THE PARAMETERS

Exact linear constraints can be specified on the parameters. Let $p_1,p_2,\ldots$ represent the values of the parameters. Then an exact linear constraint has the form

$$b_1 p_1 + b_2 p_2 + \ldots = c$$

where $b_1,b_2,\ldots$ are specified coefficients and c is a specified constant.

For example

$$p_1 + p_2 + p_3 = 1$$

and

$$2p_3 - p_5 = 3$$

are both constraints.

When constraints are used, the number of constraints must be specified in the *REGRess* paragraph; the constraints are specified in the *PARAMeter* paragraph.[8]

REGRess
 CONSTRAINT= #.   {none/prev.}
  Number of exact linear constraints on the parameters that are specified in the *PARAMeter* paragraph.

---

[8] If your BMDP programs are dated before August 1977,
  constraints are specified in a different manner (see Dixon, 1975).

PARAMeter
   CONSTRAINT=#$_1$,#$_2$,$\cdots$.   {0.0,0.0,.../prev.}   may be repeated

   Coefficients of the parameters in one constraint. The first number is the coefficient of the first parameter, etc. This statement can be repeated in the same *PARAMeter* paragraph to specify additional constraints. If any CONSTRAINT is specified, all CONSTRAINTS specified in previous *PARAMeter* paragraphs are cancelled.

   K=#.   {0.0/prev.}   may be repeated

   # is the value on the right hand side of the equal sign for the <u>preceding</u> CONSTRAINT.

   Note: The value of K is applied to the CONSTRAINT *statement preceding it. You should write your* CONSTRAINT *and K statements in pairs.*

   When constraints are specified, the upper and lower limits for some of the parameters may be violated. Any such violation is easily detected by inspecting the parameter estimates.

The two constraints, $p_1 + p_2 + p_3 = 1$ and $2p_3 - p_5 = 3$, are specified as

```
/REGRESS   CONSTRAINT=2.
/PARAMETER CONSTRAINT=1,1,1.        K=1.
           CONSTRAINT=(3)2,(5)-1.   K=3.
```

● PRINTING OBSERVED VALUES, PREDICTED VALUES AND RESIDUALS

   For each case P3R prints the predicted value (value of the function), its standard error, the value of the dependent variable, the residuals, and the observed values of the specified variables (see ⑨ in Output 14.1). You can specify whether or not to print this list and, if so, which variables to include in the list.[9] All computed values use the chosen estimates of the parameters (see note p. 466).

   If you specify

        PRINT=0.

in the *REGRess* paragraph, the residuals, predicted values and data are not printed.

   You can also specify

        PRINT=v$_1$,v$_2$,$\cdots$.

where v$_1$,v$_2$,... are names or subscripts of variables whose observed values are are to be printed for each case; the predicted value, its standard error, the

---

[9] If your BMDP programs are dated before August 1977,
    PRINT is preset to all variables and cannot be changed.

value of the dependent variable, and the residual are also printed. The values of variables not specified among $v_1, v_2, \ldots$ are <u>not</u> printed.

REGRess
   PRINT=$v_1, v_2, \cdots$.   {all variables/prev.}

   The names or subscripts of variables whose observed values are printed for each case. In addition to the observed values, the predicted value, its standard error, the value of the dependent variable and the residual are also printed. If PRINT=0 is specified, residuals, predicted values and data are <u>not</u> printed.

● SAVING THE DATA, RESIDUALS AND PREDICTED VALUES

   When DATA are saved, the predicted values and residuals from the first analysis in a problem are also saved in a BMDP File. The predicted values are saved as variable VT+1 with the name PREDICTD and the residuals are saved as variable VT+2 with the name RESIDUAL (where VT is the number of variables after transformation).

   The predicted values and residuals are computed using the chosen estimates of the parameters (see note, p. 466). If you alter the value of any variable (such as the case WEIGHT variable) in the FORTRAN subroutine, the values of these variables are also computed and saved using the chosen estimates of the parameters.

● VALUES USED IN THE GAUSS-NEWTON ALGORITHM

   The function is fitted by an iterative algorithm. The algorithm decides that a solution has been reached when

$$\left| (RSS^{(k+1)} - RSS^{(k)})/RSS^{(k+1)} \right| < C$$

for five successive values of k, where $RSS^{(k)}$ is the residual sum of squares at iteration k, and C is the value of the CONVERGENCE criterion.

   When the CONVERGENCE[10] criterion is set to a value less than zero, the maximum number of iterations is used and the parameter estimates used in the computation of the standard errors, asymptotic correlations, residuals and predicted values are from the <u>last</u> iteration; if a BMDP File is created, these residuals and predicted values are saved.

REGRess
   CONVERGE= #.   {0.00001/prev.}

   Value of the convergence criterion C as described above.

---

[10] If your BMDP programs are dated before August 1977, the minimum required abbreviation is CONVER (not CONV).

```
REGRess
    ITERATION=#.                    {50/prev.}

    Maximum number of iterations.  If convergence has not occurred by
    this number of iterations, the algorithm is terminated.

    Note:  If linear CONSTRAINTS are specified, they are solved on
    the first iteration for some of the parameters in terms of the
    other parameters; at least two iterations are required even for
    a linear function.
```

If the residual sum of squares increases between two iterations, the
increment size is halved and the residual sum of squares is recomputed and
tested against the residual sum of squares at the previous iteration. This
halving is repeated until the residual sum of squares is less than that at
the previous iteration or the maximum number of HALVINGS is reached.

At each iteration the number of increment halvings performed is printed.

```
REGRess
    HALVING= #.              {5/prev.}                    > 0
      The maximum number of increment halvings as described above.
```

TOLERANCE is used to guard against the problem of near singularity
when inverting the matrix of sums of cross products of the derivatives. A
parameter estimate is not changed at an iteration if its squared multiple
correlation with some of the other parameter estimates exceeds 1-TOLERANCE.

```
REGRess
    TOLERANCE=#.             {0.001/prev.}       .00001 < # < 1.0
      A check for near singularity as described above.  A more complete
      discussion of tolerance is given in Appendix A.11.
```

● SIZE OF PROBLEM

The maximum problem size that P3R can analyze is a function of the
number of cases (C), the total number of variables (V), and the number of
parameters (P). The following table indicates the maximum number of cases
for various combinations of P and V. Appendix B describes how to increase
the capacity of the program.

total variables V	2	3	4	5	10	20
parameters P	10	20	20	20	20	20
cases C	1700	1500	1350	1200	800	480

● COMPUTATIONAL METHOD

All computations are in single precision. Means and standard deviations are computed by the method of provisional means (Appendix A.2). The parameters are estimated by a modified Gauss-Newton algorithm (Appendix A.15).

In programs dated November 1977 or later, computations in P3R will be performed using double precision.

ACKNOWLEDGEMENT

P3R was programmed by Steve Chasen. It supersedes BMD07R, which was designed by Robert Jennrich and programmed by Paul Sampson.

PAR

14.2 Derivative-Free Nonlinear Regression

Mary Ralston, HSCF

PAR estimates the parameters of a nonlinear function by least squares using a pseudo-Gauss-Newton algorithm (Ralston and Jennrich, 1977).[11] PAR is appropriate for a wide variety of functions that are not linear in the parameters, and for which derivatives are difficult to specify or costly to compute. The nonlinear function must be specified by FORTRAN statements; the derivatives are <u>not</u> specified.

● RESULTS

We use two examples (from P3R) to illustrate the results of PAR. The data for the first example are given in Table 14.1. In Example 14.4 the sum of the two exponentials

$$f = p_1 e^{p_2 t} + p_3 e^{p_4 t}$$

is fitted to the data. The function is specified by a FORTRAN statement.

Example 14.4

```
        F=P(1)*DEXP(P(2)*X(3))+P(3)*DEXP(P(4)*X(3))
```
FORTRAN statement
to define function

```
/PROBLEM     TITLE IS 'RADIOACTIVE SULFATE DATA'.
/INPUT       VARIABLES ARE 3.
             FORMAT IS '(F8.4,F8.6,F8.0)'.
/VARIABLE    NAMES ARE COUNT,CASEWT,TIME.

/REGRESS     DEPENDENT IS COUNT.
             WEIGHT IS CASEWT.
             PARAMETERS ARE 4.

/PARAMETER   INITIAL ARE 10, -.1, 5, -.01.

/END
```
Control Language
instructions

When the function is specified by FORTRAN statements, the FORTRAN statements must be preceded by System Cards to initiate the analysis by PAR. At HSCF, the System Cards are

```
//jobname  JOB  nooo,yourname
//   EXEC  BIMEDT,PROG=BMDPAR
//FUN  DD  *
```

The FORTRAN statements are immediately followed by another System Card. At HSCF, this card is

```
//GO.SYSIN  DD  *
```

---

[11] If your BMDP programs are dated before August 1977, this program, PAR, is not available.

This System Card is followed by the Control Language instructions. The Control Language instructions are in turn followed by the data (Table 14.1). The analysis is terminated by a final System Card. At HSCF, this System Card is

> //

The System Cards are discussed in greater detail in Section 14.4.

PAR uses double precision for all computations. Therefore the double precision versions of functions should be used (e.g. DEXP, not EXP).

The *REGRess* and *PARAMeter* paragraphs are specific to PAR. In the *REGRess* paragraph we specify the DEPENDENT variable, the number of PARAMETERS and the case WEIGHT variable. In the *PARAMeter* paragraph, INITIAL values for the parameters must be stated.

The results of the analysis are presented in Output 14.4. Circled numbers below correspond to those in the output.

(1) Interpretation of the *REGRess* paragraph. Most of the values reported are preassigned values for the programs.

(2) Lower (MINIMUM) and upper (MAXIMUM) limits and the initial values specified for the parameters. As no limits were specified, asterisks are printed.

Output 14.4 An analysis of the radioactive sulfate data using PAR. The function is the sum of two exponentials. Circled numbers correspond to those in the text. Results not reproduced are indicated in italics.

```
BMDPAR - DERIVATIVE-FREE NONLINEAR REGRESSION          PROGRAM REVISED SEPTEMBER 1977
HEALTH SCIENCES COMPUTING FACILITY                     MANUAL DATE -- 1977
UNIVERSITY OF CALIFORNIA, LOS ANGELES
```

--- Control Language read by PAR is printed and interpreted ---

```
    REGRESSION TITLE

(1) REGRESSION NUMBER . . . . . . . . . . . . . . . .      0
    DEPENDENT VARIABLE. . . . . . . . . . . . . . .    COUNT
    WEIGHTING VARIABLE. . . . . . . . . . . . . . .   CASEWT
    NUMBER OF PARAMETERS. . . . . . . . . . . . . .      4
    NUMBER OF CONSTRAINTS . . . . . . . . . . . . .      0
    TOLERANCE FOR PIVOTING. . . . . . . . . . . . . 1.0E-08
    TOLERANCE FOR CONVERGENCE . . . . . . . . . . . 1.0E-05
    MAXIMUM NUMBER OF ITERATIONS. . . . . . . . .       50
    MAXIMUM NUMBER OF INCREMENT HALVINGS. . . . . .      5

    PARAMETERS TO BE ESTIMATED

           1 P(1)        2 P(2)        3 P(3)        4 P(4)
(2) MINIMUM ************  ************  ************  ************
    MAXIMUM ************  ************  ************  ************
    INITIAL   10.000000     -0.100000     5.000000     -0.010000

    USING THE ABOVE SPECIFICATIONS THIS PROGRAM COULD USE UP TO  770 CASES.
(3) NUMBER OF CASES READ. . . . . . . . . . . . .        21
```

(continued)

Output 14.4 *(continued)*

<table>
<tr><td>④</td><td colspan="2">VARIABLE
NO. NAME</td><td>MEAN</td><td>STANDARD
DEVIATION</td><td>MINIMUM</td><td>MAXIMUM</td></tr>
<tr><td></td><td>1</td><td>CCUNT</td><td>5.750695</td><td>1.711861</td><td>4.266800</td><td>15.111699</td></tr>
<tr><td></td><td>3</td><td>TIME</td><td>97.933350</td><td>60.915985</td><td>2.000000</td><td>180.000000</td></tr>
<tr><td></td><td>2</td><td>CASEWT</td><td colspan="2">NOT COMPUTED</td><td>0.004379</td><td>0.054928</td></tr>
</table>

<table>
<tr><td>⑤</td><td>ITER.
NO.</td><td>INCR.
HALV.</td><td>RESIDUAL SUM
OF SQUARES</td><td>PARAMETERS
1 P(1)</td><td>2 P(2)</td><td>3 P(3)</td><td>4 P(4)</td></tr>
<tr><td></td><td>0</td><td>0</td><td>6.116142</td><td>10.000000</td><td>-0.100000</td><td>5.000000</td><td>-0.011000</td></tr>
<tr><td></td><td>0</td><td>0</td><td>5.680311</td><td>10.000000</td><td>-0.110000</td><td>5.000000</td><td>-0.010000</td></tr>
<tr><td></td><td>0</td><td>0</td><td>5.592536</td><td>10.000000</td><td>-0.100000</td><td>5.000000</td><td>-0.010000</td></tr>
<tr><td></td><td>0</td><td>0</td><td>5.561262</td><td>11.000000</td><td>-0.100000</td><td>5.000000</td><td>-0.010000</td></tr>
<tr><td></td><td>0</td><td>0</td><td>4.992193</td><td>10.000000</td><td>-0.100000</td><td>5.500000</td><td>-0.010000</td></tr>
<tr><td></td><td>1</td><td>1</td><td>0.913285</td><td>10.102698</td><td>-0.100470</td><td>5.023928</td><td>0.001340</td></tr>
<tr><td></td><td>2</td><td>0</td><td>0.259233</td><td>7.585941</td><td>-0.166839</td><td>8.652808</td><td>-0.004084</td></tr>
<tr><td></td><td>3</td><td>0</td><td>0.110177</td><td>8.947056</td><td>-0.169415</td><td>6.950855</td><td>-0.003428</td></tr>
<tr><td></td><td>4</td><td>0</td><td>0.028216</td><td>9.058777</td><td>-0.173112</td><td>7.156355</td><td>-0.002707</td></tr>
<tr><td></td><td>5</td><td>3</td><td>0.019025</td><td>9.163389</td><td>-0.174800</td><td>7.168309</td><td>-0.002908</td></tr>
<tr><td></td><td>6</td><td>C</td><td>0.015920</td><td>10.137881</td><td>-0.189985</td><td>7.216169</td><td>-0.002973</td></tr>
<tr><td></td><td>7</td><td>5</td><td>0.015658</td><td>10.186379</td><td>-0.191123</td><td>7.233585</td><td>-0.003014</td></tr>
<tr><td></td><td>8</td><td>1</td><td>0.015283</td><td>10.686998</td><td>-0.209210</td><td>7.339658</td><td>-0.003235</td></tr>
<tr><td></td><td>9</td><td>0</td><td>0.013070</td><td>10.844036</td><td>-0.219042</td><td>7.367585</td><td>-0.003166</td></tr>
<tr><td></td><td>10</td><td>0</td><td>0.013050</td><td>10.859483</td><td>-0.219715</td><td>7.363721</td><td>-0.003158</td></tr>
<tr><td></td><td>11</td><td>0</td><td>0.013002</td><td>11.324760</td><td>-0.226622</td><td>7.331683</td><td>-0.003118</td></tr>
<tr><td></td><td>12</td><td>0</td><td>0.012934</td><td>11.195494</td><td>-0.223120</td><td>7.347094</td><td>-0.003136</td></tr>
<tr><td></td><td>13</td><td>0</td><td>0.012853</td><td>11.289281</td><td>-0.227599</td><td>7.374182</td><td>-0.003174</td></tr>
<tr><td></td><td>14</td><td>2</td><td>0.012853</td><td>11.291146</td><td>-0.227602</td><td>7.374532</td><td>-0.003175</td></tr>
<tr><td></td><td>15</td><td>0</td><td>0.012849</td><td>11.297230</td><td>-0.228215</td><td>7.377354</td><td>-0.003171</td></tr>
<tr><td></td><td>16</td><td>0</td><td>0.012848</td><td>11.305405</td><td>-0.228237</td><td>7.376182</td><td>-0.003172</td></tr>
<tr><td></td><td>17</td><td>0</td><td>0.012847</td><td>11.334945</td><td>-0.228658</td><td>7.374821</td><td>-0.003170</td></tr>
<tr><td></td><td>18</td><td>0</td><td>0.012846</td><td>11.336476</td><td>-0.228826</td><td>7.376317</td><td>-0.003172</td></tr>
<tr><td></td><td>19</td><td>0</td><td>0.012846</td><td>11.348867</td><td>-0.229183</td><td>7.379221</td><td>-0.003176</td></tr>
<tr><td></td><td>20</td><td>0</td><td>0.012845</td><td>11.346282</td><td>-0.229193</td><td>7.378816</td><td>-0.003175</td></tr>
<tr><td></td><td>21</td><td>3</td><td>0.012845</td><td>11.346608</td><td>-0.229221</td><td>7.378938</td><td>-0.003175</td></tr>
<tr><td></td><td>22</td><td>0</td><td>0.012845</td><td>11.356826</td><td>-0.229422</td><td>7.378522</td><td>-0.003175</td></tr>
<tr><td></td><td>23</td><td>0</td><td>0.012845</td><td>11.352948</td><td>-0.229367</td><td>7.378706</td><td>-0.003175</td></tr>
<tr><td></td><td>24</td><td>0</td><td>0.012845</td><td>11.353100</td><td>-0.229383</td><td>7.378853</td><td>-0.003175</td></tr>
<tr><td></td><td>25</td><td>0</td><td>0.012845</td><td>11.354609</td><td>-0.229426</td><td>7.379203</td><td>-0.003176</td></tr>
</table>

⑥ THE RESIDUAL SUM OF SQUARES (= 1.284532E-02) WAS SMALLEST WITH THE FOLLOWING PARAMETER VALUES

1 P(1)	2 P(2)	3 P(3)	4 P(4)
11.3546	-0.229426	7.37920	-3.175618D-03

⑦ ESTIMATE OF ASYMPTOTIC CORRELATION MATRIX

		P(1) 1	P(2) 2	P(3) 3	P(4) 4
P(1)	1	1.0000			
P(2)	2	-0.8139	1.0000		
P(3)	3	0.1460	-0.5028	1.0000	
P(4)	4	-0.1140	0.4187	-0.8689	1.0000

⑧ THE ESTIMATED MEAN SQUARE ERROR IS   7.5561E-04

ESTIMATES OF ASYMPTOTIC STANDARD DEVIATIONS OF PARAMETER ESTIMATES WITH   17 DEGREES OF FREEDOM ARE

⑨
1 P(1)	2 P(2)	3 P(3)	4 P(4)
0.865788	1.873086D-02	0.106594	1.362988D-04

<table>
<tr><td>⑩</td><td>CASE
NO. NAME</td><td>RESIDUAL</td><td>OBSERVED
1 COUNT</td><td>PREDICTED
1 COUNT</td><td>STD. DEV.
PREDICTED</td><td>2 CASEWT</td><td>3 TIME</td></tr>
<tr><td></td><td>1</td><td>0.603008</td><td>15.111699</td><td>14.508691</td><td>0.362641</td><td>0.004379</td><td>2.000000</td></tr>
<tr><td></td><td>2</td><td>-0.461383</td><td>11.360100</td><td>11.821483</td><td>0.171988</td><td>0.007749</td><td>4.000000</td></tr>
<tr><td></td><td>3</td><td>-0.341157</td><td>9.765200</td><td>10.106357</td><td>0.144654</td><td>0.010487</td><td>6.000000</td></tr>
<tr><td colspan="8" align="center">--- similar statistics for cases 4 to 18 ---</td></tr>
<tr><td></td><td>19</td><td>0.057188</td><td>4.496799</td><td>4.439611</td><td>0.051932</td><td>0.049453</td><td>160.000000</td></tr>
<tr><td></td><td>20</td><td>0.059359</td><td>4.360200</td><td>4.300841</td><td>0.055064</td><td>0.052600</td><td>170.000000</td></tr>
<tr><td></td><td>21</td><td>0.100391</td><td>4.266800</td><td>4.166409</td><td>0.058141</td><td>0.054928</td><td>180.000000</td></tr>
</table>

③ Number of cases read. PAR uses only complete cases in all computations. That is, if the value for any variable in a case is missing or out of range, the case is omitted from the computations. If a USE statement is specified in the *VARiable* paragraph, only the values of variables in the USE statement are checked for missing values and values out of range.

④ The mean, standard deviation, minimum and maximum for each variable. When a case WEIGHT variable is specified, as in our example, weighted means and weighted standard deviations are computed.

⑤ At each iteration PAR prints

- the number of the iteration

- the number of increment halvings (explained on p. 497)

- the residual sum of squares

$$RSS = \Sigma\ w\ (y-f)^2$$

where y is the observed value of the dependent variable in case j, f is the evaluation of the function, and w is the value of the case weight (the case weight value is 1 if there is no weighting); the summation is over all cases used in the analysis.

⑥ The minimum residual sum of squares and estimates of the parameters. Small differences between the parameter values at the last iteration and at the iteration that produces the smallest residual sum of squares can be attributed to round-off error; large differences can indicate that a saddle-point or local minimum was found. If the minimum residual sum of squares does not occur within the last (P+1) iterations (where P is the number of parameters), the last iteration is used in the remaining computations even though it is <u>not</u> the minimum.

Note: *The remaining computations use the parameter estimates printed in* ⑥.

⑦ The asymptotic correlation matrix of the parameter estimates. The matrix computation is described in Appendix A.16.

⑧ The mean square error is equal to the residual sum of squares divided by (N-p) where N is the number of cases with nonzero weights, and p is the number of independent parameters in the function.

⑨ The asymptotic standard deviations of the parameter estimates. A zero indicates a problem with the estimate: the estimate may lie on a boundary of the permissible parameter space (equal to its specified) upper or lower limit), there may be extremely high correlations among the estimated parameters, or the estimate is so poor that if it is changed the value of the function is not affected. If an estimate lies on a boundary, PAR prints a message describing the boundary.

⑩ For each case, PAR prints

- the residual, y-f

- the observed value of the dependent variable, y

- the predicted value, f, which is the value of the function

- the standard error of the predicted value (see Appendix A.16)

- the values of the independent variables and the case WEIGHT variable

● SPECIFICATIONS FOR AN ANALYSIS AND OPTIONAL OUTPUT

To fit a nonlinear function to the data you must specify

- a function in FORTRAN   p. 488

- the number of parameters in the function   p. 490

- the dependent variable   p. 490

- initial values for the parameters   p. 493

For some problems you may need to

- specify upper and lower limits for the parameters   p. 494

In addition to the above, you may also

- assign case weights   p. 490

- request plots of the residuals and predicted values
  against each other and against specified variables   p. 492

- request a normal probability plot of the residuals   p. 492

- state names for the parameters   p. 494

- specify upper and lower limits for linear combinations
  of the parameters   p. 494

- specify that only part of the data be printed   p. 496

- save the data and predicted values in a BMDP File   p. 496

- specify any of three options, MEANSQUARE, LOSS and
  PASS, that are used primarily with maximum likelihood
  estimation; they are discussed in Section 14.3   p. 499

● SPECIFYING A REGRESSION FUNCTION IN FORTRAN

Any function can be fitted to the data if you specify it by FORTRAN statements. The FORTRAN subroutine that contains the function temporarily becomes part of program PAR. The FORTRAN subroutine is called once for each case during each iteration (or halving). The calling sequence of the subroutine is

```
SUBROUTINE FUN(F,P,X,N,KASE,NVAR,NPAR,IPASS,XLOSS)
IMPLICIT REAL*8 (A-H,O-Z)
DIMENSION P(NPAR),X(NVAR)
```

where the following values should not be changed

NPAR - the number of parameters in the function

NVAR - the total number of variables (<u>not</u> the number of independent variables), the sum of the variables read and those added by transformations, if any; if USE is specified in the *VARiable* paragraph, NVAR is the largest subscript of any variable in the USE statement

KASE - the sequence number of the case for which the function is being computed

IPASS - this is used only when the function evaluation requires two passes at the data (IPASS is primarily useful with maximum likelihood estimation and is explained in Section 14.3; otherwise it can be ignored)

P(1),P(2),...,P(NPAR) - the current values of the parameters

The following values are usually not changed

X(1),X(2),...,X(NVAR) - the observed values of all the variables in the order that they appear in the data matrix

N   - the NUMBER specified in the *REGRess* paragraph. It can be used to select functions in your FORTRAN subroutine.

XLOSS - a utility or loss function to replace that of least squares as a criterion for convergence (XLOSS is primarily useful for maximum likelihood estimation and is explained in Section 14.3; otherwise it can be ignored)

The following must be evaluated in the subroutine

F   - the value of the function for this case

The rules of FORTRAN apply in the subroutine (not the rules of Control Language). The second statement, IMPLICIT REAL*8, specifies that all real values are in double precision. If you are not using an IBM 360/370 computer, you must include all real variables in a DOUBLE PRECISION statement. All FORTRAN functions can be called; double precision versions of the functions should be used.

A second example. We now reanalyze the radioimmunoassay data in Table 14.2. The empirical function appropriate to the data is

$$f = \frac{1}{p_1 x + p_2} + p_3$$

The independent variable x is the first variable. In FORTRAN we code the function as shown in Example 14.5.

Example 14.5

```
A=P(1)*X(1)+P(2)                    ⎤  FORTRAN statements
IF(A.LE.0.0) A=0.000001            ⎥  to define function
F=1.0/A+P(3)                        ⎦
```

```
/PROBLEM      TITLE IS 'INSULIN DATA'.        ⎤
/INPUT        VARIABLES ARE 2.                ⎥
              FORMAT IS '(F6.0,F6.3)'.        ⎥
/VARIABLE     NAMES ARE STANDARD,COUNT.       ⎥  Control Language
                                              ⎥  instructions
/REGRESS      DEPENDENT IS COUNT.             ⎥
              PARAMETERS ARE 3.               ⎥
                                              ⎥
/PARAMETER    INITIAL ARE 0.01, 0.1, 5.       ⎥
                                              ⎥
/END                                          ⎦
```

The System Cards required for this analysis are the same as described for Example 14.4 and are discussed in greater detail in Section 14.4. The data for this example are in Table 14.2.

The results of the analysis are presented in Output 14.5.

● DESCRIBING THE NONLINEAR FUNCTION -- THE *REGRess* PARAGRAPH

The *REGRess* paragraph describes the dependent variable and the number of parameters. It is required and can be repeated after the data to describe additional analyses of the same data (see the order of input in the summary, p. 520).

```
REGRess
    DEPENDENT=v.    {none/prev.}                        required
        Name or subscript of the dependent (predicted) variable.

    PARAMETER=#.    {none/prev.}                        required
        The number of parameters in the regression function.

    TITLE='c'.      {blank}              ≤ 160 char.
        Title for this analysis.

    NUMBER= #.      {none/prev.}
        The value of NUMBER is passed to the FORTRAN subroutine that de-
        fines the function. It can be used to select among functions coded
        in that subroutine.
```

● CASE WEIGHTs

When the error variance is not homogeneous but varies from case to case, weighted least squares estimation is more appropriate; the weight (w) for each case is proportional to the inverse of the variance. In weighed least squares, the quantity minimized is

$$\Sigma \, w \, (y-f)^2$$

where the sum is over all cases read.

Output 14.5 Analysis of the insulin data by PAR

NUMBER OF CASES READ.   14

VARIABLE			STANDARD		
NO.	NAME	MEAN	DEVIATION	MINIMUM	MAXIMUM
1	STANDARD	55.714249	69.637985	0.0	200.000000
2	COUNT	5.661283	2.773079	1.566000	9.521999

ITER.	INCR.	RESIDUAL SUM	PARAMETERS		
NO.	HALV.	OF SQUARES	1 P(1)	2 P(2)	3 P(3)
0	0	217.461414	0.010000	0.100000	5.500000
0	0	168.067877	0.010000	0.100000	5.000000
0	0	158.658378	0.011000	0.100000	5.000000
0	0	140.590615	0.010000	0.110000	5.000000
1	0	9.919630	0.002656	0.123317	1.349150
2	3	9.483507	0.002401	0.121014	1.124498
3	0	3.449059	0.001704	0.107005	−0.222941
4	0	3.157619	0.003174	0.110235	−0.029835
5	0	2.250136	0.003094	0.109053	−0.027015
6	0	0.259108	0.002668	0.108362	0.078093
7	0	0.250936	0.002635	0.108500	0.085251
8	2	0.250609	0.002642	0.108577	0.091252
9	0	0.249209	0.002687	0.108991	0.136127
10	0	0.249145	0.002693	0.108974	0.137429
11	2	0.249145	0.002693	0.108974	0.137429
12	0	0.249145	0.002693	0.108976	0.137550
13	0	0.249144	0.002694	0.108984	0.138409
14	0	0.249144	0.002694	0.108981	0.138045
15	4	0.249144	0.002694	0.108981	0.138046

THE RESIDUAL SUM OF SQUARES (=   0.249144   ) WAS SMALLEST WITH THE FOLLOWING PARAMETER VALUES

1 P(1)	2 P(2)	3 P(3)
2.693592D-03	0.108981	0.138046

ESTIMATE OF ASYMPTOTIC CORRELATION MATRIX

		P(1)	P(2)	P(3)
		1	2	3
P(1)	1	1.0000		
P(2)	2	0.7459	1.0000	
P(3)	3	0.9365	0.8828	1.0000

THE ESTIMATED MEAN SQUARE ERROR IS   2.2649E-02

ESTIMATES OF ASYMPTOTIC STANDARD DEVIATIONS OF PARAMETER ESTIMATES WITH   11 DEGREES OF FREEDOM ARE

1 P(1)	2 P(2)	3 P(3)
2.202094D-04	2.070125D-03	0.186364

CASE			OBSERVED	PREDICTED	STD. DEV.	
NO.	NAME	RESIDUAL	2 COUNT	2 COUNT	PREDICTED	1 STANDARD
1		−0.039980	9.273999	9.313979	0.087987	0.0
2		0.208020	9.521999	9.313979	0.087987	0.0
3		−0.222732	8.082000	8.304731	0.056890	5.000000
4		0.049268	8.353999	8.304731	0.056890	5.000000
5		−0.199496	7.296000	7.495496	0.054249	10.000000
6		0.022504	7.518000	7.495496	0.054249	10.000000
7		0.054465	5.863999	5.809535	0.066492	25.000000
8		0.164465	5.974000	5.809535	0.066492	25.000000
9		0.153880	4.396000	4.242119	0.061860	50.000000
10		−0.132120	4.110000	4.242119	0.061860	50.000000
11		0.048829	2.830000	2.781171	0.059216	100.000000
12		−0.107172	2.674000	2.781171	0.059216	100.000000
13		0.116027	1.797999	1.681972	0.091098	200.000000
14		−0.115972	1.566000	1.681972	0.091098	200.000000

The variance may be expressed in terms of the function f; the case weight will vary from iteration to iteration as the estimates of the parameters change.   The variable X(i), where i is the subscript of the case WEIGHT variable, can be modified in the FORTRAN subroutine describing the function.   This is known as iteratively reweighted least squares and is used in maximum likelihood estimation (Section 14.3).

In PAR, the case WEIGHTs *are specified in the* REGRess *paragraph.*

REGRess
    WEIGHT= v.   {no weight var./prev.}

    Name or subscript of the variable containing case weights. If WEIGHT is not stated or is set to zero, there are no case weights.

- *PLOTs* OF THE RESIDUALS AND PREDICTED VALUES

    In the *PLOT* paragraph you can specify the following plots:

- predicted and observed values of the dependent variable and residuals against specified variables

- residuals and residuals squared against the predicted values

- a normal probability plot of the residuals

- a detrended normal probability plot of the residuals

The residuals and predicted values plotted are those printed in the results.

These plots are illustrated in Output 13.3 (p. 388).   They are specified as follows:

PLOT
    RESIDUAL.   {no/prev.}

    The residuals (y-f) and residuals squared (y-f)^2 are plotted against the predicted values f in separate plots.

    VARIABLE= $v_1, v_2, \ldots$.   {none/prev.}

    Names or subscripts of variables against which the observed values of the dependent variable y and the predicted values f are plotted in one graph. In a second graph the residuals (y-f) are plotted against these variables.

    NORMAL.   {no/prev.}

    Normal probability plot of the residuals is printed.

                                    (continued)

```
PLOT
    DNORMAL.                    {no/prev.}

      Detrended normal probability plot of the residuals is printed.

    SIZE=#₁,#₂.                 {50,50/prev.}
```

$\#_1$ is the number of characters (width) in the horizontal axis and $\#_2$ is the number of lines (height) in the vertical axis.

● DESCRIBING THE *PARAMeters*

The *PARAMeter* paragraph is required to specify initial values for the parameters. An upper and lower limit and a name can be specified for each parameter. Upper and lower limits can also be specified for linear combinations of the parameters.

Initial values for the parameters must be specified. Here are some suggestions to help you provide reasonable initial values:

- use the solution from a similar analysis or from an analysis by a different method

- if you cannot choose an exact value, choose a reasonable range for the parameter and pick a value close to the limit nearer zero (but preferably not zero and not a specified boundary); this is the limit that is usually more precisely estimated.

- if you still cannot decide, use arbitrary nonzero numbers such as ±1, ±2, ±3,... depending on whether you think the parameters are positive or negative

```
PARAMeter
    INITIAL= #₁,#₂,···.          {none/prev.}   required, one per parameter
```

Initial values for the parameter estimates. The values must be within (but not equal to) specified lower and upper limits for the parameters. Good initial estimates are important to avoid saddle-points or local minimums of the residual sum of squares.

Note: If the final sum of squares seems too large, if there appear to be unusual features in the estimates of the parameters or residuals, or if system error messages, such as underflow, overflow or divide check, are printed, you should check

- *the FORTRAN statements that specify the function*

- *whether the function evaluated using the initial values of the parameters and at the largest or smallest data values is extremely large or small.*

If no error is found, you should try different initial values.

You can specify upper and lower limits for the parameters. Limits can be used to restrict a parameter to a given range in order to avoid a local minimum, a value of the parameter for which the function is undefined, or an interval where a change in the parameter does not affect the function (i.e., its estimated derivative is zero).

You can specify names for the parameters to be used in the printed results.

PARAMeter
  MAXIMUM= $\#_1, \#_2, \cdots$.   {none/prev.}   one per parameter
    Upper limits for the parameters.

  MINIMUM= $\#_1, \#_2, \cdots$.   {none/prev.}   one per parameter
    Lower limits for the parameters.

  NAME= $c_1, c_2, \cdots$.   {P(1),P(2),.../prev.}   one per parameter
    Names for the parameters. The preassigned names cannot be used in Control Language instructions.

In PAR you can specify that some parameters are fixed at their initial values. Then the initial value is used as the value of the parameter throughout the analysis.

PARAMeter
  FIXED=parameter names or subscripts.   {none}
    Parameters to be held fixed at their initial values.

PAR computes the function using the initial values of the parameters and then computes additional initial values of the parameters to obtain several values of the function (Appendix A.16). DELTA is used to compute the additional initial values of the parameters.

PARAMeter
  DELTA= $\#_1, \#_2, \cdots$. $\left\{ \begin{array}{l} .1*INIT(I) \text{ when } INIT(I) \neq 0 \\ .01 \text{ otherwise} \end{array} \right/ prev. \right\}$
    Step size used to compute additional starting values of the function. You will rarely need to specify DELTA.

● CONSTRAINTS ON THE PARAMETERS

Upper and lower limits for each parameter can be specified as described above.

Upper and lower limits can also be specified for linear combinations of the parameters. Let $p_1, p_2, \ldots$ represent the values of the parameters. Then the constraints have the form

$$c_1 \leq b_1 p_1 + b_2 p_2 + \ldots \leq c_2$$

where $b_1, b_2, \ldots$ are known coefficients and c_1 and c_2 are constants. For example, $p_2 \leq p_4$ can be written as

$$p_2 - p_4 \leq 0$$

When constraints are used, the number of constraints must be specified in the *REGRess* paragraph. The constraints are specified in the *PARAMeter* paragraph.

REGRess
    CONSTRAINT=#.   {none/prev.}

        Number of linear constraints on the parameters that are specified in the *PARAMeter* paragraph.

PARAMeter
    CONSTRAINT=$\#_1, \#_2, \cdots$.   {0.0,0.0,.../prev.}   may be repeated

        Coefficients of the parameters in one constraint. The first number is the coefficient of the first parameter, etc. This statement can be repeated in the same *PARAMeter* paragraph to specify additional constraints. If any CONSTRAINT is specified, all CONSTRAINTS specified in previous *PARAMeter* paragraphs are cancelled.

    LIMIT=$\#_1, \#_2$.   {$-\infty, \infty$/prev.}   may be repeated

        $\#_1$ is the lower limit and $\#_2$ is the upper limit for the linear combination of parameters specified in the <u>preceding</u> CONSTRAINT statement. If only one number is specified, it is used as a lower limit. An upper limit without a lower limit is specified as LIMIT= (2)#.

        <u>Note:</u> *The* LIMITs *are applied to the* CONSTRAINT *statement preceding it. You should write your* CONSTRAINT *and* LIMIT *statements in pairs.*

        The INITIAL *values of the parameters must satisfy the specified upper and lower limits for the parameters* <u>and</u> *for specified linear combinations of the parameters.*

- PRINTING OBSERVED VALUES, PREDICTED VALUES AND RESIDUALS

For each case, PAR prints the predicted value (value of the function), its standard error, the value of the dependent variable, the residuals and the observed values of the specified variables (see ⑩ in Output 14.4). You can specify whether or not to print this list and, if so, which variables to include in the list. All computed values use the chosen estimates of the parameters (see note p. 487).

If you specify

PRINT=0.

in the *REGRess* paragraph, no results are printed for each case. You can specify

PRINT=$v_1,v_2,\cdots$.

where $v_1,v_2,\ldots$ are names or subscripts of variables whose observed values are to be printed for each case; the predicted value, its standard error, the value of the dependent variable and the residual are also printed. The values of variables not specified among $v_1,v_2,\ldots$ are not printed.

REGRess
    PRINT=$v_1,v_2,\cdots$.   {all variables/prev.}

The names or subscripts of variables whose observed values are printed for each case. In addition to the observed values, the predicted value, its standard error, the value of the dependent variable and the residual are also printed. If PRINT=0 is specified, residuals, predicted values and data are not printed.

- SAVING THE DATA AND PREDICTED VALUES

When DATA are saved, the predicted values and their standard errors (but not the residuals) are also stored in the BMDP File. PAR allows you to save predicted values from more than one analysis of the same data. To do so you must specify in the *SAVE* paragraph the NUMBER of the analyses for which the predicted values are to be saved; otherwise only the predicted value from the first analysis is saved. The predicted values from the first analysis are saved as variable VT+1 with the name PREDICT1; standard errors of the predicted values as variable VT+2 with the name STDPRED1, the predicted values from the second analysis as variable VT+3 with the name PREDICT2 , etc.

The predicted values and the standard errors are computed using the chosen estimates of the parameters (see note, p. 487). If you alter the value of any variable (such as the case WEIGHT variable) in the FORTRAN subroutine, the values of these variables are also computed and saved using the chosen estimates of the parameters.

```
SAVE
    NUMBER=#.                        {1}

        Number of analyses (subproblems) from which the predicted values
        and their standard errors are to be saved in a BMDP File (along
        with the data).  If not specified or if set to one, only the
        results from the first analysis are saved.
```

● VALUES USED IN THE PSEUDO-GAUSS-NEWTON ITERATION

The function is fitted by an iterative algorithm. The algorithm
decides that a solution has been reached when

$$\left| (RSS^{(k+1)} - RSS^{(k)})/RSS^{(k+1)} \right| < C$$

for five successive values of k, where $RSS^{(k)}$ is the residual sum of squares
at step k, and C is the value of the CONVERGENCE criterion.

```
REGRess
    CONVERGENCE=#.                   {0.00001/prev.}

        Value of the convergence criterion C, as described above.
```

The algorithm can also be stopped if it exceeds a specified number of
iterations.

```
REGRess
    ITERATION=#.                     {50/prev.}

        Maximum number of iterations.  If convergence has not occurred
        by this number of iterations, the algorithm is terminated.
```

If the residual sum of squares increases between two iterations, the
increment size is halved and the residual sum of squares is recomputed and
tested against the residual sum of squares at the previous iteration. This
halving is repeated until the residual sum of squares is less than that of
the previous halving or the maximum number of halvings is reached.

At each iteration the number of increment halvings performed is printed.

```
REGRess
    HALVING= #.                      {5/prev.}              ≥ 0
        The maximum number of  increment halvings as described above.
```

TOLERANCE is used to guard against round-off errors in critical portions of the computations.

REGRess
    TOLERANCE=#.   {10^{-8}/prev.}

        A check for round-off errors. See Appendix A.16.

- SIZE OF PROBLEM

    The amount of data that PAR can analyze is a function of the number of cases used in the analysis (C), the largest subscript of the variables in the USE list (V), and the number of parameters estimated (total parameters - number of fixed parameters)(P). The following table indicates approximately how many cases can be used for various values of P and V.

V+P	5	10	15	20
C	930	560	400	300

Appendix B describes how to increase the capacity of the program.

- COMPUTATIONAL METHOD

    The computations are performed in double precision. The pseudo-Gauss-Newton algorithm is described in Appendix A.16.

ACKNOWLEDGEMENT

PAR was designed and programmed by Mary Ralston.

14.3 Maximum Likelihood Estimation

Parameters of a model can be estimated by the method of maximum likelihood with both P3R and PAR. We describe two methods of modifying the least squares algorithm so it can be used for maximum likelihood.

The first method is appropriate for data that are sampled from a distribution belonging to the exponential family -- such as normal, binomial, multinomial, Poisson and gamma distributions. The method provides a meaningful residual analysis and standard errors for the parameter estimates.

The second method provides estimates of the parameters only. It is appropriate for data sampled from any distribution. However, it has no residual analysis.

In our discussion we assume you are familiar with either P3R (Section 14.1) or PAR (Section 14.2).

● DATA FROM A DISTRIBUTION BELONGING TO THE EXPONENTIAL FAMILY

Jennrich and Moore (1975) show how maximum likelihood estimates of parameters from a distribution in the exponential family can be obtained from the minimization of

$$(Y-F) \; \Sigma^{-1} \; (Y-F)'$$

where

Y is a row vector containing the observed values of the dependent variable

F is a row vector containing the values of the function evaluated at the true parameter values (the expected values of the dependent variable),

and

Σ^{-1} is the inverse of the covariance matrix of Y

Usually Σ^{-1} is a diagonal matrix; each diagonal element can be replaced by a case weight equal to the inverse of the variance of the dependent variable for that case.

Let $y_1, y_2, \ldots, y_N$ be N mutually independent observed values of the dependent variable. Let the predicted value of y_j be $f(X_j, \theta)$ where X_j represents the data values of the independent variables for case j and θ represents the parameters $p_1, p_2, \ldots$ in the model. Let the weight w_j for the data in case j be

$$w_j = 1/[\text{variance}(y_j)]$$

The weight may be a function of the values of the variables and estimates of the parameters. Then in subroutine FUN we define

$$F \equiv f(\underset{\sim}{X}_j, \underset{\sim}{\theta})$$

$$X(\text{subscript of case weight variable}) \equiv w_j = w_j \, (\underset{\sim}{X}_j, \underset{\sim}{\theta})$$

and in P3R we require the partial derivatives

$$DF(I) \equiv \partial f(\underset{\sim}{X}_j, \underset{\sim}{\theta}) / \partial p_i.$$

Jennrich and Moore show that if the standard deviations are rescaled by setting the residual mean square equal to one, the standard deviations of the estimates are the usual information theory standard errors.

REGRess
    MEANSQUARE=#.   {none/prev.}

    If specified, the value of MEANSQUARE is used in place of the residual mean square to compute estimates of the asymptotic standard deviations. [12]

The data must be sampled from a distribution in the exponential family (see Lehman, 1959, p.50 for a definition). This family includes the normal, binomial, multinomial, gamma and Poisson as well as other distributions.

Jennrich and Moore assume that the parameter estimates correspond to a solution where the derivatives are zero. However, P3R and PAR use criteria for convergence based on sums of squares and <u>not</u> on the values of the derivatives. It is possible to disconnect the convergence criterion by specifying

        HALVING=0.

in the *REGRess* paragraph of PAR, or

        CONVERGENCE= -1.0.
        HALVING= 0.

in the *REGRess* paragraph of P3R, and to terminate the algorithm in P3R by specifying the maximum number of iterations. (Ten iterations are usually sufficient.)

---

[12] If your BMDP programs are dated before August <u>1976</u>, MEANSQ is not available.

A logistic model

In Appendix C.13 Jennrich illustrates how the parameters of a logistic regression can be estimated with P3R. We briefly review his example using the notation described above. The data are from Cox (1970, p. 86); at a specified time (t), a number of objects (n) are tested and the failures (s) recorded.

t	s	n
7	0	55
14	2	157
27	7	159
51	3	16

Cox fitted the data (s_i) by the logistic model

$$f_i = n_i e^{p_1+p_2 t_i}/(1 + e^{p_1+p_2 t_i})$$

If the s_i are assumed to be from independent binomial distributions, then

$$\text{var}(s_i) = f_i(n_i - f_i)/n_i$$

Therefore

$$w_i = 1/\text{var}(s_i) = n_i/[f_i(n_i - f_i)]$$

The derivatives are

$$\frac{\partial f_i}{\partial p_1} = f_i/(1+e^{p_1+p_2 t_i})$$

and

$$\frac{\partial f_i}{\partial p_2} = t_i f_i/(1+e^{p_1+p_2 t_i})$$

Therefore we specify the following FORTRAN subroutine and Control Language instructions:

Example 14.6

```
XNUMER=EXP(P(1)+P(2)*X(1))
DENOM=1.0+XNUMER
F=X(3)*XNUMER/DENOM
DF(1)=F/DENOM
DF(2)=X(1)*F/DENOM
X(4)=DENOM/F
```
FORTRAN statements to define function, derivatives, and case weight

```
/PROBLEM      TITLE IS 'COX DATA'.
/INPUT        VARIABLES ARE 4.
              FORMAT IS '(4F5.0)'.
/VARIABLES    NAMES ARE TIME,UNREADY,TESTED,CASEWT.

/REGRESS      DEPENDENT IS UNREADY.
              PARAMETERS ARE 2.
              WEIGHT IS CASEWT.
              ITERATIONS ARE 10.
              HALVING IS 0.
              CONVERGENCE IS -1.0.
              MEANSQUARE IS 1.0.

/PARAMETER    INITIAL ARE 0.0, 0.0.

/END
       7   0  55   1
      14   2 157   1
      27   7 159   1
      51   3  16   1
```
Control Language instructions

data

The System Cards required for this analysis are the same as described for Example 14.2 and are discussed in greater detail in Section 14.4.

In Example 14.6 we add to the data a fourth variable that contains case weights, which are iteratively computed. P3R checks that the sum of the case weights is positive. Therefore the case weights must not be initialized to zero.

In the *REGRess* paragraph we turn off the convergence criterion (CONVERGENCE is -1.0 and HALVING is 0), terminate the algorithm after 10 iterations and rescale the mean square error to 1.0.

The results of the analysis are given in Output 14.6. The parameter estimates used in the computation of residuals and standard errors are from the last iteration when CONVERGENCE is set to a value less than zero; the maximum likelihood estimates for the parameters are obtained from the last iteration (①) in Output 14.6).

A similar analysis can be done with PAR by omitting the two statements beginning DF(1) and DF(2) in the FORTRAN subroutine. The FORTRAN statements and Control Language instructions for PAR are

Output 14.6 Maximum likelihood. Analysis of the Cox data by P3R using
            iteratively reweighted least squares.

BMDP3R — NONLINEAR REGRESSION
HEALTH SCIENCES COMPUTING FACILITY   PROGRAM REVISED SEPTEMBER 1977
UNIVERSITY OF CALIFORNIA, LOS ANGELES   MANUAL DATE -- 1977

NUMBER OF CASES READ.   4

VARIABLE   STANDARD
NO. NAME   MEAN   DEVIATION   MINIMUM   MAXIMUM

  1   TIME   24.750000   19.362762   7.000000   51.000000
  2   UNREADY   3.000000   2.943920   0.0   7.000000
  3   TESTED   96.750000   72.499969   16.000000   159.000000

PARAMETER MAXIMA. . . . . *************** ***************
PARAMETER MINIMA. . . . . *************** ***************

ITERATION   INCREMENT   RESIDUAL SUM
 NUMBER   HALVINGS   OF SQUARES   P(1)   P(2)

    0   0   342.584473   0.0   0.0
    1   0   37.906693   -2.150285   0.013801
    2   0   8.470325   -3.504025   0.036062
    3   0   1.528115   -4.674588   0.063338
    4   0   0.657320   -5.288436   0.077877
    5   0   0.673092   -5.410882   0.080603
    6   0   0.674875   -5.415172   0.080696
    7   0   0.674875   -5.415175   0.080696
    8   0   0.674875   -5.415176   0.080696
    9   0   0.674875   -5.415176   0.080696
 ① 10   0   0.674875   -5.415176   0.080696

ASYMPTOTIC CORRELATION MATRIX OF THE PARAMETERS

                P(1)   P(2)
                  1   2

P(1)   1   1.0000
P(2)   2   -0.9101   1.0000

COMPUTED VALUE OF RESIDUAL MEAN SQUARE IS   0.337

THE SPECIFIED VALUE OF THE RESIDUAL MEAN SQUARE(1.000), NOT THE COMPUTED VALUE, IS USED IN COMPUTING STANDARD
DEVIATIONS FOR PARAMETERS AND PREDICTED VALUES.

ASYMPTOTIC STANDARD DEVIATIONS OF THE PARAMETERS ASSUMING   2 DEGREES OF FREEDOM
            P(1)   P(2)

         0.72754E 00 0.22356E-01

CASE   PREDICTED   STD DEV OF   OBSERVED
NO. LABEL   UNREADY   PRED VALUE   UNREADY   RESIDUAL   CASEWT   TIME   TESTED

  1   0.427087   0.24947   0.0   -0.427087   2.359765   7.000000   55.000000
  2   2.132166   0.97017   2.000000   -0.132166   0.475464   14.000000   157.000000
  3   6.013247   1.77660   7.000000   0.986753   0.172836   27.000000   155.000000
  4   3.427490   1.52199   3.000000   -0.427490   0.371297   51.000000   16.000000

SERIAL CORRELATION OF RESIDUALS=SUM(R(I)*R(I-1))/SQRT(SUM(R(I)**2)*SUM(R(I-1)**2))   ALL SUMS ARE FOR I=2,NUMBER
                                                                                                  OF CASES
SERIAL CORRELATION   RESIDUALS ORDERED ON
    -0.36924   CASE NUMBER

```
XNUMER=DEXP(P(1)+P(2)*X(1))
DENOM=1.0+XNUMER
F=X(3)*XNUMER/DENOM
X(4)=DENOM/F
```
FORTRAN statements to define function and case weight

```
/PROBLEM      TITLE IS 'COX DATA'.
/INPUT        VARIABLES ARE 4.
              FORMAT IS '(4F5.0)'.
/VARIABLE     NAMES ARE TIME,UNREADY,TESTED,CASEWT.

/REGRESS      DEPENDENT IS UNREADY.
              PARAMETERS ARE 2.
              WEIGHT IS CASEWT.
              HALVING IS 0.
              MEANSQUARE IS 1.0.

/PARAMETER    INITIAL ARE 0.0, 0.0.

/END
```
Control Language instructions

The System Cards required for this analysis are the same as described for Example 14.4 and are discussed in greater detail in Section 14.4.

A model of quasi-independence

P3F -- Multiway Frequency Tables (Section 11.3) -- can be used to fit a multinomial model to data in a multiway table. However, when a cell in the table has zero frequency a priori (i.e., it is known that no observation can be recorded in the cell), the method used with P3F cannot be generalized to provide standard deviations for the estimates of the parameters in the log-linear model.

We now show how P3R can be used to fit a multinomial model to data in a multiway frequency table when a cell in the table has zero frequency a priori. The data in Table 14.3 are from a sensitivity test of fibers (Frank and Pfaffman, 1969). One outcome, that corresponds to no sensitivity to any of the four stimuli, can occur when the fiber is dead. The data for this outcome are not included in the computations. The cell corresponding to this outcome is analyzed as if the outcome were a structural zero.

Table 14.3 Data on sensitivity of Chorda tympani fibers in rat's tongue to four taste stimulus sources (Frank and Pfaffman, 1969, as reported in Fienberg, 1972, and Bishop et at., 1975, p. 221).

S	Q	H: N:	Yes Yes	Yes No	No Yes	No No
Yes	Yes		2	0	1	0
Yes	No		1	3	3	2
No	Yes		3	3	0	1
No	No		3	1	4	-

Key: Shows sensitivity to   H: hydrogen chloride
                               N: sodium chloride
                               Q: quinine
                               S: sucrose

No sensitivity to any stimulus can result from a dead fiber. Therefore the cell corresponding to No for all 4 tests has no observations.

The model to be fitted to the data is the log-linear model corresponding to independence between the stimuli, i.e.,

$$f = k \exp(p_1 x_1 + p_2 x_2 + p_3 x_3 + p_4 x_4)$$

where k is a normalizing constant and the x_i's are design variables. We know that the sum of the f's over all the cells must correspond to the total frequency (N=27). This constraint can be imposed on the function by rewriting it as

$$f = \frac{N \exp(p_1 x_1 + p_2 x_2 + p_3 x_3 + p_4 x_4)}{\Sigma \exp(p_1 x_1 + p_2 x_2 + p_3 x_3 + p_4 x_4)}$$

and the derivatives of f with respect to the parameters as

$$\frac{\partial f}{\partial p_i} = f \left[x_i - \frac{\Sigma x_i \exp(p_1 x_1 + p_2 x_2 + p_3 x_3 + p_4 x_4)}{\Sigma \exp(p_1 x_1 + p_2 x_2 + p_3 x_3 + p_4 x_4)} \right]$$

where the summations are over all cells except the one containing the structural zero.

For a multinomial distribution the case weight is the inverse of the expected value of the dependent variable; i.e.

$$w = 1/f.$$

Since the covariance matrix of the dependent variable is singular, the case weights are obtained from the generalized inverse.

We therefore specify the FORTRAN statements and Control Language as

Example 14.7

```
      DIMENSION PART(4)
      IF(IPASS.EQ.2) GO TO 10
C
      IF(KASE.GT.1) GO TO 2
      DO 1 I=1,4
    1 PART(I)=0.0
      SUM=0.C
C
    2 TEMP=EXP(X(1)*P(1)+X(2)*P(2)+X(3)*P(3)+X(4)*P(4))
      SUM=SUM+TEMP
      DO 3 I=1,4
    3 PART(I)=PART(I)+X(I)*TEMP
      RETURN
C
   10 F=27.0*EXP(X(1)*P(1)+X(2)*P(2)+X(3)*P(3)+X(4)*P(4))/SUM
      X(6)=1.0/F
      DO 12 I=1,4
   12 DF(I)=F*(X(I)-PART(I)/SUM)
```

FORTRAN statements to define function, derivatives, and case weight

(continued)

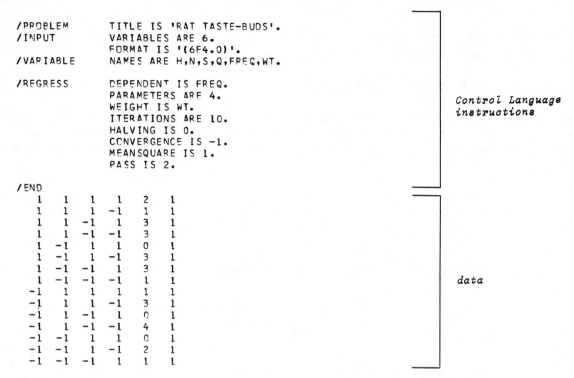

```
/PROBLEM       TITLE IS 'RAT TASTE-BUDS'.
/INPUT         VARIABLES ARE 6.
               FORMAT IS '(6F4.0)'.
/VARIABLE      NAMES ARE H,N,S,Q,FREQ,WT.

/REGRESS       DEPENDENT IS FREQ.
               PARAMETERS ARE 4.
               WEIGHT IS WT.
               ITERATIONS ARE 10.
               HALVING IS 0.
               CONVERGENCE IS -1.
               MEANSQUARE IS 1.
               PASS IS 2.

/END
     1    1    1    1    2    1
     1    1    1   -1    1    1
     1    1   -1    1    3    1
     1    1   -1   -1    3    1
     1   -1    1    1    0    1
     1   -1    1   -1    3    1
     1   -1   -1    1    3    1
     1   -1   -1   -1    1    1
    -1    1    1    1    1    1
    -1    1    1   -1    3    1
    -1    1   -1    1    0    1
    -1    1   -1   -1    4    1
    -1   -1    1    1    0    1
    -1   -1    1   -1    2    1
    -1   -1   -1    1    1    1
```

Control Language instructions

data

The System Cards required for this analysis are the same as described for Example 14.2 and are discussed in greater detail in Section 14.4.

The first four variables of the data are design variables for H, N, S and Q respectively, the fifth is the observed frequency and the sixth is the iteratively computed case weight variable.

When the statement[13]

       PASS=2.

is specified in the *REGRess* paragraph, the subroutine FUN is called twice for each case on each iteration. First P3R calls subroutine FUN once for each case, with IPASS set to 1.   On this pass

$$\sum_{(all\ cases)} \exp(p_1 x_1 + p_2 x_2 + p_3 x_3 + p_4 x_4)$$

and

$$\sum_{(all\ cases)} x_i \exp(p_1 x_1 + p_2 x_2 + p_3 x_3 + p_4 x_4) \qquad i=1,2,3,4$$

are computed. Then P3R calls subroutine FUN once for each case to compute the function value F and the derivatives DF(I) in the second pass.

When PASS is not specified in the *REGRess* paragraph, subroutine FUN is called only once for each case and the function value F and derivatives DF(I) must be computed in this one pass.

---

[13] If your BMDP programs are dated before August 1977,
    PASS is not available.

The following definition of PASS is appropriate for both P3R and PAR.

REGRess
    PASS=#.   {1/prev.}

    The number of times the data are passed to subroutine FUN. When #
    is greater than one

        - on each cycle through the cases, IPASS is set to the number of
          the cycle

        - the function (and derivatives) <u>must</u> be computed on the last cycle
          (IPASS set to #) through the cases

The results of the analysis of Example 14.7 are presented in Output 14.7.
When CONVERGE is assigned a negative value, as in our example, the estimates
of the parameters from the last iteration are used in the computation of
asymptotic standard deviations, correlations and predicted values.

A similar analysis can be obtained with PAR by increasing the number of
ITERATIONS to 25 and using the following FORTRAN statements and Control
Language instructions.

```
      IF(IPASS.EQ.2) GO TO 10
C
      IF(KASE.EQ.1) SUM=0.0
C
      TEMP=DEXP(X(1)*P(1)+X(2)*P(2)+X(3)*P(3)+X(4)*P(4))
      SUM=SUM+TEMP
      RETURN
C
   10 F=27.0*DEXP(X(1)*P(1)+X(2)*P(2)+X(3)*P(3)+X(4)*P(4))/SUM
      X(6)=1.0/F
```

FORTRAN statements to define function and case weight

```
/PROBLEM      TITLE IS 'RAT TASTE-BUDS'.
/INPUT        VARIABLES ARE 6.
              FORMAT IS '(6F4.0)'.
/VARIABLE     NAMES ARE H,N,S,Q,FREQ,WT.

/REGRESS      DEPENDENT IS 5.
              PARAMETERS ARE 4.
              WEIGHT IS 6.
              HALVING IS 0.
              MEANSQUARE IS 1.
              PASS IS 2.

/PARAMETER    INITIAL=4*0.0.

/END
```

Control Language instructions

The System Cards required for this analysis are the same as described for Example 14.4
and are discussed in greater detail in Section 14.4.

● DATA FROM ANY DISTRIBUTION

This method is appropriate for maximum likelihood estimation based on a
random sample from any distribution. The normal equations solved to maximize
the likelihood are

Output 14.7 Fitting a quasi-independent model by P3R

NUMBER OF CASES READ.   15

VARIABLE NO.	NAME	MEAN	STANDARD DEVIATION	MINIMUM	MAXIMUM
1	H	0.066667	1.032795	-1.000000	1.000000
2	N	0.066667	1.032795	-1.000000	1.000000
3	S	0.066667	1.032795	-1.000000	1.000000
4	Q	0.066667	1.032795	-1.000000	1.000000
5	FREQ	1.799996	1.320171	0.0	4.000000

PARAMETER MAXIMA. . . . . *************** *************** *************** ***************
PARAMETER MINIMA. . . . . *************** *************** *************** ***************

ITERATION NUMBER	INCREMENT HALVINGS	RESIDUAL SUM OF SQUARES	P(1)	P(2)	P(3)	P(4)
0	0	13.555552	0.0	0.0	0.0	0.0
1	0	10.054177	0.094697	0.164142	-0.183081	-0.321970
2	0	10.075403	0.099935	0.169944	-0.177120	-0.323579
3	0	10.075458	0.099935	0.169946	-0.177127	-0.323588
4	0	10.075456	0.099935	0.169946	-0.177127	-0.323588
5	0	10.075457	0.099935	0.169946	-0.177127	-0.323588
6	0	10.075461	.099935	0.169946	-0.177127	-0.323588
7	0	10.075458	0.099935	0.169946	-0.177127	-0.323588
8	0	10.075454	0.099935	0.169946	-0.177127	-0.323588
9	0	10.075459	0.099935	0.169946	-0.177127	-0.323588
10	0	10.075455	0.099935	0.169946	-0.177127	-0.323588

ASYMPTOTIC CORRELATION MATRIX OF THE PARAMETERS

		P(1) 1	P(2) 2	P(3) 3	P(4) 4
P(1)	1	1.0000			
P(2)	2	0.1270	1.0000		
P(3)	3	0.0930	0.0988	1.0000	
P(4)	4	0.0811	0.0862	0.0631	1.0000

COMPUTED VALUE OF RESIDUAL MEAN SQUARE IS   0.916

THE SPECIFIED VALUE OF THE RESIDUAL MEAN SQUARE(1.000), NOT THE COMPUTED VALUE, IS USED IN COMPUTING STANDARD DEVIATIONS FOR PARAMETERS AND PREDICTED VALUES.

ASYMPTOTIC STANDARD DEVIATIONS OF THE PARAMETERS ASSUMING   11 DEGREES OF FREEDOM
            P(1)   P(2)   P(3)   P(4)

        0.19854E 00 0.20220E 00 0.19549E 00 0.20076E 00

CASE NO.	PREDICTED FREQ	STD DEV OF PRED VALUE	OBSERVED FREQ	RESIDUAL	WT	H	N	S
1	1.324368	0.59065	2.000000	0.675632	0.755077	1.000000	1.000000	1.000000
2	2.529729	0.89515	1.000000	-1.529729	0.395299	1.000000	1.000000	1.000000
3	1.887380	0.72144	3.000000	1.112620	0.529835	1.000000	1.000000	-1.000000

--- similar statistics for cases 4 to 12 ---

CASE NO.	PREDICTED FREQ	STD DEV OF PRED VALUE	OBSERVED FREQ	RESIDUAL	WT	H	N	S
13	0.771957	0.35566	0.0	-0.771957	1.295408	-1.000000	-1.000000	1.000000
14	1.474545	0.64680	2.000000	0.525455	0.678175	-1.000000	-1.000000	1.000000
15	1.100128	0.51554	1.000000	-0.100128	0.908985	-1.000000	-1.000000	-1.000000

SERIAL CORRELATION OF RESIDUALS=SUM(R(I)*R(I-1))/SQRT(SUM(R(I)**2)*SUM(R(I-1)**2))   ALL SUMS ARE FOR I=2,NUMBER OF CASES

SERIAL CORRELATION	RESIDUALS ORDERED ON
-0.50722	CASE NUMBER

$$\sum \frac{\partial ln\ g(X_j,\theta)}{\partial p_i} = 0 \qquad i=1,2,\ldots$$

where $g(X_j,\theta)$ is the probability density of the data in case j. Let

$$f = ln\ g(X_j,\theta).$$

The normal equations can be written

$$\sum \frac{\partial f}{\partial p_i} = 0 \qquad i=1,2,\ldots$$

or

$$\sum \frac{\partial f}{\partial p_i}\,(y-f) = 0 \qquad i=1,2,\ldots$$

when $y-f$ is identically one and the summation is over all cases. If we define a new variable (and call it the dependent variable),

$$X(\text{subscript of dependent variable}) = y = f+1,$$

then $y-f$ is identically one.

Therefore the nonlinear regression programs solve the maximum likelihood normal equations if in the FUN subroutine we set

$$F = f = ln\ g(X,\theta)$$

$$X(\text{subscript of dependent variable}) = F+1$$

and (in P3R)

$$DF(i) = \frac{\partial f}{\partial p_i} = \frac{\partial ln\ g(X,\theta)}{\partial p_i}$$

Their solution yields maximum likelihood estimates for $p_1, p_2, \ldots$ and standard errors for the estimates. However, the residual analysis is meaningless because each residual $(y-f)$ is 1.

We now reanalyze the Cox data (p. 501) by this method.

We must consider each binary outcome as a separate case. Therefore each case contains a zero or a one to indicate success or failure. However, it is not necessary to replicate identical cases; we can use the weight variable to indicate frequency of outcome. The data are shown in Example 14.8.

Now let x_i be a binary outcome (zero or one) for each case. Then x_i has the binomial distribution

$$f = ln\ g(x_i,\theta) = x_i\ ln\ \theta + (1-x_i)\ ln\ (1-\theta)$$

except for a constant, where

$$\theta = e^{p_1+p_2 t} / (1+e^{p_1+p_2 t})$$

is the parameter of the binomial distribution.   Then

$$\frac{\partial f}{\partial p_1} = \frac{x_i}{\theta}\frac{\partial \theta}{\partial p_1} - \frac{1-x_i}{1-\theta}\frac{\partial \theta}{\partial p_1} = x_i - \theta$$

$$\frac{\partial f}{\partial p_2} = t(x_i - \theta)$$

We specify the FORTRAN statements and Control Language instructions as:

Example 14.8

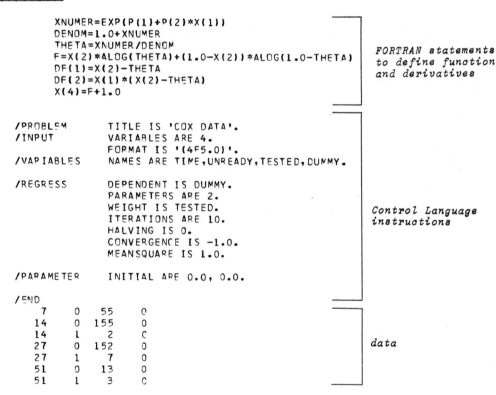

```
XNUMER=EXP(P(1)+P(2)*X(1))
DENOM=1.0+XNUMER
THETA=XNUMER/DENOM
F=X(2)*ALOG(THETA)+(1.0-X(2))*ALOG(1.0-THETA)
DF(1)=X(2)-THETA
DF(2)=X(1)*(X(2)-THETA)
X(4)=F+1.0
```

FORTRAN statements to define function and derivatives

```
/PROBLEM      TITLE IS 'COX DATA'.
/INPUT        VARIABLES ARE 4.
              FORMAT IS '(4F5.0)'.
/VARIABLES    NAMES ARE TIME,UNREADY,TESTED,DUMMY.

/REGRESS      DEPENDENT IS DUMMY.
              PARAMETERS ARE 2.
              WEIGHT IS TESTED.
              ITERATIONS ARE 10.
              HALVING IS 0.
              CONVERGENCE IS -1.0.
              MEANSQUARE IS 1.0.

/PARAMETER    INITIAL ARE 0.0, 0.0.

/END
     7     0    55    0
    14     0   155    0
    14     1     2    0
    27     0   152    0
    27     1     7    0
    51     0    13    0
    51     1     3    0
```

Control Language instructions

data

The System Cards required for this analysis are the same as described for Example 14.2 and are discussed in greater detail in Section 14.4.

The first variable in the data is TIME, the second is the binary outcome, the third is the frequency of the outcome and the last is a dummy variable. The case weight variable records the frequency. The dependent variable is recalculated at each iteration. The results of the analysis are presented in Output 14.8.

Output 14.8   Reanalysis of the Cox data by P3R using the second method
of maximum likelihood estimation. Compare these results
with those in Output 14.6 (p. 503).

```
BMDP3R - NONLINEAR REGRESSION                           PROGRAM REVISED SEPTEMBER 1977
HEALTH SCIENCES COMPUTING FACILITY                      MANUAL DATE -- 1977
UNIVERSITY OF CALIFORNIA, LOS ANGELES
```

```
NUMBER OF CASES READ. . . . . . . . . . . . .        7

VARIABLE                       STANDARD
NO. NAME           MEAN        DEVIATION      MINIMUM         MAXIMUM

  1    TIME      19.875931     10.718314      7.000000       51.000000
  2    UNREADY    0.031008      0.187227      0.0             1.000000
  4    DUMMY      0.0           0.0           -0.0            -0.0


PARAMETER MAXIMA. . . . . . . . . . . . . ***************  **************
PARAMETER MINIMA. . . . . . . . . . . . . ***************  **************

ITERATION   INCREMENT   RESIDUAL SUM
 NUMBER     HALVINGS    OF SQUARES            P(   1)         P(   2)

    0          0        387.000000            0.0            0.0
    1          0        387.000000           -2.150288       0.013802
    2          0        387.000000           -8.514508       0.155962
    3          0        387.000000           -6.481909       0.100283
    4          0        387.000000           -5.614953       0.083388
    5          0        387.000000           -5.408090       0.080216
    6          0        387.000000           -5.417967       0.080780
    7          0        387.000000           -5.414591       0.080677
    8          0        387.000000           -5.415303       0.080700
    9          0        387.000000           -5.415149       0.080695
   10          0        387.000000           -5.415184       0.080696
```

```
ASYMPTOTIC CORRELATION MATRIX OF THE PARAMETERS


                  P(   1)     P(   2)
                    1           2

P(   1)    1      1.0000
P(   2)    2     -0.9265       1.0000
```

COMPUTED VALUE OF RESIDUAL MEAN SQUARE IS   77.400

THE SPECIFIED VALUE OF THE RESIDUAL MEAN SQUARE(1.000), NOT THE COMPUTED VALUE, IS USED IN COMPUTING STANDARD
DEVIATIONS FOR PARAMETERS AND PREDICTED VALUES.

ASYMPTOTIC STANDARD DEVIATIONS OF THE PARAMETERS ASSUMING   5 DEGREES OF FREEDOM
            P(1)   P(2)

        0.79691E 00 0.24637E-01

● SPECIFYING A LOSS FUNCTION

You can specify your own loss function, such as minus the logarithm of the likelihood, to replace the least squares criterion by both P3R and PAR. You must specify LOSS in the *REGRess* paragraph, and then for each case compute XLOSS in subroutine FUN. XLOSS is then summed over all the cases and used in place of the sum of squares in the criterion for CONVERGENCE.[14]

REGRess
    LOSS.   {no/prev. }

A loss function is computed for each case in subroutine FUN. In subroutine FUN the loss function is called XLOSS. XLOSS is summed over all cases. If the minimum sum of XLOSS corresponds to the estimates that you want, the CONVERGENCE criterion can remain positive as well as the value of HALVING. Then P3R and PAR apply the criterion of convergence to the sum of XLOSS.

We recommend the use of LOSS, especially with the second method of maximum likelihood estimation.

As our last example we reanalyze the Cox data to illustrate how to use a loss function in PAR.

Example 14.9

```
XNUMER=DEXP(P(1)+P(2)*X(1))
DENOM=1.0+XNUMER
THETA=XNUMER/DENOM
F=X(2)*DLOG(THETA)+(1.0-X(2))*DLOG(1.0-THETA)
X(4)=F+1.0
XLOSS=-F*X(3)
```
FORTRAN statements to define function and derivatives

```
/PROBLEM      TITLE IS 'COX DATA'.
/INPUT        VARIABLES ARE 4.
              FORMAT IS '(4F5.0)'.
/VARIABLES    NAMES ARE TIME,UNREADY,TESTED,DUMMY.

/REGRESS      DEPENDENT IS DUMMY.
              PARAMETERS ARE 2.
              WEIGHT IS TESTED.
              MEANSQUARE IS 1.0.
              LOSS.

/PARAMETER    INITIAL ARE 0.0, 0.0.

/END
```
Control Language instructions

```
     7    0    55    0
    14    0   155    0
    14    1     2    C
    27    0   152    0
    27    1     7    0
    51    0    13    C
    51    1     3    C
```
data

The System Cards required for this analysis are the same as described for Example 14.4 and are discussed in greater detail in Section 14.4.

---

[14] If your BMDP programs are dated before August 1977, LOSS is not available.

The results are presented in Output 14.9. In our example we define
XLOSS as -F*X(3); i.e., as minus the logarithm of the likelihood multiplied
by the frequency of the likelihood (the case weight is the frequency). Since
the data are multinomial, twice the final value of the loss function is the
likelihood ratio statistic; i.e., -2 ln (maximum likelihood).

More generally, two models, one contained by the other, can be compared
by computing loss functions, -2 ln (maximum likelihood), for each model. The
difference between the loss functions provides a likelihood ratio test of
the hypothesis that the additional parameters are zero. Under the appropriate
large sample assumptions, this difference has a chi-square distribution with
degrees of freedom equal to the difference in the number of parameters in
the two models.

<u>Output 14.9</u> Reanalysis of the Cox data by PAR using a loss function

```
BMDPAR - DERIVATIVE-FREE NONLINEAR REGRESSION          PROGRAM REVISED SEPTEMBER 1977
HEALTH SCIENCES COMPUTING FACILITY                     MANUAL DATE  --  1977
UNIVERSITY OF CALIFORNIA, LOS ANGELES
```

NUMBER OF CASES READ.   7

VARIABLE NO.	NAME	MEAN	STANDARD DEVIATION	MINIMUM	MAXIMUM
1	TIME	19.875931	10.718314	7.000000	51.000000
2	UNREADY	0.031008	0.187227	0.0	1.000000
4	DUMMY	0.0	0.0	-0.0	-0.0
3	TESTED	NCT COMPUTED		2.000000	155.000000

ITER. NO.	INCR. HALV.	LOSS FUNCTION	PARAMETERS 1 P(1)	2 P(2)
0	0	305.385142	0.0	0.010000
0	0	270.067796	0.010000	0.0
0	0	268.247959	0.0	0.0
1	0	76.653071	-2.031117	0.007611
2	2	74.663518	-2.175420	0.012859
3	0	52.532254	-6.706947	0.087562
4	5	52.525842	-6.856091	0.092677
5	2	51.069111	-6.604997	0.091062
6	0	48.049263	-5.878115	0.087847
7	5	48.002807	-5.730406	0.083012
8	0	47.877357	-5.183812	0.078932
9	2	47.862700	-5.231653	0.080376
10	2	47.850837	-5.189227	0.078658
11	0	47.688867	-5.440190	0.080980
12	2	47.687708	-5.428618	0.081282
13	5	47.688858	-5.449539	0.081938
14	0	47.687897	-5.413300	0.080968
15	1	47.687478	-5.401210	0.080355
16	2	47.687388	-5.405521	0.080486
17	1	47.687297	-5.413609	0.080600
18	3	47.687291	-5.415186	0.080652
19	2	47.687288	-5.414283	0.080634

THE LOSS FUNCTION (=   47.6873   ) WAS SMALLEST WITH THE FOLLOWING PARAMETER VALUES

```
    1 P(1)        2 P(2)
  -5.41428     8.063412D-02
```

ESTIMATE OF ASYMPTOTIC CORRELATION MATRIX

```
              P(1)      P(2)
                1         2

P(1)      1    1.0000
P(2)      2   -0.9265    1.0000
```

THE ESTIMATED MEAN SQUARE ERROR IS   9.537
THE SPECIFIED VALUE OF THE MEAN SQUARE ERROR (1.000   )NOT THE COMPUTED VALUE IS USED IN COMPUTING STANDARD DEVIATIONS
FOR PARAMETERS.

ESTIMATES OF ASYMPTOTIC STANDARD DEVIATIONS OF PARAMETER ESTIMATES WITH   5 DEGREES OF FREEDOM ARE

```
    1 P(1)        2 P(2)
  0.796932     2.463822D-02
```

14.4 System Cards for P3R and PAR

When the function to be fitted to the data by P3R can be specified by function NUMBER in Control Language, the necessary System Cards at HSCF are shown in Example 14.1.

When the function to be fitted to the data by P3R or PAR is specified in the FORTRAN subroutine FUN, the subroutine must be temporarily appended to the BMDP program. We first describe how this is done in general terms, and then specify the System Cards used at HSCF and facilities that maintain the BMDP programs in a similar manner.

● GENERAL CONCEPTS

The BMDP programs are written in FORTRAN. The FORTRAN code is compiled (translated) on the computer into executable code prior to doing an analysis. Almost all computer facilities maintain the BMDP programs in executable code, greatly reducing the time used by the program (and hence its cost).

When you specify the function in FORTRAN in the SUBROUTINE FUN, the subroutine must also be compiled into executable code; the code must then be combined with that of the BMDP program prior to the analysis.

If you are not at HSCF, you should check with your computing facility consultant for the proper System Cards to use. Space is provided on the page opposite the inside back cover for you to write the cards required at your facility.

● SYSTEM CARDS USED AT HSCF (AND SIMILAR FACILITIES)

The order of the cards in the deck for P3R is

- System Cards

```
//jobname  JOB nooo,yourname
//  EXEC  BIMEDT,PROG=BMDP3R
    (Note:  Remember the T on BIMEDT)
//FUN  DD  *
```

This is followed by

- Fortran statements that define the function and its derivatives

  Note: At HSCF the first two FORTRAN *statements beginning*

      SUBROUTINE FUN...
      DIMENSION...

and the last two statements

```
    RETURN
    END
```

must *be omitted; they are provided by the computer. Check whether these statements are needed at _your_ facility.*

This is followed by

- a System Card

```
[ //GO.SYSIN  DD  *
```

followed by

- Control Language instructions and data, if on cards.

This is followed by

- System Card (to terminate program)

```
[ //
```

The order of cards for PAR is similar except the second System Card is

```
[ //EXEC  BIMEDT,PROG=BMDPAR
```

and at HSCF the first _three_ FORTRAN statements that begin

```
    SUBROUTINE FUN...
    IMPLICIT REAL*8...
    DIMENSION...
```

as well as the last two statements

```
    RETURN
    END
```

must *be omitted; they are provided by the computer. Check whether these statements are needed at _your_ facility.*

If you are reading from a BMDP File, creating a BMDP File, or reading data from a disk or magnetic tape, the System Card to describe the UNIT

```
[ //GO.FTyyF001  DD  ...
```

must be placed immediately before the

```
[ //GO.SYSIN  DD  *
```

If you specify transformations in a FORTRAN subroutine, the order must be

```
//jobname  JOB  nooo,yourname
//  EXEC  BIMEDT,PROG=BMDP3R      (or PAR)
//TRANSF  DD  *
```

This is followed by

- FORTRAN statements describing the transformations (Section 6.4)

This is followed by

- a System Card

```
//FUN  DD  *
```

and by the sequence of cards that follow //FUN DD * as described above.

The entire input deck for Example 14.2 (p. 473) using P3R is

```
//jobname  JOB  nooo,yourname             ⎤ HSCF System
//  EXEC  BIMEDT,PROG=BMDP3R              ⎦ cards
//FUN  DD  *
C
      DF(1)=EXP(P(2)*X(3))
      DF(2)=P(1)*X(3)*DF(1)               ⎤ FORTRAN statements
      DF(3)=EXP(P(4)*X(3))                ⎦
      DF(4)=P(3)*X(3)*DF(3)
      F=P(1)*DF(1)+P(3)*DF(3)
C                                         ⎤ HSCF System card
//GO.SYSIN  DD  *                         ⎦
/PROBLEM      TITLE IS 'RADIOACTIVE SULFATE DATA'.
/INPUT        VARIABLES ARE 3.
              FORMAT IS '(F8.4,F8.6,F8.0)'.
/VARIABLE     NAMES ARE COUNT,CASEWT,TIME.
                                          ⎤ Control Language
/REGRESS      DEPENDENT IS COUNT.         ⎦ instructions
              PARAMETERS ARE 4.
              WEIGHT IS CASEWT.

/PARAMETER    INITIAL ARE 10, -.1, 5, -.01.

/END
  15.1117 .004379       2
  11.3601 .007749       4
   9.7652 .010487       6
   9.0935 .012093       8
   8.4820 .013900      10
   7.6891 .016914      15
   7.3342 .018591      20
   7.0593 .020067      25
   6.7041 .022249      30
   6.4313 .024177      40                 ⎤ data from Table 14.1
   6.1554 .026393      50
   5.9940 .027833      60
   5.7698 .030039      70
   5.6440 .031392      80
   5.3915 .034402      90
   5.0938 .038540     110
   4.8717 .042135     130
   4.5996 .047267     150
   4.4968 .049453     160
   4.3602 .052600     170
   4.2668 .054928     180
//                                        ⎦ HSCF System card
```

14.5 Summary — P3R, PAR

The Control Language on this page is common to all programs. This is followed by the Control Language specific to

P3R -- Nonlinear Linear Regression	p. 520
PAR -- Derivative-Free Nonlinear Regression	p. 520

Paragraph STATEMENT[1] {Preassigned value[2]}		Definition, restriction	See pages:
/PROBlem		Required each problem	74
TITLE='c'.	{blank}	Problem title, $\leq$ 160 char.	74
/INPut		Required first problem. Either VARIABLE and FORMAT, or UNIT and CODE required.	75
VARIABLE=#.	{none/prev.}	No. of variables in input data	75
FORMAT='c'.	{none/prev.}	Format of input data, $\leq$ 800 char.	76
CASE=#.	{end-of-file/prev.}	No. of cases in data	76-77
UNIT=#.	{5(cards)/prev.}	Input unit if data are not on cards; not 1,2,6	77
REWIND.	{REWIND/prev.}	Rewind input unit	77
CODE=c.	{none}	Code to identify BMDP File	132
CONTENT=c.	{DATA}	Data or matrix in BMDP File	132
LABEL=c.	{none}	Label of BMDP File, $\leq$ 40 char.	132
/VARiable		Optional. For input from a BMDP File, items in this paragraph may be previously set, see Chapter 7.	79
NAME=c_1,c_2,···.	{X(subscript)/prev.}	Variable names, one per variable	79-80
MAXIMUM=$\#_1$,$\#_2$,···.	{none/prev.}	Upper limits, one per variable	80
MINIMUM=$\#_1$,$\#_2$,···.	{none/prev.}	Lower limits, one per variable	80
BLANK= (one only) ZERO, MISSING.	{ZERO/prev.}	Blanks treated as zeros or as missing value codes	81
MISSING=$\#_1$,$\#_2$,···.	{none/prev.}	Missing value codes, one per variable	81
USE=v_1,v_2,···.	{all variables}	Variables used in the analysis	82
LABEL=v_1,v_2.	{none/prev.}	Variable(s) used to label cases, read under A-format, one or two	83
ADD=#.	{0/prev.}	No. of variables added through transformation	99
BEFORE. or AFTER.	{BEFORE/prev.}	Data checked for limits before or after transformation	100
/TRANsform		Optional, Control Language transformations and case selection	97-105
/SAVE		Optional, required to create BMDP File	125
CODE=c.	{none}	Code to identify BMDP File, required	125-126
LABEL='c'.	{blank}	Label for BMDP File, $\leq$ 40 char.	125-126
UNIT=#.	{none}	Unit on which BMDP File is written; not 1, 2, 5 or 6	126-127
NEW.	{not new}	NEW if this is first BMDP File written in the system file	126-127

Key: # number   v variable name or subscript
'c' title, label or format   c name not exceeding 8 char., apostrophes may be required (p. 59)

[1] In BMDP programs dated before August 1977, the minimum required abbreviations are *INPUT* (not *INP*), VARIAB (not VAR), FORMAT (not FORM), CONTENT (not CONT), *VARIAB* (not *VAR*), BEFORET (not BEF), AFTERT (not AFT), *TRANSF* (not *TRAN*). If dated before February 1976, BLANK=ZERO and cannot be changed.

[2] "/prev." means that any assignment remains the same as that specified in the previous problem or subproblem until changed. Otherwise, the assignment returns to its preassigned value each time a new problem begins or the paragraph is used again.

P3R -- Nonlinear Regression

(in addition to that on p. 518)

Paragraph STATEMENT[1]	{Preassigned value}	Definition, restriction	See pages:
/REGRess		Required	469
NUMBER=#.	{none/prev.}	Code number to select function	469-471
DEPENDENT=v.	{none/prev.}	Dependent variable, required	470-471
INDEPendent=v.	{none/prev.}	Independent variable if Control Language function specified	469-471
PARAMETER=#.	{none/prev.}	Number of parameters, required	470-471
TITLE='c'.	{blank}	Title for analysis, $\leq$ 160 char.	471
WEIGHT=v.	{no weight var./prev.}	Variable containing case weights	475
CONSTRAINT=#.	{none/prev.}	Number of exact linear constraints	479
CONVERGENCE=#.	{0.00001/prev.}	Convergence criterion	481
PRINT=$v_1,v_2,\cdots$.	{all variables/prev.}	Data printed for each case	480-481
ITERATION=#.	{50/prev.}	Maximum number of iterations	481-482
HALVING=#.	{5/prev.}	Maximum number of increment halvings	482
TOLERANCE=#.	{0.001/prev.}	Check for singularity	482
MEANSQUARE=#.	{none/prev.}	If specified, used to compute asymptotic standard deviations	499-500
PASS=#.	{1/prev.}	Number of passes of data at each iteration	506-507
LOSS.	{no/prev.}	Loss function specified in FORTRAN subroutine	512-513
/PARAMeter		Optional	
INITIAL=$\#_1,\#_2,\cdots$.	{0,0,.../prev.}	Initial estimates for parameters	477-478
NAME=$c_1,c_2,\cdots$.	{P(subscript)/prev.}	Names for parameters	478-479
MAXIMUM=$\#_1,\#_2,\cdots$.	{none/prev.}	Upper limits for parameters	478-479
MINIMUM=$\#_1,\#_2,\cdots$.	{none/prev.}	Lower limits for parameters	478-479
CONSTRAINT=$\#_1,\#_2,\cdots$.	{0,0,.../prev.}	Coefficients of parameters for linear constraint, may be repeated	479-480
K=#.	{0/prev.}	Constant for linear constraint, may be repeated	479-480
/PLOT		Optional	
VARIABLE=$v_1,v_2,\cdots$.	{none/prev.}	Variables against which predicted and observed values and residuals are plotted	477
RESIDUAL.	{no/prev.}	Residuals and residuals squared plotted against predicted values	477
NORMAL.	{no/prev.}	Print normal probability plot of residuals	477
DNORMAL.	{no/prev.}	Print detrended normal probability plot of residuals	477
SIZE=$\#_1,\#_2$.	{50,50/prev.}	Length of horizontal and vertical axes	477
/END		Required	57

Key: # number v variable name or subscript
'c' title, label or format c name not exceeding 8 char., apostrophes may be required (p. 59)

[1] In BMDP programs dated before August 1977, the minimum required abbreviations are *REGRES* (not *REGR*), NUMBER (not NUMB), and CONVER (not CONV); PRINT, PASS, LOSS, CONST (in the *PARAMeter* paragraph), and K are not available; PROBIT is used in place of NORM and DNORM. If dated before August 1976, MEANSQUARE is not available.

● Order of input

		Function available in Control Language	Function specified by FORTRAN statements

(1)	System Cards, at HSCF these are	//jobname JOB nooo,yourname
		// EXEC BIMED,PROG=BMDP3R
		//SYSIN DD *
			//jobname JOB nooo,yourname
			// EXEC BIMEDT,PROG=BMDP3R
			//FUN DD *

(2)	Function specified in FORTRAN	none	FORTRAN statements, at HSCF do not include SUBROUTINE and DIMENSION statements at beginning and RETURN and END at end
(3)	System Card, at HSCF this is	none	//GO.SYSIN DD *

(4) Control Language instructions

  PROBlem paragraph, required
  INPut paragraph, required first problem
  VARiable paragraph
  TRANsform paragraph
  SAVE paragraph
  REGRess paragraph, required
  PARAMeter paragraph
  PLOT paragraph
  END paragraph, required at end of Control Language

(5) Data, if on cards

  data

(6) Control Language instructions for additional analysis of the same data, if desired

  REGRess paragraph, required
  PARAMeter paragraph
  END paragraph, required at end of each batch of Control Language

(7) System Card, at HSCF this is

  //

(6) can be repeated for additional analyses of the same data.
Control Language instructions and data (4-6) can be repeated to analyze additional problems (using the same function(s)).

PAR -- Derivative-Free Nonlinear Regression

(in addition to that on p. 518)

Paragraph STATEMENT	{Preassigned value}	Definition, restriction	See pages:
/REGRess		Required	490
DEPENDENT=v.	{none/prev.}	Dependent variable, required	490
PARAMETER=#.	{none/prev.}	Number of parameters, required	490
TITLE='c'.	{blank}	Title for analysis, $\leq$ 160 char.	490
NUMBER=#.	{none/prev.}	Code number to select function	490
WEIGHT=v.	{no weight var./prev.}	Variable containing case weights	490-492
CONSTRAINT=#.	{none/prev.}	Number of inequality constraints	494-495
PRINT=$v_1, v_2, \cdots$.	{all variables/prev.}	Data printed for each case	496
CONVERGENCE=#.	{0.00001/prev.}	Convergence criteria	497
ITERATION=#.	{50/prev.}	Maximum number of iterations	497
HALVING=#.	{5/prev.}	Maximum number of increment halvings	497
TOLERANCE=#.	{10^{-8}/prev.}	Check against roundoff errors	497
MEANSQUARE=#.	{none/prev.}	If specified, used to compute asymptotic standard deviations	499-500
PASS=1. or 2.	{1/prev.}	Number of passes of data at each iteration	506-507
LOSS.	{no/prev.}	Loss function specified in FORTRAN subroutine	512-513
/PARAMeter		Required	493
INITIAL=$\#_1, \#_2, \cdots$.	{none/prev.}	Starting values for parameter, required	493
MAXIMUM=$\#_1, \#_2, \cdots$.	{none/prev.}	Upper limits for parameters	494
MINIMUM=$\#_1, \#_2, \cdots$.	{none/prev.}	Lower limits for parameters	494
NAME=$c_1, c_2, \cdots$.	{P(subscript)/prev.}	Names for parameters	494
DELTA=$\#_1, \#_2, \cdots$.	{see p.494}	Step size for additional starting values	494
FIXED= parameter names or subscripts. {none}		Parameters whose estimates are fixed equal to INITIAL	494
CONSTRAINT=$\#_1, \#_2, \cdots$.	{0,0,.../prev.}	Coefficients of inequality constraint, may be repeated	495
LIMIT=$\#_1, \#_2, \cdots$.	{$-\infty, \infty$/prev.}	Upper and lower limits for CONSTRAINT, may be repeated	495
/PLOT		Optional	
VARIABLE=$v_1, v_2, \cdots$.	{none/prev.}	Variables against which predicted and observed values and residuals are plotted	492
RESIDUAL.	{no/prev.}	Residuals and residuals squared plotted against predicted values	492
NORMAL.	{no/prev.}	Print normal probability plot of residuals	492
DNORMAL.	{no/prev.}	Print detrended normal probability plot of residuals	492-493
SIZE=$\#_1, \#_2$.	{50,50/prev.}	Length of horizontal and vertical axes	492-493
SAVE		Specify as part of *SAVE* paragraph, p. 518	
NUMBER=#.	{1}	Number of analyses for which predicted values are saved in BMDP File	496-497
/END		Required	57

Key: #   number   v   variable name or subscript
      'c'   title, label or format   c   name not exceeding 8 char., apostrophes may be required (p. 59)

● Order of input

(1) System Cards, at HSCF these are
```
//jobname JOB nooo,yourname
//   EXEC BIMEDT,PROG=BMDPAR
//FUN DD *
```

(2) Function specified in FORTRAN
```
FORTRAN statements, at HSCF do not include SUBROUTINE, REAL*8 and
DIMENSION statements at beginning and RETURN and END at end
```

(3) System Card, at HSCF this is
```
//GO.SYSIN DD *
```

(4) Control Language instructions
```
PROBLem paragraph, required
INPut paragraph, required first problem
VARiable paragraph
TRANsform paragraph
SAVE paragraph
REGRess paragraph, required
PARAMeter paragraph
PLOT paragraph
END paragraph, required at end of Control Language
```

(5) Data, if on cards
```
data
```

(6) Control Language instructions
for additional analysis of the
same data, if desired
```
REGRess paragraph, required
PARAMeter paragraph
END paragraph, required at end of each batch of Control Language
```

(7) System Card, at HSCF this is
```
//
```

     (6) can be repeated for additional analyses of the same data
     Control Language instructions and data (4-6) can be repeated to analyze additional problems (using the same
     function(s)).

15

ANALYSIS OF VARIANCE AND COVARIANCE

In this chapter we describe three programs that estimate means, variances and regression coefficients and test hypotheses by an analysis of variance (ANOVA) or covariance. They are

P1V --	One-Way Analysis of Variance and Covariance	p. 523
P2V --	Analysis of Variance and Covariance, Including Repeated Measures	p. 540
P3V --	General Mixed Model Analysis of Variance	p. 581

P1V performs a one-way ANOVA for each dependent variable to test the equality of group means. If covariates (independent variables) are specified, an analysis of covariance is performed for each dependent variable; the coefficients of the covariates are tested for equality between groups. The equality of means (or adjusted means) between each pair of groups is tested by t statistics. If linear contrasts are specified for the group means, the significance of each contrast is tested by a t test. Scatter plots of each dependent variable, predicted value and residual against the independent variables (covariates) and of residuals against predicted values can be requested.

A one-way ANOVA can also be computed with P7D (Section 9.2) or P9D (Section 9.3). P7D can also compute an ANOVA test that does not assume the group variances are equal and can plot side-by-side histograms for the groups.

When only two groups are being computed, P3D (Section 9.1) computes two-sample t tests assuming equal or unequal group variances.

P2V performs an analysis of variance or covariance for a wide variety of fixed effects models and for repeated measures models with equal or unequal cell sizes. Fixed effects models that can be analyzed include factorial designs, Latin squares, fractional factorials, etc.; you can specify the analysis of variance components in the design.

Repeated measures models are designs in which repeated measurements are made of the same variable for each subject (or case). Split-plot models can be analyzed similarly; a plot is analogous to a subject. If there are two measurements for each subject, the analysis of the repeated measures factors is similar to a paired comparison t test. In a repeated measures model a distinction is made between variables that classify the cases into groups (grouping factors) and repeated measures of the same variable (trial factors): grouping factors may be sex, race, disease or control-treatment. A trial factor might be the time of the measurement if a measurement is repeated on each subject at fixed intervals or a treatment factor if each subject receives each treatment. Grouping factors refer to "between subject" effects and trial factors refer to "within subject" effects. A basic reference for repeated measures models is Winer (1971). In split-plot designs, factors for main plot treatments are grouping factors and subplot factors are trial factors.

Repeated measures models are a special class of mixed models. The grouping and trial factors are all fixed effect factors. A factor for subjects (cases), although not explicitly defined, is the only random effects factor. Each subject is observed at all combinations of the trial factors (i.e., is crossed with the trial factors), but at only one level of each grouping factor (i.e., is nested within the grouping factors).

P3V analyzes general mixed models using maximum likelihood estimation. Each term of the model can be specified as a fixed or random ANOVA component. Arbitrary unbalanced designs and missing cells are permitted.

● CONTROL LANGUAGE

The Control Language instructions to describe the data and variables are common to all BMDP programs and are explained in Chapter 5; the *PROBLem, INPut*[1], *VARiable* and *GROUP* paragraphs are used in the programs discussed in this chapter. If data editing or transformations are necessary, the methods described in Chapter 6 can be used. Data can be read using a FORMAT statement or from a BMDP File (Chapter 7).

A summary of the Control Language instructions common to all BMDP programs is on p. 599; summaries of the Control Language instructions specific to each program described in this chapter follow the general summary. These summaries can be used as indexes to the program descriptions.

---

[1] BMDP programs dated before August 1977 require more letters in the permissible abbreviated form (the capitalized letters). The minimum required abbreviations are specified in the footnotes to the summary (p. 599).

P1V

15.1 One-Way Analysis of Variance and Covariance

Laszlo Engelman, HSCF

P1V performs a one-way analysis of variance (ANOVA) for each dependent variable; i.e., it tests the equality of group means. If covariates (independent variables) are specified, an analysis of covariance is performed for each dependent variable; the coefficients of the covariates are tested for equality between groups. t statistics are computed to test the equality of means (or adjusted means) between each pair of groups.

If linear contrasts are specified for the group means, the significance of each contrast is tested by a t test. Scatter plots of each dependent variable, predicted value and residual against the independent variables (covariates) and residuals against predicted values can be requested.

A one-way ANOVA can also be obtained with P7D (Section 9.2). P7D also computes an ANOVA test that does not assume equal group variances and plots side-by-side histograms of the data in the groups.

● RESULTS

The Werner blood chemistry data (Table 5.1) are used to illustrate results computed by P1V. Cholesterol is usually analyzed on a logarithmic scale. In the examples in this section we transform cholesterol (CHOLSTRL) to its $\log_{10}$ (cholesterol) by stating in the *TRANSform* paragraph

/TRANSFORM LOGCHOL IS LOG(CHOLSTRL).

and ADDING one variable in the *VARiable* paragraph. We could replace the value of CHOLSTRL by its logarithm, but we choose to add a new variable with a new name (LOGCHOL) to avoid confusion in labelling the results. Control Language transformations are described in Section 6.1.

In our first example we specify that the variable used to classify cases into groups (the GROUPING variable) is BRTHPILL and that the DEPENDENT variables are LOGCHOL and CALCIUM. That is, a one-way ANOVA is to be computed for LOGCHOL and CALCIUM using the groups specified by BRTHPILL. The other Control Language instructions are described in Chapter 5.

Example 15.1

```
/PROBLEM      TITLE IS 'WERNER BLOOD CHEMISTRY DATA'.
/INPUT        VARIABLES ARE 9.
              FORMAT IS '(A4,5F4.0,3F4.1)'.
/VARIABLE     NAMES ARE ID,AGE,HEIGHT,WEIGHT,BRTHPILL,
                  CHOLSTRL,ALBUMIN,CALCIUM,URICACID,
                  LOGCHOL.
              MAXIMUM IS (6)400.
              MINIMUM IS (6)150.
              BLANKS ARE MISSING.
              LABEL IS ID.
              ADD IS 1.
              GROUPING IS BRTHPILL.

/GROUP        CODES(5) ARE       1,    2.
              NAMES(5) ARE NOPILL, PILL.

/TRANSFORM    LOGCHOL = LOG(CHOLSTRL).

/DESIGN       DEPENDENT ARE LOGCHOL,CALCIUM.

/END
```

The Control Language must be preceded by System Cards to initiate the analysis by P1V. At HSCF, the System Cards are

```
//jobname  JOB  nooo,yourname
//   EXEC  BIMED,PROG=BMDP1V
//SYSIN  DD  *
```

The Control Language is immediately followed by the data (Table 5.1). The analysis is terminated by another System Card. At HSCF, this System Card is

```
//
```

The results are presented in Output 15.1. Circled numbers below correspond to those in the output.

(1)   Number of cases read. Only complete cases are used in the analysis; i.e., cases that have no missing values or values out of range. All variables are checked unless a USE statement is specified in the *VARiable* paragraph, in which case only the variables in the USE statement are checked. In addition, if CODEs are specified for the GROUPING variable, a case is included only if the value of the GROUPING variable is equal to one of the specified CODEs.

180 of the 188 cases are used in the analysis because eight cases have one or more values missing or out of range.

(2)   The number of cases in each group is listed.

(3)   For each group the mean is printed, as well as the mean for all the cases (TOTAL). Let x_{ij} represent the jth observation in the ith group. Then the mean of the ith group is $\bar{x}_i = \sum_j x_{ij}/n_i$ where n_i is the number of cases in the group. The overall mean (TOTAL) is $\bar{x} = \sum\sum x_{ij}/N$ where $N = \sum n_i$ is the total frequency.

(4)   One-way analysis of variance (for LOGCHOL). The equality of the group means is tested by the classical one-way analysis of variance (F statistic). The degrees of freedom of the F statistic are g-1 and N-g, where g is the number of groups. The between sum of squares (between cell means) is

Output 15.1   One-way analysis of variance by P1V. Circled numbers correspond
to those in the text. Results not reproduced are indicated in
italics.

```
BMDP1V - ONE-WAY ANALYSIS OF VARIANCE AND COVARIANCE              PROGRAM REVISED SEPTEMBER 1977
HEALTH SCIENCES COMPUTING FACILITY                                MANUAL DATE --  1977
UNIVERSITY OF CALIFORNIA, LOS ANGELES
```

--- Control Language read by P1V is printed and interpreted ---

```
CONTROL LANGUAGE TRANSFORMATIONS ARE

        LOGCHOL  = LOG  (   CHOLSTRL )  .


    GROUPING VARIABLE IS. . . . . . . . . . . . .BRTHPILL

    NUMBER OF CASES READ. . . . . . . . . . . . .     188
       CASES WITH DATA MISSING OR BEYOND LIMITS . .      8
          REMAINING NUMBER OF CASES . . . . . . .      180
    NUMBER OF GROUPS FOUND. . . . . . . . . . . .       2
```

①

```
                      BEFORE TRANSFORMATION                                        INTERVAL RANGE
    VARIABLE      MINIMUM   MAXIMUM   MISSING    CATEGORY  CATEGORY    GREATER    LESS THAN
    NO. NAME      LIMIT     LIMIT     CODE       CODE      NAME        THAN       OR EQUAL TO

     5   BRTHPILL                                1.00000   NOPILL
                                                 2.00000   PILL
```

```
    NUMBER OF CASES PER GROUP
    ------------------------
```
②
```
    NOPILL     89.
    PILL       91.
    TOTAL     180.
```

```
    ****************************************************************************************************
    ****************************************************************************************************
```

```
    ESTIMATES OF MEANS
    ------------------
```

③

```
                    NOPILL    PILL       TOTAL
                      1         2           3

    CALCIUM    8      9.9977    9.9384     9.9678
    LOGCHOL   10      2.3576    2.3734     2.3656
```

```
    ONE WAY ANALYSIS OF VARIANCE FOR VARIABLE LOGCHOL
    ****************************************************************************************************
```

④ ANALYSIS OF VARIANCE

```
    SOURCE OF VARIANCE           D.F.     SUM OF SQ.    MEAN SQ.    F-VALUE        TAIL AREA PROBABILITY
    EQUALITY OF CELL MEANS          1       0.0111        0.0111     1.8265              0.1783
       ERROR                      178       1.0857        0.0061
```

```
    T-TEST MATRIX FOR GROUP MEANS ON   178 DEGREES OF FREEDOM
    --------------------------------------------------------
```

⑤
```
              NOPILL    PILL
                1         2

    NOPILL   1   0.0
    PILL     2   1.3515     0.0
```

```
    PROBABILITIES FOR THE T-VALUES ABOVE
    ------------------------------------
```

```
              NOPILL    PILL
                1         2

    NOPILL   1   1.0000
    PILL     2   0.1783     1.0000
```

--- similar results for CALCIUM follow ---

$$BSS = \Sigma n_i (\bar{x}_i - \bar{x})^2$$

and the error sum of squares is

$$ESS = \Sigma\Sigma (x_{ij} - \bar{x}_i)^2$$

The F statistic (F-value) is

$$F = \frac{BSS/(g-1)}{ESS/(N-g)}$$

The tail area probability is the probability of exceeding the value of the F statistic when the data are sampled from normal distributions with equal population variances. The probability (size of the test) can be severely affected when the groups have different population variances (Brown and Forsythe, 1974a). P7D, Section 9.2, computes a one-way ANOVA statistic that does not assume homogeneity of variances.

⑤   A t test is computed between each pair of groups to test the equality of group means. When there are no covariates this t statistic is

$$\frac{(\bar{x}_i - \bar{x}_k)/(\frac{1}{n_i} + \frac{1}{n_k})^{\frac{1}{2}}}{\{ESS/(N-g)\}^{\frac{1}{2}}}$$

The numerator is that of the two-sample t test, but the denominator uses the error mean square from the ANOVA. The probabilities computed for the t values are the probabilities of exceeding the absolute values of the t test based on a t variable with N-g degrees of freedom. The probabilities correspond to two-sided tests of the hypothesis that the means of each pair of groups are equal. These probabilities are presented for descriptive purposes. When multiple tests are performed, the procedures in Miller (1966) should be considered.

A second example. In an analysis of covariance, you must also specify the covariates. The covariates are specified in Example 15.2 as INDEPENDENT variables.

Example 15.2

```
/PROBLEM      TITLE IS 'WERNER BLOOD CHEMISTRY DATA'.
/INPUT        VARIABLES ARE 9.
              FORMAT IS '(A4,5F4.0,3F4.1)'.
/VARIABLE     NAMES ARE ID,AGE,HEIGHT,WEIGHT,BRTHPILL,
                 CHOLSTRL,ALBUMIN,CALCIUM,URICACID,
                 LOGCHOL.
              MAXIMUM IS (6)400.
              MINIMUM IS (6)150.
              BLANKS ARE MISSING.
              LABEL IS ID.
              ADD IS 1.
              GROUPING IS BRTHPILL.

/GROUP        CODES(5) ARE        1,    2.
              NAMES(5) ARE NOPILL, PILL.

/TRANSFORM    LOGCHOL = LOG(CHOLSTRL).

/DESIGN       DEPENDENT ARE LOGCHOL,CALCIUM.
              INDEPENDENT ARE AGE,HEIGHT,WEIGHT.

/END
```

The results are presented in Output 15.2. Circled numbers below correspond to those in the output.

⑥ The first DEPENDENT variable is LOGCHOL. The model fitted to the data is

$$y_{ij} = \mu_i + \beta_1(x_{1ij} - \bar{x}_1) + \beta_2(x_{2ij} - \bar{x}_2) + \ldots$$

where x_{nij} is the jth value in the ith group for the nth covariate.

The estimates of β_m ($\hat{\beta}_m$) are printed as the regression coefficients. The standard error of the estimate is printed in the second column. The t value is the ratio of $\hat{\beta}$ to its standard error; it can be used as a test of the significance of the regression coefficient.

⑦ For each group the group mean $\bar{y}_i$ is printed. The adjusted group mean is

$$\hat{\mu}_i = \bar{y}_i + \Sigma_m \hat{\beta}_m(\bar{x}_m - \bar{x}_{mi})$$

The standard error of the adjusted group mean is also printed.

⑧ The analysis of variance is now an analysis of covariance. The computational formulas are in Appendix A.17.

The analysis of covariance is patterned after the analysis described in Dixon and Massey (1969, Chapter 12).

The first test in the analysis of variance table is for the equality of the adjusted cell means, i.e., the test that μ_i are equal in the model in ⑥ . The second test is for zero slope for the covariates, i.e., the test that the coefficients β_m are zero (the μ_i can be different).

The third test in the analysis of variance table uses the model

$$y_{ij} = \mu_i + \beta_{1i}(x_{1ij} - \bar{x}_1) + \beta_{2i}(x_{2ij} - \bar{x}_2) + \ldots$$

and tests whether

$$\beta_{11} = \beta_{12} = \ldots = \beta_{1g}$$

$$\beta_{21} = \beta_{22} = \ldots = \beta_{2g}$$

   etc.

i.e., tests the equality of the coefficients for each covariate between groups. When this test is significant, the data do not fit the model in ⑥ and hence the first two tests are inappropriate.

When the third test is significant, the residual plots described on p. 531 may identify whether there are extreme values in your data or whether a transformation of the data is needed before doing a reanalysis.

⑨ The slope within each group is the regression coefficient for each covariate in the model

$$y_{ij} = \mu_i + \beta_{1i}(x_{1ij} - \bar{x}_1) + \beta_{2i}(x_{2ij} - \bar{x}_2) + \ldots$$

Output 15.2   One-way analysis of covariance by P1V

```
CONTROL LANGUAGE TRANSFORMATIONS ARE
    LOGCHOL  = LOG (   CHOLSTRL )
```

ESTIMATES OF MEANS

		NOPILL 1	PILL 2	TOTAL 3
AGE	2	32.9772	34.0876	33.5385
HEIGHT	3	64.0559	64.8678	64.4663
WEIGHT	4	129.4379	132.7140	131.0941
CALCIUM	8	9.9977	9.9384	9.9678
LOGCHOL	10	2.3576	2.3734	2.3656

(6) DEPENDENT VARIABLE IS LOGCHOL
****

COVARIATE	REG.COEFF.	STD.ERR.	T-VALUE
AGE	0.00269	0.00057	4.68296
HEIGHT	-0.00251	0.00253	-0.98909
WEIGHT	0.00033	0.00031	1.04947

(7)

GROUP	N	GRP.MEAN	ADJ.GRP.MEAN	STD.ERR.
NOPILL	89.	2.35763	2.35865	0.00783
PILL	91.	2.37336	2.37236	0.00774

ANALYSIS OF VARIANCE

(8)

SOURCE OF VARIANCE	D.F.	SUM OF SQ.	MEAN SQ.	F-VALUE	TAIL AREA PROBABILITY
EQUALITY OF ADJ. CELL MEANS	1	0.0082	0.0082	1.5294	0.2179
ZERO SLOPE	3	0.1453	0.0484	9.0126	0.0000
ERROR	175	0.9404	0.0054		
EQUALITY OF SLOPES	3	0.0163	0.0054	1.0113	0.3891
ERROR	172	0.9241	0.0054		

SLOPE WITHIN EACH GROUP
----

(9)

		NOPILL 1	PILL 2
AGE	2	0.0035	0.0019
HEIGHT	3	-0.0003	-0.0053
WEIGHT	4	-0.0001	0.0007

T-TEST MATRIX FOR ADJUSTED GROUP MEANS ON   175 DEGREES OF FREEDOM
----

(10)

		NOPILL 1	PILL 2
NOPILL	1	0.0	
PILL	2	1.2366	0.0

PROBABILITIES FOR THE T-VALUES ABOVE

		NOPILL 1	PILL 2
NOPILL	1	1.0000	
PILL	2	0.2179	1.0000

(10) The tests for adjusted group means are t tests between the adjusted means for each pair of group means. In the second panel the two-tailed probabilities are printed.

● OPTIONAL RESULTS

You can

- select groups for analysis   p. 530

- request scatter plots of each dependent variable, predicted value and residual against the independent variables (covariates), and residuals against the predicted values   p. 530

- specify contrasts for the group means to be tested for significance   p. 531

- request that any of the following be printed: the minimum and maximum values and means of all variables in each group; the covariance and correlation matrices for each group; the variance-covariance matrix for the total sample (no grouping), within groups (pooled) or between groups; and correlations between the estimated regression coefficients or between the adjusted group means   p. 535

● SPECIFYING AN ANALYSIS OF VARIANCE OR COVARIANCE

Cases are classified into groups by the values of a GROUPING variable. You must specify the GROUPING variable in the *VARiable* paragraph. When CODEs or CUTPOINTS are necessary to describe the groups or when you want to name the groups (which makes the results easier to read), you must also include a *GROUP* paragraph.

```
VARiable
    GROUPING=v.          {no grouping var./prev.}          required
        Name or subscript of variable used to classify cases into groups.  If
        the GROUPING variable has more than ten distinct values, CODEs or
        CUTPOINTS must be specified in a GROUP paragraph (Section 5.4).
```

The variables to be analyzed are described in a *DESIGN* paragraph[2], which can be repeated before the *END* paragraph to specify additional analyses of the same data. When

        /DESIGN

only is specified, a one-way analysis of variance is computed for all variables except the GROUPING variable.

---

[2] If your BMDP programs are dated before August 1977, the paragraph name is *SUBProblem* (not *DESIGN*).

You can specify the DEPENDENT variables for which the analysis of variance (no covariates) or analysis of covariance are computed. You can also specify the INDEPENDENT variables (covariates).

```
DESIGN
     DEPENDENT=v_1,v_2,···.          {all except GROUPING and
                                      INDEPENDENT variables}

     Names or subscripts of variables to be analyzed by a one-way analysis
     of variance or covariance.  Each dependent variable is analyzed
     separately.

     INDEPENDENT=v_1,v_2,···.  {none}

     Names or subscripts of variables to be used as covariates.  If none
     are specified, a one-way analysis of variance is computed.

     TITLE= 'c'.                {blank}                    ≤ 160 char.
     A title for the analysis.
```

● SELECTING GROUPS FOR THE ANALYSIS

You can select groups to be included in the analysis by specifying the GROUPs to be compared in the *DESIGN* paragraph. If GROUPs are not specified, all the groups are compared in the analysis.

```
DESIGN
     GROUP=g_1,g_2,···.        {all groups/prev.}

     Group NAMEs (from the GROUP paragraph) or group subscripts.
     A group subscript is the sequence number of the code or interval
     that defines the group (not the value of its CODE or CUTPOINT).
     The groups specified are compared by the analysis of variance or
     covariance.
```

● PLOTs PRODUCED BY P1V

To illustrate the PLOTs produced by P1V we added

     PLOT.

to the *DESIGN* paragraph.

Example 15.3

```
/PROBLEM      TITLE IS 'WERNER BLOOD CHEMISTRY DATA'.
/INPUT        VARIABLES ARE 9.
              FORMAT IS '(A4,5F4.0,3F4.1)'.
/VARIABLE     NAMES ARE ID,AGE,HEIGHT,WEIGHT,BRTHPILL,
                     CHOLSTRL,ALBUMIN,CALCIUM,URICACID,
                     LOGCHOL.
              MAXIMUM IS (6)400.
              MINIMUM IS (6)150.
              BLANKS ARE MISSING.
              LABEL IS ID.
              ADD IS 1.
              GROUPING IS BRTHPILL.

/GROUP        CODES(5) ARE       1,    2.
              NAMES(5) ARE NOPILL, PILL.

/TRANSFORM    LOGCHOL = LOG(CHOLSTRL).

/DESIGN       DEPENDENT IS LOGCHOL.
              INDEPENDENT ARE AGE,HEIGHT,WEIGHT.
              PLOT.

/END
```

In Output 15.3 the following scatter plots are printed:

(11) the observed value (O) and the predicted value (P) of the dependent variable (LOGCHOL) against each independent variable (AGE is shown) for each group separately; asterisks indicate overlap between observed and predicted values

(12) the residual (R=O-P) against the same independent variable for each group separately

(13) the residual (R) against the predicted value for each group

(14) the squared residual ($S=R^2$) against the predicted value for each group

---

DESIGN
  PLOT.   {no}

    When PLOT is specified, the following scatter plots are printed:

      - observed values of the dependent variable, predicted values, and residuals against each covariate for each group separately

      - residuals and residuals squared against the predicted values for each group separately

---

● TESTING ADDITIONAL HYPOTHESES

You can specify contrasts (linear combinations of the means μ_i); P1V tests whether each contrast is zero and whether all contrasts simultaneously are zero.

Output 15.3   Plots printed by P1V

```
CONTROL LANGUAGE TRANSFORMATIONS ARE
        LCGCHCL = LOG ( CHOLSTRL ) .
```

--- results in Output 15.2 appear here ---

```
OBSERVED, PREDICTED VALUES AND RESIDUALS OF THE DEPENDENT VARIABLE
                            VERSUS
              EACH COVARIATE FOR EACH GROUP
```

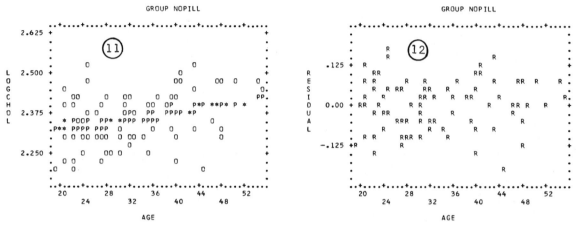

--- similar plots are printed for group PILL ---
--- similarly four plots are printed for HEIGHT and WEIGHT ---

```
PREDICTED DEPENDENT VAR. VS RESIDUALS FCR EACH GROUP.
```

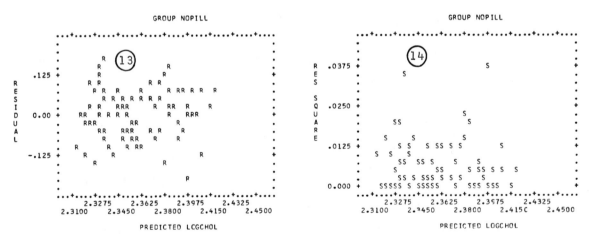

--- similar plots are printed for group PILL ---

In Example 15.4 we classify the cases according to four AGE groupings. The one-way analysis of covariance yields a highly significant F value for the test of equality of adjusted cell means (see Output 15.4). We are interested in knowing if the AGE effect is primarily linear or if it has a significant nonlinear component. Therefore in Example 15.4 we specify three CONTRASTs on the adjusted group means:

-3,	-1,	1,	3	linear effect
-1,	1,	1,	-1	quadratic effect
-1,	3,	-3,	1	cubic effect

These contrasts test hypotheses about the group means. (Although these contrasts are orthogonal in terms of their coefficients, their sums of squares may not be orthogonal if the number of observations differs between groups or if there are covariates.)

Example 15.4

```
/PROBLEM      TITLE IS 'WERNER BLOOD CHEMISTRY DATA'.
/INPUT        VARIABLES ARE 9.
              FORMAT IS '(A4,5F4.C,3F4.1)'.
/VARIABLE     NAMES ARE ID,AGE,HEIGHT,WEIGHT,BRTHPILL,
                  CHOLSTRL,ALBUMIN,CALCIUM,URICACID,
                  LOGCHOL.
              MAXIMUM IS (6)400.
              MINIMUM IS (6)150.
              BLANKS ARE MISSING.
              LABEL IS ID.
              ADD IS 1.
              GROUPING IS AGE.

/GROUP        CUTPOINTS(2) ARE      25,            35,            45.
              NAMES(2) ARE '25ORLESS', '26 TO 35', '36 TO 45', 'OVER 45'.

/TRANSFORM    LOGCHOL = LOG(CHOLSTRL).

/DESIGN       DEPENDENT IS LOGCHOL.
              INDEPENDENT ARE HEIGHT,WEIGHT.
              CONTRAST IS -3, -1,  1,  3.
              CONTRAST IS -1,  1,  1, -1.
              CONTRAST IS -1,  3, -3,  1.

/END
```

The results are presented in Output 15.4. The last panel in the results presents the contrast, its t value and the probability of exceeding t (P(T) is a two-tailed probability). The t value is computed as the ratio of $\Sigma\, c_m \hat{\mu}_m$ to its standard error where $c_1, c_2, \cdots$ are the coefficients in the contrast and $\hat{\mu}_1, \hat{\mu}_2, \cdots$ are the adjusted group means. The formula for the standard error is given in Appendix A.17.

DESIGN
  CONTRAST=#$_1$,#$_2$,$\cdots$.   {none}   may be repeated

   Coefficients used to define a contrast on the adjusted group means (or the group means if there are no covariates). CONTRAST= may be repeated in the *DESIGN* paragraph to specify additional contrasts on the adjusted group means. Each contrast is tested by a two-sided t test.

<u>Output 15.4</u> Testing specified contrasts with P1V. The results for the contrasts are in bottom right-hand panel.

```
                    CONTROL LANGUAGE TRANSFORMATIONS ARE

                        LOGCHOL  = LOG  (  CHOLSTRL )  .




                    GROUPING VARIABLE IS. . . . . . . . . . . . .AGE

                    NUMBER OF CASES READ. . . . . . . . . . . . .   188
                        CASES WITH DATA MISSING OR BEYOND LIMITS . .     8
                            REMAINING NUMBER OF CASES . . . . . . . .   180
                    NUMBER OF GROUPS FOUND. . . . . . . . . . . .     4

                            BEFORE TRANSFORMATION                      INTERVAL RANGE
                    VARIABLE   MINIMUM    MAXIMUM    MISSING   CATEGORY  CATEGORY   GREATER    LESS THAN
                    NO. NAME   LIMIT      LIMIT      CODE      CODE      NAME       THAN       OR EQUAL TO

                     2  AGE                                             25ORLESS              25.00000
                                                                       26 TO 35   25.00000   35.00000
                                                                       36 TO 45   35.00000   45.00000
                                                                       OVER 45    45.00000

                    NUMBER OF CASES PER GROUP
                    -------------------------
                    25ORLESS   50.
                    26 TO 35   59.
                    36 TO 45   41.
                    OVER 45    30.
                    TOTAL     180.


DEPENDENT VARIABLE IS  LOGCHOL
**********************************************************************************************************************


COVARIATE     REG.COEFF.    STD.ERR.      T-VALUE
  HEIGHT      -0.00183       0.00252      -0.72638
  WEIGHT       0.00037       0.00031       1.17551


GROUP       N        GRP.MEAN       ADJ.GRP.MEAN    STD.ERR.
  25ORLESS  50.       2.34059         2.34245       0.01059
  26 TO 35  59.       2.34643         2.34680       0.00960
  36 TO 45  41.       2.38815         2.38685       0.01157
  OVER 45   30.       2.41412         2.41206       0.01358


ANALYSIS OF VARIANCE

SOURCE OF VARIANCE          D.F.    SUM OF SQ.    MEAN SQ.    F-VALUE          TAIL AREA PROBABILITY


EQUALITY OF ADJ. CELL MEANS   3       0.1247       0.0416     7.6562              0.0001
ZERO SLOPE                    2       0.0077       0.0039     0.7103              0.4929
ERROR                       174       0.9446       0.0054

EQUALITY OF SLOPES            6       0.0144       0.0024     0.4341              0.8553
ERROR                       168       0.9302       0.0055


SLOPE WITHIN EACH GROUP                                       PROBABILITIES FOR THE T-VALUES ABOVE
-----------------------                                       -----------------------------------


               25ORLESS   26 TO 35   36 TO 45   OVER 45                 25ORLESS   26 TO 35   36 TO 45   OVER 45
                  1          2          3          4                        1          2          3          4

HEIGHT   3    -0.0016    -0.0044    -0.0059     0.0052       25ORLESS   1   1.0000
WEIGHT   4     0.0003     0.0003     0.0006     0.0003       26 TO 35   2   0.7611     1.0000
                                                            36 TO 45   3   0.0056     0.0085     1.0000
                                                            OVER 45    4   0.0001     0.0001     0.1564     1.0000
T-TEST MATRIX FOR ADJUSTED GROUP MEANS ON   174 DEGREES OF FREEDOM
-----------------------------------------------------------------
                                                            T-VALUES FOR CONTRASTS IN ADJUSTED GROUP MEANS
                                                            ---------------------------------------------

               25ORLESS   26 TO 35   36 TO 45   OVER 45
                  1          2          3          4        CONTRAST  GROUP     GROUP     GROUP     GROUP        T       P(T)
                                                            NUMBER   25ORLESS  26 TO 35  36 TO 45  OVER 45
25ORLESS   1    0.0
26 TO 35   2    0.3045     0.0                                  1    -3.0000   -1.0000    1.0000    3.0000    4.5542    0.0000
36 TO 45   3    2.8054     2.6611     0.0                       2    -1.0000    1.0000    1.0000   -1.0000   -0.9193    0.3592
OVER 45    4    3.9975     3.9191     1.4236     0.0             3    -1.0000    3.0000   -3.0000    1.0000   -1.0512    0.2946
```

- ADDITIONAL PRINTED RESULTS

   Additional results are requested in the *PRINT* paragraph in Example 15.5.

Example 15.5

```
/PROBLEM      TITLE IS 'WERNER BLOOD CHEMISTRY DATA'.
/INPUT        VARIABLES ARE 9.
              FORMAT IS '(A4,5F4.0,3F4.1)'.
/VARIABLE     NAMES ARE ID,AGE,HEIGHT,WEIGHT,BRTHPILL,
                      CHOLSTRL,ALBUMIN,CALCIUM,URICACID,
                      LOGCHOL.
              MAXIMUM IS (6)400.
              MINIMUM IS (6)150.
              BLANKS ARE MISSING.
              LABEL IS ID.
              ADD IS 1.
              GROUPING IS BRTHPILL.

/GROUP        CODES(5) ARE      1,    2.
              NAMES(5) ARE NOPILL, PILL.

/TRANSFORM    LOGCHOL = LOG(CHOLSTRL).

/DESIGN       DEPENDENT IS LOGCHOL.
              INDEPENDENT ARE AGE,HEIGHT,WEIGHT.

/PRINT        MAXIMUM.
              MINIMUM.
              MEAN.
              CORRELATION.
              TOTAL.
              BETWEEN.
              WITHIN.
              RREG.
              MCORRELATION.

/END
```

   The additional results are presented in Output 15.5. Circled numbers below correspond to those in the output.

(16) MINIMUM: The observed minimums for all variables in each group are printed.

(17) MAXIMUM: The observed maximums for all variables in each group are printed.

(18) MEAN: The means for all variables in each group are printed.

(19) CORRELATION: The correlations between all variables except the GROUPING variable in each group are printed. The covariances are printed if COVARIANCE is specified.

(20) TOTAL ⎫
(21) BETWEEN ⎬ are three variance-covariance matrices computed using all
            ⎪ variables (DEPENDENT and INDEPENDENT) in the analysis
(22) WITHIN ⎭

When TOTAL is specified, the variances and covariances are computed without regard to the grouping; that is, the sum of squares between two variables x and y is computed as

$$SS_{TOTAL} = \Sigma\,\Sigma\,(x_{ij} - \bar{x})(y_{ij} - \bar{y})$$

The number of degrees of freedom is N-1, where N is the number of cases.

When WITHIN is specified, the variances and covariances are computed from the pooled within-group sum of squares; that is

$$SS_{WITHIN} = \Sigma\,\Sigma\,(x_{ij} - \bar{x}_i)(y_{ij} - \bar{y}_i)$$

The number of degrees of freedom is N-g.

<u>Output 15.5</u> Optional results printed by P1V

```
CONTROL LANGUAGE TRANSFORMATIONS ARE
      LOGCHOL  = LOG (  CHOLSTRL )  .
```

```
NUMBER OF CASES PER GROUP
-------------------------
NOPILL      89.
PILL        91.
TOTAL      180.
```

```
OBSERVED MINIMA
---------------
```

(16)

		NOPILL 1	PILL 2
AGE	2	19.0000	19.0000
HEIGHT	3	57.0000	59.0000
WEIGHT	4	95.0000	94.0000
BRTHPILL	5	1.0000	2.0000
CHOLSTRL	6	155.0000	160.0000
ALBUMIN	7	3.2000	3.2000
CALCIUM	8	9.0000	8.8000
URICACID	9	2.7000	2.2000
LOGCHOL	10	2.1903	2.2041

```
OBSERVED MAXIMA
---------------
```

(17)

		NOPILL 1	PILL 2
AGE	2	55.0000	55.0000
HEIGHT	3	69.0000	71.0000
WEIGHT	4	195.0000	215.0000
BRTHPILL	5	1.0000	2.0000
CHOLSTRL	6	335.0000	390.0000
ALBUMIN	7	5.0000	4.7000
CALCIUM	8	11.1000	10.8000
URICACID	9	7.8000	9.9000
LOGCHOL	10	2.5250	2.5911

```
ESTIMATES OF MEANS
------------------
```

(18)

		NOPILL 1	PILL 2
AGE	2	32.9772	34.0876
HEIGHT	3	64.0559	64.8678
WEIGHT	4	129.4379	132.7140
BRTHPILL	5	1.0000	2.0000
CHOLSTRL	6	231.8873	239.7030
ALBUMIN	7	4.2056	4.0373
CALCIUM	8	9.9977	9.9384
URICACID	9	4.7382	4.7725
LOGCHOL	10	2.3576	2.3734

(continued)

Output 15.5 *(continued)*

CORRELATION MATRIX   GROUP NOPILL

<table>
<tr><td>⑲</td><td></td><td>AGE
2</td><td>HEIGHT
3</td><td>WEIGHT
4</td><td>CHOLSTRL
6</td><td>ALBUMIN
7</td><td>CALCIUM
8</td><td>URICACID
9</td><td>LOGCHOL
10</td></tr>
<tr><td>AGE</td><td>2</td><td>1.0000</td><td></td><td></td><td></td><td></td><td></td><td></td><td></td></tr>
<tr><td>HEIGHT</td><td>3</td><td>0.1088</td><td>1.0000</td><td></td><td></td><td></td><td></td><td></td><td></td></tr>
<tr><td>WEIGHT</td><td>4</td><td>0.2456</td><td>0.4278</td><td>1.0000</td><td></td><td></td><td></td><td></td><td></td></tr>
<tr><td>CHOLSTRL</td><td>6</td><td>0.4132</td><td>0.0303</td><td>0.0790</td><td>1.0000</td><td></td><td></td><td></td><td></td></tr>
<tr><td>ALBUMIN</td><td>7</td><td>-0.1350</td><td>C.1815</td><td>-0.2332</td><td>0.0505</td><td>1.0000</td><td></td><td></td><td></td></tr>
<tr><td>CALCIUM</td><td>8</td><td>-0.0904</td><td>C.2805</td><td>0.0374</td><td>0.3033</td><td>0.4731</td><td>1.0000</td><td></td><td></td></tr>
<tr><td>URICACID</td><td>9</td><td>0.2312</td><td>0.1205</td><td>0.2184</td><td>0.2843</td><td>0.1033</td><td>0.1482</td><td>1.0000</td><td></td></tr>
<tr><td>LOGCHOL</td><td>10</td><td>0.4048</td><td>0.0273</td><td>0.0787</td><td>0.9948</td><td>0.0333</td><td>0.2958</td><td>0.2634</td><td>1.0000</td></tr>
</table>

CORRELATION MATRIX   GROUP PILL

<table>
<tr><td></td><td></td><td>AGE
2</td><td>HEIGHT
3</td><td>WEIGHT
4</td><td>CHOLSTRL
6</td><td>ALBUMIN
7</td><td>CALCIUM
8</td><td>URICACID
9</td><td>LOGCHOL
10</td></tr>
<tr><td>AGE</td><td>2</td><td>1.0000</td><td></td><td></td><td></td><td></td><td></td><td></td><td></td></tr>
<tr><td>HEIGHT</td><td>3</td><td>0.0548</td><td>1.0000</td><td></td><td></td><td></td><td></td><td></td><td></td></tr>
<tr><td>WEIGHT</td><td>4</td><td>0.2578</td><td>0.5072</td><td>1.0000</td><td></td><td></td><td></td><td></td><td></td></tr>
<tr><td>CHOLSTRL</td><td>6</td><td>0.3137</td><td>-0.0397</td><td>0.1934</td><td>1.0000</td><td></td><td></td><td></td><td></td></tr>
<tr><td>ALBUMIN</td><td>7</td><td>-0.0062</td><td>-0.1133</td><td>-0.2158</td><td>0.1134</td><td>1.0000</td><td></td><td></td><td></td></tr>
<tr><td>CALCIUM</td><td>8</td><td>0.0784</td><td>0.0217</td><td>0.0992</td><td>0.2175</td><td>0.4301</td><td>1.0000</td><td></td><td></td></tr>
<tr><td>URICACID</td><td>9</td><td>0.1920</td><td>0.1296</td><td>0.3587</td><td>0.2695</td><td>-0.0185</td><td>0.1866</td><td>1.0000</td><td></td></tr>
<tr><td>LOGCHOL</td><td>10</td><td>0.3084</td><td>-0.0537</td><td>0.1885</td><td>0.9927</td><td>0.1154</td><td>0.2532</td><td>0.2573</td><td>1.0000</td></tr>
</table>

****
****

ESTIMATES OF MEANS

<table>
<tr><td></td><td></td><td>NOPILL
1</td><td>PILL
2</td><td>TOTAL
3</td></tr>
<tr><td>AGE</td><td>2</td><td>32.9772</td><td>34.0876</td><td>33.5385</td></tr>
<tr><td>HEIGHT</td><td>3</td><td>64.0559</td><td>64.8678</td><td>64.4663</td></tr>
<tr><td>WEIGHT</td><td>4</td><td>129.4379</td><td>132.7140</td><td>131.0941</td></tr>
<tr><td>LOGCHOL</td><td>10</td><td>2.3576</td><td>2.3734</td><td>2.3656</td></tr>
</table>

VARIANCE-COVARIANCE MATRIX   TOTAL

D.F.=   179.

<table>
<tr><td>⑳</td><td></td><td>AGE
2</td><td>HEIGHT
3</td><td>WEIGHT
4</td><td>LOGCHOL
10</td></tr>
<tr><td>AGE</td><td>2</td><td>97.9736</td><td></td><td></td><td></td></tr>
<tr><td>HEIGHT</td><td>3</td><td>2.1902</td><td>6.1609</td><td></td><td></td></tr>
<tr><td>WEIGHT</td><td>4</td><td>51.7948</td><td>24.0906</td><td>420.2422</td><td></td></tr>
<tr><td>LOGCHOL</td><td>10</td><td>0.2784</td><td>0.0011</td><td>0.2280</td><td>0.0061</td></tr>
</table>

VARIANCE-COVARIANCE MATRIX   BETWEEN

D.F.=   1.

<table>
<tr><td>㉑</td><td></td><td>AGE
2</td><td>HEIGHT
3</td><td>WEIGHT
4</td><td>LOGCHOL
10</td></tr>
<tr><td>AGE</td><td>2</td><td>55.4789</td><td></td><td></td><td></td></tr>
<tr><td>HEIGHT</td><td>3</td><td>40.5670</td><td>29.6632</td><td></td><td></td></tr>
<tr><td>WEIGHT</td><td>4</td><td>163.6814</td><td>119.6863</td><td>482.9153</td><td></td></tr>
<tr><td>LOGCHOL</td><td>10</td><td>0.7862</td><td>0.5749</td><td>2.3195</td><td>0.0111</td></tr>
</table>

VARIANCE-COVARIANCE MATRIX   WITHIN

D.F.=   178.

<table>
<tr><td>㉒</td><td></td><td>AGE
2</td><td>HEIGHT
3</td><td>WEIGHT
4</td><td>LOGCHOL
10</td></tr>
<tr><td>AGE</td><td>2</td><td>98.2124</td><td></td><td></td><td></td></tr>
<tr><td>HEIGHT</td><td>3</td><td>1.9746</td><td>6.0289</td><td></td><td></td></tr>
<tr><td>WEIGHT</td><td>4</td><td>51.1662</td><td>23.5536</td><td>419.8899</td><td></td></tr>
<tr><td>LOGCHOL</td><td>10</td><td>0.2756</td><td>-0.0021</td><td>0.2162</td><td>0.0061</td></tr>
</table>

CORRELATION MATRIX FOR THE REGRESSION COEFFICIENTS

<table>
<tr><td>㉓</td><td></td><td>AGE
2</td><td>HEIGHT
3</td><td>WEIGHT
4</td></tr>
<tr><td>AGE</td><td>2</td><td>1.0000</td><td></td><td></td></tr>
<tr><td>HEIGHT</td><td>3</td><td>0.0430</td><td>1.0000</td><td></td></tr>
<tr><td>WEIGHT</td><td>4</td><td>-0.2429</td><td>-0.4641</td><td>1.0000</td></tr>
</table>

CORRELATION MATRIX FOR THE ADJUSTED GROUP MEANS

<table>
<tr><td>㉔</td><td></td><td>NOPILL
1</td><td>PILL
2</td></tr>
<tr><td>NOPILL</td><td>1</td><td>1.0000</td><td></td></tr>
<tr><td>PILL</td><td>2</td><td>-0.0146</td><td>1.0000</td></tr>
</table>

--- analysis for CHOLSTRL appears here ---

The BETWEEN sum of squares is computed as the difference between the TOTAL and WITHIN sums of squares; that is,

$$SS_{BETWEEN} = SS_{TOTAL} - SS_{WITHIN}$$

The number of degrees of freedom is g-1.

(23) RREGRESSION: Correlations between the estimates of the regression coefficients (coefficients of the covariates) are printed.

(24) MCORRELATION: Correlations between the adjusted group means are printed.

PRINT

MINIMUM.   {no/prev.}

   Print minimums for all variables in each group.

MAXIMUM.   {no/prev.}

   Print maximums for all variables in each group.

MEAN.   {no/prev.}

   Print means for all variables in each group.

COVARIANCE.   {no/prev.}

   Print covariances between all variables in each group except the GROUPING variable.

CORRELATION.   {no/prev.}

   Print correlations between all variables in each group except the GROUPING variable.

TOTAL.   {no/prev.}

   Print variance-covariance matrix for the DEPENDENT and INDEPENDENT variables. It is computed with no grouping (see explanation above).

BETWEEN.   {no/prev.}

   Print variance-covariance matrix for the DEPENDENT and INDEPENDENT variables. It is computed from the difference between the total and pooled variance-covariance matrices (see explanation above).

WITHIN.   {no/prev.}

   Print variance-covariance matrix for the DEPENDENT and INDEPENDENT variables. It is computed from the pooled within-group sum of squares (see explanation above).

(continued)

PRINT

RREGRESSION.   {no/prev.}

Print correlations between the estimates of the coefficients of the covariates.[3]

MCORRELATION.   {no/prev.}

Print the correlations between the adjusted group means.

● SIZE OF PROBLEM

The maximum problem that can be analyzed depends on the number of groups (G) and the total number (V) of INDEPENDENT and DEPENDENT variables.

If V is less than or equal to	10	15	20	15	30
Then G can be as high as	58	27	13	27	3

Appendix B describes how to increase the capacity of the program.

● COMPUTATIONAL METHOD

All computations are performed in single precision. Means, standard deviations and covariances are computed by the method of provisional means (Appendix A.2). The computations performed by P1V are described in Appendix A.17.

ACKNOWLEDGEMENT

P1V was designed by Laszlo Engelman and programmed by Laszlo Engelman and Koji Yamasaki. It supersedes BMD01V and BMD09V; the latter program, designed by Laszlo Engelman, was the first program to use Control Language.

---

[3] If your BMDP programs are dated before August 1977, RCOR is used (not RREG).

P2V

15.2 Analysis of Variance and Covariance
Including Repeated Measures

Robert Jennrich, HSCF
Paul Sampson, HSCF

P2V performs an analysis of variance or covariance for a wide variety of fixed effects models and for repeated measures models with equal or unequal cell sizes. Fixed effects models that can be analyzed include factorial designs, Latin squares, fractional factorials, etc.; you can specify the analysis of variance components in the model.

In repeated measures models, repeated measurements are made of the same variable for each subject (or case). Split-plot models can be analyzed similarly; a plot is analogous to a subject. If there are two measurements for each subject, the analysis of the repeated measures factors is similar to a paired comparison t test. In a repeated measures model a distinction is made between variables that classify the cases into groups (grouping factors) and repeated measures of the same variable (trial factors). Grouping factors may be sex, race, disease or control-treatment. A trial factor might be the time of the measurement if a measurement is repeated on each subject at fixed intervals or a treatment factor if each subject receives each treatment. Grouping factors refer to "between subject" effects and trial factors refer to "within subject" effects. A basic reference for repeated measures models is Winer (1971). In split-plot designs, factors for main plot treatments are grouping factors and subplot factors are trial factors.

Repeated measures models are a special class of mixed models. The grouping and trial factors are all fixed effects factors. A factor for subject (cases), although not explicitly defined, is the only random effects factor. Each subject is observed at all combinations of the trial factors (i.e., is crossed with the trial factors), but at only one level of each grouping factor (i.e., is nested within the grouping factors).

P2V can analyze models that have grouping factors or trial factors or both. Other mixed models can be analyzed if the design is balanced (equal number of observations in each cell) and if you select the appropriate error term to test each analysis of variance component. Both the grouping factors and the trial factors must be crossed (not nested).

There are many aspects to the analysis of variance and covariance. We have chosen to present a number of the most frequently used designs:

Design

Grouping factors only (fixed effects models)

Two grouping factors	p.542
Two grouping factors and two covariates	p.546
Latin square	p.548
Incomplete block	p.549
Fractional factorial (2^{n-k})	p.549

Repeated measures designs

One grouping factor and one trial factor   p.549
Two grouping factors and one trial factor   p.552
Split-plot   p.555
One grouping factor and two trial factors   p.556
Two trial factors (no grouping factor)   p.559
One grouping factor, one trial factor and one covariate
    changing over trials   p.560
One grouping factor, one trial factor and one covariate
    that is constant over trials   p.562

One of the above designs may be similar to the design that you need. You can then skip the discussion of many of the other examples. We describe several examples in greater detail to explain the sums of squares and test statistics computed by P2V. If your example has any grouping factors we recommend that you read the first example, and if it has any repeated measures we recommend that you read the sixth example (one grouping factor and one trial factor).

When there are two or more trial factors, the factors must be crossed and each subject must be observed at <u>all</u> possible combinations of the trial factors. When there are two or more grouping factors, the grouping factors must also be crossed; i.e., the levels of a grouping factor must be repeated at all levels of the other grouping factor.

A covariate can be constant or it can vary across trials for a given subject. Covariates are assumed to be linearly related to the dependent variable.

A case consists of all the data for one subject (all its repeated measures are a case). There are two ways to specify a design for the analysis of variance (ANOVA) table. In the examples we illustrate both methods.

- One way uses the following Control Language item names:

  GROUPING   (the names or subscripts of the grouping factors)

  COVARIATES   (the names or subscripts of the covariates)

  DEPENDENT   (the names or subscripts of the dependent variables; when there are repeated measures (trial factors) each repeated measure is a dependent variable)

  LEVELS   (the number of levels (observations) of each trial factor)

- A second way to state the design is to specify a FORM statement. In the FORM statement G represents a grouping variable, Y the dependent variable, X a covariate and D a deleted variable (deleted variables are not used in the analysis).

- EXAMPLES

Two grouping factors

In the first example we analyze the systolic blood pressure data in Table 15.1 (Afifi and Azen, 1972, p. 166, and Kutner, 1974). There are two GROUPING factors, TREATMNT (called Drug by Kutner) and DISEASE -- with four TREATMNT groups and three DISEASE groups. Afifi and Azen and Kutner analyze the difference in systolic blood pressures (SYSINCR). In our example we use SYSINCR as the DEPENDENT variable in order to obtain the same results as Kutner; however, given the original data, one might alternatively analyze the percentage change in systolic blood pressure or perform an analysis of covariance on the final blood pressure with the original blood pressure as a covariate or perform the latter analysis using the logarithm of blood pressure.

<u>Table 15.1</u>   Data from Afifi and Azen (1972, p. 166) omitting the same cases as omitted by Kutner (1974)

TREATMENT	DISEASE	SYSINCR									
1	1	42	1	3	24	2	3	4	4	1	24
1	1	44	2	1	28	2	3	16	4	1	9
1	1	36	2	1	23	3	1	1	4	1	22
1	1	13	2	1	34	3	1	29	4	1	-2
1	1	19	2	1	42	3	1	19	4	1	15
1	1	22	2	1	13	3	2	11	4	2	27
1	2	33	2	2	34	3	2	9	4	2	12
1	2	26	2	2	33	3	2	7	4	2	12
1	2	33	2	2	31	3	2	1	4	2	-5
1	2	21	2	2	36	3	2	-6	4	2	16
1	3	31	2	3	3	3	3	21	4	2	15
1	3	-3	2	3	26	3	3	1	4	3	22
1	3	25	2	3	28	3	3	9	4	3	7
1	3	25	2	3	32	3	3	3	4	3	25
(cont'd)			*(cont'd)*			*(cont'd)*			4	3	5
									4	3	12

<u>Note:</u>   TREATMNT corresponds to drugs and is coded 1 to 4. DISEASE is coded 1 to 3. SYSINCR is the increase in systolic pressure (mmHg) due to treatment. TREATMNT is recorded in column 3, DISEASE in column 6 and SYSINCR in columns 8-9.

In the ANOVA table each grouping factor is identified by the first character of the grouping variable name; therefore the two grouping variables are given names that begin with different letters. The Control Language instructions are presented in Example 15.6. Only the *DESIGN* paragraph is specific to P2V. The other Control Language instructions are explained in Chapter 5.

Example 15.6

```
/PROBLEM      TITLE IS 'KUTNER SYSTOLIC BLOOD PRESSURE DATA'.
/INPUT        VARIABLES ARE 3.
              FORMAT IS '(3F3.0)'.
/VARIABLE     NAMES ARE TREATMNT,DISEASE,SYSINCR.

/DESIGN       DEPENDENT IS SYSINCR.
              GROUPING ARE TREATMNT,DISEASE.

/GROUP        CODES(1) ARE       1,     2,     3,     4.
              NAMES(1) ARE DRUG1, DRUG2, DRUG3, DRUG4.
              CODES(2) ARE           1,      2,      3.
              NAMES(2) ARE DISEASE1, DISEASE2, DISEASE3.

/END
```

The Control Language must be preceded by System Cards to initiate the analysis by P2V.
At HSCF, the System Cards are

```
//jobname  JOB  nooo,yourname
//   EXEC  BIMED,PROG=BMDP2V
//SYSIN DD  *
```

The Control Language is immediately followed by the data (Table 15.1). The analysis
is terminated by another System Card. At HSCF, this System Card is

```
//
```

If the FORM statement is used, the *DESIGN* paragraph is written

/DESIGN FORM IS '2G,Y'.

2G specifies that the first two variables are grouping factors, and Y specifies that the third variable is the dependent variable.

The results are presented in Output 15.6. Circled numbers below correspond to those in the output.

(1) The *DESIGN* paragraph is interpreted by P2V.

(2) Number of cases read. Only cases containing acceptable values for all
variables specified in the *DESIGN* paragraph are used in the analysis.
An acceptable value is a value that is not missing or out of range.
In addition, if CODEs are specified for any GROUPING factors (variables),
a case is included only if the value of the GROUPING factor is equal
to a specified CODE.

(3) The frequency (COUNT) of observations in each cell is printed.

(4) The mean, frequency and standard deviation of each cell for each dependent
variable are printed.

(5) An ANOVA table is printed.

The sums of squares in the one-way ANOVA are well known. The sums of
squares in the two-way, or higher, ANOVA depend upon the hypothesis of
interest unless each cell contains the same number of observations. The
hypotheses tested by P2V are the same for equal or unequal cell size problems,
and are not affected by losing some of the cases. Although the hypotheses
tested are independent, the sums of squares for unequal cell size problems

Output 15.6 A two-way analysis of variance by P2V. Circled numbers correspond to those in the text. Results not reproduced are indicated in italics.

```
BMDP2V - ANALYSIS OF VARIANCE AND COVARIANCE,           PROGRAM REVISED SEPTEMBER 1977
          INCLUDING REPEATED MEASURES                   MANUAL DATE --  1977
HEALTH SCIENCES COMPUTING FACILITY
UNIVERSITY OF CALIFORNIA, LOS ANGELES
```

--- Control Language read by P2V is printed and interpreted ---

DESIGN SPECIFICATIONS

(1)

```
        GROUP =    1   2
        DEPEND =   3
```

		BEFORE TRANSFORMATION					INTERVAL RANGE	
VARIABLE NO. NAME		MINIMUM LIMIT	MAXIMUM LIMIT	MISSING CODE	CATEGORY CODE	CATEGORY NAME	GREATER THAN	LESS THAN OR EQUAL TO
1	TREATMNT				1.00000 2.00000 3.00000 4.00000	DRUG1 DRUG2 DRUG3 DRUG4		
2	DISEASE				1.00000 2.00000 3.00000	DISEASE1 DISEASE2 DISEASE3		

(2) NUMBER OF CASES READ. 58

(3) GROUP STRUCTURE

TREATMNT	DISEASE	COUNT
DRUG1	DISEASE1	6.
DRUG1	DISEASE2	4.
DRUG1	DISEASE3	5.
DRUG2	DISEASE1	5.
DRUG2	DISEASE2	4.
DRUG2	DISEASE3	6.
DRUG3	DISEASE1	3.
DRUG3	DISEASE2	5.
DRUG3	DISEASE3	4.
DRUG4	DISEASE1	5.
DRUG4	DISEASE2	6.
DRUG4	DISEASE3	5.

(4) CELL MEANS FOR 1-ST DEPENDENT VARIABLE

TREATMNT= DISEASE =	DRUG1 DISEASE1	DRUG1 DISEASE2	DRUG1 DISEASE3	DRUG2 DISEASE1	DRUG2 DISEASE2	DRUG2 DISEASE3	DRUG3 DISEASE1	DRUG3 DISEASE2	DRUG3 DISEASE3	DRUG4 DISEASE1
SYSINCR	29.33333	28.25000	20.39999	28.00000	33.50000	18.16666	16.33333	4.40000	8.50000	13.60000
COUNT	6	4	5	5	4	6	3	5	4	5

		MARGINAL	
TREATMNT= DISEASE =	DRUG4 DISEASE2	DRUG4 DISEASE3	
SYSINCR	12.83333	14.20000	18.87930
COUNT	6	5	58

STANDARD DEVIATIONS FOR 1-ST DEPENDENT VARIABLE

TREATMNT= DISEASE =	DRUG1 DISEASE1	DRUG1 DISEASE2	DRUG1 DISEASE3	DRUG2 DISEASE1	DRUG2 DISEASE2	DRUG2 DISEASE3	DRUG3 DISEASE1	DRUG3 DISEASE2	DRUG3 DISEASE3	DRUG4 DISEASE1
SYSINCR	13.01793	5.85235	13.37161	10.97725	2.08167	12.52863	14.18919	6.91375	9.00000	10.54988

TREATMNT= DISEASE =	DRUG4 DISEASE2	DRUG4 DISEASE3
SYSINCR	10.34247	8.92748

(5) ANALYSIS OF VARIANCE FOR 1-ST DEPENDENT VARIABLE - SYSINCR

SOURCE	SUM OF SQUARES	DEGREES OF FREEDOM	MEAN SQUARE	F	TAIL PROBABILITY
MEAN	20037.49219	1	20037.49219	181.41	0.000
T	2997.42969	3	999.14307	9.05	0.000
D	415.86719	2	207.93359	1.88	0.164
TD	707.24609	6	117.87434	1.07	0.396
ERROR	5080.77734	46	110.45168		

are not in general orthogonal. Orthogonal sums of squares methods (or "sequential" methods) test hypotheses that are functions of cell sizes; P2V does not use a sequential method. For more detailed discussions, see Kutner (1974) and Speed and Hocking (1976). (The hypotheses tested by P2V for the main effects are labelled A and B by Kutner and H1 and H2 by Speed and Hocking.) They, as well as others, recommend these hypotheses for experimental data. Searle (1971, pp. 316-317) points out that sequential methods test hypotheses that depend on the cell sizes and cautions against their use.

Hypotheses tested. In our example of a two-way ANOVA, let $E(Y_{ij}) = \mu_{ij}$ where Y_{ij} is an observation of the group (i,j). The test of equality of row means is the test that

$$\Sigma_j \; \mu_{ij} = \Sigma_j \; \mu_{kj} \quad \text{for all } i,k.$$

The test of equality of column means is the test that

$$\Sigma_i \; \mu_{ij} = \Sigma_i \; \mu_{i\ell} \quad \text{for all } j,\ell.$$

The test of no interaction is the test that

$$\mu_{ij} + \mu_{k\ell} = \mu_{i\ell} + \mu_{kj} \quad \text{for all } i \neq k \text{ and } j \neq \ell.$$

The test labelled MEAN is the test that

$$\Sigma_i \; \Sigma_j \; \mu_{ij} = 0.$$

The test for MEAN is usually not of interest unless the dependent variable is the difference between two measurements.

If the model is written

$$E(Y_{ij}) = \mu + \alpha_i + \beta_j + \gamma_{ij}$$

with the usual constraints

$$\Sigma_i \; \alpha_i = 0, \quad \Sigma_j \; \beta_j = 0, \quad \Sigma_i \; \gamma_{ij} = \Sigma_j \; \gamma_{ij} = 0,$$

the hypotheses described above can also be stated as

$$\alpha_i = 0 \quad \text{for all } i$$
$$\beta_j = 0 \quad \text{for all } j$$
$$\gamma_{ij} = 0 \quad \text{for all } i,j$$

and

$$\mu = 0$$

respectively.

Computationally P2V obtains each sum of squares as the difference in the residual sums of squares of two regression models. For each grouping variable with ℓ levels P2V generates $(\ell-1)$ dummy variables. Interactions between grouping variables are represented by the products of their dummy variables. P2V first fits the regression model containing all the dummy variables for the grouping variables and their interactions and then the model containing all dummy variables but those of the main effect or interaction being tested; the difference between residual sums of squares of the two models is the sums of squares reported. A more detailed computational procedure is provided in Appendix A.18.

You can specify the effects or interactions of the grouping variables to be included in the model. Specification of the model is described on p. 571.

Two grouping factors and two covariates

In the second example we analyze the logarithm of CHOLSTRL (LOGCHOL) from the Werner blood chemistry data (Table 5.1). We specify that the COVARIATES are the logarithms of height (LOGHGHT) and of weight (LOGWGHT). The logarithms are obtained by Control Language transformations in the *TRANSform* paragraph and the three logarithms are ADDED as new variables in the *VARiable* paragraph. The two GROUPING factors are AGE (four age groupings) and BRTHPILL (two levels).

Example 15.7

```
/PROBLEM       TITLE IS 'WERNER BLOOD CHEMISTRY DATA'.
/INPUT         VARIABLES ARE 9.
               FORMAT IS '(A4,5F4.0,3F4.1)'.
/VARIABLE      NAMES ARE ID,AGE,HEIGHT,WEIGHT,BRTHPILL,
                  CHOLSTRL,ALBUMIN,CALCIUM,URICACID,
                  LOGHGHT,LOGWGHT,LOGCHOL.
               MAXIMUM IS (6)400.
               MINIMUM IS (6)150.
               BLANKS ARE MISSING.
               LABEL IS ID.
               ADD IS 3.

/TRANSFORM     LOGHGHT = LOG(HEIGHT).
               LOGWGHT = LOG(WEIGHT).
               LOGCHOL = LOG(CHOLSTRL).

/DESIGN        DEPENDENT IS LOGCHOL.
               GROUPING ARE AGE,BRTHPILL.
               COVARIATES ARE LOGHGHT,LOGWGHT.

/GROUP         CODES(5) ARE        1,    2.
               NAMES(5) ARE NOPILL, PILL.
               CUTPOINTS(2) ARE    25,         35,         45.
               NAMES(2) ARE '250RLESS', '26 TO 35', '36 TO 45', 'OVER 45'.

/END
```

Using the FORM statement, the *DESIGN* paragraph is written

/DESIGN FORM IS 'D,G,2D,G,4D,2X,Y'.

The first D deletes the first variable. The second variable (AGE) is used as a grouping factor. The third and fourth variables are also deleted. The fifth variable (BRTHPILL) is another grouping factor. The four blood chemistry measurements (variables 6 to 9) are deleted. Two new variables (10 and 11), LOGHGHT and LOGWGHT, are used as covariates. The twelfth variable (LOGCHOL) is the dependent variable.

The results are presented in Output 15.7. Circled numbers below correspond to those in the output.

⑥ Analysis of covariance for each dependent variable. The model for this analysis of covariance can be written as

$$E(y_{ij}) = \mu_{ij} + \beta_1(x_{1ij}-\bar{x}_1) + \beta_2(x_{2ij}-\bar{x}_2)$$

or equivalently

$$E(y_{ij}) = \mu + \alpha_i + \gamma_j + (\alpha\gamma)_{ij} + \beta_1(x_{1ij}-\bar{x}_1) + \beta_2(x_{2ij}-\bar{x}_2)$$

where α_i and γ_j represent the main effects and $(\alpha\gamma)_{ij}$ the interaction of the grouping variables and β_1 and β_2 are the coefficients of the covariates. The usual constraints apply to α_i, γ_j and $(\alpha\gamma)_{ij}$.

<u>Output 15.7</u> Two-way analysis of variance with two covariates by P2V

```
        CONTROL LANGUAGE TRANSFORMATIONS ARE


            LOGHGHT   = LOG  (    HEIGHT  )  .
            LOGWGHT   = LOG  (    WEIGHT  )  .
            LOGCHOL   = LOG  (    CHOLSTRL )  .




     DESIGN SPECIFICATIONS

            GROUP =    2    5
            DEPEND =   12
            COVAR =    10   11



        NUMBER OF CASES READ. . . . . . . . . . . . .      188
          CASES WITH DATA MISSING OR BEYOND LIMITS . .        6
              REMAINING NUMBER OF CASES . . . . . . . .      182

     GROUP STRUCTURE

     AGE         BRTHPILL      COUNT
     25ORLESS    NOPILL        26.
     25ORLESS    PILL          24.
     26 TO 35    NOPILL        30.
     26 TO 35    PILL          29.
     36 TO 45    NOPILL        20.
     36 TO 45    PILL          21.
     OVER 45     NOPILL        15.
     OVER 45     PILL          17.
```

ANALYSIS OF VARIANCE FOR 1-ST DEPENDENT VARIABLE - LOGCHOL

⑥

SOURCE	SUM OF SQUARES	DEGREES OF FREEDOM	MEAN SQUARE	F	TAIL PROBABILITY	BETA ESTIMATES
MEAN	0.10079	1	0.10079	18.62	0.000	
A	0.12990	3	0.04330	8.00	0.000	
B	0.00321	1	0.00321	0.59	0.442	
AB	0.01733	3	0.00578	1.07	0.364	
1-ST COVAR	0.00354	1	0.00354	0.65	0.420	-0.31080
2-ND COVAR	0.00928	1	0.00928	1.71	0.192	0.13247
ALL COVARIATES	0.00944	2	0.00472	0.87	0.420	
ERROR	0.93121	172	0.00541			

⑦ ADJUSTED CELL MEANS FOR 1-ST DEPENDENT VARIABLE

AGE =	25ORLESS	25ORLESS	26 TO 35	26 TO 35	36 TO 45	36 TO 45	OVER 45	OVER 45
BRTHPILL=	NOPILL	PILL	NOPILL	PILL	NOPILL	PILL	NOPILL	PILL
LOGCHOL	2.33968	2.34620	2.32726	2.36694	2.38733	2.38634	2.41828	2.40799

The hypotheses tested are independent, but the sums of squares may not be orthogonal. For example, the sums of squares for each covariate do not add up to the sum of squares for all covariates. The sum of squares used in the test of each hypothesis (each covariate, all covariates, each analysis of variance component) can be obtained as the difference in the residual sums of squares of two models; one in which all covariates and effects are fitted and the other in which the covariate(s) or effect of interest is set to zero.

See the previous problem for a more detailed discussion of the hypotheses tested.

The beta estimates are estimates of the coefficients of the covariates when all effects and covariates in the model are fitted.

⑦ Adjusted cell means. The adjusted mean for cell (i,j) is

$$\hat{\mu}_{ij} = \bar{Y}_{ij} + \hat{\beta}_1 (\bar{x}_1 - \bar{x}_{1ij}) + \hat{\beta}_2(\bar{x}_2 - \bar{x}_{2ij}) + \ldots$$

where $\bar{Y}_{ij}$, $\bar{x}_{1ij}$, $\bar{x}_{2ij}$ are means computed for cell $(i.j)$, $\bar{x}_1$ and $\bar{x}_2$ are means computed for all cases, and $\hat{\beta}_1$ and $\hat{\beta}_2$ are the least squares estimates of β_1 and β_2. That is, an adjusted cell mean is the mean of the dependent variable adjusted for covariates, evaluated using grand means of the covariates. The regression coefficients are assumed to be constant across groups and trials when the adjusted cell means are computed.

Latin square

Cochran and Cox (1957, p. 121) give an example of a 6x6 Latin square. Data can be read into P2V as four variables. The first three specify the levels of the factors (or grouping variables) and the fourth is the dependent variable. The design can be specified as

```
/DESIGN GROUPING ARE 1,2,3.
        DEPENDENT IS 4.
```
or as
```
/DESIGN FORM IS '3G,Y'.
```

P2V fits the data by a full factorial model (all main effects and interactions) in the grouping factors unless you specify otherwise. For a Latin square design the model will usually contain only main effects. You can state in the *DESIGN* paragraph either the effects <u>included</u> in the model

```
INCLUDED ARE 1,2,3.
```

or the effects <u>excluded</u> from the model

```
EXCLUDED ARE 12,13,23,123.
```

The choice between the two statements is a matter of convenience. Indices in the INCLUDE and EXCLUDE statements refer to the sequential order of the grouping variables (<u>not</u> to the subscripts of the grouping variables). For example, if the subscripts of the grouping variables were 2, 3 and 4, we still would write

```
INCLUDED ARE 1,2,3.
```

Incomplete blocks

John (1971, p. 135) discusses an example of a partially confounded incomplete block design. There are eight blocks. Each block contains observations at four combinations of the levels of three treatment (grouping) factors. Suppose the data are recorded as five variables such that the first variable is the block number, the next three are the levels (1 or 2) of the three treatment factors, and the last variable is the response (observation). The design can be specified either as

      /DESIGN GROUPING ARE 1 TO 4.
              DEPENDENT IS 5.
or

      /DESIGN FORM IS '4G,Y'.

As in the Latin square design above, the effects in the model must be specified; otherwise the model has more parameters than can be estimated. For John's example we specify

      INCLUDED ARE 1, 2, 3, 4, 23, 24, 34, 234.

The model contains the main effect for block, and all main effects and interactions of the three treatment factors; the model does not contain any interactions of the block effect with treatment effects.

Fractional factorial 2^{n-k}

A fractional factorial design is specified in a manner similar to the incomplete block design. John (1971, p. 154) gives a numerical example of a 2^{4-1} design where the mean effect is confounded with the fourth order interaction. Suppose the data are recorded as five variables, four design variables (grouping factors) and the dependent variable. The design is then specified either as

      /DESIGN GROUPING ARE 1 TO 4.
              DEPENDENT IS 5.
or

      /DESIGN FORM IS '4G,Y'.

In addition, the effects in the model must be specified; otherwise the model would have more parameters than could be estimated. The model for the above design contains all main effects (they are confounded with third order interactions) and three two-factor interactions (each is confounded with a second two-factor interaction). Therefore we describe the model to P2V as

      INCLUDED ARE 1,2,3,4,12,13,23.

● EXAMPLES OF REPEATED MEASURES DESIGNS

One grouping factor and one trial factor

The data (Table 15.2) are from Winer (1971, p. 525). Six subjects are divided into two groups according to the <u>method</u> (the grouping factor) used to

Table 15.2 Numerical example from Winer (1971, p. 525)

a	b₁	b₂	b₃	b₄
1	0	0	5	3
1	3	1	5	4
1	4	3	6	2
2	4	2	7	8
2	5	4	6	6
2	7	5	8	9

Note: There are two groups (a=1 and a=2). b_1, b_2, b_3, b_4
are the repeated measures for each subject (case).
The data are recorded in columns 2, 4, 6, 8 and 10
for each case.

calibrate dials. Each subject has four accuracy scores, one for each <u>shape</u>
(the trial factor) of the dials. The data for each subject comprise a case.
The analysis of the data is requested in Example 15.8.

Example 15.8

```
/PROBLEM      TITLE IS 'WINER, PAGE 525, CALIBRATION OF DIALS'.
/INPUT        VARIABLES ARE 5.
              FORMAT IS '(5F2.0)'.
/VARIABLE     NAMES ARE METHOD,ACCURCY1,ACCURCY2,ACCURCY3,ACCURCY4.

/DESIGN       DEPENDENT ARE 2 TO 5.
              LEVEL IS 4.
              GROUPING IS METHOD.
              NAME IS SHAPE.

/END
    1 0 0 5 3
    1 3 1 5 4
    1 4 3 6 2
    2 4 2 7 8
    2 5 4 6 6
    2 7 5 8 9
```

Control
Language
instructions

data

In the *DESIGN* paragraph, LEVEL=4 specifies that there are four levels
to the trial factor. Each case contains the value of the GROUPING variable
and values for <u>all</u> the trials on a subject.

Using the FORM statement, the *DESIGN* paragraph is written

```
/DESIGN FORM IS 'G,4(Y)'.
        NAME IS SHAPE.
```

G specifies that the first variable is a GROUPING factor, and 4(Y) that the
next four variables contain the values of the dependent variables (the four
levels of the trial factor SHAPE). (If 4Y is written, instead of 4(Y), the
four variables are considered to be different dependent variables, each of
which is analyzed by a separate ANOVA.)

The analysis of variance table is presented in Output 15.8.

The model for this repeated measures design is

$$y_{ijk} = \mu + \alpha_i + \pi_{k(i)} + \beta_j + (\alpha\beta)_{ij} + (\beta\pi)_{jk(i)}$$

where

α_i represents the grouping factor

$\pi_{k(i)}$ represents subjects within the grouping factor (used to obtain the error term for the grouping factor)

β_j represents the trial factor

$(\alpha\beta)_{ij}$ represents the interaction between the grouping and trial factors

and $(\beta\pi)_{jk(i)}$ represents the interaction of subjects and trial factor within the grouping factor (used to obtain the error term for the trial factor and for the interaction of subject and trial factor).

We have the usual constraints that α_i, $\pi_{k(i)}$, β_j, $(\alpha\beta)_{ij}$, and $(\beta\pi)_{jk(i)}$ each sums to zero on every index. An error term $\epsilon_{m(ijk)}$ can be added to the above model to represent experimental error within the individual observation; however, it cannot be estimated independently of $(\beta\pi)_{jk(i)}$. Winer (1971, p. 518) describes this model in more detail.

Explanation of a repeated measures analysis. Suppose there are only two measures Y_1 and Y_2 in each case (subject); i.e., the design has one trial factor with two levels. P2V computes two analyses of variance. The first is to test whether the expectation of the sum $P_0 = (Y_1+Y_2)/\sqrt{2}$ is zero. The second is to test whether the expectation of the difference $P_1 = (Y_1-Y_2)/\sqrt{2}$ is zero. This latter test is equivalent to a paired comparison t test (as computed by P3D, Section 9.1). (The denominator, $\sqrt{2}$, is chosen so that the sum of the squares of the coefficients is one.)

Output 15.8 One grouping factor and one trial factor analyzed by P2V. Only the ANOVA table is shown.

```
    DESIGN SPECIFICATIONS

          GROUP  =    1
          DEPEND =    2    3    4    5
          LEVEL  =    4


    NUMBER CF CASES READ. . . . . . . . . . . . .        6


    GROUP STRUCTURE

      METHOD        CCUNT
    *  1.0000         3.
    *  2.0000         3.
```

ANALYSIS CF VARIANCE FOR 1-ST CEPENDENT VARIABLE – ACCURCY1 ACCURCY2 ACCURCY3 ACCURCY4

SOURCE	SUM OF SQUARES	DEGREES OF FREEDOM	MEAN SQUARE	F	TAIL PROBABILITY
MEAN	477.04126	1	477.04126	111.15	0.000
M	51.04150	1	51.04150	11.89	0.026
ERROR	17.16672	4	4.29168		
S	47.45828	3	15.81943	12.80	0.000
SM	7.45830	3	2.48610	2.01	0.166
ERROR	14.83333	12	1.23611		

Now suppose we have two groups of subjects and two measures (one trial factor) for each subject. P2V again computes the sums $P_0 = (Y_1+Y_2)/\sqrt{2}$ and the differences $P_1 = (Y_1-Y_2)/\sqrt{2}$ of the two repeated measures. Two analyses of variance tables are printed by P2V. The first table is an analysis of P_0; it contains a test for the grand mean of P_0 (labelled MEAN in the results) and a test of equality of means between the two groups (a test of the group effect). The latter test is equivalent to a two-sample t test to compare the two group means for P_0. The second analysis of variance table is an analysis of P_1; it contains a test of the mean of P_1 (a test of the trial factor) and the second tests the equality of means for P_1 between the two groups (a test of the interaction between the grouping and trial factors).

Now suppose there is one grouping factor and one trial factor with three levels (repeated measures). The data will contain four variables for each subject or case -- the value of the grouping factor and three values for the dependent variable (Y_1, Y_2 and Y_3). Again P2V computes two analyses of variance. The first is for $P_0 = (Y_1+Y_2+Y_3)/\sqrt{3}$. The second can be decomposed into two parts: $P_1 = (Y_1-Y_3)/\sqrt{2}$ and $P_2 = (Y_1-2Y_2+Y_3)/\sqrt{6}$. P_1 and P_2 are the orthogonal polynomial decomposition of Y_1, Y_2, Y_3 into linear and quadratic components. (P_0 is the mean.) An analysis of variance is performed for both P_1 and P_2, but the individual analyses are not printed unless ORTHOGONAL is stated in the *DESIGN* paragraph. P2V pools the results for P_1 and P_2 by adding the sums of squares for each effect from the individual analyses. Similarly, the error sum of squares is the sum of the error sums of squares for P_1 and P_2. (We show the individual analyses in Output 15.10 .)

The ANOVA table in Output 15.8 is in two parts. The top part is the analysis of $P_0 = (Y_1+Y_2+Y_3+Y_4)/\sqrt{4}$. MEAN provides a test that the mean of P_0 is zero, which is usually not of interest. M (the first letter of METHOD) is the grouping factor; the test for M is a test of equality between the two groups defined by the grouping factor. The first ERROR reports the within-group sum of squares for P_0.

The second part of the ANOVA table presents the analysis of the trial factor (S for SHAPE) and the interaction of the trial and grouping factor (SM). As explained above, the analysis is by an orthogonal decomposition into

$$P_1 = (3Y_1+Y_2-Y_3-3Y_4)/\sqrt{20}$$
$$P_2 = (Y_1-Y_2-Y_3+Y_4)/\sqrt{4}$$
$$P_3 = (Y_1-3Y_2+3Y_3-Y_4)/\sqrt{20}$$

each of which is analyzed separately and then the sums of squares are pooled.

Two grouping factors and one trial factor

The data (Table 15.3) are from Winer (1971, p. 564). There are two GROUPING factors, ANXIETY and TENSION -- each has two levels. The experiment is repeated four times for each subject (called blocks of trials by Winer and NAMED B in Example 15.9); the number of ERRORs is recorded as the DEPENDENT variable. The data for each subject comprise a case.

Table 15.3 Numerical example from Winer (1971, p. 564)

a	b	c_1	c_2	c_3	c_4
1	1	18	14	12	6
1	1	19	12	8	4
1	1	14	10	6	2
1	2	16	12	10	4
1	2	12	8	6	2
1	2	18	10	5	1
2	1	16	10	8	4
2	1	18	8	4	1
2	1	16	12	6	2
2	2	19	16	10	8
2	2	16	14	10	9
2	2	16	12	8	8

Note: There are two grouping factors (a and b) each having
two levels. c_1, c_2, c_3, c_4 are the repeated measures
for each subject (case). The data are recorded in
columns 3, 6, 8-9, 11-12, 14-15 and 17-18.

Example 15.9

```
/PROBLEM      TITLE IS 'WINER, PAGE 564, LEARNING DATA'.
/INPUT        VARIABLES ARE 6.
              FORMAT IS '(6F3.0)'.
/VARIABLE     NAMES ARE ANXIETY,TENSION,ERRORS1,
                  ERRORS2,ERRORS3,ERRORS4.

/DESIGN       GROUPING ARE ANXIETY,TENSION.
              DEPENDENT ARE 3 TO 6.
              LEVEL IS 4.
              NAME IS B.

/GROUP        CODES(1) ARE     1,     2.
              NAMES(1) ARE   LOW, HIGH.
              CODES(2) ARE     1,     2.
              NAMES(2) ARE NONE, HIGH.

/END
```

*Control
Language
instructions*

```
1  1 18 14 12  6
1  1 19 12  8  4
1  1 14 10  6  2
1  2 16 12 10  4
1  2 12  8  6  2
1  2 18 10  5  1
2  1 16 10  8  4
2  1 18  8  4  1
2  1 16 12  6  2
2  2 19 16 10  8
2  2 16 14 10  9
2  2 16 12  8  8
```

data

Using the FORM statement, the *DESIGN* paragraph is written

```
/DESIGN FORM IS '2G,4(Y)'.
        NAME IS B.
```

The first two variables are GROUPING factors and the next four contain the
values of the dependent variable at the four levels of the trial factor.

The ANOVA table is presented in Output 15.9. There are two panels. In
the upper panel the grouping main effects and their interaction are tested;
this analysis is similar to that explained for Example 15.6 above, where

$$P_0 = (Y_1 + Y_2 + Y_3 + Y_4)/\sqrt{4}$$

is analyzed as the dependent variable. The analysis in the lower panel is
similar to that described for Example 15.8 above.

The analysis in the lower panel can be better understood if we add ORTHOGONAL   to the Control Language instructions.

Example 15.10

```
/PROBLEM       TITLE IS 'WINER, PAGE 564, LEARNING DATA'.
/INPUT         VARIABLES ARE 6.
               FORMAT IS '(6F3.0)'.
/VARIABLE      NAMES ARE ANXIETY,TENSION,ERRORS1,
                         ERRORS2,ERRORS3,ERRORS4.

/DESIGN        GROUPING ARE ANXIETY,TENSION.
               DEPENDENT ARE 3 TO 6.
               LEVEL IS 4.
               NAME IS B.
               ORTHOGONAL.

/GROUP         CODES(1) ARE    1,    2.
               NAMES(1) ARE  LOW, HIGH.
               CODES(2) ARE    1,    2.
               NAMES(2) ARE NONE, HIGH.

/END
```

The ANOVA table in Output 15.10 contains the analysis of the orthogonal components. The first and last panels are identical to those in Output 15.9. The second panel contains the sums of squares for the analysis of the linear component, B(1), the third panel that of the quadratic component, B(2), and the fourth panel that of the cubic component, B(3). Each sum of squares in the last panel is the sum of the sums of squares in the corresponding lines of the middle three panels.

Split-plot Designs

The above repeated measures analysis (Example 15.9) can also be used to obtain a split-plot analysis when the two grouping factors are the main plot or whole plot treatments and the trial factor is the subplot treatment. Often one of the main plot effects is a blocking factor. The repeated measures model described above contains an interaction of the blocking effect with the subplot treatment. If this interaction is assumed to be zero and the design is balanced (the same number of observations in each cell), you can pool the sum of squares of this interaction with the error sum of squares. For example, Snedecor and Cochran (1967, p. 370) consider a split-plot design with randomized blocks. The model is

$$Y_{ijk} = \mu + M_i + B_j + e_{ij} + T_k + (MT)_{ik} + d_{ijk}$$

where M is a main plot treatment, B is a block effect, T is a subplot treatment, e is the main plot error and d is the subplot error. If the main plot treatment (M) is recorded as the first variable, the block effect (B) as the second and subplots as the levels (say 4) of the trial factor (as described for the above repeated measures model), then the *DESIGN* paragraph may be written as

```
/DESIGN   GROUPING ARE 1,2.
          DEPENDENT ARE 3 TO 6.
          LEVEL IS 4.
          NAME IS S.
          EXCLUDE IS 12.
```

Output 15.9   Two grouping factors and one trial factor analyzed by P2V. Only the ANOVA table is shown.

```
DESIGN SPECIFICATICNS

        GRCUP =    1    2
        DEPEND =   3    4    5    6
        LEVEL =    4


    NUMBER CF CASES READ. . . . . . . . . . . . .      12


GROUP STRUCTURE

    ANXIETY    TENSION    COUNT
    LOW        NONE       3.
    LOW        HIGH       3.
    HIGH       NONE       3.
    HIGH       HIGH       3.
```

ANALYSIS OF VARIANCE FOR 1-ST DEPENDENT VARIABLE - ERRORS1 ERRORS2 ERRORS3 ERRORS4

SOURCE	SUM OF SQUARES	DEGREES OF FREEDOM	MEAN SQUARE	F	TAIL PROBABILITY
MEAN	4800.00000	1	4800.00000	465.45	0.000
A	10.08331	1	10.08331	0.98	0.352
T	8.33333	1	8.33333	0.81	0.395
AT	80.08318	1	80.08318	7.77	0.024
ERROR	82.50000	8	10.31250		
B	991.49829	3	330.49927	152.05	0.000
BA	8.41660	3	2.80553	1.29	0.300
BT	12.16658	3	4.05553	1.87	0.162
BAT	12.75002	3	4.25000	1.96	0.148
ERROR	52.16653	24	2.17360		

Output 15.10   Decomposition of the ANOVA table in Output 15.9

```
DESIGN SPECIFICATICNS

        GRCUP =    1    2
        DEPEND =   3    4    5    6
        LEVEL =    4
```

ANALYSIS OF VARIANCE FOR 1-ST DEPENDENT VARIABLE

SOURCE	SUM OF SQUARES	DEGREES OF FREEDOM	MEAN SQUARE	F	TAIL PROBABILITY
MEAN	4800.00000	1	4800.00000	465.45	0.000
A	10.08331	1	10.08331	0.98	0.352
T	8.33333	1	8.33333	0.81	0.395
AT	80.08318	1	80.08318	7.77	0.024
ERROR	82.50000	8	10.31250		
B(1)	984.14868	1	984.14868	247.84	0.000
B(1)A	1.66663	1	1.66663	0.42	0.535
B(1)T	10.41660	1	10.41660	2.62	0.144
B(1)AT	9.60004	1	9.60004	2.42	0.159
ERROR	31.76660	8	3.97083		
B(2)	6.75000	1	6.75000	3.41	0.102
B(2)A	2.99999	1	2.99999	1.52	0.253
B(2)T	0.08333	1	0.08333	0.04	0.843
B(2)AT	0.33333	1	0.33333	0.17	0.692
ERROR	15.83328	8	1.97916		
B(3)	0.59999	1	0.59999	1.05	0.335
B(3)A	3.75000	1	3.75000	6.57	0.033
B(3)T	1.66666	1	1.66666	2.92	0.126
B(3)AT	2.81666	1	2.81666	4.93	0.057
ERROR	4.56667	8	0.57083		
B	991.49829	3	330.49927	152.05	0.000
BA	8.41660	3	2.80553	1.29	0.300
BT	12.16658	3	4.05553	1.87	0.162
BAT	12.75002	3	4.25000	1.96	0.148
ERROR	52.16653	24	2.17360		

The analysis of variance table would then be similar to that in Output 15.9 (except that M replaces A, B replaces T and S replaces B). Since the above model does not contain the interactions $(MB)_{ij}$ and $(BT)_{jk}$, we can pool the sum of squares reported for BT with that for d (the ERROR in the last panel) when the design is balanced. The interactions MB and MBT are not estimated because MB is EXCLUDED.

An alternate way of analyzing this model when the design is balanced is to specify grouping factors only and choose the proper error term. For the Snedecor and Cochran model you could specify the *DESIGN* paragraph

```
/DESIGN GROUPING ARE 1,2,3.
        DEPENDENT IS 4.
        INCLUDE IS 1,2,3,12,23.
```

where variable 1 is the blocking factor, 2 the main plot treatment, 3 the subplot treatment and 4 the yield. The INCLUDE statement indicates that the model includes three main effects and two interactions. The interactions are between main plot treatments and blocks used as the error term for testing main plot treatment effects and between main plot treatments and subplot treatments.

Note that this form of input requires that you select the proper error term for testing main plot treatment and blocking effects. The tests provided by P2V are for a fixed effects model and are the proper tests for subplot treatment effects and for the interaction of main and subplot treatment effects but not the proper test for main plot or block effects.

One grouping factor and two trial factors

The data (Table 15.4) are from Winer (1971, p. 546). Subjects are grouped according to two noise levels under which they monitor three dials. Accuracy scores are obtained for calibrating each dial during three time periods. There is one GROUPING variable (NOISE) and two trial factors. Each trial factor has three levels.

Table 15.4   Numerical example from Winer (1971, p. 546).

	b_1			b_2			b_3			(Periods)
a	c_1	c_2	c_3	c_1	c_2	c_3	c_1	c_2	c_3	(Dials)
1	45	53	60	40	52	57	28	37	46	
1	35	41	50	30	37	47	25	32	41	
1	60	65	75	58	54	70	40	47	50	
2	50	48	61	25	34	51	16	23	35	
2	42	45	55	30	37	43	22	27	37	
2	56	60	77	40	39	57	31	29	46	

Note: a is a grouping variable with two levels. Period and dials are two trial factors for the repeated measures. The grouping variable (a) is recorded in column 3; the repeated measures are recorded in columns 5-6, 8-9, etc.

Example 15.11

```
/PROBLEM      TITLE IS 'WINER, PAGE 546, NOISE DATA'.
/INPUT        VARIABLES ARE 10.
              FORMAT IS '(10F3.0)'.
/VARIABLE     NAMES ARE NOISE,B1C1,B1C2,B1C3,
                        B2C1,B2C2,B2C3,
                        B3C1,B3C2,B3C3.

/DESIGN       GROUPING IS NOISE.
              DEPENDENT ARE 2 TO 10.
              LEVELS ARE 3,3.
              NAMES ARE PERIOD,DIAL.

/GROUP        CODES(1) ARE  1,  2.
              NAMES(1) ARE A1, A2.

/END
  1 45 53 60 40 52 57 28 37 46
  1 35 41 50 30 37 47 25 32 41
  1 60 65 75 58 54 70 40 47 50
  2 50 48 61 25 34 51 16 23 35
  2 42 45 55 30 37 43 22 27 37
  2 56 60 77 40 39 57 31 29 46
```

Control Language instructions

data

In Example 15.11, the LEVELs statement in the *DESIGN* paragraph states that there are two trial factors, each with three levels. The first 3 refers to the number of levels of PERIOD and the second to the number of levels of DIAL. The number of levels of the more slowly varying index (PERIOD) is stated first.

Using the FORM statement, the *DESIGN* paragraph is written

```
/DESIGN FORM='G,3(3(Y))'.
        NAME=PERIOD,DIAL.
```

The first variable is the grouping factor. The next nine variables contain the repeated measures for a subject. (3(Y)) specifies that the inner trial factor (dial calibration) has three levels and is recorded as three successive variables. 3(3(Y)) specifies that the outer trial factor (time period) has three levels and is recorded in three sets of three variables; each set varies over the three levels of the inner trial factor. The first NAME for the trial factors applies to the outer trial factor and the second NAME to the inner trial factor.

The ANOVA table is presented in Output 15.11. In the top panel the grouping variable (NOISE) is tested as described previously. The main effect of each trial factor appears in a separate panel since the appropriate error term for each effect differs (see Winer, 1971, p. 540).

The analysis of the two trial factors is again by orthogonal polynomial decomposition. Let us represent the data in the table as

	Dial		
	Y_{11}	Y_{12}	Y_{13}
Period	Y_{21}	Y_{22}	Y_{23}
	Y_{31}	Y_{32}	Y_{33}

Then let

$$P_{10} = (Y_{31}+Y_{32}+Y_{33}-Y_{11}-Y_{12}-Y_{13})/\sqrt{6} \qquad \text{linear component in Period}$$

$$P_{20} = (Y_{31}+Y_{32}+Y_{33}-2Y_{21}-2Y_{22}-2Y_{23}+Y_{11}+Y_{12}+Y_{13})/\sqrt{18} \qquad \text{quadratic component in Period}$$

P_{01} and P_{02} the corresponding linear and quadratic components in Dial

and let $P_{11}, P_{12}, P_{21}, P_{22}$ be the orthogonal decomposition of the interaction between Period and Dial; the coefficients of P_{ij} are obtained from the vector cross product of P_{i0} and P_{0j}; i.e., the product of the corresponding coefficients in P_{i0} and P_{0j}.

Then the second panel in the ANOVA table in Output 15.11 is obtained by summing the sums of squares in the analyses of P_{10} and P_{20} (the orthogonal decomposition of Period). The third panel is obtained from the analysis of P_{01} and P_{02} and the last panel from the analyses of P_{11}, P_{12}, P_{21} and P_{22}.

Output 15.11 One grouping factor and two trial factors analyzed by P2V. Only the ANOVA table is presented.

```
DESIGN SPECIFICATICNS

        GRCUP  =   1
        DEPEND =   2   3   4   5   6   7   8   9  10
        LEVEL  =   3   3


  NUMBER OF CASES READ. . . . . . . . . . . . . .        6


  GROUP STRUCTURE

   NOISE        CCUNT
   A1             3.
   A2             3.
```

ANALYSIS OF VARIANCE FOR 1-ST DEPENDENT VARIABLE - B1C1 B1C2 B1C3 B2C1 B2C2 B2C3 B3C1 B3C2 B3C3

	SCURCE	SUM OF SQUARES	DEGREES OF FREEDOM	MEAN SQUARE	F	TAIL PROBABILITY
	MEAN	105867.81250	1	105867.81250	169.99	0.000
	N	468.16235	1	468.16235	0.75	0.435
1	ERROR	2491.11060	4	622.77759		
	P	3722.33105	2	1861.16553	63.39	0.000
	PN	332.99902	2	166.49951	5.67	0.029
2	ERROR	234.88928	8	29.36116		
	D	2370.33130	2	1185.16553	89.82	0.000
	DN	50.33328	2	25.16664	1.91	0.210
3	ERROR	105.55534	8	13.19442		
	PD	10.66660	4	2.66665	0.34	0.850
	PDN	11.33328	4	2.83332	0.36	0.836
4	ERROR	127.11102	16	7.94444		

Two trial factors (no grouping factor)

We now reanalyze that data in Table 15.4 without a grouping factor.

Example 15.12

```
/PROBLEM      TITLE IS 'WINER, PAGE 546, NOISE DATA'.
/INPUT        VARIABLES ARE 10.
              FORMAT IS '(10F3.0)'.
/VARIABLE     NAMES ARE NOISE,B1C1,B1C2,B1C3,
                        B2C1,B2C2,B2C3,
                        B3C1,B3C2,B3C3.

/DESIGN       DEPENDENT ARE 2 TO 10.
              LEVELS ARE 3,3.
              NAMES ARE PERIOD,DIAL.

/END
   1 45 53 60 40 52 57 28 37 46
   1 35 41 50 30 37 47 25 32 41
   1 60 65 75 58 54 70 40 47 50
   2 50 48 61 25 34 51 16 23 35
   2 42 45 55 30 37 43 22 27 37
   2 56 60 77 40 39 57 31 29 46
```

*Control
Language
instructions*

data

Using the FORM statement, the *DESIGN* paragraph is written

```
/DESIGN FORM IS 'D,3(3(Y))'.
        NAME  = PERIOD,DIAL.
```

That is, the first variable is deleted.

The ANOVA table resulting from Example 15.12 is presented in Output 15.12 without a grouping factor. The sums of squares for P, D and PD are the same as in Output 15.11. The error sums of squares in Output 15.12 are equal to the error sums of squares plus the sums of squares of the grouping factor.

Output 15.12 Analysis of two trial factors by P2V. Only the ANOVA table is presented.

```
DESIGN SPECIFICATIONS

      DEPEND =   2   3   4   5   6   7   8   9   10
      LEVEL  =   3   3

   NUMBER OF CASES READ. . . . . . . . . . . . .        6
```

ANALYSIS OF VARIANCE FOR 1-ST DEPENDENT VARIABLE - B1C1   B1C2   B1C3   B2C1   B2C2   B2C3   B3C1
                                                                                                  B3C2   B3C3

	SOURCE	SUM OF SQUARES	DEGREES OF FREEDOM	MEAN SQUARE	F	TAIL PROBABILITY
1	MEAN	105867.81250	1	105867.81250	178.87	0.000
	ERROR	2959.27319	5	591.85449		
2	P	3722.32593	2	1861.16284	32.77	0.000
	ERROR	567.88892	10	56.78888		
3	D	2370.33130	2	1185.16553	76.03	0.000
	ERROR	155.88869	10	15.58887		
4	PD	10.66660	4	2.66665	0.39	0.817
	ERROR	138.44435	20	6.92222		

One grouping variable, one trial factor and one covariate changing over trials

This design can be used when body temperature is measured with blood pressure as a covariate on each of two days. The subjects are classified into three disease groups. Disease is the grouping factor, temperature the dependent variable, blood pressure the covariate, and days the trial factor.

Winer (1971, p. 806) presents an artificial example that has this type of design. His data (Table 15.5) are used in the following example.

Table 15.5 A numerical example from Winer (1971, p. 806)

	b_1		b_2	
a	X	Y	X	Y
1	3	8	4	14
1	5	11	9	18
1	11	16	14	22
2	2	6	1	8
2	8	12	9	14
2	10	9	9	10
3	7	10	4	10
3	8	14	10	18
3	9	15	12	22

Note: a is a grouping variable with three levels and is
recorded in column 3. The repeated measures are
recorded in columns 5-6, 8-9, 11-12 and 14-15.

Example 15.13

```
/PROBLEM      TITLE IS 'WINER, PAGE 806, NUMERICAL EXAMPLE'.
/INPUT        VARIABLES ARE 5.
              FORMAT IS '(5F3.0)'.
/VARIABLE     NAMES ARE GROUP,B1X,B1Y,B2X,B2Y.

/DESIGN       GROUPING IS GROUP.
              DEPENDENT ARE B1Y,B2Y.
              COVARIATES ARE B1X,B2X.
              LEVEL IS 2.
              NAME IS B.

/GROUP        CODES(1) ARE  1,  2,  3.
              NAMES(1) ARE A1, A2, A3.

/END
    1   3   8   4  14
    1   5  11   9  18
    1  11  16  14  22
    2   2   6   1   8
    2   8  12   9  14
    2  10   9   9  10
    3   7  10   4  10
    3   8  14  10  18
    3   9  15  12  22
```

*Control
Language
instructions*

data

When COVARIATES are stated and there is a trial factor, the COVARIATES are paired with the DEPENDENT variables. That is, the first COVARIATE is treated as the covariate for the first level of the trial factor and the second COVARIATE for the second level.

Using the FORM statement, the *DESIGN* paragraph is written

```
/DESIGN FORM = 'G,2(X,Y)'.
         NAME IS B.
```

The first variable is a grouping factor. Then there are two pairs of variables -- a covariate followed by a dependent variable. 2( ) indicates that there are two levels to the trial factor.

The ANOVA table is presented in Output 15.13. There are two panels in the ANOVA table. The top panel contains the analysis of the grouping factor and the bottom panel contains the analysis of the trial factor and of the interaction of the trial factor with the grouping factor.

Output 15.13 One grouping variable, one trial factor and one covariate analyzed by P2V. Only the ANOVA table is presented.

```
DESIGN SPECIFICATIONS

        GROUP  =    1
        DEPEND =    3    5
        CCVAR  =    2    4
        LEVEL  =    2


NUMBER OF CASES READ. . . . . . . . . . . .    9

  GROUP STRUCTURE

    GROUP      CCUNT
    A1          3.
    A2          3.
    A3          3.
```

ANALYSIS OF VARIANCE FOR 1-ST DEPENDENT VARIABLE - B1Y   B2Y

	SCURCE	SUM OF SQUARES	DEGREES OF FREEDOM	MEAN SQUARE	F	TAIL PROBABILITY	BETA ESTIMATES
	MEAN	128.78967	1	128.78967	14.51	0.013	
	G	54.25873	2	27.12936	3.06	0.136	
	1-ST COVAR	132.62947	1	132.62947	14.95	0.012	
1	ERROR	44.37048	5	8.87410			0.84747
	B	31.54651	1	31.54691	52.61	0.001	
	BG	2.33930	2	1.16965	1.95	0.236	
	1-ST COVAR	10.00198	1	10.00198	16.68	0.010	
2	ERROR	2.99804	5	0.59961			0.84524

```
POOLED REGRESSION COEFFICIENTS

   1-ST CCVARIATE        0.84629

ADJUSTED CELL MEANS  FOR  1-ST DEPENDENT VARIABLE

     GROUP  =  A1          A2           A3
          B
B1Y        1    12.65401     9.70524     12.57685
B2Y        2    16.73056    11.65401     15.67932
```

The analysis of covariance uses the same orthogonal decomposition as the ANOVA. First the covariate is averaged for each case; we denote the average of the covariate by Q_0 and that of the dependent variable by P_0. Then an analysis of covariance is performed on P_0 using Q_0 as the covariate. This is reported in the first panel.

Then the covariate is decomposed into orthogonal polynomials $Q_1, Q_2, \ldots$ in parallel with the decomposition of the dependent variable into $P_1, P_2, \cdots$. If the orthogonal polynomial decomposition is requested, a separate analysis of covariance is computed for each P_i using Q_i as a covariate. To obtain the lower panel of Output 15.13, P2V pools the covariance matrices for the polynomials of degree one and higher that contain covariances between the dependent variable, dummy variables generated for grouping variables, and the covariate(s).

This pooled estimate of the covariance matrix is used to compute an analysis of covariance for the trial factor (Appendix A.18).

The beta estimates in the ANOVA table are the coefficients of the covariate; the coefficient in the lower panel is a weighted average of the regression of P_1 on Q_1, P_2 on Q_2, etc.

The "pooled regression coefficient" (below the ANOVA table) is obtained from the weighted pooled cross-product matrix (the weights are the inverses of the error mean squares).

One grouping variable, one trial variable and one covariate that is constant over trials

This design can be used when body temperature is measured for each subject on two different days and age is used as a covariate. The subjects are classified by sexes. Sex is the grouping factor, temperature the dependent variable, age the covariate and day the trial factor.

Winer (1971, p. 803) presents an artificial example with a similar design. His data (Table 15.6) are used in the following example.

Table 15.6 A numerical example from Winer (1971, p. 803)

a	X	Y_1	Y_2
1	3	10	8
1	5	15	12
1	8	20	14
1	2	12	6
2	1	15	10
2	8	25	20
2	10	20	15
2	2	15	10

Note: a is a grouping factor, X is a covariate that is constant over trials, and Y_1 and Y_2 are two repeated measures. The grouping factor is recorded in column 3, the covariate in columns 5-6 and the repeated measures in column 8-9 and 11-12.

Example 15.14

```
/PROBLEM      TITLE IS 'WINER, PAGE 803, NUMERICAL EXAMPLE'.
/INPUT        VARIABLES ARE 4.
              FORMAT IS '(4F3.0)'.
/VARIABLE     NAMES ARE GROUP,X,B1Y,B2Y.

/DESIGN       GROUPING IS GROUP.
              DEPENDENT ARE B1Y,B2Y.
              COVARIATE IS X,X.
              LEVEL IS 2.
              NAME IS B.

/GROUP        CODES(1) ARE  1,  2.
              NAMES(1) ARE A1, A2.

/END
  1   3 10   8
  1   5 15  12
  1   8 20  14
  1   2 12   6
  2   1 15  10
  2   8 25  20
  2  10 20  15
  2   2 15  10
```

Control Language instructions

data

In the *DESIGN* paragraph two COVARIATES must be stated to match the number of repeated measures. Since the covariate is constant over trials, we repeat the subscript of the covariate.

Using the FORM statement, the *DESIGN* paragraph is written

```
/DESIGN FORM = 'G,X,2(Y)'.
        NAME IS B.
```

Since the covariate, X, is specified outside the parentheses, it is constant over trials and is used only to test between group effects.

The ANOVA table is presented in Output 15.14. The covariate does not vary across trials, therefore it is not included in the lower panel that analyzes the differences among the levels of the trial factor. Otherwise, the ANOVA table is similar to that in Output 15.13.

● OPTIONS IN P2V -- THE *DESIGN* PARAGRAPH

The *DESIGN* paragraph is required in P2V. In it you must specify the design for the analysis of variance and covariance. You may also

- name the trial factors   p. 569

- request the orthogonal decomposition of the trial factors and specify spacing of the points   p. 569

- test for compound symmetry   p. 570

- specify a model for the grouping factors   p. 571

- request that the residuals and predicted values be printed and saved in a BMDP File   p. 574

● SPECIFYING A DESIGN

General rules for the GROUP, LEVEL, DEPEND _and_ COVA _statements_

The GROUP statement lists the variables that specify the levels of the grouping factors to which a subject belongs.

The LEVEL statement is used only for repeated measures models. The number of values in the LEVEL statement is the number of trial factors; the values in the LEVEL statement specify the number of levels in each trial factor. For example, LEVEL=4,3. specifies two trial factors with four levels in the first and three levels in the second.

P2V can analyze several dependent variables in parallel; the same analysis is performed on each dependent variable. The DEPENDENT statement serves two functions in P2V.

Output 15.14 One grouping variable, one trial factor and one covariate analyzed by P2V. Only the ANOVA table is presented.

```
DESIGN SPECIFICATIONS

          GROUP  =    1
          DEPEND =    3    4
          COVAR  =    2    2
          LEVEL  =    2
```

```
    NUMBER OF CASES READ. . . . . . . . . . . . .      8
```

```
GROUP STRUCTURE

    GROUP          COUNT
    A1               4.
    A2               4.
```

ANALYSIS OF VARIANCE FOR 1-ST DEPENDENT VARIABLE - B1Y   B2Y

	SOURCE	SUM OF SQUARES	DEGREES OF FREEDOM	MEAN SQUARE	F	TAIL PROBABILITY	BETA ESTIMATES
	MEAN	400.66846	1	400.66846	32.68	0.002	
	G	44.49133	1	44.49133	3.63	0.115	
	1-ST COVAR	166.57680	1	166.57680	13.59	0.014	1.02194
1	ERROR	61.29781	5	12.25956			
	B	85.56227	1	85.56227	80.53	0.000	
	BG	0.56250	1	0.56250	0.53	0.494	
2	ERROR	6.37500	6	1.06250			

POOLED REGRESSION COEFFICIENTS

    1-ST COVARIATE   1.02194

ADJUSTED CELL MEANS FOR 1-ST DEPENDENT VARIABLE

```
        GROUP   =   A1          A2
              B
    B1Y       1    14.63323    18.36676
    B2Y       2    10.38323    13.36677
```

- It implicitly indicates the number of dependent variables.
- It specifies the variables to be used as repeated measures or as dependent variables.

Suppose T is the product of the numbers of levels of the trial factors (the number of repeated measures); if there are no trial factors, T is one. The DEPENDENT statement must list either exactly T variables or kT variables, where k is an integer. If k is greater than one, k is the number of dependent variables. When both k and T are greater than one, the variables in the DEPENDENT statement must be ordered as in the following example. Suppose k is 2 and T is 4; then the repeated measures for the first analysis are recorded in the 1st, 3rd, 5th and 7th variables listed as DEPENDENT variables and the repeated measures for the second analysis are the even-numbered variables.

For repeated measures models the order of variables specified in the DEPENDENT statement must correspond to the order implied in the LEVEL statement. If LEVEL=2,3. and DEPEND=1 TO 6., the data are read by P2V as

$$Y_{11}, Y_{12}, Y_{13}, Y_{21}, Y_{22}, Y_{23}$$

where Y_{ij} denotes the value of the dependent variable for the ith level of the first trial factor and the jth level of the second. The index corresponding to the first trial factor varies more slowly than that of the second trial factor; all levels of the second trial factor appear as blocks at each level of the first factor. DEPEND =2,3,1,4,5,6. indicates that the data are recorded in an "unnatural" order as $Y_{12}, Y_{13}, Y_{11}, Y_{21}, Y_{22}, Y_{23}$.

In a repeated measures model the number of values in the DEPENDENT statement is a whole number multiple of the product of the numbers in the LEVEL statement; e.g., if LEVEL=2,3., the number of values in the DEPENDENT statement must be a multiple of 2x3=6. If there are 12 values in the DEPENDENT statement, there are two distinct dependent variables, and an analysis of variance is made for each. If DEPEND =1 TO 12., the first dependent variable is assumed to be variables 1,3,5,7,9,11; the second to be variables 2,4,6,8,10,12.

The number of values in the COVARIATE statement is a whole number multiple of the product of the numbers in the LEVEL statement, if any.

    GROUP=1.   DEPEND=2 TO 7.   LEVEL=2,3.   COVA=8 TO 19.

indicates 12 values for covariates. Since the product of the number of levels is six, there are two distinct covariates. The first covariate is assumed to be variables 8,10,12,14,16,18; the second to be variables 9,11,13,15,17,19. In this example, the covariates are measured each time the dependent variable is measured. If there are two distinct dependent variables, the covariates are applied to both of them.

When a covariate is not measured for every level of a trial factor, the index of that covariate must be repeated in the COVARIATE statement (see Example 15.14).

    GROUP=1.   DEPEND=2 TO 7.   LEVEL=2,3.   COVA=8,9,10,8,9,10.

indicates that the covariate is measured separately for each level of the second factor (three levels) but remains unchanged for the first factor (two levels).

DESIGN
>   GROUPING= $v_1, v_2, \cdots$.   {none/prev.}
>
>   Names or subscripts of the GROUPING factors (variables). If the GROUPING variable takes on more than 10 distinct values, CODES or CUTPOINTS must be specified in a *GROUP* paragraph (Section 5.4). When CODES or CUTPOINTS are not specified, the cell means and standard deviations are not sorted before being printed.
>
>   DEPENDENT= $v_1, v_2, \cdots$.   {none/prev.}
>
>   Names or subscripts of the dependent variables, or of the variables that record an observation at any level, or combination of levels, of the trial factors. (See above for a more detailed explanation.)
>
>   LEVEL= $\#_1, \#_2, \cdots$.   {none/prev.}
>
>   Number of levels of the trial factors. LEVELs is specified only for repeated measures models. The first number is that for the slowest changing factor, the second for the next slowest changing, etc. That is, the data are organized so that all the levels of the second factor appear at each level of the first factor.
>
>   COVARIATES= $v_1, v_2, \cdots$.   {none/prev.}
>
>   Names or subscripts of the covariates. The covariates are <u>paired</u> with the repeated measures (see above for a more detailed explanation).
>
>   *Note: If any one of* GROUPING, DEPENDENT, LEVELS *or* COVARIATES *is stated, those not stated are set to none. All four are ignored if* FORM *is stated.*

General rules for the FORM *statement*

>   G = a grouping variable
>   Y = a dependent variable
>   X = a covariate
>   D = a deleted variable (a variable not used in the analysis)

The number of trial factors is indicated by the number of pairs of parentheses. Parentheses must be nested and the symbol Y must appear in the innermost nest: 4(2(Y)) is allowed but 4(Y),2(Y) is meaningless.

The number of levels of a trial factor is the number preceding the parentheses corresponding to that factor. 4(2(Y)) specifies two trial factors with four levels in the first factor and two levels in the second.

The variables in the FORM statement are in the same order as the input variables. FORM='3(2(Y)),G'. specifies that the grouping variable is the seventh variable and that the dependent variable is measured six times, corresponding to the levels of two trial factors. The data are arranged so the levels of the second factor "move fastest". For each case the variables are

$$Y_{11}, Y_{12}, Y_{21}, Y_{22}, Y_{31}, Y_{32}, G$$

where Y_{ij} is the value of the dependent variable for the ith level of the first trial factor and the jth level of the second.

The symbol D is used to indicate that a variable is not used. The statement

FORM= 'D,G,2D,2(D,Y)'.

indicates that the second variable is the grouping variable and the dependent variable is recorded as variables six and eight. The remaining variables (1,3,4,5,7) are not used.

If several dependent variables (temperature, blood pressure, weight, etc.) are to be analyzed separately, the number of distinct dependent variables should immediately precede the symbol Y: 3(2(4Y)) designates four dependent variables; each is measured at all levels of the two trial factors. Four analyses of variance are performed. The data are arranged as

$$Y_{111}, Y_{112}, Y_{113}, Y_{114}, Y_{121}, \ldots, Y_{124}, Y_{211}, \ldots$$

where Y_{ijk} is the value of the kth dependent variable for the ith level of the first trial factor and the jth level of the second factor. We say that the index corresponding to the dependent variable "moves fastest".

DESIGN
FORM='c'.   {none/prev.}

The FORM for the design. See above for an explanation. The statement can be up to 100 characters. If FORM is specified, GROUPing, LEVELs, DEPENDENT and COVARIATEs are ignored. When a GROUPing variable takes on more than ten distinct values, CODEs or CUTPOINTs <u>must</u> be specified in a *GROUP* paragraph. When CODEs or CUTPOINTs are not specified, the cell means and standard deviations are not sorted before printing.

The following statements illustrate the two ways of specifying the role of the variables; each pair specifies the same design.

GROUP=1. DEPEND=2,3,4. LEVEL=3.	FORM='G,3(Y)'.
GROUP=1,2. DEPEND=3 TO 8. LEVEL=2,3.	FORM='2G,2(3(Y))'.
GROUP=1. DEPEND=3,5,7. COVA=2,4,6. LEVEL=3.	FORM='G,3(X,Y)'.
GROUP=1,10. DEPEND=5,7,9. COVA=3,4,3,6,3,8. LEVEL=3.	FORM='G,D,X,3(X,Y),G'.
GROUP=1. DEPEND=3,4,6,7,9,10. LEVEL=3,2. COVA=2,2,5,5,8,8.	FORM='G,3(X,2(Y))'.
GROUP=1,2. DEPEND=3. (No repeated measures)	FORM='2G,Y'.
DEPEND=1 TO 3. LEVEL=3. (No grouping factor)	FORM='3(Y)'.

Not all design specifications can be given by a FORM statement. For example, there is no FORM statement equivalent to

DEPEND=1 TO 4.   COVA=5 TO 8.   LEVEL=4.

(The COVARIATES in variables 5 to 8 are paired with the levels of the trial factor.)

Complex designs

Very complex designs can also be specified. Suppose there are two grouping factors: sex and hospital. There are two trial factors: day with three levels and time with levels a.m. and p.m. There are two dependent variables: systolic and diastolic blood pressure. A separate analysis of variance will be made for each. There are three covariates: age (measured only once for each subject), weight (measured once a day), and temperature (measured each time blood pressure is taken). Altogether there are 24 variables. Data for such a design could be arranged as shown below.

GROUPS			Day 1 AM				Day 1 PM			Day 2 AM				Day 2 PM			Day 3 AM				Day 3 PM		
H	S	A	Wt	T	BPS	BPD	T	BPS	BPD	Wt	T	BPS	BPD	T	BPS	BPD	Wt	T	BPS	BPD	T	BPS	BPD
1	1																						
1	1																						
1	1																						
1	1																						
1	1																						
1	2																						
1	2																						
1	2																						
1	2																						
1	2																						
2	1																						
2	1																						
2	1																						
2	2																						
2	2																						
2	2																						
2	2																						
2	2																						

1 2 3 4 5 6 7 8 9 10 11 12 13 14 15 16 17 18 19 20 21 22 23 24

The last row of numbers above refers to the indices of the variables.

Key: H   = hospital
     S   = sex
     A   = age
     Wt = weight
     T   = temperature
     BPS = blood pressure, systolic
     BPD = blood pressure, diastolic

We could state the design as

    GROUP=1,2.
    LEVEL=3,2.
    DEPEND=6,7,9,10,13,14,16,17,20,21,23,24.
    COVA=3,4,5,3,4,8,3,11,12,3,11,15,3,18,19,3,18,22.

or more simply as

        FORM='2G,X,3(X,2(X,2Y))'.

● NAMES FOR THE GROUPING AND TRIAL FACTORS

        The first letters of the names of the grouping and trial factors are
used in the ANOVA tables. Therefore, the results can be more easily interpreted if each name begins with a distinct letter. Names for the grouping
factors are specified as variable names in the *VARiable* paragraphs. Names
for the trial factors are specified in the *DESIGN* paragraph (see Examples
15.8 to 15.14).

DESIGN
    NAME $=c_1,c_2,\cdots$.   {R,S,T,.../prev.}

    Names of trial factors (up to 4 characters each). Names are used to
    label the output and should be specified when there is more than one
    trial factor. The first NAME is for the first trial factor speci-
    fied in the LEVEL statement or the first (leftmost) trial factor in
    the FORM statement, the second for the second trial factor, etc.
    Only the first character of the name is used in the ANOVA table;
    therefore each NAME should begin with a different letter and also
    differ from the first letters of the names of the GROUPING vari-
    ables.

● ORTHOGONAL DECOMPOSITION OF TRIAL EFFECTS

        The analysis of the trial factors in a repeated measures design involves
an orthogonal polynomial decomposition for the trial factors. This is
described in detail on pp. 551-552 and in Appendix A.18. The ANOVA tables
corresponding to the ANOVA of each orthogonal polynomial are printed.

                ORTHOGONAL.

is specified in the *DESIGN* paragraph. This option is illustrated in
Output 15.10 and in the following example.

        The orthogonal decomposition is of interest only when the levels of the
trial factor are ordered (such as by time or dosage); it is not relevant when
the levels are not ordered.

DESIGN
    ORTHOGONAL.   {no/prev.}

    Print the ANOVA or analysis of covariance tables corresponding to
    the analysis of each orthogonal polynomial.

Unless you specify otherwise, the levels of each trial factor are spaced equally; i.e., 1,2,3,... . You can specify unequal spacing by a POINT statement.

DESIGN
    POINT(#)=#$_1$,#$_2$,$^{...}$.   {1,2,3... .}

    Spacing for the levels of the trial factors. # is the subscript of the trial factor; 1 specifies the first trial factor in the LEVEL or FORM statement, 2 the second, etc. #$_1$,#$_2$,... are the values assigned to the levels of the trial factor to obtain unequal spacing in the orthogonal decomposition.

- A TEST OF COMPOUND SYMMETRY

Assumptions required for the validity of F-tests in the fixed effects analysis of variance model are that the observations are mutually independent, normally distributed, and have equal variance. In the repeated measures model measures made on the same subject can be correlated. As a consequence F tests are made in a way that allows some relaxation of the assumption of complete independence. This assumption is replaced by a number of compound symmetry assumptions, one for each error term for which there is more than one degree of freedom for a trial factor. Thus F tests in an orthogonal polynomial breakdown or including only two trial levels do not require the compound symmetry assumption. In all other cases the assumption can be tested by specifying[4]

SYMMETRY.

in the *DESIGN* paragraph. These tests are based on a sphericity test found in Anderson (1958, p. 259).

These tests should be viewed with the following reservations: They have low power for small sample sizes. For large sample sizes, the test is likely to show significance although the effect on the analysis of variance may be negligible. The sphericity test can be very sensitive to outliers.

When there is reason to doubt the compound symmetry assumption, either because of the sphericity test or because of compelling theoretical considerations such as a suspected strong rapidly damping carryover effect from one trial level to the next, a conservative test can be made by reducing the degrees of freedom contributed by the trial factors (see Winer, 1971, p. 523).

---

[4] If your BMDP programs are dated before April 1977,
    SYMMETRY is not available.

DESIGN

SYMMETRY.   {no/prev.}

A test for compound symmetry using the error sum of squares of trial factors. This test is performed only if there are one or more trial factors.

To demonstrate both the use of unequal spacing and the test for symmetry, we reanalyze the data in Table 15.4 using the following Control Language instructions.

Example 15.15

```
/PROBLEM      TITLE IS 'WINER, PAGE 546, NOISE DATA'.
/INPUT        VARIABLES ARE 10.
              FORMAT IS '(10F3.0)'.
/VARIABLE     NAMES ARE NOISE,B1C1,B1C2,B1C3,
                        B2C1,B2C2,B2C3,
                        B3C1,B3C2,B3C3.

/DESIGN       DEPENDENT ARE 2 TO 10.
              LEVELS ARE 3,3.
              NAMES ARE PERIOD,DIAL.
              ORTHOGONAL.
              POINT(2) = 1,2,4.
              SYMMETRY.

/END
  1 45 53 60 40 52 57 28 37 46
  1 35 41 50 30 37 47 25 32 41
  1 60 65 75 58 54 70 40 47 50
  2 50 48 61 25 34 51 16 23 35
  2 42 45 55 30 37 43 22 27 37
  2 56 60 77 40 39 57 31 29 46
```

Control Language instructions

data

The analysis specifies two trial factors, each with three levels. The spacing for the first trial factor is left unchanged. The spacing for the second trial factor is specified as 1,2,4.

The results are presented in Output 15.15.

- ALTERNATE MODELS WHEN THERE IS MORE THAN ONE GROUPING FACTOR

When there are several grouping factors, P2V fits all possible interactions of the grouping factors unless you specify otherwise. Some designs use only a subset of the interactions; e.g., Latin squares, incomplete blocks and fractional factorials.

You can specify either the main effects and interactions to be <u>included</u> in the model or the interactions to be <u>excluded</u> from the model.[5] For example, if there are two grouping factors (Example 15.6) you can specify a model that includes only main effects by specifying

---

[5] If your BMDP programs are dated before August 1976, INCLUDE and EXCLUDE are not available.

Output 15.15   Test of compound symmetry by P2V

```
DESIGN SPECIFICATIONS

        DEPEND =   2   3   4   5   6   7   8   9   10
        LEVEL  =   3   3

    NUMBER OF CASES READ. . . . . . . . . . . . .      6
```

SUMS OF SQUARES AND CORRELATION MATRIX OF THE ORTHOGONAL COMPONENTS POOLED FOR ERROR 2 IN ANOVA TABLE BELOW

```
        427.66675       1.000
        140.22227       0.573   1.000
```

COMPOUND SYMMETRY TEST — TAIL PROBABILITY 0.2497 DEGREES OF FREEDOM   5.

SUMS OF SQUARES AND CORRELATION MATRIX OF THE ORTHOGONAL COMPONENTS POOLED FOR ERROR 3 IN ANOVA TABLE BELOW

```
         53.55528       1.000
        102.33325       0.426   1.000
```

COMPOUND SYMMETRY TEST — TAIL PROBABILITY 0.5448 DEGREES OF FREEDOM   5.

SUMS OF SQUARES AND CORRELATION MATRIX OF THE ORTHOGONAL COMPONENTS POOLED FOR ERROR 4 IN ANOVA TABLE BELOW

```
         30.19028       1.000
         19.64285      -0.505   1.000
         33.30148       0.551  -0.762   1.000
         55.30933      -0.819  -0.049  -0.107   1.000
```

COMPOUND SYMMETRY TEST — TAIL PROBABILITY 0.0838 DEGREES OF FREEDOM   5.

ANALYSIS OF VARIANCE FOR 1-ST DEPENDENT VARIABLE — B1C1   B1C2   B1C3   B2C1   B2C2   B2C3   B3C1
                                                                                                            B3C2   B3C3

	SOURCE	SUM OF SQUARES	DEGREES OF FREEDOM	MEAN SQUARE	F	TAIL PROBABILITY
1	MEAN	105867.81250	1	105867.81250	178.87	0.000
	ERROR	2959.27319	5	591.85449		
	P(1)	3720.99731	1	3720.99731	43.50	0.001
	ERROR	427.66675	5	85.53334		
	P(2)	1.33327	1	1.33327	0.05	0.836
	ERROR	140.22227	5	28.04445		
2	P	3722.32593	2	1861.16284	32.77	0.000
	ERROR	567.88892	10	56.78888		
	D(1)	2368.04517	1	2368.04517	221.08	0.000
	ERROR	53.55528	5	10.71106		
	D(2)	2.28568	1	2.28568	0.11	0.752
	ERROR	102.33325	5	20.46664		
3	D	2370.33081	2	1185.16528	76.03	0.000
	ERROR	155.88853	10	15.58885		
	PD(1,1)	0.07141	1	0.07141	0.01	0.918
	ERROR	30.19028	5	6.03806		
	PD(1,2)	3.42851	1	3.42851	0.87	0.393
	ERROR	19.64285	5	3.92857		
	PD(2,1)	6.88100	1	6.88100	1.03	0.356
	ERROR	33.30148	5	6.66030		
	PD(2,2)	0.28571	1	0.28571	0.03	0.879
	ERROR	55.30933	5	11.06186		
4	PD	10.66663	4	2.66666	0.39	0.817
	ERROR	138.44394	20	6.92220		

INCLUDE=1,2

or

EXCLUDE=12.

in the *DESIGN* paragraph. In this case the test of the main effect for each group factor is made assuming that the interaction is zero. We reanalyze the data in Table 15.1 (p. 542) using this model.

Example 15.16

```
/PROBLEM     TITLE IS 'KUTNER SYSTOLIC BLOOD PRESSURE DATA'.
/INPUT       VARIABLES ARE 3.
             FORMAT IS '(3F3.0)'.
/VARIABLE    NAMES ARE TREATMNT,DISEASE,SYSINCR.

/DESIGN      DEPENDENT IS SYSINCR.
             GROUPING ARE TREATMNT,DISEASE.
             INCLUDE = 1,2.

/GROUP       CODES(1) ARE     1,     2,     3,     4.
             NAMES(1) ARE DRUG1, DRUG2, DRUG3, DRUG4.
             CODES(2) ARE     1,     2,        3,        4.
             NAMES(2) ARE DISEASE1, DISEASE2, DISEASE3, DISEASE4.

/END
```

The ANOVA table is presented in Output 15.16. This table does not contain any interaction (TD) as does the ANOVA table in Output 15.6 (p. 544).

Output 15.16 Analysis of variance when an additive model is specified for the grouping factors

DESIGN SPECIFICATIONS

```
    GROUP =   1   2
    DEPEND =   3
```

NUMBER OF CASES READ.   58

GROUP STRUCTURE

TREATMNT	DISEASE	COUNT
DRUG1	DISEASE1	6.
DRUG1	DISEASE2	4.
DRUG1	DISEASE3	5.
DRUG2	DISEASE1	5.
DRUG2	DISEASE2	4.
DRUG2	DISEASE3	6.
DRUG3	DISEASE1	3.
DRUG3	DISEASE2	5.
DRUG3	DISEASE3	4.
DRUG4	DISEASE1	5.
DRUG4	DISEASE2	6.
DRUG4	DISEASE3	5.

ANALYSIS OF VARIANCE FOR 1-ST DEPENDENT VARIABLE - SYSINCR

	SOURCE	SUM OF SQUARES	DEGREES OF FREEDOM	MEAN SQUARE	F	TAIL PROBABILITY
	MEAN	19669.99609	1	19669.99609	176.72	0.000
	T	3063.39063	3	1021.13013	9.17	0.000
	D	418.82813	2	209.41406	1.88	0.163
1	ERROR	5788.05078	52	111.30865		

```
DESIGN

(one only)  ⎰  INCLUDE=#₁,#₂,···.    {include all main effects and inter-
            ⎱  EXCLUDE=#₁,#₂,···.     actions for grouping factors}
```

$\#_1, \#_2, \ldots$ are terms to be <u>included</u> or <u>excluded</u> from the model for the grouping factors. The grouping factors are represented by the numbers 1,2,3,... (and <u>not</u> by the subscripts of the grouping variables). Interactions are specified as 12,13,123,... etc. For example, when there are three grouping factors, both

INCLUDE=1,2,3,12,13.

and

EXCLUDE=23,123.

specify models that contain all main effects and two of the two-factor interactions. The trial factors part of the model is not affected.

● PREDICTED VALUES AND RESIDUALS

Predicted values and residuals can be printed or saved in a BMDP File to be further analyzed or plotted by other BMDP programs (e.g., P5D and P6D in Chapter 10).[6]

When there are no repeated measures, there is only one predicted value for each case (the estimate of its expected value). The residual is the difference between the observed and predicted values.

When there are repeated measures, two sets of predicted values can be estimated in terms of

- the coefficients of the orthogonal polynomials used in the computation of the sums of squares (see Appendix A.18); a predicted value and residual is computed for each orthogonal polynomial and for products of orthogonal polynomials corresponding to interactions

- the means and deviations from the means

You can choose between the two sets of parameters by stating

RESIDUALS ARE ORTH.

or

RESIDUALS ARE MEAN.

in the *DESIGN* paragraph.

The predicted values and residuals are printed when PRINT. is specified in the *DESIGN* paragraph.

---

[6] If your BMDP programs are dated before April 1977, the residuals and predicted values cannot be printed or saved.

Residuals are saved with the data in a BMDP File when you specify a *SAVE* paragraph (Section 7.1). You can save the data without the residuals if you specify

        NO RESIDUAL.

in the *SAVE* paragraph.

DESIGN
    RESIDUAL= *(one only)* MEAN,ORTH.   { MEAN /prev.}

      Method of computing residuals and predicted values.

    PRINT.   {no/prev.}

      Print the residuals and predicted values.

SAVE
    RESIDUAL.   { RESI/prev.}

      The residuals and predicted values are saved in a BMDP File
      if one is created unless you specify NO RESIDUAL.
      If saved, each case in the File contains the data, followed by the
      predicted values, followed by the residuals. See the following
      examples for how the predicted values and residuals are labelled.

When the means option is used, the residuals and predicted values are computed both for individual cells and for all marginals of the trial factors. Therefore, the number of pairs of predicted values and residuals is the product $(1+\ell_1)(1+\ell_2)\ldots$ where ℓ_1 is the number of levels of the first trial factor, etc. When the orthogonal polynomial option is selected, the number of pairs of predicted values and residuals is the product $\ell_1\ell_2\ldots$

Details of the methods of computing residuals are given in Appendix A.18. As an example, consider a design with one grouping factor, one trial factor and one covariate (measured at each level of the trial factor). The model for computing predicted values and residuals when

        RESIDUALS ARE MEAN.

is

$$y_{ijk} = \mu + \alpha_i + \beta_0 x_{i\cdot k} + \pi_{k(i)} + \gamma_j + (\alpha\gamma)_{ij} + \beta_1(x_{ijk} - x_{i\cdot k}) + (\gamma\pi)_{jk(i)}$$

where i denotes group, j denotes level of the repeated measures factor, k denotes subjects (nested in groups), $x_{i\cdot k}$ indicates that the covariate has been averaged over the levels of the repeated measures factor, $\pi_{k(i)}$ is a between subjects error component and $(\beta\pi)_{jk(i)}$ is a within subjects error component. This is the model for Example 15.13, p. 560. First, there is a predicted value and residual for the between subjects part of the model:

$$y_{i\cdot k} = \mu + \alpha_i + \beta_0 x_{i\cdot k} + \pi_{k(i)}.$$

This part of the model is a simple fixed effects model for which we compute the usual predicted value and residual. The predicted value for this part of the model is named PO and the residual is named RO. They are computed as

$$PO = \hat{\mu} + \hat{\alpha}_i + \hat{\beta}_0 x_{i \cdot k}$$

$$RO = y_{i \cdot k} - PO$$

The repeated measures part of the model can be written

$$y_{ijk} - y_{i \cdot k} = \gamma_j + (\alpha\gamma)_{ij} + \beta_1(x_{ijk} - x_{i \cdot k}) + (\gamma\pi)_{jk(i)}$$

For each level of the repeated measures factor, we have a predicted value and residual:

$$P_j = \hat{\gamma}_i + (\hat{\alpha\gamma})_{ij} + \hat{\beta}_1(x_{ijk} - x_{i \cdot k})$$

$$R_j = y_{ijk} - y_{i \cdot k}$$

Thus,

$$y_{ijk} = PO + RO + P_j + R_j$$

In the following two examples we print and save the residuals and predicted values, first using the preassigned option

RESIDUAL=MEAN.

and then specifying in the *DESIGN* paragraph

RESIDUAL=ORTH.

Example 15.17

```
/PROBLEM      TITLE IS 'WINER, PAGE 546, NOISE DATA'.
/INPUT        VARIABLES ARE 10.
              FORMAT IS '(10F3.0)'.
/VARIABLE     NAMES ARE NOISE,B1C1,B1C2,B1C3,
                        B2C1,B2C2,B2C3,
                        B3C1,B3C2,B3C3.

/DESIGN       GROUPING IS NOISE.
              DEPENDENT ARE 2 TO 10.
              LEVELS ARE 3,3.
              NAMES ARE PERIOD,DIAL.
              PRINT.

/GROUP        CODES(1) ARE  1,  2.
              NAMES(1) ARE A1, A2.

/SAVE         UNIT IS 4.
              NEW.
              CODE IS WINER.
              RESIDUAL.
/END
```

Note: The System Cards that precede the Control Language must contain a card describing where to store the BMDP File (Section 7.1). At HSCF, the System Cards are

```
//jobname JOB  nooo,yourname
//   EXEC  BIMED,PROG=BMDP2V
//FT04F001  DD  DSNAME=FS.nooo.filename,DISP=OLD
//SYSIN  DD  *
```

In addition space must be allocated for the system file (Section 7.1).

Example 15.18

```
/PROBLEM      TITLE IS 'WINER, PAGE 546, NOISE DATA'.
/INPUT        VARIABLES ARE 10.
              FORMAT IS '(10F3.0)'.
/VARIABLE     NAMES ARE NOISE,B1C1,B1C2,B1C3,
                        B2C1,B2C2,B2C3,
                        B3C1,B3C2,B3C3.

/DESIGN       GROUPING IS NOISE.
              DEPENDENT ARE 2 TO 10.
              LEVELS ARE 3,3.
              NAMES ARE PERIOD,DIAL.
              RESIDUAL = ORTH.
              PRINT.

/GROUP        CODES(1) ARE  1,  2.
              NAMES(1) ARE A1, A2.

/SAVE         UNIT IS 4.
              NEW.
              CODE IS WINER.
              RESIDUAL.

/END
```

Note: The System Cards that precede the Control Language must contain a card describing where to store the BMDP File (Section 7.1). At HSCF, the System Cards are

```
//jobname  JOB  nooo,yourname
//   EXEC  BIMED,PROG=BMDP2V
//FT04001  DD  DSNAME=FS.nooo,filename,DISP=OLD
//SYSIN  DD  *
```

In addition space must be allocated for the system file (Section 7.1).

The results are presented in Outputs 15.17 and 15.18 respectively. Note that the predicted values are labelled P followed by two numbers since there are two trial factors and that the residuals are labelled R followed by two numbers.

● TOLERANCE

The matrix of sums of cross products must be pivoted (swept) on the covariates and dummy variables for the grouping factors, if any. The tolerance limit is used to avoid pivoting when pivoting will cause a loss in accuracy in the results (Appendix A.11). The tolerance limit rarely needs to be changed.[7] For IBM 360 and 370 computers, the tolerance limit should not ordinarily be lowered.

```
DESIGN
   TOLERANCE=#.          {0.01/prev.}
   Tolerance limit for pivoting.  This rarely needs to be changed.
```

---

[7] If your BMDP programs are dated before August 1976, TOLERANCE is set to 0.01 and cannot be changed.

Output 15.17   A BMDP File is created and the residuals are printed by P2V.
(RESIDUALS=MEAN)

```
BMDP FILE WRITTEN ON UNIT 4.
        CODE. . . IS    WINER
        CONTENT . IS    DATA
        LABEL . . IS
        VARIABLES     1  NOISE      2  B1C1      3  B1C2      4  B1C3      5  B2C1
                      6  B2C2       7  B2C3      8  B3C1      9  B3C2     10  B3C3
                     11  P00       12  P10      13  P20      14  P30      15  PC1
                     16  P02       17  P03      18  P11      19  P12      20  P13
                     21  P21       22  P22      23  P23      24  P31      25  P32
                     26  P33       27  R00      28  R10      29  R2C      30  R3C
                     31  R01       32  R02      33  R03      34  P11      35  R12
                     36  R13       37  R21      38  R22      39  R23      40  R31
                     41  R32       42  R33
```

```
CASE   NOISE    P00        P10        P20        P30        P01        P02        P03        P11        P12
                P13        P21        P22        P23        P31        P32        P33        R00        R10
                R20        R30        R01        R02        R03        R11        R12        R13        R21
                R22        R23        R31        R32        R33

 1     A1     47.22209    6.55555    2.22222   -8.77777   -7.11109   -0.77778    7.88888    0.0        0.0
               0.0        0.33333   -1.00000    0.66666   -0.33333    1.00000   -0.66666   -0.77771   -0.33333
               1.00000   -0.66667   -1.66668    1.66667    0.0        1.11111   -0.55556   -0.55556   -1.22222
               2.44445   -1.22222    0.11112   -1.88889    1.77777
 2     A1     47.22209    6.55555    2.22221   -8.77777   -7.11109   -0.77778    7.88888    0.0        0.0
               0.0        0.33333   -1.00000    0.66666   -0.33333    1.00000   -0.66667   -9.66658    0.C
              -1.77778    3.88889   -0.44444   -0.11112    0.55556    0.55556   -0.11111   -0.44444   -0.77778
               0.88888   -0.11111    0.22222   -0.77777    0.55555
 3     A1     47.22209    6.55555    2.22222   -8.77777   -7.11109   -0.77778    7.88888    0.0        0.0
               0.0        0.33333   -1.00000    0.66667   -0.33333    1.00000   -0.66667   10.44450    0.0
               0.77778   -3.22223    2.11110   -1.55555   -0.55554   -1.66667    0.66667    1.00000    2.00001
              -3.33333    1.33333   -0.33334    2.66666   -2.33333
 4     A2     41.33324   13.55553   -1.77778  -11.77775   -6.66665   -3.33334    9.99999    1.11111   -0.55555
              -0.55556   -1.22222    0.44444    0.77778    0.11112    0.11111   -0.22222   -3.22217    1.33335
               0.33333   -1.66668   -1.11111    0.22221    0.88890    3.66667   -1.33333   -2.33334   -2.66667
               0.0        2.66667   -1.00000    1.33334   -0.33334
 5     A2     41.33324   13.55553   -1.77778  -11.77775   -6.66665   -3.33334    9.99999    1.11111   -0.55555
              -0.55556   -1.22222    0.44444    0.77778    0.11112    0.11111   -0.22222   -3.77773   -3.77776
               0.88889    2.88887    0.44444    2.11111   -2.55554   -0.22223   -C.55556    0.77778    0.77778
               1.11111   -1.88889   -0.55556   -0.55555    1.11111
 6     A2     41.33324   13.55553   -1.77778  -11.77775   -6.66665   -3.33334    9.99999    1.11110   -0.55555
              -0.55556   -1.22222    0.44444    0.77778    0.11112    0.11111   -0.22222    7.00003    2.44446
              -1.22223   -1.22223    0.66665   -2.33333    1.66668   -3.44444    1.88889    1.55555    1.88888
              -1.11111   -0.77778    1.55556   -0.77778   -0.77777
```

BMDP FILE CN UNIT 4 HAS BEEN COMPLETED.

ERROR TERM	SUM OF SQUARES	RECOMPUTED FROM RESIDUALS	RELATIVE ERROR
1	2491.11060	2491.10254	-0.00000
2	234.88928	234.88895	-0.00000
3	105.55534	105.55522	-0.00000
4	127.11102	127.11087	-0.00000

<u>Output 15.18</u> A BMDP File is created and the residuals are printed by P2V. (RESIDUALS=ORTH)

ANALYSIS OF VARIANCE FOR 1—ST DEPENDENT VARIABLE — B1C1   B1C2   B1C3   B2C1   B2C2   B2C3   B3C1   B3C2   B3C3   3

	SOURCE	SUM OF SQUARES	DEGREES OF FREEDOM	MEAN SQUARE	F	TAIL PROBABILITY
	MEAN	105867.81250	1	105867.81250	169.99	0.000
	N	468.16235	1	468.16235	0.75	0.435
1	ERROR	2491.11060	4	622.77759		
	P	3722.33105	2	1861.16553	63.39	0.000
	PN	332.99902	2	166.49951	5.67	0.C29
2	ERROR	234.88928	8	29.36116		
	D	2370.33130	2	1185.16553	89.82	0.000
	DN	50.33328	2	25.16664	1.91	0.210
3	ERROR	105.55534	8	13.19442		
	PD	10.66660	4	2.66665	0.34	0.850
	PDN	11.33328	4	2.83332	0.36	0.836
4	ERROR	127.11102	16	7.94444		

ERROR SUM OF SQUARES	CORRESPONDING RESIDUALS
1	R00
2	R10, R20
3	R01, R02
4	R11, R12, R21, R22

BMDP FILE WRITTEN ON UNIT   4
CODE. . . IS   WINER
CONTENT . IS   DATA
LABEL . . IS
VARIABLES

1 NOISE	2 B1C1	3 B1C2	4 B1C3	5 B2C1
6 B2C2	7 B2C3	8 B3C1	9 B3C2	10 B3C3
11 P00	12 P10	13 P20	14 P01	15 P02
16 P11	17 P12	18 P21	19 P22	20 R00
21 R1C	22 R20	23 R01	24 R02	25 R11
26 R12	27 R21	28 R22		

CASE	NOISE	P00 / R00	P10 / R10	P20 / R20	P01 / R01	P02 / R02	P11 / R11	P12 / R12	P21 / R21	P22 / R22
1	A1	141.66635	18.77940	−4.71403	−18.37114	1.64993	−0.16666	0.86602	C.28867	−1.50000
		−2.33312	0.40826	−2.12133	−2.04127	−3.53555	1.66667	−1.15470	0.00001	3.66667
2	A1	141.66635	18.77940	−4.71403	−18.37114	1.64993	−0.16667	0.86602	0.28867	−1.49999
		−28.99977	−7.34847	3.77123	−1.22475	0.23571	0.66667	−0.57734	0.57735	1.33333
3	A1	141.66637	18.77940	−4.71403	−18.37114	1.64993	−0.16667	0.86602	0.28867	−1.50000
		31.33353	6.94025	−1.64992	3.26596	3.29983	−2.33334	1.73204	−0.57736	−5.00000
4	A2	123.99977	31.02682	3.77124	−20.41238	7.07107	0.66666	0.57734	1.73205	0.66666
		−9.66653	3.67427	−0.70711	−2.44950	−0.47139	3.33334	2.30940	4.61881	−C.00000
5	A2	123.99982	31.02682	3.77124	−20.41238	7.07107	0.66666	0.57734	1.73205	0.66666
		−11.33318	−8.16493	−1.88562	3.67422	−4.47833	0.33333	0.00000	−2.30941	1.66667
6	A2	123.99979	31.02682	3.77124	−20.41238	7.07107	0.66666	0.57734	1.73205	0.66666
		21.00011	4.49075	2.59274	−1.22477	4.94974	−3.66666	−2.30941	−2.30939	−1.66666

•

BMDP FILE ON UNIT 4 HAS BEEN COMPLETED.

ERROR TERM	SUM OF SQUARES	RECOMPUTED FROM RESIDUALS	RELATIVE ERROR
1	2491.11060	2491.10669	−0.00000
2	234.88928	234.88916	−0.00000
3	105.55534	105.55530	−0.00000
4	127.11102	127.111C4	0.00000

● SIZE OF PROBLEM

P2V can analyze up to nine trial factors and nine grouping factors. The number of dependent variables plus covariates that can be analyzed is a function of the number of cells ($C=\ell_1\ell_2...$) formed by the grouping factors (where ℓ_i is the number of levels of the ith grouping factor), and the number of repeated measures ($T=t_1t_2...$) formed by the trial factors. The following table gives a rough guideline to the maximum number of dependent variables and covariates (V).

C	0	0	50	100	50
T	50	100	0	0	50
V	11	4	40	16	1

Appendix B describes how to increase the capacity of the program.

● COMPUTATIONAL METHOD

All computations are performed in single precision. Means, standard deviations and covariances are computed by the method of provisional means (Appendix A.2). The computations performed by P2V are described in Appendix A.18.

ACKNOWLEDGEMENT

P2V was designed by Robert Jennrich and Paul Sampson with major contributions from Alan Forsythe and James Frane. It was programmed by Paul Sampson.

P3V

15.3 General Mixed Model Analysis of Variance

Robert Jennrich, HSCF
Paul Sampson, HSCF

There are many approaches to analysis of variance and covariance. Most of them do not generalize easily to the unbalanced mixed model. Two that do generalize are the maximum likelihood (ML) and restricted maximum likelihood (REML) approaches to the fixed and random coefficients model. These are the approaches used in P3V (see Appendix A.19).[8] The program is designed to handle mixed models of quite arbitrary form without requiring the balance demanded by P2V (Section 15.2) and BMD08V (Dixon, 1977). On the other hand the maximum likelihood approach is not as well-studied or as widely available as the more classical approaches found in P2V and BMD08V. For this reason we recommend that this program be considered somewhat experimental in nature -- to be used in conjunction with more classical approaches and for mixed model problems that do not satisfy the balance requirements of P2V and BMD08V. REML estimates of mean and variance components agree with those obtained from classical analysis of variance (for balanced data) whenever the latter produces nonnegative variance component estimates (Jennrich, unpublished).

Our description of P3V assumes that you are familiar with the fixed and random coefficients formulation of the general mixed model (e.g., Jennrich and Sampson, 1976; Harville, 1977). An example of a mixed model is

$$y_{ijk} = \mu + \alpha_i + b_j + c_{ij} + \beta x_{ijk} + e_{ijk}$$

where

y_{ijk}	is the value of the dependent variable
μ	is a fixed effect
α_i	is a fixed effect
b_j	is a random effect (it is assumed to be sampled from a normal distribution with mean zero and variance σ_b^2)
c_{ij}	is a random effect corresponding to an interaction (it is assumed to be sampled from a normal distribution with mean zero and variance σ_c^2)
β	is the coefficient of the covariate x
e_{ijk}	is a random effect corresponding to the error (it is assumed to be sampled from a normal distribution with mean zero and variance σ_e^2)

A more general model can have several fixed effects, random effects and covariates.

---

[8] If your BMDP programs are dated before August 1977, P3V is not available.

If there are no random effects (other than e), the classical analysis can be obtained by P7D, P1V or P2V.

P3V reports the estimates and standard deviations of the fixed effects parameters, variance components, estimates of the cell means, and residuals. The log-likelihoods for the model and for submodels (that you specify) are computed.

● RESULTS

We demonstrate the results obtained with P3V by the three examples below. Our discussion raises a number of questions about the relation between conventional analysis of variance and maximum likelihood analysis as well as questions about model definition and testing strategies. We purposely try to make these questions conspicuous, a strategy we feel is appropriate since experience with maximum likelihood analysis of the general mixed model has been limited.

The model is described by a *DESIGN* paragraph in which you specify the DEPENDENT variable, variables that are COVARIATES, effects and interactions that are FIXED and how to name then (FNAME), and RANDOM effects and how to name then (RNAME). The submodels are specified in a *HYPOTHesis* paragraph in which you specify the terms in the model that are zero.

Repeated measures with one covariate

As our first example we reanalyze the data in Table 15.5 (p. 560). The data are from a numerical example (Winer, 1971, p. 806) of a repeated measures model with one covariate. The model can be written

$$y_{ijk} = \mu + \alpha_i + \beta_j + \gamma_{ij} + \beta x_{ijk} + d_{ik} + e_{ijk}$$

where α_i, β_j, γ_{ij} are fixed effects that sum to zero on all i and j and the d_{ik} and e_{ijk} represent independent normal samples from populations with variances σ_d^2 and σ_e^2.

The Control Language instructions to analyze the data are shown in Example 15.19. Note that the fixed effect μ and random component e_{ijk} are provided automatically and should not be specified.

Example 15.19

```
/PROBLEM        TITLE IS 'REPEATED MEASURES WITH COVARIATE -
                    WINER, PAGE 806'.
/INPUT          VARIABLES ARE 5.
                FORMAT IS '(5F3.0)'.
/VARIABLE       NAMES ARE GROUP,SUBJECT,TREATMNT,BLOODPRS,TEMPRTUR.

/GROUP          CODES(1) ARE 1 TO 3.
                CODES(3) ARE 1 TO 2.

/DESIGN         DEPENDENT IS TEMPRTUR.
                FIXED     IS GROUP.
                FIXED     IS TREATMNT.
                FIXED     IS GROUP,TREATMNT.
                FNAMES    ARE GROUP,TREATMNT,'GRP*TRT'.
                COVARIATE IS BLOODPRS.
                RANDOM    IS GROUP,SUBJECT.
                RNAME     IS 'SBJ*GRP'.

/HYPOTHESIS     FIXED IS 3.
/HYPOTHESIS     FIXED IS 1.
/HYPOTHESIS     FIXED IS 2.
/HYPOTHESIS     RANDOM IS 1.
/HYPOTHESIS     FIXED IS 1,3.
/HYPOTHESIS     FIXED IS 2,3.

/END
  1  1  1  3  8        2  2  2  9 14
  1  1  2  4 14        2  3  1 10  9
  1  2  1  5 11        2  3  2  9 10
  1  2  2  9 18        3  1  1  7 10
  1  3  1 11 16        3  1  2  4 10
  1  3  2 14 22        3  2  1  8 14
  2  1  1  2  6        3  2  2 10 18
  2  1  2  1  8        3  3  1  9 15
  2  2  1  8 12        3  3  2 12 22
```

Control Language instructions

data

The Control Language must be preceded by System Cards to initiate the analysis by P3V. At HSCF, the System Cards are

```
//jobname  JOB  nooo,yourname
//   EXEC  BIMED,PROG=BMDP3V
//SYSIN DD  *
```

The Control Language is immediately followed by the data (Table 15.5). The analysis is terminated by another System Card. At HSCF, this System Card is

```
//
```

The results are presented in Output 15.19. Circled numbers below correspond to those in the output.

① Number of cases read. Only cases containing acceptable values for all variables specified in the *DESIGN* paragraph are used in the analysis. An acceptable value is a value that is not missing or out of range. In addition, if CODEs are specified for any fixed effects factors, a case is included only if the value of the fixed effects factor is equal to a specified code.

② Univariate statistics for each cell. Cells are formed for all combinations of levels of the fixed effects (GROUP and TREATMNT in our example -- the level of the first fixed effect specified, GROUP, appears first in the cell index). For each cell the mean, standard deviation, coefficient of variation, and the cell count (sample size) are printed for the dependent variable and for the covariate(s) (BLOODPRS in our example).

Output 15.19 General mixed model analysis of variance by P3V. Circled numbers correspond to those in the text. Results not reproduced are indicated in italics.

```
BMDP3V - GENERAL MIXED MODEL ANALYSIS OF VARIANCE        PROGRAM REVISED SEPTEMBER 1977
HEALTH SCIENCES COMPUTING FACILITY                       MANUAL DATE -- 1977
UNIVERSITY OF CALIFORNIA, LOS ANGELES
```

--- Control Language read by P3V is printed and interpreted ---

(1) NUMBER OF CASES READ.   18

CELL INFORMATION FOR VARIABLE TEMPRTUR

(2)

CELL	MEAN	ST.DEV.	COEFF. OF VARIATION	COUNT	GROUPING VARIABLES GROUP	TREATMNT
1,1	11.66667	4.04145	0.34641	3.00000	* 1.0000	* 1.0000
1,2	18.00000	4.00000	0.22222	3.00000	* 1.0000	* 2.0000
2,1	9.00000	3.00000	0.33333	3.00000	* 2.0000	* 1.0000
2,2	10.66667	3.05505	0.28641	3.00000	* 2.0000	* 2.0000
3,1	13.00000	2.64575	0.20352	3.00000	* 3.0000	* 1.0000
3,2	16.66667	6.11010	0.36661	3.00000	* 3.0000	* 2.0000

--- univariate statistics for BLOODPRS ---

DEPENDENT VARIABLE TEMPRTUR

(3)

PARAMETER	ESTIMATE	STANDARD DEVIATION	EST/ST.DEV.	TWO-TAIL PROBABILITY (ASYMPTOTIC THEORY)
ERR.VAR.	0.3331146001	0.1570317284		
BLOODPRS	0.8462912570	0.1121652309	7.5450401306	0.0
CONSTANT	6.8194822389	0.9907456454	6.8831815720	0.0
GROUP	1.5256181238	0.7403623784	2.0606365204	0.039
GROUP	-2.4870420763	0.7485773287	-3.3223581314	0.001
TREATMNT	-1.5212988159	0.1471449164	-10.3387784958	0.0
GRP*TRT	-0.5169795080	0.2138914818	-2.4170169830	0.016
GRP*TRT	0.5469169398	0.2064081061	2.6496868134	0.008
SBJ*GRP	2.2984841011	1.1646812100		

(4) -2*LOG(MAXIMUM LIKELIHOOD) =   55.5465698242

VARIANCE-COVARIANCE MATRIX OF THE PARAMETERS

(5)

	ERR.VAR.	BLOODPRS	CONSTANT	GROUP	GROUP	TREATMNT	GRP*TRT	GRP*TRT
ERR.VAR.	0.0247							
BLOODPRS	-0.0	0.0126						
CONSTANT	-0.0	-0.0944	0.9816					
GROUP	-0.0	-0.0021	0.0157	0.5481				
GROUP	-0.0	0.0126	-0.0944	-0.2760	0.5604			
TREATMNT	-0.0	0.0063	-0.0472	-0.0010	0.0063	0.0217		
GRP*TRT	-0.0	0.0105	-0.0786	-0.0017	0.0105	0.0052	0.0457	
GRP*TRT	-0.0	-0.0084	0.0629	0.0014	-0.0084	-0.0042	-0.0255	0.0426
SBJ*GRP	-0.0123	-0.0	-0.0	-0.0	-0.0	-0.0	-0.0	-0.0

	SBJ*GRP
SBJ*GRP	1.3565

(6)

CELL	GROUPING VARIABLES GROUP	TREATMNT	DUMMY VARIABLES					
1,1	* 1.0000	* 1.0000	1.	1.	0.	1.	1.	0.
1,2	* 1.0000	* 2.0000	1.	1.	0.	-1.	-1.	0.
2,1	* 2.0000	* 1.0000	1.	0.	1.	1.	0.	1.
2,2	* 2.0000	* 2.0000	1.	0.	1.	-1.	0.	-1.
3,1	* 3.0000	* 1.0000	1.	-1.	-1.	1.	-1.	-1.
3,2	* 3.0000	* 2.0000	1.	-1.	-1.	-1.	1.	1.

(7)

CELL	OBSERVED MEAN	PREDICTED MEAN	SD.DEV. PRED.
1,1	11.6667	12.6540	0.9457
1,2	18.0000	16.7305	0.9516
2,1	9.0000	9.7052	0.9412
2,2	10.6667	11.6540	0.9457
3,1	13.0000	12.5769	0.9383
3,2	16.6667	15.6793	0.9457

VARIANCE-COVARIANCE MATRIX OF PREDICTED CELL MEANS

(8)

	1,1	1,2	2,1	2,2	3,1	3,2
1,1	0.8943					
1,2	0.7441	0.9055				
2,1	0.0122	-0.0157	0.8859			
2,2	0.0171	-0.0220	0.7784	0.8943		
3,1	-0.0073	0.0094	-0.0052	-0.0073	0.8803	
3,2	-0.0171	0.0220	-0.0122	-0.0171	0.7735	0.8943

(continued)

Output 15.19 *(continued)*

⑨ PAIRWISE TESTS FOR PREDICTED CELL MEANS

	1,1	1,2	2,1	2,2	3,1	3,2
1,1	0.0					
1,2	7.3035	0.0				
2,1	-2.2254	-5.2034	0.0			
2,2	-0.7550	-3.7386	4.1224	0.0		
3,1	-0.0577	-3.1248	2.1543	0.6899	0.0	
3,2	2.2407	-0.7933	4.4470	2.9814	6.5021	0.0

⑩ RESIDUAL ANALYSIS

CELL	OBSERVED TEMPRTUR	PREDICTED TEMPRTUR	ST.DEV. PRED.	OBSERVED- PREDICTED	ST.DEV. O-P	(O-P)/ ST.DEV.
1,1	8.0000	8.8457	1.0085	-0.8457	1.2707	-0.666
1,2	14.0000	13.7685	1.0917	0.2315	1.1999	0.193
1,1	11.0000	10.5383	0.9485	0.4617	1.3161	0.351
1,2	18.0000	18.0000	0.9366	0.0000	1.3245	0.000
1,1	16.0000	15.6160	1.0729	0.3840	1.2167	0.316
1,2	22.0000	22.2314	1.0917	-0.2314	1.1999	-0.193
2,1	6.0000	5.0506	1.0729	0.9494	1.2167	0.780
2,2	8.0000	6.1531	1.1113	1.8469	1.1818	1.563
2,1	12.0000	10.1284	0.9485	1.8716	1.3161	1.422
2,2	14.0000	12.9234	0.9832	1.0766	1.2903	0.834
2,1	9.0000	11.8210	1.0085	-2.8210	1.2707	-2.220
2,2	10.0000	12.9234	0.9832	-2.9234	1.2903	-2.266
3,1	10.0000	12.1537	0.9433	-2.1537	1.3198	-1.632
3,2	10.0000	12.7173	1.0729	-2.7173	1.2167	-2.233
3,1	14.0000	13.0000	0.9366	1.0000	1.3245	0.755
3,2	18.0000	17.7950	0.9485	0.2050	1.3161	0.156
3,1	15.0000	13.8463	0.9433	1.1537	1.3198	0.874
3,2	22.0000	19.4876	1.0085	2.5124	1.2707	1.977

CONSTRAINED MODEL - HYPOTHESIS NUMBER 1

⑪
PARAMETER	ESTIMATE	STANDARD DEVIATION	EST/ST.DEV.	TWO-TAIL PROBABILITY (ASYMPTOTIC THEORY)
ERR.VAR.	0.6240477058	0.2941789097		
BLOODPRS	0.9561385097	0.1200782227	7.9626302719	0.0
CONSTANT	5.9956278439	1.0480499202	5.7207460403	0.000
GROUP	1.5073102484	0.7583568356	1.9885993729	0.047
GROUP	-2.3771948236	0.7675437108	-3.0971450806	0.002
TREATMNT	-1.4663751896	0.1956374501	-7.4953699112	0.0
GRP*TRT	0.0	0.0		
GRP*TRT	0.0	0.0		
SBJ*GRP	2.2741467053	1.2279736733		

⑫ -2*LOG(MAXIMUM LIKELIHOOD) =   61.6279296875

VARIANCE-COVARIANCE MATRIX OF THE PARAMETERS

	ERR.VAR.	BLOODPRS	CONSTANT	GROUP	GROUP	TREATMNT	GRP*TRT	GRP*TRT
ERR.VAR.	0.0865							
BLOODPRS	-0.0	0.0144						
CONSTANT	-0.0	-0.1081	1.0984					
GROUP	-0.0	-0.0024	0.0180	0.5751				
GROUP	-0.0	0.0144	-0.1081	-0.2898	0.5891			
TREATMNT	-0.0	0.0072	-0.0541	-0.0012	0.0072	0.0383		
GRP*TRT	-0.0	-0.0	-0.0	-0.0	-0.0	-0.0	-0.0	
GRP*TRT	-0.0	-0.0	-0.0	-0.0	-0.0	-0.0	-0.0	-0.0
SBJ*GRP	-0.0433	-0.0	-0.0	-0.0	-0.0	-0.0	-0.0	-0.0

	SBJ*GRP
SBJ*GRP	1.5079

⑬ LIKELIHOOD RATIO TEST   CHI-SQUARE =   6.081

DEGREES OF FREEDOM   2

PROBABILITY   0.048

CONSTRAINED MODEL - HYPOTHESIS NUMBER 2

--- results for hypothesis 2 ---

LIKELIHOOD RATIO TEST   CHI-SQUARE =   7.343

DEGREES OF FREEDOM   2

PROBABILITY   0.025

CONSTRAINED MODEL - HYPOTHESIS NUMBER 3

--- results for hypothesis 3 ---

LIKELIHOOD RATIO TEST   CHI-SQUARE =   24.109

DEGREES OF FREEDOM   1

PROBABILITY   0.000

CONSTRAINED MODEL - HYPOTHESIS NUMBER 4

--- results for hypothesis 4 ---

LIKELIHOOD RATIO TEST   CHI-SQUARE =   12.952

DEGREES OF FREEDOM   1

PROBABILITY   0.000

CONSTRAINED MODEL - HYPOTHESIS NUMBER 5

--- results for hypothesis 5 ---

LIKELIHOOD RATIO TEST   CHI-SQUARE =   12.536

DEGREES OF FREEDOM   4

PROBABILITY   0.014

CONSTRAINED MODEL - HYPOTHESIS NUMBER 6

--- results for hypothesis 6 ---

LIKELIHOOD RATIO TEST   CHI-SQUARE =   24.659

DEGREES OF FREEDOM   2

PROBABILITY   0.000

(3) Estimates of the parameters of the model, their asymptotic standard errors, the ratios of the estimates to their standard errors (t-like statistics) and two-tailed probabilities obtained from the normal distribution. GROUP appears twice in the list of parameters -- P3V generates ℓ-1 dummy variables for a fixed effect when the fixed effect has ℓ levels (the two dummy variables for GROUP take on the values 1, 0, -1 and 0, 1, -1 at the three levels of GROUP); the estimate of the coefficient of each dummy variable is printed as a separate line in the table. Similarly, two lines that appear for GRP*TRT, the interaction of GROUP and TREATMNT, correspond to the two degrees of freedom for the interaction (see Appendix A.19).

(4) -2 $\ln$ (maximum likelihood) is minus 2 times the logarithm of the likelihood evaluated at the maximum likelihood estimates of the parameters.

(5) Variance-covariance matrix of the estimates of the parameters. Again two rows (and two columns) appear for both GROUP and GRP*TRT; they correspond to the two dummy variables generated for these effects.

(6) Dummy variables generated by P3V. The first dummy variable (the first column) contains only ones and represents the mean effect. The second and third dummy variables represent the group effects. The fourth dummy variable represents the treatment effect and the last two represent the group by treatment interactions.

(7) For each cell defined by the fixed effects P3V prints the cell mean, the predicted cell mean (using the estimated parameters and evaluated at the grand mean of the covariate), and the standard error of the predicted cell mean.

(8) Variance-covariance matrix for the predicted cell means.

(9) Pairwise tests for the predicted cell means. These are t-like ratios of the difference between each pair of means divided by the estimate of the standard deviation of their difference.

(10) Residual analysis. For each case P3V prints the

- cell to which it belongs

- observed value y of the dependent variable

- predicted value $\hat{y}$

- standard deviation of the predicted value

- residual $(y-\hat{y})$

- standard deviation of the residual

- the ratio of the residual to its standard deviation (the standardized residual)

(11) Each *HYPOTHesis* paragraph defines a submodel to be tested. The effect or effects specified in the *HYPOTHesis* paragraph are set to zero and the parameters in the model are reestimated. In the first *HYPOTHesis* paragraph in Example 15.19, the third FIXED effect is set to zero --

the third FIXED effect in the example is GRP*TRT. Therefore the parameter estimates corresponding to GRP*TRT are zero. The remaining
estimates can be compared to those of the complete model ③ to examine
the effect of setting GRP*TRT to zero.

⑫ P3V prints -2 ln (maximum likelihood) for this model. The difference
between this statistic and that in ④ is a test of the significance of
the GRP*TRT interaction.

⑬ The difference between the two values for -2 ln (maximum likelihood) is
printed. This is a likelihood ratio test of the parameters that are set
to zero (GRP*TRT in our example). Its degrees of freedom (number of
mathematically independent parameters set to zero) and tail probability
are printed. The probability is obtained from a chi-square distribution
(the asymptotic distribution of the difference) with the degrees of
freedom printed.

Similar results are obtained for the other *HYPOTHesis* paragraphs, but are
not reproduced here.

The last two *HYPOTHesis* paragraphs test whether each main effect and the
interaction are simultaneously zero. Such tests are of interest when hierarchical models are desired. (Hierarchical models include interactions only when
corresponding lower order interactions and main effects are included.) Suppose
for example that we wish to perform tests at the .01 level. Since the likelihood ratio chi-square for the group-treatment interaction was barely significant at the .05 level, we may wish to test whether the group main effect and
the group-treatment interaction are both zero. This is done by specifying
the fifth hypothesis.

Some statisticians may desire to test group effects assuming interaction
effects are zero. This can be done by comparing the model for the first hypothesis (all effects except group-treatment interaction) with the model for the
fifth hypothesis (no group effect and no interaction). This test is performed
by subtracting the corresponding values of -2 ln (maximum likelihood) or, equivalently, by subtracting the chi-square values and the corresponding degrees of
freedom.

The results for the maximum likelihood analysis by P3V can be compared
to the results for the repeated measures analysis by P2V (Output 15.13). For
both analyses, the main effect for group and the group x treatment interaction
were nonsignificant and the treatment effect was significant at the .001 level.
In P3V, the significance of the covariate is judged in terms of its asymptotic
standard error. In P2V, the significance of the covariate is assessed via
F tests separately for between group effects and for the trial effects.

A random effects model

As a second example we analyze the data in Table 15.7 from Bowker and
Lieberman (1963, p. 362). The values of the dependent variable are the life
times of electronic components tested in three randomly selected ovens at two
randomly selected temperatures.

<u>Table 15.7</u>   Life times of electronic components (Bowker and Lieberman, 1963, p. 362)

Temperature	Oven		
	1	2	3
1	237	208	192
	254	178	186
	246	187	183
2	178	146	142
	179	145	125
	183	141	136

The model for this analysis is

$$y_{ijk} = \mu + a_i + b_j + c_{ij} + e_{ijk}$$

where $i = 1,2$; $j = 1,2,3$; and $k = 1,2,3$. Here the a_i, b_j, c_{ij} and e_{ijk} are independent samples from Gaussian populations with zero means and variances σ_a^2, σ_b^2, σ_c^2, and σ_e^2 respectively. The conventional analysis of these data (as could be obtained using BMD08V) is

<u>Random Effects Model Analysis of Variance</u>

Source	Degrees of Freedom	Mean Square	Expected Mean Square	F-value	Variance Component
temp	1	13667.56	$\sigma_e^2 + 3\sigma_c^2 + 9\sigma_a^2$	99.5 **	1503.
oven	2	4823.17	$\sigma_e^2 + 3\sigma_c^2 + 6\sigma_b^2$	35.1 *	781.
temp x oven	2	137.39	$\sigma_e^2 + 3\sigma_c^2$	2.0	23.
error	12	69.78	σ_e^2		70.

* means significant at the 5% level, ** at 1%, and *** at 0.1%

To obtain maximum likelihood estimates for the parameters in the above model we specify the following Control Language instructions.

Example 15.20

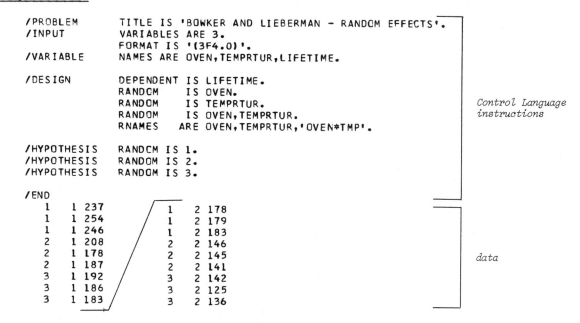

```
/PROBLEM        TITLE IS 'BOWKER AND LIEBERMAN - RANDOM EFFECTS'.
/INPUT          VARIABLES ARE 3.
                FORMAT IS '(3F4.0)'.
/VARIABLE       NAMES ARE OVEN,TEMPRTUR,LIFETIME.

/DESIGN         DEPENDENT IS LIFETIME.
                RANDOM    IS OVEN.
                RANDOM    IS TEMPRTUR.
                RANDOM    IS OVEN,TEMPRTUR.
                RNAMES    ARE OVEN,TEMPRTUR,'OVEN*TMP'.

/HYPOTHESIS     RANDOM IS 1.
/HYPOTHESIS     RANDOM IS 2.
/HYPOTHESIS     RANDOM IS 3.

/END
    1   1 237          1   2 178
    1   1 254          1   2 179
    1   1 246          1   2 183
    2   1 208          2   2 146
    2   1 178          2   2 145
    2   1 187          2   2 141
    3   1 192          3   2 142
    3   1 186          3   2 125
    3   1 183          3   2 136
```

Control Language instructions

data

The results are presented in Output 15.20. We summarize the tests of the variance components:

Maximum Likelihood Analysis for the Random Effects Model

Variance Component	Estimate	Standard Error	Degrees of Freedom	Likelihood Ratio χ^2
σ_a^2	893	1075	2	4.74
σ_b^2	664	674	1	4.00*
σ_c^2	23	47.0	1	.46
σ_e^2	70	28.3		

The number of degrees of freedom for σ_a^2 is two (rather than one) because when σ_a^2 was set equal to zero, the estimate of σ_b^2 was also zero.

The variance components for the main effects differ somewhat from the analysis of variance results but agree exactly with the maximum likelihood results given by Hartley and Vaughn (1972). In both cases, the large components are associated with the temperature and oven main effects. The χ^2 values are likelihood ratio statistics for the hypothesis that the corresponding variance component is zero. Clearly, these tests lead to less significance than the conventional analysis of variance tests, and one suspects that this may not be the best way to test the significance of a variance component.

Output 15.20 Analysis of random effects model by P3V

```
        NUMBER OF CASES READ. . . . . . . . . . . . .     18

DEPENDENT VARIABLE LIFETIME

PARAMETER          ESTIMATE            STANDARD          EST/ST.DEV.      TWO-TAIL PROBABILITY
                                       DEVIATION                         (ASYMPTOTIC THEORY)

   ERR.VAR.      69.7777777778        28.4866584901
   CONSTANT     180.3333333334        25.9904318931       6.9384508133          0.0
   OVEN         664.2788652982       674.4496845039
   TEMPRTUR     892.7998580680      1075.0786174783
   OVEN*TMP      22.7987358909        47.0256706144

-2*LOG(MAXIMUM LIKELIHOOD) =    146.9461364746

VARIANCE-COVARIANCE MATRIX OF THE PARAMETERS

                 ERR.VAR.       CONSTANT       OVEN        TEMPRTUR       OVEN*TMP

   ERR.VAR.        811.4895
   CONSTANT         -0.0          675.5024
   OVEN            -0.0000         -0.0        454882.3750
   TEMPRTUR        -0.0000         -0.0        -94041.3750   1155794.0000
   OVEN*TMP       -270.4963        -0.0         -1020.2092   -495.4041      2211.4136

RESIDUAL ANALYSIS

CELL       OBSERVED    PREDICTED     ST.DEV.      OBSERVED-     ST.DEV.     (O-P)/
           LIFETIME    LIFETIME      PRED.        PREDICTED     O-P         ST.DEV.
           237.0000    180.3333      25.9904       56.6667      31.2114      1.816
           254.0000    180.3333      25.9904       73.6667      31.2114      2.360
           246.0000    180.3333      25.9904       65.6667      31.2114      2.104
           208.0000    180.3333      25.9904       27.6667      31.2114      0.886
           178.0000    180.3333      25.9904       -2.3333      31.2114     -0.075
           187.0000    180.3333      25.9904        6.6667      31.2114      0.214
           192.0000    180.3333      25.9904       11.6667      31.2114      0.374
           186.0000    180.3333      25.9904        5.6667      31.2114      0.182
           183.0000    180.3333      25.9904        2.6667      31.2114      0.085
           178.0000    180.3333      25.9904       -2.3333      31.2114     -0.075
           179.0000    180.3333      25.9904       -1.3333      31.2114     -0.043
           183.0000    180.3333      25.9904        2.6667      31.2114      0.085
           146.0000    180.3333      25.9904      -34.3333      31.2114     -1.100
           145.0000    180.3333      25.9904      -35.3333      31.2114     -1.132
           141.0000    180.3333      25.9904      -39.3333      31.2114     -1.260
           142.0000    180.3333      25.9904      -38.3333      31.2114     -1.228
           125.0000    180.3333      25.9904      -55.3333      31.2114     -1.773
           136.0000    180.3333      25.9904      -44.3333      31.2114     -1.420


CONSTRAINED MODEL - HYPOTHESIS NUMBER  1

PARAMETER          ESTIMATE            STANDARD          EST/ST.DEV.      TWO-TAIL PROBABILITY
                                       DEVIATION                         (ASYMPTOTIC THEORY)

   ERR.VAR.      69.7777777778        28.4866584901
   CONSTANT     180.3333333333        19.4847201927       9.2551145554          0.0
   OVEN           0.0                  0.0
   TEMPRTUR     483.7222222223       783.9155255222
   OVEN*TMP     803.5000000000       584.6841898915

-2*LOG(MAXIMUM LIKELIHOOD) =    150.9493408203

VARIANCE-COVARIANCE MATRIX OF THE PARAMETERS

                 ERR.VAR.       CONSTANT       OVEN        TEMPRTUR       OVEN*TMP

   ERR.VAR.       811.4895
   CONSTANT         -0.0          379.6543
   OVEN            -0.0            -0.0         -0.0
   TEMPRTUR        -0.0000         -0.0         -0.0        614523.5000
   OVEN*TMP       -270.4963        -0.0         -0.0       -113921.7500    341855.5625

LIKELIHOOD RATIO TEST     CHI-SQUARE =      4.003

DEGREES OF FREEDOM     1

PROBABILITY      0.045
```

```
CONSTRAINED MODEL - HYPOTHESIS NUMBER  2              CONSTRAINED MODEL - HYPOTHESIS NUMBER  3
```

--- results for hypothesis 2 ---   *--- results for hypothesis 3 ---*

```
LIKELIHOOD RATIO TEST     CHI-SQUARE =     4.740      LIKELIHOOD RATIO TEST     CHI-SQUARE =     0.465

DEGREES OF FREEDOM     1                              DEGREES OF FREEDOM     1

PROBABILITY      0.029                                PROBABILITY      0.495
```

Mixed model analysis of variance

It seems natural to consider a model in which the temperature component in the above example is fixed, i.e., a mixed model of the form

$$y_{ijk} = \mu + \alpha_i + b_j + c_{ij} + e_{ijk}$$

where now both μ and α_i are fixed, the α_i sum to zero and the components b_j, c_{ij}, e_{ijk} are as before. There are at least two schools of thought regarding c_{ij}. One school assumes, as we have, that the c_{ij} are independent. The other assumes that the c_{ij} sum to zero on i. Our choice was based on a desire to make our results comparable with previously published results rather than a strong preference for one school over the other. Under the assumption that the c_{ij} are independent, the analysis of variance table using the mixed model is identical to that given for the random effects model except that the definition of σ_a^2 is changed to $\sigma_a^2 = \alpha_1^2 + \alpha_2^2$.

To obtain a maximum likelihood analysis we specify the following Control Language instructions.

Example 15.21

```
/PROBLEM      TITLE IS 'BOWKER AND LIEBERMAN - MIXED MODEL'.
/INPUT        VARIABLES ARE 3.
              FORMAT IS '(3F4.0)'.
/VARIABLE     NAMES ARE OVEN,TEMPRTUR,LIFETIME.

/GROUP        CODES(2) ARE 1,2.

/DESIGN       DEPENDENT IS LIFETIME.
              FIXED     IS TEMPRTUR.
              FNAME     IS TEMPRTUR.
              RANDOM    IS OVEN.
              RANDOM    IS OVEN,TEMPRTUR.
              RNAMES    ARE OVEN,'OVEN*TMP'.

/HYPOTHESIS   FIXED IS 1.
/HYPOTHESIS   RANDOM IS 1.
/HYPOTHESIS   RANDOM IS 2.

/END
    1   1 237      1   2 178
    1   1 254      1   2 179
    1   1 246      1   2 183
    2   1 208      2   2 146
    2   1 178      2   2 145
    2   1 187      2   2 141
    3   1 192      3   2 142
    3   1 186      3   2 125
    3   1 193      3   2 136
```

Control Language instructions

data

The results are presented in Output 15.21. We summarize the results as follows:

Maximum Likelihood Analysis for the Mixed Model

Mean or Variance Component	Estimate	Standard Error	Degrees of Freedom	Likelihood Ratio χ^2
α_1	27.6	2.26	1	11.88
σ_b^2	520.6	437.75	1	6.68
σ_c^2	7.3	26.68	1	.09
σ_e^2	70.0			

Output 15.21 Mixed model analysis by P3V

```
NUMBER OF CASES READ. . . . . . . . . . . . .       18



DEPENDENT VARIABLE LIFETIME

PARAMETER         ESTIMATE            STANDARD           EST/ST.DEV.      TWO-TAIL PROBABILITY
                                      DEVIATION                          (ASYMPTOTIC THEORY)

ERR.VAR.      69.7777777778        28.4866584901
CONSTANT     180.3333333333        13.3654705293        13.4924783707         0.0
TEMPRTUR      27.5555555556         2.2557653615        12.2156124115         0.0
OVEN         520.6419753086       437.7440521060
OVEN*TMP       7.2716049383        26.6756062595

-2*LOG(MAXIMUM LIKELIHOOD) =      139.8047790527



CONSTRAINED MODEL - HYPOTHESIS NUMBER   1


LIKELIHOOD RATIO TEST        CHI-SQUARE =        11.881

DEGREES OF FREEDOM       1

PROBABILITY        0.001


CONSTRAINED MODEL - HYPOTHESIS NUMBER   2


LIKELIHOOD RATIO TEST        CHI-SQUARE =         6.685

DEGREES OF FREEDOM       1

PROBABILITY        0.010


CONSTRAINED MODEL - HYPOTHESIS NUMBER   3


LIKELIHOOD RATIO TEST        CHI-SQUARE =         0.094

DEGREES OF FREEDOM       1

PROBABILITY        0.760
```

Treating the temperature effect as fixed clearly establishes its significance and more clearly establishes that of the random oven effect. Indeed both are now more clearly established than they were by either the conventional random or mixed model analysis of variance.

Another strategy for testing the fixed temperature effect might be based on treating

$$\hat{\alpha}_1/\hat{\text{std}}\ \hat{\alpha}_1 = 12.2$$

as a t statistic with 16 degrees of freedom. This test seems to give (if anything) even greater significance than the χ^2 likelihood ratio test.

One way to resolve the c_{ij} controversy in the mixed model is to assume $\sigma_c^2=0$ motivated by the fact that its estimate is very small. This leads to the conventional analysis of variance.

Mixed Model Analysis of Variance with no Interaction

Source	Degrees of Freedom	Mean Square	Expected Mean Square	F-value	Variance Component
temp	1	13667.56	$\sigma_e^2+9\sigma_a^2$	172.0	1509
oven	2	4823.17	$\sigma_e^2+6\sigma_b^2$	60.7	791
error	14	79.44	σ_e^2		79

Results in this table are the same as those given previously except that the interaction sum of squares has been pooled with the error sum of squares.

Clearly for testing significance with a conventional analysis of variance, the pooling that resulted from the assumption that $\sigma_c^2=0$ did a lot of good without greatly affecting the variance component estimates. The maximum likelihood analysis with $\sigma_c^2=0$ is summarized as:

Maximum Likelihood Analysis for the Mixed Model with no Interaction

Mean or Variance Component	Estimate	Standard Error	Degrees of Freedom	Likelihood Ratio
α_1	27.6	2.03	1	38.8
σ_b^2	523.6	437.59	1	26.3
σ_e^2	74.1	27.07		

As in the conventional analysis of variance, the tests become more significant when σ_c^2 is assumed to be zero. The component estimates are about the same as those in the previous maximum likelihood analysis.

● OPTIONS IN P3V

You must specify the model in a *DESIGN* paragraph   p. 594

You can specify

- the maximum number of iterations for the algorithm   p. 596
- initial values for the parameter estimates   p. 596
- whether to estimate the parameters by maximum likelihood
  or by restricted maximum likelihood   p. 595
- hypotheses to be tested   p. 596
- the number of levels for fixed effects variables   p. 597
- case weights   p. 598

● SPECIFYING THE MODEL: THE *DESIGN* PARAGRAPH

The *DESIGN* paragraph is used to specify the DEPENDENT variable, COVARIATES, FIXED effects components, RANDOM effects components, and names for the components (FNAME and RNAME respectively).

Each value of the DEPENDENT variable appears in a distinct case; there can only be one dependent variable. In P3V each repeated measure for a subject is recorded as a separate case. (This differs from P2V where multiple dependent variables can be present to represent repeated measures for a subject.)

The model is described by a sequence of FIXED and RANDOM component statements. Each component in the model (except the grand mean and the error) must be specified as either FIXED or RANDOM in separate statements; each statement corresponds to a line in an ANOVA table.

You can name the FIXED and RANDOM components by FNAME and RNAME statements respectively. Ordinarily you will probably want to give main effects the same name as the variable that defines the component. The main purpose of the FNAME and RNAME statements is to allow you to name the interactions. The names of the components are specified in the <u>same</u> sequence as that in which the components are defined. In our first example (Example 15.19) the *DESIGN* paragraph is

```
/DESIGN     DEPENDENT IS TEMPRTUR.
            FIXED     IS GROUP.
            FIXED     IS TREATMNT.
            FIXED     IS GROUP,TREATMNT.
            FNAMES    ARE GROUP,TREATMNT,'GRP*TRT'.
            COVARIATE IS BLOODPRS.
            RANDOM    IS GROUP,SUBJECT.
            RNAME     IS 'SBJ*GRP'.
```

Therefore the FNAMEs GROUP, TREATMNT and GRP*TRT are for the
GROUP, TREATMNT and GROUP x TREATMNT interactions respectively and the
RNAME SBJ*GRP is for SUBJECTs in the GROUPs component.

DESIGN
    DEPENDENT=v.   {none/prev.}   required

        Name or subscript of the dependent variable.

    COVARIATE=$v_1,v_2,\cdots$.   {none/prev.}

        Names or subscripts of the covariates.

    FIXED=$v_1,v_2,\cdots$.   {none/prev.}   may be repeated

        Names or subscripts of variables that define a fixed effects component
(main effect or interaction). Each FIXED statement corresponds to
a line in an ANOVA table.

        Note: You must specify CODES *or* CUTPOINTS *in the GROUP para-
graph (Section 5.4) for each variable in a* FIXED *statement.*

    FNAME=$c_1,c_2,\cdots$.   {FIX(subscript)/prev.}

        Names for the FIXED components. The first name is for the fixed
component defined by the first FIXED statement, the second name
for the second fixed component, etc. Note that all names are specified in one FNAMEs statement. If FNAMEs is not specified,
FIX(subscript) is used to label the results where subscript is the
sequence number of the FIX statement defining the component.

    RANDOM=$v_1,v_2,\cdots$.   {none/prev.}   may be repeated

        Names or subscripts of variables that define a random effects compo-
nent (main effect or interaction). Each RANDOM statement corresponds to a line in an ANOVA table.

    RNAME=$c_1,c_2,\cdots$.   {RAND(subscript)/prev.}

        Names for the RANDOM component. The first name is for the random
component defined by the first RANDOM statement, the second name
for the second random component, etc. Note that all names are specified in one RNAMEs statement. If RNAMEs is not specified,
RAND(subscript) is used to label the results where subscript is the
sequence number of the RAND statement defining the component.

The three examples shown for P3V have used (unrestricted) maximum likelihood estimates. P3V can also be used for restricted maximum likelihood or
REML estimates (see for example Corbeil and Searle, 1976). If data are
balanced and if the conventional analysis of variance estimates of the variance components are all nonnegative, then the conventional ANOVA estimates
are identical to the REML estimates (Jennrich, unpublished).

DESIGN
    METHOD= *(one only)* ML,REML.   {ML/prev.}

   Parameter estimates are obtained by (unrestricted) maximum likelihood estimation (ML) or by restricted maximum likelihood (REML).
   ML estimates are obtained unless REML is specified.

● INITIAL ESTIMATES FOR THE PARAMETERS

   The maximum likelihood estimates are found by iteration. You can specify
initial estimates for the parameters.

DESIGN
    PARAMETERS=$\#_1$,$\#_2$,$\cdots$.   {all 0.0 except $\sigma_e^2=1$/prev.}

   Initial estimates for the parameters. The first parameter is the
   variance of the error, σ_e^2. Next are coefficients of the covariates in
   the order stated in the COVARIATE statement (if any). These are
   followed by the fixed and random components in the sequence stated
   in the *DESIGN* paragraph. Remember that the parameters for any fixed
   effects component are the coefficients of the dummy variables; therefore if the component has more than one degree of freedom, it also
   has more than one coefficient.

● MAXIMUM NUMBER OF ITERATIONS

   The maximum number of iterations for the algorithm to obtain maximum
likelihood estimates is preassigned to 30. You can raise or lower this limit.

DESIGN
    MAXIT=#.   {30/prev.}

   Maximum number of iterations.

● SPECIFYING HYPOTHESES TO BE TESTED

   Each hypothesis to be tested (or each submodel to be evaluated) must be
specified in a separate *HYPOThesis* paragraph; no hypotheses are tested automatically. The *HYPOThesis* paragraph can be repeated to specify additional
submodels.

Each hypothesis is specified by one FIXED and/or one RANDOM statement that specify the components to be set to zero. Components are identified by the sequence number in which they are specified in the *DESIGN* paragraph. For example, the statements

$$\text{FIX} = 1,3. \qquad \text{RANDOM} = 1.$$

in the *HYPOTHesis* paragraph specifies that two fixed effects components defined in the first and third FIXED statements and the random component defined by the first RANDOM statement in the *DESIGN* paragraph are all to be set to zero.

HYPOTHesis
    FIXED=$\#_1$,$\#_2$,$\cdots$.   {none}

        The fixed components to be set to zero in the hypothesis to be tested (or submodel evaluated). Each fixed component is identified by the sequence number of the FIXED statement in which it is defined.

    RANDOM=$\#_1$,$\#_2$,$\cdots$.   {none}

        The random components to be set to zero in the hypothesis to be tested (or submodel evaluated). Each random component is identified by the sequence number of the RANDOM statement in which it is defined.

● NUMBER OF LEVELS FOR FIXED EFFECTS VARIABLES

The main effect for a fixed effects component is defined by codes, categories or levels of a grouping variable. The codes or categories can be defined by CODEs or CUTPOINTs in a *GROUP* paragraph (Section 5.4). If each value of the grouping variable corresponds to a distinct category for the fixed effect, you can specify the number of LEVELs in the *GROUP* paragraph and <u>not</u> CODEs or CUTPOINTs. Either the number of LEVELs <u>or</u> CODEs or CUTPOINTs must be specified for each grouping variable that defines a fixed component main effect.

GROUP
    LEVEL $(\#_1)$=$\#_2$.   {none}   may be repeated

        $\#_2$ is the number of levels of the variable with subscript $\#_1$. LEVEL is required for any variable that defines a fixed component main effect and for which neither CODEs nor CUTPOINTs are stated in the *GROUP* paragraph (Section 5.4).

● CASE WEIGHTS

The analysis can be weighted by the values of a case WEIGHT variable.

VARiable
    WEIGHT=v.   {none/prev.}
        Name or subscript of variable that contains case weights. If not
        specified or set to zero, there are no case weights.

● SIZE OF PROBLEM

The maximum problem that P3V can analyze is a complex function of the number of variables, covariates, groups and total number of dummy variables generated for the fixed and random effects. The following provides a rough guide to the capacity of P3V. Let vv be the total number of variables used in the analysis (the number of variables read as input and the number of dummy variables generated by P3V) and let g be the total number of groups (cells) in the ANOVA model. Then P3V can analyze the following combinations of vv and g

vv	10	20	50	75
g	100	90	65	30

Appendix B describes how to increase the capacity of the program.

● COMPUTATIONAL METHOD

The data are read in single precision. Computations are performed in double precision. The means, variances and cross products are computed by the method of provisional means (Appendix A.2). The computations performed by P3V are described in Appendix A.19. They are based on a combination Fisher-scoring and Newton-Raphson algorithm (Jennrich and Sampson, 1976).

ACKNOWLEDGEMENT

P3V was designed by Robert Jennrich and Paul Sampson with major contributions from R.L. Anderson. It was programmed by Paul Sampson.

15.4 Summary — P1V, P2V, P3V

The Control Language on this page is common to all programs. This is followed by the Control Language specific to

P1V -- One-Way Analysis of Variance and Covariance   p. 600
P2V -- Analysis of Variance and Covariance, Including
             Repeated Measures   p. 601
P3V -- General Mixed Model Analysis of Variance   p. 602

Paragraph STATEMENT[1] {Preassigned value[2]}		Definition, restriction	See pages:
/PROBlem		Required each problem	74
TITLE='c'.	{blank}	Problem title, $\leq$ 160 char.	74
/INPut		Required first problem. Either VARIABLE and FORMAT, or UNIT and CODE required.	75
VARIABLE=#.	{none/prev.}	No. of variables in input data	75
FORMAT='c'.	{none/prev.}	Format of input data, $\leq$ 800 char.	76
CASE=#.	{end-of-file/prev.}	No. of cases in data	76-77
UNIT=#.	{5(cards)/prev.}	Input unit if data are not on cards; not 1, 2, 6	77
REWIND.	{REWIND/prev.}	Rewind input unit	77
CODE=c.	{none}	Code to identify BMDP File	132
CONTENT=c.	{DATA}	Data or matrix in BMDP File	132
LABEL=c.	{none}	Label of BMDP File, $\leq$ 40 char.	132
/VARiable		Optional. For input from a BMDP File, items in this paragraph may be previously set, see Chapter 7.	79
NAME=c_1,c_2,$\cdots$.	{X(subscript)/prev.}	Variable names, one per variable	79-80
MAXIMUM=$\#_1$,$\#_2$,$\cdots$.	{none/prev.}	Upper limits, one per variable	80
MINIMUM=$\#_1$,$\#_2$,$\cdots$.	{none/prev.}	Lower limits, one per variable	80
BLANK= (one only) ZERO, MISSING.	{ZERO/ prev.}	Blanks treated as zeros or as missing value codes	81
MISSING=$\#_1$,$\#_2$,$\cdots$.	{none/prev.}	Missing value codes, one per variable	81
USE=v_1,v_2,$\cdots$.	{all variables}	Variables used in the analysis	82
LABEL=v_1,v_2.	{none/prev.}	Variable(s) used to label cases, read under A-format, one or two	83
ADD=#.	{0/prev.}	No. of variables added through transformation	99
BEFORE. or AFTER.	{BEFORE/prev.}	Data checked for limits before or after transformation	100
/TRANsform		Optional, Control Language transformations and case selection	97-105
/SAVE		Optional, required to create BMDP File	125
CODE=c.	{none}	Code to identify BMDP File, required	125-126
LABEL='c'.	{blank}	Label for BMDP File, $\leq$ 40 char.	125-126
UNIT=#.	{none}	Unit on which BMDP File is written; not 1, 2, 5 or 6	126-127
NEW.	{not new}	NEW if this is first BMDP File written in the system file	126-127

Key: #   number   v variable name or subscript
      'c' title, label or format   c name not exceeding 8 char., apostrophes may be required (p. 59)

[1] In BMDP programs dated before August 1977, the minimum required abbreviations are *INPUT* (not *INP*), VARIAB (not VAR), FORMAT (not FORM), CONTENT (not CONT), *VARIAB* (not *VAR*), BEFORET (not BEF), AFTERT (not AFT), *TRANSF* (not *TRAN*). If dated before February 1976, BLANK=ZERO and cannot be changed.

[2] "/prev." means that any assignment remains the same as that specified in the previous problem or subproblem until changed. Otherwise, the assignment returns to its preassigned value each time a new problem begins or the paragraph is used again.

P1V -- One-Way Analysis of Variance and Covariance

(in addition to that on p. 599)

Paragraph STATEMENT[1] {Preassigned value}	Definition, restriction	See pages:
VARiable	Specify as part of *VARiable* paragraph, p. 599	
GROUPing=v. {no. grouping var./prev.}	Variable used to classify cases into groups, required	529
/GROUP	Required if GROUPing variable has more than 10 distinct values	84
CODE(#)=$\#_1,\#_2,\cdots$. {10 smallest values/prev.}	Codes for variable #	84-85
CUTPOINT(#)=$\#_1,\#_2,\cdots$. {see CODE/prev.}	Cutpoints to define intervals for variable #	84-85
NAME(#)=$c_1,c_2,\cdots$. {CODEs or CUTPOINTs /prev.}	Codes or interval names for variable #	84-85
RESET. {not RESET}	If RESET, all assignments in prev. *GROUP* paragraph are reset to preassigned values	86
/DESIGN	Required, may be repeated	529
DEPENDENT=$v_1,v_2,\cdots$. {all except GROUPING and INDEP vars.}	Dependent variables	530
INDEPENDENT=$v_1,v_2,\cdots$. {none}	Covariates	530
TITLE='c'. {blank}	Title for analysis, $\leq$ 160 char.	530
GROUP=$g_1,g_2,\cdots$. {all groups/prev.}	Groups to be compared by analysis	530
PLOT. {no/prev.}	Plots against covariates and residual plots	530-531
CONTRast=$\#_1,\#_2,\cdots$. {none}	Contrast on (adjusted) groups means	531,533
/PRINT	Optional, additional results to be printed	
MINIMUM. {no/prev.}	Minimums for each group	535-538
MAXIMUM. {no/prev.}	Maximums for each group	535-538
MEAN. {no/prev.}	Means for each group	535-538
COVARIANCE. {no/prev.}	Covariance matrix for each group	535-538
CORRELATION. {no/prev.}	Correlation matrix for each group	535-538
TOTAL. {no/prev.}	Variance-covariance matrix (no grouping)	535-538
BETWEEN. {no/prev.}	Variance-covariance matrix (between groups)	535-538
WITHIN. {no/prev.}	Variance-covariance matrix (within groups)	535-538
RREGRESSION. {no/prev.}	Correlations between coefficients of covariates	535-539
MCORRELATION. {no/prev.}	Correlations between adjusted group means	535-539
/END	Required	57

Key: #   number
      v   variable name or subscript
      'c'   title

c   name not exceeding 8 chars., apostrophes may be required (p. 59)
g   group name (from *GROUP* paragraph) or subscript (not CODE or CUTPOINT)

[1] In BMDP programs dated before August 1977, *SUBP* is used in place of *DESIGN* and RCOR in place of RREG; when a *GROUP* paragraph is used, RESET is implicitly specified and cannot be changed.

- **Order of input**

    (1) System Cards, at HSCF these are
```
//jobname  JOB  nooo,yourname
//  EXEC  BIMED,PROG=BMDP1V
//SYSIN  DD  *
```

    (2) Control Language instructions
```
PROBlem paragraph, required
INPut paragraph, required first problem
VARiable paragraph, required first problem
GROUP paragraph
TRANsform paragraph
SAVE paragraph
DESIGN paragraph, may be repeated for additional analyses of the same data
PRINT paragraph
END paragraph, required at end of Control Language
```

    (3) Data, if on cards
```
data
```

    (4) System Card, at HSCF this is
```
//
```

    Control Language instructions and data (2 and 3) can be repeated for additional problems.

P2V -- Analysis of Variance and Covariance, Including Repeated Measures

(in addition to that on p. 599)

Paragraph STATEMENT[1] {Preassigned value}		Definition, restriction	See pages:
SAVE		Specify as part of *SAVE* paragraph (p. 599)	
....RESIDUAL.	{RESI/prev.}	Save residuals and predicted values	574-577
/DESIGN		Required, specify design by either FORM or GROUP,DEPEND,LEVEL and COVA.	563
GROUPING=$v_1,v_2,\cdots$.	{none/prev.}	Grouping factors	564-566
DEPENDENT=$v_1,v_2,\cdots$.	{none/prev.}	Dependent variables	564-566
LEVEL= $\#_1,\#_2,\cdots$.	{none/prev.}	Number of levels of trial factors	564-566
COVARIATE=$v_1,v_2,\cdots$.	{none/prev.}	Covariates	564-566
FORM='c'.	{none/prev.}	Design (using G,Y,X,D symbols)	566-567
NAME= $c_1,c_2,\cdots$.	{R,S,T,.../prev.}	Names of trial factors	569
ORTHOGONAL.	{no/prev.}	Orthogonal decomposition to be printed	569
POINT(#)=$\#_1,\#_2,\cdots$.	{1,2,3,...}	Spacing for levels of trial factor #, may be repeated	570
SYMMETRY.	{no/prev.}	Test of compound symmetry	570-571
(one only) {INCLUDE=$\#_1,\#_2,\cdots$ {EXCLUDE=$\#_1,\#_2,\cdots$	{include all main effects and interactions for grouping factors}	Terms to be included or excluded from the model for the grouping factors	571-574
RESIDUAL= *(one only)* MEAN,ORTH.	{MEAN /prev.}	Method of computing residuals and predicted values	574-577
PRINT.	{no/prev.}	Residuals and predicted values are printed	574-577
....TOLERANCE=#.	{0.01/prev.}	Tolerance limit	577
/GROUP		Required if any GROUPING factor has more than 10 distinct values	84
CODE(#)=$\#_1,\#_2,\cdots$.	{10 smallest values/prev.}	Codes for variable #, may be repeated	84-85
CUTPOINT(#)= $\#_1,\#_2,\cdots$.	{see CODE/prev.}	Cutpoints to define intervals for variable #, may be repeated	84-85
NAME(#)= $c_1,c_2,\cdots$.	{CODES or CUTPOINTS/prev.}	Codes or interval names for variable #, may be repeated	84-85
RESET.	{not RESET }	If RESET, all assignments in prev. *GROUP* paragraph are reset to preassigned values	86
/END		Required	57

Key: #   number   v   variable name or subscript
'c' format, title or label   c   name not exceeding 8 chars., apostrophes may be required (p. 59)

[1] If your BMDP programs are dated before April 1977, SYMMETRY is not available; the residuals and predicted values
cannot be printed or saved. If dated before August 1976, INCLUDE and EXCLUDE are not available; TOLERANCE
is set to 0.01 and cannot be changed.

- **Order of input**

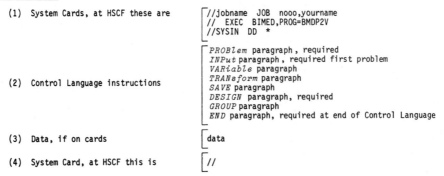

(1)	System Cards, at HSCF these are	//jobname JOB nooo,yourname
		// EXEC BIMED,PROG=BMDP2V
		//SYSIN DD *

(2)	Control Language instructions	*PROBlem* paragraph , required *INPut* paragraph , required first problem *VARiable* paragraph *TRANsform* paragraph *SAVE* paragraph *DESIGN* paragraph, required *GROUP* paragraph *END* paragraph, required at end of Control Language
(3)	Data, if on cards	data
(4)	System Card, at HSCF this is	//

Control Language instructions and data (2 and 3) can be repeated for additional problems.

P3V -- General Mixed Model Analysis of Variance

(in addition to that on p. 599)

Paragraph STATEMENT {Preassigned value}		Definition, restriction	See pages:
VARiable		Specify as part of *VARiable* paragraph (p. 599)	
WEIGHT=v.	{no case weights/prev.}	Variable containing case weights	598
/DESIGN		Required	594
DEPENDENT= v.	{none/prev.}	Dependent variable, required	594-595
COVARIATE= $v_1, v_2, \cdots$.	{none/prev.}	Covariates	594-595
FIXED= $v_1, v_2, \cdots$.	{none/prev.}	Variables that define a fixed effects component, may be repeated	594-595
FNAME= $c_1, c_2, \cdots$.	{FIX (subscript)/prev.}	Names for the FIXED components	594-595
RANDOM= $v_1, v_2, \cdots$.	{none/prev.}	Variables that define a random effects component, may be repeated	594-595
RNAME= $c_1, c_2, \cdots$.	{RAND (subscript)/prev.}	Names for RANDOM components	594-595
METHOD=*(one only)* ML,REML.	{ML/prev.}	Maximum likelihood (ML) or restricted maximum likelihood (REML)	595-596
PARAMETER= $\#_1, \#_2, \cdots$.	{all 0.0 except $\sigma_e^2=1$/prev.}	Initial estimates for the parameters	596
MAXIT=#.	{30/prev.}	Maximum number of iterations	596
/HYPOTHesis		Optional, used to specify submodels, may be repeated	596
FIXED= $\#_1, \#_2, \cdots$.	{none}	Fixed components to be set to zero	597
RANDOM= $\#_1, \#_2, \cdots$.	{none}	Random components to be set to zero	597

/GROUP		Required if there are any FIXED effects, either
		  LEVEL or CODE or CUTPOINT required for
		  each variable in FIXED component	

LEVEL(#)= $\#_1, \#_2, \cdots$.	{none}	Number of levels for variable #, may be repeated	597
CODE(#)= $\#_1, \#_2, \cdots$.	{10 smallest values/prev.}	Codes for variable #, may be repeated	84-85
CUTPOINT(#)= $\#_1, \#_2, \cdots$.	{see CODE/prev.}	Cutpoints to define intervals for variable #, may be repeated	84-85
NAME(#)= $c_1, c_2, \cdots$.	{CODEs or CUTPOINTS/prev.}	Codes or interval names for variable #, may be repeated	84-85
RESET.	{not RESET}	If RESET, all assignments in prev. *GROUP* paragraph are reset to preassigned values	86
/END		Required	57

Key: #   number   c   name not exceeding 8 chars., apostrophes may be required (p. 59)
       v   variable name or subscript

- Order of input

    (1) System Cards, at HSCF these are

```
//jobname  JOB  nooo,yourname
//  EXEC  BIMED,PROG=BMDP3V
//SYSIN  DD  *
```

    (2) Control Language instructions

```
PROBLem paragraph, required
INPut paragraph, required first problem
VARiable paragraph
TRANsform paragraph
SAVE paragraph
DESIGN paragraph, required
HYPOTHesis paragraph, may be repeated to specify additional hypotheses
GROUP paragraph
END  paragraph, required at end of Control Language
```

    (3) Data, if on cards

```
data
```

    (4) System Card, at HSCF this is

```
//
```

    Control Language instructions and data (2 and 3) can be repeated for additional problems.

16

NONPARAMETRIC ANALYSIS

In this chapter we discuss P3S -- Nonparametric Statistics. The statistics computed by P3S are appropriate for four different problems.

- The sign test and Wilcoxon signed-rank test compare the difference in location of two populations based on paired observations.

- The Mann-Whitney rank sum test and the Kruskal-Wallis one-way analysis of variance compare the differences in location of two or more populations based on independent samples from each population.

- The Friedman two-way analysis of variance compares the average ranks assigned to different objects by tests or by several judges. Kendall's coefficient of concordance is a normalization of the Friedman statistic.

- The Kendall and Spearman rank correlations estimate the correlations between two variables based on the ranks of the observations and not on the data values.

These statistics are discussed in many texts such as Conover (1971), Hájek (1969), Lehmann (1975), and Siegel (1956).

Each of the above statistics has a parallel parametric test that is based on the assumption that the data are normally distributed. The sign and Wilcoxon tests correspond to the paired t test, and the Mann-Whitney test corresponds to the two-sample t test that assumes equal variances for both populations. The t tests are discussed in P3D -- Comparison of Two Groups with t Tests (Section 9.1). The Kruskal-Wallis test corresponds to the one-way analysis of variance (see P7D, Section 9.2 or P1V, Section 15.1). The Friedman test corresponds to the test for a specific main effect in a two-way analysis of variance. The two rank correlations have a parallel in the usual product-moment correlation coefficient.

Except for dropping the assumption that the data are normally distributed, the nonparametric test statistics have assumptions similar to their parametric counterparts. For example, the Mann-Whitney test assumes that the samples are obtained from distributions that are identical under the null hypothesis; the two-sample t (with pooled variance, p. 173) makes the same assumption and also assumes that the data are normally distributed. The sizes of the Mann-Whitney test and the two-sample t test just mentioned are a function of the ratio of the scale parameters (variances) of both groups (Pratt, 1964).

P3S

16.1 Nonparametric Statistics

P3S can compute

- the sign test and Wilcoxon signed-rank test to compare matched pairs of specified variables   p. 606

- the Friedman two-way analysis of variance and Kendall's coefficient of concordance to compare any number of objects rated or scored relative to each other by several judges or tests   p. 610

- the Mann-Whitney rank-sum test to compare two independent groups and the Kruskal-Wallis one-way analysis of variance to compare two or more groups   p. 612

- the Kendall and Spearman rank correlation coefficients between pairs of specified variables   p. 613

● CONTROL LANGUAGE

The Control Language instructions to describe the data and variables are common to all BMDP programs and are explained in Chapter 5: the *PROBlem*, *INPut*[1] *VARiable* and *GROUP* paragraphs are used in P3S.

If data editing or transformations are necessary, the methods described in Chapter 6 can be used. Data can be read using a FORMAt statement or from a BMDP File (Chapter 7). If a BMDP File is read as input and a new BMDP File is created in the same problem, the two Files must be in different system files and must have different UNIT numbers.

A summary of the Control Language instructions common to all BMDP programs is on p. 618; a summary of the Control Language instructions specific to P3S follows the general summary. The summary can be used as an index to the program description.

● THE *TEST* PARAGRAPH

The *TEST* paragraph is required in P3S to specify the statistics to be computed. The *TEST* paragraph may be repeated for additional analyses of the same data. The required order of input is described in the summary (p. 619).

The *TEST* paragraph can be used to specify a TITLE for each analysis and to select the VARIABLES to be included in the computations.

---

[1] BMDP programs dated before August 1977 require more letters in the permissible abbreviated form (the capitalized letters). The minimum required abbreviations are specified in the footnotes to the summary (p. 618).

```
TEST
    TITLE='c'.                    {blank}                    ≤ 160 char.
        A title for the analysis.

    VARIABLE= v₁,v₂,···.          {all var. except the GROUPING var.}
        Names or subscripts of variables to be included in the analysis.
```

- THE SIGN AND WILCOXON SIGNED-RANK TESTS

To illustrate an analysis produced by P3S we use the data in Table 16.1 (Siegel, 1956, p. 253). The data are the relative ranks of 20 mothers (from 1 to 20) assigned by staff members. We first ask if one mother differs from another in her average ranking. It is appropriate to simultaneously test the total rankings of the mothers for equality. This is done in the second example.

<u>Table 16.1</u> Data from Siegel (1956, p. 253)

Mothers

	1	2	3	4	5	6	7	8	9	10	11	12	13	14	15	16	17	18	19	20
1	1	2	3	4	5	6	7	8	9	10	11	12	13	14	15	16	17	18	19	20
2	5	1	16	8	9	2	6	10	4	3	11	13	7	12	17	18	19	15	14	20
3	3	2	7	5	14	9	15	16	6	11	8	10	1	4	19	12	20	13	17	18
4	8	3	10	11	4	2	5	13	9	1	14	7	6	15	16	12	19	17	18	20
5	2	1	15	8	14	4	6	9	7	10	11	5	3	16	11	13	18	17	12	19
6	16	17	5	13	15	11	7	4	9	2	18	3	6	1	19	12	10	8	14	20
7	12	9	14	6	7	2	3	10	5	4	17	8	1	15	13	16	18	11	20	19
8	11	2	13	10	7	3	4	14	6	5	17	9	1	12	8	16	20	15	18	19
9	9	2	15	6	5	7	8	10	9	3	12	4	1	13	11	14	19	18	16	17
10	2	4	16	3	10	6	14	17	15	7	19	9	1	8	5	13	11	18	12	20
11	11	14	12	8	7	2	5	10	3	4	13	9	1	18	6	15	19	16	17	20
12	8	1	13	3	5	2	14	9	6	10	15	11	19	4	7	12	18	17	16	20
13	5	3	13	2	8	1	9	12	4	6	14	10	11	7	15	18	16	17	19	20

(Left margin label: J u d g e s)

<u>Note:</u> Each case contains the rankings of one judge for all 20 mothers. The first ranking is recorded in columns 2-3, the second in 5-6, etc; the number of the judge is not recorded on the data card.

In the first example we request a comparison of all possible pairs of the first four mothers; we restrict the analysis to four mothers to reduce the printed results.

In the example the observed values are ranks. The data need <u>not</u> be ranks; P3S will rank the data in order to perform the test.

The Control Language instructions are

Example 16.1

```
/PROBLEM      TITLE IS 'SIEGEL RANK DATA'.
/INPUT        VARIABLES ARE 20.
              FORMAT IS '(20F3.0)'.

/TEST         TITLE IS 'SIGN TEST AND WILCOXON TEST'.
              VARIABLES ARE 1 TO 4.
              SIGN.
              WILCOXON.

/END
```

The Control Language must be preceded by System Cards to initiate the analysis by P3S. At HSCF, the System Cards are

```
//jobname  JOB  nooo,yourname
//  EXEC  BIMED,PROG=BMDP3S
//SYSIN  DD  *
```

The Control Language is immediately followed by the data (Table 16.1). The analysis is terminated by another System Card. At HSCF, this System Card is

```
//
```

The results are reproduced in Output 16.1. Circled numbers below correspond to those in the output. The variables (mothers) are not named in the Control Language instructions. Therefore they are named X(subscript).

① The number of cases read is 13. Only complete cases are used in the computations; i.e., cases that have no missing values or values out of range. All variables are checked for acceptable values unless USE is specified in the *VARiable* paragraph (Section 5.3), in which case only the variables specified in the USE statement are checked.

Output 16.1 Sign and Wilcoxon tests by P3S. Circled numbers correspond to those in the text. Results not reproduced are indicated in italics.

```
BMDP3S - NONPARAMETRIC STATISTICS              PROGRAM REVISED SEPTEMBER 1977
HEALTH SCIENCES COMPUTING FACILITY             MANUAL DATE -- 1977
UNIVERSITY OF CALIFORNIA, LOS ANGELES
```

--- Control Language read by P3S is printed and interpreted ---

```
PERFORM SIGN TEST
PERFORM WILCOXON SIGNED RANKS TEST
```

① NUMBER OF CASES READ.   13

VARIABLE NO. NAME	MEAN	STANDARD DEVIATION	MINIMUM	MAXIMUM
1 *X(1)	7.153844	4.597937	1.000000	16.000000
2 *X(2)	4.692305	5.265999	1.000000	17.000000

--- univariate statistics for variables 3 to 18 ---

19 *X(19)	16.307648	2.626297	12.000000	20.000000
20 *X(20)	19.384583	0.960770	17.000000	20.000000

```
*   DENOTES DEFAULT VARIABLE NAME
```

(continued)

Output 16.1 *(continued)*

SIGN TEST RESULTS

③ NUMBER OF NON-ZERO DIFFERENCES

		X(1) 1	X(2) 2	X(3) 3	X(4) 4
X(1)	1	0			
X(2)	2	13	0		
X(3)	3	13	13	0	
X(4)	4	13	13	13	0

SMALLER NUMBER OF LIKE-SIGNED DIFFERENCES

		X(1) 1	X(2) 2	X(3) 3	X(4) 4
X(1)	1	0			
X(2)	2	4	0		
X(3)	3	1	2	0	
X(4)	4	6	5	3	0

LEVEL OF SIGNIFICANCE OF SIGN TEST

```
1.0000
0.2668    1.0000
0.0034    0.0225    1.0000
1.0000    0.5811    0.0923    1.0000
```

④ WILCOXON SIGNED RANKS TEST RESULTS

NUMBER OF NON-ZERO DIFFERENCES

		X(1) 1	X(2) 2	X(3) 3	X(4) 4
X(1)	1	0			
X(2)	2	13	0		
X(3)	3	13	13	0	
X(4)	4	13	13	13	0

SMALLER SUM OF LIKE-SIGNED RANKS

		X(1) 1	X(2) 2	X(3) 3	X(4) 4
X(1)	1	0.0			
X(2)	2	18.0000	0.0		
X(3)	3	10.5000	11.0000	0.0	
X(4)	4	38.0000	25.0000	11.0000	0.0

LEVEL OF SIGNIFICANCE OF WILCOXON SIGNED RANKS TEST USING NORMAL APPROXIMATION (TWO-TAIL)

```
1.0000
0.0546    1.0000
0.0144    0.0159    1.0000
0.6002    0.1520    0.0159    1.0000
```

(2) Univariate statistics for each variable

- mean
- standard deviation
- minimum observed value (not out of range)
- maximum observed value (not out of range)

(3) The sign test is computed for each pair of variables. The difference between the values of the variables in each pair is calculated for each case and the number of differences that are positive (N_+) and negative (N_-) are recorded. Let the total number of nonzero differences be $N_T = N_+ + N_-$. Then N_T is printed in the top panel of the results for the sign test. The lesser of N_+ and N_- (say N_{min}) is printed in the second panel. In the third panel P3S reports the level of significance of the sign test corresponding to a two-sided test of the hypothesis that the + and - signs of the differences are equally probable (each sign has probability ½).

When N_T is less than or equal to 25, the probability p is computed from the binomial distribution

$$p = (½)^{N_T - 1} \sum_{j=0}^{N_{min}} \frac{N_T!}{j!(N_T - j)!}$$

When N_T exceeds 25, the two-sided probability is calculated from the normal approximation

$$z = \left(N_{min} - N_T/2 + ½ \right) \Big/ (N_T/4)^{½} .$$

(4) The Wilcoxon signed rank test is computed for each pair of variables. The Wilcoxon statistic is used to test the hypothesis that two populations have the same location parameter (mean) under the assumption that both variables have the same distribution.

Let d_j be the difference between the two variables for case j. The absolute values of all nonzero d_j's are ranked; the average rank is assigned when two or more $|d_j|$'s are tied. The sum of the ranks associated with positive differences R_+ and the sum of the ranks associated with negative differences R_- are calculated. The test statistic R_{min} is the lesser of R_+ and R_-.

In the first panel of the results the number of nonzero differences is printed (N_T in (3) above). The second panel gives the value of R_{min}. In the third panel P3S reports the level of significance of the Wilcoxon signed rank test corresponding to a two-sided test of the hypothesis that the populations have the same location parameter. The probability is computed by a normal approximation for the distribution of R_{min}:

$$z = \left[R_{min} - \frac{N_T(N_T + 1)}{4} \right] \Big/ \left[\frac{N_T(N_T + 1)(2N_T + 1)}{24} \right]^{½}$$

For small sample sizes ($N \leq 20$) exact levels of significance are tabulated in Dixon and Massey (1969, Table A-19).

```
TEST
    SIGN.                    {no/prev.}

        Compute the sign test between all possible pairings of the variables.

    WILCoxON.                {no/prev.}

        Compute the Wilcoxon signed rank test between all possible pairings
        of the variables.[2]
```

● THE FRIEDMAN TWO-WAY ANALYSIS OF VARIANCE AND KENDALL'S
  COEFFICIENT OF CONCORDANCE

We use the data in Table 16.1 (Siegel, 1956, p. 233) to illustrate the
FRIEDMAN two-way analysis of variance. Each judge ranked twenty mothers
from 1 to 20. The hypothesis to be tested is that the average rank for each
mother is equal to the average rank of the other mothers.

Let R_i be the sum of the ranks for the ith variable (i=1,...,20 in our
example). The Friedman statistic is

$$X = \frac{12}{Nk(k-1)} \sum_{i=1}^{k} R_i^2 - 2N(k+1)$$

where k is the number of variables and N is the number of cases. The level
of significance of X is obtained from the chi-square distribution with k-1
degrees of freedom. This level of significance is appropriate except for
very small sample sizes.

The data read by P3S do not need to be ranks; they can be test scores
or other measures. For each case P3S ranks the results across variables.
That is, a case corresponds to a judge or test. The values each judge or
test gives to the variables are ranked by P3S.

The Kendall coefficient of concordance W is

W = X/{N(k-1)}.

The level of significance of W is the same as that of the Friedman X.

To obtain the Friedman and Kendall statistics we specify

    FRIEDMAN.

in the TEST paragraph of Example 16.2.

---

[2] If your BMDP programs are dated before August 1977,
    the minimum required abbreviation is WILCOX (not WILC).

Example 16.2

```
/PROBLEM        TITLE IS 'SIEGEL RANK DATA'.
/INPUT          VARIABLES ARE 20.
                FORMAT IS '(20F3.0)'.

/TEST           TITLE IS 'FRIEDMAN TEST AND KENDALL
                    COEFFICIENT OF CONCORDANCE'.
                FRIEDMAN.

/END
```

The results are shown in Output 16.2. For each variable the sum of the ranks are printed. This is followed by the value of X and its level of significance. Finally, the value of W is printed.

Ranks need not be used as input data. P3S ranks the values given to the variables in each case before computing the Friedman test.

TEST

FRIEDMAN.   {no/prev.}

  Compute the Friedman two-way analysis of variance and the Kendall coefficient of concordance.

Output 16.2 Friedman test performed by P3S.

```
PERFORM FRIEDMAN TWO WAY ANALYSIS OF VARIANCE TEST

NUMBER OF CASES READ. . . . . . . . . . . . .      13


FRIEDMAN TWO WAY ANALYSIS OF VARIANCE TEST RESULTS


VARIABLE        RANK
NO. NAME        SUM
  1   X(1)       93.5
  2   X(2)       61.0
  3   X(3)      154.0
  4   X(4)       87.0
  5   X(5)      111.0
  6   X(6)       57.0
  7   X(7)      103.0
  8   X(8)      143.0
  9   X(9)       92.5
 10   X(10)      76.0
 11   X(11)     181.5
 12   X(12)     110.0
 13   X(13)      71.0
 14   X(14)     141.0
 15   X(15)     163.5
 16   X(16)     189.0
 17   X(17)     226.0
 18   X(18)     202.0
 19   X(19)     214.0
 20   X(20)     254.0

FRIEDMAN TEST STATISTIC = 146.53394
LEVEL OF SIGNIFICANCE = 0.0000 ASSUMING CHI-SQUARE DISTRIBUTION WITH    19 DEGREES OF FREEDOM

KENDALL COEFFICIENT OF CONCORDANCE = 0.59325
```

● THE MANN-WHITNEY RANK SUM TEST AND KRUSKAL-WALLIS ONE-WAY ANALYSIS OF VARIANCE

The Kruskal-Wallis (1952) statistic tests the equality of the location parameters (means) for two or more independent samples.

Let N observations be classified by a GROUPING variable into g groups; the jth group contains n_j observations. All the values for each variable are ranked from 1 to N; tied values are assigned average rank for the tied values. Let R_j be the sum of the ranks for each group. The Kruskal-Wallis statistic is

$$H = \frac{12}{N(N+1)} \sum_{j=1}^{g} \frac{R_j}{n_j} - 3(N+1)$$

If values are tied, H is modified to

$$H' = H \left/ \left[1 - \frac{\Sigma^*(t_i^3 - t_i)}{N^3 - N} \right] \right.$$

where t_i is the number of observations tied with a single value, and Σ^* is the sum over all distinct values for which a tie exists.

The level of significance of H is obtained from the chi-square distribution with (k-1) degrees of freedom. This level of significance is appropriate except for very small sample sizes.

When there are only two groups, the Mann-Whitney (Wilcoxon) statistic U is also reported

$$U = R_1 - \frac{n_1(n_1+1)}{2}$$

The level of significance of U is the same as that of H and corresponds to a two-tail probability.

The Werner blood chemistry data (Table 5.1) are used to illustrate the Kruskal-Wallis and Mann-Whitney statistics. The data are classified into two groups by BRTHPILL.

Example 16.3

```
/PROBLEM      TITLE IS 'WERNER BLOOD CHEMISTRY DATA'.
/INPUT        VARIABLES ARE 9.
              FORMAT IS '(A4,5F4.0,3F4.1)'.
/VARIABLE     NAMES ARE ID,AGE,HEIGHT,WEIGHT,BRTHPILL,
                   CHOLSTRL,ALBUMIN,CALCIUM,URICACID.
              MAXIMUM IS (6)400.
              MINIMUM IS (6)150.
              BLANKS ARE MISSING.
              LABEL IS ID.
              GROUPING IS BRTHPILL.

/GROUP        CODES(5) ARE      1,   2.
              NAMES(5) ARE NOPILL, PILL.

/TEST         TITLE IS 'KRUSKAL-WALLIS TEST'.
              KRUSKAL.

/END
```

The results appear in Output 16.3. For each variable analyzed a panel of results is printed. First the frequency n_j and rank sum R_j are printed for each group. Then the Kruskal-Wallis statistic and its level of significance are printed. When there are two groups, as in our example, the Mann-Whitney statistic and its level of significance are printed.

VARiable
>GROUPING.   {no grouping var./prev.}
>
>   Name or subscript of the GROUPING variable used to classify the cases into groups. If GROUPING is not specified or is set to zero, the cases are not grouped. If the GROUPING variable takes on more than 10 distinct values or codes, CODES or CUTPOINTS must be specified in the *GROUP* paragraph (Section 5.4).

TEST
>KRUSKAL.   {no/prev.}
>
>   The Kruskal-Wallis one-way analysis of variance is computed and, if there are only two groups, the Mann-Whitney (Wilcoxon) rank sum statistic is also computed.[3]
>
>   *Note: When* KRUSKAL *is specified, the other statistics available in P3S (sign test, Wilcoxon test, Friedman two-way analysis of variance and the correlations) are not computed even if requested.*

- ## THE KENDALL AND SPEARMAN RANK CORRELATIONS

   The Kendall and Spearman rank correlations are correlations based on the ranks of the observations and not on their observed values. When the variables are categorical (take on very few values) you may prefer to use P1F (Section 11.1); P1F also computes standard errors for the correlations.

   Let $r_1, r_2, \ldots, r_N$ represent the ranks of the values of one variable and $s_1, s_2, \ldots, s_N$ the ranks of the second variable.

   The Kendall rank correlation t_b is defined as

$$t_b = \frac{P-Q}{N(N-1)}$$

where

   P = twice the number of pairs of rankings such that both $r_j > r_\ell$ <u>and</u> $s_j > s_\ell$ (agreements in rank order)

---

[3] If your BMDP programs are dated before August 1977, the minimum required abbreviation is KRUWAL (not KRU).

Output 16.3 Kruskal-Wallis test by P3S

```
GROUPING VARIABLE . . . . . . . . . . . . . . . .BRTHPILL
PERFORM KRUSKAL-WALLIS H TEST

NUMBER OF CASES READ. . . . . . . . . . . . . .      188
    CASES WITH DATA MISSING OR BEYOND LIMITS . .        8
        REMAINING NUMBER OF CASES . . . . . . . .      180
```

```
 VARIABLE            MEAN          STANDARD       MINIMUM        MAXIMUM
 NO. NAME                          DEVIATION
  2   AGE          33.538193       9.898361      19.000000      55.000000
  3   HEIGHT       64.465973       2.482127      57.000000      71.000000
  4   WEIGHT      131.093842      20.499771      94.000000     215.000000
  5   BRTHPILL      1.505514       0.501360       1.000000       2.000000
  6   CHOLSTRL    235.838211      42.743637     155.000000     390.000000
  7   ALBUMIN       4.120516       0.358715       3.200000       5.000000
  8   CALCIUM       9.967734       0.472791       8.799999      11.099999
  9   URICACID      4.755512       1.121115       2.200000       9.900000
```

```
                   BEFORE TRANSFORMATION                              INTERVAL RANGE
 VARIABLE       MINIMUM    MAXIMUM    MISSING   CATEGORY  CATEGORY   GREATER    LESS THAN
 NO. NAME       LIMIT      LIMIT      CODE      CODE      NAME       THAN       OR EQUAL TO

  5   BRTHPILL                                  1.00000   NOPILL
                                                2.00000   PILL

  6   CHOLSTRL   150.00000  400.00000
```

```
KRUSKAL-WALLIS ONE WAY ANALYSIS OF VARIANCE TEST RESULTS




 VARIABLE        2 AGE
    GROUP           FREQUENCY      RANK
 NO. NAME                         SUM
  1   NOPILL          89          7822.5
  2   PILL            91          8467.5

KRUSKAL-WALLIS TEST STATISTIC =    0.44084
LEVEL OF SIGNIFICANCE = 0.5067 ASSUMING CHI-SQUARE DISTRIBUTION WITH      1 DEGREES OF FREEDOM

MANN-WHITNEY TEST STATISTIC =   3817
LEVEL OF SIGNIFICANCE = 0.5067 (TWO-TAIL), USING NORMAL APPROXIMATION
```

--- *results for variables 3 and 4* ---

```
 VARIABLE        6 CHOLSTRL
    GROUP           FREQUENCY      RANK
 NO. NAME                         SUM
  1   NOPILL          89          7678.0
  2   PILL            91          8612.0

KRUSKAL-WALLIS TEST STATISTIC =    1.16060
LEVEL OF SIGNIFICANCE = 0.2813 ASSUMING CHI-SQUARE DISTRIBUTION WITH      1 DEGREES OF FREEDOM

MANN-WHITNEY TEST STATISTIC =   3673
LEVEL OF SIGNIFICANCE = 0.2813 (TWO-TAIL), USING NORMAL APPROXIMATION
```

```
 VARIABLE        7 ALBUMIN
    GROUP           FREQUENCY      RANK
 NO. NAME                         SUM
  1   NOPILL          89          9129.5
  2   PILL            91          7160.5

KRUSKAL-WALLIS TEST STATISTIC =    9.52726
LEVEL OF SIGNIFICANCE = 0.0020 ASSUMING CHI-SQUARE DISTRIBUTION WITH      1 DEGREES OF FREEDOM

MANN-WHITNEY TEST STATISTIC =   5124
LEVEL OF SIGNIFICANCE = 0.0020 (TWO-TAIL), USING NORMAL APPROXIMATION
```

--- *results for variables 8 and 9* ---

Q = twice the number of pairs of rankings such that both $r_j > r_\ell$ <u>and</u> $s_j < s_\ell$ (disagreement in rank order).

When rankings are tied, the formula for t_b is

$$t_b = \frac{P-Q}{\{[N(N-1)-T_1] \ [N(N-1)-T_2]\}^{\frac{1}{2}}}$$

where

$$T = \Sigma^* t_i(t_i-1)$$

and t_i is the number of observations tied with a single value and the sum Σ^* is over all distinct values for which a tie exists. T_1 is the total for the first variable and T_2 for the second variable.

The Spearman rank correlation r_s is defined as

$$r_s = \frac{6\Sigma(r_j-s_j)^2}{N^3-N}$$

When rankings are tied, r_s is modified to

$$r_s = \frac{A+B-D}{2\sqrt{AB}}$$

where

$$A = (N^3-N-T_1)/12$$

$$B = (N^3-N-T_2)/12$$

and

$$D = \Sigma \ (r_j-s_j)^2$$

and $T = \Sigma^* \ (t_i^3-t_i)$. t_i is the number of observations tied with a single value and the sum Σ^* is over all distinct values for which a tie exists. T_1 is the total for the first variable and T_2 for the second variable.

TEST

   KENDALL.   {no/prev.}

     Compute the Kendall rank correlation coefficient.[4]

   SPEARMAN.   {no/prev.}

     Compute the Spearman rank correlation coefficient.

---

[4] If your BMDP programs are dated before August 1977,
   the minimum required abbreviation is KENDALL (not KEND).

The Werner blood chemistry data (Table 5.1) are used in the following example to illustrate the Kendall and Spearman rank correlations.

Example 16.4

```
/PROBLEM       TITLE IS 'WERNER BLOOD CHEMISTRY DATA'.
/INPUT         VARIABLES ARE 9.
               FORMAT IS '(A4,5F4.0,3F4.1)'.
/VARIABLE      NAMES ARE ID,AGE,HEIGHT,WEIGHT,BRTHPILL,
                  CHOLSTRL,ALBUMIN,CALCIUM,URICACID.
               MAXIMUM IS (6)400.
               MINIMUM IS (6)150.
               BLANKS ARE MISSING.
               LABEL IS ID.

/TEST          TITLE IS 'KENDALL AND SPEARMAN CORRELATIONS'.
               KENDALL.
               SPEARMAN.

/END
```

The correlations are presented in Output 16.4.

Output 16.4 The Kendall and Spearman rank correlation coefficients computed by P3S

```
COMPUTE KENDALL RANK CORRELATION COEFFICIENT(S)
COMPUTE SPEARMAN RANK CORRELATION COEFFICIENT(S)

NUMBER OF CASES READ. . . . . . . . . . . . . .    188
    CASES WITH DATA MISSING OR BEYOND LIMITS . .      8
       REMAINING NUMBER OF CASES . . . . . . . .    180
```

KENDALL RANK CORRELATION COEFFICIENTS

		AGE 2	HEIGHT 3	WEIGHT 4	BRTHPILL 5	CHOLSTRL 6	ALBUMIN 7	CALCIUM 8	URICACID 9
AGE	2	1.0000							
HEIGHT	3	0.0654	1.0000						
WEIGHT	4	0.1847	0.3822	1.0000					
BRTHPILL	5	0.0413	0.1313	0.0413	1.0000				
CHOLSTRL	6	0.2355	−0.0175	0.0930	0.0664	1.0000			
ALBUMIN	7	−0.0475	0.0088	−0.1782	−0.1956	0.0487	1.0000		
CALCIUM	8	−0.0079	0.1324	0.0579	−0.0447	0.2061	0.3412	1.0000	
URICACID	9	0.1412	0.1094	0.1983	−0.0235	0.1579	0.0368	0.1186	1.0000

SPEARMAN RANK CORRELATION COEFFICIENTS

		AGE 2	HEIGHT 3	WEIGHT 4	BRTHPILL 5	CHOLSTRL 6	ALBUMIN 7	CALCIUM 8	URICACID 9
AGE	2	1.0000							
HEIGHT	3	0.0918	1.0000						
WEIGHT	4	0.2645	0.5050	1.0000					
BRTHPILL	5	0.0497	0.1521	0.0497	1.0000				
CHOLSTRL	6	0.3418	−0.0279	0.1387	0.0805	1.0000			
ALBUMIN	7	−0.0706	0.0116	−0.2534	−0.2307	0.0723	1.0000		
CALCIUM	8	−0.0079	0.1841	0.0875	−0.0532	0.3033	0.4674	1.0000	
URICACID	9	0.2058	0.1473	0.2857	−0.0284	0.2275	0.0532	0.1657	1.0000

● SIZE OF PROBLEM

P3S keeps the data in memory. Therefore the maximum problem that can be analyzed is a function of the number of cases and the number of variables. The size of the maximum problem also depends on the statistics to be computed. The following is a rough guide.

number of variables	10	20	50	100
maximum number of cases when				
KRUSKAL is specified	950	530	200	105
FRIEDMAN is specified	550	300	115	55
KENDALL and SPEARMAN, or SIGN and WILCOXON are specified	750	420	70	-

Appendix B describes how to increase the capacity of the program.

● COMPUTATIONAL METHOD

All computations are performed in single precision. Means and standard deviations are computed by the method of provisional means (Appendix A.2).

ACKNOWLEDGEMENT

P3S was programmed by Steve Chasen.

16.2 Summary — P3S

The Control Language on this page is common to all programs. This is followed by the Control Language specific to

P3S -- Nonparametric Statistics   p. 619

Paragraph STATEMENT[1] {Preassigned value[2]}		Definition, restriction	See pages:
/PROBlem		Required each problem	74
TITLE='c'.	{blank}	Problem title, $\leq$ 160 char.	74
/INPut		Required first problem. Either VARIABLE and FORMAT, or UNIT and CODE required.	75
VARIABLE=#.	{none/prev.}	No. of variables in input data	75
FORMAT='c'.	{none/prev.}	Format of input data, $\leq$ 800 char.	76
CASE=#.	{end-of-file/prev.}	No. of cases in data	76-77
UNIT=#.	{5(cards)/prev.}	Input unit if data are not on cards; not 1, 2, 6	77
REWIND.	{REWIND/prev.}	Rewind input unit	77
CODE=c.	{none}	Code to identify BMDP File	132
CONTENT=c.	{DATA}	Data or matrix in BMDP File	132
LABEL=c.	{none}	Label of BMDP File, $\leq$ 40 char.	132
/VARiable		Optional. For input from a BMDP File, items in this paragraph may be previously set, see Chapter 7.	79
NAME=$c_1,c_2,\cdots$.	{X(subscript)/prev.}	Variable names, one per variable	79-80
MAXIMUM=$\#_1,\#_2,\cdots$.	{none/prev.}	Upper limits, one per variable	80
MINIMUM=$\#_1,\#_2,\cdots$.	{none/prev.}	Lower limits, one per variable	80
BLANK= *(one only)* ZERO, MISSING.	{ZERO/prev.}	Blanks treated as zeros or as missing value codes	81
MISSING=$\#_1,\#_2,\cdots$.	{none/prev.}	Missing value codes, one per variable	81
USE=$v_1,v_2,\cdots$.	{all variables}	Variables used in the analysis	82
LABEL=v_1,v_2.	{none/prev.}	Variable(s) used to label cases, read under A-format, one or two	83
ADD=#.	{0/prev.}	No. of variables added through transformation	99
BEFORE. *or* AFTER.	{BEFORE/prev.}	Data checked for limits before or after transformation	100
/TRANsform		Optional, Control Language transformations and case selection	97-105
/SAVE		Optional, required to create BMDP File	125
CODE=c.	{none}	Code to identify BMDP File, required	125-126
LABEL='c'.	{blank}	Label for BMDP File, $\leq$ 40 char.	125-126
UNIT=#.	{none}	Unit on which BMDP File is written; not 1, 2, 5 or 6	126-127
NEW.	{not new}	NEW if this is first BMDP File written in the system file	126-127

Key: # number
    'c' title, label or format

v variable name or subscript
c name not exceeding 8 char., apostrophes may be required (p. 59)

[1] In BMDP programs dated before August 1977, the minimum required abbreviations are *INPUT* (not *INP*), VARIAB (not VAR), FORMAT (not FORM), CONTENT (not CONT), *VARIAB* (not *VAR*), BEFORET (not BEF), AFTERT (not AFT), *TRANSF* (not *TRAN*). If dated before February 1976, BLANK=ZERO and cannot be changed.

[2] "/prev." means that any assignment remains the same as that specified in the previous problem or subproblem until changed. Otherwise, the assignment returns to its preassigned value each time a new problem begins or the paragraph is used again.

P3S -- Nonparametric Statistics

(in addition to that on p. 618)

Paragraph STATEMENT[1] {Preassigned value}	Definition, restriction	See pages:
VARiable	Specify as part of *VARiable* paragraph, p. 618	
GROUPING=v. {no grouping var./prev.}	Variable used to classify cases into groups	612-613
/GROUP	Required if GROUPING variable has more than 10 distinct values	84
CODE(#)=$\#_1$,$\#_2$,$\cdots$. {10 smallest values/prev.}	Codes for variable #, may be repeated	84-85
CUTPOINT(#)=$\#_1$,$\#_2$,$\cdots$. {see CODE /prev.}	Cutpoints to form intervals for variable #, may be repeated	84-85
NAME(#)=c_1,c_2,$\cdots$. {CODEs or CUTPOINTs/prev.}	Codes or interval names for variable #, may be repeated	84-85
RESET. {not RESET }	If RESET, all assignments in prev. *GROUP* paragraph are reset to preassigned values.	86
/TEST	Required	605
TITLE='c'. {blank}	Title for analysis, $\leq$ 160 char.	605-606
VARIABLE=v_1,v_2,$\cdots$. {all vars./prev.}	Variables to be analyzed	605-606
SIGN. {no/prev.}	Do sign test	606-610
WILCOXON. {no/prev.}	Do Wilcoxon signed-rank test	606-610
FRIEDMAN. {no/prev.}	Do Friedman two-way analysis of variance	610-611
KRUSKAL. {no/prev.}	Do Kruskal-Wallis one-way analysis of variance	612-613
KENDALL. {no/prev.}	Compute Kendall rank correlation	613-616
SPEARMAN. {no/prev.}	Compute Spearman rank correlation	613-616
/END	Required	57

Key: # number   v variable name or subscript
     'c' title, label or format   c name not exceeding 8 char., apostrophes may be required (p. 59)

[1] In BMDP programs dated before August 1977, the minimum required abbreviations are WILCOX (not WILC), KENDALL (not KEND) and KRUWAL (not KRU).

- **Order of input**

(1) System cards, at HSCF these are
```
//jobname  JOB  nooo,yourname
//   EXEC  BIMED,PROG=BMDP3S
//SYSIN  DD  *
```

(2) Control Language instructions
```
PROBLem paragraph, required
INPut paragraph, required first problem
VARiable paragraph
GROUP paragraph
TRANsform paragraph
SAVE paragraph
TEST paragraph, required
END paragraph, required at end of Control Language
```

(3) Data, if on cards
```
data
```

(4) Control Language instructions for additional analyses of the same data, if desired
```
TEST paragraph, required
END paragraph, required after each TEST paragraph
```

(5) System Card, at HSCF this is
```
//
```

(4) may be repeated for additional analyses of the same data
Control Language instructions and data (2-4) may be repeated to analyze additional problems

17

CLUSTER ANALYSIS

In this chapter we describe three BMDP programs that form clusters of variables (characteristics) or cases (observations) or both.

P1M -- Cluster Analysis of Variables   p. 623
P2M -- Cluster Analysis of Cases   p. 633
P3M -- Block Clustering   p. 643

The methods used in these programs are discussed in Hartigan (1975).

P1M forms clusters of variables based on a measure of association or similarity between the variables (such as correlation), or on a measure of distance separating the variables. The clusters are formed by P1M according to a linkage (amalgamation) rule that can be specified. The linkage rule determines the similarity of any two clusters of variables. Initially each variable is considered a cluster that contains one variable only. At each step the two most similar clusters are joined to form a new cluster, until a single cluster is obtained that contains all the variables. P1M prints a tree diagram to illustrate the sequence of clusters formed and a summary table for the clustering process.

P2M forms clusters of cases by one of four distance criteria. The stepwise procedure to form the clusters is similar to that described above for P1M except that cases (not variables) are grouped into clusters. P2M prints either a vertical or horizontal tree diagram to describe the sequence of clusters formed. The means of the variables for the cluster formed at each step are printed.

P3M simultaneously forms clusters of both the cases and variables in a data matrix. The method of clustering variables and cases used in P3M is primarily appropriate when each variable has very few distinct values. An iterative technique is used to identify blocks (cases by variables) that have a similar pattern over a set of variables for each case. The cases in each block can be viewed as clusters of variables. P3M prints a block diagram to describe the blocks identified. It also prints two tree diagrams (one for the cases and one for the variables) to illustrate the sequence in which the cases and variables are grouped into clusters.

When the values of each variable are ordered, the variables can be grouped into factors by factor analysis (P4M, Section 18.1).

● CONTROL LANGUAGE

The Control Language instructions to describe the data and variables are common to all BMDP programs and are explained in Chapter 5: the *PROBlem*, *INPut*[1], and *VARiable* paragraphs are used in the programs discussed in this chapter.

If data editing or transformations are necessary, the methods described in Chapter 6 can be used. Data can be read using a FORMAt statement or from a BMDP File (Chapter 7). If a BMDP File is read as input and a new BMDP File is created in the same problem, the two Files must be in different system files and must have different UNIT numbers.

A summary of the Control Language instructions common to all BMDP programs is on p. 649; summaries of the Control Language instructions specific to each program described in this chapter follow the general summary. These summaries can be used as indexes to the program descriptions.

---

[1] BMDP programs dated before August 1977 require more letters in the permissible abbreviated form (the capitalized letters). The minimum required abbreviations are specified in the footnotes to the summary (p. 649).

P1M

17.1 Cluster Analysis of Variables

John Hartigan, Yale University

P1M forms clusters of variables (characteristics) based on a measure of similarity (association) between the variables. The measure of similarity can be the correlation between the variables or the absolute value of the correlation. The measure can also be a measure of distance between two variables, such as the arccosine of the correlation. The criterion used to combine variables into clusters or clusters into larger clusters can be based on the average measure of similarity (average linkage) between the variables or clusters, or the maximum similarity (single linkage) or minimum similarity (complete linkage).

The clusters are formed by P1M according to a linkage (amalgamation) rule that can be specified. The linkage rule determines the similarity of any two clusters of variables. Initially each variable is considered a cluster that contains one variable only. At each step the two most similar clusters are joined to form a new cluster, until a single cluster is obtained that contains all the variables.

● RESULTS

The data (Table 17.1) used in our examples are from Jarvik's questionnaire on smoking which was administered to 110 subjects. Each of the 12 variables (answers) is coded from 1 to 5; a high score represents a desire to smoke.

In our first example we use the preassigned option for the method of forming clusters. The Control Language instructions in Example 17.1 are described in Chapter 5.

Example 17.1

```
/PROBLEM     TITLE IS 'JARVIK SMOKING DATA'.
/INPUT       VARIABLES ARE 12.
             FORMAT IS '(12F2.0)'.
/VARIABLE    NAMES ARE CONCENTR,ANNOY,SMOKING1,SLEEPY,SMOKING2,TENSE,
                SMOKING3,ALERT,IRRITABL,TIRED,CONTENT,SMOKING4.

/END
```

The Control Language must be preceded by System Cards to initiate the analysis by P1M. At HSCF, the System Cards are

```
//jobname  JOB  nooo,yourname
//   EXEC  BIMED,PROG=BMDP1M
//SYSIN  DD  *
```

The Control Language is immediately followed by the data (Table 17.1). The analysis is terminated by another System Card. At HSCF, this System Card is

```
//
```

Table 17.1 Data from Jarvik's smoking questionnaire, administered to 110 subjects (Dr. M.E. Jarvik, unpublished)

```
3 2 1 3 2 2 1 3 2 2 3 2      4 4 5 4 5 4 5 4 4 4 4 5      1 1 2 3 2 1 2 3 1 4 2 1
4 2 5 3 5 4 5 4 5 4 3 4 4 5  2 2 3 2 2 2 3 2 2 2 2 3      2 1 3 3 4 2 3 3 1 3 2 4
5 3 4 4 5 5 5 4 5 3 4 3 4    2 2 3 2 3 2 4 2 2 3 2 3      2 2 2 2 2 2 1 2 2 2 2 1
4 2 4 3 5 4 4 4 4 3 4 3 5    2 2 3 2 4 3 3 3 2 3 3 3      1 1 3 1 3 1 3 1 1 2 2 3
4 2 4 3 4 2 4 4 2 4 3 4      4 4 4 3 4 4 4 4 3 4 4 4      2 1 3 2 3 1 3 1 1 2 1 3
3 2 3 1 3 2 3 3 3 2 3 3 4    2 2 3 2 3 2 3 2 2 2 2 3      1 1 3 1 3 1 3 1 1 1 1 3
4 2 4 2 4 3 3 3 2 3 3 4      4 2 1 2 2 3 1 4 2 3 2 1      1 1 4 1 3 1 4 1 1 1 1 4
3 2 3 2 4 2 3 3 2 3 3 4      2 1 2 3 2 2 1 3 2 3 3 1      1 1 4 3 4 1 4 1 1 3 2 4
3 2 3 2 4 4 3 3 2 3 3 4      4 3 1 3 1 3 1 3 3 3 3 1      1 1 3 1 3 1 3 1 1 1 1 3
3 2 4 1 4 3 4 2 3 3 4        2 2 4 3 4 3 4 3 2 3 3 4      1 1 4 1 4 1 5 1 1 1 2 4
5 5 1 4 1 4 1 5 4 5 5 1      2 3 4 2 4 3 4 2 3 3 3 4      1 1 1 2 4 1 5 1 1 2 2 5
1 1 2 3 3 3 3 2 1 3 1 2      4 4 3 3 3 3 3 4 3 3 3 3      1 1 4 3 3 1 4 2 1 4 2 4
2 1 3 4 4 3 4 2 1 4 1 4      4 4 4 2 3 4 2 3 3 3 3 3      1 1 3 3 3 1 3 1 1 3 2 2
2 1 3 4 4 2 3 3 1 4 1 4      2 4 3 3 2 4 3 4 3 3 4 3      1 1 3 2 3 1 2 1 1 2 2 1
2 1 4 3 4 2 4 2 1 3 1 4      3 4 2 3 2 3 2 3 3 3 3 2      2 2 2 2 3 2 3 2 2 2 2 2
3 1 3 4 4 2 3 1 4 1 4        3 3 3 2 2 4 3 2 3 3 3 2      2 2 4 3 4 3 4 3 3 4 3 4
3 2 4 4 4 2 4 3 3 4 2 4      3 4 2 3 3 4 2 3 3 3 3 2      4 4 4 4 5 4 4 4 3 4 4 5
2 2 4 3 4 2 4 3 3 4 2 5      2 1 2 2 3 2 2 3 2 2 2 2      4 5 4 3 5 4 4 4 4 4 4 4
3 2 4 4 5 2 5 3 3 4 2 5      3 2 2 3 3 3 2 3 3 4 2 2      4 4 4 4 5 4 4 4 3 4 4 5
3 2 4 4 5 3 5 3 3 3 2 5      3 2 4 2 5 3 5 3 3 3 2 5      2 3 3 2 4 3 3 3 3 3 3 3
3 3 5 4 5 2 4 3 2 4 2 5      3 2 5 3 5 3 5 3 3 4 2 5      4 3 3 4 4 3 3 4 3 4 3 4
3 1 3 3 4 2 2 3 2 4 2 4      3 3 5 5 5 3 5 4 3 5 3 5      4 4 4 3 5 4 5 5 4 4 4 5
3 1 3 1 3 2 3 2 2 1 1 3      2 2 2 1 3 2 3 2 2 1 2 1      4 3 4 4 5 3 4 5 3 5 3 4
3 2 4 2 4 2 4 3 2 2 3 4      3 2 4 2 4 4 3 3 3 2 3 4      4 3 4 3 4 4 4 4 3 4 4 5
3 2 5 2 4 2 5 2 2 3 2 5      3 3 4 3 4 4 4 3 3 3 3 4      5 1 2 4 3 1 2 5 2 4 2 3
3 2 5 2 5 3 5 2 2 3 3 5      3 3 3 5 3 3 3 4 3 5 3 3      2 2 1 1 2 2 1 2 2 3 2 1
4 3 5 3 5 4 5 4 3 3 3 5      3 2 3 3 3 2 3 2 3 2 4 3      5 2 1 3 1 1 2 4 2 4 1 1
3 2 5 2 5 2 5 3 2 3 3 5      3 2 2 2 2 3 2 3 2 3 2 3      2 2 2 1 2 1 3 2 2 2 1 2
4 3 5 3 5 3 5 4 3 3 3 5      2 2 3 3 2 2 2 2 2 2 2 3      2 2 4 3 3 1 4 2 2 3 1 5
3 2 5 1 5 3 5 3 2 3 3 5      2 4 5 4 4 2 5 3 2 4 3 5      3 2 5 4 4 2 4 2 2 4 2 5
3 2 5 2 5 3 5 3 2 3 3 5      2 1 3 1 3 2 4 2 1 1 2 3      1 1 4 1 3 2 3 2 2 2 2 2
4 2 5 3 5 3 5 4 2 3 3 5      1 2 5 2 4 2 5 2 3 3 3 3      2 1 4 1 4 2 4 2 2 2 2 4
2 1 5 2 5 1 5 3 1 3 2 5      2 2 5 4 4 2 4 4 2 5 3 3      2 2 3 2 3 2 4 2 2 3 3 3
1 2 2 2 2 2 1 3 2 3 3 2      3 2 4 4 4 1 4 3 2 4 2 5      4 1 1 4 2 1 2 4 2 4 2 2
3 2 4 3 4 2 4 2 3 3 2 4      1 1 3 1 3 2 3 1 2 2 2 3      4 2 3 3 3 2 3 3 2 3 2 4
2 2 3 2 4 2 4 2 2 3 2 4      2 2 3 1 4 2 3 1 3 2 3 2      2 2 3 1 4 2 2 2 2 3 2 1
3 2 2 3 4 2 4 3 2 4 2 4
            cont'd                        cont'd
```

The data consist of the answers to 12 questions - each coded 1 to 5 such that a high score represents a desire to smoke. The 12 questions (and their NAMEs) are concentration (CONCENTR), annoyance (ANNOY), desire to smoke - first wording (SMOKING1), sleepiness (SLEEPY), desire to smoke - second wording (SMOKING2), tenseness (TENSE), desire to smoke - third wording (SMOKING3), alertness (ALERT), irritability (IRRITABL), tiredness (TIRED), contentedness (CONTENT), desire to smoke - fourth wording (SMOKING4). The data are recorded in columns 2, 4, 6, etc. and are read using the format (12F2.0).

The results of the analysis are presented in Output 17.1. Circled numbers below correspond to those in the output.

(1) The measure of similarity used in this analysis is the absolute value of the correlation (the preassigned measure). The linkage rule is single (the preassigned rule); i.e., at each step the two clusters that are combined have the minimum single linkage (the minimum distance or maximum similarity) between any two variables that are not in the same cluster. These terms are described in more detail below and on p. 627.

(2) The number of cases read. P1M uses complete cases only in all computations; if a case has a missing value or a value out of range, the entire case is omitted. If there is a USE statement (Section 5.3), only variables in the USE statement are checked for acceptable values.

(3) The mean and standard deviation for each variable are printed.

(4) A summary table of the clusters formed.

(5) A tree showing the clusters formed at each step.

(6) An interpretation of the values in the tree.

(7) An explanation of the clustering process shown in the tree (printed only for the first problem).

The absolute value of the correlation is used in this example as the measure of similarity for the results in (4), (5), and (6). The correlations are recoded to a similarity measure between 0 and 100, where a correlation of 0.0 is recoded to zero (minimum similarity). Table (6) lists the recoded values 0, 5, 10,...,100 and the value of the correlation for which the recoded value is obtained. We call the recoded values the measure of <u>similarity</u> between each pair of variables.

Conceptually, the explanation is easier if we view each variable that is not yet in a cluster as a cluster by itself. The similarity between each pair of clusters is then computed. When more than one variable is in a cluster, the similarity between clusters is computed as the maximum over all possible pairings of variables between the two clusters. (Single linkage is the method used in our example.) At each step the two clusters with the maximum similarity, using the amalgamation rule (single linkage), are combined. The stepping terminates when only one cluster remains.

The tree diagram (5) shows the clusters that were formed during the stepping. The horizontal and diagonal lines determine the clusters. For example, CONCENTR and ALERT form one cluster; all the variables listed from CONCENTR to TIRED form a second cluster; ANNOY and IRRITABL are a third. Also, we can see that CONCENTR and ALERT form one cluster, SLEEPY and TIRED form a second cluster, and then the two clusters are combined.

Output 17.1   Analysis of the Jarvik smoking questionnaire data by P1M. Circled numbers correspond to those in the text. Results not reproduced are indicated in italics.

BMDP1M — CLUSTER ANALYSIS OF VARIABLES
HEALTH SCIENCES COMPUTING FACILITY
UNIVERSITY OF CALIFORNIA, LOS ANGELES

PROGRAM REVISED SEPTEMBER 1977
MANUAL DATE -- 1977

--- *Control Language read by P1M is printed and interpreted* ---

(1) PROCEDURE MEASURE . . . . .ABSCORR
PROCEDURE LINKAGE RULE. . . . . .MIN

(2) NUMBER OF CASES READ.   110

(3)

VARIABLE NAME	NO.	MEAN	STDEV.
CONCENTR	1	2.69	1.07
ANNOY	2	2.12	0.97
SMOKING1	3	3.36	1.13
SLEEPY	4	2.61	1.02
SMOKING2	5	3.58	1.06
TENSE	6	2.45	0.99
SMOKING3	7	3.43	1.16
ALERT	8	2.81	1.02
IRRITABL	9	2.22	0.78
TIRED	10	3.09	0.95
CONTENT	11	2.45	0.84
SMOKING4	12	3.50	1.28

(4)

VARIABLE NAME	NO.	OTHER BOUNDARY OF CLUSTER	NUMBER OF ITEMS IN CLUSTER	DISTANCE OR SIMILARITY WHEN CLUSTER FORMED
CONCENTR	1	12	12	30.07
ALERT	8	1	2	80.21
SLEEPY	4	10	2	79.82
TIRED	10	1	4	69.85
ANNOY	2	6	4	72.48
IRRITABL	9	2	2	79.61
CONTENT	11	2	3	73.92
TENSE	6	1	8	60.54
SMOKING1	3	12	4	80.98
SMOKING2	5	12	3	81.65
SMOKING3	7	12	2	84.53
SMOKING4	12	1	12	30.07

(5) TREE PRINTED OVER ABSOLUTE CORRELATION MATRIX.
CLUSTERING BY MINIMUM DISTANCE METHOD.

```
        VARIABLE
        NAME       NO.
                            ------------------------------/
CONCENTR(  1) 80/45 51/56 59 49 57/ 8 19   4 22/
                  /    /    /      /      /       /
                 /    /    /      /      /       /
ALERT   (  8)/60 69/57 60 60 59/10 22   3 20/
                 /    /    /      /      /
                ----/        /
SLEEPY  (  4) 79/35 33 24 27/13 21 12 27/
             /    /        /
TIRED   ( 10)/41 42 39 36/19 27 13 27/
             ----------/
ANNOY   (  2) 79/73/70/14 11   6 12/
                 /  /  /    /
IRRITABL(  9)/69/72/18 22 10 15/
                 /  /    /
CONTENT ( 11)/71/23 23   9 17/
                 /        /
TENSE   (  6)/22 30 12 21/
                 ----------/
SMOKING1(  3) 78 80 77/
             -------/
SMOKING2(  5) 81 81/
             ----/
SMOKING3(  7) 84/
             /
SMOKING4( 12)/
```

(6) THE VALUES IN THIS TREE HAVE BEEN SCALED 0 TO 100
ACCORDING TO THE FOLLOWING TABLE

VALUE ABOVE	CORRELATION	VALUE ABOVE	CORRELATION
0	0.000	50	0.500
5	0.050	55	0.550
10	0.100	60	0.600
15	0.150	65	0.650
20	0.200	70	0.700
25	0.250	75	0.750
30	0.300	80	0.800
35	0.350	85	0.850
40	0.400	90	0.900
45	0.450	95	0.950

--- (7) *an explanation of the clustering process* ---

The numbers superimposed on the tree diagram ⑤ are the recoded measures of similarity (the correlations recoded as shown in ⑥) between each pair of variables. The first number in each line is the measure of similarity of the variable to the left of the line with the one immediately below it, the second is with the second variable below it, etc.

The similarity between two clusters at the time they are joined is read from the table in ④. Each horizontal or diagonal line in the tree diagram ⑤ starts at one variable and ends at the intersection with a line from another variable. The cluster determined by the pair of lines is then listed beside the first variable in ④. The other boundary of the cluster is the second variable. The number of items is the number of variables in the cluster. The final column in ④ is the value of the similarity at the step when the cluster is formed.

● OPTIONAL RESULTS AND INPUT

In addition to the above results, you can

- choose the measure of similarity and the criterion (linkage rule) to combine clusters   p. 627
- request the correlation matrix of the variables   p. 630
- use a similarity or distance matrix as input to P1M.   p. 632

● THE *PROCedure* PARAGRAPH

The *PROCedure* paragraph is used to select variables for the analysis, the measure of similarity, and the linkage rule to combine (amalgamate) clusters. This paragraph can be repeated (after the data, when the data are on cards) to specify additional analyses of the same data (see the order of input in the summary, p. 650).

The MEASURE of similarity can be the value of the CORRELATION or the absolute value of the correlation (ABSCORR), or it can be obtained from a measure of distance such as the ANGLE between two variables (arccosine of the correlation) or the acute angle corresponding to the arccosine of the absolute value of the correlation (ABSANG).

The LINKAGE rule (the criterion for combining two clusters) can be the minimum distance or maximum similarity over all pairings of the variables between the two clusters (SINGLE linkage), the maximum distance or minimum similarity (COMPLETE linkage), or the average distance or similarity (AVERAGE linkage). The average similarity is the arithmetic average of the similarity (s_{ij}) using all possible pairings of the variables between the two clusters

$$\Sigma \Sigma s_{ij}/(IJ)$$

where variable (i) is contained by the first cluster and variable (j) by the second cluster, and I and J are the number of variables in the two clusters. (However, when the measure of similarity is derived from an angle, i.e., ANG or ABSANG , average similarity is computed as

$$\frac{\Sigma_i \Sigma_j s_{ij}}{\Sigma_k \Sigma_\ell s_{k\ell} \Sigma_m \Sigma_n s_{mn}}$$

where s_{ij} = cos(angle between variables i and j), and i, k, ℓ are in the first cluster and j, m, n in the second cluster.)

The following example demonstrates the *PROCedure* paragraph.

Example 17.2

```
        /PROBLEM      TITLE IS 'JARVIK SMOKING DATA'.
        /INPUT        VARIABLES ARE 12.
                      FORMAT IS '(12F2.0)'.
        /VARIABLE     NAMES ARE CONCENTR,ANNOY,SMOKING1,SLEEPY,SMOKING2,TENSE,
                         SMOKING3,ALERT,IRRITABL,TIRED,CONTENT,SMOKING4.

        /PROCEDURE    MEASURE IS ANG.
                      LINKAGE IS AVE.

        /END
```

The results are presented in Output 17.2. The tree diagram is printed over the recoded <u>correlation</u> matrix and not over the arccosine of the correlation. That is, if ANG or ABSANG is specified and the angle is obtained as a function of the correlation, the correlations are printed in the results.

PROCedure
    MEASure= *(one only)* ABSCORR,CORR,ANG,ABSANG   {ABSCORR/prev.}

    The measure of similarity used to combine variables into clusters. The definitions of these terms are given above. *Note: If* TYPE=SIMI or TYPE=DIST is specified in the *INPut* paragraph (p. 632), MEASure is not used.

    LINKAGE= *(one only)* SINGLE,AVE,COMP.   {SINGLE/prev.}

    The criterion used to combine (amalgamate) clusters.[2] The possible criteria are maximum similarity (minimum distance, SINGLE linkage), minimum similarity (maximum distance, COMPLETE linkage), or average similarity (average distance, AVERAGE linkage). AVERAGE linkage is defined above.

Variables to be analyzed can be selected either by a USE statement in the *INPut* paragraph or by a VARIABLE statement in the *PROCedure* paragraph.

---

[2] If your BMDP programs are dated before August 1977, AMALGAMATION=*(one only)* MIN,AVE,MAX. {AVE} is used in place of LINKAGE.

Output 17.2 An example of average linkage using P1M

```
PROCEDURE MEASURE . . . . . . . . . . . . . . .ANG
PROCEDURE LINKAGE RULE. . . . . . . . . . . . .AVE

NUMBER OF CASES READ. . . . . . . . . . . . .    110
```

--- means and standard deviations for each variable ---

VARIABLE NAME	NO.	OTHER BOUNDARY OF CLUSTER	NUMBER OF ITEMS IN CLUSTER	DISTANCE OR SIMILARITY WHEN CLUSTER FORMED
CONCENTR	1	12	12	61.80
ALERT	8	1	2	90.10
ANNOY	2	6	4	89.18
IRRITABL	9	2	2	89.80
CONTENT	11	2	3	87.90
TENSE	6	1	6	84.00
SLEEPY	4	10	2	89.91
TIRED	10	1	8	76.49
SMOKING1	3	12	4	92.03
SMOKING2	5	12	3	92.41
SMOKING3	7	12	2	92.26
SMOKING4	12	1	12	61.80

```
TREE PRINTED OVER CORRELATION MATRIX (SCALED 0-100).
CLUSTERING BY AVERAGE DISTANCE METHOD.
      VARIABLE
NAME       NO.
           ------------------------------------/
CONCENTR(   1) 90/78 79 74  78/72  75/54  59 52 61/
                 /         /       /            /
                /    /    /   /   /   /        /
ALERT   (   8)/78 80 80  79/80  84/55  61 51 60/
                /         /       /            /
           ----------/    /   /   /          /
ANNOY   (   2) 89/86/85/67  70/57  55 53 56/
               / /  /  /    /   /          /
              /  / /  /    /   /          /
IRRITABL(   9)/84/86/66  71/59  61 55 57/
              / /  /     /   /          /
             /  / /     /   /          /
CONTENT (  11)/85/62  69/61  61 54 58/
             /  /     /   /          /
            /  /     /   /          /
TENSE   (   6)/63 68/61  65 56 60/
               ----/    /       /
SLEEPY  (   4) 89/56  60 56 63/
                 /            /
                /            /
TIRED   (  10)/59 63 56 63/
               ----------/
SMOKING1(   3) 89 90 88/
                ------/
SMOKING2(   5) 90 90/
                ---/
SMOKING3(   7) 92/
                /
SMOKING4(  12)/
```

THE VALUES IN THIS TREE HAVE BEEN SCALED 0 TO 100
ACCORDING TO THE FOLLOWING TABLE

VALUE ABOVE	CORRELATION	VALUE ABOVE	CORRELATION
0	-1.000	50	0.000
5	-0.900	55	0.100
10	-0.800	60	0.200
15	-0.700	65	0.300
20	-0.600	70	0.400
25	-0.500	75	0.500
30	-0.400	80	0.600
35	-0.300	85	0.700
40	-0.200	90	0.800
45	-0.100	95	0.900

--- explanation of the clustering ---

```
PROCedure
    VARIABLE= v₁,v₂,···.              {all variables/prev.}
        Names or subscripts of variables to be used in the analysis.
```

● *PRINTing* CORRELATIONS

The correlation matrix is printed when CORRELATION is specified in the *PRINT* paragraph.[3]

The correlation matrix can also be printed in SHADED form: the variables are sorted into the order specified in the tree diagram and the correlation matrix is then printed with codes replacing the correlations.[4]

The following example demonstrates the above options.

Example 17.3

```
/PROBLEM      TITLE IS 'JARVIK SMOKING DATA'.
/INPUT        VARIABLES ARE 12.
              FORMAT IS '(12F2.0)'.
/VARIABLE     NAMES ARE CONCENTR,ANNOY,SMOKING1,SLEEPY,SMOKING2,TENSE,
                 SMOKING3,ALERT,IRRITABL,TIRED,CONTENT,SMOKING4.

/PRINT        CORRELATION.
              SHADE.

/END
```

The results are presented in Output 17.3. The codes used in the shaded correlation matrix are explained below the matrix.

```
PRINT
    CORRELATION.                 {no/prev.}
        Print the correlation matrix.

    SHADE.                       {no/prev.}
        Print the correlation matrix in shaded form after reordering the
        variables to correspond with the tree diagram.  The printed codes
        are formed by overprinting (printing the same line more than once);
        this may not be possible at some facilities.
```

---

[3] If your BMDP programs are dated before August 1977,
   means and standard deviations are printed only when MEAN is specified
   in the *PRINT* paragraph.

[4] If your BMDP programs are dated before February 1976,
   SHADE is not available.

Output 17.3 Optional results printed by P1M

```
PROCEDURE MEASURE . . . . . . . . . . . . . . .ABSCORR
PROCEDURE LINKAGE RULE. . . . . . . . . . . . .MIN

NUMBER OF CASES READ. . . . . . . . . . . . .    110
```

--- means and standard deviations for each variable ---

CORRELATION MATRIX

		CONCENTR 1	ANNOY 2	SMOKING1 3	SLEEPY 4	SMOKING2 5	TENSE 6	SMOKING3 7	ALERT 8	IRRITABL 9	TIRED 10
CONCENTR	1	1.0000									
ANNOY	2	0.5618	1.0000								
SMOKING1	3	0.0859	0.1438	1.0000							
SLEEPY	4	0.4570	0.3596	0.1398	1.0000						
SMOKING2	5	0.1997	0.1192	0.7851	0.2113	1.0000					
TENSE	6	0.5790	0.7047	0.2223	0.2726	0.3007	1.0000				
SMOKING3	7	0.0407	0.0604	0.8098	0.1264	0.8165	0.1200	1.0000			
ALERT	8	0.8021	0.5779	0.10C7	C.6056	0.2226	0.5939	0.0386	1.0000		
IRRITABL	9	0.5945	0.7961	0.1894	0.3365	0.2213	0.7248	0.1085	0.6054	1.0000	
TIRED	10	0.5120	0.4130	0.1987	0.7982	0.2736	0.3643	0.1386	0.6985	0.4281	1.0000
CONTENT	11	0.4921	0.7392	0.2391	C.2400	0.2352	0.7113	0.0998	0.6051	0.6974	0.3937
SMOKING4	12	0.2278	0.1218	0.7754	0.2774	0.8129	0.2139	0.8453	0.2012	0.1562	0.2714

		CONTENT 11	SMOKING4 12
CONTENT	11	1.0000	
SMOKING4	12	0.1708	1.0000

ABSOLUTE VALUES OF CORRELATIONS IN SORTED AND SHADED FORM

```
   1 CONCENTR █
   8 ALERT    ██
   4 SLEEPY   X█
  10 TIRED    X█
   2 ANNOY    ██++█
   9 IRRITABL ██+X██
  11 CONTENT  X█-+███
   6 TENSE    ██-+███
   3 SMOKING1 ....--█
   5 SMOKING2 .-.-.---██
   7 SMOKING3 .. . .███
  12 SMOKING4 -.--...-████
```

--- results of the clustering analysis appear here ---

```
THE ABSOLUTE VALUES OF
THE MATRIX ENTRIES HAVE BEEN PRINTED ABOVE IN SHADED FORM
ACCORDING TO THE FOLLOWING SCHEME
          LESS THAN OR EQUAL TO      0.1C6
  .       0.106  TO AND INCLUDING    0.211
  -       C.211  TO AND INCLUDING    0.317
  +       0.317  TO AND INCLUDING    0.423
  X       0.423  TO AND INCLUDING    0.528
  M       0.528  TO AND INCLUDING    0.634
  █       0.634  TO AND INCLUDING    0.740
  █            GREATER THAN          0.740
```

● TYPEs OF DATA THAT CAN BE ANALYZED

Input for P1M can be data or a matrix that contains either measures of similarity or measures of distance between the variables. A matrix of this form can be a covariance matrix, a correlation matrix, a matrix of angles with distance in radians, or a general similarity or distance matrix. When a matrix, other than data, is read as input, it must be input one row at a time; the FORMAT statement describes one row of the matrix.

Data can be read with a FORMAT specification or can be input from a BMDP File; the other types of input cannot be from a BMDP File. The TYPE of input must be specified when the input is not data.

INPut
    TYPE=*(one only)* DATA,COVA,CORR,ANG,SIMI,DIST.   {DATA/prev.}

      The type of input.

        DATA -- data

        COVA -- a covariance matrix

        CORR -- a correlation matrix

        ANG -- an angular distance matrix measured in radians

        SIMI -- a matrix of similarities

        DIST -- a matrix of distances

      TYPE need not be specified if data are input.

      Note: If SIMI *or* DIST *is specified,* MEASure *in the* PROCedure *paragraph is not used.*

● SIZE OF PROBLEM

P1M can analyze up to 140 variables. Appendix B describes how to increase the capacity of the program.

● COMPUTATIONAL METHOD

Means, standard deviations and correlations are computed in single precision by the method of provisional means (Appendix A.2). The method of shading the correlation matrix is similar to that of Ling (1973). The method of forming clusters is described on pp. 625 and 627.

ACKNOWLEDGEMENT

P1M was designed by John Hartigan and programmed by Howard Gilbert and Steve Chasen. Recent revisions were made by Steve Chasen.

P2M

17.2 Cluster Analysis of Cases

Laszlo Engelman, HSCF

P2M forms clusters of cases (observations) based on one of four distance measures. The distance measures are the Euclidean distance (L_2, the square root of the sum of squares of the differences between the values of the variables for two cases); the L_p distance (the sum of the pth power of the absolute difference); or the chi-square statistic or phi-square (both measure the difference of frequencies in two cases and are used when the data are counts).

Initially each case is considered to be in a cluster of its own. At each step the two clusters with the shortest distance between them are combined (amalgamated) and treated as one cluster. This process of combining clusters continues until all the cases are combined into one cluster. This algorithm is called average distance or average linkage.

P2M prints either a vertical or horizontal tree diagram to describe the sequence of clusters formed. The means of the variables for the cluster formed at each step are also printed.

● RESULTS

The data used in our examples are health indicators for eleven countries (Table 17.2).

Table 17.2 Health indicators (Harbison et al., 1970, Appendix 1, p. 8)

	DOCDNT	PHARM	NURSES	HOSPBED	ANIMAL	STARCH	LIFEEXP
ALGERIA	129	023	350	3392	21	57	35
IRAN	329	107	290	1113	24	60	51
IRAQ	241	081	235	1898	28	57	54
JORDAN	284	096	241	1712	25	49	52
LEBANON	933	192	564	4071	35	50	60
LIBYA	338	041	612	3215	24	55	57
MOROCCO	094	026	233	1516	21	57	53
SYRIA	254	07C	140	1163	13	69	52
TUNISIA	114	039	248	2967	21	57	53
TURKEY	412	057	306	1738	16	71	55
U.A.R.	483	131	454	2225	15	73	54

The health indicators measured are the relative number of doctors and dentists (DOCDNT), of pharmacists (PHARM), of NURSES and of hospital beds (HOSPBEDS), the percent of ANIMAL fat and STARCH in the diet and life expectancy (LIFEEXP). The name of country is recorded in columns 1-8, DOCDNT in 12-14, PHARM in 18-20, NURSES in 14-26, HOSPBED in 29-32, ANIMAL in 34-35, STARCH in 37-38 and LIFEEXP in 40-41; for DOCDNT , PHARM , NURSES and HOSPBED the numbers are recorded· to two decimal points. The data are read using the format (2A4,4F6.2,3F3.0)

Example 17.4

```
/PROBLEM        TITLE IS 'HEALTH INDICATOR DATA'.
/INPUT          VARIABLES ARE 9.
                FORMAT IS '(2A4,4F6.2,3F3.0)'.
/VARIABLE       NAMES ARE COUNTRY1,COUNTRY2,DOCONT,PHARM,NURSES,
                     HOSPBEDS,ANIMAL,STARCH,LIFEEXP.
                LABELS ARE COUNTRY1,COUNTRY2.

/END
```

The Control Language must be preceded by System Cards to initiate the analysis by P2M. At HSCF, the System Cards are

```
//jobname  JOB  nooo,yourname
//  EXEC  BIMED,PROG=BMDP2M
//SYSIN  DD  *
```

The Control Language is immediately followed by the data (Table 17.2). The analysis is terminated by another System Card. At HSCF, this System Card is

```
//
```

The results of the analysis are presented in Output 17.4. Circled numbers below correspond to those in the output.

(1)   The number of cases read. P2M uses only complete cases in all computations; that is, if a case has a missing value or a value out of range, the entire case is omitted. If there is a USE statement (Section 5.3), only variables in the USE statement are checked for acceptable values.

(2)   Interpretations of the Control Language instructions specific to P2M. Since none are stated in Example 17.4, preassigned values (options) are printed.

(3)   Explanation of the table in (4).

(4)   A table that lists the step-by-step amalgamation (combination) of cases into clusters.

In the first step case 4 is combined with case 3. The amalgamation distance is the distance between the cases in the cluster; the distance is defined below. When weights are not specified for the cases, the sum of case weights is the number of cases in the cluster. For each variable the mean of the cluster formed at this step is computed and printed. Therefore, in the first line the values are the means of the variables for cases 4 and 3. In the second line case 2 is added to the cluster containing cases 4 and 3; the means of the variables for the three cases are given.

(5)   A tree diagram of the clusters. Names and numbers of the cases (countries) are printed above the diagram; the cases are sorted to permit a tree to be drawn. The numbers to the left of the tree correspond to the amalgamation distances printed in (4). Each horizontal line in the tree corresponds to a cluster formed in the amalgamation process.

Output 17.4 Analysis of health indicators in Table 17.2 by P2M. Circled numbers correspond to those in the text. Results not reproduced are indicated in italics.

```
BMDP2M - CLUSTER ANALYSIS OF CASES                    PROGRAM REVISED SEPTEMBER 1977
HEALTH SCIENCES COMPUTING FACILITY                    MANUAL DATE -- 1977
UNIVERSITY OF CALIFORNIA, LOS ANGELES
```

--- Control Language read by P2M is printed and interpreted ---

(1)
```
NUMBER OF CASES READ. . . . . . . . . . . . . .     11
```
(2)
```
PRINT DISTANCE MATRIX . . . . . . . . . . . . .     NO
TYPE OF TREE PRINTED. . . . . . . . . . . . . .VERTICAL
CALCULATING PROCEDURE . . . . . . . . . . . . . SUM-SQR
STANDARDIZATION OF INPUT DATA . . . . . . . . .    YES
```

DETAILS OF THE AMALGAMATION (CLUSTERING) PROCESS

(3)
FOR EACH AMALGAMATION, THE FOLLOWING ARE PRINTED

-- THE DISTANCE BETWEEN THE TWO CLUSTERS JOINED

-- THE CASE NUMBERS FOR THE 'BOUNDARIES' OF THE NEWLY
   FORMED CLUSTER AS GIVEN IN THE CLUSTER TREE WHICH
   FOLLOWS THESE DETAILS

-- THE NUMBER OF CASES IN THE CLUSTER (SUM OF THE
   CASE WEIGHTS FOR THE CLUSTER IF CASE WEIGHT
   VARIABLE IS SPECIFIED)

-- THE (WEIGHTED) AVERAGES OF THE VARIABLES FOR THE CLUSTER
   (DIFFERENCES BETWEEN CLUSTERS CAN BE DESCRIBED IN
   TERMS OF THOSE VARIABLES WHOSE MEANS DIFFER MOST
   BETWEEN THE CLUSTERS)

(4)

AMALGAMATION ORDER	DISTANCE	CASES		SUM OF CS. WTS.	3 DOCDNT	4 PHARM	5 NURSES	6 HOSPBEDS	7 ANIMAL	8 STARCH	9 LIFEEXP
1	1.213	4	3	2.000	-0.280	0.197	-0.645	-0.475	0.705	-0.811	0.101
2	1.356	3	2	3.000	-0.186	0.317	-0.528	-0.708	0.572	-0.522	-0.005
3	1.497	9	7	2.000	-0.954	-0.900	-0.628	-0.033	-0.174	-0.316	0.101
4	1.619	10	8	2.000	0.020	-0.293	-0.746	-0.834	-1.214	1.296	0.180
5	1.775	7	2	5.000	-0.493	-0.169	-0.568	-0.438	0.273	-0.440	0.038
6	2.309	11	8	3.000	0.233	0.148	-0.228	-0.572	-1.187	1.420	0.207
7	2.526	8	2	8.000	-0.221	-C.050	-0.441	-0.488	-0.274	0.258	0.101
8	3.060	6	2	9.000	-0.192	-0.126	-0.184	-0.328	-0.210	0.167	0.172
9	3.519	2	1	10.000	-0.257	-0.222	-0.155	-0.182	-0.206	0.118	-0.121
10	5.434	5	1	11.000	0.000	0.000	0.000	0.000	0.000	0.000	0.000

```
     C N
     O          1 1
     A .  1 6 8 0 1 7 9 3 4 2 5
```
(5)
```
   S L   A L S T U M T I J I L
   A L   L I Y U . O U R O R E
   E B   G B R R A R N A R A B
   E     E Y I K . O I Q D N A
   L     R A A E R C S   A   N
   I         Y . C I   N     O
   A           O A         N
```

```
   AMALG.
   DISTANCE
            * * * * * * * * * * *
   1.213    I  I  I  I  I  I  I -+- I  I
   1.356    I  I  I  I  I  I  I  -+-- I
   1.497    I  I  I  I  I -+-    I    I
   1.619    I I -+- I   I      I    I
   1.775    I I   I  I   ---+--    I
   2.309    I I  -+--      I      I
   2.526    I I    -----+---      I
   3.060    I --------+-          I
   3.519    ---------+-           I
   5.434           -+----------
```

- OPTIONAL RESULTS

    In addition to the above results, you can
    - specify any of four criteria for distance between cases   p. 636
    - request the data and the initial distances between cases   p. 638
    - request a horizontal tree diagram   p. 638
    - specify case weights.   p. 638

- THE *PROCedure* PARAGRAPH -- THE CRITERIA TO FORM CLUSTERS

    Two types of criteria to join clusters are available. One is appropriate when the data are measurements; the other is appropriate when the data are frequency counts.

    When the data are measurements, the Euclidean distance (SUMOFSQ) between two cases or clusters (j and ℓ) is defined

$$d_{j\ell}^{(1)} = [\Sigma_i \, (x_{ij} - x_{i\ell})^2]^{\frac{1}{2}}$$

where x_{ij} is the value of the ith variable in the jth case. More generally the distance (SUMOFP) can be defined as

$$d_{j\ell}^{(2)} = [\Sigma_i \, (x_{ij} - x_{i\ell})^p]^{1/p}$$

The data values are standardized (to z-scores) before the computation of the distance unless you specify otherwise.

    When the data are frequency counts, the distance between two cases or clusters is defined as the chi-square (CHISQ) test of equality of the two sets of frequencies.

$$d_{j\ell}^{(3)} = \Sigma_i \left\{ \frac{(x_{ij}-e_{ij})^2}{e_{ij}} + \frac{(x_{i\ell}-e_{i\ell})^2}{e_{i\ell}} \right\}$$

where

$$e_{ij} = (x_{ij} + x_{i\ell}) \, \Sigma_i x_{ij}/N_{j\ell}$$

and

$$N_{j\ell} = \Sigma_i (x_{ij} + x_{i\ell}) \, .$$

The measure $d_{j\ell}^{(3)}$ can be normalized so its magnitude does not depend on the sample size $N_{j\ell}$.

The normalized statistic (PHISQ) is

$$d_{j\ell}^{(4)} = d_{j\ell}^{(3)}/N_{j\ell}$$

Initially each case is placed in a cluster by itself. At each step the two clusters with the shortest distance between them are combined (amalgamated) into one cluster. The values of the variables for a cluster are either weighted averages of the cases in the cluster (when SUMOFSQ or SUMOFP is used) or the sum of the values of the cases (when CHISQ or PHISQ is used). The weight of the new cluster is the sum of the weights of the two clusters (the weight of each case is one when no WEIGHT variable is specified). This algorithm continues, using the shortest distance each time, until all the cases are in one cluster.

PROCedure

	SUMOFSQ.	
(one only)	SUMOFP=#.	{ SUMOFSQ/prev.}
	CHISQ.	
	PHISQ.	

The criterion to combine cases and clusters. SUMOFSQ is the distance measure $d_{j\ell}^{(1)}$; the value # assigned to SUMOFP is the power p for $d_{j\ell}^{(2)}$; CHISQ is the criterion $d_{j\ell}^{(3)}$; and PHISQ is the criterion $d_{j\ell}^{(4)}$. CHISQ and PHISQ are used when the data are frequency counts.

When the criterion is SUMOFSQ or SUMOFP, it is usually preferable to standardize each variable to z-scores for the analysis. Otherwise the distance between cases will weight variables with large standard deviations more than variables with small standard deviations.

PROCedure
STANDARDIZE.   {STANDARDIZE/prev.}

The data are standardized to z-scores when the distance criterion is SUMOFSQ or SUMOFP unless you specify NO STANDARDIZE. *This option is ignored if the distance criterion is CHISQ or PHISQ.*

The cases can be weighted by the values of a WEIGHT variable.

```
PROCedure
   WEIGHT= #.                                    {no case weights/prev.}
```

> Name or subscript of the variable that contains case weights. If
> WEIGHT is not stated or is set to zero, there are no case weights
> and each case is assigned unit weight.

The following example reanalyzes the data using the sum of absolute
differences on the unstandardized data as a distance measure; this is the
distance between cases measured along the axes (grid distance).

Example 17.5

```
/PROBLEM      TITLE IS 'HEALTH INDICATOR DATA'.
/INPUT        VARIABLES ARE 9.
              FORMAT IS '(2A4,4F6.2,3F3.0)'.
/VARIABLE     NAMES ARE COUNTRY1,CCUNTRY2,DOCDNT,PHARM,NURSES,
                     HOSPBEDS,ANIMAL,STARCH,LIFEEXP.
              LABELS ARE COUNTRY1,CCUNTRY2.

/PROCEDURE    SUMOFP IS 1.
              NO STANDARDIZE.

/END
```

The results of this analysis are presented in Output 17.5. The order of
amalgamation of cases is changed, and the tree diagram differs from that of
Output 17.4.

- THE *PRINT* PARAGRAPH

The tree diagram can be printed VERTICALLY, as it appears in ⑤ in
Output 17.4, or HORIZONTALLY.[5]

The initial distances between each pair of cases can be printed; they can
also be printed in a shaded form after the cases are ordered according to the
tree diagram.

The data (standardized or unstandardized) that are used in the computations can be printed.

It is possible to suppress the printing of the table of distances and
weighted averages of the variables (④ in Output 17.4).

We request several of these options in the following example.

---

[5] If your programs are dated before August 1977,
   REGULAR is used in place of HORIZONTAL and is the preassigned option.

Output 17.5 Cluster analysis by P2M using grid distance

```
NUMBER OF CASES READ. . . . . . . . . . . . . .    11
PRINT DISTANCE MATRIX . . . . . . . . . . . . .    NO
TYPE OF TREE PRINTED. . . . . . . . . . . . . .VERTICAL
CALCULATING PROCEDURE . . . . . . . . . . . . .SUM-PWR
STANDARDIZATION OF INPUT DATA . . . . . . . . .    NO
```

DETAILS OF THE AMALGAMATION (CLUSTERING) PROCESS

FOR EACH AMALGAMATION, THE FOLLOWING ARE PRINTED

-- THE DISTANCE BETWEEN THE TWO CLUSTERS JOINED

-- THE CASE NUMBERS FOR THE 'BOUNDARIES' OF THE NEWLY
   FORMED CLUSTER AS GIVEN IN THE CLUSTER TREE WHICH
   FOLLOWS THESE DETAILS

-- THE NUMBER OF CASES IN THE CLUSTER (SUM OF THE
   CASE WEIGHTS FOR THE CLUSTER IF CASE WEIGHT
   VARIABLE IS SPECIFIED)

-- THE (WEIGHTED) AVERAGES OF THE VARIABLES FOR THE CLUSTER
   (DIFFERENCES BETWEEN CLUSTERS CAN BE DESCRIBED IN
   TERMS OF THOSE VARIABLES WHOSE MEANS DIFFER MOST
   BETWEEN THE CLUSTERS)

| AMALGAMATION | | | SUM OF | 3 | 4 | 5 | 6 | 7 | 8 | 9 |
ORDER	DISTANCE	CASES	CS. WTS.	DOCDNT	PHARM	NURSES	HOSPBEDS	ANIMAL	STARCH	LIFEEXP
1	11.800	11	10	2.000	4.475	0.940	3.800	19.815	15.500	72.000	54.500
2	13.860	7	3	2.000	1.675	0.535	2.340	17.070	24.500	57.000	53.500
3	11.710	4	3	3.000	2.063	0.677	2.363	17.087	24.667	54.333	53.000
4	16.447	3	2	4.000	2.370	0.775	2.497	15.597	24.500	55.750	52.500
5	17.380	9	6	2.000	2.260	0.400	4.300	30.910	22.500	56.000	55.000
6	20.760	10	8	3.000	3.830	0.860	3.000	17.087	14.667	71.000	53.667
7	22.350	6	2	6.000	2.333	0.650	3.098	20.702	23.833	55.833	53.333
8	30.087	8	2	9.000	2.832	0.720	3.066	19.497	20.778	60.889	53.444
9	39.445	2	1	10.000	2.678	0.671	3.109	20.939	20.800	60.500	51.600
10	63.303	5	1	11.000	3.283	0.785	3.339	22.736	22.091	59.545	52.364

```
      C N
      C           1 1
      A .  1 8 1 0 6 9 3 7 4 2 5

      S L  A S U T L T I M J I L
      A    L Y . U I U R O O R E
    E B    G R A R B N A R R A B
      E    E I . K Y I Q O D N A
      L    R A R E A S   C A   N
           I   . Y   I   C N   O
           A         A   O     N

AMALG.
DISTANCE
           * * * * * * * * * * *
   11.800  I I -+- I I I I I I I
   13.860  I I  I  I I -+- I I I
   11.710  I I  I  I I -+-- I I
   16.447  I I  I  I I  -+--- I
   17.380  I I  I  -+-    I    I
   20.760  I --+-  I      I    I
   22.350  I  I    ----+--     I
   30.087  I  ------+---       I
   39.445  ---------+-         I
   63.303           -+----------
```

Example 17.6

```
/PROBLEM       TITLE IS 'HEALTH INDICATOR DATA'.
/INPUT         VARIABLES ARE 9.
               FORMAT IS '(2A4,4F6.2,3F3.0)'.
/VARIABLE      NAMES ARE COUNTRY1,CCUNTRY2,DOCDNT,PHARM,NURSES,
                   HOSPBEDS,ANIMAL,STARCH,LIFEEXP.
               LABELS ARE CCUNTRY1,CCUNTRY2.

/PRINT         HORIZONTAL.
               DATA.
               DISTANCES.
               SHADE.

/END
```

The results are presented in Output 17.6

PRINT

 DATA.   {no/prev.}

   Print the data used in the computation. If the data are standardized, the standardized data are printed.

 DISTANCES.   {no/prev.}

   Print the initial distances between the cases. If the data are
   standardized, the distances are in terms of the standardized data.

 VERTICAL. *or* HORIZONTAL.   {VERTICAL/prev. }

   The tree diagram is printed VERTICALLY unless you specify
   HORIZONTAL.

 AMALGAMATE.   {AMALGAMATE/ prev.}

   The table of distances, case weights, and averages of the variables
   at each step is printed unless you specify NO AMALGAMATE.

 SHADE.   {no/prev.}

   Print the distance matrix in shaded form after reordering the cases
   to correspond with the tree diagram.[6] The printed codes are formed
   by overprinting (printing the same line more than once); this may
   not be possible at some facilities.

● SIZE OF PROBLEM

   P2M keeps the data in memory. Therefore the maximum size of a problem
that can be analyzed is a function of the number of variables and number of
cases. The following table provides a guide to the maximum number of cases
that can be analyzed.

---

[6] If your BMDP programs are dated before February 1976,
    SHADE is not available.

Output 17.6 Optional results printed by P2M

```
NUMBER OF CASES READ. . . . . . . . . . . . . . .           11
PRINT DISTANCE MATRIX . . . . . . . . . . . . . .          YES
TYPE OF TREE PRINTED. . . . . . . . . . . . . . .      REGULAR
CALCULATING PROCEDURE . . . . . . . . . . . . . .      SUM-SQR
STANDARDIZATION OF INPUT DATA . . . . . . . . . .          YES
PRINT INPUT DATA MATRIX AFTER STANDARDIZATION .            YES
```

STANDARDIZED INPUT DATA

CASE NO.	LABEL	COCONT 3	PHARM 4	NURSES 5	HOSPBEDS 6	ANIMAL 7	STARCH 8	LIFEEXP 9	WEIGHT
1	ALGERIA	-0.848	-1.085	0.108	1.133	-0.174	-0.316	-2.757	1.000
2	IRAN	0.003	0.559	-0.295	-1.176	0.305	0.056	-0.217	1.000
3	IRAQ	-0.371	0.050	-0.665	-0.380	0.945	-0.316	0.260	1.000
4	JORDAN	-0.188	0.343	-0.625	-0.569	0.465	-1.307	-0.058	1.000
5	LEBANON	2.573	2.223	1.547	1.820	2.065	-1.183	1.213	1.000
6	LIBYA	0.041	-0.733	1.870	0.953	0.305	-0.563	0.736	1.000
7	MOROCCO	-0.997	-1.027	-0.678	-0.767	-0.174	-0.316	0.101	1.000
8	SYRIA	-0.316	-0.165	-1.304	-1.125	-1.454	1.172	-0.058	1.000
9	TUNISIA	-0.912	-0.772	-0.578	0.702	-0.174	-0.316	0.101	1.000
10	TURKEY	0.356	-0.420	-0.188	-0.542	-0.974	1.420	0.419	1.000
11	U.A.R.	0.658	1.029	0.807	-0.049	-1.134	1.668	0.260	1.000

--- ③ *and* ④ *from Output 17.4 appear here* ---

```
   CASE             ORDER OF
NO.  LABEL       AMALGAMATION

  1 ALGERIA *******------------
  6 LIBYA         8.--------//
  8 SYRIA         7.-------//
 10 TURKEY        4.//    //
 11 U.A.R.        6./    //
  7 MOROCCO       5.----//
  9 TUNISIA       3./  //
  3 IRAQ          2.--//
  4 JORDAN        1.///
  2 IRAN          9.//
  5 LEBANON      10./
```

DISTANCES BETWEEN CASES REPRESENTED IN SHADED FORM.
HEAVY SHADING INDICATES SMALL DISTANCES.

```
CASE  CASE
 NO.  LABEL

  1 ALGERIA  ■
  6 LIBYA     ■
  8 SYRIA      ■
 10 TURKEY     ■■
 11 U.A.R.     +⊠■
  7 MORCCCO    ⋈X ■
  9 TUNISIA  -X+X ■■
  3 IRAQ      --+ ■⊠■
  4 JORDAN    ... ⊠⋈■■
  2 IRAN       ⋈⋈+⊠X■■■
  5 LEBANON            ■
```

THE DISTANCES HAVE BEEN REPRESENTED ABOVE IN SHADED FORM ACCORDING TO THE FOLLOWING SCHEME

■			LESS THAN	1.727
⊠	FROM	1.727	TO	2.082
⋈	FROM	2.082	TO	2.461
X	FRCM	2.461	TO	2.769
+	FROM	2.769	TO	2.910
-	FROM	2.910	TO	3.123
.	FRCM	3.123	TO	3.360
			GREATER THAN	3.360

INITIAL DISTANCES BETWEEN CASES

CASE NUMBER	1	2	3	4	5	6	7	8	9	10	11
1	0.0	3.97	3.84	3.82	6.83	4.07	3.52	4.40	2.99	4.30	4.75
2	3.97	0.0	1.39	1.57	5.33	3.49	2.07	2.45	2.59	2.32	2.83
3	3.84	1.39	0.0	1.21	5.10	3.11	1.73	3.01	1.85	2.78	3.54
4	3.82	1.57	1.21	0.0	5.08	3.31	2.00	3.30	2.19	3.29	3.88
5	6.83	5.33	5.10	5.08	0.0	4.44	6.48	7.10	5.82	6.09	5.33
6	4.07	3.49	3.11	3.31	4.44	0.0	3.36	4.65	2.77	3.51	3.59
7	3.52	2.07	1.73	2.00	6.48	3.36	0.0	2.37	1.50	2.50	3.82
8	4.40	2.45	3.01	3.30	7.10	4.65	2.37	0.0	2.91	1.62	2.90
9	2.99	2.59	1.85	2.19	5.82	2.77	1.50	2.91	0.0	2.68	3.62
10	4.30	2.32	2.78	3.29	6.09	3.51	2.50	1.62	2.68	0.0	1.88
11	4.75	2.83	3.54	3.88	5.33	3.59	3.82	2.90	3.62	1.88	0.0

number of variables	5	10	20
maximum number of cases when			
distance matrix is printed	500	400	300
distance matrix is not printed	630	520	370

● COMPUTATIONAL METHOD

Means and standard deviations are computed in single precision by the method of provisional means (Appendix A.2).

The method of shading the distance matrix is similar to that of Ling (1973).

The method of forming clusters is described on pp. 636-637.

ACKNOWLEDGEMENT

P2M was designed by Laszlo Engelman and programmed by Laszlo Engelman and Sandra Fu.

P3M

17.3 Block Clustering

John Hartigan, Yale University

P3M simultaneously forms clusters of both the cases and variables in a data matrix. The method of clustering variables and cases is primarily appropriate when each variable has very few distinct values. Each variable is treated as categorical or nominal (not ordered). An iterative technique is used to identify blocks (cases by variables) that have a similar pattern over a set of variables for each case. The cases in each block can be viewed as clusters of variables. P3M prints a block diagram to describe the blocks identified. It also prints two tree diagrams (one for the cases and one for the variables) to illustrate the sequence in which the cases and variables are grouped into clusters.

- RESULTS

Data from the Jarvik smoking questionnaire (Table 17.1) are used in our examples. To reduce the amount of printed output, we restrict our analysis to the first 20 cases and the first 6 of the 12 variables.

We analyze the data using the preassigned options in P3M. The Control Language instructions in Example 17.7 are described in Chapter 5.

Example 17.7

```
/PROBLEM      TITLE IS 'JARVIK SMOKING DATA'.
/INPUT        VARIABLES ARE 12.
              FORMAT IS '(12F2.0)'.
              CASES ARE 20.
/VARIABLE     NAMES ARE CONCENTR,ANNOY,SMOKING1,SLEEPY,SMOKING2,TENSE,
                  SMOKING3,ALERT,IRRITABL,TIRED,CONTENT,SMOKING4.
              USE = 1 TO 6.

/END
```

The Control Language must be preceded by System Cards to initiate the analysis by P3M. At HSCF, the System Cards are

```
//jobname  JOB  nooo,yourname
//  EXEC  BIMED,PROG=BMDP3M
//SYSIN DD  *
```

The Control Language is immediately followed by the data (first 20 cases of Table 17.1). The analysis is terminated by another System Card. At HSCF, this System Card is

```
//
```

The results of the analysis are presented in Output 17.7. Circled numbers below correspond to those in the output.

(1) Number of cases read. All acceptable values are used in the analysis (all values that are not equal to the missing value code and are not out of range).

(2) An explanation of the analysis.

Output 17.7 Block clustering by P3M. Circled numbers correspond to those in
the text. Results not reproduced are indicated in italics.

```
BMDP3M - BLOCK CLUSTERING                    PROGRAM REVISED SEPTEMBER 1977
HEALTH SCIENCES COMPUTING FACILITY           MANUAL DATE -- 1977
UNIVERSITY OF CALIFORNIA, LOS ANGELES
```

--- *Control Language read by P3M is printed and interpreted* ---

(1)   NUMBER OF CASES READ.   20

(2)   --- *explanation of the analysis* ---

(3)
```
         C O D E   F O R   E A C H   V A R I A B L E
                      1      2      3      4      5
CONCENTR  REAL     1.00   2.00   3.00   4.00   5.00
ANNOY     REAL     1.00   2.00   3.00   4.00   5.00
SMOKING1  REAL     1.00   2.00   3.00   4.00   5.00
SLEEPY    REAL     1.00   2.00   3.00   4.00
SMOKING2  REAL     1.00   2.00   3.00   4.00   5.00
TENSE     REAL     1.00   2.00   3.00   4.00   5.00
```

(4)
```
ROW PASS  THRESHOLD    COL PASS  THRESHOLD
--- ----  ---------    --- ----  ---------
 1        0.200          2       0.200
 3        0.400          4       0.400
 5        0.600          6       0.600
 7        0.800          8       0.800
 9        1.000         10       1.000
```

(5)
```
         C O D E   F R E Q U E N C I E S

VARIABLE MISSING   1    2    3    4    5
CONCENTR     0     1    4    9    4    2
ANNOY        0     5   13    1    0    1
SMOKING1     0     2    1    6   10    1
SLEEPY       0     2    3    7    8    0
SMOKING2     0     1    1    2   11    5
TENSE        0     0   10    5    4    1
```

(6)
```
T R E E   G I V I N G   J O I N I N G   S E Q U E N C E
PASS              1111111111
NUMBER    012345678901234567890
------    ---------------------
     17   --,-,-,-,--
     19   --/ I I I
     15   ----I I I
      7   ----I I I
      6   ----I I I
      1   ----I I I
     20   ----I I I
     16   --,-I I I
     14   --/ I I I
     10   ----I I I
      8   --,-I I I
      9   --/ I I I
      5   --,-/ I I
     18   --/   I I
     13   ------/ I
     12   --------I
      4   --,-----I
      2   --/     I
      3   ------,-/
     11   ------/
```

(7)
```
T R E E   G I V I N G   J O I N I N G   S E Q U E N C E
PASS              1111111111
NUMBER    012345678901234567890
------    ---------------------
ANNOY     -----,-,-,--
TENSE     -----I I I
SMOKING1  -----/ I I
CONCENTR  -------I I
SMOKING2  -------/ I
SLEEPY    ---------/
```

(8)
```
                    B L O C K   D I A G R A M
                    NUMBER OF DATA POINTS...... =   120
                    NUMBER OF BLOCKS.......... =    40
                    NUMBER OF BLOCKS,NOT SINGLE =    14

              A  T  S  C  S  S
              N  E  M  O  M  L
              N  N  O  N  O  E
              O  S  K  C  K  E
              Y  E  I  E  I  P
                    N  N  N  Y
                    G  T  G
                    1  R  2

         .------------------------------.
     17( 2                              )
     19(                 5              )
     15( 1            2        3 )
      7(      3       4        2 )
      6(         3          3 1 )
      1(         1       2  3 )
     20(      3          5           )
         '-,-, '-,
     16( (1)   (3)                    )
     14( ( )   ( ) 2                  )
         '-'   '-'
     10(      3                 1     )
         '-,      '-,
      8(    (3)      (2))
      9( 4 (-)       ( ))
         '-'       '-'
      5(                 '-,
     18(           2        4 (3))
         '-'          '-'
         ( ,------.                   )
     13( (1    3) 2                   )
         '-------'
         (                            )
     12( (1                    ) 3    )
         '-------------------'
         ( ,-, '-,,-, ,-,
      4(  (4)   (4)(5)(3)
      2( ( ) 5 ( )( )( )
         '-' '-''-''-')
         (,-------.                   )
      3(( 3      )                    )
         ((,----.                     )
     11((((5    )      1)             )
         (('-------'     )            )
         ('------------------'        )
         '--------------------------'
```

PREDICTION TABLE

(9)
```
A  T  S  C  S  S
N  E  M  O  M  L
N  N  O  N  O  E
O  S  K  C  K  E
Y  E  I  E  I  P
      N  N  N  Y
      G  T  G
      1  R  2

1  3  2  1  3  3
2  2  4  3  4  4
3  5  4  5  5  -
5  4  1  -  -  -
```

The purpose of the analysis by P3M is to identify cases that have similar patterns for subsets of the variables. To demonstrate the success of the analysis P3M reorders the cases and variables so that blocks can be identified in which the variables have the same (or almost the same) values for all the cases in the block. This block diagram ⑧ is printed and the blocks are identified. Within each block the values for each variable are constant across cases; therefore only the values of the first case are necessary to recover all the values. In the block diagram the value of the first variable for the first case is printed in each block. The prediction table ⑨ (see below) can be used to recover the other values in the block. A single value (not in the upper lefthand corner of the block), or a block within a block, represents values that are not the same as the values in the first case of the block.

Each variable is <u>recoded</u> to the range 1,2,...,9,A,B,...,Z according to one of the following options:

- If INTERVAL is not stated in the *VARiable* paragraph and the variable has 1 to 35 distinct values, the values are coded directly to 1,2,...,9,A,B,...,Z. If the variable has more than 35 distinct values, the first 35 values read are ordered and coded 1,2,...,9,A, B,...,Z; the remaining values are not used in the analysis.

- If the number of intervals is stated in the *VARiable* paragraph, the range of the variable specified will be divided into the stated number of intervals of equal length and coded. For example, if INTERVAL= (6)4 is stated, the range of the sixth variable will be divided into four intervals of equal length and the data in each interval will be coded as 1,2,3 and 4 for the first, second, third and fourth intervals, respectively.

The new codes are listed in ③ . In our example the codes correspond to the values, but need not.

Extreme outliers assign the main part of the data to a few intervals and leave intervals empty between the main data and the outliers. This reduces the chances of a successful clustering. You can partly avoid this problem by specifying MINIMUMS and MAXIMUMS in the *VARiable* paragraph.

A variable with a large number of intervals has little effect on the clustering; in general, the number of intervals should be as small as possible without making the data too coarse. An examination of the <u>table of code frequencies</u> ⑤ may indicate that there are too many codes (the number of intervals should be changed) or that there are outliers.

The <u>measure of distance</u> between two cases is the proportion of values that differ between the cases over all variables where neither value is missing. The measure of distance between variables is more complicated since values of variables are not directly comparable. If variable I is compared with variable J, a two-way table is constructed showing the frequency with which (I,J) take each pair of values (i.j), $1 \leq i, j \leq 35$. For each i, the value j is found that maximizes the frequency of occurrence of i,j. The number of values in the table not included in one of these optimal cells is the number of mismatches; the proportion of mismatches is used as the measure of distance between I and J.

P3M first reorders the data matrix. For each variable, the value that occurs most frequently is found, and the variables are reordered according to this highest frequency. For each case, P3M counts the variables whose values are modes of its frequency distribution values; the cases are ordered by this number. After the reordering, frequently occurring data values tend to lie in the upper left corner of the matrix. This helps to reduce dependence of the final clusters on input order.

The clustering algorithm. P3M clusters the cases and variables by computing a leader structure. The first case and first variable are declared leaders. On the first pass through the data, cases are declared leaders if they are not within a threshold distance of the first case or any other case declared a leader in that pass. On the second pass through the data, variable leaders are declared in a similar manner. For subsequent passes, only the leaders are used and the threshold distance is increased with each pair of passes. On the third pass, a smaller set of case leaders is identified, following the same procedure; and on the fourth pass a smaller set of variable leaders. The passes continue alternating rows and columns, and increasing the threshold distance, until finally only the first row and first column remain as leaders.

Threshold values specify the minimum distance between leaders at each pass and are stated in a table in the output ((4)). Threshold values range from zero to one; small thresholds increase the time spent in computing, but result in fewer blocks with single values (exceptions to the block cluster). The number of passes should usually be no more than twice the number of variables.

Cases are permuted so that each case follows its case leader (identified by the value in the upper left corner of each block) as closely as possible. (Only cases that were assigned to the leader on earlier passes will be between this case and its leader.) Variables are permuted similarly.

A leader structure is defined on the individual position in the data matrix as follows: for the position (3,4) corresponding to the 3rd row and 4th column, let the 2nd row be the leader of the 3rd row and the 1st column be the leader of the 4th column. If the 2nd and 3rd row are closer than the 1st and 4th columns, the leader of (3,4) is (2,4); otherwise the leader of (3,4) is (3,1). If the value at (3,4) could be predicted from the value at (2,4) or (3,1) (whichever is its leader) by using the prediction tables, this value will not be printed in the output.

Reading the output. A block diagram (8) is used to represent the clusters. P3M uses the permutation of cases (rows) and variables (columns)-- developed in the trees that give the joining sequences -- to display the leader structure of both cases and variables in blocks outlined by parentheses, commas and dashes. Values in the leader row are left blank except for the block leader, whose value is printed in the upper left corner; the blank values of the leader row can be recovered from the prediction table (9). All other values in the block are left blank if they are identical to that in the leader row. Exceptions are printed as single values or as smaller blocks. The blank values give a good visual representation of like values in parts of the data.

Missing values are represented by asterisks.

In a good cluster analysis, less than 10% of the values are printed. A block diagram with 50% of the codes printed is considered mediocre.

The <u>prediction table</u> ⑨ is used to recover codes left blank in the block diagram, and is computed during the construction of the column leaders. To recover the codes for variables in an outlined block from the leader, note which column (variable) is first in the block. Go to the same column (variable) in the prediction table and find the same code in the column that is printed in the upper left corner of the outlined block. The codes to the right of this value in the prediction table (in the same row) are those that fill in the blanks in the leader row of the block: i.e., if the upper left corner of a block begins under the third variable and contains the codes value 2, go to the third variable in the prediction table and find the row where this variable takes on value 2. The codes to the right of 3 in this row belong where the blanks are in the leader row of the outlined block.

<u>Row (case) and column (variable) leaders</u> can be found from the output trees that give the joining sequence for cases (⑥) and variables (⑦). To find the leader of a given row (or column), go right to the first slash (/), up to the first dash (-) and left to a case number or variable name, which identifies the leader. The pass number where the leader was found is at the top of the page above the top of the column before turning left. If you pick a particular pass number (a threshold level) and a row with horizontal dashes, you can read back through the hierarchy of the clustering procedure to find intermediate leaders and subclusters within clusters.

● OPTIONS

Several runs through the program, adjusting various parameters, may be necessary before a satisfactory clustering is achieved. You may adjust

- the number of intervals for various variables (they may differ from variable to variable)

- the number of passes

- the threshold levels

```
PASS
   TOTAL= #.                         {10}

      Total number of passes on the rows and columns.  More than twice the
      number of variables is rarely effective.

   THRESHOLD= #₁,#₂, ··· .    {increased linearly on every    one per
                              odd pass from 2/TOTAL to 1}     pass

      Threshold distances at each pass.  The threshold at each pass deter-
      mines the maximum distance, for that pass, at which cases or vari-
      ables will be combined.  Thresholds should be between zero and one.
```

VARiable
   INTERVALS= $\#_1$, $\#_2$, $\cdots$.   {see below}   one per variable

   The input vector INTERVALS determine the number of intervals into
   which each variable is divided. The length of each interval is
   (MAXIMUM – MINIMUM)/INTERVAL. If INTERVAL is not defined (or is
   set to zero for a variable), and the variable takes values in numbers
   1,2,...,35, the values will be coded 1,2,...,9,A,B,...,Z. If the
   variable does not take values on these numbers, the first 35 values
   read as input will be ordered and coded 1,2,...,9,A,B,...,Z.

● SIZE OF PROBLEM

   P3M keeps the data in memory. The maximum problem that it can analyze
is a function of the number of variables and the number of cases.

   The following table provides a guide to the maximum number of cases that
can be analyzed.

number of variables	5	10	20	50
maximum number of cases	720	440	240	90

   Appendix B describes how to increase the capacity of the program.

● COMPUTATIONAL METHOD

   Computations are performed in single precision.

   The method of forming the clusters is described on p. 646.

ACKNOWLEDGEMENT

   *P3M was designed by John Hartigan and programmed by John Hartigan and
Jerry Douglas. Recent revisions were made by Lanaii Kline.*

17.4 Summary — P1M, P2M, P3M

The Control Language on this page is common to all programs. This is followed by the Control Language specific to

P1M -- Cluster Analysis of Variables	p. 650	
P2M -- Cluster Analysis of Cases	p. 651	
P3M -- Block Clustering	p. 652	

Paragraph STATEMENT[1] {Preassigned value[2]}		Definition, restriction	See pages:
/PROBlem		Required each problem	74
TITLE='c'.	{blank}	Problem title, $\leq$ 160 char.	74
/INPut		Required first problem. Either VARIABLE and FORMAT, or UNIT and CODE required.	75
VARIABLE=#.	{none/prev.}	No. of variables in input data	75
FORMAT='c'.	{none/prev.}	Format of input data, $\leq$ 800 char.	76
CASE=#.	{end-of-file/prev.}	No. of cases in data	76-77
UNIT=#.	{5(cards)/prev.}	Input unit if data are not on cards; not 1, 2, 6	77
REWIND.	{REWIND/prev.}	Rewind input unit	77
CODE=c.	{none}	Code to identify BMDP File	132
CONTENT=c.	{DATA}	Data or matrix in BMDP File	132
LABEL=c.	{none}	Label of BMDP File, $\leq$ 40 char.	132
/VARiable		Optional. For input from a BMDP File, items in this paragraph may be previously set, see Chapter 7.	79
NAME=$c_1,c_2,\cdots$.	{X(subscript)/prev.}	Variable names, one per variable	79-80
MAXIMUM=$\#_1,\#_2,\cdots$.	{none/prev.}	Upper limits, one per variable	80
MINIMUM=$\#_1,\#_2,\cdots$.	{none/prev.}	Lower limits, one per variable	80
BLANK= (one only) ZERO, MISSING.	{ZERO/ prev.}	Blanks treated as zeros or as missing value codes	81
MISSING=$\#_1,\#_2,\cdots$.	{none/prev.}	Missing value codes, one per variable	81
USE=$v_1,v_2,\cdots$.	{all variables}	Variables used in the analysis	82
LABEL=v_1,v_2.	{none/prev.}	Variable(s) used to label cases, read under A-format, one or two	83
ADD=#.	{0/prev.}	No. of variables added through transformation	99
BEFORE. or AFTER.	{BEFORE/prev.}	Data checked for limits before or after transformation	100
/TRANsform		Optional, Control Language transformations and case selection	97-105
/SAVE		Optional, required to create BMDP File	125
CODE=c.	{none}	Code to identify BMDP File, required	125-126
LABEL='c'.	{blank}	Label for BMDP File, $\leq$ 40 char.	125-126
UNIT=#.	{none}	Unit on which BMDP File is written; not 1, 2, 5 or 6	126-127
NEW.	{not new}	NEW if this is first BMDP File written in the system file	126-127

Key: # number   v variable name or subscript
'c' title, label or format   c name not exceeding 8 char., apostrophes may be required (p. 59)

[1] In BMDP programs dated before August 1977, the minimum required abbreviations are *INPUT* (not *INP*), VARIAB (not VAR), FORMAT (not FORM), CONTENT (not CONT), *VARIAB* (not *VAR*), BEFORET (not BEF), AFTERT (not AFT), *TRANSF* (not *TRAN*). If dated before February 1976, BLANK=ZERO and cannot be changed.

[2] "/prev." means that any assignment remains the same as that specified in the previous problem or subproblem until changed. Otherwise, the assignment returns to its preassigned value each time a new problem begins or the paragraph is used again.

P1M -- Cluster Analysis of Variables

(in addition to that on p. 649)

Paragraph STATEMENT[1] {Preassigned value}	Definition, restriction	See pages:
INPut	Specify as part of _INPut_ paragraph, p. 649	
TYPE= _(one only)_ DATA,COVA,CORR,ANG,SIMI,DIST. {DATA /prev.}	Type of input if not data	632
/PROCedure	Optional	
MEASure= _(one only)_ ABSCORR,CORR,ANG,ABSANG. {ABSCORR/prev.}	Measure of similarity used to cluster variables	627-628
LINKAGE= _(one only)_ SINGLE,AVE,COMP. {SINGLE /prev.}	Linkage rule to amalgamate clusters	627-628
VARIABLE=$v_1,v_2,\cdots$. {all variables/prev.}	Variables to be clustered	628-630
/PRINT	Optional	
CORRELATION. {no/prev.}	Print correlations	630
SHADE. {no/prev.}	Print correlation matrix in shaded form	630
/END	Required	

Key: v   variable name or subscript

[1] In BMDP programs dated before August 1977, the minimum required abbreviation is VARIAB (not VAR); AMALG= _(one only)_ MIN,MAX,AVE. {AVE /prev.} is used in place of LINKAGE . MEAN. is required in the _PRINT_ paragraph to obtain means and standard deviations of the variables. If dated before February 1976, SHADE is not available.

● Order of input

   (1) System Cards, at HSCF these are

            //jobname JOB nooo,yourname
            // EXEC BIMED,PROG=BMDP1M
            //SYSIN DD *

   (2) Control Language instructions

            PROBlem paragraph, required
            INPut paragraph, required first problem
            VARiable paragraph
            TRANsform paragraph
            SAVE paragraph
            PROCedure paragraph
            PRINT paragraph
            END paragraph, required at end of Control Language

   (3) Data, if on cards

            data

   (4) Control Language instructions
        for additional analyses of the
        same data, if desired

            PROCedure paragraph, required
            END paragraph, required after each _PROCedure_ paragraph

   (5) System Card, at HSCF this is

            //

   Control Language instructions and data (2-4) can be repeated for additional problems.

P2M -- Cluster Analysis of Cases

(in addition to that on p. 649)

Paragraph STATEMENT[1] {Preassigned value}		Definition, restriction	See pages:
/PROCedure		Optional	636-637
(one only) { SUMOFSQ. SUMOFP=#. CHISQ. PHISQ. }	{SUMOFSQ/prev.}	Criterion to combine cases	636-637
STANDARDIZE.	{STANDARDIZE if SUMOFSQ or SUMOFP; no otherwise}	Standardized data used in analysis	637
WEIGHT=v.	{no case weights/prev.}	Variable containing case weights	637-638
/PRINT		Optional	
DATA.	{no/prev.}	Print data used in analysis	638-640
DISTANCES.	{no/prev.}	Print initial distances between cases	638-640
VERTICAL. or HORIZONTAL.	{VERTICAL/prev.}	Print tree diagram vertically or horizontally	638-640
AMALGamate.	{AMALGAMATE/prev.}	Print table of distances, case weights and averages at each step	638-640
SHADE.	{no/prev.}	Print distance matrix in shaded form	638-640
/END		Required	57

Key: # number
      v variable name or subscript

[1] In BMDP programs dated before August 1977, REGULAR is used in place of HORIZONTAL and is the preassigned option. If dated before February 1976, SHADE is not available.

- Order of input

  (1) System Cards, at HSCF these are
```
//jobname  JOB  nooo,yourname
//   EXEC  BIMED,PROG=BMDP2M
//SYSIN DD *
```

  (2) Control Language instructions
```
PROBLem paragraph, required
INPut paragraph, required first problem
VARiable paragraph
TRANsform paragraph
SAVE paragraph
PROCedure paragraph
PRINT paragraph
END paragraph, required at end of Control Language
```

  (3) Data, if on cards
```
data
```

  (4) System Card, at HSCF this is
```
//
```

   Control Language instructions and data (2 and 3) can be repeated for additional problems.

P3M -- Block Clustering

(in addition to that on p. 649)

Paragraph STATEMENT {Preassigned value}	Definition, restriction	See pages:
VARiable	Specify as part of *VARiable* paragraph, p. 649	
INTERVAL=$#_1$,$#_2$,···. {first 35 different values}	Number of intervals, one per variable	648
/PASS	Optional	
TOTAL=#. {10}	Number of passes of rows and columns	647
THRESHOLD=$#_1$,$#_2$,···. {increases linearly on every odd pass from 2/ TOTAL to 1.0}	Thresholds, one per pass	647
/END	Required	57

Key: # number

- Order of input

   (1) System Cards, at HSCF these are

```
//jobname  JOB  nooo,yourname
//   EXEC  BIMED,PROG=BMDP3M
//SYSIN  DD  *
```

   (2) Control Language instructions

```
PROBlem paragraph, required
INPut paragraph, required first problem
VARiable paragraph
TRANsform paragraph
SAVE paragraph
PASS paragraph
END paragraph, required at end of Control Language
```

   (3) Data, if on cards

```
data
```

   (4) System Card, at HSCF this is

```
//
```

Control Language instructions and data (2 and 3) can be repeated for additional problems.

18

MULTIVARIATE ANALYSIS

The term "multivariate analysis" encompasses a variety of statistical procedures. In this chapter we discuss four BMDP programs used for multivariate analysis.

P4M -- Factor Analysis   p. 656
P6M -- Canonical Correlation Analysis   p. 685
P6R -- Partial Correlation and Multivariate Regression   p. 697
P7M -- Stepwise Discriminant Analysis   p. 711

P4M performs a factor analysis of a correlation or covariance matrix. Initial factor extraction is by principal components, maximum likelihood, Kaiser's Second Generation Little Jiffy, or iterated principal factor analysis. Several methods of rotation are available, including varimax and direct quartimin. Factor scores are computed for each case. Mahalanobis distances are computed from the centroid of all cases for the factor scores, original data, and the residuals of the original data regressed on the factor scores. Input to P4M can be data, a correlation or covariance matrix, factor loadings, or factor score coefficients.

P6M performs a canonical correlation analysis between two sets of variables. It computes and prints the canonical correlations, coefficients for the canonical variables, canonical variable scores, and correlations of the original variables with the canonical variables (loadings). It also prints the eigenvalues associated with each pair of canonical variables and Bartlett's test for the significance of the remaining eigenvalues.

P6R computes the partial correlations of a set of variables after removing the linear effects of a second set of variables. The computation of the partial correlations includes the computations of the regression coefficients for predicting one set of variables from another set of variables (multivariate regression). P6R prints the partial correlations, regression coefficients and their standard errors, squared multiple correlations and residuals.

P7M performs a discriminant analysis between two or more groups. The variables used in computing the linear classification functions are chosen in a stepwise manner. Both forward or backward selection of variables is possible; at each step the variable that adds most to the separation of the groups is entered into (or the variable that adds the least is removed from) the discriminant function. The important group differences can be specified as contrasts: these contrasts guide the selection of the variables. Group classifications are evaluated and a classification table is printed. A jackknife-validation procedure may be requested to reduce the bias in the group classifications.

Multivariate methods are also available in other BMDP programs: The equality of the means of several variables in two groups is tested in P3D (Section 9.1). Cluster analysis (Chapter 17) provides methods of looking for data patterns, the similarity of cases and the similarity of variables. Multiway frequency tables are analyzed by P3F (Section 11.3).

Multivariate methods are sensitive to the assumptions of the analysis. P4M and P7M compute the Mahalanobis distance from each case to the overall mean (P4M) or to its group mean (P7M); the Mahalanobis distance can be used to examine the data for outliers or extreme values. Before a multivariate analysis is performed, the data should be screened for errors and distributional assumptions by the methods described in Chapters 8 and 9. The pattern of missing values in the data can be examined with PAM (Section 12.2); PAM can also replace the missing values by estimates based on the acceptable values.

● CONTROL LANGUAGE

The Control Language instructions to describe the data and variables are common to all BMDP programs and are explained in Chapter 5: the *PROBlem*, *INPut* and *VARiable* paragraphs are used in the multivariate programs; P7M also uses the *GROUP* paragraph.[1]

If data editing or transformations are necessary, the methods described in Chapter 6 can be used. Data can be read using a FORMAT statement or from a BMDP File (Chapter 7). These programs can also begin an analysis from a matrix of results, e.g., covariances or correlations. The forms of data input are discussed in each program description.

---

[1] BMDP programs dated before August 1977 require more letters in the permissible abbreviated form (the capitalized letters). The minimum required abbreviations are specified in footnotes to the summary (p. 734).

A summary of the Control Language instructions common to all BMDP programs is on p. 734; summaries of the Control Language instructions specific to each multivariate program follow the general summary. These summaries can be used as indexes to the program descriptions.

P4M

18.1 Factor Analysis

James Frane, HSCF
Robert Jennrich, HSCF

P4M performs a factor analysis of a correlation or covariance matrix. Initial factor extraction is by principal components, maximum likelihood, Kaiser's Second Generation Little Jiffy, or iterated principal factor analysis. Several methods of rotation are available, including varimax and direct quartimin. Factor scores are computed for each case. Mahalanobis distances are computed from the centroid of all cases for the factor scores, original data, and the residuals of the original data regressed on the factor scores. Input to P4M can be data, a correlation or covariance matrix, factor loadings, or factor score coefficients.

Frane and Hill (1974,1976) describe the use and interpretation of results of analyses by P4M.

● RESULTS

The Jarvik smoking questionnaire data (Table 17.1) are used to illustrate a factor analysis by P4M. In Example 18.1 we specify only Control Language instructions that describe the data and variables (these instructions are discussed in Chapter 5). For all options specific to P4M we use preassigned values.

Example 18.1

```
/PROBLEM      TITLE IS 'JARVIK SMOKING DATA'.
/INPUT        VARIABLES ARE 12.
              FORMAT IS '(12F2.0)'.
/VARIABLE     NAMES ARE CONCENTR,ANNOY,SMOKING1,SLEEPY,SMOKING2,TENSE,
                 SMOKING3,ALERT,IRRITABL,TIRED,CONTENT,SMOKING4.

/END
```

The Control Language must be preceded by System Cards to initiate the analysis by P4M. At HSCF, the System Cards are

```
//jobname  JOB  nooo,yourname
//  EXEC  BIMED,PROG=BMDP4M
//SYSIN  DD  *
```

The Control Language is immediately followed by the data (Table 17.1). The analysis is terminated by another System Card. At HSCF, this System Card is

```
//
```

The results of the analysis are presented in Output 18.1. Circled numbers below correspond to those in the output.

① Interpretation of the Control Language instructions specific to P4M. Since no instructions are stated in Example 18.1, preassigned values or options are printed.

<u>Output 18.1</u> Factor analysis by P4M. Circled numbers correspond to those in the text. Results not reproduced are indicated in italics.

```
BMDP4M - FACTOR ANALYSIS                          PROGRAM REVISED SEPTEMBER 1977
HEALTH SCIENCES COMPUTING FACILITY                MANUAL DATE -- 1977
UNIVERSITY OF CALIFORNIA, LOS ANGELES
```

--- Control Language read by P4M is printed and interpreted ---

①
```
WEIGHT VARIABLE . . . . . . . . . . . . . . .
UNROTATED FACTORS ARE PRINCIPAL COMPONENTS.
NUMBER OF FACTORS IS LIMITED TO THE NUMBER OF EIGENVALUES GREATER THAN    1.000
TOLERANCE LIMIT FOR MATRIX INVERSION. . . . . .   0.00010
VARIMAX ROTATION IS PERFORMED.
GAMMA . . . . . . . . . . . . . . . . . . . .     1.0000
MAXIMUM NUMBER OF ITERATIONS FOR ROTATION . . .      50
CONVERGENCE CRITERION FOR ROTATION. . . . . . .  0.0000100
KAISER'S NORMALIZATION. . . . . . . . . . . . .     YES
```

DATA AFTER TRANSFORMATIONS FOR FIRST   5 CASES
CASES WITH ZERO WEIGHTS AND MISSING DATA NOT INCLUDED.

②

CASE LABEL	CASE NUMBER	WEIGHT 8 ALERT	1 CONCENTR 9 IRRITABL	2 ANNOY 10 TIRED	3 SMOKING1 11 CONTENT	4 SLEEPY 12 SMOKING4	5 SMOKING2	6 TENSE	7 SMOKING3
	1	1.00000 3.00000	3.00000 2.00000	2.00000 2.00000	1.00000 3.00000	3.00000 2.00000	2.00000	2.00000	1.00000
	2	1.00000 4.00000	4.00000 3.00000	2.00000 4.00000	5.00000 4.00000	3.00000 5.00000	5.00000	4.00000	5.00000
	3	1.00000 5.00000	5.00000 3.00000	3.00000 4.00000	4.00000 3.00000	4.00000 4.00000	5.00000	5.00000	4.00000
	4	1.00000 4.00000	4.00000 3.00000	2.00000 4.00000	4.00000 3.00000	3.00000 5.00000	5.00000	4.00000	4.00000
	5	1.00000 4.00000	4.00000 2.00000	2.00000 4.00000	4.00000 3.00000	3.00000 4.00000	4.00000	2.00000	4.00000

③ NUMBER OF CASES READ.   110

UNIVARIATE SUMMARY STATISTICS

④

VARIABLE	MEAN	STANDARD DEVIATION	COEFFICIENT OF VARIATION	SMALLEST VALUE	SMALLEST STANDARD SCORE	FIRST CASE FOR SMALLEST	LARGEST VALUE	LARGEST STANDARD SCORE	FIRST CASE FOR LARGEST
1 CONCENTR	2.69091	1.07298	0.398744	1.0000	-1.58	12	5.0000	2.15	3
2 ANNOY	2.11818	0.97427	0.459957	1.0000	-1.15	12	5.0000	2.96	11
3 SMOKING1	3.36364	1.13111	0.336275	1.0000	-2.09	1	5.0000	1.45	2
4 SLEEPY	2.60909	1.02353	0.392295	1.0000	-1.57	6	5.0000	2.34	60
5 SMOKING2	3.58182	1.06126	0.296291	1.0000	-2.43	11	5.0000	1.34	2
6 TENSE	2.44545	0.99158	0.405480	1.0000	-1.46	33	5.0000	2.58	3
7 SMOKING3	3.42727	1.16098	0.338747	1.0000	-2.09	1	5.0000	1.35	2
8 ALERT	2.80909	1.01814	0.362445	1.0000	-1.78	73	5.0000	2.15	3
9 IRRITABL	2.21818	0.78263	0.352825	1.0000	-1.56	12	4.0000	2.28	11
10 TIRED	3.09091	0.95346	0.308473	1.0000	-2.19	23	5.0000	2.00	11
11 CONTENT	2.45455	0.84198	0.343027	1.0000	-1.73	12	5.0000	3.02	11
12 SMOKING4	3.50000	1.27610	0.364601	1.0000	-1.96	11	5.0000	1.18	2

CASE NUMBERS ABOVE REFER TO DATA MATRIX BEFORE ANY CASES HAVE BEEN DELETED DUE TO MISSING DATA.
CASES WITH ZERO WEIGHTS ARE NOT INCLUDED.

CORRELATION MATRIX

⑤

		CONCENTR 1	ANNOY 2	SMOKING1 3	SLEEPY 4	SMOKING2 5	TENSE 6	SMOKING3 7	ALERT 8	IRRITABL 9	TIRED 10	CONTENT 11	SMOKING4 12
CONCENTR	1	1.000											
ANNOY	2	0.562	1.000										
SMOKING1	3	0.086	0.144	1.000									
SLEEPY	4	0.457	0.360	0.140	1.000								
SMOKING2	5	0.200	0.119	0.785	0.211	1.000							
TENSE	6	0.579	0.705	0.222	0.273	0.301	1.000						
SMOKING3	7	0.041	0.060	0.810	0.126	0.816	0.120	1.000					
ALERT	8	0.802	0.578	0.101	0.606	0.223	0.594	0.039	1.000				
IRRITABL	9	0.595	0.796	0.189	0.337	0.221	0.725	0.108	0.605	1.000			
TIRED	10	0.512	0.413	0.199	0.798	0.274	0.364	0.139	0.698	0.428	1.000		
CONTENT	11	0.492	0.739	0.239	C.240	0.235	0.711	0.100	0.605	0.697	0.394	1.000	
SMOKING4	12	0.228	0.122	0.775	0.277	0.813	0.214	0.845	0.201	0.156	0.271	0.171	1.000

SQUARED MULTIPLE CORRELATIONS (SMC) OF EACH VARIABLE, WITH ALL OTHER
VARIABLES

⑥

	SMC
1 CONCENTR	0.70351
2 ANNOY	0.74250
3 SMOKING1	0.73312
4 SLEEPY	0.68377
5 SMOKING2	0.78201
6 TENSE	0.66472
7 SMOKING3	0.82062
8 ALERT	0.80208
9 IRRITABL	0.71437
10 TIRED	0.72627
11 CONTENT	0.69130
12 SMOKING4	0.80294

(continued)

Output 18.1 *(continued)*

COMMUNALITIES OBTAINED FROM 3 FACTORS AFTER 1 ITERATIONS.
THE COMMUNALITY OF A VARIABLE IS ITS SQUARED MULTIPLE CORRELATION (COVARIANCE) WITH THE FACTORS.

⑦
```
    1 CONCENTR    0.6601
    2 ANNOY       0.7956
    3 SMOKING1    0.8391
    4 SLEEPY      0.8474
    5 SMOKING2    0.8561
    6 TENSE       0.7804
    7 SMOKING3    0.8941
    8 ALERT       0.8258
    9 IRRITABL    0.7978
   10 TIRED       0.8453
   11 CONTENT     0.7715
   12 SMOKING4    0.8698
```

⑧
```
FACTOR    VARIANCE EXPLAINED    CUMULATIVE PROPORTION OF TOTAL VARIANCE
   1           5.426                         0.452
   2           2.997                         0.702
   3           1.361                         0.815
   4           0.560                         0.862
   5           0.363                         0.892
   6           0.302                         0.917
   7           0.241                         0.937
   8           0.200                         0.954
   9           0.158                         0.967
  10           0.146                         0.979
  11           0.137                         0.991
  12           0.110                         1.000
```

THE VARIANCE EXPLAINED BY EACH FACTOR IS THE EIGENVALUE FOR THAT FACTOR.

TOTAL VARIANCE IS DEFINED AS THE SUM OF THE DIAGONAL ELEMENTS OF THE CORRELATION (COVARIANCE) MATRIX.

UNROTATED FACTOR LOADINGS (PATTERN)
FOR PRINCIPAL COMPONENTS

⑨
```
                   FACTOR    FACTOR    FACTOR
                     1         2         3

CONCENTR     1      0.742    -0.309     0.117
ANNOY        2      0.755    -0.361    -0.309
SMOKING1     3      0.491     0.763    -0.124
SLEEPY       4      0.611    -0.117     0.679
SMOKING2     5      0.561     0.735    -0.030
TENSE        6      0.770    -0.232    -0.366
SMOKING3     7      0.417     0.847    -0.055
ALERT        8      0.808    -0.337     0.244
IRRITABL     9      0.783    -0.302    -0.306
TIRED       10      0.702    -0.138     0.577
CONTENT     11      0.748    -0.256    -0.382
SMOKING4    12      0.540     0.757     0.070

             VP     5.426     2.997     1.361
```

THE VP FOR EACH FACTOR IS THE SUM OF THE SQUARES OF THE ELEMENTS OF THE COLUMN OF THE FACTOR LOADING MATRIX
CORRESPONDING TO THAT FACTOR. THE VP IS THE VARIANCE EXPLAINED BY THE FACTOR.

⑩ ORTHOGONAL ROTATION, GAMMA =   1.0000

```
ITERATION   SIMPLICITY
            CRITERION
    0       -1.900373
    1       -6.017688
    2       -6.019553
    3       -6.019557
```

ROTATED FACTOR LOADINGS (PATTERN)

⑪
```
                   FACTOR    FACTOR    FACTOR
                     1         2         3

CONCENTR     1      0.601     0.034     0.546
ANNOY        2      0.867     0.021     0.209
SMOKING1     3      0.131     0.907     0.007
SLEEPY       4      0.117     0.116     0.906
SMOKING2     5      0.141     0.905     0.128
TENSE        6      0.859     0.147     0.144
SMOKING3     7      0.005     0.945     0.010
ALERT        8      0.590     0.030     0.691
IRRITABL     9      0.863     0.085     0.214
TIRED       10      0.249     0.143     0.873
CONTENT     11      0.862     0.117     0.125
SMOKING4    12      0.061     0.910     0.195

             VP     3.802     3.443     2.538
```

THE VP FOR EACH FACTOR IS THE SUM OF THE SQUARES OF THE ELEMENTS OF THE COLUMN OF THE FACTOR PATTERN MATRIX
CORRESPONDING TO THAT FACTOR. WHEN THE ROTATION IS ORTHOGONAL, THE VP IS THE VARIANCE EXPLAINED BY THE FACTOR.

(continued)

Output 18.1 *(continued)*

ROTATED FACTOR LOADINGS

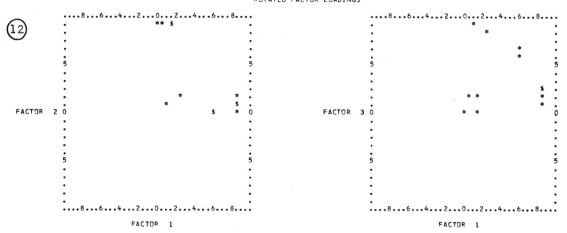

(12)

FACTOR 2

FACTOR 1

FACTOR 3

FACTOR 1

OVERLAP IS INDICATED BY A DOLLAR SIGN. SCALE IS FROM -1 TO +1.

SORTED ROTATED FACTOR LOADINGS (PATTERN)

(13)

		FACTOR 1	FACTOR 2	FACTOR 3
ANNOY	2	0.867	0.0	0.0
IRRITABL	9	0.863	0.0	0.0
CONTENT	11	0.862	0.0	0.0
TENSE	6	0.859	0.0	0.0
CONCENTR	1	0.601	0.0	0.546
SMOKING3	7	0.0	0.945	0.0
SMOKING4	12	0.0	0.910	0.0
SMOKING1	3	0.0	0.907	0.0
SMOKING2	5	0.0	0.905	0.0
SLEEPY	4	0.0	0.0	0.906
TIRED	10	0.0	0.0	0.873
ALERT	8	0.590	0.0	0.691
VP		3.802	3.443	2.538

THE ABOVE FACTOR LOADING MATRIX HAS BEEN REARRANGED SO THAT THE COLUMNS APPEAR IN DECREASING ORDER OF VARIANCE
EXPLAINED BY FACTORS. THE ROWS HAVE BEEN REARRANGED SO THAT FOR EACH SUCCESSIVE FACTOR, LOADINGS GREATER
THAN 0.5000 APPEAR FIRST. LOADINGS LESS THAN C.2500 HAVE BEEN REPLACED BY ZERO.

FACTOR SCORE COEFFICIENTS
THESE COEFFICIENTS ARE FOR THE STANDARDIZED VARIABLES, MEAN ZERO AND STANDARD DEVIATION ONE.

(14)

		FACTOR 1	FACTOR 2	FACTOR 3
CONCENTR	1	0.09301	-0.03935	0.16307
ANNOY	2	0.27541	-0.03385	-0.09242
SMOKING1	3	0.01728	0.27403	-0.07719
SLEEPY	4	-0.17902	-0.01809	0.48035
SMOKING2	5	-0.00784	0.26672	-0.01128
TENSE	6	0.28382	0.00873	-0.13400
SMOKING3	7	-0.03190	0.29001	-0.04754
ALERT	8	0.05389	-0.04844	0.24844
IRRITABL	9	0.27036	-0.01415	-0.09178
TIRED	10	-0.12227	-0.01241	0.42845
CONTENT	11	0.29053	0.00039	-0.14409
SMOKING4	12	-0.05440	0.26711	0.04592

FACTOR SCORE COVARIANCE (COMPUTED FROM FACTOR STRUCTURE AND FACTOR SCORE COEFFICIENTS)

(15)

		FACTOR 1	FACTOR 2	FACTOR 3
FACTOR	1	1.000		
FACTOR	2	-0.000	1.000	
FACTOR	3	0.000	0.000	1.000

THE DIAGONAL OF THE ABOVE MATRIX CONTAINS THE SQUARED MULTIPLE CORRELATIONS OF EACH FACTOR WITH THE VARIABLES.

(continued)

Output 18.1 *(continued)*

ESTIMATED FACTOR SCORES AND MAHALANOBIS DISTANCES (CHI-SQUARES) FROM EACH CASE TO THE CENTROID OF ALL CASES
FOR ORIGINAL DATA (12 D.F.) FACTOR SCORES (3 D.F.) AND THEIR DIFFERENCE (9 D.F.).
EACH CHI-SQUARE HAS BEEN DIVIDED BY ITS DEGREES OF FREEDOM.
CASE NUMBERS BELOW REFER TO DATA MATRIX BEFORE DELETION OF MISSING DATA.

(16)

CASE LABEL	CASE NO.	CHISQ/DF 12	CHISQ/DF 3	CHISQ/DF 9	FACTOR 1	FACTOR 2	FACTOR 3
	1	1.432	1.212	1.505	0.167	-1.899	0.014
	2	1.113	1.063	1.130	1.114	1.341	0.389
	3	1.333	1.238	1.365	1.357	0.511	1.269
	4	0.715	0.593	0.755	0.781	0.848	0.670

--- similar statistics for cases 5 to 105 ---

CASE LABEL	CASE NO.	CHISQ/DF 12	CHISQ/DF 3	CHISQ/DF 9	FACTOR 1	FACTOR 2	FACTOR 3
	106	0.423	0.783	0.303	-0.388	0.652	-1.331
	107	0.451	0.288	0.505	-0.288	0.106	-0.878
	108	1.459	2.926	0.970	-1.067	-1.752	2.138
	109	0.530	0.199	0.640	-0.337	-0.295	0.629
	110	2.035	0.488	2.550	-0.066	-0.765	-0.935

FACTOR SCORE COVARIANCE (COMPUTED FROM FACTOR SCORES)

(17)

	FACTOR 1	FACTOR 2	FACTOR 3
FACTOR 1	1.000		
FACTOR 2	0.000	1.000	
FACTOR 3	-0.000	-0.000	1.000

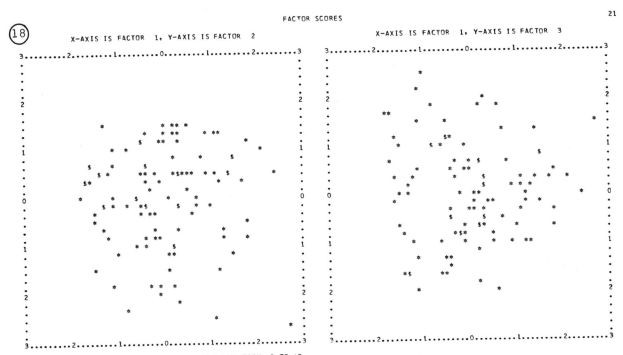

FACTOR SCORES

(18)

OVERLAP IS INDICATED BY A DOLLAR SIGN. SCALE IS FROM -3 TO +3.
FACTOR SCORES GREATER THAN 3 ARE PLOTTED AS 3. FACTOR SCORES LESS THAN -3 ARE PLOTTED AS -3.

(2) Data for the first five cases are printed. The number of cases printed can be specified.

(3) Number of cases read. P4M uses only complete cases in all computations. That is, if the value of any variable in a case is missing or out of range, the case is omitted from all computations. If a USE statement is specified in the *VARiable* paragraph, only the values of variables in the USE statement are checked for missing value codes and values out of range.

(4) Univariate summary statistics

- mean

- standard deviation

- coefficient of variation

- smallest observed value (not out of range)

- smallest standard score

- first case at which smallest observed value occurs

- largest observed value (not out of range)

- largest standard score

- first case at which largest observed value occurs

If case weights are specified, weighted means and standard deviations are computed.

(5) Correlation matrix.

(6) Squared multiple correlation (SMC) of each variable with all other variables.

(7)
(8) The eigenvalues of the factors in (8) are listed (under the heading "variance explained"). The preassigned criterion for the number of factors is the number of factors with eigenvalues greater than one (see third line of (1)). Therefore, in (7) communalities are obtained for <u>three</u> factors (those with eigenvalues greater than one). The communality of a variable is its squared multiple correlation with the factors extracted.

The cumulative proportion of total variance in (8) is the sum of the variance explained (eigenvalues) up to and including the factor divided by the sum of all the eigenvalues. A successful factor analysis explains a large proportion of variance with a very few factors.

(9) Unrotated factor loadings (pattern) for principal components. These loadings are the eigenvectors of the correlation matrix multiplied by the square roots of the corresponding eigenvalues. They are the correlations of the principal components with the original variables. The eigenvalues (VP) are printed at the bottom of each column.

⑩ Orthogonal rotation is performed. Gamma is preassigned to 1 because varimax rotation is performed. At each iteration the simplicity criterion G (p. 670) is printed.

⑪ Rotated factor loadings (pattern) -- coefficients of the factors after rotation. The sum of squares of the coefficients are printed below each column (VP). When the rotation is orthogonal, as in this example, VP is the variance explained by the factor and the rotated loadings are the correlations of the variables with the factors.

⑫ Plots of the rotated factor loadings. The loadings for one factor are plotted against those of another factor.

⑬ Sorted rotated factor loadings. The variables are reordered so the rotated factor loadings for each factor are grouped. Loadings less than 0.25 are set to zero. If a variable has two loadings greater than 0.5, it is ordered according to the larger of the two. This sorted presentation shows that CONCENTR and ALERT are in two factors; the other variables are each primarily in a single factor. The three factors appear to be "mood," "smoking" and "fatigue."

⑭ Factor score coefficients. The rotated factor loadings are multiplied by the factor correlations to obtain the factor structure (identical to factor loadings in the orthogonal case). The factor structure matrix contains the correlations of the factors with the variables. The factor structure is multiplied by the inverse of the correlation (or covariance) matrix of the original variables to obtain the factor score coefficients. These factor score coefficients are for the standardized variables.

⑮ Factor score covariances. The factor structure matrix is multiplied by the factor score coefficients to obtain the covariances of the factor scores. When the method of initial factor extraction is principal components (no communality estimates and only one iteration, as in our example), the factor score covariance matrix is the same as the factor correlation matrix. Otherwise, the diagonal of this covariance matrix contains the squared multiple correlations of each factor with the variables. This matrix is the identity matrix in our example because the initial extraction is by principal components and the rotation is orthogonal.

⑯ Estimated factor scores and Mahalanobis distances. Factor scores are obtained by multiplying the standard scores for the original variables by the factor score coefficients. The three factor scores are listed in the last three columns.

The three columns labelled CHISQ/DF are Mahalanobis distances divided by degrees of freedom. The first column contains the Mahalanobis distance of the case to the mean of all cases, which is computed using the inverse of the correlation (or covariance) matrix and the standard scores. Its degrees of freedom is the number of variables (12). The second column contains the Mahalanobis distance of the factor scores for each case, which is computed using the factor scores and the inverse of the factor score covariance matrix. The difference between these two Mahalanobis D^2's (before dividing by the degrees of freedom) is the Mahalanobis D^2 for the residual space; i.e., the subspace of the original variables that is orthogonal to the factor scores. The third column contains this Mahalanobis D^2 divided by the appropriate degrees of freedom.

For large samples from a multivariate normal distribution, these three distances divided by their degrees of freedom are distributed approximately as chi-square divided by degrees of freedom. Large distances indicate multivariate outliers. For a discussion of detecting outliers in multivariate data, see Hawkins (1974).

(17) The factor score covariance matrix. This is recomputed using the factor scores, and serves as a check for numerical accuracy.

(18) Plots of the factor scores; one factor against the other.

● OPTIONAL RESULTS AND INPUT

In addition to the results shown in Output 18.1, the following can be printed: standard scores, correlation matrix in shaded form after the variables are sorted according to their factor loadings, covariance matrix, inverse of the correlation (or covariance) matrix, partial correlations, factor structure matrix under oblique rotation, and residual correlations.   p. 673

You may specify

- the factor analysis form (correlation or covariance), after subtracting (or not subtracting) the mean   p. 664
- the method of initial factor extraction   p. 664
- the initial communality estimates   p. 665
- the criterion for the number of factors   p. 669
- the method of rotation   p. 669

You may also

- eliminate some of the printed results   p. 673
- specify the number of factors to be plotted   p. 677
- specify a variable that contains case weights   p. 677
- save many of the matrices in BMDP Files to be further analyzed by this or other BMDP programs   p. 678
- begin the analysis from data, a covariance or correlation matrix, loadings or factor score coefficients   p. 681
- compute factor scores for one set of data using factors defined by another analysis   p. 682

● THE MATRIX TO BE FACTORED

You may choose to factor the correlation matrix, covariance matrix, the correlation matrix about the origin (i.e., assuming variable means are zero) or the covariance matrix about the origin. If a choice is not specified, the correlation matrix is factored.

FACTOR
    FORM= *(one only)* CORR,COVA,OCORR,OCOVA.   {CORR/prev.}

    The matrix to be factored.

        CORR: the correlation matrix
        COVA: the covariance matrix
        OCORR: the correlation matrix about the origin
        OCOVA: the covariance matrix about the origin

● THE METHOD OF INITIAL FACTOR EXTRACTION

Four methods of initial factor extraction are available: principal components (PCA) and iterated principal factor analysis (PFA), discussed in Harman (1967); maximum likelihood factor analysis (MLFA), discussed by Lawley and Maxwell (1971); and Kaiser's (1970) Second Generation Little Jiffy (LJIFFY).

Principal components analysis (PCA) is recommended for a first analysis or when the common factor model is not appropriate for the data. Maximum likelihood factor analysis (MLFA) is recommended when the common factor model is known to be appropriate, when the number of variables is 60 or less, and when the correlation matrix is nonsingular. Kaiser's Second Generation Little Jiffy also requires a nonsingular correlation matrix; it consists of image analysis followed by orthoblique rotation. Principal factor analysis (PFA) is appropriate for data known to follow the common factor model and can also be used with a singular correlation matrix; however, it is generally considered inferior to MLFA and LJIFFY.

If a method is not specified, PCA is used.

FACTOR
    METHOD = *(one only)* PCA,MLFA,LJIFFY,PFA.   {PCA/ prev.}

    The method of initial factor extraction.[2]

        PCA: principal component analysis
        MLFA: maximum likelihood factor analysis
        LJIFFY: Kaiser's Second Generation Little Jiffy
        PFA: principal factor analysis

---

[2] If your BMDP programs are dated before August 1977,
    the minimum required abbreviation is METHOD (not METH).

When MLFA or PFA is specified, the maximum number of iterations can be specified. In addition, the convergence criterion (EPS) for PFA can be changed.

FACTOR
    ITERATE=#.   {25/prev.}   PFA or MLFA only

    Maximum number of iterations performed.[3]

    EPS=#.   {0.001/prev.}   PFA only

    Convergence criterion for iteration on communalities. The iteration continues to the number of times specified for ITERATE, or until the estimated communalities from two successive iterations differ by EPS or less.

● TOLERANCE

    The inverse of the correlation or covariance matrix is computed by stepwise pivoting. The TOLERANCE limit is used to determine whether to pivot on a variable. If the TOLERANCE limit is not met for any variable, the computations continue when METHOD is PCA or PFA but terminate when METHOD is MLFA or LJIFFY.

FACTOR
    TOLERANCE=#.   {.0001/prev.}

    Tolerance limit.[4] If the squared multiple correlation of any variable exceeds 1.0 - TOLERANCE, that variable is considered to be a linear combination of the other variables and pivoting is not performed for that variable. When METHOD is MLFA or LJIFFY, the program terminates if any variable does <u>not</u> pass the tolerance limit.

● THE INITIAL COMMUNALITY ESTIMATES

    Communality estimates can be specified as one of three Control Language options or as a list of values, one for each variable. The three Control Language options are

    UNALT: the diagonal of the correlation (or covariance) matrix remains unaltered

---

[3] If your BMDP programs are dated before August 1977,
    the minimum required abbreviation is ITERATE (not ITER).

[4] If your BMDP programs are dated before April 1977,
    TOLERANCE is preassigned to .0001 and cannot be changed.

SMCS: the diagonal of the correlation (or covariance) matrix is replaced by the squared multiple correlations of each variable with the remaining variables (if the covariance matrix is factored, the squared multiple correlations are multiplied by the corresponding variances)

MAXROW: the diagonal elements of the correlation (or covariance) matrix are replaced by the maximum absolute row values of the correlation matrix (if the covariance matrix is factored, these values are multiplied by the corresponding variances)

FACTOR
   COMMUNALITY= *(one only)* UNALT,SMCS,MAXROW.   {UNALT for PCA;
   or COMMUNALITY=$\#_1,\#_2,\cdots$.   SMCS otherwise}

    The initial estimates of the communalities

       UNALT: unaltered
       SMCS: squared multiple correlations
       MAXROW: maximum value in row

   Or you may specify a list of values, $\#_1,\#_2,\ldots$ (one per variable used), as the estimates. If USE is specified in the *VARiable* paragraph, the first value is for the first variable in the USE list, etc.

In Example 18.2 we specify that the initial factor extraction is by maximum likelihood.

Example 18.2

```
/PROBLEM     TITLE IS 'JARVIK SMOKING DATA'.
/INPUT       VARIABLES ARE 12.
             FORMAT IS '(12F2.0)'.
/VARIABLE    NAMES ARE CONCENTR,ANNOY,SMOKING1,SLEEPY,SMOKING2,TENSE,
                SMOKING3,ALERT,IRRITABL,TIRED,CONTENT,SMOKING4.

/FACTOR      METHOD IS MLFA.

/END
```

The additional results are presented in Output 18.2. Circled numbers below correspond to those in the output.

(19) The preassigned value for the communality estimates is SMCS when the METHOD of initial factor extraction is MLFA.

(20) The eigenvalues are computed from the original correlation matrix. These are the eigenvalues of the correlation matrix (without communalities substituted for the diagonal elements).

(21) The algorithm for maximum likelihood factor extraction is described in Appendix A.21.

㉒ Interpretations for the remaining results are similar to those for the results in Output 18.1 (from ⑦ to the end). The results differ slightly from Output 18.1 because of the different method of initial factor extraction. Some of the remaining results are not presented.

Output 18.2 Some results of a maximum likelihood factor analysis by P4M

```
WEIGHT VARIABLE . . . . . . . . . . . . . . . . .
INITIAL COMMUNALITIES ARE SQUARED MULTIPLE CORRELATIONS OR COVARIANCES.
MAXIMUM LIKELIHOOD FACTOR ANALYSIS IS PERFORMED.
NUMBER OF ITERATIONS FOR INITIAL FACTOR EXTRACTION   25
NUMBER OF FACTORS IS LIMITED TO THE NUMBER OF EIGENVALUES GREATER THAN    1.000
TOLERANCE LIMIT FOR MATRIX INVERSION. . . . . .    0.00010
VARIMAX ROTATION IS PERFORMED.
GAMMA . . . . . . . . . . . . . . . . . . . . .    1.0000
MAXIMUM NUMBER OF ITERATIONS FOR ROTATION . . .      50
CONVERGENCE CRITERION FOR ROTATION. . . . . . . 0.0000100
KAISER'S NORMALIZATION. . . . . . . . . . . . .     YES
```

--- ② *to* ⑥ *from Output 18.1 appear here* ---

⑲ COMMUNALITY ESTIMATES ARE SQUARED MULTIPLE CORRELATIONS (COVARIANCES).

EIGENVALUES OF UNALTERED CORRELATION MATRIX

⑳
```
    5.426     2.997     1.361     0.560     0.363     0.302     0.241     0.200     0.158     0.146
    0.137     0.110
```

ITERATION FOR MAXIMUM LIKELIHOOD

㉑

ITERATION	MAXIMUM CHANGE IN SQRT(UNIQUENESS)	LIKELIHOOD CRITERION TO BE MINIMIZED	STEP HALVINGS
		0.969191	
1	0.120209	0.900708	2
2	0.061833	0.836862	0
3	0.012304	0.834094	0
4	0.000609	0.834089	0
5	0.000002		

```
AN ASTERISK (IF ANY) AFTER THE ITERATION NUMBER INDICATES
THAT APPROXIMATE DERIVATIVES WERE USED.
```

```
CANONICAL CORRELATIONS
        0.9790
        0.9668
        0.9082
```

㉒

```
COMMUNALITIES OBTAINED FROM  3 FACTORS AFTER    5 ITERATIONS.
THE COMMUNALITY OF A VARIABLE IS ITS SQUARED MULTIPLE CORRELATION (COVARIANCE) WITH THE FACTORS.
```

```
     1 CONCENTR   0.5753
     2 ANNOY      0.7457
     3 SMOKING1   0.7630
     4 SLEEPY     0.7596
     5 SMOKING2   0.8011
     6 TENSE      0.7110
     7 SMOKING3   0.8784
     8 ALERT      0.7561
     9 IRRITABL   0.7551
    10 TIRED      0.8043
    11 CONTENT    0.6993
    12 SMOKING4   0.8352
```

(continued)

Output 18.2   *(continued)*

FACTOR	VARIANCE EXPLAINED	CUMULATIVE PROPORTION OF TOTAL VARIANCE
1	4.793	0.399
2	3.162	0.663
3	1.129	0.757

TOTAL VARIANCE IS DEFINED AS THE SUM OF THE DIAGONAL ELEMENTS OF THE CORRELATION (COVARIANCE) MATRIX.

UNROTATED FACTOR LOADINGS (PATTERN)
FOR MAXIMUM LIKELIHOOD CANONICAL FACTORS

		FACTOR 1	FACTOR 2	FACTOR 3
CONCENTR	1	0.529	0.543	0.027
ANNOY	2	0.527	0.599	-0.329
SMOKING1	3	0.732	-0.466	-0.097
SLEEPY	4	0.518	0.389	0.583
SMOKING2	5	0.790	-0.419	-0.023
TENSE	6	0.579	0.490	-0.369
SMOKING3	7	0.722	-0.596	-0.040
ALERT	8	0.587	0.622	0.157
IRRITABL	9	0.574	0.562	-0.332
TIRED	10	0.590	0.448	0.506
CONTENT	11	0.552	0.507	-0.370
SMOKING4	12	0.789	-0.456	0.066
	VP	4.793	3.162	1.129

THE VP FOR EACH FACTOR IS THE SUM OF THE SQUARES OF THE ELEMENTS OF THE COLUMN OF THE FACTOR LOADING MATRIX
CORRESPONDING TO THAT FACTOR.   THE VP IS THE VARIANCE EXPLAINED BY THE FACTOR.

ORTHOGONAL ROTATION, GAMMA =   1.0000

ITERATION	SIMPLICITY CRITERION
0	-0.611441
1	-5.852844
2	-5.864646
3	-5.864750
4	-5.864750

ROTATED FACTOR LOADINGS (PATTERN)

		FACTOR 1	FACTOR 2	FACTOR 3
CONCENTR	1	0.595	0.051	0.468
ANNOY	2	0.839	0.030	0.204
SMOKING1	3	0.128	0.864	0.023
SLEEPY	4	0.164	0.116	0.848
SMOKING2	5	0.144	0.874	0.127
TENSE	6	0.818	0.142	0.146
SMOKING3	7	0.007	0.937	0.011
ALERT	8	0.597	0.039	0.631
IRRITABL	9	0.840	0.090	0.204
TIRED	10	0.283	0.137	0.840
CONTENT	11	0.817	0.111	0.142
SMOKING4	12	0.068	0.893	0.183
	VP	3.604	3.264	2.216

THE VP FOR EACH FACTOR IS THE SUM OF THE SQUARES OF THE ELEMENTS OF THE COLUMN OF THE FACTOR PATTERN MATRIX
CORRESPONDING TO THAT FACTOR.   WHEN THE ROTATION IS ORTHOGONAL, THE VP IS THE VARIANCE EXPLAINED BY THE FACTOR.

--- *the remainder of the results is analogous to* (12)
to (18) *in Output 18.1* ---

● The Number of Factors

A maximum NUMBER of factors can be specified.[5] In addition, the number of factors can be limited by requiring that the eigenvalues be greater than a CONSTANT.

FACTOR
    NUMBER=#.   {no. of variables}

       The maximum number of factors obtained.

    CONSTANT=#.   {1.0/prev.}

       The factors obtained are restricted to those with eigenvalues greater than CONSTANT. When the covariance matrix is factored, the limit is applied to the CONSTANT times the average variance of the variables.

       The number of factors for PCA, MLFA and LJIFFY is determined from the eigenvalues of the unaltered correlation matrix; for PFA from the eigenvalues of the correlation matrix after the substitution of communality estimates at each iteration.

● The METHOD of Rotation

P4M allows both orthogonal and oblique rotation. If principal component analysis is your primary aim, rotation is not necessary. The option to omit rotation is

       METHOD=NONE.

in the *ROTATE* paragraph.

ROTATE
    METHOD= *(one only)* VMAX,DQUART,QRMAX,   {VMAX unless LJIFFY
           EQMAX,ORTHOG,DOBLI,ORTHOB,NONE.   is specified/prev.}

       The method of rotation.[6]

          VMAX: varimax

          DQUART: direct quartimin rotation for simple loadings (Jennrich and Sampson, 1966; this is the recommended method for oblique rotation)

          QRMAX: quartimax

          EQMAX: equamax

                                    (continued)

---

[5] If your BMDP programs are dated before August 1977, the minimum required abbreviation is NUMBER (not NUMB).

[6] If your BMDP programs are dated before August 1977, the minimum required abbreviation is METHOD (not METH).

(continued from previous page)

> ORTHOG: orthogonal with gamma (see below)
>
> DOBLI: direct oblimin with gamma (see below)
>
> ORTHOB: orthoblique (this is the preassigned value for LJIFFY (Kaiser, 1970) and is available <u>only</u> with LJIFFY)
>
> NONE: no rotation

Rotations are performed to minimize the <u>simplicity criterion</u> G (Harman, 1967, Chapters 14 and 15).

$$ G = \sum_{i \neq j} \left[\sum_{k=1}^{p} a^2_{ki} \, a^2_{kj} - \frac{\Gamma}{p} \left(\sum_{k=1}^{p} a^2_{ki} \right) \left(\sum_{k=1}^{p} a^2_{kj} \right) \right] $$

where

$i, j = 1,\ldots,m$

m = number of factors

p = number of variables

(a_{ij}) = is the matrix of factor loadings for orthogonal and direct oblimin rotation and is the factor structure for indirect oblimin

The value of Γ can be specified (or implied by means of the preassigned value). For orthogonal rotation, low values of Γ (e.g., $\Gamma=0$) emphasize "simplifying" the rows of a loadings matrix, and large values (e.g., $\Gamma=1$) emphasize simplifying the columns (Harman, 1967, p. 304). For direct oblimin, increasing Γ causes factors to be <u>more</u> highly correlated (more oblique). Commonly used names of methods of rotation are given in the following table:

Γ	Type of Rotation	
	Orthogonal	Oblique direct oblimin
0	quartimax	direct quartimin (simple loadings)
1	varimax	
m/2	equamax	

More details concerning methods of rotation are found in Jennrich and Sampson (1966), Harman (1967) and Kaiser (1970). The last reference also includes the orthoblique method.

ROTATE
> GAMMA=#. $\begin{Bmatrix} 1.0 \text{ for ORTHOG} \\ 0.0 \text{ for DOBLI} \end{Bmatrix}$ only for ORTHOG and DOBLI
>
> Value of gamma.

The rotation terminates when the maximum number of iterations is reached or when the relative change in the value of G (defined above) between two successive iterations is less than CONSTANT.

ROTATE
    MAXIT=#.   {50/prev.}

   Maximum number of iterations for rotation.[7]

   CONSTANT=#. {0.00001/prev.}

   Convergence criterion for rotation. The convergence criterion is satisfied when the relative change in G between two successive iterations is less than CONSTANT.

• KAISER'S NORMALIZATION

   Kaiser's normalization (Harman, 1967, p.306) is performed unless

        NO NORMAL.

is specified.

ROTATE
    NORMAL.   {NORMAL/prev.}

   Kaiser's normalization is performed unless NO NORMAL is specified.[8]

The following example demonstrates the results of an oblique rotation.

Example 18.3

```
/PROBLEM     TITLE IS 'JARVIK SMOKING DATA'.
/INPUT       VARIABLES ARE 12.
             FORMAT IS '(12F2.0)'.
/VARIABLE    NAMES ARE CONCENTR,ANNOY,SMOKING1,SLEEPY,SMOKING2,TENSE,
                SMOKING3,ALERT,IRRITABL,TIRED,CONTENT,SMOKING4.

/ROTATE      METHOD IS DQUART.

/END
```

Some of the results are presented in Output 18.3. Circled numbers correspond to the notes below.

(23) Direct oblimin rotation is performed. The simplicity criterion is described on p. 670.

---

[7] If your BMDP programs are dated before August 1977, the minimum required abbreviation is MAXITR (not MAXIT).

[8] If your BMDP programs are dated before August 1977, the minimum required abbreviation is NORMAL (not NORM).

Output 18.3 Some results from a factor analysis using oblique rotation

```
WEIGHT VARIABLE . . . . . . . . . . . . . . . . .
UNROTATED FACTORS ARE PRINCIPAL COMPONENTS.
NUMBER OF FACTORS IS LIMITED TO THE NUMBER OF EIGENVALUES GREATER THAN      1.000
TOLERANCE LIMIT FOR MATRIX INVERSION. . . . .      0.00010
DIRECT QUARTIMIN ROTATION FOR SIMPLE LOADINGS IS PERFORMED.
GAMMA . . . . . . . . . . . . . . . . . . . . .      0.0
MAXIMUM NUMBER OF ITERATIONS FOR ROTATION . . . .       50
CONVERGENCE CRITERION FOR ROTATION. . . . . . .   0.0000100
KAISER'S NORMALIZATION. . . . . . . . . . . . .      YES
```

--- ② to ⑨ from Output 18.1 appear here ---

㉓ DIRECT OBLIMIN ROTATION, GAMMA =   0.0

```
ITERATION   SIMPLICITY
            CRITERION
    0       4.970519
    1       2.951623
    2       1.207235
    3       0.730899
    4       0.708151
    5       0.707762
    6       0.707759
```

㉔ ROTATED FACTOR LOADINGS (PATTERN)

		FACTOR 1	FACTOR 2	FACTOR 3
CONCENTR	1	0.506	-0.046	0.459
ANNOY	2	0.887	-0.054	0.028
SMOKING1	3	0.083	0.912	-0.080
SLEEPY	4	-0.123	0.044	0.961
SMOKING2	5	0.062	0.901	0.050
TENSE	6	0.887	0.080	-0.049
SMOKING3	7	-0.057	0.960	-0.050
ALERT	8	0.455	-0.061	0.621
IRRITABL	9	0.877	0.012	0.031
TIRED	10	0.028	0.065	0.893
CONTENT	11	0.897	0.050	-0.069
SMOKING4	12	-0.044	0.907	0.142
VP		3.643	3.411	2.356

THE VP FOR EACH FACTOR IS THE SUM OF THE SQUARES OF THE ELEMENTS OF THE COLUMN OF THE FACTOR PATTERN MATRIX CORRESPONDING TO THAT FACTOR. WHEN THE ROTATION IS ORTHOGONAL, THE VP IS THE VARIANCE EXPLAINED BY THE FACTOR.

㉕ FACTOR CORRELATIONS FOR ROTATED FACTORS

		FACTOR 1	FACTOR 2	FACTOR 3
FACTOR	1	1.000		
FACTOR	2	0.170	1.000	
FACTOR	3	0.446	0.174	1.000

㉖ SORTED ROTATED FACTOR LOADINGS (PATTERN)

		FACTOR 1	FACTOR 2	FACTOR 3
CONTENT	11	0.897	0.0	0.0
TENSE	6	0.887	0.0	0.0
ANNOY	2	0.887	0.0	0.0
IRRITABL	9	0.877	0.0	0.0
CONCENTR	1	0.506	0.0	0.459
SMOKING3	7	0.0	0.960	0.0
SMOKING1	3	0.0	0.912	0.0
SMOKING4	12	0.0	0.907	0.0
SMOKING2	5	0.0	0.901	0.0
SLEEPY	4	0.0	0.0	0.961
TIRED	10	0.0	0.0	0.893
ALERT	8	0.455	0.0	0.621
VP		3.643	3.411	2.356

THE ABOVE FACTOR LOADING MATRIX HAS BEEN REARRANGED SO THAT THE COLUMNS APPEAR IN DECREASING ORDER OF VARIANCE EXPLAINED BY FACTORS. THE ROWS HAVE BEEN REARRANGED SO THAT FOR EACH SUCCESSIVE FACTOR, LOADINGS GREATER THAN 0.5000 APPEAR FIRST. LOADINGS LESS THAN 0.2500 HAVE BEEN REPLACED BY ZERO.

--- the remainder of the results is analogous to ⑭ to ⑱ in Output 18.1 ---

(24) Rotated factor loadings (pattern). The results differ from (11) in Output 18.1. Since the rotation is not orthogonal, VP is not the variance explained by the factor, but large values of VP still indicate important factors and small values indicate unimportant factors.

(25) Factor correlations for rotated factors. These are the correlations between the factors. When the rotation is orthogonal this matrix is the identity matrix and is not printed.

(26) Sorted rotated factor loadings (pattern). See (13) (p. 662) for a description of sorted rotated factor loadings.

● SELECTING THE PRINTED RESULTS

The *PRINT* paragraph is used to specify the results you want printed. You can also specify the number of cases to be printed from the original data matrix (five is the preassigned number).

In addition, you can request STANDARD scores, COVARIANCE matrix, INVERSE of the correlation (or covariance) matrix, PARTIAL correlations of each pair of variables removing the effects of all other variables, factor structure matrix (FSTR) when oblique rotation is performed, and RESIDUAL correlation matrix. The correlation matrix can be printed in SHADED form after sorting the variables according to the factors.[9]

Example 18.4 is an expansion of Example 18.1, and illustrates how to request several of the above results.

Example 18.4

```
/PROBLEM      TITLE IS 'JARVIK SMOKING DATA'.
/INPUT        VARIABLES ARE 12.
              FORMAT IS '(12F2.0)'.
/VARIABLE     NAMES ARE CONCENTR,ANNOY,SMOKING1,SLEEPY,SMOKING2,TENSE,
                 SMOKING3,ALERT,IRRITABL,TIRED,CONTENT,SMOKING4.

/PRINT        STANDARD.
              SHADE.
              PARTIAL.
              RESIDUAL.

/END
```

In Output 18.4 we reproduce results that are not printed in Output 18.1. Circled numbers below correspond to those in Output 18.4.

(27) Standard scores. For each value, $z_{ij} = (x_{ij}-\bar{x}_i)/s_i$ is computed and printed, where x_{ij} is the value of the ith variable in the jth case.

---

[9] If your BMDP programs are dated before February 1976, SHADE is not available.

(28) Partial correlations. These are the correlations between each pair of variables after removing the linear effects of all the other variables. This matrix is equivalent (except for the signs of the off-diagonal elements) to the "anti-image" correlation matrix.

(29) Residual correlations. The residual correlations are $R-AA'$, where R is the original correlation matrix, A the initial loadings matrix and A' is the transpose of A.

(30) Correlations in shaded form. The variables are reordered according to the sorted rotated factor loadings. The values of the correlations are replaced by the codes listed in the output and the shaded correlation matrix is printed.

Output 18.4 Optional results printed by P4M

```
WEIGHT VARIABLE . . . . . . . . . . . . . . . .
UNROTATED FACTORS ARE PRINCIPAL COMPONENTS.
NUMBER OF FACTORS IS LIMITED TO THE NUMBER OF EIGENVALUES GREATER THAN     1.000
TOLERANCE LIMIT FOR MATRIX INVERSION. . . . . .   0.00010
VARIMAX ROTATION IS PERFORMED.
GAMMA . . . . . . . . . . . . . . . . . . . . .   1.0000
MAXIMUM NUMBER OF ITERATIONS FOR ROTATION . . .      50
CONVERGENCE CRITERION FOR ROTATION. . . . . . . 0.0000100
KAISER'S NORMALIZATION. . . . . . . . . . . . .     YES
```

--- (2) to (4) *from Output 18.1 are printed* ---

(27) STANDARD SCORES   VARIABLE INDICES

LABEL	NO.	WEIGHT	1	2	3	4	5	6	7	8	9	10	11	12
	1	1.000	0.3	-0.1	-2.1	0.4	-1.5	-0.4	-2.1	0.2	-0.3	-1.1	0.6	-1.2
	2	1.000	1.2	-0.1	1.4	0.4	1.3	1.6	1.4	1.2	1.0	1.0	1.8	1.2
	3	1.000	2.2	0.9	0.6	1.4	1.3	2.6	0.5	2.2	1.0	1.0	0.6	0.4
	4	1.000	1.2	-0.1	0.6	0.4	1.3	1.6	0.5	1.2	1.0	1.0	0.6	1.2
	5	1.000	1.2	-0.1	0.6	0.4	0.4	-0.4	0.5	1.2	-0.3	1.0	0.6	0.4

--- similar standard scores for cases 6 to 105 ---

	NO.	WEIGHT	1	2	3	4	5	6	7	8	9	10	11	12
	106	1.000	-0.6	-1.1	0.6	-1.6	0.4	-0.4	0.5	-0.8	-0.3	-1.1	-0.5	0.4
	107	1.000	-0.6	-0.1	-0.3	-0.6	-0.5	-0.4	0.5	-0.8	-0.3	-1.1	-0.5	0.4
	108	1.000	1.2	-1.1	-2.1	1.4	-1.5	-1.5	-1.2	1.2	-0.3	1.0	-0.5	-1.2
	109	1.000	1.2	-0.1	-0.3	0.4	-0.5	-0.4	-0.4	0.2	-0.3	-0.1	-0.5	0.4
	110	1.000	-0.6	-0.1	-0.3	-1.6	0.4	-0.4	-1.2	-0.8	-0.3	-0.1	-0.5	-2.0

--- (5) *and* (6) *from Output 18.1 are printed* ---

(28) PARTIAL CORRELATIONS

		CONCENTR 1	ANNOY 2	SMOKING1 3	SLEEPY 4	SMOKING2 5	TENSE 6	SMOKING3 7	ALERT 8	IRRITABL 9	TIRED 10	CONTENT 11	SMOKING4 12
CONCENTR	1	1.000											
ANNOY	2	0.118	1.000										
SMOKING1	3	-0.066	0.019	1.000									
SLEEPY	4	-0.056	0.174	-0.055	1.000								
SMOKING2	5	-0.008	-0.242	0.250	-0.053	1.000							
TENSE	6	0.106	0.201	-0.006	-0.031	0.230	1.000						
SMOKING3	7	-0.133	0.123	0.299	-0.036	0.350	-0.134	1.000					
ALERT	8	-0.606	-0.090	-0.097	0.168	0.074	0.068	-0.011	1.000				
IRRITABL	9	0.145	0.448	0.023	-0.018	0.068	0.231	0.075	0.016	1.000			
TIRED	10	-0.075	-0.029	0.086	0.641	0.087	-0.079	-0.048	0.305	0.052	1.000		
CONTENT	11	-0.199	0.375	0.159	-0.241	0.030	0.239	-0.104	0.315	0.098	0.081	1.000	
SMOKING4	12	0.241	-0.006	0.207	0.180	0.250	0.017	0.476	-0.048	-0.142	-0.041	0.015	1.000

THE ELEMENTS OF THIS MATRIX ARE THE PARTIAL CORRELATIONS
OF EACH PAIR OF VARIABLES, PARTIALED ON ALL OTHER VARIABLES
(I.E., HOLDING ALL OTHER VARIABLES FIXED).

--- (7) *to* (9) *from Output 18.1 are printed* ---

(continued)

Output 18.4 *(continued)*

RESIDUAL CORRELATIONS

(29)

		CONCENTR 1	ANNOY 2	SMOKING1 3	SLEEPY 4	SMOKING2 5	TENSE 6	SMOKING3 7	ALERT 8	IRRITABL 9	TIRED 10
CONCENTR	1	0.340									
ANNOY	2	-0.074	0.204								
SMOKING1	3	-0.028	0.010	0.161							
SLEEPY	4	-0.112	0.066	0.013	0.153						
SMOKING2	5	0.014	-0.049	-0.055	-0.026	0.144					
TENSE	6	-0.021	-0.073	-0.024	0.024	0.028	0.220				
SMOKING3	7	-0.000	0.034	-0.048	0.008	-0.042	-0.025	0.106			
ALERT	8	0.070	-0.078	-0.008	-0.093	0.024	-0.017	0.001	0.174		
IRRITABL	9	0.002	-0.002	-0.002	0.031	-0.005	-0.060	0.021	-0.054	0.202	
TIRED	10	-0.120	0.011	0.030	-0.038	-0.002	-0.002	-0.006	-0.056	0.013	0.155
CONTENT	11	-0.098	-0.036	0.020	0.012	-0.008	-0.064	-0.016	0.007	-0.083	0.053
SMOKING4	12	0.054	0.009	-0.059	-0.011	-0.045	-0.000	-0.017	0.004	-0.016	-0.043

		CONTENT 11	SMOKING4 12
CONTENT	11	0.228	
SMOKING4	12	-0.012	0.130

ORTHOGONAL ROTATION, GAMMA =   1.0000

ITERATION	SIMPLICITY CRITERION
0	-1.900373
1	-6.017688
2	-6.019553
3	-6.019557

--- (11) to (13) *from Output 18.1 are printed ---*

(30) ABSOLUTE VALUES OF CORRELATIONS IN SORTED AND SHADED FORM

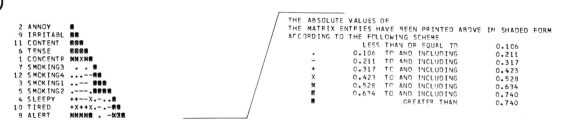

```
    2 ANNOY      ▪
    9 IRRITABL   ▪▪
   11 CONTENT    ▪▪▪
    6 TENSE      ▪▪▪▪
    1 CONCENTR   ▪▪X▪▪
    7 SMOKING3    . . ▪
   12 SMOKING4   ...-▪▪
    3 SMOKING1   ..-- ▪▪▪
    5 SMOKING2   .---.▪▪▪▪
    4 SLEEPY     ++--X.-..▪
   10 TIRED      +X++X.-.-▪▪
    8 ALERT      ▪▪▪▪▪ . -X▪▪
```

THE ABSOLUTE VALUES OF
THE MATRIX ENTRIES HAVE BEEN PRINTED ABOVE IN SHADED FORM
ACCORDING TO THE FOLLOWING SCHEME

	LESS THAN OR EQUAL TO	0.106
.	0.106 TO AND INCLUDING	0.211
-	0.211 TO AND INCLUDING	0.317
+	0.317 TO AND INCLUDING	0.423
X	0.423 TO AND INCLUDING	0.528
▪	0.528 TO AND INCLUDING	0.634
▪	0.634 TO AND INCLUDING	0.740
▪	GREATER THAN	0.740

--- (14) to (18) *from Output 18.1 are printed ---*

PRINT

   CASE= #.   {5/prev.}

     Number of cases for which data are printed.

   FSCORE= #.   {all factors}

     Number of factors for which factor scores are printed.

   STANDARD.   {no/prev.}

     The standard scores are printed.

   COVARIANCE.   {no/prev.}

     The covariance matrix is printed.

   CORRELATION.   {CORRELATION/prev.}

     The correlation matrix is printed unless NO CORRELATION is
     specified.

   INVERSE.   {no/prev.}

     The inverse of the correlation (or covariance) matrix is printed.

   PARTIAL.   {no/prev.}

     The partial correlations of each pair of variables are printed after
     removing the linear effects of all other variables. These partial
     correlations are the negatives of the "anti-image correlations."

   FSTR.   {no/prev. }

     The factor structure matrix is printed when oblique rotation is
     performed.

   RESIDUAL.   {no/prev.}

     Residual correlations are printed. The residual correlations are
     $R-AA'$, where R is the correlation matrix, A the initial loadings
     matrix and A' the transpose of A.

   SHADE.   {no/prev.}

     The correlation matrix is printed in shaded form after the variables
     are sorted according to the factor loadings.

    Rotated factor loadings are printed twice (see ⑪ and ⑬ in
Output 18.1). At the second printing loadings less than LOLEV in absolute
value are replaced by zero and the variables are sorted according to the
levels of loadings greater than HILEV. Since HILEV affects the sorting
of the variables according to the factor loadings, it also affects the
SHADED correlation matrix. The SHADED correlation matrix can be printed
without sorting the variables if you specify HILEV=10 or some other large
value.

```
PRINT
    HILEV= #.              {0.5/prev.}
```

Value considered as a high factor loading. Variables are sorted for each factor according to loadings greater than HILEV.

```
    LOLEV=#.               {0.25/prev.}
```

Value considered as a low factor loading. Values less than LOLEV are replaced by zero in the second printing of the rotated factor loadings.

● THE *PLOT* PARAGRAPH

Two kinds of plots printed by P4M are illustrated in Output 18.1.
- plots of the rotated factor loadings ⑫
- plots of the factor scores ⑱

You can also request plots of the unrotated factor loadings.

```
PLOT
    INITIAL=#.             {0}
```

Number of unrotated factors for which factor loadings are plotted.[10] For each pair of factors the loadings of one factor are plotted against those of the other.

```
    FINAL=#.               {4}
```

Number of rotated factors for which factor loadings are plotted. For each pair of factors the loadings of one factor are plotted against those of the other.

```
    FSCORE=#.              {3}
```

Number of factors for which factor scores are plotted. For each pair of factors the scores of one factor are plotted against those of the other.

● CASE WEIGHTs

The data in each case can be weighted by the values of a WEIGHT variable. Weights are used when the variance is not homogeneous over all cases (the weight is the inverse of the variance), or to represent the frequencies of cases that are repeated in the data (the weight is the frequency of the case), or to remove the influence of some cases (with weight zero) while still obtaining their factor scores and Mahalanobis distances.

---

[10] If your BMDP programs are dated before August 1977,
the minimum required abbreviation is INITIAL (not INIT).

The variable containing the case WEIGHT is specified in the *VARiable* paragraph. Case weights affect the computations of the means, variances and covariances (see Section 2.1).

VARiable
    WEIGHT=v.   {no weight var./prev.}

    Name or subscript of the variable containing the case weights. Values of the case weight should be zero or positive (but never negative). If WEIGHT is not specified or is set to zero, there are no case weights.

- SAVING RESULTS IN A BMDP FILE

    Many of the results computed by P4M can be stored in a BMDP File for input to subsequent analyses. The results that can be saved include

DATA:	the data and factor scores (both the data and the factor scores for each case are written into the BMDP File -- first the data and then the factor scores, which are named FACTOR1, FACTOR2, etc.)
COVA:	the covariance matrix, variances, means, sample size and sum of weights (this is equivalent to saving a correlation matrix; the correlation matrix can be used in an analysis that reads the covariance matrix as input and vice versa)
UFLD:	unrotated factor loadings
RFLD:	rotated factor loadings
FCOR:	factor correlations
FSCF:	factor score coefficients

SAVE
    CONTENT= *(one or more)* DATA,COVA,UFLD,RFLD,
             FCOR,FSCF.   {DATA}

    The data or matrices to be saved in a BMDP File.[11] DATA includes both data and factor scores. The factor scores appear <u>after</u> the data in each case and are named FACTOR1, FACTOR2, etc.

        COVA: covariance matrix
        UFLD: unrotated factor loadings
        RFLD: rotated factor loadings
        FCOR: factor correlations
        FSCF: factor score coefficients

The following example illustrates the order in which the BMDP Files are formed.

---

[11] If your BMDP programs are dated before August 1977,
      the minimum required abbreviation is CONTENT (not CONT).

Example 18.5

```
/PROBLEM        TITLE IS 'JARVIK SMOKING DATA'.
/INPUT          VARIABLES ARE 12.
                FORMAT IS '(12F2.0)'.
/VARIABLE       NAMES ARE CONCENTR,ANNOY,SMOKING1,SLEEPY,SMOKING2,TENSE,
                    SMOKING3,ALERT,IRRITABL,TIRED,CONTENT,SMOKING4.

/SAVE           UNIT IS 4.
                NEW.
                CODE IS JARVIK.
                CONTENT IS DATA,COVA,UFLD,RFLD,FCOR,FSCF.

/END
```

Note: The System Cards that precede the Control Language must contain a card describing where to store the BMDP File (Section 7.1). At HSCF, the System Cards are

```
//jobname  JOB  nooo,yourname
//  EXEC  BIMED,PROG=BMDP4M
//FT04F001  DD  DSNAME=FS.nooo.filename,DISP=OLD
//SYSIN  DD  *
```

In addition space must be allocated for the system file (Section 7.1).

The messages verifying that the BMDP Files are written in Output 18.5. Note that the data and factor scores (DATA) are in the last BMDP File formed. The message that this File is completed appears after the estimated factor scores and Mahalanobis distances are printed.

Output 18.5 Results that can be saved in BMDP Files by P4M. Results not reproduced are indicated in italics.

```
WEIGHT VARIABLE . . . . . . . . . . . . . . . .
UNROTATED FACTORS ARE PRINCIPAL COMPONENTS.
NUMBER OF FACTORS IS LIMITED TO THE NUMBER OF EIGENVALUES GREATER THAN      1.000
TOLERANCE LIMIT FOR MATRIX INVERSION. . . . . .    0.00010
VARIMAX ROTATION IS PERFORMED.
GAMMA . . . . . . . . . . . . . . . . . . . . .    1.0000
MAXIMUM NUMBER OF ITERATIONS FOR ROTATION . . .      50
CONVERGENCE CRITERION FOR ROTATION. . . . . . . 0.0000100
KAISER'S NORMALIZATION. . . . . . . . . . . . .      YES

REQUESTED OUTPUT BMDP FILE
    UNIT    =    4
    CODE    = JARVIK
    LABEL   =
    CONTENT =
              DATA        (INPUT DATA MATRIX AND FACTOR SCORES)
              COVA        (COVARIANCE MATRIX)
              UFLD        (UNROTATED FACTOR LOADINGS)
              RFLD        (ROTATED FACTOR LOADINGS)
              FCOR        (FACTOR CORRELATION MATRIX)
              FSCF        (FACTOR SCORE COEFFICIENTS)
```

--- ② *from Output 18.1 is printed* ---

```
NUMBER OF CASES READ. . . . . . . . . . .    110

BMDP FILE WRITTEN ON UNIT 4
                  CODE. . . IS     JARVIK
                  CONTENT . IS     COVA
                  LABEL . . IS
                  VARIABLES    1  CONCENTR    2  ANNOY      3  SMOKING1   4  SLEEPY     5  SMOKING2
                               6  TENSE       7  SMOKING3   8  ALERT      9  IRRITABL  10  TIRED
                              11  CONTENT    12  SMOKING4

BMDP FILE ON UNIT  4 HAS BEEN COMPLETED.
```

(continued)

Output 18.5   *(continued)*

--- ③   to   ⑨   *from Output 18.1 is printed* ---

```
BMDP FILE WRITTEN ON UNIT    4
                    CODE. . . IS     JARVIK
                    CONTENT . IS     UFLD
                    LABEL . . IS
                    VARIABLES    1  CONCENTR    2  ANNOY      3  SMOKING1    4  SLEEPY     5  SMOKING2
                                 6  TENSE       7  SMOKING3   8  ALERT       9  IRRITABL  10  TIRED
                                11  CONTENT    12  SMOKING4
```

BMDP FILE ON UNIT 4 HAS BEEN COMPLETED.

--- ⑩   to   ⑬   *from Output 18.1 are printed* ---

```
BMDP FILE WRITTEN ON UNIT    4
                    CODE. . . IS     JARVIK
                    CONTENT . IS     RFLD
                    LABEL . . IS
                    VARIABLES    1  CONCENTR    2  ANNOY      3  SMOKING1    4  SLEEPY     5  SMOKING2
                                 6  TENSE       7  SMOKING3   8  ALERT       9  IRRITABL  10  TIRED
                                11  CONTENT    12  SMOKING4
```

BMDP FILE ON UNIT 4 HAS BEEN COMPLETED.

```
BMDP FILE WRITTEN ON UNIT    4
                    CODE. . . IS     JARVIK
                    CONTENT . IS     FCOR
                    LABEL . . IS
                    VARIABLES    1  FACTOR1    2  FACTOR2    3  FACTOR3
```

BMDP FILE ON UNIT 4 HAS BEEN COMPLETED.

--- ⑭   *from 18.1 is printed* ---

```
BMDP FILE WRITTEN ON UNIT    4
                    CODE. . . IS     JARVIK
                    CONTENT . IS     FSCF
                    LABEL . . IS
                    VARIABLES    1  CONCENTR    2  ANNOY      3  SMOKING1    4  SLEEPY     5  SMOKING2
                                 6  TENSE       7  SMOKING3   8  ALERT       9  IRRITABL  10  TIRED
                                11  CONTENT    12  SMOKING4
```

BMDP FILE CN UNIT 4 HAS BEEN COMPLETED.

--- ⑮   *from 18.1 is printed* ---

```
BMDP FILE WRITTEN ON UNIT    4
                    CODE. . . IS     JARVIK
                    CONTENT . IS     DATA
                    LABEL . . IS
                    VARIABLES    1  CONCENTR    2  ANNOY      3  SMOKING1    4  SLEEPY     5  SMOKING2
                                 6  TENSE       7  SMOKING3   8  ALERT       9  IRRITABL  10  TIRED
                                11  CONTENT    12  SMOKING4  13  FACTOR1    14  FACTOR2   15  FACTOR3
```

```
ESTIMATED FACTOR SCORES AND MAHALANOBIS DISTANCES (CHI-SQUARES) FROM EACH CASE TO THE CENTROID OF ALL CASES
FOR ORIGINAL DATA ( 12 D.F.) FACTOR SCORES (  3 D.F.) AND THEIR DIFFERENCE (  9 D.F.).
EACH CHI-SQUARE HAS BEEN DIVIDED BY ITS DEGREES OF FREEDOM.
CASE NUMBERS BELOW REFER TO DATA MATRIX BEFORE DELETION OF MISSING DATA.
```

```
    CASE   CHISQ/DF CHISQ/DF CHISQ/DF   FACTOR   FACTOR   FACTOR
LABEL  NO.     12       3        9         1        2        3

      1      1.432    1.212    1.505     0.167   -1.899    0.014
      2      1.113    1.063    1.130     1.114    1.341    0.389
      3      1.333    1.238    1.365     1.357    0.511    1.269
```

--- *similar statistics for cases 4 to 107* ---

```
    108      1.459    2.926    0.970    -1.067   -1.752    2.138
    109      0.530    0.199    0.640    -0.337   -0.295    0.629
    110      2.035    0.488    2.550    -0.066   -0.755   -0.935
```

BMDP FILE ON UNIT 4 HAS BEEN COMPLETED.

--- ⑰   *and*   ⑱   *from Output 18.1 are printed* ---

● FORMS OF INPUT

P4M can start an analysis from data, from a covariance or correlation matrix, or from orthogonal factor loadings or factor score coefficients.

If your input is data, you can skip the following discussion. If your input is not data, you must specify the TYPE of input unless it is from a BMDP File and the CONTENT of the BMDP File corresponds to one of the permissible TYPEs defined below.

```
INPut
    CONTENT= c.                    { DATA }     used only when input is from a
                                                BMDP File

      If the input is not DATA, CONTENT must be specified.  It must
      be identical to the CONTENT stated in the SAVE paragraph when
      the BMDP File was created.

    TYPE= (one only) DATA,CORR,      {determined by CONTENT if
          COVA,LOAD,FSCF             input is from a BMDP File; DATA
                                     otherwise}

      Type of input.  TYPE need not be specified when the input is data
      or when the input is from a BMDP File whose CONTENT corresponds
      to one of the names listed above.  If input is factor loadings
      (LOAD), the factors are assumed to be orthogonal.
```

When the input is <u>not</u> from a BMDP File and TYPE is CORR or COVA, either a square matrix or a lower triangular matrix can be read as input. A lower triangular matrix has one element (the diagonal) in the first row, two elements in the second, etc.

```
INPut
    SHAPE= (one only) SQUARE,LOWER.     {SQUARE/prev.}

      Shape of the matrix when the input TYPE is CORR or COVA and is
      not read from a BMDP File.  Each row of the matrix must begin in a
      new record.  The format describes the longest row.
```

When the input is <u>not</u> from a BMDP File and TYPE is LOAD or FSCF, the factors are read one at a time; that is, a factor in LOAD or FSCF corresponds to a case in DATA. The number of factors must be specified.

```
INPut
    FACTOR=#.                {none}

      Number of factors when the input TYPE is LOAD or FSCF and input
      is not read from a BMDP File.  If TYPE is LOAD, the factors are
      assumed to orthogonal.
```

When input is a <u>correlation or covariance matrix from a BMDP File</u>, you can obtain factor scores if the data are on the same BMDP File as the matrix with the same BMDP File code. To match up variables from the data with the variables in the correlation or covariance matrix, the SCORE statement must be given. This option avoids recomputing the covariance or correlation matrix without losing the ability to obtain factor scores when you are using several methods of factoring.

When <u>factor loadings or factor score coefficients are input from a BMDP File</u>, factor scores can be obtained if the data and covariance matrix are in the same system file with the same code. This allows you to try several methods of rotation and to obtain factor scores without recomputing the covariance matrix or initial loadings. Moreover, by using this option, scores for one set of subjects can be obtained using factor score coefficients computed from another set of subjects. Factor scores can also be obtained for one set of variables using the factor score coefficients computed from another set of variables; e.g., factor scores for posttreatment variables can be obtained using factor score coefficients from a pretreatment factor analysis of the same variables. To match variables from the covariance matrix with variables from the loadings or coefficients, the USE statement can be used. To match variables from the data with variables in the loadings or coefficients matrix, the SCORE statement must be given.

VARiable
   SCORE=$v_1,v_2,\cdots$.   {none}

      Variables used for factor scores. This is used only when input is from a BMDP File and the data are <u>not</u> read as input. The SCORE statement signals P4M that factor scores are to be computed and that the data are in a BMDP File in the same system file with the same CODE as the covariance matrix, factor loadings or factor score coefficients read as input.

To demonstrate the use of the SCORE statement, a COVARIANCE matrix stored in a BMDP File is read as input in Example 18.5. The CODE for both the covariance matrix and the data is JARVIK, and both matrices are in the same system file on UNIT number 4.

Example 18.6

```
/PROBLEM      TITLE IS 'JARVIK SMOKING DATA'.
/INPUT        UNIT IS 4.
              CODE IS JARVIK.
              CONTENT IS COVA.

/VARIABLE     SCORES ARE 1 TO 12.

/END
```

Note: The System Cards that precede the Control Language must contain a card describing where to find the BMDP File (Section 7.3). At HSCF, the System Cards are

```
//jobname  JOB  nooo,yourname
//   EXEC  BIMED,PROG=BMDP4M
//FT04F001  DD  DSNAME=FS.nooo.filename,DISP=OLD
//SYSIN  DD  *
```

where filename is the name given to the system file when the BMDP File was created.

The results are presented in Output 18.6; they are identical to those in Output 18.1 except that the panel of univariate statistics is not printed.

Output 18.6 Starting a factor analysis from a covariance matrix

```
INPUT FORMAT
        BMDP FILE . . . . . CODE. . . IS    JARVIK
                           CONTENT . IS    COVA
                           LABEL . . IS
                           VARIABLES   1  CONCENTR   2  ANNOY     3  SMOKING1   4  SLEEPY    5  SMOKING2
                                       6  TENSE      7  SMOKING3  8  ALERT      9  IRRITABL  10  TIRED
                                      11  CONTENT   12  SMOKING4


VARIABLES TO BE USED
              1  CONCENTR    2  ANNOY      3  SMOKING1    4  SLEEPY     5  SMOKING2
              6  TENSE       7  SMOKING3   8  ALERT       9  IRRITABL  10  TIRED
             11  CONTENT    12  SMOKING4

NUMBER OF VARIABLES TO BE USED. . . . . . . . .   12

WEIGHT VARIABLE . . . . . . . . . . . . . . .
UNROTATED FACTORS ARE PRINCIPAL COMPONENTS.
NUMBER OF FACTORS IS LIMITED TO THE NUMBER OF EIGENVALUES GREATER THAN     1.000
TOLERANCE LIMIT FOR MATRIX INVERSION. . . . . .    0.00010
VARIMAX ROTATION IS PERFORMED.
GAMMA . . . . . . . . . . . . . . . . . . . . .    1.0000
MAXIMUM NUMBER OF ITERATIONS FOR ROTATION . . .      50
CONVERGENCE CRITERION FOR ROTATION. . . . . . .  0.0000100
KAISER'S NORMALIZATION. . . . . . . . . . . .      YES

TOTAL DEGREES OF FREEDOM TO BE USED IN COMPUTATIONS     110

THE FOLLOWING VARIABLES WILL BE USED FOR COMPUTING FACTOR SCORES.

         1  CONCENTR
         2  ANNOY
         3  SMOKING1
         4  SLEEPY
         5  SMOKING2
         6  TENSE
         7  SMOKING3
         8  ALERT
         9  IRRITABL
        10  TIRED
        11  CONTENT
        12  SMOKING4


CORRELATION MATRIX
```

		CONCENTR 1	ANNOY 2	SMOKING1 3	SLEEPY 4	SMOKING2 5	TENSE 6	SMOKING3 7	ALERT 8	IRRITABL 9	TIRED 10	CONTENT 11	SMOKING4 12
CONCENTR	1	1.000											
ANNOY	2	0.562	1.000										
SMOKING1	3	0.086	0.144	1.000									
SLEEPY	4	0.457	0.360	0.140	1.000								
SMOKING2	5	0.200	0.119	0.785	0.211	1.000							
TENSE	6	0.579	0.705	0.222	0.273	0.301	1.000						
SMOKING3	7	0.041	0.060	0.810	0.126	0.816	0.120	1.000					
ALERT	8	0.802	0.578	0.101	0.606	0.223	0.594	0.039	1.000				
IRRITABL	9	0.595	0.796	0.189	0.337	0.221	0.725	0.108	0.605	1.000			
TIRED	10	0.512	0.413	0.199	0.798	0.274	0.364	0.139	0.698	0.428	1.000		
CONTENT	11	0.492	0.739	0.239	0.240	0.235	0.711	0.100	0.605	0.697	0.394	1.000	
SMOKING4	12	0.228	0.122	0.775	0.277	0.813	0.214	0.845	0.201	0.156	0.271	0.171	1.000

--- the remainder of the results is the same as in Output 18.1 ---

- ### SIZE OF PROBLEM

    P4M can analyze up to 100 variables with 10 factors unless maximum likelihood factor analysis is requested, in which case only 60 variables can be analysed. Appendix B describes how to increase the capacity of the program.

- ### COMPUTATIONAL METHOD

    The data are read in single precision. All computations are performed in double precision. Means, standard deviations and covariances are computed by the method of provisional means (Appendix A.2). When case weights are used, the statistics are adjusted so that the average nonzero weight is one.

    The description of many of the formulas is given in the program descriptions. Appendix A.21 describes the method of maximum likelihood factor analysis.

    The inverse of the correlation or covariance matrix is computed by stepwise pivoting (Appendix A.11). Eigenvalues are obtained by means of Householder tridiagonalization and Reinsch's (1973) TQLRAT version of QR. Eigenvectors are obtained by inverse iteration.

    The method of shading the correlation matrix is similar to that of Ling (1973).

ACKNOWLEDGEMENT

P4M was designed by James Frane with major contributions from Robert Jennrich and Paul Sampson. It was programmed by James Frane with major contributions from Paul Sampson. It supersedes BMD08M, which was developed by Robert Jennrich and Paul Sampson.

P6M

18.2 Canonical Correlation Analysis

James Frane, HSCF

P6M performs a canonical correlation analysis between two sets of variables. It computes and prints the canonical correlations, coefficients for the canonical variables, canonical variable scores, and correlations of the original variables with the canonical variables (loadings). It also prints the eigenvalues associated with each pair of canonical variables and Bartlett's test for the significance of the remaining eigenvalues.

● RESULTS

The Jarvik smoking questionnaire data (Table 17.1) are used in a canonical analysis by P6M. In Example 18.7 we specify the two sets of variables between which the canonical correlations are computed. The remaining Control Language instructions are common to all BMDP programs and are discussed in Chapter 5.

Example 18.7

```
/PROBLEM      TITLE IS 'JARVIK SMOKING DATA'.
/INPUT        VARIABLES ARE 12.
              FORMAT IS '(12F2.0)'.
/VARIABLE     NAMES ARE CONCENTR,ANNOY,SMOKING1,SLEEPY,SMOKING2,TENSE,
                  SMOKING3,ALERT,IRRITABL,TIRED,CONTENT,SMOKING4.

/CANONICAL    FIRST ARE SMOKING1,SMOKING2,SMOKING3,SMOKING4.
              SECOND ARE CONCENTR,ANNOY,SLEEPY,TENSE,
                  ALERT,IRRITABL,TIRED,CONTENT.

/END
```

The Control Language must be preceded by System Cards to initiate the analysis by P6M. At HSCF, the System Cards are

```
//jobname  JOB  nooo,yourname
//   EXEC  BIMED,PROG=BMDP6M
//SYSIN  DD  *
```

The Control Language is immediately followed by the data (Table 17.1). The analysis is terminated by another System Card. At HSCF, this System Card is

```
//
```

The results of the analysis by P6M are presented in Output 18.7. Circled numbers below correspond to those in the output.

① Interpretation of Control Language instructions specific to P6M. Except for specifying the two sets of variables, all options are preassigned.

② Data for the first five cases. The number of cases printed can be specified; five is the preassigned number.

<u>Output 18.7</u> Canonical correlation analysis by P6M. Circled numbers correspond to those in the text. Results not reproduced are indicated in *italics*.

```
BMDP6M - CANONICAL CORRELATION ANALYSIS
HEALTH SCIENCES COMPUTING FACILITY                        PROGRAM REVISED SEPTEMBER 1977
UNIVERSITY OF CALIFORNIA, LOS ANGELES                     MANUAL DATE  --  1977
```

--- Control Language read by P6M is printed and interpreted ---

① FIRST SET OF VARIABLES
      3 SMOKING1   5 SMOKING2   7 SMOKING3   12 SMOKING4

   SECOND SET OF VARIABLES
        1 CONCENTR   2 ANNOY   4 SLEEPY   6 TENSE   8 ALERT
        9 IRRITABL   10 TIRED   11 CONTENT

```
NUMBER OF VARIABLES IN FIRST SET. . . . . . . .      4
NUMBER OF VARIABLES IN SECOND SET . . . . . . .      8
TOTAL NUMBER OF VARIABLES USED. . . . . . . . .     12
MAXIMUM NUMBER OF CANONICAL VARIABLES . . . . .      4
MINIMUM CANONICAL CORRELATION TO BE USED. . . .    0.0
WEIGHT VARIABLE . . . . . . . . . . . . . . . .
PRECISION . . . . . . . . . . . . . . . . . . .   DOUBLE
TOLERANCE FOR MATRIX INVERSION. . . . . . . . .  0.0100000
EIGENVALUE LIMIT. . . . . . . . . . . . . . .    0.0
APPROX. NUMBER OF VARIABLES WHICH CAN BE ANALYZED   120
```

DATA AFTER TRANSFORMATIONS FOR FIRST   5 CASES
CASES WITH ZERO WEIGHTS AND MISSING DATA NOT INCLUDED.

②

CASE LABEL	NUMBER	WEIGHT 6 TENSE	3 SMOKING1 8 ALERT	5 SMOKING2 9 IRRITABL	7 SMOKING3 10 TIRED	12 SMOKING4 11 CONTENT	1 CONCENTR	2 ANNOY	4 SLEEPY
1	1.00000	1.00000	2.00000	1.00000	2.00000	3.00000	2.00000	3.00000
	2.00000	3.00000	2.00000	2.00000	3.00000			
2	1.00000	5.00000	5.00000	5.00000	5.00000	4.00000	2.00000	3.00000
	4.00000	4.00000	3.00000	4.00000	4.00000			
3	1.00000	4.00000	5.00000	4.00000	4.00000	5.00000	3.00000	4.00000
	5.00000	5.00000	3.00000	4.00000	3.00000			
4	1.00000	4.00000	5.00000	4.00000	5.00000	4.00000	2.00000	3.00000
	4.00000	4.00000	3.00000	4.00000	3.00000			
5	1.00000	4.00000	4.00000	4.00000	4.00000	4.00000	2.00000	3.00000
	2.00000	4.00000	2.00000	4.00000	3.00000			

③ NUMBER OF CASES READ.   110

UNIVARIATE SUMMARY STATISTICS

④

VARIABLE	MEAN	STANDARD DEVIATION	COEFFICIENT OF VARIATION	SMALLEST VALUE	LARGEST VALUE	SMALLEST STANDARD SCORE	LARGEST STANDARD SCORE	SKEWNESS	KURTOSIS
3 SMOKING1	3.36364	1.13111	0.336275	1.00000	5.00000	-2.09	1.45	-0.36	-0.57
5 SMOKING2	3.58182	1.06126	0.296291	1.00000	5.00000	-2.43	1.34	-0.40	-0.63
7 SMOKING3	3.42727	1.16098	0.338747	1.00000	5.00000	-2.09	1.35	-0.42	-0.63
12 SMOKING4	3.50000	1.27610	0.364601	1.00000	5.00000	-1.96	1.18	-0.54	-0.79
1 CONCENTR	2.69091	1.07298	0.398744	1.00000	5.00000	-1.58	2.15	0.10	-0.81
2 ANNOY	2.11818	0.97427	0.459957	1.00000	5.00000	-1.15	2.96	0.89	0.33
4 SLEEPY	2.60909	1.02353	0.392295	1.00000	5.00000	-1.57	2.34	0.01	-0.80
6 TENSE	2.44545	0.99158	0.405480	1.00000	5.00000	-1.46	2.58	0.26	-0.79
8 ALERT	2.80909	1.01814	0.362445	1.00000	5.00000	-1.78	2.15	0.02	-0.48
9 IRRITABL	2.21818	0.78263	0.352825	1.00000	4.00000	-1.56	2.28	0.06	-0.63
10 TIRED	3.09091	0.95346	0.308473	1.00000	5.00000	-2.19	2.00	-0.31	-0.25
11 CONTENT	2.45455	0.84198	0.343027	1.00000	5.00000	-1.73	3.02	0.19	-0.16

VALUES FOR KURTOSIS GREATER THAN ZERO INDICATE DISTRIBUTIONS
WITH HEAVIER TAILS THAN THE NORMAL DISTRIBUTION.

(continued)

Output 18.7 *(continued)*

CORRELATIONS

⑤

		SMOKING1	SMOKING2	SMOKING3	SMOKING4	CONCENTR	ANNOY	SLEEPY	TENSE	ALERT	IRRITABL	TIRED	CONTENT
		3	5	7	12	1	2	4	6	8	9	10	11
SMOKING1	3	1.000											
SMOKING2	5	0.785	1.000										
SMOKING3	7	0.810	0.816	1.000									
SMOKING4	12	0.775	0.813	0.845	1.000								
CONCENTR	1	0.086	0.200	0.041	0.228	1.000							
ANNOY	2	0.144	0.119	0.060	0.122	0.562	1.000						
SLEEPY	4	0.140	0.211	0.126	0.277	0.457	0.360	1.000					
TENSE	6	0.222	0.301	0.120	0.214	0.579	0.705	0.273	1.000				
ALERT	8	0.101	0.223	0.039	0.201	0.802	0.578	0.606	0.594	1.000			
IRRITABL	9	0.189	0.221	0.108	0.156	0.595	0.796	0.337	0.725	0.605	1.000		
TIRED	10	0.199	0.274	0.139	0.271	0.512	0.413	0.798	0.364	0.698	0.428	1.000	
CONTENT	11	0.239	0.235	0.100	0.171	0.492	0.739	0.240	0.711	0.605	0.697	0.394	1.000

SQUARED MULTIPLE CORRELATIONS OF EACH VARIABLE IN SECOND SET WITH ALL OTHER VARIABLES IN SECOND SET

⑥

VARIABLE		
NUMBER	NAME	R-SQUARED
1	CONCENTR	0.68425
2	ANNOY	0.72147
4	SLEEPY	0.67121
6	TENSE	0.63869
8	ALERT	0.79529
9	IRRITABL	0.70704
10	TIRED	0.71877
11	CONTENT	0.67799

SQUARED MULTIPLE CORRELATIONS OF EACH VARIABLE IN FIRST SET WITH ALL OTHER VARIABLES IN FIRST SET

⑦

VARIABLE		
NUMBER	NAME	R-SQUARED
3	SMOKING1	0.71036
5	SMOKING2	0.74227
7	SMOKING3	0.79150
12	SMOKING4	0.76658

⑧

EIGENVALUE	CANONICAL CORRELATION
0.27278	0.52229
0.14128	0.37588
0.05779	0.24040
0.01882	0.13719

NUMBER OF EIGENVALUES	BARTLETT'S TEST FOR REMAINING EIGENVALUES		
	CHI-SQUARE	D.F.	SIGNIFICANCE
0	56.31	32	0.00502
1	23.66	21	0.30975
2	8.05	12	0.78129
3	1.95	5	0.85637

BARTLETT'S TEST ABOVE INDICATES THE NUMBER OF CANONICAL
VARIABLES NECESSARY TO EXPRESS THE DEPENDENCY BETWEEN THE
TWO SETS OF VARIABLES. THE NECESSARY NUMBER OF CANONICAL
VARIABLES IS THE SMALLEST NUMBER OF EIGENVALUES SUCH THAT
THE TEST OF THE REMAINING EIGENVALUES IS NON-SIGNIFICANT.
FOR EXAMPLE, IF A TEST AT THE .01 LEVEL WERE DESIRED,
THEN   1 VARIABLES WOULD BE CONSIDERED NECESSARY.
HOWEVER, THE NUMBER OF CANONICAL VARIABLES OF PRACTICAL
VALUE IS LIKELY TO BE SMALLER.

CANONICAL VARIABLE LOADINGS (CORRELATIONS OF CANONICAL VARIABLES WITH ORIGINAL VARIABLES)

⑨

		CNVRF1	CNVRF2	CNVRF3	CNVRF4
		1	2	3	4
SMOKING1	3	-0.445	-0.534	-0.659	0.286
SMOKING2	5	-0.728	-0.384	-0.151	0.548
SMOKING3	7	-0.289	-0.270	-0.473	0.787
SMOKING4	12	-0.639	0.056	-0.565	0.518

		CNVRS1	CNVRS2	CNVRS3	CNVRS4
		1	2	3	4
CONCENTR	1	-0.721	0.356	-0.013	-0.311
ANNOY	2	-0.303	-0.141	-0.384	-0.401
SLEEPY	4	-0.600	0.347	-0.377	0.260
TENSE	6	-0.700	-0.333	0.001	-0.178
ALERT	8	-0.730	0.156	0.149	-0.361
IRRITABL	9	-0.457	-0.337	-0.115	-0.072
TIRED	10	-0.691	0.027	-0.256	0.072
CONTENT	11	-0.532	-0.440	-0.308	-0.558

③ Number of cases read. Cases included in the computations are those that contain acceptable values for all the variables used in the analysis; cases are omitted from all computations when the value of any variable used in the analysis is missing or out of range.

④ Univariate statistics

- mean
- standard deviation
- coefficient of variation
- smallest observed value (not out of range)
- largest observed value (not out of range)
- smallest standard score
- largest standard score
- skewness
- kurtosis

In Section 2.1 these univariate statistics are defined and the effect of case weights on their computation is described.

⑤ Correlation matrix.

⑥ Squared multiple correlations (R^2) of each variable in the second set with all other variables in the second set.

⑦ Squared multiple correlations (R^2) of each variable in the first set with all other variables in the first set.

⑧ Eigenvalues are found for the canonical correlation problem (for the matrix $R_{xx}^{-\frac{1}{2}} R_{xy} R_{yy}^{-1} R_{yx} R_{xx}^{-\frac{1}{2}}$ defined in Appendix A.22). Anderson (1958), Cooley and Lohnes (1971) and Morrison (1967) discuss canonical correlation analysis.

- The eigenvalues are printed.

- The canonical correlations are the square roots of the eigenvalues.

- Bartlett's (1947) test for the significance of the k smallest eigenvalues is printed, where k can be 1, 2, etc. The uppermost line (chi-square = 56.31) tests whether the eigenvalues differ significantly from zero; this is a test that the correlations between the two sets of variables are zero. A significant chi-square indicates that the two sets of variables are not independent. The next line (chi-square = 23.66) tests whether all eigenvalues but the largest differ significantly from zero; this is a test of whether the first canonical variable is sufficient to describe the dependence between the two sets of variables. The number of canonical variables of practical value is less than or equal to the smallest number of eigenvalues for which Bartlett's test for the remaining eigenvalues is nonsignificant.

⑨ Canonical variable loadings. These are the correlations of the canonical variables with the original variables. CNVRF1 is the name assigned by P6M to the 1st canonical variable in the first set; CNVRF2 to the 2nd, etc. CNVRS1 is the name assigned to the 1st canonical variable in the second set, etc. These correlations are analogous to unrotated factor loadings.

● OPTIONAL RESULTS AND INPUT

In addition to the above results you can

- print the covariance matrix, the matrix of canonical variables and the regression coefficients for the canonical variables   p. 690

- plot original and canonical variables in bivariate plots   p. 691

- assign weights to the cases   p. 694

- save the data and the canonical variables or a covariance matrix in a BMDP File for input to other BMDP programs   p. 694

- start the analysis from data, a covariance matrix, or a correlation matrix   p. 695

● THE *CANONical* PARAGRAPH

The variables included in each set of variables must be specified in the *CANONical* paragraph. Each set should contain at least two variables; otherwise a regression program (Chapter 13) should be used.

The number of canonical variables to be obtained can be stated explicitly. If not stated the number is determined by the program as being all canonical variables whose correlations are greater than CONSTANT. (CONSTANT is preset to zero).

In addition, you can specify the tolerance for matrix inversion, whether the computations are to be in single or double precision, and whether covariances and correlations are computed about the mean or about the origin.

```
CANONical
    FIRST=v₁,v₂,····          {none}                required

    Names or subscripts of variables in the first set of variables.
    At least two variables must be specified.

    SECOND=v₁,v₂,····         {none}                required

    Names or subscripts of variables in the second set of variables.
    At least two variables must be specified.
                                                    (continued)
```

CANONical

   NUMBER=#.   {number of variables in smaller set}

      Maximum number of canonical variables to be obtained.[12]

   CONSTANT=#.   {0.0/prev.}

      Canonical variables obtained must have a canonical correlation
      that exceeds CONSTANT.

   PRECISION= *(one only)* SINGLE,DOUBLE. {DOUBLE/prev.}

      Precision used in the computations.

   TOLERANCE=#.   {0.01/prev.}   between 0.0 and 1.0

      Tolerance for matrix inversion. Inversion is performed by stepwise
      pivoting. A variable is not pivoted if its squared multiple corre-
      lation with already pivoted variables exceeds 1-TOLERANCE , or if
      pivoting causes an already pivoted variable to have a squared
      multiple correlation with other pivoted variables that exceeds
      1- TOLERANCE . For IBM 360 and 370 computers TOL should not be
      less than 0.01 for single precision and not less than 10^{-7} for
      double precision.

   ZERO.   {no/prev.}

      Covariances and correlations are computed about the origin and
      not about the mean. This is a rarely used option.

● THE *PRINT* PARAGRAPH

   The number of cases for which the data are printed can be specified.

   In addition to the correlation matrix and the canonical variable loadings
printed in Output 18.7, P6M can print the covariance matrix, the canonical
variables and the regression coefficients for the canonical variables. These
results are requested in Example 18.8.

Example 18.8

```
/PROBLEM      TITLE IS 'JARVIK SMOKING DATA'.
/INPUT        VARIABLES ARE 12.
              FORMAT IS '(12F2.0)'.
/VARIABLE     NAMES ARE CONCENTR,ANNOY,SMOKING1,SLEEPY,SMOKING2,TENSE,
                  SMOKING3,ALERT,IRRITABL,TIRED,CONTENT,SMOKING4.

/CANONICAL    FIRST ARE SMOKING1,SMOKING2,SMOKING3,SMOKING4.
              SECOND ARE CONCENTR,ANNOY,SLEEPY,TENSE,
                  ALERT,IRRITABL,TIRED,CONTENT.

/PRINT        MATRICES ARE CORR,CANV,COEF,LOAD.

/END
```

---

[12] If your BMDP programs are dated before August 1977,
      the minimum required abbreviation is NUMBER (not NUMB).

Output 18.8 Optional results printed by P6M

--- ② to ⑧ in Output 18.7 are printed ---

COEFFICIENTS FOR CANONICAL VARIABLES FOR FIRST SET OF VARIABLES

⑩

		CNVRF1 1	CNVRF2 2	CNVRF3 3	CNVRF4 4
SMOKING1	3	0.378543E-01	-0.976451E 00	-0.965493E 00	-0.900841E 00
SMOKING2	5	-0.109321E 01	-0.646536E 00	0.134105E 01	0.182999E 00
SMOKING3	7	0.119115E 01	-0.173899E 00	+0.333693E-01	0.145194E 01
SMOKING4	12	-0.704060E 00	0.128569E 01	-0.660196E 00	-0.214955E 00

STANDARDIZED COEFFICIENTS FOR CANONICAL VARIABLES FOR FIRST SET OF VARIABLES
(THESE ARE THE COEFFICIENTS FOR THE STANDARDIZED VARIABLES - MEAN ZERO, STANDARD DEVIATION ONE.)

		CNVRF1 1	CNVRF2 2	CNVRF3 3	CNVRF4 4
SMOKING1	3	0.043	-1.104	-1.092	-1.019
SMOKING2	5	-1.160	-0.686	1.423	0.194
SMOKING3	7	1.383	-0.202	-0.039	1.686
SMOKING4	12	-0.898	1.641	-0.842	-0.274

COEFFICIENTS FOR CANONICAL VARIABLES FOR SECOND SET OF VARIABLES

		CNVRS1 1	CNVRS2 2	CNVRS3 3	CNVRS4 4
CONCENTR	1	-0.441692E 00	0.745510E 00	-0.470381E 00	-0.163811E 00
ANNOY	2	0.801410E 00	0.461495E 00	-0.605503E 00	-0.739549E 00
SLEEPY	4	-0.250790E 00	0.581216E 00	-0.685988E 00	0.615867E 00
TENSE	6	-0.692552E 00	-0.380734E 00	0.421877E 00	0.448775E 00
ALERT	8	0.140028E 00	0.204741E 00	0.150159E 01	-0.685341E 00
IRRITABL	9	0.900002E-01	-0.795294E 00	0.425982E 00	0.113746E 01
TIRED	10	-0.327905E 00	-0.616256E 00	-0.246355E 00	0.172116E 00
CONTENT	11	-0.402041E 00	-0.595032E 00	-0.971468E 00	-0.795208E 00

STANDARDIZED COEFFICIENTS FOR CANONICAL VARIABLES FOR SECOND SET OF VARIABLES
(THESE ARE THE COEFFICIENTS FOR THE STANDARDIZED VARIABLES - MEAN ZERO, STANDARD DEVIATION ONE.)

		CNVRS1 1	CNVRS2 2	CNVRS3 3	CNVRS4 4
CONCENTR	1	-0.474	0.800	-0.505	-0.176
ANNOY	2	0.781	0.450	-0.590	-0.721
SLEEPY	4	-0.257	0.595	-0.702	0.630
TENSE	6	-0.687	-0.378	0.418	0.445
ALERT	8	0.143	0.208	1.529	-0.698
IRRITABL	9	0.070	-0.622	0.333	0.890
TIRED	10	-0.313	-0.588	-0.235	0.164
CONTENT	11	-0.339	-0.501	-0.818	-0.670

CANONICAL VARIABLES (CASE NUMBERS REFER TO DATA BEFORE DELETION OF CASES)

⑪

LABEL	CASE NO.	WEIGHT	CNVRF1	CNVRF2	CNVRF3	CNVRF4	CNVRS1	CNVRS2	CNVRS3	CNVRS4
	1	1.0000	-0.1954	1.8242	1.2321	-1.3620	0.1247	1.1330	-0.5973	-0.9229
	2	1.0000	-0.6712	-0.8597	-0.7208	0.7465	-2.5299	-1.3010	0.2394	-0.1880
	3	1.0000	-1.1961	-0.9950	0.9382	0.4104	-2.5714	0.9062	1.3725	0.0831
	4	1.0000	-1.9002	0.2907	0.2780	0.1954	-2.1278	-0.7060	1.2109	0.6072
	5	1.0000	-0.1029	-0.3485	-0.4028	0.2274	-0.8327	0.8508	-0.0588	-1.4278

--- *canonical variables for cases 6 to 105* ---

	106	1.0000	-0.1029	-0.3485	-0.4028	0.2274	0.5286	-0.8461	1.3204	0.2293
	107	1.0000	0.9525	1.2745	-0.7784	0.9452	1.0792	0.1966	0.0289	0.1056
	108	1.0000	0.9958	1.6503	1.1987	0.0899	-0.7903	1.9462	0.4103	0.2740
	109	1.0000	-0.2387	1.4484	-0.7450	-0.5067	-0.2428	1.8573	-0.3426	-0.1194
	110	1.0000	-0.4109	-2.8813	2.6100	-1.1308	1.0021	-1.0009	0.4685	-0.3382

NUMERICAL CONSISTENCY CHECK

⑫

THE FOLLOWING VARIANCES OF CANONICAL VARIABLES SHOULD ALL BE EQUAL TO ONE

CANONICAL VARIABLE	VARIANCE	RELATIVE ERROR
CNVRF1	0.100000D 01	0.115186D-14
CNVRF2	0.100000D 01	0.187350D-14
CNVRF3	0.100000D 01	0.148492D-14
CNVRF4	0.100000D 01	0.151268D-14
CNVRS1	0.100000D 01	-0.177636D-14
CNVRS2	0.100000D 01	0.119349D-14
CNVRS3	0.100000D 01	0.265066D-14
CNVRS4	0.100000D 01	-0.133227D-14

--- ⑨ *in Output 18.7 is printed* ---

The additional matrices are printed in Output 18.8. Circled numbers below correspond to those in the output.

⑩ Coefficients of the canonical variables for the first set of variables.

The second panel contains the standardized coefficients; i.e., coefficients for the standardized variables (with mean zero and standard deviation one).

The two panels are then repeated for the second set of variables.

⑪ Values of the canonical variables for each case.

⑫ A numerical consistency check.

PRINT
    CASE= #.   {5/prev.}

   Number of cases for which data are printed.

    MATRICES= *(one or more)*   CORR,COVA,COEF,CANV,LOAD.
                        {CORR,LOAD}

   Matrices to be printed.

        CORR: correlations
        COVA: covariances
        COEF: coefficients of the canonical variables
        CANV: values of the canonical variables
        LOAD: canonical variable loadings.

   When any matrix is specified, only the specified matrices are printed.

● THE *PLOT* PARAGRAPH

   Any variable or canonical variable can be plotted against any other variable or canonical variable. The canonical variables are named

        CNVRF1, CNVRF2, etc. for variables in the first set

   and CNVRS1, CNVRS2, etc. for variables in the second set.

   To illustrate these plots we specify

Example 18.9

```
/PROBLEM      TITLE IS 'JARVIK SMOKING DATA'.
/INPUT        VARIABLES ARE 12.
              FORMAT IS '(12F2.0)'.
/VARIABLE     NAMES ARE CONCENTR,ANNOY,SMOKING1,SLEEPY,SMOKING2,TENSE,
                 SMOKING3,ALERT,IRRITABL,TIRED,CONTENT,SMOKING4.

/CANONICAL    FIRST ARE SMOKING1,SMOKING2,SMOKING3,SMOKING4.
              SECOND ARE CONCENTR,ANNOY,SLEEPY,TENSE,
                 ALERT,IRRITABL,TIRED,CONTENT.

/PLOT         XVARS ARE CNVRS1, CONCENTR.
              YVARS ARE CNVRF1, CNVRS1.
              SIZE IS 40,25.

/END
```

The plots are printed in Output 18.9.

Output 18.9 Plots printed by P6M after the results in Output 18.7.

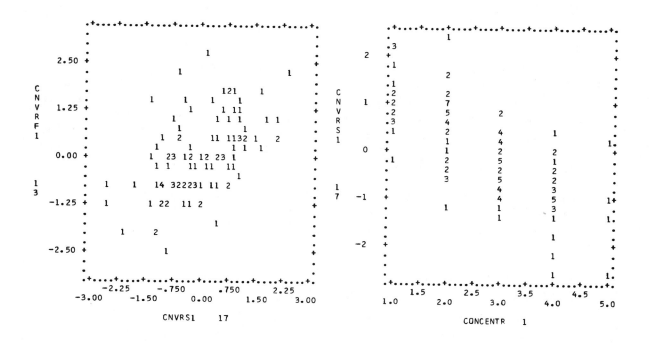

```
PLOT
    YVARIABLE= v₁,v₂,···.              {none}

    Names or subscripts of variables to be plotted vertically (along
    the Y-axis).

    XVARIABLE= v₁,v₂,···.              {none}

    Names or subscripts of variables to be plotted horizontally (along
    the X-axis).

    Note:  Both original and canonical variables can be specified.  The
    first YVARIABLE  is plotted against the first XVARIABLE , the
    second against the second, etc.

    SIZE=#₁,#₂.                        {50,50/prev.}

    #₁ is the number of characters (width) in the horizontal axis and
    #₂ is the number of lines (height) in the vertical axis.
```

● CASE WEIGHTs

     The data in each case can be weighted by the values of a WEIGHT vari-
able. Weights are used when the variance is not homogeneous over all cases
(the weight is the inverse of the variance), or to represent the frequencies
of cases that are repeated in the data (the weight is the frequency of the
case), or to remove the influence of some cases (with weight zero) from the
computations of the canonical correlations while still allowing computation
of their canonical variable scores.

     The variable containing the case WEIGHT is specified in the *VARiable*
paragraph. The effect of case weights on the computations of the means,
variances and covariances is described in Section 2.1.

```
VARiable
    WEIGHT=v.                         {no weight var./prev.}

    Name or subscript of the variable containing the case weights.
    Values of the case weight should be zero or positive (but never
    negative).  If WEIGHT is not specified or is set to zero, there
    are no case weights.
```

● SAVING RESULTS IN A BMDP FILE

     Both the data (including canonical variables) and the covariance
matrix can be saved in a BMDP File and used as input to subsequent analyses.

SAVE
   CONTENT=*(one or both)* DATA, COVA.   {DATA}

   The data (including canonical variables) or the covariance matrix or both can be saved in a BMDP File.[13] If DATA is specified, each case contains the variables, followed by the first set of canonical variables and then the second set of canonical variables; the variables in the first set are named CNVRF1, CNVRF2, etc. and those in the second set CNVRS1, CNVRS2, etc.

   Note: If a BMDP File is being created, an extra System Card is necessary (Section 7.1).

● FORMS OF INPUT

   P6M can start an analysis from data or from a covariance or correlation matrix.

   If your input is data, you can skip the following discussion. If your input is not data, you must specify the TYPE of input unless it is from a BMDP File and the CONTENT of the BMDP File corresponds to one of the permissible TYPEs defined below.

INPut
   CONTENT= c.   { DATA }   used only when input is from a BMDP File

   If the input is not DATA, CONTENT must be specified. It must be identical to the CONTENT stated in the *SAVE* paragraph when the BMDP File was created.

   TYPE= *(one only)* DATA,COVA,CORR.   {determined by CONTENT if input is from a BMDP File; DATA otherwise}

   Type of input. TYPE need not be specified when the input is data or when the input is a covariance or correlation matrix from a BMDP File.

   When the input is <u>not</u> from a BMDP File and TYPE is CORR or COVA, either a square matrix or a lower triangular matrix can be read as input.[14] A lower triangular matrix has one element (the diagonal) in the first row, two elements in the second, etc.

---

[13] If your BMDP programs are dated before August 1977,
   the minimum required abbreviation is CONTENT (not CONT).

[14] If your BMDP programs are dated before April 1977,
   only data can be read as input if a BMDP File is <u>not</u> used.

> INPut
>   SHAPE= *(one only)* SQUARE,LOWER.   {SQUARE/prev.}
>
>   Shape of the matrix when the input TYPE is CORR or COVA and is
>   <u>not</u> read from a BMDP File. Each row of the matrix must begin in a
>   new record. The format describes the longest row.

- SIZE OF PROBLEM

    P6M can analyze approximately 80 variables when double precision is
specified and 110 variables in single precision. Appendix B describes how to
increase the capacity of the program.

- COMPUTATIONAL METHOD

    The data are read in single precision. All computations are performed
in double precision unless you request single precision. Means, standard
deviations, skewness and kurtosis are computed by the method of provisional
means (Appendix A.2). Means, skewness and kurtosis are always computed in
double precision. If single precision is specified, cross-product deviations
are computed in double precision and accumulated in single precision with
floating rounded store. When weights are used, the statistics are adjusted
so that the average nonzero weight is one.

    The computational procedure for the canonical analysis is described in
Appendix A.22.

ACKNOWLEDGEMENT

    *P6M was designed and programmed by James Frane. It supersedes BMDO9M,
which was developed by Robert Jennrich and Paul Sampson.*

P6R

18.3 Partial Correlation and Multivariate Regression

James Frane, HSCF

P6R computes the partial correlations of a set of variables after removing the linear effects of a second set of variables. The computation of the partial correlations includes the computations of the regression coefficients for predicting one set of variables from another set of variables (multivariate regression). P6R prints the partial correlations, regression coefficients and their standard errors, squared multiple correlations, and residuals.

● RESULTS

The Werner blood chemistry data (Table 5.1) are used to illustrate the results from P6R. In Example 18.10 the four blood chemistry measurements (CHOLSTRL, ALBUMIN, CALCIUM, URICACID) are specified as the DEPENDENT variables and the three physical measurements (AGE, HEIGHT and WEIGHT) as the INDEPENDENT variables. The remaining Control Language instructions are described in Chapter 5.

Example 18.10

```
/PROBLEM     TITLE IS 'WERNER BLOOD CHEMISTRY DATA'.
/INPUT       VARIABLES ARE 9.
             FORMAT IS '(A4,5F4.0,3F4.1)'.
/VARIABLE    NAMES ARE ID,AGE,HEIGHT,WEIGHT,BRTHPILL,
                 CHOLSTRL,ALBUMIN,CALCIUM,URICACID.
             MAXIMUM IS (6)400.
             MINIMUM IS (6)150.
             BLANKS ARE MISSING.
             LABEL IS ID.

/REGRESS     DEPENDENT ARE CHOLSTRL,ALBUMIN,CALCIUM,URICACID.
             INDEPENDENT ARE AGE,HEIGHT,WEIGHT.

/END
```

The Control Language must be preceded by System Cards to initiate the analysis by P6R. At HSCF, the System Cards are

```
//jobname  JOB  nooo,yourname
//  EXEC  BIMED,PROG=BMDP6R
//SYSIN  DD  *
```

The Control Language is immediately followed by the data (Table 5.1). The analysis is terminated by another System Card. At HSCF, this System Card is

```
//
```

The results of the analysis are presented in Output 18.10. Circled numbers below correspond to those in the output.

(1) Interpretation of the Control Language instructions specific to P6R. Some of the listed options are preassigned.

② Data for the first five cases are printed. The number of cases printed can be specified.

③ Number of cases read. Cases included in the computations are those that contain acceptable values for all the variables used in the analysis; cases are omitted from all computations when the value of any variable used in the analysis is missing or out of range.

④ Univariate statistics

- mean
- standard deviation
- coefficient of variation
- smallest observed value (not out of range)
- largest observed value (not out of range)
- smallest standard score
- largest standard score
- skewness
- kurtosis

In Section 2.1 the univariate statistics are defined and the effect of a case weight on their computations is described.

Output 18.10   Partial correlation analysis by P6R. Circled numbers corres-
               pond to those in the text. Results not reproduced are indicated
               in italics.

```
BMDP6R - PARTIAL CORRELATION AND MULTIVARIATE REGRESSION        PROGRAM REVISED SEPTEMBER 1977
HEALTH SCIENCES COMPUTING FACILITY                             MANUAL DATE -- 1977
UNIVERSITY OF CALIFORNIA, LOS ANGELES
```

--- Control Language read by P6R is printed and interpreted ---

```
① INDEPENDENT VARIABLES ARE
        2  AGE          3  HEIGHT        4  WEIGHT

   DEPENDENT VARIABLES ARE
        6  CHOLSTRL     7  ALBUMIN       8  CALCIUM        9  URICACID

   NUMBER OF INDEPENDENT VARIABLES . . . . . . . .     3
   NUMBER OF DEPENDENT VARIABLES . . . . . . . . .     4
   TOTAL NUMBER OF VARIABLES USED. . . . . . . . .     7
   WEIGHT VARIABLE . . . . . . . . . . . . . . . .
   PRECISION . . . . . . . . . . . . . . . . . . .  DOUBLE
   TOLERANCE FOR MATRIX INVERSION. . . . . . . .  0.0100000

   APPROX. NUMBER OF VARIABLES WHICH CAN BE ANALYZED    119
```

```
② DATA AFTER TRANSFORMATIONS FOR FIRST    5 CASES
   CASES WITH ZERO WEIGHTS AND MISSING DATA NOT INCLUDED.

     CASE
   LABEL    NUMBER    WEIGHT    2 AGE      3 HEIGHT    4 WEIGHT    6 CHOLSTRL    7 ALBUMIN    8 CALCIUM    9 URICACID

   2381       1      1.00000   22.00000   67.00000   144.00000    200.00000     4.30000      9.80000      5.40000

   1610       3      1.00000   25.00000   62.00000   128.00000    243.00000     4.10000     10.40000      3.30000

    561       5      1.00000   19.00000   64.00000   125.00000    158.00000     4.10000      9.90000      4.70000

   2519       6      1.00000   19.00000   67.00000   130.00000    255.00000     4.50000     10.50000      8.30000

    225       7      1.00000   20.00000   64.00000   118.00000    210.00000     3.90000      9.50000      4.00000
```

```
③ NUMBER OF CASES READ. . . . . . . . . . . . . .    188
   CASES WITH DATA MISSING OR BEYOND LIMITS . .        8
   REMAINING NUMBER OF CASES . . . . . . . . .      180
```

(continued)

<u>Output 18.10</u>   *(continued)*

UNIVARIATE SUMMARY STATISTICS

④

VARIABLE	MEAN	STANDARD DEVIATION	COEFFICIENT OF VARIATION	SMALLEST VALUE	LARGEST VALUE	SMALLEST STANDARD SCORE	LARGEST STANDARD SCORE	SKEWNESS	KURTOSIS
2 AGE	33.53889	9.89801	0.295120	19.00000	55.00000	-1.47	2.17	0.40	-0.99
3 HEIGHT	64.46667	2.48211	0.038502	57.00000	71.00000	-3.01	2.63	-0.12	-0.04
4 WEIGHT	131.09444	20.49982	0.156374	94.00000	215.00000	-1.81	4.09	1.06	1.94
6 CHOLSTRL	235.83889	42.74377	0.181241	155.00000	390.00000	-1.89	3.61	0.46	0.06
7 ALBUMIN	4.12056	0.35872	0.087057	3.20000	5.00000	-2.57	2.45	-0.07	-0.36
8 CALCIUM	9.96778	0.47280	0.047433	8.80000	11.10000	-2.47	2.39	-0.03	-0.58
9 URICACID	4.75556	1.12111	0.235748	2.20000	9.90000	-2.28	4.59	1.18	2.92

VALUES FOR KURTOSIS GREATER THAN ZERO INDICATE DISTRIBUTIONS
WITH HEAVIER TAILS THAN THE NORMAL DISTRIBUTION.

CORRELATIONS

⑤

		AGE 2	HEIGHT 3	WEIGHT 4	CHOLSTRL 6	ALBUMIN 7	CALCIUM 8	URICACID 9
AGE	2	1.000						
HEIGHT	3	0.089	1.000					
WEIGHT	4	0.255	0.473	1.000				
CHOLSTRL	6	0.365	0.011	0.146	1.000			
ALBUMIN	7	-0.079	-0.006	-0.235	0.057	1.000		
CALCIUM	8	-0.009	0.143	0.065	0.255	0.453	1.000	
URICACID	9	0.209	0.125	0.304	0.274	0.030	0.166	1.000

⑥ SQUARED MULTIPLE CORRELATIONS OF EACH INDEPENDENT VARIABLE WITH ALL OTHER INDEPENDENT VARIABLES
(MEASURES OF MULTICOLLINEARITY OF PREDICTOR VARIABLES)
AND TESTS OF SIGNIFICANCE OF MULTIPLE REGRESSION
DEGREES OF FREEDOM FOR F-STATISTICS ARE   2 AND   177

VARIABLE NO. NAME	SMC	F-STATISTIC	SIGNIFICANCE (P LESS THAN)
2 AGE	0.06645	6.30	0.00228
3 HEIGHT	0.22522	25.73	0.00000
4 WEIGHT	0.26991	32.72	0.00000

⑦ SQUARED MULTIPLE CORRELATIONS(SMC) OF EACH DEPENDENT VARIABLE WITH THE INDEPENDENT VARIABLES
AND TESTS OF SIGNIFICANCE OF MULTIPLE REGRESSION
DEGREES OF FREEDOM FOR F-STATISTICS ARE   3 AND   176

VARIABLE NO. NAME	SMC	F-STATISTIC	SIGNIFICANCE (P LESS THAN)
6 CHOLSTRL	0.13920	9.49	0.00001
7 ALBUMIN	0.06957	4.39	0.00527
8 CALCIUM	0.02087	1.25	0.29301
9 URICACID	0.11080	7.31	0.00012

PARTIAL CORRELATIONS OF DEPENDENT VARIABLES REMOVING LINEAR EFFECTS OF INDEPENDENT VARIABLES

⑧

		CHOLSTRL 6	ALBUMIN 7	CALCIUM 8	URICACID 9
CHOLSTRL	6	1.000			
ALBUMIN	7	0.117	1.000		
CALCIUM	8	0.284	0.474	1.000	
URICACID	9	0.209	0.116	0.163	1.000

⑤   Correlation matrix.

⑥   Squared multiple correlations (SMC or R^2) of each independent variable with all other independent variables. This is a measure of the multicollinearity of the independent (predictor) variables (for a discussion see Gunst and Mason, 1977). The SMC is transformed to an F statistic that has (I-1) and (N-1) degrees of freedom, where I is the number of independent variables and N is the number of cases analyzed.

⑦   Squared multiple correlations (SMC) of each dependent variable with the independent variables. The SMC is transformed to an F statistic with I and (N-I-1) degrees of freedom. These are tests of significance of the regression of each dependent variable on the independent variable.

⑧   Partial correlations between the dependent variables after removing the linear effects of the independent variables. In this example, these partial correlations do not differ greatly from the original correlations in ⑤ due to the relatively low correlations of the dependent variables with the independent variables.

● OPTIONAL RESULTS AND INPUT

In addition to the above results, you can

- print the covariances, partial covariances, residuals for each dependent variable, regression coefficients and their tests of significance, and the covariance and correlations of the regression coefficients   p. 702

- plot variables and/or residuals against each other   p. 706

- print a normal probability plot of the residuals   p. 706

- weight the data in each case   p. 707

- save the data and residuals, the covariance matrix, or the partial covariance matrix in a BMDP File to use as input to other BMDP programs   p. 708

- start the analysis from data, a covariance matrix or a correlation matrix   p. 709

● THE *REGRess* PARAGRAPH

The *REGRess* paragraph is required.[15] It is used to specify the DEPENDENT and INDEPENDENT variables. If the problem has only one DEPENDENT variable you should use one of the regression programs in Chapter 13.

---

[15] If your BMDP programs are dated before August 1977, the minimum required abbreviation is *REGRES* (not *REGR*).

```
REGRess
    DEPENDENT= v₁,v₂,···.              {none}              required
```

Names or subscripts of the dependent variables.

```
    INDEPENDENT= v₁,v₂,···.            {none}              required
```

Names or subscripts of the independent variables.

Note: The partial correlations of the variables in the DEPENDENT *statement are computed, removing the linear effects of the variables in the* INDEPENDENT *statement.*
Exception: If either the DEPENDENT *or* INDEPENDENT *statement is not present, the correlation and covariance matrices will be produced for the variables indicated in whichever statement is present. If neither statement is present, the correlation and covariance matrices will be produced for all variables in the* USE *statement of the* VARiable *paragraph.*

Usually covariances and correlations are computed around the mean. You may want to compute them about the origin (i.e., as if the means were known to be zero).

```
REGRess
    ZERO.                             {not ZERO /prev.}
```

If ZERO is specified, the covariances and correlations are computed about the origin. *Note: This is a rarely used option.*

Computations can be done in either single or double PRECISION. TOLERANCE is used in the matrix inversion to guard against singularity.

```
REGRess
    PRECISION=(one only) SINGLE, DOUBLE.    { DOUBLE /prev.}
```

Computations are performed in double precision unless otherwise specified.

```
    TOLERANCE= #.           {0.01/prev.}    between 0.0 and 1.0
```

Tolerance for matrix inversion. Matrix inversion is performed by stepwise pivoting. A variable is not pivoted if its squared multiple correlation (R^2) with already pivoted variables exceeds 1.0-TOLERANCE or if pivoting it will cause the R^2 of any variable already pivoted with the remaining pivoted variables to exceed 1.0- TOLERANCE. For IBM 360 and 370 computers, TOLERANCE should not be less than 0.01 when the computations are done in single precision.

● THE *PRINT* PARAGRAPH

You can specify the number of cases for which the data are listed; the data for five cases are listed if the number is not stated.

You can select the matrices to be printed. The Control Language instructions in the *PRINT* paragraph in Example 18.11 are used to obtain the matrices available in P6R that were not printed by the analysis specified in Example 18.10.

Example 18.11

```
/PROBLEM      TITLE IS 'WERNER BLOOD CHEMISTRY DATA'.
/INPUT        VARIABLES ARE 9.
              FORMAT IS '(A4,5F4.C,3F4.1)'.
/VARIABLE     NAMES ARE ID,AGE,HEIGHT,WEIGHT,BRTHPILL,
                  CHOLSTRL,ALBUMIN,CALCIUM,URICACID.
              MAXIMUM IS (6)400.
              MINIMUM IS (6)150.
              BLANKS ARE MISSING.
              LABEL IS ID.

/REGRESS      DEPENDENT ARE CHOLSTRL,ALBUMIN,CALCIUM,URICACID.
              INDEPENDENT ARE AGE,HEIGHT,WEIGHT.

/PRINT        MATRICES ARE CORR,PART,COVAPART,CREG,
                  RREG,COEF,STANC,TTEST,RESI.

/END
```

The results are presented in Output 18.11. The matrices that were not printed in Output 18.10 are described below. Circled numbers below correspond to those in Output 18.11.

⑨ Partial covariances of the dependent variables after removing the linear effects of the independent variables. The diagonal of the matrix contains the residual mean squares (RMS) for the regression of the dependent variable on the independent variables. The partial covariance is related to the partial correlation by $cov_{ik} = corr_{ik} \cdot \sqrt{RMS_i RMS_k}$ where i and k are variable subscripts.

⑩ The covariances of the estimates of the regression coefficients are proportional to the inverse of the matrix of cross products of deviations for the independent variables. This inverse is printed in ⑩. It must be multiplied by the residual mean square of each dependent variable to obtain the covariances of the estimates for the dependent variable. The residual mean square can be obtained from the diagonal of the partial covariance matrix in ⑨.

⑪ Correlations of the estimates of the regression coefficients.

⑫ Regression coefficients for predicting the dependent variables from the independent variables. Each column in the output contains the coefficients for a dependent variable. The standard errors of the regression coefficients are printed in the second panel.

<u>Output 18.11</u> Optional results printed by P6R. These results are printed
after the results in Output 18.10.

(9) PARTIAL COVARIANCES OF DEPENDENT VARIABLES REMOVING LINEAR EFFECTS OF INDEPENDENT VARIABLES
(DIAGONAL CONTAINS RESIDUAL MEAN SQUARES)

		CHOLSTRL 6	ALBUMIN 7	CALCIUM 8	URICACID 9
CHOLSTRL	6	0.159951E 04			
ALBUMIN	7	0.163423E 01	0.121770E 00		
CALCIUM	8	0.536129E 01	0.780566E-01	0.222602E 00	
URICACID	9	0.890839E 01	0.432441E-01	0.820059E-01	0.113668E 01

(10) COVARIANCES FOR ESTIMATES OF REGRESSION COEFFICIENTS.

FOR EACH DEPENDENT VARIABLE, THE COVARIANCES OF THE REGRESSION COEFFICIENTS ARE OBTAINED BY MULTIPLYING THE MATRIX BELOW BY THE RESIDUAL MEAN SQUARE FOR THAT DEPENDENT VARIABLE. THE RESIDUAL MEAN SQUARE IS OBTAINED FROM THE DIAGONAL OF THE PARTIAL COVARIANCE MATRIX.

		AGE 2	HEIGHT 3	WEIGHT 4
AGE	2	0.610823E-04		
HEIGHT	3	0.997340E-05	0.117038E-02	
WEIGHT	4	-0.809975E-05	-0.683191E-04	0.182083E-04

CORRELATIONS FOR ESTIMATES OF REGRESSION COEFFICIENTS

(11)

		AGE 2	HEIGHT 3	WEIGHT 4
AGE	2	1.000		
HEIGHT	3	0.037	1.000	
WEIGHT	4	-0.243	-0.468	1.000

REGRESSION COEFFICIENTS FOR PREDICTING DEPENDENT VARIABLES (COLUMNS) FROM INDEPENDENT VARIABLES (ROWS)

(12)

		CHOLSTRL 6	ALBUMIN 7	CALCIUM 8	URICACID 9
AGE	2	0.150586E 01	-0.573597E-03	-0.105425E-02	0.158066E-01
HEIGHT	3	-0.103747E 01	0.195152E-01	0.273779E-01	-0.813286E-02
WEIGHT	4	0.178744E 00	-0.515375E-02	0.527286E-04	0.151227E-01
INTERCEPT		0.228784E 03	0.355734E 01	0.823126E 01	0.276721E 01

STANDARD ERRORS FOR REGRESSION COEFFICIENTS

		CHOLSTRL 6	ALBUMIN 7	CALCIUM 8	URICACID 9
AGE	2	0.313E 00	0.273E-02	0.369E-02	0.833E-02
HEIGHT	3	0.137E 01	0.119E-01	0.161E-01	0.365E-01
WEIGHT	4	0.171E 00	0.149E-02	0.201E-02	0.455E-02
INTERCEPT		0.807E 02	0.704E 00	0.952E 00	0.215E 01

(13) STANDARDIZED REGRESSION COEFFICIENTS FOR PREDICTING COLUMN VARIABLES FROM ROW VARIABLES
(THESE ARE THE COEFFICIENTS FOR THE STANDARDIZED VARIABLES — STANDARD DEVIATION ONE.)

		CHOLSTRL 6	ALBUMIN 7	CALCIUM 8	URICACID 9
AGE	2	0.349	-0.016	-0.022	0.140
HEIGHT	3	-0.060	0.135	0.144	-0.018
WEIGHT	4	0.086	-0.295	0.002	0.277
INTERCEPT		5.352	9.917	17.410	2.468

(continued)

Output 18.11   *(continued)*

T-STATISTICS FOR REGRESSION COEFFICIENTS   DEGREES OF FREEDOM =   176

(14) FOR EACH DEPENDENT VARIABLE, THE T-STATISTIC FOR EACH INDEPENDENT VARIABLE IS FOR THE
SIGNIFICANCE OF THAT INDEPENDENT VARIABLE GIVEN THE OTHER INDEPENDENT VARIABLES.

		CHOLSTRL 6	ALBUMIN 7	CALCIUM 8	URICACID 9
AGE	2	4.82	-0.21	-0.29	1.90
HEIGHT	3	-0.76	1.63	1.70	-0.22
WEIGHT	4	1.05	-3.46	0.03	3.32
INTERCEPT		2.84	5.05	8.65	1.29

SIGNIFICANCE LEVELS (TWO-TAIL) FOR T-STATISTICS

		CHOLSTRL 6	ALBUMIN 7	CALCIUM 8	URICACID 9
AGE	2	0.000	0.834	0.775	0.059
HEIGHT	3	0.449	0.104	0.092	0.824
WEIGHT	4	0.296	0.001	0.979	0.001
INTERCEPT		0.005	0.000	0.000	0.200

(15) NAMES FOR RESIDUALS ARE CREATED BY THE PROGRAM USING R FOLLOWED
BY THE FIRST SEVEN CHARACTERS OF THE CORRESPONDING VARIABLE NAME.

RESIDUALS (CASE NUMBERS REFER TO DATA BEFORE DELETION OF CASES)

LABEL	CASE NO.	WEIGHT	RCHOLSTR 10	RALBUMIN 11	RCALCIUM 12	RURICACI 13
2381	1	1.000	-18.1414	0.1899	-0.2500	0.6523
1610	3	1.000	18.0135	0.0067	0.4909	-1.2938
561	5	1.000	-55.3401	-0.0512	-0.0700	0.2626
2519	6	1.000	43.8786	0.3160	0.4476	3.8114
225	7	1.000	-3.5948	-0.2867	-0.4686	-0.3473

--- residuals for cases 8 to 182 ---

1250	183	1.000	-13.3523	0.1185	-0.3460	0.5955
1789	184	1.000	3.1088	0.4140	0.5205	1.6969
575	186	1.000	-46.1832	-0.0739	0.7377	-0.5935
2271	187	1.000	35.1310	0.1999	0.3104	-0.6734
39	188	1.000	-58.2387	-0.3211	-1.0260	0.5963

NUMERICAL CONSISTENCY CHECK

RESIDUAL MEAN SQUARES ARE COMPUTED FROM BOTH COVARIANCE MATRIX AND RESIDUALS, AND
RELATIVE DIFFERENCE (DIFFERENCE DIVIDED BY SMALLER OF TWO ESTIMATES) IS COMPUTED.

	RESIDUAL MEAN SQUARES COMPUTED FROM		
	COVARIANCE MATRIX	RESIDUALS	RELATIVE DIFFERENCE
RCHOLSTR	0.159951D 04	0.159951D 04	0.355380D-16
RALBUMIN	0.121770D 00	0.121770D 00	0.125364D-14
RCALCIUM	0.222602D 00	0.222602D 00	0.374061D-15
RURICACI	0.113668D 01	0.113668D 01	-0.586034D-15

(13) Standardized regression coefficients. These regression coefficients are for the standardized variables (mean zero and standard deviation one). The standardized regression coefficients are the ordinary coefficients divided by the standard deviations of the dependent variables and multiplied by the standard deviations of the independent variables.

(14) t statistics for the regression coefficients. These are the ratios of the estimates of the regression coefficients to their standard errors. Two-tail significance levels for the t statistics are printed in the second panel.

(15) Residuals. The values of the residuals for each dependent variable for each case are printed. *P6R generates names for the residuals. Each name consists of the letter R followed by the first seven letters of the name of the dependent variable. For example, RCHOLSTR is the name assigned to the residual for* CHOLSTRL.

```
PRINT
  CASE= #.                          {5/prev.}
    Number of cases for which data are listed.

  MATRICES=(one or more)  CORR, COVA, PART, COVAPART, CREG,
                          RREG, COEF, STANC, TTEST, RESI.
                              {CORR, PART}

    The matrices to be printed.¹⁶
      CORR: correlations ((5) in Output 18.10)

      COVA: covariances

      PART: partial correlations ((8) in Output 18.10)

      COVAPART: partial covariances ((9) in Output 18.11)

      CREG: covariances of the regression coefficients ((10) in Output 18.11)

      RREG: correlations of the regresion coefficients ((11) in Output 18.11)

      COEF: regression coefficients and their standard errors ((12) in
            Output 18.11)

      STANC: standardized regression coefficients ((13) in Output 18.11)

      TTEST: t tests for regression coefficients ((14) in Output 18.11)

      RESI: residuals for each dependent variable ((15) in Output 18.11)
    If any matrix is specified, only those matrices specified are printed.
```

---

¹⁶ If your BMDP programs are dated before August 1977, use INVCV in place of CREG, and INVCR in place of RREG.

● THE *PLOT* PARAGRAPH

    Any variable or residual can be plotted against any other variable or residual. The residuals can also be plotted in a normal probability plot.

    In the set of residuals for each dependent variable the residuals are named R followed by the first seven letters of the variable name. We illustrate the use of the residual names by plotting the residuals of CHOLSTRL (named RCHOLSTR) against the residuals of ALBUMIN (named RALBUMIN) and the values of CHOLSTRL against values of ALBUMIN.

Example 18.12

```
/PROBLEM      TITLE IS 'WERNER BLOOD CHEMISTRY DATA'.
/INPUT        VARIABLES ARE 9.
              FORMAT IS '(A4,5F4.0,3F4.1)'.
/VARIABLE     NAMES ARE ID,AGE,HEIGHT,WEIGHT,BRTHPILL,
                  CHOLSTRL,ALBUMIN,CALCIUM,URICACID.
              MAXIMUM IS (6)400.
              MINIMUM IS (6)150.
              BLANKS ARE MISSING.
              LABEL IS ID.

/REGRESS      DEPENDENT ARE CHOLSTRL,ALBUMIN,CALCIUM,URICACID.
              INDEPENDENT ARE AGE,HEIGHT,WEIGHT.

/PLOT         XVAR = RCHOLSTR, CHOLSTRL.
              YVAR = RALBUMIN, ALBUMIN.
              SIZE IS 40,25.

/END
```

    The two plots are presented in Output 18.12.

Output 18.12 Plots printed by P6R

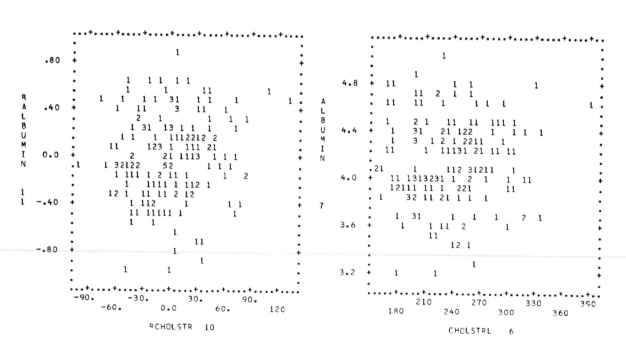

```
PLOT
    XVAR= v₁,v₂,...  .                {none}
```
   Names or subscripts of the variables or residuals to be plotted horizontally (along the X-axis).

```
    YVAR= v₁,v₂,...  .                {none}
```
   Names or subscripts of the variables or residuals to be plotted vertically (along the Y-axis).

   *Note: Each variable or residual in XVAR is plotted against the corres-
   ponding variable or residual in YVAR. The names of the residuals
   are R followed by the first seven letters of the name of the dependent
   variable.*

```
    SIZE= #₁,#₂.                     {50,50/prev.}
```
   $\#_1$ is the number of characters (width) in the horizontal axis and
   $\#_2$ is the number of lines (height) in the vertical axis.

```
    NORMAL.                          {no/prev.}
```
   Print a normal probability plot of the residuals.[17]

- CASE WEIGHTS

   The data in each case can be weighted by the values of a WEIGHT variable. Weights are used when the variance is not homogeneous over all cases
   (the weight is the inverse of the variance), to represent the frequencies
   of cases that are repeated in the data (the weight is the frequency of the
   case), or to remove the influence of some cases (with zero weights) while
   still computing their residuals.

   The variable containing the case WEIGHT is specified in the *VARiable*
   paragraph. The effect of case weights on the computations of the means,
   variances and covariances is described in Section 2.1.

```
VARiable
    WEIGHT=v.            .           {no weight var./prev.}
```
   Name or subscript of the variable containing the case weights.
   Values of the case weight should be zero or positive (but never
   negative). If WEIGHT is not specified or is set to zero, there
   are no case weights.

---

[17] If your BMDP programs are dated before August 1977,
    use PROBIT in place of NORMAL.

• SAVING RESULTS IN A BMDP FILE

The data (including residuals), covariance matrix and partial covariance matrix can be saved in a BMDP File for input to subsequent analyses.

SAVE
>   CONTENT=*(one or more)*   DATA,COVA,COVAPART.   {DATA}

>   The data (including residuals), the covariance matrix or the partial covariance matrix can be saved in a BMDP File.[18] If DATA is specified, each case contains the data followed by the residuals; the residuals are named R followed by the first seven letters of the name of the dependent variable.

We illustrate saving the data and the partial covariance matrix in Example 18.13.

Example 18.13

```
/PROBLEM     TITLE IS 'WERNER BLOOD CHEMISTRY DATA'.
/INPUT       VARIABLES ARE 9.
             FORMAT IS '(A4,5F4.0,3F4.1)'.
/VARIABLE    NAMES ARE ID,AGE,HEIGHT,WEIGHT,BRTHPILL,
                 CHOLSTRL,ALBUMIN,CALCIUM,URICACID.
             MAXIMUM IS (6)400.
             MINIMUM IS (6)150.
             BLANKS ARE MISSING.
             LABEL IS ID.

/REGRESS     DEPENDENT ARE CHOLSTRL,ALBUMIN,CALCIUM,URICACID.
             INDEPENDENT ARE AGE,HEIGHT,WEIGHT.

/SAVE        UNIT IS 4.
             NEW.
             CODE IS WERNER.
             CONTENT IS DATA,COVAPART.

/END
```

> *Note:* The System Cards the precede the Control Language must contain a card describing where to store the BMDP File (Section 7.1). At HSCF, the System Cards are
>
> ```
> //jobname  JOB  nooo,yourname
> //  EXEC  BIMED,PROG=BMDP6R
> //FT04F001  DD  DSNAME=FS.nooo.filename,DISP=OLD
> //SYSIN  DD  *
> ```
>
> In addition space must be allocated for the system file (Section 7.1).

The messages verifying that the BMDP Files are written are shown in Output 18.13. In the BMDP File containing the data (DATA), each case consists of the data for the case followed by the residuals.

---

[18] If your BMDP programs are dated before August 1977,
the minimum required abbreviation is CONTENT (not CONT).

● FORMS OF INPUT

P6R can start an analysis from data or from a covariance or correlation matrix.

If your input is data, you can skip the following discussion. If your input is not data, you must specify the TYPE of input unless it is from a BMDP File and the CONTENT of the BMDP File corresponds to one of the permissible TYPEs defined below.

INPut
   CONTENT= c.   { DATA }   used only when input is from
                                                              a BMDP File

   If the input is not DATA, CONTENT must be specified. It must be identical to the CONTENT stated in the *SAVE* paragraph when the BMDP File was created.

   TYPE= *(one only)* DATA,COVA,CORR.   {determined by CONTENT if
                                         input is from a BMDP File;
                                         DATA otherwise}

   Type of input. TYPE need not be specified when the input is data or when the input is a covariance or correlation matrix from a BMDP File.

Output 18.13   BMDP Files created by P6R

```
REQUESTED OUTPUT BMDP FILE
    UNIT    =          4
    CODE    = WERNER
    LABEL   =
    CONTENT =
            DATA
            COVAPART
```

--- results of the analysis are printed ---

PARTIAL CORRELATIONS OF DEPENDENT VARIABLES REMOVING LINEAR EFFECTS OF INDEPENDENT VARIABLES

```
          CHOLSTRL ALBUMIN  CALCIUM  URICACID
              6        7        8        9

CHOLSTRL  6   1.000
ALBUMIN   7   0.117    1.000
CALCIUM   8   0.284    0.474    1.000
URICACID  9   0.209    0.116    0.163    1.000

  BMDP FILE WRITTEN ON UNIT      4
                        CODE. . . IS      WERNER
                        CONTENT . IS      COVAPART
                        LABEL . . IS
                        VARIABLES     10  RCHOLSTR   11  RALBUMIN   12  RCALCIUM    13  RURICACI

BMDP FILE ON UNIT  4 HAS BEEN COMPLETED.
```

```
NAMES FOR RESIDUALS ARE CREATED BY THE PROGRAM USING R FOLLOWED
BY THE FIRST SEVEN CHARACTERS OF THE CORRESPONDING VARIABLE  NAME.

  BMDP FILE WRITTEN ON UNIT      4
                        CODE. . . IS      WERNER
                        CONTENT . IS      DATA
                        LABEL . . IS
                        VARIABLES     1  ID       2  AGE       3  HEIGHT     4  WEIGHT    5  BRTHPILL
                                      6  CHOLSTRL 7  ALBUMIN   8  CALCIUM    9  URICACID 10  RCHOLSTR
                                     11  RALBUMIN 12  RCALCIUM 13  RURICACI

BMDP FILE ON UNIT  4 HAS BEEN COMPLETED.
```

When the input is <u>not</u> from a BMDP File and TYPE is CORR or COVA, either a square matrix or a lower triangular matrix can be read as input.[19] A lower triangular matrix has one element (the diagonal) in the first row, two elements in the second, etc.

INPut
   SHAPE= *(one only)* SQUARE,LOWER.   { SQUARE/prev.}

   Shape of the matrix when the input TYPE is CORR or COVA and is <u>not</u> read from a BMDP File. Each row of the matrix must begin in a new record. The format describes the longest row.

● SIZE OF PROBLEM

A maximum of 100 variables can be analyzed in double precision, and 150 in single precision. Appendix B describes how to increase the capacity of the program.

● COMPUTATIONAL METHOD

The data are read in single precision. All computations are performed in double precision unless you request single precision. Means, standard deviations and the covariance matrix are computed by the method of provisional means (Appendix A.2). Means, skewness and kurtosis are always computed in double precision. If single precision is specified, cross-product deviations are computed in double precision and accumulated in single precision with floating rounded store. When weights are used, the statistics are adjusted so that the average nonzero weight is one.

The computations performed by P6R are described in Appendix A.11, except that P6R can have more than one specified dependent variable.

ACKNOWLEDGEMENT

P6R was designed and programmed by James Frane.

---

[19] If your BMDP programs are dated before April 1977, only data can be read as input if a BMDP File is <u>not</u> used.

P7M

18.4 Stepwise Discriminant Analysis

Robert Jennrich, HSCF
Paul Sampson, HSCF

P7M performs a discriminant analysis between two or more groups. The variables used in computing the linear classification functions are chosen in a stepwise manner. Both forward and backward selection of variables are possible; at each step the variable that adds the most to the separation of the groups is entered into (or the variable that adds the least is removed from) the discriminant function. The important group differences can be specified as contrasts; these contrasts guide the selection of the variables. Group classifications are evaluated and presented in a classification table. A jackknife-validation procedure may be requested to reduce the bias in the group classifications.

● RESULTS

The Fisher iris data (Table 18.1) are used to illustrate the stepwise discriminant analysis by P7M. In Example 18.14 the data and variables are described in Control Language instructions and IRISTYPE is specified as the variable that classifies the cases into three groups -- SETOSA, VERSICOL and VIRGINIC.

Example 18.14

```
/PROBLEM      TITLE IS 'FISHER IRIS DATA'.
/INPUT        VARIABLES ARE 5.
              FORMAT IS '(4F3.1,F3.0)'.
/VARIABLE     NAMES ARE SEPALLEN,SEPALWID,PETALLEN,PETALWID,IRISTYPE.
              GROUPING IS IRISTYPE.

/GROUP        CODES(5) ARE 1 TO 3.
              NAMES(5) ARE SETOSA,VERSICOL,VIRGINIC.

/END
```

The Control Language must be preceded by System Cards to initiate the analysis by P7M. At HSCF, the System Cards are

```
//jobname  JOB  nooo,yourname
//   EXEC  BIMED,PROG=BMDP7M
//SYSIN  DD  *
```

The Control Language is immediately followed by the data (Table 18.1). The analysis is terminated by another System Card. At HSCF, this System Card is

```
//
```

The results are presented in Output 18.14. Circled numbers below correspond to those in the output.

① Interpretation of options specific to P7M. Many of the options in this example are preassigned. The GROUPING variable (IRISTYPE) is specified in Example 18.14.

Table 18.1 Fisher iris data (Fisher, 1936). Length and width of sepals (SEPALLEN and SEPALWID) and petals (PETALLEN and PETALWID) on 50 flowers from each of three types of iris (IRISTYPE).

1	2	3	4	5
50	33	14	02	1
64	28	56	22	3
65	28	46	15	2
67	31	56	24	3
63	28	51	15	3
46	34	14	03	1
69	31	51	23	3
62	22	45	15	2
59	32	48	18	2
46	36	10	02	1
61	30	46	14	2
60	27	51	16	2
65	30	52	20	3
56	25	39	11	2
65	30	55	18	3
58	27	51	19	3
68	32	59	23	3
51	33	17	05	1
57	28	45	13	2
62	34	54	23	3
77	38	67	22	3
63	33	47	16	2
67	33	57	25	3
76	30	66	21	3
49	25	45	17	3
55	35	13	02	1
67	30	52	23	3
70	32	47	14	2
64	32	45	15	2
61	28	40	13	2
48	31	16	02	1
59	30	51	18	3
55	24	38	11	2
63	25	50	19	3
64	32	53	23	3
52	34	14	02	1
49	36	14	01	1
54	30	45	15	2
79	38	64	20	3
44	32	13	02	1
67	33	57	21	3
50	35	16	06	1
58	26	40	12	2
44	30	13	02	1
77	28	67	20	3
63	27	49	18	3
47	32	16	02	1
55	26	44	12	2
50	23	33	10	2
72	32	60	18	3

cont'd

48	30	14	03	1
51	38	16	02	1
61	30	49	18	3
48	34	19	02	1
50	30	16	02	1
50	32	12	02	1
61	26	56	14	3
64	28	56	21	3
43	30	11	01	1
58	40	12	02	1
51	38	19	04	1
67	31	44	14	2
62	28	48	18	3
49	30	14	02	1
51	35	14	02	1
56	30	45	15	2
58	27	41	10	2
50	34	16	04	1
46	32	14	02	1
60	29	45	15	2
57	26	35	10	2
57	44	15	04	1
50	36	14	02	1
77	30	61	23	3
63	34	56	24	3
58	27	51	19	3
57	29	42	13	2
72	30	58	16	3
54	34	15	04	1
52	41	15	01	1
71	30	59	21	3
64	31	55	18	3
60	30	48	18	3
63	29	56	18	3
49	24	33	10	2
56	27	42	13	2
57	30	42	12	2
55	42	14	02	1
49	31	15	02	1
77	26	69	23	3
60	22	50	15	3
54	39	17	04	1
66	29	46	13	2
52	27	39	14	2
60	34	45	16	2
50	34	15	02	1
44	29	14	02	1
50	20	35	10	2
55	24	37	10	2
58	27	39	12	2

cont'd

47	32	13	02	1
46	31	15	02	1
69	32	57	23	3
62	29	43	13	2
74	28	61	19	3
59	30	42	15	2
51	34	15	02	1
50	35	13	03	1
56	28	49	20	3
60	22	40	10	2
73	29	63	18	3
67	25	58	18	3
49	31	15	01	1
67	31	47	15	2
63	23	44	13	2
54	37	15	02	1
56	30	41	13	2
63	25	49	15	2
61	28	47	12	2
64	29	43	13	2
51	25	30	11	2
57	28	41	13	2
65	30	58	22	3
69	31	54	21	3
54	39	13	04	1
51	35	14	03	1
72	36	61	25	3
65	32	51	20	3
61	29	47	14	2
56	29	36	13	2
69	31	49	15	2
64	27	53	19	3
68	30	55	21	3
55	25	40	13	2
48	34	16	02	1
48	30	14	01	1
45	23	13	03	1
57	25	50	20	3
57	38	17	03	1
51	38	15	03	1
55	23	40	13	2
66	30	44	14	2
68	28	48	14	2
54	34	17	02	1
51	37	15	04	1
52	35	15	02	1
58	28	51	24	3
67	30	50	17	2
63	33	60	25	3
53	37	15	02	1

Key: 1 - SEPALLEN, 2 - SEPALWID, 3 - PETALLEN, 4 - PETALWID, 5 - IRISTYPE

The three groups of iris (IRISTYPE) are Setosa, Versicolor and Virginica. All variables but IRISTYPE are recorded to 1/10 of a centimeter. The data are recorded in columns 2-3, 5-6, 8-9, 11-12 and 15.

<u>Output 18.14</u> Stepwise discriminant analysis by P7M. Circled numbers corres-
pond to those in the text. Results not reproduced are indicated
in italics.

```
BMDP7M  -  STEPWISE DISCRIMINANT ANALYSIS.          PROGRAM REVISED SEPTEMBER 1977
HEALTH SCIENCES COMPUTING FACILITY                  MANUAL DATE  --  1977
UNIVERSITY OF CALIFORNIA, LOS ANGELES
```

--- Control Language read by P7M is printed and interpreted ---

① TOLERANCE. 0.010
   F-TO-ENTER 4.000   4.000
   F-TO-REMOVE. 3.996   3.996
   METHOD   1
   MAXIMUM FORCED LEVEL . . .   0
   MAXIMUM NUMBER OF STEPS. .   10
   GROUPING VARIABLE.   5
   NUMBER OF GROUPS   3
   PRIOR PROBABILITIES. . . .   0.33333   0.33333   0.33333

		BEFORE TRANSFORMATION					INTERVAL RANGE	
VARIABLE		MINIMUM	MAXIMUM	MISSING	CATEGORY	CATEGORY	GREATER	LESS THAN
NO.	NAME	LIMIT	LIMIT	CODE	CODE	NAME	THAN	OR EQUAL TO
5	IRISTYPE				1.00000	SETOSA		
					2.00000	VERSICOL		
					3.00000	VIRGINIC		

② NUMBER OF CASES READ.   150

   MEANS

③
GROUP =	SETOSA	VERSICOL	VIRGINIC	ALL GPS.
VARIABLE				
1 SEPALLEN	5.00600	5.93600	6.58800	5.84333
2 SEPALWID	3.42800	2.77000	2.97400	3.05733
3 PETALLEN	1.46200	4.26000	5.55200	3.75800
4 PETALWID	0.24600	1.32600	2.02600	1.19933
5 IRISTYPE	1.00000	2.00000	3.00000	2.00000
COUNTS	50.	50.	50.	150.

--- standard deviations and coefficients of variation
are printed in separate panels ---

```
************************************************************************************************
```

STEP NUMBER   0

④
VARIABLE	F TO REMOVE	FORCE LEVEL	TOLERANCE	*	VARIABLE	F TO ENTER	FORCE LEVEL	TOLERANCE
	DF= 2 148			*		DF= 2 147		
				*	1 SEPALLEN	119.264	1	1.000000
				*	2 SEPALWID	49.160	1	1.000000
				*	3 PETALLEN	1180.160	1	1.000000
				*	4 PETALWID	960.007	1	1.000000
```

*(continued)*
```

Output 18.14 *(continued)*

⑤ STEP NUMBER   1
VARIABLE ENTERED   3 PETALLEN

VARIABLE	F TO FORCE REMOVE LEVEL DF= 2 147	TOLERANCE	* * * * * *	VARIABLE	F TO FORCE ENTER LEVEL DF= 2 146	TOLERANCE
3 PETALLEN	1180.161 1	1.000000		1 SEPALLEN	34.323 1	0.428216
				2 SEPALWID	43.035 1	0.857180
				4 PETALWID	24.766 1	0.765300

U-STATISTIC OR WILKS' LAMBDA   0.0586283   DEGREES OF FREEDOM   1   2   147
APPROXIMATE F-STATISTIC   1180.161   DEGREES OF FREEDOM   2.00   147.00

F - MATRIX   DEGREES OF FREEDOM =   1 147

	SETOSA	VERSICOL
VERSICOL	1056.87	
VIRGINIC	2258.26	225.34

CLASSIFICATION FUNCTIONS

GROUP = VARIABLE	SETOSA	VERSICOL	VIRGINIC
3 PETALLEN	7.89469	23.00368	29.98038
CONSTANT	-6.86962	-50.09642	-84.32411

****

--- results for steps 2 and 3 ---

STEP NUMBER   4
VARIABLE ENTERED   1 SEPALLEN

VARIABLE	F TO FORCE REMOVE LEVEL DF= 2 144	TOLERANCE	* * * * *	VARIABLE	F TO FORCE ENTER LEVEL DF= 2 143	TOLERANCE
1 SEPALLEN	4.721 1	0.347993				
2 SEPALWID	21.936 1	0.608860				
3 PETALLEN	35.590 1	0.365126				
4 PETALWID	24.904 1	0.649314				

U-STATISTIC OR WILKS' LAMBDA   0.0234386   DEGREES OF FREEDOM   4   2   147
APPROXIMATE F-STATISTIC   199.145   DEGREES OF FREEDOM   8.00   288.00

F - MATRIX   DEGREES OF FREEDOM =   4 144

	SETOSA	VERSICOL
VERSICOL	550.19	
VIRGINIC	1098.27	105.31

CLASSIFICATION FUNCTIONS

GROUP = VARIABLE	SETOSA	VERSICOL	VIRGINIC
1 SEPALLEN	23.54416	15.69820	12.44584
2 SEPALWID	23.58786	7.07252	3.68529
3 PETALLEN	-16.43063	5.21145	12.76655
4 PETALWID	-17.39839	6.43422	21.07909
CONSTANT	-86.30843	-72.85257	-104.36826

⑥ CLASSIFICATION MATRIX

GROUP	PERCENT CORRECT	NUMBER OF CASES CLASSIFIED INTO GROUP -		
		SETOSA	VERSICOL	VIRGINIC
SETOSA	100.0	50	0	0
VERSICOL	96.0	0	48	2
VIRGINIC	98.0	0	1	49
TOTAL	98.0	50	49	51

JACKKNIFED CLASSIFICATION

GROUP	PERCENT CORRECT	NUMBER OF CASES CLASSIFIED INTO GROUP -		
		SETOSA	VERSICOL	VIRGINIC
SETOSA	100.0	50	0	0
VERSICOL	96.0	0	48	2
VIRGINIC	98.0	0	1	49
TOTAL	98.0	50	49	51

(continued)

Output 18.14   *(continued)*

SUMMARY TABLE

⑦

STEP NUMBER	VARIABLE ENTERED	REMOVED	F VALUE TO ENTER OR REMOVE	NUMBER OF VARIABLES INCLUDED	U-STATISTIC	APPROXIMATE F-STSTISTIC		DEGREES OF FREEDOM
1	3 PETALLEN		1180.1597	1	0.0586	1180.161	2.00	147.00
2	2 SEPALWID		43.0353	2	0.0369	307.104	4.00	292.00
3	4 PETALWID		34.5686	3	0.0250	257.503	6.00	290.00
4	1 SEPALLEN		4.7211	4	0.0234	199.145	8.00	288.00

⑧

INCORRECT CLASSIFICATIONS

MAHALANOBIS D-SQUARE FROM AND POSTERIOR PROBABILITY FOR GROUP -

GROUP SETOSA		SETOSA	VERSICOL	VIRGINIC
CASE				
1		0.2 1.000	90.7 0.000	181.6 0.000
6		1.3 1.000	84.0 0.000	170.1 0.000
10		2.3 1.000	113.7 0.000	210.0 0.0
18		2.8 1.000	67.5 0.000	145.7 0.000
26		4.0 1.000	113.2 0.000	210.2 0.0

--- similar statistics for remaining cases in SETOSA ---

GROUP VERSICOL		SETOSA	VERSICOL	VIRGINIC
CASE				
3		105.3 0.000	2.2 0.996	13.1 0.004
8		131.7 0.000	8.4 0.960	14.8 0.040
9	VIRGINIC	130.9 0.000	8.7 0.253	6.5 0.747
11		99.2 0.000	1.3 0.998	13.8 0.002
12	VIRGINIC	149.0 0.000	8.4 0.143	4.9 0.857

--- similar statistics for remaining cases in VERSICOL ---

GROUP VIRGINIC		SETOSA	VERSICOL	VIRGINIC
CASE				
2		208.6 0.0	27.3 0.000	1.9 1.000
4		207.9 0.0	31.7 0.000	4.5 1.000
5	VERSICOL	133.1 0.000	5.3 0.729	7.2 0.271
7		173.2 0.000	26.6 0.000	11.0 1.000
13		159.0 0.000	12.8 0.003	1.2 0.997

--- similar statistics for remaining cases in VIRGINIC ---

EIGENVALUES

⑨

32.19192   0.28539

CANONICAL CORRELATIONS

0.98482   0.47120

VARIABLE	COEFFICIENTS FOR CANONICAL VARIABLES	
1 SEPALLEN	0.82938	0.02410
2 SEPALWID	1.53447	2.16452
3 PETALLEN	-2.20121	-0.93192
4 PETALWID	-2.81046	2.83919
CONSTANT	2.10510	-6.66147

GROUP	CANONICAL VARIABLES EVALUATED AT GROUP MEANS	
SETOSA	7.60760	0.21514
VERSICOL	-1.82505	-0.72790
VIRGINIC	-5.78255	0.51277

--- ⑩ *plot of group means ---*

POINTS TO BE PLOTTED

⑪

GROUP	MEAN COORDINATES		SYMBOL FOR CASES	SYMBOL FOR MEAN
SETOSA	7.61	0.22	A	1
VERSICOL	-1.83	-0.73	B	2
VIRGINIC	-5.78	0.51	C	3

GROUP SETOSA

CASE	X	Y	CASE	X	Y	CASE	X	Y	CASE	X	Y	CASE	X	Y
1	7.67	-0.13	44	6.93	-0.71	64	7.13	-0.79	92	7.70	1.46	126	7.78	0.58
6	7.21	0.36	47	6.83	-0.54	65	8.06	0.30	96	7.61	-0.01	135	7.22	-0.11
10	8.68	0.88	51	6.76	-0.51	68	6.82	0.46	97	6.56	-1.02	136	7.33	-1.07
18	6.25	0.44	52	8.08	0.76	69	7.19	-0.36	101	7.49	-0.27	137	5.66	-1.93
26	8.61	0.40	54	6.56	-0.39	72	9.16	2.74	102	6.81	-0.67	139	8.08	0.97
31	6.76	-0.76	55	6.77	-0.97	73	8.13	0.51	107	7.69	-0.01	140	8.02	1.14
36	7.99	0.09	56	7.96	-0.16	79	7.37	0.57	108	7.92	0.68	144	7.50	-0.19
37	8.33	0.23	59	7.57	-0.81	80	9.13	1.22	113	7.34	-0.95	145	7.59	1.21
40	7.24	-0.27	60	9.85	1.59	88	9.47	1.83	116	8.40	0.65	146	7.92	0.21
42	6.41	1.25	61	6.86	1.05	89	7.06	-0.66	125	8.58	1.83	150	8.31	0.64

(continued)

Output 18.14 *(continued)*

GROUP VERSICOL

CASE	X	Y	CASE	X	Y	CASE	X	Y	CASE	X	Y	CASE	X	Y
3	-2.55	-0.47	30	-1.00	-0.49	71	0.31	-1.32	100	-0.90	-0.90	121	0.48	-0.80
8	-3.50	-1.68	33	-1.11	-1.75	77	-1.62	-0.47	104	-1.42	-0.55	122	-1.55	-0.59
9	-3.72	1.04	38	-2.93	0.03	85	-0.22	-1.58	106	-1.86	0.32	129	-2.67	-0.64
11	-2.29	-0.33	43	-1.27	-1.21	86	-2.01	-0.91	110	-1.16	-2.64	130	-0.38	0.09
12	-4.50	-0.88	48	-2.40	-1.59	87	-1.18	-0.54	114	-2.14	0.09	131	-2.42	-0.09
14	-1.09	-1.63	49	-0.29	-1.80	93	-1.75	-0.82	115	-2.48	-1.94	134	-1.96	-1.15
19	-2.43	-0.97	62	-1.20	0.08	94	-1.96	-0.35	117	-1.33	-0.16	141	-2.26	-1.59
22	-2.45	0.80	66	-2.77	0.03	95	-2.10	1.19	118	-3.84	-1.41	142	-1.44	-0.13
28	-1.46	0.03	67	-0.78	-1.66	98	-1.19	-2.63	119	-2.26	-1.43	143	-2.46	-0.94
29	-1.80	0.48	70	-2.59	-0.17	99	-0.61	-1.94	120	-1.26	-0.55	148	-3.52	0.16

GROUP VIRGINIC

CASE	X	Y	CASE	X	Y	CASE	X	Y	CASE	X	Y	CASE	X	Y
2	-6.80	0.58	23	-6.85	2.43	46	-4.37	-0.12	81	-6.29	0.47	112	-6.33	-1.38
4	-6.65	1.81	24	-7.42	-0.17	50	-5.28	-0.04	82	-5.00	0.19	123	-6.85	0.83
5	-3.82	-0.94	25	-4.68	-0.50	53	-4.08	0.52	83	-3.94	0.61	124	-5.20	1.14
7	-5.11	1.99	27	-5.65	1.68	57	-5.11	-2.13	84	-5.61	-0.34	127	-6.85	2.72
13	-4.97	0.82	32	-4.68	0.33	58	-6.52	0.30	90	-9.17	-0.75	128	-4.44	1.35
15	-5.07	-0.03	34	-5.18	-0.36	63	-4.08	0.19	91	-4.76	-2.16	132	-5.45	-0.21
16	-5.51	-0.04	35	-5.81	2.01	74	-6.80	0.86	103	-6.27	1.65	133	-5.66	0.83
17	-6.80	1.46	39	-5.22	1.47	75	-6.52	2.45	105	-6.23	-0.71	138	-5.96	-0.09
20	-5.89	2.35	41	-5.72	1.29	76	-5.51	-0.04	109	-5.36	0.65	147	-6.76	1.60
21	-6.61	1.75	45	-7.58	-0.98	78	-4.58	-0.86	111	-6.32	-0.97	149	-7.84	2.14

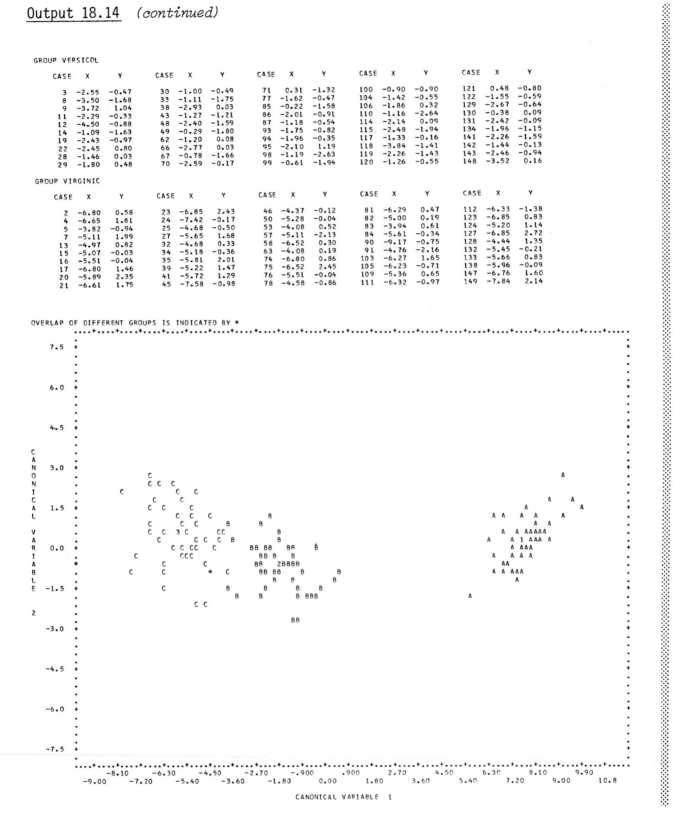

OVERLAP OF DIFFERENT GROUPS IS INDICATED BY *

CANONICAL VARIABLE 1

② Number of cases read. P7M uses complete cases only in all computations. That is, if the value of any variable in a case is missing or out of range, the case is omitted from all computations. If a USE statement is specified in the *VARiable* paragraph, only the values of variables in the USE statement are checked for missing value codes and values out of range. When CODEs are specified for the GROUPing variables, only cases with a specified code are used.

③ Means, standard deviations and coefficients of variation for each variable in each group and for all groups.

The pooled (within-groups) standard deviation is

$$\{\Sigma\,(N_k-1)s_k^2/\,\Sigma\,(N_k-1)\}^{\frac{1}{2}}$$

where s_k^2 is the variance and N_k is the sample size of the kth group.

④ Step 0 is the step before any variable is entered into the discriminant function. P7M prints the F-to-enter for each variable. At step 0 the F-to-enter for a variable corresponds to the F statistic computed from a one-way analysis of variance (ANOVA) on the variable for the groups used in the analysis. The degrees of freedom correspond to those of the one-way ANOVA; i.e., $(g-1)$ and $\Sigma(N_k-1)$ where g is the number of groups.

The force level is discussed on p.725 and tolerance on p. 731.

⑤ The variable with the highest F-to-enter at step 0 (PETALLEN) is entered into the discriminant functions; this is the variable that discriminates the best between groups. At step 1 the following are computed:

- F-to-remove for the variable in the equation (this is equal to the F-to-enter at step 0)

- F-to-enter for each variable not in the equation (this is equal to the F statistic corresponding to the one-way ANOVA on the residuals of the variable; i.e., at each step the F-to-enter is computed from a one-way analysis of covariance where the covariates are the previously entered variables)

- Wilks' Λ or U statistic (this is a multivariate statistic that tests the equality of group means for the variable(s) in the discriminant function)

- Approximate F statistic (this is a transformation of Wilks' Λ that can be compared with the F distribution; at step 1 the F statistic is the one-way ANOVA between the group means for the variable entered)

- F matrix (this contains F values computed from the Mahalanobis D^2 statistics that test the equality of group means for each pair of groups; the test is for only the variables in the discriminant functions)

- Classification functions (the classification function can be used to classify cases into groups; the case is assigned to the group with the largest value of the classification function)

⑥ At the last step, in addition to the results printed at each step, P7M prints the

- classification matrix (each case is classified into a group according to the classification functions; the number classified into each group and the percent of correct classifications are printed)

- jackknifed classification matrix (each case is classified into a group according to the classification functions computed from all the data except the case being classified; see Lachenbruch and Mickey, 1968)

⑦ Summary table. This contains a one line summary of each step including the F-to-enter (or remove) for the variable entered (or removed), the U statistic and the approximate F statistic.

⑧ Classification of each case. For each case Mahalanobis D^2 is computed to each group mean. The posterior probability for the distance of a case from a group is the ratio of $\exp(D^2)$ for the group over the sum of $\exp(D^2)$ for all groups. Prior probabilities, if assigned, affect these computations. Outliers can be identified as cases with large D^2 from their group means. For large samples from a multivariate normal distribution, the D^2 from a case to its group mean is approximately distributed as a chi-square with degrees of freedom equal to the number of variables selected.

Each case incorrectly classified is noted in the output (cases 5, 9 and 12).

⑨ Eigenvalues of the matrix $W^{-\frac{1}{2}}BW^{-\frac{1}{2}}$ are computed where $\underset{\sim}{B}$ is the between-groups sums of cross products and $\underset{\sim}{W}$ is the pooled (within-groups) sum of squares (see Appendix A.23 for a more precise definition). The eigenvalues, canonical correlations between the variables entered and dummy variables representing the groups, and the coefficients for the canonical variables are printed. The first canonical variable is the linear combination of variables entered that best discriminates among the groups (largest one-way ANOVA F statistic), the second canonical variable is the next best linear combination orthogonal to the first one, etc. The canonical variables are adjusted so that the (pooled) within-group variances are one and their overall mean is zero. The canonical variables are evaluated at the group means.

⑩ The group means only are plotted in a scatter plot. The axes are the first two canonical variables. (This plot is not reproduced in Output 18.14).

⑪ The group means and all cases are plotted in a scatter plot. The axes are the first two canonical variables. In this plot group A (SETOSA) is well differentiated from the other two groups. Group B (VERSICOL) slightly overlaps group C (VIRGINIC). *Note: If there is only one canonical variable a histogram is plotted.*

A discriminant analysis can be severely affected by the presence of an outlier. Such an outlier can sometimes be identified in this plot.

● OPTIONAL RESULTS

You must specify how to group the cases. In addition, you can

- assign prior probabilities to the groups   p. 721

- specify the order (or partial order) of entry of variables
  into the discriminant functions   p. 725

- specify the criterion to enter and remove variables
  from the discriminant function; both forward and backward
  stepping are possible   p. 725

- direct the entry by specifying contrasts that define the
  distances to be maximized between groups   p. 727

- specify JACKKNIFE in the *DISCRiminant* paragraph;
  this results in the computation of the Mahalanobis distance
  (and resulting posterior probability) for each case from
  all the other cases in its group   p. 730

- specify the maximum number of steps and the tolerance
  limit   p. 731

- specify the results to be printed   p. 731

- specify the groups used in the plots and the type of
  canonical plot   p. 730

- save both the data and canonical variables in a BMDP File
  for input to other programs   p. 732

● CLASSIFYING CASES IN GROUPS

To classify cases into groups you must specify a GROUPING variable
in the *VARiable* paragraph (as in Example 18.14).

VARiable
   GROUPING = v.   {no grouping var./prev.}   required

   The name or subscript of the variable used to classify cases into
   groups. To make the printed results easier to read, we suggest that
   you specify group NAMEs in the *GROUP* paragraph (Section 5.4).

   *Note: P7M requires either a GROUP paragraph or that the number
   of groups be specified in the INPut paragraph. A GROUP paragraph is required when each value (code) of the GROUPING variable does not designate a distinct group.*

INPut
   GROUP = #.   {none/prev.}

   Number of groups to be formed. This specification is required if
   neither CODEs nor CUTPOINTs are specified for the GROUPING
   variable.

● SELECTING GROUPS FOR THE ANALYSIS

   If the discriminant analysis is performed for a subset of groups, the groups to be analyzed are specified in a USE statement in the *GROUP* paragraph. Groups not included in the USE statement are classified into groups according to the classification function, but are <u>not</u> used in estimating the classification function.

   The USE statement is a convenient way to validate your classification function. You can subdivide the cases in each group into two separate groups; one group can then be used to estimate the classification function and the other group can be classified according to the function.

   In Example 18.15 we demonstrate how random subsamples can be selected from each group to form subgroups that are not used to estimate the discriminant function. The subgroups are then used to validate the classification function.

<u>Example 18.15</u>

```
/PROBLEM      TITLE IS 'FISHER IRIS DATA'.
/INPUT        VARIABLES ARE 5.
              FORMAT IS '(4F3.1,F3.0)'.
/VARIABLE     NAMES ARE SEPALLEN,SEPALWID,PETALLEN,PETALWID,IRISTYPE.
              GROUPING IS IRISTYPE.

/TRANSFORM    PROB     = RNDU(783217).
              NEWGROUP = IRISTYPE + 3.
              TRUE     = PROB LE 0.2.
              IRISTYPE = NEWGROUP IF TRUE.

/GROUP        CODES(5) ARE 1 TO 6.
              NAMES(5) ARE SETOSA,VERSICOL,VIRGINIC,
                      NEWSET,NEWVERS,NEWVIRG.
              USE = 1 TO 3.

    /END
```

   The GROUPING variable is IRISTYPE. In the *TRANsform* paragraph random subsamples are chosen so that 20% of the cases are allotted to 3 new groups. First a uniform random number is generated between zero and one (783217 is a starting value for the random number generator). The temporary variable NEWGROUP is set to IRISTYPE+3.   TRUE is set to true when PROB is less than 0.2; i.e., with a probability of 20%. IRISTYPE is set to NEWGROUP if TRUE is true (i.e., if the uniform random number is less than 0.2).   That is, for each case a uniform random number is generated and, when it is less than 0.2, IRISTYPE is set to IRISTYPE+3 (group 1 becomes group 4, etc.).

   In the *GROUP* paragraph we specify that <u>six</u> (not three) codes are possible and name the new groups formed: NEWSET (from SETOSA), NEWVERS (from VERSICOL) and NEWVIRG (from VIRGINIC).

In Output 18.15 we present the classification functions and classification matrix. Only three groups (USE=1 TO 3 in the *GROUP* paragraph) are used to estimate the classification function. But the cases in all six groups are classified according to the function. All the cases in NEWSET are correctly classified into SETOSA, 12 of the 13 cases in NEWVIRG are classified correctly, and all 10 cases in NEWVERS are correctly classified.

GROUP
    USE=$g_1,g_2,\cdots$.   {all groups/prev.}

> Names or subscripts of <u>groups</u> used in estimating the classification functions. Cases with acceptable values for the GROUPING variable but that are <u>not</u> in these groups will be classified by the function but will <u>not</u> be used in computing the cross-products matrix nor in estimating the classification function.

● PRIOR PROBABILITIES

Unless stated otherwise, a case is assumed a priori to have equal probability of being in any group. If prior probabilities are stated, they affect only the constant term of the classification function and the computation of the posterior probabilities.

GROUP
    PRIOR=$\#_1,\#_2,\cdots$.   {equal prior prob./prev.}

> Prior probabilities for each group. The first number is the prior probability for the first group, the second for the second group, etc. This is according to order specified in CODEs, CUTPOINTS or to order of input *(not according to the order in the* USE *statement of the GROUP paragraph).*
>
> The prior probabilities of the groups USED in the analysis should add to unity. Unequal prior probabilities affect the computation of the constant term in the classification function and of the posterior probabilities (see Appendix A.23); they do not affect the F statistic, Wilks' Λ or the selection of variables.
>
> *When the number of groups differs between two problems, the preassigned value for the second problem is "equal prior probabilities" and not previous problem (prev.).*

<u>Output 18.15</u> Cross validation of a discriminant function with P7M

```
CONTROL LANGUAGE TRANSFORMATIONS ARE

        PROB     = RNDU (    783217 ) .
        NEWGROUP = IRISTYPE +   3.0000 .
        TRUE     = PROB   LE   .20000 .
        IRISTYPE = NEWGROUP IF TRUE   .

    TEMPORARY NAMES USED IN TRANSFORMATIONS
        PROB    NEWGROUP TRUE


    VARIABLES TO BE USED
            1 SEPALLEN    2 SEPALWID    3 PETALLEN    4 PETALWID    5 IRISTYPE

    TOLERANCE. . . . . . . . .    0.010
    F-TO-ENTER . . . . . . . .    4.000    4.000
    F-TO-REMOVE. . . . . . . .    3.996    3.996
    METHOD . . . . . . . . . .        1
    MAXIMUM FORCED LEVEL . . .        0
    MAXIMUM NUMBER OF STEPS. .       10
    GROUPING VARIABLE. . . . .        5
    NUMBER OF GROUPS . . . . .        6
    PRIOR PROBABILITIES. . . .    0.33333    0.33333    0.33333    0.33333    0.33333    0.33333
```

```
                   BEFORE TRANSFORMATION                                INTERVAL RANGE
    VARIABLE      MINIMUM    MAXIMUM    MISSING    CATEGORY  CATEGORY   GREATER    LESS THAN
    NO. NAME      LIMIT      LIMIT      CODE       CODE      NAME       THAN       OR EQUAL TO

    5   IRISTYPE                                   1.00000   SETOSA
                                                   2.00000   VERSICOL
                                                   3.00000   VIRGINIC
                                                   4.00000   NEWSET
                                                   5.00000   NEWVERS
                                                   6.00000   NEWVIRG

        NUMBER OF CASES READ. . . . . . . . . . . . .    150
```

```
    MEANS

        GROUP =   SETOSA     VERSICOL   VIRGINIC   NEWSET     NEWVERS    NEWVIRG    GPS.USED
    VARIABLE
    1 SEPALLEN   5.02143    5.87750    6.62703    4.92500    6.17000    6.47692    5.80840
    2 SEPALWID   3.43571    2.76500    3.00811    3.38750    2.79000    2.87692    3.07731
    3 PETALLEN   1.46428    4.24750    5.57297    1.45000    4.31000    5.49231    3.67731
    4 PETALWID   0.23810    1.33500    2.02432    0.28750    1.29000    2.03077    1.16218
    5 IRISTYPE   1.00000    2.00000    3.00000    4.00000    5.00000    6.00000    1.95798

    COUNTS       42.        40.        37.        8.         10.        13.        119.
```

--- results for steps 0, 1 and 2 are printed ---

```
STEP NUMBER    3
VARIABLE ENTERED    4 PETALWID

    VARIABLE        F TO  FORCE  TOLERANCE  *   VARIABLE        F TO  FORCE  TOLERANCE
                   REMOVE LEVEL             *                  ENTER LEVEL
             DF=  2  114                    *            DF=  2  113
    2 SEPALWID   47.072   1    0.758357     *   1 SEPALLEN   3.792   1    0.329800
    3 PETALLEN   25.680   1    0.695746     *
    4 PETALWID   27.866   1    0.669123     *

U-STATISTIC OR WILKS' LAMBDA    0.0236785    DEGREES OF FREEDOM    3    2    116
APPROXIMATE F-STATISTIC          208.948     DEGREES OF FREEDOM    6.00    228.00

    F - MATRIX        DEGREES OF FREEDOM =    3  114


            SETOSA    VERSICOL VIRGINIC NEWSET    NEWVERS
VERSICOL   576.34
VIRGINIC  1103.31    104.85
NEWSET       0.36    178.30    355.55
NEWVERS    222.91      0.43     46.42   116.94
NEWVIRG    570.49     56.35      0.67   274.03    35.44

CLASSIFICATION FUNCTIONS

        GROUP =    SETOSA     VERSICOL    VIRGINIC
    VARIABLE
    2 SEPALWID    33.15436   12.92362     8.41314
    3 PETALLEN     2.05212   16.62949    21.19389
    4 PETALWID   -22.56166    6.36792    23.33980

    CONSTANT     -56.86957  -58.53294   -96.43256
```

(continued)

Output 18.15 *(continued)*

CLASSIFICATION MATRIX

GROUP	PERCENT CORRECT	NUMBER OF CASES CLASSIFIED INTO GROUP –		
		SETOSA	VERSICOL	VIRGINIC
SETOSA	100.0	42	0	0
VERSICOL	92.5	0	37	3
VIRGINIC	97.3	0	1	36
NEWSET	0.0	8	0	0
NEWVERS	0.0	0	10	0
NEWVIRG	0.0	0	1	12
TOTAL	96.6	50	49	51

JACKKNIFED CLASSIFICATION

GROUP	PERCENT CORRECT	NUMBER OF CASES CLASSIFIED INTO GROUP –		
		SETOSA	VERSICOL	VIRGINIC
SETOSA	100.0	42	0	0
VERSICOL	92.5	0	37	3
VIRGINIC	94.6	0	2	35
NEWSET	0.0	8	0	0
NEWVERS	0.0	0	10	0
NEWVIRG	0.0	0	1	12
TOTAL	95.8	50	50	50

SUMMARY TABLE

STEP NUMBER	VARIABLE ENTERED REMOVED	F VALUE TO ENTER OR REMOVE	NUMBER OF VARIABLES INCLUDED	U-STATISTIC	APPROXIMATE F-STATISTIC	DEGREES OF FREEDOM	
1	3 PETALLEN	920.8586	1		920.859	2.00	116.00
2	2 SEPALWID	39.1414	2	0.0593	248.740	4.00	230.00
3	4 PETALWID	27.8658	3	0.0353	208.948	6.00	228.00
				0.0237			

	INCORRECT CLASSIFICATIONS	MAHALANOBIS D-SQUARE FROM AND POSTERIOR PROBABILITY FOR GROUP –		

GROUP	SETOSA		SETOSA	VERSICOL	VIRGINIC
CASE					
1			0.2 1.000	84.6 0.000	170.6 0.000
6			0.3 1.000	83.0 0.000	166.5 0.000
10			2.1 1.000	110.4 0.000	202.7 0.0
18			3.1 1.000	61.5 0.000	134.5 0.000
26			0.3 1.000	95.8 0.000	184.5 0.000
124			167.7 0.000	17.5 0.000	0.7 1.000
128			143.8 0.000	12.2 0.007	2.4 0.993
133			176.1 0.000	19.0 0.000	0.4 1.000
147			208.9 0.000	37.9 0.000	11.0 1.000
149			223.1 0.0	40.4 0.000	6.3 1.000

GROUP	NEWSET		SETOSA	VERSICOL	VIRGINIC
CASE					
42		SETOSA	4.5 1.000	68.0 0.000	140.4 0.000
64		SETOSA	1.8 1.000	74.1 0.000	157.4 0.000
65		SETOSA	0.1 1.000	92.7 0.000	180.5 0.000
69		SETOSA	0.5 1.000	80.9 0.000	166.0 0.000
73		SETOSA	0.5 1.000	97.1 0.000	185.8 0.000
92		SETOSA	1.9 1.000	90.3 0.000	172.2 0.000
97		SETOSA	2.8 1.000	71.1 0.000	153.5 0.000
108		SETOSA	0.5 1.000	90.2 0.000	175.5 0.000

GROUP	NEWVERS		SETOSA	VERSICOL	VIRGINIC
CASE					
14		VERSICOL	74.4 0.000	1.6 1.000	27.0 0.000
30		VERSICOL	75.7 0.000	0.5 1.000	20.9 0.000
62		VERSICOL	81.5 0.000	0.9 1.000	17.0 0.000
70		VERSICOL	98.1 0.000	0.8 0.993	10.7 0.007
71		VERSICOL	55.6 0.000	4.3 1.000	37.6 0.000
93		VERSICOL	89.9 0.000	1.2 1.000	17.1 0.000
104		VERSICOL	80.2 0.000	0.3 1.000	18.9 0.000
118		VERSICOL	130.0 0.000	4.8 0.795	7.5 0.205
119		VERSICOL	93.0 0.000	3.2 1.000	20.6 0.000
120		VERSICOL	80.2 0.000	0.3 1.000	18.9 0.000

GROUP	NEWVIRG		SETOSA	VERSICOL	VIRGINIC
CASE					
4		VIRGINIC	207.4 0.0	34.0 0.000	5.2 1.000
7		VIRGINIC	180.4 0.000	27.4 0.000	6.6 1.000
15		VIRGINIC	150.1 0.000	10.3 0.014	1.8 0.986
20		VIRGINIC	175.1 0.000	25.5 0.000	4.6 1.000
27		VIRGINIC	188.3 0.000	28.3 0.000	5.6 1.000
57		VERSICOL	149.8 0.000	14.1 0.576	14.7 0.424
76		VIRGINIC	158.4 0.000	12.3 0.004	1.4 0.996
84		VIRGINIC	159.0 0.000	12.2 0.006	2.0 0.994
90		VIRGINIC	294.2 0.0	58.5 0.000	16.7 1.000
91		VIRGINIC	150.3 0.000	10.1 0.388	9.2 0.612
127		VIRGINIC	212.4 0.0	38.9 0.000	6.7 1.000
132		VIRGINIC	165.5 0.000	13.6 0.002	0.9 0.998
138		VIRGINIC	175.9 0.000	18.9 0.001	3.7 0.999

(continued)

Output 18.15 *(continued)*

```
EIGENVALUES

                31.20006     0.31156

CANONICAL CORRELATIONS

                0.98435      0.48739

VARIABLE      COEFFICIENTS FOR CANONICAL VARIABLES

    2 SEPALWID     2.17813     2.57506
    3 PETALLEN    -1.65802    -1.00248
    4 PETALWID    -3.82359     3.14622

CONSTANT          3.83798    -7.89431

GROUP       CANONICAL VARIABLES EVALUATED AT GROUP MEANS
    SETOSA         7.98323     0.23404
    VERSICOL      -2.28642    -0.83211
    VIRGINIC      -6.59025     0.63391
    NEWSET         7.71299     0.27964
    NEWVERS       -2.16353    -0.97197
    NEWVIRG       -6.76688     0.39725

POINTS TO BE PLOTTED

GROUP         MEAN       SYMBOL      SYMBOL
           COORDINATES   FOR CASES   FOR MEAN

    SETOSA    7.98   0.23     A          1
    VERSICOL -2.29  -0.83     B          2
    VIRGINIC -6.59   0.63     C          3
    NEWSET    7.71   0.28     D          4
    NEWVERS  -2.16  -0.97     E          5
    NEWVIRG  -6.77   0.40     F          6
```

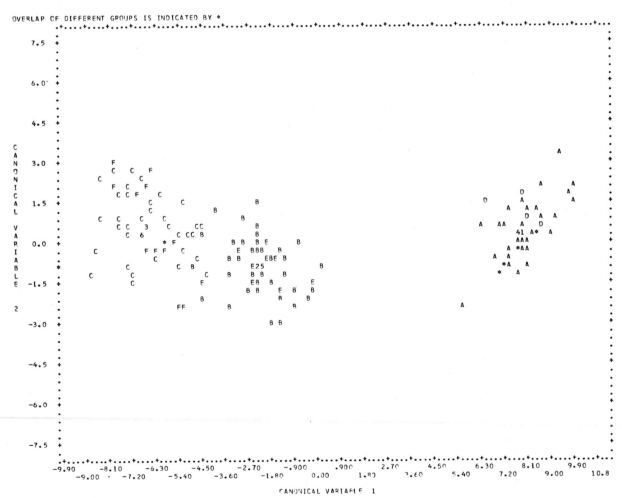

OVERLAP OF DIFFERENT GROUPS IS INDICATED BY *

● ORDERING THE ENTRY OF VARIABLES

All variables except the GROUPING variable are considered to be independent variables.

The LEVEL statement in the *DISCriminant* paragraph can be used to specify a complete or partial ordering, which divides the variables into groups containing one (complete ordering) or more (partial ordering) variables.

In the LEVEL statement you can assign positive numbers (integers) or zero to the variables. Variables assigned zero are excluded from the analysis. Variables assigned a positive value are entered into the equation -- variables with smaller values are entered before variables with larger values. Variables with the same value compete for entry according to the METHOD specified. P7M begins stepping with the lowest positive value of LEVEL and enters all possible variables with that LEVEL (provided they pass the F-to-enter and tolerance limit) before considering variables at the next higher level. Variables not assigned any value for LEVEL are set to a value greater than the maximum value assigned (one if no LEVEL statement is present).

When variables are eliminated by setting LEVEL=0, the F-to-enter statistic is printed for these variables at each step. When variables are eliminated from the analysis by omitting them from the USE statement in the *VARiable* paragraph, not even their F-to-enter is computed and printed.

DISCriminant
  LEVEL= $\#_1, \#_2$.   {highest level specified + 1}   one per variable

  The first number is the level assigned to the first variable read as input, the second to the second variable read as input, etc. If LEVEL is not stated, all variables except the grouping variable are assigned a level of one. LEVEL determines the order of entering variables into the classification function (see above). If LEVEL is stated for some variables but not all of them, the remaining variables are assigned to the next level greater than the maximum assigned.

  FORCE =#.   {0/prev. }

  If FORCE is greater than zero, variables with LEVEL less than or equal to FORCE are entered into the classification function without regard to the F-to-enter limit, and cannot be removed from the function once entered.

● REMOVING VARIABLES FROM THE CLASSIFICATION FUNCTION

Either of two criteria can be used to remove variables from the classifiction function:

   - a variable is removed if its F-to-remove is less than the F-to-remove limit

- a variable is removed to obtain a smaller Wilks' Λ than was previously obtained at an earlier step with the same number of variables in the function

---

DISCriminant
   METHOD=1.*or* 2.   {1/prev.}

   Method of removing variables from the classification: 1, by an F-to-remove limit; 2, to obtain a smaller Wilks' Λ than was previously obtained at an earlier step with the same number of variables.[20]

● FORWARD AND BACKWARD STEPPING

   The discriminant analysis begins with no variables in the classification function. Variables are entered or removed one at a time according to the criterion used. After all variables are entered that can be entered according to the criterion, they can be removed from the classification function according to a second set of F-to-enter and F-to-remove limits. An example of forward and backward stepping is given for P2R (Example 13.5); it is done in the same way for P7M.

DISCriminant
   ENTER= $\#_1,\#_2$.   {4.0,4.0/prev.}

   F-to-enter limits. The first number is used when entering variables into the classification function until no more variables can be entered. The second number (if it is larger than the first) is then used for backward stepping to remove variables. If only one number is specified, the second number is set equal to the first by the program.

   REMOVE= $\#_1,\#_2$.   {3.996,3.996/prev.}

   F-to-remove limits. The first number is used when entering variables into the classification function until no more variables can be entered. The second number (if it is larger than the first) is then used for backward stepping to remove the variables. REMOVE must be less then ENTER , or a variable could be continuously entered and removed at alternate steps. If only one number is specified, the second number is set equal to the first by the program.

---

[20] If your BMDP programs are dated before August 1977,
     the minimum required abbreviation is METHOD (not METH).

● DIRECTING THE STEPPING BY CONTRASTS

You can specify one or more contrasts to direct the stepping. For example, we reanalyze the Fisher iris data (Table 18.1) by specifying a contrast on the groups

CONTRAST IS 0,1,-1.

in the *DISCriminant* paragraph. The above contrast specifies that the difference we want to maximize is between the second and third groups.

The Control Language instructions are given in Example 18.16.

Example 18.16

```
/PROBLEM        TITLE IS 'FISHER IRIS DATA'.
/INPUT          VARIABLES ARE 5.
                FORMAT IS '(4F3.1,F3.0)'.
/VARIABLE       NAMES ARE SEPALLEN,SEPALWID,PETALLEN,PETALWID,IRISTYPE.
                GROUPING IS IRISTYPE.

/GROUP          CODES(5) ARE 1 TO 3.
                NAMES(5) ARE SETOSA,VERSICOL,VIRGINIC.

/DISCRIMINANT CONTRAST IS 0, 1, -1.

/PLOT           CONTRAST.

/END
```

CONTRAST is stated in the *PLOT* paragraph to obtain a plot of the canonical variables based on the specified contrasts.

Results are presented in Output 18.16

The F-to-enter limits are the F statistics for the tests that the contrast(s) is zero. This is described in greater detail in Appendix A.23.

Since only one contrast is specified for this example, only one canonical variable is estimated. Instead of a bivariate canonical plot, a histogram of the canonical variable is plotted in Output 18.16.

DISCriminant
 CONTRAST=$\#_1$,$\#_2$,$\cdots$.   {none/prev.}   may be repeated

 Coefficients of a contrast used to direct the stepping. $\#_1$ is the coefficient for the first group, $\#_2$ for the second group, etc. (according to the CODES, CUTPOINTS or order of input -- *not according to the order in the GROUP USE statement*). The coefficients should sum to zero. CONTRAST= may be repeated to specify additional contrasts. If more than one contrast is specified, all the specified contrasts are used to direct the stepping. If CONTRASTS are not specified, they are generated to test the equality of all group means. When any CONTRAST is specified, the CONTRASTS specified in a previous *DISCriminant* paragraph are cancelled.

(continued)

<u>Output 18.16</u> Stepwise discriminant analysis by P7M directed by a contrast

```
TOLERANCE. . . . . . . . .      0.010
F-TO-ENTER . . . . . . . .      4.000      4.000
F-TO-REMCVE. . . . . . . .      3.996      3.996
METHOD . . . . . . . . . .          1
MAXIMUM FORCED LEVEL . . .          0
MAXIMUM NUMBER OF STEPS. .         10
GROUPING VARIABLE. . . . .          5
NUMBER OF GROUPS . . . . .          3
PRIOR PROBABILITIES. . . .    0.33333    0.33333    0.33333
```

```
                    BEFORE TRANSFORMATION                           INTERVAL RANGE
VARIABLE          MINIMUM    MAXIMUM    MISSING    CATEGORY  CATEGORY   GREATER    LESS THAN
NO. NAME          LIMIT      LIMIT      CODE       CODE      NAME       THAN       OR EQUAL TO

 5   IRISTYPE                                      1.00000   SETOSA
                                                   2.00000   VERSICOL
                                                   3.00000   VIRGINIC


NUMBER OF CASES READ. . . . . . . . . . . . .        150
```

--- means, standard deviations and coefficients of variation are printed ---

```
STEP NUMBER   0

   VARIABLE        F TO   FORCE  TOLERANCE  *    VARIABLE           F TO   FORCE   TOLERANCE
                  REMOVE  LEVEL             *                      ENTER  LEVEL
                  DF=  1  148                *                      DF=  1  147
                                             *    1 SEPALLEN      40.103    1      1.000000
                                             *    2 SEPALWID       9.016    1      1.000000
                                             *    3 PETALLEN     225.347    1      1.000000
                                             *    4 PETALWID     292.490    1      1.000000
```

--- results for steps 1 to 3 ---

```
STEP NUMBER   4
VARIABLE ENTERED   2 SEPALWID

   VARIABLE        F TO   FORCE  TOLERANCE  *    VARIABLE           F TO   FORCE   TOLERANCE
                  REMOVE  LEVEL             *                      ENTER  LEVEL
                  DF=  1  144                *                      DF=  1  143
   1 SEPALLEN      6.355    1   0.347993    *
   2 SEPALWID      5.211    1   C.6C8860    *
   3 PETALLEN     28.914    1   0.365126    *
   4 PETALWID     48.692    1   0.649314    *
```

```
U-STATISTIC OR WILKS' LAMBDA    0.2547542    DEGREES OF FREEDOM     4     1      147
APPROXIMATE F-STATISTIC           105.313    DEGREES OF FREEDOM     4.00    144.00
```

```
 F - MATRIX         DEGREES OF FREEDOM =     4   144

           SETOSA     VERSICOL
VERSICOL    550.19
VIRGINIC   1098.27     105.31
```

```
CLASSIFICATION FUNCTIONS

         GROUP =   SETOSA       VERSICOL       VIRGINIC
VARIABLE
   1 SEPALLEN      23.54416      15.69820       12.44584
   2 SEPALWID      23.58786       7.07252        3.68529
   3 PETALLEN     -16.43063       5.21145       12.76655
   4 PETALWID     -17.39839       6.43422       21.C7909

CONSTANT         -86.30843     -72.85257     -104.36826
```

```
CLASSIFICATION MATRIX

GROUP      PERCENT    NUMBER OF CASES CLASSIFIED INTC GROUP -
           CORRECT
                      SETOSA   VERSICOL VIRGINIC
SETOSA     100.0        50        0        0
VERSICOL    96.0         0       48        2
VIRGINIC    98.0         0        1       49

TOTAL       98.0        50       49       51
```

```
JACKKNIFEC CLASSIFICATION

GROUP      PERCENT    NUMBER OF CASES CLASSIFIED INTO GROUP -
           CORRECT
                      SETOSA   VERSICOL VIRGINIC
SETOSA     100.0        50        0        0
VERSICCL    96.0         0       48        2
VIRGINIC    98.0         0        1       49

TOTAL       98.0        50       49       51
```

Output 18.16 *(continued)*

SUMMARY TABLE

STEP NUMBER	VARIABLE ENTERED	REMOVED	F VALUE TO ENTER OR REMOVE	NUMBER OF VARIABLES INCLUDED	U-STATISTIC	APPROXIMATE F-STSTISTIC	DEGREES OF FREEDOM	
1	4 PETALWID		292.4905	1	0.3345	292.490	1.00	147.00
2	3 PETALLEN		19.6385	2	0.2948	174.607	2.00	146.00
3	1 SEPALLEN		16.9447	3	0.2640	134.766	3.00	145.00
4	2 SEPALWID		5.2108	4	0.2548	105.313	4.00	144.00

EIGENVALUES

2.92535

CANONICAL CORRELATIONS

0.86328

VARIABLE   COEFFICIENTS FOR CANONICAL VARIABLES

1 SEPALLEN	0.78419
2 SEPALWID	0.81671
3 PETALLEN	-1.82164
4 PETALWID	-3.53109

CONSTANT   4.00143

GROUP   CANONICAL VARIABLES EVALUATED AT GROUP MEANS

SETOSA	7.19488
VERSICOL	-1.52373
VIRGINIC	-5.67115

POINTS TO BE PLOTTED

GROUP	MEAN COORDINATES		SYMBOL FOR CASES	SYMBOL FOR MEAN
SETOSA	7.19	0.0	A	1
VERSICOL	-1.52	0.0	B	2
VIRGINIC	-5.67	0.0	C	3

GROUP SETOSA

CASE	CAN.V	CASE	CAN.V	CASE	CAN.V	CASE	CAN.V	CASE	CAN.V
1	7.36	44	6.83	64	7.04	92	6.91	126	7.25
6	6.78	47	6.68	65	7.60	96	7.26	135	6.92
10	8.02	51	6.61	68	6.37	97	6.56	136	7.31
18	5.83	52	7.48	69	6.97	101	7.23	137	5.98
26	8.10	54	6.38	72	7.92	102	6.70	139	7.42
31	6.68	55	6.75	73	7.61	107	7.34	140	7.31
36	7.60	56	7.64	79	6.87	108	7.35	144	7.21
37	7.88	59	7.47	80	8.34	113	7.29	145	6.88
40	6.99	60	8.92	88	8.49	116	7.82	146	7.50
42	5.75	61	6.23	89	6.94	125	7.64	150	7.74

GROUP VERSICOL

CASE	CAN.V	CASE	CAN.V	CASE	CAN.V	CASE	CAN.V	CASE	CAN.V
3	-2.29	30	-0.81	71	0.69	100	-0.59	121	0.69
8	-2.83	33	-0.53	77	-1.40	104	-1.19	122	-1.30
9	-3.86	38	-2.81	85	0.26	106	-1.87	129	-2.35
11	-2.09	43	-0.85	86	-1.64	110	-0.31	130	-0.39
12	-4.03	48	-1.81	87	-0.97	114	-2.07	131	-2.28
14	-0.55	49	0.26	93	-1.42	115	-1.79	134	-1.52
19	-2.03	62	-1.17	94	-1.76	117	-1.22	141	-1.68
22	-2.57	66	-2.65	95	-2.36	118	-3.24	142	-1.33
28	-1.40	67	-0.24	98	-0.35	119	-1.73	143	-2.07
29	-1.86	70	-2.42	99	0.00	120	-1.03	148	-3.41

GROUP VIRGINIC

CASE	CAN.V	CASE	CAN.V	CASE	CAN.V	CASE	CAN.V	CASE	CAN.V
2	-6.66	23	-7.26	46	-4.14	81	-6.14	112	-5.62
4	-6.89	24	-7.03	50	-5.02	82	-4.82	123	-6.79
5	-3.36	25	-4.31	53	-4.05	83	-3.94	124	-5.31
7	-5.47	27	-5.89	57	-4.24	84	-5.25	127	-7.35
13	-4.99	32	-4.57	58	-6.31	90	-8.53	128	-4.64
15	-4.83	34	-4.83	63	-3.95	91	-3.90	132	-5.14
16	-5.24	35	-6.14	74	-6.74	103	-6.48	133	-5.65
17	-6.92	39	-5.42	75	-6.96	105	-5.73	138	-5.66
20	-6.32	41	-5.85	76	-5.24	109	-5.31	147	-6.93
21	-6.83	45	-6.94	78	-4.12	111	-5.74	149	-8.12

HISTOGRAM OF CANONICAL VARIABLE

```
                                                                 A
                                                              A  AA
                                                              A  AA
                  C                         B                 A  AA
      C           C           C         B   B  B              AAAAAA
      C           C     C     C         B   B BB            A  AAAAA
     CC     CC C  C              C      B  B BB   BB        A  AAAAA
    CCC CC CCCCC   CCC   C  B    BBBBBBB B BB  B  B       A  A  AAAAAAAAA
 C C  CCCCCCCCCCCCCCCCCCCCBB BB BBBBBBBBBBBBBBBBBB  B      AA AAAAAAAAAAAA  A
 ..+....+....3....+....+....+....+....+.2..+....+....+....+....1....+....+..
 -8.1     -6.3      -4.5      -2.7      -.90       .90      2.7       4.5       6.3       8.1       9.9
      -7.2      -5.4      -3.6      -1.8       0.0       1.8       3.6       5.4       7.2       9.0
```

> *When* CONTRAST *are specified, the computation of the F-to-enter, F-to-remove and Wilks' Λ are affected; the coefficients of the classification functions, the classification matrix and Mahalanobis distances are not directly affected; they depend only on the set of variables selected and* not *on the values of the contrasts.*
>
> *The effect of specifying* CONTRASTS *is described in Appendix A.23.*

PLOT

   CONTRAST.   {no/prev.}

When contrasts are specified in the *DISCriminant* paragraph and CONTRAST in the *PLOT* paragraph[21], the canonical variables and the plot of the canonical variables use the contrasts specified in the *DISCriminant* paragraph. Otherwise, the coefficients for the canonical variables are obtained from the matrix $W^{-\frac{1}{2}}BW^{-\frac{1}{2}}$.

   CANONICAL.   {yes/prev.}

A plot of the canonical variables is printed unless NO CANONICAL is specified. The canonical variables plotted are determined by whether or not CONTRAST is specified in the *PLOT* paragraph. If there is only one canonical variable, a histogram is printed.

   GROUP=g_1,g_2,$\cdots$.   {all groups/prev.}   may be repeated

Groups to be plotted in the canonical variable plot. Each GROUP= statement describes a separate plot. g_1,g_2,... are the NAMEs or subscripts of the groups.

● MAHALANOBIS D^2 AND POSTERIOR PROBABILITIES

Mahalanobis D^2 and the posterior probability are computed for each case after the final step of the discriminant analysis. D^2 is the distance from each case to each group mean. Both the group mean and the cross-products matrices use the case in the computation of the cross products.

When JACKKNIFE is specified in the *DISCriminant* paragraph each case is eliminated in turn from the computation of the group means and cross products; D^2 and the posterior probability are computed for the distance from the case to the groups formed by the remaining cases (Lachenbruch and Mickey, 1968). In the output the distances and posterior probabilities are labelled "jackknifed distances and posterior probabilities."

---

[21] If your BMDP programs are dated before August 1977,
    CANON has the meaning that CONTRAST now has and a plot is always printed.

DISCriminant
  JACKKNIFE.   {no/prev. }

  When JACKKNIFE is specified, Mahalanobis distances and the posterior
  probabilities for each case are computed without using the case in the
  computation of the group mean and pooled within-group covariance
  matrix.

● MAXIMUM NUMBER OF STEPS

DISCriminant
  STEP=#.   {2(no. of var.)/prev.}

  Maximum number of steps in the analysis.

● TOLERANCE

  Variables are <u>not</u> entered into the classification function unless they
can pass the TOLERANCE limit.

DISCriminant
  TOLERANCE=#.   {0.01/prev.}   between 0.001 and 1.0

  Tolerance limit. No variable is entered into the classification
  function whose squared multiple correlation (R^2) with already
  entered variables exceeds 1-TOLERANCE, or whose entry will cause
  the tolerance of an already entered variable with the other variables to exceed 1-TOLERANCE.

● CONTROLLING THE PRINTED RESULTS

  The *PRINT* paragraph is used to request that additional results be
printed -- or that selected results <u>not</u> be printed.

PRINT
  WITHIN.   {no/prev.}

  The within-groups covariance matrix is printed.[22]

  STEP.   {yes/prev.}

  If NO STEP is specified, the results are <u>not</u> printed at every step;
  they are printed at only Step 0 and the last step.

                                              (continued)

---

[22] If your BMDP programs are dated before February 1976,
     WITHIN is not available.

PRINT

CLASSIFICATION= #$_1$,#$_2$,$\cdots$.   {none/prev.}

Steps at which the classification matrix and the jackknifed classification matrix are printed. They are printed automatically after the
last step.

POSTERIOR.   {yes/prev.}

Mahalanobis D^2 and posterior probabilities are printed at the last
step unless NO POSTERIOR is specified.[23]

POINT.   {yes/prev.}

The values of the canonical variables used in the plot are printed
unless NO POINT is specified. [24]

● SAVING THE DATA AND CANONICAL VARIABLES IN A BMDP FILE

When a BMDP File is created, both the data and the canonical variables
are saved. The canonical variables are named CNVR1, CNVR2, etc. and placed
immediately after the data for each case.

The BMDP File can then be read as input to other BMDP programs.

SAVE

NCAN=#.   {see below}   # $\leq$ no. of groups - 1

The number of canonical variables to be saved in a BMDP File. If
not specified, the number of canonical variables saved is equal to
the number of CONTRASTS specified in the *DISCriminant* paragraph,
or is one less than the number of groups used in the analysis if no
CONTRASTS are specified (but not more than the number of variables
selected). If NCAN is greater than the number of contrasts, the
first set of canonical variable(s) contains the canonical variables
evaluated for the contrasts ordered by the size of the eigenvalues,
and the remaining set contains the residual variables (variables
orthogonal to those corresponding to the set of contrasts).

---

[23] If your BMDP programs are dated before February 1976,
POSTERIOR is always requested.

[24] If your BMDP programs are dated before February 1976,
POINT is always requested.

● SIZE OF PROBLEM

The maximum size of a problem that P7M can analyze is a complicated function of the number of variables (V), the number of groups (G) and the number of cases (C). We indicate the maximum number of cases (C) for various combinations of G and V.

G	2	2	3	5	10
V	10	50	50	50	50
C	1800	1350	1150	859	450

Appendix B describes how to increase the capacity of the program.

● COMPUTATIONAL METHOD

The data are read in single precision. All computations are performed in double precision.

The computational procedure is described in Appendix A.23. See also Jennrich (1977b).

ACKNOWLEDGEMENT

P7M was designed by Robert Jennrich and Paul Sampson and programmed by Paul Sampson. It supersedes BMD07M.

18.5 Summary — P4M, P6M, P6R, P7M

The Control Language on this page is common to all programs. This is followed by the Control Language specific to

P4M --	Factor Analysis	p. 735
P6M --	Canonical Correlation Analysis	p. 737
P6R --	Partial Correlation and Multivariate Regression	p. 738
P7M --	Stepwise Discriminant Analysis	p. 739

Paragraph STATEMENT[1] {Preassigned value[2]}		Definition, restriction	See pages:
/PROBLem		Required each problem	74
TITLE='c'.	{blank}	Problem title, $\leq$ 160 char.	74
/INPut		Required first problem. Either VARIABLE and FORMAT, or UNIT and CODE required.	75
VARIABLE=#.	{none/prev.}	No. of variables in input data	75
FORMAT='c'.	{none/prev.}	Format of input data, $\leq$ 800 char.	76
CASE=#.	{end-of-file/prev.}	No. of cases in data	76-77
UNIT=#.	{5(cards)/prev.}	Input unit if data are not on cards; not 1, 2, 6	77
REWIND.	{REWIND/prev.}	Rewind input unit	77
CODE=c.	{none}	Code to identify BMDP File	132
CONTENT=c.	{DATA}	Data or matrix in BMDP File	132
LABEL=c.	{none}	Label of BMDP File, $\leq$ 40 char.	132
/VARiable		Optional. For input from a BMDP File, items in this paragraph may be previously set, see Chapter 7.	79
NAME=$c_1,c_2,\cdots$.	{X(subscript)/prev.}	Variable names, one per variable	79-80
MAXIMUM=$\#_1,\#_2,\cdots$.	{none/prev.}	Upper limits, one per variable	80
MINIMUM=$\#_1,\#_2,\cdots$.	{none/prev.}	Lower limits, one per variable	80
BLANK= (one only) ZERO, MISSING.	{ZERO/ prev.}	Blanks treated as zeros or as missing value codes	81
MISSING=$\#_1,\#_2,\cdots$.	{none/prev.}	Missing value codes, one per variable	81
USE=$v_1,v_2,\cdots$.	{all variables}	Variables used in the analysis	82
LABEL=v_1,v_2.	{none/prev.}	Variable(s) used to label cases, read under A-format, one or two	83
ADD=#.	{0/prev.}	No. of variables added through transformation	99
BEFORE. or AFTER.	{BEFORE/prev.}	Data checked for limits before or after transformation	100
/TRANsform		Optional, Control Language transformations and case selection	97-105
/SAVE		Optional, required to create BMDP File	125
CODE=c.	{none}	Code to identify BMDP File, required	125-126
LABEL='c'.	{blank}	Label for BMDP File, $\leq$ 40 char.	125-126
UNIT=#.	{none}	Unit on which BMDP File is written; not 1, 2, 5 or 6	126-127
NEW.	{not new}	NEW if this is first BMDP File written in the system file	126-127

Key: # number   v variable name or subscript
'c' title, label or format   c name not exceeding 8 char., apostrophes may be required (p. 59)

[1] In BMDP programs dated before August 1977, the minimum required abbreviations are *INPUT* (not *INP*), VARIAB (not VAR), FORMAT (not FORM), CONTENT (not CONT), *VARIAB* (not *VAR*), BEFORET (not BEF), AFTERT (not AFT), *TRANSF* (not *TRAN*). If dated before February 1976, BLANK=ZERO and cannot be changed.

[2] "/prev." means that any assignment remains the same as that specified in the previous problem or subproblem until changed. Otherwise, the assignment returns to its preassigned value each time a new problem begins or the paragraph is used again.

P4M -- Factor Analysis

(in addition to that on p. 734)

Paragraph STATEMENT[1] {Preassigned value}		Definition, restriction	See pages:
INPut		Specify as part of *INPut* paragraph, p. 734	
CONTENT=c.	{DATA}	DATA, CORR, COVA, LOAD, FSCF can be read from BMDP File	681
TYPE= (one only) DATA,CORR,COVA,LOAD,FSCF.	{DATA or CONTENT from BMDP File}	Type of input if not data	681
SHAPE= (one only) SQUARE,LOWER.	{SQUARE/prev.}	Shape of matrix if TYPE=CORR or COVA	681
FACTOR=#.	{none}	Number of factors when TYPE=LOAD or FSCF	681
VARiable		Specify as part of *VARiable* paragraph, p. 734	
WEIGHT=v.	{no case weights/prev.}	Variable containing case weights	677-678
SCORE=$v_1,v_2,\cdots$.	{none}	Variables used for factor score (only if input is not data)	682
SAVE		Specify as part of *SAVE* paragraph, p. 734	
CONTENT= (one or more) DATA,COVA,UFLD,RFLD, FCOR,FSCF.	{DATA}	Data and results saved in BMDP File	678
/FACTOR		Optional, initial factor extraction	
FORM= (one only) CORR,COVA,OCORR,OCOVA.	{CORR/prev.}	Factor analysis form	664
METHOD= (one only) PCA,MLFA,LJIFFY,PFA.	{PCA/prev}	Method of initial factor extraction	664
ITERATE=#.	{25/prev.}	Maximum number of iterations for factor extraction	665
EPS=#.	{0.001/prev.}	Convergence criterion when METHOD=PFA.	665
TOLERANCE=#.	{.0001/prev.}	Tolerance limit	665
COMMUNALITY= (one only) UNALT,SMCS,MAXROW. COMMUNALITY=$\#_1,\#_2,\cdots$.	{UNALT for PCA, SMCS otherwise/prev.}	Initial communality estimates	665-666
NUMBER=#.	{no. of variables}	Maximum number of factors	669
CONSTANT=#.	{1/prev.}	Factors correspond to eigenvalues > CONSTANT	669
/ROTATE		Optional, factor rotation	
METHOD= (one only) VMAX,DQUART,QRMAX,EQMAX, ORTHOG,DOBLI,ORTHOB,NONE.	{VMAX unless LJIFFY/prev.}	Method of rotation	669-670
GAMMA=#.	{1.0 for ORTHOG ; 0.0 for DOBLI}	Gamma, only for ORTHOG and DOBLI	670
MAXIT=#.	{50/prev.}	Maximum number of iterations	671
CONSTANT=#.	{0.00001/prev.}	Convergence criterion for rotation	671
NORMAL.	{NORMAL/prev.}	Kaiser's normalization	671
/PRINT		Optional	
CASE=#.	{5/prev.}	Number of cases for which data are printed	673-676
FASCORE=#.	{all}	Number of factors for which factor scores are printed	673-676
STANDARD.	{no/prev.}	Print standard scores	673-676
COVARIANCE.	{no/prev.}	Print covariance matrix	673-676
CORRELATION.	{CORR/prev.}	Print correlation matrix	673-676
INVERSE.	{no/prev.}	Print inverse of corr. or covar. matrix	673-676
PARTIAL.	{no/prev.}	Print partial correlations	673-676
FSTR.	{no/prev.}	Print factor structure matrix (oblique rotation)	673-676
RESIDUAL.	{no/prev.}	Print residual correlations	673-676
SHADE.	{no/prev.}	Print shaded correlations after reordering	673-676
HILEV.	{0.50/prev.}	High factor loadings value	676-677
LOLEV.	{0.25/prev.}	Low factor loadings value	676-677
/PLOT		Optional	
INITIAL=#.	{4}	Number of unrotated factors for factor loadings plots	677
FINAL=#.	{4}	Number of rotated factors for factor loadings plots	677
FSCORE=#.	{3}	Number of factors for factor score plots	677
/END		Required	57

Key: # number   c name not exceeding 8 char., apostrophes may be required (p. 59)
     v variable name or subscript

[1] If your BMDP programs are dated before August 1977, the minimum required abbreviations are CONTENT (not CONT), METHOD (not METH), ITERATE (not ITER), NUMBER (not NUMB), MAXITR (not MAXIT), NORMAL (not NORM), INITIAL (not INIT). If dated before April 1977, TOLERANCE is preassigned to .0001 and cannot be changed. If dated before February 1976, SHADE is not available.

(continued)

● <u>Order of input</u>

(1) System Cards, at HSCF these are
```
//jobname  JBO  nooo,yourname
//  EXEC  BIMED,PROG=BMDP4M
//SYSIN  DD  *
```

(2) Control Language instructions
```
PROBlem paragraph, required
INPut paragraph, required first problem
VARiable paragraph
TRANsform paragraph
SAVE paragraph
FACTOR paragraph
ROTATE paragraph
PRINT paragraph
PLOT paragraph
END paragraph, required at end of Control Language
```

(3) Data, if on cards   data

(4) System Card, at HSCF this is   //

Control Language instructions and data (2 and 3) can be repeated for additional problems.

P6M -- Canonical Correlation Analysis

(in addition to that on p. 734)

Paragraph STATEMENT[1] {Preassigned value}	Definition, restriction	See pages:
INPut	Specify as part of *INPut* paragraph, p. 734	
CONTENT=c. {DATA}	DATA,COVA,CORR can be read from BMDP File	695
TYPE= *(one only)* DATA,COVA,CORR. {DATA or CONTENT from BMDP File}	Type of input if not data	695
SHAPE= *(one only)* SQUARE,LOWER. {SQUARE}	Shape of matrix if TYPE=CORR or COVA	695-696
VARiable	Specify as part of *VARiable* paragraph, p. 734	
WEIGHT=v. {no case weights/prev.}	Variable containing case weights	694
SAVE	Specify as part of *SAVE* paragraph, p. 734	
CONTENT= *(one or both)* DATA,COVA. {DATA}	Data and results saved in BMDP File	694-695
/CANONical	Required	689
FIRST=$v_1,v_2,\cdots$. {none}	Variables in first set, required	689
SECOND=$v_1,v_2,\cdots$. {none}	Variables in second set, required	689
NUMBER=#. {number of variables in smaller set}	Maximum number of canonical variables	689-690
CONSTANT=#. {0.0/prev.}	Canonical variables only for those with corr. > CONSTANT	689-690
PRECISION= *(one only)* SINGLE,DOUBLE. {DOUBLE/prev.}	Precision for computations	689-690
TOLERANCE=#. {0.01/prev.}	Tolerance	689-690
ZERO. {no/prev.}	Covariances computed assuming means are zero	689-690
/PRINT	Optional	
CASE=#. {5/prev.}	Number of cases for which data are printed	690-692
MATRICES= *(one or more)* CORR,COVA,COEF,CANV,LOAD. {CORR,LOAD}	Matrices to be printed	690-692
/PLOT	Optional	
XVAR=$v_1,v_2,\cdots$. {none}	Variables for X-axes of plots	692-694
YVAR=$v_1,v_2,\cdots$. {none}	Variables for Y-axes of plots	692-694
SIZE=$\#_1,\#_2$. {50,50/prev.}	Size of plots	692-694
/END	Required	57

Key: # number   c name not exceeding 8 char., apostrophes may be required (p. 59)
      v variable name or subscript

[1] If your BMDP programs are dated before August 1977, the minimum required abbreviations are CONTENT (not CONT) and NUMBER (not NUMB). If dated before April 1977, only data can be read as input if a BMDP File is not used.

- Order of input

    (1) System Cards, at HSCF these are
```
//jobname JOB nooo,yourname
//  EXEC  BIMED,PROG=BMDP6M
//SYSIN DD *
```

    (2) Control Language instructions
```
PROBlem paragraph, required
INPut paragraph, required first problem
VARiable paragraph
TRANsform paragraph
SAVE paragraph
CANONical paragraph, required
PRINT paragraph
PLOT paragraph
END paragraph, required at end of Control Language
```

    (3) Data, if on cards   [data

    (4) System Card, at HSCF this is   [//

    Control Language instructions and data (2 and 3) can be repeated for additional problems.

P6R -- Partial Correlation and Multivariate Regression

(in addition to that on p. 734)

Paragraph STATEMENT [1]　{Preassigned value}	Definition, restriction	See pages:
INPut	Specify as part of *INPut* paragraph, p. 734	
CONTENT=c.　{DATA}	DATA,COVA,CORR can be read from BMDP File	709
TYPE=(one only) DATA,　{DATA, or CONTENT from 　COVA,CORR.　BMDP File}	Type of input if not data	709
SHAPE=(one only) SQUARE,LOWER.　{SQUARE/prev.}	Shape of matrix if TYPE=CORR or COVA	710
VARiable	Specify as part of *VARiable* paragraph, p. 734	
WEIGHT=v.　{no case weights/prev.}	Variable containing case weights	707
SAVE	Specify as part of *SAVE* paragraph, p. 734	
CONTENT=(one or more) DATA,COVA,COVAPART.　{DATA}	Data and results saved in BMDP File	708
/REGRess	Required	700
DEPENDENT=v_1,v_2,$\cdots$.　{none}	Dependent variables, required	700-701
INDEPENDENT=v_1,v_2,$\cdots$.　{none}	Independent variables, required	700-701
ZERO.　{no/prev.}	Covariances computed assuming means are zero	701
PRECISION=(one only) SINGLE,DOUBLE.　{DOUBLE/ prev.}	Precision of computations	701
TOLERANCE=#.　{0.01/prev.}	Tolerance	701
/PRINT	Optional	
CASE=#.　{5/prev.}	Number of cases for which data are printed	702-705
MATRICES=(one or more) CORR,COVA, 　PART,COVAPART,CREG,RREG, 　COEF,STANC,TTEST,RESI.　{CORR,PART}	Results to be printed	702-705
/PLOT	Optional	
XVAR=v_1,v_2,$\cdots$.　{none}	Variables for X-axes of plots	706-707
YVAR=v_1,v_2,$\cdots$.　{none}	Variables for Y-axes of plots	706-707
SIZE=$\#_1$,$\#_2$.　{50,50/prev.}	Size of plots	706-707
NORMAL.　{no/prev.}	Normal probability plot of residuals	706-707
/END	Required	57

Key:　# number
　v　variable name or subscript

[1] If your BMDP programs are dated before August 1977, the minimum required abbreviations are CONTENT (not CONT) and *REGRES* (not *REGR*); in the MATRICES statement use INVCV in place of CREG and INVCR in place of RREG; PROBIT is used in place of NORMAL . If dated before April 1977, only data can be read as input if a BMDP File is <u>not</u> used.

● <u>Order of input</u>

(1)　System Cards, at HSCF these are
```
//jobname  JOB  nooo,yourname
//   EXEC  BIMED,PROG=BMDP6R
//SYSIN  DD  *
```

(2)　Control Language instructions
```
PROBLem paragraph, required
INPut paragraph, required first problem
VARiable paragraph
TRANsform paragraph
SAVE paragraph
REGRess paragraph, required
PRINT paragraph
PLOT paragraph
END paragraph, required at end of Control Language
```

(3)　Data, if on cards
```
data
```

(4)　System Card, at HSCF this is
```
//
```

Control Language instructions and data (2 and 3) can be repeated for additional problems.

P7M -- Stepwise Discriminant Analysis

(in addition to that on p. 734)

Paragraph STATEMENT[1] {Preassigned value}		Definition, restriction	See pages:
INPut		Specify as part of *INPut* paragraph, p. 734	
GROUP=#.	{none/prev.}	Number of groups, required if more than 10 groups and no *GROUP* paragraph	719
VARiable		Specify as part of *VARiable* paragraph, p. 734	
GROUPING=v.	{none/prev.}	Variable used to group cases, required	719
/GROUP		Required if GROUPING variable has more than 10 distinct values	719
CODE(#)=$\#_1,\#_2,\cdots$.	{10 smallest values/prev.}	Codes for variable #	84-85
CUTPOINT(#)=$\#_1,\#_2,\cdots$.	{see CODE/ prev.}	Cutpoints to form intervals for variable #	84-85
NAME(#)=$c_1,c_2,\cdots$.	{CODES or CUTPOINTS/ prev.}	Code or interval names for variable #	84-85
USE=$g_1,g_2,\cdots$.	{all groups/prev.}	Groups used for within-group cross-product matrix	720-721
PRIOR=$\#_1,\#_2,\cdots$.	{1.0/number of groups/prev.}	Prior probabilities used to compute posterior probabilities	721
SAVE		Specify as part of *SAVE* paragraph, p. 734	
NCAN=#.	{no. of groups - 1/prev.}	Number of canonical variables included with data in BMDP File.	732
/DISCriminant		Optional	
LEVEL=$\#_1,\#_2,\cdots$.	{highest + 1}	Ordering of variables for stepping	725
FORCE=#.	{0/prev.}	Level through which variables are forced into function	725
METHOD=1. *or* 2.	{1/prev.}	Method of deleting variables	725-726
ENTER=$\#_1,\#_2$.	{4.0,4.0/prev.}	Lower limit for F-to-enter	726
REMOVE=$\#_1,\#_2$.	{3.999,3.999/prev.}	Upper limit for F-to-remove	726
CONTRAST=$\#_1,\#_2,\cdots$.	{equality of group means/prev.}	Contrast used to direct stepping, may be repeated	727-730
JACKKNIFE.	{no/prev.}	Posterior prob. and D^2 computed excluding each case in turn	730-731
STEP=#.	{2(no. of var.)/prev.}	Maximum number of steps	731
TOLERANCE=#.	{0.01/prev.}	Tolerance	731
/PRINT		Optional	
WITHIN.	{no/prev.}	Print pooled within-group covariance matrix	731
STEP.	{STEP/ prev.}	Print results at each step	731
CLASSIFICATION=$\#_1,\#_2,\cdots$.	{none/prev.}	Steps at which classification matrix is printed	732
POSTERIOR.	{POST /prev.}	Posterior prob. and D^2 are printed	732
POINT.	{POINT/prev.}	Values of canonical variables are printed	732
/PLOT		Optional	
CONTRAST.	{no/prev.}	Canonical variables are based on specified contrasts	730
CANONICAL.	{CANON/prev.}	Canonical variables are plotted	730
GROUP=$g_1,g_2,\cdots$.	{all groups/prev.}	Groups to be plotted in one plot, may be repeated	730
/END		Required	57

Key: # number   g group name or group subscript (not CODE or CUTPOINT)
      v variable name or subscript

[1] If your BMDP programs are dated before August 1977, the minimum required abbreviation is METHOD (not METH); CANON in the *PLOT* paragraph has the meaning that CONTRAST now has and a plot is always printed. If dated before February 1976, WITHIN is not available; POSTERIOR and POINT are always requested.

(continued)

● Order of input

(1) System Cards, at HSCF these are

```
//jobname  JOB   nooo,yourname
//  EXEC   BIMED,PROG=BMDP7M
//SYSIN  DD *
```

(2) Control Language instructions

PROBLem paragraph, required
INPut paragraph, required first problem
VARiable paragraph, required first problem
GROUP paragraph
TRANsform paragraph
SAVE paragraph
DISCriminant paragraph
PRINT paragraph
PLOT paragraph
END paragraph, required at end of Control Language

(3) Data, if on cards

```
data
```

(4) System Card, at HSCF this is

```
//
```

Control Language instructions and data (2 and 3) can be repeated for additional problems.

19

SURVIVAL ANALYSIS

In this chapter we discuss

P1L -- Life Tables and Survival Functions.

The techniques described in this program are appropriate when measuring the time to occurrence of some event or response; for example, survival time (i.e., the response is death), or time to recurrence of a disease. Because many of the techniques were originally motivated by survival studies, we use the language of such problems in this chapter. Many other types of studies with a time-to-response outcome (e.g., time to conception, time on a job, time to failure) may be treated similarly.

The ability to use data from cases for which the response has not yet occurred distinguishes the techniques discussed in this chapter from other statistical methodology. This kind of data is called incomplete or censored data, and may arise from loss to follow-up (that is, the patient may have moved away, or refused to participate in the study), death from causes other than the one under study, or no response before the end of the study (withdrawn alive).

A typical problem might be to assess the effect of an experimental drug on animal survival in a laboratory study. A fixed number of animals are treated at the start of the experiment; length of time from treatment to death is recorded for each animal. Frequently the study ends after a specified proportion of animals die, or after a certain time period has elapsed. The observations from animals that survive to the end of the study are censored at a common time. By contrast, in clinical studies patients usually enter the study at different times; therefore the lengths of follow-up time differ among patients.

Special techniques are required to analyze data with censored observations. The methods presented here assume that censored observations are not related to the individuals' true times to response. P1L provides estimates of the survival distribution for censored data. A major advantage of the techniques described is the use of all patient follow-up information (although unequal) in estimating the survival probabilities. The output from P1L includes

- estimates of the survival function using the actuarial-type life table (Cutler-Ederer)

- estimates of the survival function based on the product-limit (Kaplan-Meier) estimate

- the Mantel-Cox and Breslow statistics to test the equality of survival distributions for different patient groups (these statistics are the analogues of nonparametric rank statistics that are appropriate to censored data)

When there are no censored observations, you can analyze the data using a variety of techniques, such as regression (Chapter 13), analysis of variance (Chapter 15) or nonparametric statistics (Chapter 16).

P1L

19.1 Life Tables and Survival Functions

Jacqueline Benedetti, HSCF
Karen Yuen, HSCF

P1L estimates the survival (time-to-response) distribution of patients who have been observed over varying periods of time.[1] The data can arise from experiments in which all subjects enter the study either concurrently or at different times. In the latter case, all patients are observed for unequal amounts of time. A major advantage of the techniques described in this program is the use of all patient follow-up information (although unequal) in estimating the survival probabilities.

Two estimates of the survival distribution are available; the product-limit (Kaplan-Meier, 1958) estimate based on individual survival times, and the actuarial life-table (Cutler-Ederer, 1958) that groups the data by time interval. When each interval contains only one observation, the two estimates are identical.

The survival curves can be reported for all the patients, or separately for subsets of the patients. For example, separate estimates may be desired for patients in different treatment groups. The equality of the survival distributions for the patient groups can be tested by two nonparametric rank tests.

● CONTROL LANGUAGE

The Control Language instructions to describe the data and variables are common to all BMDP programs and are explained in Chapter 5: the *PROBlem, INPut, VARiable* and *GROUP* paragraphs are used in P1L.

If data editing or transformations are necessary, the methods described in Chapter 6 can be used. Data can be read using a FORMAT statement or from a BMDP File (Chapter 7). If a BMDP File is read as input and a new BMDP File is created in the same problem, the two Files must be in different system files and must have different UNIT numbers.

A summary of the Control Language instructions common to all BMDP programs is on p. 769; a summary of the Control Language instructions specific to P1L follow the general summary. This summary can be used as an index to the program description.

● RESULTS

The primary types of results available are illustrated in the following two examples. In our examples the response is death.

---

[1] If your BMDP programs are dated before August 1977, P1L is not available.

Life Table Analysis

A life table is a method of summarizing the results of a study by grouping the times to response into time intervals. For each time interval the table records the number of subjects who are still in the study at the start of the interval, the number responding during the interval, and the number censored (lost to follow-up or withdrawn). From these numbers the probability of a response in an interval is estimated.

For example, suppose that the times to response are grouped into yearly intervals. A subject who showed a response (died) in his sixth year in the study would be counted as entering and leaving each of the first five years, but counted as entering the sixth year and showing a response in it; he would not appear in any computation for the seventh year and later. Similarly if a subject terminates participation in the study (either the study ends or he discontinues the follow-up) in the sixth year, he is counted as entering and leaving each of the first five years, but counted as entering the sixth year and then as withdrawn or lost (depending on the cause).

Two types of probabilities may be of interest. One is the conditional probability of showing no response in an interval (surviving) given that a subject has entered the interval. The second is the probability of showing no response (surviving) from the start of the study to any given interval. The latter is known as the survival distribution. These probabilities serve much the same purpose as a histogram or cumulative distribution function in describing data.

Example 19.1 illustrates the life table technique applied to lung cancer data analyzed by Prentice (1973) and presented in Table 19.1. The data represent survival times and patient characteristics from subjects enrolled in a lung cancer study. The survival information is provided by two variables. The first is patient's time on study (SURVIVAL), the second is a categorical variable called STATE that indicates whether the time represents a death (coded 1), or a censored observation (coded 0). That is, patients coded as 0 were alive when last observed.

In addition to the Control Language instructions common to all programs (Chapter 5), P1L requires a *FORM* paragraph that indicates the structure of the survival time variables. In this example, SURVIVAL provides the patient's total time on study and STATE provides the STATUS of the patient, that is, whether the patient is a loss to follow-up, etc. RESPONSE indicates which values of the STATUS variable represent true responses. More than one code may be possible. For example, different causes of death may be individually coded, yet all represent the response under study (i.e., death). All other valid codes are treated as censored.

Table 19.1 Survival in days of lung cancer patients (Prentice, 1973)

Survival	State	Treatment	Cell Type		Survival	State	Treatment	Cell Type		Survival	State	Treatment	Cell Type
72	1	1	1		112	1	0	1		3	1	1	2
411	1	1	1		999	1	0	1		95	1	1	2
228	1	1	1		11	1	1	1		24	1	0	2
231	0	0	1		25	0	1	1		18	1	0	2
242	1	0	1		144	1	1	1		83	0	0	2
991	1	0	1		8	1	1	1		31	1	0	2
111	1	0	1		42	1	1	1		51	1	0	2
1	1	0	1		100	0	1	1		90	1	0	2
587	1	0	1		314	1	1	1		52	1	0	2
389	1	0	1		110	1	1	1		73	1	0	2
33	1	0	1		82	1	1	1		8	1	0	2
25	1	0	1		10	1	1	1		36	1	0	2
357	1	0	1		118	1	1	1		48	1	0	2
467	1	0	1		126	1	1	1		7	1	0	2
201	1	0	1		8	1	1	2		140	1	0	2
1	1	0	1		92	1	1	2		186	1	0	2
30	1	0	1		35	1	1	2		84	1	0	2
44	1	0	1		117	1	1	2		19	1	0	2
283	1	0	1		132	1	1	2		45	1	0	2
15	1	0	1		12	1	1	2		80	1	0	2
87	0	0	1		162	1	1	2					
(cont'd)					*(cont'd)*								

Key: survival time, state (1=dead, 0=censored),
treatment (1=standard, 0=test),
cell type (1=squamous, 2=adeno).
The time of survival is recorded in columns 1-3; the
other variables are recorded in columns 6, 9 and 12.

Example 19.1

```
/PROBLEM      TITLE IS 'PRENTICE DATA'.
/INPUT        VARIABLES ARE 4.
              FORMAT IS '(4F3.0)'.
/VARIABLE     NAMES ARE SURVIVAL,STATE,TREAT,CELL.

/FORM         TIME IS SURVIVAL.
              STATUS IS STATE.
              RESPONSE IS 1.

/END
```

The Control Language must be preceded by System Cards to initiate the analysis by P1L. At HSCF, the System Cards are

```
//jobname JOB nooo,yourname
// EXEC BIMED,PROG=BMDP1L
//SYSIN DD *
```

The Control Language is immediately followed by the data (Table 19.1). The analysis is terminated by another System Card. At HSCF, this System Card is

```
//
```

The results appear in Output 19.1. Circled numbers below correspond to those in the output.

(1) Number of cases read. Cases that contain acceptable values for all variables specified in *FORM* and *ESTimate* paragraphs are used in the analysis. A case is omitted from all computations when the value of any variable used in the analysis is missing or is out of range. If

CODEs are specified for a GROUPING variable, a case is included only if the value of the GROUPING variable is equal to one of the specified codes.

(2) Time intervals. The range of survival times is divided into ten equally spaced intervals. Therefore, as in this example, intervals may not be whole numbers. The number or width of intervals can be specified (p. 753).

The survival experience of the patients is summarized by interval. All 62 patients began the study, and hence entered the first interval, 0 - 99.9. Three patients were censored in that interval (i.e., were alive, but were on the study for less than 99.9 days at the time of analysis). Thirty-four patients died within 99.9 days of entry into the study. Hence 62-3-34 = 25 patients enter the next interval; that is, have survival times greater than 99.9 days.

(3) Number of patients exposed to the risk of dying during the interval. This is estimated by

$$r_i = n_i - \tfrac{1}{2} c_i$$

where

n_i = number of patients entering the interval

c_i = number censored in the interval (due to patients that are either lost to follow-up, or withdrawn)

It is assumed that censored observations occur randomly (from a uniform distribution) in the interval. Hence, patients who are censored are considered to be at risk for half the interval. Based on the number of patients at risk, the conditional probability of dying in the interval is calculated. This is estimated by

$$q_i = d_i / r_i$$

where d_i = the number dying in the interval. q_i is the probability that an individual will die in the interval, given that he enters the interval. Implicit in this calculation is the assumption that the risk of dying is constant over the entire interval. The conditional probability of surviving is given by $p_i = 1 - q_i$.

(4) The cumulative survival function: This is the estimate, P_i, of the cumulative proportion, surviving to the <u>beginning</u> of the ith interval, and defined as

$$P_i = p_{i-1} P_{i-1} ,$$

where $P_1 = 1$.

This estimate is based on the fact that survival to the ith interval requires that one survive to the (i-1)st. This is the usual life table estimate. Its approximate standard error, obtained from Greenwood's (1926) formula, is defined as

$$\text{s.e. } (P_i) \simeq P_i \left\{ \sum_{j=1}^{i-1} \left(q_j \Big/ r_j p_j \right) \right\}^{\tfrac{1}{2}}$$

This estimate may considerably underestimate the variance when the amount of censoring is high (Gross and Clark, 1975).

(5) The hazard function (also called the failure rate, the instantaneous death rate, or the force of mortality) is estimated at the midpoint of each interval; i.e.,

$$\lambda_i = \frac{2q_i}{h_i(1+p_i)}$$

with approximate standard error

$$\text{s.e.} \ (\lambda_i) \approx \left[\frac{\lambda_i^2}{r_i q_i} \left\{ 1 - \left[\frac{h_i \lambda_i}{2} \right]^2 \right\} \right]^{\frac{1}{2}}$$

This estimate may considerably underestimate the variance when the amount of censoring is high (Gross and Clark, 1975).

The death density function (probability of death per unit time) estimated at the midpoint of each interval i is given by

$$f_i = \frac{P_i - P_{i+1}}{h_i} = \frac{P_i q_i}{h_i}$$

where h_i is the width of the ith interval.

The approximate standard error of the estimate is

$$\text{s.e.} \ (f_i) = \left(\frac{P_i q_i}{h_i} \right) \left(\sum_{j=1}^{i-1} \frac{q_j}{r_j p_j} + \frac{p_i}{r_i q_i} \right)^{\frac{1}{2}}$$

The above two functions are alternate ways of describing survival data. These estimates are most useful for detecting patterns suggestive of parametric models that may describe the data. For example, a constant estimate of the hazard function over each interval is suggestive of an exponential distribution. Other forms of the hazard, and their inter-pretation are discussed in books such as Gross and Clark (1975).

(6) Estimates of the quantiles of the survival function. That is, the estimated times at which 75%, 50% (median survival) and 25% of the patients are still alive. To estimate median survival, for example, let $[t_i, t_{i+1})$ be the interval for which $P_i \geq \frac{1}{2}$ and $P_{i+1} < \frac{1}{2}$. Then the estimate of median survival (the 50% quantile) is given by

$$Q_{50} = (t_i - t_0) + \frac{(P_i - \frac{1}{2})}{f_i}$$

where t_0 is the time at which the first interval begins (usually zero). The approximate standard error is

$$\text{s.e.} \ (Q_{50}) \cong 1/(2f_i r_1^{\frac{1}{2}})$$

<u>Output 19.1</u> Life table analysis by P1L. Circled numbers correspond to those in the text. Results not reproduced are indicated in italics.

BMDP1L — LIFE TABLES AND SURVIVAL CURVES
HEALTH SCIENCES COMPUTING FACILITY
UNIVERSITY OF CALIFORNIA, LOS ANGELES

PROGRAM REVISED SEPTEMBER 1977
MANUAL DATE — 1977

--- Control Language read by P1L is printed and interpreted ---

NUMBER OF CASES READ.   62   (1)

LIFE TABLE AND SURVIVAL ANALYSIS

INTERVAL	ENTERED (2)	WITHDRAWN	LOST	DEAD	EXPOSED	PROPORTION DEAD (3)	PROPORTION SURVIVING	CUMULATIVE SURVIVAL (4)	HAZARD (S.E.) (5)	DENSITY (S.E.)
0.0 - 99.90	62	3	0	34	60.5	0.5620	0.4380	1.0000	0.0078	0.0056
								0.0	0.0012	0.0000
99.90 - 199.80	25	1	0	11	24.5	0.4490	0.5510	0.4380	0.0058	0.0020
								0.0638	0.0017	0.0000
199.80 - 299.70	13	1	0	4	12.5	0.3200	0.6800	0.2414	0.0038	0.0008
								0.0563	0.0019	0.0000
299.70 - 399.60	8	0	0	3	8.0	0.3750	0.6250	0.1641	0.0046	0.0006
								0.0498	0.0026	0.0000
399.60 - 499.50	5	0	0	2	5.0	0.4000	0.6000	0.1026	0.0050	0.0004
								0.0419	0.0034	0.0000
499.50 - 599.40	3	0	0	1	3.0	0.3333	0.6667	0.0615	0.0040	0.0002
								0.0337	0.0039	0.0000
599.40 - 699.30	2	0	0	0	2.0	0.0	1.0000	0.0410	0.0	0.0
								0.0280	0.0	0.0
699.30 - 799.20	2	0	0	0	2.0	0.0	1.0000	0.0410	0.0	0.0
								0.0280	0.0	0.0
799.20 - 899.10	2	0	0	0	2.0	0.0	1.0000	0.0410	0.0	0.0
								0.0280	0.0	0.0
899.10 - 999.00	2	0	0	2	2.0	1.0000	0.0	0.0410	0.0200	0.0004
								0.0280	0.0000	0.0000

(6)

QUANTILE	ESTIMATE	STANDARD ERROR
75TH	44.44	11.427
MEDIAN (50TH)	88.88	11.427
25TH	195.41	51.314

SUMMARY TABLE

TOTAL	DEAD	WITHDRAWN	LOST	PERCENT CENSORED
(7) 62	57	5		0.0806

PATTERN OF CENSORED DATA

```
     *    ***             *
  .+....+....+....+....+....+....+....+....+....+....+....+....+....+....+....+....+....+....+....+....+.
     50.0      150.      250.      350.      450.      550.      650.      750.      850.      950.
  0.00     100.      200.      300.      400.      500.      600.      700.      800.      900.      1000
```

(8) PATTERN OF TRUE RESPONSE TIMES

```
     ***** *** **** *  ** **    *  *    *  **    *            *                              **
  .+....+....+....+....+....+....+....+....+....+....+....+....+....+....+....+....+....+....+....+....+.
     50.0      150.      250.      350.      450.      550.      650.      750.      850.      950.
  0.00     100.      200.      300.      400.      500.      600.      700.      800.      900.      1000
```

(continued)

Output 19.1 *(continued)*

⑨
CUMULATIVE PROPORTION SURVIVING

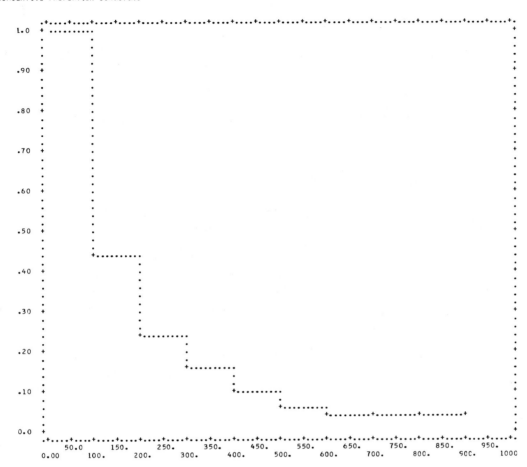

⑦   A summary of the total number of patients dying, and the number and percentage of censored observations.

⑧   Plots of the individual censoring times and times of response. These are useful for comparing censoring patterns between groups, or for examining patterns of censoring within a group. For example, a treatment with numerous early losses may indicate lack of patient acceptance of the particular therapy.

⑨   A plot of the estimated cumulative survival function. This is a step function that decreases at times corresponding to the <u>beginning</u> of each interval. The size of the plot can be specified.

The Product-limit Estimate

P1L provides a second estimate of survival using the product-limit (Kaplan-Meier) estimate which is an estimate of the cumulative survival distribution. When there is no censoring the product-limit estimate is the same as a cumulative histogram (empirical distribution function). The product-limit and life table estimates are identical when the intervals of the life table contain at most one observation each. The product-limit estimate has the advantage of giving results that are independent of the choice of intervals.

Example 19.2 illustrates the results produced by the product-limit estimate. All Control Language instructions are the same as for Example 19.1 except for the *ESTimate* paragraph.

Example 19.2

```
/PROBLEM      TITLE IS 'PRENTICE DATA'.
/INPUT        VARIABLES ARE 4.
              FORMAT IS '(4F3.0)'.
/VARIABLE     NAMES ARE SURVIVAL,STATE,TREAT,CELL.

/FORM         TIME IS SURVIVAL.
              STATUS IS STATE.
              RESPONSE IS 1.

/ESTIMATE     METHOD IS PRODUCT.

/END
```

The results of this example are presented in Output 19.2. Circled numbers below correspond to those in the output.

⑩   The N observed survival times are ordered ($t_1 \leq t_2 \ldots \leq t_N$) and printed. If names are assigned to the status codes in the *GROUP* paragraph, the appropriate name is printed for each response time; otherwise, the assumed codes are DEAD and CENSRD.

(11) The estimate of the survival curve is printed at each unique time of death. It is estimated as

$$P(t) = \prod_{t_i < t} \frac{(N-i+1-\delta_i)}{(N-i+1)}$$

where $\delta_i = \begin{cases} 1 \text{ if } t_i \text{ represents a death (true response)} \\ 0 \text{ if } t_i \text{ is a censored observation.} \end{cases}$

Output 19.2   Product-limit estimate by P1L

NUMBER OF CASES READ.   62

PRODUCT-LIMIT SURVIVAL ANALYSIS

CASE LABEL	CASE NUMBER	TIME (10)	STATUS	CUMULATIVE SURVIVAL (11)	STANDARD ERROR
8	1	DEAD			
16	1	DEAD	0.9677	0.0224	
43	3	DEAD	0.9516	0.0273	
56	7	DEAD	0.9355	0.0312	
27	8	DEAD			
36	8	DEAD			
53	8	DEAD	0.8871	0.0402	
33	10	DEAD	0.8710	0.0426	
24	11	DEAD	0.8548	0.0447	
41	12	DEAD	0.8387	0.0467	
20	15	DEAD	0.8226	0.0485	
46	18	DEAD	0.8065	0.0502	
60	19	DEAD	0.7903	0.0517	
45	24	DEAD	0.7742	0.0531	
12	25	DEAD	0.7581	0.0544	
25	25	CENSRD			
17	30	DEAD	0.7416	0.0556	
48	31	DEAD	0.7251	0.0568	
11	33	DEAD	0.7086	0.0578	
38	35	DEAD	0.6921	0.0588	
54	36	DEAD	0.6757	0.0597	
28	42	DEAD	0.6592	0.0604	
18	44	DEAD	0.6427	0.0611	
61	45	DEAD	0.6262	0.0618	
55	48	DEAD	0.6097	0.0623	
49	51	DEAD	0.5933	0.0627	
51	52	DEAD	0.5768	0.0631	
1	72	DEAD	0.5603	0.0634	
52	73	DEAD	0.5438	0.0637	
62	80	DEAD	0.5273	0.0638	
32	82	DEAD	0.5109	0.0639	
47	83	CENSRD			
59	84	DEAD	0.4938	0.0640	
21	87	CENSRD			
50	90	DEAD	0.4762	0.0641	
37	92	DEAD	0.4586	0.0641	
44	95	DEAD	0.4409	0.0641	
29	100	CENSRD			
31	110	DEAD	0.4226	0.0640	
7	111	DEAD	0.4042	0.0638	
22	112	DEAD	0.3858	0.0635	
39	117	DEAD	0.3674	0.0630	
34	118	DEAD	0.3491	0.0625	
35	126	DEAD	0.3307	0.0619	
40	132	DEAD	0.3123	0.0611	
57	140	DEAD	0.2939	0.0602	
26	144	DEAD	0.2756	0.0592	
42	162	DEAD	0.2572	0.0580	
58	186	DEAD	0.2388	0.0567	

CASE LABEL	CASE NUMBER	TIME	STATUS	CUMULATIVE SURVIVAL	STANDARD ERROR
15	201	DEAD	0.2205	0.0552	
3	228	DEAD	0.2021	0.0536	
4	231	CENSRD			
5	242	DEAD	0.1819	0.0519	
19	283	DEAD	0.1617	0.0499	
30	314	DEAD	0.1415	0.0476	
13	357	DEAD	0.1213	0.0449	
10	389	DEAD	0.1010	0.0417	
2	411	DEAD	0.0808	0.0379	
14	467	DEAD	0.0606	0.0334	
9	587	DEAD	0.0404	0.0277	
6	991	DEAD	0.0202	0.0199	
23	999	DEAD	0.0	0.0	

MEAN SURVIVAL TIME = 158.00   S.E. = 30.453

(12) | QUANTILE | ESTIMATE |
|---|---|
| 75TH | 30.00 |
| MEDIAN (50TH) | 84.00 |
| 25TH | 186.00 |

Thus, P(t) is a step function that changes at each distinct time of death. If tied observations occur, deaths are assumed to occur slightly before censored observations.

$$\text{s.e. } (P(t)) \; \tilde{=} \; [P(t)] \left\{ \sum_{t_i < t} \frac{\delta_i}{(N-i)(N-i+1)} \right\}^{\frac{1}{2}}$$

(12) Estimates of the mean and quantiles of the distribution.

The estimated mean is

$$\hat{\mu} = \sum_{i=1}^{N} P(t_{i-1})(t_i - t_{i-1})$$

where the summation is over all times of death. When the patient who is longest on the study is a censored observation, $\hat{\mu}$ underestimates the true mean, and a warning is printed in the output. An estimate of the variance of $\hat{\mu}$ is also printed. See Appendix A.20 for its formula. Formulas for the quantiles of the distribution are also given in Appendix A.20.

● OPTIONAL RESULTS AND INPUT

In addition to the results and input forms given in Examples 19.1 and 19.2, the input data may be structured in several forms and various output options specified.

You may

- input data containing dates or times   p. 762

- input data arranged as a life table   p. 765

- plot survival curves, log-survival curves, hazard functions and density functions   p. 755

- select patient groups based on the value of a prognostic factor or treatment   p. 758

- test equality of survival curves between these groups   p. 760

You may also specify

- the time units used in the analysis   p. 761

- multiple response codes   p. 762

- which censored status codes represent losses   p. 762

- the width or number of intervals used in the life table   p. 753

- prognostic variables whose values are printed with the product-limit estimate   p. 754

● THE *ESTimate* PARAGRAPH

The *ESTimate* paragraph is used in P1L to specify the method of the analysis that is desired, and the statistics and plots to be printed. The *ESTimate* paragraph may be repeated for additional analyses of the same data.

Examples 19.1 and 19.2 demonstrate the Control Language instructions necessary to compute the survival curves using two methods: the actuarial life table and the product-limit estimate. These are specified by the METHOD parameter.

```
ESTimate
   METHOD= (one only) LIFE,PROD.                    {LIFE/prev.}

      When PROD is specified, the survival distribution is estimated
      by the product-limit estimate. Otherwise, the life table method is
      used.
```

● PRINTING THE PRODUCT-LIMIT ESTIMATES

The product-limit estimate is calculated at individual survival times, whereas the life table utilizes the data grouped into intervals. When the number of observations is large, the output from the product-limit estimate may be excessive. You may omit printing either estimate by stating

NO PRINT.

This is especially useful if you are mainly interested in obtaining plots (p. 755) or test statistics (p. 760).

```
ESTimate
   PRINT.                    {PRINT/prev.}

      The survival distribution estimate is printed unless NO PRINT
      is stated.
```

● INTERVALS FOR THE LIFE TABLE

Analysis by the life table technique (METHOD=LIFE) groups observations into intervals of time. When no further specifications are made, the range of observed survival times is divided into 10 equally spaced intervals. A more suitable choice of interval may be obtained in one of three ways: you may specify the number of intervals desired by the PERIOD statement -- this divides the data into the requested number of equally spaced intervals; you may choose to define the width of the interval; or you may specify exact intervals, particularly if you wish to have them of unequal width. The use of too few intervals is discouraged (<10), since the larger the interval the less likely it is that the force of mortality is the same throughout the interval.

```
ESTimate
                    PERIOD=#.                    {PERIOD=10/prev.}
      (one only)    WIDTH=#.
                    CUTPOINT=#₁,#₂,···.
```

When the METHOD is LIFE, specify one of the following:

PERIOD=#.

Number of intervals desired; the range of observation is divided into intervals of equal width.

WIDTH=#.

The range of observations are divided into as many intervals as are needed with a given width.

CUTPOINTS= $\#_1,\#_2,$···.

Cutpoints for dividing the range for time into intervals. Each cutpoint represents the upper limit of a time interval. The last interval contains all times greater than the last cutpoint.

When METHOD is PROD, the above are ignored.

● VARIABLES PRINTED WITH THE PRODUCT-LIMIT ESTIMATE

It is often desirable to associate individual observations with values of possible prognostic variables. For example, you may want to know whether all early deaths were among elderly patients or among patients with a particular cell type. Since the product-limit estimate prints a separate line for each case, you can request that the values of certain variables also be printed. We illustrate this capability in Example 19.3.

Example 19.3

```
      /PROBLEM      TITLE IS 'PRENTICE DATA'.
      /INPUT        VARIABLES ARE 4.
                    FORMAT IS '(4F3.0)'.
      /VARIABLE     NAMES ARE SURVIVAL,STATE,TREAT,CELL.

      /FORM         TIME IS SURVIVAL.
                    STATUS IS STATE.
                    RESPONSE IS 1.

      /ESTIMATE     METHOD IS PRODUCT.
                    VARIABLE IS CELL.

      /GROUP        CODES(4) ARE        1,       2.
                    NAMES(4) ARE SQUAMOUS, ADENOCA.

      /END
```

The results of this example are shown in Output 19.3. The last column lists the values of CELLTYPE for individual cases. An examination of these variables may provide valuable information about their possible relationship to survival time.

ESTimate
    VARIABLE= v_1, v_2, v_3, v_3.   {none}

    Names or subscripts of variables to be printed when the product-limit estimate is specified. A maximum of 4 variables may be printed. If CODEs (or CUTPOINTs) and NAMEs are specified in a *GROUP* paragraph (Section 5.4) for one or more of these variables, the specified NAMEs are printed in the output and not the values of the variable(s).

● PLOTs

    Plots of the survival curve and associated functions are provided by P1L. For either method of estimation, you may obtain plots of the survival curve, log-survival, or the cumulative hazard. The latter two are especially useful for suggesting possible parametric models for the survival function. Other functions frequently used to suggest parametric models are the hazard and the death density, which can be plotted when the life table estimate is used.

<u>Output 19.3</u> Printing an additional variable with the product-limit estimate

PRODUCT-LIMIT SURVIVAL ANALYSIS

CASE LABEL	CASE NUMBER	TIME	STATUS	CUMULATIVE SURVIVAL	STANDARD ERROR	CELL
	8	1	DEAD			SQUAMOUS
	16	1	DEAD	0.9677	0.0224	SQUAMOUS
	43	3	DEAD	0.9516	0.0273	ADENOCA
	56	7	DEAD	0.9355	0.0312	ADENOCA
	27	8	DEAD			SQUAMOUS
	36	8	DEAD			ADENOCA
	53	8	DEAD	0.8871	0.04C2	ADENOCA
	33	10	DEAD	0.8710	0.0426	SQUAMOUS

--- similar results for the remaining cases ---

ESTimate
>   PLOT= *(one or more)* SURV,LOG,CUM,HAZ,DEN.   { SURV /prev.}

>   Plot one or more of the following:

>   SURV -- the cumulative survival function P(t) estimated by either the life table or product-limit method

>   LOG -- the natural logarithm of the survival function $\ln$ P(t)

>   CUM -- the cumulative hazard function ($-\ln$ P(t))

>   HAZ -- the hazard function if METHOD=*LIFE*

>   DEN -- the death density function if METHOD=*LIFE*

>   If any plots are specified, only those specified are printed.

We use the data from Table 19.1 to illustrate the output obtained from requesting plots.

Example 19.4

```
/PROBLEM      TITLE IS 'PRENTICE DATA'.
/INPUT        VARIABLES ARE 4.
              FORMAT IS '(4F3.0)'.
/VARIABLE     NAMES ARE SURVIVAL,STATE,TREAT,CELL.

/FORM         TIME IS SURVIVAL.
              STATUS IS STATE.
              RESPONSE IS 1.

/ESTIMATE     PLOTS ARE HAZ,CUM.

/END
```

Since no METHOD is specified in the *ESTimate* paragraph, the life table analysis is performed. Output 19.4 presents the plots requested.

The hazard function is often used to detect possible parametric descriptions of the data. Because the hazard rate often appears irregular, the cumulative hazard, $-\ln$ P(t), is often preferred. A discussion of the interpretation of such plots may be found, for example, in Gross and Clark (1975) and Nelson (1972). When a parametric model seems appropriate for your data, you can also analyze the data using P3R or PAR (Chapter 14).

You can specify the size of the plots to be printed.

ESTimate
>   SIZE=$\#_1$,$\#_2$.   {100,50/prev.}

> $\#_1$ is the number of characters (width) in the horizontal axis and
> $\#_2$ is the number of lines (height) in the vertical axis.

Output 19.4 Plots printed by P1L

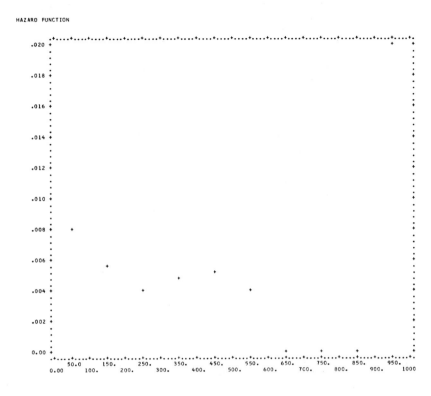

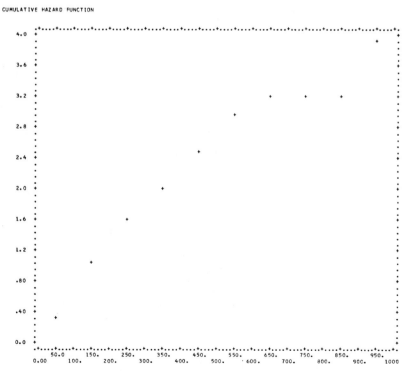

● GROUPS

    Estimates of the survival curve may be obtained separately for different groups of patients. For example, in the Prentice data, one might wish to estimate survival separately by treatment, or by cell type.

    Example 19.5 illustrates the analysis obtained when the patients are divided by treatment group.

Example 19.5

```
/PROBLEM        TITLE IS 'PRENTICE DATA'.
/INPUT          VARIABLES ARE 4.
                FORMAT IS '(4F3.0)'.
/VARIABLE       NAMES ARE SURVIVAL,STATE,TREAT,CELL.

/FORM           TIME IS SURVIVAL.
                STATUS IS STATE.
                RESPONSE IS 1.

/ESTIMATE       METHOD IS PRODUCT.
                GROUP IS TREAT.

/GROUP          CODES(3) ARE    0,        1.
                NAMES(3) ARE TEST, STANDARD.

/END
```

    The results of this example are presented in Output 19.5. For each level of the grouping variable a separate estimate of the survival distribution is printed.

    The summary table presents individual entries for each group as well as for overall patient information. Plots of censoring times and death times are given for individual groups. This is particularly useful for monitoring the patterns of censoring between groups.

    The plot for each category of the grouping variable appears in the same plot frame. The character used for plotting is the first letter of the code name (if specified) in the *GROUP* paragraph. Otherwise, the letters A,B,C,... are used.

ESTimate
  GROUPING= v.   {no grouping}

    Name or subscript of variable to be used to classify cases into groups. A separate analysis is performed for each level of the grouping variable. If GROUPING is not specified or is set to zero, all data are in one group. If the GROUPING variable takes on more than 10 distinct values, you must specify CODEs or CUTPOINTS for it in a *GROUP* paragraph.

Output 19.5 Product-limit analysis for two groups

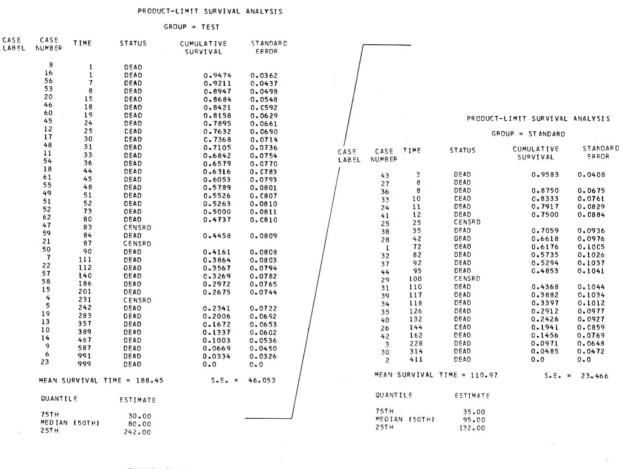

PRODUCT-LIMIT SURVIVAL ANALYSIS

GROUP = TEST

CASE LABEL	CASE NUMBER	TIME	STATUS	CUMULATIVE SURVIVAL	STANDARD ERROR
8	1	DEAD			
16	1	DEAD	0.9474	0.0362
56	7	DEAD	0.9211	0.0437
53	8	DEAD	0.8947	0.0498
20	15	DEAD	0.8684	0.0548
46	18	DEAD	0.8421	0.0592
60	19	DEAD	0.8158	0.0629
45	24	DEAD	0.7895	0.0661
12	25	DEAD	0.7632	0.0690
17	30	DEAD	0.7368	0.0714
48	31	DEAD	0.7105	0.0736
11	33	DEAD	0.6842	0.0754
54	36	DEAD	0.6579	0.0770
18	44	DEAD	0.6316	0.0783
61	45	DEAD	0.6053	0.0793
55	48	DEAD	0.5789	0.0801
49	51	DEAD	0.5526	0.0807
51	52	DEAD	0.5263	0.0810
52	73	DEAD	0.5000	0.0811
62	80	DEAD	0.4737	0.0810
47	83	CENSRD		
59	84	DEAD	0.4458	0.0809
21	87	CENSRD		
50	90	DEAD	0.4161	0.0808
7	111	DEAD	0.3864	0.0803
22	112	DEAD	0.3567	0.0794
57	140	DEAD	0.3269	0.0782
58	186	DEAD	0.2972	0.0765
15	201	DEAD	0.2675	0.0744
4	231	CENSRD		
5	242	DEAD	0.2341	0.0722
19	283	DEAD	0.2006	0.0692
13	357	DEAD	0.1672	0.0653
10	389	DEAD	0.1337	0.0602
14	467	DEAD	0.1003	0.0536
9	587	DEAD	0.0669	0.0450
6	991	DEAD	0.0334	0.0326
23	999	DEAD	0.0	0.0

MEAN SURVIVAL TIME = 188.45   S.E. = 46.053

QUANTILE	ESTIMATE
75TH	30.00
MEDIAN (50TH)	80.00
25TH	242.00

PRODUCT-LIMIT SURVIVAL ANALYSIS

GROUP = STANDARD

CASE LABEL	CASE NUMBER	TIME	STATUS	CUMULATIVE SURVIVAL	STANDARD ERROR
43	3	DEAD	0.9583	0.0408
27	8	DEAD		
36	8	DEAD	0.8750	0.0675
33	10	DEAD	0.8333	0.0761
24	11	DEAD	0.7917	0.0829
41	12	DEAD	0.7500	0.0884
25	25	CENSRD		
38	35	DEAD	0.7059	0.0936
28	42	DEAD	0.6618	0.0976
1	72	DEAD	0.6176	0.1005
32	82	DEAD	0.5735	0.1026
37	92	DEAD	0.5294	0.1037
44	95	DEAD	0.4853	0.1041
29	100	CENSRD		
31	110	DEAD	0.4368	0.1044
39	117	DEAD	0.3882	0.1034
34	118	DEAD	0.3397	0.1012
35	126	DEAD	0.2912	0.0977
40	132	DEAD	0.2426	0.0927
26	144	DEAD	0.1941	0.0859
42	162	DEAD	0.1456	0.0769
3	228	DEAD	0.0971	0.0648
30	314	DEAD	0.0485	0.0472
2	411	DEAD	0.0	0.0

MEAN SURVIVAL TIME = 110.97   S.E. = 23.466

QUANTILE	ESTIMATE
75TH	35.00
MEDIAN (50TH)	95.00
25TH	132.00

SUMMARY TABLE

	TOTAL	DEAD	WITHDRAWN	LOST	PERCENT CENSORED
TEST	38	35	3		0.0789
STANDARD	24	22	2		0.0833
TOTALS	62	57	5		

PATTERN OF CENSORED DATA

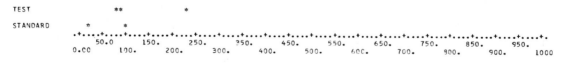

PATTERN OF TRUE RESPONSE TIMES

● TEST STATISTICS

You may wish to test whether the survival curves obtained for the group defined by the GROUPING variable are equal. Two such statistics appropriate for censored data can be requested; they are analogues of nonparametric rank tests.

The first test was proposed by Mantel (1966). When there are no censored observations it is essentially an exponential scores test (or Savage statistic); that is, it uses scores based on the exponential distribution. When there are censored data, the statistic assumes that the underlying distributions are the same for the censored observations in the groups being tested.

The second statistic is analogous to the Kruskal-Wallis (or generalized Wilcoxon) test. The statistic used in P1L was proposed by Breslow (1970) for the case in which censoring patterns may differ in the comparison groups. The Breslow test tends to give greater weight to early times to response than does the Mantel test.

We use the data from Table 19.1 to illustrate the use of these statistics.

Example 19.6

```
/PROBLEM      TITLE IS 'PRENTICE DATA'.
/INPUT        VARIABLES ARE 4.
              FORMAT IS '(4F3.0)'.
/VARIABLE     NAMES ARE SURVIVAL,STATE,TREAT,CELL.

/FORM         TIME IS SURVIVAL.
              STATUS IS STATE.
              RESPONSE IS 1.

/ESTIMATE     METHOD IS PRODUCT.
              GROUP IS TREAT.
              STATISTICS ARE BRESLOW,MANTEL.

/GROUP        CODES(3) ARE    0,       1.
              NAMES(3) ARE TEST, STANDARD.

/END
```

The results are given in Output 19.6. The individual survival times are used in the calculation of these statistics (see Appendix A.20).

Both statistics are asymptotically distributed as chi-square. Because the effective sample size is related to the actual number of deaths, a high degree of censoring may affect the distribution of the tests. For discussions of small sample properties and use of the statistics, see Tarone and Ware (1977), or Lee, Desu and Gehan (1975).

ESTimate
  STATISTICS= *(one or both)* MANTEL,BRESLOW.   {none/prev.}

  MANTEL specifies that the generalized Savage (Mantel-Cox) test is
  computed to test the equality of survival curves defined by GROUP.
  BRESLOW specifies that Breslow's version of the generalized
  Wilcoxon statistic be computed.

● The *FORM* Paragraph

The *FORM* paragraph is required by P1L to describe the structure of the survival time variables. The form of such data may occur in many ways. Commonly used structures may be directly input to the program. Data occurring in other forms may be transformed (Chapter 6) to one of these structures.

Time

You may wish to specify the unit of time that you would like printed in the output. Or, if your data are in the form of dates (see p. 762), you may wish to choose the appropriate scale for the calculation of the survival curve.

```
FORM
    UNIT= (one only) DAY,WEEK,MONTH,YEAR.              {MONTH}

        or UNIT=c.

    Unit for labelling the time scale in the output.  If DAY, WEEK,
    MONTH, or YEAR are specified, and the data are in the form of
    dates, the specified UNIT will be used in the calculations.
```

Time-status Input

In this form of input, which is illustrated in Examples 19.1 - 19.6, one variable contains the time that the subject is observed (to the response or until he is withdrawn or lost to follow-up), while a second variable indicates whether a response is observed or censoring is assumed. This <u>status</u> variable may contain numerous codes, one (or more) to indicate the occurrence of a response and up to 9 types of censored observations. Censoring commonly is due to loss to follow-up (e.g., the patient has moved or dropped out of the study) and withdrawals (the patient is still alive at the end of the study or at the time of analysis). Separate codes may exist for different causes of death. These may be treated as responses (deaths), or as censored observations. All censored values are treated identically in the analysis.

Output 19.6 Comparison of groups by P1L. Only the test statistics are shown.

TEST STATISTICS

	STATISTIC	D.F.	P-VALUE
GENERALIZED WILCOXON (BRESLOW)	0.009	1	0.9229
GENERALIZED SAVAGE (MANTEL-COX)	0.770	1	0.3803

All eligible codes (i.e., not equal to the missing value code or out
of range) not listed in RESPONSE are assumed to be censored.

If multiple codes are specified in RESPONSE, the names DEAD1,DEAD2,...
appear in the summary tables, and in the output of the product-limit estimate.
Multiple censored observations are named CENSRD1,CENSRD2,..., where CENSRD1
corresponds to the smallest code encountered in the data which is not specified
in RESPONSE, CENSRD2 is the second, etc. The correspondence between names
and codes is given in the summary table. If NAMEs are given to the CODEs of
the STATUS variable in the GROUP paragraph, the names are used to label the
results.

You may also identify values of the codes representing censored observations that are losses. This is frequently useful in understanding the data,
but in no way influences the analysis.

All eligible codes not listed in either RESPONSE or LOSS are censored.
When names are not specified for the values of STATUS in the GROUP paragraph, default names for values in LOSS are LOST1,LOST2,... .

Date-status Input

This form of input is similar to the time-status input. Instead of a
time-on-study variable, the data are presented as two sets of dates; one set
providing the month, day and year of ENTRY onto the study, the second set
providing the date of TERMINATION. P1L automatically converts these two
sets of dates into a time-on-study variable, which is assumed to be in
months, unless otherwise specified.

For example, if your date of ENTRY is recorded in variables 4 (month), 5 (day) and 6 (year) and date of TERMINATION is recorded in variables 7 (month), 8 (day) and 9 (year), you would specify

        ENTRY=4,5,6.
        TERMINATION=7,8,9.

in the *FORM* paragraph. P1L can also analyze the data if you record only two date variables, such as month and year. For example, if your date of ENTRY is recorded in variables 5 (month) and 6 (year), you would specify

        ENTRY=5,(3)6.

and TERMINATION would be similarly specified.

You may want to use this type of analysis when the response is recorded in minutes (or seconds). To do so, you would specify only the first variable for ENTRY and the first for TERMINATION. You would then specify UNIT=MINUTE. Then all the statistics will be computed correctly and time differences in the output will be labelled MINUTE.

FORM
   ENTRY=v_1,v_2,v_3.   {none}

   Names or subscripts of the variables representing month, day and year of patient entry into the study. Note the <u>order is required</u>. You can specify one, two or three variables; for example, month and year is specified as ENTRY=v_1,(3)v_3.

   TERMINATION=v_1,v_2,v_3.   {none}

   Names or subscripts of variables representing month, day and year of termination. Note the <u>order is required</u>.

STATUS, RESPONSE and LOSS specifications are as in the time-status input form. Note that if both the year of entry and termination are in the 1900's, only the last two digits need be present (e.g., 77 instead of 1977). If one date is earlier than 1900, both years must be given in their entirety.

Artificial dates for the survival times in Table 19.1 are presented in Table 19.2. We illustrate the input of these data to P1L in Example 19.7.

Table 19.2 Artificial dates giving rise to the survival times in Table 19.1

Month	Day	Year	MonthT	DayT	YearT	State		Month	Day	Year	MonthT	DayT	YearT	State
7	15	76	7	18	76	1		1	1	72	4	5	72	1
6	1	75	6	9	75	1		12	1	73	3	11	74	0
12	10	75	12	18	75	1		12	1	73	3	21	74	1
1	1	74	1	11	74	1		12	1	73	3	28	74	1
6	1	75	6	12	75	1		12	1	73	3	29	74	1
4	3	75	4	15	75	1		4	15	75	8	19	75	1
5	1	74	5	26	74	0		4	15	75	8	25	75	1
10	1	75	11	5	75	1		3	1	74	7	23	74	1
1	1	76	2	12	76	1		3	1	74	8	10	74	1
7	1	73	9	11	73	1		1	1	72	8	16	72	1
7	1	73	9	21	73	1		9	15	73	7	26	74	1
1	1	72	4	2	72	1		6	1	75	7	16	76	1

(continued)

Key: Date of entry is recorded as the first three variables. Date of termination is recorded as variables 4 to 6. The seventh variable is state (0 censored, 1 dead). The data are recorded in columns 3-4, 7-8, 11-12, etc.

Example 19.7

```
/PROBLEM      TITLE IS 'STANDARD TREATED - PRENTICE DATA'.
/INPUT        VARIABLES ARE 7.
              FORMAT IS '(7F4.0)'.
/VARIABLE     NAMES ARE ENTMONTH,ENTDAY,ENTYEAR,
                 TERMONTH,TERDAY,TERYEAR,STATE.

/ESTIMATE     METHOD IS PRODUCT.

/FORM         ENTRY       IS ENTMONTH,ENTDAY,ENTYEAR.
              TERMINATION IS TERMONTH,TERDAY,TERYEAR.
              STATUS IS STATE.
              RESPONSE IS 1.
              UNIT IS DAY.

/END
```

Control Language instructions

7	15	76	7	18	76	1		1	1	72	4	5	72	1
6	1	75	6	9	75	1		12	1	73	3	11	74	0
12	10	75	12	18	75	1		12	1	73	3	21	74	1
1	1	74	1	11	74	1		12	1	73	3	28	74	1
6	1	75	6	12	75	1		12	1	73	3	29	74	1
4	3	75	4	15	75	1		4	15	75	8	19	75	1
5	1	74	5	26	74	0		4	15	75	8	25	75	1
10	1	75	11	5	75	1		3	1	74	7	23	74	1
1	1	76	2	12	76	1		3	1	74	8	10	74	1
7	1	73	9	11	73	1		1	1	72	8	16	72	1
7	1	73	9	21	73	1		9	15	73	7	26	74	1
1	1	72	4	2	72	1		6	1	75	7	16	76	1

data

The results from this example (Output 19.7) are identical to the results obtained for the standard group in Output 19.5.

Specifying the Termination Date of the Study

Frequently, TERMINATION is only present when a patient dies or is lost to follow-up, and no date is punched for a patient still alive at the end of the study or the time of analysis. You may specify a cut-off, or analysis date which will be treated as the date of censoring for patients still on-study. The appropriate status code for those individuals will be generated by P1L.

FORM
    CENSOR=#$_1$,#$_2$,#$_3$.   {none}

   Numbers indicating the date (month, day and year) when the study terminates or the date for the analysis. This is used only with date-status input and is necessary only when there is no date of TERMINATION for some of the censored observations.

Life Table Input

Survival data are frequently grouped for presentation in reports. Such grouped data may be input to P1L, but only the life table analysis will be computed. Suppose, for example, that the data in Table 19.1 had been summarized as in Table 19.3. Each case represents one line of the life table from

Output 19.7 An analysis by P1L using the artificial dates in Table 19.2

```
                          PRODUCT-LIMIT SURVIVAL ANALYSIS

                              GROUP = STANDARD
  CASE      CASE
  LABEL   NUMBER      TIME      STATUS      CUMULATIVE   STANDARD
                                            SURVIVAL     ERROR

            43          3        DEAD        0.9583       0.0408
            27          8        DEAD
            36          8        DEAD        0.8750       0.0675
            33         10        DEAD        0.8333       0.0761
            24         11        DEAD        0.7917       0.0829
            41         12        DEAD        0.7500       0.0884
            25         25        CENSRD
            38         35        DEAD        0.7059       0.0936
            28         42        DEAD        0.6618       0.0976
             1         72        DEAD        0.6176       0.1005
            32         82        DEAD        0.5735       0.1026
            37         92        DEAD        0.5294       0.1037
            44         95        DEAD        0.4853       0.1041
            29        100        CENSRD
            31        110        DEAD        0.4368       0.1044
            39        117        DEAD        0.3882       0.1034
            34        118        DEAD        0.3397       0.1012
            35        126        DEAD        0.2912       0.0977
            40        132        DEAD        0.2426       0.0927
            26        144        DEAD        0.1941       0.0859
            42        162        DEAD        0.1456       0.0769
             3        228        DEAD        0.0971       0.0648
            20        314        DEAD        0.0485       0.0472
             2        411        DEAD        0.0          0.0

         MEAN SURVIVAL TIME = 110.97          S.E. =   23.466

            QUANTILE          ESTIMATE

            75TH               35.00
            MEDIAN (50TH)      95.00
            25TH              132.00
```

Output 19.1; that is, each case summarizes survival experience for a single interval. The first variable represents the number of individuals entering the interval, the second the number of losses, the third the number of withdrawals, and the final variable the number of deaths. The input of these data to P1L is illustrated in Example 19.8.

Table 19.3   Life table from Output 19.1

ENTER	LOST	WITHDRAWN	DEAD
62	3	0	34
25	1	C	11
13	1	0	4
8	0	0	3
5	0	0	2
3	0	C	1
2	0	0	0
2	0	0	0
2	0	0	0
2	0	0	2

Key: ENTER   -- number entering interval
      LOST   -- number lost to follow-up during interval
      WITHDRAWN -- number withdrawn during interval
      DEAD   -- number dying during interval

The data are recorded in columns 3-4, 8, 12, and 15-16.

Example 19.8

```
/PROB          TITLE IS 'PRENTICE,DATA'.
/INPUT         VARIABLES ARE 4.
               FORMAT IS '(4F4.0)'.
/VARIABLE      NAMES ARE ENTER,LOST,WITHDRAW,DEAD.

/FORM          NENTER IS ENTER.
               NLOST  IS LOST.
               NWITH  IS WITHDRAW.
               NDEAD  IS DEAD.

/END
   62    3    0   34
   25    1    C   11
   13    1    0    4
    8    0    0    3
    5    0    0    2
    3    0    C    1
    2    0    0    0
    2    0    0    0
    2    0    0    0
    2    0    0    2
```

Control Language instructions

data

The *FORM* paragraph specifies which variables contain the number of patients entering an interval and the numbers lost, withdrawn, and dying during the interval. For these data NWITH could have been omitted since the variable contains only zeros. If NENTER is omitted, P1L assumes that the initial number of individuals in the study is the total number of patients in variables NDEAD, NLOST and NWITH.

FORM

 NENTER=v.   {sum of NDEAD + NLOST + NWITH}

  Name or subscript of variable that contains the number of patients
  who entered each interval.

 NDEAD=v.   {none}

  Name or subscript of variable that contains the number of patients
  who died in each interval.

 NLOST=v.   {none}

  Name or subscript of variable that contains the number of patients
  who were lost in each interval.

 NWITH=v.   {none}

  Name or subscript of variable that contains the number of patients
  who were withdrawn in each interval.

The results from Example 19.8 (Output 19.8) are identical to those in Output 19.1 with one exception. In Example 19.8 the intervals are labelled 0-1, 1-2, etc. If you have a variable that contains the lower limit for each interval, it may also be input.

Output 19.8 Life tables analysis by P1L beginning from data input as a life table

LIFE TABLE AND SURVIVAL ANALYSIS

INTERVAL	ENTERED	WITHDRAWN	LOST	DEAD	EXPOSED	PROP DEAD	PROP SURV	CUM SURV (S.E.)	HAZARD (S.E.)	CUM HAZARD	DENSITY (S.E.)
0.0 - 1.0	62	3	0	34	60.5	0.5620	0.4380	1.0000 0.0	0.0078 0.0012	0.3299	0.0056 0.0000
1.0 - 2.0	25	1	0	11	24.5	0.4490	0.5510	0.4380 0.0638	0.0058 0.0017	1.0797	0.0020 0.0000
2.0 - 3.0	13	1	0	4	12.5	0.3200	0.6800	0.2414 0.0563	0.0038 0.0019	1.5958	0.0008 0.0000
3.0 - 4.0	8	0	0	3	8.0	0.3750	0.6250	0.1641 0.0498	0.0046 0.0026	2.0148	0.0006 0.0000
4.0 - 5.0	5	0	0	2	5.0	0.4000	0.6000	0.1026 0.0419	0.0050 0.0034	2.5003	0.0004 0.0000
5.0 - 6.0	3	0	0	1	3.0	0.3333	0.6667	0.0615 0.0337	0.0040 0.0039	2.9703	0.0002 0.0000
6.0 - 7.0	2	0	0	0	2.0	0.0	1.0000	0.0410 0.0280	0.0 0.0	3.1703	0.0 0.0
7.0 - 8.0	2	0	0	0	2.0	0.0	1.0000	0.0410 0.0280	0.0 0.0	3.1703	0.0 0.0
8.0 - 9.0	2	0	0	0	2.0	0.0	1.0000	0.0410 0.0280	0.0 0.0	3.1703	0.0 0.0
9.0 - 10.0	2	0	0	2	2.0	1.0000	0.0	0.0410 0.0280	0.0200 0.0000	3.8866	0.0004 0.0000

FORM
   INTERVAL=v.   {see below}

     Name or subscript of variable that contains the lower limit for
     each interval. If INTERVAL is not stated, the integers 0,1,2,...
     are assigned.

     Survival-type data may occur in many other forms. You can use the
TRANsformation paragraph or FORTRAN transformations via the BIMEDT
procedure to put the data into one of the above forms for analysis
(Chapter 6).

● SIZE OF PROBLEM

     P1L can obtain a life table estimate for as many as 2500 cases when there
are 20 intervals in the life table and 10 groups are being simultaneously
analyzed. It can obtain the product-limit estimate for as many as 1850 cases
if there is no censoring and up to 3000 cases if there is extensive censoring.
Appendix B describes how to increase the capacity of the program.

● COMPUTATIONAL METHOD

     All computations are performed in single precision. The formulas for the
standard errors and the test statistics are in Appendix A.20.

ACKNOWLEDGEMENT

    *P1L was designed by Jacqueline Benedetti and Karen Yuen with major
contributions from Virginia Clark, Robert Elashoff and Ray Mickey. It was
programmed by Lawrence Young. It supersedes BMD01S and BMD11S.*

Control Language on this page is common to all programs. This is followed by the Control Language specific to

P1L -- Life Tables and Survival Functions   p. 770

Paragraph STATEMENT[1] {Preassigned value[2]}		Definition, restriction	See pages:
/PROBlem		Required each problem	74
TITLE='c'.	{blank}	Problem title, $\leq$ 160 char.	74
/INPut		Required first problem. Either VARIABLE and FORMAT, or UNIT and CODE required.	75
VARIABLE=#.	{none/prev.}	No. of variables in input data	75
FORMAT='c'.	{none/prev.}	Format of input data, $\leq$ 800 char.	76
CASE=#.	{end-of-file/prev.}	No. of cases in data	76-77
UNIT=#.	{5(cards)/prev.}	Input unit if data are not on cards; not 1, 2, 6	77
REWIND.	{REWIND/prev.}	Rewind input unit	77
CODE=c.	{none}	Code to identify BMDP File	132
CONTENT=c.	{DATA}	Data or matrix in BMDP File	132
LABEL=c.	{none}	Label of BMDP File, $\leq$ 40 char.	132
/VARiable		Optional. For input from a BMDP File, items in this paragraph may be previously set, see Chapter 7.	79
NAME=$c_1,c_2,\cdots$.	{X(subscript)/prev.}	Variable names, one per variable	79-80
MAXIMUM=$\#_1,\#_2,\cdots$.	{none/prev.}	Upper limits, one per variable	80
MINIMUM=$\#_1,\#_2,\cdots$.	{none/prev.}	Lower limits, one per variable	80
BLANK= (one only) ZERO, MISSING.	{ZERO/prev.}	Blanks treated as zeros or as missing value codes	81
MISSING=$\#_1,\#_2,\cdots$.	{none/prev.}	Missing value codes, one per variable	81
USE=$v_1,v_2,\cdots$.	{all variables}	Variables used in the analysis	82
LABEL=v_1,v_2.	{none/prev.}	Variable(s) used to label cases, read under A-format, one or two	83
ADD=#.	{0/prev.}	No. of variables added through transformation	99
BEFORE. or AFTER.	{BEFORE/prev.}	Data checked for limits before or after transformation	100
/TRANsform		Optional, Control Language transformations and case selection	97-105
/SAVE		Optional, required to create BMDP File	125
CODE=c.	{none}	Code to identify BMDP File, required	125-126
LABEL='c'.	{blank}	Label for BMDP File, $\leq$ 40 char.	125-126
UNIT=#.	{none}	Unit on which BMDP File is written; not 1, 2, 5 or 6	126-127
NEW.	{not new}	NEW if this is first BMDP File written in the system file	126-127

Key: # number   v variable name or subscript
     'c' title, label or format   c name not exceeding 8 char., apostrophes may be required (p. 59)

[1] In BMDP programs dated before August 1977, the minimum required abbreviations are *INPUT* (not *INP*), VARIAB (not VAR), FORMAT (not FORM), CONTENT (not CONT), *VARIAB* (not *VAR*), BEFORET (not BEF), AFTERT (not AFT), *TRANSF* (not *TRAN*). If dated before February 1976, BLANK=ZERO and cannot be changed.

[2] "/prev." means that any assignment remains the same as that specified in the previous problem or subproblem until changed. Otherwise, the assignment returns to its preassigned value each time a new problem begins or the paragraph is used again.

P1L -- Life Tables and Survival Functions

(in addition to that on p. 769)

Paragraph STATEMENT {Preassigned value}	Definition, restriction	See pages:
/ESTimate	Optional, may be repeated	753
METHOD= *(one only)* LIFE,PROD. { LIFE/prev.}	Compute life table or product-limit estimate	753
PRINT. {PRINT/prev.}	Print survival distribution estimate	753
(one only) { PERIOD=#. {PERIOD=10/prev.} / WIDTH=#. / CUTPOINT=#$_1$,#$_2$,$\cdots$.	The intervals for the life table when METHOD=LIFE	753-754
VARIABLE=v$_1$,v$_2$,v$_3$,v$_4$. {none}	Variables printed with product-limit estimate	754-755
PLOT= *(one or more)* SURV,LOG,CUM,HAZ,DEN. {SURV/prev.}	Types of plots	755-756
SIZE=#$_1$,#$_2$. {100,50/prev.}	Width and height of plots	756
GROUPING=v. {no grouping}	Variable used to classify cases into groups	758
STATISTIC= *(one or both)* MANTEL,BRESLOW. {none/prev.}	Statistics to test equality of survival curves	760
/GROUP	Required if GROUPING var. specified and it has more than 10 distinct values	84
CODE(#)=#$_1$,#$_2$,$\cdots$. {10 smallest values/prev.}	Codes for variable #	84-85
CUTPOINT(#)=#$_1$,#$_2$,$\cdots$. {see CODE/prev.}	Cutpoints to define intervals for variable #	84-85
NAME(#)=c$_1$,c$_2$,$\cdots$. {CODES or CUTPOINTS/prev.}	Codes or interval names for variable #	84-85
RESET. {not RESET }	If RESET, all assignments in prev. *GROUP* paragraph are reset to preassigned values	86
/FORM	Required	761
UNIT= *(one only)* DAY,WEEK,MONTH,YEAR. or UNIT=c. {MONTH }	Unit to label time scale	761
TIME= v. {none}	Variable that contains the survival times	761-762
STATUS=v. {none}	Variable containing status of patient	761-762
RESPONSE= #$_1$,#$_2$,$\cdots$. {first code of STATUS}	Values of STATUS variable that are responses	761-762
LOSS= #$_1$,#$_2$,$\cdots$. {none}	Values of STATUS variable that are losses	762
ENTRY= v$_1$,v$_2$,v$_3$. {none}	Month, day, year of patient entry	762-763
TERMINATION=v$_1$,v$_2$,v$_3$. {none}	Month, day, year of patient termination	762-763
CENSOR=#$_1$,#$_2$,#$_3$. {none}	Date when study terminates or date of analysis	765
	The following are used when a life table is used as input:	
NENTER=v. {sum of NDEAD+NLOST+NWITH}	Variable containing no. of patients entering interval	765-767
NDEAD=v. {none}	Variable containing no. of patients dying in interval	765-767
NLOST=v. {none}	Variable containing no. of patients lost in interval	765-767
NWITH=v. {none}	Variable containing no. of patients withdrawn during interval	765-767
INTERVAL=v. {0,1,2,...}	Variable containing lower limits for intervals	767-768
/END	Required	57

Key: # number
v variable name or subscript

- Order of input

    (1) System Cards, at HSCF these are
    ```
    //jobname  JOB  nooo,yourname
    // EXEC  BIMED,PROG=BMDP1L
    //SYSIN DD  *
    ```

    (2) Control Language instructions
    ```
    PROBlem paragraph, required
    INPut paragraph, required first problem
    VARiable paragraph
    TRANsform paragraph
    SAVE paragraph
    ESTimate paragraph, may be repeated
    GROUP paragraph
    FORM paragraph, required
    END paragraph, required at end of Control Language
    ```

    (3) Data, if on cards
    ```
    data
    ```

    (4) System Card, at HSCF this is
    ```
    //
    ```

Control Language instructions and data (2 and 3) can be repeated for additional problems.

APPENDIX A

CONTENTS

Section		Page
A.1	Random Numbers	772
A.2	Method of Provisional Means	774
A.3	Hotelling's T^2 and Mahalanobis D^2 (P3D)	776
A.4	Bartlett's Statistic (P9D)	778
A.5	Tests and Measures in the Two-way Frequency Table (P1F)	778
A.6	Stepwise Identification of Extreme Cells (P2F)	793
A.7	Standard Errors for Unsaturated Log-linear Models (P3F)	796
A.8	Orthogonal Polynomials in P3F	797
A.9	Estimating (Smoothing) the Missing Value Correlation Matrix	798
A.10	Replacing Missing Values (PAM)	799
A.11	Linear Regression -- Estimating the Coefficients	800
A.12	Residual Analysis in P9R	803
A.13	Regression on Principal Components (P4R)	805
A.14	Polynomial Regression (P5R)	806
A.15	Nonlinear Least Squares (P3R)	808
A.16	Derivative-free Nonlinear Regression (PAR)	811
A.17	One-way Analysis of Variance and Covariance (P1V)	815
A.18	Analysis of Variance and Covariance, Including Repeated Measures (P2V)	818
A.19	General Mixed Model Analysis of Variance (P3V)	823
A.20	Survival Functions (P1L)	827
A.21	Maximum Likelihood Factor Analysis (P4M)	829
A.22	Canonical Analysis (P6M)	830
A.23	Stepwise Discriminant Analysis (P7M)	833
A.24	Using BMDP Programs from a Terminal	840

A.1 RANDOM NUMBERS

You can generate both uniform and normal random numbers, either by Control Language instructions in the *TRANsform* paragraph or by FORTRAN statements in the FORTRAN transformation subroutine. Below we describe both random number generators and how to use them by FORTRAN statements. In Section 6.3 we describe how to use them by Control Language instructions.

● UNIFORM RANDOM NUMBER GENERATOR

The FORTRAN code used in the uniform random number generator is

```
        FUNCTION RANDOM(I)
        M1=65539
        M2=4101
        M3=261
C           M1=2**16+3
C           M2=2**12+5
C           M3=2**8+5
        I=M3*I
        L=M1
        IF(I.LT.0)L=M2
        I=I*L
        IF(I.LT.0) I=I+2147483647+1
        RANDOM=FLOAT(I)*.4656613E-9
        RETURN
        END
```

Let I be a large odd integer. Then I is multiplied by (2^8+5) and again by either $(2^{12}+5)$ or $(2^{16}+3)$. This yields an integer (mod 2^{31}, still called I). This integer is now turned into a uniform random number (RANDOM) by dividing by 2^{31} (multiplying by 0.4656613×10^{-9}).

Therefore the integer that you specify in the Control Language instruction y=RNDU(i) is the initial value of I. To obtain each new random number I is multiplied as explained above and normalized to lie between zero and one.

To use FUNCTION RANDOM(I) in a FORTRAN subroutine you must specify an initial value for the random number generator in a data statement; e.g.,

    DATA IRAND/562345/

(IRAND should be odd) and then use RANDOM(IRAND); in your FORTRAN statements; i.e.,

    Y=RANDOM(IRAND)

stores the random number in Y. Y can be a subscripted variable, such as X(3) or it can be used in an expression to compute the value for a variable, such as

    X(2)=Y+5.0

● NORMAL RANDOM NUMBERS

Pairs of normal random numbers are generated from pairs of uniform random numbers by the Box and Muller (1958) method. That is, if r_1 and r_2 are two uniform random numbers, then

$$z_1 = (-2 \log_e r_1)^{\frac{1}{2}} \cos (2\pi r_2) \quad \text{and}$$
$$z_2 = (-2 \log_e r_1)^{\frac{1}{2}} \sin (2\pi r_2)$$

are a pair of statistically independent random numbers from a normal distribution with mean zero and variance one. The uniform random number generator described above is part of the normal random number generator subroutine.

In Control Language instructions the i in RNDG(i) has the same role as in RNDU(i).

The normal random number generator can be part of your FORTRAN transformation statements. Its calling sequence is

        CALL RANDG(N,Z,XBAR,SIGMA,IRAND)

where

N   is the number of normal random numbers that you want

Z   is a vector containing the random numbers

XBAR   is the mean of the normal population (i.e., 0.0 if random
        numbers from the standard normal distribution are wanted)

SIGMA   is the standard deviation of the normal population (i.e.,
        1.0 for the standard normal distribution)

IRAND   is a large odd integer used to start the generator

An example

In Section 6.3 we give an example of generating normal random numbers from the standard normal distribution with probability 0.7, and from the normal with mean zero and standard deviation 3 with probability 0.3. Using FORTRAN statements we could write

```
DATA   IRAND/567213/
Y=RANDOM (IRAND)
CALL  RANDG (1, X(1), 0.0, 1.0, IRAND)
1F(Y.GT.0.7) X(1)=3.0*X(1)
```


A warning

If you want to use either or both random number generators in FORTRAN statements for more than one problem (i.e., more than one *PROBlem* paragraph), you must initialize the first value of the random number generator as described below; otherwise you may get the same sequence of random numbers in each analysis. Use the following two FORTRAN statements.

```
COMMON/NUMBER/IRAND
```

$$IF(NPROB.EQ.1.AND.KASE.EQ.1)IRAND=572311$$

That is, the value of IRAND must be stored in a COMMON block (called NUMBER) and initialized at the first case of the first problem. Do not use a DATA statement for IRAND. (In many facilities overlays are used for BMDP programs. If overlays and a data statement are used IRAND is reset to its original value at each new *PROBlem* paragraph.)

A.2 METHOD OF PROVISIONAL MEANS

Many BMDP programs compute the mean, variance or sum of squares, skewness, kurtosis and covariance. All but the mean require that deviation about the mean be used in the computations. If the data are kept in computer memory it is possible to first compute the mean and then compute each deviation. However, this restricts the number of cases that can be analyzed.

A provisional means algorithm is used to avoid keeping the data in memory or reading the data twice. This algorithm produces more accurate results than a formula such as $\Sigma x_i^2 - (\Sigma x_i)^2/N$ for the sum of squares.

● MEANS AND VARIANCES

In the provisional means algorithm the mean $\bar{x}$ and sum of squares of deviations (S^2) for each variable are computed recursively as

$$d_j = w_j(x_j - \bar{x}_{j-1})$$

$$W_j = W_{j-1} + w_j$$

$$\bar{x}_j = \bar{x}_{j-1} + d_j/W_j$$

$$S_j^2 = S_{j-1}^2 + d_j(x_j - \bar{x}_j)$$

where

x_j is the jth observation

w_j is the weight for case j (if no case weight is specified, $w_j = 1$)

W_j is the sum of the weights for the first j cases

$\bar{x}_j$ is the mean of the first j cases

S_j^2 is the sum of squares of deviations for the first j cases

Only cases with acceptable data and a nonzero weight are used.

The mean is $\bar{x}_N$ and the variance $s^2 = S_N^2/[(N-1)W_N/N]$.

● SKEWNESS AND KURTOSIS

Skewness (g_1) and kurtosis (g_2) are computed in a similar manner when no case weights are specified, or all case weights are either zero or one; Spicer (1972) describes a similar algorithm. When case weights are specified that are not zero or one, skewness and kurtosis are not computed.

● COVARIANCES AND CORRELATIONS

All BMDP programs (except P8D and PAM) that compute the covariance between two variables use only cases for which both variables have acceptable values. Most programs are even more restrictive and use only cases that contain acceptable values for all the variables in the covariance matrix. We now describe how covariances are computed in all programs except P8D and PAM, which use a slightly modified algorithm.

The formula for the covariance between variable i and k is

$$cov_{ik} = \Sigma\, w_j(x_{ij}-\bar{x}_i)(x_{kj}-\bar{x}_k)/[(N-1)\Sigma\, w_j/N]$$

where

x_{ij} is the jth observation for variable i

$\bar{x}_i$ and $\bar{x}_k$ are the means of the variables computed from the cases used in the analysis

w_j is the weight of the jth case (1 if no case weights are specified)

N   is the number of observations used in the computation with non-zero weight

Then the covariance is computed recursively as

$$d_{ij} = w_j(x_{ij}-\bar{x}_{i(j-1)}) \quad ; \quad d_{kj} = w_j(x_{kj}-\bar{x}_{k(j-1)})$$

$$W_j = W_{j-1} + w_j$$

$$\bar{x}_{ij} = \bar{x}_{i(j-1)} + d_{ij}/W_j \quad ; \quad \bar{x}_{kj} = \bar{x}_{k(j-1)} + d_{kj}/W_j$$

and

$$S^2_{ikj} = S^2_{ik(j-1)} + d_{ij}(x_{kj} - \bar{x}_{kj})$$

where

W_j is the sum of the weights for the first j cases

$\bar{x}_{ij}$ is the mean of the first j cases for variable i

S^2_{ikj} is the sum of squares of cross-products for the first j cases

Then the covariance between variables i and k is

$$S^2_{ikN}/[(N-1)W_N/N],$$

the variance of variable i is

$$S^2_{iiN}/[(N-1)W_N/N] \, ,$$

and the correlation between variables i and k is

$$S^2_{ikN}/(S^2_{iiN} \, S^2_{kkN})^{\frac{1}{2}} \, .$$

Each program description specifies the cases that are used in the computations.

A.3 HOTELLING'S T^2 AND MAHALANOBIS D^2 (P3D)

The pooled within-groups covariance between each pair of variables (say x and y) is computed using only cases for which both x and y are acceptable values; i.e., are not equal to the missing value codes and not out of range. If COMPLETE is specified in the *TEST* paragraph, only cases for which the values of all the variables are acceptable are used in the analysis.

Let (x_{ij}, y_{ij}) be the values of x and y for the jth case in the ith group. Then

$$\bar{x}_i = \Sigma_j x_{ij}/n_i$$

is the mean of x in the ith group where n_i is the number of pairs of acceptable values (x_{ij}, y_{ij}). When two groups are being compared, the pooled within-groups covariance is c_{xy} computed using data from <u>only</u> the two groups.

$$c_{xy} = \frac{\sum\limits_{i=1}^{2} \sum\limits_{j=1}^{n_i} (x_{ij} - \bar{x}_i)(y_{ij} - \bar{y}_i)}{\sum\limits_{i=1}^{2} (n_i - 1)}$$

If there is only one group, the summation over i is omitted.

Let $\underset{\sim}{C} = (c_{k\ell})$ be the covariance matrix computed between all pairs of variables in the analysis and $\underset{\sim}{C}^{-1} = (c_{k\ell})^{-1}$ be the inverse of the covariance matrix.

Mahalanobis D^2 is computed only if the sample size n_i in each group is greater than 1. Let $\underset{\sim}{\bar{X}}_1$ represent a column vector of means for the first group and $\underset{\sim}{\bar{X}}_2$ for the second group. Then to compare two groups

$$D^2 = (\underset{\sim}{\bar{X}}_1 - \underset{\sim}{\bar{X}}_2)' \; \underset{\sim}{C}^{-1} \; (\underset{\sim}{X}_1 - \underset{\sim}{X}_2)$$

where the prime indicates matrix transposition

$$T^2 = D^2 \Big/ \left(\frac{1}{h_1} + \frac{1}{h_2} \right)$$

where h_1 and h_2 are the harmonic means of the sample sizes n_1 and n_2 respectively used in computing the covariance for each pair of variables. If COMPLETE is specified, n_1 and n_2 are constant for all pairings and $h_1 = n_1$ and $h_2 = n_2$. Otherwise

$$h_1 = \left[\sum_{\text{all pairings}} \frac{1}{n_1} \Big/ \frac{v(v+1)}{2} \right]^{-1}$$

where v is the number of variables. h_2 is similarly defined. Lastly,

$$F = T^2 \frac{(h_1 + h_2 - v - 1)}{v(h_1 + h_2 - 2)}$$

When there is only one group

$$D^2 = \underset{\sim}{\bar{X}}_1' \; \underset{\sim}{C}^{-1} \; \underset{\sim}{\bar{X}}_1 \quad , \quad T^2 = h_1 D^2$$

and

$$F = T^2 \frac{(N_1 - v)}{v(N_1 - 1)}$$

A.4 BARTLETT's STATISTIC (P9D)

Bartlett's statistic for homogeneity of group variances is computed using only groups having nonzero variances. The formula is

$$M = (N-g) \ln \left[\Sigma (n_i-1) s_i^2 / (N-g) \right] - \Sigma (n_i-1) \ln (s_i^2)$$

where

g = the number of groups with nonzero variances

n_i = frequency of the ith group

N = Σn_i

s_i^2 = variance of group i

The level of significance of Bartlett's statistic is computed by approximating M by an F statistic (Dixon and Massey, 1969, p. 308)

$$F = f_2 M / [f_1 (b-M)]$$

where

$$f_1 = g-1 \quad , \quad f_2 = (g+1)/A^2 \quad ,$$

$$A = \frac{1}{3(g-1)} \left[\Sigma \frac{1}{n_i-1} - \frac{1}{N-g} \right] \quad \text{and} \quad b = f_2/(1 - A + 2/f_2) .$$

The F statistic is compared with the F distribution with f_1 and f_2 df.

A.5 TESTS AND MEASURES IN THE TWO-WAY FREQUENCY TABLE (P1F)

● NOTATION

Let $(a_{ij}; i = 1,\ldots,R; j = 1,\ldots,C)$ be the frequency counts in the R x C two-way contingency table. Let

$$r_i = \Sigma_j a_{ij}, \quad c_j = \Sigma_i a_{ij} \quad \text{and} \quad N = \Sigma_i \Sigma_j a_{ij}$$

represent the row totals, column totals and table total respectively. Also let

$$A_{ij} = \sum_{k>i} \sum_{\ell>j} a_{k\ell} + \sum_{k<i} \sum_{\ell<j} a_{k\ell}$$

$$D_{ij} = \sum_{k>i} \sum_{\ell<j} a_{k\ell} + \sum_{k<i} \sum_{\ell>j} a_{k\ell}$$

$$P = \sum_i \sum_j a_{ij} A_{ij}$$

$$Q = \sum_i \sum_j a_{ij} D_{ij}$$

Therefore, A_{ij} is the sum of the frequencies in cells in which both indices are greater, or both indices are less than (i,j), and D_{ij} is the sum of frequencies in cells in which one index is greater and the other is less than (i,j). Hence P is twice the total number of agreements in the order of the subscripts between all pairs of observations, and Q is twice the total number of disagreements.

● ASYMPTOTIC STANDARD ERRORS (ASEs)

Two ASEs are computed for each measure. One (labeled ASE1 in the output) is appropriate to use in setting confidence limits on the parameters. It is obtained by the method of Goodman and Kruskal (1972) based on multinomial sampling conditional on the total table frequency N (except for the Goodman and Kruskal τ and λ^* and the tetrachoric r_t). This ASE is denoted s_1 since it is the ASE derived by assuming the alternate hypothesis H_1 is true; i.e., the measure is not zero.

The second ASE, denoted s_0, is a modification by Brown and Benedetti (1977a) that is more appropriate to test the null hypothesis H_0 that the measure is zero. In the output, T-VALUE is the ratio of the statistic to this ASE (s_0).

The formulas to compute s_1 (ASE1) for Yule's Q and Y and ln(cross-product ratio) appear in Kendall and Stuart (1967); and for γ, Somer's D, λ, λ^*, τ appear in Goodman and Kruskal (1963, 1972). The formula for s_1 in the tetrachoric r_t is from Pearson (1913). The remaining ASEs, including all those under the null hypothesis, are derived according to Brown and Benedetti (1977a).

Guidelines to the use of these ASEs both to test if the measure is zero and to set confidence limits for the measure are given by Brown and Benedetti (1977a, 1976).

All but three ASEs are derived based on multinomial sampling conditional on the total table frequency. Two exceptions are the Goodman and Kruskal τ and λ^* whose ASEs are derived based on multinomial sampling conditional on the row or column totals. The third is the tetrachoric correlation.

The formulas for s_1 and s_0 follow the definition of the measure. Many measures can be written as a ratio v/w where v is the numerator and w the denominator. The notation v and w is used in the formulas for s_1 and s_0.

● STATISTICS

Chi-Square (χ^2)

This is the classical chi-square test of independence between two categorical variables:

$$\chi^2 = \sum_i \sum_j [(a_{ij} - e_{ij})^2/e_{ij}] , \quad df = (R - 1)(C - 1)$$

where $e_{ij} = r_i c_j/N$. The significance level of χ^2 is also given.

Likelihood Ratio Chi-Square (G^2)

This is a test of independence between rows and columns based upon a likelihood ratio approach. In general the results are similar to that of the usual χ^2, but this one is computationally more expensive.

$$G^2 = 2 \sum_i \sum_j a_{ij} \; ln \; (a_{ij}/e_{ij}), \quad df = (R - 1)(C - 1)$$

where

$$e_{ij} = r_i c_j/N$$

The significance level of G^2 is also given.

Yates' Corrected Chi-Square (χ_y^2)

When the contingency table is 2x2, a chi-square that includes a correction for continuity is also computed

$$\chi_y^2 = \begin{cases} \dfrac{N(|a_{11}a_{22} - a_{12}a_{21}| - \frac{N}{2})^2}{r_1 r_2 c_1 c_2} & \text{if } |a_{11}a_{22} - a_{12}a_{21}| > \dfrac{N}{2} \\ 0 & \text{otherwise} \end{cases}$$

The significance level of χ_y^2 is also given.

Fisher's Exact Probability

For the 2x2 table, the exact probability of any configuration under the assumption of independence between rows and columns can easily be calculated.

$$Pr(a_{11}, a_{12}, a_{21}, a_{22}) = \frac{r_1! r_2! c_1! c_2!}{N! a_{11}! a_{12}! a_{21}! a_{22}!}$$

conditioned on the row and column totals.

The <u>direction</u> of the 1-TAIL probability is chosen as follows:

If $a_{11} a_{22} \leq a_{12} a_{21}$

choose the minimum of a_{11} and a_{22}; otherwise, choose the minimum of a_{12} and a_{21}. For example, let cell (1,1) be the cell so chosen. Then the probability that a value of cell (1,1) is equal to or less than a_{11} is

$$P_1 = \sum_{x=0}^{a_{11}} Pr(a_{11} - x, a_{12} + x, a_{21} + x, a_{22} - x)$$

Assuming that a_{11} was chosen, the other tail probability is computed as follows:

$$P_2 = \sum Pr(a_{11} + y, a_{12} - y, a_{21} - y, a_{22} + y)$$

where the sum is over y such that

$$Pr(a_{11}, a_{12}, a_{21}, a_{22}) \geq Pr(a_{11} + y, a_{12} - y, a_{21} - y, a_{22} + y)$$

and y>0; i.e., over all terms in the second tail whose probability does not exceed that of the observed outcome $(a_{11}, a_{12}, a_{21}, a_{22})$

PROB(1 - TAIL) = p_1

PROB(2 - TAIL) = $p_1 + p_2$

Note that PROB(1 - TAIL) is chosen as the tail with lesser probability in it. Given that a one-sided hypothesis is tested, check if this tail corresponds to the tail required by the hypothesis. If it does not, then for the hypothesis being tested, PROB(1 - TAIL) $\geq$ 0.5, which is a nonsignificant result.

Phi (ϕ)

The value of χ^2 depends not only on the relative frequency in each cell but also on the total sample size N. A measure that is independent of N is

$$\phi = (\chi^2/N)^{\frac{1}{2}}$$

For a 2x2 table, ϕ may be positive or negative according to the formula

$$\phi = (a_{11}a_{22} - a_{12}a_{21})/(r_1 r_2 c_1 c_2)^{\frac{1}{2}}$$

The significance level of the test that $E(\phi) = 0$ may be obtained from the corresponding significance level for χ^2.

Maximum Value of Phi (ϕ_{max})

In a 2x2 table, the maximum possible absolute value of ϕ given the row and column totals is less than or equal to 1. This value is calculated.

If $a_{11}a_{22} < a_{12}a_{21}$, then $\phi_{max} = -[(r_1 c_1)/(r_2 c_2)]^{\frac{1}{2}}$ or $-[(r_2 c_2)/(r_1 c_1)]^{\frac{1}{2}}$

whichever is less than 1 in absolute value

otherwise $\phi_{max} = [(r_1 c_2)/(r_2 c_1)]^{\frac{1}{2}}$ or $[(r_2 c_1)/(r_1 c_2)]^{\frac{1}{2}}$

whichever is less than 1

Note that if $\phi < 0$, then ϕ_{max} is the lower bound; i.e., $\phi_{max} < 0$.

Contingency Coefficient (C)

Another transformation of χ^2 which does not depend on the sample size N is

$$C = [\chi^2/(N + \chi^2)]^{\frac{1}{2}} = [\phi^2/(1 + \phi^2)]^{\frac{1}{2}}$$

The significance level of the test for $E(C) = 0$ may be obtained from the significance level of χ^2.

Maximum Value of the Contingency Coefficient (C_{max})

C is always less than or equal to one. For the 2x2 table this maximum value is calculated

$$C_{max} = [\phi^2_{max}/(1 + \phi^2_{max})]^{\frac{1}{2}}$$

Cramer's V

Another transformation of χ^2 (which reduces to ϕ for the 2x2 table) is

$$V = \left[\frac{\chi^2}{N(m-1)}\right]^{\frac{1}{2}} \qquad \text{where } m = \text{minimum } (R,C)$$

Yule's Q and Y

For a 2x2 table, Yule defined the measure of association Q

$$Q = \frac{a_{11}a_{22} - a_{12}a_{21}}{a_{11}a_{22} + a_{12}a_{21}}$$

The standard errors of Q are

$$s_1^2 = \frac{1}{4}(1-Q^2)^2 \left[\frac{1}{a_{11}} + \frac{1}{a_{12}} + \frac{1}{a_{21}} + \frac{1}{a_{22}} \right]$$

$$s_0^2 = \frac{1}{4} \left[\frac{N^3}{(a_{11}+a_{12})(a_{11}+a_{21})(a_{12}+a_{22})(a_{21}+a_{22})} \right]$$

Yule also defined a measure of colligation y

$$Y = \frac{\sqrt{a_{11}a_{22}} - \sqrt{a_{12}a_{21}}}{\sqrt{a_{11}a_{22}} + \sqrt{a_{12}a_{21}}}$$

The standard errors of Y are

$$s_1^2 = \frac{1}{16}(1-Y^2)^2 \left[\frac{1}{a_{11}} + \frac{1}{a_{12}} + \frac{1}{a_{21}} + \frac{1}{a_{22}} \right]$$

$$s_0^2 = \frac{1}{16} \left[\frac{N^3}{(a_{11}+a_{12})(a_{11}+a_{21})(a_{12}+a_{22})(a_{21}+a_{22})} \right]$$

Both Q and Y are -1 when a_{11} or a_{22} is equal to zero, 1 when a_{12} or a_{21} is equal to zero, and zero when $a_{11}a_{22} = a_{12}a_{21}$ (i.e., the cross-product ratio is one).

Cross-Product Ratio (α)

For a 2x2 table, the cross-product (or odds) ratio is defined as
$\alpha = (a_{11}a_{22})/(a_{12}a_{21})$

This is 1 when χ^2 is 0 and 0 or ∞ when one of the cells has zero frequency. Since its distribution is extremely asymmetric under the hypothesis of independence between rows and columns, but that of $ln(\alpha)$ is symmetric, the LN (CROSS-PRODUCT RATIO) is also given as well as its ASE.

The standard errors of $ln(\alpha)$ are

$$s_1^2 = \frac{1}{a_{11}} + \frac{1}{a_{12}} + \frac{1}{a_{21}} + \frac{1}{a_{22}}$$

$$s_0^2 = \frac{N^3}{(a_{11}+a_{12})(a_{11}+a_{21})(a_{12}+a_{22})(a_{21}+a_{22})}$$

Tetrachoric correlation (r_t)

The tetrachoric correlation is the correlation of a bivariate normal distribution that exactly duplicates the 4 cell probabilities in a 2x2 table. It is found by solving the following equations implicitly for r_t.

$$\begin{array}{|cc|} \hline a & b \\ \\ c & d \\ \hline \end{array}$$

$$\Phi(z_1) = \frac{a + c}{N}$$

$$\Phi(z_2) = \frac{a + b}{N}$$

$$\int_{-\infty}^{z_2} \int_{-\infty}^{z_1} \phi(z_1, z_2, r_t) dz_1 dz_2 = \frac{a}{N}$$

where $\Phi(z)$ is the Gaussian cdf with zero mean and unit variance and $\phi(z_1, z_2, r_t)$ is the bivariate normal with mean zero, variance one and correlation r_t.

The bivariate normal integral is approximated by an infinite series in r_t (Everitt, 1910) and r_t is found implicitly by iteration. When the infinite series does not converge within 100 terms ($|r_t| > 0.9$), Gaussian quadrature is used to evaluate the integral.

If a single cell is zero, the tetrachoric correlation can be defined as unity (or -1.0). We prefer to modify the cell to be ½ and then solve for r_t. The tetrachoric correlation should then be considered as any value from the computed value up to unity. Our justification is that the pattern of frequencies is duplicated by the choice of r_t; yet since frequencies are ordinal, the underlying probability is estimated with uncertainty equal to 1/(2N) in each cell. Therefore, setting the zero cell to ½ yields a lower bound for the estimate of the correlation (Brown and Benedetti, 1977b).

The formula for s_1^2 is from Pearson (1913).

$$s_1^2 = \frac{1}{N^3} \left(\frac{1}{\phi(z_1,z_2,r_t)} \right)^2 \left\{ \frac{(a+d)(b+c)}{4} + (a+c)(b+d)\Phi_2^2 + (a+b)(c+d)\Phi_1^2 \right.$$

$$\left. + 2(ad-bc)\Phi_1\Phi_2 - (ab-cd)\Phi_2 - (ac-bd)\Phi_1 \right\}$$

$$s_0^2 = \left(\frac{1}{\phi(z_1,z_2,0)} \right)^2 \frac{(a+b)(a+c)(b+d)(c+d)}{N^5}$$

where $\Phi_1 = \Phi[(z_1-r_t z_2)/(1-r_t^2)^{\frac{1}{2}}] - 0.5$ and $\Phi_2 = \Phi[(z_2-r_t z_1)/(1-r_t^2)^{\frac{1}{2}}] - 0.5$

and

$$\phi(z_1, z_2, r_t) = \frac{1}{2\pi(1-r_t^2)^{\frac{1}{2}}} \quad \exp \left\{ - \frac{z_1^2 - 2r_t z_1 z_2 + z_2^2}{2(1-r_t^2)} \right\}$$

Gamma (γ)

Gamma is a measure of the monotone relationship between two ordered variables (Goodman and Kruskal, 1954). It is estimated by

$$G = (P - Q)/(P + Q)$$

The standard errors of G are

$$s_1^2 = 16[\Sigma \Sigma \ a_{ij}(QA_{ij} - PD_{ij})^2]/(P+Q)^4$$

$$s_0^2 = 4[\Sigma \Sigma a_{ij}(A_{ij} - D_{ij})^2 - (P-Q)^2/N]/(P+Q)^2$$

Kendall's Tau-B (τ_b)

Kendall's τ_b is a correlation measure of the monotone relationship between two ordered variables that compares the number of agreements in the ordering of the indices between pairs of observations with the number of disagreements. Siegel (1956) gives the following estimate when many ties are expected.

$$t_b = \frac{(P - Q)}{\{[N(N-1) - \Sigma_i r_i(r_i-1)][N(N-1) - \Sigma_j c_j(c_{j-1})]\}^{\frac{1}{2}}} \equiv \frac{v}{w}$$

The standard errors of t_b are

$$s_1^2 = \{\Sigma\Sigma a_{ij}[2w(A_{ij}-D_{ij}) + t_b(r_i(N^2-\Sigma c_j^2) + c_j(N^2-\Sigma r_i^2))]^2$$

$$- Nt_b^2(2N^2-\Sigma r_i^2-\Sigma c_j^2)^2\}/w^4$$

$$s_0^2 = 4[\Sigma \Sigma a_{ij}(A_{ij}-D_{ij})^2 - \frac{(P-Q)^2}{N}]/w^2$$

where $w'_{ij} = - \frac{N}{w} [r_i(N^2-\Sigma c_j^2) + c_j(N^2-\Sigma r_i^2)]$

Stuart's Tau-C (τ_c)

A similar measure to τ_b, which uses a different denominator, is τ_c. It is estimated by

$$t_c = (P - Q)/N^2 \cdot [m/(m-1)]$$

where $m = \min(R,C)$.

The two standard errors of t_c are similar.

$$s_1^2 = s_0^2 = \frac{4}{N^4} \left(\frac{m}{m-1}\right)^2 \Sigma \Sigma a_{ij}(A_{ij} - D_{ij})^2$$

Product Moment Correlation (r)

The ordinary correlation coefficient is computed using the cell entries as frequencies and cell indices as the observed values.

$$r = \frac{\Sigma_i \Sigma_j a_{ij}(i-\bar{i})(j-\bar{j})}{[\ \Sigma_i r_i(i-\bar{i})^2 \Sigma_j c_j(j-\bar{j})^2]^{\frac{1}{2}}} \equiv \frac{v}{w}$$

where $\bar{i} = \Sigma_i i r_i/N$ and $\bar{j} = \Sigma_j j c_j/N$

The standard errors of r are

$$s_1^2 = \frac{1}{w^4} \Sigma \Sigma a_{ij} \{w(i-\bar{i})(j-\bar{j}) - \frac{v}{2w}[(i-\bar{i})^2 \Sigma c_j(j-\bar{j})^2 + (j-\bar{j})^2 \Sigma r_i(i-\bar{i})^2]\}^2$$

$$s_0^2 = \frac{1}{w^2}\{ \Sigma \Sigma a_{ij}(i-\bar{i})^2(j-\bar{j})^2 - \frac{v^2}{N} \}$$

Spearman Rank Correlation Coefficient (r_S)

The Spearman rank correlation coefficient, r_S, is computed using the cell entries as frequencies and the cell indices to order the cells. The formula for ties (Siegel, 1956) has been rewritten in our notation.

$$r_S = \frac{\Sigma_i \Sigma_j a_{ij}[\ \underset{k<i}{\Sigma} r_k + \frac{r_i}{2} - \frac{N}{2}]\ [\ \underset{\ell<j}{\Sigma} c_\ell + \frac{c_j}{2} - \frac{N}{2}\ ]}{\frac{1}{12}[N^3 - N - \Sigma_i(r_i^3 - r_i)]\ [N^3 - N - \Sigma_j(c_j^3 - c_j)]^{\frac{1}{2}}}$$

The standard errors of r_S are

$$s_1^2 = \frac{1}{N^2 w^4} \Sigma \Sigma a_{ij}(wv'_{ij} - vw'_{ij} - \frac{w}{N}\Sigma \Sigma a_{ij}v'_{ij} + \frac{v}{N}\Sigma \Sigma a_{ij}w'_{ij})^2$$

$$s_0^2 = \frac{1}{N^2 w^2} \Sigma \Sigma a_{ij}(v'_{ij} - \frac{1}{N}\Sigma \Sigma a_{ij}v'_{ij})^2$$

where $R(i) = 2\underset{k<i}{\Sigma} r_k + r_i - N$ $\qquad C(j) = 2\underset{\ell<j}{\Sigma} c_\ell + c_j - N$

$$v = \frac{1}{4}\Sigma \Sigma a_{ij}R(i)C(j) \qquad \text{and} \qquad w = \frac{1}{12}[(N^3 - \Sigma r_i^3)(N^3 - \Sigma c_j^3)]^{\frac{1}{2}}$$

$$v'_{ij} = N[\frac{1}{4} R(i)C(j) + \frac{1}{4} \Sigma_{j'}a_{ij'}C(j') + \frac{1}{4} \Sigma_{i'}a_{i'j}R(i')$$

$$+ \frac{1}{2} \Sigma_{j'} \sum_{i'>i} a_{i'j'}C(j') + \frac{1}{2} \Sigma_{i'} \sum_{j'>j} a_{i'j'}R(i')]$$

$$w'_{ij} = - \frac{N}{96w} [(N^3 - \Sigma r_i^3)c_j^2 + (N^3 - \Sigma c_j^3)r_i^2]$$

Somers' D (d_{asym})

Somers' d is an asymmetric version of τ_b. It is appropriate when one ordered index is to be predicted from knowledge of the second ordered index.

$$d_{j|i} = (P - Q)/(N^2 - \Sigma_i r_i^2) \quad ; \quad d_{i|j} = (P - Q)/(N^2 - \Sigma_j c_j^2)$$

The standard errors of $d_{j|i}$ are

$$s_1^2 = \frac{4}{(N^2 - \Sigma r_i^2)^4} \Sigma \Sigma a_{ij}[(N^2 - \Sigma r_i^2)(A_{ij} - D_{ij}) - (N - r_i)(P - Q)]^2$$

$$s_0^2 = \frac{4}{(N^2 - \Sigma r_i^2)^2} \Sigma \Sigma a_{ij}(A_{ij} - D_{ij})^2$$

The ASEs of $d_{i|j}$ are obtained by permuting the indices.

Tau-Asymmetric (τ_{asym})

Goodman and Kruskal (1954) propose another measure of association in addition to λ. This measure, τ, compares random proportional prediction of an index with conditional proportional prediction based upon knowledge of the second index.

$$\tau_{j|i} = \frac{N \Sigma_i \Sigma_j (a_{ij}^2/r_i) - \Sigma_j c_j^2}{N^2 - \Sigma_j c_j^2} \equiv \frac{v}{w} \quad ; \quad \tau_{i|j} = \frac{N \Sigma_i \Sigma_j (a_{ij}^2/c_j) - \Sigma_i r_i^2}{N^2 - \Sigma_i r_i^2}$$

The ASEs of $\tau_{j|i}$ (or $\tau_{i|j}$) are obtained by assuming multinomial sampling in each row (or column).

$$s_1^2 = \frac{4}{w^4} \left\{ w^2N^2 \Sigma \Sigma \frac{a_{ij}^3}{r_i^2} + (v-w)^2 \Sigma_j c_j^3 + 2 w(v-w)N \Sigma \Sigma \frac{a_{ij}^2 c_j}{r_i} \right.$$

$$- w^2N^2 \Sigma_i \frac{1}{r_i^3} (\Sigma_j a_{ij}^2)^2 - (v-w)^2 \Sigma_i \frac{1}{r_i} (\Sigma_j a_{ij}c_j)^2$$

$$\left. + 2w(v-w)N \Sigma_i \frac{1}{r_i^2} (\Sigma_j a_{ij}^2)(\Sigma_j a_{ij}c_j) \right\}$$

$$s_0^2 = \frac{4}{w^2} \left\{ N^2 \Sigma \Sigma \frac{a_{ij}^3}{r_i^2} + \Sigma c_j^3 - 2N \Sigma \Sigma \frac{a_{ij}^2 c_j}{r_i} - N^2 \Sigma_i \frac{1}{r_i^2} (\Sigma a_{ij}^2)^2 \right.$$

$$\left. - \Sigma_i \frac{1}{r_i} (\Sigma_j a_{ij} c_j)^2 + 2N \Sigma_i \frac{1}{r_i^2} (\Sigma_j a_{ij}^2)(\Sigma_j a_{ij} c_j) \right\}$$

The ASEs of $\tau_{i|j}$ are obtained by permuting the indices.

Lambda-Asymmetric (λ_{asym})

Lambda is a measure of predictive association that measures the degree of success with which one index can be used to predict the second index (Goodman and Kruskal, 1954). No ordering of indices is assumed.

$$\lambda_{j|i} = \frac{\Sigma_i max_j \, a_{ij} - max_j \, c_j}{N - max_j \, c_j} \quad ; \quad \lambda_{i|j} = \frac{\Sigma_j max_i \, a_{ij} - max_i \, r_i}{N - max_i \, r_i}$$

The standard errors of $\lambda_{j|i}$ are

$$s_1^2 = \frac{1}{(N-c_\ell)^2} \left\{ \Sigma \Sigma a_{ij} [\delta_{ij}^{in} - \delta_j^\ell + \lambda \, \delta_j^\ell]^2 - N\lambda_{j|i}^2 \right\}$$

$$s_0^2 = \frac{1}{(N-c_\ell)^2} \left\{ \Sigma \Sigma a_{ij} [\delta_{ij}^{in} - \delta_j^\ell]^2 - \frac{(\Sigma_i a_{in} - c_\ell)^2}{N} \right\}$$

where ℓ is the index of column such that c_ℓ is the maximum

a_{in} is the maximum in row i

$\delta_{ij}^{in} = 1$ if $j = n$ and zero otherwise, $\quad \delta_j^\ell = 1$ if $\ell = j$ and zero otherwise

The ASEs for $\lambda_{i|j}$ are obtained by permuting the indices.

Lambda-Symmetric (λ)

This is a symmetric version of the previous statistics.

$$\lambda = \frac{\Sigma_i \, max_j \, a_{ij} + \Sigma_j \, max_i \, a_{ij} - max_j \, c_j - max_i \, r_i}{2N - max_j \, c_j - max_i \, r_i}$$

The standard errors of λ are

$$s_1^2 = \frac{1}{(2N-c_\ell-r_k)^2} \left\{ \Sigma\Sigma \, a_{ij}[(\delta_{ij}^{in} + \delta_{ij}^{mj} - \delta_j^\ell - \delta_i^k) + \lambda\,(\delta_j^\ell + \delta_i^k)]^2 - 4N\lambda^2 \right\}$$

$$s_0^2 = \frac{1}{(2N-c_\ell-r_k)^2} \left\{ \Sigma\Sigma \, a_{ij}[\,\delta_{ij}^{in} + \delta_{ij}^{mj} - \delta_j^\ell - \delta_i^k]^2 - \frac{(\Sigma_i a_{in} + \Sigma_j a_{mj} - c_\ell - r_k)^2}{N} \right\}$$

where, in addition to the notation for λ_{asym},

k is the index of row such that r_k is the maximum

a_{mj} is the maximum in column j

$\delta_{ij}^{mj} = 1$ if i = m and zero otherwise

$\delta_i^k = 1$ if k = i and zero otherwise

Lambda-Star-Asymmetric (λ_{asym}^*)

A modification of Lambda-Asymmetric that is not affected by differing row (or column) marginals is λ^* where

$$\lambda_{j|i}^* = \frac{\Sigma_i(\max_j a_{ij})/r_i - \max_j \Sigma_i(a_{ij}/r_i)}{R - \max_j \Sigma_i(a_{ij}/r_i)} \equiv \frac{v}{w}$$

$$\lambda_{i|j}^* = \frac{\Sigma_j(\max_i a_{ij})/c_j - \max_i \Sigma_j(a_{ij}/c_j)}{C - \max_i \Sigma_j(a_{ij}/c_j)}$$

The ASEs for $\lambda_{j|i}^*$ (or $\lambda_{i|j}^*$) are derived based on multinomial sampling in each row (or column).

$$s_1^2 = \frac{1}{w^2} \; \Sigma\Sigma \frac{a_{ij}}{r_i^2} [(\delta_{ij}^{in} - \delta_j^\ell) + \lambda_{j|i}^* \, \delta_j^\ell]^2 - \Sigma_i \frac{1}{r_i^3} [(a_{in} - a_{i\ell}) + \lambda_{j|i}^* \, a_{i\ell}]^2$$

$$s_0^2 = \frac{1}{w^2} \; \Sigma\Sigma \frac{a_{ij}}{r_i^2} \; (\delta_{ij}^{in} - \delta_j^\ell)^2 - \Sigma_i \frac{1}{r_i^3} (a_{in} - a_{i\ell})^2$$

where

a_{in} is the maximum frequency in row i

ℓ is the column j for which $\Sigma_j a_{ij}/r_i$ is a maximum

The ASEs of $\lambda_{i|j}^*$ are obtained by permuting the indices.

Uncertainty Coefficient-Asymmetric

This is an asymmetric measure of association between two unordered variables based on an information theory approach that reflects the relative reduction of uncertainty about one factor when the second factor is known.

$$U_{j|i} = \frac{U_j + U_i - U_{ij}}{U_j} \equiv \frac{v}{w} \quad , \qquad U_{i|j} = \frac{U_j + U_i - U_{ij}}{U_i}$$

where

$$U_{ij} = - \Sigma_i \Sigma_j \frac{a_{ij}}{N} \log \frac{a_{ij}}{N} \quad , \quad U_j = -\Sigma_j \frac{c_j}{N} \log \frac{c_j}{N} \quad , \quad U_i = -\Sigma_i \frac{r_i}{N} \log \frac{r_i}{N}$$

The standard errors of $U_{j|i}$ are

$$s_1^2 = \frac{1}{N^2 w^4} \Sigma \Sigma a_{ij} \left[(U_i - U_{ij}) \log \frac{c_j}{N} + U_j \left(\log \frac{a_{ij}}{N} - \log \frac{r_i}{N} \right) \right]^2$$

$$s_0^2 = \frac{1}{N^2 w^2} \left\{ \Sigma \Sigma a_{ij} \left(\log \frac{c_j}{N} + \log \frac{r_i}{N} - \log \frac{a_{ij}}{N} \right)^2 - N(U_j + U_i - U_{ij})^2 \right\}$$

The ASEs of $U_{i|j}$ are obtained by permuting the indices.

Uncertainty Coefficient-Symmetric

A symmetric measure related to the above asymmetric measures is

$$U = \frac{U_j + U_i - U_{ij}}{(U_j + U_i)/2}$$

This measure has been normalized so that U may range between zero and one. U is frequently defined without the 1/2 in the denominator (see Brown, 1975).

The ASEs of U are

$$s_1^2 = \frac{4}{N^2 (U_j + U_i)^4} \Sigma \Sigma a_{ij} \left[U_{ij} \left(\log \frac{r_i}{N} + \log \frac{c_j}{N} \right) - (U_j + U_i) \log \frac{a_{ij}}{N} \right]^2$$

$$s_0^2 = \frac{4}{N^2 (U_j + U_i)^2} \left\{ \Sigma \Sigma a_{ij} \left(\log \frac{r_i}{N} + \log \frac{c_j}{N} - \log \frac{a_{ij}}{N} \right)^2 - \frac{(U_j + U_i - U_{ij})^2}{N} \right\}$$

<u>McNemar's Test of Symmetry</u> (χ^2_{MC})

This is a test of symmetry which is calculated for square tables (R=C) only.

$$\chi^2_{MC} = \sum_{i<j} \sum \frac{(a_{ij} - a_{ji})^2}{a_{ij} + a_{ji}}$$

The significance level of χ^2_{MC} is also given. The degrees of freedom are R(R-1)/2.

<u>Test of Linear Regression</u>

Let the frequency table be 2 x k (2 rows and k columns) and a set of k coefficients (z_j) assigned, one to each column. The regression of a_{ij}/c_j on z_j is performed and the following χ^2 test with 1 df is computed (Cochran, 1954).

$$\chi^2 = \frac{\left[\sum c_j \left(\frac{a_{1j}}{c_j} - \frac{r_1}{N}\right)(z_j - \tilde{z})\right]^2}{\sum c_j(z_j - \tilde{z})^2} \cdot \frac{N^2}{r_1 r_2}$$

where $\tilde{z} = \dfrac{\sum c_j z_j}{N}$

<u>Smoothed Values</u> (Mosteller, 1968)

Let R' and C' be the number of nonzero rows and columns respectively. The cell frequencies are then successively altered by the following algorithm until convergence is reached or 25 iterations have been performed. The kth iteration is

At step k

$$a_{ij}^{(2k+1)} = a_{ij}^{(2k)}/R'r_i^{(2k)} \quad , \quad a_{ij}^{(2k+2)} = a_{ij}^{(2k+1)}/C'c_j^{(2k+1)}$$

Convergence occurs when

$$0.99 < R'r_i^{(2k+2)} < 1.01 \quad \text{and} \quad 0.99 < C'c_j^{(2k+2)} < 1.01$$

for all i and j.

Note that due to zero cell frequencies (as in the case of only one nonzero element in a row), this algorithm may not converge.

● AUTOMATIC COLLAPSING AND ADDING A CONSTANT TO EACH CELL

Collapsing

If the expected value of any cell in the table is less than a user-specified value (MIN>0), the program automatically collapses the corresponding row or column, depending on which has the smaller marginal total. This row (column) is combined with the adjacent row (column) that has the smaller total. This process is repeated until the expected values of all cells in the collapsed table are greater than MIN.

There are many possible criteria for collapsing. Since automatically performed collapsing can lead to an undesired combination of categories, it is suggested that the user examine the individual tables and specify the desired collapsing by using CODEs, CUTPoints and NAMEs in the CATEGory paragraph.

The following statistics are calculated on the collapsed table: Pearson's χ^2, likelihood ratio χ^2, ϕ, C and Cramer's V. All other statistics are calculated on the original table. Note that if the table is collapsed to a 2x2 table, Yates corrected χ^2 is not computed.

If a row or a column of the table contains only zero frequencies it is ignored, and all statistics are computed on the reduced table defined by the nonzero rows and columns. Thus, collapsing need not be requested to remove levels of indices that contain all zeros.

Delta

The cells of a table may be augmented by a user-specified value DELTA. The following statistics are computed on the modified table: Pearson's χ^2, Yates corrected χ^2, likelihood-ratio χ^2, ϕ, C, Cramer's V, the cross-product ratio, Yule's Q and Y, tetrachoric correlation, McNemar's test and the test of the regression coefficient. Tables of the expected values, differences and residuals are also affected by the value of DELTA. All other computations are performed on the original table. Rows and columns that are completely zero are not used in the computation. If collapsing is requested, the value DELTA is added to the frequencies of the collapsed table.

2 x 2 Tables

The following statistics are computed only when the input table is 2 x 2 (they are not computed for a larger table that collapses to 2 x 2): Yates corrected $\overline{\chi^2}$, Fisher's exact test, ϕ_{max}, Yule's Q and Y, the cross-product ratio and the tetrachoric correlation r_t.

Collapsing is not performed on a table that is originally 2 x 2.

A.6 STEPWISE IDENTIFICATION OF EXTREME CELLS (P2F)

● DEFINITION OF CRITERIA

Let $(i,j) \in E$ represent the cells eliminated before the ith cell or declared empty a priori. Form the pseudo-frequency table $\{a_{ij}^{*}\}$ where

$$a_{ij}^{*} = a_{ij} \qquad (i,j) \notin E$$

$$a_{ij}^{*} = e_{ij}^{*} \qquad (i,j) \in E$$

where a_{ij} is the observed frequency and e_{ij}^{*} is the fitted value based on the quasi-independent model. That is, the expected (fitted) values replace the observed frequencies for eliminated and empty cells. Let r_{i}^{*}, c_{j}^{*} and N^{*} be the row, column and total frequency for this table. Then it can be shown that the expected value for any cell in this table $r_{i}^{*}c_{j}^{*}/N^{*}$ is equal to the fitted values e_{ij} when $(i,j) \notin E$ and e_{ij}^{*} when $(i,j) \in E$.

When E contains only one cell (I,J), the fitted value for this cell is

$$e_{ij}^{'} = \frac{(r_{I} - a_{IJ})(c_{J} - a_{IJ})}{(N - r_{I} - c_{J} + a_{IJ})}$$

In order to approximate the fitted value which a cell will have after being eliminated we rewrite $e_{ij}^{'}$ as

$$e_{IJ}^{'} = \frac{(r_{I}^{*} - a_{IJ}^{*})(c_{J}^{*} - a_{IJ}^{*})}{(N^{*} - r_{I}^{*} - c_{J}^{*} + a_{IJ}^{*})}$$

It should be noted that once any cell has been excluded, this is not exact since the elimination of any cell changes the fitted values of all cells previously excluded and therefore r_{I}^{*}, c_{j}^{*} and N^{*} are also modified. Therefore there are differences between the value of the criterion to delete a cell and that to reenter the cell at the step at which the cell is eliminated.

Using the above notation, we define the criteria as:

CHISQ:
Let χ^{2} be the value of the χ^{2} test of independence based on the non-eliminated cells; i.e., $(i,j) \notin E$. The change in χ^{2} caused by increasing a single cell (I,J) by Δ is

$$\delta_{IJ} = \Delta \left\{ S_{++}^{*} - 1 - \frac{(N^{*}+\Delta)}{c_{J}^{*}(c_{J}^{*}+\Delta)} S_{+J}^{*} - \frac{(N^{*}+\Delta)}{r_{I}(r_{I}+\Delta)} S_{I+}^{*} \right. $$

$$\left. + \frac{(N^{*}+\Delta)}{(r_{I}^{*}+\Delta)(c_{J}^{*}+\Delta)} \left(\frac{\Delta a_{IJ}^{*}}{r_{I}^{*}c_{J}^{*}} + 2a_{IJ}^{*} + \Delta \right) \right\}$$

where $S_{++}^* = \Sigma_i \Sigma_j a_{ij}^* /(r_i^* c_j^*)$, $S_{I+}^* = \Sigma_j a_{IJ}^2 /c_j^*$, $S_{+J}^* = \Sigma_i a_{iJ}^2 /r_i^*$

To test an eliminated cell for reentry: $\quad \Delta = a_{IJ} - a_{IJ}^* \quad (I,J) \in E$

To select a cell for elimination: $\qquad\qquad \Delta = e_{IJ}' - a_{IJ} \quad (I,J) \notin E$

As the value of the criterion, $(\chi^2 + \delta_{IJ})$ is printed.

LRCHI:
Let G^2 be the value of the likelihood ratio test for independence based on the noneliminated cells. The change in G^2 caused by changing a single cell (I,J) from the value d_{IJ} to b_{IJ} is

$$\delta_{IJ} = 2[b_{IJ} \; ln \; b_{IJ} - d_{IJ} \; ln \; d_{IJ} - (r_I^* + \Delta) \; ln \; (r_I^* + \Delta) - r_I^* \; ln \; r_I^*$$

$$- (c_J^* + \Delta) \; ln \; (c_J^* + \Delta) + c_J^* \; ln \; c_J^* + (N^* + \Delta) \; ln \; (N^* + \Delta) - N^* \; ln \; N^*]$$

where $\Delta = b_{IJ} - d_{IJ}$

To test an eliminated cell for reentry: $\quad d_{IJ} = a_{IJ}^*, \; b_{IJ} = a_{IJ} \quad (I,J) \in E$

To test a cell for elimination: $\qquad\quad d_{IJ} = a_{IJ}, \; b_{IJ} = e_{IJ}' \quad (I,J) \notin E$

As the value of the criterion, $(G^2 + \delta_{IJ})$ is printed.

DIF:
The criterion for all cells is

$$a_{ij} - r_i^* c_j^* /N^*$$

STAN:
The criterion for all cells is

$$(a_{ij} - r_i^* c_j^* /N^*)/(r_i^* c_j^* /N^*)^{1/2}$$

ADJ:
The criterion for all cells is

$$(a_{ij} - r_i^* c_j^* /N^*)\Big/\left[\frac{r_i^* c_j^*}{N^*} \left(1 - \frac{r_i^*}{N^*}\right)\left(1 - \frac{c_j^*}{N}\right)\right]^{1/2}$$

QUSTAN:
The criterion for all cells is

$$(a_{ij} - e_{ij}')/e_{ij}'^{1/2}$$

QUADJ:
Let $\Delta = a_{ij}^* - e_{ij}'$. The criterion for all cells is

$$(a_{ij} - e_{ij}')\Big/\left[\frac{(r_i^* + \Delta)(c_j^* + \Delta)}{(N^* + \Delta)} \left\{1 - \frac{(r_i^* + \Delta)}{(N^* + \Delta)} \right\} \left\{1 - \frac{(c_j^* + \Delta)}{(N^* + \Delta)}\right\}\right]^{1/2}$$

- ALGORITHMS TO ESTIMATE EXPECTED VALUES FOR QUASI-INDEPENDENT MODELS

The expected values under the model of quasi-independence are estimated by an algorithm of Brown (1974) when the number of excluded cells (including those identified as extreme) is less than R + C - 1. Otherwise they are estimated by an algorithm of Goodman (1968).

Brown's algorithm at the kth step is

$$e_{ij}^{\prime(k)} = \frac{(r_i^{*(k-1)} - e_{ij}^{\prime(k-1)})(c_j^{*(k-1)} - e_{ij}^{\prime(k-1)})}{N^{*(k-1)} - r_i^{*(k-1)} - c_j^{*(k-1)} + e_{ij}^{\prime(k-1)}}$$

$$r_i^{*(k)} = r_i^{*(k-1)} + e_{ij}^{\prime(k)} - e_{ij}^{\prime(k-1)}$$

$$c_j^{*(k)} = c_j^{*(k-1)} + e_{ij}^{\prime(k)} - e_{ij}^{\prime(k-1)}$$

$$N^{*(k)} = N^{*(k-1)} + e_{ij}^{\prime(k)} - e_{ij}^{\prime(k-1)}$$

for all the empty cells. To check of convergence has occurred, test if

$$\text{Max} \left| e_{ij}^{\prime(k)} - \frac{r_i^{*(k)} c_j^{*(k)}}{N^{*(k)}} \right| < \epsilon$$

for some suitably chosen ϵ (CONVERGENCE) where the maximum is over all excluded cells. The starting values are: the expected value of the cell before exclusion; 0 if the cell is empty; or the expected value calculated by a previous step in a stepwise routine for the identification of extreme cells.

After convergence, the fitted (expected) values of all the cells are computed by

$$e_{ij}^* = \frac{r_i^* c_j^*}{N^*}$$

where r_i^*, c_j^* and N^* are the modified row and column marginals and the total frequency of the fitted values found by the above algorithm.

Goodman's algorithm to find the quasi-independent expected values adjusts the row and column marginal totals. Express the estimated expected value as

$$\hat{e}_{ij}^* = \hat{\alpha}_i \hat{\beta}_j$$

Let

$$\hat{r}_i = \Sigma_j a_{ij}, \quad \hat{c}_j = \Sigma_i a_{ij}$$

be the sums of the observed frequencies over the included cells. At the first step, calculate the R values for α_i.

$$\alpha_i^0 = \hat{r}_i / \Sigma_j \delta_{ij}$$

where δ_{ij} is 0 if cell (i,j) is excluded; 1 otherwise. At the 2mth step $(m \geq 1)$, calculate the C values for $\hat{\beta}_j$.

$$\hat{\beta}_j^{2m-1} = \hat{c}_j / \Sigma_i \delta_{ij} \hat{\alpha}_i^{2m-2}$$

At the $(2m+1)$th step, calculate the R values

$$\hat{\alpha}_i^{2m} = \hat{r}_i / \Sigma_j \delta_{ij} \hat{\beta}_j^{2m-1}$$

The above iteration is continued until the maximum difference between steps is less than CONVERGENCE. Then the expected values for the cells are calculated as

$$\hat{e}_{ij}^* = \hat{\alpha}_i \hat{\beta}_j$$

A.7 STANDARD ERRORS FOR UNSATURATED LOG-LINEAR MODELS (P3F)

Lee (1977) provides a method of finding standard errors for an unsaturated model when the expected values of each cell can be expressed in closed form (i.e., the model is direct). When the model is not direct, he proposes that the standard errors be evaluated for a direct model having the indirect model as a subset. Preferably the direct model should differ from the indirect one by as few terms as possible. This provides upper bounds for the standard errors.

P3F tests if the model is direct by

    (a) deleting all redundant terms from the model so that it is defined by the minimal set of marginals

    (b) deleting all factors that appear in only one term or in all terms

    (c) if there are two terms or less, the model is direct

    (d) if (a), (b) and (c) have produced any change in the model, return to (a); otherwise the remaining model is indirect

When the model is indirect, a direct model containing it is found as follows:

Let the model remaining after iterating through steps (a) - (d) be the kernel of the indirect model. Generate all models containing two configurations and determine which models contain the kernel as a submodel. Choose the model of lowest order that contains the kernel as a submodel. If more than one model of the lowest order is found, the first model found is used (unfortunately the model may not be unique). Form the direct model containing the union of the original model and the model chosen above. This is the direct model used to compute the asymptotic variances. This model is printed.

A.8 ORTHOGONAL POLYNOMIALS IN P3F

Let $x_{ijk\ell} = \ln F_{ijk\ell}$ where $F_{ijk\ell}$ is the expected (fitted) value for cell (i,j,k,ℓ) and let a plus (+) in the subscript indicate summation over the index replaced by the plus, i.e., $x_{ij++} = \sum_k \sum_\ell x_{ijk\ell}$.

For each factor with M levels, M-1 orthogonal polynomials are generated. The computations of the coefficients can best be shown by two examples. Let $c_i, i=1,\ldots I$ be the values of the polynomial of any given order. Then the coefficient of the polynomial is

$$\frac{1}{gJKL} \Sigma_i c_i x_{i+++}$$

where $g = \Sigma_i |c_i|$ and x_{i+++}.

Let $d_j, j=1,\ldots,J$ and $e_k, k=1,\ldots K$ be values of the polynomials of any order for indices j and k. Then the coefficient of the polynomial product is

$$\frac{1}{g'L} \Sigma_i \Sigma_j \Sigma_k c_i d_j e_k x_{ijk+}$$

where $g' = \Sigma_i \Sigma_j \Sigma_k |c_i d_j e_k|$.

When the model is saturated, the asymptotic standard error s is estimated by

$$s^2 = \frac{1}{(gJKL)^2} \Sigma_i \, c_i^2 / f_{i+++}$$

in the first case and

$$s^2 = \frac{1}{(g'L)^2} \Sigma_i \, \Sigma_j \, \Sigma_k \, (c_i d_j e_k)^2 / f_{ijk+}$$

in the latter case where $f_{ijk\ell}$ is the observed value in cell (i,j,k,ℓ).

A.9 ESTIMATING (SMOOTHING) THE MISSING VALUE CORRELATION MATRIX (PAM)

After the covariance matrix is computed, it is converted to a correlation matrix. The eigenvalues of this correlation matrix are computed if the ALLVALUE option is selected or if the eigenvalues are requested in the *PRINT* paragraph. Some of these eigenvalues may be negative if the ALLVALUE option is selected. If any eigenvalues are negative, the correlation matrix is reestimated using the positive eigenvalues and their corresponding eigenvectors: First the matrix

$$A = V'EV$$

is computed where V is the matrix of eigenvectors of the positive eigenvalues and E is the diagonal matrix of positive eigenvalues. Then the reestimated correlation matrix B is computed from A by the usual method of converting a covariance matrix to a correlation matrix. The reestimated covariance matrix is obtained from B by multiplying the rows and columns of B by the original standard deviations.

A.10 REPLACING MISSING VALUES (PAM)

To substitute means for missing values, the data are read from a temporary unit and missing values are replaced by means.

If the simple linear regression method is used, the vector of maximum correlations and indices of variables of maximum correlations are computed. Then the data are read and estimates are made using simple linear regression of each missing variable on the variable with which it is most highly correlated. If the variable of maximum correlation is also missing, the available variable that has the highest correlation is found and used. If a grouping variable is specified, the standard deviations computed from the pooled within-groups covariance matrix and the appropriate group means are used in the regression.

When either SINGLE, TWOSTEP or STEP is specified, variables are chosen on the basis of the highest partial correlation or F-to-enter, as in P2R (there is no F-to-remove, so once variables are entered they remain). Tolerance is checked (Appendix A.11). If TWOSTEP is specified, or if only one step of STEP is needed, the correlation matrix is not altered. If more than three predictors are chosen pivoting is performed on the correlation matrix, as in P2R. To prevent accumulated round-off error a fresh copy of the correlation matrix is used after pivoting rather than using reverse pivots. If a grouping variable is specified the appropriate group means are used in the regressions.

When the multiple regression method is used, the correlation matrix is inverted in a stepwise manner under control of a tolerance such that pivoting is not performed for any variable whose squared multiple correlation with previously pivoted variables exceeds 1-tolerance. The data are then read from a scratch file one case at a time. A copy of the inverse is reverse pivoted for any variables that are missing and for which pivoting was previously performed. Pivoting will also be performed for any variables that are available for that case and for which pivoting was not previously performed due to tolerance, but can now be pivoted. Mahalanobis distances are computed from the case to the center of all cases in its group (as in P7M) using the variables that were originally available. If a grouping variable is specified, the appropriate group means are used in the regression.

When a grouping variable is specified and its value is missing for a case, the grouping variable is estimated using the classification functions from a standard discriminant analysis (similar to P7M) based on the available variables for that case. If other variables are missing, they are estimated using the means of the group into which the case has been classified. Estimation for a missing grouping variable is available only for the regression method.

A.11 LINEAR REGRESSION -- ESTIMATING THE COEFFICIENTS

A multiple linear regression equation can be written as

$$E(y_j - \bar{y}) = \beta_1 (x_{1j} - \bar{x}_1) + \ldots + \beta_p (x_{pj} - \bar{x}_p)$$

In matrix notation this can be written as

$$E(\underset{\sim}{Y}') = \underset{\sim}{X}' \underset{\sim}{\beta}'$$

where

$\underset{\sim}{Y} = (y_j - \bar{y})$ is a row vector of length N

$\underset{\sim}{X} = (x_{ij} - \bar{x}_i)$ is a pxN matrix

$\underset{\sim}{\beta} = (\beta_i)$ is a row vector of length p

Then the estimate $\underset{\sim}{b}$ of $\underset{\sim}{\beta}$ is

$$\underset{\sim}{b}' = (\underset{\sim}{X}\underset{\sim}{X}')^{-1} \underset{\sim}{X}\underset{\sim}{Y}' \ .$$

In this section we explain how $\underset{\sim}{b}$ is obtained numerically by "sweeping" the matrix $\underset{\sim}{X}\underset{\sim}{X}'$ of cross products of deviations. Sweeping is a method of inverting the matrix of cross products of deviations so that at each step (as each variable is entered into the regression equation), the coefficients $\underset{\sim}{b}$, the partial correlations, the multiple correlation and tolerance, and the residual sum of squares are computed as part of the matrix inversion (see also Jennrich, 1977a).

● SWEEPING AND ESTIMATES OF THE COEFFICIENTS

In BMDP programs, regression equations are usually computed by sweeping a matrix $\underset{\sim}{C}$ of sums of cross-products of deviations:

$$\underset{\sim}{C} = \sum_{1}^{N} (\underset{\sim}{x}_j - \underset{\sim}{\bar{x}})' (\underset{\sim}{x}_j - \underset{\sim}{\bar{x}})$$

where $\underset{\sim}{x}_j$ denotes the data for case j, $\underset{\sim}{\bar{x}}$ denotes the vector of sample means and N is the sample size. If case weights are used $\underset{\sim}{C}$ is the weighted sum of cross-products. If a ZERO intercept is used, $\underset{\sim}{C}$ is the sum of products $\sum \underset{\sim}{x}_j \underset{\sim}{x}_j'$.

The same results (except for minor differences in round-off error) are obtained whether a covariance or correlation matrix or the matrix of cross-products of deviations is used.

A basic reference for sweeping is Dempster (1969, p. 62). In BMDP, sweeping is used both to obtain regression equations and to do matrix inversion. Sweeping is most easily described in the context of stepwise regression (P2R).

Suppose we have p independent variables so that $\underset{\sim}{C}$ is a p+1 x p+1 matrix with dependent variable as variable p+1. At step one of stepwise regression, an independent variable is chosen, say variable k. The matrix $\underset{\sim}{C}$ is swept on variable k to produce a matrix $\underset{\sim}{C}*$, where

$$C^*_{ij} = C_{ij} - C_{ik}C_{kj}/C_{kk} \qquad \text{for } i \neq k, \, j \neq k$$

$$C^*_{kj} = C_{kj}/C_{kk}$$

$$C^*_{ik} = C_{ik}/C_{kk}$$

$$C^*_{kk} = -1/C_{kk}$$

Note that $\underset{\sim}{C}^*$ is symmetric.

At this point, $C^*_{p+1,k}$ is the <u>regression coefficient</u> for predicting the dependent variable p+1 from variable k. (The intercept is computed separately.) Also, $C^*_{p+1,p+1}$ is the <u>residual sum of squares</u> from regressing the dependent variable (p+1) on variable k. The <u>partial correlation</u> of a pair of variables i and j for $i \neq k$ and $j \neq k$ can be computed as

$$r_{ij \cdot k} = \frac{C^*_{ij}}{\sqrt{C^*_{ii}C^*_{jj}}}$$

The estimate of the variance of the regression coefficient is proportional to $C^*_{p+1,p+1}C^*_{kk}$. In the computer, C^*_{ij} is stored in the same place that C_{ij} was stored so $\underset{\sim}{C}$ is overwritten as $\underset{\sim}{C}^*$ is computed. If we let $\underset{\sim}{C}$ represent the computer FORTRAN array rather than the mathematical array, we define sweeping on variable k algorithmically as

$$C_{ij} = C_{ij} - C_{ik}C_{kj}/C_{kk} \qquad \text{for } i \neq k, \, j \neq k$$

$$C_{kj} = C_{ij}/C_{kk}$$

$$C_{ik} = C_{ik}/C_{kk}$$

$$C_{kk} = -1/C_{kk}$$

At step two, we choose another variable, say ℓ and sweep as we did for variable k. At this point $C_{p+1,p+1}$ contains the residual sum of squares for regressing the dependent variable p+1 on variables k and ℓ; $C_{p+1,k}$ and $C_{p+1,\ell}$ are the regression coefficients; the partial correlation of variables i and j (i and $j \neq k$ or ℓ) is

$$\frac{C_{ij}}{\sqrt{C_{ii}C_{jj}}}$$

The estimated covariance matrix of the regression coefficients (assuming an intercept) is

$$\frac{-C_{p+1,p+1}}{n-3} \begin{pmatrix} C_{kk} & C_{k\ell} \\ C_{\ell k} & C_{\ell\ell} \end{pmatrix}$$

where -3 is replaced by -2 if there is no intercept.

At an arbitrary step, suppose that sweeping has been performed for variables 1 to k. Let

$$\underset{\sim}{C} = \begin{pmatrix} -A_{kk} & B'_{kq} \\ B_{qk} & D_{qq} \end{pmatrix}$$

where q = p-k+1. $\underset{\sim}{A}$ is the inverse of the cross product of deviations for the variables that have been swept (entered into the equation). $\underset{\sim}{B}$ contains the <u>regression coefficients</u> for predicting variables k+1 to p+1 from variables 1 to k. The estimate of the <u>covariance matrix of the regression coefficients</u> for predicting variable i (k < i $\leq$ p+1) is

$$\frac{C_{ii}}{N-k-1} \underset{\sim}{A}$$

where the term -1 is dropped if there is no intercept. $\underset{\sim}{D}$ is the sum of cross-products of the residuals of the variables that have not been swept regressed on the variables that have been swept; the diagonal of $\underset{\sim}{D}$ contains the residual sum of squares for each nonswept variable. The <u>partial correlations</u> for variables k+1 to p+1 adjusting for the linear effects of variables 1 to k are obtained by converting $\underset{\sim}{D}$ to a correlation matrix. Thus the variables for which sweeping has been performed can be considered as independent variables and the remaining variables are dependent variables. Sweeping a variable changes a variable from being dependent to independent. Sweeping is also reversible. If a reverse sweep is performed, a variable changes its status from independent to dependent.

The inverse of a matrix is obtained by sweeping all variables. More precisely, the inverse is equal to the negative of the result of sweeping all variables.

● TOLERANCE

Sometimes the matrix $\underset{\sim}{C}$ is singular or nearly singular. In this case C cannot be inverted or cannot be inverted with satisfactory numerical accuracy. A deeper problem, say in the context of regression, is that the regression coefficients have poor statistical properties whenever the covariance matrix of the independent variables is nearly singular since the estimated variance of the regression coefficient for a particular independent variable is inversely proportional to one minus the squared multiple correlation of that independent variable with all other independent variables. One minus this squared multiple correlation is called the <u>tolerance</u> for that variable. The reciprocal of the tolerance is called the <u>variance inflation factor</u>. In practice, if one independent variable has a high squared multiple correlation with the other independent variables, it is extremely unlikely that the independent variable in question contributes significantly to the regression equation. For these reasons, BMDP programs always perform regression analysis (and matrix inversion) in a stepwise manner in such a way that at any step no variable is added to the list of independent variables if either

- its squared multiple correlation with already included independent variables exceeds one minus the tolerance limit

- including the variable would cause the squared multiple correlation for an already included variable to exceed one minus the tolerance limit

Variables that do not pass the tolerance test are considered redundant. When the solution of an ill-conditioned problem is necessary, a program like P9R (with METHOD=NONE.) that uses double precision should be used.

A.12 RESIDUAL ANALYSIS IN P9R

Residuals for each case are computed as

$$(y-\bar{y}) - b_1(x_1-\bar{x}_1) - \ldots - b_p(x_p-\bar{x}_p)$$

where

   y = dependent variable

   b_i = regression coefficient for the ith independent variable x_i

The standard error of a residual for a case with positive weight is computed as the square root of

$$\left[\frac{1}{w} - \frac{1}{N} - (\underset{\sim}{x}-\underset{\sim}{\bar{x}})\underset{\sim}{C}^{-1}(\underset{\sim}{x}-\underset{\sim}{\bar{x}})'\right] RMS$$

where

   $\underset{\sim}{C}^{-1}$ is the inverse of the matrix of cross products of deviations of the independent variables ($\underset{\sim}{A}$ in Appendix A.11)

   N is the number of cases with nonzero weight

   w is the case weight

   RMS is the residual mean square

and the terms $1/N$ and $\underset{\sim}{\bar{x}}$ are dropped if there is no intercept.

The standard error of a residual with zero weight is computed as the square root of

$$\left[1 + \frac{1}{N} + (\underset{\sim}{x}-\underset{\sim}{\bar{x}})\underset{\sim}{C}^{-1}(\underset{\sim}{x}-\underset{\sim}{\bar{x}})'\right] RMS$$

Standardized residuals are obtained by dividing each residual by its standard error.

The Mahalanobis distance from the case to the centroid of all cases in the space defined by the independent variables is

$$(N-1)(\underset{\sim}{x}-\bar{\underset{\sim}{x}})\underset{\sim}{C}^{-1}(\underset{\sim}{x}-\bar{\underset{\sim}{x}})'$$

where the terms -1 and $\bar{\underset{\sim}{x}}$ are dropped if there is a ZERO intercept.

Weighted residuals are computed by multiplying the residual by the square root of the weight for cases with positive weights and are the same as the ordinary residual for cases with zero weights.

For cases with positive weight, the deleted residual is obtained by dividing the ordinary residual by

$$1 - \frac{w}{N} - w(\underset{\sim}{x}-\bar{\underset{\sim}{x}})\underset{\sim}{C}^{-1}(\underset{\sim}{x}-\bar{\underset{\sim}{x}})'$$

where the terms w/N and $\bar{\underset{\sim}{x}}$ are dropped if there is no intercept. The deleted residual is the residual which would have been obtained had the case been given a zero case weight. For cases with zero weights, the deleted residual is the same as the ordinary residual.

Cook's (1977) distance is defined for cases with positive case weight as

$$\frac{r*^2 v}{(p+1)RMS}$$

where r* denotes the deleted residual; where the term +1 is dropped if the intercept is zero, and

$$v = w(\frac{1}{N} + d)$$

where the term 1/N is dropped if there is a ZERO intercept and where d is the Mahalanobis distance divided by N-1 (or by N if there is a zero intercept). For a case with a zero case weight, Cook's distance is defined as the value that would have been computed had the case been given a case weight of one.

A.13 REGRESSION ON PRINCIPAL COMPONENTS (P4R)

The eigenvalues (λ_k) and eigenvectors (a_{ki}) of the covariance or correlation matrix (C) of the independent variables are computed using the Jacobi method, and the principal component scores (z_{kj}) are obtained as

$$z_{kj} = \sum_i a_{ki}(x_{ij} - \bar{x}_i) \qquad\qquad j=1,\ldots,N; \; k=1,\ldots,p$$

where N is the number of cases and p is the number of independent variables, or

$$z_{kj} = \sum_i a_{ki}\left(\frac{x_{ij}-\bar{x}_i}{s_i}\right) \quad , \text{ if standardization is requested.}$$

The regression coefficients (β_k) of the components, and the correlations ($r_{z_k y}$) of the principal component scores (z_k) with the dependent variable ($y=x_d$) are computed as

$$\beta_k = \frac{\sum_i a_{ki} C_{id}}{\lambda_k}$$

where C_{id} is the covariance of variable i with $y = x_d$, or

$$\beta_k = \left(\sum_i a_{ki} R_{id}\right) \frac{s_d}{\lambda_k} \quad , \quad \text{if standardization is requested}$$

where R_{id} is the correlation of variable i with $y = x_d$, and then

$$r_{z_k y} = \beta_k \cdot \frac{\sqrt{\lambda_k}}{s_y}$$

The regression coefficients of the variables (b_i) are computed.

$$b_i = \sum_k a_{ki}\beta_k$$

or

$$b_i = \frac{\sum_k a_{ki}\beta_k}{s_i} \quad , \text{ if standardization is requested.}$$

The residual sum of squares, total F and F for the component are computed.

$$RSS_d = \sum_j (y_j - \bar{y})^2$$

$$RSS_k = RSS_{k-1} - (N-1)\beta^2_k \lambda_k$$

$$FTOT_k = \frac{(RSS_d - RSS_k)/k}{RSS_k/(N-1-k)}$$

$$F_k = \frac{(RSS_{k-1} - RSS_k)}{RSS_k/(N-1-k)}$$

A.14 POLYNOMIAL REGRESSION (P5R)

Let w_j, x_j and y_j denote the weight, independent variable value and dependent variable value for the jth case where $j=1,\ldots,N$. For any two N-vectors $\underset{\sim}{u}$, $\underset{\sim}{v}$, let

$$[\underset{\sim}{u},\underset{\sim}{v}] = \sum_{j=1}^{N} w_j u_j v_j \qquad \text{(the weighted inner product of } \underset{\sim}{u} \text{ and } \underset{\sim}{v})$$

Orthogonal polynomials values ($\underset{\sim}{P}_s$) for degrees $s=1,\ldots,r$ are computed recursively by the Forsythe (1957) method normalized so that the (weighted) sum of squares for each is one. The computation of the $\underset{\sim}{P}_s$ is described later.

The regression coefficients for the fitted orthogonal polynomials are given by

$$\hat{\gamma}_s = [\underset{\sim}{P}_s,\underset{\sim}{y}] ; \qquad s=0,\ldots,r$$

Those for the fitted polynomial in x of degree s are given by

$$\hat{\beta}_t = \sum_{q=0}^{s} b_{tq} \hat{\gamma}_q ; \qquad t=0,\ldots,s$$

The residual values of the dependent variable after fitting a polynomial of degree $s=0,\ldots,r$ are

$$\hat{\underset{\sim}{e}}_s = \underset{\sim}{y} - \hat{\gamma}_0 \underset{\sim}{1} - \hat{\gamma}_1 \underset{\sim}{P}_1 - \ldots - \hat{\gamma}_s \underset{\sim}{P}_s$$

The residual sum of squares and mean square are

$$RSS_s = [\hat{\underset{\sim}{e}}_s, \hat{\underset{\sim}{e}}_s] \quad \text{and}$$

$$RMS_s = RSS_s/(N-s-1)$$

The standard errors and covariances for polynomials of degree s are estimated by

$$\hat{s.e.}(\hat{\gamma}_p) = RMS_s^{\frac{1}{2}} ; \qquad p=0,\ldots,s$$

$$\hat{cov}(\hat{\beta}_p, \hat{\beta}_q) = \sum_{t=0}^{s} b_{pt}b_{qt}RMS_s ; \qquad p,q=0,\ldots,s$$

$$\hat{s.e.}(\hat{\beta}_p) = [\hat{cov}(\hat{\beta}_p, \hat{\beta}_p)]^{\frac{1}{2}}; \qquad p=0,\ldots,s$$

An analysis of variance table is computed in the form

Degree	df	Mean Square	F
0	1	MS_0	MS_0/RMS_s
1	1	MS_1	MS_1/RMS_s
$\vdots$	$\vdots$	$\vdots$	$\vdots$
s	1	MS_s	MS_s/RMS_s
Residual	N-s-1	RMS_s	

where

$$MS_t = \hat{\gamma}_t^2 ; \qquad t=0,\ldots,s$$

The goodness-of-fit estimates

$$F_s = \frac{(RSS_s - RSS_r)/(r-s)}{RSS_r/(N-r-1)}$$

with r-s and N-r-1 degrees of freedom computed for each degree s=0,...,r-1.

- COMPUTATION OF ORTHOGONAL POLYNOMIAL VALUES (FORSYTHE, 1957)

    Let $q_{0,j} = 1$ and $q_{1,j} = x_j - \bar{x}$ where x_j is the observed value of the independent variable for case j and

$$\bar{x} = \sum_j w_j x_j / \sum_j w_j$$

is the weighted mean. The orthogonal polynomials are computed recursively using the relation

$$q_{s+1,j} = q_{1,j}P_{s,j} - \alpha_{1s}P_{s,j} - \alpha_{2s}P_{s-1,j} \qquad s=1,2,\ldots,r-1$$

where

$$|q_s| = \{\Sigma_j w_j q_{s,j}^2\}^{\frac{1}{2}}$$

$$P_{s,j} = q_{s,j}/|q_s| \quad \text{(normalized values)} \quad \text{where } P_{0,j} = 1/N$$

$$\alpha_{1s} = \Sigma_j w_j(x_j-\bar{x})P_{s,j}^2$$

$$\alpha_{2s} = \Sigma_j w_j(x_j-\bar{x})P_{s-1,j}P_{s,j}$$

$$r = \text{maximum degree of polynomial}$$

Let $b_{0s},\ldots,b_{ss}$ denote the coefficients for the expansion of the sth degree orthogonal polynomial in powers of x. The coefficients of the (s+1)th degree orthogonal polynomial are computed by letting

$$b_{00} = 1/|q_0|, \quad b_{01} = -\bar{x}/|q_1|, \quad b_{11} = 1/|q_1|$$

and then

$$b_{i,s+1} = (b_{i-1,s} - \bar{x}b_{is} - \alpha_{1s}b_{is} - \alpha_{2s}b_{i,s-1})/|q_{s+1}| \; ; \quad i=0,\ldots,s+1$$

where

$$b_{h,j} = 0 \quad \text{for } h < 0 \text{ or } h > j$$

A.15 NONLINEAR LEAST SQUARES (P3R)

P3R minimizes the weighted residual sum of squares

$$RSS = \Sigma \, w[y-f(\underset{\sim}{x},\underset{\sim}{p})]^2$$

where the summation is over the N complete cases subject to linear constraints, if any are specified, of the form

$$\Sigma_i b_{\ell i}p_i = c_\ell$$

For each case

> x is the vector of values of the independent variables
>
> y is the value of the dependent variable
>
> w is the case weight
>
> $f(x,p)$ is the value of the function evaluated using the values of the parameters $p = (p_1, p_2, \ldots, p_m)$

Initially the system of linear constraints (if specified) is solved in terms of a subset of the parameters. Let m be the number of parameters in the subset and m' the original number (m'=m when there are no linear constraints). To simplify the notation we let the m parameters be $p_1, p_2, \ldots p_m$. Therefore

$$p_\ell = \sum_{i=1}^{m} b_{\ell i} p_i + c_\ell \qquad\qquad m + 1 \leq \ell \leq m'$$

Minimizing the residual sum of squares

The vector p that minimizes the RSS is obtained through iteration (Jennrich and Sampson, 1968). At each iteration the function is approximated by a first order Taylor series expansion; i.e.,

$$y = f(x, p^{(0)}) + \sum z_i(p_i - p_i^{(0)})$$

where the superscript (0) specifies the current value of the parameters and $z_i = \partial f(x, p^{(0)})/p_i$, i=1,2,...,m are the partial derivatives. (When there are linear equality constraints, more linear terms are necessary.) Then for any $p^{(0)}$ the above can be written as a linear equation in the z_i, and the coefficient of z_i can be found as in linear regression. The new estimate of p_i is $p_i^{(0)}$ plus the estimated coefficient of z_i.

The following are computed for each case

$$z_i = \partial f(x,p)/\partial p_i \qquad i=1,2,\ldots,m$$

$$e = y - f(x,p)$$

or, if there are any linear equality constraints,

$$z_i = \frac{\partial f(x,p)}{p_i} + \sum_{\ell=m+1}^{m'} b_{\ell i} \frac{\partial f(x,p)}{\partial p_\ell} \qquad i=1,2,\ldots,m$$

and

$$e = y - f(x,p) + \sum_{\ell=m+1}^{m'} \frac{\partial f(x,p)}{\partial p_\ell} [p_\ell - \sum b_{\ell i} p_i - c_\ell]$$

P3R then forms the matrix ($\underset{\sim}{A}$) of weighted sums of cross products of $z_1, z_2, \ldots, z_m, e$; i.e., $A = (a_{ij})$ where $z_{m+1} = e$ and $a_{ij} = \Sigma \, w z_i z_j$.

Using the Gauss-Jordan algorithm for matrix inversion, the matrix $\underset{\sim}{A}$ is swept on its diagonal elements (except $a_{m+1, m+1}$) in a stepwise manner. At each step the index of the pivoting element is the r which maximizes $a_{m+1, r}/a_{rr}$ such that the TOLERANCE limit is not violated (Appendix A.11). If any of the first m diagonal elements of $\underset{\sim}{A}$ are left unpivoted because they fail the TOLERANCE test, corresponding elements of the last row of $\underset{\sim}{A}$ are set to zero.

Let $\hat{p}_i$ be the provisionally estimated value; i.e., $\hat{p}_i = p_i^{(0)} + a'_{i(m+1)}$ where a'_{ij} is the value of a_{ij} after pivoting the matrix $\underset{\sim}{A}$. The updated values are then chosen as

$$p_i = \hat{p}_i + d\,(\hat{p}_i - p_i^{(0)})$$

where $0 < d \leq 1$ and d is chosen so that the p_i's satisfy their upper and lower limits if specified (if d < a small constant, one or more parameters are left unchanged from previous values). If there are linear constraints

$$p_\ell = \Sigma \, b_{\ell i} p_i + c_\ell \qquad m + 1 \leq \ell \leq m'.$$

Upper and lower limits for these parameters may be violated; these violations can be found by inspecting the parameter estimates.

A new value of RSS is computed. If the new RSS is greater than the previous RSS, d is halved and new values of the p_i are obtained. Increment halving continues until the new RSS is not larger than the previous RSS or the maximum number of HALVINGS is reached. If the maximum number of HALVINGS is reached, P3R continues using the values at the last halving.

Iterations are performed until the CONVERGENCE criterion is satisfied or the maximum number of ITERATIONS is reached.

Asymptotic standard deviations

The asymptotic covariance of p_i and p_j is $s^2 a'_{ij}$ where a'_{ij} is the pivoted value of a_{ij} and $s^2 = RSS/(N-m'')$ where m'' is the number of independent (pivoted) parameter estimates ($m'' \leq m$). a_{ij} is zero if either a_{ii} or a_{jj} is unpivoted. If a value is specified for MEANSQUARE, then s^2 is the specified value; otherwise s^2 is computed using the smallest RSS if CONVERGENCE is positive or the last RSS if CONVERGENCE is negative.

If there are linear constraints the asymptotic variances and covariances of the remaining parameters are obtained from those of the subset of m parameters.

The standard error of the predicted value for a case is

$$s \, \{ \, \Sigma \, \Sigma \, z_k a'_{ij} z_j \, \}^{\frac{1}{2}}$$

A.16 DERIVATIVE-FREE NONLINEAR LEAST SQUARES (PAR)

PAR finds the minimum of the function

$$Q(\underset{\sim}{p}) = \Sigma w(y - f(\underset{\sim}{x},\underset{\sim}{p}))^2$$

(where the summation is over all cases) subject to constraints each of which can be written as

$$\underset{\sim}{b}_\ell{}'\underset{\sim}{p} \geq c_\ell$$

Such constraints include MINIMUMS and MAXIMUMS on the parameters as well as the additional CONSTRAINTS and corresponding LIMITs, all of which are specified in the *PARAMeter* paragraph.

For each case

$\underset{\sim}{x}$	is the vector of values of the independent variables
y	is the value of the dependent variable
w	is the case weight
$f(\underset{\sim}{x},\underset{\sim}{p})$	is the value of the function evaluated using the values of the parameters $\underset{\sim}{p} = (p_1, p_2, \ldots, p_m)$

Overview of the procedure

If there are no boundary constraints each iteration consists of approximating $f(\underset{\sim}{x},p)$ by a linear function of p and solving the resulting linear regression problem to get a new estimate of $\hat{p}$. The linear function $\ell(x,p)$ equal to $f(x.p)$ at $p^{(1)},\ldots,p^{(m'+1)}$ (estimates of $\hat{p}$ computed in previous $\tilde{m}'+1$ iterations, where m' is the number of parameters to be estimated) is used to approximate $f(\underset{\sim}{x},p)$. The $\underset{\sim}{p}$ which minimizes

$$Q^\star(\underset{\sim}{p}) = \Sigma\ w(y - \ell(\underset{\sim}{x},\underset{\sim}{p}))^2$$

is found and used to replace the oldest member of the set $p^{(1)},\ldots,p^{(m'+1)}$ and the revised set of parameter vectors is passed to the next iteration.

If there are boundary constraints on the parameters, the procedure described above is modified so that in each iteration an attempt is made to find a new estimate that satisfies all of the boundary constraints and decreases the value of $Q^\star$. Unlike the unconstrained case, if $f(\underset{\sim}{x},p)$ happens to be a linear function of p, the constrained minimum may not be located in one iteration. Within each iteration the boundary constraints are divided into two sets -- the active constraints (those for which $b_\ell{}'p^{(m+1)} = c_\ell$) and the inactive constraints ($b_\ell{}'p^{(m+1)} \geq c_\ell$). The direction of the new estimate is constrained to be along boundaries formed by some of the active constraints if not doing so would lead to the violation of some of the active constraints. Then if necessary, the step length is shortened so that all of the inactive constraints are satisfied by the new estimate. LaGrange multipliers are used to compute the constrained minimum of $Q^\star$.

Generating the starting values

The m+1 starting parameter vectors needed by the algorithm are generated from the INITIAL and DELTA parameters in the *PARAMeter* paragraph as follows:

$$p_i^{(k)} = \text{INIT}(i) + \delta_{ik}\text{DELTA}(i)$$

where δ_{ik} is the Kronecker delta.

If any parameters are designated as FIXED in the *PARAMeter* paragraph only m'+1 starting values are computed where m' is the number of parameters to be estimated. If any of the $p^{(k)}$ violate a boundary constraint the magnitude of DELTA(k) is decreased so that $p^{(k)}$ lies halfway between $p^{(m'+1)}$ and the nearest boundary.

The regression function is evaluated for each starting vector. Then the starting vectors are renumbered so that

$$Q(\underset{\sim}{p}^{(k)}) \geq Q(\underset{\sim}{p}^{(k+1)}) \text{ for } k=1,\ldots,m'$$

Description of one iteration when there are no boundary constraints

Let

$\underset{\sim}{y}$ = n component vector of values of the dependent variable

$\underset{\sim}{f}(\underset{\sim}{p})$ = n component vector valued function of values of the regression function for each case

$\underset{\sim}{\Delta P}$ = m' x m' matrix with columns $p^{(k)} - p^{(m'+1)}$

$\underset{\sim}{\Delta F}$ = n x m' matrix whose columns are $\underset{\sim}{f}(\underset{\sim}{p}^{(k)}) - \underset{\sim}{f}(\underset{\sim}{p}^{(m'+1)})$

$\underset{\sim}{W}$ = n x n diagonal matrix of case weights

Step 1

Form the (m'+1) x (m'+1) matrix

$$\underset{\sim}{A} = \begin{pmatrix} \underset{\sim}{\Delta F}'\underset{\sim}{W}\underset{\sim}{\Delta F} & [\underset{\sim}{y} - \underset{\sim}{f}(\underset{\sim}{p}^{(m'+1)})]'\underset{\sim}{W}\underset{\sim}{\Delta F} \\ \underset{\sim}{\Delta F}'\underset{\sim}{W}[\underset{\sim}{y}-\underset{\sim}{f}(\underset{\sim}{p}^{(m'+1)})] & 0 \end{pmatrix}$$

Step 2

A stepwise regression modification of the Gauss-Jordan algorithm for matrix inversion is used to pivot on the first m' diagonal elements of $\underset{\sim}{A}$. At each step the index of the pivoting element is the r which maximizes $a_{m'+1,r}^2/a_{rr}$ among all of the unpivoted a_{rr} such that the TOLERANCE limit is not violated.

Step 3

Let $\underset{\sim}{\alpha}$ denote the vector containing the first m' elements of the (m'+1)th column of A. If any of the first m' diagonal elements of A were not used as pivots the corresponding elements of $\underset{\sim}{\alpha}$ are set equal to zero. $\underset{\sim}{\delta}$ is computed from $\underset{\sim}{\delta} = \Delta P \underset{\sim}{\alpha}$. Then $\underset{\sim}{p}^{(m'+2)} = \underset{\sim}{p}^{(m'+1)} + \underset{\sim}{\delta}$ and $\underset{\sim}{f}(\underset{\sim}{p}^{(m'+2)})$ are computed.

Step 4

An attempt is made to find a point that decreases $Q(\underset{\sim}{p})$. If $Q(\underset{\sim}{p}^{(m'+2)}) > Q(\underset{\sim}{p}^{(m'+1)})$, Q is evaluated at a sequence of points (up to step HALVING) in which the step length is successively halved and the direction alternates between $\underset{\sim}{\delta}$ and $- \underset{\sim}{\delta}$.

The set of parameter vectors to be passed to the next iteration is determined as follows:

Let r be the first subscript such that $|\alpha_r| > .00005$. Then for k=r,...,m'+1 let

$$\underset{\sim}{p}^{(k)}_{new} = \underset{\sim}{p}^{(k+1)}_{old}$$

and if r>1 for k=1,...,r-1

$$\underset{\sim}{p}^{(k)}_{new} = (\underset{\sim}{p}^{(k)}_{old} + \underset{\sim}{p}^{(m'+2)}_{old}) / 2$$

This completes one iteration. Iterations are repeated until the convergence criterion is satisfied, or the maximum number of iterations is reached.

Boundary constraints

For each constraint a "tolerance" is computed as

$$t_{\ell} = \sum_{i=1}^{m} | b_{\ell i} \text{DELTA}(i)| \cdot \text{TOLERANCE}$$

A constraint will be considered satisfied as an equality (i.e., active) if

$$|\underset{\sim}{b}_{\ell}' \underset{\sim}{p} - c_{\ell}| \le t_{\ell}$$

An inequality constraint will be considered satisfied by $\underset{\sim}{p}$ if

$$\underset{\sim}{b}_{\ell}' \underset{\sim}{p} - t_{\ell} \ge c_{\ell}$$

At each iteration the constraints are divided into active and inactive constraints. Let s denote the number of active constraints at the current iteration.

For each active constraint, A (in Step 1 above) is augmented with a row and column whose first m' elements are the components of the vector $b_\ell' \Delta P$ and remaining elements are zero. Pivoting as described in Step 2 is performed on this augmented matrix. Values of $b_\ell' \delta$ are found among the last s elements of the (m'+1)th column of A. To constrain δ so that $p^{(m'+1)} + \delta$ will satisfy the active inequality constraints pivoting is performed as follows:

a. For r = m'+2,...,m'+s+1 pivot on $a_{r,r}$ if

    - r has not been used as a pivot index and

    - $a_{m'+1,r} < -t_{(r-m'-1)}$

Repeat until no r satisfies the criteria used for pivoting.

b. If $a_{m'+1,m'+1}/D < $ TOL, pivot on $a_{r,r}$ and return to part a, where r denotes the first integer, such that

    - r was used as a pivot index in part a

    - $\dfrac{a_{m'+1,r}}{a_{rr}} > t_{(r-m'-1)}$

Compute $\delta^* = \Delta P \alpha$, and $\delta = d\delta^*$ where $0 < d \leq 1$ and d is the largest number such that $p^{(m'+2)} = p^{(m'+1)} + \delta$ satisfies all of the inactive constraints. Then compute $f(p^{(m'+2)})$.

Step 4 is performed as described above except:

- If δ points in a direction interior to any active boundary, the direction is not reversed.

- The step length in the reverse direction is shortened if not doing so would violate an inactive constraint.

Asymptotic standard deviations and correlations

The asymptotic covariance matrix of p is estimated by

$$\hat{\Sigma} = s^2 \Delta P (\Delta F' \Delta F)^{-1} \Delta P'$$

where ΔF and ΔP are the values in the last iteration

$$s^2 = Q(\hat{p})/(n'-m'')$$

where

    n' = number of cases with nonzero weight
    m'' = number of independent (pivoted) parameter estimates
    $\hat{p}$ = the vector that gives the smallest value of Q if this is one
       of the last m'+1 estimates or the final value.

or if MEANSQ is specified

$$s^2 = \text{MEANSQ}.$$

The standard deviation of the predicted value $\hat{f}(\underset{\sim}{x},\underset{\sim}{p})$ is estimated by

$$s(\underset{\sim}{g}(\underset{\sim}{x})'(\Delta\underset{\sim}{F}'\Delta\underset{\sim}{F})^{-1}\underset{\sim}{g}(\underset{\sim}{x}))^{\frac{1}{2}}$$

where $g_k(\underset{\sim}{x}) = f(\underset{\sim}{x},\underset{\sim}{p}^{(k)}) - f(\underset{\sim}{x},\underset{\sim}{p}^{(m'+1)})$

A.17 ONE-WAY ANALYSIS OF VARIANCE AND COVARIANCE (P1V)

The model analyzed is

$$y_{ij} = \mu_i + \beta_1(x_{1ij} - \bar{x}_1) + \ldots + \beta_p(x_{pij} - \bar{x}_p) + e_{ij}$$

where

$i = 1,\ldots,g$ (the group index)

$j = 1,\ldots,n_i$ (the case index in group i)

x_{kij} = the value of the kth variable for case j in group i

Assume that all g groups are to be compared, the first p variables are the covariates, and the (p+1)st variable is the dependent variable. The grand means ($\bar{x}_k$), the between group sum of cross products ($b_{k\ell}$), the pooled within group sum of cross products ($w_{k\ell}$), and the total sum of cross products ($a_{k\ell}$) are given by

$$\bar{x}_k = \frac{1}{N} \sum_{i=1}^{g} n_i \bar{x}_{ki} \qquad\qquad (N = \sum_{i=1}^{g} n_i)$$

$$b_{k\ell} = \sum_{i=1}^{g} n_i (\bar{x}_{ki} - \bar{x}_k)(\bar{x}_{\ell i} - \bar{x}_\ell)$$

$$w_{k\ell} = \sum_{i=1}^{g} (x_{kij} - \bar{x}_{ki})(x_{\ell ij} - \bar{x}_{\ell i})$$

$$a_{k\ell} = b_{k\ell} + w_{k\ell}$$

The between, within and total covariance matrices are obtained by dividing

$$(b_{k\ell}),\ (w_{k\ell}),\ (a_{k\ell})$$

by their degrees of freedom, g-1, N-g and N-1 respectively.

The regression coefficients are estimated by

$$\hat{\beta}_{k\ell} = \sum_{\ell=1}^{p} w^{k\ell}\ w_{\ell,p+1} \qquad\qquad \text{for } k=1,\ldots,p$$

where

$(w^{k\ell})$ is the inverse of the p x p matrix $(w_{k\ell})$

The error variance is estimated by

$$\hat{\sigma}^2 = (w_{p+1,p+1} - \sum_{k=1}^{p} \hat{\beta}_k w_{k,p+1})/(N-g-p)$$

The correlation matrix of the $\hat{\beta}_k$ is given by

$$\text{corr}(\hat{\beta}_k,\hat{\beta}_\ell) = w^{k\ell}/(w^{kk}w^{\ell\ell})^{\frac{1}{2}}$$

The estimates of the standard deviations of the $\hat{\beta}_k$ are given by

$$\hat{\text{s.d.}}\ (\hat{\beta}_k) = \sqrt{w^{kk}}$$

and the corresponding t statistics by

$$t_k = \hat{\beta}_k/\text{s.d.}\ (\hat{\beta}_k)$$

The estimates of the adjusted group means are given by

$$\hat{\mu}_i = \bar{y}_i + \sum_{k=1}^{p} \hat{\beta}_k(\bar{x}_k - \bar{x}_{ik})$$

Let δ be the Kronecker delta, h and i the indices of two groups and

$$d_{hi} = \frac{1}{n_h} \delta_{hi} + \sum_k \sum_\ell (\bar{x}_k - \bar{x}_{kh})w^{k\ell}(\bar{x}_\ell - \bar{x}_{\ell i})$$

The correlations of the adjusted group means are given by

$$\hat{\text{corr}}(\hat{\mu}_h,\hat{\mu}_i) = d_{hi}/(d_{hh}d_{ii})^{\frac{1}{2}}$$

and the estimates of their standard deviations are given by

$$\hat{s.d.} (\hat{\mu}_i) = \hat{\sigma} \sqrt{d_{ii}}$$

Pairwise t statistics for equality of adjusted group means are given by

$$t_{hi} = (\hat{\mu}_h - \hat{\mu}_i)/\hat{\sigma} (d_{hh} + d_{ii} - 2d_{hi})^{\frac{1}{2}}$$

Let $c_1,\ldots,c_g$ denote a set of t test contrast coefficients. An estimate of the corresponding contrast is given by

$$\hat{\gamma} = \sum_{i=1}^{g} c_i \hat{\mu}_i$$

An estimate of its standard deviation is given by

$$\hat{s.d.} (\hat{\gamma}) = \hat{\sigma} \left(\sum_{h=1}^{g} \sum_{i=1}^{g} c_h d_{hi} c_i \right)^{\frac{1}{2}}$$

Let $\tilde{w}_{p+1,p+1}$ denote the value of the (p+1)st diagonal element of the (p+1) x (p+1) matrix $(w_{k\,k})$ which results from performing Gauss-Jordan pivots on the first p diagonal elements. Define $\tilde{w}_{i,p+1,p+1}$ and $\tilde{a}_{p+1,p+1}$ in the same way. The analysis of variance table is

Source	df	Sum of Sq.	Mean Sq.	F-value
Eq. of adj. group means	df_1	SS_1	SS_1/df_1	MS_1/MS_3
Zero slopes	df_2	SS_2	SS_2/df_2	MS_2/MS_3
Error	df_3	SS_3	SS_3/df_3	
Eq. of slopes	df_4	SS_4	SS_4/df_4	MS_4/MS_5
Error	df_5	SS_5	SS_5/df_5	

where

$$df_1 = g-1 \qquad SS_1 = \tilde{a}_{p+1,p+1} - \tilde{w}_{p+1,p+1}$$

$$df_2 = p \qquad SS_2 = \sum_{k=1}^{p} \hat{\beta}_k w_{k,p+1}$$

$$df_3 = n-g-p \qquad SS_3 = \tilde{w}_{p+1,p+1}$$

$$df_4 = df_3 - df_5 \qquad SS_4 = \tilde{w}_{p+1,p+1} - \sum_i w_{i,p+1,p+1}$$

$$df_5 = \Sigma \ (n_i - p - 1) \qquad SS_5 = \underset{i}{\Sigma} \ \tilde{w}_{i,p+1,p+1}$$

The analysis of variance table for one-way analysis of variance consists of the first and third lines of the above table. The equality of slopes test is not performed if the within cross product of deviations for covariates

$$[(w_{k\ell i}) \qquad k,\ell = 1,\ldots,p]$$

for any group i, is singular.

A.18 ANALYSIS OF VARIANCE AND COVARIANCE INCLUDING REPEATED MEASURES (P2V)

We consider the case of several group factors, $g_1,\ldots,g_a$, and several trial factors $t_1,\ldots,t_b$. Let y_{st} be the response of subject s to trial combination $t = (t_1,\ldots,t_b)$. Similarly let x_{stv} be the vth covariate value for subject s on trial combination t; and for ease of exposition, let

$$x_{s,t,p+1} = y_{st}$$

It is assumed that the response and the covariates have been measured for each subject on each trial combination, although the covariates may be constant across some or all trials. The outline below is explained in the steps that follow.

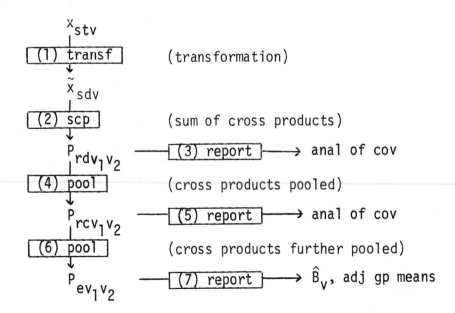

Step 1

For each subject s and variable v, the values x_{stv} across trials are transformed into orthogonal polynomial components $\tilde{x}_{sdv}$. Here, $d = (d_1,\ldots,d_b)$ denotes a degree combination. Specifically

$$\tilde{x}_{sdv} = \Sigma_{t_1} \cdots \Sigma_{t_b} \; \Pi_{d_1 t_1} \cdots \Pi_{d_b t_b} \; x_{stv}$$

where

$\Pi_{d_j t_j}$ = the value of the orthogonal polynomial of degree d_j at t_j

Each trial factor t_j is assumed to range over equally spaced points unless otherwise specified by a POINT statement.

Step 2

For each degree combination d, an analysis of covariance is performed on the data $\tilde{x}_{sdv}$ producing a sum of cross products $P_{rdv_1v_2}$ for each pair of variables x_{v_1} and x_{v_2} and each analysis of variance component r defined by the group factors $g_1,\ldots,g_a$. This step and the next are described in greater detail below.

Step 3

The sums of cross products $P_{rdv_1v_2}$ are used to produce a standard analysis of covariance for each degree d.

Step 4

The cross products $P_{rdv_1v_2}$ are pooled over all degree combinations $d = (d_1,\ldots,d_b)$ that belong to the same analysis of variance component c defined by the trial factors $t_1,\ldots,t_b$. For this purpose, c may be represented by a list of zeros and ones so that

$c = (0,1,0,1)$

represents a $t_2 \times t_4$ interaction. With this convention

$$P_{rcv_1v_2} = \underset{d\varepsilon c}{\Sigma} \; P_{rdv_1v_2}$$

where $d\varepsilon c$ whenever $d = (d_1,\ldots,d_b)$ and $c = (c_1,\ldots,c_b)$ have exactly the same zeros.

Step 5

For each analysis of variance component c defined by the trial factors, the pooled cross products $P_{rcv_1v_2}$ are used to produce a standard analysis of covariance.

Step 6

Let e denote the error component defined by the group effects. The pooled cross products $P_{ecv_1v_2}$ are further pooled across the trial components c. This pooling is weighted by the reciprocals of the error mean squares MS_{ec} reported in the previous step. To be more specific, the pooled cross products are given by

$$P_{ev_1v_2} = \Sigma_c \, MS_{ec}^{-1} \, P_{ecv_1v_2}$$

Step 7

Let $\tilde{P}_{ev_1v_2}$ denote the result of performing pivots on the first p diagonal elements of $P_{ev_1v_2}$ (Jennrich and Sampson, 1968). Then

$$\hat{\beta}_v = \tilde{P}_{e,v,p+1}$$

are the pooled regression coefficient estimates that are used to compute the adjusted group means

$$\bar{y}_{gt}^* = \bar{y}_{gt} + \sum_{v=1}^{p} \hat{\beta}_v (\bar{x}_v - \bar{x}_{gtv})$$

for each group combination $g = (g_1, \ldots, g_a)$ and trial combination $t = (t_1, \ldots, t_b)$. Here $\bar{x}_{gtv}$ and $\bar{y}_{gt}$ denote the average of x_{stv} and y_{st} over all subjects s in group combination g; and $\bar{x}_v$ denotes the average of x_{stv} over all subjects s and trial combinations t.

Step 8

Using the regression coefficient estimates

$$\hat{\beta}_{cv} = P_{e,c,v,p+1}$$

obtained after pivoting in Step 5 and the analysis of variance component residuals x^*_{sdv} obtained by subtracting the group effects from the results $\tilde{x}_{sdv}$ of Step 1, the transformed residuals

$$\tilde{e}_{sd} = x^*_{s,d,p+1} - \sum_{v=1}^{p} x^*_{sdv} \hat{\beta}_{cv}$$

are computed for each subject s and degree combination d. Thus for each value of d, c is chosen so dϵc. The transformed fits are

$$\tilde{v}_{sd} = \tilde{y}_{sd} - \tilde{e}_{sd} \quad .$$

To obtain the untransformed fits and residuals, extend the definition of $\pi_{d_jt_j}$ so that it equals π_{d_j1} whenever $t_j=0$ and let

$$\pi_{dt} = \pi_{d_1t_1} \, \pi_{d_2t_2} \cdots \pi_{d_bt_b}.$$

Then the untransformed fits and residuals are given by

$$\hat{v}_{st} = \sum_{d \epsilon t} \pi_{dt} \tilde{v}_{sd}$$

$$\hat{e}_{st} = \sum_{d \epsilon t} \pi_{dt} \tilde{e}_{sd}$$

where $d \epsilon t$ means that d has exactly the same zeros as t (as in Step 4).

● COVARIANCE ANALYSIS

As indicated in the previous section, the core computations are covariance analyses; many of them are executed, and all of them are similar in form. Although the covariance analyses are applied to transformed data, there is no need to make that distinction here, nor do the trial indices need to appear, because the analyses are applied only across groups. Accordingly, let

$$g_1, \ldots, g_a, \ x_1, \ldots, x_p, \ x_{p+1}$$

denote the group factors and variables. As above, $y = x_{p+1}$ is the dependent variable. The fitted model form is

$$y = \mu_{r_1} + \ldots + \mu_{r_q} + \beta_1 x_1 + \ldots + \beta_p x_p + e$$

where $r_1, \ldots, r_q$ are all possible subsets of the factors $g_1, \ldots, g_a$ unless otherwise specified by an INCLUDE or EXCLUDE statement. A typical r_j has the form $r_j = (g_{i_1}, \ldots, g_{i_k})$. For each factor g_i in r_j, the component

$$\mu_{r_j} = \mu_{g_{i_1} \cdots g_{i_k}}$$

is assumed to sum to zero over all values of g_i corresponding to fixed values of all the other g_i in r_j.

● SUMS OF CROSS PRODUCTS (SCP)

This corresponds to Step 2 above. For each $v_1, v_2 = 1, \ldots, p+1$ and each $r = r_1, \ldots, r_q$, the residual cross products $P_{rv_1v_2}$ for the residuals in x_{v_1} and x_{v_2} after fitting all components $\mu_{r_1}, \ldots, \mu_{r_q}$ except μ_r are obtained together with the residual cross products $P_{ev_1v_2}$ after fitting all components $\mu_{r_1}, \ldots, \mu_{r_q}$. This is done by linear regression after generating the appropriate dummy variables to represent each component $\mu_{r_1}, \ldots, \mu_{r_q}$. To simplify the analysis, it is assumed that the observed levels of the grouping factors are sufficient to uniquely define the components $\mu_{r_1}, \ldots, \mu_{r_q}$. The computation proceeds by computing all cross products for all variables and dummy variables across all subjects. The residual cross products $P_{rv_1v_2}$ are obtained by means of pivots on the appropriate diagonal elements of this large cross product matrix.

Cross products are computed in single precision after means have been subtracted.

- REPORT

This corresponds to Steps 3, 5 and 7 above. For each $r = r_1,\ldots,r_q$, view $P_{rv_1v_2}$ as a $(p+1) \times (p+1)$ matrix and let $\tilde{P}_{rv_1v_2}$ be the result of pivoting on the first p diagonal elements of $P_{rv_1v_2}$. If it is not possible to do this without encountering a diagonal zero (which can happen when the original covariates in the General Procedure are constant across trials) as many pivots as possible are performed. The pivoted cross products $\tilde{P}_{rv_1v_2}$ are used to report an analysis of covariance.

The error sums of squares

$$SS_e = \tilde{P}_{e,p+1,p+1}$$

has degrees of freedom

$$df_e = n - m - p'$$

where

   n = total number of subjects times the number of orthogonal polynomials (degree combinations d) that are pooled for the
   covariance analysis
   m = total number of dummy variables generated above
   p' = number of covariates for which it was possible to perform the
   pivots in the previous paragraph

The sum of squares due to the analysis of variance component μ_r, $r = r_1,\ldots,r_q$, is

$$SS_r = \tilde{P}_{r,p+1,p+1} - SS_e$$

and has degrees of freedom df_r equal to the number of dummy variables required to represent μ_r. For each covariate x_v which was not eliminated because it corresponds to a diagonal zero, the sum of squares is

$$SS_{x_v} = \left(\tilde{P}_{e,v,p+1}\right)^2 \Big/ |P_{evv}|$$

and has one degree of freedom $df_{x_v} = 1$. Let $r = r_1,\ldots,r_q$, e, or any non-eliminated covariate $x_1,\ldots,x_p$. The mean square for the analysis of co-variance component r is

$$MS_r = SS_r/df_r$$

and the F statistic for the corresponding hypothesis is

$$F_r = MS_r/MS_e$$

A.19 GENERAL MIXED MODEL ANALYSIS OF VARIANCE (P3V)

The basic procedure is that described by Jennrich and Sampson (1976) although a slightly different parameterization is used here. Examples given in the text (Section 15.3) may help to clarify the points of major interest to the user.

The general model is the same as that treated by Hartley and Rao (1967), Rao (1972), Hemmerle and Hartley (1973) and Harville (1977).

$$y = X\alpha + U_1b_1 + \ldots + U_cb_c + e$$

where

X is an n by p matrix of known values

α is a p vector of unknown parameters

U_i is an n by q_i matrix of known values

b_i is a q_i vector of random values from $N(0,\sigma_i^2)$, and

e is an n vector of random values from $N(0,\sigma^2)$.

The random vectors $b_1,\ldots,b_c$ and e are assumed independent. The parameters $\sigma_1^2,\ldots,\sigma_c^2,\sigma_e^2$ are called "variance components" and similarly the components $\alpha_1,\ldots,\alpha_p$ of α are called "mean components".

The first column of X is a one vector; the next columns of X are dummy variables, if any, generated according to the specified design; and the last columns are covariates provided explicitly by the user. If I is a grouping variable the specification

       FIX = I.

in the *DESIGN* paragraph will generate $\ell-1$ dummy variables

$$x_i^{(r)} = \delta_{ir} - \delta_{i\ell}; \qquad r=1,\ldots,\ell-1$$

where i denotes an arbitrary value (level) of I, ℓ is the total number of levels of I, and δ_{ir} denotes the Kroneker delta. If J is another grouping variable with m levels the specification

FIX = I,J.

will generate $(\ell-1)(m-1)$ dummy variables

$$x_{ij}^{(r,s)} = x_i^{(r)} x_j^{(s)}; \qquad r=1,\ldots,\ell-1; \qquad s=1,\ldots,m-1$$

where i and j denote arbitrary values of I and J. This provides a mechanism for parameterizing main effects and interactions for the fixed effects. A third order interaction would take the form

FIX = I,J,K.

Similarly the columns of the matrices U_k are dummy variables generated under user specification. If I is a grouping variable the specification

RAND = I.

will generate ℓ dummy variables

$$\mu_i^{(r)} = \delta_{ir}; \qquad r=1,\ldots,\ell$$

where ℓ is the number of levels of I. If J is another grouping variable with m levels, the specification

RAND = I,J.

will generate ℓm variables

$$\mu_{ij}^{(r,s)} = \delta_{ir}\delta_{js}; \qquad r=1,\ldots,\ell; \qquad s=1,\ldots,m.$$

Each specification RAND = "something" defines a matrix U_k and corresponding variance component σ_k^2. There need be no variance components other than σ^2. When this is the case the problem becomes a simple fixed effects general linear hypothesis problem.

Turning to the estimation procedure, let

$$\theta = (\alpha_1,\ldots,\alpha_p,\sigma_1^2,\ldots,\sigma_c^2,\sigma^2)$$

denote the complete parameter vector and let $\lambda(\theta)$ denote the corresponding log-likelihood of y. The estimation procedure is based on a combination Fisher-scoring and Newton-Raphson algorithm. The first step is a scoring step

$$\Delta\theta = -\mathcal{J}^{-1}(\theta)s(\theta).$$

Here $s(\theta) = d\lambda/d\theta$ is the Fisher score vector and $\mathcal{J}(\theta) = \text{cov}_\theta s(\theta)$ is the corresponding information matrix. Scoring steps are continued until $\Delta\lambda<1$ at which point Newton-Raphson steps

$$\Delta\theta = -\left(\frac{d^2\lambda}{d\theta d\theta}\right)^{-1} s(\theta)$$

begin.   Boundary constraints

$$\sigma_e^2 \geq 0; \quad \sigma_k^2 \geq 0; \qquad k=1,\ldots,c$$

and singularity problems are handled by partial sweeping strategies similar to those employed in P3R. (Appendix A.15). The assumed initial values for the parameters are

$$\sigma_e^2 = s^2; \quad \alpha_k = \sigma_\ell^2 = 0; \quad k = 1,\ldots,p; \quad \ell = 1,\ldots,c$$

where s^2 is the sample variance of y. A considerable effort is devoted to making the number of computations required per iteration depend only on the number of levels of the fixed and random effects (except e) rather than on total sample size n (Hemmerle and Hartley, 1973).

Standard errors for the maximum likelihood estimates $\hat{\alpha}_1,\ldots,\hat{\alpha}_p,\hat{\sigma}_1^2,\ldots,\hat{\sigma}_c^2$, and $\hat{\sigma}^2$ are obtained from the appropriate diagonal elements of $\mathcal{J}^{-1}(\hat{\theta})$. Maximum likelihood estimates for the expected values $\mu_1,\ldots,\mu_n$ of the observations $y_1,\ldots,y_n$, namely

$$\hat{\mu} = X\hat{\alpha}$$

are computed together with the fitted residuals

$$\hat{e} = y - \hat{\mu}.$$

The standard errors for $\hat{\mu}_1,\ldots,\hat{\mu}_n$ are obtained from the appropriate diagonal elements of

$$\hat{\text{cov}}\ \hat{\mu} = X\ \hat{\text{cov}}\ \hat{\alpha}\ X'$$

where $\hat{\text{cov}}\ \hat{\alpha}$ is the appropriate submatrix of $\mathcal{J}^{-1}(\hat{\theta})$.

An estimate of the common standard deviation of the observations y_i is obtained from

$$\hat{\text{var}}\ y_i = \hat{\sigma}_1^2 + \ldots + \hat{\sigma}_c^2 + \hat{\sigma}^2.$$

Finally, estimates of the standard errors of the fitted residuals $\hat{e}_1,\ldots,\hat{e}_n$ are obtained from

$$\text{var}\ \hat{e}_i = \hat{\text{var}}\ y_i - \hat{\text{var}}\ \mu_i$$

These estimates and standard errors are printed for each case together with the standardized residuals $\hat{e}_i/\hat{\text{std}}\ \hat{e}_i$.

For each combination of values of the grouping variables, say I and J, a predicted (adjusted) cell mean

$$\mu_{ij}^* = x_{ij}\ \hat{\alpha}_1 + \bar{x}\ \hat{\alpha}_2$$

is computed. Here x_{ij} denotes the dummy variable values from X corresponding to any pair of values of I and J, $\bar{x}$ denotes the mean vector over all cases for all of the covariates in X, and $\hat{\alpha}_1$ and $\hat{\alpha}_2$ correspond to the fixed effects estimates and coefficients of the covariates respectively. Letting C denote the matrix with rows $(x_{ij}, \bar{x})$, standard errors for the μ_{ij}^* are obtained from the appropriate diagonal elements of

$$\hat{\text{cov}}\ \mu^* = C\ \hat{\text{cov}}\ \hat{\alpha}\ C'.$$

The elements of this matrix are also used to construct pairwise tests

$$(\mu_{ij}^* - \mu_{i'j'}^*) / \hat{\text{std}}(\mu_{ij}^* - \mu_{i'j'}^*)$$

for the equality of pairs of adjusted cell means.

Finally a specification such as

FIX = 2.

in an *HYPOTHesis* paragraph will produce a likelihood ratio test of the hypothesis that the second set of fixed components specified in the *DESIGN* paragraph is zero. If, for example, the second specification in the *DESIGN* paragraph had been FIX = I,J a test for zero interaction would be obtained. A specification such as

RAND = 3.

in an *HYPOTHesis* paragraph will give a likelihood ratio test for $\sigma_3^2 = 0$, where σ_3^2 is the third variance component defined in the *DESIGN* paragraph. These tests are obtained by fitting the appropriate restricted models and subtracting log-likelihoods. Degrees of freedom are differences of the numbers of parameters fitted.

● RESTRICTED MAXIMUM LIKELIHOOD ESTIMATION (REML)

Restricted maximum likelihood estimates are computed in two stages. First the variance components $\gamma = (\sigma_1^2, \ldots, \sigma_C^2, \sigma_e^2)$ are estimated by maximizing the likelihood of the least squares residuals y.X obtained from the regression of y on X. This likelihood does not depend on the mean components α, which are estimated by maximizing the likelihhod of y with respect to α, holding the variance components γ fixed at the values $\hat{\gamma}$ obtained in the first stage. The required estimates of cov $\hat{\alpha}$ and cov $\hat{\gamma}$ are obtained from the inverses of the appropriate information matrices $\mathcal{I}(\hat{\alpha})$ and $\mathcal{I}(\hat{\gamma})$ evaluated at the REML estimates $\hat{\alpha}$ and $\hat{\gamma}$. All these are obtained by means of a minor modification of the unrestricted algorithm. Likelihood ratio χ^2 statistics are obtained by subtracting the log-likelihoods of y evaluated at the appropriate REML estimates.

A.20 SURVIVAL FUNCTIONS (P1L)

Let the N observed times to response (survival times) or time on study (if the observation is censored) be ordered

$$t_1 \leq t_2 \leq \cdots \leq t_N$$

Associated with each t_i is a δ_i such that

$$\delta_i = \begin{cases} 1 & \text{if } t_i \text{ is a response} \\ 0 & \text{if } t_i \text{ is a censored observation} \end{cases}$$

The <u>product-limit estimate</u> of the survival curve is given by

$$P(t) = \prod_{t_i < t} \frac{N-i+1-\delta_i}{N-i+1}$$

The corresponding estimate of the standard error is

$$\text{s.e. } (P(t)) \simeq P(t) \left\{ \sum_{t_i < t} \frac{\delta_i}{(N-i)(N-i+1)} \right\}^{\frac{1}{2}}$$

Let the times corresponding to a response (i.e. $\delta_i = 1$) be represented by

$$T_1 \leq \cdots \leq T_D$$

where D is the total number of responses. Then the estimated <u>mean survival time</u> is

$$\hat{\mu} = \sum_{i=1}^{D} P(T_i)(T_i - T_{i-1})$$

where $P(T_i)$ is the product-limit estimate based on all the data at T_i. The estimated variance of $\hat{\mu}$ is

$$\hat{\text{var}} (\hat{\mu}) = \sum_{j} \frac{S_j^2}{(N-j)(N-j+1)}$$

where

$$S_j = \sum_{i=j}^{D} P(T_{i-1})(T_i - T_{i-1}) .$$

An estimate of the 50th quantile (i.e., the median) is given by

$$P_{0.5} = \inf \{t: P(t) \geq 0.5\}$$

Estimates for other quantiles are obtained in a similar manner.

Comparing groups: The Mantel and Breslow statistics

Let k by the number of groups. The null hypothesis is that the groups have the same survival distribution.

At time T_i, let n_{ij} be the number of subjects in group j still in the study (that is, whose observation time t is greater than or equal to T_i). Let x_{ij} be the number of subjects responding at exactly time t_i in group j. (If there are no tied response times, x_{ij} is zero for all but one group; $x_{ij}=1$ for the group where the response occurs.)

Conditioned on the n_{ij} and the sum $x_{i+} = \Sigma \, x_{ij}$, the vector

$$\underset{\sim}{x_i} = (x_{i1},\ldots,x_{ik})$$

has a k-1 dimensional hypergeometric distribution with mean vector

$$E(\underset{\sim}{x_i}) = (E(x_{i1}),\ldots,E(x_{ik}))$$

where $E(x_{ij}) = n_{ij}x_{i+}/N_{i+}$

The covariance matrix $\underset{\sim}{V_i}$ has elements

$$cov(x_{ij},x_{ij}') = \frac{n_{ij}(\delta_{jj'} - n_{ij'}/n_{i+})x_{i+}(n_{i+} - x_{i+})}{n_{i+}(n_{i+} - 1)}$$

where

$$\delta_{jj'} = \begin{cases} 1 & \text{if } j=j' \\ 0 & \text{otherwise} \end{cases}$$

Let

$$\underset{\sim}{E} = \Sigma \, E(\underset{\sim}{x_i})$$
$$\underset{\sim}{O} = \Sigma \, \underset{\sim}{x_i}$$
$$\underset{\sim}{V} = \Sigma \, \underset{\sim}{V_i}$$

The Mantel-Cox test (generalized Savage test) is

$$\chi^2_M = (\underset{\sim}{O}-\underset{\sim}{E})' \; \underset{\sim}{V}^{-1} \; (\underset{\sim}{O}-\underset{\sim}{E})$$

which is asymptotically distributed as χ^2 with k-1 df.

Now let

$$w_{ij} = n_{i+}x_{ij} - x_{i+}n_{ij} = n_{i+}(x_{ij} - x_{i+}n_{ij}/n_{i+}) \text{ , and } W_i = \sum_j w_{ij} \text{ .}$$

Hence the vector $\underset{\sim}{W} = (W_1,\ldots W_{k-1})$ has mean zero and covariance

$$\underset{\sim W}{V} = \Sigma \, n^2_{i+}\underset{\sim}{V_i}$$

The statistic

$$\chi^2_B = \underset{\sim}{W}' \; \underset{\sim W}{V}^{-1} \; \underset{\sim}{W}$$

is the Breslow (generalized Wilcoxon) statistic, which is asymptotically distributed as χ^2_{k-1}.

Note that χ^2_M differs from χ^2_B in the method of weighting the observations.

A.21 MAXIMUM LIKELIHOOD FACTOR ANALYSIS

Maximum likelihood factor analysis is discussed by Lawley and Maxwell (1971). The algorithm used here was developed by R.I. Jennrich and P.F. Sampson at the Health Sciences Computing Facility.

Let R be the sample correlation matrix. The normal theory maximum likelihood estimates are computed for the factor loading matrix Λ and the unique standard deviation matrix Ψ (square roots of one minus the communality for each variable) in the factor analytic decomposition

$$\Sigma = \Lambda \Lambda' + \Psi^2$$

where Σ is the population correlation matrix. (Maximum likelihood factor analysis is scale free so it does not matter whether the correlation or covariance matrix is used.) Here Ψ is diagonal and the loadings Λ are canonical (Rao, 1955).

The program uses a Newton-Raphson iteration

$$\Delta\Psi = -(f''_{ij})^{-1}(f'_i)$$

to minimize a function f of Ψ which is a negative slope affine transformation of the conditional maximum of the likelihood for the sample given Ψ (cf. Jennrich and Robinson, 1969; Clarke, 1970; Jöreskog and van Thillo, 1971).

In terms of the eigenvalues

$$\gamma_1 \leq \gamma_2 \leq \cdots \leq \gamma_p$$

and vectors

$$w_1,\ldots,w_p$$

of $\Psi R^{-1}\Psi$, the function

$$f = \sum_{m=k+1}^{p} (\log \gamma_m + \gamma_m^{-1} - 1)$$

where k is the number of factors and p the number of variables.

The required derivatives $f'_i = \partial f/\partial\Psi_i$ and $f''_{ij} = \partial^2 f/\partial\Psi_i\partial\Psi_j$ are given by

$$f'_i = \sum_{m=k+1}^{p} (1 - \gamma_m^{-1})w_{im}^2$$

and

$$f''_{ij} = \sum_{m=k+1}^{p} \nu_{im}\nu_{jm} \sum_{n=1}^{k} \frac{\gamma_m + \gamma_n - 2}{\gamma_m - \gamma_n} w_{in}w_{jn} + \tfrac{1}{2} \delta_{ij} \sum_{m=k+1}^{p} (3\gamma_m^{-1} - 1) \nu_{im}^2$$

where

$$-\nu_m = 2\gamma_m^{-1}R^{-1}\Psi w_m$$

If, as frequently occurs during the initial steps, (f_{ij}'') is not positive definite, it is replaced by a matrix of approximate second order derivatives

$$f_{ij}'' = (\sum_{m=k+1}^{p} \nu_{im}\nu_{jm})(\sum_{m=k+1}^{p} w_{im}w_{jm})$$

If the value of f is not decreased by the step $\Delta\Psi$, the step is halved (i.e., $\Delta\Psi$ is replaced by $\frac{1}{2}\Delta\Psi$) and halved again until the value of f decreases or ten halvings fail to produce a decrease. Stepping continues until all values of $\Delta\Psi_i$ are less than the convergence criterion or the number of steps equals its prescribed maximum.

Using the converged value of Ψ, the eigenvalue problem

$$\Psi^2\nu_m = \gamma_m R^{-1}\nu_m , \qquad m = 1,\ldots,p$$

is solved and the estimated columns of Λ are computed using

$$u_m = \rho_m R^{-\frac{1}{2}}\nu_m , \qquad m = 1,\ldots,k$$

where $\rho_m = (1 - \gamma_m)^{\frac{1}{2}}$ is the estimated canonical correlation. The advantage of this parameterization is that it converges smoothly even in Heywood cases -- when some of the diagonal components of Ψ are zero.

A.22 CANONICAL ANALYSIS (P6M)

The covariance matrix is computed by the method of provisional means (Appendix A.2). If computations with means assumed to be zero are desired, the products of the means are added back into the covariance matrix and means are set to zero.

The covariance matrix is converted to a correlation matrix and all computations are then made in terms of standardized variables (mean zero, standard deviation one).

Denote the correlation matrix by

$$R = \begin{pmatrix} R_{XX} & R_{XY} \\ R_{YX} & R_{YY} \end{pmatrix}$$

where X denotes the smaller of the two sets of variables. R is stored as a triangular matrix (R is symmetric so only the lower half need be used).

The matrix

$$\begin{pmatrix} 0 & R_{XY} \\ R_{YX} & R_{YY} \end{pmatrix}$$

is pivoted on each of the Y variables to obtain

$$\begin{pmatrix} -R_{XY}R_{YY}^{-1}R_{YX} & R_{XY}R_{YY}^{-1} \\ R_{YY}^{-1}R_{YX} & -R_{YY}^{-1} \end{pmatrix}$$

Pivoting is performed in a stepwise manner such that no variable is pivoted whose squared multiple correlation with previously pivoted variables exceeds 1 - TOL, where TOL is specified in the *CANONical* paragraph. TOL thus determines the effective rank of the set of Y variables. Rows and columns corresponding to nonpivoted variables are set to zero.

The eigenvalue-eigenvector problem

$$R_{XY}R_{YY}^{-1}R_{YX}\beta = \lambda R_{XX}\beta$$

is then solved for the eigenvalues $\lambda_1 \geq \lambda_2 \geq ... \geq \lambda_m > 0$ where m is the smaller of the effective ranks of the two sets of variables; the corresponding eigenvectors are $\beta_1,...,\beta_m$. This eigenvector-eigenvalue problem is solved in three stages. First, the problem is transformed to the problem

$$R_{XX}^{-\frac{1}{2}}R_{XY}R_{YY}^{-1}R_{YX}(R_{XX}^{-\frac{1}{2}})'\beta* = \lambda \beta*$$

$R_{XX}^{-\frac{1}{2}}$ is obtained by stepwise pivoting in such a way that no variable is pivoted whose squared multiple correlation with previously pivoted variables exceeds 1 - TOL. Rows and columns corresponding to nonpivoted variables are set equal to zero. Next, eigenvalues and eigenvectors are obtained for the transformed problem. Eigenvalues are obtained by tridiagonalization and Reinsch's (1973) TQLRAT version of QR. Eigenvectors are obtained first for the tridiagonalized matrix and then for the original matrix by inverse iteration. The eigenvectors are normalized so that $\beta_i^{*'}\beta_i^* = 1$. Lastly, β is obtained as

$$\left(R_{XX}^{-\frac{1}{2}}\right)'\beta* .$$

Canonical correlations are the square roots of the eigenvalues

$$\rho_i = \sqrt{\lambda_i} \qquad i = 1,\ldots,m$$

The coefficients for the canonical variables for the set of X variables are the eigenvectors β_i

$$B_X = (\beta_1,\ldots,\beta_m)$$

The coefficients for the canonical variables for the set of Y variables are obtained by dividing the eigenvectors by their corresponding canonical correlations and then multiplying by $R_{YY}^{-1}R_{YX}$

$$B_Y = R_{YY}^{-1}R_{YX}(\beta_1/\rho_1,\ldots,\beta_m/\rho_m)$$

Canonical variable scores for each case are obtained by multiplying the standard scores for the original variables by the canonical variable coefficients

$$\begin{pmatrix} v_X \\ v_Y \end{pmatrix} = \begin{pmatrix} B_X \\ B_Y \end{pmatrix} Z$$

where Z denotes the standard scores for the case.

Canonical variable loadings are the correlations of the original variables with the canonical variables. They are also the regression coefficients for predicting the standardized variables from the canonical variables. As such they may be of value in semantically interpreting the canonical variables. These loadings are analogous to unrotated factor loadings.

Loadings for X variables on canonical X variables are obtained by multiplying the canonical X variable coefficients by R_{XX}

$$A_{XX} = B_X R_{XX}$$

Loadings for Y variables on canonical Y variables are obtained by multiplying the canonical Y variable coefficients by R_{YY}

$$A_{YY} = B_Y R_{YY}$$

A.23 STEPWISE DISCRIMINANT ANALYSIS

The following notations will be used:

p   = number of variables available

q   = number of variables entered at a given step

t   = total number of groups

g   = number of groups used to define the discriminant functions

n_i = number of cases in group i

n   = total number of cases in the g defining groups

x_{ijr} = value of variable r in case j of group i

h   = number of hypotheses (contrasts)

h_{ki} = coefficient for group i in hypothesis k

p_i = prior probability for group i

Assume for simplicity that the first g of the t groups are used to define the classification functions.

Step 1

The data are read and the method of provisional means (Appendix A.2) is used to compute the group means

$$\bar{x}_{ir} = \sum_{j=1}^{n_i} x_{ijr}/n_i \qquad \begin{array}{l} i = 1,\ldots,t \\ r = 1,\ldots,p \end{array}$$

group standard deviations

$$s_{ir} = \left(\sum_{j=1}^{n_i} (x_{ijr} - \bar{x}_{ir})^2/(n_i-1) \right)^{\frac{1}{2}} \qquad \begin{array}{l} i = 1,\ldots,t \\ r = 1,\ldots,p \end{array}$$

and pooled within groups sums of cross-product deviations

$$w_{rs} = \sum_{i=1}^{g} \sum_{j=1}^{n_i} (x_{ijr} - \bar{x}_{ir})(x_{ijs} - \bar{x}_{is}) \qquad \begin{array}{l} r = 1,\ldots,p \\ s = 1,\ldots,p \end{array}$$

The latter are used to compute the within group correlations

$$r_{ij} = w_{ij}/(w_{ii}w_{jj})^{\frac{1}{2}} \qquad \begin{array}{l} i = 1,\ldots,p \\ j = 1,\ldots,p \end{array}$$

Step 2

Let H = (h_{ki}) be the h by g matrix of hypothesis contrasts. If no contrasts are specified, h is set to g-1 and

$$h_{ki} = \begin{cases} 1 & i \le k \\ -k & i = k + 1 \\ 0 & \text{otherwise} \end{cases}$$

These contrasts test the equality of all g group means.

The stepwise procedure is defined in terms of the matrices

$$W = (w_{rs})$$

and

$$M = W + \overline{X}'H'(HN^{-1}H')^{-1}H\overline{X}$$

where $\overline{X} = (\overline{x}_{ir})$ is a g x p, and N is the diagonal matrix $\lfloor n_1, \ldots, n_g \rfloor$ of group sizes. The entry and removal of variables is <u>defined</u> in terms of the results of sweeping on the diagonal elements of W and M (the computations themselves proceed somewhat more efficiently).

Assuming for simplicity that the first q variables have already been swept, write

$$W = \begin{bmatrix} W_{11} & W_{12} \\ W_{21} & W_{22} \end{bmatrix} \qquad M = \begin{bmatrix} M_{11} & M_{12} \\ M_{21} & M_{22} \end{bmatrix}$$

where W_{11} and M_{11} are q x q. At each step let

$$A = \begin{bmatrix} -W_{11}^{-1} & W_{11}^{-1}W_{12} \\ W_{21}W_{11}^{-1} & W_{22}-W_{21}W_{11}^{-1}W_{12} \end{bmatrix}$$

$$B = \begin{bmatrix} -M_{11}^{-1} & M_{11}^{-1}M_{12} \\ M_{21}M_{11}^{-1} & M_{22}-M_{21}M_{11}^{-1}M_{12} \end{bmatrix}$$

B is not actually computed, since only the diagonal elements are needed. These diagonal elements are computed from the matrix

$$\begin{bmatrix} A & T \\ T' & C \end{bmatrix}$$

which is defined at step zero to be

$$\begin{bmatrix} W & \overline{X} \\ \overline{X}' & 0 \end{bmatrix}$$

and is updated at each step by sweeping or reverse sweeping the diagonal elements of A. The diagonal elements of B are computed using the fact that

$$B = Q'Q + A$$

where

$$Q = (H(N^{-1} - C)H')^{-\frac{1}{2}} H'T'.$$

The following statistics are computed at each step

(a) F values for testing differences between each pair of groups:

$$F_{ij} = \frac{(n - g - q + 1)n_i n_j}{q(n_i + n_j)} \, D_{ij}^2/(n-g) \qquad\qquad i,j = 1,\ldots,g$$

where

$$D_{ij}^2 = (n-g)(\overline{X}_i - \overline{X}_j)' \, W_{11}^{-1} \, (\overline{X}_i - \overline{X}_j)$$

is the (squared) Mahalanobis distance between groups i and j and where $\overline{X}_i$ is the vector of means for group i for the q variables that have been entered. D_{ij}^2 is computed as

$$(n-g)(2c_{ij} - c_{ii} - c_{jj})$$

(b) F values for each variable

If variable r has been entered

$$F_r = \frac{a_{rr} - b_{rr}}{b_{rr}} \qquad \frac{n - g - q + 1}{h}$$

with h and n - g - q + 1 degrees of freedom

If variable r has not been entered

$$F_r = \frac{b_{rr} - a_{rr}}{a_{rr}} \qquad \frac{n - g - q}{h}$$

with h and n - g - q degrees of freedom

(c) Wilks' Λ-statistic for the hypothesis defined by H

$$\Lambda = \det(W_{11})/\det(M_{11})$$

with $(q, h, n - g)$ degrees of freedom. Λ is computed by initially setting it equal to one and updating it at each step by multiplying its previous value by a_{rr}/b_{rr} where r is the index of the variable entered or removed at the step.

(d) The F approximation to Λ (Rao, 1973, p. 556)

$$F = \frac{1 - \Lambda^{1/s}}{\Lambda^{1/s}} \cdot \frac{m*s + 1 - hq/2}{hq}$$

where

$$m* = n - g - \tfrac{1}{2}(q - h + 1)$$

$$s = \begin{cases} \left(\dfrac{h^2 q^2 - 4}{h^2 + q^2 - 5}\right)^{\frac{1}{2}} & h^2 + q^2 \neq 5 \\[2em] 1 & h^2 + q^2 = 5 \end{cases}$$

The numbers of degrees of freedom for F are hq and $(m*s+1 - hq/2)$. The approximation is exact if either h or q is 1 or 2.

(e) Tolerance values

$$t_r = a_{rr}/w_{rr} \qquad\qquad r = q + 1,\ldots,p$$

Step 3

To move from one step to the next, a variable is removed or added according to the first of the following rules which applies.

Rule 1   If METHOD=1 is specified in the DISCriminant paragraph and one or more entered variables are available and have F values less than the F-to-remove threshold, the one with the smallest F value is removed.

Rule 2   If METHOD=2 is specified and one or more entered variables are available, the one with the smallest F value is removed if by its removal Wilks' Λ will be smaller than it was when the same number of variables were previously entered.

Rule 3   If one or more nonentered variables are available, with tolerance above the tolerance threshold and are either at a forced level or have F values above the F-to-enter threshold, the one with the highest F value is entered.

Variables in forced levels are available only if their level is equal to the working level, if they are not entered, and if they have tolerance above the tolerance threshold.

Variables in nonforced levels are considered available only if their level is less than or equal to the working level and, for nonentered variables, if their tolerance is above the tolerance threshold. (See Appendix A.11 for a discussion of tolerance.)

The working level begins at 1 and moves to the next level when none of the rules apply. If the specified maximum level has already been reached, the specified maximum number of steps has been reached, or the specified maximum number of variables has been entered; the stepping terminates.

Step 4

When the stepping is complete, or when the number of variables entered is equal to one of the numbers indicated in the PRINT paragraph, the following are computed and printed except for (b) and (c) which are printed only when the stepping is complete:

(a) Group classification function coefficients, which are defined as

$$\hat{\beta}_i = (n - g) \, W_{11}^{-1} \, \overline{X}_i \qquad \text{(a } q \times 1 \text{ vector)} \qquad i = 1, \ldots, g$$

and the corresponding constants

$$\hat{\alpha}_i = \log p_i - \tfrac{1}{2}(n - g) \, \overline{X}_i' \, W_{11}^{-1} \, \overline{X}_i \qquad i = 1, \ldots, g$$

where

p_i is the prior probability for group i

Note that $W_{11}^{-1} \, \overline{X}_i$ is computed as a submatrix of T and $\overline{X}_i' \, W_{11}^{-1} \, \overline{X}_i = -c_{ii}$.

(b) The squared Mahalanobis' distance of case j in group i from the mean of group k

$$D_{ijk}^2 = (n - g) \sum_{r=1}^{q} \sum_{s=1}^{q} (x_{ijr} - \overline{x}_{kr}) \, a_{rs} \, (x_{ijs} - \overline{x}_{ks}) \qquad \begin{array}{l} i = 1, \ldots, t \\ j = 1, \ldots, n_i \\ k = 1, \ldots, g \end{array}$$

or if requested in the *PRINT* paragraph, the cross validation or jackknife distance, $_*D_{ijk}^2$, obtained by withholding this case from all computations except the evaluation of the distance function.

The computing formulas are

$$D^2_{ijk} = (n-g)e$$

$$*D^2_{ijk} = (n - 1 - g)(e + a^2/b - \delta_{ik}/(n_i[n_i-1]))$$

where

$$e = f + 2(c_i - c_k) - c_{ii} + c_{kk}$$

$$a = \delta_{ik}/n_k + c_i - c_k - c_{ik} + c_{ii}$$

$$b = 1 - 1/n_i - f$$

δ_{ik} is the Kronecker delta

$$c_k = X'_{ij}W^{-1}_{11}\bar{X}_k \quad \text{(where } W^{-1}_{11}\bar{X}_k \text{ has been computed as a submatrix of T)}$$

$$c_{ij} = -\bar{X}'_i W^{-1}_{11}\bar{X}_j \quad \text{(already computed in C)}$$

$$f = \sum_{r=1}^{q} \sum_{s=1}^{q} (x_{ijr} - \bar{x}_{ir})a_{rs}(x_{ijs} - \bar{x}_{is})$$

$$= (X_{ij} - \bar{X}_i)'W^{-1}_{11}(X_{ij} - \bar{X}_i)$$

$$X_{ij} = (x_{ij1},\ldots,x_{ijq})'$$

(c) The posterior probability that case j from group i came from group k

$$P_{ijk} = P_k \exp(-\tfrac{1}{2}D^2_{ijk}) \bigg/ \sum_{r=1}^{q} P_r \exp(-\tfrac{1}{2}D^2_{ijr}) \qquad \begin{array}{l} i = 1,\ldots,t \\ j = 1,\ldots,n_i \\ k = 1,\ldots,g \end{array}$$

If JACKKNIFE is requested, the D's are replaced by *D's in the above formula. A classification matrix that gives the number of cases n_{ik} in group i whose posterior probability P_{ijk} was largest for group k is printed.

Step 5

The eigenvalue problem

$$H\bar{X}W^{-1}_{11}\bar{X}'H'u_i = H(-C)H'u_i = \lambda_i H N^{-1}H'u_i, \quad \text{where } \bar{X} \text{ is a g x q matrix of variable means for all groups}$$

is solved for eigenvalues $\lambda_1 \geq \ldots \geq \lambda_h$ and eigenvectors $u_1, \ldots, u_h$ normalized so that

$$u_i' \; H \; N^{-1} H' u_i = 1$$

The coefficients $\hat{\gamma}_i$ of the ith canonical discriminant function defined by H are given by

$$\hat{\gamma}_i = W_{11}^{-1} \; \bar{X}' \; H' \; u_i \sqrt{\frac{n-g}{\lambda_i}} \qquad\qquad i = 1, \ldots, h$$

If h < q and if required, q - h additional canonical functions will be computed corresponding to zero eigenvalues. For each $i = h+1, \ldots, q$ in turn a random q-vector v_i is generated and orthogonalized by Gramm-Schmidt to $\hat{\gamma}_1, \ldots, \hat{\gamma}_{i-1}$. Then

$$\hat{\gamma}_i = W_{11}^{-1} \; V_i / (V_i' \; W_{11}^{-1} \; V_i)^{\frac{1}{2}} \qquad\qquad i = h+1, \ldots, q$$

The cumulative proportion of explained dispersion is computed as

$$v_i = \sum_{j=1}^{i} \lambda_j / \sum_{j=1}^{h} \lambda_j \qquad\qquad i = 1, \ldots, h$$

The canonical variables (values of the canonical functions)

$$f_{ijr} = \sum_{s=1}^{q} \hat{\gamma}_{rs} (x_{ijs} - \bar{x}_s) \qquad\qquad \begin{array}{l} i = 1, \ldots, t \\ j = 1, \ldots, n_i \end{array}$$

for r = 1,2 are computed and plotted. All requested values of f_{ijr} are written on Save File.

The canonical correlations are computed from the eigenvalues as

$$\rho_i = \sqrt{\frac{\lambda_i}{1+\lambda_i}}$$

A.24 SPECIAL OPTION FOR TERMINAL USERS

When Control Language instructions are submitted through a terminal, some systems automatically generate sequence numbers in columns 73-80 of each line of Control Language instructions. These sequence numbers can interfere with the interpretation of the instructions. If your BMDP programs are dated after August 1977, you can avoid this problem by stating the number of columns (characters) in each line that are to be read and interpreted. For example, if the sequence numbers begin in column 73, then state

        /CONTROL   COLUMN=72.   /END

Both the *CONTROL* and *END* paragraphs should be stated in the first line and stated <u>before</u> any other Control Language instructions. Your other Control Language instructions (to describe the data, variables and analysis) begin in the next line.

CONTROL
   COLUMN=#.   {80/prev.}

   Maximum number of characters per line that contain Control Language instructions. Required only if the system automatically inserts a sequence number or other identification at the end of each line.

   The *CONTROL* paragraph followed by an *END* paragraph must be specified as the first line of Control Language instructions.

APPENDIX B

B.1   INCREASING THE CAPACITY OF A BMDP PROGRAM

At the end of each program description, a section entitled SIZE OF PROBLEM gives example(s) of the maximum number of cases, variables, groups, etc. (whichever are relevant) that can be analyzed by the program. If your problem does not exceed the capacity of the program (and most problems do not), this Appendix can be omitted. If your data exceed the capacity of the program, you can either do the analysis in parts or increase the capacity of the program.

In this section we describe how to increase the capacity of the program. In the following section (Appendix B.2) we give detailed formulas from which you can estimate the capacity needed.

Each program allots 15000 locations (computer words) to store the matrices used in the analysis. The matrices used include the data (if the data are kept in memory), a vector of means, a covariance or correlation matrix or any vector or matrix computed during the analysis. Once you estimate the number of locations needed, you can easily modify the BMDP program to use more than 15000 locations.

In each BMDP program there is a subroutine with five FORTRAN statements:

```
SUBROUTINE IBSIZE
COMMON/MEMORY/N,L,IB(15000)
N=15000
RETURN
END
```

In this subroutine N is the number of locations for the matrices (15000) and IB is the vector that contains N locations. To increase the capacity of the program, for example to 18000 words, you need to modify this subroutine to be

```
SUBROUTINE IBSIZE
COMMON/MEMORY/N,L,IB(18000)
N=18000
RETURN
END
```

Note that there are two changes: IB(18000) and N=18000.

The following order of input is used at HSCF to modify the SUBROUTINE IBSIZE.

```
//jobname  JOB   nooo,yourname                        ⎤
//   EXEC  BIMEDT,PROG=BMDPxx,REGION=182K             ⎥  HSCF System Cards
//TRANSF  DD   *                                       ⎦
       RETURN                                         ⎤
       END                                            ⎥
       SUBROUTINE IBSIZE                              ⎥  FORTRAN
       COMMON/MEMORY/N,L,IB(18000)                    ⎥  statements
       N=18000                                        ⎦
//GO.SYSIN  DD  *                                      ⎦  HSCF System Card

       Control Language instructions                  ⎤  from program
       and data (if on cards)                         ⎦  description

   //                                                  ⎦  HSCF System Card
```

The REGION statement on the second system card tells the computer that your job requires 182K bytes of computer memory. This is an increase of 12K bytes over the 170K bytes that would ordinarily be sufficient for the BIMEDT procedure. The increase is computed as $(18000-15000) \times 4 = 12000 = 12K$.

Essentially we are using the same procedure as is used when transformations are specified in FORTRAN (the BIMEDT procedure, Section 6.4). At HSCF the first two records of the FORTRAN transformation subroutine are supplied automatically, therefore the first two FORTRAN statements shown above (RETURN, END) are necessary to terminate the FORTRAN transformation subroutine. (If we were specifying any transformations by FORTRAN statements, they would precede the RETURN and END statements.)

There is no RETURN and END statements after N=18000 since they are supplied automatically at HSCF.

If at your facility you must supply the SUBROUTINE TRANSF statement when specifying transformations in FORTRAN, then your procedure to increase the capacity of a program is as follows: Use the same System Cards as if you were specifying transformations by FORTRAN statements. Then in place of the FORTRAN subroutine to specify transformations, supply the entire SUBROUTINE IBSIZE from the first card (SUBROUTINE IBSIZE) to the last card (END). If you also want to specify transformations in FORTRAN, then add the SUBROUTINE TRANSF.

B.2 PROGRAM LIMITATIONS

At the end of each program description we give an example of how many variables or combination of variables and cases can be analyzed by the program. The exact formula for the maximum number of variables, cases, groups, etc. that can be analyzed by a program is very complex. The only time these formulas are of interest is when your problem exceeds the maximum size that can be analyzed. At times when your problem is too large, it can be analyzed in segments; otherwise, you may need to increase the capacity of the program as described in Appendix B.1.

In this appendix we give a detailed formula that you can use to estimate the number of locations (computer words) necessary to store the vectors and matrices used in the analysis.

First we describe the notation. Then one or two formulas are presented for each program; we present a simplified formula that is almost sure to be conservative (estimate too many locations) when the detailed formula is very complex.

- NOTATION

    The following notation is used in many of the formulas

    M   - number of locations needed to analyze the data (When $M \leq 15,000$, the data can be analyzed by the BMDP program without change; when $M > 15,000$, the capacity of the program must be increased as described in Appendix B.1.)

    VI   - number of variables read as input (specified in the *INPut* paragraph or recorded in the BMDP File)

    VT   - number of variables after transformations (the sum of VI and the number of variables added by transformation, ADD in the *VARiable* paragraph)

    VM   - max (VI, VT)

    VU   - number of variables used in the analysis (specified by a USE statement in the *VARiable* paragraph or VT if no USE statement is present)

    CI   - number of cases read as input

    CU   - number of cases used in the analysis (such as number of complete cases if complete cases only are used or number of cases with USE set to one by case selection)

    GN   - number of groups

    NGV - number of grouping or category variables

    NCAT - total number of categories in all grouping variables (the sum of the CODEs specified + the intervals specified by CUTPOINTS + 10 times the number of grouping or categorical variables for which CODEs or CUTPOINTS are not specified)

NT   - number of Control Language transformation statements (each OMIT or DELETE statement generates the equivalent of a Control Language transformation for <u>each</u> case omitted or deleted)

NLCL - number of <u>characters</u> in the Control Language instructions after redundant <u>blanks</u> are eliminated

All programs allot the following number of locations for basic information (such as NAMEs of variables, transformations, etc.)

$$Q = 8 \cdot VM + 6 \cdot NT + NLCL/4$$

and if there are grouping or categorical variables, they allot an additional

$$G = 2 \cdot VT + 6 \cdot NGV + 3 \cdot NCAT$$

In our conservative formulas Q is often replaced by $8 \cdot VM + 300$ and G by $2 \cdot VT + 700$, or both by $10 \cdot VM + 1000$.

Scatter plots and normal probability plots are printed by many programs; e.g., those that perform regression and multivariate analysis. In general, the plots reuse the same locations as the analysis, and as many plots are formed at one time as there are memory locations available. Each plot requires $(NH + 11)(NW + 15)/4$ locations where NH is the height (number of lines in the vertical axis) and NW is the width (number of characters in the horizontal axis). The data are reread as many times as necessary to form all the plots requested. (P3R and PAR keep the data in memory; therefore they form one or at <u>most</u> two plots at a time).

The formulas for the individual programs appear on the pages shown below.

Program	Page	Program	Page	Program	Page
P1D	844	P3F	848	P3R	850
P2D	844	P1L	849	P4R	851
P3D	845	P1M	849	P5R	851
P4D	845	P2M	849	P6R	851
P5D	845	P3M	849	P9R	851
P6D	846	P4M	849	PAR	851
P7D	847	P6M	850	P1S	852
P8D	847	P7M	850	P3S	852
P9D	847	PAM	850	P1V	852
P1F	847	P1R	850	P2V	853
P2F	848	P2R	850	P3V	853

<u>P1D</u> The conservative formula is

$$M = 30 \cdot VM + 1000$$

and the detailed formula is

$$M = Q + G + 15 \cdot VM + 5 \cdot VT + NCAT + 11 \cdot NGV + 40$$

<u>P2D</u> The conservative formula is

$$M = 2 \text{ (number of distinct values in the data)} + 8 \cdot VM + 2000$$

In more detail the space required is:

To estimate the space you need, consider that storage is initially allocated for each selected variable sufficient to store 24 distinct values and their frequencies; for variables with more than 24 distinct values, additional storage is allocated in blocks sufficient to store 50 more values and their frequencies.

M = space as described above + Q

P3D The conservative formula is

$$M = 10 \cdot VM + 26 \cdot VU \cdot GN + H + 1000$$

and the detailed formula is

$$M = Q + G + GN + 26 \cdot VU \cdot GN + H$$

where GN = number of groups (2 if there is no grouping variable)

$$H = \begin{cases} 0 & \text{if NO HOTEL and NO CORR} \\ VU^2 \cdot GN + \dfrac{(VU+1)^2 \cdot VU \cdot GN}{4} & \text{if HOTEL or CORR} \end{cases}$$

P4D The conservative formula is

$$M = 76 \cdot VM + 300$$

and the detailed formula is

$$M = 65 \cdot VU + VT + 9 \cdot VM + NLCL/4$$

P5D P5D forms as many plots as possible at one time and reads the data as many times as necessary to form all plots. The following formulas assume that all plots are formed simultaneously.

The conservative formula is

$$M = 13 \cdot VM + \sum_i NCI + \sum_i 9 \cdot NPV \cdot NPT \cdot NPG + H + 2000$$

and the detailed formula is

$$M = Q + G + \max(2 \cdot VT, VM) + VT + \max_i NPV + 2 \max_i NPG + VM$$
$$+ \sum_i NCI + 2 \cdot GN \cdot NICAT + \sum_i 9 \cdot NPV \cdot NPT \cdot NPG + H$$

where

$\max\limits_i$ and $\sum\limits_i$ are the maximum and summation respectively over all *PLOT* paragraphs

and

NCI = number of categories (lines in the plots) summed over all variables specified to be plotted in a *PLOT* paragraph

NPV = number of variables specified to be plotted in a *PLOT* paragraph

NPT = number of types of plots specified to be plotted in a *PLOT* paragraph

$$NPG = \text{total number of groups (in all GROUP statements)} \\ \text{specified in a } PLOT \text{ paragraph}$$

$$H = \begin{cases} (NH+11) \cdot (NW+15)/4 + 30 & \text{if any of CUM, NORM,} \\ & \text{DNORM or HALFNORM} \\ & \text{is specified} \\ 0 & \text{otherwise} \end{cases}$$

NW   = number of characters in horizontal axis (width)

NH   = number of lines in vertical axis (height)

GN   = number of groups (10, if there is a grouping variable but neither CODEs nor CUTPOINTs are specified)

NICAT = number of variables to be plotted for which CODEs and CUTPOINTs are not specified

<u>P6D</u> P6D forms as many plots as possible at one time and rereads the data as many times as necessary to form all the plots. The following formulas are based on forming all plots simultaneously.

The conservative formula is

$$M = 14 \cdot VM + \max_i (NH + 11)(NW + 15)/4 + \sum_i H + 2000$$

and the detailed formula is

$$M = Q + G + \max (VI, 2 \cdot VT) + VT + \max_i NPVX + \max_i NPVY + \max_i NPG$$
$$+ VM + \max_i 2 \cdot NG \cdot NPVM + \max_i (NH + 11) \cdot (NW + 15)/4$$
$$+ \sum_i H + 40$$

where

$\max_i$ and $\sum_i$ are the maximum and summation respectively over all *PLOT* paragraphs

and

NH   = number of characters in the horizontal axis (width)

NW   = number of lines in the vertical axis (height)

$$H = \begin{cases} 16 \cdot NPG \cdot \min (NPVX, NPVY) & \text{if PAIR} \\ 16 \cdot NPG \cdot NPVX \cdot NPVY & \text{if CROSS} \end{cases}$$

NPG   = number of groups specified in GROUP statements in a *PLOT* paragraph

NPVX = number of XVARIABLES

NPVY = number of YVARIABLES

NPVM = max (NPVX, NPVY)

P7D P7D keeps the data in memory. The conservative formula is

$$M = 10 \cdot VM + (VT+1)(CU+11) + 1000$$

and the detailed formula is

$$M = Q + G + (VT+1)(CU+11) + 300 .$$

P8D The conservative formula is

$$M = 8 \cdot VM + H + 300$$

and the detailed formula is

$$M = Q + H + 300$$

where

$$H = \begin{cases} VU(\tfrac{1}{2} \cdot VU + 15) & \text{if TYPE is COMPLETE} \\ VU(4 \cdot VU + 8) & \text{if TYPE is CORPAIR} \\ VU(3 \cdot VU + 8) & \text{if TYPE is COVPAIR or ALLVALUE} \end{cases}$$

If ROW or COLUMN is specified, then

$$H = \begin{cases} NRC (NRC + 1)/2 & \text{if TYPE is COMPLETE} \\ 8 \cdot NR \cdot NC & \text{if TYPE is CORPAIR} \\ 6 \cdot NR \cdot NC & \text{if TYPE is COVPAIR or ALLVALUE} \end{cases}$$

where
      NR is the number of rows selected
      NC is the number of columns selected, and
      NRC is the total number of distinct row and column variables

P9D P9D analyzes up to 4 variables at a time and rereads the data as often as necessary to analyze all the variables.

The conservative formula is

$$M = 14VM + NGV(50 + NG) + 12(NCAT + CL) + 1000$$

and the detailed formula is

$$M = P + Q + 4 \cdot VT + NGV(50 + MG) + 3i(NCAT + CL) + 300$$

where

      MG = number of marginal specifications

      CL = total number of cells (the product of the numbers of levels of the grouping variables)

      i = 1, 2, 3 or 4 depending on the maximum number of variables that can be analyzed at one time

P1F A conservative formula is

$$M = 28 \cdot VM + 11 \cdot NTAB + \Sigma \, NCELL + \max (NCELL + 8 \cdot NR + NC)$$
$$+ H_1 + 2500$$

and the detailed formula is

$$M = Q + G + 18 \cdot VM + 3 \cdot NCAT' + 11 \cdot NTAB + \Sigma \, NCELL$$
$$+ \max (NCELL + 8 \cdot NR + NC) + H_1 + H_2 + H_3 + 440$$

where
  Σ and max are the summation and maximum over all tables

  VM   = total number of variables (including those specified by DEFINE statements)

  NCAT' = total number of categories (codes or intervals) for all variables; when no CODEs or CUTPoints are assigned in the *CATEGory* paragraph for a variable; it is assumed to have 10 codes

  NTAB = total number of tables requested (each level of each CONDITION variable is a separate table)

  NCELL = $(NR + 6)(NC + 6)$ where NR and NC are the number of rows and columns respectively in the table

  $H_1 = \begin{cases} \text{number of cells in table if multiway table input is used} \\ 0 \text{ otherwise} \end{cases}$

  $H_2 = \begin{cases} \text{VM if any DEFINE statements are specified} \\ 0 \text{ otherwise} \end{cases}$

  $H_3 = \begin{cases} \text{number of coefficients in COEFFICIENT statements} \\ 0 \text{ otherwise} \end{cases}$

<u>P2F</u> A conservative formula is

$$M = 25 \cdot VM + 20 \cdot NTAB + \Sigma\ NCELL + \max\ (3 \cdot NCELL + 8 \cdot NR + NC)$$
$$+ H_1 + 2500$$

and a detailed formula is

$$M = Q + G + 15 \cdot VM + 3 \cdot NCAT' + 20 \cdot NTAB + \Sigma\ NCELL$$
$$+ \max\ (3 \cdot NCELL + 8 \cdot NR + NC) + 21 \cdot NSTEP + H_1$$
$$+ H_2 + H_4 + 440$$

where
  $H_4 = 2 \cdot$ total number of cells specified in EMPTY statements
  and the other terms are defined as in P1F above.

<u>P3F</u> A conservative formula is

$$M = 29 \cdot VM + 47 \cdot NTAB + X + H_1 + 2500$$

and a detailed formula is

$$M = Q + G + 19 \cdot VM + 3 \cdot NCAT' + 47 \cdot NTAB + X + H_1 + H_2 + H_5 + 250$$

where

  $X = \begin{cases} \Sigma\ NCELL & \text{when forming tables} \\ 4\ \max\ NCELL & \text{when analyzing table} \end{cases}$

  NCELL = number of cells in table (product of the number of levels of each dimension)

  H_5 = number of models specified + $2 \cdot$ number of terms specified in all models

  and the other terms are defined as in P1F above.

P1L The conservative formula is

$$M = 16 \cdot VM + 3 \cdot CU + H + 3000$$

and the detailed formula is

$$M = Q + G + 6 \cdot VM + 3 \cdot CU + 50 \cdot GN + H + 2500$$

where

$$H = \begin{cases} NPER \cdot (6 + 4 \cdot GN) + GN \cdot (10 + 2 \cdot GN) & \text{if LIFE table} \\ 2 \cdot NKM & \text{if PRODUCT- limit analysis} \end{cases}$$

and

NPER = number of intervals in life table
NKM = number of distinct uncensored survival times

P1M The conservative formula is

$$M = 17 \cdot VM + VT(VT + 1)/2 + 300$$

and the detailed formula is

$$M = Q + 8 \cdot VT + VT(VT + 1)/2 + VM$$

P2M P2M keeps the data in memory. The conservative formula is

$$M = 8 \cdot VM + H + 500$$

and the detailed formula is

$$M = Q + H + 300$$

where

$$H = \begin{cases} CU(VU + 21) & \text{if the distance matrix is printed} \\ CU(VU + 14) & \text{otherwise} \end{cases}$$

P3M P3M keeps the data in memory. The conservative formula is

$$M = 50 \cdot VM + CI(7 + VU) + B + 300$$

and the detailed formula is

$$M = Q + P + 3 \cdot VT + 5 \cdot CU + VU(4 + CI + C) + VU^2$$
$$+ \max (2 \cdot CU, VT) + B$$

where

B = number of blocks x 4 $(B \geq 8)$

P = number of passes

C = maximum number of codes for any variable $(C \leq 35)$

The maximum number of blocks B is nearly $VU \cdot CU/4$. The number of blocks formed is reduced by specifying a fewer number of passes. P3M forms only as many blocks as there are locations available in memory.

P4M The detailed formula is

$$M = 8 \cdot VM + 17 \cdot VU + 2 \cdot VU \cdot FN + 2 \cdot FN^2$$
$$+ \max (VU^2 + VU, 9028) + \max (VU, FN^2 + FN) + 90$$

where FN = number of factors

P6M The conservative formulas are

$$M = 14 \cdot VM + 15 \cdot VU + VU^2 + 2 \cdot VQ^2 + 100 \qquad \text{if double precision}$$

$$M = 14 \cdot VM + 13 \cdot VU + VU(VU+1)/2 + VQ^2 + 100 \quad \text{if single precision}$$

where VQ is the number of variables in the smaller set

P7M A conservative formula is

$$M = 56 \cdot VM + VU^2 + 7VU \cdot GN + 4 \cdot CU + 1500$$

and the detailed formula is

$$M = Q + G + VU^2 + 5VU \cdot GN + 2 \cdot VIN(GN-1) + 7 \cdot VT + 10 \cdot GN^2$$
$$+ 35 \cdot VU + 4 \cdot VM + 4 \cdot CU + 26 \cdot GN + H_1 + H_2$$

where
$$H_1 = \begin{cases} 2500 & \text{if the CANONICAL variables are plotted} \\ 0 & \text{otherwise} \end{cases}$$

$$H_2 = \begin{cases} GN \cdot CU & \text{if POSTERIOR probabilities are printed} \\ 0 & \text{otherwise} \end{cases}$$

VIN = number of variables in the discriminant function

PAM The detailed formula is

$$M = G + 14 \cdot VM + 19 \cdot VU + 4 \cdot GN + 10 \cdot VU \cdot GN + 2 \cdot VU^2 + 1000$$

P1R A conservative formula is

$$M = 23 \cdot VM + VU(VU+1)/2 + 1000$$

and the detailed formula is

$$M = Q + G + VU(VU+1)/2 + 5 \cdot VT + 8 \cdot VU + 3 \cdot NP$$

where NP = number of plots

P2R A conservative formula is

$$M = 18VM + VU(VU+1)/2 + 1000$$

and the detailed formula is

$$M = Q + 12 \cdot VU + VU(VU+1)/2 + 3 \cdot NP + H + 20$$

where
NP = number of plots
$$H = \begin{cases} 11 + VU & \text{if FLOAT is specified} \\ 0 & \text{otherwise} \end{cases}$$

P3R P3R keeps the data in memory. Before the analysis P3R prints how many cases can be used in the analysis (C). If the number of cases in your data (CI) exceeds C, you can estimate the number of locations required as $M = (CI/C) \cdot 15000$.

A conservative formula is

$$M = 16 \cdot VM + CU(VT+5) + 1000$$

and a detailed formula is

$$M = Q + CU \cdot (VT+5) + 2 \cdot VM + 3 \cdot VT + \max(2 \cdot VT + 2, VI)$$
$$+ 12 \cdot NP + NP(NP+3)/2 + 48 + H_1 + H_2$$

where

NP = number of parameters

$$H_1 = \begin{cases} 3 \cdot NC + NC(NC+3)/2 + 2 \cdot NP \cdot NC & \text{if NC constraints are specified} \\ 0 & \text{if there are no constraints} \end{cases}$$

$$H_2 = \begin{cases} VT + 2 & \text{if BMDP File is created} \\ 0 & \text{otherwise} \end{cases}$$

P4R A conservative formula is

$$M = 25VM + 3 \cdot VM^2 + 300$$

and the detailed formula is

$$M = Q + VM \cdot (3 \cdot VM + 17)$$

P5R A conservative formula is

$$M = 8 \cdot VM + 10 \cdot CU + H_1 + 1200$$

and the detailed formula is

$$M = Q + 10 \cdot CU + 3 \cdot D^2 + H + 200$$

where

$$H_1 = \begin{cases} 2 \cdot CU & \text{if case weights are specified} \\ 0 & \text{otherwise} \end{cases}$$

D = degree of polynomial

P6R $\quad M = 13 \cdot VM + 15 \cdot VU + VU^2 + 300 \qquad$ if double precision

$\quad M = 13 \cdot VM + 13 \cdot VU + VU(VU+1)/2 + 300 \quad$ if single precision

P9R $\quad M = 14 \cdot VM + VU^2 + 10 \cdot VU + 300 \qquad\qquad$ if METHOD=NONE

$\quad M = 14 \cdot VM + VU(VU+1)(VU+2)/3 + 6VU^2 + 56VU + 300 \quad$ otherwise

PAR PAR keeps the data in memory. Before the analysis PAR prints how many cases can be used in the analysis (C). If the number of cases in your data (CI) exceeds C, you can estimate the number of locations required as $M = (CI/C) \cdot 15000$.

A conservative formula is

$$M = 15 \cdot VM + CU(5+2PT+2VM) + 35PT + 8PT^2 + 300$$

and a detailed formula is

$$M = Q + CU \cdot (5+2PE+2VS) + 7 \cdot VT + 10PT + 24PE + 3PE^2 + 2PE \cdot CON$$
$$+ BE + 2 \cdot BE \cdot PE + BE^2 + 300$$

where

$$PT = \text{total number of parameters}$$

$$PE = \text{number of parameters estimated}$$

$$VS = \begin{cases} \text{largest variable subscript in USE statement} \\ VT \quad \text{otherwise} \end{cases}$$

$$CON = \text{number of specified constraints}$$

$$BE = \text{maximum number of boundaries encountered during iteration}$$

P1S A conservative formula is

$$M = 31\ VM + 500$$

and a detailed formula is

$$M = Q + 3 \cdot VM + 20 \cdot VT + 100$$

P3S P3S keeps the data in memory. The detailed formula is

$$M = Q + 2 \cdot VT + VU + (VT+2) \cdot CU + H_1 + H_2 + H_3 + H_4 + H_5 + 40$$

where

$$H_1 = \begin{cases} 3(VU+1)VU/2 + VT & \text{if SIGN test} \\ 0 & \text{otherwise} \end{cases}$$

$$H_2 = \begin{cases} VU \cdot (VU+1)/2 + 2 \cdot CU + VT & \text{if KENDALL} \\ 0 & \text{otherwise} \end{cases}$$

$$H_3 = \begin{cases} VU(VU+1)/2 + 2 \cdot CU + VT & \text{if SPEARMAN} \\ 0 & \text{otherwise} \end{cases}$$

$$H_4 = \begin{cases} 3 \cdot (VU+1) \cdot VU/2 + \max(VT, 3 \cdot CU) & \text{if WILCOXON} \\ VT \cdot (CU+2) & \text{if FRIEDMAN} \\ \max(2 \cdot VT, 3 \cdot CU) + CU \cdot VT & \text{if both WILCOXON and FRIEDMAN} \\ 0 & \text{otherwise} \end{cases}$$

$$H_5 = \begin{cases} G + GN + CU & \text{if KRUSKAL-WALLIS} \\ 0 & \text{otherwise} \end{cases}$$

P1V A conservative formula is

$$M = 19 \cdot VM + 12VU + 18GN + 8VU \cdot GN + VU^2 \cdot (GN+1) + 1000$$

and a detailed formula is

$$M = Q + G + 5 \cdot VM + 4 \cdot VT + 7 \cdot VU + 13 \cdot GN + 8 \cdot VU \cdot GN$$
$$+ VU^2 \cdot (GN + 1) + 5 \max(VU, GN) + 60$$

<u>P2V</u> The detailed formula is

$$M = Q + G + NVV(NTP + 2) + NDV\left[NTP(NX+NY) + NDV/2\right]$$
$$+ NX \cdot NY(NTP + 2^{NT} + 1) + NY \cdot NTE + 2GN(NX + NY + NG)$$
$$+ NT \cdot NTP + (NX + NY)(7 \cdot NTP + 2) + NTSS + NTS + 3VM$$
$$+ 16GN + 3NDV + 3NTP + 9 \cdot NXY + NTS + 2^{NT+1} + GN$$
$$+ 14 \cdot NCM + NY$$

where

NX   = number of covariates

NY   = number of dependent variables (separate analyses on each)

NTP = number of repeated measures (product of number of levels of the trial factors)

NVS = number of variables saved

NTS = sum of number of levels of the trial factors

NDV = number of dummy variables generated for the grouping factors (GN if the INCLUDE or EXCLUDE options are not used)

NG   = number of grouping variables

GN   = number of groups defined by the grouping variables

NTSS = sum of squares of the number of levels of the trial factors

NVV = $(NX + NY)(NX + NY + 1)/2$

NTE = number of lines in the ANOVA table

NCM = number of components corresponding to each error term in the ANOVA table

NXY = NX + NY

NT   = number of trial factors

<u>P3V</u> A detailed formula is

$$M = Q + G + NV^2 + NR^2 + GN^2 + GN \cdot NV + NP^2 + 25 \cdot NP + 12 \cdot VT$$
$$+ 18 \cdot NV + 9 \cdot GN + 11 \cdot NR + NN$$

where

NR = number of dummy variables generated by P3V in the random part of the model

NV = total number of variables including covariates and generated dummy variables

NP = number of parameters (one for each fixed dummy variable, covariate and variance component)

NN = NH · NC where NH is the number of hypotheses and NC is the number of components

GN = number of cells in the fixed part of the model

APPENDIX C

CONTENTS

Section		Page
C.1	Detecting Outliers with Stepwise Regression (P2R)	855
C.2	It Wasn't an Accident (F-to-enter, F-to-remove)	855
C.3	Scaling for Miniumum Interaction Using BMDP6M	856
C.4	Computing Predictions	857
C.5	Tolerance in Regression Analysis	857
C.6	Random Case Selection	857
C.7	Ridge Regression Using BMDP2R	858
C.8	Analysis of Multivariate Change Scores	859
C.9	Checking Order of Cards in a Data Deck	859
C.10	Alternate Form for BMDP Control Language	859
C.11	First Steps	860
C.12	Using P1D to Identify and List Cases Containing Special or Unacceptable Values	861
C.13	Maximum Likelihood Estimation by Means of P3R	862
C.14	Multivariate Analysis of Variance and Covariance Using P7M	863
C.15	Analysis of the Pattern of Missing Data	863
C.16	The Iterated Least Squares Method of Estimating Mean and Variance Components Using P3R	864
C.17	Quick and Dirty Monte Carlo	865
C.18	Lagged Variables Using Transformation Paragraph	865
C.19	Cross Validation in BMDP9R	866
C.20	Residual Analysis in BMDP9R	866

C.1   Detecting Outliers with Stepwise Regression
By M.R. Mickey, Health Sciences Computing Facility, UCLA

Stepwise regression can be used for detecting outliers – cases for which the value of the dependent variable is relatively poorly accounted for by an appropriate regression equation. The residuals may not indicate an aberrant value if the case causes the fitted regression plane to lie reasonably close to the outlier point. One needs to consider the plane fitted with the case not included in the calculation. This case deletion is in effect readily accomplished by augmenting the set of independent variables by an additional set, one corresponding to each case. The values of the additional variables are zero with the exception that the value of the variable corresponding to a given case is 1 for that case. In effect one augments the X-matrix with an identity to produce (X,I) as the matrix of independent variables. A deck setup using BMDP2R, is shown below.

```
// EXEC BIMEDT, PROG=BMDP2R
//TRANSF DD *
      DO 1 I=1,21
   1  X(I+2)=0.0
      X(K+2)=1.0
//SYSIN DD *
PROBLEM TITLE='DETECTING OUTLIERS
WITH STEPWISE REGRESSION'./
INPUT VARIABLES=2.FORMAT='(F2.0,F3.0)'.
CASES=21./
VARIABLE ADD=21.NAMES=AGE,GESELL./
REGRESS DEPENDENT=2.LEVELS=1,0,21*2./
END/
 1595
 2671
 1083
  991
15102
 2087
 1893
11100
 8104
 2094
 7113
  996
 1083
 1184
11102
10100
12105
10100
12105
 4257
17121
 1186
10100
FINISH/
//
```

The augmenting variables are entered stepwise at a level of forcing that prohibits them from entering until the original independent variable has been accounted for. The F-to-enter for the augmenting variables then supplies an indicator of the aberrancy of the cases relative to the regression structure. The entering of an augmenting variable is equivalent to deleting the corresponding case.

Further details are given in: Mickey, Dunn and Clark (1967). Note on the use of stepwise regression in detecting outliers. *Computers and Biomedical Research*, 1, 105-111.

C.2   It Wasn't an Accident
By A.B. Forsythe, Supervising Statistician, Health Sciences Computing Facility, UCLA

Several users of the stepwise regression and discriminant function analysis programs have asked why we use the terms F-to-enter and F-to-remove throughout the writeup and output, rather than simply calling them F values. Some have suggested that we could ask the user for the level of significance (α) and have the program convert it to the appropriate F values. The computer programing to do this is simple enough but the statistics are difficult. Since the program is selecting the "best" variable, the usual F tables do not apply. The appropriate critical value is a function of the number of cases, the number of variables, and, unfortunately, the correlation structure of the predictor variables. This implies that the level of significance corresponding to an F-to-enter depends upon the particular set of data being used. For example, with several hundred cases and 50 potential predictors, an F-to-enter of 11, would roughly correspond to α = 5% if all 50 predictors were uncorrelated. The usual use of the F table would erroneously suggest a value of 4.

There is nothing wrong with the F table. It was constructed for testing the significance of a preselected variable and not the "best" variable out of many. However, the F-to-enter and F-to-remove are still useful values for guiding the regression program's variable selection, but the probability statements are tough.

References

Forsythe, A.B., P.R.A. May and L. Engelman (1970). Computing advantage scores by multiple regression. In *Psychopharmacology and the Individual Patient*. Wittenborn, Soloman, Goldberg and May, Eds. Raven Press, 116-123.

Forsythe, A.B., P.R.A. May and L. Engelman (1971). Prediction of multiple regression. *Journal of Psychiatric Research* 8, 119-126.

Forsythe, A.B., L. Engelman, R. Jennrich and P.R.A. May (1973). A stopping rule for variable selection in multiple regression. *Journal of the American Statistical Association*, 68, 75-77.

Anderson, R.L., D.M. Allen and F.B. Cady (1972). Selection of predictor variables in linear multiple regression. In *Statistical Papers in Honor of George W. Snedecor*, T.A. Bancroft, Ed. Ames, Iowa, University of Iowa Press.

C.3 Scaling for Minimum Interaction Using BMDP6M
By Robert I. Jennrich, Dept. of Biomathematics, UCLA

At times one wishes to scale categorical responses in an otherwise classical analysis of variance in such a way that the resulting model is as additive (has as little interaction) as possible. For example, consider a pair of treatments used at three hospitals to inhibit postoperative infection resulting from colon surgery. The infection may be totally inhibited (A), mild (B), or severe (C). Assume that a total of 18 patients experience infections as recorded in the following table:

	H_1	H_2	H_3
T_1	A B C	A B B	C A B
T_2	C B A	A B A	C C A

We wish to assign values to A, B and C to minimize the size of the interaction relative to that of the main effects which is equivalent to minimizing the

$$\text{relative interaction} = \frac{\text{interaction sum of squares}}{\text{total sum of squares}}$$

This is an eigenvalue problem that can be solved by means of canonical correlation. Let a_{ij}, b_{ij}, c_{ij} be the proportions of A's, B's and C's in the i,j cell. Clearly, minimizing the relative interaction is equivalent to maximizing

$$\frac{\text{total main effect sum of squares}}{\text{total sum of squares}}$$

This is equivalent to finding a variable

$$y = Aa + Bb + Cc$$

which has maximum multiple correlation with an arbitrary basis x,y,z of the total main effect space – in other words the first canonical variable of a,b,c relative to x,y,z. Since correlations are unaffected by additive constants we may assume that

$$x_{ij} = \delta_{i1}, \; y_{ij} = \delta_{1j}, \; z_{ij} = \delta_{2j}$$

where δ_{ij} is the Kronecker delta. For the same reason we may assume that A = 0 and perform a canonical analysis of x,y,z versus

b,c. The coefficients B and C of b and c in the definition of the first canonical variable provide a set of values of A, B and C which minimize the relative interaction.

Larger tables, more letters and more dimensions may be treated in the same way. Cell frequencies need not be equal. For the table given above the input data could be

x	y	z	b	c
1	1	0	.333	.333
1	0	1	.667	.0
1	0	0	.333	.333
0	1	0	.333	.333
0	0	1	.333	.0
0	0	0	.0	.667

Using BMDP6M gives the optimum values

$$A = 0, B = -1.352, C = 2.981$$

and a squared canonical correlation

$$\rho^2 = 0.891$$

which means that 89% of the total variance is in main effects and 11% in the interaction. The optimized cell means are

.543	-.901	.543
.543	-.451	1.987

This table may be obtained from the first canonical variable values by appropriate translation and scaling. The required input is

```
PROBLEM TITLE='SCALING FOR MINIMUM RELATIVE
    INTERACTION'./
INPUT VARIABLES=5.FORMAT='(5F5.0)'./
VARIABLE NAMES=R,C1,C2,'B(I,J)','C(I,J)'./
CANONICAL FIRST=R,C1,C2.SECOND='B(I,J)','C(I,J)'./
PRINT MATRIX=CANV, COEF./        END/
  1  1  0.3333.3333
  1  0  1.6667.0
  1  0  0.3333.3333
  0  1  0.3333.3333
  0  0  1.3333.0
  0  0  0.0    .6667
```

The program produces standardized canonical coefficients. These must be divided by standard deviations to obtain the required coefficients.

An alternative approach might have been to minimize the interaction sum of squares directly after setting A = 0 and C = 1 to eliminate zero solutions. The difficulty here is that the solution may have small main effects as well as small interaction which is not satisfactory.

C.4 Computing Predictions
By Laszlo Engelman, Health Sciences
Computing Facility, UCLA

The equations of a model may be evaluated on a set of cases other than those used to determine the parameters of the model. This is accomplished by assigning zero weight to cases you do not want to affect the computations of the regression coefficients.

Suppose for the first 100 cases the dependent variable is recorded and for the next 50 you wish to predict the dependent variable. Your input could be

```
PROBlem      TITLE='PREDICTION'./
INPUT        VARIABles=5.
             FORMAT='(5F7.0)'.
             CASEs=150./
VARIABle     ADD=1.
             WEIGHT=6./
TRANSFormation
             X(6)=KASE LE 100./
REGRESsion.../
END/

    .  (data matrix)
    .

FINISH
```

The above example sets the weight variable (6th variable) equal to 1 for the first 100 cases and to 0 for the next 50 cases.

Using an open-ended transformation method, the above can be accomplished by stating

```
X(6)=1.0
IF(KASE.GT.100)X(6)=0.0
```

If knowledge of the outcome variable is coded in the data by some other scheme, appropriate coding can be devised to accommodate the scheme. For example, if X(1), the dependent variable, is zero only when it is not known, one can use the open-ended transformation.

```
X(6)=1
IF(X(1).EQ.0)X(6)=0
```

to set the weight to zero or one.

C.5 Tolerance in Regression Analysis
By Laszlo Engelman, Health Sciences
Computing Facility, UCLA

Many BMD and BMDP program writeups refer to a concept called "tolerance" and ask the user to state a "limit for tolerance." The meaning of this concept is discussed below.

The concept is mentioned in programs that deal with the prediction of a dependent variable using several independent variables. Although the concept is relevant in nonstepwise procedures, we discuss its use in a stepwise regression program.

Suppose a regression computation proceeds in a stepwise manner: at each step one more independent variable is added to the set of variables to be used in the prediction of the dependent variable. Let's denote the dependent variable by y and the variables already selected to be predictors by $x_1, x_2, ..., x_q$. At the next step a new variable, x_{q+1} will be selected, but only if it passes a test — if its tolerance is greater than the tolerance limit.

But what is the "tolerance of the new predictor x_{q+1}"? It is the proportion of the variability in x_{q+1} not explained by $x_1, x_2, ..., x_q$; it is one minus the squared multiple correlation of x_{q+1} with the previously accepted predictors. That is, the tolerance of x_{q+1} is

$$1 - R^2_{x_{q+1} \cdot x_1, x_2, \ldots, x_q}$$

When the tolerance of x_{q+1} is small (e.g., $< .001$) the variable is unlikely to be of any significant help in the prediction and will cause the standard errors of the regression coefficients to be large. Furthermore, since a small tolerance means a large multiple correlation, which indicates that x_{q+1} is very close to being expressible as a linear combination of $x_1, x_2, ..., x_q$, admitting x_{q+1} as a predictor could cause serious computational accuracy problems. If computers were infinitely accurate, tolerance would still be useful to guard against results being overly dependent on the inaccuracy (truncation or rounding) in the recorded data.

C.6 Random Case Selection
By Laszlo Engelman, Health Sciences
Computing Facility, UCLA

Random sub-sampling, a frequently used analytical technique, can be accomplished with the BMDP programs. The example below randomly selects approximately 1/4 of the cases to be included in the computations.

```
PROBlem      TITLE='RANDOM SAMPLES'./
INPUT        VARIABles=5.
             FORMAT='(5F7.0)'.
             CASEs=982./
TRANSFormation
             R=RNDU(152319).
             USE=R LT .25./
END/

    .
    .  (data matrix)
    .

FINISH/
```

The first transformation generates a uniform (0-1) random value; the second selects the case if the generated random value is less than .25.

C.7 Ridge Regression Using BMDP2R

Maryann Hill, Health Sciences Computing Facility, UCLA

In a regression analysis when the independent variables are highly correlated, the data are often said to be ill conditioned. The resulting regression coefficients may be quite unstable and not useful for future predictive purposes on a new sample. Ridge regression is a technique that is used to "tame" the estimates of regression coefficients, to portray sensitivity of the estimates to the particular set of data being used, and to obtain point estimates with smaller mean square error (although the estimates will be biased).

In the regression model $Y = Z\beta + e$, the ridge estimate of the coefficient vector β is

$$\hat{\beta}^* = (Z'Z + \lambda I)^{-1} Z'Y$$

where Z is the matrix (n cases by p variables) of the standardized independent variables and Y is the vector of the standardized dependent variable. The usual least squares estimate is obtained when $\lambda = 0$.

Plotting the resulting coefficients for a number of values of λ gives an indication of the stability of the coefficients. You hope to find the value of λ where the coefficients begin to smooth out and no longer make sudden changes (e.g., switching signs). The estimates of the coefficients eventually approach zero as λ goes to infinity.

By adding "dummy" cases to the end of the standardized data file and using the zero intercept option (TYPE=0), you can try this technique with your own data using BMDP2R. The "dummy" cases determine the amount added to the diagonal of the $Z'Z$ matrix. Add one "dummy" case for **each** of the p independent variables with $\sqrt{(n-1)\lambda}$ as the value of the corresponding variable and zeros for the remaining variables. Note that the $Z'Z$ matrix is (n-1) times the correlation matrix. It is useful to think of ridge regression in terms of the correlation matrix; the size of the value added to the diagonal elements of the correlation matrix is then comparable from problem to problem. In this context values of λ less than one are of most interest.

Example: Hoerl (1962) discussed a ridge technique in an article dealing with the measurement of the performance of a chemical process. He specified a relationship between three highly correlated process variables and a response variable, added random noise to the response variable and then analyzed the data. Although the specified relationship had all positive coefficients, the usual least squares solution produced inflated coefficients – one of which was negative. He then applied a ridge technique to these data showing the taming effect on the coefficients and producing solutions closer to the "true" values.

To see the effect of $\lambda = .16$ on the regression coefficients for the Hoerl data, we compute $\sqrt{(n-1)\lambda} = \sqrt{9 \times .16} = 1.2$ and submit the following cards for the HSCF system:

```
//   EXEC BIMEDT,PROG=BMDP2R
//TRANSF DD  *
      IF(KASE.GT.10)GO TO 1
      X(1)=(X(1)-1.82)/.4022
      X(2)=(X(2)-1.86)/.4088
      X(3)=(X(3)-1.88)/.4492
      X(4)=(X(4)-28.9)/4.0213
  1   CONTINUE
/*
//GO.SYSIN DD  *
PROBLEM TITLE IS RIDGE./
INPUT VARIABLES ARE 4.
      FORMAT IS '(4F4.1)'./
REGRESSION DEPENDENT IS 4.
      ENTER IS .001.  REMOVE IS 0.
      TYPE IS ZERO./
END/
   11 11 11 223
   14 15 11 223
   17 18 20 292
   17 17 18 270
   18 19 18 285
   18 18 19 304
   19 18 20 311
   20 21 21 314
   23 24 25 328
   25 25 24 340
   12  0  0   0
    0 12  0   0
    0  0 12   0
/*
//
```

Using the sample $\bar{x}$ and s to standardize the independent variables, $X(1),X(2),X(3)$ and the dependent variable, $X(4)$ for 10 cases

10 cases of raw data

3 dummy cases

Inserting different values of $\sqrt{(n-1)\lambda}$ and rerunning the program, we obtain and plot ridge estimates of the coefficient for each λ (see figure). (**Note:** A number of problems can be run together and the BIMEDT procedure can be used to change the values of the dummy cases in each problem.)

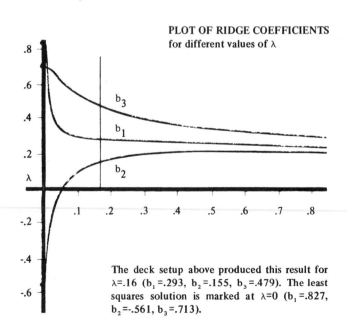

PLOT OF RIDGE COEFFICIENTS
for different values of λ

The deck setup above produced this result for $\lambda = .16$ ($b_1 = .293$, $b_2 = .155$, $b_3 = .479$). The least squares solution is marked at $\lambda = 0$ ($b_1 = .827$, $b_2 = -.561$, $b_3 = .713$).

You will also want to plot the residual sum of squares versus λ. The most desirable coefficients hopefully will correspond to that value of λ where the residuals have not started to increase rapidly, but yet the values of the coefficients have settled down.

References

Hoerl, A.E. (1962). Application of ridge analysis to regression problems. *Chem. Eng. Prog.* 58, 54-59.

Hoerl, A.E. and R.W. Kennard (1970). Ridge regression: biased estimation for nonorthogonal problems. *Technometrics* 12, 55-67.

Hoerl, A.E. and R.W. Kennard (1970). Ridge regression: applications to nonorthogonal problems. *Technometrics* 12, 69-82.

C.8 Analysis of Multivariate Change Scores
James W. Frane, Dept. of Biomathematics, UCLA

Changes in subjects from pretreatment to posttreatment on a large number of variables may be analyzed in a number of ways using BMDP programs. The first way is by using **P3D** which includes t tests for each variable and Hotelling's T for all the variables simultaneously. Two other methods can also be used to gain insight into the changes.

Factor analysis: The large number of change scores may be reduced to a smaller number of factors by using the factor analysis program **P4M**. Data must be preprocessed, e.g., by **P1S** (Multipass Transformations). First change scores and their standard deviations are computed. Next, the change scores are divided by their standard deviations. Means should **not** be subtracted. These "standardized" data are used as input to **P4M**. In **P4M**, specify that the covariance matrix around the origin is to be factor analyzed. This is done by stating FORM IS OCOVAR in the FACTOR paragraph. Salient factors will be identified by variables whose changes are large and highly correlated.

Stepwise selection of variables: Whereas factor analysis summarizes a large number of variables by means of derived factors which involve all the variables, stepwise regression achieves a summary by means of an artful selection of variables. To analyze change scores using **P2R**, an additional variable is created which is identically equal to one. This added variable is the dependent variable in a regression with zero intercept and the change scores are the independent variables. At step zero, the F-to-enter values are equal to the squares of the t-statistics for testing zero change which would be obtained in **P3D**. At any step in **P2R**, the F statistic for regression is the same as the F statistic for Hotelling's T in **P3D** which would be obtained for the set of variables entered in the regression in **P2R**. Variables that are not entered are variables whose changes can be explained by the variables which have entered the regression. This procedure is also equivalent to a "one group discriminant analysis" in which a sample of change scores is compared to a theoretical group with zero mean.

C.9 Checking Order of Cards in a Data Deck
James W. Frane, Dept. of Biomathematics, UCLA

When there are several cards per subject or experimental unit, the proper ordering of cards in a data deck is essential. Each card should include a case identification number and a card number. The order of cards in a deck can be checked and deviant cards flagged by using BMDP1D. Suppose that you have two cards per subject, that the case identification number appears as variables 1 and 21, and that the card number (1 or 2) is recorded as variables 2 and 22. The following deck setup can then be used:

```
PROBLEM   TITLE IS 'CHECK ORDER OF CARDS'./
INPUT     VARIABLES ARE 40.
          FORMAT IS '(20F4.0)'./
VARIABLE  MINIMUMS ARE (2)1,(21)0,2.
          MAXIMUMS ARE (2)1,(21)0,2.
          AFTERT./
TRANSF    X(21) IS X(21)-X(1)./
PRINT     MAXIMUM.
          MINIMUM./
END/
```

In the VARIABLE paragraph, we state that the minimum and maximum values for the second identification variable (variable 21) are precisely zero; i.e., before subtracting the first case identification variable, the second case identification variable was the same as the first. In order to be sure that the cards for a subject are in order, we specify that the minimum and maximum values of the card number variables (2 and 22) are precisely 1 and 2. We specify AFTERT because the limits must be checked after variable 21 is transformed. The effect of the PRINT paragraph is to print the data for any deviant cases.

C.10 Alternate Form for BMDP Program Control Language
James W. Frane, Dept. of Biomathematics, UCLA

The BMDP program control language does not have any rules regarding the card columns in which keywords and parameter values are to be placed. This eliminates many errors in problem specification. However, BMDP control language does have a syntax. Uniform arrangement of control language eliminates many syntax errors. Consider the following control language:

```
/PROBLEM   TITLE IS 'STRUCTURED CONTROL
           LANGUAGE'.
/INPUT     VARIABLES ARE 5.
           FORMAT IS '(5F4.0)'.
/VARIABLE NAMES ARE SEX, HEIGHT, WEIGHT, AGE,
           HEARTRATE.
           GROUPING IS SEX.
/END
```

Note: a) The virgule (/) appears at the beginning of each paragraph rather than at the end. The virgule always appears in column one and no other character except blank appears in column one.

b) Paragraph names go in columns two through eleven.

c) The statements (sentences) begin in column twelve.

d) Only one statement goes on a card.

Although these rules are **not necessary**, many users find them a **convenient** means of avoiding control language errors. In particular, it is easy to see that one virgule is present for each paragraph, to see which paragraphs are present, to see which sentences are used, and to verify that each sentence ends with a period.

C.11 First Steps

W.J. Dixon, Health Sciences Computing Facility, UCLA

Students reading standard textbooks on statistics (including my own) or books on computers may easily gain the notion that a statistical analysis done on the computer is a fairly simple one-step operation – one need only decide on the form of analysis, punch the data cards and submit the problem to the computer via a packaged program with specified control statements. However, real life is not so simple. An analysis of real data for a real problem is usually much more complex. Many things should be considered in the early stages of the analysis:

- The data will almost always contain missing values and erroneous entries that arise from keypunch errors or other transcribing errors: the pattern and extent of missing values should be studied and decisions should be made about what to do with them; erroneous entries should be found and procedures should be specified for dealing with them.

- Data distributions may not be as advertised – often they are not normal, are probably not symmetric, have tails high enough to be uncomfortable for least squares procedures, and contain a few wandering values that defy correction but are not believable: transformations and/or trimming procedures may need to be considered to deal with these problems.

- It may not be possible to specify the most appropriate analysis until the data are examined in a variety of ways.

- The question of whether the data are a homogeneous group or need to be stratified should be resolved.

- A decision should be made as to whether the data sufficiently satisfy the assumptions of later analyses that are planned to follow.

So what should you do?

A general discussion in the absence of real data with real problems may not be very enlightening because problems with different data sets differ widely. It may help, however, to know what size the problem may be when planning a data analysis for a study with many variables (more than ten or twenty) and many cases (more than 200). An exploratory examination of the data dealing with the problems stated above can be expected to demand at least ten times more effort than an analysis of the main research hypothesis for which the study was launched. Larger data sets or those with many missing values are almost entirely exploratory; they can keep someone with a large responsive computer busy for weeks, or perhaps years. At each stage of the screening, analysis uncovers information that affects the subsequent steps in the analysis (for example, the need for stratification on age, sex, diagnosis, the need for transformation, etc.).

The BMDP Manual issued in 1975 has a discussion of these problems starting on page 1. A number of the examples associated with the D programs are included in the manual and illustrate the screening operations suggested above. How other programs are used to serve screening or exploratory functions is also more fully explained in the manual. The P-programs are, in general, easy to use for screening since many of them are constructed to allow the designation of subgroups, which can be analyzed separately, and supply printer graphics that allow one to more easily examine differences in the subgroups. For example, programs P5D and P6D allow the graphical identification of subgroups with different alphabetic letters (see BMDP Manual, page 174). A recent paper by D.J. Finney discussing the importance of screening data has just appeared in *Biometrics* 31, 1975, pp. 375-386. His title is: "Numbers and data."

Which programs could be used in a sequence of analyses for screening data with 15 variables recorded for 400 cases?

- P4D needs no format and gives a column-by-column summary of the data. It lists all data in various forms (garbage included) so long as it is legal. This permits a simple first screening of the data file. Usually this program is run several times, once listing the data as they exist and then additional runs are made with certain types of values replaced with specified characters.

- P2D supplies basic frequency counts, uncovers more keypunch errors, identifies how many values fall outside acceptable minimum and maximum limits, and reveals various distributional anomalies for each variable in turn (errors that are evident from these distributions can then be corrected).

- P5D allows the pictorial visualization of each variable with histograms and plots for subgroups as well as for the entire group; probit plots allow an assessment of normality.

- P6D provides crossplots of two variables, which allows an examination of the interrelation of pairs of variables and may make further errors evident.

- P1F tabulates two-way contingency tables with a variety of descriptors of the relationship between two variables; such tables are frequently used in the screening phase of analysis to reveal the presence of impossible values in the data.

- P7D provides histograms of each variable for designated subgroups or strata from which you can observe the character of changes in the distributions from strata to strata, such as basic information for anticipated regression or other multivariate procedures.

- P3M provides multidimensional histograms, etc.

See article on P1D (below) for detailed examples of using that program for screening purposes.

C.12 Using P1D to Identify and List Cases Containing Special or Unacceptable Values
Maryann Hill, Health Sciences
Computing Facility, UCLA

Even the most thorough univariate data screening may fail to reveal the presence of inconsistencies or incorrect values in the data; blunders or outliers in the data may be identified if one variable is examined with another variable. For example, an adult weighing 195 pounds is not too unusual until you notice that the corresponding height is five feet. Knowledge of the data structure and internal relations can be used to complete a better data screening. Scatter plots and two-way tables help identify problems. However, if the data file is large it is difficult to identify the extreme or illogical cases. Investigators want to locate such cases quickly and to be able to examine other variables for that case.

P1D can be used to print only the cases containing such problems. A listing of such cases is obtained by using transformations to create new variables that represent the problems of interest, stating minimum, maximum and/or missing values for the new variables, and then requesting that cases with extreme values be printed.

Two-way tables confirm the existence of inconsistencies, such as a male coded as a birth control pill user. Here such a two-way table (code values are indicated) might appear as

			Pill User	
			1 yes	2 no
SEX	1	Male	X	
	2	Female		

Counts found in the "male" – "pill yes" cell indicate a miscoding or recording error. In order to identify cases with this mistake, create a new variable, NEW1=10xSEX + PILL. The new variable now contains codes 11,12,21,22 corresponding to each cell; 11 is the code for the problem cell. Stating a minimum code of 12 makes the value 11 fall outside the acceptable range. P1D has the option to list cases outside stated limits.

A particular response to a survey question may limit the range of answers to another question or require that it be skipped. This type of inconsistency can also be detected with a two-way table:

		Type of Drug		
		not applicable	type A	type B
		0	1	2
DRUG	1 yes			
TAKEN	2 no		X	X

Counts found in the marked cells are unacceptable. Here the transformation NEW2=10xDRUG + TYPE, results in a code for each cell: 10,11,12,20,21,22. Cases with codes 21 or 22 need to be examined. They can be listed by stating a maximum of 20 and requesting that cases with larger values be printed.

A scatter plot of systolic blood pressure versus diastolic blood pressure reveals such errors as a systolic reading less than a diastolic one. To locate this error we generate a new variable NEW3 = SYSTOLIC - DIASTOLIC and request that any case with a value of NEW3 less than zero be printed. At the same time we might be concerned about readings differing by more than 60 units so a maximum value of 60 can also be stated.

P1D program control instructions for listing the problem cases discussed above are

```
PROB/
INPUT    VARIABLES ARE 7.
         FORMAT IS '(A4,6F5.0)'./

VARIABLE NAMES ARE ID, SEX, PILL, DRUG, TYPE,
         SYSTOLIC, DIASTOLIC, NEW1, NEW2, NEW3.
         LABEL IS ID.  ADD = 3.  AFTERT.
         MIN = (8)12, (10)0.  MAX = (9)20, 60./

TRANSF   NEW1 = 10 * SEX.
         NEW1 = NEW1 + PILL.
         NEW2 = 10 * DRUG.
         NEW2 = NEW2 + TYPE.
         NEW3 = SYSTOLIC - DIASTOLIC./

PRINT    MIN.    MAX./
END/
```

NEW1, NEW2 and NEW3 are the three new variables ADDed through the TRANSFormation paragraph. AFTERT indicates that the check for extreme values should be made after the transformations are performed. Cases with the new codes falling outside the stated limits are listed with their ID number as a label, along with the data values for variables one through ten. The words TOO LARGE, TOO SMALL or MISSING are printed instead of the actual value out of range. In the above example the unacceptable new codes were extremes. If a code of interest falls in the middle, the MISSing option can be used to print out such cases. The output example below lists only unusual cases.

CASE NO.	LABEL	SEX	PILL	DRUG	TYPE	SYSTOLIC	DIASTOLIC	NEW1	NEW2	NEW3
3	368	1	2	2	0	90	125	12	20	TOO SMALL
25	403	1	1	1	2	150	120	TOO SMALL	12	30
53	1072	2	1	2	1	130	95	21	TOO LARGE	35

A listing of a subpopulation may be obtained in a similar manner. For example, the following transformations may be used to obtain female pill users who take Drug A and have a systolic blood pressure over 200.

```
A =  SEX EQ 2.         B =  PILL EQ 1.
C =  TYPE EQ 1.        D =  SYSTOLIC GT 200.
E =  A AND B.          F =  C AND D.
NEW4 =  E AND F.
```

A through F are "temporary" variables and do not need to be counted in the VARIABLE ADD list nor named in the VARIABLE NAME list. These are logical transformations (p. 67 of the BMDP Manual). The value of D is 1 (true) if the blood pressure is over 200, and 0 (false) if it is 200 or lower. The value of E is 1 if both A and B are true, zero if either or both are false. NEW4 is 1 (true) only if A, B, C and D are all true. Otherwise NEW4 is 0 (false). Declaring 1 to be a MISSING value for NEW4 and requesting PRINT MISSING will cause a listing of the desired subpopulation to be printed.

C.13 Maximum Likelihood Estimation by Means of P3R

Robert I. Jennrich, Dept. of Biomathematics, UCLA

Mickey and Britt (1974) show how to use BMDX85, a precursor of BMDP3R, to maximize a log-likelihood of the form

$$\log L = \sum_{i=1}^{n} \log \ell(x_i, \theta)$$

and thereby produce maximum likelihood estimates. Here the $\ell(x_i, \theta)$ are likelihoods of independent observations x_i that depend on a parameter vector θ that is to be estimated. To do this they minimized

$$-\log L = \sum_{i=1}^{n} f^2(x_i, \theta)$$

with respect to θ by using BMDX85 with

$$f(x_i, \theta) = \sqrt{-\log \ell(x_i, \theta)}$$

and $y_i = 0$. We illustrate another method that is restricted to exponential models but proceeds in a very intuitive way and provides standard error as well as parameter estimates. Assume that $y_1, ..., y_n$ is a sequence of observations whose means μ_i and covariances σ_{ij} depend on a parameter vector θ. If the matrix (σ_{ij}) is diagonal or at least has a diagonal pseudoinverse with diagonal elements σ^{ii}, we estimate θ using P3R with

$$y_i = y_i, \quad f(x_i, \theta) = \mu_i(\theta), \quad w_i = \sigma^{ii}$$

Used in this way, P3R becomes an iteratively reweighted Gauss-Newton algorithm in which the weights w_i vary from iteration to iteration. Jennrich and Moore (1975) show that when the y_i have a regular exponential distribution (as happens when sampling from Poisson, binomial, multinomial, gamma and other populations) P3R used as suggested becomes a scoring algorithm and the estimates obtained are maximum likelihood estimates. Moreover the standard errors produced are the usual information theory standard errors, provided the specified residual variance option is used to set the latter equal to one. This means that much of the auxiliary output that is nominally intended for a least squares analysis is applicable to a maximum likelihood analysis as well.

To illustrate, the following table contains some quantal response data from Cox (1970, p. 86)

t_i	s_i	n_i	$\hat{\mu}_i$	$\widehat{std}\,\hat{\mu}_i$
7	0	55	0.43	0.25
14	2	157	2.13	0.97
27	7	159	6.01	1.78
51	3	16	3.43	1.52

The s_i represent the number of ingots heated for time t_i in a sample size n_i that were not ready for rolling. Under the assumption that the s_i have independent binomial distributions $B(n_i, \pi_i(\theta))$, the use of P3R with

$$y_i = s_i, \quad f_i = n\pi_i, \quad w_i = (n_i \pi_i (1-\pi_i))^{-1}$$

gives maximum likelihood estimates and information theory standard errors corresponding to any parameterization for the $\pi_i(\theta)$.

Cox used the logistic model

$$\pi_i(\theta_1, \theta_2) = \frac{e^{\theta_1 + \theta_2 t}}{1 + e^{\theta_1 + \theta_2 t}}$$

For this specific model, P3R gave estimates

$$\hat{\theta}_1 = -5.415, \quad \hat{\theta}_2 = 0.0807$$

and standard errors

$$\widehat{std}\,\hat{\theta}_1 = 0.7275, \quad \widehat{std}\,\hat{\theta}_2 = 0.02236$$

which agree with the precision obtained by Cox. Part of the additional output of the program includes estimates of the expected cell frequencies $\mu_i = n_i \pi_i$ with their appropriate standard errors. These are displayed in the table above. The input requires six FORTRAN statements for the FUN routine:

```
T = EXP(P(1)+P(2)*X(1))
D = 1+T
F = X(3)*T/D
DF(1) = F/D
DF(2) = X(1)*F/D
X(4) = D/F
```

The input for the remainder of the program is

```
PROBLEM    TITLE = 'COX DATA'./
INPUT      VARIAB = 4.   CASES = 4.
           FORMAT = '(4F5.0)'./
REGRES     DEPEND = 2.  PARAM = 2.   WEIGHT = 4.
           ITER = 10. HALF = 0. CONVER = -1.0.
           MEANSQ = 1.0./
PARAMETER INITIAL = 0.0,0.0./
END/
    7   0     55    1
   14   2    157    1
   27   7    159    1
   51   3     16    1
```

The Jennrich and Moore reference cited above gives further applications to Poisson and multinomial models including contingency table analysis.

References Cox, D.R. (1970). *Analysis of Binary Data*. London, Methuen.

Jennrich, R.I. and R.H. Moore (1975). Maximum likelihood estimation by means of nonlinear least squares. Princeton Univ., Educational Testing Service.

Mickey, M.R. and P.M. Britt (1974). Obtaining linear scores from preference pairs. *Comm. Statist.* 3, 501-511.

C.14   Multivariate Analysis of Variance and Covariance Using P7M
James Frane, Health Sciences Computing Facility, UCLA

Multivariate analysis of variance and covariance are the primary objectives of BMD11V and BMD12V, but they are also part of the stepwise discriminant analysis programs BMD07M and BMDP7M. The first two programs are used primarily for hypothesis testing. The last two are intended to answer broad questions such as: I have measured several variables on several groups of subjects, what can you tell me about the relationship of the variables to group membership? Which groups are similar? Which variables are highly correlated? Which subjects are outliers?

Wilks' Λ for multivariate analysis of variance, the classification table, the Mahalanobis' distances, the posterior probabilities, the F-to-enter and F-to-remove values, the canonical variables and their plots, etc. all help to answer these questions.

To see how multivariate analysis of variance and covariance are performed, we begin by discussing F-to-enter values. At step zero, the F-to-enter value for a variable is the F statistic for a one-way univariate analysis of variance. At step one, each F-to-enter value for the nonentered variables is the F statistic for a one-way univariate analysis of covariance where the covariate is the variable that has entered. At step q, the F-to-enter for a nonentered variable is the F statistic for a one-way univariate analysis of covariance where the covariates are the variables that have already entered.

It also happens that the ratio of the Wilks' Λ values for step q and step q+q' is the Wilks' Λ for a multivariate analysis of covariance where the covariates are the first q variables entered and the dependent variables are the next q' variables entered. To determine the significance of Wilks' Λ for this multivariate analysis of covariance, Rao's F approximation can be used (see BMDP manual, page 424). The degrees of freedom for Λ are q',g, and n-g-q, where g is the number of groups and n is the total number of cases. (However, if contrasts are stated in P7M, the second number of degrees of freedom is the number of contrasts.)

If you have a specific multivariate analysis of covariance problem, the covariates can be made to enter first and then the dependent variables. This is done in P7M by using the LEVELs statement in the DISCriminant paragraph; e.g.,

LEVELs = 1,1,1,2,2,0.

could be used for a multivariate analysis of covariance where the first three variables are the covariates, the next two are the dependent variables, and the sixth (with level zero) is the grouping variable. The FORCE statement can also be used to assure that all covariates and dependent variables are entered. You may also wish to force in the covariates and allow the dependent variables to enter as they wish to provide a subset of the dependent variables. If the dependent variables are forced first, you can obtain a subset of the covariates.

When P7M runs with its assumed options, a one-way multivariate analysis is computed. Multiway analyses of variance and covariance can be performed at the cost of running the program several times.

In this case, CONTRast statements are specified to define the effect to be tested. For example, suppose we have six groups:

1. eastern male
2. southern male
3. western male
4. eastern female
5. southern female
6. western female

The contrast 1, 1, 1, -1, -1, -1 would be used to test the main effect for sex and the contrasts 1, -1, 0, 1, -1, 0 and 0, 1, -1, 0, 1, -1 could be used to test the main effect for geographic region. Note that variables related to differences in sex may not also be related to differences in geographic region and so different variables may be chosen in P7M for the different sets of contrasts.

When contrasts are used the canonical variables are computed for the contrasts also. If contrasts are stated for geographic region in the above example, the plot of the canonical variables will show the maximum separation of subjects according to geographic region.

C.15   Analysis of the Pattern of Missing Data
James Frane, Health Sciences Computing Facility, UCLA

Missing data occur in many studies. In the analysis of data with many values missing, it is frequently assumed that the pattern of missing values is random, or at least does not adversely affect the results of the analysis. In practice such assumptions are often false. A number of methods can be used to analyze the pattern of missing values and to assess its affect.

Factor analysis can be used on the pattern of missing values in the following way. The original variables are first transformed to binary variables by replacing available data by one, and missing data by zero. The matrix of zeros and ones is then factored. Salient factors correspond to groups of variables whose patterns of missing values are highly correlated. **Cluster analysis** can also be used in this manner.

Regression analysis can be used to see how the pattern of missing data for a variable is related to the other variables. All the variables can be studied simultaneously as follows. First use BMDP8D (Missing Data Correlation). In BMDP8D add as many variables as there are original variables. The new variables are the same as those used in the factor analysis. Save the correlation matrix in BMDP8D and use this matrix as input to BMDP6R (Partial Correlation and Multivariate Regression). In BMDP6R, state that the independent variables are the original variables and the dependent variables are the binary variables.

One can also use **canonical correlation**. In BMDP6M, state that the first set of variables consists of the original variables and the second set consists of the binary variables.

C.16 The Iterated Least Squares Method of Estimating Mean and Variance Components Using P3R

R.L. Anderson and R.I. Jennrich,
Health Sciences Computing
Facility, UCLA

Program P3R provides a convenient means of implementing R.L. Anderson's iterated least squares method. Consider a normal random vector y whose mean $\mu = \mu(\alpha)$ depends on a vector α of "mean components" and whose covariance matrix $\Sigma = \Sigma(\sigma^2)$ depends on a vector σ^2 of "variance components." We begin with a set of statistics $\bar{y}_1, \ldots, \bar{y}_p$ that are sufficient for α, and a second set $MS_1, \ldots, MS_q$ that are sufficient for σ^2. The general procedure is to fit both sets of statistics to their expectations using the inverses of their covariance matrices as weights. This will produce maximum likelihood estimates and information theory standard errors.

To illustrate the procedure, consider the unbalanced two-stage nested model developed by Anderson and Crump (1967) and further explored by Thompson and Anderson (1975). The sampling process involves k_1 classes with one sample per class and k_2 classes with two samples per class. The model is

$$y_{ij} = \alpha + a_i + b_{ij} \; ; \; i = 1, \ldots, k_1 + k_2$$

$$j = \begin{cases} 1 & ; i \leq k_1 \\ 1,2 & ; i > k_1. \end{cases}$$

The a_i are $NID(0, \sigma_a^2)$, the b_{ij} are $NID(0, \sigma_b^2)$, and the a_i are independent of the b_{ij}. The means

$$\bar{y}_1 = \sum_{i \leq k_1} y_{i_1}/k_1, \quad \bar{y}_2 = \sum_{i > k_1} \sum_j y_{ij}/2k_2$$

are sufficient for α and the following sums of squares are sufficient for σ_a^2 and σ_b^2:

$$SSM_1 = k_1 (\bar{y}_1 - \alpha)^2 \; , \quad SSM_2 = 2k_2 (\bar{y}_2 - \alpha)^2$$

$$SSA_1 = \sum_{i \leq k_1} (y_{i_1} - \bar{y}_1)^2 \; , \quad SSA_2 = 2 \sum_{i > k_1} (\bar{y}_{i\bullet} - \bar{y}_2)^2$$

$$SSB_2 = \sum_{i > k_1} \sum_j (y_{ij} - \bar{y}_{i\bullet})^2$$

where $\bar{y}_{i\bullet} = \sum_{j=1}^{2} y_{ij}/2$, $i > k_1$. Note that SSM_1 and SSM_2 depend on α. We summarize these statistics as means and mean squares.

df	Mean or Mean Sq	Expectation	Variance
1	MSM_1	$\sigma_b^2 + \sigma_a^2$	$2EMS^2/df$
$k_1 - 1$	MSA_1	$\sigma_b^2 + \sigma_a^2$	$2EMS^2/df$
1	MSM_2	$\sigma_b^2 + 2\sigma_a^2$	$2EMS^2/df$
$k_2 - 1$	MSA_2	$\sigma_b^2 + 2\sigma_a^2$	$2EMS^2/df$
k_2	MSB_2	σ_b^2	$2EMS^2/df$
	$\bar{y}_1$	α	$\sigma_b^2/k_1 + \sigma_a^2/k_1$
	$\bar{y}_2$	α	$\sigma_b^2/2k_2 + \sigma_a^2/k_2$

The procedure is to fit the expectations in the third column to the mean squares and means in the second column using (since everything in sight is independent) the reciprocals of the variances in the fourth column as weights. Using P3R for this purpose and the data (Davies, 1954, p. 117)

851	863	854	863	869	875	845	869	857	869
					869	857	869	857	881

where $k_1 = 5$ and $k_2 = 5$, the required P3R setup for the FUN routine is:

```
X(7)=X(2)
IF(X(5).NE.0.0)  X(7)=X(5)*(X(2)-P(3))**2
F=P(1)*X(3)+P(2)*X(4)
DF(1)=X(3)
DF(2)=X(4)
DF(3)=0.0
X(6)=X(1)/(2*F**2)
IF(X(1).NE.0.0) GO TO 1
F=P(3)
DF(1)=0.0
DF(2)=0.0
DF(3)=1.0
X(6)=1.0/(P(1)/X(3)+P(2)/X(4))
1 CONTINUE
```

The required program control information is:

```
/PROBLEM TITLE='ITERATED LEAST SQUARES'.
/INPUT VARIABLE=7. FORMAT='(F2.0,F7.0,5F3.0)'.
/REGRESSION DEPEND=7. PARAM=3. WEIGHT=6. ITER=10.
         HALV=0.CONVER= -1.0. MEANSQ=1.0.
/PARAMETER INITIAL=1.0,1.0,1.0.
/END
```

And the required data are:

```
1 860.0  1 1   5 1
4  54.0  1 1     1
1 864.8  1 2  10 1
4 212.4  1 2     1
5  32.4  1 0     1
  860.0  5 5     1
  864.8 10 5     1
```

Here

$$\bar{y}_1 = 860.0 \quad , \quad MSA_1 = 54.0$$

$$\bar{y}_2 = 864.8 \quad , \quad MSA_2 = 212.4 \quad , \quad MSB_2 = 32.4 \; .$$

These were computed by hand but could have been obtained through using a program such as P7D. The program converged in 5 iterations from "arbitrary" starting values $\alpha = \sigma_a^2 = \sigma_b^2 = 1$ to give the results:

Component	Estimate	Standard Error
σ_b^2	30.23	18.9
σ_a^2	52.65	35.7
α	862.64	2.73

See the July 1975 *BMD Communications* for further comments on using P3R for iteratively reweighted least squares fitting.

References

Davies, O.L. (1954). *The Design and Analysis of Industrial Experiments*, New York, Hafner.

Anderson, R.L. and P.P. Crump (1967). Comparison of designs and estimation procedures for estimating parameters in a two-stage nested process. *Technometrics* 9, 499-516.

Thompson, W.O. and R.L. Anderson (1975). A comparison of designs and estimators for the two-stage nested random model. *Technometrics* 17, 37-44.

C.17 QUICK AND DIRTY MONTE CARLO
James Frane, Health Sciences Computing Facility, UCLA

Sometimes it is desirable to get a quick idea of the sensitivity of a statistic to departures from the usual underlying assumptions. The following setup can be used in BMDP3D to assess the sensitivity of the ordinary two-sample t test to the assumption of equal variances. BMDP3D reports both the usual Student's t and a t test based on separate variances.

```
/PROBLEM     TITLE IS 'MONTE CARLO'.
/INPUT       VARIABLES ARE 0.  CASES ARE 100.
/VARIABLES   ADDED ARE 3.  GROUPING IS 1.
/TRANSF      X(1) IS KASE GT 75.
             X(2) IS RNDG(1794831).
             TEMP IS X(2)*2.
             X(2) IS TEMP IF X(1).
             X(3) IS RNDG(49819327).
             TEMP IS X(3)*2.
             X(3) IS TEMP IF X(1).

/FINISH
```

In this example, data are generated randomly for two statistically independent variables and two groups (N_1 = 75, N_2 = 25) with the variances in the second group four times those of the first group. (The alternative form of control language is used in the example, where the "/" appears at the beginning of each paragraph rather than at the end.)

More complex Monte Carlo experiments can be made easily by using the BIMEDT procedure. In the following example, 100 statistically independent variables are generated for two groups. The p-values for the t tests obtained for these 100 variables should constitute a random sample from the uniform distribution. However, since the variances are unequal, the p-values will not have a uniform distribution.

```
// EXEC BIMEDT,PROG=BMDP3D
// TRANSF DD *
        DATA IST/19748217/
        X(1)=0.
        IF(KASE.GT.75) X(1)=1.
        SIGMA=1.
        IF(KASE.GT.75) SIGMA=2.
        CALL RANDG(100,X(2),0.,SIGMA,IST)
//SYSIN DD *
/PROBLEM
/INPUT       VARIABLES ARE 0.  CASES ARE 100.
/VARIABLES   ADDED ARE 101.  GROUPING IS 1.
/FINISH
//
```

The same methods can be used in any of the BMDP programs. The random number generator invoked above is part of the BMDP package; you could also use any other random number generator in the BIMEDT procedure.

These methods are quick and dirty. They are not intended to be used for extensive Monte Carlo experiments since special purpose programs would be more efficient.

C.18 LAGGED VARIABLES USING TRANSFORMATION PARAGRAPH
Alan B. Forsythe, Health Sciences Computing Facility, UCLA

We have been asked how to generate lagged variables without recreating the data set or using the FORTRAN transformation option in the BMDP programs. A lagged variable has as its value for case i the value of the variable at case i-1 (lag 1). For example, if we wish to estimate the weekly incidence of a disease as a linear function of the incidence the previous two weeks, we could have as our model

$$\text{Incidence (week i)} = \alpha + \beta_1 \text{ Incidence (week i-1)}$$
$$+ \beta_2 \text{ Incidence (week i-2)} + \epsilon.$$

Our data could be one weekly incidence per card. We do not want to repunch the deck to put the previous two weeks data on the cards. Here is the program control information for a linear regression program:

```
PROBLEM TITLE IS 'LAGGED REGRESSION'./
INPUT VARIABLE IS 1. FORMAT IS '(F3.2)'./
VARIABLE NAMES ARE INCIDENC, LAG1, LAG2, TEMP.
     ADDED ARE 3.
     USE ARE INCIDENC, LAG1, LAG2./
TRANSFORMATION LAG2=LAG1. LAG1=TEMP. TEMP=INCIDENC.
     USE=KASE GT 2./
REGRESSION DEPENDENT IS INCIDENC./
END/
```

Notes:
   (1)   The USE statement in VARIABle paragraph discards the variable named TEMP.

   (2)   The TRANSFORMATION USE=KASE GT 2. discards the first two cases since they do not have the data for both previous weeks.

C.19   Cross Validation in BMDP9R
by J.W. Frane

The ultimate assessment of the merit of a regression equation is how well it fits new data. P9R allows easy evaluation of a regression equation by means of the case weight variable. The input data are divided into two groups: the training set from which the regression equation is computed and a cross valida- tion set. Cases in the training set are given weight equal to one. Cases in the cross validation set are given weight zero. P9R computes the residual mean square for the cases with posi- tive weight and the average squared residual for the cases with zero weight.

The case weights can be assigned randomly to divide a single sample into two parts. The following setup will divide a sample into two roughly equal parts.

```
/ PROBLEM      TITLE IS 'CROSS VALIDATION'.
/ INPUT        VARIABLES ARE 10.
              FORMAT IS '(10F4.0)'.
/ VARIABLE     ADD IS 1.
              WEIGHT IS 11.
/ REGRESS      DEPENDENT IS 1.
              INDEPENDENT ARE 2 TO 10.
/ PRINT        MATRICES ARE CORR,RESID.
/ TRANSFORM    TEMP IS RNDU(5793171).
              X(11) IS TEMP LT .5.
/ END
```

The first transformation statement stores a uniform random number between zero and one in the temporary variable TEMP. The second transformation statement uses the logical operator "less than" to set X(11) equal to one if TEMP is less than one-half and to set X(11) equal to zero otherwise.

If the first fifty cases comprise the training set, and the remaining cases comprise the cross validation set, we could use the transformation statement

```
X(11) IS KASE LE 50.
```

C.20   Residual Analysis in BMDP9R
by J.W. Frane

The primary purpose of BMDP9R - All possible Subsets Regress- sion is to identify good subsets of variables. There are sev- eral aspects of being "good." One aspect is to obtain a good fit in terms of a large squared multiple correlation by only using a small subset of the available predictor variables. This aspect is handled by the Furnival-Wilson algorithm (Technometrics, 1974) for identifying "best" subsets.

Another desirable feature is that there be no outlier residu- als. Most regression programs compute residuals and many pro- vide plots or other analyses of the residuals. However, for small and moderate sample sizes, ordinary residuals do not al- ways provide an adequate assessment of the sensitivity of the regression equation to the individual cases. BMDP9R provides several indications of the quality of the fitted regression equation. After computing the ordinary residual for each case, we compute the "deleted" residual. The regression coefficients used in computing the deleted residual are defined in terms of the other cases. That is, the effect of a case is removed from the regression equation when its deleted residual is computed. When you request the plot of the deleted residual versus the ordinary residual you will notice that most of the points lie more or less on a straight line. There may be a few points that are relatively far from this line. The data for such points can then be checked.

We also compute the standardized (Studentized) residual for each case by dividing each residual by its standard error. For large sample sizes, the standard error for a residual is usu- ally very close to the square root of the residual mean square. Some statistical packages use this as their defini- tion of a standardized residual. Thus their standardized re- sidual is merely a linear rescaling of the ordinary residual. When proper standard errors are used for each case, the trans- formation is not monotonic; i.e., the largest standardized re- sidual need not correspond to the largest ordinary residual. Outliers can easily be missed if only the ordinary residual is reported. When requested, a normal probability plot for the standardized residual is printed.

In our April, 1977 update, we added a new statistic for each case that indicates the extent to which the computed regres- sion equation would change if the case were deleted (R.D Cook, Technometrics, Feb., 1977, 15-18). This statistic combines the standardized residual with the distance from the case to the center of cases in the space of the predictor variables. A case can have a large influence on the regression equation if it has a large standardized residual or a large distance or if it has moderately large standardized residual and dis- tance.

Although BMDP9R is designed to select a subset of variables, you can also request a specific equation. To do so, add

```
METHOD IS NONE.
```

to the REGRESS paragraph. This instructs the program to use all the independent variables and not to search for any "best" subsets.

APPENDIX D

How To:

Request Copies of the BMD and BMDP Programs

Obtain Additional Manuals

Report Difficulties and Suspected Errors

Obtain *BMD Communications*

Obtain HSCF Technical Reports

● COPIES OF THE BMD AND BMDP PROGRAMS

Health Sciences Computing Facility distributes both the BMD and BMDP programs. The programs are written in FORTRAN (to maximize portability) and distributed on tape as FORTRAN card images. The BMDP programs are also distributed as load modules for IBM 360/370 computers.

Since there are some differences in FORTRAN from computer to computer, we have established redistribution centers for other computer systems.

Requests for copies of the IBM version of the BMDP programs must be made on one of our request forms. For our Tape Copy Request Brochure, call or write:

> BMDP Program Librarian
> Health Sciences Computing Facility
> AV-111, CHS
> University of California
> Los Angeles, CA 90024
> (213) 825-5940

Current addresses and telephone numbers of the redistribution centers for other computer systems are included in the Tape Copy Request Brochure. Note that versions obtained from redistribution centers are not as recent as those obtained from us. As of August 1977 there are redistribution centers for the following computer systems:

> CDC 6000/CYBER
> Honeywell
> Univac 1100 series
> Univac 70/90 series
> PDP-11
> HP-3000
> Riad-20

-867-

ICL System 4 and 2900 series
Hitachi Hitac series
Fujitsu Facom series
Xerox Sigma 7
Telefunken TR 440

We encourage users of other computer equipment to become redistribution centers and so avoid duplication of effort.

- ## THE BMD AND BMDP MANUALS

The BMD and BMDP Manuals can be ordered from

University of California Press
2223 Fulton Street
Berkeley, CA 94720
(415) 642-4243

A copy of the manual is supplied with each Tape Copy from HSCF.

- ## DIFFICULTIES AND SUSPECTED ERRORS

We are most anxious to improve the quality of the BMDP programs. To report an error, please send a complete listing of the input and output to

Supervisor, BMDP Programming
Health Sciences Computing Facility
AV-111, CHS
University of California
Los Angeles, CA 90024

- ## BMD COMMUNICATIONS

BMD Communications is a newsletter that contains notices of updates to the BMDP programs and manual, and short articles that discuss the programs (see Appendix C). It is currently issued approximately twice a year at no charge. To be put on the mailing list, please send a note to

BMDP Program Librarian
Health Sciences Computing Facility
AV-111, CHS
University of California
Los Angeles, CA 90024

- ## HSCF TECHNICAL REPORTS

Health Sciences Computing Facility publishes a series of technical reports, some of which discuss uses of the programs. Many of the reports are subsequently published in journals. The unpublished reports are available for a nominal cost from

BMDP Program Librarian
(see above address)

The reports must be prepaid. The reports currently available are:

1. Keypunching with Program Drum Control for IBM026 and 029 (1974) - Suzanne Prakel (9 pp., $.50).

2. Novel Uses of BMD Programs: Canonical Correlation Analysis of Contingency Tables (1970) - Ray Mickey (6 pp., $.50).

8. Annotated Computer Output for Factor Analysis Using Professor Jarvik's Smoking Questionnaire (1974) - James Frane and MaryAnn Hill (46 pp., $1.50).

9. Maximum Likelihood Estimation by Means of Nonlinear Least Squares (1975) - Robert I. Jennrich and Roger H. Moore (33 pp., $1.50).

15. Chi-Square Probabilities for 2x2 Tables (1975) - D. Goyette and M. Mickey (133 pp., $2.50).

16. Methods for Detecting Nonrandom Association of Metaphase Chromo-somes (1975) - M.A. Spence, A.B. Forsythe, M. Nesbitt, U. Francke (10 pp., $1.00).

17. Side Inch I (1973) - Dolores Adams (172 pp. output, $3.00).

18. Side Inch II (1974) - MaryAnn Hill and Dolores Adams (215 pp output, $3.50).

19. Experimental Data Sets (1975) - Alan Forsythe, Editor (293 pp. output, $4.00)

24. LSD: Linear System Function and Derivatives Subroutine (1976) - R.I. Jennrich and A.D. Thrall (16 pp., $1.00).

26. A Class of James-Stein Regression Estimators: Some Relations to Ridge Regression (1977) - P.O. Anderson (18 pp., $1.00).

27. The Effect of Population Skewness of Confidence Intervals Determined from Mean-Like Statistics (1977) - N.J. Johnson (13 pp., $1.00).

28. Randomization or Minimization in the Treatment Assignment of Patient Trials: Validity and Power (1977) - A.B. Forsythe and F.W. Stitt (9 pp., $1.00).

The entire list of Technical Reports is available from the BMDP Program Librarian.

REFERENCES

Afifi, A.A. and S.P. Azen (1972). *Statistical Analysis: A Computer-Oriented Approach*. New York Academic Press.

Anderson, R.L., D.M. Allen and F.B. Cady (1972). Selection of predictor variables in linear multiple regression. In *Statistical Papers in Honor of George W. Snedecor*, T.A. Bancroft, Ed. Ames, Iowa, University of Iowa Press.

Anderson, R.L. and P.P. Crump (1967). Comparison of designs and estimation procedures for estimating parameters in a two-stage nested process. *Technometrics* 9, 499-516.

Anderson, T.W. (1958). *An Introduction to Multivariate Statistical Analysis*. New York, Wiley.

Andrews, D.F., P.J. Bickel, F.R. Hampel, P.J. Huber, W.H. Rogers, J.W. Tukey (1972). *Robust Estimates of Location: Survey and Advances*. Princeton, Princeton University Press.

Armitage, P. (1971). *Statistical Methods in Medical Research*. Oxford, Blackwell Scientific Publications.

Bartlett, M.S. (1947). Multivariate analysis. *J. Roy. Statist. Soc.* 9, Series B, 176-197.

Beale, E.M.L. and R.J.A. Little (1975). Missing values in multivariate analysis. *J. Roy. Statist. Soc.* 37, Series B, 129-145.

Benedetti, J.K. and M.B. Brown (1976). Alternate methods of building log-linear models. *Proceedings of the 9th International Biometric Conference*, Volume 2, 209-227.

Bishop, Y.M.M., S.E. Fienberg and P.W. Holland (1975). *Discrete Multivariate Analysis: Theory and Practice*. Cambridge, Mass., MIT Press.

Bowker, A.H. and G.J. Lieberman (1963). *Engineering Statistics*. Englewood Cliffs, New Jersey, Prentice-Hall.

Box, G.E.P. and M.A. Muller (1958). A note on the generation of random normal deviates. *Ann. Math. Statist.* 29, 610-613.

Breslow, N. (1970). A generalized Kruskal-Wallis test for comparing k samples subject to unequal patterns of censorship. *Biometrika* 57, 579-594.

Brown, M.B. (1974). The identification of sources of significance in two-way contingency tables. *Appl. Statist.* 23, 405-413.

Brown, M.B. (1976). Screening effects in multidimensional contingency tables. *Appl. Statist.* 25, 37-46.

Brown, M.B. and J.K. Benedetti (1976). Asymptotic standard errors and their sampling behavior for measures of association and correlation in the two-way contingency table. I. Testing the null hypothesis; II. Power and confidence limits. Technical Report No. 23, Health Sciences Computing Facility, UCLA.

Brown, M.B. and J.K. Benedetti (1977a). Sampling behavior of tests for correlation in two-way contingency tables. *J. Amer. Statist. Assoc.* 72, 309-315.

Brown, M.B. and J.K. Benedetti (1977b). On the mean and variance of the tetrachoric correlation coefficient. *Psychometrika* 42, in press.

Brown, M.B., M. Doron and A. Laron (1974). Approximate confidence limits for the concentration of insulin in radioimmunoassays. *Diabetologia* 10, 23-25.

Brown, M.B. and A.B. Forsythe (1974a). The small sample behavior of some statistics which test the equality of several means. *Technometrics* 16, 129-132.

Brown, M.B. and A.B. Forsythe (1974b). Robust tests for the equality of variances. *J. Amer. Statist. Assoc.* 69, 364-367.

Brownlee, K.A. (1965). *Statistical Theory and Methodology in Science and Engineering*. New York, John Wiley and Sons.

Clarke, M.R.B. (1970). A rapidly converging method for maximum likelihood factor analysis. *Brit. J. Math. Statist. Psych.* 23, 43-52.

Cochran, W.G. (1954). Some methods for strengthening the common χ^2 tests. *Biometrics* 10, 417-441.

Cochran, W.G. and G.M. Cox (1957). *Experimental Designs*, 2nd ed. New York, Wiley.

Conover, W.J. (1971). *Practical Nonparametric Statistics*. New York, Wiley.

Cook, R.D. (1977). Detection of influential observations in linear regression. *Technometrics* 19, 15-18.

Cooley, W.W. and P.R. Lohnes (1971). *Multivariate Data Analysis*. New York, Wiley.

Corbeil, R.R. and S.R. Searle (1976). Restricted maximum likelihood (REML) estimation of variance components in the mixed model. *Technometrics* 18, 31-38.

Cox, D.R. (1970). *The Analysis of Binary Data*. London, Methuen.

Cox, D.R. (1972). Regression models and life tables. *J. Roy. Statist. Soc.* 34, Series B, 187-220.

Cramer, H. (1946). *Mathematical Methods of Statistics*. Princeton, Princeton University Press.

Cutler, S.J. and F. Ederer (1958). Maximum utilization of the life table method in analyzing survival. *J. Chron. Dis.* 8, 699-713.

Daniel, C. (1959). Use of half-normal plots in interpreting factorial two-level experiments. *Technometrics* 1, 311-341.

Daniel, C. and F.S. Wood (1971). *Fitting Equations to Data*. New York, Wiley.

Davies, O.L. (1954). *The Design and Analysis of Industrial Experiments*. New York, Hafner.

Dempster, A.P. (1969). *Elements of Continuous Multivariate Analysis*. San Francisco, Addison-Wesley.

REFERENCES

Dixon, W.J., Ed. (1975). *BMDP Biomedical Computer Programs*. Los Angeles, Univ. of Calif. Press.

Dixon, W.J., Ed. (1977). *BMD Biomedical Computer Programs*. Los Angeles, Univ. of Calif. Press.

Dixon, W.J. and F.J. Massey, Jr. (1969). *Introduction to Statistical Analysis*, 3rd ed., New York, McGraw-Hill.

Dixon, W.J. and J.W. Tukey (1968). Approximate behavior of the distribution of Winsorized t (Trimming/Winsorization 2). *Technometrics* 10, 83-98.

Everitt, P.F. (1910). Tables of the tetrachoric functions for fourfold correlation tables. *Biometrika* 7, 437-451.

Fienberg, S.E. (1972). The analysis of incomplete multiway contingency tables. *Biometrics* 28, 177-202.

Fisher, R.A. (1936). The use of multiple measurements in taxonomic problems. *Ann. Eugen.* 7, 179-188.

Fleiss, J.L. (1973). *Statistical Methods for Rates and Proportions*. New York, Wiley.

Forsythe, A.B., L. Engelman, R. Jennrich and P.R.A. May (1973). A stopping rule for variable selection in multiple regression. *J. Amer. Statist. Assoc.* 68, 75-77.

Forsythe, A.B., P.R.A. May and L. Engelman (1970). Computing advantage scores by multiple regression. In *Psychopharmacology and the Individual Patient*. J.R. Wittenborn, S.C. Goldberg and P.R.A. May, Eds., Raven Press, Chap. 8, 116-123.

Forsythe, A.B., P.R.A. May and L. Engelman (1971). Prediction of multiple regression. *J. Psychiatric Res.* 8, 119-126.

Forsythe, G.E. (1957). Generation and use of orthogonal polynomials for data fitting with a digital computer. *J. Soc. Ind. Appl. Math.* 5, 74-88.

Frane, J.W. (1976). Some simple procedures for handling missing data in multivariate analysis. *Psychometrika* 41, 409-415.

Frane, J.W. and M. Hill (1974). Annotated Computer Output for Factor Analysis using Professor Jarvik's Smoking Questionnaire. Technical Report No. 8, Health Sciences Computing Facility, UCLA.

Frane, J.W. and M. Hill (1976). Factor analysis as a tool for data analysis. *Commun. Statist. - Theor. Meth.*, A5, 487-506.

Frank, M. and C. Pfaffman (1969). Taste nerve fibers: A random distribution of sensitivities to four tastes. *Science* 164, 1183-1185.

Furnival, G.M. and R.W. Wilson (1974a). Regression by leaps and bounds. *Technometrics* 16, 499-511.

Furnival, G.M. and R.W. Wilson (1974b). Regression by leaps and bounds -- A program for finding the best subset regressions (computer program). New Haven, Yale University and U.S. Forest Service, Nov. 11, 1974.

Goodman, L.A. (1968). The analysis of cross-classified data. *J. Amer. Statist. Assoc.* 63, 1091-1131.

Goodman, L.A. and W.H. Kruskal (1954). Measures of association for cross-classification. *J. Amer. Statist. Assoc.* 49, 732-764.

Goodman, L.A. and W.H. Kruskal (1963). Measures of association for cross-classification. III. Approximate sampling theory. *J. Amer. Statist. Assoc.* 58, 310-364.

Goodman, L.A. and W.H. Kruskal (1972). Measures of association for cross-classification. IV. Simplification of asymptotic variances. *J. Amer. Statist. Assoc.* 67, 415-421.

Greenwood, M. (1926). The natural duration of cancer. Reports on public health and medical subjects 33. H.M. Stationary office, London.

Gross, A. and V. Clark (1975). *Survival Distributions: Reliability Applications in the Biomedical Sciences.* New York, Wiley.

Gunst, R.F. and R.L. Mason (1977). Advantages of examining multicollinearities in regression analysis. *Biometrics* 33, 249-260.

Haberman, S.J. (1972). Log-linear fit for contingency tables, algorithm AS 51. *Appl. Statist.* 21, 218-224.

Haberman, S.J. (1973). The analysis of residuals in cross-classified tables. *Biometrics* 29, 205-220.

Hájek, J. (1969). *Nonparametric Statistics.* San Francisco, Holden-Day.

Harbison, F.H., J. Maruhnic and J.R. Resnick (1970). *Quantitative Analysis of Modernization and Development.* Princeton, Princeton University, Industrial Relations Section, Research Report Series No. 115, Appendix 1, p. 8.

Harman, H.H. (1967). *Modern Factor Analysis*, 2nd ed. Chicago, Univ. of Chicago Press.

Hartigan, J.A. (1975). *Clustering Algorithms.* New York, Wiley.

Hartley, H.O. and J.H.K. Rao (1967). Maximum likelihood estimation for the mixed analysis of variance model. *Biometrika* 54, 93-108.

Hartley, H.O. and W.K. Vaughn (1972). A computer program for the mixed analysis of variance model based on maximum likelihood. In *Statistical Papers in Honor of George W. Snedecor.* T.A. Bancroft, Ed. Ames, Iowa State University Press.

Harville, D.A. (1977). Maximum likelihood approaches to variance component estimation and to related problems. *J. Amer. Statist. Assoc.* 72, 320-340.

Hawkins, D.M. (1974). The detection of errors in multivariate data using principal components. *J. Amer. Statist. Assoc.* 69, 340-344.

Hemmerle, W.J. and H.O. Hartley (1973). Computing maximum likelihood estimates for the mixed A.O.V. model using the W transform. *Technometrics* 15, 819-831.

Hocking, R.R. (1972). Criteria for selection of a subset regression: which one should be used. *Technometrics* 14, 967-970.

Hoerl, A.E. (1962). Application of ridge analysis to regression problems. *Chem. Eng. Prog.* 58, 54-59.

Hoerl, A.E. and R.W. Kennard (1970a). Ridge regression: biased estimation for nonorthogonal problems. *Technometrics* 12, 55-67.

Hoerl, A.E. and R.W. Kennard (1970b). Ridge regression: application to nonorthogonal problems. *Technometrics* 12, 69-82.

REFERENCES

Jennrich, R.I. (1977a). Stepwise regression. In *Statistical Methods for Digital Computers*, K. Enslein, A. Ralston and H.S. Wilf, Eds. New York, Wiley, Chap. 4.

Jennrich, R.I. (1977b). Stepwise discriminant analysis. In *Statistical Methods for Digital Computers*, K. Enslein, A. Ralston and H.S. Wilf, Eds., New York, Wiley, Chap. 5.

Jennrich, R.I. and P.B. Bright (1976). Fitting systems of linear differential equations using computer generated exact derivatives. *Technometrics* 18, 385-392.

Jennrich, R.I. and R.H. Moore (1975). Maximum likelihood estimation by means of nonlinear least squares. In *Proceedings of the Statistical Computing Section, Amer. Statist. Assoc.* 57-65.

Jennrich, R.I. and S.M. Robinson (1969). A Newton-Raphson algorithm for maximum likelihood factor analysis. *Psychometrika* 34, 111-123.

Jennrich, R.I. and P.F. Sampson (1966). Rotation for simple loadings. *Psychometrika* 31, 313-323.

Jennrich, R.I. and P.F. Sampson (1968). Application of stepwise regression to nonlinear least squares estimation. *Technometrics* 10, 63-67.

Jennrich, R.I. and P.F. Sampson (1976). Newton-Raphson and related algorithms for maximum likelihood variance component estimation. *Technometrics* 18, 11-17.

John, P.W.M. (1971). *Statistical Design and Analysis of Experiments*. New York, MacMillan.

Jöreskog, K.G. and M. van Thillo (1971). New rapid algorithms for factor analysis by unweighted least squares, generalized least squares and maximum likelihood. Research Memorandum, 71-S. Princeton, Educational Testing Service.

Kaiser, H.F. (1970). A second generation Little Jiffy. *Psychometrika* 35, 401-415.

Kaplan, E.L. and P. Meier (1958). Nonparametric estimation from incomplete observations. *J. Amer. Statist. Assoc.* 53, 457-481.

Kasser, I. and R.A. Bruce (1969). Comparative effects of aging and coronary heart disease and submaximal and maximal exercise. *Circulation* 39, 759-774.

Kendall, M.G. and A. Stuart (1967). *The Advanced Theory of Statistics*, Vol. 2, 2nd ed., New York, Hafner.

Kronmal, R.A. and M. Tarter (1973). The use of density estimates based on orthogonal expansions. In *Exploring Data Analysis -- The Computer Revolution in Statistics*, W.J. Dixon and W.L. Nicholson, Eds. Berkeley, Univ. of Calif. Press, Chap. 8.

Kruskal, W.H. and W.A. Wallis (1952). Use of ranks in one-criterion variance analysis. *J. Amer. Statist. Assoc.* 47, 583-621.

Kutner, M.H. (1974). Hypothesis tesing in linear models (Eisenhart Model I). *Amer. Statist.* 28, 98-100.

Lachenbruch, P. and R.M. Mickey (1968). Estimation of error rates in discriminant analysis. *Technometrics* 10, 1-11.

Larsen, W.A. and S.J. McCleary (1972). The use of partial residual plots in regression analysis. *Technometrics* 14, 781-790.

Lawley, D.N. and A.E. Maxwell (1971). *Factor Analysis as a Statistical Method*, 2nd ed. New York, American Elsevier.

Lee, E.G., M.M. Desu and E.H. Gehan (1975). A Monte Carlo study of the power of some two-sample tests. *Biometrika* 62, 425-432.

Lee, S.K. (1977). On the asymptotic variances of u-terms in log-linear models of multidimensional contingency tables. *J. Amer. Statist. Assoc.* 72, 412-419.

Lehman, E.L. (1959). *Testing Statistical Hypotheses*. New York, Wiley.

Lehmann, E.L. (1975). *Nonparametrics: Statistical Methods Based on Ranks*. San Francisco, Holden-Day.

Ling, R.F. (1973). A computer generated aid for cluster analysis. *Communications of ACM* 16, 355-361.

Mantel, N. (1966). Evaluation of survival data and two new rank order statistics arising in its consideration. *Cancer Chemotherapy Reports* 50, 163-170.

Mantel, N. and W. Haenszel (1959). Statistical aspects of the analysis of data from retrospective studies of disease. *J. Natl. Cancer Inst.* 22, 719-748.

Mickey, M.R. and P.M. Britt (1974). Obtaining linear scores from preference pairs. *Comm. Statist.* 3, 501-511.

Mickey, M.R., O.J. Dunn and V. Clark (1967). Note on the use of stepwise regression in detecting outliers. *Comp. Biomed. Res.* 1, 105-111.

Miller, R.G., Jr. (1966). *Simultaneous Statistical Inference*. New York, McGraw-Hill.

Morrison, A.S., M.M. Black, C.R. Lowe, B. MacMahon and S.Y. Yuasa (1973). Some international differences in histology and survival in breast cancer. *Intl. J. Cancer* 11, 261-267.

Morrison, D.F. (1967). *Multivariate Statsitical Methods*. New York, McGraw-Hill.

Mosteller, F. (1968). Association and estimation of contingency tables. *J. Amer. Statist. Assoc.* 63, 1-28.

Nelson, W. (1972). Theory and applications of hazard plotting for censored failure data. *Technometrics* 14, 945-966.

Pearson, K. (1913). On the probable error of a coefficient of correlation as found from a fourfold table. *Biometrika* 9, 22-27.

Pratt, J.W. (1964). Robustness of some procedures for the two-sample location problem. *J. Amer. Statist. Assoc.* 59, 665-680.

Prentice, R.L. (1973). Exponential survivals with censoring and explanatory variables. *Biometrika* 60, 279-288.

Prescott, P. (1975). An approximate test for outliers in linear regression. *Technometrics* 17, 129-132.

Ralston, M. and R.I. Jennrich (1977). Derivative-free nonlinear regression. In *Proceedings of Computer Science and Statistics: Tenth Annual Symposium on the Interface*, in press.

REFERENCES

Rao, C.R. (1955). Estimation and tests of significance in factor analysis. *Psychometrika* 20, 93-111.

Rao, C.R. (1972). Estimation of variance and covariance components in linear models. *J. Amer. Statist. Assoc.* 67, 112-115.

Reinsch, C.H. (1973). Algorithm 464. Eigenvalues of a real, symmetric, tri-diagonal matrix. *Communications of ACM* 16, 689.

Scheffé, H. (1959). *The Analysis of Variance.* New York, Wiley.

Searle, S.R. (1971). *Linear Models.* New York, Wiley.

Siegel, S.S. (1956). *Nonparametric Statistics for the Behavioral Sciences.* New York, McGraw-Hill.

Snedecor, G.W. and W.G. Cochran (1967). *Statistical Methods*, 6th ed. Ames, Iowa State University Press.

Speed, F.M. and R.R. Hocking (1976). The use of R( )-notation with unbalanced data. *Amer. Statist.* 30, 30-33.

Spicer, C.C. (1972). Algorithm AS 52. Calculation of power sums of deviations about the mean. *Appl. Statist.* 21, 226-227.

Svalastoga, K. (1959). *Prestige, Class and Mobility.* London, Heineman.

Täljedal, I.B. and S. Wold (1970). Fit of some analytic functions to radio-immunoassay standard curves. *Biochem. J.* 119, 139-143.

Tarone, R.E. and J. Ware (1977). On distribution-free tests for equality of survival distributions. *Biometrika* 64, 1, 156-160.

Thompson, W.O. and R.L. Anderson (1975). A comparison of designs and estimators for the two-stage nested random model. *Technometrics* 17, 37-44.

Werner, M., R.E. Tolls, J.V. Hultin and J. Mellecker (1970). Sex and age dependence of serum calcium, inorganic phosphorus, total protein, and albumin in a large ambulatory population. In *Fifth International Congress on Automation, Advances in Automated Analysis*, Vol. 2, 59-65.

Winer, B.J. (1971). *Statistical Principles in Experimental Design*, 2nd ed. New York, McGraw-Hill.

Woolf, B. (1955). On estimating the relation between blood group and disease. *Ann. Hum. Genet.* 19, 251-253.

INDEX

SYMBOLS

@, 66
' (apostrophe), 59-60, 66
Б (blank), 67
c, 59-60
'c', 59-60
C_p, 423
g, 175, 227
ϕ, 261, 263, 781-2
χ^2, see chi-square test
#, 58-60
/, 57
//, see System Cards, end-of-file
=, 58

A

abbreviations in Control Language, 61
acceptable value, 8
accuracy, 13
    see also tolerance
actuarial, see life table
ADD variables, 99
adjusted
    cell mean, 527, 548
    group means, 527
        contrast on, 531-3
        correlation between, 816
adjusted R^2, 403, 422
AFTER, 100
all possible subsets, 418-22
    see also regression
amalgamation, see linkage
    distance, 634, 636-7
analysis of covariance, 521-2
    model, 527, 547
    multivariate, 859
    one-way, 526-9
    two-way, 546-8
analysis of variance, 521-2
    fractional factorial, 549
    Friedman two-way, 610
    incomplete block, 549
    Kruskal-Wallis one-way, 612
    Latin square, 548
    mixed model, 581, 591-4, 823
    model, 20
    multivariate, 859
    one-way, 188-190, 201-2, 523-6
    repeated measure, 540-1, 551-2
    split-plot, 554
    two-way, 191-3, 542-6
    with covariates, see analysis of
        covariance
anti-image correlation, 674
apostrophe, use of, 59-60, 66
ARE, 58
ASE, 267, 779-80, 783-90
assignment
    repeated, of numbers, 65
    statements, 58-61
association
    marginal and partial, 303-5, 313-4
    measures of, 261, 264
assumed value, see preassigned value
assumption, see preassigned value
asymptotic correlation of parameter
    estimates, 466

autocorrelation, see serial correlation,
    lagged variable

B

Б (blank), 67
backward stepping
    in discriminant analysis, 726
    in regression, 406-7
bar graph, see histogram
Bartlett
    statistic (test for variances), 202,
        778
    test for eigenvalues, 688
BEFORE, 100
Behrens-Fisher, see two-sample t test
best subset in regression, 418
    criterion to select, 423-4
beta estimate, 548
BIMEDT procedure, 106-8
binary, 110, 130
bivariate plot, see scatter plot
biweight, 150-1
blank
    as missing value code, 81
    in Control Language, 64
block diagram, 646-7
BMDP File, 123-135
    allocating space for, 127-8
    available in programs, 14
    contents of, 130-1
    copying data from, 135
    covariance or correlation matrix, 131
    creating, 125-9
    data in, 130
    definition of, 125
    location of, 126-7
    need for, 123-4
    System Cards for, 128-9, 133-4
    use of, 132-4
bound, see limit
Breslow statistic, 760, 828
Brown-Forsythe statistic, 188-9
BY, 64-5

C

c, 'c', 59-60
canonical
    correlation, 23, 688, 830-2
        in discriminant analysis, 839
    variable
        in discriminant analysis, 718
        loading, 832
        score, 832
case, 8-9
    as used in analysis, 8-9, 14, 82
    classified into groups, 84-6
    complete, 8-9
    deleting, 103-4
    label, 83
    number of, 76-7
    omitting, 103-4
    print, see print case
    selection, 9, 14, 103-4
    sequence (KASE), 97, 106
    weight, 13, 14

categorical data, 245
CATEGory paragraph, 84-6
cell indices and frequency counts as
    input, 271-6
censored data, 741-2
char., character
characters
    illegal, 159-161
    types of, 159-161
    recoding nonnumeric, 109
chi-square test
    in two-way frequency table, 252, 261,
        262, 780
    of quasi-independence, 289
classification
    function, 717, 837
    matrix, 718
        jackknifed, 718
classifying cases into groups, 84-6
cluster analysis, 21-2, 621-2
CODE
    for BMDP File, 125-6, 132
    for groups or categories, 84-5
coding sheet, 47-50
coefficient
    of concordance, 610
    of variation, 10
        computed in programs, 14
    regression, 375-6, 381
    standardized regression, 383
collapsing two-way frequency tables,
    258-9, 792
command in Control Language, 58
comment in Control Language, 66
communality, 661, 665-6
complete case, 8-9
compound symmetry, 570-1
concordance, coefficient of, 610
conditional probability, 744, 746
constraint
    linear, 479
    inequality, 494-5
CONTENT of BMDP File, 125-6, 132
contingency
    coefficient, 261, 263, 782
    table, see frequency table, multi-
        way frequency table
contrast
    in discriminant analysis, 727-8
    on cell means, 531-3
Control Language, 56-66
    apostrophe, 59-60, 66
    blanks in, 64
    command, 58
    comment, 66
    definition, 62-3
    error, 69-70
    implied list, 64-5
    matching elements, 65-6
    misspelling, 66, 69
    numbers, 65
    paragraph, 57
    preassigned value, 62
    punctuation, 56-7
    remark, 66
    repeated assignment of numbers, 65
    repeated paragraphs, 66
    repeated sentences, 65
    repetition of values, 64
    reserved words and symbols, 66
    sentences, 57-61
    statement, 58-61

syntax, 56-7
tab feature, 65
transformation, 97-105
Cook's distance, 427, 804
copy data from BMDP File, 135
correlation, 10-11
  canonical, 23, 688
  computation of, 775-6
  computed in programs, 14
  matrix by group, 179-82
  matrix of regression coefficients,
    383-5, 412, 426-7, 802
  missing value, 334-5, 337-8, 352-3,
    798
  multiple, 11, 14, 381, 700
  partial, 11, 14, 23, 404, 700
  product-moment, 11, 14
  rank, 261, 264, 613-5
  saved in BMDP File, 131
  serial, 384, 468
  tetrachoric, 263-4, 784-5
count, see frequency, sample size
covariance, 10
  computation of, 775-6
  computed in programs, 14
  matrix by groups, 385
  see also analysis of covariance,
    correlation
covariate, 527
Cramer's V, 261, 263, 782
cross-product ratio, 261, 263, 783
cross section of frequency table, 245,
  253-4
cross tabulation, see frequency table
cross validation, 425, 720-1, 866
crossed, 541
cumulative
  frequency plot, 221-2
  histogram, 222-3
cutpoint, 84-5

D

D², see Mahalanobis distance
data, 8
  checking before or after transforma-
    tion, 100
  checking, see also missing value, limit
  copy or punch, from BMDP File, 135
  editing, 95-110
  screening, 15-25, 95-110, 860
  used in analysis, 8-9, 14, 82
  see also case, variable
death density function, 747
death rate, instantaneous, 747
default, see preassigned value
definition in Control Language, 62-3
DELETE cases, 103-4
deleted
  cell, 285, 288-9
  residual, 427
dendogram, see tree diagram
dependent variable, 381
discriminant analysis, 24-5, 711-9, 833-9
distance, see Mahalanobis distance, cluster
  analysis
double precision, 13,14

E

editing, data, 95-110
eigenvalue, 661
  analysis, see factor analysis
eigenvector, 661
END paragraph, 57
end-of-file, 68, 76-7
equality of proportions, 261, 262
errors, common, 69-70
= (equal), 58
estimate of location, see mean, median,
  mode, robust; see also missing value
excluded value, 137
  see also case selection
expected value
  from log-linear model, 301
  in two-way frequency table, 250, 256-8
  under quasi-independence, 289, 290
  see also predicted value

exponential function, see nonlinear
extreme value, see outlier, value out of
  range

F

F-to-enter, 404, 406-7, 855
  in discriminant analysis, 717, 835
F-to-remove, 403, 406-7, 855
  in discriminant analysis, 717, 835
F test
  for variances, 173
  see also analysis of variance,
    Bartlett's test, Levene's test
factor
  analysis, 22-3, 661-73
    iterative principal, 664
    maximum likelihood, 664, 829-30
  extraction, 664-5
  loading, 661, 662
  rotation, 669-70
  score, 662
    coefficient, 662
    covariance, 662
  structure, 662
failure rate, 747
file, see BMDP File, system file
filename, 126
FINISH paragraph, 57
Fisher's exact test, 262, 781
fixed effect, 581
force of mortality, 747
format, 51-3, 70
  A-type, 52
  F-type, 51-2
  nonstandard, 110
  X, 52
FORTRAN
  errors, 70
  transformation, 106-9
forward stepping
  in discriminant analysis, 726
  in regression, 406-7
fractional factorial, 549
Freeman-Tukey residuals, 268-70
  in multiway table, 316-7
frequencies, equality of cell, 201
frequency
  cumulative, 150
  cumulative, plot, 221-2
  of codes or intervals, 143-4
  of codes or values, 150
  of single column data, 156-7
  of nonnumeric codes, 158-9
  sample size, 10, 14
frequency table, 245-7
  adjusted marginals, 270, 791
  collapsing, 258-9
  cross section of, 245, 253-4
  departure from independence, 282-5
  empty (excluded) cells, 281-2, 288-9
  form two-way, 252-3
  input of, 271-6
  multiway, see multiway frequency table,
    log-linear model
  residuals, 268-70
  tables of percentages, 256-8
  tests and measures, 260-7
  tests of independence, 262
  two-way, 248-50
Friedman two-way analysis of variance, 610
function, see regression, transformation

G

g, 175, 227
G², see likelihood ratio chi-square
gamma, 261, 264, 670, 785
geometric mean, 117-8
goodness-of-fit, see chi-square test,
  likelihood ratio chi-square
GROUP paragraph, 84-6
group, 9
  name, 84-5
  subscript, 227

grouping
  factor, 540
  variable, 9
groups
  comparison of, see analysis of variance,
    t test
  plotted, 224-7, 235-6

H

Hampel estimate, 150-1
harmonic mean, 117-8
hazard function, 747
  cumulative, 756
heteroscedasticity, 16
hierarchical, 302
histogram, 217-9
  available in programs, 14, 215-6
  cumulative, 222-3
Hotelling's T², 177, 776-7
HSCF, Health Sciences Computing Facility,
  UCLA

I

ill-conditioned, 803
  see also tolerance
implied test, 64-5
incomplete block, 549
incomplete data, 741-2
  see also missing value
independence in two-way frequency table, 262
independent variable, 381
INPut paragraph, 75-8
input
  nonstandard, 110
  types of, 14
  see also data, case, variable
intercept, 390-1
interquartile range, 147
intervals, 84-5
inversion, matrix, 676, 702, 800-3
IS, 58
item name, 58
  abbreviation, 61
  incorrect or extra, 66
  subscript, 60
iteratively reweighted least squares, 475

J

jackknife in discriminant analysis, 730-1
JCL, see System Cards
Job Control Language, see System Cards
jobname, 67

K

Kaiser's Second Generation Little Jiffy,
  664
Kaplan-Meier estimate, 750-2
KASE, 97, 106
Kendall
  coefficient of concordance, 610
  rank correlation, 261, 264, 613-5, 785
keypunching, 49
Kruskal-Wallis one-way analysis of
  variance, 612
kurtosis, 10
  computation of, 775
  computed in programs, 14
  standard error of, 10, 149

L

label
  case, 83
  for BMDP File, 125-6, 132
lagged variable, 865

SYSTEM CARDS REQUIRED TO USE BMDP PROGRAMS

<u>At HSCF</u>   <u>Fill in those needed at your facility</u>

● Standard deck (all programs but P1S, PAR and possibly P3R)

```
job card                //jobname  JOB  nooo,yourname
program ID              //  EXEC  BIMED,PROG=BMDPxx
end of system cards     //SYSIN  DD  *
```

```
┌─────────────────────────────────┐
│ Control Language instructions and │
│ data (if on cards) are placed     │
│ here -- see program description   │
└─────────────────────────────────┘
```

```
end of job              //
```

If you are using a tape or disk (as for a BMDP File), insert

```
    //FTyyF001  DD  DSNAME=FS.nooo.filename,DISP=OLD
```

before

```
    //SYSIN  DD  *
```

....

● When transformations are specified by FORTRAN statements
  (Section 6.4) or for P1S

```
job card                //jobname  JOB  nooo,yourname
program ID (note the T) //. EXEC  BIMEDT,PROG=BMDPxx
FORTRAN statement       //TRANSF  DD  *
```

```
┌──────────────────────┐
│ FORTRAN statements    │
└──────────────────────┘
```

```
Control Language is next //GO.SYSIN  DD  *
```

```
┌─────────────────────────────────┐
│ Control Language instructions and │
│ data (if on cards) are placed     │
│ here -- see program description   │
└─────────────────────────────────┘
```

```
end of job              //
```

If you are using a tape or disk (as for a BMDP File), insert

```
    //GO.FTyyF001  DD  DSNAME=FS.nooo.filename,DISP=OLD
```

before

```
    //GO.SYSIN  DD  *
```

....

● When using PAR or P3R and specifying the function by FORTRAN
  statements

```
job card                //jobname  JOB  noo,yourname
program ID (note the T) //  EXEC  BIMEDT,PROG=BMDPxx
FORTRAN statement       //FUN  DD  *
```

```
┌──────────────────────┐
│ FORTRAN statements    │
└──────────────────────┘
```

```
Control Language is next //GO.SYSIN  DD  *
```

```
┌─────────────────────────────────┐
│ Control Language instructions and │
│ data (if on cards) are placed     │
│ here -- see program description   │
└─────────────────────────────────┘
```

```
end of job              //
```

If you are using a tape or disk (as for a BMDP File), insert

```
    //GO.FTyyF001  DD  DSNAME=FS.nooo.filename,DISP=OLD
```

before

```
    //GO.SYSIN  DD  *
```